SCHOOL AND SOCIETY

EDITED BY J. McKEEN CATTELL

VOLUME XXIX

JANUARY-JUNE, 1929

WITH WHICH HAS BEEN COMBINED THE

EDUCATIONAL REVIEW

Edited by WILLIAM McANDREW

NEW YORK
THE SCIENCE PRESS
1929

THE SCIENCE PRESS PRINTING COMPANY
LANCASTER, PA.

CONTENTS AND INDEX

VOLUME XXIX—JANUARY-JUNE, 1929

NAMES OF CONTRIBUTORS ARE PRINTED IN SMALL CAPITALS

Achievement, Scholastic, and Character, H. J. STEERE, 707
ADAMS, J., Literature by Infection, 429
ADAMS, S. C., The Parent-Teacher Movement, 474
Adult Education, in Turkey, 110; at Columbia University, 140
ALLTUCKER, M. M., Tenure and Training of City School Superintendents, 649
American, Association for the Advancement of Science, Address, Vice-president of Section of Education, 1; New York Meeting, 10; -Scandinavian Foundation, 636, 830
Angell, President, on Yale University Affairs, 321
Anti-evolution Laws and Religious Neutrality, A. O. LOVEJOY, 133
Appointments, at Yale Univ., 635; at Columbia, 636
Appropriations, N. Y. State Dept. of Education, 186; Legislative, for Univ. of North Carolina, 250
Architects, Education of, 829
Argentina, Educational Visitors from, 150
Articulation, Commission, H. S. WEET, 345; Educational, J. DEWEY, 399
Arts College, Education in, L. J. BENNETT, 69
Athletics, and Scholarship, M. E. HUTCHINSON, 151; Going Straight in, G. NORLIN, 205
Attendance, School, in London, 434
Australia, South, Education in, 320
Averill, L. A., The Hygiene of Instruction, 165

BAGLEY, W. C., The Profession of Teaching, 101
Baird, A. C., Public Discussion and Debate, 463
Baldwin, Bird, Resolutions on the Death of, 437
BALLOU, F. W., Federal Aid to Education, 406
BARKER, A. W., Our Eye-minded Girls, 490
Barnes, C. C., Directive-Study Sheets in American History, 463
BASSETT, S. J., Sex Differences, 397
BENNETT, L. J., Education in the Arts College, 69
Beta Hypothesis of Learning, J. Q. HOLSOPPLE and I. VANOUSE, 15; R. P. CARROLL, 543
Bibliographical and Int. Library Congress, 320
Biology, Middle-school, J. G. NEEDHAM, 183
Boeckel, F. B., Between War and Peace, 31
Bogardus, E., Immigration and Race Attitudes, 32
BONSER, F. G., Industrial Arts Education, 392
Book, List with Personality, E. M. CUSHMAN, 491; Reviews, W. S. MONROE and M. R. HULL, 521
Books, Better, Review of, 23, 163, 297, 459, 585, 620; of 1928, J. L. WHEELER, 230; and Literature, 392
Boston University and the Sargent School, 670
Bowdoin College, Institute of Social Sciences at, 412
BOYD, J. A., Personality *vs.* Methods, 489
BOYNTON, F. D., Dept. of Superintendence, 140; Education: What Program? What Price? 269
Boys, Congenial Work for, R. WELLING, 14; in Industry, 60; Club in Urban High School, R. H. MAHONEY, 89; Continuation School, N. Y. State, 506, 799
BRANNON, M. A., The State and the State University, 683
Branom, M. E., A Teacher's Geography, 462
Brazil, Summer School, 139
Bridges, H. J., Taking the Name of Science in Vain, 173
British, Students in America, 8; Institute in Paris, 51; Boys in American Preparatory Schools, 215; Branch of the International School of Vedic, 275; National Union of Teachers, 480; Prime Minister on Education, 602; Broadcasting, 646; Board of Education, 678; School at Ypres, 798; Labor Government and Education, 843; Columbia, Library Extension in, 799
Brooklyn Botanic Garden and the Schools, 435
Brooks-Bright Essays, 28
Brookwood Labor College, 92
BRUSH, H. R., Student Tourist Third Class, 561
BUCKINGHAM, R. B., Philosophy and Organization of Research, 755
Building, School, J. M. GWINN, 339
Buildings, Rural Junior High-school, 381
Bureau of Education, J. W. CRABTREE, 664
Business, and Education, C. F. TAEUSCH, 723; Leadership in, W. T. FOSTER, 734
BUTTERFIELD, E. W., Who is Dishonest? 360

California Assoc. Supervisors of Child Welfare and Attendance, 51
Camenisch, S. C., Chicago Practice Tests, 624
Canada, The Colleges of, V. MASSEY, 369
Canadian, National Council of Education, 366; Universities, Registration, R. WALTERS, 375
Carnegie, Pensions, 574; United Kingdom Trust, 665; Scholarships for Librarians, 668
Carr, W. G., Education for Citizenship, 591
CARREON, M. L., Professional Training, 243
CARROLL, R. P., Beta Hypothesis of Learning, 543
Censorship of Student Publications, H. G. DOYLE, 197
CHAMPLIN, C. D., Who is Practical in Education? 700
Chase, President, and Univ. of N. C., 678
Chicago, Principals' Club, 33; World's Fair at, 669; Public Schools, Appropriations for, 832; Univ. of, Children's Medical Center at, 277; Presidency, 566; Retirement of Members of Faculties, 771
Child, Welfare, and Attendance, Assoc., 51; in Irish Free State, 536; Health Day in N. Y. City, 538; Development, Research in, A. GESELL, 765
Children, in Cities and Suburbs, 114; Communicable Diseases among, 410; Heckscher Foundation for, 605
Children's Medical Center at Univ. of Chicago, 277; Fund of Michigan, 539; Labor in Ecuador, 603
China, An Official Language for, 111; Educational Conditions, 736
City Club, Portland, The Platoon Plan, 169
Clarkson College of Technology, 771

Coe, G. A., The Motives of Men, 174
College Students, Observation of the, J. H. FURBAY, 13
Colleges, American Assoc. of, R. WALTERS, 126; and Secondary Schools, New England Assoc. of, R. WALTERS, 519
Collegiate Educational Research, M. E. HAGGERTY, 653
Colorado, Univ. of, Summer Quarter, 114
Columbia University, Deutsches Haus, 112; Adult Education at, 140; Real Estate Leases of, 220; and Greenwich House, 410; Home Study Dept., 483; Gift of Mr. Harkness, 507; Appointments and Promotions, 636; Summer Session, 670, J. J. Coss, 842
Commercial Education in Sweden, 112
Commonwealth Fund, 395; Fellowships, 667
Compulsory Education and State Laws, 276
Conferences, Educational, Foreign, 52
Cooper, J. M., Religious Outlines for Colleges, 298
COOPER, W. J., The U. S. Dept. of Education, 317
Copyright Law Amendment, K. FENNING, 282
Cornell University, Messenger Lectures, 279
Coss, J. J., Columbia Summer Session, 842
Counseling, Freshman, P. W. HOLADAY, 234
CRABTREE, J. W., The Future of the Bureau of Education, 664
CROW, L. D., Parent, Teacher and Student Cooperation, 553
Cuban Physical Training Institute, 666
Curriculum, Liberal Arts, H. P. RAINEY, 258; in College of Liberal Arts and Sciences, Illinois, W. SHUMWAY, 572
CURTIS, H. S., The Drama in Education, 793
CUSHMAN, E. M., Book List with Personality, 491

DAVIS, B. E., Mrs. Dorsey, 194
DAVIS, M. C., Education in Mexico, 547
DAY, F. P., Eliphalet Nott, 625
Day, President, Installation, 606
Deans of Men, 436
Dearborn, W. F., Intelligence Tests, 171
Des Moines, Trouble at, 634; Conference of Bureau of Education, 740
DEWEY, J., Educational Articulation, 399
Discussion, 13, 57, 121, 149, 195, 227, 256, 282, 330, 360, 388, 417, 441, 489, 513, 543, 571, 612, 642, 675, 700, 746, 776, 808, 838
Diseases, Communicable, among Children, 410
Dishonest, Who Is? E. W. BUTTERFIELD, 360
Dissertations, University, L. HEYL, 808
Ditson Bequest to Musical Education, 769
Dormitory Values for Students, E. L. MOULTON, 362
Dorsey, Mrs., B. E. DAVIS, 194
DOYLE, H. G., Student Publications, 197
Drama in Education, H. S. CURTIS, 793
Drum, W. N., A Preview of Teaching, 35

EATON, T. H., What Education is Rural? 75
Ecological and Economic Studies, D. F. MILLER, 571
Economics, Home, American Association, 770
Ecuador, Children's Labor in, 603
Edison, Mr., Selection of Able Students, 604
Education, in 1928, 14; What Program? What Price? F. D. BOYNTON, 269; Dept. of, A, 846
Educational, Events, 8, 50, 79, 110, 138, 186, 215, 247, 275, 320, 351, 379, 408, 434, 480, 504, 536, 563, 602, 632, 665, 691, 736, 767, 797, 828; Notes and News, 11, 54, 83, 115, 142, 190, 221, 251, 279, 324, 355, 383, 413, 438, 484, 509, 540, 567, 606, 637, 670, 696, 741, 772, 802, 833; Research and Statistics, 15, 65, 96, 131, 151, 201, 234, 264, 336, 366, 397, 424, 446, 495, 521, 553, 577, 618, 649, 681, 707, 751, 784, 815, 847; Supervision, 34
EELLS, W. C., A Centennial History of Education, 57; Freshmen and Sophomores, 258; Professional Magazines, 446
Eldridge, S. and C. D. Clark, Major Problems of Democracy, 594
Employment, Teacher, H. R. MAHLER, 331
Engineering, Summer School, 113
England, Educational, Broadcasting in, 646; Policy, 750
English, Rural Schools, 329; Teachers, Conference at Northwestern University, 565
Ethical Training of Children, E. R. GREGORY, 778
Eugenics, *A bas*, A. S. PEARSE, 612
Examination Board, College Entrance, R. WALTERS, 551
Examinations in Switzerland, 59
Exceptional Boy, 188

FARRAND, M. L., Amer. Assoc. of Univ. Professors, 129
Federal Aid to Education, F. W. BALLOU, 406
Fellowship, Opportunities for Foreign Study, A. M. PALMER, 118; New Education, Fifth International Conference of, 275
Fellowships, for Study in France, 563; Commonwealth Fund, Awards, 667
FENNING, K., Copyright Law Amendment, 282
Fontaine, E. C., Teaching in the Secondary School, 36
Foreign, Educational Conferences, 52; Countries, Education in, 79; Students in Great Britain, 505; Holiday Courses, 550; Vacation Study, A. M. PALMER, 644
Forensic Honor Society, 693
FOSTER, W. T., Leadership in Business, 734
France, Student Ambassadors to, R. A. MICKEL, 363; Fellowships for Study in, 563
FREDERICK, R. W., The Term Report as a College Teaching Device, 256
FREEMAN, F. S., Intelligence Test Ranks and College Grades, 784
French Schools, Overstudy in, 691
Freshman, What He Wants to Know, L. RAINES, 577
Freshmen and Sophomores, W. C. EELLS, 258
FURBAY, J. H., Do College Students Observe? 13

Gander, Sauce for the, 519
GATES, A. I., Educational Psychology, 1
GAVIT, J. P., Definition of Intelligence, 228
Geneva, Conference, C. H. WILLIAMS, 442; School of International Studies, 504
German Minority in Upper Silesian Schools, 247
GESELL, A., Research in Child Development, 765
GEYER, E. M., The New University, 333
GIBSON, J. E., A Student Loan Fund in Mississippi, 224
Gifts, Philanthropic, in 1928, 94
Girls, Our Eye-minded, A. W. BARKER, 490
Glueck, E. T., The Community Use of Schools, 620
GOODNOW, F. J., Commemoration Day Address, 527
Government and Education, 781, 783
Graduate Study at Harvard University, 575

GRANT, A. and W. H. COWLEY, Supply and Demand of Educational Workers, 618
GRAVES, F. P., What a Teacher Should Expect from the School, 557
GRAY, J., State Superintendents, 838
Great Britain, County Libraries and Education in, 79; Education in 1928, 228; Health of School Children, 379; Foreign Students, 505
Greenan, J. T., Citizenship, 31
Greenwich House and Columbia University, 410
GREGORY, E. R., Ethical Training of Children, 778
Grizzell, E. D., Education: Principles and Practice, 621
Grover, K., The Story of May-day, 299
GRUBE, H. and S. R. ELLIS, The Nursery School and Moral Education, 534
Guérard, A. L., The Life and Death of an Ideal, 459
Guggenheim, Exchange Fellowships, 770; Murry and Leonie Foundation, 833
Gullible, Education for, H. G. SHIELDS, 122
GWINN, J. M., School Building Program, 339

H., E. E., Administrative Women in Education, 423
Hagedorn, H., The Dreams of Zach Peters, 32
HAGGERTY, M. E., Collegiate Educational Research, 653
Haiti, The Schools of, 737
Hall Bequest to Colleges of the Near East, 9
Handwriting, Ability in, M. WITTLER, 847
Harkness, Mr., Gift to Columbia University, 507
HARTMANN, G. W., Initial Performance and Ultimate Achievement, 495
Hartshorne and May, Studies in Deceit, 172
Harvard, Univ., Dormitories, 9; House Plan, 140; Residential Colleges, 124, 262; Degree of Master of Education, 189; Graduate Study, 575; Teachers' Assoc., 354, 723; Chemical Laboratories, 483; Study of Languages and Literature, 539; Council on Hispano-American Studies, 694; Graduate School, Language Requirements, 739; Summer School, 801
Hazeltine, M. E., Anniversaries and Holidays, 299
Hazing in American Colleges, V. M. SIMS, 201
Health Day, Child, in N. Y. City, 538
HECKER, J. F., Industry and Education in Soviet Russia, 515
Heckscher Foundation for Children, 605
HENRY, E. A., College Library Expenditures, 746
HENRY, R. L., The "Talkies," 149
Hepner, W. and F., Junior Citizens in Action, 32
HEYL, L., University Dissertations, 808
High School, Teaching in, W. J. KLOPP, 705
High-school, Drop-outs, F. P. OBRIEN, 642; Education, Statistics on, O. L. TROXEL, 441; Students, Selection by Mr. Edison, 604
History of Education, W. C. EELLS, 57
HODGSON, J. G., University Libraries, 825
HOLADAY, P. W., Freshman Counseling, 234
Holland, Public Playing Fields in, 767
Holley, C. E., Elementary Teacher's Technique, 167
Hollingworth, L. S., Psychology of the Adolescent, 297
Holloway, W. J., Curriculum Making, 170
HOLSOPPLE, J. Q. and I. VANOUSE, The Beta Hypothesis of Learning, 15
Honors Work in School and College, J. PARK, 812
Hoover, President, on Education and Public Health, 323
House Plan at Harvard University, 140
How to Study, E. S. JONES, 702
Howard University, 249
Human Relations, Inst. of, at Yale Univ., 219, 564
HUNSICKER, L., Overlapping of Professional Courses, 776
Hunter College, 424
HUTCHINSON, M. E., Athletics and Scholarship, 151

Illiteracy, Reduction of, in the Orient, 50
Improvement of Teaching, G. S. WYKOFF, 58
India, Patna University, 138; Education in, 261; New Universities, 408
Indian, Affairs, 80; Schools, Administration, 217
Industrial Arts Education, F. G. BONSER, 392
Industry, Boys in, 60
Instalment Buying, T. NYLANDER, 330
Insurance, Group, at Yale University, 81; Endowment, L. PIKE, 810
Intelligence, Definition of, J. P. GAVIT, 228; Test Ranks and College Grades, F. S. FREEMAN, 784
Inter-American, Educational, Conference, 216; Federation, 409; Education, 784
International, Bureau of Education, C. MORLEY, 283; Studies, Geneva School of, 504
Investment Problem, Teacher's, A. V. SHAW, 729
Ireland, Northern, Country Schools of, 186
Irish Free State, Child Welfare in, 536

Jerusalem and Saloniki, Universities of, 50
Johns Hopkins Univ., Degrees in Education, 508; Commemoration Day Address, F. J. GOODNOW, 527
JONES, E. S., How to Study, 702
Junior College Graduates, G. M. OKERLUND, 676

Kansas, Univ. of, Summerfield Scholarships, 800
Kelty, M. G., Teaching American History, 301
KEPPEL, A. R., A Phase of Record Keeping, 840
Keys, N., The Improvement of Measuring, 462
KLOPP, W. J., Teaching in the High School, 705
Koos, L. V., The Questionnaire in Education, 467

Ladies, Shall We Join the? W. A. NEILSON, 469
Language, Official, for China, 111; Values, Foreign, J. WARSHAW, 417
Learned Societies, Amer. Council of, Grants, 668; and Fellowships, 830
Lectures, Messenger, at Cornell Univ., 279
Legislation, School, 391
LENNES, N. J. and I. B. FEE, Variability of Individual Performance, 264
LENTZ, T. F., JR., Sex Differences in School Marks, 65
Levine, A. J. and L. Marks, Testing Intelligence and Achievement, 466
Librarians, Carnegie Scholarships for, 668; World Conference of, 828
Libraries, County, and Education in Gt. Britain, 79; and Bibliographies, World Congress, 692; Universities, J. G. HODGSON, 825
Library, Assoc., Amer., Nomination of Officers, 249, 637; International, and Bibliographical Congress, 320; Observation in, D. C. TROTH, 336; American, in Paris, 614; Expenditures, College, E. A. HENRY, 746; Extension in British Columbia, 799; Conference, Summer, at Univ. of Wis., 831
Lindeman, E., Adult Education, 465
Literature by Infection, J. ADAMS, 429

Little, President, and the Univ. of Michigan, 198
London, Univ. of, American Graduate Students in, D. A. ROBERTSON, 121; Medical Schools, Women Students in, 351; School Attendance in, 434; Schools, 494; County Council, Educational Estimates, 632; Children, Eyesight of, 692
LOVEJOY, A. O., Anti-evolution Laws and Religious Neutrality, 133
Lowell, President, Twenty Years of, 677

MCANDREW, W., Matters of Moment, 17, 153, 288; Review of Better Books, 23, 163, 297, 459; Review of Professional Books, 585, 620; Educational Pilgrimage, to Antioch, 449; to Atlanta, 579; Editorial Comment, 709
MacClintock, P. L., Literature in the Elementary School, 304
MCGINNIS, W. C., Professional Improvement and Salaries, 545
MCNEIL, R. H., Training on College Newspapers, 419; Virginia Polytechnic Institute's Service to the State, 779
Magazines, Professional, What Do Prospective Educators Read? W. C. EELLS, 446
Mahan, T. J., Citizenship, 29
MAHLER, H. R., Teacher Employment, 331
MAHONEY, R. H., Boys' Club in Urban High School, 89
Massachusetts, Legislature, 693
MASSEY, V., The Colleges of Canada, 369
Mathews, S., Jesus on Social Institutions, 32
MAY, E. P., Wellesley Graduates, 147
Measurement Movement, Educational, C. W. ODELL, 751
Measures, Self-scored, L. N. YEPSEN, 681
Menge, E. J., The Laws of Living Things, 622
Mexico, Educational Movements in, M. C. DAVIS, 547
Michigan, Children's Fund of, 539; Univ. of, Resignation of President, 115; School of Music of, 187; and President Little, 198; and High Schools, Cooperation between, I. M. SMITH, 420; Courses in Education, 437; Summer Session, 565
MICKEL, R. A., Student Ambassadors to France, 363
Middle States and Md., Accredited Schools of, 481
Mifflin, Lloyd, Memorial Home for Teachers, 351
Military Schooling, 518
MILLER, D. F., Ecological and Economic Studies, 571
MILLER, G. A., Hindu-Arabic Numerals, 390
Mississippi, Student Loan Fund, J. E. GIBSON, 224
MONROE, W. S. and M. R. HULL, Book Reviews, 521
Monroe, W. S., Directing Learning in the High School, 305; and Others, Ten Years of Educational Research, 297
MOON, G. R., Reliability of Rating Schemes, 366
MORLEY, C., Int. Bureau of Education, 283
MOULTON, E. L., Dormitory Values for Students, 362
Music Week, 381
Musical Education, Ditson Bequest to, 769

National Educ. Assoc., Atlanta Meeting, 680; Dept. of Superintendence, 61, 125, 140, 269, 309, 339, 399; Dept. of Supervisors, 95, 189, 695; Council of Education of, J. K. NORTON, 819
Natural History, Allegany School of, 353; American Museum of, 539
NEEDHAM, J. G., Middle-school Biology, 183
NEILSON, W. A., Shall We Join the Ladies? 469
Negro Elementary and Secondary Education, 481
New, York, City, Schools, Short Time in, 82; School Teachers, Salaries, 217; Building Program, 382; Child Health Day, 538; Million Pupils of, 814; State, Dept. of Educ., Appropriations, 186; Earnings of Continuation School Boys, 248; Savings, 506; Rural Schools in, 322; College for Teachers, 436; Normal School Buildings, 481; Guidance Counselors and Bureaus, 634; Continuation School Boys, 799; Univ. Junior High-school Conference, 412; Honorary Degrees, 802; Jersey, State Educational Survey, 218
News, Education Becomes, 615
Newspapers, College, Training on, R. H. MCNEIL, 419
NORLIN, G., Going Straight in Athletics, 205
North Carolina, Univ. of, Legislative Appropriations, 250; and President Chase, 678
Northwestern Univ., F. A. Austin Scholarship Foundation, 382; Conference of English Teachers, 565
NORTON, J. K., National Council of Education, 819
Nott, Eliphalet, F. P. DAY, 625
Numerals, Hindu-Arabic, G. A. MILLER, 390
Nursery School, and Child Development, R. S. WOODWORTH, 497; and Moral Education, H. GRUBE and S. R. ELLIS, 534; of Western Reserve Univ., 769
Nursing, School of, Yale Univ., 188; Western Reserve Univ., 353
NYLANDER, T., Instalment Buying, 330

Oberlin College, E. H. WILKINS, 334
OBRIEN, F. P., Cooperative Research, 642
O'BRIEN, R. E., Roman Catholic Schools, 595
ODELL, C. W., Educational Measurement Movement, 751
Ohio State Educational Conference, 232
OKERLUND, G. M., Junior College Graduates, 676
Ontario, Education in, 768
Oregon, Univ. of, Summer Session, 482
Orient, Reduction of Illiteracy in, 50
Orleans, J. and G. Sealy, Objective Testing, 306
Outlook, Educational, 59
Overlapping of Professional Courses, L. HUNSICKER, 776
Oxford, Univ. of, Rhodes House at, 633

PALMER, A. M., Foreign Fellowship Opportunities, 118; Foreign Vacation Study, 644
Pan-American Countries, Exchange of Literature, 216
Parent, Teacher and Student Cooperation, L. D. CROW, 553; -Teacher, Movement, S. C. ADAMS, 474; Work of, F. V. WATKINS, 599
Paris, British Institute, 51; Club for Women Students, 409; American Library, B. STEVENSON, 614
PARK, J., Honors Work in School and College, 812
Park, M. G., Problem Outline in Introduction to Teaching, 589
Parks, National, Educational Features of, 380
Patna, The University of, 138
PEARSE, A. S., *A bas* Eugenics, 612
Peking Union Medical College, 797
Pennsylvania, Univ. of, Schoolmen's Week at, R. W., 446; and Valley Forge, 507

Pensions, Mothers', T. E. SULLENGER, 424; Carnegie, 574
Performance, Individual, Variability of, N. J. LENNES and I. B. FEE, 264; Initial, and Ultimate Achievement, G. W. HARTMANN, 495
Period Education in Erewhon, A. D. WEEKS, 675
Personality *vs.* Methods, J. A. BOYD, 489
Personnel, Workers, Seminar for, D. H. T., 493; Public, Administration, Bureau of, 694
Philosophy, Chicago Doctors of, M. O. WILSON, 815
Photoplay, College Course on, 219
Physical Training Institute, Cuban, 666
Physicians, School, Amer. Assoc. of, 564
PIKE, L., Insurance Endowment, 810
PIRNIE, J. A., Educational Research, 123
Pittsburgh Survey, 537
Playground and Recreation Assoc. of Amer., 354
Playing Fields, Public, in Holland, 767
Politics and Schools, 392
Portugal, National Education Board in, 536
Practical in Education, Who is? C. D. CHAMPLIN, 700
PRESSEY, L. C., The Women in "American Men of Science," 96
Princeton University, New Buildings, 321
Prizes for Essays on Highway Safety, 604
Profession of Teaching, W. C. BAGLEY, 101
Professional Training in Education, M. L. CARREON, 243
Professors, University, Salaries of, 285
PROTZMAN, M. I., Student Rating of College Teaching, 513
Psychology, Educational, A. I. GATES, 1
Putnam, Herbert, and the Library of Congress, 484

Quotations, 14, 59, 92, 124, 150, 198, 228, 261, 285, 329, 366, 391, 424, 443, 494, 518, 549, 574, 614, 646, 677, 749, 783, 843

Radio Education, 740, 749, 831
RADOSAVLJEVICH, P. R., Tolstoy's Experimental School, 175, 208
RAINES, L., What a Freshman Wants to Know, 577
RAINEY, H. P., Liberal Arts Curriculum, 258
Rating, Schemes, Reliability of, G. R. MOON, 366; of College Teaching by Students, M. I. PROTZMAN, 513
Record Keeping, A. R. KEPPEL, 840
Registrars, Seventh Annual Institute for, 277; Amer. Assoc. of, 616
Reports, 60, 94, 125, 199, 230, 262, 286, 334, 395, 444, 550, 575, 678, 750, 781, 845
Research, Educational, J. A. PIRNIE, 123; Fund, of Dept. of Superintendence, 125; The Subvention of, G. M. WHIPPLE, 443; Cooperative, F. P. OBRIEN, 642; Philosophy and Organization of, B. R. BUCKINGHAM, 755
Residential Colleges at Harvard and Yale, 124, 262
Retirement of Professors, 199
Rhodes, Trust, 505; House at Univ. of Oxford, 633
ROBERTSON, D. A., Amer. Graduate Students in London, 121
ROBINSON, F. B., President's Address before the Association of Urban Universities, 237
Rockefeller Foundation, 53, 768
Roman Catholic Elementary Schools, R. E. O'BRIEN, 595
Rugg, H. and A. Shumaker, The Child-centered School, 163
Rural, Education, T. H. EATON, 75; Schools, in N. Y. State, 322; English, 329; Junior High-school Buildings, 381; High Schools, 434
RUSSELL, C., Westfield Conference for Young Teachers, 648
Russia, Soviet, Industry and Education in, J. F. HECKER, 515
Rutgers University, Reorganization of, 278
RYAN, W. C., JR., The Department of Superintendence, 309; American Secondary Education, 787

Safety, Highway, Prizes for Essays on, 604
Salaries, of Professors, 10, 285; of N. Y. City School Teachers, 217; and Professional Improvement, W. C. MCGINNIS, 545; Teachers, Index of, 603
Saloniki and Jerusalem, Universities of, 50
Sargent School and Boston University, 670
SCHEIDEMANN, N. V., Earliest Recorded Objective Test, 702
Schmidt, G. A., Vocational Education in Agriculture, 303
Scholarship of Applicants for Teaching Positions, M. A. STEINER, 388
Scholarships, Summerfield, at Univ. of Kansas, 800
SCHUTTE, T. H., Educational Waste, 195
Science and Mathematics Teachers, Central Assoc. of, 95
Scott, Z., R. Congdon, H. Peet and L. Frazee, Open-Door Language Series, 305
Secondary Education, American, W. C. RYAN, JR., 787
Self-help for College Students, 738
Sex Differences, in School Marks, T. F. LENTZ, JR., 65; in History Retention, S. J. BASSETT, 397
SHAW, A. V., The Teacher's Investment Problem, 729
SHIELDS, H. G., Education for the Gullible, 122
SHUMWAY, W., Curriculum in College of Liberal Arts and Sciences at Univ. of Illinois, 572
Sight-saving Classes, 738
SIMS, V. M., Hazing in American Colleges, 201
SMITH, I. M., Cooperation between the High Schools and the University of Michigan, 420
Snedden, D., Educational Sociology, 586
Social Science Research Council Fellows, 444
Societies and Meetings, 61, 95, 126, 232, 446, 519, 551, 616, 648, 680
Southern California, Univ. of, Summer School, 278; Dept. of Philosophy, 695
Spain, Student Disorders in, 380; Progressive Education in, 549
Spanish Universities, 563
Special Correspondence, 89, 118, 147, 194, 224, 258, 283, 333, 363, 420, 442, 491, 515, 547, 572, 614, 644, 702, 747, 779, 812, 842
Standardization of High Schools and Colleges, 352
Stanford Univ., Appointments, 81; Reorganization, 286
State, Laws and Compulsory Education, 276; and the State University, M. A. BRANNON, 683
STEERE, H. J., Character and Scholastic Achievement, 707
STEINER, M. A., Scholarship of Applicants for Teaching Positions, 388
STEVENSON, B., American Library in Paris, 614
Stillman, B. W., Training Children to Study, 300
Stone, C. R., Silent and Oral Reading, 168
SULLENGER, T. E., Mother's Pensions, 424
Summer School, for Engineering, 113; Univ. of Colorado, 114; Brazil, 139; Univ. Southern Calif., 278; N. Y. State College for Teachers, 436; Univ. of Oregon, 482; Univ. of Michigan, 565;

Columbia Univ., 670, J. J. COSS, 842; Harvard Univ., 801
Superintendence, Dept. of, Cleveland Meeting, 61; F. D. BOYNTON, 140; W. C. RYAN, JR., 309; Address of President, 269, 339; J. DEWEY, 399; Atlanta Meeting, 801; Research Fund, 125
Superintendents, City, M. M. ALLTUCKER, 649; State, Appointing, J. GRAY, 838
Supervision, Cooperative, F. L. WRIGHT and J. L. BRACKEN, 747
Supervisors of Instruction, Conference, 95, 189, 695
Supply and Demand of Educational Workers, A. GRANT and W. H. COWLEY, 618
Support, Federal and Local, of Schools, 845
Survey, Educational, New Jersey, 218; Pittsburgh, 537
Survival Rates of Pupils in Public Schools, 537
Sweden, Commercial Education in, 112
Switzerland, Examinations in, 59

T., D. H., Seminar for Personnel Workers, 493
TAEUSCH, C. F., Business and Education, 723
"Talkies," R. L. HENRY, 149
Teacher, What He Should Expect from the School, F. P. GRAVES, 557
Teaching, Improvement of, G. S. WYKOFF, 58
Tenure and Training of City School Superintendents, M. M. ALLTUCKER, 649
Term Report as a College Teaching Device, R. W. FREDERICK, 256
Test, Objective, Earliest Recorded, N. V. SCHEIDEMANN, 702
Time Expenditure by High-school Teachers, M. WALKER and H. R. LASLETT, 131
Tolstoy's Experimental School, P. R. RADOSAVLJEVICH, 175, 208
Tourist Third Class, Student, H. R. BRUSH, 561
Trans-Mississippi West, A. T. W., 548
Trojan Air College, 411
TROTH, D. C., Observation in the Library, 336
TROXEL, O. L., Statistics on High-school Education, 441
Turkey, Adult Education in, 110

Union College, 614
United States Dept. of Education, W. J. COOPER, 317
University, Professors, Amer. Assoc. of, M. L. FARRAND, 129; Club, American, of New York, 322; The New, E. M. GEYER, 333
Urban Universities, Assoc. of, President's Address, F. B. ROBINSON, 237

Valedictorians and Salutatorians in American Colleges, R. D. WELLONS, 643
Van Waters, M., Parents on Probation, 166
Vedic, International School of, British Branch of, 275
Ventilation of Schoolrooms, 443
Virginia Polytechnic Institute, R. H. MCNEIL, 779
Vocational, Training, Federal Appropriations, 139; Guidance and Placement, Cleveland Meetings, 190

W., A. T., The Trans-Mississippi West, 548
W., R., Schoolmen's Week at the University of Pennsylvania, 446
Wales, Intermediate Education in, 737
WALKER, M. and H. R. LASLETT, Time Expenditure by High-school Teachers, 131
Wallin, J. E. W., Education of Handicapped Children; Clinical and Abnormal Psychology, 623
Walsh, L. and M., History and Organization of Education in Pennsylvania, 168
WALTERS, R., Assoc. of Amer. Colleges, 126; Registration in Canadian Universities, 375; New England Assoc. of Colleges and Secondary Schools, 519; College Entrance Examination Board, 551
WARSHAW, J., Foreign Language Values, 417
WASHBURNE, C., Winnetka, 37
Waste, Educational, T. H. SCHUTTE, 195
WATKINS, F. V., Parent-Teacher Work, 599
Week, Education, American, 506
WEEKS, A. D., Period Education in Erewhon, 675
WEET, H. S., The Articulation Commission, 345
Wellesley Graduates, Occupations of, E. P. MAY, 147
WELLING, R., Congenial Work for Boys, 14
WELLONS, R. D., Valedictorians and Salutatorians in American Colleges, 643
Wesleyan University, Bennett Lectures, 82
West Point, Entrance to, 739
Western Reserve Univ., School of Nursing, 353; Nursery School, 769
Westfield Conference for Young Teachers, C. RUSSELL, 648
WHEELER, J. L., Educational Books of 1928, 230
WHIPPLE, G. M., The Subvention of Research, 443
Wickham, E. K., Children's Behavior and Teachers' Attitudes, 592
Wiley, J. A., Silent Reading and Study, 33
WILKINS, E. H., Oberlin College, 334
WILLIAMS, C. H., The Geneva Conference, 442
WILSON, M. O., Chicago Doctors of Philosophy, 815
Winnetka, C. WASHBURNE, 37
Wisconsin, Univ. of, Experimental College of, 750; Summer Library Conference, 831
WITTLER, M., Ability in Handwriting, 847
Women, in "American Men of Science," L. C. PRESSEY, 96; in College Libraries, J. I. WYER, 227; Administrative, E. E. H., 423
WOODWORTH, R. S., The Nursery School and Child Development, 497
World, Federation of Education Associations, 248; Congress on Libraries and Bibliographies, 692
World's Fair at Chicago, 669
WRIGHT, F. L. and J. L. BRACKEN, Cooperative Supervision, 747
WYER, J. I., Women in College Libraries, 227
WYKOFF, G. S., Improvement of Teaching, 58

Yale Univ., Group Insurance, 81; Residential Colleges, 124; School of Nursing, 188; Institute of Human Relations, 219, 564; Dept. of Education, 251; President Angell on Affairs at, 321; Appointments, 635
Yard, R. S., Our Federal Lands, 306
YEPSEN, L. N., Self-scored Measures, 681
Ypres, British School at, 798

Zirbes, L., Practice in Reading, 33

SCHOOL AND SOCIETY

EDITED BY J. McKEEN CATTELL

WITH WHICH IS COMBINED THE

EDUCATIONAL REVIEW

EDITED BY WILLIAM McANDREW

Volume XXIX SATURDAY, JANUARY 5, 1929 Number 732

RECENT ADVANCES IN EDUCATIONAL PSYCHOLOGY[1]

By Professor A. I. GATES

TEACHERS COLLEGE, COLUMBIA UNIVERSITY

At the request of the president of the American Association for the Advancement of Science, I shall attempt in this paper to survey in semi-popular form the outstanding contributions of scientific study in the fields with which I am least unfamiliar. The paper will deal briefly with recent investigations of the objectives of education, the processes of teaching and learning, the characteristics of human nature, their measurement and educational significance and trends in the formulation of principles in the general science of educational psychology.

Investigations of Educational Objectives

Educational endeavor is probably most definite and fruitful when it is guided by intelligible objectives. Until recently it has been customary to assume that the task of determining the aims and purposes of education is the special function of philosophy. According to the traditional point of view, philosophy and science represent distinct enterprises, each making its contributions by means of unique methods. Although some of the sciences still declare that problems of values and purposes lie outside of their scope, the sharp demarcation of philosophy and science is breaking down, at least in education. Indeed, an important recent advance, worthy of note on this occasion, is the increase in mutual understanding and cooperation of these two groups of workers. The activities of philosopher and scientist in education have become so closely correlated, in fact, that any effort to distinguish them sharply results in exaggeration. Thus the statement that in education the philosopher is the person who thinks without actually doing experiments invites the converse assertion that the scientist is the person who does experiments without actually thinking. More and more the philosophy of education is becoming an outgrowth of the science in the form of generalization and hypotheses and more and more the science is endeavoring to put into effect for purposes of appraisal the suggestions of philosophy.

The prevailing philosophy emphasizes social usefulness as the objective of education and the utilization of natural interests and individual aptitudes of pupils as the means. This point of view is a generalization of the results of studies of the needs of

[1] Address of the retiring chairman and vice-president, Section of Education, American Association for the Advancement of Science, New York, December 29, 1928.

social life on the one hand and the characteristics of human learning on the other. The social criterion of educational values found justification in those early scientific studies which disclosed the fallacies of faculty psychology and its corollary, mental discipline, and which led to the discovery of common elements as the basis of the transfer of experience and to the notion of social utility as a source of motivation. Recent years have witnessed new applications of scientific methods to the study of the characteristics and needs of society, as a means of determining more definitely the objectives of education. Although it is still in the initial stage, this vigorous movement constitutes, perhaps, one of the most significant of recent advances in the science of education.

The problem of determining what particular adjustments and resources are essential to a fruitful participation in life has, within recent years, led to scores of studies designed to ascertain precisely the uses to which specific facts and skills may be put in the affairs of different classes of people. These studies have already shown that many facts and skills essential for constructive family, social, civic and economic life are not provided by existing educational agencies. Thus, recent studies by Rugg and others have shown that many concepts and intellectual experiences essential to a constructive participation in the solution of current social, economic and civic problems are not provided by the school or other agencies. Similar studies have shown, on the other hand, that much that is now taught satisfies no genuine need in the lives of most people. Thus, a recent study by Bowden indicates that 85 per cent. of the arithmetic, beyond the four operations of simple addition, subtraction, multiplication and division, now taught in the typical school, is of practically no utility to 75 per cent. of the adult population.

Studies designed to ascertain what facts and skills are valuable at the present day and what ones are now taught must be supplemented by investigations of which of these will and will not be useful in the future. To the prediction of the requirements of the future, scientific methods are now being applied. Investigators in this field at once discovered the inadequacy of available technique of sociological research for accomplishing their many purposes, especially the prediction of social, economic and political trends. The result has been a lively endeavor to develop better methods of investigation. Indeed, the most significant aspect of recent work by educationists is the indication that improved techniques for sociological study may be rapidly developed.

Investigations of Teaching and Learning

The problem of what to teach, with which the new type of alliance of students of the philosophy and science of education seems to be mainly concerned, is intimately tied up with the question of how to teach. Three years ago Dean Henmon and others deplored what then appeared to be a serious neglect of experimental studies of the learning and teaching processes. It is gratifying to say that since that time scientific workers have shown a renewed activity in these fields of research. In nearly every direction, studies of learning have been extended.

There has been, in the first place, an extension in the range of ages of subjects studied. Baldwin, Gesell and others have carried researches of learning to the cradle and Thorndike and others have pursued them nearer than ever before toward the grave. These investigators have so impressively demonstrated the hitherto unappreciated capacity of individuals at both extremes to learn more and better than they now do that new types of educational agencies for infants and adults both seem to be needed. The ability of infants to acquire various emotional and motor adjustments, likes and dislikes, temperamental and volitional habits has so impressed several students that the time-honored theory of instinctive behavior, supported by such master scientists as Darwin and James, has been bluntly denied. The most fundamental adjustments and dispositions of the child, they declare, are not based upon instincts or native tendencies but upon habits acquired in infancy. While the majority of authorities consider that habit formation is greatly influenced by native endowment, they nevertheless acknowledge the importance of adequate guidance in infancy as a means of planting the seeds from which desirable temperamental, volitional and character traits may grow.

To the many persons who have assumed that the period from six to sixteen or twenty is the prime of life for acquiring information and skill, the work of Thorndike and others on adult learning has been something of a revelation, as well as a source of satisfaction to those of us who have passed the age long considered ideal. Thorndike's studies indicate that the zenith of power for acquiring information, ideas and the more subtle skills comes in the early twenties. The decade from twenty to thirty is superior to any other; the decade from thirty to forty is at least equal to the span from ten to twenty, and even at forty-five, a man can hold his own with his son at the presumably versatile and receptive age of fifteen. If middle-age can equal youth at youth's own intellectual specialty, adulthood may continue doggedly to claim superiority in its field of alleged supremacy —general and practical judgment.

The facts revealed by recent studies of adult learning not only justify the present interest in providing for the entire citizenry institutional opportunities and guidance for continuing actively to learn until old age, but they also challenge the wisdom of our present system of concentrating schooling entirely in the fewest possible years and bringing it to an abrupt, and too often, a final conclusion at sixteen, or some other legally prescribed age. To secure the advantages of education in the more potent years of the late teens and early twenties, to make schooling more useful and desirable by relating it more directly to the needs of practical life and to increase the probability of a sound start in undertaking the full responsibilities of the world's work, a gradual transition from the control of the school to life at large seems desirable. The success of work under guidance as a final stage in the preparation of the physician, the lawyer, the school superintendent and others suggests the value of some form of internship in community life under guidance of the school. If the student physician who is in the top five per cent. in intelligence, is over twenty-five years of age and has received the longest and most rigid training still needs a considerable period of guidance after securing his degree, the average person, who is much younger, less intelligent and less practically trained, when he completes his schooling, would seem even more seriously to need a period of internship in his life's work.

INVESTIGATIONS OF TECHNIQUES OF TEACHING AND LEARNING

Within the last two years there have been gratifying advances in the study of the principles underlying efficiency in learning.

In certain recent studies of the influence of various factors on the rate and limits of learning, such as those published in the last Yearbook of the National Society for the Study of Education, it appears that *differences* in native aptitude among learners play a very prominent rôle in achievement, whereas various *differences* in methods, teachers, time allotments, per capita expenditures, home study and the like, as they now exist in general practice, exert a relatively small influence. These results have led certain educationists to conclude hastily that native capacities alone fully determine a pupil's level of achievement and that, conversely, methods, materials and teachers exert a trivial influence. This interpretation is quite unjustified. The studies show merely that certain factors superficially different are really substantially the same in the vital characteristics. To prove that two methods are equal is not to demonstrate that both are impotent. A survey of the whole field of study of methods of learning, furthermore, will reveal the fact that there are vital features in which variations in procedure produce marked differences in the efficiency of learning. Thus while Thorndike found in a general survey that the transfer value of learning depended more on the intelligence of the pupil than on the nature of the subject pursued, Woodrow found that, irrespective of intelligence, the transfer of improvement from the same subject varied greatly with the methods of instruction and study adopted. Again, while Mosher found that the conventional phonetic method and non-phonetic methods in reading gave substantially equal results, Courtis found that a new method of teaching primary reading produced results greatly superior to those obtained from current methods. There are, in other words, many methods, differing greatly in appearance that vary but slightly in potency; and other methods, even less obviously unlike, which differ greatly in effectiveness.

New Conceptions of the Learning-Teaching Process

For some time, the outcomes of research have been pointing toward a new conception of teaching and learning. According to the traditional point of view, education involved the selection of facts and skills which instructors were to teach and pupils were to learn. Effort and strain on the part of both teacher and pupil were assumed to be necessary features of education. The radically new point of view to which accumulated evidence points has been voiced in several forms in recent years but nowhere more clearly than in an address by John Dewey read in March of this year and from which I quote.

"The question of method (now) takes on a new . . . form. It is no longer a question of how the teacher is to instruct and how the pupil is to study. The problem is to find what conditions must be fulfilled in order that study and learning will naturally and necessarily take place, what conditions must be present so that pupils will make the responses which can not help having learning as their consequences. The pupil's mind is no longer to be on study or learning. It is given to doing the things that the situation calls for, while learning is the result."

As I see them, research activities have recently been directed with increasing definition toward the discovery of the conditions which will "naturally and necessarily" evoke the responses and establish the insight, skill, appreciation and habits desired. It is becoming increasingly clear that the same principles are to be followed whether the problem is to arrange a complex social situation so as to induce a desired type of conduct reaction or to organize a book page, so as to call into life a useful form of reaction to words or figures. Thus recent research shows that reading, arithmetic or history is mastered most effectively not by drilling upon phonetics, multiplication tables or columns of facts and definitions, but by providing materials so arranged that the activities called for appeal to the pupil as eminently worth while and so organized mechanically that the desired learnings can not fail to result. This new point of view calls for an intimate knowledge of the reaction tendencies of children and the elements in the mechanical or objective situation which determine the character of the response. It may be freely predicted that this new conception of method, like the social efficiency theory of educational objectives, will bring about marked changes in the textbooks and other material, in the technique of the teacher and in the character of student activities.

Studies of Results of Present Educational Systems

Among the many significant recent contributions must be included several comprehensive studies of the results obtained from schooling as it is now conducted. H. F. Clark's efforts to ascertain the financial returns from investing different numbers of years in school; Haggerty's studies of the general cultural outcomes of different college courses and Thorndike's investigations of the influence of various high-school subjects upon intellectual abilities have yielded results of greatest significance. That schooling of the present type beyond a certain point (which doubtless varies widely among different individuals) may be an extravagance that benefits neither the individual nor society seems not unlikely. That many courses in college and other schools fail to justify their claim of advancing cultural values seems probable. That such subjects as Latin, mathematics and the physical sciences as now taught in high school excel very slightly, if at all, such subjects as civics or biology, or even stenography, manual arts or cooking, in increasing "general ability to think with all kinds of data" seems very probable, indeed. If such findings are verified by further research, a need for and, fortunately, also to some extent, the character of reform in the curriculum and in educational guidance will be indicated.

Studies of Educational Diagnosis and Measurement

Scientific study has revealed enormous variations among individuals in the abilities essential to the acquisition of social, vocational, civic, ethical, recreational, physical and intellectual resources. To enable each child to develop in the happiest and socially most productive manner requires an educational program differentiated both in degree and kind. Means of determining during the elementary school period the type and amount of further education that will best advance the interests of the individual and society is one of the most crucial of present needs. The last two years have witnessed important advances in the measurement of human performance and in the development of techniques essential for educational diagnosis and prognosis.

Improvements in instruments for appraising achievement in the familiar school subjects and skills from kindergarten to the university have been accompanied by more conspicuous advances in gauging conduct, emotional, volitional and appreciative reactions. The work of May and Hartshorne has shown the feasibility of measuring a child's status on a scale ranging from greatest honesty or reliability to the greatest dishonesty or deceit. If it is possible accurately to measure these aspects of behavior which the subject is likely to try to conceal, the outlook for measuring other forms of conduct seem promising indeed. Lehman and Witty have opened up a field of measuring capacities and inclinations in children's avocational activities. Rogers and others have made possible an approach to scientific guidance in athletics and sports. Thurstone, Burt, and others have shown the way to achieve practically useful measures of the appreciative, emotional and volitional capacities and abilities. The achievement of these workers within the last few years is sufficient, I believe, to justify the statement that our leaders in the field of measurement, if provided with reasonable financial resources, could, in a short time, devise practically useful tests of any known human ability, interest, appreciation or special talent.

The workers in the field of human measurement have recently made some extremely important technical and theoretical advances. The achievements of Thorndike, Courtis, Kelley, Terman and Freeman are particularly notable. Thorndike has discovered methods of disentangling the factors of rate, accuracy, difficulty, range and the like, several of which have previously been represented in unknown proportions and relation in the scores of most tests. Courtis and others have devised means of determining the functional relations of speed and accuracy, of combining them and of predicting variations in one brought about by changes in the other. Although the phenomena which the psychologists study are influenced by several variables not as yet fully detected and measured, such studies as those of Courtis and Thorndike promise eventually to yield functional laws similar, in all essentials, to those found in physics.

Spearman in England and Kelley in America, both utilizing new and ingenious but different statistical methods, have added greatly to our knowledge of the nature of the fundamental factors underlying human abilities and aptitudes. Spearman would base the practical program of prognosis of abilities upon the measurement of a small number of general factors, a larger number of group factors found in a series of activities and a still larger number of special abilities specific to particular tasks. Kelley has undertaken the most essential and hitherto baffling task of reducing the almost numberless socially valuable activities involved in industrial, scholastic, esthetic and recreational life to a small number of types or components. To reduce all forms of achievement to a few constituent factors would bring the task of appraising human abilities within the range of practical accomplishment. Kelley's work, indeed, promises to result in one of the useful contributions in the history of human measurement.

Advances in Educational Guidance and Prognosis

To achieve the objectives of education, it it necessary not only to determine the abilities, skills, habits or inclinations a pupil now possesses, but also to predict the outcomes of future education. Prognosis and guidance depend upon our ability to estimate in quantitative terms the degree of capacity implied by a measure of performance. The problem of measuring native capacity or potentiality has been clouded by the popular conception that acquired ability is one thing and native talent another and that, consequently, a test of the former can not be a measure of the latter. Since, in practice, it is true that we must always measure acquired ability or conduct, it would seem, therefore, that we can not gauge capacity. Recent research, however, seems to show that when certain educative influences are equal, individual differences in native *aptitude* will be revealed by measures which portray differences in *ability*. The practical problem of measuring capacity, then, is not one of discovering tests of functions uninfluenced by education or experience, but one of finding under what conditions educative influences are nearly enough equal to result in making a measure of acquired ability a useful indication of capacity and of making allowances for the significant environmental variations that may be found among the children in a typical American community. Terman and Freeman have taken an active part in investigating this problem in connection with various mental, motor and volitional traits. The results of a list of nearly two hundred studies on some phase of this problem which they have made or assembled during the last three years indicate that there is no insurmountable technical difficulty to be faced in appraising the constitutional equipment underlying capacity or potentiality. Indeed, in the case of most intellectual and motor functions the task seems easier than many of us had previously feared.

Although prognosis of educational and vocational outcomes falls far short of the validity of prediction in some of the physical sciences, it compares favorably with foresight in some of the older biological fields. It is probably true, for example, that the intellectual status which a child of seven will attain at twenty can be predicted more accurately than can his physical health, stamina, or weight and nearly as accurate as his height.

Advances in Educational Diagnosis and Remedial Work

In the field of diagnosis of special human disabilities, a field in which medicine has achieved the most notable advances, rapid strides have also been made. In substantially all essentials, the diagnosis of defects in musical talents by Seashore, of disabilities in reading by Gray or of susceptibility to nervous disturbances by Wells is similar to the diagnostic technique used by physicians. The taking of case histories, the use of mechanical instruments and functional tests, the theory of syndrones or patterns of symptomatic deficiencies are essentially the same. It appears, moreover, that competent students thoroughly trained by Judd and Buswell could diagnose difficulties in arithmetic skills or that those thoroughly trained by C. T. or W. S. Gray could diagnose disabilities in reading or those trained by Horn could analyze troubles in spelling with a degree of thoroughness and accuracy equal to the average physician's analysis of the causes of disorders of digestion or circulation among school children. Prescription of remedial treatment for certain educational ills by experts seems now to be as definite and valid as prescription for improving many of the more complex physical disorders.

Recent Trends in Methods of Research

As professional services in medicine became more useful when the questionnaire about subjective symptoms was replaced by objective instruments or procedures such as the electric cardiograph and the chemical analysis of the secretions of the stomach, so in education, practice may hope to be improved by the development of objective measures of psychological characteristics. And quite as knowledge of physiological functions and their interrelations was obtained mainly by objective methods of research, so a better understanding of mental functions and their associations is likely to be achieved by means of quantitative data. To observe that Courtis, Kelley, Thorndike, Symonds and others in this country are rounding out systems of educational psychology based almost exclusively on quantitative rather than on the traditional mixture of observational, subjective analytic, semi-experimental and test methods, is to detect a significant sign of the times. The work of Spearman in England has in some respects been more striking. He has, for the first time in history, published a system of principles of psychology based entirely upon statistical analysis of the results of mental and educational tests.

It would be misleading, however, to imply that all of our creditable systems of working hypotheses are based on statistical analyses of the results of mental and educational tests. There has, in fact, been a marked increase in the number of investigators who prefer experimental analysis by means of rigid and complete control of smaller numbers of subjects to statistical evaluations of groups. The Gestalt psychology, which was developed chiefly in Germany and is being tested for and applied to education by Ogden and others in this country, depends chiefly on experimental rather than statistical techniques. In America there has been a notable increase in experimental work by a group of investigators whose point of view is considerably broader but no less scientific than that of the so-called Behaviorists. On the other hand, the contributions of such subjectivists as Freud are regarded more as the highly suggestive speculations of novelists and biographers than as products of science. There is clearly a tendency in educational psychology to consider seriously only those explanatory systems which have a substantial basis in quantitative and verifiable data.

Trends in Systematic Accounts of Educational Psychology

As the result of a marked disposition of scientific workers to specialize in one or another method of attack, there is now appearing a larger number of really distinctive systems of explanatory principles than we have ever had before. Since progress in the science is made by extensive tests and applications of rival hypotheses, this specialization is constructive and desirable.

But, if the leading men in science can not tell which of the several different systems of principles is most valid, it would seem that the professional workers would be in a state of embarrassing uncertainty in their practice. Due to the fact that application usually lags considerably behind discovery of a principle, the conflict of theories has a less disturbing effect on practice than might be expected. As in medicine and other professions, the existence of several rival theories may have wholesome effects. The resulting uncertainty may tend to correct an attitude of complacency and dogmatism which has been an unfortunate characteristic of the school man of the past. It may even arouse those engaged in professional work to cooperate with investigators in the search for true principles of guidance. Indeed, there is some evidence that the appearance of rival theories in recent years has greatly stimulated research in the professional field.

Advances in Use of School as a Laboratory

One of the most significant movements in recent times has been the opening of the doors of the schools to scientific investigations. As nearly as I can ascertain, the number of public and private institutions maintaining a research department devoted in whole or part to scientific investigations has nearly doubled in the last three years. Already many of these schools have made important contributions. Not only have they tested rival theories by applying them to practice in the natural school setting, but they have also uncovered fresh hypotheses which command the attention of the general science. The public, moreover, in an increasing measure, is willing not only to tolerate experimentation in the schools but even to support it. The statement that "the school is the greatest laboratory of democracy," which we have heretofore made with a kind of poetic license, is perhaps approaching literal validity.

EDUCATIONAL EVENTS

BRITISH STUDENTS IN AMERICA

The British Committee of Award of the Commonwealth Fund Fellowships has announced that it is now prepared to receive applications for the fellowships to be awarded in 1929. It is reported that after four years' working the scheme has been so successful that the directors of the fund in New York have increased the number of ordinary fellowships from 20 to 30.

The ordinary fellowships are tenable at an approved American university for two years. They are open to persons of British descent domiciled in England, Scotland, Wales or Ireland who are graduates of recognized universities therein and are unmarried and not more than thirty years of age. Women as well as men may apply. Provision amounting to approximately £600 per annum will be made for the total expenditure involved during the tenure of a fellowship. Applications must be forwarded through the authorities of the university or college of which the candidate is, or was, a member.

The committee also announces this year five fellowships for graduates of Dominion universities and three fellowships for persons of British descent holding appointments under the British Government, the Government of India, or the Government of a British Dominion, Colony, Protectorate or Mandated Territory.

The committee has issued a report of the working of the plan in 1928. It states that the number of candidates during the year was 100 (75 men, 25 women). With two exceptions, applications were received from every university in Great Britain and Ireland, and candidates from nearly all the universities were interviewed.

The committee is anxious to help returning fellows, so far as lies in its power, to secure posts for which they are fitted, and to cooperate whenever possible with the University Appointments Boards or with individual heads and professors in the universities. The secretary of the committee will give information at any time in regard to the qualifications of any fellows approaching the completion of the tenure of one of the fellowships.

THE HALL BEQUEST TO COLLEGES OF THE NEAR EAST

THE residue of the estate of the late Charles M. Hall, "father of aluminum," amounting to $10,000,000, will be distributed by his trustees to higher educational institutions of the Near East and the Orient, the trustees announced, according to the Associated Press.

Their action is in line with the stipulation in Mr. Hall's will that the money be used for "educational purposes in Japan, Continental Asia, Turkey and the Balkan states of Europe." He left to the trustees, Arthur V. Davis, of Pittsburgh, and Homer H. Johnson, of Cleveland, decision as to the manner of distribution, either as endowment to existing institutions or independent of them. The trustees said they made their decision after consultation with educational leaders who had made a special study of relations between the United States and the Near and Far East.

The twenty-one institutions among which the money is to be distributed were announced as:

Kobe College Corporation, St. Luke's International Hospital and College for Nursing and Cooperating Board for Christian Education in Chosen, Inc., all in Japan.

American College, Madura and Allahabad Agricultural Institute in India.

American University of Beirut, American College for Girls at Constantinople, Robert College of Constantinople, International College of Smyrna, Sofia American Schools, Athens College in Greece, Anatolia College, Thessalonica Agricultural and Industrial Institute and Albanian-American School of Agriculture, all in the Near East.

Oberlin-Shansi Memorial Association, Harvard-Yenching Institute, Lingnan University, West China Union University, University of Nanking, Fukuen Christian University and Shantung University, all in China.

The Harvard-Yenching Institute for Chinese Studies, incorporated in Massachusetts, which has received from Mr. Hall's estate a separate endowment of its own of several millions, is to hold and administer part of the endowments of the Chinese institutions named.

Mr. Hall, a resident of Niagara Falls, N. Y., died in 1914. He was the inventor of the process by which aluminum is made. He was a major stockholder in the Aluminum Company of America and allied corporations.

THE DORMITORY HOUSES OF HARVARD UNIVERSITY

IT is reported in the daily papers that the "house" plan will be put in force throughout Harvard College with funds of about $10,000,000 promised by Edward S. Harkness, of New York City, a Yale graduate, whose $3,000,000 financed the first "house" at Harvard, now being set up. Architects and engineers are at work on plans for splitting the college's 3,000 students up into small social groups, and providing separate quarters for each of these, and Mr. Harkness has promised to finance the change. It is estimated that the buildings will cost from $8,000,000 to $10,000,000.

The plans for the first "house" specified a group of dormitories, dining-halls and common room, in which a cross-section of the student body selected from the three upper classes would live with resident tutors. In extending the plan to the whole student body some of the more recently constructed dormitories in the Harvard Yard will be used.

In regard to the report that in the first place a similar offer had been refused by Yale University, the following statement has been issued: "The officers of Yale University note with regret the appearance in the public press of Sunday, December 30, of an article purporting to be based on interviews with the secretary and other officials of the university to the effect that Mr. Edward S. Harkness, '97, had never made to Yale an offer similar to that which he is reported to have made to Harvard for the erection of small residential quadrangles. In order to correct this misstatement and to do justice to Mr. Harkness, who has been a constant benefactor of Yale, the university desires to state that Mr. Harkness did proffer a gift to Yale, with a time limit attached, to permit of a subdivision of the undergraduate body into small residential groups. The university was unfortunately unable to reach a decision concerning this plan within the time set, whereupon Mr. Harkness's very generous offer lapsed."

THE SALARIES OF PROFESSORS

An Associated Press despatch, dated from New Haven on December 17, states that the present salary of members of the Yale faculty is between one third and two thirds of the $15,000 or $16,000 a year taken as a standard for the economic level for a professor, according to a report on income and living costs of the faculty prepared by Professor Yandell Henderson and Maurice R. Davie.

President James Rowland Angell in a foreword to the report, which was prepared for the Yale Chapter of the American Association of University Professors, says in part:

The problem presented by academic salaries is, in many ways, the most urgent now confronting American education. Plenty of competent men are quite ready to live themselves on extremely modest stipends in return for the intrinsic rewards which they find in a scholarly life. But they rightfully hesitate to subject their children to the limitations of the under privileged in a time of general financial prosperity.

The report is based on a questionnaire to which 63 per cent. of the Yale faculty replied.

Professors Henderson and Davie took as a standard for the economic level for a professor after twenty-five years of service "the amount of money necessary to maintain a home in a ten-room house which he owns free of mortgage, to keep one servant and pay for some occasional service, and to provide an education for his children in preparatory school, college and professional school on an equality with that obtained by the general run of students in this university; life at this level now costs about $15,000 or $16,000 a year." Full professors received between $5,000 and $8,000 a year; associate professors from $4,000 to $5,000 and assistants $3,000 to $4,000.

THE AMERICAN ASSOCIATION FOR THE ADVANCEMENT OF SCIENCE

The American Association and some sixty scientific societies met in New York from December 27 to January 2. The registered attendance was about 5,000, which includes only a part of the members of the associated societies. Dr. Robert A. Millikan, director of the Norman Bridge Laboratory and chairman of the executive committee of the California Institute of Technology, was elected president to succeed Dr. Henry Fairfield Osborn, president of the American Museum of Natural History. Vice-presidents and chairmen of the sections were elected as follows:

Section A—E. T. Bell, professor of mathematics, California Institute of Technology.

Section B—C. E. Mendenhall, professor of physics, University of Wisconsin.

Section C—S. C. Lind, director of the school of chemistry, University of Minnesota.

Section D—Harlow Shapley, professor of astronomy, Harvard University and director of the Harvard College Observatory.

Section E—G. F. Kay, professor and head of the department of geology and dean of the college of liberal arts, University of Iowa.

Section F—Professor C. M. Child, professor of zoology, University of Chicago.

Section G—J. Arthur Harris, head of the department of botany, University of Minnesota.

Section H—A. V. Kidder, Phillips Academy.

Section I—Madison Bentley, professor of psychology, Cornell University.

Section K—H. L. Rietz, professor of mathematics, the State University of Iowa.

Section L—Henry O. Taylor, New York City.

Section M—H. F. Moore, professor of engineering materials, University of Illinois.

Section N—Ludwig Hektoen, head of the department of pathology of the University of Chicago, and director of the McCormick Institute for Infectious Diseases.

Section O—M. F. Miller, professor of soils, University of Missouri.

Section Q—Frank N. Freeman, professor of educational psychology, University of Chicago.

EDUCATIONAL NOTES AND NEWS

DR. KARL S. LASHLEY, psychologist of the behavior research fund of the Institute of Juvenile Research at Chicago, has been elected president of the American Psychological Association. Dr. Lashley will deliver his presidential address before the International Psychological Congress, which meets in New Haven in September, the annual meeting of the association for 1929 having been merged with the congress.

THE American Society of Naturalists has elected as president Dr. George H. Parker, professor of zoology and director of the laboratory at Harvard University. The American Geological Society has elected Dr. Heinrich Ries, professor of economic geology in Cornell University.

PROFESSOR MORRIS R. COHEN, since 1912 professor of philosophy in the College of the City of New York, has been elected president of the eastern section of the American Philosophical Society. Dr. E. G. Spaulding, professor of philosophy at Princeton University, was elected vice-president, and Charles W. Hendel, of Princeton University, secretary and treasurer.

A DINNER was given on December 22 in honor of the resigning dean and the dean-elect of the school of medicine of Western Reserve University, Dr. Carl A. Hamann and Dr. Torald Sollmann. A decorated sheepskin was presented to Dr. Hamann, containing resolutions adopted on his retirement by trustees and faculty of his institution.

THE American Association of University Women, which raised $200,000 to provide radium for the research work of Mme. Marie Curie, and which in support of this work pays her the income from the balance of the fund amounting to over $50,000, have voted that in case of death the income shall be paid to her daughter, Mme. Irene Curie-Joliot, who has been working with Mme. Curie for fifteen years.

DR. JOSEPH GÜRTLER, a former university professor, has been elected president of the Austrian National Assembly in place of Herr Miklas, who has become president of the Austrian Republic.

DR. PERCIVAL R. COLE, vice-president of Teachers' College of Sydney, Australia, has been named visiting Carnegie professor of international relations at the University of Hawaii for the second semester of the present academic year and for the summer school in 1929.

H. C. WANG, of Tsing Hua University, Peking, fellow in international law of the Carnegie Corporation, has been appointed lecturer in the university.

ERNEST MINOR PATTERSON, professor of economics in the Wharton School of the University of Pennsylvania, has been given leave of absence to enable him to serve as visiting professor at the Post-Graduate Institute of International Studies at Geneva, Switzerland, during the second term of the current academic year.

DEAN ROBERT WILLIAMS, professor of philosophy of Albion College, Michigan, has been named acting president of Ohio Northern University at Ada, Ohio, during a year's leave of absence of President Albert E. Smith.

THREE new members have been elected to the board of trustees at Boston University. They are Frank G. Allen, lieutenant-governor of

Massachusetts; Mr. J. B. L. Hornberger, a retired business man of Pittsburgh, Pennsylvania, and Mr. William T. Rich, a Boston business man, of the firm of Chase and Sanborn.

Membership of the committee of the school survey of Boston has been selected as follows: By the mayor, President A. Lawrence Lowell, of Harvard University; by the Boston Chamber of Commerce, Carl Dreyfus; by the Real Estate Exchange of the city, Francis R. Bangs; by the Labor Union, Frank P. Fenton; by the Parent-Teachers Association, Mrs. Willard D. Woodbury, the local president; by the schools, Arthur L. Gould, assistant superintendent; Walter F. Downey, principal of the English High School, and Archer M. Nickerson, of a Junior High School; by the School Board, Michael H. Sullivan, a Boston lawyer, who is president of the committee.

Herbert Spencer, formerly of the University of Pittsburgh, has been elected principal of the Henry Clay Frick Training School for Teachers of the city of Pittsburgh. He succeeds Dr. H. B. Davis, who died on September 14.

J. Freeman Guy, superintendent of Bellevue, Pennsylvania, schools, has been elected an associate superintendent of the Pittsburgh schools at a salary of $7,500.

Dr. Donald A. Laird, director of the Colgate Psychological Laboratory, has been appointed chief of the scientific staff of the Personnel Analysis Bureau of Chicago. Dr. Edward C. Stoy, recently of the Carnegie Institute of Technology, is deputy chief. The bureau provides a personnel psychological test service for business and professional men and women. No vocational guidance or employment testing work is undertaken, the bureau referring requests for such service to individual psychologists.

Dr. Arnold Gesell delivered an address at the New York Academy of Medicine on December 13, on "The Developmental Diagnosis of Infant Behavior and Its Significance for Clinical Pediatrics."

Norman Angel, who is making a brief visit to the United States, will lecture during January on "Education for Public Service," under the auspices of the United Parents Association of New York City.

Ernest Thompson Seton, naturalist, lecturer and author, who has spent many years studying and teaching woodcraft in this country, has been engaged as a special lecturer for the 1929 Summer Session Nature Camps of The Pennsylvania State College, according to an announcement made by Dr. George R. Green, professor of nature education and director of the camp, which is situated in Stone Valley, sixteen miles from the college, near the geographic center of Pennsylvania and is surrounded by highly interesting geological formations. Two camps will be conducted during the session, the first from June 27 to July 18, and the second from July 17 to August 17.

The Royal Historical Society, London, celebrated the sixtieth anniversary of its foundation at a dinner on December 7, at which Dr. Abraham Flexner was the principal speaker.

Dr. David Bancroft Johnson, founder and president of Winthrop College for Women, died on December 26, at the age of seventy-two years.

The Reverend John H. Fasy, S.J., professor of ethics at Fordham University, died on December 23, at the age of forty-one years.

Dr. W. H. Ottman, for many years professor of history at William Penn Charter School, died on December 25 at the age of fifty-five years.

William Dunlap Knox, for forty years county superintendent of schools in South Carolina, has died at the age of eighty-one years.

The Carnegie Corporation has made a grant of $50,000 to the American Historical Association to finance the first year of a nation-wide survey of history and other studies in high schools by the committee of the society on history and other social studies in the schools. Professor A. C. Krey, of the University of Minnesota, states that the survey is planned with a view to a reorganization of these studies and that it contemplates a five-year study of the high schools of the country. A committee of fifteen is proposed to oversee and direct the investigation. Members of the committee who cooperated with Dr. Krey in drawing up the plan for the investigation are: John S. Bassett, professor of history at Smith College; Guy

Stanton Ford, dean of the graduate school of the University of Minnesota; Ernest Horn, director of research in elementary education of the University of Iowa; Henry Johnson, head of the department of the teaching of history, Teachers College, Columbia University; William E. Lingelbach, professor of history, of the University of Pennsylvania; L. C. Marshall, formerly head of the department of economics, University of Chicago, now at the Johns Hopkins University; C. E. Merriam, head of the department of political science at the University of Chicago and former president of the American Political Science Association; Jesse H. Newlon, director of the Lincoln School in Teachers College.

DR. M. LYLE SPENCER, president of the University of Washington; Dr. C. E. Friley, president of the American Association of Collegiate Registrars, and Professor E. D. Randolph, chairman of the local committee, University of Washington, have sent out to the presidents, deans and other officials of colleges and universities who may be interested in the problems involved in the reorganization of the first two years of college work an invitation to attend a conference to be held at Seattle, Washington, on April 19, to consider the questions involved in the reorganization of the first and second years of college work. The local committee has already received promises of cooperation from the representatives of a number of universities who are leaders in the experiments that are being conducted in this field. In order that the local committee in charge of the arrangements may know what members of your staff are interested in this question, will you kindly send the names and addresses of such persons to Professor E. D. Randolph, University of Washington, Seattle. As the program develops, full information will be sent to all those whose addresses are supplied to the committee on organization. The proposed conference is sponsored jointly by the University of Washington and the American Association of Collegiate Registrars.

DR. MILAN GROLL, the Yugoslav minister for education, has consulted the Anglo-Yugoslav Society in London with regard to the foundation of an English college in Yugoslavia for the education of Yugoslav boys in the English language and on English lines. The London *Times* reports that the advice of the society has been favorable, and that practical details are now being considered. It is probable that arrangements will be made for an English schoolmaster of experience to go to Belgrade to discuss the matter with the Yugoslav educational authorities. The idea is that the college should be a boarding school on the lines of an English public school, which would be placed in charge of an English headmaster, and in which English ideas of training with the help of sports would be applied.

DISCUSSION

DO COLLEGE SCIENCE STUDENTS KNOW HOW TO OBSERVE?

JUST how much does the entering college student know about everyday science? This is a question for not only the lay individual who wishes to speculate, but for the science educator who would build a class-program that begins where the student is acquainted.

In order to determine the status of the students entering college biology courses with at least one high-school course in biology, a list of questions was recently given to several hundred such students—representative students from thirty-four states—and the following results were obtained (percentages are nearest whole figure):

Forty-five per cent. state that an oyster is a fish.

Ninety-five per cent. state that a robin's breast is red (one student says "flesh-colored.")

Ten per cent. believe that earthworms "rain down."

Thirty-eight per cent. believe that dragons exist (most of them stated that dragons are found in swamps and forests of the tropics).

Five per cent. believe that warts are a result of handling toads.

Eighty-five per cent. do not know what the theory of evolution teaches: twenty-five per cent. say it teaches that man descended from monkeys;

fifteen per cent. say he descended from other anthropoid apes; ten per cent. say that he descended from gorillas. Several say that man is said to have descended from other mammals. One student wrote, "evolution is the theory that man descended from Heaven." A few state that it says fish are ancestors of man. Another says "evol. teaches that animals descended from fossils."

Sixty per cent. believe that evolution contradicts the creation account in Genesis.

Twenty per cent. believe that evolution does not contradict the creation account in Genesis.

Twenty per cent. are doubtful whether or not the two accounts can coincide.

Ninety per cent. believe that stars are five-pointed in shape.

Eighty-five per cent. believe that a whale is a fish.

Ninety per cent. believe that a bat is a bird.

Eighty per cent. believe that sponges are plants.

Sixty-five per cent. state that corals are plant formations.

Seventy per cent. say that bacteria are animals.

Fifty-five per cent. say that goiter is a disease of the muscles of the neck (one says that "it is something like rheumatism, only it gets you in the neck.")

Five per cent. state that the longest bone in the body is the backbone.

Sixty per cent. did not know that grasshoppers could fly.

Ninety-five per cent. say that the best way to lift a rabbit is by his ears.

Sixty per cent. believe that bees gather "honey" from flowers.

Eighty per cent. could not give a definition of an animal which would distinguish it from a plant. (One, "something that moves on feet"; another, "a living organism requiring food and water"; another, "a beast.")

Five per cent. believe that butterflies are born from butterfly eggs.

The most impressive feature of these results is the evident lack of observation of simple, everyday sights—a pitiful inability to observe, to question or to interpret what is seen about them.

When we science teachers become aware of the facts, we must revise some of our teaching methods if we produce really scientific-minded students. We must certainly emphasize cultivation of the ability to question, to analyze and to interpret; but the big task, evidently, is to teach the student first to *observe*!

J. H. FURBAY

DEPARTMENT OF BIOLOGY,
TAYLOR UNIVERSITY,
UPLAND, INDIANA

CONGENIAL WORK FOR BOYS

I NOTE that Dr. Gilbert J. Raynor, principal of the Alexander Hamilton High School, asserts that 50 per cent. of the high-school students in New York City are unprepared to do the required work. That is why a large proportion leave school with the stamp of failure. He also says they often fail miserably with harmful effects on their attitude toward the world at large and constituted authority in particular. And the remedy he suggests is more vocational training.

The trustees of the George Junior Republic have always been so deeply imbued with the truth of this that they require both shop work and school work and the students are marked on each. So many alleged "tough" cases have developed into fine characters that quite outside of our intention we have come to be known as a sort of reformatory whereas originally we had no such plan (nor have we at any time more than a very small proportion of difficult cases).

Is there any magical trick about giving a youngster who is almost nauseated with the printed page all day long some congenial shopwork which uses another set of brain cells and thus freshens up his nervous system?

RICHARD WELLING,
Trustee and late President,
George Junior Republic

QUOTATIONS

EDUCATION IN 1928

THE most outstanding educational achievement in 1928 has been the increase of public interest in education.

It was particularly noticeable in the eighth annual observance of American education week, November 5 to 11, under the joint auspices of the American Legion and the National Education Association. American education week is of inestimable value in acquainting the people of the country with the work, aims, ideals and needs of the schools.

The teaching profession itself is responsible for most of the advances made in education. The task of guiding the growth of 28,000,000 young lives now in schools belongs to the teacher. Therefore much attention has been given in the last year to raising the standards of teacher training. This movement has been led by the American Association of Teachers Colleges, a department of the National Education Association.

Last February the association made, for the first time in the history of American education, a list of accredited teacher-training institutions. It is hoped that this will have on the teaching profession an effect similar to the accrediting of medical schools by the American Medical Association.

Never before has there been so much general interest in safeguarding the mental health of school children. It is significant that approximately twenty courses have been introduced into our colleges and universities to train visiting teachers, workers who are equipped with an understanding of psychology, mental hygiene and social adjustment.

The visiting teacher will in time replace the attendance officer. Instead of maintaining a police force to keep children in school we shall draw them there by the intelligent and friendly guidance of teachers who understand the problems of childhood.

There has been a marked advance in the use of educational devices for vitalizing teaching. The year 1928 has seen the beginning of Dr. Damrosch's radio hour for school children once each week. Visual education has been given new impetus by the improvement of teaching films.

An effort to serve all the children is seen in the larger support for continuation programs for pupils who must begin at an early age to earn money. Provision is made whereby these pupils may find remunerative employment and still enjoy some of the benefits of free schooling. Added to this program there is the evening school offering educational opportunities to adult men and women who missed them in former years.

The outlook for a United States Department of Education with a secretary in the President's Cabinet to carry on necessary research and scientific fact finding has never been more promising.

We are rapidly moving toward the goal of the National Education Association—"A fair start in life for every child."—*Statement to the Associated Press by Uel W. Lamkin, president of the National Education Association.*

EDUCATIONAL RESEARCH AND STATISTICS

A NOTE ON THE BETA HYPOTHESIS OF LEARNING

DUNLAP[1] cites as an instance leading to his revision of the law of frequency his correction of a typewriting error by voluntarily practising the word as incorrectly written. The following experiment, although it shows qualitatively nothing more than his correction of "hte" had already shown, eliminates the possibility of accident with respect to that particular observation.

The subjects were a night-school typewriting class of forty students who were just beginning to transcribe from their shorthand notes. Instructions were given that there was to be no erasing, no letters struck over and no attempt to correct in any way; the first copy was to be turned in in every case.

The dictation was so planned that words often misspelled were used frequently. The papers were not returned and nothing was said about errors of any kind. The errors were checked, and when one was found in any person's paper on four occasions it was recorded as a constant error for him. The student was then asked to spell the word orally. If he could spell it correctly the mistake was classed as a constant automatic error and used in the experiment.

[1] "A Revision of the Fundamental Law of Habit Formation," *Science*, April 6, 1928.

Of the forty students eleven were found, during a period of eight weeks, who had made at least four such constant automatic errors. Two of the eleven made eight such errors.

The words for each student were then divided by chance into two groups of two each for nine students and two groups of four each for the two who made eight such errors.

Each student's attention was then called to the fact that he was consistently misspelling the words, and he was asked to type, spelling as he had misspelled them, eight lines the width of the page of each of the first two words. The instructions, which were usually considered "funny" or "mysterious," were repeated, and the practice supervised to see that the student wrote just what he was asked to write and nothing more. The other pair of words was assigned for the same amount of practice of the usual kind, that is, practice in which the word is correctly spelled. There were very few errors in either type of practice, hence they are disregarded.

Dictation was given after practice in such a way that each of the words practised was used at least four times. Table 1 shows the kind of

TABLE 1

Subject	Words practiced as correctly spelled		errors after practice
A	parcel	(parcil)	0
	received	(recieved)	2
B	necessary	(neccessary)	4
	shipped	(shiped)	0
C	their	(thier)	0
	occasioned	(occassioned)	4
	items	(ittems)	0
	transit	(transet)	0
D	immediately	(emmediately)	2
	instance	(instanse)	1
E	source	(sourse)	1
	owing	(ouing)	1
F	errors	(errers)	2
	reduce	(reduse)	0
	there	(their)	0
	account	(acount)	0
G	guarded	(gaurded)	2
	belief	(beleif)	4
H	account	(accuont)	1
	shipped	(shiped)	0
I	slight	(sleight)	1
	design	(desing)	2
J	opportunity	(oportunity)	0
	referred	(refered)	0
K	through	(thruogh)	1
	shown	(shoun)	2
		Total	30

Subject	Words practiced as misspelled		errors after practice
A	agreed	(agread)	0
	shipments	(shippments)	0
B	reduce	(reduse)	0
	possibly	(posibly)	0
C	fulfill	(fullfill)	0
	necessary	(neccessary)	0
	owing	(oweing)	0
	occasioned	(occassioned)	0
D	because	(becuase)	0
	receipt	(reciept)	0
E	shipped	(shiped)	0
	their	(thier)	0
F	certainly	(certinly)	0
	immediately	(imediately)	0
	possibly	(posibly)	0
	value	(valeu)	0
G	allowance	(alowance)	0
	adjusting	(ajusting)	0
H	not	(mot)	0
	cancel	(cansel)	0
I	dropped	(droped)	0
	shipped	(shiped)	0
J	write	(wright)	0
	develop	(develope)	0
K	disappoint	(dissapoint)	0
	quantity	(quanity)	0
		Total	0

errors made and the frequency of occurrence in the four uses of each word after practice. It will be seen that all except one of the eleven students made errors in words which were practised as correctly spelled and that not a single one of the eleven students made an error in any word which was practiced as incorrectly spelled. Note that Subject C made errors in all four uses of the word "occasioned" after practice when the word was practised correctly, but after practice in misspelling not a single error occurred. An examination of the kind of errors made and corrected shows little except that errors in double letters were the kind which seemed to predominate in the mistakes remedied by practice in correct spelling. This, however, might be merely an accident.

The only real difficulty in the interpretation of these data lies in the fact that they seem "too good to be true." In psychological experiments on learning, there are few instances in which the results in the experimentally varied situation differ from the results of the "control" situation so completely as these do.

JAMES QUINTER HOLSOPPLE
IRENE VANOUSE

CLEVELAND, OHIO

EDUCATIONAL REVIEW

Edited by WILLIAM McANDREW

MATTERS OF MOMENT

We Are Certainly Reading More.—One thing is certain: We school people are reading more. I well remember a series of meetings of the Brooklyn Teachers Association when the study of professional material was being pushed by Brooklyn's popular schoolmaster, Walter Gunnison. A prominent member of the faculty of the Boys' High School read a paper on the futility of professional study. He said he had made a canvass of all his colleagues and it was their unanimous opinion that the reading of books on psychology or instruction had not helped them in their teaching one iota. The sockdolager (American for *coup de grâce*) of that meeting was given by the brilliant president of the Packer Collegiate Institute, Dr. Truman J. Backus, who said, "I never read a book on pedagogy in my life, thank God." That was thirty-six years ago. In my mind's ear I can hear the crackling applause that seemed to come from every pair of hands in that large audience of teachers.

What We Teachers Clap Hands At.—Did you ever make a study of our applause? It would be interesting to take a sonometer to various educational meetings and get the relative responses to various propositions. I heard a speaker tell Grand Rapids school people that they would be better off at a motion-picture show than attending teachers' meetings. The plaudits were notably hearty. I was at a meeting in Erie when the chairman of an institute announced that because of the absence of one of the speakers the session would close forty-five minutes ahead of time. The hand-clapping was full of fervor. Rabbi Hirsch used to proclaim public-school teaching a woeful failure. His public-school-teacher audience was loud in approval. It is a curious fact that a speaker who trounces, pummels and wallops teaching the hardest gets the noisiest commendations from educators. In Chicago I heard an advocate of the child-directed school smothered with commendatory sounds when he berated the typical public school as a barbarous straight-jacket to atrophy the abilities of children. In the same hall, within a month, the same audience greeted by enthusiastic manual acclaim the words of a speaker ridiculing the new-educationists as soft-hearted irresponsibles who would let a child play himself into incompetence for taking up the work of the world. The platform orator who desires applause can get it from us by hammering something. If it is a new thing that seems to require a revision of our thought and practice we'll give him a glad hand. If he sets up a straw teacher and punishes her, or if he belittles our business, we'll cheer him. As I recall the meetings I have attended for the past forty years I hear successive rounds of applause for the fine old educational mastodons who opposed certificates for teachers, compulsory education laws, retirement systems, tenure, reading circles, manual training, laboratory science, promotional examination for teachers, longer training-school courses, plan-books, and, in short, almost everything that our fathers didn't have.

Year after year I have attended educational dinners at which we were supplied with doggerel to sing ridiculing forward movements in our line of service or intimating that we are the most abused and downtrodden of all the public servants.

Somebody turned the tables at the last Inland-Empire Convention in Spokane. The committee engaged a male quartette to entertain the school men and women at the banquet.

The director of these singers, not finding anything suitable for an educational convention, composed the words and music of a dirge. As solo, duet, trio, four-part music, with antiphonal effect, as fugue, as contrapuntal arrangement, as melody, and plain recitative, those tuneful rascals repeated these jibes over and over:

Oh, pity the poor teachers—
Six hours in one place,
Five days a week,
Forty weeks a year,
Saturdays off,
Summers free,
Oh, pity the poor teachers
They need your sympathy.

And, as usual, we applauded this. We are so considerate we'll give anybody who presents any absurdity, in a gentlemanly manner, all the hand-clapping he wants. We would applaud the Devil.

Accordingly, considering the persistence of a childish insouciance, I am bold to say that the growth of the habit of reading books appertaining to the improvement of teaching is highly creditable to the men and women who work in our schools. That Brooklyn Teachers' Association which glorified the distinguished educator who never read a book on education now maintains, every season, courses of reading and study creditable to a university and given official recognition as equivalent to college study. New York, which used to applaud the lampooners of reading educational periodicals, now has a magazine, *High Points*, filled entirely with progressive articles written by public-school teachers. Chicago, which, in the days of Edward Cooley, had its organized teachers fighting all his provisions for professional reading and study, has its *Public School Journal* in the hands of every teacher. Its book reviews, its constructive articles, its whole contents, are the work of the members of the city school staff.

In the days when Truman Backus thanked God he had never read a book on pedagogy, Appleton's was issuing its long series of professional volumes. Heath had a "Teachers' Library." The Kelloggs had one. Without losing sleep you could read every teacher-book on the market. You can not, now, unless you neglect everything else, go through the volumes issued yearly by a score of houses interested in works on instruction, supervision and the philosophy of education.

Keeping Track of Trends.—Some analysis, some preview, of the contents of these books is a boon to him who must budget his time. These bibliologoi have apparently become considered by the publishers as worth-while people, for the packages of books sent off each week to Dr. Rose, their patriarch, can be measured by the cord. I find a perusal of the club's minutes, in spite of my objection to being told quite so pointedly what I ought to read, a handy summary of educational news as affecting trends, projects and view-points.

For instance, in this month's proceedings, I get a suggestion upon university reform which leads me to read Max McConn's "College or Kindergarten" with such pleasurable profit that I would send a box of Scottish oatmeal cakes for the next collation of the club. What they say about Denison's "Emotion as the Basis of Civilization" set me to reading it. They are right in their estimate of it. You will find in their discussions some pertinent thoughts on school prizes, a sheaf of observations on training for citizenship, some surprisingly complete remarks on the teaching of reading, a tart comment on supervision and much fresh new matter on teaching in general.

It seems to me a perusal of this set of reviews by teachers and principals will save a great deal of continued use of methods proved to be due for the discard.

Guess Where This Happened.—An editorial commentator in an organ of a teachers' association hails with congratulations the beginning of a new era in cooperation between teachers and the officers of the state departments of schools. During the three-days' discussions the appreciation of teachers' and superintendents' points of view became more evident than ever before. There were difficulties on the administrative side which had not been appreciated by teachers. Artificial barriers were removed. There will be a more effective understanding of common problems. The teachers were most sympathetically received. Their views received the utmost consideration, especially when constructive proposals were advanced. The main purpose of the conference was the amendment of the state courses of study. It raised the question of the restrictive influence of the curriculum on teachers' initiative and whether the time had not come for the abolition of state requirements. Some were in favor of the merest skeleton of a course of study. Others thought that a statement of the accomplishment required at the end of the course was enough, with the liberty to each school to reach that stage in the manner best suited to local needs, thus throwing more responsibility on teachers and evoking a more effective response. It was soon seen from the discussion that there were practical difficulties due to shifting school population which made desirable a measure of uniformity for each school grade. Eventually it was agreed that a uniform curriculum is still required, but that this should be an elastic one to interfere as little as possible with the originality of the teacher. There should be handbooks of outlines for the different grades but they should be prepared with the assistance of teachers. The present English syllabus was considered the best of all, for it gives the widest latitude. The geometry syllabus was settled in the most drastic manner. It was cut out altogether. It was considered that boys get all the geometry they need from their drawing and manual work, while the pitiful case of girls, struggling with a subject in which they have no interest, was proof against any arguments that could be put forward for the defense of geometry. Arithmetic, as has always been the case, proved the bone of greatest contention. The delegates wanted drastic reductions. These included the entire excision of the metric system, the highest common divisor, the least common multiple and elaborate puzzles with four-decked fractions. The association wanted clerks in large schools to save the principal from routine work which keeps him from his real duties. It wanted power given to teachers to require official examination of children presumed to be mentally defective. It asked that fixed desks and seats, screwed to the floor, be supplanted by movable chairs and tables. It recorded that the continuous child-accounting blanks, giving a complete school history of each child, were not worth the labor involved. It asked that teachers' living quarters be built near the rural schools. These and many other requests and opinions were patiently answered in detail by the officers of the state department. The delegates fought hard for their contentions. The outcome, says the editor, clearly proves the value of the association to its members. Some teachers at times express a doubt as to the value of joining, but this conference must show them the great advantage of union. The improvement of teachers' conditions, the grant of greater responsibility to them, obligate them to a greater response. It is not beyond the bounds of possibility that the Teachers' Association will, in time, be charged with the task of keeping its membership clear of those who are not acting in accordance with the highest dictates of professional conduct. At first, the work of the association was handicapped with heavy discouragements. It persevered. Now we can record that it is imbued with the professional spirit. We have a real cooperation of teachers with officials to solve their joint problems.

What state association do you think is referred to? New York? Michigan? Pennsylvania?

Radio Won't Do.—What you have just read is from the organ of the Transvaal Teachers' Association, published in Johannesburg, South Africa. If the paragraph had been so headed, the chances are you would have passed it by unread, preferring to attend to matters of nearby current interest. But the educational magazines that come to this desk from overseas, from New Zealand, from India, from Czecho-Slovakia and elsewhere show attention to the same problems that are demanding the notice of our own workers in Oregon or Massachusetts. For example, this same Transvaal paper has a summary of the experiments with phonograph records and radio in the schools. Can they replace the teacher? it inquires. Not yet. The knell of the teacher was thought to have been rung when syllabuses so complete were devised that Lancastrian monitors could hear and check the recitations. One combined policeman and clerk could care for a school of a thousand children. Now come the gramophone and wireless. History and geography lessons can be caught by thousands of classrooms from a central broadcasting studio. The well-known French minister of education can come back and, looking at his watch, declare that at this moment the whole educational system of the country is listening to a broadcast on the rivers of Europe. But the experiments in Kent have shown that you can not correlate any wireless service, however good, with the individual needs of a multiplicity of classes. For music and spoken language the gramophone is of immense help when you can control the time of its use. Wireless lessons have proved of much advantage for set occasions, for giving distant schools the advantage of hearing a distinguished speaker, with fresh ideas, and the distinct skill needed to interest and benefit children. But, when all is considered, the radio can occupy only a small portion of the school time-table. You must have a live personality observing the whole audience and, according to its capacity, passing lightly over one point, questioning on another, repeating, varying, illustrating, and, when the lesson has extended to the point of weariness, stopping, and turning to something fresh. The best of life is entwined with emotions and sentiments. Children are persons, not buckets. They need the companionship of a vivifying personality. Ether waves can never supplant the living presence of a fine man or woman.

Jazz, South Africa, and World Peace.—I could give you the substance of an excellent article by Transvaalian Alan Howgrave-Graham on music appreciation, which would effectively remind you that mere singing exercises devoted to good selections enable children in their grown-up days better to appreciate music and to make their living less forlorn. Appreciation lessons, says he, should be concentrated especially upon reproduction of orchestral music, omitting, of course, jazz and other irritant poisons. I could give you the whole of this Transvaal paper's inspiring article on international understanding in the schools. Frederick J. Gould writes it. It is the spirit, not the machinery, of the League of Nations that needs to be impressed upon the children. We must have a conception of past and present humanity. The old geography concerned itself with the mechanical facts of rivers, areas, etc. The new geography treats of the drama of human order and progress, human labor and aspirations. The new history stresses industry, art, science, law and civic betterment in preference to war. The children will admire and compare the beautiful buildings, pictures, sculptures, costumes, gardens and music of many lands. The new science gives grateful recognition to the widening of our knowledge effected by Linnaeus, Humboldt, Pasteur, Edison, Marconi, and shows the oneness of all mankind. We should show our youth how a small body of emigrants called Pilgrims assembled in the cabin of the anchored *Mayflower* off Cape Cod and signed a compact and resolved "to enact statutes and frame such just and equal laws as shall be thought most meet and convenient for the general good of the colony." Our Transvaal friend is cosmopolitan. Our business, he continues, is with ideals, the newest aspirations in political, educational and esthetic development. We must make plain the fact that a national ideal is not a patented conception. It is important to point out that it is held in common with other nations. If we proudly say, "An Englishman's word is his bond," it does not mean dishonesty is the type of other men. We must cultivate the very honorable pleasure of recognizing the excellences of other peoples. The honesty of the Albanian, the courtesy of the Spaniard, the industry of the Belgian. The Hebrew exhortation, "Let us now praise famous men," may be extended to, "Let us now praise famous nations." In that spirit we could point to an assembly of twenty countries in Louvain and see Nicholas Murray Butler, an American, putting an inscription on the new library: "Enmity burned me; American kindness restored." In that spirit we may cite to our children, and they to us, a thousand illustrations from Germany, from Austria, from France, from the world at large. We teach ideals. They are the signs of the upward and onward spirit, though we know that all nations are still slow pupils in the academy of which the patient rector is Love. Mankind, capable of oriental massacre, 1914 B. C., and world slaughter, A. D. 1914, defies and annuls its coarser instincts in seasons of the ascendency of heart and reason. Let the teacher give honorable notice of these better times, of pacts and alliances of generosities between nations. The record runs like a golden thread through the histories of Egypt, Asia, Greece, Rome and Europe, to The Hague Conference of 1899, to the League of Nations and the later pacts, from Grotius to Woodrow Wilson. These are the ideals to make familiar to the generation which is in the schools.

School-fights Across the Sea.—So, the South African teacher is pretty close to us. You feel it in the account of a farewell dinner and dance tendered by teachers to Mr. and Mrs. H. S. Scott, on the occasion of his retirement from the position of director of education for Transvaal. Mr. Morris, chairman of the Education Association, made a neat address of congratulation and good-bye:

> Mr. Scott began under circumstances not altogether auspicious. He has shown that the criticisms aimed at his appointment were groundless and the misgivings expressed concerning his suitability for the post unfounded. His course has been among many rocks, some hidden. He has sacrificed none of his freight. Schools were never

better in the Province. He may look with pardonable pride upon the present school system.

Then, of course, the victim of the dinner responded:

What fights we have had! The teachers fought the government; they fought each other. They had no scarcity of headlines in the papers. When there was nobody left to fight against, there was fighting on general principles to keep in practice. It came so that when there was quiet I was uneasy for fear that there was nothing doing.

Doesn't that remind you of dear old Chicago?

Grave and Gay in School Affairs.—This Transvaal school journal seems to me a refreshing sheet. There are many pages of letters from teachers. One tells us that those who consider their work drudgery and think their real delight begins only when Friday evening comes can not teach their children the great joy of work. A man or woman, she says, who has a jealous grudge is not fit to train children in the world's great need, peace and good-will.

How do you like this for South African humor? The inspector asked the teacher what her day's plan of work had been. She told him she had carried out a splendid plan of correlation. She began the opening exercises by reading the parable of the fig tree. For arithmetic she set problems on bushels of figs. For nature-study they learned the growth and uses of the fig tree. For geography they discussed all the countries where fig trees grow. Now, says the narrator, in that room there was a boy who had the gift of tongues. The inspector heard him whisper to his neighbor, "Oh, damn the fig tree."

Every page bears the exhortation and promise: "Support our advertisers and they will support you." The readers are told that the proprietress of Maison Camille is hair-dresser to the association and gives it a discount of 10 per cent. "The Louvre" has been officially appointed hosiers to the association and will give one pair of ladies' artificial silk stockings free. Henry Simpson, Ltd., is engagement-ring specialist to the organization. S. Greaves & Co. hold a similar appointment for wedding gifts. Tickets for South Africa may be bought of the American Express Co., offices everywhere.

World Trends in Education.—Now that we have led you this little way into the educational affairs of a distant part of the world, should we not venture further? Teachers College, New York, has issued the fourth educational yearbook of the International Institute and thereby completed accounts of the school systems of forty-three countries. Dr. I. L. Kandel rightly says these books should be considered more than mere descriptions. They should furnish the student of education with some notion of the major problems with which the world is to-day confronted. Taken in connection with the three earlier volumes, which covered England, France, Germany, Canada and twenty-six other nations, the present book enables you to understand the content, methods, administration and problems of the whole globe. The editor calls our attention to the spread of the idea of democracy in education and to the growing tendency of society to supply the best opportunities for individual capacities. Everywhere apprenticeship and craftsmanship are declining. Highly mechanized industries are spreading. The old organization of education on a class basis perpetuates a pitiful tradition that literary education is the best preparation for a vocation. Along with it, in other countries than ours, is found embarrassment due to the crowding of literary courses by those who hope through them to find more genteel, white-collar employment. Dr. Kandel believes that easing the elementary curricula by dropping considerable book-work and supplanting it by manual training is tending to give labor a higher esteem and to instil into the minds of older pupils an appreciation of the place of industry in modern society. Where traditional secondary schools are governed largely by requirements set by the universities or by a static concept of culture, they still ignore the needs of the majority whose education is not to be continued. Such schools persist in opposition to teaching the existence of contemporary economic conditions.

Changes Everywhere.—The unrest in secondary education is world wide. America took the first step toward revising the courses and added new subjects to the traditional high-school course. She recognized vocational education as deserving as much attention for children of high-school age as is given to the traditional curriculum. France appears to be undertaking a similar reform. In Germany there is a tendency to supply parallel courses of high-school grades adapted to different aptitudes of pupils.

In Belgium the ministry of science and art, responsible to parliament, has authority over the school system. He is assisted by consultative committees of teachers and by a body of school inspectors, men and women. Kindergartens, elementary schools, intermediate schools, athénées, universities, and special schools, as of industry, agriculture, commercial and professional institutions, compose the system. Local school boards appoint the teachers, who are required to be of Belgian nationality and holders of the professional certificates specified by law. Salaries are fixed by the school boards, but must not fall below the legal minimum. The scale is the same for men and women. Attendance on public or private instruction is compulsory. Vocational education is not standardized. Each school regulates itself. Retired teachers are paid a sum reached by dividing the average salary of the last five years by the age of the teacher and multiplying the quotient by the years of service.

Similar facts and more are given for Denmark, Hungary, Iraq (Mesopotamia), Lithuania, Mexico, Russia, Serbia, Croatia, Slovenia, Spain and Turkey.

Professor C. Richard, of Lycée Buffon, Paris, continues an account of the educational system of France, supplementing three articles in earlier yearbooks of this International Institute.

Editor Rheinhold Lehman, of the Leipzig *Times and School Reform,* performs a similar service for Germany. Director W. H. Perkins, Warwickshire, does this for England; Carson Ryan, Swarthmore College, for the United States. This fourth yearbook maintains the high standard of the previous volumes. In these books Paul Monroe, George Counts, Thomas Alexander, Lester Wilson, Milton Del Manzo and Editor Kandel are performing a high-grade service for the educational progress of the world. This set of reports is an essential part of a good educational library.

A REVIEW OF BETTER BOOKS

HOI BIBLIOLOGOI

When all the clotheshangers, the result of the Stevedore's fertile brain and cunning hands, were filled, when every one of Lady Alice's folding luxuries with the embroidered canvas held manly grace or comely femininity, which is to say when the bibliologoi were all seated, Papa Rose, the potentate, read a letter from the editor of the *Educational Review* announcing its acquisition by SCHOOL AND SOCIETY, and expressing the hope that we would continue our mission of persuading the heathen to search the scriptures of the prophets of our profession.

"Shall we continue?" inquired our patriarch, "to ask our archivist to send reports of our symposiums to the magazine, now that it is under other auspices?"

"Have there been any libel suits begun by authors or publishers?" asked Polly.

"None of record," said the Professor.

"Is our stenographer feeling shorthanded?" inquired Carolina.

"Yes, in the proper sense," said we. "Your endurance of my omissions and acceptance of commissions gives me the sense of the glad hand."

"I have developed quite a liking for seeing our names in print once a month," confessed the Signpost.

"—— and to having a record in real print," added Luther.

"Until every teacher has a professional library," suggested the General, "and every school system a bibliological club, we ought to persevere in the mission of telling the world how good the educational books are. The expert reviewer has made his place. If any one will print the ideas of amateurs let the project be encouraged."

"I move *imprimamus*," said Luther the Literary.

Seconded, thirded, everybodied and carried.

The College Absurdity constructively criticized: McConn.—The reviews were continued by the General, who said in part:

"Here's a man[1] who puts forth a proposition that strikes you as ridiculous, absurd and impossible. He laughs at it himself. Then he begins to rationalize, to penetrate, to balance pros and cons, and ends by convincing and persuading you not only that the scheme is workable but that it is inevitable and led up to by the most serious writers who have tackled the problem. This genial genius is Max McConn, dean of Lehigh University. No extra-collegiate critic surpasses him in satirical depiction of the expensive joke known as the American college. No defender of it says more authoritative praise of the hard-working, respectable and self-sacrificing citizens who fill its chairs and executive offices. He treats the matters about which he is not sure with a diffidence that makes you love him. He handles the recognized failures of higher education with an earnestness that commands your respect. Here is a man thinking and criticizing who awakens no antagonism by cocksureness, a professor who adopts no superiority, a specialist with an expanding breadth of view. His theme is the American college.

"It was established and for two hundred years was conducted to serve by producing men to minister to higher needs. This purpose has been smothered. Woodrow Wilson said that the college had become a country club. A favorite characterization by professors is that it is regarded as a kindergarten, a place to play and be to some degree affected by the imposition of learning. Who allowed it to become so? Professors and administrators, who are usually ex-professors, are inclined to be timid. The academic life naturally selects instructors who are students, thinking, not acting. The born doers, the leaders, reformers, go-getters, scorn taking a professorship. Whatever the college originally was for, those who seek its advantages have their own purposes: bread and butter, prestige, kindergarten enjoyment, and, occasionally, culture. This last seems becoming obsolete. But Dean McConn is sure, from his daily conversations with young men, that it is recrudescent in the newer generation.

"Why not reorganize the discipline and 'flunk out' all the kindergartners who come to play and haven't the brain or the will to study? It would be inhumane. But the play groups, with their fine clothes, motor cars, luxurious fraternity houses and expensive living, dominate the campus. They develop a defensive contempt for the severe intellectual labor of which they are incapable. The proper attitude toward books and study is an insouciant neglect. A decent respect for the intent of endowments, a provision for the still considerable number of

[1] Max McConn, "College or Kindergarten," The New Republic, N. Y. 275 pp. $1.00.

youth who feel an urge to learn and to serve, require the establishment of real colleges, scholars' institutions for culture, for civic ministry. Dean McConn's discussion of who should go to such an establishment, how they should be selected, what they should be taught, and how, and by whom, what the living should be, the extra-curriculars, the athletics, will stir in most schoolmen lively aspirations which they had known long since and lost awhile. As for me, after seeing, year after year, the keen edge of ambition of my high-school youngsters dulled by the very institution which they sought with expectation of a life of productive endeavor, after wasting many hours at meetings of athleticsgetrunken alumni of my old alma mater, after being dragooned into buying tickets to burlesque shows by my college's traveling dramatic companies, I'm for Dean McConn's project all the way through. The air is full of brickbats aimed at our monumental educational monstrosity, a waster of youth, a system of tomfoolery, a dishonest hypocrisy. Here's a man gathering the missiles and building them into a solid structure. None of the features he proposes are new or untried. None have failed, not one.

"What about the majority of boys and girls, the superkindergartners, who now warp college into the form it has taken? McConn is fair to them. He sees in their clubs and sports, their smart periodicals and snappy dramatics, an educational content of no little value. Let us have higher schools to satisfy the parents of these youngsters—stadia, theaters, playgrounds, fraternity houses, ivy and architecture. Let the present extra-curriculars constitute the essential core of the course. Put in English composition and literature, foreign dittos, social sciences and the fine arts. Admit on certification from approved schools, preferably private, and let the foundation be known as The Gentleman's College. Let it, in its catalogue, announce its special purpose with entire honesty, saying it does not propose to develop musty pedants or visionary intellectuals, but to prepare normal young people for positions of leadership in the social and business world.

"What is here proposed is to some degree what we have gone some way toward in the lower schools. It is grouping according to aptitudes. It is succeeding so well that McConn's intelligent and brilliant application of the principle to college is the clearest sort of logic. Solid and sensible as his work is, it twinkles with a wit and humor that place it on the list of brightest outputs of the year. If any one doubts this, take as a sample the chapter on coeducation. If this isn't the most concise piece of refutation most charmingly done that you have come across I'll open the leaves of New Republic books for any one who disagrees with me. These publishers still issue their books uncut. It's an atavism and complacency that should, in these days of the measurers, be subjected to a count in order to compute the time wasted by readers in doing machine work by hand."

A thrilling treatise on the culture of loyalties: Denison.—The report of Peter, the Reader, was next:

"I commend to your attention this handsome volume.[2] It treats with engaging and amiable detail a proposition occasionally tossed off without much proof—the idea that our heart rather than our head decides our conduct. Mr. Denison enlarges the notion so as to cover the careers of whole nations and races. By nursing the fear, the awe, the admiration and wonder of men, the priest builds up religion. Pomp and ceremony, color and noise, are summoned to his aid. He suffuses a clan, a tribe, a nation, an empire, with the satisfactions of imagination and desire. King and priest are one. He is the visible symbol of the emotions of the realm. Through the origins of the family, of religion, of the tribe, of the nation, of Egypt, of Persia, of China, of India, of Japan and of Africa, the author carries this fascinating concept, giving to those remote civilizations a closer hold upon you as you realize that he is developing a big idea full of significance for our world future. The strong man proclaims himself god or son of the god. National unity develops on this idea. Divine descent, divine right, holds the reverence and obedience of the

[2] J. H. Denison, "Emotion as the Basis of Civilization," Charles Scribner's Sons, N. Y. 555 pp. $5.00.

subjects. A ruler constrains the whole populace to fulfil his purpose. The nation builds, it paints, it writes, according to his taste. There is no initiative. The patriarchal system produces a static civilization. Then certain races display a forward drive of individual wills. In order to resist destruction by other peoples the people must in certain fields have a common will. Hence came their assemblies in which after weighing proposals of individual wills they adopted a common conclusion. Their laws did not rest on fear and awe as did those of the priest-king. I commend to you the brilliant discourse on the democracy of the Greeks, their dread of one-man power, the tyrannies and cruelties that sprang from it. It and the government of Rome here get a pertinence of uncommon degree. How Christianity adopted the idea of a single ruler and won the emotions by imposing ceremonial, assumed a monopoly of the truth and failed to unify the world, is startlingly narrated. Christianity proclaimed universal brotherhood and practiced such bitter intolerance against outsiders as to make the world suspicious. Mohammed comes with his vision of world unity and warms the emotions of the South and East. Wherever the faithful are, in the grim solitude of the desert, in vast assemblies in a crowded city, they kneel and bow to Mecca, uttering the same words of adoration for the same true god and of loyalty to his prophet, feeling that millions at that precise moment are doing the same. With unflagging interest the underlying theory of this book is carried through the Middle Ages to the development of modern nationality. The formation of Anglo-Saxon ideals is treated with steady brilliancy. How principles were born, rose, sank and arose again, and must be nursed into health and vigor, as, for instance, chivalry and the sense of honor, is portrayed with luminosity. The patriarchal type of civilization reaches a culmination in tyranny and oppression. The pendulum swings to fraternalism. The weaker emotion of brotherhood fails to hold. Love for the strong man restores the monarchy. Now comes America and gathers up the experiences of earlier republics and works them into forms that make possible democracy on a large scale. The old religious cultures which had held nations together are found so useless that the constitution renounces them all and proceeds without any state religion. A few great pioneers saw and proclaimed that authority in government is vested in the people and not in a king; authority in knowledge is founded on search and reason and not on sacred lore; authority in religion and morals is vested in the conscience and not in any pope or sacred book. These are the fundamentals on which democracy is based and are certain to overcome every patriarchal government when they are accepted—all other governments had been a matter of slower growth. The American statesmen created all at once a new scheme and moved into it. There was no king to give them a charter. They drafted a document themselves and swore allegiance to it. This was their basis of unity, as heretofore allegiance to a king had been the bond. This invention has been, since then, so frequently used that we are prone to forget how startling it was. What details of that constitution need repairing the author reviews with lucidity. Our representative government fails to represent the people. Large minorities have no voice in the conduct of our common affairs. The small vote at elections chooses representatives who are not representative. A well-organized and vociferous minority may control government for selfish ends. It should be arranged that smaller classes, workers, professions, should have adequate means of expression so that at least their desires would be known by the legislatures. The domestic tranquillity and general welfare proposed by the constitution have fallen short of realization. The citizen at large has not given to self-government that attention and thought which the founders intended and expected. We do not train our youth in those things which we know to be essential to good government. Our public-school men and women, like the rest of the population, are too prone to rely on custom and tradition as means of making young Americans into the patriotic and fore-sighted statesmen the Revolutionary men were. Other nations have used the religious emotions as means of unity. Napoleon had little belief in God, but he summoned the pope to anoint him with sacred oil. Mussolini has the Tribuna declare, 'In the new government there is to be the leader who can not be confined within the law but who is given us by the will of God.' Democracy is based on the assumption that men are intelligent and will be led by reason to work for the general welfare. But man is not controlled by intelligence or by generous instincts. His feelings and desires direct him. If he is to be rightly governed by himself and his fellows, he and they must have their emotions properly educated. The stability of an autocracy depends upon the awe and reverence of the people toward the ruler; the steadiness of democracy rests on the loyalty of citizens to their mutual agreement or constitution. Emotions of loyalty to a king are easily awakened. They are personal. Loyalty to a constitution depends on a sense of honor and is much harder to get. In a monarchy the emotions are warmed by ceremonial and old effective propaganda. In a democracy there are no intelligently directed emotional cultures. Those of the Catholic church are of a patriarchal system and subversive of democracy; those of the Protestant sects are independent, divisional and subversive of unity. As we study the history of nations and see the tremendous effects produced by emotional cultures we can not but feel that it is possible to cultivate emotions adapted to the forms of a democracy which would add a hundredfold to the excellence of the nation and prevent the great evils of political corruption and disregard of law that are now creeping over us like an insidious disease.

"These quotations give you some idea of the spirit of the work. With admirable sturdiness it proposes the culture of a national ideal, a culture that will make us feel that we are really one, suffering one another's pain, rejoicing in one another's happiness. It is the ideal of the founders. It is the generosity, the public spirit, of a Washington.

"Men have worked together to create a state where justice, brotherhood and peace abide. It should be possible, here, to arouse and maintain an emotion, an ideal, of the American State where there is fair play for all with no unnecessary pain and privation, with mutual sympathy and understanding between all groups, the strong aiding and strengthening the weak. America started with an inspiring declaration of principles. Our representatives are not always so devoted to the general welfare as to their own, but we have developed a sense of honor beyond that of some other peoples. Men in India, given charge of the barriers at railway crossings, won't open them unless you pay them a fee. Natives in Egypt, paid to distribute the irrigating water, are commonly caught shutting it off from farms whose owners will not come across with personal gifts. Dishonest and selfish representatives and servants of democracy have furthered a feeling of resentment toward authority. Respect for father or husband or policeman has grown weak. Modern youth objects to doing right under compulsion, whether it is fear of punishment on earth or dread of hell hereafter. On the other hand, it has a respect for good sportsmanship, and here, maybe, is the survival of the flower of chivalry, the sense of honor. In the school, in the boy scouts, in the college, in the motion-picture houses, in the radio service, in the periodical press, there are the means of cultivating those loyalties on which democracy may find a sure foundation. The patriarchal system can not succeed with us. We have outgrown it. The fratriarchal scheme is not succeeding well—we are too numerous and too diverse. The fact that we coalesce in groups is significant. The refined are drawn together by similar tastes and manners. The noisy soup-eater with egg stains on his vest will never be invited to intimacy with their circle. Nor should he. The progressive thinkers in science or religion or politics will not make welcome the propounder of outworn platitudes. People differ so much that great devotions are impossible in large numbers. Let us recognize, therefore, in the organization of our society the strength that is inherent in group organization. These bodies are of different values to the state. They should be recognized in our civic organization not as hereditary or exclusive castes but as open to all when reaching qualification. Otherwise democracy and its principle of equality is likely to wreck society and progress by clinging to a falsehood. Any scheme treating men as equal in particulars in which they are superior or inferior is doomed to failure as would be that of educating high-school children in a primary grade. The true meaning of democracy is equality of opportunity: in just treatment, in rights to personal possessions, in particular not interfering with the progress of others. Unintelligent democracy tends to reduce everything, government, art, literature, morals, to the vulgar level of mediocrity. We need a constant process of lifting men to higher levels of achievement. It would mean the continued advance of our standards in business, art, education and character. This plan of recognition of groups Mr. Denison calls anepsiarchal.

"I am taking more time than usual. From these samples you must conclude that here is a book greatly worth your perusal. It is a history of civilization unified by a big central idea. It unites what is in most of our minds in the shape of scattered memories and gives them a coherent vitality with large portents for the future. It maintains its thesis by specific instances from a remarkable range of world movements. It strides with a sure majesty toward the expanding ideal of brotherhood. Most men believe in it. It is disseminated through press and drama, art and literature, conversation and the increase of service clubs. It is penetrating every corner of the earth, borne upon the waves of the radio. There is being created a world spirit. It is the only possibility of happiness for all. It is the goal toward which we are progressing as the old selfish passions are gradually submerged, as the howl of the primitive beast-man is lost in the tones of human sympathy. Out of the welter of discord arises a note of the harmony that is to be. It can be heard in the deep roar of the nation's industry, the blare of ten thousand whistles, the sounds in a million homes, the clatter of pans, the happy voices of children, the cheery greetings of hospitality. Clearer and higher, chanting of harmony, and beauty, and kindliness, the mysterious power that throbs in the heart of all mankind announces that sublime event toward which the whole creation moves."

Prize-giving defeating its purposes.—Carolina was next:

"I think one of the going plans for international understanding is the Brooks-Bright encouragement to study. Every year, seniors in secondary schools are encouraged to study some aspect of our foreign relations. Two students are selected each year after their essays have been rated and are given a trip to Europe. They are helped there to make their visit profitable. You can get particulars by writing to Professor Edward M. East, Harvard University. This handsome little publication[3] contains six of the best essays on the effect of the increase of American and British population upon international relations. Wars have come from the need of a growing country to provide homes and sustenance for its increasing numbers. Two boys of New York City, one from Boston, one from New London, one from Saratoga, California, one from Topeka, have their essays printed here, their portraits and pictures of their schools. The disquisitions seemed to me well worth reading. Young Cameron Mackenzie has a striking discussion of the ease with which emotional ties, hands-across-the-sea, can be broken by yellow newspapers. The youngsters have done a commendable amount of wide study. Their style is good; their diction clever and graceful."

"I am not sure," remarked the General, "that writing or doing any individual school work for personal prizes should be encouraged. I am not a bigot, I hope, and I know that the usage is of long standing, and supported by public-spirited citizens and commendable organizations. We, in Chicago, like the school folks in New York, seem to be reaching the conclusion that personal rewards for public service, for essays, for posters, for athletic prowess, are not conducive to the purest motives. For the general welfare, not personal advantage, the originators of our country said we should set up the state. They chose education as one of the state functions to further this ideal. Writing an essay for a prize for oneself is more of a selfish than of a generous performance. You must balance the general good of getting many boys to study a valuable

[3] "Brooks-Bright Essays," The Macmillan Co., N. Y. 95 pp. 72 cents.

subject impelled by a self-rewarding motive against the personal overloaded reward to one boy given a trip to Europe. John's essay is worth, say, 90 on the basis of 100 maximum. Henry's is worth 89. So John gets 100 reward and Henry gets 0."

"How would you spur youth to good deeds?" asked Martin of Tours.

"How do you spur yourself?" returned the General. "What impelled Washington or Lincoln, or the thousands of ministers of the gospel? What impels that not inconsiderable number of men and women teachers who can and who know they can make more money and get more of the world's notice in some other pursuit? Without any effusive, hypocritical gushing, we are bound to say, are we not, that plain duty, or service, to use the word that Rotarians, Kiwanians, Lambs, Boosters, Elks and Moose put into their creeds—service that churches have glorified for generations—is what we are obligated to regard, rather than prizes, trophies, honorable mentions and pictures in the school paper."

"Would you abolish emulation as a school force?" asked Dr. Batwell.

"Why, certainly. Whence came it? The Jesuit schools saddled it upon education. It has run its course in 'head boy,' 'tail boy,' spelling-down matches, tablets with the names of honor students, Arista lists and valedictorians. It is a device to foster envy and to violate the American principle of equality, abolition of artificial distinctions among us. If you are not strong enough to abolish it, as that wonderful Sanderson did in Oundle School, hook it up with general welfare and specify that prizes competed for shall be for groups or schools, not for persons."

"Illustrate," said Martin.

"Like the Union League prizes for the study of the character of Washington," said the General. "They used to be medals with the name of the prize-winner. Uncle John Benham has changed them to a bust or a picture given to the school whose boy or girl writes the best essay. Richard Welling, the New Yorker, who devotes himself to pushing high schools into realizing that their main business is citizenship before Latin, or algebra or any other subject, offers prizes to the school and not to the student. Everybody should study and write upon the theme that is so essentially a public-education requisite, but everybody should do it under circumstances that put him in the position of working for a larger interest than his own advantage."

An obligation shamefully side-stepped, Civic teaching: Mahan.—Polly, the Political, brought to the meeting a collection of books on citizenship. These she described as follows.

"Thomas Jefferson Mahan, Ph.D.,[4] has given the alleged teaching of civics a good jolt. The public schools were instituted chiefly to preserve the principles of the Republic. The statesman whose name this author's parents selected recommended a system of schools based on the proposal to educate each generation in our political fundamentals, to teach youth what is going on now and to imbue each with a desire to make his part of it go on right. The projects of Washington, Franklin, Adams and Madison; the adoption of a system of making the childless as well as parents pay for the education of the coming citizen; the promise of legislators who forced the common-school laws through against earnest opposition in every state; all had in mind a scheme of instruction chiefly political. From time to time the laymen makers of laws have jogged the schoolmasters to attend to the paramount duty of civic training. Dr. Mahan finds the obligation notoriously neglected. Democracy, he says, can't achieve its goal unless every citizen is properly trained to work in that direction. We have assumed that teaching the machinery of government will automatically make the student a good citizen. We have neglected duties and responsibilities. The so-called civic instruction of our schools is vague and indefinite. It has no adequate purpose. It is remote from the needs of the community. It is of little or no practical value.

"How does Mr. Mahan justify this humiliating charge? His investigation is a model of its kind. On the assumption that the schools are supported by the people and belong to them,

[4] Thomas Jefferson Mahan, "An Analysis of the Characteristics of Citizenship," Press of Teachers College, N. Y. 44 pp. $1.50.

not to us teachers, he set out to find a large number of good citizens in various parts of the United States. He began with forty-eight members of four business men's clubs in his own city and twenty professors in the Teachers College. 'Name for me, each of you,' he said, 'four good citizens not including yourself.' From the 272 names thus secured he chose the eighty most frequently named. He interviewed each one at length, asking these questions and recording the answers.

What duties of good citizenship do you perform or believe you should?

What are the difficulties you meet?

What are the ten most important traits of good citizenship?

"Dr. Mahan then selected a hundred cities in four classes according to size and location. He wrote to their superintendents of schools asking each for the names of ten good citizens. That was the number, wasn't it, considered large enough to save the rottenest city in the world from destruction by Jehovah. Fifty-eight superintendents were able, each, to find ten good men in their towns. Mahan put the same questions to these citizens. Two hundred of them were civic enough to answer. So now the doctor had an analysis of the American citizen as conceived, *Anno Republicae* 152. It is one of the most interesting lists you ever saw. The paramount duty, mentioned 180 times, is to render civic service. 'To vote' comes second with 150 counts. At the foot of the list are, 'choose best representatives' and 'refrain from gossip.' You really must examine these duties in the book itself. They are as essential for every teacher to know as are the lists of defects and satisfactory points which our vocational advisers are continuously collecting from employers. The traits specified by Dr. Mahan's correspondents number 88, beginning with honesty, 210 votes, and ending with leadership, five. Forty-four difficulties were recorded, running from lack of information, 71, to neglect of obligations, five.

"Meantime the enquiring Mahan has put 350 high-school students through a similar investigation. He lists their answers. They give the first vote to 'patriotism and loyalty'; the second to 'education'; the lowest choice is 'interest in government.' You note from his tables that the duties, traits and obstacles to good citizenship which the presumed best grown-ups conceive are not to any important degree those which high-school boys say they believe in. This would seem to show what the need of instruction is. Whence cometh instruction? 'Ask the authorities,' answers Mahan, and quotes them. Samuel Parker says the text-books do; Hall-Quest says we depend on the book and follow it in minute detail. Harold Rugg, George Strayer, Brother Bobbitt and Henry Morrison record the same sad story.

"'Come then,' exhorts the relentless Mahan, 'let us tabulate the text-books.' He does not give their titles and authors; there's a tender soul for you! But if you are suspicious of his authenticity he'll tell you their names if you write to him. His facts are amazing, astounding, pitiable, disgraceful, inglorious and scandalous. In these texts the amount of space devoted to treatment of the items named by the 280 selected citizens as important in citizenship runs at 5 per cent., 3 per cent., 6 per cent. and so forth, 10 per cent. being the highest; 5.64 per cent., the average. The most frequent duty of citizens, as named by them, is civic service. Only two of the texts treat it; one, with two pages; the other, with half a page. To corrupt politics one text-book devotes half a page; another, one page; all the others, none. Brother Buchner, of Baltimore, who wrote that clarion-toned book, 'Of What Use are Common People?' will be struck by this point, for he took up with a prominent publisher the proposition to issue a civic text that would incline pupils to learn the truth about such rottenness as is known to exist in city, state and national government. We instruct the traveler as to dangers as well as safe roads. We warn our hygiene classes against harms as well as describe the wholesome things. Our civic teaching is a political anesthesia to the effect that our institutions are perfect and all's right with our world. An important reason for graft is this school-taught patriotism. Mahan's study shows the prominence of ignorance as an obstacle to good citizenship. Well, the publisher was apparently uninterested in such a treatise as Buchner proposed and which, if anybody can, he would make vibrate with good, hot, indignation such as the old Romans nursed into effective action.

"My time is up. I am loath to close, for I have not told you all of the benefits of this snug little volume. Its analyses are safe starting-points for chapters and exercises in a real civics curriculum or text. Here's praying that some one who knows how to write, some one in whom the fires of our American Revolution still glow, some one who has vibrations in tune with the spirits of the glorious originators of this Republic may compose a school manual on the basis here furnished." (Applause.)

A Godsend for the Civics Teacher: Greenan.—"John Greenan, whose spirited book on the problems of democracy was complimented by being excluded from Chicago high schools by a two-by-four official because it gave both sides of controversial subjects, issues a companion work.[5] It opens with a quotation from Bishop Oldham which ought to please our mayor:

> America First.
>
> Not in pride, arrogance and disdain of other races.
>
> Not in treading again the old, worn, bloody pathway which ends in chaos and disaster.
>
> But in blazing a new trail along which, please God, other nations will follow where wars shall be no more.

"Master Greenan says supplementary readings must be selected, from live, present-day material and be short enough to show that we recognize that we can't get the long home study that we might wish. We must compete with ball games, movies, radios, and use the slogan of our competitors: 'Make it snappy.' Accordingly John has clipped from the current civic magazines forty-eight articles on democracy, immigration, presidential campaigns, city politics, lobbies, educational funds, Volsteadism, war, peace, imperialism, Philippines, family problems, divorce, farms, crime, railroad rates, labor, capital and tariff. You listen to Lowden, Borah, Hoover, Smith, Coolidge, Commons, Hapgood, Rockefeller, Green and men like them. The selections are classified in a logical order and each is given a careful and broad-minded introduction to help bring the matter into an integrated body of thought. The bibliography, the 'laboratory exercises,' the questions, make this a godsend to teachers who are working overtime to find current material of civic value."

War Facts, Peace Arguments for Teachers: Boeckel.—"Florence Boeckel is education director of the National Council for Prevention of War. She has compiled a handbook for peace-workers.[6] Its aim is to focus the large volume of more or less intense desire of the people of the world to graduate from the old, expensive and unintelligent methods of settling disputes between nations. Naturally, and thereby especially pertinent to us, the book starts with education. That's right. Our main business is peace, construction, progress, building, perfecting. I do not see how any one can give any thought to the ordinary aspirations and intent of teaching without realizing that teachers are constitutionally and inevitably opposed to war, which, in such awful proportion, destroys the work on which we spend our lives. When any newspaper or prominent member of a community upholds warlike preparations and throws contempt upon people who oppose these activities it is well for us to remember that our national association of teachers, which is the largest society in the world, is officially on record for making war an outlaw. The greatest newspaper in our city had a spell of excitement over our sanity a while ago and printed editorials on 'yellow schools.' An excited school-board damned and banned a history syllabus prepared by our whole teaching force because there was provided instruction upon the cost and wastefulness of war. Miss Boeckel devotes a hundred and seventeen pages to quotation of our various resolutions, text-book provisions, and so forth, and supplies detailed suggestions for teaching international tranquillity through geography, history, civics, even by domestic science, mathematics and athletics. No school subject is neglected. Miss Boeckel's work is valuable because of its logical and orderly arrangement of supremely important affairs, but the extracts she has collected and interspersed throughout the volume give it a glow and fervor that make its study amply rewarded."

The mission of Jesus was not political: Mathews.—"To those reformers who are too prone to use some pronouncement of Jesus as

[5] John T. Greenan, "Readings in American Citizenship," Houghton Mifflin Co., Boston. 436 pp. $1.90.

[6] Florence Brewer Boeckel, "Between War and Peace," The Macmillan Co., N. Y. 591 pp. $2.50.

authority for their proposed legislation, Dr. Shailer Mathews's new book[7] makes gentle remonstrance. Christ nowhere gives political teaching. His attitude toward the state and politics is seen in his own life. Others, like Plato and Mohammed, weighted their philosophy and religion with political teachings that were either so ideal as to be impracticable or so practicable as eventually to be outgrown. Although the Jews hungered for political leadership, although the Romans finally executed Jesus on the charge of it, he rejected it and held himself sternly to the duties of a preacher of good-will. What the revolutionary disturbances were in Jesus's time, how the revolutionary spirit affected him, what his teachings were on the family, on marriage, on wealth, on the state and on the church, are reviewed here with the author's frequent demonstration of how these teachings were not for building a system but to develop an attitude of brotherliness. Dean Mathews, as many of you know from personal acquaintance, is easy and pleasant to follow. The whole of this book is of steady interest."

How to Stop Hating the Foreigner among us: Bogardus.—"A favorite platform speaker of some few years ago, an Illinois schoolmaster, William Hawley Smith, used to say that there's nothing in the world more interesting than folks. Emory Bogardus has produced a folk study[8] that touches all of us. He inquires what our attitudes are to the Negro, the Armenian, the Jew, the Mexican, the Englishman, in our midst. Our nationality involves a bewildering array of behavior-patterns and values. Some are relatively fixed; others are fluid. Our immigrant is a native of one country; for the time being a part of another. He is a human person with loves and hates, trust and suspicion, in a turmoil. In the South the Negro is one of the most disconcerting conundrums in spite of efforts being made to solve it. In the East the diverse races threaten community relationships. In the West the Japanese problem is an incitement to animosities. Professor Bogardus searches our race antipathies and predilections, measuring their weight as affecting forty lineages. Likes and dislikes differ in various regions. Antipathies of teachers, employers, workmen, women, means of abatement, and so on, are treated in a refreshing variety of incident and comment so as to produce a readable and instructive work."

Civics for the younger children: The Hepners.—"Walter and Frances Hepner give us a civics reader for the younger children.[9] It is in story form with the up-to-date usage of motivating each lesson by putting the questions first. The Minter twins have spirited adventures: forming a citizens' club, learning about municipal health and fire-prevention, Jane Addams, Red Cross, postal usages, presidents and service. It is a jolly and wholesome little book, full of movement and equipped with an abundance of questions, plans and themes for class discussions that go straight to the heart of the whole problem: good-will, sense of honor, general welfare, unselfishness."

Real romance in civic study: Hagedorn.—"I had another book of citizenship, but I lent it to Peter. He hasn't returned it, so I can't tell you the number of pages and the cost. Maybe the archivist who sends our proceedings to the magazine will supply this conventional information. I call your attention to Herman Hagedorn's engaging story.[10] The skilful author introduces Zach, who is trying hard to study his civics, who wishes his teacher would make things as interesting as his mother does, and who succumbs to the dullness of his book and goes to sleep. Then come to him the thoughts his mother had provoked. Zach is launched into adventure, performance and progress, himself sharing in the big historical events which brought us our civic blessings. There is something about Hagerdorn's temperament that gives

[7] Shailer Mathews, "Jesus on Social Institutions," The Macmillan Co., N. Y. 158 pp. $1.50.

[8] Emory S. Bogardus, "Immigration and Race Attitudes," D. C. Heath & Co., New York. 268 pp. $1.80.

[9] Walter and Frances Hepner, "Junior Citizens in Action," Houghton Mifflin Co., New York. 257 pp. 60 cents.

[10] Herman Hagedorn, "The Dreams of Zach Peters," John C. Winston Co., Philadelphia.

him a grip on young readers. I have tried this Peters story on several children. They are enthusiastic about it."

This ended the contributions of Polly, the Political.

There is nothing about reading omitted: Wiley.—Principal Philip Manzer, Philip, the Philanthropic, took up the subject of reading:

"If there is any defect or excellence in the teaching of reading that Professor Wiley, of State Teachers College, Iowa, hasn't captured and put into his collection,[11] I who have taught and supervised this subject for many a year can not think of it. Every difficulty I have encountered, every device I have learned or invented, is here in this little encyclopedia of the subject. It's a treasure chest, sure enough. The excellences of oral reading and by what practice to get them, how to keep reading aloud from preventing real reading, closing the mouth tight, preventing the impediment of whispering and lip moving, the useful device of holding something in the mouth, the need of varying bodily postures, the prevention of eye fatigue, the desirability of a worth-while content in practice and corrective drills, the way to cure mind-wandering, the phenomenon of reading a page without knowing what it's about, the method of noting essentials in a paragraph, exercises in translating written directions into action, the waste of too much teacher-help, the almost unknown attention to training pupils to doubt what they see in print and thus to know how to read a newspaper, the very valuable ability to guess what points are going to come up in examination, and hundreds of other facts, habits and requisites germane to reading and study are covered in this compendium of specific lessons. Professor Wiley says he writes for those intending to teach reading, for those who are already teaching it, for college students who flounder in the abundance of print they are required to wade through, and for superintendents who need to know why their system does not make readers and students. To my mind every teacher who is concerned with the learning process of her pupils—for reading is the core of all instruction—will find this manual a boon. If I were one of those nabobs who, we are told, make a practice of owning philosophers and learned men to keep the royal mind supplied with the means of knowing what is wanted I would subsidize this expert diagnostician and trainer to give me the power to use what I call my mind to the best advantage."

A tabulation of reading practices: Zirbes.—"One other valuable addition to the library of the teacher of reading is Dr. Laura Zirbes's comparison[12] of the various practices now used to train the young in this chief of the scholar's arts. Her inventory of what the teachers do is a time-saver for any one who teaches. Her list of objectives is provocative of progress and refreshment. So are her parallel columns of good and poor planning, good and poor courses, good drills and poor ones in the same school system, evaluation of teaching and supervisory experiments. This is a book that will save teacher, principal and superintendent the slow and wearing process of trial and error. Get it, keep it handy. Take draughts of it at intervals. It will pay."

Chicago Schoolmasters mildly self-critical.—The Viking Maid held up a blue volume and thus commented:

"Again the Chicago Principals' Club contributes a book[13] devoted to the professional task of stiffening their service. A modest, anonymous member contributes an animated introduction reminding us that a principals' organization is obligated to maintain high professional standards. You get these by knowing what the science of education is. If your club is professional, the general public will approve it. Politics will yield to what is best for the schools. To hold professional standards, results must be attained based on scientific procedure. Opinion will not suffice. You must test and report facts. The standing of a professional organization is established by evidence of this

[11] J. A. Wiley, ''Practice Exercises in Silent Reading and Study,'' published by the author, Cedar Falls, Iowa. 368 pp. $2.00.

[12] Laura Zirbes, ''Comparative Studies of Current Practice in Reading,'' press of Teachers College, N. Y. 229 pp. $2.00.

[13] ''The Chicago Principals' Club,'' Third Yearbook, Club Headquarters, 315 Plymouth Court. 196 pp. $1.00.

sort. What is this club's reputation? Is it content to let instruction remain as it is? Or is the club promotive of studies for the improvement of teaching? They tell us the schools are behind the procession. For example, how are the schools dealing with the problems of citizenship? We've got to find out very soon how to get at the larger problems. So proceeds this snappy writer of a pointed preface. One might seem to see between these lines a mild and cautious protest against the outrageous overlords of the Chicago schools who, after the work of a great committee of teachers, selected by votes of the principals for superior competency, relentlessly and without reason threw into the discard exactly such a study as the writer of the introduction extols. Thousands of dollars expended in printing the contributions of thousands of the best workers in Chicago were thrown away. A committee of the most strenuous, generous, industrious, patriotic sort, without any thanks, is kicked out of the board rooms for what? For having been appointed under a previous president. If for no other reason than to mitigate the contempt at large for Chicago schools this work of the principals is a timely project. It organizes material for reading; it works out standards of achievement in arithmetic; develops lessons for the deaf and proposes reorganization of the kindergarten. I should like to propose the work for crowning by us when our awards are made at the end of the year."

"Are you one of the authors of it?" asked Polly, the Political.

"I decline to answer, on advice of counsel," retorted the Viking.

Pussyfoot Supervision: Brueckner, Hosic and Others.—The Signpost was first at the bat, saying:

"Twenty contributors, of whom thirteen are professors of education, give us their views on supervision.[14] It no longer has to argue its right to exist, says Professor Burton, of the University of Wisconsin. All the tests of what pupils know and can do show that those whose teachers were guided and followed up ranked ahead of those whose teachers were not. When any productive process is performed in parts by different workers as in a graded school or a post office or a hospital, organization is essential; direction prevents waste of time and effort. I glean from the various chapters that teaching is especially backward among productive services on account of a common feeling of distaste for being supervised and because of a tendency of supervisors to want a thing to be done because the supervisor orders it. Colonel Hamilton, our Revolutionary Alexander, considered the best army one composed of obedient soldiers who do not think. In this book William Kilpatrick discourses approvingly of democracy in supervision. 'Seldom will the supervisor wish to settle anything on authority but will be willing democratically to trust a fresh democratic study.' Brother Bobbitt sounds the same note: 'The thing is not to tell teachers what to do but rather to clarify and quicken their vision so that they can see for themselves what to do.' They remind one of superintendents' opinions collected by Lotus Coffman, indicating that the main business of the supervisor is to sympathize and not to interfere. Comrade Curtis, in this volume, is not so squeamish. 'Teachers,' he says, 'are not the only possessors of inalienable natural rights and needs. Education is established and paid for by society for definite purposes other than jobs for teachers. The superintendent is the community's responsible agent to get its work done. He must have complete control. No sophistries about democracy can lessen the superintendent's duty to make decisions, to guide, direct and control.' I am wondering whether the persistence of schools in continuing their neglect of demonstrated ways of efficient teaching, a weakness noted by so many authors who have been reviewed here, is not due to an overplus of sentimentality regarding us, the teachers. With all the definite results of research determining better and poorer procedures of instruction why must a superintendent wait for us to make a democratic search for method? If I were a superintendent I would say, 'Here, you, listen to this. Here's the way spelling is now being taught with the best returns. Our patrons are entitled to this. Use it.' I'd send my inspectors into the schools. Where I found a dear old lady still dawdling

[14] "Educational Supervision," First Yearbook, National Conference on Educational Method, press of Teachers College, N. Y. 270 pp. $1.10.

along with the method of 1840, I'd put her on the carpet."

"That," shot Anna, the Arguer, "is why you are not a superintendent."

"Why is it," asked the Signpost, smiling at his assailant, "that physicians are so much more up-to-date than we in the use of proven treatments?"

"They aren't," interposed Dr. Batwell. "After Lister had reduced by antiseptic precautions the mortality in his hospital ward to an amazing extent the surgeons of the other wards went on in the old way with their murderous methods. Only Lister's students used and spread his technique."

"That's another argument for hard, unsympathetic supervision," retorted the Signpost. "It was Judge Andrew S. Draper, educator, who had the honesty to tell the people that the teachers were wasting the lives of the children. The trouble with our schools to-day is that in too many cases the head man acts as though his title were sympathizer not superintendent. He plans for popularity, not for performance. His discourse at our meetings is pap, sweet stuff, best-teachers-in-the-world bouquets, when he might be giving the people what they pay for: the best training discovered by experimenters in our line."

"Come back to book, thou caustic Cato," said Carolina.

"Quite right. The primary fact this volume stresses is that the majority of teachers are inadequately trained. They don't know what has been found elsewhere to be best. It is absolutely essential to provide expert and unifying supervision. If any opposition has been justified, it has been by faulty supervision, not by the supreme value of academic initiative or freedom. We are not free. Acceptance of engagement and receipt of payment bind us in obligation to a system controlled by a superintendent. How supervision is done in various schools, how supervisors are trained, how principals waste time, how they lie about their day's work, how research is pinning them down to productive service and supplanting the overworked inspirational appeal, how good teaching may be evaluated, how supervision is appraised, constitute the bulk of the collection. It's a good book, despite its timid spots and willingness to wait for better service until the supervisor can coax the teachers not to be hurt by getting out of the rut. It's the first yearbook. I wish they had secured a few supervisors of other than schools to write a chapter or two. Maybe the second volume will give us that. But let us thank Chairman Brueckner and Editor Hosic. It's a good start."

Putting purpose into performance: Drum.—The Signpost continued:

"A large trouble with us, says Warren Nevin Drum,[15] is that we are not thinking of the outcomes that should ensue from the activities we direct. I had a principal once who had us teachers fill out slips a day ahead, one for each lesson, recording what mental power we planned to strengthen in our hopefuls by means of the tasks required. I remember one of us wrote 'attention' on one hundred and ninety-five slips to cover the whole year and then dismissed the matter from her mind. We had a superintendent who urged us to stop speaking of an arithmetic class but to program a period for accuracy, reliability and persistence. There was a school of a good deal of note in rural New York which abandoned subjects and called them 'influences.' Latin and its teacher were 'the classic influence,' and so forth. I heard the late Hugo Münsterberg vent much sarcastic ridicule against bothering with aims in teaching. The German schoolmasters, the best in the world, he said, had no aims. It seems that Hugo stemmed no tide. Aims, purposes, objectives, dot the pages of all the educational literature I meet. I feel that if my boss should come into my class and find us all rolling down the wind without a good bright aim fluttering at our masthead he ought to make us go ashore to some supply house and get one.

"Dean Drum gets an aim for us derived from the historic development of education. School is the intentional agency set up by society to perpetuate civilization through the transmission of its acquired controls to each oncoming generation. Don't soothe yourself by concluding that this means acquainting the youth with the

[15] Warren Nevin Drum, "A Preview of Teaching," Ginn & Co., N. Y. 337 pp. $1.80.

acquisitions of the past. One of the important transmissions is a drive for progress. My best teaching is not with the things that were but with the desire for the things that ought to be. Mr. Drum avoids a not uncommon haziness I have regretted in some educational books read. He starts various discussions with a distinct definition of what he means. His illustrations especially delight me due to a predilection for a famous old book my father gave me, Todd's 'Student's Manual.' The citations in the present volume remind me of it. They are unstilted, unforced, concerned with familiar things. Thus does my author survey for me the physical and mental bases of education, its purposes, its organization to achieve them, my responsibilities, my discipline, study, pupil conferences, drills, appreciation, and lastly—a surprise—it is entitled 'As Others See Us.' I need not give you samples of it. One part is as good as another and all of it is prime."

Mastery of teaching: Fontaine.—The Post's last report was as follows:

"We were told here that Charles Holley's new book on modern principles for the elementary teacher makes no bones of telling us that we are too slow in making our guide what numerous investigations have shown to be efficient and economical ways. My author, Clarke Fontaine,[16] is another confessed reformer who doesn't attempt to soothe us by saying we are doing pretty well. He is a state inspector of high schools. He has to hear and appraise the work of teachers. It isn't good enough. He gives verbatim reports of high-school exercises of the sort going on everywhere and says, 'This won't do. There's no reason why you should potter like this. You're merely treadmilling. Wake up. Use your brains. Make up your mind before you start to-day's lesson in Latin what worth-while changes it should make in the children who are put through it. Consider what management of the exercise is likely to produce those changes. From time to time stiffen your mind by reading up-to-date conclusions on the manner of performing your specific subject. Occasionally apply standard measurements to find out how much your ministrations have improved your flock.' Young teachers, he says, and those of ripe experience continue to hear lessons and to treat subject-matter as ground to be covered. He's for the paidocentric teaching about which Harold Rugg writes a whole set of books. You'll search long before you'll find a cleaner-cut disquisition as to how to spend that forty or sixty minutes in which a class is in your presence and under your direction. This chapter, by diagram, example and reasoning from principles, is worth a high-school director's learning by heart and delivery to a staff meeting. From actual exercises managed by teachers in his bailiwick Inspector Fontaine supplies a wealth of aids such as we are commonly asking, concrete examples of the way work should be done. The how and the why of the socialized recitation, the laboratory method in literature, history and civics, the preponderating importance of study over recitation, and the ways to engender habits of work are handled in a masterly manner. Here is, at last, a bold and honest statement given with startling frankness: 'Home-study is largely a myth. It is practically impossible for you to secure it for the majority of your pupils.' To continue to give out home-work as if it could be secured, to build high-school procedure on learning that depends on home-work, to have promotions on it, to hold back and to drive out of high school those who fail, to continue expecting high school to be a sifting concern for only the fittest is to forget the obligations of democracy. We are in the race between catastrophe and education. Every normal youth belongs in high school. It's the high school's business to fit itself to all the children of adolescent age. This is a good, brave book, based on broad views. It has a patriotic philosophy and a drive toward teaching that has clear aims and a mastery of method rather than a subjection to it."

The afterfeast (nafeest) of this session was Netherlandish, furnished by Lady Alice as reminiscent of the Roses' summer in Katwyk. There were sandwiches (tusschen anderen plaatsen met kaas), chocolade, cakes (koeken) called zwaluwen (swallows), in the shape of little birds. There were candies (suikergoeden), brought from Leijden. Full of these and of good cheer, hoi bibliologoi went to their homes.

[16] E. Clarke Fontaine, "Ways to Better Teaching in the Secondary School," Ginn & Co. N. Y. 271 pp. $1.60.

SCHOOL AND SOCIETY

EDITED BY J. McKEEN CATTELL
WITH WHICH IS COMBINED THE
EDUCATIONAL REVIEW
EDITED BY WILLIAM McANDREW

Volume XXIX | Saturday, January 12, 1929 | Number 733

WINNETKA

By CARLETON WASHBURNE
WINNETKA, ILLINOIS

There is a small city, a suburb of Chicago, that is well named Winnetka. For "Winnetka" is an American Indian word meaning "beautiful land." Winnetka lies on the shore of Lake Michigan where once an oak forest grew. It is a suburb of beautiful homes, each surrounded by garden and lawn, shrubs and usually some of the old forest oaks. Its often winding streets are lined with elms and maples. There are no factories. There are no flats and apartment buildings. People move to Winnetka in order to have a good place in which their children may grow up to happy, clean, effective manhood and womanhood. Most Winnetka men work in Chicago's offices and factories. They are business and professional people with rather good incomes from their work, able to afford a little or a large home, with some ground around it.

There are poorer people, too, in Winnetka, although there are seldom any who are destitute. A town of twelve thousand people must have its garbage collectors, its ditch diggers, its street sweepers, the workers in the local laundry, the clerks in the local stores. These people live in Winnetka in smaller homes, but still with a bit of garden and lawn.

Both rich and poor send their children to the Winnetka public schools.

Three of these are elementary schools for children between the ages of five and eleven. One is a junior high school for children of twelve and thirteen. From the junior high school the children go to a township high school, a large centralized institution for the children of Winnetka and three other suburbs somewhat similar in their general character.

Winnetka's school buildings are modern, clean, well-aired, well-lighted, attractive to look at, attractive to be in. Each is surrounded by trees and shrubs and grass, and has ample space for the children to play. Inside they are well equipped with movable furniture. The rooms, especially for the little children, are homelike, with flowers, curtains, goldfish and birds. Let us go into one of these buildings and watch the children at work.

We go to the kindergarten. Its large bay window to the south contains a window seat, on which the teacher is sitting, surrounded by children listening to a story. Round tables, large enough for a dozen or fifteen children each, stand in the main part of the room. Soon the children are at these tables, molding things with clay, drawing with crayons, building with blocks. Some children are in the little workroom just off the main kindergarten. Here with coping saws and beaver board they are making toys—a boy is taking a box and nailing a back on it to make a chair or a girl is making a bed for her dolls. The children are moving about freely, to a large extent choosing their own activities. There is much of the spirit of Montessori in the kindergarten, but few if any of the Montessori materials. Some of Froebel's gifts can be seen, but they are being used by the children merely as playthings.

After forty or fifty minutes of free activities the children come together for a song and some rhythms. Then with the teacher they go out to gather different kinds of seeds if it is fall, or buds if it is spring. Or they visit the local stores and see how things are sold, or go to the dairy and watch the milk being bottled.

The kindergarten has no academic aims. It exists in Winnetka, as in many places in America, to give the children training in social attitudes, in ability to get along with one another, in proper habits of health. It exists, too, to give children a chance to create, a chance to be themselves as fully as possible.

Let us step into a first-grade room, a room for six-year-old boys and girls.

The children are seated at little tables, enameled cream-color and covered with fringed, colored burlap cloths on which the children have embroidered designs. As we look around the room we see paintings made by the children, illustrations of stories they have heard, pictures of things they have seen on their field trips. These paintings are on large sheets of paper, about eighteen by twenty-four inches in size. Each is mounted in a crude lath frame made by the children themselves and freely decorated by them.

We see the children at work, each doing his own individual task. One is learning to recognize phrases, another to recognize separate words; a third is applying his knowledge of words to the reading of a story in his primer. Few children are doing exactly the same things.

The devices are such that each child can teach himself and correct his own work. Their absorption as they bend over their tasks or their relaxation as they stop to chat with one another, is wholly childlike. The teacher is going about among them, sitting with this one a while, encouraging that one, taking a small group together and explaining some of their work. The whole atmosphere of the room is one of informality and pleasant, serious work.

Then perhaps it is time for milk. The children pass the little bottles around, and each child drinks through a straw while the teacher reads them a story.

Now it is time to work on the little farm that the children are making. They have been out to a real farm in the country and have seen the barn and the cows and chickens and pigs. They want a make-believe farm in their classroom. They are full of ideas as to ways of making it. One boy has brought a large box from home, which will make the beginning of a barn. Some have modeled little animals from plasticene or clay. Others have drawn pictures of what they would like their model farm to be like. All have ideas. All pool them in the discussion. They reach decisions and get to work with saw, and hammer, and paint brush, and clay, again wholly absorbed.

Let us spend a large part of a day in a fourth-grade room, watching the activities of nine-year-old children. We get there in the morning before the children come.

The children enter the room informally. Each sits at his seat and takes from his drawer some piece of work. As we go about among the children we find that most of them are perhaps doing arithmetic. A few are working on other subjects. We stop at the desk of Charles, the son of the local butcher. Like almost all the children, he is rosy-cheeked, decently dressed, natural and unrepressed. He is beginning the subject of long division. He looks at his book and finds a simple explanation written in language he can understand. The explanation carries him only one step forward. It shows him how he can write down what he has heretofore been doing mentally in short division. It contains several worked-out examples. Charles covers each of these with a piece of paper and tries to work them himself. Then he compares his work with the work in the book.

After one or two unsuccessful attempts he gets the knack and turns to the page of exercises. The first of these comes under a heading A. He works through this A assignment, perhaps occasionally glancing back at the explanation if he feels himself in doubt. When he finishes the eight or ten examples that make up this assignment, he finds at the bottom of the page a note: "For answers, see page 9." On page 9 he finds all the examples worked out for him. He compares his work. Two of his examples are wrong. He turns back to the page of exercises and does the B assignment: five more examples of the same kind as those he has been attempting. Again he looks to page 9 to see if his answers are right and if his work is properly set down. This time he has made no errors, so he skips C and D and turns to Step 2 on the next page of his book. Step 2 is presented as follows:

At our school bazaar the fourth-grade children took orders for 96 garden markers. There were 32 children. How many markers should each child make to complete the order?

To find the answer you would have to divide 96 by 32. Have you ever worked an example like this? How many times does 3, the first number in your divisor, go into 9? 3 goes into 9, 3 times; so 32 will probably go into 96, 3 times. Place the 3 directly above the 6 of the 96. In long division it is very important to place the figures in your answer correctly.

This is right: $\begin{array}{r} 3 \\ 32\overline{)96} \end{array}$ This is wrong: $\begin{array}{l} 3 \\ 32\overline{)96} \end{array}$

Now multiply 32 by 3. Try to do the multiplication in your head. Write the answer, 96, like this:

$$\begin{array}{r} 3 \\ 32\overline{)96} \\ 96 \end{array}$$

Subtract 96 from 96. Write the remainder, 0, under the 6.

$$\begin{array}{r} 3 \\ 32\overline{)96} \\ 96 \\ \hline 0 \end{array}$$

Each child should make 3 garden markers.

Try this one: $21\overline{)42}$

It is explained, in the book, step by step.

In doing the following examples, remember to (1) divide; (2) multiply; (3) subtract; (4) be careful to place your answer correctly.

Do this example: $20\overline{)40}$. Look at the first example at the top of page 8 to see if your work is right.

On page 8, at the top, the child finds three worked out examples, then an A assignment of ten examples for him to attempt, a B assignment of five, a C of five and a D of five. After the A assignment appears this instruction: "If you have made any mistakes in A, first correct your mistakes, then work B." And after the B assignment appears this: "If B is all right, you may skip C and D, but if you made any mistakes in B, correct these mistakes, then work C."[1]

Charles works unmindful of the clock or of the other children. He is deeply absorbed because he is starting on a fresh process. He finds himself a little puzzled as to parts of the explanation. He steps to another child and asks for help, selecting a child who is farther advanced than himself. Perhaps he is not satisfied. Then he asks the teacher.

Let us look around at the other children. One of them is completing his compound multiplication in arithmetic. Another is ahead of Charles. He has finished the first eight steps of his long division and is giving himself a practice test. This test will bear examining in some detail.

It consists of seven examples, one to correspond with each step of actual long divi-

[1] "Washburne Individual Arithmetic." Book Six. Carleton Washburne and Marion Carswell. World Book Company.

sion work. One is very simple, with no difficulties whatever. Another contains a nought in the answer. Another has a remainder. And so on. As the child completes the test he finds these directions: "Compare your answers with the answers on page 30. If your work is correct, ask your teacher for a real test." He turns to page 30 to correct his work. He finds the following directions and answers:

Suppose you did not get 4 for your first answer. The (111) under the 4 tells you to turn to page 111 in your Correction Book. Work 5 examples there. When you have corrected your work, you may take Form 2 of the Practice Test.

4 (111) 4_{r4} (114) 36_{r2} (117) 90_{r9} (119)

1_{r8} (113) 70 (118) 84 (115)

The child has made mistakes in the fourth and sixth examples, those involving a nought at the end. He goes quietly to the teacher's desk and gets a Correction Book. He turns to page 119 and page 118 and does the indicated work. Then he goes back to his own book and does Form 2 of the practice test. Form 2 is identical in the elements it covers with Form 1, but the actual answers are different. This time the child makes no mistakes and asks the teacher for a real test. The teacher hands him a Test Book, in which no answers are given, but in which there is a test that corresponds exactly with the form that he has just taken. There are no trick examples. There is no example which contains a single difficulty that was not contained in the test the child gave himself. That test covered completely and diagnostically the first eight steps of his work in long division. The real test covers the same steps. He finishes the test and puts it on the teacher's desk for her to correct. Then perhaps he turns to his reading.

Helen has just received back from her teacher a test in compound multiplication that she took yesterday. The test is not marked as to its quality. Two of the examples, however, are circled, and after each is written the number of the page in the Correction Book, where the child will find additional exercises of the same sort as those which she missed in her test. Helen takes a copy of the Correction Book from the teacher's desk and works the assignments indicated. She corrects the work herself and finds that she still is making mistakes. She turns back to the original explanation in her own book, but perhaps can not yet see what is wrong with her work. (No matter how carefully the material is prepared, an occasional child will need direct help from the teacher.) Her hand goes up and the teacher soon comes to her and gives her the necessary help.

At every moment the teacher is down among the children, working with them, helping this one over a difficulty, stimulating that one, putting these two who are a bit lazy into competition with each other, supervising the work of another—teaching every moment, but never lecturing to the class as a whole, or hearing class recitations.

The arithmetic period lasts perhaps forty minutes. Some children have stopped their arithmetic before the time was up. A few have been working on language or reading or history and geography. These children are those who are classified as self-reliant and therefore may budget their own time; or perhaps they are children who are ahead in their arithmetic and behind in some other topic, and have therefore been told by the teacher to spend more time on the subject in which they are slower, less on the one in which they are faster. The period closes, but Charles is oblivious to the fact. The teacher glances at him, notices that he is absorbed in his new undertaking, and does not interrupt. The other children quietly take out their language books and begin similar individual work in them.

Again there are practice exercises so arranged that the child who learns a new step quickly may skip additional drill and go to the next step, while the child who makes mistakes the first time has a second, or third, or even a fourth opportunity to practice, so that he may *master* that step before going on to the next. Again we find the children at all sorts of different points in their work. Here is a child who has begun fifth-grade work, although still sitting in the fourth-grade room. Here is another who has not quite completed her third-grade work. Each child is going at his own rate. Each child when he reaches a practice test is checking himself and practicing where he finds himself weak. Each child when he completes a practice test is taking a complete diagnostic test given by the teacher. These diagnostic tests, like the practice tests and teaching material, have been prepared by a group of teachers working together and have been revised over and over to fit the needs of the children. The tests have been made, *not for the purpose of marking children, but for the purpose of finding out where each child needs help.* They are therefore not dreaded, but are asked for. The test is the way the child can prove to himself and the teacher that he is ready to go on to the next unit of work. A failure on the test simply means the necessity for practicing on his weak points, but no further retardation in progress.

Each test is made in several forms, all equivalent. The teacher may give one form to one child, a different form to another, but there is little danger of children trying to pass on to one another the answers to these tests. They know what the tests are going to contain in advance, for their practice tests contain exactly the same elements. There is no temptation to cheat.

Now it is playtime. The children in this room and those from one or two other rooms go out to the playground together. A trained playground director awaits them. She helps them to organize themselves into teams for some form of competitive game. As they play she helps to bring home to them the ideal of sportsmanship, of good fellowship, of team play. The playground is not merely a place for recreation, not merely a place for physical development. It is also a place where ideals are inculcated, where children learn to be social minded, where they learn the value of persistence and of team work.

Playtime is over. These children return to their rooms, while other children go to the playground.

The children sing—not songs written especially to teach children singing, but fine old folk songs from Germany, from Russia, from Spain, from England, or songs by some of the great masters. They sing for the joy of singing, wasting no time on drills in "do, ra, me, fa." Such drills are reserved for those who are going to specialize in music and may be given higher in the grades.

Then perhaps the teacher reads aloud to the children a story or some poems, and they discuss them together. This work is for appreciation, not for mastery of knowledges or skills. It is quite free, it is entirely unmarked, it has nothing to do with promotion.

Assembly time has come. The children go into the assembly room, where two or three hundred of their fellows are gathered. Yesterday one of the rooms had presented a play that it had worked out. To-morrow the assembly will be given over to a talk with a stereopticon. But to-day is a business meeting.

The meeting is presided over by an eleven-year-old girl, who has been elected chairman. The secretary, a boy, reads the minutes of the last meeting; a few routine matters are cleared out of the way; then the chairman asks if there is any new business. Our friend Charles, from the fourth grade, rises in his place. "In the last business meeting in our room," he says, "we discussed the question of water pistols in school. A lot of the children have been bringing water pistols and squirting water on each other on the playground or in the halls. The children in our room don't think we ought to allow it any more." Charles sits down. A fifth-grade boy stands and is recognized by the chairman. "We talked about it in our room, too, and we decided that it would be all right to bring water pistols to school if we only used them on one part of the playground and everybody who wanted to play with water pistols went to that part of the playground. I don't think that we should keep everybody from having water pistols just because some children don't want them. I don't see what harm they are, any way."

A girl stands up. "The boys fill their water pistols with dirty water. It's likely to have germs in it and to make us sick. It gets our clothes all dirty, too. I don't think we ought to allow any water pistols in the school."

A boy: "We might ask the janitor to set out some pails of clean water and have a rule that everybody would have to fill his water pistol from those pails of clean water instead of from puddles or from any dirty water. Then if we kept all the shooting of the water pistols to one part of the playground, I can't see that it would do any harm."

Charles speaks again: "The water wouldn't stay clean if everybody filled his pistol in it. And the children who wanted to play with water pistols would hide behind the children who didn't want to so as not to get shot with the water, and I don't think the thing would work at all. I move that water pistols be kept away from the school and the playground."

The motion is seconded. There is a little more discussion. Then a vote. A large majority votes against the water pistols. (From that time on no water pistols appear in school—the children usually obey their self-imposed rules.)

The children go home for luncheon.

It is afternoon. Our fourth-grade children are returning to their seats. Each one is taking out his work. It is spelling this time. Let us see what Charles is doing.

He has a spelling book in which certain words are checked. We find that all the words for the first half of the year were dictated to him and all the other pupils in the room in September, before the children had had a chance to study them. All words missed by any child were checked in that child's speller, thereby making an individual word list for each pupil. Charles has studied six of these checked words the preceding day. He now hands the list of these six words to his partner, Walter, who has moved his desk closer to Charles for the spelling period. Walter dictates to Charles the six words that Charles studied yesterday. Charles writes the words. Then Charles dictates to Walter a similar list of the words that Walter studied yesterday. The two boys correct their own work with each other's help. Then each sets about the studying of a new group of words for to-morrow. The words that are checked in Charles's book are not the same as those checked in Walter's, for they missed different words in the pre-test in September. While the children are studying, the teacher is down among them giving them devices for learning to spell their words correctly, encouraging them, helping them. On Friday each child will review all his words for the week, and on Monday the partners will dictate these review lists. The teacher will then correct the papers and will note in each child's speller the words which he has succeeded in getting right on a weekly review test. Were we to visit the room again at the beginning of the next semester, we would find that all the checked words of the previous semester are reviewed by each child.

Now it is reading time. Each child is reading his own book. The children have all been tested as to their reading ability. No child has a book which is too difficult for him.[1] No two children have the same book. Each child reads individually. The teacher goes about among them, letting them read one at a time to her. But they read aloud to her alone, not to the rest of the class. She gives each one drill where he needs it. Most of them need little or none. Charles has finished his book and it writing a composition on it—a book review which serves the double purpose of showing the teacher that he understands his book and of being an exercise in English composition. Another child is taking a brief oral test on a book she has finished, the teacher having a test card with which to make such testing easy. A third is simply handing in a book slip stating that the book has been read. This child does not know whether or not she will be tested on the particular book. As a matter of fact, the teacher has seen her reading it, absorbed, and knows no test is necessary.

And now it is time for social science.

Instead of remaining in the fourth grade —which is just beginning this subject—let us step into a sixth-grade room and watch the eleven-year-olds at work.

In social science for the first time we find all the children working on the same general topic. Some, it is true, have nearly finished reading the story of the Vikings, others are nearer the beginning.

[1] Books are selected on the basis of reading tests, from the Winnetka Graded Book List, by Carleton Washburne and Mabel Vogel. Rand McNally and Company. 1928.

This Viking study includes both the history and geography of these bold Norsemen, for one can not understand the Vikings without knowing something of the country in which they lived. Throughout the Winnetka schools history and geography are a single subject, not two separate subjects. People's lives must be lived somewhere. To participate in their lives with them involves geography as well as history.

As we look at the material, we find it written simply, dramatically, interestingly. We find that the picturization of the life of that different civilization is made so vivid that the child is experiencing it himself.

As he reads about the Vikings, the child draws maps or fills in maps, showing where they lived, showing the topography of their country and showing their journeys. As soon as any child completes a topic he comes to a practice test by which he can check up his own knowledge of the subject. Having satisfied himself through this practice test that he knows the essential facts, he asks the teacher for a real test, which is again complete and diagnostic, as in the case of other individualized subjects.

But social science—history and geography—is not only an individual subject. It is not merely an amassing of facts. Important as it is that children shall know certain basic facts, it is still more important that they shall have an experience in social living, that they shall have stimulus to creative work. It is in order to make it possible to use social science in this way that the children do not proceed strictly individually in this one subject. If a child completes a topic before his fellows, he may use his surplus time for arithmetic or language or spelling or reading or, if he wishes to do so, for additional work on this particular topic. The child who is unusually slow in mastering the topic may borrow some time from his more completely individualized subjects, so as not to hold the rest of the group back. The fact that all academic subjects, except social science, are completely individualized makes it possible, without violating the principle of individual mastery, to have all children on the same general topic in this one field. Let us watch this sixth-grade group.

They are studying the life of the Vikings. They are trying to imagine themselves living in those days of adventure. They have decided to have a "Viking Day," and to this end they have already begun to make their room over into a Viking feast hall. At one end there is a throne, on which the Viking Chief will sit. Two girls are making tapestries to hang beside the throne. Each boy is soon at work on his shield, making his own design. A group here is making a Viking boat. Another group has gone down to the lumber yard to borrow some lumber for a Viking feast table. A few girls are planning together what they can have for their Viking feast. They are reading in books about what the Vikings ate. The art supervisor drops in and gives the children suggestions and help in the designs of their tapestry or the shields, and answers the eager questions of some of the girls concerning the costumes they are making. Perhaps the children sing as they work, an old Norse folk-song which they have learned in their music period, because the music supervisor knows that the children are interested in the Vikings. They plan to sing this song at their feast.

One boy is telling some of his friends of a plan for making drinking horns. "My father works at the stockyards," he says. "He can bring us some steers' horns. We can paint them and use them to drink our mead."

In such an activity as this, ample opportunity is given for the widest range of ingenuity and initiative. Each child is encouraged to vary from his fellows, to express himself, to create. Yet all are utilizing their special interests or abilities for the welfare of the group enterprise.

The Viking feast hall is not for the purpose of teaching children about the Vikings. The amount of time they will spend on this one project is entirely disproportionate to the amount of valuable information they will get from it. It is the *outcome* of their reading concerning the Vikings—the *outcome* of their factual work, rather than a means to the mastery of facts. To teach facts exclusively through such projects would be to limit very seriously the things with which children become familiar. Much learning can be done more economically through the direct means of reading and study. Out of this reading and study, however, may grow ideas for action. These are given full play and are made the basis for creative expression and a training in group cooperation.

A reference outline is kept in each school room, in which the teacher will find suggestions from the supervisors as to types of activities, as to sources of reading for the teacher and the children and as to ways in which the playground, music, art and socialized activities departments may be of assistance. This outline is merely suggestive and helpful. Each teacher and each group of children work out their own group and creative activities.

The day ends all too soon and the children leave the school, eagerly talking about their plans.

Finally, let us visit the junior high school. In many ways it seems much like the lower grade schools. Again the children have periods when they are doing individual work, where each child strives for mastery of certain knowledges or skills, where no child leaves a job until he has it completed, where no child remains on a job after he has it mastered. Again we see carefully prepared, complete diagnostic tests for each unit of work. Again we find self-dependence. Again we find a total absence of lectures and recitations. Again we find the spontaneity and naturalness which always accompany the freer kind of education.

But in the junior high school the work is departmentalized. The children are with one teacher for arithmetic, with another for English, with another for shop, with another for social science. We find the junior high school building equipped for printing, for art metal craft, for woodworking and turning, for pottery making, and all forms of art and craft work. We find a library with children learning how to run it. We find, of course, an assembly room and a gymnasium and a large playground. And there is the cooking room, the sewing room, the general science laboratory—all the characteristic rooms that one would find in the best of American junior high school buildings—the children circulating from one room to another.

In one of these rooms, however, there is a class that deserves more than passing attention. It is called "biology" and it does include the study and appreciation of the development of life on this earth from the amoeba to man. But it devotes a good deal of time and attention to human life. In it the children learn, in an entirely frank way, how human reproduction takes place. They are taught the functions and care of the reproductive organs and are given the opportunity to ask freely any questions they wish. There is no evasion. There are no circumlocutions. The whole atmosphere of the class is clean, open, scientific.

It is also idealistic. Sex is taught not merely as a biological function, but also as a function of far-reaching personal and social significance. Questions of conduct are freely discussed. The class often becomes one in ethics as well as in biology.

All seventh-grade children are required to take this course. The boys and girls have it at different periods of the day. A parent, by applying personally at the school and agreeing to give equally complete instruction at home, may have a child excused, but this rarely occurs—it is usually possible to show a parent that to forbid the class to a child is to stimulate his curiosity. But the possibility of getting a child excused prevents any concerted opposition to the course among parents. Most parents are in hearty sympathy with the course.

The results of this course in biology—which has been given now for nine years—are wholly good. There is a notable cleanness of mind and action on the part of the children who have had it.

Throughout the school most of the children move from room to room according to a program, when the bell rings. Some children, however, do not. We find some staying in a room after the bell rings or continuing their work in the shop instead of going to arithmetic. As we inquire into this, we find that the children are divided into the self-reliant group and the supervised group. Children who are supervised must follow the daily program unless they get special permission from their teacher to do otherwise. Self-reliant children may budget their own time, as is done under the Dalton Plan.

To be rated as self-reliant, a child first fills out a blank, stating why he believes that, given freedom, he will use it wisely. This blank is submitted to all of his teachers, to his social problems class, to the student council and to the children who are already classified as self-reliant. All these children ballot without discussion of the merits and faults of the applicant. Those who are already in the self-reliant groups write their reasons for their vote in each case. The faculty reaches the final decision. If the decision is adverse, the specific reasons are taken up with the child alone by the principal of the school, so that the child may overcome whatever faults are indicated. He may apply again for self-reliant rating at any time he wishes. Sooner or later he will probably succeed in reaching his goal if he really wants to. And most children want to, because it means higher standards and more freedom through greater responsibility.

Many of the self-reliant children follow the standard daily program, simply because they find it convenient and well balanced. But those who wish to modify the arrangement of their time are free to do so.

In the junior high school some subjects are socialized. If there is to be a discussion in social science, all children, both self-reliant and supervised, must be present for the discussion. No self-reliant pupil will handicap others by being absent when his presence is needed. Therefore pupils intending to absent themselves speak to the teacher in advance in order that such embarrassment may be avoided. Especially in arithmetic, in grammar, in the individual work in science, in cooking or sewing or shop, in art and printing, the self-reliant child makes his own daily program and is his own master.

As we follow a particular child around, we find that about half of his day is spent in academic classrooms, mastering knowledges and skills, and that about half his day is spent in some elective or special courses or some courses involving social experience. We find him on the playground, participating in team games. We find him in music appreciation courses or in the band or the orchestra or the glee club. We find that he is taking some form of creative work. We find that altogether he has had a choice of some twenty-five or thirty elective and special courses, from which he has selected those which seemed to meet his needs and interests best. He has, too, certain courses which are required of all children, courses dealing in the common essentials of knowledge and skill, courses in which he must reach mastery of each step before proceeding to the next, and courses which are therefore strictly individual as to the child's progress.

The teacher's bookkeeping throughout all schools—elementary and junior high—if we stop to speak to one of the teachers, turns out to be rather simple. Each teacher has a list of all the tests covering knowledge and skill subjects which every child must pass. These are written across the top of her blank book. Down the side are written the children's names. As a child passes a test without errors, a date is entered after his name and under the name of the test. This record gives a graphic representation of the status of the children, some children having a long row of dates after their names, some a short row, some children a long period of time between tests, others a short period. At a glance the teacher can tell how far advanced every child in her class is.

And all the children themselves have records called goal cards, by which they watch their own progress.

On the back of these goal cards is an attitude chart, filled out by the teacher and child in consultation with each other. A segment of such an attitude chart is reproduced herewith. If the child and teacher together agree that the middle paragraph most nearly describes the child's attitude in regard to group spirit, a short horizontal line is placed after this little paragraph at the close of the first six weeks of school. If at the close of the following six-weeks period they agree that there has been improvement, but not to such a high degree as to make the next to the highest paragraph descriptive of the child's attainment, the horizontal line is placed higher, but still opposite the middle paragraph. Then let us suppose that at the end of the third six-weeks period, the next to the

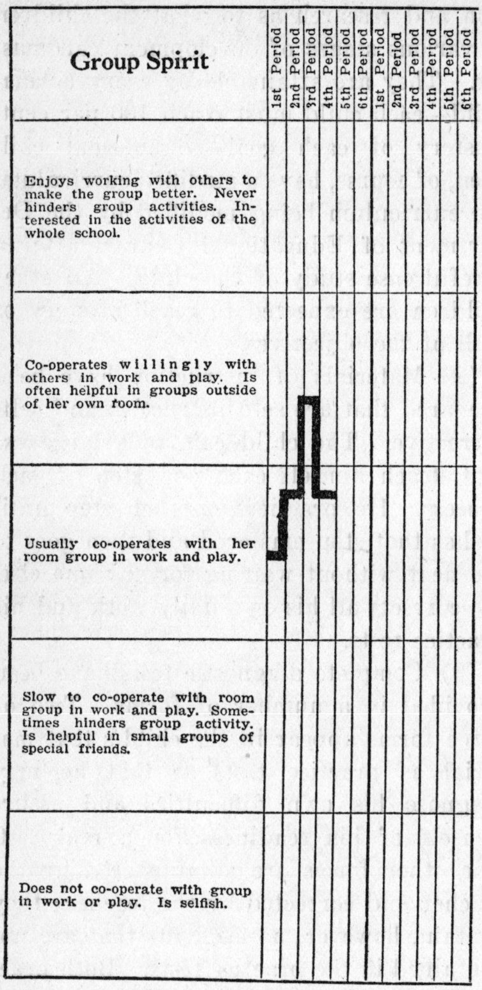

highest paragraph seems better to describe the child's group spirit. Perhaps at the close of the fourth period the child and teacher agree that the group spirit has dropped somewhat—perhaps the child has been a little complacent and has ceased his effort—the third paragraph again is descriptive of the child's group spirit, so the horizontal line for this period drops. We thus get a graph of the child's attitude during the course of the year, as shown on the sample segment.

There are similar groups of paragraphs to indicate the child's self-reliance, initiative, work spirit, orderliness, courtesy and any special interests or abilities.

The purpose of this attitude chart is to keep before the mind of the child certain definite ideals and to give him the habit of taking stock of himself once every six weeks to see how nearly he has attained these ideals. A second purpose is to keep both the child and parent aware of the fact that the development of desirable attitudes is as important a part of school work as is the mastery of academic subject-matter.

The goal card, with the *amounts* of work accomplished indicated on one side, the attitude chart on the other, takes the place of the old-time report card. But it keeps the parents in much more intimate contact with the schools.

No schools can long succeed without the support of the parents. Winnetka parents are therefore kept in close touch with the schools—partly through the goal cards, partly through much-encouraged school visiting, partly through the local press, but perhaps most of all through an active, well-organized parent-teacher association.

This association sponsors meetings in each classroom between the teacher and the parents of her pupils, and between the parents and the school authorities in each school building, and in the village as a whole. At these meetings there is the greatest possible opportunity for questioning.

Criticisms are always welcomed. The particular grievance of the parent is carefully investigated and a report made on this investigation. Criticism of methods in general or of standards or of curriculum content are made the basis for scientific study and research. If such research shows the criticism merited, the organization of the schools is accordingly altered. If the research justifies present procedure, the critics are answered with facts.

This policy—and the fact that the children are happy in school and do above-average work in the high school after they graduate—has kept the bulk of Winnetka parents whole-heartedly back of the schools. There are occasional irreconcilables, of course, but they form so small a minority that there has been no contest in a school board election for at least nine years. The schools are absolutely free from politics, the board members being the ablest, broadest-visioned men and women that the community can draft for this service. And the school board never interferes in professional questions—it settles general policies, and gives the superintendent and his teachers freedom to make the schools good places for children to learn and to develop.

Let us conclude this informal account of the Winnetka schools by abstracting from the schoolroom activities we have been observing the underlying principles of the individual technique, in accordance with which the Winnetka schools have been organized.

First of all, the curriculum is divided into two distinct parts. One part consists of those knowledges and skills in which we are trying to make children like-minded. The other consists of stimuli and opportunities for creative work under social conditions.

We want all children to be able to spell alike. We want all children to get the same answer for a sum in addition. We want all children to have the same notion as to the general locality of Paris. We want all children to have the same person and the same general achievement in mind when we mention Columbus. Since children differ very widely in their ability to grasp such facts and skills, a technique has been evolved to make it possible for each child to grasp them at his own rate. This technique consists of three steps, as follows:

(1) The objectives, or goals, are very specifically stated. They are determined as far as possible on the basis of research as to genuine social needs. They are organized according to the results of observation and research as to what the children at various stages of development can master. They are attainable by every normal child—each child must reach 100 per cent. mastery of each goal. Subnormal children, of course, have a modified curriculum, the curriculum being modified by the Department of Educational Counsel after a careful case study of the child. All other children are expected to reach mastery of each of the objectives.

(2) Materials of instruction have been prepared that are self-instructive and self-corrective. The child can, to a large extent, teach himself each new step of each process. He practices on each step until he has that step mastered and then goes to the next without waiting for any one else. He corrects all his own daily work and his practice tests.

(3) Complete diagnostic tests have been provided in a number of forms. Two or three forms appear in the child's text material as practice tests so that he may diagnose his own difficulties and assure himself of his readiness for a real test. The other forms are administered by the teacher and corrected by the teacher; they contain, however, no elements that are not contained in the practice tests. Both practice tests and real tests are keyed in such a way as to refer the child to the specific remedial exercises which he needs in order to overcome the difficulties which the test reveals. The tests are marked only by an indication of where the child will find the necessary practice work in order to reach mastery. A child having missed one test does the indicated practice work, then takes another form of the same test.

About half the morning and half the afternoon are consumed by the individual mastery of the knowledge and skill subjects. In these, promotion from grade to grade is individual, continuous and by subjects. It does not involve any change of classroom. The room in which a child sits is determined by his social age—the age of the children with whom he can best associate in the half of the morning and of the afternoon that are left free for group and creative activities.

These group and creative activities are frequently centered around the children's work in social science or literature. They also include, however, appreciation of music, art and literature, self-governing assemblies, playground activities, shop work, the writing, editing, illustrating and printing of a self-supporting school newspaper, and a wide variety of other means for stimulating creative work on the part of the child and for developing in him a social consciousness.

The purpose of the group and creative activities is never academic. There is no attempt to teach subject-matter through these activities, although there is necessarily frequent correlation between the socialized work and the individual work. Such correlation as exists, however, is incidental and unforced.

Creative work is a direct stimulus to the child to vary from his fellows. It is the exact opposite of the work for mastery of knowledge or skill in common with his fellows, although it may make use of the latter or may stimulate it. Variation is essential to evolution. Schools in the past have not given sufficient time or attention to the need for variation among pupils. In the Winnetka schools, through creative work, there is an attempt to stimulate variation, originality and initiative.

Too much stress on individualism, however, would make society centrifugal to an extent that would be disruptive. A social consciousness is most seriously needed at the present stage of the world's development. The children are therefore given their creative work to a large extent in a social setting, where each child is contributing his particular ability or interest to the welfare of a group enterprise—dramatizations, discussions, games and group projects of all sorts tend to give this social consciousness.

It will be remembered that as we went around among the rooms in the Winnetka schools we found no recitations and infrequent class explanations. Class explanations have given way to self-instructive materials. Recitations have given way on the one hand to complete diagnostic tests, on the other hand to group and creative activities.

The Winnetka schools are not a finished product. Rather they are an educational laboratory in which new methods of education are being tried out and the results carefully measured. Scientific research is applied constantly to the various activities in an attempt to discover whether they are resulting in the knowledge or skill or attitude for which they are intended. The detailed procedure varies from year to year, even from month to month, as our scientific understanding of education grows.

The scientific approach to education in Winnetka heads up in two well organized, well equipped departments—the Research Department and the Department of Educational Counsel.

The Research Department, headed by Mabel Vogel Morphett, carries forward investigations on problems that affect general school procedure—what shall go into the curriculum, at what stage of children's development can they best learn the various topics, what methods are most effective, etc. These problems almost invariably originate with teachers—usually in grade meetings. They are often attacked directly by the teachers, the Research Department being reserved for problems requiring rather elaborate or technical work.

The Department of Educational Counsel, headed by Frances Dummer, is a child guidance clinic. Its investigations are into the adjustment of individual children. The psychiatrist, psychologist, physician and counselors pool their findings and recommend procedures by which each child referred to them may be properly adjusted.

Both these departments are integral parts of the school system. Both continually modify the detailed practices of the schools.

Through all the experimentation, however, these principles guide the work of the Winnetka schools: Every child has a right to master those knowledges and skills which he will probably use in life; every child has the right to live naturally, happily and fully as a child; human progress depends on the development of each individual to his full capacity; and the welfare of human society requires the development of a vital social consciousness in each individual.

It is fitting, is it not, that the schools in the "beautiful land," Winnetka, should attempt to be places where children live happily, where they have freedom to create, freedom to live socially, freedom to express themselves as children, and where at the same time they are fitted in a thorough, scientific way for participation in the life which surrounds them?

EDUCATIONAL EVENTS

THE UNIVERSITIES OF SALONIKI AND JERUSALEM

Two universities of the Near East that have recently come into existence, one at Saloniki and the other at Jerusalem, are described in a bulletin recently issued by the U. S. Bureau of Education.

The University of Saloniki began with 15 professors and 100 students. It offers the classical studies. A chair of Hebrew was created and a professor appointed in 1927. The intention is to transfer to the University of Saloniki the Superior School of Agriculture, now under the faculty of physics and mathematics of the University of Athens, and to create in 1929 a veterinary section.

The new university is a governmental organization financed by a tax of 3 per cent. on the customs duty of the merchandise imported through Saloniki, by gifts, the tuition fees of students and aid from the Central Government. All professors are appointed by the ministry at Athens.

The Hebrew University at Jerusalem, formally opened on April 1, 1925, after 40 years or more of intermittent effort and planning, began as a number of institutes intended mainly for research. While it welcomes all students without regard to sex, race, religion or social station, and the hope is that its work will be of benefit to all mankind, the purposes of its founding were more specifically to bring an inspiring influence into the life of the Jewish peoples and their civilization; to provide a working place for Jewish scholars and scientists; to contribute to the revival of Hebrew; and to aid in the material development of Palestine. The language of instruction is Hebrew.

At present the university consists of a chemical institute and a microbiological institute, both inaugurated in 1924. An institute of Jewish studies, a school of oriental studies, an institute of Palestine natural history and a department of hygiene were opened in 1926. An institute of mathematics is in process of organization.

The Jewish population of Palestine is growing rapidly, and its youth is knocking at the door of the university in numbers that will go on increasing every year. The number of Jewish students in Europe in search of a hospitable university is also growing and as the world's economic conditions are adjusted, more and more of them will attend the University of Jerusalem as a few have done already for graduate and research work.

THE REDUCTION OF ILLITERACY IN THE ORIENT

According to a bulletin issued by the U. S. Bureau of Education attempts to reduce illiteracy in different countries were made immediately following the war and were continued through the years thereafter. If any great reduction is made for the entire world, it must take place in those countries where the percentage of illiteracy is highest. In China, India, the Soviet Union, and the Orient in general the authorities have awakened to the dangers of illiteracy, and for several years have been making efforts to extend at least the rudiments of education to the entire population.

In India almost every province is displaying great activity; and it is a testimony to the clear vision of those who now direct instructional policy that in most places attention is being turned to a concerted attack upon illiteracy.

Few of the provinces of India have compulsory education laws. Bombay led the way with a bill in 1918; a number of other provinces followed in 1919 and 1920. The introduction of the compulsory principle is hampered by financial stringency and native prejudice, but the timidity of the authorities is disappearing and compulsion is being introduced, especially in the municipal areas.

It is now realized by many local governments that a very large part of the education needed in India is adult education. So far as the town population is concerned, there is a great scope for the university extension movement. But the main problem attending adult education in India is that of reaching the country districts.

The report of the work of stamping out illiteracy in the Union of Soviet Republics for 1925–26 shows that there were 49,804 schools for semi-literates and illiterates with an attendance of 1,599,755.

The first great step toward the eradication of illiteracy in China was made during the literary revolution of 1917–1919, when the much less intricate spoken language, Pei-hua, was substituted as a literary medium for the old, very difficult classical language. The adoption of Pei-hua immensely simplified the process of learning the written language, and made it more nearly possible to give some instruction in reading and writing to the 200,000,000 adolescents and adults that had passed the school age and had been denied the opportunity for schooling. By careful study 1,000 of the most frequently used characters in Pei-hua were selected and arranged in a "foundation character course," a mastery of which gives the common man a foundation knowledge of the language, and enables him to write simple letters, keep accounts and read Pei-hua literature intelligently. The average time necessary to complete the course is ninety-six hours.

THE BRITISH INSTITUTE IN PARIS

LORD CREWE, Lord Derby and Lord Hardinge of Penshurst, all three former British ambassadors to France, together with Lord Revelstoke, have issued an appeal on behalf of the British Institute in Paris, which has been founded for the benefit of British students in that city. The Guild, the first part of the scheme, was opened in January last, largely as the result of liberal donations from many sources. In their letter Lords Crewe, Derby, Hardinge and Revelstoke say:

> The time has now arrived for the completion of the scheme for the British Institute in Paris. A sum of £20,000 has been expended on the non-residential side of the scheme, and a centre for educational classes in French and English is now working most satisfactorily at the Guild of the British Institute, 6 rue de la Sorbonne, where a general library and a reading-room are available for visitors.
>
> But in order to erect a suitable College of Residence at the Cité Universitaire, the additional sum of at least £100,000 is needed. Of this amount, about £45,000 is in hand. An anonymous donor has promised the sum of £10,000, payable under covenant by instalments over a term of years, on condition that the sum of £100,000 is reached. Under this system a donor saves income-tax and supertax in respect of his donation, provided it is paid by instalments extending over a period exceeding six years. Thus the eventual cost to a donor of £1,000 who is subject to the highest rate of supertax now in force is only £500, and the net yearly cost is only £71 8s 7d. Promises of several donations on this basis have been received.
>
> We appeal to all lovers of French culture, and to those who realize the need of British students being provided with good lodging under supervision amid the corporate life of the Cité Universitaire, to help us to complete the scheme within the period of three months during which the whole of the free site is at our disposal.

THE CALIFORNIA STATE ASSOCIATION OF SUPERVISORS OF CHILD WELFARE AND ATTENDANCE

THE association recently completed its organization by the meeting of the council at Del Monte in connection with the superintendents' convention. This council, composed of two representatives from each of the organized sections—San Francisco Bay, Southern, Central and Northern—organized by electing the following officers:

President: Mr. Edward Albert, of Alameda.
Vice-President: Mr. Jack Byfield, of Bakersfield.
Secretary-Treasurer: Miss Stella Linscott, of Napa.

It is stated that the increased demands upon supervisors for certification calls for well-trained men and women and naturally adds to the responsibilities of the position. To meet these responsibilities, it is essential that the closest cooperation obtain, hence, the need of section organizations, similar to those of teachers, and then the state council that shall act as a clearing house for the various sections.

The purpose of the organization is said to be to promote the work of child welfare and school attendance throughout the State of California by

1. Providing means for the dissemination of progressive ideas concerning school attendance;
2. Maintaining high standards for the proper training of Supervisors of Child Welfare and Attendance;
3. Cooperating fully with all social agencies interested in the welfare of the child;
4. Furthering legislation in behalf of child welfare and school attendance.

The committee on legislation composed of Stella Linscott, Edward Albert, John R. Hunt, Jack Byfield, E. C. Giffen and Mrs. Lillian B. Hill, of the State Department, met at the same time and adopted a program of changes in attendance laws to be presented to the next Legislature for consideration.

FOREIGN EDUCATIONAL CONFERENCES

THE program for the Geneva conference of the World Federation is being planned about the theme, "International Understanding and Good Will through Education." All departments will, therefore, have an international aspect in their discussions and papers. Much attention will be given to a consideration of how the spirit of international cooperation and good-will can be introduced into the schools. The official languages of the conference will be English, French and German. Interpreters will be provided who will translate the addresses into the language asked for by the majority present at any particular session or into the language announced beforehand as the official language of that section. A communication from Miss Constance Morley, secrétaire du congrès, Comité Local d'Organisation, Bureau International d'Education, states that the International Bureau of Education is making an earnest effort to secure representatives and interested groups of teachers to attend the Geneva meeting from as many countries as possible both in Europe and in Asia.

The eleventh International Economic Course will be held at Rotterdam from August 19 to 31, 1929, during the two weeks preceding the International Congress for Commercial Education at Amsterdam, and following the World Federation of Education Associations, which will meet in Geneva during the latter part of July and in August, 1929. The course will be organized by a local committee presided over by Dr. R. Mees, president of the general council of the Commercial University of Rotterdam, and will be managed on the plans which have proved so efficacious at former courses. Visitors will be given as comprehensive a survey of Dutch economic life as possible and they will likewise have an opportunity of becoming acquainted with various aspects of Dutch national and intellectual life. The course will begin on August 19, and will last a fortnight. Lectures will be given every morning, and the afternoons will be reserved for excursions. At the lectures, after a general introduction on the Netherlands and Rotterdam, those aspects of Dutch political economy will be treated which are of particular importance to the country and of special interest to strangers. The lectures will be in German, French or English. The number of participants will probably be limited to 150. The visitors will be taken by competent guides to the port of Rotterdam, to the adjacent industrial district, to the mouth of the Rhine, the Hook of Holland and to the Dutch plains with their extensive orchards, kitchen gardens and unique waterways. A visit to The Hague will give an opportunity of seeing the Palace of Peace, where the International Court of Justice now has its seat.

A conference of British and American students will be held in Merton College, Oxford, in the summer, under the auspices of the Carnegie Endowment for International Peace. The choice of undergraduates in American schools will be based on scholarship, personality and collegiate activity, and students must be members of the International Relations Clubs, affiliated with the Carnegie Endowment. The endowment is offering a competition based on papers to be written on renunciation of war and the acceptance of peaceful change and arbitration, disarmament and international cooperation. The two best papers will receive a prize of $600 to cover the cost of the trip, and the winners will represent the American students on the floor of the conference. The trip, according to the Carnegie Endowment, is planned for the study of international relations and exceptional opportunities will be offered for meeting distinguished international personalities and for serious study of international organization and international problems as well as for contact with students of foreign universities. The group, which sails on July 5, will be accompanied by Professor Clyde Eagleton, of New York University, and Miss Amy Hemingway Jones, national secretary of the International Relations Clubs. After the conference in England, the students will visit The Hague Court, the University of Leiden and will stop at Delft, Amsterdam, Brussels and Paris. At Paris they will be the guests of the University City and the Endowments, and will make trips to Versailles and Fontainebleau.

THE ROCKEFELLER FOUNDATION

THE Rockefeller Foundation and the Laura Spelman Rockefeller Memorial have been consolidated into a new philanthropic corporation, also to be known as the Rockefeller Foundation, with total net assets of $264,602,447. The General Education Board is not affected by the consolidation.

A statement issued by Raymond B. Fosdick, chairman of a special committee on the readjustment of the relations of the Rockefeller boards, stated that "among the reasons for the consolidation was the desire to avoid overlapping in the work done by the two consolidating corporations and to insure greater unity and cooperation in carrying out the programs which have heretofore been administered under the two boards independently."

An order approving the consolidation was signed by Supreme Court Justice Mitchell on petition of George E. Vincent, president of the foundation, and Arthur Woods, acting president of the memorial. The written consent of Frank P. Graves, state commissioner of education, was also filed with the court.

The petition set forth that the assets of the foundation totaled $158,090,543.04 and of the memorial $65,127,535.42, giving the new foundation assets of a book value of $203,298,503.46. The actual market value of the securities held by the consolidating corporations, however, was listed at $273,841,262.10 and other assets listed are valued at $39,332,368.16, thus furnishing the new fund with assets of an actual value of $313,173,180.26. The liabilities assumed by the new foundation total $48,671,183.15.

The first act of the trustees of the new foundation was to set aside from the principal the sum of $35,000,000 to provide for outstanding obligations. This left a net capital fund with a book value of $168,298,503.24 and an actual value of $278,173,180.26, but with liabilities still outstanding of $13,671,183.15.

The old Rockefeller Foundation owned bonds with a book value of $28,791,100.59 and a market value of $29,773,747.51; stocks with a book value of $98,811,060.82 and a market value of $163,803,476.84; land, buildings and equipment worth $422,973.63, and cash, secured loans and receivables amounting to $30,065,408.04. Its liabilities aggregated $21,781,605.23. The foundation received in 1928 $9,175,550.13 from interest, dividends and gifts.

The Laura Spelman Rockefeller Memorial included in its holdings bonds with a book value of $38,332,806.13 and a market value of $44,519,199.75; stocks with a book value of $17,950,742.80, and a market value of $35,744,838, and cash, secured loans and receivables totaling $8,843,986.49. The income of the memorial in 1928 was $4,693,069.18. Its liabilities totaled $26,889,577.92.

The members and officers of the new Rockefeller Foundation follow: Members: James R. Angell, Trevor Arnett, John W. Davis, David

EDUCATIONAL NOTES AND NEWS

Dr. Henry Crew, professor of physics at Northwestern University, was reelected president of the American Association of University Professors at the recent New York meeting. Professor H. C. Warren, of Princeton University, was elected vice-president to succeed Professor Marion P. Whitney, of Vassar College. Professor H. W. Tyler, of the Massachusetts Institute of Technology, was reelected secretary, and Professor Joseph Mayer, of Tufts College, treasurer. New members of the council are as follows: B. H. Bode, the Ohio State University; A. L. Bondurant, the University of Mississippi; M. T. Bogert, Columbia University; H. S. Conard, Grinnell College; H. G. Doyle, George Washington University; P. O. Ray, the University of California; F. K. Richtmyer, Cornell University; Joseph Stebbins, the University of Wisconsin; H. S. White, Vassar College, and H. V. Wilson, the University of North Carolina.

At the meetings of the American Psychological Association held at Columbia University, New York City, on December 27, 28 and 29, the following elections were announced: President, Dr. K. S. Lashley, Institute for Juvenile Research, Chicago; secretary (1929–1931), Professor Carl C. Brigham, Princeton University; representatives on the division of anthropology and psychology, National Research Council, Professor Samuel W. Fernberger, University of Pennsylvania, and Professor Walter Miles, Stanford University; representative on the Social Science Research Council, Professor Floyd H. Allport, Syracuse University; representatives on the council of the American Association for the Advancement of Science, Dr. Walter V. Bingham, Personnel Research Federation, and Professor Robert M. Ogden, Cornell University. At the business meeting of the association it was voted to omit the usual annual meeting in December, 1929, and to merge this with the ninth International Congress of Psychology to be held at Yale University in September under the presidency of Dr. J. McKeen Cattell. The presidential address of Dr. Lashley will be given at that time.

Dr. E. M. Johnson, of the University of Minnesota, was elected president of the American Association of Teachers of Journalism at the annual convention at Ann Arbor, which was held in conjunction with the American Association of Schools and Departments of Journalism. V. McKenzie, of the University of Washington, was elected vice-president, and John O. Simmons, of Syracuse University, was reelected secretary-treasurer; R. S. Mann, of the University of Missouri, and C. D. Johnson, of Baylor University, were elected additional members of the executive committee. It was voted to hold the next annual convention at Baton Rouge, Louisiana, with a dinner in New Orleans.

Albert L. Colston, principal of the Brooklyn Technical High School, was elected president of the newly formed American Association of Technical High Schools and Institutes at the recent convention in Detroit. Other officers elected were: J. F. Powers, of the East Technical High School, Cleveland; E. G. Allen, of the Cass Technical High School, Detroit; William F. Kirkland, of the Toronto Technical High School, and John Wood, of the Ridge Technical High School, Cambridge, Mass.

DR. JOHN SHAPLEY, Mores professor in the fine arts at New York University, has been elected president of the College Art Association.

J. L. HOLTSCLAW, principal of the Detroit High School of Commerce, has been elected president of the National Commercial Teachers Association.

THE dinner of the school of education of New York University will be held in connection with the meeting of the Department of Superintendence, at Hotel Cleveland, on February 29. The subject to be discussed is "Education for Special Groups." Dr. Henry Turner Bailey, director of the Cleveland School of Art and of the John Huntington Polytechnic Institute, will speak on "Educational Provisions for the Gifted"; Alexander S. Lyman, general attorney, New York Central Railroad and secretary of the council, New York University, on "Education for Commerce and Industry"; Dr. John J. Tigert, president of the University of Florida, on "Education of the Handicapped"; Dr. John W. Withers, dean of the school of education, on "Education for the Professions."

AT the eighth annual meeting of the Chicago Botany Alumni held in New York on the evening of December 27, there was presented to the University of Chicago $25,000 to be known as the John M. Coulter Research Fellowship Fund. It was hoped that Professor Coulter, who died on December 24, would be present. This sum for the fellowship had resulted from the contributions of 130 doctors and 75 other alumni and past students of the department of botany over which Dr. Coulter had presided for so many years. The interest only of this fund is to be used for an annual pre-doctorate fellowship tenable in any branch of plant science at the department of botany, University of Chicago. The presentation was made by Professor R. B. Wylie, of the Iowa State University, and accepted on behalf of the University of Chicago by Dr. Max Mason, of the Rockefeller Foundation, former president of the University of Chicago.

FRANCIS H. HERRICK was given a dinner on December 1, commemorating "the fortieth year of his service to Western Reserve University and the fortieth anniversary of the establishment of the department of biology." Some one hundred of his colleagues joined in honoring him on this occasion and brief addresses were given by the president, Dr. Robert E. Vinson, representing the university; by Harold Clark, representing the Cleveland Museum of Natural History, and by Dr. Henry B. Ward, representing the biologists of the country, and to these Professor Herrick responded.

J. RUSSELL SMITH, professor of economic geography at Columbia University, is the recipient of the medal of the Harmon Foundation awarded to the "author of an article of signal benefit in stimulating constructive opinion in social or industrial fields." The award consists of a gold medal and $500. The award to Dr. Smith was based on his article, "Plan or Perish," published in the *Survey Graphic* for July, 1927, in which he discussed the situation in the Mississippi Valley leading up to the flood disaster and offered a plan for the control of a great river at high water.

HERR FRIEDRICH DÖRNHÖFFER, director of the Bavarian State Museums and Galleries, and Professor August L. Mayer, the collector and art historian, have been appointed corresponding members of the commissions for ancient and modern art of the Royal Belgian Museums. It is said that this is the first act of recognition of German intellectual and artistic leaders by Belgium since the war.

A DINNER was given on January 4 at the University Club, New York City, to celebrate the election of Robert C. Post to the board of trustees of the Stevens Institute of Technology, to succeed the late Colonel George Harvey. Dr. John Johnston, chief of the research department of the United States Steel Corporation, formerly professor at Yale University, was the principal speaker.

DR. EDWARD T. DEVINE has been appointed director of the Bellevue-Yorkville health demonstration to fill the position left vacant by the resignation of Dr. Leverett D. Bristol. Dr. Devine has held posts with the New York Charity Organization Society, the New York School of Social Work and the American Red Cross. He was for twenty-one years editor of *The*

Survey and professor of social economy at Columbia University for fourteen years.

Professor Geoffrey Atkinson was appointed dean of Amherst College at a recent meeting of the executive committee of the board of trustees to succeed Dean Thomas C. Esty, who resigned. Professor Atkinson was graduated from Amherst in 1913 and has since taught Romance languages.

Mrs. Dorothy McSparran Arnold has been appointed assistant dean in the Washington Square College of New York University.

Mitchell Gratwick, who recently resigned his position as assistant dean of freshmen at Harvard College, will in September become headmaster of the Nicholas Country Day School of Buffalo, New York.

E. S. Russell, formerly superintendent of schools at Simsbury, Conn., has become director of the teacher-training school at New Haven. Mr. Paul D. Collier, of Port Arthur, Texas, has succeeded Mr. Russell as superintendent.

Professor Thomas H. Briggs, of Teachers College, Columbia University, who is on sabbatic leave this year, sailed on January 10 with Mrs. Briggs for several months in Sicily, where he will be engaged in writing. Professor and Mrs. Briggs spent the fall semester in California.

Dean William E. Smyser, of Ohio Wesleyan University, has been granted a leave of absence for the academic year 1929–30. The leave will be the first which Dean Smyser has had in his twenty-eight years at Ohio Wesleyan. A resolution of appreciation has been passed by the trustees.

Professor J. A. Yates, of the Kansas State Teachers' College at Pittsburgh, is on a year's leave of absence as a student at the University of Kentucky, Lexington, Ky.

Assistant Director Gabriel R. Mañalac, of the Bureau of Education, Manila, has been detailed to visit a number of the leading elementary and secondary schools in the United States, giving special attention to administration, supervision and vocational instruction. He left Manila on October 6 and will probably return to the Philippines in time to be at the next summer assembly, conferences and conventions of teachers, principals and superintendents in Baguio during April and May.

Vice-governor and Mrs. Eugene A. Gilmore returned to the Philippines on October 29, after seven months' leave spent in the United States and Europe. Mr. Gilmore, who is at the same time secretary of public instruction, was granted another year's extension of his leave by the University of Wisconsin at the request of Governor-General Henry L. Stimson.

Professor Adolphe Ferrière, the distinguished Swiss educator of the J. J. Rousseau Institute in Geneva, has returned to Europe after having spent some weeks in Turkey on invitation of the Director of Public Education in Smyrna and the adjoining provinces where he made sixteen addresses to large and enthusiastic groups of teachers. Professor Ferrière has educated a number of leading Turkish educators, and through them and his books is widely known in Turkey, where many of the advanced ideas he has so strongly propounded at Geneva are being put into effect. His interpreter and guide during his time in Smyrna was a former pupil, Professor Mustafa Rahmy Bey, of the International College and the Normal School for Girls in Smyrna, who by translation and otherwise has done much to spread modern educational ideals.

Dr. Montessori will hold the fourteenth international training course of the Montessori system of education in London, beginning next April and lasting for about four months.

Professor Truman Kelley, of Stanford University, lectured recently under the auspices of the Harvard Graduate School of Education on "Mental Structure and its Bearing upon Problems of Inheritance and Education."

Professor Frank Alfred Golder, of Stanford University, an authority on Russia and director of the Hoover war library, has died at the age of fifty-one years.

The Reverend Dr. Simon Peter Long, president of the Chicago Lutheran Bible School and known as author, lecturer and pastor of the Lutheran Church, died on January 4, aged sixty-eight years.

WILLIAM HENRY VAN DER SMISSEN, professor at the University of Toronto, died on January 2, aged eighty-five years. He was a member of the university senate and professor emeritus of German in University College.

ANNA CAROLINE MAXWELL, for thirty years director of the school of nursing at the Presbyterian Hospital, New York City, died on January 2, at the age of seventy-seven years.

THOMAS K. MCCLELLAND, principal of the Speedway and Alexander Street's public schools, of Newark, New Jersey, and for twenty-five years a teacher in the Newark schools, died on December 13, as the result of injuries received when struck by an automobile.

W. W. RUPERT, superintendent of the Pottstown public schools for thirty-seven years, died on January 6, in his seventy-eighth year. He retired several years ago.

IN his first message to the legislature Mr. Franklin D. Roosevelt, newly elected governor of New York State, states that the chief mandatory increase in the coming budget "will be the additional sum, running probably to $9,000,000, for the extension of educational facilities throughout the state. Under the present methods of apportioning state funds to rural school districts, the poorer districts in many instances fail to receive their fair share. The method of apportionment should be simplified and made to conform more closely to the relative wealth of the districts."

THE endowment fund for the six American Colleges in the Near East has reached $10,250,000, according to Albert W. Staub, American director of the campaign to secure $15,000,000 for this purpose. Before July 1 the whole must be raised or several large contingent gifts will be lost. Mr. Staub announced that since New Year's an anonymous gift of $60,000 has been received to establish a chair of Arabic at the American University of Beirut. He also said that Dr. Charles F. Thwing, chairman of the Cleveland committee, had agreed to raise $80,000 to endow the presidency of Athens College. William G. Mather, a trustee, has already contributed $10,000 to this institution.

DISCUSSION

1929 AS A CENTENNIAL YEAR IN THE HISTORY OF EDUCATION

IN continuation of previously published lists[1] of centennial dates in the history of education, the following list of important 1929 centennial dates is presented. Additional details regarding the events mentioned may be found in the standard encyclopedias and histories of education.

529 All pagan schools, including the influential University of Athens, closed by imperial edict of the Christian emperor of Rome, Justinian.

529 Saint Benedict, wealthy Roman, founded monastery of Monte Cassino, first of thousands of European monasteries of the Benedictines, the order to which the world is largely indebted for the preservation of learning during the Middle Ages. See Longfellow's poem, "Monte Cassino."

929 Death at Bagdad of Albategni, important contributor to development of trigonometry and one of the first of the many prominent Arabian astronomers.

1229 "Cessatio" or strike at University of Paris on account of death of two students at hands of city authorities. Exodus of masters and students resulting in establishment of rival universities at Angers and Orleans.

1229 As a result of an invitation from King Henry III of England (issued at Reading, July 16), some of the striking masters and students from University of Paris settled at Cambridge, virtually reviving that institution after a period of inactivity.

1429 Death of John Gerson, chancellor of the University of Paris, who attempted to reform the university curriculum by the banishment of scholastic subtleties and the introduction of guidance and moral spirit among the students.

1629 Birth of Huygens, Dutch physicist and mathematician, one of the greatest scientists of the seventeenth century.

1729 First establishment in the United States of the Order of the Ursulines, Catholic teaching order for elementary education.

[1] See SCHOOL AND SOCIETY, 24: 457; 25: 168, and 27: 237, for similar lists of centennial dates for 1926, 1927 and 1928.

1729 Publication at Boston of "Arithmetick: Vulgar and Decimal," written by Professor Isaac Greenwood, of Harvard College, the first arithmetic and the first elementary text-book written by an American author and printed in English in America. Three copies in existence, two in Harvard library, and one in Library of Congress.

1829 Publication in the Kasan *Messenger* (Russia) of paper by Lobachevsky on "New Elements of Geometry, with a Complete Theory of Parallels," based upon denial of Euclidean postulate of parallel lines. First publication of the foundations of non-Euclidean geometry.

1829 Organization by Mexico of higher Lancastrian schools for the Mexican state of Texas.

1829 Beginning of publication of Bowditch's translation of Laplace's "Mécanique Céleste," which gave powerful stimulus to advancement of mathematical learning in the United States and which, according to Edward Everett, "may be considered as opening a new era in the history of American science."

1829 Organization at Boston of the "Society for the Diffusion of Useful Knowledge," with promotion of public education as one of its important objects.

1829 Organization at Cincinnati of the "Western Academic Institute and Board of Education," important and influential society in the development of education in Ohio and the West.

1829 Enactment of first general school law for the state of New Jersey.

1829 Establishment of a high school at Burlington, Vermont.

1829 Opening of Georgetown College, Kentucky.

1829 Illinois College founded by a group of Yale students.

1829 First issue of the *School Magazine*, published at Boston, with W. C. Woodbridge as editor.

1829 First issue of the *American Quarterly Register and Journal of the American Education Society*, published at Andover, Mass.

1829 Publication of Samuel R. Hall's "Lectures on School-keeping," first professional book in English issued in America and widely influential in the improvement of teaching.

WALTER CROSBY EELLS

SCHOOL OF EDUCATION,
STANFORD UNIVERSITY

ON THE IMPROVEMENT OF TEACHING

Two or three years ago, Professor Eugene C. Bingham, of Lafayette College, in discussing the merits of research and teaching, made the statement that "the *first* function of a college is to teach its students."[1] One might go even further and say that "the first function of a college is *good* teaching." Assuming, then, the really self-evident truth of this statement, I should like to propose a method—neither novel nor radical—whereby college teaching may be improved.

This is simply a variation of the student-criticism-of-instructor method. We have at present in some colleges and universities the rating sheets, which students fill out anonymously and on which they "rate" their teachers on such qualities as knowledge of subject, interest in subject, force of presentation, and the like. But these "rating sheets" do not seem to go quite far enough. There is a tendency, in most cases, for the student to use too high a figure, and there is little opportunity for concrete destructive and constructive criticisms.

As a supplement, then, to these "rating sheets," or even as an independent means of measuring teaching, I propose a method whereby a paper is received from each student, written either within or outside the classroom, discussing in some detail each of the following points:

(1) A constructive criticism of the content of the course.

(2) A destructive criticism of the content of the course.

(3) A constructive criticism of the teacher and the methods he used in teaching the course.

(4) A destructive criticism of the teacher and his methods.

Students should be told at the beginning of the semester that they will be asked to write on these subjects at the end of the term. The papers should, naturally, be anonymous, and they should not be read until all grades for the semester have been recorded. Furthermore, they should be turned over to an intelligent stenographer, who should make a digest of their content and list the various criticisms which have been made under the four general head-

[1] Eugene C. Bingham, "Research in Colleges," *Science*, 61: 174, 1925.

ings. Copies of this digest should be sent to the head of the department and to the instructor concerned, so that both will know the strength and weakness of the course and teacher and can work together on plans for improvement.

Such a method is entirely practicable. Several of my colleagues recently made use of the parts dealing with destructive criticisms. Their students were entirely frank, and called their attention to a number of mannerisms of which they, themselves, were unaware. For instance, one instructor learned that he spoke in a monotone, that his voice was not audible in every part of the room, that his assignments were too long, that he was too easy with his grades, that his indirectness in facing his class destroyed much of the effectiveness of his subject-matter, that certain assignments were utterly uninteresting, that the method was not varied enough, and that certain divisions of the work were treated with too much, others with too little detail.

GEORGE S. WYKOFF

PURDUE UNIVERSITY

QUOTATIONS

THE EDUCATIONAL OUTLOOK

THE educational trends and achievements of 1928 provide the only safe basis for a reliable estimate on the educational outlook for 1929. According to this view, the unprecedented progress in 1928 becomes the foundation for still greater gain in 1929.

The people as a whole are more than ever before showing confidence and pride in their schools. They turn the cold shoulder to college and foundation presidents who would limit high school and college opportunities to the talented and to the few in order to reduce the costs of education. The people are giving enthusiastic support to school authorities through parent-teacher associations and through civic and other organizations. Citizens understand teachers better and teachers understand citizens better.

The provision in cities and states for retirement allowances for the more adequate teacher-tenure regulations have increased teaching efficiency throughout the nation. The legal and medical professions now place the teaching profession on a par with their own. There is excellent team work in the profession.

The conditions which followed the war created difficult problems in education as well as in business, industry and social life. There is a clear demand for higher standards of ethics in every phase of modern activity. Teachers, like the other groups, are working on these problems. There is an effort to create higher standards and to keep them free from partisan or commercial influences. The public will never again allow selfish agencies, patent medicine advertisers or social agitators to invade the schools with their propaganda.

The stage is set for a rapid advance in education. There are more than 4,000,000 young people in high schools and more than 1,000,000 in colleges. In 1929, the following items will stand out in the record of growth and achievement: Relating the work of the school to the work and the needs of the home and community; carrying forward the movement for more extensive character training in the schools; improvement of courses of study and a better articulation between subjects and courses and between schools on different levels; growth of professional spirit on the part of teachers; increased attention to the philosophy of teaching, and shaping educational policies, methods and all work to meet the needs of the child.—*James W. Crabtree, Secretary National Education Association, in an Associated Press dispatch.*

EXAMINATIONS IN SWITZERLAND

SWISS educationists, like the educationists of other countries, are feeling their way towards the solution of the examination problem. Not much has been done in abolishing examinations for the selection of pupils for the secondary schools; the adoption of other methods appears rather in the awarding of the matriculation certificate.

Swiss primary education, fortunately or unfortunately as the case may be, is left entirely to the cantonal authorities. As there is only the vaguest attempt at federal control conditions prevailing in these schools are bound to differ widely with regard to the standard and the kind of work done. This does not apply to the secondary schools that prepare for the universities or for the technical high school, which is a federal university. As their curriculum has to cover a certain prescribed ground, the secondary schools must obviously restrict their numbers to pupils that seem fit for the more advanced work.

This selection is made in the majority of Swiss secondary schools by an entrance examination which combines a written test in different subjects with an interview in the same subjects. The latter is generally given preponderance over the result of the written examination. In case of doubt the candidate is given a chance to prove his mettle in a so-called probationary term. In some cases the headmaster relies on the record brought from the last school attended, but some find this unsatisfactory as the method of keeping records is not yet systematic enough.

As there are in Swiss secondary schools no scholarships in the English sense of the word there is not the same need as in England for competitive examination. Financial help does not depend on the outcome of any test-paper, a free place being given to any pupil applying for it, provided he shows promise in his work. In awarding the matriculation certificate, however, the Swiss authorities have departed from the ordinary examination system. In the first place most of the state secondary schools and a few private ones (there are, of course, only a few private schools) are entitled to award their pupils the matriculation certificate on the completion of their course. To prevent an indiscriminate use of this right an agreement has been reached between the universities on the one hand and the boards of the various secondary schools on the other. Scholastic institutions desiring to come under the above agreement have to fulfil certain minimum demands as regards the number of subjects taught and the standard of the work done, and they are subject to inspection by the federal board of secondary education.

Pupils are to some extent weeded out during the school course. If a pupil fails to secure a sufficient percentage in his year's work he is sent down—a procedure more easily carried out where the majority of schools are run by the state. The examination at the end of the school career, set by the staff and corrected by the staff, is followed by an interview in at least four subjects which may vary according to the type of school. The interview is supervised by members of the school board. For the matriculation certificate the year's marks count at least one half, sometimes even two thirds, and the examination results count for the rest. To eliminate still further the danger of putting a premium on mere memory work examiners are particularly required to try to ascertain the candidate's judgment and his power of reasoning rather than the amount of knowledge he has acquired. This last stipulation, and the fact that the school work of the candidate is taken into account, should go far to make examinations what they should be—an effort to gauge the mental ripeness of the future student. To entrust the examination to the secondary school puts indeed no mean responsibility on its shoulders; on the other hand, as experience shows, confidence in a man calls forth the will to justify the trust placed in him.—*London Times Educational Supplement.*

REPORTS

BOYS IN INDUSTRY

THAT the working boy 14, 15, 16 or 17 years of age is not the irresponsible individual many people are wont to believe; that he does stick to one job; that he is not given to idleness, and that there is a close connection between the last grade he completes in school and the number of positions he holds during his early working years are facts brought out in a study of employed boys in the state of New York, recently completed by the Industrial Education Bureau of the State Education Department.

The study was concerned with 75,000 employed boys ranging in age from 14 to 17 years and employed throughout the state. Because these boys have gone to work before completing high school, the law requires that they attend a day part-time or continuation school four hours a week, either on their own or their employers' time. The school is held between 8 A. M. and 5 P. M. and the instruction given combines both cultural and practical education in the general, commercial and industrial fields.

That these boys show a marked tendency to keep the first positions they secure is indicated by the fact that of the total number studied, 44 per cent. had held but one job since leaving full-time school. Furthermore, 29 per cent. of the boys had held but two jobs since leaving full-time school and 13.6 per cent. three jobs. Combining these figures shows that 87 per cent. of the boys had held three jobs or less since leaving full-time school. In some cases the boys had only been out of school a few weeks and in no case had the period been over three years. These figures indicate that the labor turnover of the employed boy of work permit age in industry compares very favorably with that of older age groups in industrial life.

Another favorable point regarding the employed boy attending part-time school is that he is willing to work. The study shows that less than 1 per cent. of the boys reporting had never worked. This also compares favorably with older age employed groups. In this connection the law itself helps to keep the unemployed boy off the streets and stimulates him into finding a job by requiring his attendance upon part-time school for a period of 20 hours a week during unemployment. Normal healthy boys who are not at work should certainly be required to go to school.

There was found to be a close relationship between the number of jobs the boy held and the last grade he completed in full-time school, provided the fifth and sixth grade graduates were omitted from consideration. This group includes a large proportion of overage and backward pupils many of whom drift from job to job all the time.

For working boys who had completed the eighth grade, 44 per cent. were found to be in their first job and for those who had completed one year in high school before going to work, 48 per cent. were still in their first positions. The percentage continues to rise as more grades are completed. Fifty-five per cent. of boys completing second-year high school and 61 per cent. of those completing three years of high school had held only one job. These percentages show the close connection between education and the number of jobs a boy going out into industry will hold. It is evident from this study that the schooling the boy receives in the upper grades gives him a market value which enables him to secure a better job than does the boy who leaves school in the lower grades. He also realizes the value of a good position and is more inclined to hold it.

SOCIETIES AND MEETINGS

THE TENTATIVE PROGRAM FOR THE CLEVELAND MEETING OF THE DEPARTMENT OF SUPERINTENDENCE[1]

SUNDAY, FEBRUARY 24, 1929

The ministers of Cleveland and of the nation are invited to discuss Sunday morning the convention thesis, namely, "How Can the Public Schools Better Serve Democracy, Increasingly Produce a Higher Type of Citizen?"

3:15 P. M.: Vesper Service.

Place: Music Hall, Public Auditorium.

Speaker: Rev. Joel B. Hayden, pastor, Fairmount Presbyterian Church, Cleveland.

[1] Reprinted by courtesy of the editor from *The Journal of the National Education Association* for February.

Music: Glendale Choral Club, Cleveland, under the direction of Russell V. Morgan, director of music, Cleveland Public Schools.

MONDAY, FEBRUARY 25, 1929

9:00 A. M.: How Can the Convention Thesis be Answered through a Better Financing of Public Education?

Singing: Led by Albert Edmund Brown, dean, Ithaca Institution of Public School Music, Ithaca, N. Y.

Unison Prayer: Led by the president of the department.

Presiding: Robinson G. Jones, superintendent of schools, Cleveland, Ohio.

Address of welcome: E. M. Williams, president of the Board of Education, Cleveland, and president of the Sherwin-Williams Paint Company.

President's address: Frank D. Boynton, superintendent of schools, Ithaca, N. Y., and president of the Department of Superintendence.

Our chief concern with the future school building program: Joseph M. Gwinn, superintendent of schools, San Francisco, Calif.

How is education to be financed in view of the increasing cost? George D. Strayer, professor of school administration, Teachers College, Columbia University, New York City.

Report of the Committee on Lay Relations: M. G. Clark, superintendent of schools, Sioux City, Iowa.

2:15 P. M.: Discussion Groups.

The theme for these groups will be the same as discussed during the morning, but divided between the speakers named and discussion from the floor. This plan will be followed each afternoon.

The following discussion groups will meet:

Group 1, county superintendents, J. W. Sweeney, superintendent of Elk County schools, St. Mary's, Pa., chairman. Education and finance—Paul R. Mort, Teachers College, Columbia University, New York City; Financing the rural schools—C. E. Rarick, professor of rural education, Kansas State Teachers' College, Hays, Kansas; Proper rural facilities—Ernest Burnham, Department of Rural Education, Western State Teachers' College, Kalamazoo, Mich.; Summary of theme—John A. H. Keith, state superintendent of public instruction, Harrisburg, Pa.

Group 2, cities of less than 10,000 population, L. H. Bugbee, superintendent of schools, West Hartford, Conn., chairman. Other speakers include: J. C. West, Bemidji, Minn.; H. H. Davis, Columbus, Ohio; Arthur Deamer, Cedar Rapids, Iowa; H. M. Roland, Washington, N. C.; C. F. Hedges, Neenah, Wis.

Group 3, cities over 10,000 and less than 50,000 population, Wilbur H. Lynch, superintendent of schools, Amsterdam, N. Y., chairman. Can building costs be cut? If so, how?—Roy R. Roudebush, assistant superintendent of public instruction, Indianapolis, Ind.; To what extent should school funds be used for activities not strictly classed as school work?—M. G. Neale, dean, school of education, University of Missouri, Columbia, Mo.; The cause of increase in school costs—Louis P. Benezet, superintendent of schools, Manchester, N. H.; If the state supplies money for local school expenses, how far is the state justified in supervising schools? —William W. Fairchild, superintendent of schools, Rutland, Vt.

Group 4, cities of 50,000 to 100,000 population, L. W. Mayberry, superintendent of schools, Wichita, Kans., chairman. What education should be publicly financed?—Frank G. Pickell, Montclair, N. J.; How a city of 100,000 people profits from an adequate statewide financing system—Paul R. Mort, New York City; Economies effected through efficient business management—Homer Shepherd, Knoxville, Tenn.; Practical economies which are put into effect in cities of 100,000 people—M. C. Lefler, Lincoln, Nebr.

Group 5, cities larger than 100,000 and less than 200,000 population, George N. Child, superintendent of schools, Salt Lake City, Utah, chairman. The attitude of the public mind toward taxation—A. L. Threlkeld, Denver, Colo.; The relationship between financial support of education and results—C. B. Glenn, Birmingham, Ala.; Why school costs have increased in recent years—R. L. Jones, Memphis, Tenn.; Financial economies in school administration—P. C. Packer, Iowa City, Iowa.

Group 6, cities of over 200,000 population, Frank Cody, superintendent of schools, Detroit, Mich., chairman. National aid for education—Frank W. Ballou, Washington, D. C.; State aid for education—J. A. H. Keith, Harrisburg, Pa.; The pay-as-you-go plan for capital costs—H. C. Morrison, Chicago, Ill.; A continuous publicity program—R. G. Jones, Cleveland, Ohio.

Group 7, Music Education, Will Earhart, director of music, Pittsburgh Public Schools, Pittsburgh, Pa., chairman. Values of music education in the present age—Walter Van Dyke Bingham, New York City; The place of music in the high-school curriculum—John T. Bogan, Chicago, Ill.; What company should music keep? an inquiry as to the appropriateness of music in college and college preparatory courses—Will Grant Chambers, State College, Pa.; The answer given by high schools and colleges, a report of present practise as disclosed by a recent survey—Peter W. Dykema, New York City.

Group 8, Assistant and district superintendents of schools, Frank M. Underwood, assistant superintendent of schools, St. Louis, Mo., chairman. Other speakers include: W. H. Martin, Kansas City, Mo.; E. B. Cauthorn, Dallas, Tex.; Mary A. S. Mugan, Fall River, Mass.; Edwin L. Miller, Detroit, Mich.; H. M. Buckley, Cleveland, Ohio.

7:35 P. M.: Demonstration of Physical and Health Education by Cleveland Children.

Half-hour music program, Cleveland Public Schools.

Program of physical and health education, arranged by the staff of physical and health education workers in the Cleveland Public Schools.

TUESDAY, FEBRUARY 26, 1929

9:15 A. M.: The Articulation of the Units of American Education.

Singing: Led by Russell V. Morgan, director of music, Cleveland Public Schools.

The work of the Commission on Articulation of Educational Units: Herbert S. Weet, superintendent of schools, Rochester, N. Y., chairman.

Waste in American education through lack of coordination of the units of American education: John Dewey, professor of philosophy and dean of Columbia University, New York City.

The problem of articulation as seen by the college and professional schools: Edward C. Elliott, president, Purdue University, Lafayette, Ind.

The necessity of coordinating educational activities with public affairs: Leonard P. Ayres, Cleveland Trust Company.

Business meeting: Reports of committees and nomination of officers.

2:15 P. M.: Discussion Groups.

Group 1, Joint meeting with the National Council of Kindergarten Supervisors and National Council of Primary Education; topic, Problems and progress in the articulation of the kindergarten and the primary grades. Julia Letheld Hahn, director of kindergarten and primary grades, San Francisco, Calif., chairman.

Group 2, The new types of organization of school units, George Melcher, superintendent of schools, Kansas City, Mo., chairman. The advantages and disadvantages of the 6–4–4 plan of organization—William J. Cooper, state superintendent of public instruction, Sacramento, Calif.; Discussion led by John Sexson, superintendent of schools, Pasadena, Calif., and Samuel J. Slawson, superintendent of schools, Johnstown, Pa.; The Texas junior high school—M. H. Moore, superintendent of schools, Fort Worth, Texas; The possibilities of the four-year junior college—James M. Wood, president, Stephens College, Columbia, Mo.

Group 3, Where can time best be economized in reorganization of educational units?, Charles H. Judd, professor of education, University of Chicago, chairman. Other speakers include: Fred J. Kelly, Moscow, Idaho; Samuel P. Capen, Buffalo, N. Y.; C. R. Mann, Washington, D. C.; David Allen Robertson, Washington, D. C.

Group 4, Accrediting agencies and college entrance requirements, J. B. Edmonson, professor of education, University of Michigan, Ann Arbor, Mich., chairman. Other speakers include: Jesse Newlon, New York City; Lewis Wilbur Smith, Berkeley, Calif.; Jesse B. Davis, Boston, Mass.; George M. Wiley, Albany, N. Y.

Group 5, Advantages and disadvantages of the six-year high school for the larger city and smaller community, R. E. Tidwell, state superintendent of public instruction, Montgomery, Ala., chairman. The six-year high school in the American public school system—C. O. Davis, Ann Arbor, Mich.; The six-year high school in the larger urban community—C. R. Foster, Indiana, Pa.; The six-year high school in the rural community—A. W. Yawberg, Cleveland, Ohio.

Group 6, Articulating school with life, Paul C. Stetson, superintendent of schools, Dayton, Ohio, chairman. Educational processes of the adjustment of youth to life—Howell Cheney, South Manchester, Conn.; Articulating the school with the home—Mrs. S. M. N. Marrs, president National Congress of Parents and Teachers, Austin, Texas; Robert L. Cooley, Milwaukee, Wis.

Group 7, Articulation problems in the field of adult education, Carroll R. Reed, superintendent of schools, Bridgeport, Conn., chairman. Administration and organization in smaller communities—W. C. Smith, Albany, N. Y.; Administration and organization in larger communities—William J. Bogan, Chicago, Ill.; Curriculum and method in larger cities—Alonzo G. Grace, Cleveland, Ohio; Curriculum and method in smaller communities—Paul J. Kruse, Ithaca, N. Y.; Randall J. Condon, Cincinnati, Ohio.

Group 8, The guidance program as a means to articulation of the units of American education, John H. Bosshart, superintendent of schools, South Orange, N. J., chairman. The effect of guidance upon articulation from unit to unit and within units—R. D. Allen, assistant superintendent of schools, Providence, Rhode Island; The effect of guidance upon the articulation of the organization—W. E. Givens, superintendent of schools, Oakland, Calif.; The effect of guidance upon the articulation of the curriculum—E. N. Ferriss, Cornell University, Ithaca, N. Y.; The effect of guidance upon teacher training for better articulation—C. D. Cooper, principal of the State Normal School, Brockport, N. Y.; Better articulation through guidance and its effect upon morale and scholarship—Elizabeth E. Packer, acting principal, New Trier Township High School, Winnetka, Ill.

Group 9, Articulation of teacher training agencies with the other units of American education, John W. Withers, dean of the school of education, New York University, New York City, chairman. Summary and interpretation of the report of the committee on the articulation of teacher training agencies—John W. Withers; The state department of education in relation to articulation of teacher training agencies within the state—Ned H. Dearborn, state department of education,

Albany, N. Y.; The university school of education in relation to other teacher training agencies within the state—D. C. Phillips, University of Missouri, Columbia, Mo.; Arts colleges as teacher training agencies—R. H. Jordan, Cornell University, Ithaca, N. Y.; Articulation of state agencies for teacher training with the field staffs of their service areas—from the standpoint of the school superintendent—T. W. Gosling, superintendent of schools, Akron, Ohio; from the standpoint of the president and faculty of the teacher training agency—Charles Foster, State Teachers College, Indiana, Pa.; General discussion from the floor—led by Arvie Eldred, superintendent of schools, Troy, N. Y.

7:35 P. M.: Joint Meeting with the American Educational Research Association.—The Importance of Research as a Basis for Public School Administration, Arthur B. Moehlman, chairman.

Functional administration and research: M. R. Keyworth, superintendent of schools, Hamtramck, Mich.

Function and value of public school research departments: W. W. Theisen, assistant superintendent of schools, Milwaukee, Wis.

The research function of state departments: J. Cayce Morrison, assistant commissioner for elementary education, State Education Department, Albany, N. Y.

University research and its value to public school administration: M. R. Trabue, professor of education, University of North Carolina, Chapel Hill, N. C.

WEDNESDAY, FEBRUARY 27, 1929

9:15 A. M.: How Can the Public Schools Better Serve Democracy by a Better Trained and a Better Selected Teaching Staff?

What a superintendent has a right to expect of an institution training teachers for the elementary schools: E. C. Hartwell, superintendent of schools, Buffalo, N. Y.

What a superintendent has a right to expect of an institution training teachers for the secondary schools: Charles S. Meek, superintendent of schools, Toledo, Ohio.

What a rural school has a right to expect of an institution training teachers for the rural schools: Julian E. Butterworth, professor of education, Cornell University, Ithaca, N. Y.

What a teacher has a right to expect in help, guidance, and professional stimulus from the school engaging her services: Frank Pierrepont Graves, state commissioner of education, Albany, N. Y.

2:15 P. M.: Discussion Groups—How Can the Public Schools better Serve Democracy by a more Careful Selection of Candidates for Teacher Training Institutions, Better Basal Training, Better Conditions for Improvement in Service, and Correspondingly Better Compensation?

Group 1, County Superintendents, J. W. Sweeney, chairman. Improvement of teachers—N. Searle Light, director, division of rural education, State Department of Education, Hartford, Conn.; Training teachers in service—Kate V. Wofford, superintendent, Laurens County Schools, Laurens, S. C.; Vitalizing teaching through motive—Marie Sorum, superintendent, Emmet County Schools, Estherville, Iowa; Summary of theme—A. E. Winship, editor, *Journal of Education,* Boston, Mass.

Group 2, Cities of less than 10,000 population, L. H. Bugbee, chairman. Other speakers include: E. W. Ireland, Stratford, Conn.; L. P. Hollis, Greenville, S. C.; J. P. Vaughan, Chisholm, Minn.; C. R. Coblentz, Eaton, Ohio; E. C. MacInnis, Jefferson, Wis.; I. H. Hart, Cedar Rapids, Iowa.

Group 3, Cities of over 10,000 and less than 50,000 population, Wilbur H. Lynch, Amsterdam, N. Y., chairman. Are the universities making adequate provision for liberal citizenship education in their programs for preparation of secondary teachers?—J. O. Creager, dean, College of Education, University of Arkansas, Fayetteville, Ark.; Salaries in teacher training institutions, are they sufficient to secure the best service?—Roy P. Wisehart, state superintendent of public instruction, Indianapolis, Ind.; To what extent are employers responsible for the success or failure of the young teacher?—John B. Heffelfinger, superintendent of schools, Newton, Kansas; Selective teacher training—Sheldon E. Davis, president, State Normal College, Dillon, Mont.

Group 4, Cities of over 50,000 and less than 100,000 population, L. W. Mayberry, Wichita, Kans., chairman. Better training for entrance—David E. Weglein, Baltimore, Md.; Training after entrance—A. H. Hughey, El Paso, Tex.; Rewards for training—Clyde B. Moore, Cornell University; Will training and rewards develop a profession—Harry DeW. DeGroat, Cortland, N. Y.

Group 5, Cities over 100,000 and less than 200,000 population, George N. Child, Salt Lake City, Utah, chairman. Requisite qualifications of the beginning teacher and how to secure them—G. W. Frasier, Greeley, Colo.; The active teacher a constant student—Why, what, when, where?—P. P. Claxton, Tulsa, Okla.; The place, kind, and amount of supervision requisite for improved teaching service—E. W. Butterfield, Concord, N. H.; The relationship between salary schedules and teacher service—E. S. Evenden, New York City.

Group 6, Cities of over 200,000 population, Frank Cody, Detroit, Mich., chairman. What counts in the selection of teachers?—R. L. Jones, Memphis, Tenn.; How long should be the basal training for a teacher?—M. C. Potter, Milwaukee, Wis.; What training should be given while in service—C. W. Washburne, Winnetka, Ill.; How stimulate continuation of training while in service? —Fred M. Hunter, Denver, Colo.

Group 7, Physical and health education, Frederick Rand Rogers, Albany, N. Y., chairman. The organization of school medical service—Frederick W. Maroney, Atlantic City, N. J.; Education of the physical vs. education through the physical—Jesse Feiring Williams, Columbia University, New York City; Administrative policies in health education—Albert J. Stoddard, Schenectady, N. Y.

Group 8, Training for administration, Zenos E. Scott, Springfield, Mass., chairman. The responsibility which a profession and the Department of Superintendence must assume for establishing standards for its members—Fred Engelhardt, Minneapolis, Minn.; Current practises in selecting school administrative officers—E. E. Lewis, Columbus, Ohio; The extent to which qualifications for school administrative officers should be legally standardized in states and the United States—Augustus O. Thomas, Augusta, Me.; Professional training of school administrative officers—Thomas W. Gosling, Akron, Ohio.

7:30 P. M.

This evening is reserved for college dinners.

THURSDAY, FEBRUARY 28, 1929

9:15 A. M.: How Can the Convention Thesis be Answered through Character Education?

Music program.

The scientific investigation of problems of character education: William F. Russell, dean of Teachers College, Columbia University, New York City.

Handicaps of character education in the United States: William C. Bagley, professor of education, Teachers College, Columbia University, New York City.

Character education from the point of view of the philosophy of education: John J. Tigert, president, University of Florida, Gainesville, Fla.

Reports of committees.

2:15 P. M.

Music program: Cleveland Public Schools.

Introduction of Uel W. Lamkin, president of the National Education Association and president of Northwest Missouri State Teachers College, Maryville, Mo.

Introduction of the new U. S. Commissioner of Education.

Introduction of the newly elected president of the Department of Superintendence.

Address: Hon. Daniel A. Reed, congressman from the forty-third district, New York state, and chairman of the Committee on Education in the House of Representatives.

Address: Paul V. McNutt, dean of the law school, University of Indiana, and national commander of the American Legion.

EDUCATIONAL RESEARCH AND STATISTICS

SEX DIFFERENCES IN SCHOOL MARKS WITH ACHIEVEMENT TEST SCORES CONSTANT

Do girls get more credit for the same work than boys? Are teachers in the elementary schools in assigning marks subject to spurious social influences unrelated to academic achievement, and are the girls more capable of exerting such influence than boys? The superiority of girls on school marks in some instances, when considered with the relative equal showing of the two sexes on objective intelligence tests, has challenged considerable thought. One explanation of this phenomenon has been found in the notion that girls are more industrious and make better use of their intelligence. A second explanation has been suggested in the affirmative answer to the two questions above, namely, that due to the subjective manner of assigning marks, girls have a natural, though somewhat unfair, advantage over the boys. In order to throw some light upon the validity of these two assumptions, a study has been made of 390 pupils, 188 girls and 202 boys, in grades two to six, in a mid-western suburban system.[1] The comparison was made between the semester marks in the several subjects for each pupil for the first half of the school year 1927–28 and scores on the Stanford achievement test given February, 1928, very shortly after the beginning of the second semester. Table I gives a

[1] The writer wishes to acknowledge his indebtedness to Miss Fannie Moxley, who assembled the raw data for this problem and who did considerable of the computation.

picture of the data without transmuting either the school marks or the raw scores of the Stanford achievement test.

cent. below on Stanford achievement tests, which gives them relatively an 8 per cent. superiority on school marks as compared to their

TABLE I

	II	III	IV	V	VI	Grades
Girls	33	32	27	50	46	Number of cases
Boys	34	30	38	51	49	
Girls	192	266	490	543	736	Average Stanford achievement score
Boys	217	241	522	591	708	
	Per cent.	Per cent.	Per cent.	Per cent.	Per cent.	
Girls	80	72	96	81	82	Percentage A's, B's, & C's made as semester marks
Boys	80	57	91	80	71	
Girls	0	+15	+5	+1	+11	Girls' superiority over boys' on school marks
Boys	160	223	452	542	632	S.A.T. score reached or exceeded by that percentage of boys = to percentage of A's, B's and C's made by boys
Girls	72	75	74	52	73	Percentage of girls R. or Exc. S.A.T. score noted in previous row
Girls	−8	+18	−17	−28	+2	Girls' superiority over boys' on S.A.T. score
	Per cent.	Per cent.	Per cent.	Per cent.	Per cent.	
Girls	+8	−3	+22	+29	+9	Girls' superiority on marks relative to their superiority on S.A.T. score

Table I is to be interpreted as follows: In the second grade we find thirty-three girls and thirty-four boys whose median Stanford achievement scores are, respectively, 192 and 217. Of all semester grades made by the girls, 80 per cent. were C's or better, and an equal percentage was made by the boys, showing the superiority of the girls over the boys in grade two to be zero on school marks. The Stanford achievement test score reached or exceeded by 80 per cent. of the boys is 160. The percentage of girls reaching or exceeding this score is 72, showing the boys to be 8 per cent. superior to the girls on standardized tests, or, stated from the point of view of the girls, their superiority on the Stanford achievement test is −8 per cent., as over against a zero percentage of superiority on school marks. That is, they are even with the boys on school marks, and 8 per cent. below on Stanford achievement tests, which gives them relatively an 8 per cent. superiority on school marks as compared to their relative superiority on Stanford achievement tests. Similarly, grade four shows the girls getting 5 per cent. more A's, B's and C's than the boys, whereas 17 per cent. less reach or exceed the score of 452 on the standardized tests. They would thus have an advantage of 22 per cent. on school marks, if achievement were constant. In the third grade, the boys show a relative 3 per cent. superiority on school marks, whereas, in the fifth and sixth grades, the girls show a relative superiority of 29 per cent. and 9 per cent. A general inspection of columns three and four of Table I shows the boys superior to the girls in average Stanford achievement scores in three grades out of five, whereas on the basis of school marks they do not surpass the girls in any grade—the general tendency being very distinctly for the girls to get higher school marks in proportion to their achievement as shown by the Stanford achievement tests.

Table II presents the same material a little more adequately, inasmuch as the comparisons are made on the percentage of one group reaching or exceeding the median of the other group. In order to make this comparison it was necessary to reduce the school marks from letters to numbers. A+ was given twelve points credit, A given eleven, A− given ten, B+ given nine, etc.

Looking at grade two, Table II, we see that the median on school marks for boys is 15.5, and that 58 per cent. of the girls reached or exceeded this median, giving them an 8 per cent. superiority on absolute school marks. The median Stanford achievement score for the second-grade boys is 193.5, a score reached or exceeded by only 39 per cent. of the girls, giving them a superiority on Stanford achievement tests of −11. This is nineteen points below their superiority on school marks, or, conversely stated, their relative superiority on school marks is +19 per cent. In the third grade it is −12½ per cent., that is, 12½ per cent. lower than the boys. In the fourth grade it is +54 per cent., in the fifth grade +22 per cent. and in the sixth grade +8 per cent. Comparing the 188 girls with the 202 boys, in all five grades, we find the girls getting 8 per cent. higher rating on school marks, and 8 per cent. lower rating on the Stanford achievement test, making a total advantage of 16 per cent. In order to make this comparison for all grades, the Stanford achievement test score of each pupil was reduced to plus or minus deviation from the grade norms, and the sum of the transmuted school marks was divided by the number of subjects taken, in order to make comparison fair between individuals in different grades. A rough inspection of Table II shows the girls making higher school marks in four out of five classes, but higher Stanford achievement scores in practically only one class out of five.

Because of the way the data have been assembled and treated, it is rather difficult, and it ap-

TABLE II

Grade	II	III	IV	V	VI	Total
Number of cases	67	62	65	101	95	390
Median of school marks for boys	15.5	17.0	33.5	34.5	38.5	5.01
Percentage of girls reaching or exceeding median of boys on school marks	Per cent. 58	Per cent. 62½	Per cent. 80	Per cent. 44	Per cent. 59	Per cent. 58
Superiority of girls on school marks	Per cent. 8	Per cent. 12½	Per cent. 30	Per cent. −6	Per cent. 9	Per cent. 8
Median S.A.T. score for boys	193.5	225	528	601.5	687.5	+1.245
Percentage of girls reaching or exceeding median of boys on S.A.T.	Per cent. 39	Per cent. 75	Per cent. 26	Per cent. 22	Per cent. 51	Per cent. 42
Superiority of girls on S.A.T.	Per cent. −11	Per cent. 25	Per cent. −24	Per cent. −28	Per cent. 1	Per cent. −8
Relative superiority of girls on school marks	Per cent. +19	Per cent. −12½	Per cent. +54	Per cent. +22	Per cent. +8	Per cent. +16

pears to the writer rather useless, to attempt to ascertain the probable error of these findings. This is partly due to the fact that a major factor in the phenomenon is very apparently the teacher, and the study involves only ten teachers. Leaving the certainty of the findings, however, for further investigation, one is tempted on the basis of the data here available to make the following suggestions: (1) The discrepancies between grades, even though a single grade represents more than one teacher in some cases, suggests the probability of a very great difference among teachers in this tendency to favor the girls in awarding school marks. Further study along this line might result in a significant technique for understanding and measuring significant differences in teachers. It would be interesting to look for a tendency on the part of particular teachers to favor girls in preference to boys, semester after semester. With such a sex differentiating coefficient ascertained, it may be possible to discover other factors correlated with and responsible for the favoritism, such as age and tenure of teacher, and possible emotional factors, compensatory sex consciousness, sex jealousy, etc. (2) While the major interpretation placed here upon these data is that we have a measure of favoritism toward girls, some may wish to consider the alternative interpretation, namely, that the standardized tests for some reason or other place the girls at a handicap. We have been frequently told and cautioned that these new type examinations do not measure all that is measured by the essay examination, and there has been a tendency to give as much or more credit to estimates of daily classroom work as to final examinations. According to these data it would look as though one of the things measured by the essay examination, not measured by the new type examination, is the smiling and friendly disposition or whatever it is that causes the girls to get a higher mark than boys, with achievement constant. (3) In line with one of our most important findings relative to heretofore measured traits, namely, that differences in groups are greater than differences between groups, we might well suspect that this error which we find in the subjective marking of the teachers as indicated in the discrepancy between marks and standardized scores, is only an index to the total error to be found when we consider all pupils regardless of sex. If teachers are in error 16 per cent. in the relative credit given to one half of the school population, one shudders to think of the total amount of error for all pupils. We have had very surprising intimations of the amount of this error from the low reliability of scoring essay examinations, but such data to date do not tell the whole story for two reasons: (a) A score on a particular essay examination paper is one thing; a term mark for a subject is another. (b) Our present measures of unreliability do not tell us much about certain constant errors from such sources as handwriting, physical stigmata, general friendliness, sex, etc. Certainly no one will minimize the importance of such assets as friendly disposition and attitude of cooperativeness, but the question here raised is, Have we unwittingly and unwisely mixed it with academic achievement and falsely credited it under the label of the academic? (4) The question of individual difference in ability to get more or less credit for the same achievement suggests the possibility of a measure here of some sort of social intelligence or social technique of considerable value in vocational guidance and other prognosis. Such a measure might eventually be developed out of the ratio between a pupil's rank on school marks and his rank on a Standardized achievement test both in terms of S. D. This ratio or index might eventually be developed as a measure of a tendency known in the army as "hand-shaking." The reliability of such a measure could very easily be estimated by any one having data similar to that used in this study, but running over two or more semesters instead of one.

Is this differentiation between the sexes true similarly or inversely for other levels of school; junior high, senior high, college? Do men teachers show the same bias as women teachers? All teachers in this study are women. What precautions can teachers take to prevent sex or other kinds of favoritism, aside from resorting to objective tests? As the data stand they constitute an additional indictment of subjective grading, still the practice in most of our schools.

Theo. F. Lentz, Jr.

Washington University,
St. Louis

SCHOOL AND SOCIETY

EDITED BY J. McKEEN CATTELL

WITH WHICH IS COMBINED THE

EDUCATIONAL REVIEW

EDITED BY WILLIAM McANDREW

Volume XXIX | SATURDAY, JANUARY 19, 1929 | Number 734

THE DEPARTMENT OF EDUCATION IN THE LIBERAL ARTS COLLEGE

By Professor L. J. BENNETT

OHIO WESLEYAN UNIVERSITY

THE PROBLEM

A FEW years ago the American liberal arts college was a happy institution. "Academic quiet" is a fair description of the atmosphere in which it lived. Its curriculum was simple; its stated aim was single. Its student body was fairly homogeneous and not too large. Many of its graduates entered the business world and were accepted without question; others entered the professional schools. A large proportion of its graduates, sometimes a majority of them, and many non-graduates, became teachers in the secondary schools, peacefully, without undue difficulties of certification and often without the formality of any certification. In the high schools these young people developed curricula which reflected the work they had taken in the colleges, and set up the aim of preparing as many as possible of their pupils to enter these same colleges. No one seemed to question the system and citizens sometimes spoke proudly of the local high school as "our college."

Now all this is changed. No longer may the college offer a unified curriculum. No longer will the public schools accept for teachers whatever product the colleges have to offer. The public insists upon determining the elements of the curricula of its secondary schools according to its own notions of the local needs. Professors of education have appeared in the faculties of the liberal arts colleges. Many of them have been critical of the college as to its aims, curricula and methods of teaching. The liberal arts professors have resented with much bitterness this enforced intrusion of these newcomers with "heretical" ideas. As the enrolment in the high schools has increased by rapid strides in recent years so has the demand for high school teachers increased and with it the number of professors of education. In the larger universities a separate "college of education" has been the result, but in the greater number of smaller schools the maximum development has been the "department of education." At the same time the public through its legislatures and state departments of education has been increasing constantly its demands on the colleges in the way of requirements for the obtaining of a state certificate or license.

So rapid have been these changes, and so rapid has been the increased enrolment in the colleges due to the rapid growth of the high schools, that in a great many of the older-type liberal arts colleges great confusion of both purpose and conduct has arisen. With this confusion, in many cases, there has been a corresponding increase in mutual criticism between the liberal arts and the education professors, not only in amount but in bitterness. The public recently has been attracted by the confusion and has made quite a market for magazine articles that champion one or the other side of the controversy. While this current literature of "coruscating expletives and phosphorescent rhetoric" has served more to amuse the public than enlighten it, within many college walls it has added to the confusion and created bitterness where it did not exist before. One much esteemed friend of the writer's who is a dean of education, contemplating the situation, has suggested Pippa's "All's right with the world" should be paraphrased to "All's *riot* with the college." It is hardly as serious as that, yet, outside of the magazines. But it is conceivable that in some institutions it might become so, if the discussion attendant upon reorganization of curricula and the meeting of the vocational demands of all sorts made by the new elements that have come into the colleges with the rapid increase of enrolment does not very soon become less emotional and more thoughtful. Some are so gloomy as to predict the ultimate disappearance of the liberal arts college from the field of American education, what with the demands of the professional schools from above, the crowding into its field of the junior college from below, the expansion of the two-year normal school into the teachers college with its four-year curriculum, and the college's own confusion of purposes in the attempt to meet the new vocational demands of all sorts that are being made upon it.

Thus this question of "right" or "riot" in the college is one of vast importance not only to the American liberal arts college but to the public as well. The institution, without an exact parallel in any other important country in the world, has meant much to the peculiar development of American ideals and citizenship. We can not afford to let it go. There is still a very important place in our educational scheme for those liberal and cultural subjects that are not only necessary for the happiness of the individual but, through their integrating value, for the perpetuation of democracy, both governmental and social.

And so we have the problem, how may the present confusion of thought and emotional stress existing in many of the liberal arts colleges be allayed and a method of constructive readjustment set up in their place? The achievement of a mutual understanding between the departments of education and the other departments in the faculties of those liberal arts colleges doing teacher training on a professional basis is only one phase of the larger problem; we shall confine the discussion to this one phase as being of sufficient magnitude and importance for the limits of this article. We shall discuss, first, the *causes* of the mutual misunderstanding, second, some of the evil *results* that follow, and, third, suggest some possible *remedies*.

CAUSES

Merely to call attention to some of these will suffice to suggest remedies to the mind of the thoughtful reader. Others will need more careful examination.

Both history and psychology indicate that the human mind does not receive new ideas readily when they appear to be inconsistent or in conflict with long established notions. The "academic mind" has been no exception to this principle. We may cite the appearance of the early sophists in Athens, the commotion caused at Paris by Abelard with his new spirit of inquiry and his new and bold method of disputation, the hostility or indifference of many of the universities towards the early humanists, and the centuries-long struggle of the natural sciences in modern times for a place in the sun beside the older "liberal" arts. All of these "new" movements were regarded upon their appearance as attempted intrusions into the sacred precincts of the hallowed ancient culture. In all of them were said to lie a base utilitarianism and a charlatan appeal to the multitude. Jealousy often arose as the result of the popular acceptance of the newer movements. Academic halls echoed with gloomy predictions of the disappearance of culture, the downfall of religion and morality, and even the decay of civilization. As history repeats itself, may we hope the present chapter ends as happily as have the previous ones, that mutual respect and comprehension take the place of criticism, jealousy, mutual contempt and open hostility.

On the other hand, "new" movements have been characterized by a certain "youthful" enthusiasm on the part of their leaders for the reform of the world, resulting too often in a thoughtless challenge to all that was good in the old order, unseemly personal ambitions, the exploitation of students, a certain aloofness and unwarranted assumption of the superiority of whatever was "new" and "modern." There has always been at the outset a lack of acquaintance and personal association on the part of the leaders of both sides. Readjustment and peaceful adaptation have come only as personal contacts were established, and comprehension has arisen only from a thoughtful study of each side to the controversy by the other.

But there are some features of the present conflict that have their foundation in the peculiar causes of it. In the first place, the vocational preparation of high school teachers has been forced upon the liberal arts colleges largely by legislation. The alternatives have been, either train teachers as the state as employer desires or close the college doors to a vast number of applicants for admission. Force is always a source of anger, and particularly in America. The sensing of this outside pressure which has seemed to the colleges like interference has added much to the heat of academic opposition.

Moreover, there have been much uncertainty and shifting of the requirements by legislatures and state departments of education. Much of this has had its origin in the fact that educational theory in the field of teacher training is still in a state of uncertainty as to its curricula and methods, although its purposes have become quite clear. There is much contention between the teachers of the training or "practice" schools and the teachers of educational theory for "more time," and the result has been the constant adding, dropping or making elective of various subjects. To this has been added the continual increasing of the amount and adequacy of student teaching in the "practice" school, a source of much confusion to the schedule of the college proper. These difficulties are increased for the larger liberal arts colleges which draw students from a number of different states. The variability among the states in requirements constitutes a real problem for the departments of education and the general administrative officers of such colleges that are trying hard to meet the demands of these out-of-state students who desire to prepare to "teach at home."

There is an apparent incompatibility between liberal and vocational education. An able college president stated recently that these two ideas could not exist in the same institution. Yet the fact is, they do so exist, and must exist together in the education of even the same individual. A vocational education without an adequate accompanying cultural development results in machine-like attitudes in the conduct of the vocation in later life; whereas an extended cultural education in advance of and separated from any preparation for a vocation is an economic impossibility for a large proportion of those enrolled in the modern college, and especially those who expect to enter public school teaching.

Some of the trouble has arisen from the peculiar nature of the work of the professors of education. In the first place, they are held responsible by the requirements of their work for the discussion of the *aims* of education. This leads to an inquiry on the part of the students into the validity of many elements of the college curriculum. Unwisely, too often, the professors of education have indulged needlessly and sometimes discourteously in this discussion of the aims of certain liberal arts departments in their own colleges.

The same thing is true in the discussion of *methods* of teaching that must take place in education classes. But one point here is too often overlooked by students and instructors alike in these discussions, and that is the fact that there are often differences in the adequacy and desirability of certain methods in high schools and colleges. That is, high school "method" and college "method" have many differences on both psychological and administrative grounds. The constant discussion in education class of methods of teaching and learning reaches the ears of liberal arts professors, and sometimes enters into their discussions in faculty meetings. To them it seems like a jargon of words and the false idea arises that method is being substituted for subject matter. This erroneous impression is sometimes increased by the thoughtless over-statements of members of the department of education. The very natural result has been that men who have at heart the accomplishment of the aims of liberal education have looked upon the whole scheme of professional education of teachers as an attack upon standards of scholarship. The impression is heightened by the fact that the requirements of teacher training force many students to omit taking desired elective courses in favorite fields or with favorite and able professors in the major or other subjects. How false this idea is, and how inconsistent it is with the aims of teacher training, will be pointed out later.

In some of the larger liberal arts colleges that have been overwhelmed by a very rapid and recent increase in the enrolment of persons with average economic status and with the idea of education for some sort of utilitarian and vocational value as the uppermost aim back of the attempt to obtain higher education, there is sad need of a vocational guidance program that shall impartially and early in the student's college career begin a study of needs, attitudes and capacities. Much confusion arises from the coming of students in the final year of college work to a realization of a desire to prepare for high school teaching. The confusion is just as great in the departments of education as in the subject matter departments; in each group all sorts of readjustments must be made. In those colleges where systematic vocational and educational guidance is begun with the freshmen or even with the applicants for college entrance, this source of confusion and misunderstanding between "education" and liberal arts is disappearing.

The type of training the average holder of the Ph. D. degree in a liberal arts field has received is no doubt a factor of much importance in creating a dislike for discussions of methods of teaching. When we invent another degree of equal rank with the Ph. D., to be based on preparation for teaching rather than the present elaborate preparation for research, but founded upon the same high requirements of general scholarship as the Ph. D., and maintain a separate staff of research workers who need do little or no teaching, we shall have made long strides toward a better understanding on the part of liberal arts instructors of what all the "educationist's" discussion of "methods" is about. This is not to say there are not a great many liberal arts men who are excellent teachers and masters of the finest methods of teaching on the college level. But too often there has been nothing of consequence in their graduate preparation to make them such students and masters of methods. They have acquired their skill by the application of their native keen mental "alertness" to learning, often unconsciously, by observation, by trial and error, by imitation, and sometimes by conscious experimentation, the fine art of teaching; it is such teachers that give rise to the idea that superior teachers are "born, not made." On the other hand, there can be no denial that many teachers in the colleges hold in contempt the idea of the existence of such entities as economy of teaching, and economy of learning, and place the whole responsibility upon the student for the assimilation of whatever is offered, however it may be offered.

There is still one more specific cause of the ill feeling that exists that must be mentioned. The majority of teachers of "education" have, previous to their graduate study and entrance into college teaching, been teachers for several years in the public high schools. The liberal arts professors assume that these people have attained no more than the low level of scholarship that is supposed to be the possession of the average public high school teacher. No one seems to have any idea that such a person could be in any measure a specialist in any subject-matter field. On the other hand, the professor of education too often assumes just as erroneously that liberal arts professors are "impractical" scholars, without teaching skill of any sort, and with no experience outside academic walls. This mutual low rating of the personnel of the "other side" is unquestionably the source of much needless trouble and confusion.

Results

But why be so concerned with the situation? A perpetual Armageddon of argument and criticism might be a healthy thing for the faculty. No one can suffer much. In most states the legislative requirements for teacher training are enforced so rigidly that the average liberal arts college can not disgorge itself of the department of education without a resultant disastrous loss of enrolment and tuition. On the other hand, the liberal arts professors are in such overwhelming majority that no one can seriously interfere with the courses, methods and equipment they deem desirable or necessary.

But the college does not exist for the professors or the trustees, although we sometimes forget the fact. The students constitute the real "center," and it is upon them the damage that may result from confusion and bitterness falls. Angry or misguided liberal arts professors advise students against taking education courses, hold these courses up to ridicule and insist the state has no right to determine the qualifications of its employees and can not enforce its demands. Consequently, students who intend to teach put off the planning of courses in education until too late to meet the requirements, or take the education courses in a state of mental rebellion or cynicism that militates against the happiness of the student and his maximum efficiency in the education classes. Other students are given bad advice sometimes by education professors, and evolve an attitude of disregard for some or all of the work in liberal arts, are satisfied with a low level of scholastic attainment and often fail in actual teaching as the result.

The quarrel has put the liberal arts college in a false light in some communities. It is made to appear still to rest its claim to recognition as a vital educational force on the discarded doctrine of formal discipline. It sometimes is supposed to be entirely opposed to the acceptance of any responsibility for any sort of vocational training on its part; when this notion takes hold of the public supporting a college, there is a quiet turning away from it of many of its students who seek the specialized training offered to undergraduates by the state universities, and a quiet withdrawal of much of its financial support. It is unlikely that many liberal arts colleges in the country take this extreme stand. Those institutions that accept a certain amount of vocational and pre-vocational education as a part of their legitimate function would do well to adjust their internal differences or at least keep much of the discussion attendant upon readjustment from the public press until the readjustment has been completed.

REMEDIES

Many of the means of readjustment and of the cures for the state of mind back of the confusion have already been suggested in connection with the discussion of specific causes above. It yet remains to examine one or two of the proposed and other possible remedies. One suggestion frequently made is the administrative action of placing all the courses in education in a fifth and graduate year, to be taken after the completion of the four-year A.B. course. There are two very cogent objections to this procedure. First, the present economic status of those who most commonly seek to become teachers is a serious bar. Nor does the present wage scale for public school teachers warrant such a course. It is quite conceivable that the rapidly increasing per capita wealth of the country may, through a wider distribution of wealth, negate this objection in the course of time. But a second objection lies in the very nature of teacher training. Preparation for teaching consists to a very large degree in the acquisition of the subject-matter courses taught by the liberal arts departments. Every subject in the curriculum, practically, lends itself in some degree to this end. Moreover, students of the theory of teacher training are a unit in insistence upon making this acquisition of subject-matter scholarship as nearly simultaneous with the study of psychology and method as practicable. The teachers colleges and normal schools combine the teaching of subject matter and method in a given study in the same course in order to keep the association of the two as close as possible in the mind of the student. In this respect teacher training differs in method from that of the other professions to quite a large extent.

So this suggestion of getting "education" out of the way of the liberal arts college by kicking it up into the graduate school is not consistent with the requirements of teacher training of persons making their initial preparation for teaching.

On the psychological and personal side, there must arise a different attitude on the part of both sides to the controversy. The professors of education, being the proponents of a new aim to be added to the old one of the liberal arts college, bear the obligation for initiating efforts to bring about a better understanding. Let them practice restraint in criticism, the fullest courtesy in all their dealings with the aspects of the controversy, and be patient to explain the purposes of their work.

They should make it so clear it can never be forgotten again by the liberal arts professors that those engaged in the preparation of teachers fully recognize the fundamental importance of adequate scholarship as an absolutely necessary basis of teacher training, and that the acquisition of this scholarship is one of the fundamental elements in the process. This can be exemplified abundantly by pointing out the fact that the directors of student teaching and the state departments of education insist that no student be permitted to begin so-called "practice teaching" until an adequate subject-matter foundation has been laid in the major field in which the student is to obtain his "practice." Furthermore, in most states, the state department of education insists that the teacher in the field teach only in those branches in which he has had a subject-matter major or minor while in college, so far as is practicable.

On the other hand, may it be hoped the liberal arts professor will meet the professor of education half way in an attempt to explain dispassionately the aims and content of his own work, and will seek further to understand the real meaning of the newer department of education.

While each professor on the college faculty must bear his individual share of responsibility for the improvement of conditions, the college administration and the heads of departments should lead the way. If "riot" is not to prevail over "right," every effort should be made to bring about friendly discussion of and thoughtful research into the problems presented by the controversy in question. Group discussion should take the place of the private criticism and even bitter recrimination that too often now exist. Personal association between the leaders of the opposite sides not only should be encouraged but provided for in every way possible. Much misunderstanding results from lack of personal acquaintanceship.

Bitter feeling and emotional outburst have no place in the discussion of such an important matter as the readjustment of the liberal arts college to the new requirements of teacher training. Both sides will gain much by approaching these discussions in a spirit of gentility and good breeding and mutual respect and consideration. Then, in the words of Professor L. B. Richardson, "The anxious fears of those who are continually on guard lest something with the taint of vocationalism should slip into the curriculum of the liberal college, hardly would be justified either in theory or in fact. With the purpose of the institution as a guide, keeping firmly to its spirit, that college which has the advantage of sane common sense can hardly go astray. The result will be neither a mass of cultural material with no direct application to the future work of the individual, nor the aggregate of special information with no illumination from the great world of thought outside, but a judicious combination of the two, each vivified by continual contact with the other."

WHAT EDUCATION IS RURAL?

By Professor THEODORE H. EATON
CORNELL UNIVERSITY

I

To discuss rural education intelligibly one must postulate *rural* and *education.*

(1) Among the factors governing life in America (*a*) some obtain everywhere. These are the common or generic elements of a democratic civilization—folkways, mores, ethos, institutions, technical products and natural phenomena. (*b*) Under conditions of centralized industry and density of population such become

in the margins modified and supplemented to constitute a differential mode of living, which we call urban. (c) Similarly, under conditions of decentralized industry and sparsity of population a differential mode arises, which we call *rural*. Under these conditions is developed a *rural environment* of customs, ethical conduct, group spirit, group organs, technical utilities and incidence of "the open," distinguishable from the generic elements of civilization found everywhere, and contrasting with those peculiar to the urban mode of life. This is *rus*. Rural people are those whose differential traits are products of reaction to the stimuli of *rus*.

(2) Education is (a) a process of learning directed to ends of desired traits in the individual (*i.e.*, of attitude, of knowledge, of conduct). This process is (b) a means to perpetuation and reconstruction of social organization in accord with an ideal (*e.g.*, "achieved democracy"). It is a vehicle of social integrity and social progress.

II

There are three "schools of thought," each tending to determine the category of rural education by a different criterion. The first holds that rural education is "education for rural life." Aim or *objective* is the criterion of classification—as in the case of "professional education." The second holds that the use of stimuli of the rural environment, or deriving from it, gives us rural education. The criterion is the "medium of instruction"—as in the case of "classical education." The third holds that rural education is the education of rural people. The criterion is the learner or pupil—as in the case of "immigrant education."

(1) If education is a directed process of learning, there is no education unless there is design; and there can be no design except in reference to an end. Design, then, is the essence of education, as distinguished from accidental or incidental learning, and design derives from the object to be accomplished. Hence it is logical that such education as is set up in terms of ends contributive to rural life should be called rural education. But the view does not imply that the rural school should prepare children for careers as "*rural* citizens."

The criterion admits to rural education certain areas of education that commonly, by the criterion of objectives, are assigned to other fields. For example, rural leaders have suggested that rural life should profit more from the education of city people in respect to certain features of rural economy than it profits from the preparation of prospective farmers in high schools. Thus, a knowledge on the part of urban voters of the unequal incidence of the general property tax upon the wealth of the rural population might make for improvement of the system of taxation in rural areas. That might well result in the solution of a significant and characteristic difficulty in rural living. But there are those who hold that teaching to such ends belongs to civic education and not to rural education. Perhaps the conflict may be in some measure avoided by placing the rural objective proper in a design of objectives set up to further an aim of general reference to rural life. On that basis the case mentioned, because the objective is not referable to rural life as such, is not a case of rural education. But the criterion of "rural objectives" still leaves a large marginal area of education in doubt.

(2) The criterion of "medium of instruction" has had some influence, too, in the matter of rural education. The argument runs thus: "The subject-matter which the teacher presents to the pupils" is the subject-matter which the pupils learn; it is their education. Hence, if the "subject-matter" is rural, the education is rural education, no matter who the pupils may be, or what the uses to which the education is designed. Granted that the objective in education is the source of the design which characterizes the process; yet the design *is* in the selection and organization of stimuli to learning; and those stimuli are the "medium of instruction." The medium, then, is the essence of the educative process. If it is rural, the process is rural education.

A student of educational theory may, by careful consideration of the nature of subject-matter, pick flaws in the argument; but still find a trace of pertinence in it. One may point out that the same stimuli may enter into different designs of education; yet not deny that there are elements of truth in the contention.

The second criterion for determining what education is rural is not, then, meaningless.

(3) An inquirer gathers overwhelmingly the impression that the foregoing views are of little moment to the professional group of educators. For them rural education is the education of the people of *rus*. The criterion is the rurality of the pupil. There are, of course, minor limits to its application. For example, if one son of a prosperous farmer goes to a "centralized rural school," and there "masters the number combinations" under a flash-card system, that is rural education. But if another son is sent to board with his aunt in the city and masters the same combinations under the same system in a city school, that is another story.

Now a "rural school" is a public school maintained in a political subdivision of less than twenty-five hundred population. Such schools, whether of one room, one teacher, two grades and four pupils, or of twenty rooms, twenty teachers, twelve grades and four hundred pupils, do educate in the main rural children, and do furnish the most extensive and accessible facilities for education among the people of *rus*. Hence, by virtue of the last criterion, they become the dominant, if not the exclusive, agencies for rural education.

III

Truth is not always achieved by compromise. Yet throwing the light from three points at once upon the dim field of rural education may enable clearer definition. In that light any process or agency of rural education should reveal (1) a design in accord with a "rural objective" that points to the accomplishment of a larger aim in improvement of rural life; (2) a rural "medium of instruction" as essential in the design; (3) pupils who have rural traits. The objective from which the design derives is conditioned by the qualifications of the pupil and by resources in stimuli to directed learning. Hence the design itself is a resultant of the composition of three factors rather than a derivative of one exclusively. With this in mind it may be worth while to examine briefly the claims of several agencies.

The rural elementary school: Its major aim is that of all elementary schools in a democracy. The essential objectives contributive to that aim are not rural. The media of instruction in the main are not and need not be rural. But the pupils are rural. Nevertheless, the rural elementary school has certain "rural objectives." These derive, not from the prospective "rural citizen," but from the life of the boy and girl now, to-day, this month, this year, as members of a rural family, a rural neighborhood, a rural community—as dwellers in "the open." These objectives may fit into the pattern of education "for citizenship in a democracy," or they may not; but they do fall into the pattern of "education for life"—which is now, as well as to come. Each of them calls for a design appropriate to its accomplishment, and in that design "rural materials" will find a significant place. The rural elementary school is, then, responsible for *some* rural education.

The rural high school: The major aim is, as with the elementary school, not rural. But selection and differentiation have proceeded further than in the elementary school, so that functions of preparation for differing modes of adult life appear. This is evidenced particularly by courses in agriculture—and occasional attempts at country life curricula—and to a less extent in courses in homemaking. In such cases there is a design of objectives referable to an ideal of *rus*, and most of those objectives are distinctly rural. Each of them, in turn, calls for an appropriate design of directed learning in which the stimulating media are largely rural. Again, in the high school, objectives that are rural grow out of the present rural living of pupils. Since social participation of clearly rural character is likely to be greater among those of high-school age than among younger children, such objectives make greater demands upon the high school than upon the elementary school. Hence the implications for use of the "rural medium" are direct and extensive. Finally, the pupils of the rural high school are in general rural. Thus, according to our composite criterion, the rural high school is more fully an agency of rural education than the elementary school. But its chief function is neither in theory, nor by long odds in practice, rural education.

The agricultural college is not clearly definable in terms of aim. It is, however, as a college, an institution of education for those of superior learning capacity. In certain particulars of function it points to preparation of "leaders" in the reconstruction and improvement of *rus*. These leaders may be exemplars of rural modes of living—as "high level" farmers and rural citizens; they may be agents dwelling *in rure,* and contributing to its welfare through service or teaching—such as managers of "co-operatives," county agricultural agents, county home demonstration agents; or they may be agents of rural improvement not necessarily dwelling *in rure,* but contributing indirectly through research, publication, etc.—such as specialists in cattle feeding, specialists in marketing, specialists in home economics, editors of the rural press. It is, as a college, perhaps, characteristically a professional school for those who look to lives of service contributive to rural welfare. As such its main objectives fall into the category of rural, and in the designs appropriate to their attainment the use of rural "materials" is largely involved. As such, too, it deals preponderantly with rural pupils. Whether or not the agricultural college deserves to be called an institution for rural education, it has far more of the characteristics of such than either the rural elementary school or the rural high school.

Most characteristically rural, perhaps, of all existent educational agencies is the "cooperative extension work" of the U. S. Department of Agriculture, with its county agricultural agents, its county home demonstration agents, its county club leaders. Not all the work is education—some of it is service to rural people, not a little is entertainment of rural people. Dominantly, however, its design is in accord with constructive development of rural life according to an ideal of *rus;* secondarily, its design is toward alleviation of present difficulties in rural life. Its objectives are in large part rural, and the components of particular designs to their accomplishment (*e.g.,* in "extension projects and sub-projects") largely rural "media of instruction." The clientele is, of course, predominantly rural.

IV

The argument points to the general conclusion that rural education, as such, is not coextensive with "the problem of the rural schools." The conclusion is in no way derogatory to the importance of "the problem of the rural school." Under a policy of "equalization of educational opportunity," that problem is second to none in significance. It is implied, however, that rural education tends to be lost from sight when it is confused with the rural school. A survey of publications and "programs" under the heading, "Rural Education," will confirm the implication in fact.

The argument points further to many relatively specific corollaries—some negative, some positive; some of academic interest only, some of practical interest. Such may be suggested by the following list:

(1) Teaching:

(*a*) Teaching pupils in rural elementary schools to spell the words of the Ayres' list is not rural education.

(*b*) Teaching pupils in rural schools to avoid contamination of wells and springs is rural education.

(2) Supervision:

(*a*) Supervising the teaching of handwriting in rural elementary schools is not rural education.

(*b*) Supervising the teaching of ''home garden work'' in rural schools is rural education.

(3) Administration:

(*a*) In a county of which the largest center is a village of one thousand, the county superintendent of schools is not characteristically an administrator of rural education.

(*b*) In that county the ''4-H club leader,'' who organizes and directs the work of local leaders of boys' and girls' ''4-H clubs,'' is an administrator of rural education.

(4) Qualifications of ''educators'':

(*a*) To be qualified to teach, supervise, administer rural schools is not the same as to be qualified in rural education.

(*b*) To be qualified in rural education is not the same as to be qualified for teaching, supervision or administration of rural schools.

EDUCATIONAL EVENTS

PROVISION FOR EDUCATION IN SEVERAL FOREIGN COUNTRIES

RECENT appropriations for education made from national funds by the several central governments, as shown in the budgets proposed, estimated and actual, were, after 1919, in comparison with other years, on a fairly high level, both in absolute amounts and in their relation to the total expenditures for all governmental purposes. In Europe especially this was remarkable.

According to a bulletin issued by the U. S. Bureau of Education, those countries that put their finances on a sound basis after the war, balanced their budgets and stabilized their currencies or brought them again to par, were forced either by their own governments or by outside agencies to pursue policies of the strictest economy. In some countries the different departments of government were conducted on strict monthly allowances. The newly formed states were, of course, faced with the necessity of establishing an entire financial system. Even in these circumstances, education and other human welfare activities were supported generously.

In England and Wales the board of education estimated for the year 1925–26 an expenditure of £58,250,000 on elementary education and £12,000,000 on higher education.

In Belgium the Ministry of Science and Arts reports that the communes, provinces and national government expended for primary education in 1925, 24,439,100 francs. The subsidies given to schools of secondary education in 1925 were 39,498,708 francs.

The older countries of Europe are generally setting apart the greatest sums for debt service and national defense, and education comes third in the list. However, in the Netherlands the largest single item in the budget is for education; in Norway it is second, after debt service; in Sweden, second after defense. In France, Italy, Denmark and Hungary, education is third; in Bulgaria, it is fourth.

The newly created national entities of Europe are having to spend freely for developmental work, such as building roads and railroads, and establishing means of rapid communication. Education in these countries usually holds fourth place in the budget.

In the far-eastern countries large budget deficits seldom occur, as the governments are conservative in their estimates. In Japan, in 1924, the allocation for education was 73,591,000 yen, or 14 per cent. of the total expended.

The budget for Siam, in 1924–25, carried an appropriation for education of 1,390,319 tical (the rate of exchange for a tical is about thirty-seven cents).

The Federated Malay States, in 1924, expended £210,155 for education; during the same period the Commonwealth of Australia through its separate states appropriated £9,082,858.

The South American republics, while under the necessity of making large expenditures to develop their natural resources, materially increased the annual appropriations for education.

In 1926, Argentina budgeted 135,321,710 paper pesos for education; Bolivia, 4,511,305 Bolivianos; Chile, 140,663,638 paper pesos; Colombia, 3,530,896 pesos; Ecuador, 6,708,062 sucres; Paraguay, 44,336,948 paper pesos; Peru, 1,559,432 libras; Uruguay, 6,525,000 pesos; Venezuela, 5,397,478 bolivars.

COUNTY LIBRARIES AND EDUCATION IN GREAT BRITAIN

THE report for the year 1927–28 of the Carnegie United Kingdom Trust on County Libraries in Great Britain and Ireland states, according to the London *Times*, that the chief event of the year was the official recognition of county libraries as a section of the Library Association. This is described as a definite advance which gives the service its due status.

By the end of last July fifty-two county librarians had joined the Library Association and twenty-three counties were institutional members. The service has developed with remarkable rapidity and is now an important factor in the social and educational development of the less populous areas. More than twelve million people are now provided with books through fifteen thousand local centers, and the trustees' local grants amount to about £400,000.

Reference is made to the extension of the service by Scottish seaboard counties to the staffs of lighthouses. A grant of £5 per lighthouse was made by the trust towards the cost of the additional books required, and the Northern Lighthouse Board makes an annual grant of 10s. per light in return for the special service. As many lighthouses are remote even from villages the provision is particularly desirable, and information received shows that it is greatly appreciated. Sixty-four of the eighty lights in Scotland are being served. The remainder are either within easy reach of an ordinary shore library or are in Argyll, which as yet possesses no county library. In England and Wales lightships and rock lighthouses are served by the British Sailors' Society working in conjunction with Trinity House. Shore lights in these two countries receive, in some cases, special collections from the appropriate county library, but there is as yet no definite arrangement between the lighthouse authority and the county such as exists in Scotland.

In a chapter on education the report remarks:

> It is probably fair to say that at no time in the history of the public library has organized education received so much deliberate and direct service from the public library as it is receiving to-day. It is equally fair to say that the county library is as active, if not as a whole more active, in this matter as the borough library—a fact which is natural, since students and schools in the less populous areas are more dependent on the library, and because the county library is a function (except in Ireland) of the education authority. Moreover, in certain respects the county library is essentially more elastic in its methods, in that success depends upon its sending out for periods of months the largest possible consignments to the places where they are wanted; the borough librarian of necessity, and perhaps even more by tradition, keeps a much tighter grip on the books, and therefore deals with individuals (not groups) on the basis of the fortnight lending period (which is of little use to a school or a class).

THE ADMINISTRATION OF INDIAN AFFAIRS

THE following statement was presented to President Coolidge recently by a deputation headed by Mr. Charles J. Rhoads, of Philadelphia, Pennsylvania, president of the Indian Rights Association.

As members of the Indian Rights Association we are here, first, to express our appreciation of the progress your administration has made in the improvement of the Indian Service.

The survey of the service by the Institute for Government Research, which was done at the request of your Secretary of the Interior, Dr. Work, is, we all feel, the most complete, comprehensive and sane review of the Indian Administration and its needs that has ever been made, and we congratulate you on this most sincerely.

The institute's report stresses the necessity for an immediate increase of appropriation to combat the spread of disease, to save life, to raise the standard of the service personnel and to greatly improve all facilities which are now notoriously bad.

It shows that the personnel of the service is sadly insufficient as respects numbers, and, with certain marked exceptions, lamentably inefficient, if it is to be judged by standards maintained in other departments of the government. The turnover is as high as 67 per cent. a year—among the trained nurses employed by the government, we understand it is as high as 140 per cent. a year. These conditions are for the most part due to the insufficient salaries paid by the government and to bad living conditions on the reservations.

Hospitals are without medical facilities, schools are overcrowded and unsanitary. The government has been attempting to feed children at a cost of eleven cents a day, and this in institutions where the dietary has not been properly supplemented by farm produce. Children and adults have not been properly cared for in the hospitals, and trachoma and tuberculosis are exacting a terrible toll in blindness and death—a toll that would be lessened if an adequate health service were maintained.

These are only a few of the facts disclosed by the Meriam report. It calls for a large increase in congressional appropriations—an emergency appropriation of at least $1,000,000 to increase the quantity and improve the quality of the food available for children in the boarding schools, and an immediate appropriation of $5,000,000 more for the general improvement of the service.

These recommendations call for immediate action on the part of Congress, and it is the opinion of the institute that the present budget of the Indian bureau should be doubled if the service is to be put upon a satisfactory basis.

We feel that this is a national emergency and that it is worthy of your personal attention. We ask that you urge upon Congress and the Bureau of the Budget that adequate funds be appropriated to put the Indian Service on a plane that will be in keeping with the progressive steps already taken by your administration.

In closing, I wish to express our appreciation of your courtesy in granting us this interview, to assure you of our desire to cooperate with you in this work which you have undertaken, and to file with you a more detailed memorandum, together with a copy of the institute survey with a summary thereof.

GROUP INSURANCE AT YALE UNIVERSITY

PRESIDENT JAMES ROWLAND ANGELL, of Yale University, has announced that the university has offered a comprehensive program of group insurance to the faculty, administrative heads and to the clerical and service staff of the university. A substantial portion of the premium will be paid by the university. The amount of insurance involved in the entire plan is approximately $5,000,000. This is one of the largest programs of group insurance in any university or college.

The amounts of insurance for the members of the faculty and of the administrative staff are based upon a classification of positions, with a minimum of $5,000 and a maximum of $10,000 of insurance. The insurance was effective for every one on December 19, 1928, and the entire premium was paid for one month by the university. After January 19 the insurance will remain in force only for those who have expressed willingness to contribute their share towards the premium. The balance of the premium will be paid by the university.

In a letter announcing this insurance plan to the faculty, President Angell said:

> I believe this plan will mean much in years to come to members of our faculty and their families. Excellent protection is provided at extremely small cost, and I am sure that the matter deserves the most serious consideration. I intend to avail myself of this opportunity, and sincerely trust that each member of our faculty may likewise be disposed to secure this insurance on his life.

The employees of the clerical and other departments have been insured each for $1,000, the whole premium being paid by the university.

The arrangements for the insurance coverage were made by Lewis S. Welch, Incorporated, of New Haven. The business was placed through Wallace and Spencer, the New Haven general agents of the Connecticut General Life Insurance Company.

APPOINTMENTS AT STANFORD UNIVERSITY

TWENTY appointments to the Stanford University summer quarter teaching staff were announced recently by President Ray Lyman Wilbur, following confirmation of nominations by the board of trustees.

Dr. Thomas William MacQuarrie, president of the State Teachers College at San Jose, California, has been named as acting professor on the school of education teaching staff for summer quarter. Dr. MacQuarrie, who holds his A.B., A.M. and Ph.D. degrees from Stanford University, was professor of education at the University of Southern California before going to San Jose State Teachers College.

Among other appointments to the teaching staff of the school of education is that of Walter Lewis Bachrodt, city superintendent of schools of San Jose. Mr. Bachrodt has been named acting associate professor as has William Francis Redding, head of the guidance department, Providence, R. I., public schools.

Arnold Clarence Argo, for the past seven years principal of the Sequoia Union High School, Redwood City, California, and William George Carr, former professor of education at Pacific University, Oregon, have been appointed as acting assistant professors in the school of education for the summer quarter. Mr. Carr has recently been appointed assistant in research of the National Education Association, Washington, D. C., and is the author of "Education for World Citizenship."

Others appointed as acting assistant professors in the school of education are Roscoe David Case, superintendent of city schools, Brush, Colorado; Miss Alice Cecelia Cooper, head of the English department of the Modesto Junior College, California; Harrison F. Heath, instructor in the San Jose State Teachers College; Mrs. Leona Hadley McCully, of the Palo Alto High School, California; Miss Nancy Gertrude Milligan, director of elementary education in the Pasadena City Schools, California; Clarence Robert Stone, of Berkeley, California.

Professor Edgar Colby Knowlton, of Ohio Wesleyan University, has been appointed as acting professor of English for the summer quarter of 1929. Knowlton is a graduate of Harvard University. Professor Henning Larsen, of the University of Iowa, has also been named as acting associate professor of English for the summer term.

Professor Friedrich von der Leyen, of the University of Cologne, has been chosen as acting professor of German for the summer quarter. He was educated at the Gymnasium Charlottenburg and the Universities of Marburg, Leipzig and Berlin. Since 1920 he has been professor of philology at the University of Cologne, and is author of many published works on literary and philological subjects.

Miss Louise Gode, a native of Bremen, Germany, and a graduate of the Lyceum and Oberlyceum of Bremen, who has been teaching German for three years at Barnard College, has been appointed as acting instructor in German for the summer.

Two appointments on the teaching staff of the Department of Physical Education for Women have been confirmed for the summer quarter and include the appointment of Miss Eleanor Davis, director of physical education for women at Colorado College, as acting director of physical education for women and the appointment of Miss Wilma Fenner, Stanford, M.A., 1928, as acting instructor in physical education for women.

Dr. Karl K. Darrow, of the Bell Telephone Laboratories, has been appointed as acting professor of physics for the summer quarter. Dr. Darrow has been a student at the Universities of Paris and of Berlin and has been with the Bell Telephone Laboratories since 1925.

During the summer quarter Professor Robert Redfield, of the University of Chicago, will be an acting assistant professor of psychology. He is now assistant professor of anthropology at the University of Chicago. Professor Robert Holmes Seashore has also been named as acting assistant professor of psychology. During the past year he has been an associate professor of psychology at the University of Oregon and was National Research Council Fellow at Stanford for two years previous.

THE BENNETT LECTURES OF WESLEYAN UNIVERSITY

THE Bennett Lectures, on the George Slocum Bennett Foundation, will take the form of a conference on modern literature this year and will be given in Memorial Chapel at eight o'clock, February 11, 13, 15, 17 and 19. It is expected that each speaker will give an informal address in the chapel in the evening, to which the public is invited, after which there will probably be a smoker in one of the fraternity houses, where undergraduates may meet the speaker. The following morning about ten o'clock, at the Eclectic House, there will be an opportunity for not over fifteen interested men to spend an hour or more with the lecturer. These conferences will be under the direction of Professor Wilbert Snow.

There has been some adjustment in the list of speakers, due to the impossibility of securing one or two of those originally proposed.

The first lecture of the series, February 11, will be on "Poetry" by Robert Frost, poet, former professor of English and now poet in residence at Amherst. From 1921 to 1923, Mr. Frost held the position of poet in residence at the University of Michigan. On February 13, Jesse Lynch Williams, novelist and short-story writer, will lecture on "The Craft of Writing." In 1917, his three-act comedy, "Why Marry?" was awarded the Pulitzer prize for the best American play produced that year. On February 15, Walter Prichard Eaton, author and lecturer on dramatic topics, will speak on "What is Modern Drama?" Mr. Eaton is a graduate of Harvard University. On February 17, Walter Hampden, the actor, will lecture on "The Stage." Will Irwin, the author, will probably speak on February 19.

The smokers will probably be arranged as follows: in connection with Mr. Frost's lecture, February 11, Alpha Delta Phi fraternity; Mr. Williams's lecture on the 13th, Psi Upsilon fraternity; Mr. Eaton's lecture on the 15th, Chi Psi fraternity; Will Irwin's lecture on the 19th, Beta Theta Pi fraternity.

SHORT TIME IN NEW YORK CITY SCHOOLS

A SURPRISING increase in short time in the high schools is shown in the statistical report of school register and attendance for the month of November, made public at the Board of Education and summarized in the New York *Sun*. This report, as compiled by the bureau of statistics, shows there were 29,547 high-school students on a short-time schedule in the city on November 30, or 9,620 more than on the same date a year ago. There was an increase over the preceding month of more than 4,000 short-time students.

The annual increase in high school short time was only slightly less than the increase in register during the year. The high-school register on November 30 last was 142,686 students, 9,940 more than on the same date in 1927.

Elementary school short time, however, decreased by nearly 12,000 students, a large gain in the campaign to reduce congestion in these schools. On November 30 there were 791,362 elementary pupils on register, of whom only 37,350 were on a short-time schedule. These figures show an increase in register of 920 pupils and a decrease in short time of 11,400 pupils. The reduction is due largely to the opening of a number of new elementary schools and to the work of the committee on more complete use of school buildings, headed by District Superintendent James J. Reynolds.

The training schools reported a register of 5,281 students, a decrease in the year of 1,148 students; the vocational schools, with a register of 4,576 students, increased 678 in register; the truant schools, with a register of 357, increased ten in register. The total register of all day schools aggregated 1,029,966 students, a gain of 13,295 students in the city schools during the year.

The tabulation of register and short-time pupils on November 30, showing the gain or loss by boroughs in the elementary, junior high and senior high schools, is given in the report which follows.

ELEMENTARY SCHOOLS

Borough	Nov. 30 Register	Gain or Loss	Nov. 30 Short Time	Gain or Loss
Manhattan	173,649	−10,198	....	....
The Bronx	141,033	+ 5,149	6,815	+ 3,659
Brooklyn	327,053	− 639	21,221	− 4,264
Queens	126,188	+ 6,395	8,287	−10,103
Richmond	23,439	+ 213	1,027	− 692
City	791,362	+ 920	37,350	−11,400

JUNIOR HIGH SCHOOLS

Borough	Nov. 30 Register	Gain or Loss	Nov. 30 Short Time	Gain or Loss
Manhattan	33,792	− 147	....	....
The Bronx	19,861	+ 1,294	1,402	− 60
Brooklyn	29,773	+ 1,578	....	....
Queens	2,172	+ 792	....	....
Richmond	No junior high schools			
City	85,598	+ 2,926	1,402	− 60

HIGH SCHOOLS

Borough	Nov. 30 Register	Gain or Loss	Nov. 30 Short Time	Gain or Loss
Manhattan	39,062	− 1,129	8,385	+ 625
The Bronx	23,903	+ 3,014	5,979	− 769
Brooklyn	56,767	+ 2,934	6,369	+ 2,752
Queens	19,455	+ 2,178	8,814	+ 7,012
Richmond	3,499	+ 360	....	....
City	142,686	+ 9,940	29,547	+ 9,620

EDUCATIONAL NOTES AND NEWS

THE nomination of William J. Cooper, State Superintendent of Public Instruction of California, for U. S. Commissioner of Education was submitted to the Senate by President Coolidge on January 12.

DEAN ROBERT WILLIAMS, of Albion College, was elected acting president of Ohio Northern University at a meeting of the board of trustees of that institution on December 28. He will take up his work in June of this year, when President Albert E. Smith begins a year's leave of absence, and will become president in June, 1930.

PROFESSOR WILLIAM A. NITZE, chairman of the department of Romance languages at the University of Chicago, has been elected president of the Modern Language Association. Professor Nitze was a member of the special committee on reorganization of the association, and it is expected that he will direct efforts to change some of its policies.

URSEL NARVER, of Portland, Oregon, until recently president of the Associated Students of Oregon State College, was elected president of the National Student Federation of America at the fourth annual congress of that body at the University of Missouri.

EDUCATIONAL leaders in Virginia gave a banquet on January 9 in honor of E. C. Glass, who has been for fifty years superintendent of the Lynchburg schools.

DR. CHRISTIAN GAUSS, dean of the college of Princeton University since 1925 and chairman of the department of modern languages since 1913, has been appointed to the Class-of-1900 Professorship of Modern Languages.

DR. FRANK CLIFFORD WHITMORE has been appointed dean of the school of chemistry and physics at the Pennsylvania State College, effective on July 1. He assumes his new position after having been for four years head of the department of chemistry at Northwestern University, where he has been a member of the chemistry department since 1920. Dr. Whitmore succeeds Dean G. L. Wendt, who has been appointed assistant to the president of the college in charge of research. Dr. Whitmore has taught at Harvard University, Williams College, the Rice Institute and the University of Minnesota. He is a director of the American Chemical Society and was director of the second session of the Institute of Chemistry held at Northwestern University last summer. During the year 1927–28 he was chairman of the division of chemistry and chemical technology of the National Research Council.

DR. JOSEPH TRELOAR WEARN, associate professor of medicine in the Harvard Medical School, associate director of the Thorndike Memorial Laboratory and visiting physician of the Boston City Hospital, has been appointed director of medicine at Lakeside Hospital and head of the department of medicine of the School of Medicine of Western Reserve University. Dr. Wearn will fill the vacancy left in June, 1927, by the death of Dr. Charles Franklin Hoover, who had occupied the chair of medicine since 1909.

DR. J. V. BREITWIESER, dean of the school of education, has been appointed exchange lecturer from the University of North Dakota to the University of Manitoba in the annual international good-will series of the colleges.

DR. O. J. PETERSON has been appointed head of the department of mathematics at the State Teachers College at Emporia, Kansas.

THOMAS GRIFFITH TAYLOR, authority on Australian and Antarctic geography and geology, who has been associate professor of geography at the University of Sydney, has been appointed professor of geography at the University of Chicago as a permanent member of the faculty. Professor Roman Dyboski, professor of English literature in the University of Cracow, Poland, will teach in the university during the winter quarter.

DR. EVERETT L. AUSTIN, associate professor of rural education at Ball Teachers College, has been named dean of men. Professor C. E. Palmer resigned from this position in order to devote his entire time to the department of music, of which he is the head.

DR. EDWIN A. SHAW, professor of education in Tufts College, has been elected chairman of the Somerville, Massachusetts, school committee. Dr. Francis J. Fitzpatrick has been elected vice-chairman.

THE resignation of Dr. Eugene A. Bishop, assistant professor and acting head of the department of sociology in the college of liberal arts at the University of New Hampshire, has been accepted.

PROFESSOR A. A. TITSWORTH has retired after forty-two years of service in the mathematical department of Rutgers University.

THE executive council of the American Historical Association announces that Ivy Lee has been appointed chairman of the national committee in charge of raising the American Historical Research fund of $1,000,000. Mr. Lee succeeds the late Senator Albert J. Beveridge as chairman of the committee.

THE REVEREND WILLIAM H. MCMASTER, president of Mount Union College, was recently elected president of the Ohio Council of Churches at a meeting of that organization held at Columbus. He succeeds Governor-elect Myers Y. Cooper, president of the council for the past three years.

LAIRD BELL, a Chicago lawyer; George Otis Smith, director of the U. S. Geological Survey, and Ernest E. Quantrell, investment banker of New York City, have been elected members of the board of trustees of the University of Chicago.

WILLIAM BARCLAY PARSONS has been chosen for the thirteenth time as chairman of the trustees of Columbia University. Vacancies in standing committees have been filled as follows: Education committee, Jackson E. Reynolds, '99, to succeed Stephen G. Williams, '81; building and grounds, Gano Dunn, '91, to succeed Albert W. Putnam, '97; finance, Willard V. King, '89, to succeed Jackson E. Reynolds, '99; honors, Chief Judge Benjamin N. Cardozo, '89, to succeed the late Newbold Morris, '89; legal affairs, John G. Milburn, to succeed himself.

THE staff of the educational department of the Memorial Art Gallery, Rochester, N. Y., has been enlarged by the addition of Miss Sarah Kitchen, who has been engaged for a special art educational project in connection with Wednesday children's museum hours, Saturday afternoon picture story hours and Sunday sketching hours. The expansion was made possible by two gifts which provide for Miss Kitchen's salary, one from an anonymous donor, and the other from the class of 1918 of the University of Rochester.

THE Cincinnati *School Index* reports that members of the board of education of Minneapolis have visited Cincinnati to confer with Associate Superintendent Roberts, of the local school system, with respect to the Minneapolis superintendency. Mr. W. F. Webster, now superintendent at Minneapolis, wishes to retire. The Minneapolis board, it is understood, has had conferences with several educators, among them Mr. Roberts, with the view of having their names considered in connection with the vacancy. Mr. Roberts has been in the Cincinnati school system for nearly thirty years, beginning as a teacher in the elementary schools.

DR. JAMES F. MCKERNON, retiring president of the New York Post-Graduate Medical School and Hospital, was the guest of honor on January 9 at a dinner at the Hotel Biltmore attended by 500 members and guests of the faculty association of the school. Dr. McKernon has been connected with the Post-Graduate Medical School for thirty years and has been elected honorary president. Tribute to Dr. McKernon's services, both at the Post-Graduate Medical School and as head of its medical unit in France during the war, was paid by Dr. J. T. M. Finney, of the Johns Hopkins University, surgeon-in-chief of the A. E. F.; Dr. Livingston Farrand, president of Cornell University; the Reverend Dr. Karl Reiland, rector of St. George's Episcopal Church, and Dr. Edward H. Hume and Dr. Arthur F. Chase, of the Post-Graduate faculty. Dr. Marshall C. Pease presided.

PROFESSOR EDWIN R. A. SELIGMAN, head of the department of economics at Columbia University, has been appointed visiting Carnegie professor of international relations to Havana by the Carnegie Endowment for International Peace. Dr. Seligman, who will leave on his mission on January 27, will lecture at the University of Havana, where he will discuss economics and finances apropos of the establishment of a new fiscal system in Cuba.

PROFESSOR EDWIN S. KEMMERER, of Princeton University, left New York City on January 9 on his way to join a commission of experts which will sail from San Francisco on January 18 for China, where they will reorganize the finances of the country. Dr. Kemmerer has served as a financial expert in Mexico, Guatemala, Chile, Poland, Ecuador and Bolivia. He was a member of the United States Trade Commission in South America in 1922, headed a commission of financial experts in Colombia in 1923, was a member of the Gold Standard Commission for the Union of South Africa in 1924 and 1925, and served as an expert to the Dawes commission in 1925.

AMONG the passengers who sailed on January 13 for Spain was the official delegation of the executive council of the new City University of Madrid, which has visited the principal cities in this country studying university conditions. The delegation was headed by Viscount Casa Guilar, secretary of the university and personal physician to the King. Other members were Dr. Mariano Gomez Ulla, head of the medical service of the Spanish Army, Dr. Nicolas Canto and Dr. Severiano Bustamante, also of the Army Medical Corps. Miguel de Zarraga, American correspondent for Madrid newspapers, was appointed as special delegate.

Frederic J. Gurney, for thirty-five years assistant recorder of the University of Chicago, has retired from active service at the age of seventy-two years and will spend the next few months in travel in the Near East. Mr. Gurney's son is teaching in a missionary school at Resht, Persia. Mr. Gurney has been succeeded by Mr. Ernest C. Miller, registrar of Tulane University, and previously registrar of the University of North Dakota.

President Edmund D. Soper, of Ohio Wesleyan University, addressed the meeting of the Board of Foreign Missions of the Methodist Episcopal Church at Detroit on January 17 on "Interpreting the New Attitude towards Other Faiths."

Congressman Daniel A. Reed, of New York, states that he will be unable to speak before the Department of Superintendence at Cleveland on February 28, as announced in the program printed in School and Society last week. Mr. Reed asks to be excused because of pressing matters to be taken up in the Congress at the end of the present session, which will prevent his absence from Washington.

Miss Frances Perkins, who was recently reappointed New York State commissioner of labor by Governor Franklin D. Roosevelt, delivered on January 8 the first of a series of lectures on "Industry and Social Welfare" arranged by Columbia University's Institute of Arts and Sciences. The subject of the lecture was "Humanizing Industry."

Dr. A. D. Lindsay, master of Balliol College, University of Oxford, is delivering on Friday evenings beginning on January 4 a series of five lectures on "The Conditions of Democracy" on the William J. Cooper Foundation of Swarthmore College.

Dr. David Crenshaw Barrow, chancellor emeritus of the University of Georgia, died on January 11, aged seventy-seven years.

Professor Dietrich Schaefer, the German historian, died in Berlin on January 12.

A gift of $500,000 has been made to Princeton University by Thomas D. Jones, '76, and by his niece, Miss Gwethalyn Jones, of Chicago. The fund is to be used for endowment and erection of a building for work in mathematics, to be known as the Henry Burchard Fine Mathematical Hall. About two years ago Mr. Jones endowed the Henry Burchard Fine professorship of mathematics, which is now held by Professor Oswald Veblen.

By the will of the late Benjamin Duke, $580,000 is given to the Angier B. Duke Memorial, Inc., at Durham, N. C., a membership corporation, with the purpose of maintaining a loan fund and a scholarship fund for Duke and such other universities as its directors may choose. The corporation was founded in 1925 with a $1,000,000 gift from Mr. Duke in memory of his son, Angier B. Duke. Its directors are the trustees of the Duke Endowment Fund, established by his late brother, James B. Duke, benefactor of Duke University.

Dartmouth is named as the ultimate beneficiary of the estate of Mrs. Jeannette I. Cummings, widow of Horace S. Cummings, who died December 12. The bulk of the estate, estimated in excess of $500,000, is to be turned over to the college on the death of Mrs. Cummings's sister for the erection of a memorial to her husband.

A bequest of $225,000 for building a new wing to Yale Medical School is contained in the will of the late Dr. Thomas F. Smallman, a Brooklyn surgeon. The bequest is effective after the death of the widow, Mrs. Jane U. Smallman, who inherits the income from the $225,000 during her life. The proposed wing is to be known as "The Jane Smallman Wing for the Treatment of the Sick."

A $300,000 trust fund has been left to the Boy Scouts of Albany by the will of the late George C. Hawley, of that city. Mr. Hawley became interested in the Boy Scout movement in Albany eight years ago, and his gifts since that time had been frequent. Previous gifts included a sixty-acre camp site, which he equipped with a water system, several buildings, boats and general camping equipment. He also made a practice of furnishing the camp with fresh vegetables from his own garden.

THE new Tokio Imperial University library, rebuilt following the earthquake of 1923 with a gift of $2,000,000 from John D. Rockefeller, Jr., has been dedicated. The building is modern in every respect and is designed to stand through quakes many times more severe. The library is equipped with 600,000 volumes already and this number is expected to increase with further gifts. Marquis Tokugawa gave the entire contents of his famous Nanki library of 100,000 books. Several of the Imperial University professors made trips to the United States and Europe to acquire more. The New York City Library Association, Harvard University and Yale University each sent over 4,000 books, and there were large numbers contributed by the British, German, Italian and Swiss governments. It is planned to make the new plant a cultural center where students from abroad may gather with Japanese scholars and carry on research work.

BY the will of the late Arthur Astor Carey, of Cambridge, Massachusetts, a trust fund of more than $1,000,000 is bequeathed to the Mount Prospect School for Boys in Waltham, Massachusetts. The trust fund originated in 1869 with John Jacob, Henry and William Astor and C. F. Southmayd, and in 1920 was valued at $1,000,000.

THE General Convention of the Protestant Episcopal Church of America has voted to raise $1,000,000 by March, 1929, to build the St. Luke's International Medical Center in Tokyo, as a commemoration by the American people of the coronation of the emperor of Japan, which took place in November.

A CHURCH boarding school for boys, representing an outlay of more than $1,000,000, is to be established in Delaware as the gift of A. Felix du Pont. Application is being made for a charter by the Delaware Church School Association, which will have title to the property. As a first step Mr. du Pont has bought the Comegy Farm, about two miles from Middletown, comprising a tract of 350 acres, as a site for the building, which is expected to cost at least $500,000. A similar sum is to be used for endowment. While there is no intention to restrict enrolment to boys of the Episcopal denomination, the purpose is frankly to maintain a school in which the religious element in education will be emphasized and the teaching so directed as to influence the student body to become efficient in Christian service.

THE trustees of the Rockefeller Foundation have placed about $170,000 at the disposal of the University of Utrecht. The money will be used to establish a new school of physiology under the direction of Professor Noyon.

DURING his recent visit to Buenos Aires, President-elect Hoover, on behalf of the Associated Harvard Clubs, presented to the University of Buenos Aires, represented by President Ricardo Rojas, a fellowship of $2,000 a year at Harvard University. According to the text of a resolution by the Associated Harvard Clubs on November 23, it is intended to foster good-will and mutual understanding between the oldest university in North America and the largest and one of the oldest in South America. The fellowship will bring a student to Harvard for two years, beginning in 1929. The gift, which provides for advanced study for two years, will be known as the Harvard Fellowship. It will be open to all men in the University of Buenos Aires, for that institution, unlike American colleges, has only graduate schools of professional character.

IN order to meet the demand for professional Jewish social workers, the fifteen-month curriculum of the Training School for Jewish Social Work will be enlarged to a full-two-year course. The decision to inaugurate the change was made at a recent meeting of the Board of Trustees, which includes Mr. Felix M. Warburg, chairman, Dr. Lee Frankel, I. Edwin Goldwasser, Moses J. Stroock, Mrs. Sydney Bork, Dr. Solomon Lowenstein, Harry Glucksman, Judge Horace Stern and Maurice J. Karpf, director of the school. It was also announced that the school will apply for a permanent charter from the State Board of Regents. It has been operating under a temporary charter granted in April, 1925. Since its beginning 200 students have been graduated and all have been placed in positions in community organizations.

The Museum Journal reports that the Children's Laboratories, of New Rochelle, New York, begun in December, 1927, by Mrs. Marguerite E. Schwarzman, has entered upon its second year with the active support of a newly formed board of directors. During the first experimental year it was found that a larger staff was necessary in order to suitably expand the three types of work which the laboratories participate in, namely: weekly classroom work with children in the neighboring schools; lectures both for children and adults, and the work in the laboratories. The laboratories are located in a small white cottage in a country setting, furnished to resemble a home rather than a school room. Both space limitations and the nature of the experiment make it impossible to accommodate more than twenty children at a time. These come to the laboratories usually by appointment. To meet the demand for private instruction, classes of ten meet one hour every week for thirty weeks. These classes supplement the material exhibited, making field trips, collecting and preparing specimens as a part of their work.

THE fourth annual session of the "Seminar in Mexico" will be held in Mexico City, from July 13 to August 3, 1929. This seminar is under the auspices of the Committee on Cultural Relations with Latin America, of which John Dewey is honorary chairman; Henry Goddard Leach is chairman; Catharine Waugh McColloch and John A. Lapp are vice-chairmen, and Walter Frank is treasurer. This committee seeks to further mutual understanding and appreciation between the peoples of the Americas. The program will include general lectures on the life of Mexico, to be given by leaders in the political, business and cultural life of the country; round-table discussions specializing upon various phases of Mexico; lectures upon the historical and archeological backgrounds of Mexico; trips to nearby cities and towns. Ample time will be allowed for rest and recreation. Membership is limited to those whose business or professional connections equip them to contribute to the discussions and enable them to reach a large audience upon their return. Applications for membership should be sent to Hubert C. Herring, 307 East 17th Street, New York City.

THE New York *Times* reports that protests have been made against the appointment of Walter L. Fisher as trustee of the University of Illinois on the ground that he is a pacifist and that his sponsor, State Representative Anna Wilmarth Ickes, is a pacifist. The question was raised as to whether Mr. Fisher's appointment is part of a program of opposition to military training at the university. In answer both Mr. Fisher and Mrs. Ickes denied they are pacifists. David L. Shillinglaw, State Commander of the American Legion, and General Milton J. Foreman sent communications to Governor-elect Louis L. Emmerson asking that he, in his present position as secretary of state, withhold the certificate of appointment pending an investigation. Mr. Fisher, who is a Chicago lawyer and president of a labor bank, was appointed by Governor Small last week to succeed Mrs. Ickes as a trustee. She resigned on Monday to become a member of the legislature. Mr. Fisher, who is a son of Walter L. Fisher, secretary of the interior during President Taft's administration, said he was evidently being mistaken for his brother, Arthur W. Fisher, who was a conscientious objector during the war.

Two educational bills have been brought before the New York Legislature for consideration. They were proposed by Senator J. Griswold Webb and Assemblyman Irving F. Rice, of Cortland, chairmen of the two education committees. It is estimated they would make necessary an appropriation of approximately $6,000,000. An analysis of the bills from the Department of Education, given out by the introducers, explained the measures in this way: One of the bills makes provision for school districts employing but one teacher and gives to each such district the difference between a four-mill tax upon actual valuation of the taxable property of such district and $1,500. It also provides that no such district shall receive less than $425. This bill would make it possible for every one-teacher school district in this state to furnish a $1,500 program by levying a four-mill tax on actual valuation. The other bill extends to school districts employing two, three or four teachers the so-called equalization quota, which is now given to districts employing five or more teachers. These two bills furnish a comprehensive plan for the apportionment of state funds upon the basis of wealth and the number of children to be educated and should completely equalize both the tax rate and educational opportunity throughout the state, giving to the financially weak districts an abundance of state funds.

A NEW student-loan plan is under consideration at Columbia University, whereby a $500,000 fund will be used to supply students with enough money for an entire four-year college career. The university is already loaning money to more than 400 students at the rate of $75,000 to $80,000 a year. In explaining the project under consideration by trustees of the university, Nicholas McDowell McKnight, secretary of the appointments office, which handles loans, said that within three years the university hopes to have a $500,000 fund to supply students with $2,500 or $3,000 each to provide tuition money for four years. The present system of small loans is not convenient for such purposes, he added. Columbia's system has been to loan money for tuition only for five years at 5 per cent. Most of the loans go to juniors, seniors and second-year graduates, thus cutting down risks of care-free and overambitious freshmen. Medical, engineering and law students are the most frequent borrowers, with women taking as much money as men in proportion to the enrolment.

ACCORDING to the State Department of Health, 350 communities in New Jersey are carrying on a continuous child hygiene program under its supervision. There are 116 child hygiene nurses, nineteen of whom are paid entirely by the State department of health, eighty-six entirely by municipalities, and eleven partly by the State and municipalities. These nurses, the department notes, made thousands of visits to expectant mothers and to mothers of infants and older children. In the preschool clinics, 2,392 children were immunized against diphtheria and more than 9,000 Schick tests and immunization tests were made among school children in the communities where these nurses are employed.

FACTS gathered by the Bureau of Education give an indication of the number of blind people there are in the United States and the steps that are being taken toward their education. It shows that there are eighty institutions in the United States in which the blind are taught. Of these forty-seven are State institutions, twenty-one are schools or classes in city school systems, five are institutions wholly supported by private funds, five others are private institutions, partly or largely aided by state funds, while one is a school in the Philippine Islands, and one a school in Porto Rico. In 1927 there were 6,084 pupils in these schools, who were being taught by 863 instructors. In kindergarten classes there were 336 pupils; in classes corresponding to grades one to four there were 2,179 pupils; in grades corresponding to five to eight there were 1,977; and in high schools there were 1,236. The libraries of these institutions contain 157,380 volumes printed in the Braille raised type.

SPECIAL CORRESPONDENCE

THE BOYS' CLUB IN AN URBAN HIGH SCHOOL

IN a number of secondary schools throughout the country, the students' general association is proving a very satisfactory agency for the development of student morale and the promotion of good school citizenship. Principals and teachers take reasonable pride in the character of student assemblies and business meetings conducted under the auspices of such organizations; they are justified in their faith that students are entitled to participate in school government and to assume a measure of responsibility for the academic and non-academic activities of the school community. From its very nature, however, the students' general association or any other student-body organization may prove inadequate for other than a limited number of social-civic purposes that relate to the school as a whole—purposes that can usually be served by school assemblies. To meet the demands of the student body for legitimate forms of activity not available through such a comprehensive and coordinating body as the students' general association, or the various departmental clubs in the school, boys' clubs and girls' leagues have been found quite effective, and in many communities are proving most successful. Frequently, the vice-principal or vocational counselor is faculty adviser of the boys' club; the dean of girls is the obvious adviser of the girls' league. Where these two organizations function well, increased opportunity exists to rally the boys and girls and to provide social activities that respond to the interests of the adolescent and that are at the same time wholesome and desirable from the educational standpoint.

That student activities of this character need no defense is readily admitted by most investigators on the place of extra-curricular activities in education. To quote Professor Fretwell:[1]

> While the aims of pupils and teachers may differ, every wise teacher recognizes that these volunteer pupil organizations are based on the instinctive tendencies of the pupils, and that it is the business of the teacher to arrange the situation so that the pupils will want better clubs and develop the ability to satisfy this improved want. . . . Wise leaders, teachers or pupils, see that such organizations are based on instinctive tendencies of gregariousness, of love of approval, of rivalry, of mastery, of altruistic effort, and so afford an opportunity for activities that may be fundamentally educative. These leaders know that outside of regular school classes pupils are going to have organizations of some kind and that these organizations are going to exercise a tremendous influence on the life of the individual and on the life of the school. These leaders know, every parent and every one in a position of authority in and out of school must know, that this extra-curricular phase of school life can not be neglected. . . . We have learned that a positive, constructive program of what to do, worked out by teachers and pupils together, is one that captures the imagination and wins the allegiance of both teachers and pupils.

To meet the needs of boys, with whom this paper is concerned, the boys' club may serve a useful purpose and may, indeed, make generous contributions to the recognized objectives of education. In the belief, therefore, that the reader may be interested in a statement concerning the practical side of boys' work rather than a discussion of "boyology," the writer will give in the following paragraphs an account of the aims and activities of the club with which he is most familiar, namely, the Boys' Club of the Morgan Gardner Bulkeley High School, of Hartford, Connecticut. At this school, it should be said, a students' general association does not exist. There is, however, an alert student council; and membership in the athletic association is held by the vast majority of the students.

What the Bulkeley Boys' Club stands for is stated as follows in the constitution of the club: "The purpose of this organization shall be to develop in its members an enthusiasm for the highest ideals in scholarship, sportsmanship, fellowship and character. It shall endeavor to create among the boys of Bulkeley High School a public opinion that shall at all times rally to the support of the school when the opportunity to serve is offered." This article appears on the reverse side of the membership cards of the club; and under it is printed the club pledge: "I promise to give my best to the club that the above aims may be realized." Space below is reserved for the member's signature.

At the outset membership in the club was limited to students who had completed successfully the work of the lower freshman class. The experience of the past two years, however, has made the club officers and advisers feel that the restriction was unwise. Eligibility, therefore, was extended to every boy in the school upon the opening of the school in September, 1928, with the result that the membership increased from the 225 of the previous year to 305. Approximately 50 per cent. of the boys in the school joined; it was not expected that every boy would become a member. Dues are twenty-five cents a year. Since considerable profit is derived from the annual dance and other activities of the club, it is possible to keep the dues at this very moderate figure.

Five officers are elected in the spring of each year. In them is vested a large measure of responsibility for the success of the club. Thus far the officers selected have for the most part

[1] "The Place of Extra-curricular Activities in Education," a paper read before the Harvard Teachers' Association, March 14, 1925.

proven worthy; experience to date indicates that the members select as their president leaders not inferior to the president of the student council. The duties of the officers are clearly specified in the constitution of the club. The executive committee meets at no specified time; committee meetings are called whenever the business of the club demands attention. As a rule, not less than seven or eight meetings are called each semester. The president presides, and the faculty adviser is regularly present.

Preliminary to the membership drive in the fall of each year it seems advisable to hold a general boys' rally in the school auditorium. The speakers should include the president of the club, the faculty adviser and the principal of the school. Every effort should be made to make this meeting as enthusiastic as possible. Subsequently room representatives should be either appointed by the executive committee or elected by vote in the session rooms through the school at large; then the membership drive begins. It is expected that room representatives will complete the canvass within a week. Club posters and a "thermometer" prove most valuable during the drive week. The school paper contributes valuable publicity. The drive complete, the club is ready for the year's work.

Under ordinary circumstances, three supper meetings are held each semester. Supper tickets at forty or fifty cents each are placed on sale several days before the supper; the room representatives assume charge of the ticket sale. Members of the girls' league cooperate to make the suppers a success by decorating the school cafeteria and by serving as waitresses. An orchestra composed of members of the club furnishes music for the supper.

After the supper the members recess briefly and proceed to the assembly hall, where the business meeting is held. Here the members have an opportunity to manifest their civic interest in matters relating to the welfare of the club and the school. Ordinarily, a prominent citizen is invited to address the gathering on a topic that holds real interest for boys. After the address comes the evening's entertainment. For this purpose skits, stunts, one-act plays, movies, vocal and instrumental numbers, mock trials and debates readily win favor. After the entertainment a few remarks bearing on the work of the club are made by the faculty adviser; frequently the principal is called upon to say a few words. The club song is sung, and the meeting is then adjourned.

To maintain interest in the regular meetings, the program should be varied and worth while. One of the most successful meetings of the Bulkeley club comes on the evening of the father-son dinner. On that evening, short talks are given by fathers and sons, and both groups contribute to the entertainment. One meeting a year features student speakers only, and they are received with genuine interest. At a meeting of the club a few months ago, boys prepared talks on the following topics: "Making the Student Council Effective," "The Bulkeley Athletic Association," "Real Values at Bulkeley," "Social Activities at Bulkeley," "Qualities in Men which Boys Admire," "What the Younger Boys Think of the Boys' Club," "Impressions of a Post-Graduate" and "Impressions of an Amateur Actor." The first topic was handled by the president of the student council; the last by an outstanding member of the dramatic club. Thus the boys were in every case able to discuss topics which bore upon their own interests and activities. Frequently the boys themselves suggest topics that are most appropriate.

The club hopes to inaugurate in the near future a faculty-student night, with contributions both light and serious from both teachers and boys. It goes without saying that the men teachers are regularly invited to all the club activities. Their cooperation is especially valuable at the annual field day of the club, and their presence at the club's dance is always welcomed.

As an evidence of the interest of the club in school athletics, football badges and other insignia are sold each fall; school spirit is thus enkindled and considerable profit is available for the club itself or for the promotion of school athletics. As an evidence of the club's interest in school citizenship, a good citizenship prize of five dollars is awarded at each graduation to the boy member of the graduating class who, in the course of his four years at high school, has given evidence by his leadership, character and devotion to all the school stands for that he merits such an award. The faculty council names the recipient of this prize. And as an evidence of its interest in the order and morale of the school, the club is ready to second the efforts of the student council and thus cooperate in making its regulations effective.

If any boys' club is to prosper, it must have able faculty direction. Indeed, it is not too much to say that the main responsibility for the success of the club rests upon the faculty adviser. His rôle is one of guidance and cooperation; domination is almost as unwise as a frank *laissez-faire* policy. He should understand boys, and should appreciate their points of view, attitudes, interests, problems and ambitions. It is essential that friendly, frank and helpful relationships prevail between member and adviser; and if the latter has the gift of inspirational leadership, it is difficult to place limits upon what the club may achieve, for, as Superintendent Boynton, of Ithaca, is so fond of pointing out, at every stage in history youth has never failed to follow inspirational leadership. The experienced faculty adviser is aware, too, that some of the greatest satisfactions of life come from *working with* boys. In a very true sense, his function is a guidance function, and in the light of this fact it has frequently been suggested that the duties of faculty adviser and vocational counselor be vested in one person.

The duties of the faculty adviser are, of course, numerous. Club programs must be given his approval, club finances must be carefully inspected, club officers must be trained in parliamentary procedure, club correspondence and publicity require a certain amount of supervision, entertainment rehearsals must be coached when necessary, and the club should always be able to profit by his helpful counsel. His assistance may be withdrawn only when the boys are apparently able to execute a given plan independently and successfully. The faculty adviser may wisely delegate to the club officers any matters that they give promise of handling fairly well; it is their club, and they should be encouraged to assume responsibilities that are not beyond their powers. Adherence to such a policy is much more difficult for the adviser than a policy of domination; but the effort involved is justified if it promotes good citizenship and democratic living among the youth in our schools.

The boys' club is perhaps one of the best answers the high school can offer to the challenge of the so-called boy problem. It gives the school a hold upon the boy and enables the school to make of him a worthier member of society. It appeals to his inner impulses without resorting to preachment or aiming to reform him; the school puts its faith in the boy, and the response of the boy is eloquent proof that the faith has not been wrongly placed.

ROBERT H. MAHONEY

BULKELEY HIGH SCHOOL,
HARTFORD, CONN.

QUOTATIONS

BROOKWOOD LABOR COLLEGE AND THE AMERICAN FEDERATION OF LABOR

THE recent condemnation of the Brookwood Labor College by the American Federation of Labor brings to the foreground the question of the future of adult education in connection with the labor movement. The issue is rendered especially acute because of the way in which the condemnation was effected; it was a scholastic lynching. Methods were employed which are not tolerated to-day in so-called "capitalistic" private institutions, where accused persons are entitled to a hearing before condemnation can ensue. This phase of the matter has received attention in the press, but the extent to which the future of workers' education in this country is involved has not had corresponding publicity. Nor has the bearing of the Brookwood incident upon the prospects of organized labor itself under its present political management come to the notice of any large part of the public.

* * * * *

In connection with the educational phase of the matter, it is significant that the motion of condemnation of Brookwood was sponsored at New Orleans by Mr. Mahon, president of the

Street Railway Employees' Union. Mr. Mahon is the man who, in behalf of that union, signed an agreement with Mr. Mitten which guaranteed immunity to the company unions of the Philadelphia traction interests controlled by that gentleman. The *quid pro quo* was that Mr. Mitten would not oppose regular unions in any further traction developments in other cities in which he had a controlling voice, provided those unions adopted the standards already in force in Mr. Mitten's company unions. It happens that Mr. Muste, the head of Brookwood, had incurred the antagonism of Mr. Mahon by public criticism of the policy involved in the agreement. Another point of educational import is the influential position occupied by Mr. Woll as chairman of the education committee of the American Federation of Labor, its only permanent committee. He is now engaged in gathering under his brooding wings the Workers' Education Bureau, having introduced a resolution that this bureau have a board of directors entirely elected by the American Federation of Labor and international unions. At present three out of eleven are approved by the executive council of the American Federation of Labor. Even more important is the fact that the resolution, if and when adopted, would deprive state and city federations, local unions and district councils, together with labor schools and colleges, from representation. If he succeeds in getting this measure through the next convention of the Workers' Bureau (an organization formed by liberal labor elements independently of the American Federation of Labor), he can congratulate himself that labor education has been made safe for the political machine of the federation which he so skilfully conducts. At present, some of the labor schools are conducted by men who are Brookwood graduates. The condemnation of Brookwood is a warning to them that they may be next in line. Will Mr. Woll's next step be to discipline them? Any activities of his in this direction will be worthy of attention.

It can not be too generally understood that the condemnation of Brookwood is no isolated event. It is a part of the policy to eliminate from the labor movement the schools and influences that endeavor to develop independent leaders of organized labor who are interested in a less passive and a more social policy than that now carried on by the American Federation of Labor in its close alliance with the National Civic Federation. Opposition to the official political machine of the former is to be interpreted as enmity to organized labor itself; that any opposition is ascribed to Bolshevist sympathies is in line with the resort to cheap epithets currently employed to discredit any liberal movement. What will become of the organized labor movement in case such policies continue to grow?—John Dewey in *The New Republic.*

The more intelligent leaders of labor must admit, however, that regardless of any technical defense which may be set up, it is a great misfortune when the activities of the federation bring forth condemnation from persons occupying positions in the nation's esteem such as John Dewey occupies. To deny that labor need pay any attention to what he says is to deny that labor need attend to its status in informed public opinion. When labor concerns itself with education, it concerns itself with a fundamental social activity in which Dr. Dewey is an acknowledged expert, and which affects, directly or indirectly, the entire community. Nor can any body of citizens with the pretensions of organized labor live by and for itself alone. No other group in the life of the nation is so insulated that it can justifiably resent all observation or criticism. We may grant the right of autonomy and self-government in the unions, without foregoing the right to disagree with them, especially when they reach out from technical industrial matters into matters of special public concern like education. Nor does labor itself act as if it were self-sufficient when it has to ask for public support in legislative, judicial and sometimes even in industrial controversies. If the manner of the federation's action in regard to Brookwood, as inspired by Mr. Woll, is a correct indication of the nature of his mind, he is ill-suited to keep the good-will of any one interested in fair play, to say nothing of those concerned with education. It is an important question for labor whether it should, in its own interest, entrust to him in the future so much influence over its decisions.—*The New Republic.*

REPORTS

PHILANTHROPIC GIFTS IN 1928

THE year just ended was distinguished by the philanthropy of American men of wealth. The total is estimated at $2,330,600,000. A compilation of the John Price Jones Corporation, reporting to the Associated Press, shows a steady increase in recent years as follows:

Year	Total Benefactions
1921	$1,719,000,000
1922	1,787,760,000
1923	1,859,310,000
1924	2,000,320,000
1925	2,068,570,000
1926	2,192,680,000
1927	2,219,700,000

The largest benefactions were those of Payne Whitney. It was found that he had given $60,000,000 to libraries, hospitals and other institutions. Of this nearly $26,000,000 went to create a trust fund to promote educational and scientific progress, details concerning which have already been reported in SCHOOL AND SOCIETY.

Next in size were the Rockefeller donations, totaling about $30,000,000. The Laura Spelman Rockefeller Memorial voted $5,000,000 to be devoted to the Great Smoky Mountains National Park, $1,000,000 for the University of Chicago to be used in teaching religion and $2,000,000 for Brookings Institute, Washington. John D. Rockefeller, Jr., agreed to pay the cost of restoring the historic town of Williamsburg, Va., at a cost estimated between $4,000,000 and $5,000,000. He gave $2,000,000 to the City University of Paris and a like amount for a museum in Jerusalem. The Rockefeller Foundation gave $3,500,000 conditionally to Cambridge University, England. The General Education Board promised $3,000,000 to Harvard and $1,416,666 to Cornell. There were numerous smaller donations.

Many of the largest contributions went toward the assistance of education and allied research. George C. Booth, of Detroit, gave $6,500,000 to Cranbrook Foundation for an educational and cultural center. Edward S. Harkness is reported to have given $10,000,000 to Harvard. James G. Cutler left $2,650,000 to the University of Rochester. Chauncey M. Depew left $1,000,000 to Yale. Yale also received $1,000,000 from Abram E. Fitkin, of New York. Julius Rosenwald promised $2,000,000 to the University of Chicago. A. P. Giannini gave $1,500,000 to the University of California; Leonard D. and Arthur J. Baldwin, of East Orange, N. J., gave $1,500,000 to convert Drew Theological Seminary of Madison, N. J., into a university.

M. C. Taylor, of New York, gave $1,500,000 to Cornell University. Mr. and Mrs. Albert D. Lasker gave $1,000,000 to the University of Chicago. The Charles M. Hall estate gave $2,000,000 to Harvard for education in the Orient. Mrs. Annie C. Kane, of New York, gave $1,000,000 to Columbia, and the same amount to the Home for Incurables. James Ward Packard gave $1,200,000 to Lehigh University. Edwin Webster Sanborn left $1,500,000 to Dartmouth College, to which institution also the F. Augustus Schermerhorn estate gave $1,158,000.

John J. Raskob gave $1,000,000 to create the Bill Raskob Foundation for poor children and orphans. R. R. Fogel left $1,500,000 to the Pacific Hebrew Orphan Asylum and Home Society, San Francisco. Fred J. Fisher, of Detroit, gave $1,000,000 to the Little Sisters of the Poor. Milton S. Hershey gave $2,000,000 to be used in the construction of a community center in the town of Hershey, site of his factories near Harrisburg, Pa.

One of the largest benefactions to hospitals was that of $5,000,000 left to St. Luke's Hospital here by the late Mrs. Mary Ann Fitzgerald. Uri T. Hungerford gave $2,600,000 to the Charlotte Hungerford Hospital at Torrington, Conn. Mrs. John I. Kane left $1,000,000 to New York Orthopaedic Dispensary and Hospital. The New York Public Library will receive the principal of the $1,300,000 estate of the late John R. Slattery, left in trust for his widow.

Felix M. Warburg gave $1,000,000 to the American Jewish Joint Agricultural Corporation for the establishment of Jewish agricultural colonies in Russia. The late Morris Schinasi, cigarette manufacturer, bequeathed $1,000,000 for the erection of a hospital at Magnesia, Asia Minor, where he was born. Mr. and Mrs. George Blumenthal gave $1,000,000 to the Metropolitan Museum to acquire art treasures.

Julius Rosenwald gave $2,000,000 to the Rosenwald Fund, bringing it to more than $20,000,000, all of which must be spent within twenty-five years for the betterment of humanity.

SOCIETIES AND MEETINGS

THE CLEVELAND MEETING OF THE NATIONAL CONFERENCE OF SUPERVISORS AND DIRECTORS OF INSTRUCTION

THE program has been arranged as follows:

TUESDAY, FEBRUARY 26

Assembly Hall, Hotel Hollenden, 9: 30 A. M.

Mary A. S. Mugan, president of the conference, presiding.

Topic: Next Steps in Supervision.

(1) From the standpoint of the elementary supervisor: Julia L. Hahn, director of kindergarten and printing grades, San Francisco.

(2) From the standpoint of the elementary school principal: Arthur S. Gist, principal of training school and director of practice teaching, State Teachers College, San Francisco.

(3) From the standpoint of the supervisor of rural schools: I. Jewell Simpson, assistant state superintendent of schools of Maryland, Baltimore.

(4) A balanced program of supervision: James F. Hosic, professor of education, Teachers College, Columbia University, New York.

Annual Business Meeting.

WEDNESDAY, FEBRUARY 27

Assembly Hall, Hotel Hollenden, 9: 00 A. M.

Mary A. S. Mugan, president of the conference, presiding.

Topic: Scientific Method in Supervision as Presented in the Second Yearbook of the Conference.

(1) Introduction and presentation of the yearbook: Leo J. Brueckner, professor of elementary education, University of Minnesota.

(2) Teachers' difficulties as a basis for supervision: Douglas Waples, Graduate Library School, University of Chicago.

(3) Survey techniques for the experimental determination of the values of materials and methods: Paul T. Rankin, director of research, Detroit public schools.

(4) Teacher participation in curriculum construction: Prudence Cutright, director of instructional research, Minneapolis public schools.

(5) Appraisal and summary—suggested uses for the yearbook: Ernest Horn, professor of education, State University of Iowa.

LUNCHEON MEETING

Lattice Room, Hotel Statler, 12: 00

A. S. Barr, first vice-president of the conference, presiding.

Informal address by Mary A. S. Mugan, president; James F. Hosic, secretary-treasurer; William H. Burton and J. Cayce Morrison, members of the executive committee.

This will be a family gathering for members of the conference, for the discussion of policies and future plans of the organization. Admission by membership card.

THE CENTRAL ASSOCIATION OF SCIENCE AND MATHEMATICS TEACHERS

ABOUT five hundred members were present at the twenty-eighth annual meeting of the Central Association of Science and Mathematics Teachers, which was held at the University of Chicago, on November 30 and December 1. Addresses were given before the general conference by:

Professor Otis W. Caldwell, Columbia University.

Professor Louis C. Karpinski, University of Michigan.

John Mills, member of the Technical Staff, Bell Telephone Laboratories.

Professor W. D. Harkins, the University of Chicago.

Jerome Lederer, M.E., president of Aerotech, Inc.

Dr. W. T. Bovie, Northwestern University Medical School.

The association is composed of six sections: Biology, chemistry, general science, geography, mathematics and physics. Papers were given before each of these sections on November 30.

Recently the association under the leadership of its past president, Mr. W. F. Roecker, was incorporated and purchased the magazine *School Science and Mathematics*. This magazine has been the official journal of the association, but it has been managed and published under the private ownership of Mr. Charles M. Turton and Mr. Glen W. Warner, of Chicago.

School Science and Mathematics has always had a wide circulation. Its influence in secondary school science and mathematics teaching has long been recognized by leading educators. Every effort will be made under the new management to maintain its former high standard. Mr. Glen W. Warner, of Crane Junior College, Chicago, will continue as the editor of the journal, and Mr. W. F. Roecker has been elected business manager.

The officers elected at the annual meeting are:

President, Ada L. Weckel, head of the biology and geography department, Oak Park and River Forest Township High School, Oak Park, Illinois.

Vice-President, Walter G. Gingery, principal of the George Washington High School, Indianapolis, Indiana.

Secretary, W. F. Roecker, head of the science department, Boys' Technical High School, Milwaukee, Wisconsin.

The next annual meeting will be held in Chicago, November 29 and 30, 1929.

EDUCATIONAL RESEARCH AND STATISTICS

THE WOMEN WHOSE NAMES APPEAR IN "AMERICAN MEN OF SCIENCE" FOR 1927

SOME little material has been published regarding American men of science, covering such facts as place of birth, institution in which graduate training was obtained, and so on. However, there appears to have been no study simply of the women active in scientific work. The present paper attempts some study of this group. The results concern the 687 women included in the 1927 edition of "American Men of Science." These results will be summarized under the following headings: (1) birthplace, (2) age, (3) education, (4) major interest and (5) present location.

(1) *Birthplace.*—The first table shows: (a) the number of these women born in each state; (b) similar figures for the 601 leading scientific men[1] as given by Dr. Cattell, and (c) the frequency of scientific women per million population in each state (the census of 1880 being the basis, since these women average forty-two years in age). The results show the North Atlantic states to lead in total number of women, with the North Central states a quite close second. This reverses the situation for the men.

TABLE I

BIRTHPLACE (BY STATE) OF 687 AMERICAN WOMEN OF SCIENCE AND 601 AMERICAN MEN OF SCIENCE

	Number		Per million population in 1880	
	Women	Men		
North Atlantic	(273)	(200)	(19)	(14)
Maine	10	6	15	9
New Hampshire	13	7	38	20
Vermont	9	6	27	18
Massachusetts	64	48	36	27
Rhode Island	15	1	56	4
Connecticut	14	16	23	27
New York	77	67	15	13
New Jersey	16	8	11	6
Pennsylvania	55	41	13	10
South Atlantic	(42)	(42)	(5.5)	(5.5)
Delaware	3	2	21	14
Maryland	11	13	12	14
Dist. Columbia	3	3	17	17
Virginia	5	8	3	5
West Virginia	6	4	10	6
North Carolina	7	5	5	4
South Carolina	4	4	4	4
Georgia	1	3	.7	2
Florida	2	0	7	0

The greatest number of women were born in Massachusetts, New York, Pennsylvania and Illinois. These four states produced 36 per cent. of the total. In proportion to population,

[1] The 601 "leading scientists" are, of course, much more highly selected than the women with whom they are being compared, but they appeared to be the only group available for such comparisons.

TABLE I—(*Continued*)

BIRTHPLACE (BY STATE) OF 687 AMERICAN WOMEN OF SCIENCE AND 601 AMERICAN MEN OF SCIENCE

	Number		Per million population in 1880	
	Women	Men		
South Central	(20)	(18)	(2)	(2)
Kentucky	9	5	6	3
Tennessee	2	4	1	3
Alabama	0	2	0	2
Mississippi	0	2	0	2
Louisiana	4	1	4	1
Texas	5	1	3	.7
Oklahoma	0	1	0	4
Arkansas	0	2	0	2
North Central	(230)	(230)	(12)	(13)
Ohio	34	47	11	15
Indiana	11	18	6	9
Illinois	52	45	17	15
Michigan	20	13	12	8
Wisconsin	20	24	15	18
Minnesota	15	14	19	18
Iowa	28	27	18	17
Missouri	17	21	8	10
North Dakota	2	1	11	5
South Dakota	3	3	22	22
Nebraska	11	6	24	13
Kansas	17	11	17	11
Western	(51)	(20)	(29)	(11)
Montana	1	2	26	51
Wyoming	5	2	250	100
Colorado	12	1	60	5
New Mexico	3	0	30	0
Arizona	0	0	0	0
Utah	1	3	7	21
Nevada	0	0	0	0
Idaho	3	0	94	0
Washington	7	0	93	0
Oregon	2	1	12	6
California	17	11	21	14
Foreign	26	68		
Canada	21	18		
Not given	24	5		

however, New Hampshire, Vermont, Rhode Island and Massachusetts are outstanding.[2]

[2] The large numbers for Wyoming, Idaho and Washington are unsound, since the number per million was reckoned from the 20,000 or so people in these states in 1880.

(2) *Age.*—The age of the women in "American Men of Science" is summarized in the table below. Sixty-six women did not give their age. The youngest was twenty-seven, and the oldest eighty-four. The median age is forty-two; 32 per cent. of the women fall between thirty-five years of age and forty-four.

TABLE II

THE DISTRIBUTION OF AGES OF WOMEN IN "AMERICAN MEN OF SCIENCE"

80–84	3
75–79	7
70–74	17
65–69	25
60–64	30
55–59	50
50–54	67
45–49	99
40–44	107
35–39	111
30–34	86
25–29	19
Not given	66
Total	687

(3) *Education.*—The education received by these women presents several interesting facts. The first degree was an A.B. for 476 of the cases, 68 per cent. of the total; the B.S. was next frequent, with 150 cases. One must not, however, at once conclude that the A.B. is superior as a foundation for scientific work; the greater number of A.B. degrees is probably simply due to the relatively undeveloped status of the B.S. program twenty years ago when the average

TABLE III

UNDERGRADUATE DEGREE OF WOMEN IN "AMERICAN MEN OF SCIENCE"

A.B.	476
B.S.	150
B.L.	10
Miscellaneous	25
No degree	26
Total	687

woman of this group was doing her undergraduate work.

The writer was surprised to observe that there were twenty-six women who had never received any college degree.

The natural next question is as to the colleges which seem most to stimulate women to a scientific career. The institutions from which there were five or more women graduates in "American Men of Science" are listed in order below. It is evident at once that the women's colleges of the East stand out as being the chief contributors of these scientific women. In fact, the five colleges—Vassar, Smith, Mount Holyoke, Wellesley and Bryn Mawr—together furnish 25 per cent. of all the women listed. A third fact of interest concerning this first degree is that it was obtained in 61 per cent. of the cases from a privately endowed institution. The large state universities make a relatively slight contribution in proportion to their size. Why these conservative eastern "nunneries" should thus distinguish themselves over the western coeducational universities is not clear. It is not the writer's impression (and she has had opportunities to observe the work in both types of institution) that the teaching in the eastern girls' colleges is better. Probably a number of factors have operated. The students at Vassar, Smith, Bryn Mawr were fifteen or twenty years ago a group with a very different economic and social background as compared with the "coeds" of that time in the mid-west. These and other factors tended to make a select group intellectually. They more often had sufficient means to facilitate graduate work. They had fewer opportunities to marry. The centers for graduate work were then largely in the East. In short, the writer doubts whether these eastern schools deserve any great credit for these facts—but the findings are of distinct interest.

TABLE IV

INSTITUTIONS FROM WHICH FIVE OR MORE OF THE 687 WOMEN RECEIVED THEIR UNDERGRADUATE DEGREES

Vassar	47	Illinois	10
Smith	41	Iowa	10
Mount Holyoke	39	Stanford	10
Cornell	34	Minnesota	9
Chicago	28	Brown	7
Columbia	27	Toronto	7
Wellesley	24	Radcliffe	7
Bryn Mawr	19	Missouri	7
Nebraska	19	Colorado	6
Goucher	18	Oregon	5
Michigan	18	Pennsylvania	5
Kansas	16	Northwestern	5
Wells	14	Ohio State	5
Wisconsin	14	Other institutions	177
Oberlin	12	No degree	24
California	12		
Washington	11	Total	687

Now as to the graduate degrees held by these women. The type of graduate degree (a) is shown in Table V. There are 128 who held no advanced degree. The outstanding degree is obviously the Ph.D.

TABLE V

GRADUATE DEGREES HELD

No further degree	128
M.A.	14
Ph.D.	492
M.D.	35
LL.D.	3
D.L.	1
Sc.D.	14
Total	687

Another item of interest concerning this degree is (b) the institutions in which it was

TABLE VI

INSTITUTIONS FROM WHICH FIVE OF MORE WOMEN RECEIVED AN ADVANCED DEGREE

Chicago	87	Minnesota	15
Columbia	80	Iowa	13
Cornell	39	Radcliffe	11
Yale	36	Clark	10
Johns Hopkins	31	Stanford	10
Bryn Mawr	28	George Washington	8
Pennsylvania	25	Ohio State	7
California	22	Mount Holyoke	6
Wisconsin	19	Other institutions	76
Michigan	18	No. adv. degree	128
Illinois	18		
		Total	687

obtained. The following table shows the institutions from which five or more of these women obtained their advanced degrees. Chicago and Columbia alone contribute 30 per cent. of all advanced degrees.

It appears at once that the list is very short. The women tend to center in relatively few institutions. Of the 559 holding an advanced degree 483 received it in institutions listed above.

The year in which the degree was obtained (c) may be of some interest. The table below indicates that 128 of the women received their degree within the last five years, and 225 of them within the last ten years. Only seventeen received an advanced degree thirty or more years ago.

TABLE VII

Year in which Advanced Degree was Obtained*

Within last 5 years	128
From 6– 9 years ago	127
" 10–14 " "	86
" 15–19 " "	67
" 20–24 " "	30
" 25–29 " "	28
" 30–34 " "	15
Over 35 " "	2
	483

* Includes only those obtaining degrees from institutions in which five or more such women had studied.

(4) *Major Interest.*—The subjects in which the women in "American Men of Science" are specializing are given below. These subjects are identical with those listed for the investigations previously made, except that home economics and hygiene have been added as separate groups. The writer suspects that hygiene has been included under physiology, and home economics more than likely under chemistry, in previous analyses. The two chief fields of interest appear to be botany and psychology, with zoology as a close third. In fact, these three subjects are the major interest of 52 per cent. of all the women listed. All three of these subjects are in the general field of biological science. One can not be sure whether the openings for women are better in these fields or whether women take to these subjects more readily than to non-biological science. In the case of psychology this situation is very likely due to the opportunities for women in this general field, for as clinicians in school systems in many places a woman is preferred to a man. The same explanation, however, could hardly hold in the case of botany and zoology.

TABLE VIII

Major Field of Interest of 687 American Women of Science

Anatomy	9
Anthropology	18
Astronomy	21
Botany	122
Chemistry	75
Geology	20
Home Economics	11
Hygiene	17
Mathematics	55
Pathology	19
Physics	29
Physiology	54
Psychology	122
Zoology	115
Total	687

TABLE IX

Showing the Present Occupational Status of American Women of Science

College president	1
Dean	4
Professor	115
Associate professor	76
Assistant professor	98
Instructor	64
Research	35
Assistant	35
Curator	2
Fellow	4
Total academic	434
Position not in colleges	171
No position	82
Total	687

(5) *Present Location.*—The present location of these women and their professional status, in case they are teaching, are presented in tables IX and X. There are 82 women who have no present position; 171 are placed in laboratories and clinics that have no connection with universities; the remaining number—434—are teaching in colleges or universities. Of the 434 who are teaching, 294 are of professorial rank or better. This fact would indicate that these women were being reasonably successful in their teaching careers.

The list of institutions in which these women are located shows again the preponderance of the privately endowed institution; 70 per cent. of these positions are in endowed schools. It suggests also that the five outstanding women's colleges of the East tend to absorb their own graduates. Thus there were previously shown to be 25 per cent. of the women who graduated from one of these five colleges; there are 20 per cent. who are located there. Although the actual situation is not recorded, the writer suspects that many of the graduates returned to their alma mater, while many of the others simply exchanged one women's college for another. Of all the 434 women, only 30 per cent. are located in state-supported universities.

TABLE X

PRESENT LOCATION OF THE 434 WOMEN WHO ARE TEACHING FOR THOSE INSTITUTIONS IN WHICH FIVE OR MORE WOMEN ARE LOCATED

Columbia	23
Smith	22
Wellesley	22
California	21
Mount Holyoke	18
Vassar	18
Minnesota	14
Johns Hopkins	10
Chicago	8
Iowa	8
Bryn Mawr	7
Cornell	7
Wells	7
Stanford	6
New York University	6
Wisconsin	5
Harvard Medical	5
Carnegie Institute	5
Goucher	5
	217
Miscellaneous	217
Total	434

There is one other item of interest concerning these women. Seventy-two of the 687 are married; of these seventy-two, thirty-eight are married to men who are also in "American Men of Science." From facts already presented one would conclude that these scientific women certainly do not tend to marry, inasmuch as the median age of these women is forty-two and only seventy-two are married at present. It also appears that when these women do marry they are as likely as not to marry a man who is also a scientist.

(6) *Summary.*—There appear to be a few outstanding facts in this investigation:

(a) The North Atlantic and North Central states produced 503—or 73 per cent.—of the 687 women listed in "American Men of Science." The most productive states, in gross numbers, are New York and Massachusetts. In proportion to population, the most productive states are New Hampshire, Vermont and Rhode Island.

(b) The average age of the 687 women is forty-two.

(c) These women usually received a B.A. for an undergraduate degree—and the greater proportion from the endowed women's colleges of the East. The typical advanced degree is the Ph.D., which is obtained over half the time in an endowed institution. Just half the advanced degrees have been obtained within the past ten years.

(d) The women show an overwhelming majority interested in biological science.

(e) Of the 687 women, 434 are teaching—294 with a rank of assistant professor or higher; 70 per cent. of those teaching are located in endowed institutions.

(f) Of the entire 687 women, only seventy-two—or 10 per cent.—are married.

LUELLA COLE PRESSEY
THE OHIO STATE UNIVERSITY

SCHOOL AND SOCIETY

EDITED BY J. McKEEN CATTELL

WITH WHICH IS COMBINED THE

EDUCATIONAL REVIEW

EDITED BY WILLIAM McANDREW

Volume XXIX | Saturday, January 26, 1929 | Number 735

THE PROFESSION OF TEACHING IN THE UNITED STATES[1]

By Professor WILLIAM C. BAGLEY

TEACHERS COLLEGE, COLUMBIA UNIVERSITY

THE development of American education has been beset from the outset by handicaps and obstacles, many of which undoubtedly confront our fellow-workers in other countries, but some of which are indigenous, so to speak, to our own soil, growing out of our own peculiar traditions and *mores:* our deep-seated and thoroughly dynamic ideals of local self-government; the diverse standards of our conglomerate population; the sharply contrasting needs and interests of our urban and rural people; our fondness for quantity-production and our delight in numerical magnitudes; our distrust of the expert; our zeal in making laws and our zest in breaking them; and a host of other factors and forces, many of which work in quite opposite directions, but all of which have cooperated to make extremely difficult the development of an educational system which would be constructively effective on a nation-wide basis.

And yet these unique factors in our problem, even though they have constituted serious handicaps to educational effort, have also been, perhaps for that very reason, a stimulating challenge, the continued response to which has resulted in progress of a most substantial sort, with promises for the future that should give hope and inspiration to those in other countries who are facing problems similar in difficulty although in many instances quite different in kind.

The advancement in the status of the teacher's calling, while the most recent of the large developments in American education, is in some respects the most significant and promises for the future the most far-reaching results. It is also, I believe, a development quite unprecedented in the history of education and, so far as I know, it is unparalleled in other countries.

In reviewing the handicaps that have beset this development, it goes without saying that many of them are not at all peculiar to our country. Something akin to contempt for the work of teaching, especially in the lower schools, has found expression, I suppose, in all ages and in all climes. It was the Englishman, Bernard Shaw, who coined the famous epigram, "Those who can, do; those who can not, teach." The immortal Boswell, in a ponderous effort to explain why Samuel Johnson was so complete and pitiable a failure as a teacher of youth, ventured the following sage reflection:

[1] A lecture given December 18, 1928, in the course, "American Educators," offered especially for foreign students by the International Institute of Teachers College.

The art of communicating instruction, of whatever kind, is much to be valued; and I have ever thought that those who devote themselves to this employment, and do their duty with diligence and success, are entitled to very high respect from the community, as Johnson himself often maintained. Yet I am of the opinion that the greatest abilities are not only not required in this office, but render a man less fit for it.

While this patronizing attitude of thinly veiled contempt for the work of teaching is no new thing and not at all confined to our own country, I believe that it has constituted a far more serious handicap to the development of our profession here than it has elsewhere.

In the first place, until recently, the teaching-personnel of our public schools has been transient and unstable. Twenty years ago, the average period of service of the public-school teacher was not more than four years, which meant that tens of thousands of teachers remained only one, two or three years in the service. The occupation was distinctly recognized in most communities as temporary, and those who from force of circumstances were compelled to make it a life work were naturally regarded with something akin to pity. For the able and ambitious, teaching was openly taken up as a stepping-stone to what both the teacher and the public thought of as worthier callings. One of the early university professors of education, in whose classes I sat thirty years ago, laughingly referred to public-school teachers as a group made up chiefly of immature women and feeble men.

Along with this condition, of course, went the parallel fact that the teachers as a whole were pitifully unprepared for their work. Twenty years ago, more than a majority of the public-school teachers had had no education beyond the high school, and more than ten thousand were limited in their education to what the elementary school provided.

Although every state maintained professional schools for teachers, not one in four of those employed in the public schools was a product of such an institution. As short a time ago as 1916, Judd and Parker asserted in an official bulletin of the Bureau of Education that the United States gave less attention to the training of teachers than did any other civilized nation. With brief tenure and lack of training quite naturally went meager compensation, and in a country where occupations won public regard in direct proportion to the material rewards that they provided, this condition was in itself a sufficient stigma to the teacher's calling.

Closely related to the handicaps which transiency, instability, low training standards and meager preparation placed in the way of professional development was the unequal competition with other occupations for talented recruits. This was most serious, of course, in connection with the problem of drawing able men into the profession. Not only did the vast development of business and industry multiply the opportunities for building huge individual fortunes, but the spectacular achievements of our captains of industry, finance and organization caught the public imagination, bringing to successful efforts in those fields a measure of renown and popular adulation beside which even the material rewards were of quite subordinate value.

There are one or two incidents in my own life that may give a concrete setting to the conditions to which I have referred. Some forty years ago I was a schoolboy in the city of Detroit. As cities went, even in those days, Detroit was an unpretentious, rather conservative urban center, surpassed in wealth, population and promise by nearly a score of American cities. One day in the early nineties, while walking along one of the streets of the city, I saw a little group gathered around a queer-looking conveyance drawn up alongside the curb. I joined the crowd, and found that the object of their interest was what we then called a horseless carriage. A young man was rather frantically engaged in overhauling the machinery, every now and again making a desperate effort to get the clumsy contraption to show some signs of life. As long as I watched, his efforts were rewarded only by a wheezy cough from the crude engine, echoed, of course, by the jeers of the crowd. That jeering crowd little dreamed that the scene which they were witnessing for the first time would be reenacted within the next thirty years on ten thousand city streets and country roads by hundreds of thousands of exasperated drivers of self-propelled vehicles; still less did they dream that the evolution of that clumsy, horseless carriage would cause their city to outdistance all but three of its competitors in population and wealth and make it the world center for the most highly organized branch of modern industry; least of all did they dream that the young man who was struggling so desperately to conjure a vital spark in that newfangled internal-combustion engine was in all likelihood the man who, within three decades, would be recognized and acclaimed as the type and symbol of American genius at its own unique best.

It is not at all to be wondered at that the marvelous expansion of American industry, with its overwhelming rewards of wealth and fame for successful effort, should have cast a shadow over fields of endeavor less spectacular, less appealing to the concrete imagination of the public, less obviously creative of new values. It is small wonder that, with competition of this sort, the latter fields were unable to attract so large a share of superior talent as has been the case in many other countries. The relative paucity of our national contributions to pure science, to literature, music and the other fine arts, and to statesmanship of the first order may be explained at least in part by this factor. Obviously an occupation so modestly rewarded as teaching and one that offers so few opportunities for renown would have, under these conditions, a relatively low place in public esteem.

The effect of all this upon the morale of the teaching group may be readily inferred. Those who remained for any length of time in the profession acquired, in many cases, an inferiority complex of large dimensions. They openly regretted that they had not taken up another occupation. Just as openly, they advised young people against teaching as a career and commiserated one another over their hard lot. About eight years ago in visiting the college in Michigan where I spent my undergraduate days, I called on one of the two or three of my former instructors who still survived. He asked me what I had been doing over the years and where I was located. I told him that I had been teaching and was still engaged in that occupation. Then he asked me where I had come from when I entered college. He shook his head sadly when I told him, and then, with a sincere sigh of pity, he said, "And just think what you might have become if you had only gone back to Detroit and entered the automobile business." I left his office and my old college with a deep sense of my failure to reflect any worthy credit on my *alma mater*.

I could multiply concrete examples of this sort from my own experience and that of my friends, but enough has been said to indicate one of the most serious obstacles that the development of a real profession of teaching has confronted in our country. With what I have said regarding the instability, inadequate training and transiency of the great rank and file of teachers, this may give us a sufficient background against which to project the advances that our profession has made.

To-day, many of the conditions to which I have referred are radically different from what they were fifteen, ten, even five years ago. The period of service of the average teacher has been extended from four or five years to at least eight or nine years. The level of training has advanced to a much higher plane—where fifteen years ago the median public-school teacher had no more than a high-school education at most, to-day it is probable that 60 per cent. of these teachers have had two years or more in advance of high-school graduation. In several states the proportion is nearly 100 per cent. The number of college graduates in the public-school service has also shown a remarkable increase. The enrolment in our normal schools and teachers' colleges has doubled in the past five years, and the output of these professional schools is now so large that, for the first time in our history, there is an actual surplus of trained teachers in most of the cities and in some of the states.

This condition has led to significant advances in the standards of our professional schools. Many of the former two-year normal schools have advanced the requirements for elementary-school teachers to three years and some are now on a full four-year basis. Paralleling these advances there has been a really remarkable development within the profession, some of the outstanding trends of which I shall mention a little later. In public esteem, too, the teacher's calling has made significant advances.

Like most profound changes, these developments have been brought about in part by conscious and deliberate purposing, and in part by the fortunate operation of forces and factors that are largely beyond either individual or social control. Let us consider first these latter, impersonal factors.

Primarily, of course, one must recognize the unprecedented material prosperity of our country. This has made possible both a wider extension of educational opportunity and a keener demand for better schools and better teachers. As a result, the level of teachers' salaries has advanced significantly, and is still advancing in spite of a tendency toward the stabilization of wage and salary levels in other occupations. Teaching can now compete with other callings on terms much more nearly equal than have prevailed heretofore.

This, however, does not tell the whole story, for the contrasts with the spectacular rewards of business and industry still persist. Yet for some reason the influence of this contrast is less noticeable to-day than it was only a few years ago. This may be due to a recognition on the part of the public that these huge material rewards in the very nature of things can go to only a very few of the most capable or the most fortunate, while the rank and file must necessarily fare much more modestly.

Back of all this, however, is another set of facts, the full significance of which we are probably not yet in a position to grasp. The leaven of the Industrial Revolution, which has been responsible for so many fundamental social changes, is still working, and working in a more thoroughgoing fashion in our country than anywhere else. The report of the American Federation of Labor, recently published, reveals the astounding fact that, in spite of the vast development of American industry in the present decade, the number of persons actually engaged in manufacturing has decreased by approximately a million since 1920. In other words, the improvement of automatic machinery has not only kept pace with the expansion of industry; it has sent a million workers to seek other means of earning a living. In this country, too, much more than in other countries, the influence of the Industrial Revolution has profoundly affected agriculture. Power-driven machinery has apparently replaced no fewer than 800,000 farm workers since 1920.

As a mere layman in economics, it would be presumptuous in me to attempt an interpretation of these facts. I can not escape the conclusion, however, that they are related in a very direct way to the opportunities that our profession has recently enjoyed to augment its numbers, advance its standards and stabilize its service. If I am right in my inferences, these developments in invention and industrial organization are actually driving men and women out of industry and farming into the white-collar occupations. Not only have the traditional professions grown in numbers—there are 250,000 more professional workers now than in 1920, according to the Federation's report—but a veritable multitude of other white-collar occupations are advancing toward a professional status in the sense that specific and often prolonged courses of education are willingly undertaken by those seeking either employment or advancement. Banks, department stores, the great hotel syndicates, insurance companies and public service corporations are developing elaborate schools for the training of their personnel. In at least one of the big insurance companies the vice-president in charge of education is one of the highest paid and most highly respected of the executives. With this emphasis upon specialized training, there has naturally been a corresponding emphasis upon an extended and thoroughgoing general education which shall serve as a background for the specialized courses; hence another reason why the high-school enrolment has trebled in fifteen years and why the college enrolment has doubled in ten years.

May I say parenthetically that it is of the utmost significance to education that this recent turn of the Industrial Revolution has not only reduced the proportion of workers needed in industry and farming, but has also increased the numbers needed in the white-collar occupations? The development of type-setting machinery, for example, made it possible for one operator to do the work of four compositors, and thus reduced the demand for the old-time printer, but the economy and efficiency of the new process greatly multiplied the demand for writers, editors, illustrators and advertising specialists. In fact, every department of automatic machines for mass-production has opened new fields of useful employment almost all of which have meant a stepping-up of the intellectual level of the work involved. Within the past decade this change has been going on with unprecedented acceleration; hence the heavy demands now made upon the schools and colleges are something more than a mere reflex of our economic prosperity; in a very real sense, they are the expression of a tremendously enlarged need on the part of millions of people for a type of instruction and discipline that will mean for them a genuine intellectual advance. Hence the recent controversy in our field regarding the possibilities of raising through education the mass-levels of effective intelligence is concerned with something more than a merely academic question. Upon the issue that this controversy involves hangs the future of our industrialized civilization.

I have suggested that the recent development of our profession has been conditioned in part by impersonal forces, largely economic in character, which have operated to expand the field of our service, to increase the demands made upon us and to give us more and better recruits. The net result has been an almost complete transformation of the conditions under which we have been working. May I impress particularly the fact that, so far as its outward manifestations are concerned, this transformation has come very suddenly—almost overnight, so to speak? Many of our fellow-workers are still rubbing their eyes and wondering whether it is not all a dream. Others are still, in a manner of speaking, fast asleep—working on programs which reflect needs that seemed genuine enough a few years ago, but which can now be seen as based upon quite erroneous assumptions regarding the trends of contemporary civilization; programs, for example, that would keep the farm boys on the farms to compete with gasoline engines and combined harvesters; and programs for premature vocational training based on the theory that the white-collar occupations are overcrowded when they are apparently the only occupations that have not been seriously overcrowded in the past few years and are to-day the occupations in which there are evidences of the greatest expansion.

It need hardly be said that the situation which confronts us is fairly unique to our own country. Other nations undoubtedly need heavier emphasis upon agricultural and trade education and less emphasis upon intellectual education. Be that as it may, it is clear enough that some of our own students of education have made some rather bad guesses during the past two decades and that some of them are still repeating their stereotyped pleas even though the need for their particular variety of reform no longer exists. On the other hand, it is equally true that the progress of our profession has been influenced in a very powerful positive fashion by the students of education. While they have undoubtedly made mistakes in some of their efforts to define social problems and to construct programs that would work toward the solution of these problems, they have played an important part in laying the foundations upon which a real and great profession of teaching is even now arising.

For upward of thirty years, a steadily increasing number of men and women have been devoting their lives to the serious study of the educational problem. The pioneers of this group were a few scattering school executives who conceived of their duties as comprehending something beyond the machinery of organization and the routine of administration, and who set a splendid example of constructive leadership and truly creative effort. One of these men was William Torrey Harris, who infused into the city school system of St. Louis a vigorous new life and who later served with distinction as the federal commissioner of education. Another was Francis W. Parker, who, as head of the schools of Quincy, Massachusetts, was the founder in America of what we now call the progressive school of educational theory; another was William H. Maxwell, the first superintendent of the schools of Greater New York. A fourth was Calvin Kendall, for many years superintendent of schools in Indianapolis and during the latter part of his life commissioner of education for the State of New Jersey.

Among the early colleagues and companions of these executives were the first professors of education in the colleges and universities. The real development of these departments of education may be dated from about 1890. Two years before, Clark University had been founded under the leadership of Stanley Hall, and during the following decade Clark was a nursery of educational ideals and enthusiasms. Then came the development of Teachers College under James E. Russell, and at the University of Chicago the pioneer work of John Dewey. From Clark and Columbia and Chicago men and women in increasing numbers went out to other colleges and universities either to establish or to remodel on a true university basis the departments of education. State universities, like those of Wisconsin, Iowa, Minnesota, California and Illinois, became in their turn centers of instruction, research and inspiration directed toward the problems of teaching and learning, of administration and supervision in the public schools. Private and endowed institutions like Peabody, Stanford, Yale and Harvard assumed their share of the great task.

The influence of this development of the university study of education upon the profession of teaching has been profound. In the first place, it has provided for the professional education of teachers a substantial body of knowledge. The recency of this development is exemplified by the fact that many of the men who have done the pioneer work are still in their prime. Some of them indeed have already addressed you in this course, and others will address you. Dr. Thorndike spoke to you last week of the work that has been done here and at other centers in the strictly scientific study of education, but with the modesty of the true scientist, he did not tell you of the mighty part that he has played in it.

A second influence of the university study of education has been a new access of self-respect on the part of the teaching personnel. The inferiority complex, to which I referred as one of the handicaps to our professional development, is gradually but certainly giving place to a sense of professional pride and dignity, tempered as it should be and as I hope it always will be, by a keen sense of the complexities of our problem and of the serious responsibilities which one must assume who would do even the humblest work in the field of teaching.

A third influence is one of the most significant of all. The university study of education has played a most important part in integrating the teaching profession. As Dean Russell told you a few weeks ago, something akin to the old-world caste distinction between the education of the masses and the education of the classes has persisted even in our unit system which otherwise so closely articulates the elementary and secondary schools. With us, the distinction has been one primarily of training and material rewards. The elementary-school teacher has represented a narrower and briefer training than the high-school teacher and even now receives in most of our school systems a distinctly lower salary. It has been a popular belief, shared by many members of the profession itself, that the work of teaching increases in difficulty, dignity and importance as one goes up the age scale. The university study of education has probably done more than anything else to reveal the fallacy of this popular belief, and to correct the injustice that has been done to the younger children in our schools by a deliberate policy which uses the lower grades as the testing ground for the immature and inexperienced teachers, the permanent abode of the weak and the indolent, and the final resting-place of the old and decrepit. To-day there is a growing conviction that no phase or field of teaching can lay valid claim to being more difficult or more important than any other phase. Discriminations and distinctions as to salaries are breaking down, as, for example, in the gradual extension of the single-salary schedule which does away with all distinctions except those that are based upon training, experience and meritorious service.

This general movement has been a powerful force in integrating our profession vertically, so to speak. Other forces have been operating to integrate the profession horizontally or geographically. Chief among these are our educational organizations. Foreign students sometimes wonder why, with our lack of any centralized educational authority in the nation as a whole, with the lack even of highly centralized state systems, our schools all over the country are in fundamental ways very much alike, dominated by the same aims and ideals, following fairly similar programs of study, governed by essentially uniform standards. The answer is simple. While our school systems are essentially local, the teaching profession is essentially national. For seventy years the educational leaders of the nation have met annually to discuss their common problems, but it has been only within the past twenty years that the state and national organizations have really represented the profession as a whole. To-day these organizations are made up of, and controlled very largely by, the rank and file of elementary and secondary teachers. The National Education Association has grown in active membership from 10,000 to 200,000 in a single decade. Its policies are now determined by a representative assembly made up largely of delegates elected by the state associations. Many of the latter, in turn, are controlled by similar representative assemblies elected by district and local associations. The total enrolment in all of these organizations aggregates nearly three quarters of a million, which means that three out of every four members of our profession can have a vote and a voice in determining where our profession will go and how it will get there—in formulating our collective ideals and devising the means of realizing them through collective action. To this end the national association employs a headquarters staff with a personnel of more than one hundred men and women, including expert research workers, editors, legislative agents, publicity agents and specialists in the major educational fields. Several of the state organizations have similar staffs, and practically all of them employ full-time secretaries and publish official journals. May I emphasize the fact that this development has taken place almost entirely within a single decade?

One of the striking characteristics of this and other phases of our professional development has been the clear-cut tendency toward a thoroughgoing democracy. Not only are the distinctions between the elementary-school service and the high-school service being obliterated, but the equally unfortunate distinctions between the classroom teacher and the executive and supervisory officials are being minimized. In our professional organizations, as in our classes in education, all the workers in our field can meet on a common footing.

This tendency, which has been abetted by many of the administrators themselves, merits an especial emphasis in a discussion of the profession of teaching in the United States. It is distinctly a conscious effort to counteract in education some of the admitted evils that elaborate organization has brought about in business and industry. In the latter fields, the magnification of the executive and supervisory officers in contrast with those who do the first-hand work has perhaps been inevitable. Quite naturally, as our school systems expanded, a similar hierarchy of administrative authority was established, and the distinctions involved in this administrative hierarchy became in effect professional distinctions. To be transferred from the first-hand work of teaching boys and girls to an executive or administrative post was generally, and still is in many places, looked upon as a professional promotion. Under these conditions a large city school system became quite analogous to a great factory with its board of directors, its superintendent, managers, foremen, bosses and "hands." In school work, the classroom teachers were the "hands."

Now whatever may be the advantages or the dangers of such a hierarchy in business and industry, it works veritable mischief when applied to education. A simple contrast will, I think, make this clear.

If I buy an automobile I am not particularly concerned, except from a humanitarian point of view, with the workmen who have actually put it together. I can be reasonably certain that a few highly competent engineers designed the car, that a few others devised elaborate machinery for making and testing the various parts, and that a competent hierarchy of executives, superintendents, managers, foremen and bosses formed a responsible overhead for supervising its construction. The factory hands who operated the automatic machinery, screwed up the nuts, clinched the cotter-pins and sprayed on the paint and varnish: these may have been morons or they may have been near-geniuses; they may have had no interest whatsoever in their work beyond their pay-checks or they may have been true craftsmen with a fine pride in good workmanship; they may have been human automata going through their motions with as little real understanding of what it all meant as the machines that they operated, or they may have been men of keen insight, seeing their work in clear relation to the completed product. To me, merely as a purchaser of an automobile, it would make little difference. I can trust the machinery of production and testing under the supervision of the overhead. In fact, I can be fairly certain that if any one of the factory-hands were a near-genius and tremendously interested in his work for its own sake and able to see his work clearly in its relation to the completed product, he would very quickly be taken from the ranks and promoted to the overhead.

So much if I should buy an automobile. When I send my children to school, however, my attitude toward the person who does the actual, first-hand work of their education is almost completely reversed. It is true that I would wish plans and specifications of that education to be well drawn by highly competent students of the problem; I would like the text-books to be authoritative and well-written; I would like the tests to be objective and accurate; I would like an organization that would guarantee a healthful school environment. But above all I would want for my children a real teacher. No virtues of the "overhead" could compensate for a teacher who had no interest in his work, who saw nothing beyond his pay-check, who found no joy and felt no pride in doing his work as well as it could be done irrespective of the material rewards that it brought, who had no vision of what it meant and no understanding of what his efforts contributed to the completed product.

One of the prominent objectives of our profession at the present time is to give to those who do the actual first-hand work of teaching an adequate recognition. Within the past ten years there has been a distinct tendency toward the participation of classroom teachers in the construction of educational policies and programs. In some school systems, councils elected by the teachers have a recognized function in the government of the schools. Probably the most characteristic expression of this tendency, however, is found in the work that is now going on all over the country in the revision and construction of curricula by groups of classroom teachers.

While practices such as these tend to dignify the actual first-hand work of teaching, they have, I think, an even deeper significance. They represent a quite new type of control for public education—and a type of control which has vast possibilities for the future. It goes without saying that some of the results will be disappointing. There must necessarily be groping and stumbling and blundering; but in the end the progress that is made is likely to be both substantial and enduring.

And this I take it is the fundamental justification of democracy as a mode of social control. Autocratic leadership gets results more quickly; and, under extremely competent leadership, the results may mean genuine progress. But dependence upon autocratic leadership suffers under two handicaps. In the first place, a really competent leader may not appear for years or even generations; in the second place, progress which is made possible only by a dictatorship is not likely to be sustained when the strong hand loses its grip. Given a reasonably high level of trained intelligence, the democratic group will be able to carry on even if competent leadership does not appear; and although its progress may be slow, it is much more likely to be certain and sustained.

I have attempted to present in general outline the development of the profession of teaching in the United States. I have called attention to some of the typical handicaps that this development has encountered; to the economic forces which have transformed in a striking fashion some of these handicaps; to the contributions that the students of education have made to our professional development; and to some of the factors that have worked toward professional solidarity and integration. I have probably set forth certain of the characteristics of our profession as though they were full-fledged achievements rather than ideals and aspirations many of which are still far from realization. My aim has been, however, to portray substantial trends, in the future fruition of which some of our dreams may come true. Certain it is that the present situation is full of promise. Whether this great army of teachers, now numbering in all branches of education upward of a million men and women, can think together and work together toward the fulfilment of this promise is another question. There are, of course, social forces and economic factors that will constitute handicaps in the future as similar forces and factors have been handicaps in the past. But personally I am optimistic; the transformation that I have myself witnessed in thirty years is so thoroughgoing that I can not but believe that another generation will carry us much further on the road to better things. It is literally true that through our profession every significant unit in our vast population can be touched and quickened. It is within our power as an organized and responsible group to make the American school the greatest single constructive force in American life. I have every faith that our profession will prove neither recreant nor inadequate to its great trust and its great opportunity.

EDUCATIONAL EVENTS

ADULT EDUCATION IN TURKEY

ELEANOR I. BURNS, dean of the Constantinople Women's College at Stamboul, has sent to SCHOOL AND SOCIETY a copy of a communiqué from the governor of Stamboul in regard to the opening of adult schools for the teaching of the new alphabet. Miss Burns writes:

Similar orders have been given by governors all over Turkey, so that beginning January 1, 1929, it can truly be said, "Adult Turkey goes to school."

All schools or business houses with more than twenty-five employees are required to open classes for the employees, and can be closed for failure to comply with the order. Police are rounding up all citizens registered in their districts and are to serve as truant officers.

But though force will be used if needed, there is real desire on the part of adult Turkey to go to school. The few recalcitrants are more than counterbalanced by those over forty or foreigners, who are eager to enter the classes. With a stroke of a pen illiteracy is to be past history in Turkey;

yet this is not simply a "magnificent gesture" but a thoroughgoing undertaking, carried on with zeal by the Ghazi, ministers, deputies and best of all the Turkish people.

The communiqué from the governor is as follows:

(1) In conformity with article 52 of the special regulation of November 24, 1928, national schools will be formed, beginning January 1, 1929.

(2) All Turkish citizens, from 16–40 years, who do not know how to read and write the new characters, and are not attending school, nor connected with an official organization, are required to learn the new writing at the national school opened in the zone in which they reside.

(3) All such persons should present themselves to the local council to register and indicate whether or not they know the former Arabic writing.

(4) Those who know the Arabic writing are required to follow the new course for two months, whereas those who do not know the former characters must attend for four months in separate classes.

(5) If heads of families wish to teach the new characters to their families and relatives, they too must present themselves to the local council in order to be examined. In any case their families will be examined at the end of each course and if the examination shows neglect either on the part of the head of the family acting as teacher, or on the part of the members of the family, legal proceedings will follow.

(6) All who know the new characters are excused from attending the national schools, but they must present themselves to the commission for examination, Monday and Thursday, from 2–5 P. M. They will be given a certificate which they must show the local council of their zone in order that necessary annotation can be made on the registers. This must be done within a month, and to the certificate should be attached a photograph with a duplicate filed at the commission.

There follows the list of 28 schools in which these classes will be held, and in conclusion the governor urges them to follow with zeal the course of progress toward civilization traced out by the Ghazi, their "grand guide."

AN OFFICIAL LANGUAGE FOR CHINA

THE Ministry of Education in the national government, as reported in the New York *Times,* has announced a program to popularize the use of mandarin as the official and, eventually, the only language in all China.

The presence of numerous dialects in various parts of the country long has been one of the chief barriers to unity. A person coming from Canton, for example, can not speak intelligibly with a man from Shanghai. If both are educated, they usually speak in mandarin, the language of the scholars and of Peking. The word "mandarin" means official in Chinese. A mandarin in the old days was a magistrate. Hence the mandarin language was the official court language.

To-day, whenever a man of prominence makes an address he prefers to speak in mandarin. Otherwise, it is explained, his audience might think him uneducated and unworthy of his high office. Even students in high schools and colleges in Shanghai and the South of China do not all speak mandarin, although the majority of them doubtless can understand in a general way when spoken to in the official tongue.

It is also a fact, according to the *Times,* that many students returning to China from American universities when speaking to other students from a different section of China invariably talk in English. Now and then they may lapse into their own dialect or speak mandarin, if they can, but it is interesting to note that when they do this almost invariably they accompany their words with a drawing of the Chinese character in the air or on some convenient surface.

The written language, of course, is universally the same throughout China. The characters, that is, are the same. There may be some shades of meaning in various sections of the country that differ a bit from others, but on the whole the generalization that the written language is the same stands.

The use of "pidgeon English" is well-nigh universal among the lower classes. For example, many of the servants on board the transpacific liners, American and otherwise, are Chinese. These Chinese "boys" may come from any section of China. And when, as often occurs, a Shanghai "boy" wants to go on an errand while his ship is in port in Hongkong, or if a Cantonese or other Kwantung man comes aboard and speaks to a Chinese cabin boy or other servant, they speak in "pidgeon English."

This peculiar and at times picturesque jargon has grown up along the China coast in the past century. It is not, as is generally supposed, a result only of the Chinese efforts to learn a useful brand of English, but has grown out of efforts on both sides to reach some spoken method of expression readily comprehensible to the other.

The expressions are made by the use of English words or perversions of English words, true. But the form is in the main a direct translation of the Chinese expression for the same meaning. For example, if one wants a ricsha, he tells the Chinese boy something like this: "My wantchee one piecie ricsha." Now, that isn't as far from what the Chinese would say in his own language as one might think. This "language" has used English as its basis, on a substructure of Chinese grammatical construction—if any.

The problem of teaching the Chinese masses to speak what to them must perforce be a new language—and that is what mandarin is to them—is a big one. But the authorities in the Ministry of Education feel that a start must be made, and hence a National Language Unification Preparatory Committee has been appointed.

COMMERCIAL EDUCATION IN SWEDEN

COMMERCIAL schools in Sweden vary greatly in scope and character. Many of them are private institutions, but according to information received at the United States Bureau of Education, the Swedish national government now inspects and gives grants in aid to 7 commercial colleges, 4 communal commercial schools, 7 private commercial schools, 46 apprentices' schools with commercial courses and 15 higher elementary schools that offer instruction in commercial subjects. The attendance at the strictly commercial schools is 1,527 pupils; at the apprentices' and higher elementary schools, 3,986, including those taking courses other than commercial.

The commercial colleges (Handelsgymnasier) normally give a two-year course based on an average course of six years in the secondary school. The student that enters the commercial college will ordinarily have had 4 years of primary training and 6 of secondary and will be about 17 years of age. From 32 to 38 hours weekly are devoted to compulsory subjects of instruction: The linguistics, comprising Swedish, English, German and French; and the purely commercial subjects such as bookkeeping, office work, the theory of business, commercial arithmetic, commercial law, economic geography with knowledge of commodities, political economy, shorthand, typewriting, handwriting, engrossing, etc.

The communal and private commercial schools generally give a one-year course on somewhat lower levels than that of the commercial colleges and admit students that have had elementary and continuation-school instruction only. The apprentices' schools are intended to provide youth with theoretical knowledge of their several trades at the same time that they are gaining professional skill by being employed at practical work in those trades. The instruction is arranged in two one-year classes with eight to twelve hours of teaching per week. Each commune decides whether and to what extent it will establish apprentices' schools and, having done so, it may enforce obligatory school-attendance for youth between the ages of 15 and 18. Instruction in the higher elementary schools extends 1, 2, 3 or 4 years beyond the six-year elementary course and may include commercial subjects.

The government grant is given to a commercial college if the municipalities of the district in which it is located contribute at least one third the amount the government provides. To commercial schools and schools for apprentices the grant is a certain amount per teaching hour and not more than one half the expense of the material; to the higher elementary schools it is a certain amount for each class.

The two commercial universities, one each at Stockholm and Gothenburg, admit graduates of a secondary school or those having an equivalent education, and grant the degrees *graduate in economics* and *certificated commercial teacher*. The courses are so arranged that it should be possible for the student to pass his final examinations after two years of study.

THE NEW "DEUTSCHES HAUS" OF COLUMBIA UNIVERSITY

THE "Deutsches Haus" of Columbia University, replacing the cultural center closed when

America entered the world war, will be opened at an international ceremony on January 29. The German ambassador, Baron von Prittwitz, and Baroness von Prittwitz will be among a large number of distinguished Germans and Americans who will attend.

Modernistic German interior decoration has been employed to give "atmosphere" to the five story structure at 423 West 117 Street, the former home of Dr. Talcott Williams, late director emeritus of the school of journalism. The building was purchased by the Columbia trustees at the suggestion of President Butler and given over to the department of Germanic languages for administration as an American center for the study of German culture and as another one of the university cultural centers established in the interest of international understanding and good-will.

"The new German house will cooperate directly with several organizations in Germany which now offer guidance to resident American students of its literature, arts and sciences," Professor Frederick W. J. Heuser, who has been appointed director, said:

They are the Amerika Institut, in Berlin, Vienna and Munich, the first of which has the largest library on the United States in Europe; the Carl Schurz Association of Berlin and the Munich Deutsche Akademie, each of which has made a gift of several thousand books to the Haus; as well as other prominent schools and educational authorities throughout Germany and Austria.

To Columbia's colony of undergraduate, graduate and research students of German language and literature, the Deutsches Haus will serve as a social and academic center. It will have rooms for a limited number of advanced students, an apartment for a visiting professor, and a library of about 5,000 volumes dealing with the culture and civilization of post-war Germany and Austria.

There will be kept a permanent exhibit of the most recent German publications in the field of science, art, literature, technology and occasional small exhibits of German etchings and paintings. The entire third floor has been turned into a library.

A SUMMER SCHOOL FOR TEACHERS OF ENGINEERING

THE Society for the Promotion of Engineering Education announces that the annual session of its summer school for engineering teachers will be devoted to the study of methods of teaching mechanical engineering and will be held at Purdue University, Lafayette, Indiana, from June 27 to July 18, inclusive. The summer schools are an outgrowth of the comprehensive study of engineering education made by the society during the past five years. The school has the principal purpose of bringing about improved methods of instruction in engineering through intensive study of the methods of teaching particular subjects or divisions of engineering curricula. The sessions are attended by teachers from all parts of the country who rank in experience from young instructors to professors and deans. The work is conducted partly through lectures and discussions devoted to educational principles in general and to particular subjects; through a demonstration of teaching procedures, and through intensive study by members of the group of educational problems.

The session of 1929 will be attended by seventy-five teachers. The staff has been chosen from among the foremost teachers and practitioners of mechanical engineering of the country and also includes a number of executives of industrial firms. A portion of the program of the 1929 session will be held at the Hawthorne, Illinois, plant of the Western Electric Company where the party will study manufacturing and production methods and administrative and personnel problems. All of the members of the school and of the staff will live together for the period of the work in one of the Purdue dormitories with the object of promoting an *esprit de corps* among the teachers. Dean A. A. Potter, of Purdue, will serve as the local director of the session, and the general summer-school enterprise is under the direction of Mr. H. P. Hammond, associate director of investigation, Society for the Promotion of Engineering Education, 33 West 39th Street, New York, to whom applications to attend may be sent.

THE SUMMER QUARTER OF THE UNIVERSITY OF COLORADO

A CONFERENCE on western history during the first week of the summer quarter of the University of Colorado will be sponsored by Dr. James F. Willard, head of the resident history faculty, Director Milo G. Derham has announced. Professors F. L. Paxson, Wisconsin, and F. J. Turner, formerly of Harvard, and other distinguished scholars are planning to attend the sessions.

One hundred seventy-five faculty members have been employed for the two terms, whose dates are June 14 to July 20, and July 20 to August 23. New instructors include: Frank W. Cady, professor of English literature, Middlebury College, Vermont; Leslie Lewis, English literature, University of Oregon; Cecil C. North, professor of sociology, Ohio State University; William A. Oldfather, professor of Latin, University of Illinois; Charles W. Odell, associate director of educational research, Illinois; Phillip A. Parsons, dean of the school of social work, Oregon.

Glenn F. Thistlethwaite, head coach at Wisconsin, will conduct a two-weeks' football school the first term. Willard N. Grein, director of physical education for the public schools of Denver, will repeat his work of last summer in coaching football and in physical education in public schools.

The French and Spanish houses will be conducted as usual, and under the supervision of Professor Edwin B. Place, of the department of Romance languages.

As usual the recreation department will have a schedule of short trips near Boulder during the week, and automobile trips and peak climbs during the week-ends. The Arapaho glacier will be featured both terms, and Long's Peak, highest peak in northeastern Colorado, will be climbed.

CHILDREN IN CITIES AND SUBURBS

MANY children in factory towns, few children in residential towns, is the condition in the metropolitan area, according to the report on population to be published in a few days by the Regional Plan of New York and Its Environs and summarized in the New York *Times*.

The analysis of age groups throughout the region, made as a basis for planning school and recreation requirements of the towns and cities in the district, shows that Perth Amboy, N. J., one of the chief manufacturing cities in the area, has the greatest percentage of children, while East Orange, a residential city, with a relatively small percentage of its population engaged in manufacturing, has the lowest percentage of children.

The analysis, based on the last federal census, shows that 37 per cent. of the population in the region within fifty miles of Manhattan is under the age of twenty years. This age group ranks in different parts of the region from 30 per cent. of the total population in East Orange to 46 per cent. in Perth Amboy, with 36 per cent. in New York City and 33 per cent. in Manhattan.

Bayonne, with high industrial concentration, ranks second in the percentage of children, with 45 per cent., according to the report. The four boroughs of New York City other than Manhattan all greatly exceed Manhattan in the proportion of children, with an average of about five more in each 100 population. Also, the findings say, of those gainfully employed in the four other boroughs, just about 5 per cent. more are employed in manufacturing than in Manhattan.

It is evident that the proportion of children of primary school age and of young people of the age for which outdoor recreation is almost as necessary as education has to be considered in estimating for school sites and recreation areas.

The Regional Plan also reports that Manhattan leads the other boroughs in the percentage of single and widowed persons, while the other boroughs have a stronger attraction for families.

It appears that people who want to live in family homes have to betake themselves to the suburbs. Adults who live singly are most likely to be content near the crowded centers where they work and where the distractions outside the home are to be found more easily.

The reasons that make the suburbs relatively desirable for people with families are too obvious to call for explanation. Near the centers of activity the destruction of old self-contained houses, in which families of moderate means could pay rents and bring up children a few years ago, expresses an aspect of the suburban trend that is the obverse of that seen in the outlying developments.

THE RESIGNATION OF THE PRESIDENT OF THE UNIVERSITY OF MICHIGAN

Dr. Clarence Cook Little's resignation as president of the University of Michigan was accepted by the board of regents on January 21. In accepting the resignation the board of regents expressed regret in a resolution reading:

His high ideals of educational standards, his initiative, his constructive aspirations, his frankness, courage and sincerity have made the severing of relationships a heartfelt loss to us all. We trust the future may have for him the richest rewards.

The text of Dr. Little's letter follows:

For some time two things have been increasingly apparent.

First, that my methods of handling situations dealing with interests of private donors, political interest, "local" interests and alumni interests are not consistent with policies which the Board of Regents deems wise.

Second, that I shall, I hope, be more effective in scientific research and teaching than in administration.

I therefore request that my resignation be accepted to take effect September 1, 1929, and that I be given a leave of absence from June 30, 1929, to August 31, 1929, or before that if the regents desire it.

I further ask two things:

First, that the university college be established only if the Board of Regents is whole-heartedly in favor of the principles and if it is approved by the deans, or if my successor is definitely in favor of it and will personally sponsor it.

Only in these ways can it have a fair chance of success. It would seem needlessly hard on the students to launch it under circumstances likely to doom it to failure.

Second, that the present legislative program be placed in charge of the dean of administration acting for the present and of a committee of the regents.

I hope that the regents will agree with me, in the absence of personal feeling, and will realize that I wish to acknowledge their great kindness to me personally at all times.

The chief assets possessed by any executive are the ingrained principles which activate his policies. These, right or wrong, necessitate the above course of action in spite of great personal regret on my part that such is the case.

EDUCATIONAL NOTES AND NEWS

Dr. Morgan L. Combs, from 1927 to 1929 director of the division of research and surveys of the Virginia State Department of Education, has been elected president of the State Teachers College at Fredericksburg, Virginia.

The Rev. Dr. W. H. P. Faunce, president of Brown University, celebrated on January 16 the seventieth anniversary of his birthday.

Dean William F. Russell, of Teachers College, has been appointed chairman of the committee on the celebration of the one hundred and seventy-fifth anniversary of Columbia University. He has also been made a member of the advisory committee on educational policy of the university.

Nathan Hayward, president of the American Dredging Company, has been elected president of Franklin Institute of Philadelphia. He is a native of Boston and is a graduate of Harvard University and the Massachusetts Institute of Technology.

G. H. Sanberg, superintendent of schools at Rochester, Minnesota, has been elected president of the Minnesota Education Association.

The American Society of Civil Engineers has chosen Anson Marston, dean of engineering at Iowa State College, as its sixtieth president. The election took place at the annual convention in New York.

The Howland Memorial prize, awarded by Yale University "in recognition of some achievement of marked distinction in the field of literature or fine arts or the science of government," has been awarded to Sir Arthur Salter, K.C.B., director of the economic and finance section of the League of Nations. The prize carries with it a medal, which was to be presented formally to Sir Arthur at exercises held in William L. Harkness Hall on January 25. He was expected to speak on "Economic Interdependence as Opposed to Political Nationalism."

DR. CHARLES HOMER HASKINS, since 1912 professor of history and political science at Harvard University and from 1912 to 1924 dean of the graduate school of arts and sciences, has been elected to the Henry Charles Lea chair of medieval history.

PROFESSOR JOHN S. P. TATLOCK, since 1926 chairman of the department of English at Harvard University, has resigned to become professor of English in the University of California. Professor John T. Murray will take his place at Harvard as chairman of the department.

DR. ABRAHAM FLEXNER has been appointed American visiting lecturer to Belgium under the auspices of the C. R. B. Educational Foundation for the year 1929. Dr. Flexner will lecture during February at the four Belgian universities. His lecture subjects are "Medical Education" and "The Idea of a Modern University."

DR. A. S. PEARSE, of Duke University, will serve as visiting professor of biology in Keio University, Tokyo, Japan, from February 1, 1929, to May 15, 1930, for the Rockefeller Foundation. He will then spend a couple of months in research in Siam and India and return by way of London about September 15, 1930.

DR. ERNEST E. IRONS, dean of Rush Medical College, will be visiting lecturer in January to the school of tropical medicine of the University of Porto Rico, San Juan, as will Professor Edwin O. Jordan, of the University of Chicago. Dr. Jordan will lecture on food poisoning, the epidemiology of paratyphoid infection and the epidemiology of influenza.

DR. LEROY A. KING, professor of educational administration at the University of Pennsylvania, has been appointed as a member of the Pennsylvania State Council of Education by Governor John S. Fisher. Dr. King succeeds Francis R. Cope, Jr., Dimock.

SUPERINTENDENT JAMES H. RISLEY, of Pueblo, Colorado, was presented with a life membership in the National Education Association by the teachers of Pueblo at a recent meeting. On this occasion the principal of the Thatcher School, Max D. Morton, made an address in which he recounted Mr. Risley's achievements during his eight years of service as superintendent of the Pueblo schools, which was followed by a speech of acceptance by Mr. Risley.

LLOYD P. STERNER, superintendent of the Bloomsburg, New Jersey, schools, retired on November 3, on the seventieth anniversary of his birthday and on the completion of thirty-nine years' association with the schools of the district. A testimonial dinner was given in his honor by the teachers of the system, when he was presented with a purse of gold. The Kiwanis and Rotary Clubs also entertained in his honor, presenting him with a gold watch and chain.

ERNEST M. TOWNSEND has been appointed assistant state commissioner of education in charge of elementary schools in New Jersey.

THOMAS D. EASON, state supervisor of teacher training of Virginia, has been elected secretary to the State Board of Education to succeed Dabney S. Lancaster, who has become dean of men at the University of Alabama.

A CHANGE in the organization of the school system in Lakewood, Ohio, took place on January 7, 1929, when the board of education elected George W. Grill assistant superintendent in charge of business affairs. Lakewood in common with many other Ohio cities has operated for a great many years under the dual plan of administration, superintendent of schools and clerk-treasurer working on a coordinate basis. This move places complete executive administration of the school system under the direction of Superintendent of Schools Julius E. Warren.

F. K. W. DRURY, assistant librarian of Brown University Library in Providence, has been appointed executive assistant to the board on the library and adult education of the American Library Association to succeed L. L. Dickerson.

DR. WILLIAM M. MARSTON, instructor in psychology at New York University, has gone to Hollywood, where under the direction of Carl Laemmle he will assist in the production of the "Universal" films.

PROFESSOR B. R. ANDREWS, of Teachers College, Columbia University, has been asked to serve as a member of the National Committee on Employer-Employee Relationships in the Home, which is organizing research in this field. The committee held a preliminary conference in Washington on December 8.

DR. ESTELLA FORD WARNER has been appointed director of the Marion County child health demonstration at Salem, Oregon, to succeed Dr. William DeKleine, who resigned to become associated with the American Red Cross in Washington, D. C.

PROFESSOR WALTER S. MONROE, director of the bureau of educational research of the University of Illinois, has a leave of absence from January to May, which he and Mrs. Monroe are spending in California and the southwest.

PIERO PARINI, general secretary of the Foreign Fascist Organization, arrived in New York on January 21. He came here to study American school systems and educational methods.

M. PAUL HAZARD, of the Collège de France, who is lecturing at Harvard University this year as an exchange professor, spoke recently at Mount Holyoke on "The Union of the Arts, Painting, Music and Poetry in French Romanticism."

COUNT CARLO SFORZA arrived in New York on January 21. He will give a course at Wesleyan University during the second half of the academic year on recent diplomatic developments in Europe.

THE Instituto de las Espanas and the American Association of Teachers of Spanish recently held an informal reception in honor of the Argentine Cultural Commission of Educators at Columbia University. The visiting commission, numbering eighteen, consists of Professor Ernesto Nelson, who is conducting the party; Professors Carlos A. Abeledo, Juan Bordarampe, Carlos Cossio, Elvira V. Lopez, Victor Mercante, Ernesto A. Wells Molinelli, Ventura Morera, Ernestina L. de Nelson, Eulogio Sanz and Atilio Vadone. Others in the group are Carlos Cucullo, civil engineer; Josefina A. Wells Molinelli and Helma Georgina Rojo, teachers of English; Erasmo Justo Munoz, electrical expert; Estela V. de Semino, teacher; Ramón Garcia and Eduardo R. Prayones, students.

DR. JOHN J. LOFTUS, president of the New York Principals Association, addressed the principals of elementary schools of Michigan on January 18 at a state conference of educators held at the State Normal College at Ypsilanti. The topic of his address was "Quo Vadis."

DR. C. C. CRAWFORD, who is professor of education at the University of Southern California, will teach courses during the summer sessions at the University of Michigan.

COLONEL WIRT ROBINSON, U.S.A., retired, for many years professor of chemistry, mineralogy and geology at the West Point Military Academy, died suddenly of heart disease in Washington on January 9, in his sixty-fifth year.

THE death is announced of Charles J. Taylor, for many years head of the painting and illustration department of fine arts of the Carnegie Institute of Technology.

SOPHIE IRENE LOEB, known for her work as an author, lecturer and in child welfare, died on January 18, in Memorial Hospital, New York City. She was fifty-three years old.

M. A. CASSIDY, since 1901 superintendent of the schools of Lexington, Kentucky, died on December 22 at the age of seventy-two years.

DR. J. K. LIGHT, a former teacher and principal in the New Jersey schools, died recently. Dr. Light was a student at Yale University and Berlin University. He served in educational fields in various states for a period of forty years, during which time he was assistant principal of the Jersey City High School from 1894 to 1903.

PRESIDENT LOWELL has received from Mr. Edward S. Harkness a letter in which he says: "According to the estimates which you submitted to me, Harvard University requires $11,392,000 to carry out its plans for subdividing the undergraduate body into small residential groups. This amount includes $1,500,000 for endowment in connection with the plan. I shall be glad to give to Harvard University, for the above purpose, this sum of $11,392,000."

THIRTY money gifts aggregating $423,938, including an anonymous gift of $175,000 to be applied toward the erection of a dormitory for the use of students of the Medical School, are announced by President Nicholas Murray Butler, of Columbia University, following a meeting of the trustees. The next largest gift, $112,500, was received from the General Education Board and is to be expended under the direction of President Butler in meeting the cost of carrying forward and publishing researches under the general supervision of the Columbia University council on research in the humanities. The School of Dental and Oral Surgery benefits to the extent of $80,000. Of this, $50,000 was received from an anonymous donor. The balance, $30,000, was received from Dr. Henry W. Gillett, of New York, to be applied toward his proposed gift of $100,000 to the Dental School.

WESLEY COLLEGE, University of North Dakota, has received a gift of $40,000 for a new building to be named Robertson Hall, in honor of President E. P. Robertson. The donors are Mr. and Mrs. John M. Hancock, of New York, and their children. The gift is made with the understanding that $60,000 be added to the endowment of Wesley from other sources.

FORMAL transfer of the Spence School, New York City, from private ownership to the control of trustees, was marked by a dinner at the Hotel Plaza on January 11 given by the principal, Miss Charlotte S. Baker, and the associate principals, Miss Helen Clarkson Miller and Miss Grace A. McElroy, in honor of the recently formed board of trustees, the first in the history of the school. The Spence School was founded forty years ago by the late Miss Clara B. Spence and since then has been privately owned and directed.

ANNOUNCEMENT has been made by the Philadelphia Fidelity Company, trustees, that the estate of the late Dr. William Curran, who died nearly fifty years ago, now amounts to more than $1,000,000 and produces a net annual income of $54,320. Seeking to carry out the provisions of the will, the trustees, together with the Presbyterian Church, of which Dr. Curran was a member, petitioned Judge Frank Smith, in the Court of Common Pleas, to grant a charter for the Curran Foundation.

THE Institute of International Education requests that professors who expect to spend a sabbatical year in Europe will send in their names and the countries they wish to visit to the institute as soon as possible. There are occasionally some interesting opportunities to accept invitations to attend various conferences, or to give addresses. At the present time a request has come from Germany for a list of American professors who expect to be in that country during 1928–1929 and who would be willing to lecture in their field of work. Regret is expressed that no honorarium can be given but hospitality and traveling expenses within Germany are offered.

THE Senate of Calcutta University has denied the recommendations of the recently appointed committee regarding reorganization and carried a resolution affirming that reorganization on the lines of the Sadler Commission's report can alone serve the best interests of the university. The resolution further proposed that the senate should in future be elected as to nine tenths of its membership, with one tenth nominated by the government. The early creation of a board of secondary education was suggested, but, after debate, it was decided to leave open the question by what authority the board should be called into existence. The Sadler Commission, which presented its report in 1919, recommended a drastic reorganization of Indian education, with the object of raising the standard of admission to the universities and suggested that a board of secondary and intermediate education should be constituted to supervise the examination system. It also proposed that the constitution of Calcutta University should be revised in such a way as to combine due representation of public opinion with provision for supervision by the government.

SPECIAL CORRESPONDENCE

SOME FOREIGN STUDY FELLOWSHIP OPPORTUNITIES

WITH the inauguration this year of the Austro-American student exchange, the foreign study exchange fellowship activities of the Institute of International Education have been extended to include six European countries: Austria, Czechoslovakia, France, Germany, Hungary and Switzerland. Under these exchanges a limited number of fellowships and scholarships are offered each year to American students who wish to study abroad. These fellowships and scholarships have been established as an international exchange in appreciation of those offered by American colleges and universities to the nationals of the countries concerned.

The fundamental idea behind these foreign study opportunities for American students is to make it possible for America to broaden her horizon and to promote international good-will through a better mutual understanding between the United States and foreign countries. That the furtherance of this ideal is being realized is clearly manifest in the activities of those who have returned after an enjoyment of these opportunities, and the increasing breadth of vision and of interest in international affairs on the part of our people generally and of our youth particularly.

This year 211 graduate students are engaged in advanced study in American colleges and universities and in foreign universities on the exchange fellowships and other foreign study opportunities administered by the Institute of International Education.

Eighty-two American college graduates are spending the year abroad on exchange fellowships, one in Austria, five in Czechoslovakia, twenty-five in France, forty-one in Germany, four in Hungary and six in Switzerland. One hundred and seven nationals of these countries are now studying at institutions of higher learning in the United States; one is from Austria, eight from Czechoslovakia, nineteen from France, fifty from Germany, nine from Hungary, two from Italy and eighteen from Switzerland. More than sixty representative American colleges and universities are cooperating in this international student exchange movement. In addition to the exchange fellowships twenty-one Americans are studying in France and one in Germany on the other foreign study graduate fellowships administered by the institute.

A candidate applying for one of these foreign study fellowships must (1) be a citizen of the United States or of one of its possessions; (2) at the time of making the application be a graduate of a college, university or professional school of recognized standing, or at the time of entering upon the scholarship have met this requirement; (3) be of good moral character and intellectual ability, and of suitable personal qualities; (4) present a certificate or other evidence of good health; (5) possess ability to do independent study and research; and (6) have a practical reading, writing and speaking knowledge of the language of instruction in the particular country.

These opportunities are open both to men and to women. Preference in selection is given to candidates under thirty years of age.

Scholarship and fellowship holders must have sufficient money of their own to cover traveling, vacation and incidental expenses. Certain steamship lines allow a reduction in steamship rates to the fellows and scholars, and in some instances free visas may be secured.

FOR STUDY IN AUSTRIA

Through arrangements made by the Austro-American Institute of Education in Vienna, six fellowships, each covering room and board, as well as tuition in the Austrian institutions of higher learning, are offered to American students who desire to study in Austria.

A practical reading, writing and speaking knowledge of German is essential for the proper enjoyment of these opportunities. American fellows are required to reside in Vienna, Graz, Salzburg or Leoben during the entire academic year, arriving at the time of official opening about October 15 and remaining for about ten months. The living accommodations are provided in the homes of selected Austrian citizens who are deeply interested in the promotion of cultural relations between Austria and the United States.

Applications for these fellowships must be submitted on or before March 1.

FOR STUDY IN CZECHOSLOVAKIA

The Czechoslovak Ministry of Education offers, through the American Czechoslovak Student Exchange, several fellowships of 15,000 Czechoslovak crowns each (equivalent to about $500, which approximately covers the cost of room, board and tuition) to American students who wish to study in Czechoslovakia. These fellowships are available for study at Charles University, the University of Technological Sciences, the Arts Academy and the Commercial College in Prague, at the Masaryk University and the Institute of Technology in Brno, and at the Komensky University in Bratislava.

A practical knowledge of either the Czech or the Slovak language is required of candidates, adequate for understanding lectures delivered in one of these languages. Preference in selection is given to applicants who have successfully pursued Slavonic studies in an American college or university—primarily to those who intend to become teachers in the subject of Slavonic languages, or whose major interest is in history or a scientific field.

American fellows are required to reside in Prague, in Brno or in Bratislava during the entire academic year from the first of September through June. Scholarship allowances are given only for the time actually spent in Czechoslovakia; payments of the allowance are made by the Czechoslovak Ministry of Education.

Applications for these fellowships must be submitted on or before March 1.

For Study in France

The Ministry of Public Instruction and the universities of France offer, through the Franco-American Student Exchange, a number of scholarships covering board, lodging and tuition, and some providing free tuition only. These scholarships are offered for study at the Universities of Bordeaux, Grenoble, Lyon, Paris, Strasbourg and Toulouse, at the École Normale Supérieure de Sèvres for women, and at the École Supérieure de la Métallurgie et de l'Industrie des Mines in Nancy for men.

Applicants must have a practical ability to use French books, both in general subjects and in their own special field, and be able to speak French and understand lectures delivered in French. Applicants are reminded that the standard of work in French universities is very high and to profit by it American students should have already completed a year of graduate work.

Applications for these scholarships must be submitted on or before February 1.

For Study in Germany

The German universities, through the Akademischer Austauschdienst, the representative in Germany of the American-German Student Exchange, have established a number of fellowships covering board, lodging and tuition. This exchange is a movement toward developing international friendship and good-will by creating a tradition of cooperation and reciprocity between the United States and Germany through the study of the institutions and psychologies of the two countries. These fellowships are available for study at the Universities of Berlin, Bonn, Breslau, Frankfurt, Kiel, Köln, Leipzig, Marburg, Munich and Tübingen, and at the various technological institutes in Berlin, Danzig and Dresden.

A practical reading, writing and speaking knowledge of German is essential to the complete enjoyment of these opportunities. A summer spent at one of the summer courses in Germany before entering upon the fellowship has been found extremely desirable for improving facility in the use of the language.

American fellows are required to report at the universities to which they are assigned at the time of official opening (about October 15) and to reside in Germany for at least ten months. They may express preferences for certain universities, but these preferences must be supported by adequate reasons for the choice. Assignments will be made after consideration of the subjects of study chosen by the candidates.

Applications for these fellowships must be submitted on or before February 15.

For Study in Hungary

The Hungarian Ministry of Education offers to American students, through the American-Hungarian Student Exchange, several scholarships covering tuition, lodging in the Nicholas Horthy College for men and in the Elizabeth College for women, and lunch and dinner at one of the students' messes. These scholarships are available at the University of Budapest, the University Faculty of Economic Sciences, the Polytechnic High School, the Veterinary College and the Music Academy, all in Budapest.

A sufficient knowledge of Hungarian to enable the student to understand lectures is required. Graduates of medical schools who propose to do graduate work and pupils of music may be admitted without a knowledge of Hungarian, provided they have an adequate knowledge of German.

American scholars are required to reside in Budapest during the entire academic year, from early September until the end of June. Scholarship allowances are given only for the time actually spent in Budapest.

Applications for these scholarships must be submitted on or before March 15.

FOR STUDY IN SWITZERLAND

The universities of Switzerland offer a number of tuition scholarships to American students through the Swiss-American Student Exchange. In several instances these scholarships are supplemented by stipends covering board and lodging, or their equivalent, provided in the communities in which the universities are located. These scholarships are available for study at the Universities of Basle, Berne, Freiburg, Geneva, Lausanne, Neuchatel and Zurich and at the Eidgenössische Technische Hochschule in Zurich and the Handelshochschule in St. Gallen.

Evidence of a good working knowledge of either French or German, preferably both, dependent upon the language of the institution attended, is required of candidates. A knowledge of both languages is, of course, very desirable.

American scholars are required to report at the universities to which they are assigned at the time of official opening (about October 15) and to reside in Switzerland until the end of the academic year, which is usually about the middle of July. During the long vacation periods, especially between terms (March 1 to April 15), exceptional opportunity is afforded to visit in Switzerland and the surrounding countries of Europe.

Applications for these fellowships must be submitted on or before March 1.

ADDITIONAL OPPORTUNITIES

In addition to the opportunities mentioned above, the Institute of International Education administers the American Field Service Fellowships for advanced study in French universities, the Germanistic Society Fellowship for study of German culture, and the Scholarships for the Junior Year Abroad. The institute also arranges for the placement of a number of American men in postes d'assistant d'Anglais in French lycées and écoles normales.

Application blanks and further information about these opportunities and about the international exchange fellowships and scholarships may be obtained by addressing the writer at the Institute of International Education, 2 West 45th Street, New York City.

ARCHIE M. PALMER,
Assistant Director

DISCUSSION

THE SUCCESS OF AMERICAN GRADUATE STUDENTS IN THE UNIVERSITY OF LONDON

THE best single criterion whereby to measure the efficiency of an American college is the record made by its alumni in graduate schools, especially those of the Association of American Universities. The experience of this association's committee on classification of universities and colleges has clearly shown this to be true. On account of my work with this committee I have been interested in using every possible means to get at the efficiency of a college through the record of its graduates. Recently I wrote to some of my friends among the officers of universities abroad for the purpose of securing from these foreign universities such records as have been made by American graduate students. The first return has been received from Dr. Edwin Deller, of the University of London.

University College, together with the London School of Economics, receives most of the American students who enter the University of London.

Thirty-two American graduate students were in attendance at University College and the London School of Economics of the University of London: thirteen men and nineteen women. For the session of 1925–26 there were fourteen: three men and eleven women. For 1926–27 there were nineteen: eight men and eleven women. During 1927–28, six: two men and four women. Five men and two women were in attendance for two years.

Among the several faculties these students were distributed as follows:

	1925–26	1926–27	1927–28
Arts	6	7	4
Medical sciences	4	4	0
Sciences	4	8	2

The courses or special fields chosen by the students were: Biochemistry, two; chemistry, two; embryology, one; English, six; German, one; history, four; philosophy, one; phonetics, two; physiology, eight; psychology, three; statistics, four.

Of the thirty-two who pursued work in the University of London during the period of 1925–28, six received the degree of Ph.D., and one received the degree of D.Sc.

The American universities represented were: Brown University, one; Bryn Mawr College, five; Columbia University, six; Cornell University, one; Harvard University, four; the Johns Hopkins University, one; Princeton University, two; Radcliffe College, one; Smith College, one; University of California, one; University of Chicago, three; University of Minnesota, two; University of Vermont, one; University of Wisconsin, one; Vassar College, one; Yale University, one.

The highest American degrees held by the students were: Ph.D., eight; M.A., nine; M.D., six; B.A., seven; no degrees reported, three.

All interested in American education, but especially the above-named universities, will be gratified by the comment of the provost of University College: "In all cases their work and progress were satisfactory."

DAVID A. ROBERTSON

EDUCATION FOR THE GULLIBLE

QUITE a bit has been said about the high cost of selling, the social uselessness of salesmen and the waste in advertising, and yet it continues. The influence of Stuart Chase's "Tragedy of Waste" and the later Chase and Schlink's "Your Money's Worth" has not been little. Outcries such as these are challenges, but only challenges. I have noted no falling off in the Listerine sales or in the demand for Murine or what have you. The problem of maldistribution is so huge that the giant needs constant battering. What of it? If one takes that view, nothing can be done but simply to accept the situation. But, if one is blessed with an urge, a bit of deep-seated evangelism, a feeling that there is some hope, then—the cure-all—education.

Education for the gullible! More tangibly put, education in sales-resistanceship. Once we have developed a race imbued with the fundamental concepts of sales-resistanceship (I shall not attempt to name them), the nostrum monger will die a natural and quick death. Some hopeful signs are appearing. We have beginnings in education for the consumer. The more alert and socially minded home economics departments of our larger high schools and colleges have, in part at least, paid some attention to the problem of getting the most for your money. But where can you find work being done in sales-resistanceship?

The plastic age is the place to begin. Here is a job for the social study and commercial departments of our high schools, our people's colleges. The social study departments have too long concerned themselves with the extolling of a bookish history, although some of the courageous ones are breaking away from that, and the commercial departments of the typical large high school have in the past taken the job of turning out stenographers and typists, mere clerical mills. The social composition of this particular division of secondary education is such that it is a strategic place in which to apply antidotes for the ill effects of high-pressure salesmanship. Hence my somewhat naïve suggestion that the prosaic commercial department take on this task. Besides, since some of them offer courses in salesmanship (yes, even on the high-school level), there really develops a reciprocal duty for any school offering such work to give offsetting courses in sales-resistanceship.

From the standpoint of social values, which would it most profit the bright high-school youngster or the docile college freshman to know: the concept of marginal utility or the result of an experiment proving that there is no necessary relationship between price and quality? Or Adam Smith's canons of taxation compared with a thoroughgoing knowledge of how to detect spurious advertising? Certainly if one accepts the doctrine that education is preparation for complete participation in life, much may be presented favoring the immediate introduction of courses in sales-resistanceship on the several levels of education. It might even take on the august sacredness of an entrance requirement.

If the well-known statement of ex-President Eliot to the effect that the major purpose of an education was to "know a good man when he saw one" it would seem that this thing could take tangible form in our program of sales-resistanceship education. The power to detect honest salesmen and the ability to silence with speed and certainty the glib and brass-tongued fellow would be an ability of no small price.

With whole armies of pedagogues engaged in job analyses, testing techniques and other scientific procedures, the problem of building a course in sales-resistanceship appears within the bounds of possibility. Successful training in salesmanship in some instances has been based on a method of analyzing in great detail the processes of selling. This is done by carefully noting what successful salesmen in various fields do and how their success is achieved. The educational pioneer in the field of sales-resistanceship might by one method or another obtain (possibly from the salesmen themselves, although there are some dubious ethical principles involved) the names of several hard and super-hard prospects. Then, by a system of careful and thorough analysis, that courageous educationalist would have objective data concerning the make-up of hardy sales resisters. This technique could be applied to meet any local situation.

If most of our real education (real in the sense of actual) comes through advertising and other informal channels, the educational scheme must have some device to serve as a counter-irritant for such advertising and salesmanship as are socially useless. Sensibly conceived, sales-resistanceship would do the trick. The real issue behind this whole question of illth is the question of the reduction of gullibility.

HAROLD GUSTAV SHIELDS
UNIVERSITY OF CHICAGO

A VITAL CONSIDERATION FOR EDUCATIONAL RESEARCH

THE article entitled, "Do College Students Know and Understand the Lord's Prayer?" by Lester R. Wheeler, in the issue of SCHOOL AND SOCIETY for December 8, raises an important point in the field of educational research: that of choice of material on which the investigation is to be based. In the case at hand, the subject-matter is the Lord's Prayer. It deserves, because of its nature, the highest respect of every one, no matter to what faith one is pledged, but as a basis for research as to the ability of a group to interpret that which has been memorized, it does not possess the proper characteristics.

By the laws of Tennessee the students are compelled to repeat the Lord's Prayer so frequently that it becomes a matter of form. When it is given in unison the individual does not have the real opportunity to give thoughtful expression to the words, but must hurry on to the next phrase or be left behind by the rest of the group. Is it surprising that this repetition has brought a more definite understanding of the words than of the thought contained?

The score cards used presented the views of ten ministers, representing five denominations. Apparently a fair representation, but who can say that the Lord's Prayer has one, two, ten or fifty meanings? It is so highly figurative that individual interpretations will naturally vary. For this reason, I criticize the choice of matter on which to base any conclusions of educational value.

The writer has placed his emphasis on the fact that the prayer has been repeated so many times, and he has not considered the nature of the selection. He seems quite disturbed that the prospective teachers do not seem to agree on the meaning and will not be qualified to teach it to their pupils. Here he seems to commit the error, committed before in Tennessee, of telling trained educators what to teach. Bible reading is a common practice, but when one tries in a public school to tell others what a figurative selection means, he is attempting a real task.

We are compelled to notice that the title refers to "college students," but the research was conducted in a state that makes specific requirements and among 540 students. It is misleading and suggestive of hasty conclusions. The writer refers to the failure of the church to teach the students the "wider and more subtle meaning" of the well-known passage. By so doing, he presents the characterization of the material that I have mentioned. He realized too late that the subtle meanings make the prayer improper material for the test.

The writer's final statement is the repetition of a truth that has been known for a long time, but I sincerely feel that his research has not added proof to that known. My criticisms of the report of his research are as follows: (1) General title for a specific case. (2) Faulty choice of subject-matter for the test. (3) Failure to bring out new facts of educational value, reasonably expected, to be worthy of the name educational research.

JAMES A. PIRNIE

ROBINSON SEMINARY,
EXETER, N. H.

QUOTATIONS

RESIDENTIAL COLLEGES AT HARVARD AND YALE

AT the November meeting of the Yale Corporation recommendations were presented providing for new residential quadrangles for undergraduates, of whom about 750 are without adequate dormitory accommodations, to be erected as soon as the sites decided on for them can be made available and the funds secured for their construction. This action, as ratified at the meeting of the corporation in December, calls for the early provision, as an initial step, of four such quadrangles: of which two can be erected, it is hoped, in the near future.

The need for some such solution of Yale's over-crowded undergraduate schools has been under serious consideration ever since the increase in numbers that followed the war had shown that Yale life to-day had lost important benefits to the students that were theirs when classes were smaller. In 1914 the late Professor George Burton Adams proposed a "Third College," which was to give a type of education between that of the college and scientific school. The reconstruction of 1919–20, however, took the select course from Sheffield and added it to the college as a non-Latin Ph.B. course. Conditions having become more acute since then partly owing to this change and partly to larger entrance classes, the university has been considering various plans for relief. Several have been under discussion and the result was the corporation's decision stated above, which will now go into effect as sites and funds become available.

In the meanwhile Harvard University seems to have been facing much the same conditions of student population and was studying its plans for relief. Both Yale and Harvard had come to the same general conclusion, that the English small-college-unit plan was best adapted to American college conditions. Harvard had therefore decided to begin a reorganization of its college in small residential units, when funds could be procured. Learning of this (according to a statement in the Boston *Globe* of December 27 last, which at this writing has not been affirmed or commented upon officially by Harvard) Edward S. Harkness, '97, offered to Harvard $3,000,000 as the initial fund for carrying out its plan. This gift to Harvard by Mr. Harkness—of whose help in emergencies and of whose many undertakings for Yale on his own initiative, Yale and Yale men are most appreciative and owe him much—is a fine gift to American education and has pleased Yale men everywhere.

We should leave the matter at this point but for two misunderstandings that have come from newspaper statements about this gift—one that makes it appear that Mr. Harkness offered this great gift to Harvard without giving Yale a similar opportunity; the other that Yale had declined such an offer. In fairness to Mr.

Harkness, Harvard and Yale, *The Alumni Weekly* feels that such misstatements should be corrected.

Mr. Harkness had long held the belief that undergraduates at Yale University should be housed in small residential quadrangles, each containing from 150 to 200 students, and each equipped with its own dining halls, proctors' rooms and commons. This idea he had discussed with officers of the university, at the same time expressing his desire to cooperate with the university in financing the cost of such a project. This plan, and other proposals, such as those for the establishment of an "Honors College" and for the division of the undergraduate group into several colleges, were taken under consideration by a faculty committee which based its procedure on its desire to submit comprehensive recommendations on all of these proposals and their bearing on each other. Largely because of the enforced absences for long periods of the officers of the university and many of the leading members of the faculty in connection with the endowment fund, the work of this committee was delayed, so that a complete report could not be made by July 1, 1928, the time set by Mr. Harkness for a final decision on his proposal. The offer therefore lapsed, as was explained in a public statement by the university early this week.

The problem itself, however, of a better student-residential organization at Yale, continued to be given thorough study through the summer and fall, and, as stated above, came to a head at the December meeting of the Yale Corporation when the decision was reached to erect four new undergraduate quadrangles and to start work on the first two of these as soon as funds were in hand.—*The Yale Alumni Weekly.*

REPORTS

THE MILLION DOLLAR RESEARCH FUND OF THE DEPARTMENT OF SUPERINTENDENCE

THE following letter has been addressed to the members of the Department of Superintendence:

You will remember that at the Boston Meeting of the Department of Superintendence the "Committee on Financing Educational Research" submitted a report recommending "the creation of a permanent $1,000,000 Fund to be invested in safe securities with the income to be used for educational research on such studies as the department may from time to time authorize and direct to be made."

The committee further recommended that:

"In creating a permanent fund for this purpose, no paid solicitors be employed and no large gifts be sought. We believe it should be a genuine cooperative undertaking by which the superintendents themselves, through sacrifice and devotion to the public welfare, should undertake to create through many small gifts from the friends of public education a fund sufficient to produce an annual income of $40,000 to be devoted to such research as will help to make public education more fruitful, more efficient in administration, and more genuinely democratic in meeting the needs of all the children. Larger gifts, if they are offered without conditions which will make them unacceptable, may be received, but always with the understanding that they are to be used in such manner as the executive committee may direct to advance the general welfare.

"With a membership in the department of over 3,100, which ought to become 4,000 in a short time, we believe it will be comparatively easy to raise $1,000,000, if each member in his own community among his friends and acquaintances will undertake to raise $250 for this purpose. We recommend that the attempt be made to raise the fund in this manner, upon a democratic, nation-wide basis."

A number of subscriptions to the amount of $250 each have already been paid in, and the trustees of the National Education Association have agreed to take charge of the fund and to administer it in accordance with the terms of the report.

We hope to be able to report at the Cleveland meeting that the $1,000,000 fund is in sight. The membership of the department is now 3,684. The committee will undertake to raise the balance of the fund from sources outside the department, if the members will get back of the undertaking to the extent of $250 each.

We are proposing that each member of the department assume responsibility for $250, to be paid in five annual instalments. Many will prefer to pay the entire amount themselves; others will be able through their Parent-Teacher Associations, and through local friends of education, to secure what they may not wish to pay personally, each member being entirely free to handle the matter as he desires. By this plan there would be created during the first year a fund of $200,000, which at 4 per cent. would yield an income of $8,000, the second year $400,000 with an income of $16,000. In five years the full million dollars would be reached, with an annual income of $40,000, which would enable the department to carry on a continuous study of the problems of school administration from funds entirely within its own control and independent of any outside influence or the implications or suspicion of obligation to any interest except the public welfare.

We are enclosing pledge cards, and are asking that they be filled and returned to Mr. S. D. Shankland, executive secretary of the department, 1201 Sixteenth Street, Washington, D. C.; an addressed envelope is enclosed for this purpose. Will you please give this matter your early attention, in order that the committee may be able to report the results at the business meeting in Cleveland on Tuesday morning, February 26?

Let's do the job and get it off our hands. It can be done and done easily if every member will assume his small share of the responsibility.

Sincerely yours,

Randall J. Condon,
Chairman

Frank W. Ballou
Charles H. Judd
Lamont F. Hodge

Frank D. Boynton,
President Department of Superintendence and Member of Committee.

January 12, 1929.

SOCIETIES AND MEETINGS

THE ASSOCIATION OF AMERICAN COLLEGES

The Association of American Colleges went south for the first time in its history, holding its fifteenth annual meeting at Chattanooga, Tennessee, January 10 to 12. About 275 of the more than 400 member colleges were represented by well over 300 presidents, deans and professors.

For the first time also the association went outside the field of education by passing unanimously a resolution in favor of the Kellogg peace treaty and telegraphing its approval to the secretary of state. As to two other matters—anti-evolution legislation and district conference regulations dealing with commercialism in athletics—the association declined to take specific action, the point being made that the purpose of the association is "inclusive and cooperative rather than exclusive and standardizing and that legislation and regulations are not within its province."

There was, however, plenty of discussion of the situation as to anti-evolution legislation, including the address of Dr. William L. Poteat, president emeritus and professor of biology in Wake Forest College, in which he said:

> The demagogue and the propagandist are having a rollicking time with this nation of seventh graders. Remember the frank admission of publishers that public-school texts on science are changed on the demand of fundamentalist opinion. Remember this propaganda of obscurantism is just begun. Florida, Kansas, Oklahoma and Colorado are scheduled to follow the lead of Arkansas. For the youth of all America fetters are now forging, and unless the colleges and universities interpose with address and vigor to protect the helpless against the misinformed, we can expect nothing but disloyalty and execration when these fetters come to be broken, as they surely will.

Present tendencies in college athletics were discussed in a paper by Professor Bert E. Young, of Indiana University, and in remarks by President H. M. Gage, of Coe College, who presented and advocated endorsement of the new athletic regulations of the North Central Association. Without reference to these or other specific regulations the association passed a resolution as follows:

> The acceptable college encourages high-class athletics as an ally of educational efforts. This association stands against such abuses as commercialism, professionalism and sensational exploitation of college teams by promoters within or without the college. The tone of athletics must be in harmony with the general tone required of a member institution. The management and control of the athletics of an institution should be vested in a small, effective and responsible body chosen from the chief administrative officers, espe-

cially the president, the deans and the athletic committee, with the full support of the trustees.

A Preliminary Joint Session

The general theme of the meeting was announced as "The College Teacher." This same theme was considered at a joint session on the morning of January 10, preceding the association meeting, under the auspices of the Educational Associations and the Council of Church Boards of Education. Papers on "What Constitutes a Good College Teacher" were presented by Dr. Robert L. Kelly, President Guy E. Snavely, of Birmingham-Southern College; President Rees E. Tulloss, of Wittenberg College, and Professor Charles H. Judd, director of the School of Education, University of Chicago. Dr. Judd charged that "the American colleges have steadfastly held to the mythological faith that good teachers are the product of chance. I should like to be as emphatic as I can in the assertion that good teachers are always and invariably products of conscious effort. . . . The time has come when institutions must take a hand in the production of teachers."

The Annual Dinner

There were about 330 persons in attendance at the annual dinner of the Association of American Colleges, held at the Read House on the evening of January 10. The program included singing by students in the music department of the University of Chattanooga.

Trevor Arnett, president of the association, gave, as a part of his presidential address, the results of a study of college teachers' salaries. He showed that, in 302 colleges throughout the country, "the average salary paid to teachers of the rank of instructors and upwards" increased from $2,279 in 1919–20 to $2,958 in 1926–27, an increase of 29.8 per cent. The average salary ranged from $3,385 for New England to $2,660 for the southern states; this latter figure is an advance of 33.4 per cent. over 1919–20, the largest for any geographical division. Mr. Arnett pointed out that, on the basis of the 1914–15 dollar, the average nominal salary of $2,958 is a real average salary of $1,825, so that teachers "were but slightly better off in 1927 than were like workers in 1914."

Of 11,361 teachers who replied, 7,557 reported that they supplemented their regular salaries for the nine months' session by other earnings, which equaled 23.8 per cent. of their regular salaries. "The earnings range from a few dollars to $10,000 or more. The median is $522. Only a fourth make $1,000 or more and but 7.7 per cent. as much as $2,000 or more."

The range of the college salary scale is narrow, Mr. Arnett found. "No one receives a salary over $15,000, and but one per cent. of the teachers receive more than $7,000 per year. . . . Certain of the leading universities and colleges, both large and small, have secured funds for salary increases and are paying to their leading professors salaries of $7,000 to $10,000 per year.

Mr. Arnett closed with these queries:

(1) Whether the salary range for college teachers should not be widened by making the upper limit flexible so as to provide salaries large enough to attract able men.

(2) Whether it would not be well for colleges and universities to add a sufficient sum to the regular salaries of the faculties to enable them to control outside work.

(3) Whether waiving the principle of permanent tenure in return for higher salaries would not be an advantage to the teaching profession.

The second speaker at the dinner was Dr. Poteat, who spoke "In Praise of Ignorance," ironically in reference to "the heated controversies in certain religious circles about irrelevant matters long ago settled by responsible men of science," and seriously in reference to "the crucial questions in all fields of physical nature, no less than those of personality" in which "the great scientists—we may ignore the minor scientists—admit their limitations."

The third dinner speaker, for whom the college delegates rose as the guest of honor, was Viscount Vincent Massey, minister from the Canadian government at Washington. Mr. Massey touched upon the characteristics which Canadian and American colleges have in common:

First, our colleges for the most part are residential communities; secondly, they exist to teach the humanities; and, thirdly, they endeavor to train the character as well as to educate the mind. This trinity of objects is, of course, common to secondary schools the world over, but in the realm of higher education I believe these are the peculiar possession of the American and British systems.

Mr. Massey discussed problems which confront Canadian and American faculties alike, "probably the greatest of which is due to a virtue which all North Americans possess—an unquenchable desire for education."

THE TRAINING OF COLLEGE TEACHERS

At the morning session of January 11, President Ernest H. Wilkins, of Oberlin College, gave the report of the commission on the enlistment and training of college teachers. The commission recommended that the Association of American Colleges should request the leading graduate schools of the country:

(1) To ascertain the proportion of their own doctorial graduates engaged in college teaching.

(2) To ascertain the proportion of their present doctoral candidates intending to engage in college teaching.

(3) To restudy individually the question as to whether they are doing all they can to train students for college teaching.

The commission further suggests:

(4) That no graduate school admit to candidacy for the doctorate any student intending to engage in college teaching who has not a wide background of intellectual interest and experience.

(5) That efforts be made to give to each graduate student intending to engage in college teaching an adequate training in methods of teaching as applied to the department of knowledge in which the student is working.

(6) That each graduate school should offer to students intending to engage in college teaching an adequate and varied optional course in the instructional and administrative problems of the American college.

(7) That for those graduate students who are intending to engage in college teaching there be an optional quantitative relaxation of the research requirement; and

(8) That heads of departments in graduate schools regard it as a part of their task to acquaint themselves with all readily ascertainable evidence as to the teaching ability of their graduate students.

The commission also made certain recommendations as to the development of the teaching ability of newly appointed instructors. Late in the meeting the association acted favorably on the recommendations of the commission. Among those taking part in the discussion were President James L. McConaughy, of Wesleyan University; Dean Marshall S. Brown, of New York University; Dean Otis E. Randall, of Brown University; Dr. Kelly, presenting a letter from President W. P. Few, of Duke University; Dean Melvin E. Haggerty, of the University of Minnesota; President D. L. Marsh, of Boston University; President J. A. Apple, of Hood College, and Dean R. A. Kent, of Northwestern University.

REPORTS OF OTHER COMMISSIONS

That "a cordial feeling between this association and the American Association of University Professors" has been established was reported by President W. W. Boyd, of the Western College for Women, as chairman of the commission on academic freedom and academic tenure. The commission, feeling "that there is little more that can be done at the present," recommended that it be discharged. This was done.

Dr. Charles R. Mann, director of the American Council on Education, gave the report of the commission on surveys, in which were chronicled experiments in improving the mechanism of college administration and operation and other experiments toward developing objective measures of the product of college operations. In closing, Dr. Mann dealt with the general theme of the meeting and made four points as follows:

(1) There are great teachers in every walk of life.

(2) The great teacher's personality and methods are unique. You can't define a teacher, therefore, in terms of personality.

(3) The great teacher is revealed by the changes he works in people.

(4) The distinctive acts of a great teacher are *first*, that he decentralizes responsibility; *second*, that he stimulates persistent thinking; *third*, that he fosters religious faith. These three give you objective measures for judging a teacher.

The report of the commission on personnel technique based on questions sent out by President L. B. Hopkins, of Wabash College, as chairman, was presented by Dean Herbert E. Hawkes, of Columbia College.

To the question, do you have a group of faculty members to advise students, 256 colleges answered yes and 66 answered no. As to the giving of medical service to students, 280 answered yes, and 39 no. Psychological tests (215 different forms of test) are used at 271 colleges; 49 colleges do not use such tests. Personnel records apart from records in the office of the registrar are kept at 174 colleges; 136 reported that they do not keep separate records. To the question, does any agency in the institution know the quality of scholastic work during and before the end of any semester, 312 colleges replied yes and nine replied no. Some agency carrying on research in education or personnel was reported by 152 colleges, while 163 wrote that they have no such agency. A total of 186 institutions replied yes to the question, is there any member of the administration or faculty who utilizes information from all six of the indicated sources?

President Frederick C. Ferry, of Hamilton College, gave the report of the commission on college architecture and college instruction in the fine arts, announcing the forthcoming book on college architecture by Charles Z. Klauder, sponsored by the Carnegie Corporation and to be published by Charles Scribner's Sons.

Various ways in which schools and colleges are cooperating to raise intellectual standards were described by Dean Raymond Walters, of Swarthmore College, in a report which he presented as chairman of the commission on faculty and student scholarship.

"Experimentation with the College Teacher's Problems" was the subject of a presentation by Dean Melvin E. Haggerty, of the College of Education, University of Minnesota, in which he told of four types of such experimentation. These new ventures show, Dean Haggerty said, that "the diversity and rapidity of change in college education exceeds all previous experience in this country," and that college administrators are determined to "substitute facts for platitudes" and to "drive out educational superstition with knowledge and understanding."

BUSINESS MATTERS

A detailed report on work of the executive committee and of the executive secretary for the first year was presented by Dr. Robert L. Kelly. A tribute to Dr. Kelly's service in founding the Association of American Colleges in 1914 and to his activity since as "a great educational statesman" was paid by President Albert N. Ward, of Western Maryland College, and, upon President Ward's motion, the association voted an appropriation of $500 to Dr. Kelly to take a vacation and to recuperate from his recent illness of influenza.

The report of the treasurer, Warden Bernard I. Bell, of St. Stephen's College, showed receipts for the year of $22,518 and disbursements of $15,990. The total assets of the association were indicated as $6,927.

The membership fee was increased from $25 to $50 a year, upon motion of the committee on resolutions, made by the chairman, President D. J. Cowling, of Carleton College. Other action, taken upon motion of this committee, included creation of a department of educational research; recommendation of the "uniform trust for public uses"; acceptance of the Carnegie Corporation's invitation to become the agency of promoting plans for the improvement of public libraries; warning against fraudulent "degree-mill" colleges, and approval of the World Student Union.

Officers for 1929–30 were elected as follows:

President: President Guy E. Snavely, of Birmingham-Southern College.

Vice-President: President William Mather Lewis, of Lafayette College.

Executive secretary: Dr. Robert L. Kelly, New York City.

Treasurer: Warden Bernard I. Bell, St. Stephen's College.

Additional members executive committee: President Ada L. Comstock, of Radcliffe College, and Trevor Arnett, of the General Education Board.

RAYMOND WALTERS

SWARTHMORE COLLEGE

THE AMERICAN ASSOCIATION OF UNIVERSITY PROFESSORS

THE decision to establish an appointment service for college and university teachers was perhaps the most important action taken by the American Association of University Professors at its fifteenth annual meeting held at the Casa Italiana, Columbia University, on December 31 and January 1. No such noncommercial general appointment service for college teachers exists at the present time. Headquarters for the service will be 26 Jackson

Place, Washington, D. C., where a permanent office is to be opened by the association early in 1929. The appointment service will be available only to members of the association but it was also voted to establish a non-voting junior membership for graduate students and those not yet eligible as active members. The report on the appointment service was presented by Professor Joseph Mayer, of Tufts, chairman of the special committee on the subject.

Freedom of teaching in science was discussed at some length and it was voted to appoint a committee to cooperate with the American Association for the Advancement of Science in the preparation of a pamphlet on this subject for general circulation.

The testimony presented to the Federal Trade Commission on efforts to utilize college teachers as agents of propaganda was considered, but it was deemed inappropriate to express a formal opinion until the commission has made its final report. The council was requested, however, to keep the matter under attention and to recommend such action by the association as the facts may call for.

The report of the committee on academic freedom and tenure, presented by Professor H. R. Fairclough, of Amherst, stated that: "As a result of the existence and activity of this committee the general conditions of academic freedom and tenure throughout the country are undoubtedly more satisfactory than they were a generation ago. Much, however, still remains to be done. We seldom have legal power of redress but we do have a powerful weapon in the publicity we can give to offending institutions." Twenty-nine cases have been handled by the committee during the past year.

Practice and principles of appointment and promotions were analyzed and discussed at length by the chairman of the committee on that subject, Professor Hardin Craig, of Stanford.

The report of the committee on the organization and conduct of local chapters was presented by its chairman, Professor Edward S. Allen, of Iowa State College. He made many recommendations of policy for the guidance of chapter officers and suggestions for procedure by which the local organizations may play a more lively part in their respective communities. He stressed the fact that "this is the only association which unites college and university teachers of all subjects from the whole country for informal discussion." A peculiarly interesting piece of chapter activity was reported by Professor Yandell Henderson, of Yale, a study of "Income and Living Costs of a University Faculty," made by the Yale Chapter at the request of the president of the university and published by the Yale University Press. The study indicates, Professor Henderson pointed out, not only that the salaries of professors are lower than they should be but that they will remain so until the size of the faculty is stabilized in each institution. The present tendency, he said, is to use any increase in appropriation for salaries to increase the size of the faculty.

Two delegates from the Association of American Colleges addressed the association, President Boyd, of Western College for Women, and President Lewis, of Lafayette. Both expressed their satisfaction in the increasingly cordial relations between the association of teachers and the association of administrators.

The directors of the American Council on Education and the Institute of International Education described recent activities of their respective bodies.

A report from the chairman of the association's committee on cooperation with Latin American universities, Dr. L. S. Rowe, indicated promising developments in that field.

Members active in the foundation and development of the association discussed its present problems at the annual dinner held Monday night at the Columbia University Faculty Club.

Professor H. C. Warren, of Princeton, was elected vice-president of the association. Ten members of the council were elected: Professors B. H. Bodie, Ohio State; M. T. Bogert, Columbia; A. L. Bondurant, Mississippi; H. S. Conard, Grinnell; H. G. Doyle, George Washington; P. O. Ray, California, Berkeley; F. K. Richtmyer, Cornell; Joel Stebbins, Wisconsin; H. S. White, Vassar; H. V. Wilson, North Carolina.

MARGARET L. FARRAND
SMITH COLLEGE

EDUCATIONAL RESEARCH AND STATISTICS

TIME EXPENDITURE BY HIGH-SCHOOL TEACHERS

MUCH has been written in education magazines and said in teachers' institutes and conventions about the importance of time budgets for teachers. A few tabulations of data on this subject have been published, but the problem is ever a new one and somewhat irksome in anticipation. This is no less true of the teacher just about to enter upon the work of her first position than of the teacher who has taught for some years and, perhaps, acquired some bad or at least unsatisfactory teaching habits through passivity and unprogressiveness. The importance of renewed emphasis on time budgets for teachers is shown when only thirty-seven out of 102 teachers at a county institute in the far west declared that they had ever made a time budget for themselves, and only eleven out of these thirty-seven declared that they had adhered to their budgets for half of a school year or longer. Whether this condition is more true in the west than in the east and more true of beginning than of experienced teachers is a matter of conjecture at the present time.

The purpose of this little investigation was to find the amounts of time actually spent on their several activities by the teachers of a small high school, typical of hundreds throughout the United States. The method of procedure was simply the preparation of charts on which were listed the usual activities of high-school teachers, with spaces for the time spent at each activity for each half day of the week. These were sent during different weeks to the three teachers who composed the entire faculty of a small high school and who, because they were friends of one of the writers, might be expected to fill out the charts carefully and accurately. They were asked to fill in the time spaces after each activity each half day in order that the accounts might be more accurate. At the end of the week the charts were returned to the writers by the teachers.[1] These teachers—two young women and one young man—had had an average of two years of teaching experience. Their work represented a wide range of school duties and related activities. Their extra-curricular and community duties were unfairly heavy, as they are so often in the small high school in the somewhat isolated community. In the state in which the high school is located, it is considered a good high school and is accredited by the state department of education. The teachers are graduates of accredited colleges.

The average amount of time spent on strictly school work by each teacher in this little school was eight hours and forty minutes—a very fair amount even when augmented by the added hour and forty minutes each day that was spent by each teacher on extra-curricular activities, but not with the additional added hour and eight minutes of community work each day of the school week. These teachers felt somewhat that they were overworked and that they did not have time enough to do their legitimate work well, but this would not have been the case if they had been allowed to confine themselves more exclusively to their school work. A different distribution of their waking hours would have made their work more profitable, and pleasant as well.

Two of these teachers did not read any books or magazines on education during the period charted; one did no general reading, and one prepared no lesson plans. Such a chart as this intimates the teacher's relation to and interest in his teaching as well as the number of hours which he works.

The condition of the school system is indicated by the heavy extra-curricular duties and by the absence of any form of teachers' meetings. The outlook of the community is intimated in its heavy demand for participation in community work by the teachers.

It may, then, be advisable to repeat for the benefit of older teachers in these typical communities as well as for the beginning teachers that time budgets are valuable as protection against excessive demands on their time. A

[1] The charts sent to the teachers covered different weeks. Each teacher wrote, however, that the week covered had been an unusual week, although none was immediately preceding or succeeding holidays.

Distribution of waking time of three teachers

	Average time per day I	II	III	Total of three per week	Per cent. total waking time*	Per cent. eight-hour work day
Classroom teaching	3:45	3:45	5:00	62:30	26.2	52.1
Preparing lessons	1:27	:59	:00	12:10	5.1	10.2
Correcting papers	:04	:45	:00	4:05	1.7	3.4
Grades, records, reports	:00	:21	:10	2:25	1.0	2.1
Conferences with pupils and parents	:00	:15	:15	2:30	1.0	2.0
Conferences with teachers	:00	:00	:00	:00	.0	.0
Teachers' meetings	:00	:00	:00	:00	.0	.0
Taking class roll	:05	:05	:10	1:40	.7	1.4
Supervision study hall	1:12	1:30	1:03	18:45	7.8	15.6
Attending school assemblies	:19	:15	:09	3:35	1.5	3.0
Professional reading	:00	:25	:00	2:05	.9	1.7
Extra-curricular activities	1:22	1:36	2:00	24:50	10.0	20.0
P. T. A. meetings	:00	:06	:00	:30	.2	.4
General reading	:04	:54	:00	4:50	2.0	
Church–SS work	:00	:00	:00	:00	.0	
Community work	1:48	:48	:36	3:12	1.3	
Committee meetings	:20	:09	:04	2:45	1.2	
Society and clubs	:00	:24	:00	1:20	.8	
Lunch	:30	:45	:45	10:00	4.2	
Recreation—rest	2:12	1:50	3:00	35:10	14.6	
Time to self other than recreation	:00	2:26	:00	12:10	5.1	
Time spent at school	7:15	7:55	7:06			
No. classes taught	4⅗	5	5⅘			
No. pupils taught	42	48	78			
School work on Saturday	7:00	2:05	:00			
School work on Sunday	2:00	:20	:00			

* Basis taken as sixteen hours. This leaves 3:15 unaccounted for each day by each teacher.

time budget may enable them to devote sufficient amounts of their time to teaching so that they do it satisfactorily to themselves. A great many beginning teachers have only vague ideas of the communities in which they will work and the demands that will be made upon them. If they enter—as many do—upon their work with unconsidered ideas of the suitable division of time among their professional, social and recreational activities, they may—as many do—suffer complete or partial failure where it is not at all necessary, acquire bad habits of teaching or turn from teaching in disgust.

Even though a time budget may not be satisfactory in its first construction, its very reconstruction and modification will lead to thought about the problem of the distribution of time and will assist in the development of a helpful philosophy of teaching. The teacher who has a time budget is able to see clearly whether he may assume new voluntary engagements safely or may convince others that additional demands on his time are unfair.

Obviously the time budget must be somewhat flexible from week to week. It must be used by the teacher—not allowed to use him. On the other hand, it should be adhered to and built up for the weeks of the school year for use in succeeding years. Such a development yields a sense of security and freedom in taking time for things which are out of the routine, that is, assists in creating a feeling of justifiable freedom.

Mary Walker
H. R. Laslett

Corvallis, Oregon

SCHOOL AND SOCIETY

EDITED BY J. McKEEN CATTELL
WITH WHICH IS COMBINED THE

EDUCATIONAL REVIEW

EDITED BY WILLIAM McANDREW

Volume XXIX   Saturday, February 2, 1929   Number 736

ANTI-EVOLUTION LAWS AND THE PRINCIPLE OF RELIGIOUS NEUTRALITY

By Professor ARTHUR O. LOVEJOY
THE JOHNS HOPKINS UNIVERSITY

It is, of course, evident that those who are primarily interested in propaganda for the theory of evolution have no reason to regret the enactment of "anti-evolution" laws. It has often been said by others, and it is doubtless true, that nothing could do so much to advertise the subject and to arouse the intellectual curiosity of youth concerning the theory as such efforts to keep them from a knowledge of it. The promoters of such legislation may know little about biology, but they know less about human nature. They probably have, in the last five years, done more than all the schoolmasters and professors to set boys and girls to inquiring, reading and talking about evolution. But the suggestion which is sometimes heard that university teachers ought on this account to take a *laissez-faire* attitude towards the whole movement seems to me a mistake. There is something at issue of much more general and fundamental significance than the acceptance or rejection by a certain number of young persons of a particular biological hypothesis; it is the maintenance of the integrity, dignity and efficiency of the American state universities, and the assurance that they will be so conducted that competent scholars can serve in them without sacrifice of their intellectual self-respect or disloyalty to their professional obligations. It would very likely be a good thing for evolutionism as a doctrine to pass such laws that the dispensing of information about it would be driven wholly into the hands of biological bootleggers; but it would not be good for universities—or for science. What is at issue in this matter is not a scientific hypothesis but an educational principle; at bottom the issue is that of the limits of the right of a sovereign democracy to control the content of the teaching in the institutions—and specifically in the universities—which it maintains at its own expense for the education of its own youth. The question of the teaching of evolution is merely the momentary form which this larger issue has taken on.

Now behind the movement for anti-evolution legislation there is one contention—a supposed principle of political philosophy—which bears upon this issue. It is not this, indeed, which chiefly inspires the movement; but it is to this principle that the advocates of such legislation chiefly appeal in their arguments; and by their acceptance of it, also, their actual program is very definitely limited. The argument, which is genuinely plausible and deserving of serious consideration, is put thus in one of the organs of the fundamentalist movement, in reply to the question: "Why Bar Evolution from State Schools?"

Because evolution, speaking as it does concerning creation and the Creator, the miracles of the Bible and the philosophy of life, is properly classed with religions.

Because state schools have no right to teach religion of any kind.

Because teaching religion of any sort in the state schools is a step towards the union of church and state.

Because the evolutionist has no more right to ask the state schools to teach his religion than the Christian fundamentalist has to ask the state to teach his belief. Towards all religions civil law should take a neutral attitude.

Because debarring evolution from the public schools has not infringed in any way upon the right of evolutionists to think, speak and write upon this subject as they choose, so long as they do not use state funds, secured by taxation, with which to do it.[1]

According to this reasoning it is the opponents of this type of legislation who demand the teaching of a religious dogma in tax-supported institutions and reject the separation of church and state. The charge often brought against the advocates of anti-evolution laws is retorted upon those who make it. The retort is a perfectly natural one; no doubt, to a great many good citizens it appears a perfectly just one. Even Mr. Walter Lippmann, in his fair-minded and thought-provoking little book "American Inquisitors," has suggested that Mr. Bryan in this matter was an entirely consistent follower of Thomas Jefferson. There is, he acutely points out, between Jefferson's Bill for Establishing Religious Freedom, adopted by the General Assembly of Virginia in 1786, and the Anti-Evolution Act adopted by the General Assembly of Tennessee in 1925,

a strange agreement. . . . On one vital matter both laws appeal to the same principle, though they aim at diametrically opposite ends. The Virginia statute says that "to compel a man to *furnish contributions of money* for the propagation of opinions which he disbelieves is sinful and tyrannical." . . . The Tennessee legislators were merely applying this principle. They disbelieved in the evolution theory, and they set out to free their constituents of the sinful and tyrannical compulsion to pay for the propagation of an opinion which they disbelieved. . . . The political leader who in his generation professed to be Jefferson's most loyal disciple, asked whether, if it is wrong to compel people to support a creed they disbelieve, it is not also wrong to compel them to support teaching which impugns the creed in which they do believe.

That is, as Mr. Lippmann insists, an argument which we must fairly meet. It is, doubtless, often put forward insincerely. But it is a view which might well be, and in many cases probably is, honestly held. I wish to consider on this occasion, not whether the principle of religious neutrality, which is the essence of the argument, is valid as a piece of political philosophy, but what it really means and what consequences can be legitimately drawn from it with respect to the teaching of any given science, such as biology, in state institutions, and especially in state universities—assuming that there are to be state universities and that the science in question is to be included in their course of study. One thing is immediately evident: if *this* is the ground upon which legislation on the matter is defended, that legislation must be strictly limited to the maintenance of such neutrality in these institutions. The argument obviously does not justify the requirement of any specified *positive* teaching on questions about which differences of theological or philosophical belief prevail among taxpayers, or the imposition of any religious tests for academic appointments. Now the statute most recently adopted seems to be intentionally drawn so as to keep within the limits of this principle; and it will help to clarify the matter if we note just what it is that this statute prohibits and permits.

The Arkansas law declares it to be

unlawful for any teacher or other instructor in any university, college, normal, public school, or other institution . . . which is supported in whole or in

[1] From *The Crusaders' Champion.*

part from public funds derived by state or local taxation to teach the theory or doctrine that mankind ascended or descended from a lower order of animals [or] to adopt or use a text-book that teaches the theory . . . that mankind descended or ascended from a lower order of animals.

Precisely what can this language be reasonably construed to mean?

(1) The law does not propose any credal requirement for the tenure of teaching positions. It does not demand that a teacher shall hold any specified belief on the subject in question.

(2) The law is purely prohibitive, not prescriptive. It forbids what it calls the "teaching" of a certain theory; it does not require that any one shall teach that this theory is false or that any alternative theory is true.

(3) This law (unlike that in Tennessee) does not set up any religious document or theological formula even as a negative criterion of what may be taught in state schools and universities. It does not, in particular, say: "Nothing which is in conflict with the first chapter of Genesis, construed in the natural or literal sense of its terms, shall be taught." The first chapter of Genesis appears, for example, to assert in plain terms that the world was made in six days. There are, presumably, some taxpayers in Arkansas, including, perhaps, the framers of the anti-evolution law, who believe this assertion to be true. Nevertheless there is nothing in the statute which forbids the denial of it by a teacher in a state institution.

(4) Specifically, the Arkansas law does not prohibit the teaching of the "theory of evolution," *i.e.*, the doctrine of the transformation of species through natural descent, in the case of organisms other than man.

(5) What "teaching" with respect to man the framers of the law intended to prohibit is not wholly clear from the language used. If a distinction is recognized (as it presumably is by the authors of the law) between man's body and his mental and moral constitution, and the latter is regarded as his distinctively human attribute, there is nothing in the stature which would have any bearing upon the question of man's bodily descent; and the teaching of biology would consequently be wholly unaffected.

(6) Nevertheless, it is probable that the intent of the law is to prohibit the "teaching" that man is "descended," in the physiological sense, from any non-human ancestors. To this single prohibition the legal content of the statute appears to reduce.

(7) It remains to ask what is to be understood by the expression "to teach the theory or doctrine that" man is so descended. The word "teach" is an ambiguous one, eminently unsuitable for use in a statutory definition of a criminal act. At least five senses of it, and as many conceivable interpretations of the prohibition contained in the statute, may be distinguished.

(1) "Teaching the theory" in question might mean defining or expounding it, informing students that such a theory has been advanced and explaining to them what it asserts. If the term were understood in this sense, the intent of the law, and its effect if enforced, would be to exclude from the public educational institutions of the state all modern text-books in biology, anthropology, philosophy, psychology and sociology, and to require teachers, even in the state university, to avoid all mention, however impartial, of one of the most generally held and pervasive of scientific hypotheses. The enforcement of such a provision could mean nothing less than the exclusion of all the branches of biological science relating to man from the courses of study in the state university and other public institutions. For, if a science

is to be dealt with at all—at least in a university—the whole range and variety of current hypotheses concerning its problems must obviously be presented frankly and accurately; and it is difficult to see how a self-respecting university teacher could accept or hold a position in an institution in which he was not permitted to deal with his subject in this manner. But it seems clear that the statute can not legitimately be interpreted in so absurd a sense. It is not a law to prohibit the mention or exposition of the theory to which it refers.

(2) It may, perhaps, be suggested that the law, while permitting definition or exposition of the theory, prohibits mention of the arguments advanced by those who believe in it. But the language of the statute certainly does not require, nor, so far as I can see, does it permit, such an interpretation. You do not "teach the theory that the sun revolves about the earth," when you set forth the reasons which led to the acceptance of the Ptolemaic astronomy.

(3) If the law permits the exposition both of the theory itself and of the arguments commonly offered by its adherents, does it forbid mention of the fact that the great majority of contemporary biologists and anthropologists accept such a theory? Clearly not; the statute is neither by title nor content one to prohibit the giving of information concerning the prevailing tendencies of opinion among biologists.

(4) Shall we then say that what is really required is that the teacher shall never—even when asked—allow his students to know what his own opinion is about the descent of man? This, again, would seem to be an unnecessary and therefore inadmissible interpretation. There is nothing to justify the charge that the statute ought to be entitled: "A law to require teachers to conceal their personal opinions on certain subjects." If it be said that the object of the law is to permit only teachers who disbelieve in the evolutionary descent of man to let their own opinions be known, the law would in that case conflict with the principle of academic neutrality upon which it is ostensibly grounded. It would virtually limit teaching appointments to those adhering to a particular religious doctrine.

(5) There remains, then, only one sense which can legitimately be given to the word "teach," in laws of this character: the sense in which it is synonymous with "inculcate." What such a statute, strictly construed, may be presumed to prohibit is propaganda, the teaching of a certain theory as an undisputed or indisputable dogma, the attempt to convert students to a specific opinion. Any teacher who has occasion to deal directly with the subject of man's descent would, as it appears to me, fully comply with the provisions of such a law if he should lay before his students, when the study with which they are concerned requires it, an accurate exposition of the evolutionary theory of the descent of man, a statement of the arguments of its advocates, and also any arguments of a scientific or philosophical character which have been urged against it, an indication of the prevailing state of scientific opinion on the subject, and a reminder that to some religious believers the theory is inadmissible because it is in conflict with their theological convictions—and should then leave the student to reach his own conclusion by the use of his own intelligence and conscience. If the student's religious beliefs appear to him to require rejection of the hypothesis in question, no attempt could—in conformity with the law—be made to dissuade him from doing so, nor could he be refused promotion, or the like, because of his attitude; while the teacher would be equally free to hold his own opinion, and would be under no obligation to hide it from the knowledge of others.

Thus reasonably interpreted, such a law as has been adopted in Arkansas is likely to do no great educational mischief, and it may even bring some educational advantages. The dogmatic temper, and even a kind of superstition, is not unknown in the teaching of science; the tendency of the law should be to discourage all kinds of dogmatism in the presentation of the topic in question, and to place the whole matter in the arena of free inquiry, free discussion and individual judgment. This, assuredly, is a result much to be desired. And where nothing more than this is required, a conscientious teacher may, it appears to me, properly hold that no restrictions are imposed which the ethical code of his profession obliges him to reject.

I do not suggest that this is the result desired by most of those who have promoted such legislation. Free inquiry and undogmatic discussion are probably the last things which many of them would wish to bring about. What I am pointing out is, first, that nothing more than this is unequivocally required by such a statute as has been analyzed; and second, that nothing more can be justified by the principle of neutrality to which its proponents appeal—unless that principle be understood to demand the exclusion of the "teaching," not of a theory, but of certain *subjects*—of a whole group of important sciences—in state institutions. For you can not teach a science and omit exposition and discussion of theories held by large numbers of specialists in it; nor can you, in the name of "neutrality," demand that a science be presented only by teachers who reject a particular theory—and specifically, the theory which experts in the subject almost universally hold. States may, of course, if they wish, eliminate the biological sciences —as in the interest of "religious neutrality," they have eliminated theological studies from the curricula of public institutions; but if they are not prepared to go to that length, there is no way in which they can permit the teaching of those sciences while imposing restrictions in excess of those indicated in the above interpretation of the Arkansas law. Any further restrictions would amount to a departure from neutrality, and the setting up of sectarian tests of orthodoxy.

It is to be observed that if the principle of neutrality is valid, it can not be limited to the teaching of a particular theory. It purports to define a moral or political right of the individual taxpayer, and the only law which would embody it consistently would be one making it unlawful for teachers in institutions supported by taxation to "teach" any theory to which any taxpayer —or at the least, any body of taxpayers having formulated principles—objects. And this consideration makes it the more evident that the term "teaching" must be construed in the sense here suggested. Taken in any other sense, neutrality in teaching would require, for example, either that the subjects of physiology, medicine and hygiene be excluded altogether from state schools and universities, or else that in the teaching of them no mention be made of the occurrence or the physical causes of disease; otherwise the supposed rights of Christian Scientist taxpayers would be violated. In one city in California, according to Dr. Maynard Shipley, the former interpretation has been given to the principle by a school board. But, of course, the consequences of the principle, so construed, would not stop here; out of deference to one group of taxpayers or another, many of the natural sciences, and a great part of history, would be eliminated or eviscerated. The demand for neutrality, in short, if it means more than the demand that instruction shall be an accurate presentation of the results of observation or experiment and an undogmatic canvassing of the principal hypotheses presented for the interpretation of those results, leads to pure absurdity.

To those, then, who defend legislation forbidding the "teaching" of any specified theory in tax-supported institutions on the ground that such institutions must be neutral on questions about which taxpayers are divided, one must answer, first of all, that the only kind of neutrality which would not render these institutions educational, or rather, uneducational absurdities—which, in other words, would not virtually destroy them—consists in full liberty of inquiry and discussion and opinion for both student and teacher. The only restriction which it would impose upon the teacher would be that he should treat with courtesy and respect any religious or political beliefs held by any student, and that, instead of dogmatically imposing his personal views upon the student, he should encourage the latter to think for himself and to arrive at his own views through critical reflection upon carefully ascertaind facts. Few university teachers, certainly, would take exception to such requirements. But they are requirements which it is difficult to enforce by legal process; legislative attempts to define them so precisely, in terms of concrete acts, as to bring them effectively within the scope of the criminal code, must necessarily be futile. Even if they could be so defined, such legislation—if consistent with the only rational interpretation of the principle of neutrality—would not make, and does not make, for the essentially obscurantist and sectarian ends which are manifestly aimed at by most of those who invoke that principle for the justification of their legislative programs.

EDUCATIONAL EVENTS

THE UNIVERSITY OF PATNA

SINCE the settlement during Sir Henry Wheeler's Governorship of Bihar and Orissa of the long-discussed problem of a site, the University of Patna is said by the *London Times Educational Supplement* to have made steady progress. A great teaching center has been growing on the banks of the Ganges, and the authorities responsible have not forgotten the great traditions of ancient days when Nalanda was the most celebrated seat of Buddhist learning in the world.

The latest addition to the buildings of the university is the Science College, which was opened by the Viceroy last month. Expressing the confidence that the university would go from strength to strength, Lord Irwin paid a tribute to Sir Sultan Ahmed, who has been the vice-chancellor for the past five years, and is now serving on the Hartog Auxiliary Committee of the Simon Commission. Sir Sultan Ahmed, in his address on the same day at convocation, advised the graduates to apply their energies to the educational advancement of the country and the eradication of social evils, instead of allowing politics to monopolize their activities. He suggested that the solution of educational and social problems would also be the solution of many political problems of the country.

One of the mistakes of collegiate education in India as shaped nearly a century ago was said to be its too exclusively literary character. Lord Irwin held that no university to-day in a scientific age is complete without its equipment for scientific research, as one of the many branches which go to make the whole tree of human knowledge. Such equipment is especially needed in India, with its great material resources to be developed, its industrial possibilities, its agricultural and engineering problems to be solved.

Lord Irwin said that, situated as it is in a busy and crowded center, Patna University should be the focus of thought of different communities, different creeds, different interests. There should be found the play of mind on mind, the habit of independent thought, the scholarship whose hallmark it was that it knew its own limitations of knowledge. This would encourage the students to think out their position and not to rest content without solid foundations for the convictions they professed.

THE ORGANIZATION OF A SUMMER SCHOOL FOR NORTH AMERICAN STUDENTS IN BRAZIL

DR. CARLOS DELGADO DE CARVALHO, of the Brazil Research School in Rio de Janeiro, Brazil, is in this country for the purpose of discussing with scholars and educators the possibility of organizing in Rio de Janeiro a summer session for North American students. The courses to be offered will be on the history, geography, institutions and social conditions of Brazil. Moreover, the courses will be given in English. The regular courses in any one of these subjects will be of fifteen hours' duration but general surveys of these subjects, consisting of about five lectures, will be organized for the benefit of the student tourists who, it is hoped, will be interested in these subjects as part of their travels in Latin America. The longer courses are organized primarily for teachers who, it is hoped, will be interested in those subjects to a sufficient extent to justify the giving of the courses.

The tour of Mr. Hoover in South America, the establishment of the Pan-American Airship Lines from Florida to Argentina and the general interest aroused in Latin America at the present time justify the belief on the part of the Brazilian scholars and educators interested in the movement that the establishment of such a summer session at Rio de Janiero serves a real and valuable purpose.

It must not be forgotten that, when we have our summer, Brazil has its mildest weather when the temperature is about 65° F. Moreover, our vacation corresponds with their period of greatest school activity. This Brazil Research School will organize excursions to surrounding places of interest. Those familiar with the geography of Rio de Janeiro know how many such places there are. It is expected that visitors attending such a summer session will enjoy their stay.

Teachers, students and others interested in the proposed plan can secure further information by addressing Dr. Carlos Delgado de Carvalho at the Institute of International Education, 2 West 45th Street, New York City.

FEDERAL APPROPRIATIONS FOR VOCATIONAL TRAINING

ACCORDING to the *U. S. Daily,* Congress would be authorized to appropriate as much as $6,000,000 annually in additional funds for training farm boys and girls in agriculture and home economics on a permanent cooperative program with the states under a bill which the House Committee on Rules approved January 23 for consideration.

The bill passed the Senate on April 9, 1928. The action of the committee followed a hearing at which Representative Reed (Rep.), of Dunkirk, N. Y., chairman of the House Committee on Education, advocated the bill.

Under the terms of the bill Congress would be empowered to enter upon this program:

> Appropriation of $500,000 for the fiscal year ending June 30, next, and then, for each year thereafter, a sum exceeding by $500,000 the sum appropriated for each preceding year, and annually thereafter there is permanently authorized to be appropriated for each year the sum of $6,000,000.
>
> One half of such sums would be allotted to the states and territories in the proportion that their farm population bears to the total farm population of the United States, exclusive of the insular possessions, according to the United States Census last preceding the end of the fiscal year in which any such allotment is to be made, and shall be used for salaries of teachers, supervisors and directors of agricultural subjects in such states and territories.
>
> The other half of these sums would be allotted to the states and territories in the proportion that their rural population bears to the total rural population of the United States, exclusive of the insular possessions, according to the same census arrangement, and to be used for salaries of teachers, supervisors and directors, development and improvement of home economics subjects in those states.

The bill also provides authorization for an appropriation of $100,000 annually to the Federal Board for Vocational Education, for carrying out the purposes of this proposed legislation.

Representative Reed told the committee on rules that under the Smith-Hughes Act there is a permanent and continuing appropriation of $6,000,000 annually, of which $3,000,000 is for agriculture and $3,000,000 for trade and industry. Twenty per cent. of the second $3,000,000, or $600,000, he said may be used for home economics. The cooperation between the federal government and the states is on a fifty-fifty basis. The states are now spending for vocational education $2.65 for each dollar of federal funds used.

ADULT EDUCATION AT COLUMBIA UNIVERSITY

The extent of the growth of adult education in recent years is seen in the record of the university extension department of Columbia University, according to Professor James Chidester Egbert, director of university extension and the school of business of Columbia University. He says:

In 1910 when we began giving extension courses for adults we had but 800 students on our rolls. To-day, nineteen years later, we have more than 15,000 students.

To find a pupil sixty years old or more among them is not an uncommon experience and we have a great many who are in their forties. The courses are planned primarily for mature students whose chief interest lies outside of the university and who have leisure to pursue only a few courses in the late afternoon or at night. For these students the sole condition is that they show their ability to pursue the work with success. All the courses are open to both men and women.

This work of adult education by Columbia University is divided into three groups. First, there are the regular university extension courses. These are carried on at Morningside Heights in Manhattan, at the Brooklyn Law School and at the Young Women's Christian Association Building, Newark, N. J. Other centers, in addition to these, are planned for the near future.

The second group consists of those taking home study courses. These courses are mainly for people whose business or home ties do not permit them to attend evening lectures.

The third group, under the direction of the Institute of Arts and Sciences of Columbia University, represents an achievement in adult education. It consists of a program of intellectual entertainment in lectures and concerts, held at the McMillin Academic Theater and Earl Hall, Columbia University, and of a series of short lectures also conducted at the McMillin Academic Theater. The combination consists of two hundred lectures, concerts and plays. Lectures covering ten popular liberal arts courses, which are non-academic and open to all adults, are held every evening, Sundays and holidays excepted, at 8:15, from mid-October to the end of April. Those wishing to join at the mid-season are permitted to do so.

The opportunity for further adult education which this vast program offers to individuals, literary clubs and organizations of various kinds, and as continuation courses for groups of employees of large corporations, can not be overestimated.

THE HARVARD "HOUSE" PLAN

According to press dispatches from Cambridge accurate estimates of what it will cost Harvard University to effect a complete subdivision of the college into small residential groups or houses were learned from authoritative sources and the total amount of money to be given by Edward S. Harkness, of New York, for the completion of the house plan will be $11,300,000. The preliminary estimates have been turned in to the Harvard authorities and that figure has been set.

Under the plans, as they have been drawn up by the architects, three new groups of buildings will be erected in the vicinity of the present freshman dormitories along the Charles River. One of these will be erected behind Gore Hall, another on Memorial Drive below McKinlock Hall toward Boston and the third on the plot of land now occupied by the power station, at the corner of Memorial Drive and Boylston Street, Cambridge.

These groups of buildings will be the first three units of the house plan. Then, it is expected, that the freshman dormitories will form the basis of two more units. Smith and Standish Halls will be grouped together as one house, and Gore and McKinlock Halls will be grouped together for another. The dormitories on Mount Auburn Street, known as the "gold coast," including Claverly, Randolph and Russell Halls and Westmorly Court, will be made into one or two houses, according to the needs of the plan.

Actual details of the new buildings to supplement the present dormitories in order to adapt them to the house plan are not yet known. The work done up to the present has consisted solely of figuring out the costs of putting the plan through, and this part of the work has not been completed.

THE CLEVELAND CONVENTION

The fifty-ninth annual session of the Department of Superintendence will be held in Cleveland, February 24 to 28, inclusive.

The program has been built around a central thesis, namely, "How can the Public Schools Better Serve Democracy, Increasingly Produce a Higher Type of Citizen?" In this one terse sentence we have stated the goal of American education, cited a major objective of the church and expressed the hope of good citizens everywhere.

Each day's program will deal with some phase of this thesis and will undertake to answer in part the question therein raised in order that the critics of public education may have their objections considered and the public get a better knowledge of how its present program came to be, what service is rendered and the cost of that service.

For example: Monday's theme will be: "How can the Ideal Standard set up in the Convention Thesis be Realized by a Better Financing of Education?" The first general session will deal with this part of the problem. In the afternoon, nine discussion groups will continue the discussion. In the evening a mass demonstration of service will be given by thousands of Cleveland children illustrating the work in physical and health education.

Tuesday's program will deal with "How can We Realize our Goal by a Better Articulation of the Units of Education?" The general session will treat this phase of the problem of American education. In the afternoon, nine other discussion groups will continue the discussion under nine very distinctive heads or topics. In the evening we will undertake to show how the goal may be reached through research and a joint meeting with the American Educational Research Association has been arranged.

Wednesday's program will discuss the ideals of the convention thesis under "How Education may be Improved through a Better Teaching Staff." This discussion at the general session Wednesday morning will consider a better selection of candidates for teacher-training institutions, a more severe weeding as they are in training, modern and more difficult courses—academic as well as professional—and better conditions and compensation for the better material. Nine other discussion groups will continue the discussion in the afternoon.

The climax comes on Thursday. The theme for this day is: "How can We Realize the Thesis Ideal by a Better Plan for Character Education?" Three of the best-known men in education have been selected for this discussion at the morning general session, students of this phase of education, and platform men of great ability. In the afternoon the discussion will continue. At that time the president of the National Education Association, the new United States Commissioner of Education and the president of the American Legion will close the convention.

On the general sessions program, and the twenty-seven discussion groups, every speaker has been selected with care. Before he was invited it was ascertained that he had accomplished something well worth passing on in the field he is to discuss. With less than half a dozen instances out of over one hundred and fifty possibilities, are there "repeaters." There will be many "new faces" with something behind them. Each discussion group has a theme and speakers equally strong as those in the program of the general sessions.

Advertising and propaganda have been rigidly excluded. Ours is an educational convention. It will cost the people of the country a round half million. It is definitely up to every schoolman in attendance to see to it that the money which his community contributes will be returned many fold to his community. The opportunity will be there. The rest is up to the individual.

The ministers of Cleveland have been personally invited to preach on the convention thesis at their morning service on February 24. Through the religious press and the Associated Press, this invitation has been extended to the ministers of America. Each member participating in the program has been asked to invite the ministers of his community to participate. Every one who reads this statement is asked to solicit the aid of the clergy, the "Uplift Faculty" of the youth of America, to join hands with us in the common objective of making the youth of this generation into a higher type of citizen.

FRANK D. BOYNTON, *President,*
Department of Superintendence, N. E. A.

ITHACA, N. Y.,
JANUARY 25, 1929

EDUCATIONAL NOTES AND NEWS

DR. FRANCIS L. PATTON, for many years president of Princeton University, celebrated his eighty-sixth birthday at his home in Bermuda on January 22.

THE REVEREND DR. ARLO AYRES BROWN, president of the University of Chattanooga, has been elected president of Drew University in Madison, N. J. He will succeed the Reverend Ezra S. Tipple, who resigned as head of the institution last November, effective upon the selection of a successor.

DR. LAWRENCE J. MEADER will be formally installed as president of Russell Sage College at Troy, New York, on February 22.

PRESIDENT GUY E. SNAVELY, of Birmingham-Southern College, was elected on January 12 president of the American Association of Colleges.

PROFESSOR RUDOLPH ALTROCCHI, chairman of the department of Italian at the University of California, was elected president of the American Association of Teachers of Italian at its recent meeting in Toronto.

DR. J. B. EDMONSON, professor of secondary education and director of the division of university inspection of high schools, has been appointed dean of the school of education of the University of Michigan. The office has been filled since September by an administrative committee selected by the board pending the appointment of a dean, upon the grant of leave of absence to former Dean Allen S. Whitney, whose resignation becomes effective at the close of the present school year. Dr. Edmonson received his bachelor's degree from Michigan in 1906, obtaining his doctorate from Chicago in 1925.

DR. ALBERT S. HURST has resigned his post as dean of Teachers College, Syracuse University, which he has held since 1920. Dr. Hurst expressed more than a year ago his desire to return to his original professorship. His resignation will take effect at the close of the academic year in June. He has been connected with the university for twenty-two years.

GEORGE H. LAMSON, head of the zoological department of the Connecticut Agricultural College, has been appointed dean of the division of agricultural science, *vice* Dr. E. W. Sinnott, whose resignation was recently announced.

PROFESSOR FRANK N. BRYANT, head of the department of business mathematics at Syracuse University, has been elected director of admissions and secretary of the board of admissions, succeeding Dr. Eugene F. Bradford.

W. W. MCKECHNIE has been appointed secretary to the Scottish Education Department, in succession to Sir George Macdonald, who retired from the public service on December 31.

L. B. BENNY has been appointed principal of the Portsmouth Municipal College. He has been principal of Bournemouth Municipal College since September, 1927.

PERCY MACKAYE, dramatist, whose plays have been staged by the leading producers in the United States, England and Germany, has received an appointment to the faculty of Rollins College.

AT Yale University, Professor Edward Prokosch, chairman of the department of German, New York University, has been appointed professor of German; M. Albert Gabriel Feuillerat, of the University of Rennes, France, professor of French, and Professor W. Hubert Greaves, of the University of Toronto, professor of public speaking in the Divinity School.

DR. JAMES F. NORRIS, professor of organic chemistry in the Massachusetts Institute of Technology, has been appointed visiting professor of chemistry at Bowdoin College for the second semester. This arrangement has been made possible through the generosity of Mrs. William J. Curtis, New York, who established a fund in memory of her husband, a member of the class of 1875 and for many years chairman of the finance committee of the college.

PROFESSOR WOLFGANG KOEHLER, of Berlin, will be the non-resident lecturer in psychology at Cornell University during the second term. He will assume his work as lecturer on April 20 and will lecture at Cornell for six weeks.

During this period he will take charge of the course in systematic psychology and will hold a series of informal conferences with graduate students and members of the university faculty.

DR. FRANKLIN W. BARROWS has resigned after ten years' service as assistant state medical inspector of schools in the New York State Education Department. Dr. Barrows now becomes medical health supervisor in New Rochelle.

IN honor of thirty-one years of continuous service as superintendent of the city schools, and as a tribute to his service, the city teachers of Great Falls, Montana, recently presented Mr. Largent with a life membership in the National Education Association. Mr. Largent has presented his resignation from the superintendency effective in August.

AN oil portrait of Dr. William H. Nichols, vice-president of the New York University Council, donor of the Nichols Chemistry Building and a graduate of the class of 1870, was presented to New York University on January 10 at an informal gathering in the council room at the Washington Square Center of the university. The portrait is the gift of Mrs. William H. Nichols and is the work of George R. Boynton. The members of the council, deans and officers of the university were present at the ceremony. Dr. Elmer Ellsworth Brown, chancellor of the university, made the presentation on behalf of Mrs. Nichols.

PRESIDENT WALLACE W. ATWOOD, president of Clark University and director of the school of geography, has received the diploma from the Swedish Anthropological and Geographical Society to which he has recently been elected as foreign member.

OWEN D. YOUNG has accepted appointment on an advisory board formed by the regents of the University of the State of New York to take up a project for a new building to house the New York State Museum.

DR. ISAAC A. ABT, head of the department of pediatrics at Northwestern University's Medical School, has returned after six months' study and travel in Europe.

PROFESSOR WILLIAM B. MUNRO, of the department of government of Harvard University, and Assistant Professor Arthur Burkhard, of the Germanic department, will be on leave of absence during the first half of the academic year 1929–30.

DR. EMMA MARSHALL DENKINGER has resigned as dean of Wheaton College in order to continue research work in England.

DR. LIVINGSTON FARRAND, president of Cornell University, left Ithaca on January 29 for a three weeks' archeological journey which will take him to Guatemala and other points in Central America and the West Indies. While in Guatemala Dr. Farrand will inspect the many evidences of an earlier civilization in which that country abounds. He will be accompanied by Dr. Louis Knudson, plant physiologist, of Cornell, and Professor H. F. Bosworth, former dean of the college of architecture. They will return to Ithaca on February 20.

WILBUR T. CLEMENS, for several years head of the department of sociology of Syracuse University, has been appointed to direct courses in educational evangelism to be given by the Greater New York Federation of Churches in cooperation with Columbia University Extension School.

THE first of a series of three lectures on "The New China" will be given by Dr. Jeremiah Whipple Jenks, research professor of government at New York University, on February 4. Dr. Jenks also will lecture on February 6 and 8. While these lectures are given primarily for the benefit of the faculty members and students of the university, the general public is invited.

DR. TRUMAN L. KELLEY, of Stanford University, recently lectured at the University of Minnesota on "The Mental Process of Discovery" and "The Use of Human Judgments in the Investigation of Future Values," and at the University of Iowa on "The Interrelationship between Method of Research and Field of Investigation."

DR. WILLIAM C. BAGLEY, of Teachers College, Columbia University, recently addressed the members of the Psychology Club of the Jamaica Training School for Teachers on "Progress Made in Psychology in 1928."

Dr. A. Monroe Stowe, professor of education at Randolph-Macon Woman's College, who during the academic year 1927–28 made a cooperative survey of the curricular needs of Washington and Lee University, will address the Association of Virginia Colleges on February 8 and 9 on "Cooperative College Curriculum Reconstruction."

Dr. Henry Fairfield Osborn, president of the American Museum of Natural History, spoke on the evening of January 9 in the University Playhouse, Washington Square College, under the auspices of the New York University Philosophical Society. His topic was "The Borderland between Science and Philosophy."

Dr. John Dewey, member of the Laureate Chapter of Kappa Delta Pi, an honor society in education, will address the society at its annual dinner February 26 at the Hotel Cleveland, Cleveland, Ohio. With this address the society inaugurates its lectureship to which eminent educators and scientists will be invited as speakers. Kappa Delta Pi now has a membership of nearly 10,000 in its 55 chapters.

A dinner was recently given at the Union League Club in commemoration of the seventy-fifth anniversary of the founding of Lincoln University, the pioneer institution in America for the higher education of the Negro. Dr. John M. T. Finney, of Baltimore, president of the board of trustees; Dr. Robert R. Moton, principal of Tuskegee Institute, Alabama, and Dr. William Hallock Johnson, president of the university, were the speakers.

Dr. Edward H. Griffin, who was dean of the college at the Johns Hopkins University from 1889 until his retirement in 1915, died on January 22 at the age of eighty-five years.

Sylvanus Morris, professor of law and formerly dean of the law school of the University of Georgia, died suddenly on January 24, at the age of seventy-five years.

Professor Wilfred H. Sherk, head of the department of mathematics of the University of Buffalo since 1913, died suddenly on January 28. He was fifty-five years of age.

Dr. John D. Logan, head of the department of English in Marquette University, died on January 24 at the age of sixty years.

Marien Foye Carter, dean of the Savage School for Physical Education, New York, and pioneer in physical health educational circles, died on January 27. She had been dean of the school since its organization in 1898.

Dr. James T. Mackey, principal of the Henry Snyder Junior High School of Jersey City, died suddenly on January 25 at the age of sixty-eight years. In point of service Dr. Mackey was the oldest principal in Jersey City schools, having taught and supervised for more than thirty-five years.

Professor M. J. M. Hill, emeritus professor of mathematics in the University of London, died on January 11 at his residence at Golders Green at the age of seventy-two years. He retired from the Astor chair of mathematics at University College, London, in 1924, after forty years of service to the college and to the university.

Dr. F. C. Ferry, president of Hamilton College, was elected president of the New York State Association of Education, organized on January 29 by representatives of New York colleges and universities at a meeting in Hunter College. The association, which replaces an organization of the same kind that disbanded some time ago, will hold its annual meetings in conjunction with the Educational Convocation at Albany, held each year by the Board of Regents. The programs of the meetings will be planned by a committee consisting of Dr. Frederick B. Robinson, president of City College, *chairman;* Dr. Henry T. Moore, president of Skidmore College, and Dr. James Sullivan, of the State Department of Education, at whose call the association assembled. In addition to electing officers the members of the association discussed junior colleges, honorary degrees, credits for extension courses and standards for summer sessions.

The Ohio State University Press announces the establishment of a new educational journal to be known as the *Journal of Higher Education.* It is the hope of the press that the magazine will be a national medium of publication for materials dealing with the educational and personnel aspects of higher education. It will be under the editorial direction of W. W.

Charters, of the Ohio State University, and a group of widely known associate editors. The business management of the journal is under the direction of W. E. Pearce, university publisher. The first issue will appear in September, 1929.

THE series of articles on "Urban Influences on Higher Education in England," recently published in this magazine by President Kolbe, of the Polytechnic Institute of Brooklyn, forms the first part of a book entitled "Urban Influences on Higher Education in England and the United States," which has just been published by the American Association for Adult Education in their series, "Studies in Adult Education" (The Macmillan Company, 1928). This is said to be the first sustained effort to trace the development of a particular urban type of higher education in the two great English-speaking nations.

THE HONORABLE ELIHU ROOT, secretary of state from 1905 to 1909 and member of the Permanent Court of Arbitration at the Hague; Mr. J. L. Garvin, editor of the London *Observer* and of the "Encyclopaedia Britannica," and Mr. William Allen White, editor of the *Emporia Gazette,* have consented to act in 1929 as a committee of judges for the annual *Yale Review* award of two thousand dollars. The award will be made this year to the author of the article on a current question in national or international affairs, appearing in the present volume of *The Yale Review,* which the committee deems "most deserving of this special recognition for its excellence." This volume of *The Yale Review* will close with the summer issue, published in June, 1929, and the decision of the judges will be announced in the autumn issue, published in September.

THE Valley Forge Military Academy, formerly known as the Devon Park Hotel, was destroyed by fire early on January 18 with a loss estimated at $500,000. This is covered by insurance.

THE will of Henry C. Munger, of Plainfield, N. J., provides charitable bequests of $960,000. Mount Holyoke receives $200,000 and Northfield School, $100,000.

A GIFT of $100,000 has been made by Dr. and Mrs. W. Wilbur Beckett to the endowment fund of the school of medicine of the University of Southern California.

PRESIDENT M. G. BRUMBAUGH and J. J. Oller, president of the board of trustees, have made possible the erection of a president's home at Juniata College. President Brumbaugh has given $25,000 and Mr. Oller, $10,000.

ARRANGEMENTS have been completed whereby the department of zoology at the University of Texas will have $135,000 to be used in the development of graduate instruction and research during the next eight years. Approximately one half of this sum will be given by the General Education Board; the rest will be raised by the university. The zoological staff plans to use a portion of this fund for technical assistance and for fellowships.

THE projected institute of biology at Harvard University, which has been brought within reach of the university by a gift of $2,000,000 from the International Education Board and which will include not only a building in which the university's various branches of biology, now scattered, can be brought together and enlarged, but also provision for the endowment and development of biological research, will take definite shape in the spring, when, it is hoped, actual construction of the building will begin. The project will cost at least $6,000,000. The International Education Board offered to add another $1,000,000 when the university has raised an additional amount of $3,000,000. The committee on the building, composed of representatives of the various biology divisions in the university, has prepared and submitted to Dr. Lowell the building plans, stating the requirements for departmental space. Of the $6,000,000 for the institute, $4,000,000 will be devoted to the endowment and development of biological research by an addition of new men to the staffs of the various departments.

WILLIAM H. KINGSLEY, treasurer of New York University, announces that the Centennial Fund of New York University, of which Percy S. Straus is chairman, has been enlarged by gifts amounting to $371,310 since the annual meeting of the council of the university last October. The largest gift, $250,000, was received from Dr. William H. Nichols, to be applied immediately toward the construction of a new building for the university's School of Education. In making the gift Dr. Nichols stipulated that the full amount be returned eventually to the general endowment fund of the university. An anonymous donor gave $24,007 for the purchase of books for the research library of the Washington Square College. Dr. Lucius Littauer gave an additional $7,500 for study of the prevention and cure of pneumonia, under the direction of Dr. William H. Park, of the Medical College. In the last three years Mr. Littauer has given $55,500 to the university for this purpose. Other gifts included $1,000 from William M. Kingsley toward the construction of the new School of Education building, and $2,000 from Paul M. Warburg for the faculty fund.

THE new library of the University of Rochester being built at a cost of $1,500,000 is nearing completion. The building will have a capacity of 1,000,000 volumes, with extensions which would accommodate an additional 1,000,000. It is said to be one of the most fully equipped university libraries in this country. The library will have four floors, with a book tower of 19 levels, 188 feet high, adjoining it. Eleven levels in the tower will have a capacity of 45,000 volumes each, and seven circular stacks will hold 22,000 each. With the extra space supplied by the basement the tower section will accommodate 1,000,000 volumes. The main part of the building will have reading rooms for special courses, faculty and seminary libraries, browsing rooms, general reference rooms and stack rooms with a capacity of more than 50,000 volumes.

A CABLEGRAM from Paris reports that an international center for psychological research, the first of its kind in the world, will be erected on a site donated by the French government at the chateau of Louis XIV in Sceaux, six miles south of Paris. The announcement is attributed to Dr. Serge Yourievitch, vice-president of L'Institut Générale Psychologique. Dr. Yourievitch sailed on January 30 for New York to study American laboratory equipment and endeavor to interest American psychologists in the enterprise. The site at Sceaux consists of 500 acres and it is hoped that 100,000,000 francs (almost $4,000,000) will be spent for buildings and laboratories. Part of this fund is expected from various governments. Dr. Yourievitch stated that the center has been planned on a cooperative basis for various types of research work now carried on by universities and laboratories scattered over the world.

HARRY PAYNE WHITNEY has offered up to $750,000 to the American Museum of Natural History for the construction of a new wing to house collections of bird life, provided the city contributes equally.

A GIFT of $1,000,000, to be administered in the "cause of better understanding among all mankind," announced on January 17 in celebration on Sunday of his seventieth birthday by Lucius N. Littauer, glove manufacturer, former representative in congress of New York City and Gloversville, N. Y. In his deed of gift, Mr. Littauer states: "I trust that you will devote the funds at your disposal to altruistic activities of every nature, charitable, humanitarian, educational, religious and communal; that in the advancement and promotion of such activities, you will include research and publication, the establishment and maintenance of altruistic agencies and institutions, and the aid of any such agencies and institutions already established, the functions of which tend to advance the public welfare. The care of the sick, the young, the aged, the helpless; the encouragement of recreation and self-improvement for all people should always merit your consideration and assistance."

THREE quarters of the $2,000,000 Coolidge fund for the Clarke School for the Deaf at Northampton, Mass., has been raised, according to an announcement made by Earl P. Charlton, of Fall River, national chairman of the fund. "Of the $1,500,000 now given or pledged," he stated, "$255,000 in contingent gifts and $50,000 is contingent upon our raising the full amount by March 4. To claim these gifts is an additional spur to prompt giving by those who wish to share in making this fund a success."

A CONTRIBUTION of $150,000 has been promised by Mr. John D. Rockefeller, Jr., toward the fund of $600,000 still needed to complete the buildings of the Fieldston School, New York City, the new pre-professional and high school of the Ethical Culture School. The amount originally raised for the school was $1,000,000, of which Mr. Rockefeller donated $250,000, but the sum was found insufficient and a campaign for an additional $600,000 has been started. Mr. Rockefeller's gift was made on condition that the remaining $450,000 be raised by June 29, 1930. Almost $200,000 of this has been pledged. Although the school is not fully completed, part of the new plant was opened last October, and the school is now being conducted with about 460 pupils and a faculty of sixty.

BY the will of the late Elihu B. Taft, attorney, who died on January 13, his estate, valued at about $100,000, is offered to Burlington, Vt., for the erection of a schoolhouse.

IN response to a constantly increasing demand, the Polytechnic Institute of Brooklyn has recently supplemented its graduate courses in chemistry by the establishment of a Graduate School of Chemistry and Engineering, offering courses leading to the degrees of master of science in chemistry, master of civil engineering, master of electrical engineering and master of mechanical engineering. One hundred and twenty-eight graduate students, representing thirty-eight American and five foreign institutions, are enrolled in the various courses. The majority of the students are engineers in the great industrial plants of the metropolitan area; the remainder are employees in municipal, state and federal departments or are teachers of science in schools and colleges.

As a result of the success that has attended the experiment of assigning teachers to the Brooklyn Children's Museum to give lectures to the school children of that borough, the New York City board of superintendents on October 11 decided to try a similar plan of cooperation with the American Museum of Natural History for the benefit of school children residing in the Boroughs of Manhattan and the Bronx. Accordingly the board of superintendents asked the board of education to approve the establishment of three additional substitute teaching positions in Public School No. 93, Manhattan, so that these teachers may be assigned to work with public school pupils in connection with the Natural History Museum. Associate Superintendent Joseph M. Sheehan, in recommending the extended program of cooperation with the museum authorities of the city, reported that the plan in Brooklyn, where several substitute teachers have been assigned since May, 1925, to work in connection with the Children's Museum of the Brooklyn Institute of Arts and Science "has been extraordinarily successful."

SPECIAL CORRESPONDENCE

THE OCCUPATIONS OF WELLESLEY GRADUATES

NINETY members (30 per cent.) of the class of 1928 which left Wellesley last June have found their niches and are at work in the big world, according to a recent report of Dr. Alice I. Perry Wood, director of the Personnel Bureau of Wellesley College. Of these, twenty-eight are teaching in schools and colleges and the other sixty-two are engaged in occupations which vary from research to advertising, with salaries ranging from $500 for part-time work to $1,800. Of the other 70 per cent., fifty-seven are studying, here and abroad, subjects ranging from nursing to philosophy. Two are at Oxford, three at the Sorbonne, one at the University of Grenoble, and two at the University of Florence. Three members of the class of 1928 have taken up the study of law. Some are married, some engaged, some staying at home, some traveling. Of the 298 members of the class only twenty-six who want positions have not yet found them.

Of those that are working, it is significant to note that only 30 per cent. are teaching, while 69 per cent. are working at different occupations, including social work, library work, secretarial and clerical work, drafting, technics, editorial work, selling—a range so wide it is hard to scan. Perhaps there is no more certain way of estimating the changes in the attitude toward occupations for women in the last fifty years than to look over the history of the occupational or personnel bureau of a large woman's college such as Wellesley. The question "After College What?" requires far deeper consideration than it did fifty years ago when women's colleges were young and when their graduates were destined, as a group, to be teachers. Back in the seventies teaching was practically the only respectable profession for women, and the pioneers of those first college days entered it, not only as a matter of course but because they wished to have a part in the broadening of educational opportunities for women. Of the seventeen alumnae of the class of 1880 who answered the questionnaire sent out by the Personnel Bureau recently, nine were employed. Seven of these are engaged in education, one is a doctor and another a librarian. Since 1900, however, the percentage of teachers among employed alumnae hovers around and below 50 per cent., a much lower percentage.

The growth of the college and the widening of the vocational field for women have been simultaneous. Of course one must consider that in the class of 1880 there were twenty-seven students, while in 1923 there were 278, and that the greater numbers represent so many added types of students and correspondingly varied interests, and a greater range of occupations after college. It is interesting to note the steadily diminishing figures for the teaching profession in successive classes:

	Teaching	Number of graduates
1900–04	135	718
1905–09	163	1,183
1910–14	208	1,406
1915–19	243	1,534
1920–21	193	687
1922	81	389
1923	55	278
1924	59	359
1925	64	351
1926	49	340
1927	34	332

The Personnel Bureau at Wellesley is a highly organized and efficient machine. It is the central repository which accumulates such facts as scholarship, psychological tests, honors, health records, contacts and extra-curricular activities which will help in sympathetic placing and vocational advice. The collection of this material is facilitated by the Personnel Board, made up of the president of the college, and the three deans of freshmen, college and residence, the director of the Personnel Bureau, the college physicians, the college recorder, the professor of the psychology department and the associate in the Personnel Bureau. This board brings into close cooperation the administrative centers of the college, and acts as a central clearing house for information concerning the individual students. A cumulative record card is kept, in the Personnel Bureau, for every student, containing her history year by year during her college career. Photographs taken before freshman year are appended to this card to be supplanted later by a senior photograph. In order to have the most complete knowledge of the individual, the Personnel Bureau requests from members of the faculty personality ratings based on the following characteristics: appearance, power of comprehension, memory, cooperativeness, integrity, temperament, healthiness of mental life, sense of humor. Blanks for these ratings are sent out every year, so that the bureau has these estimates of individual students every year for every course. The interview also figures highly in the student's personnel care. Each student has a personal interview every year with an officer of the Personnel Bureau. According to Dr. Wood, the old process of interviewing seniors and helping them in a choice of a vocation was quite unsatisfactory. "The inadequacy of this process is seen after a very slight acquaintance with the helplessness of many of our seniors, and the dismay with which some of them try to fit their courses to some occupation, when they have chosen them along lines of popular courses, popular professors or room-mate's advice." That vocational guidance begun during the freshman year and continued through a student's four years will help the average girl to plan her college life more intelligently and more purposefully is Dr. Wood's firm belief.

It is not to be gathered from this article that Wellesley is leaning toward the vocational school. Its atmosphere and aims are academic, but it can not overlook the fact that its graduates are engaged in all kinds of work and that an astonishingly small number are unemployed and unmarried. Therefore, the college is doing its best, realizing the large part it plays in the lives of its students and graduates, to help the women who pass through its doors to evaluate their capabilities and thus to take up intelligently their careers.

ELIZABETH P. MAY

DISCUSSION

THE CULTURAL INFLUENCE OF THE "TALKIES"

The talkies will make Hollywood the slang center of the United States. . . . A wisecrack recorded in Hollywood will be heard in all corners of the country months before the same quip could travel from town to town across the continent with a road show or a vaudeville troupe.

WADE WERNER, prophesying in a newspaper article appearing in the California capital of moviedom on December 8, 1928, broadcasts this comforting news to the world at large. The prospect which his words conjure up should be particularly interesting to the teachers of the children in American schools. What influence are the talking movies to have on the speech habits of those who hear them? What is going to happen to the American-English language and to American culture generally once every small-town movie house is equipped to reproduce night after night the language which the current cult of realism in all things literary will demand of successful screen plays?

The outlook is by no means assuring. Judging by the past there is little to indicate that moving-picture producers will be actuated by any principles of social responsibility which extend beyond tangible results in the box office. The written conversations already necessary for the silent pictures have never been models of good English. Their influence, however, has been small because the emphasis in the movies has always been on action rather than on speech. It has not mattered much what the actors said—though there has been a brave attempt at making the lips of the players seem to say what the screen (an instant later) recorded in the written words. What the actors *did* carried the drama, and the occasional direct conversations, aside from a few borrowings from the vaudeville stage, have probably not had an appreciably bad effect on national habits of speech. Alongside the comic strips, the movies up to the present moment have been relatively harmless. They have not ranked with illiterate or foreign home environment, with street and playground associations, with the vaudeville shows, or with cheap books and magazines as influences which make for degeneration of the language and the consequent lowering of the general cultural standard.

In the last years of this third decade of a wonder-working century we are witnessing the end of the first phase of the moving-picture industry. Apparently no one is quite sure what the second phase will be—one writer suggests that the movies are committing suicide.[1] But whatever the second phase is, it will be upon us shortly; it has already arrived in our large cities, and it will reach down to touch the whole population of America, urban and rural, just as the first phase has done. The unique contribution of the "new movies" will clearly be the spoken word synchronized with the dramatization of events on the screen. The speech level of the Hollywood "lot" seems likely to be reproduced millions of times in the ears of millions of people, including practically 100 per cent. of the children of the country from the kindergarten to college.

No one can doubt that this tremendous reiteration of the spoken word under conditions tending greatly to emphasize a certain style of language will have its effect on the speech habits of impressionable young people who have no mind-set or philosophy to resist it. Nor can we hope that the producers will make willingly any altruistic effort to raise the level of the great majority of "talkies" above the vaudeville-show patter of the present moment. There is no particular incentive for the makers of commercial pictures, with or without the talking accompaniment, to do anything more than appeal to the rather low group tastes of the masses of people, reproducing for them their own language with appropriate profane, suggestive and obscene decorations such as have delighted the "groundlings" since Shakespeare's time. We may expect no higher standard in the "out-loud" movies than we have previously had in the pictures themselves. We may look forward to no noticeably higher ideal in the "realistic" talking movies than we have had in recent stage successes which have masqueraded behind the amusingly naïve contention that "This is pure art" the most daringly profane and pornographic literature since the drama of

[1] Gilbert Seldes, "The Movies Commit Suicide," *Harper's Magazine*, November, 1928.

the Restoration Period in England—a span of two centuries and a half.

Mr. Werner says on this point:

Modern stage plays with a high profanity content can not be made into talking pictures without considerable deletion of language likely to excite the scissor muscles of the screen censors. Even original movie dialogue has to be carefully composed to satisfy picturegoers accustomed to stage profanity, without offending censors *not yet ready* [the italics are not Mr. Werner's] to allow such profanity on the talking screen.

James Gleason, the author of "Is Zat So?" and other plays, who is writing talking-picture dialogue now, is working out a vocabulary of expletives which sound nearly enough like the cusswords of the up-to-date stage to pacify the spectator who would rebel at substitutions like "My Goodness!" or "Dear Me!" and yet are utterly innocent of profanity in themselves.

Perhaps censorship will save the moral situation, although it is not impossible that the censors who are "not yet ready" for the last word in profane speech will find it as hard to keep profanity out of the "talkies" as other types of censorship have in the fields of the novel and the modern drama. Whatever the event in that direction, he is indeed a sanguine observer of the present-day trend who believes that we shall hear good English from the talking movies. Inherent in the situation is the plain demand of the mass mind for something easy and for something broadly humorous. Slang, profanity, even obscenity have always satisfied that demand and probably always will. It is, of course, altogether true that the language level of any people can not rise higher than its cultural and intellectual level. It is a question—still debatable it is to be hoped—whether in America our average cultural and intellectual plane is above the movie and vaudeville standard of the present moment.

RALPH L. HENRY

CARLETON COLLEGE

QUOTATIONS

EDUCATIONAL VISITORS FROM ARGENTINA

EDUCATIONAL exchanges have for the most part followed East and West lines. The cultural influences of Southern Europe have, however, also passed through the tropics and found fertile and extensive territory below the equator and its later exchanges have followed chiefly the sea paths of the pioneers. It is significant, therefore, that a group of educators have come all the way from Argentina to acquaint themselves at first hand with what is going forward in the United States in the varied fields of teaching. Among them is Dr. Ernesto Nelson, supervisor of secondary education, with three doctors of medicine to inquire into methods of instruction in the medical schools, three doctors of chemistry and an electrical engineer, besides professors of pedagogy, English history and other university subjects and teachers in the elementary and secondary schools.

While young men and women have come from South America to study in our universities, this is, so far as is remembered, the first considerable group of teachers that has come. They have distinguished precedent. Over eighty years ago Dr. Sarmiento visited the educational institutions of Europe and America and was especially influenced by Horace Mann. Returning to Argentina, he succeeded in establishing a department of education, of which he later became minister. He came back to America again in 1865 as minister to the United States and remained till 1868, when he was chosen president of the Argentine Republic. During his administration he gave first attention to education. One of his books had to do with "The Schools, the Basis of Prosperity in the United States." Another was a life of Abraham Lincoln.

The coming of this group adds new strands to the early tenuous connections established by one man, and gives promise of a closer cultural relationship along North and South lines. It is not a one-sided exchange as is manifested by the coming of a Justice of the Appellate Court of Argentina, a Dr. Alfredo Colmo, as a "visiting professor," to give a course of lectures at Columbia University. The educational entente has a basis of interest each in the other, without which it could not flourish.—*The New York Times*.

EDUCATIONAL RESEARCH AND STATISTICS

COLLEGE ATHLETICS AND SCHOLARSHIP[1]

THIS study was made at the suggestion of the Carnegie Foundation for the Advancement of Teaching, and the technique used is that suggested in the article "College Athletics and Scholarship" found in the twenty-second annual report of this society.

In the first place the two following principles were laid down: (1) An athlete is a male undergraduate mentioned in the college year book as having been a member of a varsity or freshman team, even if he was not awarded a letter.

(2) A non-athlete is any other male member of the group.

The class examined was the one entering Cornell College in September, 1922, and February, 1923, and graduating in June, 1926 (normally). The following limitations were set upon the students examined:

(a) Only men were considered.
(b) Men who graduated with the class (June, 1926) but did not enter with the class (September, 1922, or February, 1923) were disregarded.
(c) Men dropping out before completing one semester were disregarded.
(d) Men entering with twenty or more hours of advanced work were disregarded.
(e) Men entering with their class but who did not finish until 1927 were also considered.

Six sports were considered: football, baseball, track, cross country, basketball and wrestling. The freshmen had teams only in football and basketball. A total of forty athletes and sixty-seven non-athletes were examined. A series of ten questions was asked in regard to these athletes and non-athletes. Below are the ten questions and with each question the answer in summary form.

Question 1. What percentage obtained degrees?

Answer:	Athletes	43 per cent.
	non "	33 per cent.
	non "	30 per cent.
	Difference	10 per cent.

Question 2. What percentage were on probation sometime during their course?

Answer:	Athletes	53 per cent.
	Difference	23 per cent.

Question 3. What was the average number of years spent in college?

Answer:	Athletes	3.08 years
	non "	2.43 "
	Difference	.65 "

Question 4. What was the average number of hours carried?

Answer:	Athletes	15.61 semester hours
	non "	14.52 " "
	Difference	1.09 " "[2]

Question 5. What was the average grade?[3]

Answer:	Athletes	1.34
	non "	.98
	Difference	.36[2]

Question 6. What was the average intelligence score?[4]

Answer:	Athletes	124.87
	non "	121.68
	Difference	3.19[2]

Question 7. How do the various sports rank in the grades of those participating in them?

Answer: Rank	Sport	Grade
1	Cross country	1.31
2	Track	1.14
3	Basketball	1.07
4	Baseball	1.01
5	Average athlete	.98
6	Two or more sports	.97
7	Wrestling	.95
8	Football	.92

Question 8. How do the various sports rank in intelligence scores?

Answer: Rank	Sport	Score
1	Track	126.06
2	Average athlete	124.87
3	Football	124.45
4	Basketball	122.55
5	Two or more sports	122.24
6	Cross country	118.00
7	Wrestling	116.00
8	Baseball	110.00

1 An abstract of a study made at Cornell College, Mount Vernon, Iowa.

2 This difference has no significance statistically, being less than three times its probable error.

3 The literal grades A, B, C, D, E, F were translated into the numerical grades 3, 2, 1, 0, −1, −2 respectively.

4 On entrance to Cornell College, each of these students took an intelligence test issued by the American Council on Education.

Interesting comparisons can be made between these intelligence scores and the average scholastic grades made in the various sports. Track men did well in both; football men were high in intelligence but low in grades, while wrestlers were low in both. The athletes as a whole, the track, football and basketball men and those engaging in two or more sports all ranked higher in intelligence scores than the non-athletes.

Question 9. What proportion took hard and easy courses and how did their grades compare therein?

Answer: In order to rank the courses as hard and easy sixty-three of them were considered, and for each course the percentage of students that received higher grades than their average semester grade was calculated. These courses had a wide range of percentages, so, following the normal frequency curve, the courses were divided in five groups and rated as hard, medium hard, average, medium easy and easy, respectively. For instance, there were two courses in which none of the students received higher grades than their average semester grades, while in another course there was 88 per cent. of the students who received a grade higher than their average grade. The first two courses were, of course, rated as hard and the last as easy. There were seven hard, ten medium hard, thirty average, ten medium easy and six easy courses.

In the hard courses 17 per cent. of the athletes and 11 per cent. of the non-athletes were enrolled.

In the easy courses 15 per cent. of the athletes and 10 per cent. of the non-athletes were enrolled.

	Grades: Hard courses	Grades: Easy courses
non-Athletes	1.31	2.18
"	.68	1.74
Difference	.63	.44[2]

Question 10. What percentage hovered about the passing or danger line?

Answer: Two steps were used in determining the passing line: *First:* The courses most widely taken by the men were selected, *i.e.*, the courses in which at least sixteen of the men in this class were enrolled.[5]

Second: The percentages of the athletes and non-athletes taking these popular courses with a grade of either C or D were calculated.

Grade	Athletes Per cent.	non-Athletes Per cent.
C	51.5	45.9
D	16.9	15.9
Total	68.4	61.8

GENERALIZATIONS FROM THESE DATA

(1) The data are based on too small a number of students for any very significant conclusions to be made.

(2) The athletes stay in college somewhat longer than the non-athletes and a larger proportion of them graduate.

(3) The difference in scholarship between the athletes and non-athletes is negligible.

(4) Some of the sports apparently produce lower grades in their participants than others, but we have no assurance that the same results would take place in some other college or in another class in the same college.

(5) Those students participating in two or more sports are rather low in scholarship.

(6) Intelligence and scholarship do not always correlate among athletes.

(7) Athletes, as a whole, are no more "dumb-bells" than the rest of the students.

(8) Athletes seem to be a trifle more fond of the easy courses than do the non-athletes.

(9) Athletes do not dodge the hard courses as much as the non-athletes do.

(10) Too many students, both athletes and non-athletes, are just "getting by" in the popular courses.

(11) Very little difference in the percentage of athletes and non-athletes getting C's or D's in the popular courses.

(12) No evidence to show that participation in athletics at Cornell College during the years 1922–26 caused the grades of those participating to fall materially below those not participating.

(13) Further evidence needed before we can dogmatically say that the college athlete is a poorer or better student than his non-athletic brother.

MARK E. HUTCHINSON
CORNELL COLLEGE,
MOUNT VERNON, IOWA

[5] See "College Athletics and Scholarship," *op. cit.*, page 64, footnote 1, for method used. The men students at Cornell from 1922–27 averaged about 330 annually.

EDUCATIONAL REVIEW

Edited by WILLIAM McANDREW

MATTERS OF MOMENT

Schoolmasters and Europe.—This is the season when every fair-sized city has a series of lectures upon European trips. Some have lantern slides; some have pictures passed around. The schoolman's mail brings alluring circulars inviting to mountains high and cities populous. In the past ten years my cousin Harriet has toured through every civilized country of the globe without leaving Chicago. She took a boat to Benton Harbor once and was miserably seasick from the time she left the Municipal Pier until the friendly breakwater at the mouth of the St. Jo. received her in his sheltering arm. She threw away her return ticket and bought a place in a jostling autobus.

Seasickness.—If you ever have experienced the all-gone sensation of that upset of the nervous system which the continuing and unreasonable pitching and tossing of a vessel brings to pass, by means, the wise ones say, of disturbance of the liquids in the semicircular canals of the ear, the organs of equilibrium, you will not condemn my lady cousin for her adherence to America first—land, not water, where my fathers died. Even so short a trial as the crossing from Dover to Calais engenders such moanings of despair, such abandonment of hope, patience and philosophy, that men who have endured, with Roman patience, sieges of bodily pain, wail like ill-trained children.

Mrs. Annie Hitchcock found it desirable to make many crossings of the Atlantic but always with woeful attacks of the dread disturbance. Sometimes a week or ten days in a hotel in the nearest European city was required before she could be up and about. On one voyage, she says, having engaged a woman nurse for the trip over, that useful companion proposed the belladonna plaster. Mrs. Hitchcock tried it. Miracle! Not an unhappy hour, not a meal missed. On one returning voyage, as the ship was leaving Southampton, our lady made the acquaintance of a girl teacher who had saved and borrowed money enough to cover the long-dreamed-of excursion. "I'll be deathly sick," she said. "On the calmest days I lay in my berth and inhaled the ship smell, the sickening odor of the kitchen, of damp cloths and bilge-water. I am elected for seven days of concentrated misery." Mrs. Hitchcock furnished an extra belladonna plaster. Magic, again! Our little teacher spent the days as blithely as if on shore and valiantly ate into the table profits of the steamship company. I have a relative, a woman of slender architecture, who inevitably was rocked into wretchedness by the cradle of every deep she tried: the crossing to Havana, the short voyage from New York to Norfolk and even the simple night journey of the Fall River Line. None of the specifics perpetually advertised in travel-journals were of any comfort to her. She learned of the Hitchcock device. I have seen her on a wallowing voyage of almost constant storms cheerily promenading the deck or sitting before the rack-protected table in the dining saloon with all the windows battened tight against the spray, she partaking of twenty-two meals out of a total of twenty-two afforded. I heard two women and one man to whom this cheerful Samaritaness had given plasters say they had usually been seasick but on this occasion felt fine all the way over. I, myself, told all of this to the ship's doctor of the *Ryndam* who did not laugh at it but remarked that it was quite probable that osmosis from a belladonna or an opium plaster would give the nerves the needed correction to prevent the common upset. Of course I did not ask any other physician. You know what happens to one idea when a second doctor has a whack at it. But in the proper fashion of the true researcher I will not generalize but keep within the facts, to wit:

Number reporting having used belladonna plasters	6
Number reporting escape from seasickness	6
Median	6
Correlation	Per cent., 100
Number seen by me who said they were wearing 'em	5
Number of such whom I saw daily unailing	5
Average	5
Correlation	Per cent., 100
Number of physicians questioned	1
Number saying the plaster should be efficacious	1
Per cent.	100

On the morning of the sailing of your vessel, before she leaves the wharf, you retire to the privacy of your stateroom or of your hotel chamber. You remove from the belladonna side of your plaster the tissue protector. Confidently and cheerily you place the comforter upon your skin at the area commonly called the pit of the stomach. You place your hands over it and stand in the position of the pink-faced worthy portrayed in M. Vibert's picture, "After a Good Dinner at the Abbot's." Meantime while the warmth necessary for adhesion is functioning, you say aloud: "Great is osmosis. Every day in every way this shall do better and better." Common politeness requires you, out of consideration for the eleven fellow travelers and one doctor to whom I have introduced you, to remind yourself that the percentage of plasteric failures is 0, and that you owe a duty to the ancient and honorable guild of crossers of the sea. Closer than a brother will this preserver of composure cling, even through your daily baths, until, at last, on terra firma once more, there comes the quick sharp pang of parting.

Who go abroad?—What reason is there, anyhow, why you should get yourself to Europe? The duty lies in the fact of your present condition of undevelopment. Even the stupidest traveler tells you, "Life means more to me since I went." Until you have been over your mind is but a Mikado's empire of the old days, isolated, too narrow, stunted, meager, contracted, strangled. There is a complex of inadequacy which nowadays is aggravated by noting what a large number of your acquaintances are superior to you in this regard. You know that you owe to your community, to your profession, to your service, that expanded broadmindedness which is made easier than ever in our epoch by no less than fifteen first-class transatlantic steamship lines offering hundreds of comfortable vessels. It is worth saving for; it justifies undertaking every sort of honest supplementary employment to add to your salary; it warrants reducing comforts to-day and cutting living expenses down, also staying away from shows. It is worth borrowing some money at reasonable rates. If any philanthropic, lucky person wants to donate something to your school, shoo him away from the idea of prize essays and other rewards for children doing their regular duty. Get him to establish a travel fund whereby teachers may be helped to make a journey to the Old World.

The cost.—My neighbor and his wife visited Holland, Germany, Switzerland,

France, England and Scotland, leaving New York July 4, landing there September 7, for $812, the two of them. George Stonehill, Chicago, told me yesterday that himself and wife can live comfortably abroad when not on railroad trains at $2.90 per day, the two, *tout compris*—which, he says, means, room, two beds, hot and cold running water, heat, light, breakfast, luncheon, dinner and use of a bath. At this rate it is foolish to arrive at your American port of departure before the time of sailing. The worst financial exasperation of the journey is the steamers' fare. All of them waste an enormous amount of food for which you pay. They have imitated and surpassed one another until the most modest of them confronts simple-living Americans with elaborate courses every meal, an offering of bouillon and sandwiches between breakfast and luncheon, a perambulating collation in the middle of the afternoon, a late repast after dinner, a buffet open all the time from which free food is daintily dispensed. There is no reason for this lavish ostentation. What could be saved in expense of it, cut from the price of your ticket, would reduce your liability to illness and bring you home a happier and a less portly citizen.

An estimate of the cost is easy these days. The American Express Company, with agencies everywhere in the United States, has developed a travel service remarkably detailed as to costs. This company has diagrams of all the ships, fare-tables for railroads and omnibuses all over the world, and a corps of the best-mannered, accommodating men-behind-the-counter to be found anywhere. The company has gathered up the extras which formerly disconcerted budgets made beforehand. It will advise you that the following fees for the ship's company are common: $5 for the man who waits on you at table, $5 for the one who fills your bathtub with salt water every morning, $5 for the room steward who brings you orange-juice and coffee before you get up, $5 for the man on deck who tucks your rug around you, $1.50 for the use of the rug, $1.50 for the rent of the chair, $1 for the band. Everybody seems to pay these fees. The steamship companies could do it if they cut down their table. Everybody eats too much on board as well as on shore.

When you travel by train you always entrust your baggage to official porters. They meet you at the entrance to the station, they find a compartment and seat for you. When your train enters a station you raise a window and call a porter. You pay what amounts to four cents, American money, for each valise carried; eight cents, each, for the large, heavy ones. In an American railway terminal you may preserve your dignity and your handbag in spite of the expensive colored gentlemen who scorn anything short of a quarter of a dollar, but in Europe, no one without enduring withering contempt of all the world may do without the help of these uniformed carriers. Even if I had no bag it seems to me I ought to hand a coin to one of these gentle men, for, believe me, they are the incarnation of politeness, faithfulness, help and good nature.

The American Express Company will tell you another comforting thing. Hotel tips have ceased to be the annoying and mortifying nuisance of the old days. Your bill includes heat, light, lodging and the delicate offering they call breakfast. In place of the confusing puzzle of what to give the various hotel employees you get a "service charge," 10 per cent. added to your bill. The same is true in the restaurants. If some belated hostelry or eating-place in some back country region leaves the tipping to you, give the cashier 10 per cent. and tell him it's for service.

Oh, those passports!—There is an unescapable formality that reminds you of Franklin Giddings's definition of educational administration: "the systematic way of doing things that ought not to be done at all." Add as many days more than six weeks as you can to the period allowed our Department of State for determining whether it is safe for the peace of the world to let you leave the country. Away back in antiquity there may have been some use in passports. Now they are plain red tape—contributions to the salaries of useless officials, nothing else. Next, there are the visas. The American consul of every land you want to visit puts his O. K. upon the document and taxes you. Every European nation is beckoning to American visitors with one hand and picking their pockets of passport fees with the other. Nevertheless, one chivalrous element is in the business. They want you to bring the partner of your joys and sorrows. Accordingly, one passport does for man and wife. So, hasten to the town photographer and for this belated wedding journey let the bride and groom be pictured on unmounted paper two and three quarters inches square, on which, with black ink, you sign your name, sending the print in duplicate to the honorable, the Secretary of State. Isn't it silly? One reason for the European prejudice against Americans is the distressing portraits of them hurriedly taken and exhibited on passports. As you love your country have enough exposures until madame and you approach some degree toward respectability of looks.

Before the war passports had gone with other relics of the Guelphs and Ghibellines. The state departments do not know it's over. But take the trouble to hunt up some schoolmasters and note the earnest unanimity with which English, German, French and the other teachers are giving peace, toleration and the League of Nations the top line of things taught.

Running over.—You deserve to suffer self-reproach if you overspend after your first week abroad. Spending is business and must be guided by business methods. The best and simplest traveler's bookkeeping I ever saw was that which Oliver Harkness, a Brooklyn schoolman, inflicted on himself. In his pocket notebook he had penned a table of equivalents. For instance, he had francs translated according to their value at that time into American currency:

F1	.0375
F2	.075
F3	.1125
F4	.15

and so forth, up to 100 francs; then 200, 300, and so on up to 5,000 francs. It takes an ordinary teacher fifty minutes to make such a table and is excellent exercise in multiplication, or addition and penmanship. It goes on one page of a pocket notebook three by five inches in area. Within a week five fellow travelers had copied brother Oliver's handy tables. If I were advertising anything I wanted passengers to have I would print a table like that of schoolmaster Harkness with my advertising matter upon it and hand it to every one who gets off the boat.

Mr. Harkness kept his cash account in American money, using columns headed:

No. of days from July 3 ....
Date ....
Spent to-day ....
Total spent..................
Average per day ....
Total cost of entire trip at this rate
Balance on hand ....

Here was fact and foresight on one sheet. For persons who, like teachers, have the ragged edge of bankruptcy always within visible distance, such a daily review of financial standing prevents the corrosion of the value of the last days of a journey, a distress which is as discreditable as it is unnecessary.

What to take.—One doesn't need so many items of equipment as he usually thinks he should take. The letter of credit issued by the American Express Company can be cashed, part at a time, almost anywhere. The company's travelers' checks are good in every town. The ship's purser will trade you enough small change for your landing port to get you to a hotel. He has lists of all of them from the *de luxe* ones to the modest quarters where you can be comfortable without spendthrift's remorse.

A bag holding heavier clothing and an overcoat for use on shipboard can be left without cost in the office of the steamer line in Europe and shipped at small expense to your port of departure when you embark for return. A light raincoat and umbrella are desirable. You can get laundry done in twenty-four hours everywhere. A small repair kit for clothing and its human contents is essential. But no sensible person takes from city to city more than can be carried in valises that will be carried in the racks of a compartment.

Ocean ennui.—Take no stock in the words of those that tell you that the pure restfulness of the ocean air and the glorious hues of sea and sky is one of the greatest delights of the voyage. You'll get sensibly tired of it. Everybody does who has nothing else. Clarence Wilder, who, for ten or more years, has conducted parties abroad, tells me that after the third day at sea the monotony so irritates his men and women that at half past three it reaches to such heights of fretting and complaint that he takes a book and disappears into some undiscoverable retreat until dinner time. Then his fussing constituency get over their griefs. John Finley, before sailing, accumulates a stock of tasks that must be done. He makes his daily program suitable to a high intelligence quotient: his morning, afternoon and evening brisk walk of so many circuits of the deck, his obligated working hours, and his allowance for relaxation. No ocean voyage bores him. If you should make a list of books you really want to read, if you should make some accurate estimate of how many of them you can cover in the six hours a day you intend to be industrious, if you will then discard 20 per cent. of your collection and take the rest on board (you will find some additions in the ship's library you know to be good for you), you can leave all your books in the suit case with your heavy clothing and make the crossing and return with the satisfaction of an honest man of foresight who doesn't squander the priceless gift of time. Otherwise, what have you? A laborious search for something to do, a fatuous effort to stretch trivial conversation over an area too big for it, a filling of your mind with gossip of which you would be heartily ashamed on shore, a straining of your digestive machinery due to eating as an occupation to kill time.

The diary and notebook.—Unless you write a journal of your trip you get a small proportion of the profit and joy it is able to give. A recognition of this fact is a good measure of your intelligence. It was Dr. Weir Mitchell, eminent Philadelphia mental hygienist, who persuaded, with health-giving results, his patients to take daily exercise in painting with words and representing by drawing the things around them with intent to discover the picturesque.

Your trip is a study; it is an education. It is worth the serious and constructive activities of mind you would expect to employ in a course of art or sociology or geography or language or literature. Select, then, a well-bound notebook, a thick one, as nearly as may be of the common size of books in your library, in order that hereafter it may sit with them on the shelf and may endure without being subjected to the mortification of being chucked into a pile of miscellanies on account of its unwieldy size and unsatisfactory binding. Charlie Richards went to the trouble of having a journal especially made for him, with 300 pages, loose leaves, strong linen paper, in a stout cover. Each time he pasted a picture into it he thickened the binding edge of the leaf with a strip the thickness of the paper. When he reached home the binder made the leaves into a book as thick through the back as through the front. To Charles his "Complete Works" are an enduring delight.

As to parties.—You are given opportunities to join travel parties supposed to be held together from the time you leave until the day of putting foot once more upon your home land. The manager computes your entire expense and arranges all details of sleeping places, meals and sights. By becoming one of his flock you are shown precisely what he decides you should see. Watch-dog guides worry you away from what interests you and chase you back into the herd. You see more things, mostly what you don't care for, and you digest less of what you take in. If there are accounts of party trips omitting the distress of inescapable nuisances, free from the strain of being enjoined to "move on," the narrators are practicing artistic omission. Even the extended journey you make with your intimate friend is a severe discipline. Judge Watson, who has been married forty years and who, last summer, took his one and only wife abroad, said, "It was the first European experience for either of us. My life partner has the sweetest temper vouchsafed to any woman. I am reputed an even-dispositioned companion, but on the tenth day we fell out over another art gallery and the inside of another church was almost enough to cause a separation. Most companionships are saved by adequate periods of separation, but to be together every hour in the day for weeks at a time is to run great risks of breaks in affection." Judge and Mrs. Watson made an arrangement for alternating responsibilities, day by day. "Sunday," he said, "belongs to madame. I'll take her to every blooming shop and church and gallery she names. Then Monday belongs to me. I'll amble along the quays, see the water works and explore the places where the real work of the present-day world is done. If she cares to ramble with me I am pleased. If she chooses to rest in the hotel it is agreeable. To-morrow is her day again." Two men traveling together, two women pooling their interests, can save themselves from irritation, from rips in the peplum of friendship, by an arrangement of that kind.

The guide-book.—Of course one saves a lot of waste by using good guide-books. They cost six dollars apiece if in the English language. If read on the way over they have the zest of anticipation, but every one, unless he has the mind of a Macaulay, forgets most of the bewildering details by the time he comes, in the body, close to the attractions described. The happiest travelers soon learn, unblushingly, to read the guide-book on the very spot. John Beveridge will not leave his room until he has reread the chapter covering the location he is in. He notes the things he wants to see. He arranges them in an order best for going from one to another, selects the street-car lines, and sallies forth comforted by a consciousness of foresight.

All the guide-books I ever saw omit most of the things to which the tastes of an American mere man would attract him. Oscar Burbank, Grand Rapids teacher, had a day for Marseilles. He had read, a few years before, of the opening of a marvelous waterway by which the commerce of Lyons, Valence and the other industrial cities of the Rhone can be brought, without the costly transfer to sea-going vessels, right up to the Marseilles wharves. Marseilles chapters in the guide-books say nothing of this triumph of our own day. They enlarge upon the monuments, the cathedral, the arc de triomphe, the museums, the Palais Longchamp, the zoological garden, the Chateau d'eau, and the Chateau d'If. No one in the hotel where Oscar stopped seemed able to answer his anxious question: "Où est le canal de Marseille et Rhone?" The man who sold maps couldn't tell. By hanging around the Chamber of Commerce Oscar found a business man who sketched a pencil diagram of the coast and told him where to get a trolley car for l'Estaque, six miles up the shore. Alighting from the car on a seaside beach, our Oscar put again his anxious query, "Où est le canal, le canal de Marseille au Rhone?" To which the skipper of a little power-boat answered, "It's half an hour from here, mister, and I'll take you into it and back for ten francs, thirty-seven cents, American." "I got more pure joy out of that little ride," says Oscar, "than all the Pierre Pujet sculptures and paintings and architecture in Marseilles contributed. We puffed along among steamers from Norway, Australia, Greece, New York and Algeria. We went among the clumsy dredges which the French have not outgrown. We passed big barges loading cement from the works away up on the mountain sides at the end of dizzy inclined railways, and then, *Voila! le canal!* The most remarkable canal in the world, coming out of the bottom of a limestone cliff, with noble stone piers on both sides. A tug and two barges came out of the tunnel. We went in under its generous stone arch. For over four miles this watery avenue pierces this mountain, straight to the low land beyond. The semicircular little patch of light is the opening at the other end. A tow-path of masonry runs the entire length on the right hand; another, on the left. A tablet at the portal tells how the president of the French Republic opened it in 1921. I am so gratified in finding it at last that I would wish to have an inscription added that happy Oscar Burbank visited it in 1928."

His narration moved Harry Goodison, of the Springfield high school, to say that the best thing for him in Strasbourg was not the cathedral, outside or in, but a walk on the tow-path of a canal alive with all sorts and conditions of barges. They are locking through, they are coming in from confluents originating in some unknown back country. Straight and dignified or sweeping in noble curves and lined with trees, they unite in a wide basin where the trim, able-looking, long tow-boats gather them into flotillas, and there is the opening into the Rhine far above Mainz and the conventional tourist route from Cologne. In spite of all the guide-books, most men born in our time would like to see how a city gets its water, what its industries are and how it arranges its transportation.

For instance.—Those are the things that make Rotterdam so attractive to a man. You get a taste of its quality when you board one of its steamers in New York harbor. The Holland America line makes weekly sailings. If you have a dread of dirty boats favored by cockroaches, served by stewards who excite your doubts as to the thoroughness of their washings, the cleanliness of these trim steamers with the green-and-white bands around their funnels will put them into your category of the experiences with no regrets. Perfect ministry to the comfort of passengers has been studied and perfected with Dutch thoroughness. Dean Lough selected the *Ryndam* of this line for the seat of his floating university which sailed around the world. Because of his wide culture and human interest, the ship's captain, Mynheer John Lieuwen, was put on the list of professors. Captain John could fill a chair of philosophy, sociology, geography and industry anywhere. The ships of this line will let you off at Southampton, or Boulogne, but you had better stay on board until you can walk ashore to the Wilhelminakada in the most fascinating port in the world—the old town of the dam on the river Rotte.

Go to the first stationer's or book-shop and buy a map, five cents American; and a dictionary of both languages, twenty-five cents. They advantage you 1,000 per cent. Resolve not to shout when trying to make yourself understood. Your language already has the reputation of being an unmusical tongue. Don't confirm the distaste for it by harsh noises. You are now on a continent which has perfected through centuries the refinement of speech and manners. You will live, for many days, the recipient of courtesies shown in your country only to the boss by participants of the patronage. The concierge in the little coop at the entrance of the hotel is a gentleman. It's his occupation to welcome you, discover your desires, satisfy them, be your directory and dictionary. You can properly make him your financial adviser. He loves his business, including you. You do not fee him. He's in the 10 per cent.

The curious disturbances which burn in your interior mind need not fret you if you devote a few minutes to turning a cold stream of thought on them. A desperate complex of shortcomings suffuses you as you realize that you know less than not only a few eminent personages like Mr. Mencken and Dr. Straton but than every one around you. But you may remind yourself that each person you come in contact with has met hundreds of Americans more ignorant and more poverty-blessed than you. A silence, a dignity, a gentle attitude of amusement, is not hard to assume. In a little while it will grow habitual and give you the supreme content of the *integer vitae*.

A sample.—Rotterdam lies upon the Maas which starts in France as the Meuse. By various cuttings it appropriates much water of the Rhine and other streams and gives the largest ships an exit to the North Sea. The city honors Caland, the engineer who worked out this enterprise. His monument rises near the post-office and the city hall. Up and down and roundabout, the town is pierced by animated canals lined with wide quays. Everything from everywhere is unloaded upon them and carried into the picturesque buildings in the upper stories of which reside the proprietors. Coffee, apples, baskets, automobiles, brooms, oranges, fish, soap, wood, iron, machinery and an amazing profusion of flowers line the waterways. The bank of the Maas is a business street shaded by great trees and therefore named the Boomjies. The barges penetrate into the heart of the city, threading their way between high walls and through low tunnels. You stand in an open court and hear voices below you. A canal is hidden under your feet. Rotterdam is a Venice of industry. Rotterdam works. A day in Rotterdam is worth a week in Paris, where the frequency of the sign "American Bar" insults you a dozen times a day, where rascals, spotting you as a stranger, try to sell you pornographic pictures or guide you to places where artificial wickedness is on exhibition for foreigners. There are at least four excellent and moderate-priced hotels in Rotterdam in which you can have rooms with glass doors opening upon the waterways. An industrial motion picture show continuously passes. There are ships from all quarters of the globe; there are the amazingly long Rhine-arks from the whole length of that busy stream; there are the farm boats from every part of the Netherlands; there are the elegant little office motors which tend the commercial houses up and down the Maas; there is the service named "The here and there," a line of water buses that will take you anywhere. The Rotterdam boat-builders early developed a grace of line and harmony of proportion which no maker there violates. Be it tug-boat, barge, launch or sailer, the Holland vessel, hull and upperworks, satisfies the eye. On one of these, by a little personal inquiry, seated on a packing box or pile of freight, you can ride till noon or dinner time through a country such as you dreamed of in your youth, a land of windmills, pretty farms, little villages, tall churches, quaint bridges, and can get a tram or train back to your balcony over the water.

The diary once more.—This brings us back again to the journal. You want to bring a fountain pen and one of those traveler's ink-wells of metal with a double corking arrangement which interferes with the affinity of ink for white shirts. You need a strong compact with yourself that you will bring your journal up to date each day. As Mary Kelty, of Madison, remarks, this keeps your jeweled beads of memory on a string. Otherwise a large part of the enjoyment and benefit of your journey slips through your fingers and is lost forever. It does take some force of character to write a travel journal in a strange city. You dread to lose an hour during which you might be absorbing new impressions. Consider the travelers' journals you have read—their regrets that "on this day I lazily and stupidly omitted to write my notes. The events and experiences are a blurred memory." According to the best researchers: If ten hours of sight-seeing be counted 100, eight hours, plus two of writing a journal, are 157. What Bayard Taylor did, who was the top-notch American traveler of your father's time, was to jot down facts and impressions in a little pocket notebook all day long and at night, in his chamber, elaborate them in his permanent journal. Henry James's fascinating "Little Tour in France" was similarly made. You will get a peculiar satisfaction from your gain in proficiency. At first your journal reads like a weak dilution of the guide-book or of a catalogue. Then yourself says to you, "This is not me"—or, if your early pedantry influences you, "This is not I." Then, day by day the desire to create something of your own grows stronger until you find the knack of recording an interfusion of your surroundings with yourself, a progressive changing of you from what you were when you left home to what you shall be when you return. Your diary is indispensable to making your trip do that for which you undertook it.

Smothered in imitation.—What I am getting to, as you see, is that a journey to Europe is no hit-or-miss passing of the time but something worthy of your best intelligence and foresight in planning and execution. There are yet so many foolish people in the world that you will be surrounded by the suggestion of omitting to use your brains in the way you know is best, you'll get scant encouragement to manage your sight-seeing in accordance with your individual needs.

The tourist atmosphere leads travelers to visit what other voyagers have seen, to flock with the crowd. That is the reason we wasted our youth studying Latin and algebra. It was being done by so many.

Take the art galleries, for instance. In many of them a guide whose vain repetitions as the heathens use has turned him into an incarnation of boredom will insist upon your proceeding through every room. In an hour museumitis permeates you. The muscles about your eyes ache; a pain in back and shoulders has you. The utter stupidity of crowding so many paintings under one roof appals you. If you had to live in rooms so decorated you would shout yourself into insanity. The interior of churches is worse. We have a weight of solemnity upon us. We are oppressed by low voices and whispers. The guide is an exaggerated development of the nuisance who shows you the family album. Be sensible and courageous therefore and select one church and one art gallery. Take an early day when your endurance is at its best and get out of each the best there is in it for you. The rest are all alike enough to have no claim on you. You will not be brought to the intensity of the man Frank Cody, of Detroit, tells about. This was a New York judge of the supreme court whose daughter had faithfully taken him to everything he ought to see. Frank heard him, settling himself into an armchair in the Bible Hotel in Amsterdam, exclaiming "Thank God I've finished the last picture gallery." George Bartlett, of Brooklyn, cut loose from a party in Leyden and went to a public school. The boys read to him, in English, accounts of the wheat fields of North Dakota. George's personally conducted confrères envied him for twenty-four hours. Similar was the experience of Charley Skinner, of Philadelphia. The conductor told him that no travelers navigated the Seine. Charley conducted inquiries on his own account and spent a whole day upon the front deck of an unadvertised steamer winding through a lovely land. Mark Whitman's happiest remembrance of Paris is a day with a workingman's picnic at Charenton, where the Marne canal comes into the Seine. He touched the Parisian's Paris. Two days in that city and five spent exploring provincial France will better satisfy you than a week in the capital, where everybody is seeing the same stock sights as is everybody else.

Some real France.—For you can rise up early in the morn and at 7:30 take a seat next the window in a car of the Paris, Lyons, and Mediterranean Railway. You'll find a book in the rack describing everything, mile by mile, on the route. The very center of France is yours. You shall have rivers, canals, roads, farms, mountains, plains and cities. At noon you are at Dijon with an hour to taste it. At four you have Lyons and the Rhone. At seven, while it is still light, you may get out at Avignon and cross the square to the charming Hotel Crillon managed with a polite regard for your purse. In the twilight you may walk in ten minutes to the superb old garden of the popes and, looking over the rushing river, see your walled town completely satisfying your boyish imaginings conceived by your reading of Froissart, Grimm and Jack the Giant Killer. From Avignon, next morning, runs a perfect open-air autobus to Uzes, a perfect hill town, walled and castled; around to Nimes with the amphitheater and temple of the Romans, to their superb aqueduct across the Gard; and back to your starting-place before dinner. Another day of France from the car window brings you back to Paris by another route.

The return voyage.—You have to book a September return voyage before you leave America. To believe that there is added entertainment in using different lines going and coming is childish. But if you have a better and a poorer service, of course you should have the better coming home, a dessert to a good repast. You get your clothing and your books out of storage. You wish you had known as many useful things when starting as now you do, and you resolve with Spartan nobility to abstain forever from the vulgar boasting which begins "When I was abroad."

A REVIEW OF BETTER BOOKS

By HOI BIBLIOLOGOI

THESE are the chronicles of the thirty-second sitting of a teachers' council organized by Pater Johannes Rose and self-christened hoi Bibliologoi, the discussers of books. Their purpose was originally more selfish, but by the suggestion of SCHOOL AND SOCIETY they have been ordained educational missionaries devoted to alluring teachers into the fruitful field of professional reading. With the exception of the paterfamilias, who merely moderates the meetings, none of us ever reviewed books before we joined. We are amateurs, much busied with over-heavy school tasks in a hard-pressed school system. We have a reasonable supply of humility complexes, albeit they are endangered by certain authors and publishers who assure us we are interesting and sane. We are of that bourgeoisy Philistinism which only knows what it likes. We read more books than we mention, selecting for the edification of our fellows only those that we think worthy of remark.

For the thirty-second meeting we had a crisp winter evening. The Roses' studio was cheery with a wood fire on the grate.

Rugg, refreshingly rebellious.—When all the wraps were hung upon the Stevedore's ingenious folding rack and every Bibliologos was seated in the easy folding chairs, the moderator launched the Lady Carolina into the sea of conversation, who said:

"We had Stanwood Cobb's work reviewed here. I have another book on the liberated school.[1] It has a refreshing atmosphere of animation, enthusiasm, confidence, triumph, vigor, courage, verve and ardor, balanced by caution and modesty. It begins with a survey of American educational history, done with a refreshing lack of the ponderosity that dulled the beginning pages of many of the older books on the growth of our schools. It ascribes to Sanders Pierce, William James and John Dewey the substructure of a thoroughgoing rational philosophy of conduct. After 1900, littler professors of education evolved social efficiency as the supreme goal of education. Harold Rugg says he is going to preface a library of critical estimate of our civilization and training by writing a book on "The American Mind and the Reconstruction of the School." The present educational situation is two conflicting concepts: society and self. They generate two methods: conformity and self-expression. Wm. T. Harris campaigned against the Procrustean bed of grades. The educational leaders concentrated on administration. When the superintendent visited another city he brought home a satchel full of blanks. The college professors made the text-books. The curriculum consisted of a program of narrow and useless school subjects determined by the contents of the texts. For forty years the schools have worked, tied by the bonds of college entrance requirements.

[1] Harold Rugg and Ann Shumaker, "The Child-centered School." World Book Co., Yonkers, N. Y. 359 pp. $1.80.

University faculties dominated the outlines of committees of ten or whatever the number. Meantime a second group gained recognition, the scientific students of educational processes. Both of these types worked to improve, not to reform, the existing system. The third group had the true revolutionaries: Francis Parker, John Dewey, William Kilpatrick and their kind, true revolutionaries, creators, who cut through the superficial details of administration and saw a new school. They discarded the current schemes of subjects, text-books, recitations, fixed furniture and large classes. They experimented. Conspicuous among educational makeshifts was the nation-wide movement to reorganize the middle grades which Messrs. Judd, Johnston and others pushed in their journals and on the stump. More than five hundred cities built junior high schools. This was administrative rearrangement, superficial, not fundamental. These well-meaning but timorous organizers merely knocked out one piece of the educational structure after another and hammered new props in place. Under the sponsorship of the universities, rigid prescriptions for secondary and upper elementary schools were laid down. Reading matter produced in England before 1800 made up most of the literature. There was almost no attention to anything produced in America after the Civil War. There was a strangle hold on the materials of instruction. It is becoming increasingly clear that nothing short of an educational revolution will undo the harm. Came the scientific students of education. Following the epoch-making work of William James, Wilhelm Wundt, J. McKeen Cattell and others, the procedures of the biometricians were taken into the field of education. Came the questionnaire and the survey. Standardized tests entered the classroom. Rarely did the educational technicians question the existing order. They were concerned with makeshifts. They failed to see the whole child and the unity of childhood with adult life. Unhampered by the restrictions of the school, American progress outside went on. We now have a great, sprawling, national scheme of education.

"This condensed account, lacking the verve and swing of the two animated authors, introduces you to the new articles of faith which glow in the pages; freedom *vs.* control, child initiative, child interest, self-activity, creative self-expression, personality and social adjustment. You have, here, the programs of work, the criticisms upon them stated and answered. You have some altogether fascinating chapters on the arts, rhythm, music as expression, the child as creative artist, the child as poet, the children's theater and creative group-life. This, then, says Harold or Ann, is the Educational Revolution which has blazed up over the concept of freedom. In the short space of thirty years the brittle shell of conformity has been blasted through and new educational foundations have been sunk in the earth of freedom. The current transformation in educational theory is nothing short of a revolution. The child-centered schools have routed the concept of discipline and have implanted firmly that of growth."

"I'm for 'em," said the General when Carolina had finished her review. "I have joined every revolution since I began to teach, and they have been many. I was a Spencerite in 1880 and belonged to the new education. I joined the revolution of Charles Ham and Henry Belfield here in Chicago and marched under the new education banner of mind, heart and hand. I revoluted with the Herbartians and with the Montessorians. I skirmished for Miss Aitken's new education and dear old Colonel Parker's, and Preston Search's and John Kennedy's and Francis Burke's and Edward Bok's. I was a revolutionist for vertical handwriting and spelling reform, socialized recitation, supervised study, work-study-play platoons, project method and the I.Q. Dear old Homer Bevans called me a man milliner because I changed my style so much, but I have a philosophy for justification. Change is life. What though there have been, even in our own day, a score of new educations, each successive band of crusaders shouting, 'Here at last is the true gospel.' If we didn't have 'em to break the shells of formalism that grow in time over each successive system we would ossify. If the innovator didn't hammer our established systems he couldn't break the incrustation. I'm for Harold the Dauntless. He has convictions; he argues like a gentleman. I'll bet he doesn't say a spiteful thing against a living soul."

"No," continued Carolina, "But he says that 95 per cent. of us are not artist-teachers but artisans, constant talkers, exhibitionists on platforms. The teacher speaks; what she says goes. She organizes the thinking; she impresses her individuality and her ideas on the pupils. Sir John Gorst declared that Americans have lost the power of independent thought. He lays it to our system of schools. Alfred Harmsworth called us a race of new Chinese, all cast in the same mould. He believed our educational methods responsible."

"And Alfred Mosely," interpolated Peter the Reader, "paid the expenses of British teachers to visit our schools because he found Americans most able to think for themselves."

"I have in my district," said Martin of Tours, "parents whose children attended the new education schools. I have never heard more bitter reproaches than these fathers make against the waste of time and the crippling of intelligence due to the joyous following of childish desires."

"And I," said Henry the Humanist, "know several fathers and mothers who favor the Francis Parker school because their children learn so well."

"Call in the testers," suggested the one we call our Geometer. "Let them take Eddie Maguire's public school and Harold Rugg's Lincoln school. Let them get from unprejudiced parents an outline of what children ought to be. Let them devise an inspection and score to see which children are really better trained. Until you give us some specific tabulation we are only where we were when Rousseau or Froebel or Spencer or Horace Mann or James Rice or Edward Bok or Mr. Livesy published their warm stuff berating us all."

"My book agrees to that," replied the reviewer. "It says, 'even the sympathetic believers in this new education feel that their writing is essentially description and self-congratulation. It is to be regretted that we have not produced adequate measures of the outcomes of the new education.' Ring for the Duke of Buckingham, Columbus, Ohio, who with St. Paul says we must prove all things."

Banishing the boredom of school: Averill.— The next offering was by our Martin of Tours: "From Professor Averill,[2] who teaches psychology in the state normal school in Worcester, Massachusetts, I get a fine grist of suggestions. There are healthy states of mind, and there are too many curable disorders of it interfering with the efficient work of the world. Many of them develop in school children. If we knew more about these ailments and the conditions of mental soundness we would find teaching more satisfying. There are innumerable schoolrooms, says this author, in which the wrong attitude of children toward daily tasks is favored. In many a school the teacher is a mediocre workman content to accept the second best or even the tenth best of what her pupils are capable of doing. Strong and clear objectives are too rarely evident. Too long have our schools been places for exercising the thinking capacities of teachers instead of pupils. The type of teacher found all too frequently in the service achieves little for enlightened and progressive ideals."

"I'd like to ask a question," said Anna, who has now for two years borne the title of head wrangler with no annoyance thereat. "Isn't this lambasting of the schools being overdone? It seems to me that most of the books on teaching we have had reviewed here have fallen into the cheap performance of running down the whole American system from kindergarten to college. Educational orators on the platform throw their reprimands at us. If we treated our children in this way we'd never teach them anything."

"I think it's a good thing," ventured the Signpost. "It's an antidote to the super-sweets the superintendents fill the teachers with."

"Isn't it a legitimate move to form a desire to read the books?" asked Martin. "The doctor can't get you to buy his medicine unless he shows you that you are sick. Consider, for in-

[2] Lawrence Augustus Averill, "The Hygiene of Instruction." Houghton Mifflin Co., Boston. 287 pp. $1.80.

stance, Professor Averill's situation. He attempts in his normal school to bring through his course those high-school graduates who are going to teach. They never, says he, have had any systematic instruction in how to study. They seem to have developed the same memoriter unthinking methods that Averill's teachers let him use when he went to school. Mr. George Carman, head of our big Lewis Institute here, started with a scheme by which each class period was allowed as much time for study as for reciting and all under the teacher of the particular subject. He couldn't find teachers able to work it. What's the use of our objecting to these criticisms if they are true? If enough of them continue to be printed maybe the profession will wake up to the fact that one reason why it is not more respected is because it is too complacent. Take for instance Professor Averill on the dawdling teacher. Slow and sluggish class management limits the advance below what it ought to be. It generates and confirms habits and attitudes of carelessness, sloth and indolence. Thorndike's researches find that children have too little to do rather than too much. They are afflicted with boredom, ennui, which has the same effect as fatigue and is mistaken for it. We had here in Chicago a self-appointed committee of teachers protesting against the platoon schools and the accuracy requirement in arithmetic on the ground that these would drive the children too hard. Professor Averill cites opening exercises with repeated dronings of overlearned songs and ceremonies as drugging the children to sleep at the very beginning of the day. You can't doze over his book. It is full of animation. He shows that life, movement, exercise, activity, are the necessities of healthy youth. He gives the characteristic tonics needed for classes in one subject after another—reading, spelling, writing, and the rest. He treats the hygiene of discipline, of character, of bodily health, of habit, the problem children, the new education, the new teacher, the child-guidance clinic. I will not permit your discussion to leave the impression that this is a negative or complaining book. It isn't. It is positive, constructive, persuasive and cheery."

Preparing the parent: Van Waters.—The Viking Maid reported substantially as follows:

"Now that you have, during the past several meetings, heard many competent women set you right as to our changeful young folks, listen to another capable lady help you to help parents. Most of us have heard Miriam Van Waters when she has spoken in Chicago and are glad she has given us in permanent form[3] gleanings from her experience and conclusions. A repeated caution prevailing through her work is that youth is not adult. If the scientific study of the past few years has shown anything it is that to judge children by adult standards is unfair and wicked. A few of our schools and some of our courts have grasped this discovery. It is as important as that of Copernicus. Most of the adult world ignores it with the result of destroying millions of children. Understanding of the world of youth can not be gained from reading nor from observation nor from memory. Our own childhood is so far away that memory of it is too dim for use. Whosoever guides the young must undergo the process which Jesus called being born again. The best advice is that of one of the best of our educators, William Burnham: 'Let the child alone and set him a good example.' Respect for parents is not inherent; it must be won. You have to analyze yourself and put in such ingredients of character as will make you respectable. What makes the well-mannered, considerate children that leaven our school classes? Imitation of courteous, sympathetic, unselfish parents.

"Most of the evil, most of the beautiful, most of the cowardly, most of the daring acts to which we seem impelled by circumstances are due to reverberations from childhood and largely traceable to parental behavior. One generalization we can make about the life stories of delinquents is that they have been subjected to upheavals, quarrels of adults. This is only of late years coming to be understood. The average adult is no more qualified to understand a child than he is to make deep-sea soundings. A child has rights, duties, responsibilities, needs and points of view which must be respected. So has an

[3] Miriam Van Waters, "Parents on Probation." New Republic, N. Y. 333 pp. $1.00.

adult. Neither should dominate. These things should be pooled. To do this takes great skill. The task belongs to mother. It requires knowledge of the biological and social requirements of infancy, childhood, youth, maturity and old age. It requires rebuilding of homes until children will not be enslaved to the comfort and tastes of adults. This gives you something of the measure of the Van Waters book. Observant, experienced, trained, sympathetic, constructive, moving toward a sane and lovely ideal of our living together, she progresses through the bewildering problems of sex, of honor, of religion, of good and bad things done by children, parents and teachers, 'to the glorious adventure of growing up.' Perpetual patience, sympathy, affection, adjustment, are her specifics. Parents must be educated. Fifty-four modern books, each best one marked with a star, are cited to that end. Force and violence have failed ingloriously. The complexities of life must not baffle us. Centuries of tradition hamper us. But they are putting up their shutters, going out of business; they are bankrupt. Slowly the attitude of the artist and the scientist is making its way into parenthood. The great thing is to have continued faith in the respectability of human life."

A hearty and cheery review of modern teaching: Holley.—Peter the Reader said this:

"I have a new book[4] on the newer ways to perform our service. It is one of the Century series of educational handbooks. Charles Holley wrote it, another Illinois professor of education. He starts it with a bang. 'To some,' he says, 'it may seem that teaching has markedly changed in the last thirty years. Along some lines it has. Yet teachers are making the same mistakes with my children that teachers inflicted on me when I was in school.' Holley is for the joy of achievement and the right of self-expression. It is surprising how many of the new-education special-school people fail to note that this is stressed in all the teaching books coming from the press and is not an idea patented by any faculty of the Joysome School or the Nishative Academy. Most of the applied problems in our text-books, says Dr. Holley, appeal to the natural desire of children to achieve. Children are so constituted that the agreeable type of experience is the one they will persist in following. Use this. It's foolish to give school tasks as penalties. Lois Meek's experiments show a marvelous power gained by succeeding. It's not so much lack of intelligence or lack of interest that retards progress as it is a sense of failure. Find the failure. Help the lame dog over the stile. Enjoy his victory with him. We are in the success business, not recording and scolding mistakes. This is a pleasingly human book. It is sympathetic. Inferiority complexes are generated in school by repeated failures in arithmetic when the progress of the class is too rapid for the gait of some. The mass treatment which fails to see individual difficulties breeds the complexes. The opposite defect, swelled head, superiority complex, is cultivated by too much praise and prominence. Holley tells us how to develop the learning morale, enthusiasm for lessons and faith in the master. Morale's main sustenance is continuing success. In the school where I work there are teachers who make it a point never to let any really important essential of the lesson go unconquered by any pupil. Mr. Hamilton is organizing the whole Oak Park school system on this mastery program. It is the keynote of Henry Morrison's epoch-making book on high-school teaching. Holley's treatment of conduct, discipline, individual care, grouping, socialized recitation, drill, thinking, emotional training, ideals, attitudes, individuality, projects, problems, study habits, measurements, is all flavored with this cheerful and constructive philosophy. The book is hearty from start to finish. After the well-illustrated exposition of the general principles of teaching, the author applies them in detail to reading, literature, history, creative expression, and all the usual divisions of an elementary course of study. I can not find that the buffets of the new educationists have any case for attacks on us when our own people are producing works like this."

[4] Charles Elmer Holley, "Modern Principles and the Elementary Teacher's Technique." The Century Co., N. Y. 131 pp. $1.50.

The mastery of reading: Stone.—Thus spoke Polly the Political:

"About fifteen years ago Principal Clarence Stone found that the reading done in the middle and upper grades was much inferior to accomplishment in other subjects. He tried various ways of bettering it. He found assistance and inspiration in the work of our Chicagoan, Dr. Charles Judd. He learned much from teachers in his own town, St. Louis. He put into a book what he considered essentials of an adequate effectiveness of reading instruction. And, now, five years later, his publishers issue a new and enlarged edition.[5] Here you will find, applied to classroom situations, recent conclusions resulting from scientific experimentation. The eye-span and pauses, rate and comprehension, vocalization and inner speech, get short but clear presentation. About the end of the third grade the average pupil gets ideas from print faster than he can articulate the words. In the seventh grade he senses them twice as fast as he can speak. If you give too much pronouncing of words (oral reading) after the third grade you interfere with learning to read. If you keep it up into the higher grades you prevent some pupils from ever really learning to read at all. That is, you fasten on them lip-movements, whispering, etc., that make the acquisition of meaning a slow, laborious, imperfect process. Mr. Stone concludes this part of his presentation with a direct shot at you, when he lists 'facts you should know,' and when he asks, 'what is the average silent-reading rate suitable for your class?' etc. What the attainments ought to be at the end of different grades, how to decide by tests what these really are, how to treat individual defects and superiorities, gives Mr. Stone's work the businesslike quality of knowing what is needed and how to get it, a knowledge, the absence of which in the teaching he observed before he wrote the book, induced him to undertake the work. Having felt the embarrassment of supervising teaching when his own lack of knowledge handicapped him, this author now writes with the advantage of knowing what points need to be stressed and what can be left to one's general common sense. I like his footnotes. They tell where he got some of the ideas which make his work practical. I like his particularity in telling what goals different reading exercises should aim to reach. I like his insistence on appreciation and enjoyment. It seems to me his lists for reading in the different grades are the ones I should have made had I been sufficiently skilful. Every selection seems to me the one that will engage and benefit the children of the age intended. He has a collection of common deficiencies in teaching reading and quotes experts on each. He turns reading lessons into exercises in thinking, in study, in picturing, in enjoying, in acting. He gives an abundance of actual lessons and of tests for various stages of progress. In my opinion his book is entitled to rank as a standard work. I found it easy and pleasant reading and thoroughly sound."

The epic struggle in Pennsylvania schools: The Walshes.—Principal Manzer was next.

"Here is a study[6] which I found intensely interesting. Louise and Mathew Walsh, of that beautiful town, Indiana, up in the Pennsylvania mountains, have written an account of the struggles of the schoolmaster of the Keystone State from William Penn's time till now. You have no idea of the herculean task of getting common schools established and of keeping them in a first-rate condition in that commonwealth. The peculiar temperament of the Quakers, the agglomeration of Dutch, Swedes, Germans, Scotch-Irish, Huguenots, English, Welsh, Negroes, Mennonites, Dunkers, Shakers, Schwenkfelders, Aminites, Seventh-day Baptists, Separatists, Labadists, Lutherans, United Brethren, Catholics, Episcopalians, Methodists, New Borns, Rousdorfers, New Moons, Gechtelians, Moravians, Quietists, Lebellians, twenty-two distinct German sects in Lancaster County alone; the accepted duty of making education a religious function held by many churches; the positive objection to schooling, a trait of many

[5] Clarence R. Stone, "Silent and Oral Reading." Houghton Mifflin Co., Boston. 332 pp. $2.00.

[6] Louise and Mathew Walsh, "History and Organization of Education in Pennsylvania." State Teachers College, Indiana, Pennsylvania. 276 pp. $1.50.

sects who hold that it interferes with godliness, have given the common schools a rocky road indeed. The Walshes have brought into a connected narrative striking incidents of the colonial period, the advanced educational theories of the Revolution, the amazing delay in getting them put into practice, the effect of the Bell-and-Lancaster wave, the bewildering adoption and repeal of free-school laws, reactions against supervision, down to the appointment of our Illinoisian, John Keith, as state superintendent of Pennsylvania public instruction. The authors cover the Finegan tragedy with hearty approval of his businesslike and professional administration. As I read those astounding pages of step after step of indisputable advance in the efficiency of the schools to be followed by the state-wide howl against the 'carpet-bagger superintendent' and by attacks from the state grange, which far more than any other group was benefiting by the new program, and then by the hostility of my fallen idol, Pinchot, I am ready to hate the dear old state of Pennsylvania, the cradle of our liberties, who has never grown up and out of her swaddling clothes. But this is I, not the Walshes. Their history is history, not propaganda. They string their good, bad and mixed events along in a continuous story, listing the page and paragraph of the archives from which they quote. They portray Penn, the Quaker, Pastorius, Christopher Sower, Christopher Dock, Thad Stevens, Wickersham, Schaeffer, Finegan and others, as portraits, not as ideal studies. With no apparent desire to tell you so, they convince you that the educational struggle of that historic state is a great epic in which real heroes, hundreds of them forgotten, as is the reward of our school warriors, fought their good fight and went down to defeat before embattled ignorance and stupidity. For their long and arduous labor in collecting and sifting their material, for their remarkably convenient arrangement of it—four or five catch titles on every page—and for their unbiased presentation of the story, these Walshes must be classed with the long line of school-missionaries giving themselves unstintedly to the cause."

Platoonery, Portland, Oregon, City Club.— The next was our Semaphore, Doctor Post:

"Here is an innocent little pamphlet[7] that looks quite harmless but is capable of causing cackle galore in Chicago where the word 'platoon' is enough to throw into fits hundreds of people who don't know the difference between a platoon school and a common council.

"From it I learn that the Portland City Club appointed a committee which undertook to ascertain the nature of the platoon plan, to study its results, and to tell what's the matter with it. This committee studied four platoon and four non-platoon schools for two months, and then arrived at a systematic plan to conduct their investigation as a whole. Only when principals and teachers of any school expressed themselves as ready to go on the platoon plan was it undertaken. They began with two schools. In six months four more asked to come in, and so on, until thirty-two were constituted. Only grades four to eight were platooned, but on requests of teachers and parents, the plan, adapted to the ages and school accommodations of the younger children, was put into operation in lower grades as well. The committee addressed itself to the bugaboo which our self-appointed critics of platoonery raised here: that the mothering of children is necessary and is dissipated by the plan. Portland reports the principals as convinced that the platoon caused no deprivation of any valuable service of this sort. Most of the teachers appear, says the report, to find nothing of serious value taken away by the reduction of mothering. Some, however, think the loss important. Maybe, says this Portland committee, mothering is not a need of the child but a yearning of the teacher. Somebody ought to introduce John Watson to the Portlanders to show them that the main trouble with present-day children is overmothering. Dr. DeBusk in Portland made a fatigue study of children in both kinds of schools and found a slight advantage in the platooners. In the matter of pupil failures the difference wasn't much. In the platoons 7.5 per cent. failed; in

[7] "The Platoon Plan in the Portland Schools." City Club, Portland, Oregon. 23 pp. 25 cents.

the regular schools, 8.3 per cent. The Portland Teachers Association made some investigations of its own. 'Are you happy?' they asked 476 platoon workers; 369 said that they were. There were no control groups selected for answering this question. We must assume, therefore, that of the teachers in the common type of school 100 per cent. are happy."

"Why so?" asked Anna.

"Because they have not been subjected to change," said the Signpost. "Girl alive! Don't you know teachers are human, and don't you know Carruther's studies of discontent show that whenever any new regulation is made for hospital workers, postal employees, soldiers, teachers, any organized body, the amount of preference for present conditions is almost unanimous. It is the result of outside domination. If teachers or postal servants or any organization ask the powers-that-be to make the new regulations, the petitioners will show that 100 per cent. are unhappy from lack of the change. If a Chicago committee of teachers, not the school board, had discovered platoon schools or junior high schools, and had persuaded the teachers' associations to fight for 'em and had won, every school staff would be unhappy until it got platoons."

"I move," said Euclid, "we put the Post back on the road. In these days of probing everything by actual measurement no member of this club should call a thing good or bad unless he can tell how many degrees good and how many medians bad."

"Oh, very well," said the Signpost. "If my views, the result of long and careful studies of human nature, are worth as little as that I'll let the Portland City Club take up your time. The report covers the various strengths and weaknesses of school work, comparing platoon with old-line teaching. The new schools have given a distinct gain in nature-study and in library service; the auditorium periods vary greatly in value due to fitness and incompetence of teachers. On the whole this feature is a distinct gain; so is the physical training. Eighty-two per cent. of the teachers favor the plan in preference to the old; the children are happier. The cost of maintenance is about the same. It offers educational opportunities which seem superior to the old scheme. It will increase in favor as it becomes adjusted."

How curriculum revision affects teachers: Holloway.—The offering of Luther the Literary was this:

"Everybody here has a fresh memory of the Chicago organization for revising the curriculum. Teacher volunteers were relieved from classroom service and met in frequent assemblies to agree on general principles and to block out the details. Invitations were issued to the entire teaching staff to contribute suggestions, comments, details. We were told that a curriculum made for our city by those who live in it and who know its children was likely to work better than any imposed on us by superintendents or by college entrance boards. Here is a book[8] that shows how such participation affects teaching. Dr. Holloway got permission of Maryland authorities to test by experiment the effect of teacher curriculum making in ten counties. His report is a remarkable application of measurement to a plan that has usually been the subject of a great deal of talking in the mist. I wish there were time to quote all the careful steps and detailed estimates of results in teachers and pupils. Dr. Holloway tested before and after. He tested control groups where no teachers worked in making a new course. Here is what he reports.

"During the work the curriculum makers did not lag behind the other teachers in professional spirit and teaching power.

"In the years immediately following they improved at a faster rate than the others.

"The children taught by the curricularii made greater gains in school work.

"The course-of-study revisers did very much more professional reading than they ever had done in any year before and more than other teachers.

"The supervisors studied more and were of more valuable help to all teachers.

"The book is full of spicy comment. After a careful reading of it I am prepared to say that if a perfect curriculum were in vogue in a

[8] William J. Holloway, ''Participation in Curriculum Making as a Means of Supervision.'' Press of Teachers College, N. Y. 54 pp. $1.50.

school system and was made by a perfect superintendent the system would be justified in throwing it away and having the teachers take a year to make a new one."

"Why not," asked the Argumentative, "have no course at all, but let each teacher make her own every day and develop initiative?"

"Or," said the Signpost, "why not have the children make it hourly *à la l'education nouvelle?*"

"If you are capable of taking anything seriously," answered Luther, "it is because in union there is strength. A curriculum to function has to be thought about. Thought is generated by discussion. One teacher does not discuss much with herself and children's discussion is as the fitful summer breeze."

Testor retestus: Dearborn.—Dr. Batwell was next:

"Dr. Walter Fenno Dearborn, of Harvard University, takes up the case of intelligence testing[9] with the belief that it and the supposition behind it have generated serious misconceptions. Intelligence tests have aided in the meeting of some problems. They have failed to advance the solution of others. We have those who hold that one's intellectual ability can be shown by these tests to be hereditary and not susceptible of much improvement by training. Dr. Dearborn doesn't find the facts or arguments to convince him that this is so. As I have been leading boys for many years along the straight and narrow path of Euclidean demonstration, I have, of course, come to long for the orderly mind. Eureka! Dearborn! He marches from point to point with the precision of a demonstration in geometry. He tackles each of the apostles of intelligence testing who has given us teachers the chill of hopelessness of ever being able to increase the stock of mental power in any boy. He takes his keen scalpel and politely carves their arguments into shreds and carefully, without rudeness, lays cuttings in the basket. Dearborn argues like a gentleman. He reminds me of that master of courteous debate, the late revered Charles W. Eliot. With dignity, with precision, with a wealth of diagram, illustration and exact quotation, Dearborn travels to the conclusion that it is not possible from any knowledge that has been obtained and cited to differentiate the relative effects of nature and nurture on human intelligence. You will be clarified and comforted by a study of this text. You will agree that there is much more agreement as to who is intelligent than as to what intelligence is. The author gives nine formulations of prominent definers. You will find, toward the end of the volume, that his own conception is this: intelligence is the resultant of all the faculties of the mind.

"By no means unimportant are the striking by-products you will gather along this roadmaker's main path. For instance, some of our restless reformers here have hit upon large schools as a next point of attack for our teachers' organizations. I get a sensible whoa for any beforehand assumption on this point by noting in this book that D. A. Emerson, in SCHOOL AND SOCIETY, January, 1925 (No. 524), shows that the smaller the high school the larger is the percentage of high marks given pupils by their teachers. But, says our author, the pupils from the smaller schools are, as has been shown in various ways, actually, on the average, inferior in attainment to those from the larger schools. Teachers in smaller schools are more generous in their grading.

"One of the most important suspicions I derive from a study of this work is that intelligence does depend a great deal more on the kind of teaching a child gets and gives to himself than on any other consideration. The wave of intelligence testing that swept over us carried the notion of fixed intellectual endowment with which we are born and which neither parents, teachers nor ourselves can, by taking any thought, increase. On the contrary, the opposite cheering proposition is demonstrated here, that what the intelligence tests measure is definitely affected by what parents and teachers do. A boy may be brightened, he may be dulled, and many are, by us. As men have fought to preserve their notions of freedom of the will, the battle now is waged for freedom of the intellect. If the tests seem to show what is contrary to this idea, it may be that the tests are imper-

[9] Walter Fenno Dearborn, "Intelligence Tests, Their Significance for School and Society." Houghton Mifflin Co., Boston. 336 pp. $2.20.

fect. Life is full of mistakes of examiners. Pasteur, Linnaeus, Edison, Beecher, Humboldt, Leibig, Seward, were officially rated dunces by their teachers. Harvard's best boy seems to have notoriously repudiated his rating. Intelligence tests, as at present constituted, recognize chiefly the sort of abilities that school and college prefer. We fail to crown, when they are students, those who subsequently attain eminence as writers, composers, artists, scientists and men of affairs. Maybe we don't know yet the rudiments of training human powers. It is more than thirty years since the problem of laggards in the schools was pushed to the front in educational literature and conventions. We were told we taught subjects, not children. Attention to retardation has since been a feature of school systems everywhere. This book says that there is still as much retardation as ever. But to argue from this that intelligence is, therefore, unimprovable is no more valid than to argue that we haven't improved our teaching. To say the mind can not be made over may be merely a confession that we are not skilful enough to do it. Whatever our hesitation should be in believing that the results of intelligence testing may justify a narrowing of the prospects of any child, we can still use the tests as an aid in grouping. Dr. Dearborn assures us that their employment as, for instance, in Chicago junior high schools may aid, but they are not legitimately the sole basis for grouping.

"A very valuable precept derivable from various portions of this book is the exhortation to fit our courses and instruction, week by week, to the capacities of different children so that pupils will experience more of the blessings of success than of the disappointment of failure. If I grasp aright the spirit of this delightful club of ours, a tendency nurtured by our superbly optimistic Lord and Lady Rose, it is that teachers are managers of success rather than correctors of mistakes. The books reviewed here, including this one, sound that cheery note. The experimenters are beginning to tell us they can demonstrate by figures that the teacher who sees that the largest number of children are encouraged to let no task be abandoned in failure is the one whose youngsters gain most in their independent persistence and victory. It certainly is true in mathematics study. We have good testimony that it works everywhere. Dearborn's chapters on the classwork for feeble-minded children really glow with hope. His repudiation of the doctrine of original and inherited sin, his rejection of the intelligence tester's opinion that mankind shows the average of a thirteen-year-old development—his whole book is to me a delight. Here is a scientist with all the caution that belongs, who combines with it a human sympathy and cheer that warms you to him."

Teaching honesty and then finding pupils more dishonest than before: Hartshorne and May.—Our Anna of the Doubting Mind said this:

"The surveyors, God bless 'em, are going into the unstaked wilderness of character teaching and are trying to set up some landmarks on which we can base our lines of limitation and definition. The American Religious Education Association, five years ago, resolved to further a scientific investigation of the question: How is religion being taught and with what effect? Professors, researchers and school executives were enlisted, and now after five years' work, Messrs. May and Hartshorne report on their investigations.[10] They take in hand the common vice of school, cheating. They analyze deception, cite the situations in which it is evident, discuss methods of correction, and try various measures of its amount as practiced by boys, by girls, by Protestants, by Catholics, by Jews. They consider the factors which affect it: sex, age, race, home, associates, occupation, heredity, training, motion pictures, suggestions. They find that in some schools cheating seems almost universal in the classes of some teachers and absent from the pupils of others. They find whole schools infested by it and others comparatively immune. They found classes who, in 1925, were the most dishonest of all those tested, becoming under another teacher, in 1926, the most trustworthy. They compared pupils of similar homes who were attending schools of the traditional and schools of the progressive types. The progressives deceived

[10] Hartshorne and May, ''Studies in Deceit.'' The Macmillan Co., N. Y. 306 pp. $5.00.

less. Maybe the newer type of schools were so conducted that in cheating you couldn't get any advantage from it. The tendency to deceive is about as prevalent among Protestant children who are enrolled in Sunday school as it is in those who are not. The same thing is true of Jewish children who attend their own religious schools. I can not find that any different conclusion is reached with regard to Catholic children. In trying to find, in the case of children of all denominations, which ones received religious instruction in Sunday schools, the investigators were hampered by the fact that the children lied about this fact.

"The whole matter is in a primitive stage. We have no conclusive or nearly satisfactory tests or experiments on the efficiency of method of training in honesty. Professor Trow, of the University of Michigan, used Forbush's "Honesty Book" as a basis for teaching three classes, while three others were untaught. The Sim's honesty test showed that the combined scores of those who had been taught honesty indicated a slight increase in deception. The untaught group showed a somewhat greater increase in the same vice. The teaching did not decrease falsification. The conclusion of the whole matter is full of interest to all of us. I would advise you to study the whole work. No conclusive experiments have been undertaken by which education of character has been successfully demonstrated. No one is honest or dishonest 'by nature.' The mere urging of honest behavior, no matter how much it is 'emotionalized' has no necessary relation to the control of conduct. This does not imply that teaching ideals is not desirable or necessary, but that prevailing ways of doing it are ineffective and possibly harmful. In other words, this is one of the big problems about which we don't yet know much, while every decent one of us realizes it is of such great importance that as much attention and help should be given to study in this direction as is bestowed upon the search for a cure for cancer."

Watson, Darrow, Mencken, falsity and ruin: Bridges.—Our last contribution was the General's.

"I commend to you two good books on the large problems of present human trends. Both repudiate the tendencies following the teachings of John Watson, Clarence Darrow and Mr. Mencken. Horace Bridges[11] finds them cocksure of fallacies as absurd as those of Billy Sunday and William J. Bryan, against whom they lead the reaction. In theorizing about life they deny that there are any standards that can legitimately be applied or that there is any possibility of deflecting the course of human affairs from the line of predestined unfolding. Like Mr. Mencken, while they work hard to show us that whatever is is wrong, they protest that there is no right by contrast with which the wrongness of the present wrongness can be demonstrated. Their philosophy is on an intellectual level with the theology of Dr. Straton and Dr. Sunday. The most of the people we know consider the life of man a glorious adventure. But there is a great multitude of youth not possessed of conclusions like those of middle life or old age. Our universities abound with students dazzled by the brilliance and awed by the seeming authority of certain powerful popular writers. They feel that they can not trust anything of the teaching of the past. They suppose it proven that man is a mere animal mechanism, and that neither religion nor morals, neither metaphysics nor spiritual philosophy, has anything to offer that can be accepted by a mind really free and determined to keep itself untainted by superstition. Watson's experimental results have value. He has given an effective impetus toward a genetic study of habit formation. His doctrines are false and ruinous. In much of the conclusions put forth as established by experiment is a hidden canker of a depreciated estimate of the worth of life, of the dignity of man. It has spread with the diffusion of work on science and with the circulation of misconceptions of the meanings of scientific record. The inexpert public has, unawares, imbibed them. Science has been misrepresented and maligned. With orderly process Dr. Bridges proceeds to review the causes

[11] Horace James Bridges, "Taking the Name of Science in Vain." The Macmillan Co., N. Y. 272 pp. $2.50.

of present disturbances, the unbelief in man, in freedom, in moral evolution. He considers the adequacy of art, of literature, of satire, the one-sidedness of Sinclair Lewis and Eugene O'Neill. He enlarges on man as a social being, on his rights, his duties, his patriotism, his nationalism and his world obligations. Out of it comes a clean conclusion of an open road ahead to travel which is to maintain dignity, faith and a progress toward a superb destiny."

World woe, cowardice and the return to manliness: Coe.—"The second stirring treatment of similar themes is that of George Coe,[12] who has been admired and praised in this club heretofore when we reviewed his "What Ails our Youth?" Dr. Coe accepts our time as a period of spiritual depression. We are highly organized, industrially focused, scientifically managed, psychologically analyzed, rich in things, but distracted and ethically upset. Enormous power has been added to us but we don't know what to do with it. We can throw our voice thousands of miles and have nothing to say. We can set type with lightning speed, print sheets by the hundred thousand and have nothing worth recording. Mostly a sense of disillusionment pervades our powers. There is a growing skepticism of the worth of the common man. It is becoming almost popular to sneer at democracy. A partly blatant America-first patriotism, partly furtive nationalism, has displaced the bland and expansive political consciousness of the last generation. In all our history we were never moved by fears so much as now. Never were forward-looking proposals ever so regularly confronted with the objection, 'You can not change human nature.' America is a child with lots of playthings but fidgeting and dissatisfied. Is it the depression due to a great war? Is it a by-product of modern science? Is it a consequence of the new psychology of behaviorism or of psychoanalysis? Has it been put over on the populace by the O'Neills, the Menckens, the Lewises, who find it remunerative to exaggerate the selfish and the sensual side of life? Now follows an enquiry as to what the war did to our belief in man. It was no sudden meteorite dropping upon us from outside our system of everyday life. It was a direct and to-be-expected growth of our commercial, economic, industrial procedures and ethics. Men did not assume nobility in man in 1913. They did not glorify it in 1915. But it was present. A mass of Americans responded to the idealism of the 'Fourteen Points.' Weigh this, and add the fact that war-makers can not get us to fight another nation without first frightening us or artificially working up our hatred by lying. We behold moral confusion and, on the whole, a downward trend in our regard for our own qualities. Why is it that the universal horror of this war does not lead to repentance for war-making? Why don't we turn over a new leaf? Practically nobody wants war, but something prevents us from having robust confidence in our ability to avoid the fatal steps. After penetrating and pungent diagnosis of our present social malady comes a masterly prescription for the self-healing that is imperative. The fun our genial doctor pokes at the behaviorists, psychologists, analysts, is delicious, albeit he gives them credit for what, other than nonsense, they have given us. Read and rejoice in his cheery chapter on what capacities children reveal for us; enjoy 'Human nature in the school'; absorb his version of the good old schoolboy favorite, 'lives of great men all remind us, we can make our lives sublime.' You are now in the swing of the cure. Through the rest of the chapters walks the good Samaritan pouring myrrh and oil on the wounds. I do not exaggerate when I call this an inspired book. Its balance of wit and wisdom, satire and seriousness, its creation of healthy certainty brings you to the end of it with a glow of satisfaction."

There was much bantering discussion which produced so little worthy of record that the Recorder put away his book and pencils and helped our lovely ladies spread the coffee cakes upon the great platters, pour the hot cakes and sort the cheeses, after which the isometric feast disappeared amidst a gentle and refined merriment.

[12] George A. Coe, "The Motives of Men." Charles Scribner's Sons, N. Y. 265 pp. $2.25.

SCHOOL AND SOCIETY

EDITED BY J. McKEEN CATTELL

WITH WHICH IS COMBINED THE

EDUCATIONAL REVIEW

EDITED BY WILLIAM McANDREW

Volume XXIX | Saturday, February 9, 1929 | Number 737

THE SPIRIT OF TOLSTOY'S EXPERIMENTAL SCHOOL[1]

By PAUL R. RADOSAVLJEVICH

NEW YORK UNIVERSITY

I

One fancies, indeed, that experiments in education would not be necessary; and that we might judge by the understanding whether any plan would turn out well or ill. But this is a great mistake. Experience shows that often in our experiments we get quite opposite results from what we have anticipated. We see, too, that since experiments are necessary, it is not in the power of one generation to form a complete plan of education.

So spoke Kant of the Philanthropin, the famous experimental school of Basedow at Dessau in Germany. And so we may say that Tolstoy's experiment at his estates, called Yasnaya Polyana, has been by no means a useless one. The most recent experimental schools here and abroad ("Doing-School," "Dalton Plan," "Winnetka Plan," "L'Ecole Rénovée," "Ecole sur mesure," "Arbeitsschule," "Tatschule," "Produktivschule," "Gemeinschaftsschule," "Lebensschule," "L'Ecole Active," "Decroly School," "Creative School," "Troudovaya Shkola," "Montessori School," "Freie Schule," etc.) are more or less applications of Tolstoy's suggestions for boys and girls to do things. He says:

Let them do all they can for themselves—carry their own water, fill their own jugs, wash up, arrange their own rooms, clean their boots and clothes, lay the table. Believe me, that, unimportant as these things may seem, they are a hundred times more important for your children's happiness than a knowledge of French or of history. These things train the children to simplicity, to work and to self-reliance. If you can add work on the land, if it be but a kitchen garden, that will be well. Believe me, that without that condition there is no possibility of moral education, a Christian education or consciousness of the fact that men are not naturally divided into the classes of masters and slaves, but that they are all brothers and equals.

Count Leo Tolstoy is not only a great figure in modern literature but one of the most significant reformers and educators in the world. Prince Peter A. Kropotkin prophesies with confidence that "some day Tolstoy's ideas of education will become the starting-point of educational reform work much deeper than the reforms of Pestalozzi and Froebel." Right now our American educational Solons and experimentalists or innovators ought to listen to the following two great educational postulates of Tolstoy. The first demand of Tolstoy refers to the school as an implement of education and, at the same time, an experiment on the young generation, constantly giving new results. He says:

Only when an experiment is the basis of a school, only when every school is, so to speak,

[1] A tribute on the centennial of the birth of the great Russian educator at Yasnaya Polyana: 1828–1928.

a pedagogical laboratory, only then will the school not fall behind universal progress, and the experiment will be able to lay firm foundations for the science of education.

The second demand of Tolstoy refers to the school as one of those organic parts of the state which can not be viewed and valued separately, because its worth consists only in a greater or lesser correspondence to the remaining parts of the state. He says:

The school is good only when it takes cognizance of the fundamental laws by which the people live. A beautiful school for a Russian village of the steppe, which satisfies all the wants of its pupils, will be a very poor school for a Parisian; and the best school of the seventeenth century will be an exceedingly bad school in our time; and, on the other hand, the very worst school of the Middle Ages was for its time better than the best of our time, because it better corresponded to its time, and at least stood on a level with the general education, if not in advance of it, while our school stands behind it.

The problems of education interested Tolstoy for over forty years, and it was as a schoolmaster in his native village as long ago as 1862 that he first gave signs of his ideas on government and society. In his "Appeal to the Tzar and his Assistants" (1901) Tolstoy urged removal of all barriers to education, besides liberation of the mouzhiks (Russian peasantry), abolition of secret police organizations and abolition of all limitations of religious freedom. The Tzar was deaf to Tolstoy's proposals and perished tragically. No doubt, Tolstoy foretold the coming of a bloody revolution, but he thought that it might be avoided if the reforms he urged were granted. It is a fact that the monument to Tolstoy's greatness grows more imposing as time goes on. This article will dwell only on his educational arguments, with special reference to his experiment which is under the spell of his two fundamental convictions, *viz.*, (1) that the only method of education is experiment, and (2) that the only criterion of education is liberty. When the Tzar Alexander II liberated the serfs, Tolstoy as a good landlord immediately set to work at the education of the mouzhik children so that they might be fitted for their newly acquired liberty. In a two-story stone house he established a free school with four teachers besides himself. A little bell, hung over the doorway, rang at about eight o'clock every morning, and half an hour later the children appeared. There were in all about forty pupils, but rarely more than thirty at a time. The girls formed 6 per cent. of the whole, being from three to five in number. Seven to thirteen years was the normal age of the boys. In addition to these every year there were three or four grownups who came to the school for a month, or sometimes the whole winter, to make up for the lack of opportunity to study during their boyhood.

But not satisfied with only this form of activity, Tolstoy also edited an educational journal, *The School at Yasnaya Polyana* (for the months of November and December, 1862), in which he gave the results of his experience for the benefit of those in other parts of Russia who were enlisted in the same noble enterprise. This work attracted just as wide attention as all other literary works of the great Slavic man of genius. It is probably true that Tolstoy is very hard to understand, for he was an original character, a Russian, a mystic and an introspectionist *par excellence*. In so far as we can learn there are no translations of his works that are perfectly reliable. Either they are a poor bungle or else they are so highly doctored and adjusted that one can not get at the man Tolstoy. Some of the translations of his works are like Pope's translation of Homer's "Iliad" which quite truly has been called Pope's "Iliad." It may be that Tolstoy's greatness becomes more lucid when interpreted by some follower than in his own words, though some of the great ones who visited him were rather disappointed. Rolland and the men of the periodical *Europe* recently paid tribute to the genius and creative energy of that strange Russian figure by publishing a memorial issue of their review, which is an outstanding contribution to the doctrines of non-resistance and non-violence advocated by the philosopher of Yasnaya Polyana.

In so far as we are concerned, we shall not attempt any close estimate of his work in education, and yet one might take certain of his theories and set them into the foreground. But here one is met by a great difficulty. Tolstoy did not take very seriously some of his school work, and he also spoke lightly of it in some of his books, and as we read the works of the Russian Rousseau we find that he made that impression on others. He shows the influence of Greek and French freedom in thinking, but, so far as we are able to judge, he does not stand on the same level with Jean Jacques Rousseau and the Greeks in his thinking. We feel that Tolstoy appears greater when he stands against a Russian background than against a Greek, a French or a German one. For a man economically free to get his own education and his knowledge of the past and the present in education, Tolstoy seems more like a transient experimenter. Even his school journal lasted only about a year.

It is no doubt true that Tolstoy did not accomplish more than a tenth of what he undertook, but one should not be too hard on a dreamer and an experimenter, for we have generally been too willing to cast such followers into a pit. It is being said that "a one-man school seldom succeeds," and yet it is a fact that all our public schools are modeled on the plan of private, individual schools. New ideas can not be developed without cooperation, and it is plain that Tolstoy did not get such cooperation. His school was feared and regarded with no little suspicion both by the Russian state and by the Russian (Greek Orthodox) church. But it is said no one ever proved that Tolstoy was insincere in what he tried to do by educating the serfs. I believe we ought not to be too hard in pressing Tolstoy to tell us objectively if his educational ideas were realized at Yasnaya Polyana. Plato in his "Republic" writes: "I want to know whether ideas are ever realized in fact. Is not speech more than action, and must not the actual, whatever a man may think, fall short of the truth? What do you say? I agree." In weighing and considering, rather than in praising or condemning the spirit of Tolstoy's experimental school, I vividly recall a sentence of his:

> One might succeed in explaining to the dullest of men the most difficult of problems, if he had no previous conception in regard to it; but it is impossible to explain to the cleverest of men even the simplest matters, if he is perfectly sure that he knows everything about them.

We intend to set down some examples of Tolstoy's procedure and state, as far as possible, what was his theory in education, *e.g.*, as shown in his school at Yasnaya Polyana.

II

Absolute *freedom* is Tolstoy's ideal in education, and he would apply it to children almost as fully as to adults. He says:

> That the pupils should come to learn of their own accord, when they desire it, is a *conditio sine qua non* of all fruitful teaching just as in the feeding it is a *conditio sine qua non* that the eater should be hungry.

The simple organization of Tolstoy's school corresponds to the simplicity of its ideal. There is no program order of school organization. It is modified every year, day and hour. For example, there may be four lessons before noon, but sometimes only three or two. The teacher may begin with arithmetic, pass over to geometry and finish with grammar; but sometimes the teacher and pupils are so carried away with the subject that the period may last three hours instead of one.

Generally, the classes begin about 9 A. M. and end at 8–9 P. M. The subjects during the day are: mechanical and graded reading, composition, penmanship, grammar, sacred history, Russian history, drawing, mechanical drawing, singing, mathematics, talks on the natural sciences and religion. In the evening are given singing, graded reading, talks, physical experiments and composition. There are no beginners. The lowest class reads, writes and solves problems in the first three arithmetical operations. The favorite subjects in the evening course are reading and experiments. But not all are admitted to the class in experiments, only the oldest and best, and the more intelligent ones of the second class.

The children bring nothing with them, neither text-books nor copybooks; nor have they anything to carry in their heads. No home lessons are given, and therefore the children are not obliged to remember any lessons. They do not think of their classes until they have begun. All that they bring with them is their impressionable nature and their conviction that to-day it will be as jolly in school as it was yesterday. One of the peculiarities of Tolstoy's school is that if the pupils want to go home at any time they are allowed to do so. Tolstoy gives the following dramatic account of a scene such as occurs once or twice a week:

> At times when the classes are uninteresting . . . and the children are tired, or before the holidays, when the ovens at home are prepared for a hot bath, two or three boys will suddenly rush into the room during the second or third afternoon class-hour, and will hurriedly pick out their caps.
>
> "What's up?"
>
> "Going home."
>
> "And studies? There is to be singing yet."
>
> "The boys say they are going home," says one, slipping away with his cap.
>
> "Who says so?"
>
> "The boys are gone!"
>
> "How is that?" asks the perplexed teacher who has prepared the lesson. "Stay!"
>
> But another boy runs into the room, with an excited and perplexed face.
>
> "What are you staying here for?" he angrily attacks the one held back, who, in indecision, pushes the cotton batting back into his cap. "The boys are way down there—I guess as far as the blacksmith's."
>
> "Have they gone?"
>
> "They have."
>
> And both run away, calling from behind the door: "Good-bye, Ivan Ivanovich!"

Such scenes are rather mortifying to the teacher, but he submits to them because they give a deeper meaning to the five, six or even seven classes voluntarily attended each day by the children. The desire to learn is strong enough in pupils to make them undergo many vexations in order to satisfy it. But truancy did not exist in Tolstoy's village school. Maybe if attendance at school were presented to pupils not as a duty but as a privilege, they might prize it more highly, and if it were shown that they could go home when they liked, the very sense of liberty would make them want to stay. It would bring into play not the authority, but the attraction of the master.

The children sit down whenever they please. They may sit on the benches, tables, window-sill, floor or in the armchair. The girls do not mingle with the boys. They always sit down near each other. Before the teacher has arrived the children gather near the porch, pushing each other off the steps, or go skating on the frozen crust of the smooth road, while some go to the schoolrooms. If it is cold, they read, write or play, while waiting for the master. No attempt whatever is made to enforce order, for, according to Tolstoy, "children should learn to keep order themselves." He describes the following scene:

> The teacher comes to the room, where on the floor lie screaming children, shouting, "The heap is not large enough!" or "You are choking me, boys!" or "That will do! Don't pull my hair!" and so forth.
>
> "Peter Mikhaylovich!" a voice at the bottom of the heap calls out to the teacher as he enters, "tell them to stop!"
>
> "Good morning, Peter Mikhaylovich!" shout the others, continuing their game.
>
> The teacher takes the books and gives them to those who have gone with him up to the bookcase; those who are lying on top of the heap, without getting up, also ask for books. The heap becomes smaller by degrees. The moment the majority have books, the rest run to the bookcase and cry: "Me too, me too. Give me yesterday's book, and me the *Koltsovian* book," and so forth. If there are two left who, excited from the struggle, still keep rolling on the floor, those who have books cry out to them:
>
> "Do not bother us! We can't hear a word! Stop now!"
>
> The excited boys submit, and most out of breath take hold of their books, and only at first, while sitting at their books, keep swinging their legs from unalloyed excitement. The martial spirit takes flight, and the reading spirit reigns in the room.
>
> With the same enthusiasm with which he was pulling Mitka's hair, he is now reading the *Koltsovian* book (so they call Koltsov's works with us), almost clenching his teeth, his eyes aflame and seeing nothing about him but his book. It will take as much effort to tear him away from the book as it took before to get him away from fighting. . . .
>
> I have never noticed any one whispering, or pinching his neighbor, or giggling, or snorting into his hand or complaining against another. When a pupil who has been studying with a sexton or in a country school comes to me with such a complaint, we say to him "Why don't you pinch back?"

Let us summarize the spirit of such educational school policy.

(1) Freedom is here to the extent of anarchy—in the good sense (called philosophic).

(2) All are socially equal: "Good morning, Peter Mikhaylovich!" is good enough for any real democrat.

(3) Tolstoy does not rule by objective force (though he did pull a pupil's hair for stupidity on one occasion).

(4) Natural human sense and desire rule the school.

(5) There is a sense of the need and the reason for order.

(6) The reaction is gradual, and two of the pupils have to be called by their fellows to stop fighting.

(7) There is self-government—certainly nothing better.

(8) A very little furniture (the children sit where they please, on a bench, on a window-sill or on the floor, etc.).

(9) Perfect order during instruction (no whispering, pinching or laughing).

(10) Irregular hours for lessons. (Sometimes the pupils themselves cry: "More, more!" and scold those who are tired of the subject. "If you are tired, go to the babies," they will call out contemptuously.)

(11) Classes last from one to three hours; interest controls.

(12) The children do not have to come to school, to remain at school or to pay attention at school.

Tolstoy claims that disorder on the surface is useful and necessary, however strange and irksome it may seem. Disorder or free order appears frightful to us only because we are accustomed to an entirely different system. The use of force is founded upon an inconsiderate and disrespectful interpretation of human nature. We are not able to see that the confusion will die down like a fire and that then we shall have an order better and more stable than we could get by coercion. Children should be treated as reasoning and reasonable beings and they will find out through experience that order is necessary.

In theory Tolstoy is right. The only hitch is this: his pupils were Russians, and not temperamental Irish or Mexicans. And furthermore most teachers are not Tolstoys, genuine educators and moulders, but simply mechanicians and drill-masters. Though we are inclined to think that in certain schools, of the Dewey type, for example, certain results are usually obtained, Tolstoy unfortunately does not say how long he had to wait and work for the result set forth in his writing. As Tolstoy remarks, "Most of our trouble is due to bad education." Victor Hugo declared in his "Les Misérables," "There are no bad mettles, but there is a bad culture." It is probably true that human nature pure and simple is not so bad as the orthodox dogmatists would have us believe. To think that human nature is good and true is a better dogma than to think that all men are born children of the devil. The actual fact, in all probability, lies somewhere between these extremes. Nobody really knows. In his famous "Resurrection" Tolstoy strikes a trenchant blow at a superstition common to past as well as modern psychology when he says:

> One of the first wide-spread superstitions is that every man has his own special, definite qualities; that a man is kind, cruel, wise, stupid, energetic, apathetic, etc. Men are not like that. We may say of a man that he is more often kind than cruel, oftener wise than stupid, oftener energetic than apathetic, etc., or the reverse; but it would be false to say of one man that he is kind and wise, of another that he is wicked and foolish. And yet we classify mankind in this way. And it is untrue. Men are like rivers: the water is the same in each, and like in all, but every river is narrow here, is more rapid there, here slower, there broader, now clear, now cold, now dull, now warm. It is the same with men. Every one carries within him the germs of every human quality, and sometimes one manifests itself, sometimes another, and the man often becomes unlike himself, while still remaining the same man. In some people these changes are very rapid.

Tolstoy held to the idea of letting children alone while they fought out their own battles, thus enabling them to reach a better understanding. He held that to step into a row as a *deus ex machina* and settle the affair and to compel the combatants to forgive and to kiss each other is a mistake. Tolstoy, here, is mixing things. In the first place children do not always hit upon the best possible solution, either in lessons or in passions. Indeed, even adults do not. Tolstoy unfortunately fails to introduce the help that children need to assist them in working out the passing problem. At this point the great Russian takes Rousseau too seriously and too blindly.

It is fair to say that the main force in Tolstoy's theory of education is liberty. In the completest sense possible, all his work is based on liberty. We submit the following statements as an indication of the place of this doctrine in Tolstoy's theory of education.

(1) Let the children select what and how they wish to learn.

(2) The results are good for the pupils, the teachers and the evolution of method.

(3) The teachers do not ascribe the failure of their teaching to the laziness, conduct, stupidity, deafness and stuttering of their pupils but to themselves, and so they try to find a solution.

(4) The children learn readily and eagerly. They want lessons for the evening.

(5) The children are quite free in class, and this, of course, is the chief condition of successful teaching.

(6) Natural relations always arise between teachers and pupils.

(7) In friendly relations the teacher learns to know and understand his pupils fully. (After school Tolstoy would often take a walk with them in the snow, some-

times going to the edge of the woods where the danger of wolves forbade further wandering; he would tell them stories and lead them into the discussion of the deepest questions, in which these peasant boys showed as much intelligence as learned and educated men; for a long time they walk on, talking thus seriously, one of the boys holding Tolstoy's hand affectionately.)

(8) The method is made to fit and please the pupil instead of the teacher.

(9) In fifteen years the method grew closer and closer to the pupil, and the teachers felt the need of learning.

(10) The pupil is placed in the foreground for education by the simplest and easiest path and not by some method once and forever fixed.

Tolstoy claimed "a certain pedagogic tact," and we grant it. He is right, no doubt, in thinking that rigid discipline of the schools, the lack of freedom and initiative, the constant demand for silence and obedience and the refusal to allow the pupils to criticize the lessons that they receive have a certain stupefying effect.

In 1845, sixty-five "lickings" a day were common in Boston and so it was in Tolstoy's day. History in the form of dates and names was next in importance to the whackings that the children got on hands and back. Thus it used to be, but now whipping is the exception. The schools are better and education is on a higher plane, very largely through a greater liberty. Tolstoy's day of liberty, equality and fraternity may some day arrive. Freeing the child in body and mind is the principal work of the schools.

Tolstoy was very careful to compare his school with that of the village. We have now worked out the following contrasts:

A. *In Village School:*	B. *In Tolstoy's School:*
1. The teacher always selects the method easiest for him.	1. The teacher always selects the method easiest for the pupil.
2. The easier it is for the teacher, the less satisfactory it is for the pupil.	2. The easier it is for the pupil, the harder it is for the teacher.
3. Some methods are good for the teacher and bad for the pupil.	3. Some methods are hard for the teacher and good for the pupil.
4. The village school does not recognize the individual differences and natural aptitudes between pupils.	4. Tolstoy's school recognizes the individual differences and natural aptitudes between pupils.

As for *examinations,* Tolstoy regarded them as a superstition of the Middle Ages. We think of the examinations as belonging to an age of education when memorizing played an essential part. To recite was to know and to think and this ancient superstition is not uncommon to this day. Many almost never reason but they "try to think," *i.e.,* to recall the words of a speech formerly committed to memory. For the examination in the sense of just memorizing and committing to memory Tolstoy had no use. Examinations are often ends in themselves and the pupil does not learn philosophy or history, but he does learn to answer questions—a totally useless branch of study. No man needs more material at ready recall than is necessary to carry on thinking. The rest of his material may go on file for purpose of illustration. Tolstoy detested insincerity and false foundations in thinking and education. We shall undertake to mention four:

(1) The child learns in order not to be punished.

(2) The child learns in order to earn a reward.

(3) The child learns in order to do better than others.

(4) The child or young man learns in order to obtain an advantageous position in the world.

It is highly probable that we should go to school to learn how to think accurately and as resourcefully as possible in life's most common and even in life's most trying and puzzling situations. Tolstoy's long school day and his story telling are very true to the best life of the school. It is highly probable that most lesson periods are too short for the right sort of mental growing and understanding, but often too long in pumping for facts held in memory. The imagination is not appealed to often enough. Just here Dewey would stress the importance of imagery. It is probable that one reason why people go to the movies is that they have such a poor movie show of their own. The person who can not readily imagine can not see very much when it comes to a final summation.

III

Tolstoy used his experimental school as a laboratory for experiments rather than as a mere deviation from the established public school system which tends to mechanize, automatize, petrify and ossify, or to boost this or that educational philosophy. In the field of education, too, he exhibits a profound habit of questioning all traditions and customs in all realms of thought and activity, and of making them answer for themselves. Tolstoy, like all great reformers, was first a doubter. To doubt means to investigate; to investigate means to think; to think means to look for the truth—and the truth will save us all. After all, people are not wicked but duped. Ignorance is one of the main causes of all human misunderstandings, which are the result of the lack of grasping another's point of view. While altogether disapproving punishment, Tolstoy admits that the habit of punishing was so ingrained in him and the teachers of his school that they indulged in it once or twice, but the result was to convince him that it was a grave error.

One day a Leyden jar disappeared from the laboratory. Another day pencils and books began to vanish mysteriously. The best pupils blushed and stammered when questioned about it as if they had been guilty, but it was only the idea of being suspected that affected them so. Finally the culprits were discovered. Two boys from a neighboring village had hidden their booty in a small box. The disclosure was a great satisfaction to the school, removing terrible suspicion from other children.

Tolstoy in his embarrassment submitted the case to the pupils of his school. He asked them to suggest the kind of punishment. Some suggested whipping, and asked to be allowed to do the whipping themselves. Others recommended placing a placard bearing the word "thief" on each of the guilty pair. This suggestion was accepted and a little girl was called in to sew the obnoxious word upon their coats. The rest of the pupils looked on with malicious glee, and some of the boys could not help mocking at the two poor transgressors, begging that they might be led through the village and carry the placard until the next holiday. The two boys cried bitterly, and one of them cast wicked and savage glances at his exulting classmates. As he went home, with his head bent down and eyes on the ground and with the gait of a criminal, the boys followed in a crowd and tormented him so cruelly and unnaturally that they appeared to be possessed by an evil spirit. Tolstoy noticed that from that time on that boy became less studious and ceased to participate in the games of the other pupils. A little later this boy stole some coppers from one of his teachers. Once more the placard was fastened upon him, and the same brutal scenes were repeated. Tolstoy reasons as follows:

> I began to admonish him, just as all educators admonish; a grownup boy, a good talker, who was present, began to admonish him, too, repeating the words which he, no doubt, had heard from his father, an innkeeper.

"You steal once, and you steal a second time," he spoke, solemnly declaiming his words, "and it becomes a habit, and leads to no good."

I began to feel vexed. I was almost enraged against the thief. I looked at the face of the punished boy, which now was even paler, more suffering and more cruel than before; I for some reason thought of prisoners in jail, and I suddenly felt ashamed and felt such loathing for myself that I tore off the stupid label, told him to go wherever he pleased, and suddenly convinced myself, not through reasoning, but with my whole being, that I had no right to torment the unfortunate boy, and that I could not make of him what I and the innkeeper's son would like to make of him. I convinced myself that there were secrets of the soul, hidden from us, upon which only life can act, and not moral precepts and punishment.

What nonsense! The boy has stolen a book. By a whole complicated road of feelings, thoughts, faulty ratiocinations, he was led to take a book belonging to somebody else, which he for some reason locked up in a chest, and I paste on him a piece of paper with the word "thief," which means something entirely different! What for? To punish him by shaming him? What for? What is shame? How do we know that shame destroys the inclination toward thieving? May be it only encourages it. May be that which was expressed in his face was not at all shame. Indeed, I know for sure that it was not shame, but something quite different, which might have slept forever in his soul, and which it was good to evoke. May be there, in the world which is called real, in the world of the Palmerstons, Cayenne [it should be remembered that Tolstoy wrote this in the early sixties]—in the world where not that is reasonable which is reasonable, but that which is real—let people, who themselves have been punished, invent rights and duties to punish. Our world of children —of simple, independent men—must remain pure from self-deception and the criminal faith in the legality of punishment, free from that self-deception and belief that the feeling of revenge becomes just the moment you call it punishment.

In one word, Tolstoy claims that the school has no right and ought not to punish or reward the pupils. Tolstoy follows Rousseau and the naturalistic school in his thinking.

(To be concluded)

MIDDLE SCHOOL BIOLOGY IN CHINA[1]

By JAMES G. NEEDHAM
CORNELL UNIVERSITY

IN the common schools of the nation children should have a chance to learn what every one needs to know about the life of the world we live in. They should learn the common names of common plants and animals: of trees, grain crops, vegetables, flowers and weeds; of domesticated animals, pets, birds, food fishes and common insects; for these are the things we must live with and live by. They feed us and clothe us, they serve or injure us, they provide the material for our arts and crafts. They supply us with wholesome comforts. They en-

[1] Professor Needham spent the academic year 1927–8 in China, where, on behalf of the China Foundation for the Promotion of Education and Culture, he lectured on biological subjects, and visited and conferred with teachers of biology in fifteen Chinese universities. He found the biological work of university courses very similar to that done in America, taught by men of fairly good training (many of them, indeed, his own pupils) and with fairly good equipment. But their pupils are ill prepared. The weakest point in China's biological teaching program is below the universities in the middle schools and in the lower grades. Both biology and nature study appear in their printed programs; but there is hardly any life in the biology, and nature study quite avoids the study of nature—a condition that has not yet wholly passed in America. The teachers lecture, often from the old lecture notes of their own student days, or read to their pupils from books about things that live in Europe or in America, but not in China. Professor Needham spent a large part of the year in collaboration with Professor S. C. Lee, of the National Normal University, Peking, working on a program of middle school biology, based wholly on Chinese materials. That book is now being printed in Chinese. The following paragraphs are from Professor Needham's Introduction. The principles here concisely stated grew out of his long teaching experience in America.

tertain us and they educate us. They furnish the physical basis for the imagery of our poetry and classics.

Children should learn the activities of common plants and animals. They should observe the growth habits and flowering and fruiting habits of plants; they should learn the brooding and nesting habits of animals, their modes of locomotion, walking, running, jumping, swimming, flying, their voices and sense perceptions, for in all these activities we of the human species are partakers.

Children should learn to observe the changes that go on in infancy and growth of living creatures. They should note the changes of days and seasons, for in such changes human beings also are involved.

Such knowledge is very practical. It is a part of a liberal education. It should be an important part of the school program.

There are some general practices that should be observed in the teaching of biology whatever the grade of the work. Five of these relating to the approach to the subject may be stated as follows:

(1) Living plants and animals should be studied before dead ones, for biology with life left out is not the sort to interest and hold the mind of the normal youth.

(2) Whole plants and animals should be observed before dissection and analysis are begun.

(3) Native and local plants and animals should be studied in preference to foreign ones.

(4) Forms big enough for easy examination should be used before microscopic ones are taken up.

(5) Simple methods and apparatus should be used before complex ones; eyes before lenses and simple lenses before compound microscopes; fingers before forceps; knives before scalpels and scalpels before microtomes.

Nature study is the study of nature, and not reading about things or hearsay or lecturing. If in the elementary schools pupils have had some real nature study they will come up to the middle schools with their eyes opened to see the life of their environment, with their wits sharpened to appreciate the grace and beauty of the plants and animals about them, and with some idea of the practical value of a knowledge of living things. This is basic knowledge. If they come up without it, the middle schools will have to supply it.

The natural order of inquiry of the child's mind is somewhat as follows:

I. First comes the age of *discovery*—of random observations. The natural questions about a plant or an animal are such as these:

(1) What is its name?
(2) How is it known (recognition characters)?
(3) Where does it live?
(4) What does it do?
(5) What is it good for?

These are elementary questions. Good nature study will answer them.

II. Then comes the age of beginning *analysis*—when such questions as these naturally arise:

(1) What are its allies? (elementary concepts of grouping).
(2) What are its parts? (beginning anatomy).
(3) What are their functions? (beginning physiology).
(4) How does it develop? (beginning embryology).
(5) What can be done with it?

Such questions as these should find their answers in middle-school biology.

III. Then comes the age of *interpretation*, when such questions as these demand answers:

(1) What is its basic substance?
(2) What are the essential elements and processes of its organization?
(3) What are its biological affinities?
(4) What are the laws and processes of its development?
(5) What is its philosophical significance?

These are not elementary ideas. They belong to college biology and should not be introduced too early.

If questions arise as to correlation of subjects studied and how to avoid repetition, let it be remembered that repetition is not to be avoided. Proper repetition reinforces the lessons and deepens the interest in them. As in other subjects—reading, writing, arithmetic, etc.—repetition is the rule. All repeat; all use the same things over and over again, but they are used in further construction, further upbuilding of knowledge. So if the frog has been made the subject of nature study lessons it is not thereby at all disqualified for use in middle school and college. The middle-school teacher should first make sure that the elementary questions (such as in Group I) have been answered and then should proceed further to examine structure and function and life history in greater detail, introducing the aid of books and lenses and laboratory tools in moderation and teaching the making of experiments with the living animal to explain its powers and activities and the making of simple preparations of specimens for permanent record.

What is made the subject of study is often unimportant. The essential thing is that it be real *study of the living thing* and not mere hearsay or reading or lecturing about the thing.

The rigidity of the school program with its fixed hours and lock-step procedure is quite unfavorable for gaining the greatest benefit from the study of living nature. The best opportunities for learning biology are not always in the laboratory. They are often found in the street, in the meadow or by the pond; and the activities of plants and animals rarely conform well to the hours of the school program. Therefore, we recommend that biology teachers allow such pupils as show an aptitude for biology to make studies and collections individually and outside of regular school hours. Let them report the results of such studies to the class. Such work will often be of the highest value and should receive school credit.

It is a monstrous abuse of the science of biology to teach it only in the laboratory. "Life is adjustment to the order of nature."[2] Life belongs in the fields, in the ponds, on the mountains and by the seashore. Its wonderful fitness to place and conditions can be rightly understood only when seen in the natural setting. Students of all grades should be encouraged to go out-of-doors and see this fitness for themselves. Thus and thus only will they learn the rôles played by members of natural society.

The way to encourage such study afield is to give credit for it in the record of the classes. Surely it is as worthy of credit as are observations on bones and blood. The way to insure that no unfair advantage is taken of freedom of time for personal observations afield is to require definite report of observations made. Such report may take the form of (a) notes and drawings of things observed or (b) specimens collected and brought to the class exercises in proper containers. The entire class will often find much interest in oral reports by its members of field observations when these are illustrated by the specimens that have been observed.

Collecting the materials for the class exercises should be largely done by members of the class. The teacher will hardly have time to do it all, so great is the burden of classes usually imposed on him; and if he had time it is not fair that he should do it all and so deprive his pupils of that contact with living nature that is often the best part of a biological education. The way to get it done by the pupils is to give them credit for doing it, the same as for any other good work. The teacher should look ahead and see what is going to be needed, and should plan his course to fit the local opportunities and the season. He should then clearly state what specimens of plants or animals are needed, and when; should tell in what kind of places they are to be found, and how collected. The school should provide collecting apparatus and containers. And credit should be promised according to the results severally obtained, just as for work done in class. Foresight and planning will then be the chief work of the teacher; collecting and arranging materials will be done by the class, greatly to its own educational profit.

It is what students do that educates them. Therefore, the good teacher will test his materials and methods by the reactions of his students. He will endeavor to find things that are of interest because of their activity, their beauty and their practical value. He will find tasks simple enough for satisfactory performance by his pupils and difficult enough to call forth competitive effort in their doing. The test of good teaching will lie in the attitude of the pupil at the end. The pupil should come forth having a little real first-hand knowledge and an appetite for more.

[2] W. K. Brooks.

EDUCATIONAL EVENTS

THE COUNTRY SCHOOLS OF NORTHERN IRELAND

THE Educational Supplement of the London *Times* reports that some time ago the Advisory Council of Education was asked by the Ministry to report on the best method of stimulating an interest in country life through the country schools and to state whether a rural bias in the curriculum is desirable and, if so, whether it can best be secured solely through the medium of school gardening and nature study, or whether the teaching of other subjects such as English, geography and arithmetic can be adapted to this end. The council's reply has now been received and circulated to education committees, managers and teachers with an expression of the ministry's cordial approval and a request that action may be taken as far as possible in accordance with the suggestion put forward by the council.

The council recognizes that it is not the school influence which is mainly responsible for the drift to the towns and that the tendency can not effectually be combated by the schools unaided. It is admitted, however, that something can be done in the schools to foster an interest and a pride in the life of the countryside. The council states that the selection of the right type of teacher is of primary importance.

As to the curriculum, the *Times* states that the council is against any attempt to give formal instruction in agriculture, and would rely chiefly on encouraging the teacher to adapt the daily lessons to the local environment. It would give a further stimulus to the provision of school gardens and the teaching of gardening and it suggests that inspectors of the Department of Agriculture should be invited to visit the schools and give advice and encouragement. Again, in regard to nature study, the teachers are to be encouraged to act on their own initiative, to modify and adapt the prescribed program to fit local conditions and to make use of country excursions teaching their pupils that their intelligence can be applied to other things as well as books.

On the question of giving a rural bias to the teaching of arithmetic, English and geography, the council judges it to be unnecessary to provide special rural arithmetic text-books. It is sufficient if the teacher is encouraged to accustom his pupils to apply the rules to such problems as daily perplex the farmer and his wife. In geography the council recommends a study of local topography together with local history and local monuments. As for English, they condemn the existing rural readers as being dull and too obviously written with a purpose, and they suggest the compilation of an interesting set of selections from standard works.

The council recommends playing fields, organized games and the development of the activities of Boy Scouts and Girl Guides. These things are said to be often neglected in the country because they are not there, as in the towns, clearly necessary for the health of the children, and the importance of an organized social life is not generally recognized. But the chief cause of the flight from the countryside is probably not the economic motive, though the council is inclined to give this precedence. It would seem to be rather a natural craving for variety and excitement, and these can be supplied even in the country by an organized social life, which should have its beginnings in the schools.

APPROPRIATIONS RECOMMENDED BY GOVERNOR ROOSEVELT FOR THE NEW YORK STATE DEPARTMENT OF EDUCATION

THE Department of Education comprises the division of administration, the section of mandatory allowances for the support of common schools, academic quotas, continuation schools, etc., the two state normal colleges, nine normal schools, college of agriculture, college of home economics, veterinary college and drill hall at Cornell, agricultural experiment station at Geneva, six secondary schools of agriculture, the school of clay working and ceramics at Alfred, the nautical school, the motion picture division, the college of forestry at Syracuse University and the support, care and education of the deaf, dumb and blind.

The decrease in the education department (administration) is $26,169.19. The personal service of the administration has increased $31,-905; this provides five new positions amounting to $12,360; three of these positions are for the expansion of rural education, and there are regular increases to the various members of the education staff amounting to $19,245. It has been the custom for two or three years past to attempt to equalize the salaries of the lower-paid employees in this department, and instead of attempting to do it at one time it has been spread over a period of years, and the increase to the regular staff there is not very large when you consider that it covers increases to a group containing approximately 750 persons.

Maintenance and operation in the administration has a decrease of $9,400; this is mainly made up of a special item of last year that provided an appropriation for new bookcases in the library.

Immediately available sets forth a decrease of $42,174.19. This is an amount that was appropriated by the legislature of 1928 but which it will not be necessary to equal this year.

Construction sets forth a decrease of $6,500; last year an appropriation was made to complete the construction of the grill in the State Library.

The various education statutes provide for certain increments to carry on education work throughout the state, and in this class comes the support of common schools, academic quotas, books, apparatus and works of art, attendance of academic pupils, non-resident tuition, the training of teachers, state scholarships, rehabilitation of physically handicapped, support and instruction of the deaf, dumb and blind, and grants to libraries. There is a total increase under this heading of $7,990,860. Of this amount the largest increase is in the support of common schools; this appropriation increased $7,616,000 over the appropriation of 1928. Continuation schools are closely allied to the support of common schools; this increased $173,115; academic quotas increased $30,000; supplying of books, apparatus and works of art increased $50,000; non-resident tuition increased $90,000, and state aid to physically handicapped children increased $50,000.

The increase in the state colleges and normal schools is $112,253.97; of this amount $108,590 is an increase in personal service. Most of this increase is provided for by statute, that is, an increment for good and meritorious teaching service each year, and for a two-year course in training teachers for rural schools at New Paltz, Potsdam and Geneseo Normal Schools.

The maintenance and operation has increased $14,640; this increase is mainly made up of educational supplies and a more complete library in each of the normal schools.

The immediately available item has decreased $2,091.03 and is explained by the fact that it was not necessary to make this appropriation this year.

Construction decreased $9,000. Last year it was necessary to make appropriations of $115,-000; this year the recommendations are $106,-000, of this amount $100,000 is for the State College for Teachers at Buffalo.

THE SCHOOL OF MUSIC OF THE UNIVERSITY OF MICHIGAN

WE learn from *The Michigan Alumnus* that the board of regents decided at its meeting on January 21 to make the present University School of Music and its complete administrative organization one of the divisions of the university. Under the new arrangement, which will go into effect with the fall term of 1929–1930, students in the School of Music will have all the rights and privileges of any other division of the university. It will also be possible for the School of Music to offer lower tuition charges in accordance with those of the other colleges, with the financial aid which affiliation with the university will make possible. The action also provides for an exchange of credit with other colleges or schools of the university, the exact amount to be determined by the dean of the division in which the student is enrolled. Degrees in the future will be granted through the university at the general graduation exercises held each June.

About a year ago President Little appointed a committee of the Board of Regents to meet with a committee representing the Board of Directors of the school to work out a plan for the proposed unification. Hitherto the School of Music has operated on the basis of a private school, although in reality cooperating to some extent with the university. The School of Music organization will remain intact, retaining its present administrative staff and faculty. Charles A. Sink is president and Earl V. Moore musical director.

A new building to house the school will be constructed by the university as soon as funds are made available by the Legislature. However, no definite time was suggested for the consummation of this project, although the present building on Maynard Street passes into the hands of the university. According to the new arrangement it is understood that the university will provide a sum not to exceed $60,000 yearly to aid the new division in paying the salary expenses of its staff.

ENDOWMENT OF THE YALE UNIVERSITY SCHOOL OF NURSING BY THE ROCKEFELLER INSTITUTE

THE Yale School of Nursing has received a gift of $1,000,000 for endowment from the Rockefeller Foundation. "Coming as it does at the end of a five-year trial period," President Angell said, in making the announcement, "this gift is of great significance. It means that a novel experiment has proved a success, and an educational program for nurses, comparable to that offered in medicine, law and engineering, is placed on a stable and permanent basis. It means further that nursing is now recognized to be of sufficient importance to warrant the existence of a school organized from the point of view of educating the nurse rather than primarily for the purpose of providing a hospital with nursing service."

Among the features of the plan are the high admission requirements; a curriculum which emphasizes a thorough study of fundamental as well as practical training; payment of a substantial tuition fee by the student, and furnishing of maintenance by the hospital during the period of service in the wards.

When the Yale School of Nursing was organized in 1923, under the supervision of Miss Annie Goodrich, the training schools in this country were graduating some 17,000 students a year and many graduates were finding it difficult to earn a living. The purpose of the Yale School, therefore, was to offer better educational opportunities rather than to increase the number of graduate nurses. Two years of college work were required for admission. A course of study was arranged to cover twenty-eight months. It was stipulated that the student should spend such time in the hospital ward as the mastery of bedside-care demanded. Students are rotated from one service to another so that each may have experience in all of the departments, including internal medicine, surgery, obstetrics and gynecology and psychiatry. With the practical work is coordinated the study of fundamental subjects, including bacteriology, anatomy, physiology, psychology, sociology and economics. The preventive aspect of disease is always emphasized.

The Yale School of Nursing is one of the two in this country organized as independent schools in a university and planned to be equal in standing with the other professional schools of the institution. There are at present 116 students enrolled, and more than half of these hold college degrees. Affiliates from other schools are admitted to courses not given in their own institution, but they are not awarded degrees or diplomas. A six-weeks' course was also offered this year to 24 graduate nurses from all parts of the country who were selected by the Rockefeller Foundation to study the methods adopted by the school.

THE EXCEPTIONAL BOY

DISTINGUISHED engineers and others, encouraged by the success of previous efforts, will again aid in the search for the "best discoverable boy" of 1929, to study at the Massachusetts Institute of Technology beginning next fall. Among the committee which will seek to determine the most likely candidate for technical study in any of the institute's departments are Dr. Samuel Wesley Stratton, president of the institute; Edward P. Warner, assistant secretary of the navy for aeronautics; Gerard Swope, president of the General Electric Company; Elisha Lee, vice-president of the Pennsylvania Railroad; Frank W. Lovejoy, general manager of the Eastman Kodak Company; Frank B.

Jewett, vice-president of the American Telephone and Telegraph Company; James P. Munroe, president of the Munroe Felt and Paper Company; Arthur D. Little, president of Arthur D. Little, Inc.; William E. Nickerson, vice-president of the Gillette Safety Razor Company, and Ellery Sedgwick, editor of the *Atlantic Monthly*.

This committee, assembled by the *Youth's Companion*, which offers the scholarship, will give final consideration to the qualifications of young men between the ages of 17 and 22, who have shown outstanding ability, and will award a four-year scholarship to at least one of them. Entrants will be required to write a short essay on the subject "Why I Should Like a Technical Education." Those who successfully pass will later be considered on the basis of ability shown in presenting projects in science or engineering which they have themselves conceived and executed.

A similar search last year resulted in the choice of two boys for the honor—Elwood W. Schafer, of Cleveland, Ohio, and Rodney D. Chipp, Jr., of New York City. Both submitted original technical projects showing unusual scientific ability. They are now students at Massachusetts Institute of Technology. The success of the plan went far toward convincing authorities that this nation-wide search for students of unusual ability opened a new field in educational research.

REQUIREMENTS FOR THE DEGREE OF MASTER OF EDUCATION AT HARVARD UNIVERSITY

As registration begins at the School of Education for the second half-year it is announced that teachers and other students of education in the neighborhood of Boston are enabled to secure the degree of master of education in the Harvard Graduate School by several new means. These changes are in line with the recent decision to make the master of education degree a work of two years' time.

The total requirement of study for the degree is sixteen half-courses, the equivalent of two years. In addition to the work in courses, candidates for the degree take a general examination at the conclusion of their program of study and meet an apprenticeship requirement.

The recent votes of the faculty concern credit for courses at other institutions, credit for extension courses and the admission of part-time students to courses they wish to take as auditors. These changes are made to fit the needs of students who are unable to take two full and continuous years of work at the school. A student who spends one full and continuous year in residence at the school may receive credit, in the discretion of the administrative board, for eight half-courses of work done at another institution.

Students whose work is done entirely on part-time may combine courses taken during the academic year with courses taken in the summer school and extension course. Not more than four courses taken by extension will be credited under any plan.

The general examination will require a sequence of regular work, but the course credits have no necessary relation to the candidate's success in the general examination. The committee of examiners will shortly issue a general statement on the scope and character of the examination itself.

The new two-year program for the Ed.M. offers to any teacher or prospective teacher an unusual opportunity to secure a thorough preparation for professional service. Experienced teachers may meet the apprenticeship requirements by credit for their regular work in school positions.

THE NINTH ANNUAL MEETING OF THE CONFERENCE OF SUPERVISORS AND DIRECTORS OF INSTRUCTION

THE ninth annual meeting of the National Conference of Supervisors and Directors of Instruction, formerly the National Conference on Educational Method, will be held in Cleveland on February 26 and 27. There will be two sessions and a luncheon.

The first program—that on Tuesday morning—will be devoted to the topic, "Next Steps in Supervision." The program on Wednesday morning will be given over to a discussion of the second Yearbook of the conference, prepared by Professor L. J. Brueckner and his committee on "Scientific Method in Supervision." The Yearbook is made up of twenty-two chapters devoted primarily to the exposition of newer and more objective techniques in the study of teaching. The Yearbook will be ready for distribution shortly before the convention.

On Wednesday at noon there will be a luncheon for members only at the Statler Hotel. Dr. Burton, of the University of Chicago, and Dr. Morrison, assistant commissioner for elementary education in the State of New York, will speak. Afterwards there will be a discussion of the policies of the conference.

The most important business to come before the conference at this time will be the question of final vote of confirmation of the affiliation of the conference with the National Education Association. In accordance with a resolution passed at the meeting in Cambridge in February, 1928, a petition was circulated requesting that the conference be made a regular department of the National Education Association. Four hundred signers were secured. The petition, together with a revision of the constitution to adapt it to the general policies of the parent organization, were submitted to the executive committee of the National Education Association at the meeting in Minneapolis in July. The petition was unanimously accepted, subject to a further vote of confirmation after the final action of the conference itself at its next annual meeting.

CLEVELAND MEETINGS ON VOCATIONAL GUIDANCE AND PLACEMENT

THE annual meetings of organizations interested in vocational guidance, placement, employment management and educational personnel practice will bring a large number of educators, executives and research workers to Cleveland, February 20 to 23, just preceding the sessions of the Department of Superintendence of the National Education Association. Included in this group are the National Vocational Guidance Association, the National Association of Appointment Secretaries, the National Committee of Bureaus of Occupation, the National Association of Deans of Women, the College Personnel Officers, the Personnel Research Federation, and individual representatives from the American Management Association, the Deans of Men, the American Association of Collegiate Registrars, the American Council on Education and other interested societies.

These groups are cooperating to avoid duplication in programs and also to make it possible to share the unique features of each organization by holding open meetings and some joint sessions. The programs will be attractive to vocational counselors, specialists in occupational information, placement officers, employers and employment managers, deans, registrars, teachers, psychologists and personnel workers. The common points in the separate programs show a growing realization both of the diverse responsibility for counseling, and of the fact that problems of adjustment in and out of school concern a great many administrative officers as well as specialists.

A joint meeting of all the organizations will be held on Saturday morning, February 23, under the auspices of the Personnel Research Federation. A report of the study, "Careers of 15,000 Business and Professional Women," now being made at the University of Michigan will be given. Dr. Margaret Elliott, assistant professor of personnel management, will report the part dealing with "Problems of Occupational Classification," and Dr. Grace E. Manson, research associate in the school of business administration, will present "Educational Background and Occupation Progress," which deals with the relationship between education and earnings within this large and representative group of women. Dr. Harold A. Edgerton, of the Ohio State University, is to report on "A Follow-up Study Through College of 2,000 Freshmen." Dr. Edward K. Strong, Jr., of Stanford University, will speak on the "Measurement of Vocational Interests." As a final summing up of these cooperative meetings, Dean Francis F. Bradshaw, of the University of North Carolina, is to lead a discussion of the possibility of coordination of efforts of all groups interested in personnel, placement and vocational guidance.

EDUCATIONAL NOTES AND NEWS

PROFESSOR JOHN DEWEY, of Columbia University, will leave for Scotland early in March to deliver a course of Gifford lectures at the University of Edinburgh. Dr. Dewey expects to be abroad for six months.

PROFESSOR CHARLES A. BEARD, the historian, formerly professor in Columbia University, will lecture for several weeks beginning in the latter part of March at Harvard University, under the auspices of the department of government.

ACCORDING to newspaper reports, Mr. Newton D. Baker, of Cleveland, has been offered the presidency of the Johns Hopkins University, of which institution he is one of the trustees. Dr. R. Lyman Wilbur, president of Stanford University, is reported to have received leave of absence from the trustees in order that he may accept the secretaryship of the Department of the Interior in Mr. Hoover's cabinet.

A DINNER to Dr. Clarence C. Little, who recently resigned as president of the University of Michigan, will be given on the evening of February 15 at the Hotel Commodore by graduates of the university.

DR. JAMES M. KIERAN took up on February 1 his work as president of Hunter College, where he has been acting president since December. The formal induction of Dr. Kieran will probably take place in March.

CARL P. BLACKWELL on December 10 became dean of agriculture and director of the experiment station of the Oklahoma Agricultural and Mechanical College at Stillwater. He was previously agronomist for the National Fertilizer Company.

THE Kent State Normal College, Kent, Ohio, will formally install Dr. James O. Engelman as president on March 22 and 27, and will at the same time dedicate a new training school building and a new library.

DR. ROBERT ANDREWS MILLIKAN, director of the Norman Bridge Laboratory of the California Institute of Technology, and Dr. Albert A. Michelson, professor of physics at the University of Chicago, will receive the gold medals awarded by the Society of Arts and Sciences for distinguished work in science. Presentations will take place at a dinner at the Biltmore Hotel, New York City, on February 22.

PORTRAITS of Dr. William H. Nichols, the late William A. White and the late Charles E. Perkins, the three chief benefactors of the Polytechnic Institute of Brooklyn, were recently unveiled in the office of the president of the institute. Mr. Charles E. Potts, chairman of the corporation, acted as master of ceremonies and spoke briefly of the life and work of each benefactor. Dr. Nichols (Polytechnic, 1868), formerly chairman of the board of the General Chemical Company and chairman of the corporation of the Polytechnic, is perhaps the leading figure in the world's chemical industry. He is still vice-chairman of the Polytechnic Corporation and has been the chief force in establishing the Polytechnic on its present basis. The late William A. White, of Brooklyn (Polytechnic, 1859), was celebrated both for his wide philanthropy and his library, one of the finest private collections in the world, containing rare Shakespeariana and early editions of Keats and Blake, and other valuable books, which he knew thoroughly and loved both as a scholar and a connoisseur. The late Charles E. Perkins, also of Brooklyn, was a leader in the manufacture of textiles and made the Polytechnic the residuary legatee of his estate. The portraits of Dr. Nichols and Mr. Perkins were painted by George R. Boynton; that of Mr. White by Henry Stanley Todd. The unveiling of the portraits and the reception that followed were attended by relatives and friends of the benefactors, members of the corporation, officials of the institute and representatives of the faculty.

DR. ORTON LOWE, head of the English department at Miami University and for many years director of English in the Pennsylvania State Department of Public Instruction, has been chosen director of the summer institute of English education of the Pennsylvania State College. Among those who will lecture at the session are: Joseph Hergesheimer, Pennsylvania novelist and short story writer; Edward Davison, English poet; Vachel Lindsay, one of America's major poets; Professor John Macy, of Columbia University; Miss Helen L. Cohen, head of the English department of Washington Irving High School, New York City, and author of a number of books on plays and the theater, and Mrs. Marjorie S. Douglas, writer and critic of short stories.

Professor Daniel C. Knowlton, of Yale University, an authority on visual instruction in the elementary schools, will be among the visiting professors next month at the school of education of Boston University, under the co-operative program sponsored by both the school of education and the Massachusetts Elementary Principals' Association.

At Teachers College, Columbia University, Charles I. Lambert has been appointed professor of psychiatric education, and H. Shelton Smith, professor of education. Adelaide T. Case has been promoted to be associate professor of education.

In the absence of Dr. L. A. Headley, chairman of the department of education at Carleton College, Professor John Phelan will be acting department head. Mr. Clyde C. Hillis, who recently received his M.A. in education at Indiana University, will take Professor Headley's classes for the semester.

Harvey H. Davis, formerly director of the division of records and statistics of the St. Louis, Mo., board of education, has become assistant professor in the school administration department of the Ohio University.

Shaw Livermore, formerly assistant dean of the School of Business at Harvard University, and more recently associated with the firm of Tucker, Anthony and Company, of Boston, has been appointed assistant professor of economics in the University of Buffalo.

S. B. Butler, superintendent of schools of Madison County, Alabama, has announced his candidacy for the office of state superintendent of education in 1930.

William H. Hanlon, superintendent of schools of Contra Costa County, California, has been elected president of the bay section of the California Teachers' Association for the next year.

E. S. Russell, formerly superintendent of schools at Simsbury, Conn., has become director of the teacher-training school at New Haven, Conn. Mr. Paul D. Collier, of Port Arthur, Texas, has succeeded Mr. Russell as superintendent.

William A. Frayer, professor of European history and member of the faculty of the University of Michigan for eighteen years, has resigned to become president of the Bureau of University Travel, with headquarters in Newton, Massachusetts.

Thomas W. Lamont, the banker, has accepted the chairmanship of the newly formed Diphtheria Prevention Commission of New York City, which has been organized with clinics scattered over the city.

Professor William Hovgaard, of the Department of Naval Architecture and Marine Engineering at Massachusetts Institute of Technology, has been named a member of the committee on ship construction recently appointed by the United States Department of Commerce.

Dr. Oliver C. Lockhart, head of the department of economics and finance in the University of Buffalo, has been granted leave of absence from January, 1929, to January, 1930, to accompany Professor E. W. Kemmerer as a member of the Commission of Financial Advisers to the Government of China. During his absence Dr. Ralph C. Epstein will be acting head of the department.

President Ernest Martin Hopkins, of Dartmouth College, expects to leave Hanover in the near future for a vacation of several months.

Sally Jean Lucas, who was asked by Governor-General Stimson, of the Philippine Islands, to visit that country for the purpose of developing a health education program for the schools of the islands, sailed from Seattle on January 12 for Manila and will remain there for three months. She will also consult with educational and health authorities in the promotion of programs in Japan. She has given similar service in the Panama Canal Zone and also has visited Belgium and recommended a program for the schools of that country.

Professor Oliver M. Washburn, of the art department of the University of California, is planning a group tour of Europe and the Mediterranean region.

T. J. McCormack, superintendent of the LaSalle-Peru Township High School and director of the LaSalle-Peru-Oglesby Junior College, at LaSalle, Illinois, has been granted a leave of absence for five months, which he will spend in study and travel in Europe.

Dr. Aldred Scott Warthin, professor of pathology, has been appointed Henry Russel lecturer at the University of Michigan. Previous Henry Russel lecturers are Professor Moses Gomberg, in 1926; Professor Frederick G. Novy, in 1927, and Professor Henry Arthur Sanders, in 1928. The Henry Russel award has gone in past years to Assistant (now Associate) Professor Carter Goodrich, of the department of economics, in 1926; Assistant Professor Albert Hyma, of the department of history, in 1927, and Assistant Professor Laurence M. Gould, of the department of geology, now with the Byrd Antarctic Expedition, in 1928. The winner of the award for 1929 will be announced at the time of the lecture in May. The Henry Russel lectureship and the Henry Russel award have been established with the endowment fund bequeathed to the university by the late Mr. Henry Russel, of Detroit. The purpose of Mr. Russel's bequest was stated to be the increase of the salaries of the teaching staff, and since by itself the income of the fund was not enough to raise salaries substantially, the regents in 1925 decided to assign the income annually in equal portions to two members of the faculties, one, the lecturer, to be nominated by the executive board of the Research Club for distinguished attainment as a scholar; the other, the recipient of the award, to be one of the younger members of the faculties, chosen for his attainments in his subject and his promise of future distinction.

Dr. Kurt Koffka, professor of research in psychology at Smith College, will give four lectures on "The Gestalt Theory" at the New School for Social Research, New York City, on Tuesday evenings, at 8: 20 P. M., beginning on February 12.

The Honorable Charles Evans Hughes was the principal speaker at a dinner of Brown alumni on February 1.

Professor George Herbert Mead, professor of philosophy in the University of Chicago, has been chosen Carus Lecturer before the American Philosophical Association for the year 1929. The lectures have been previously given by Professor John Dewey, of Columbia University, and Professor Arthur Lovejoy, of the Johns Hopkins University.

Alexander D. Lindsay, master of Balliol College, Oxford, will deliver the annual Godkin lectures for 1928–29 at Harvard University on February 5 and 7. He will lecture on "Some New Forms of Public Opinion."

Frederick George Young, dean of the school of sociology at the University of Oregon, formerly head of the department of economics and sociology, and later dean of the graduate school from its founding, at the University of Oregon, secretary of the Oregon State Historical Society and editor of its *Quarterly,* died in Eugene, on January 4. Philip A. Parsons, dean of the School of Social Work in Portland, has been appointed acting dean of the School of Sociology.

James Phinney Munroe, the manufacturer, long identified with the interests of the Massachusetts Institute of Technology, of which he was a graduate, died on February 2, in his sixty-seventh year. Mr. Munroe was president of the alumni association of the Massachusets Institute of Technology from 1894 to 1897, and as a life member of the corporation of the institute had been its secretary. From 1899 to 1908 he was managing editor of the *Technology Review.* Mr. Munroe was chairman of the Lexington School Committee, chairman of the Massachusetts Commission for the Blind and the vice-president of the North Bennett Street Industrial School. He also had been a member of the Lexington Historical Society, of which he was president in 1898; the National Society of Vocational Education, of which he was president in 1910 and 1911; the Boston Chamber of Commerce, where he had been chairman of the committee on education. He was vice-chairman of the Federal Board of Vocational Education from 1917 to 1921, and in 1917 he was chairman of the Massachusetts Institute of Technology commission for national service.

A GIFT of $250,000 by an anonymous donor, to establish the "Charles Henry Markham Fund" in honor of the chairman of the board of the Illinois Central Railroad, is announced by the Board of Trustees of the University of Chicago. This fund will support teaching, research and clinical activities of the departments of medicine and surgery.

SPECIAL CORRESPONDENCE

IN HONOR OF MRS. DORSEY

FIFTEEN thousand people had gathered in the great Shrine Temple. The organ broke forth in the march as six hundred dignitaries of state university, city, college and public schools filed to their seats on the stage, almost all of them wearing the cap and gown of academic degree. The vast audience broke into applause as the speakers and honored guest appeared in a second group, to take their place on the rostrum and conduct the ceremonies of dedication. It was a unique occasion. The governor of the state, the superintendent of public instruction, the deans or presidents of sixteen colleges and universities of California were there to represent their constituency, as was also the mayor of Los Angeles and the president of the city council. They were not gathered to pay homage to a war hero, to a prize-fighter, a movie actor or even a Lindbergh. They gathered there to do honor to the little woman who has led the schools of Los Angeles. The occasion was cast around the unveiling and dedication of a portrait of Susan Miller Dorsey to the city of Los Angeles. The portrait was painted by John Hubbard Rich, of that city, and represented the expenditure of three thousand dollars which had been subscribed by the devoted teachers of the schools as a token of love and esteem for this old-fashioned woman, new-type teacher; admiration which she has aroused in their hearts during the thirty-two years she has served the schools and children of Los Angeles. There were tears in the eyes of many as little Lucy Bonne epitomized the sentiments of all by reciting touchingly a poem intended to precede the floral offering brought by a hundred children. The invocation by Dr. John Smape breathed the sentiment that the people had gathered to honor a woman who has the religion of culture and the culture of religion, who exemplifies both culture and religion. A telegram was read by the chairman of the evening, John Cooper, state superintendent of public instruction of California and commissioner-elect of the U. S. Bureau of Education. The message was from the National Education Association expressing appreciation officially from that body of the work Mrs. Dorsey has done for education. It concluded with the statement that "You are honoring America's greatest educator." Governor Young paid high tribute to the genius of the woman honored and read a resolution passed by the state board of education in recognition of her surpassing service in the cause of education. Mayor Cryer, of Los Angeles, told how the citizens of that great city have found Mrs. Dorsey endowed more than the rest in tact, grace and womanly qualities which remind us all of our obligation to live lives of service and devotion.

Dean W. W. Kemp, of the School of Education of the University of California, gave the chief address of the day in which he outlined in vivid word picture the ways in which this woman has in so simple a manner accomplished so much. He said in part:

In the not far distant past the custom has been to catapult superintendents from office. It is a glorious thing to so decorate a city superintendent of schools. I take it it is getting safer for superintendents. Her career spans all the important decades of public-school development. She has had a major part during the last two decades in elaborating our system of public schools. She combines several characteristics which have made her great. Her glorious womanhood, her social vision and sympathy, high scholarship, artistry in the classroom, coupled with undoubted executive ability, have wrought her success. These qualities were the five-pointed star of destiny which guided Mrs. Dorsey to the Phi Beta Kappa key for high scholarship in Vassar, to a teachership there a year after her graduation, to service in social work in

Los Angeles in the early years of her residence here, and later in the classroom of the Los Angeles High School, where she soon became vice principal. It was this quintet of stellar qualities that guided her through the seven years of hard work as assistant superintendent of the Los Angeles schools, and again were her cloud by day and pillar of fire by night during the past nine glorious years when she has been called upon to meet the greatest demands ever made on a school system, due to the unbelievable, unprecedented growth of the city of Los Angeles. Although a classical student by training, the Los Angeles schools have, under Mrs. Dorsey's leadership, developed three nationally known vocational institutions in the form of the million dollar Frank Wiggins trade school, the metropolitan part-time school, and the Jacob Riis school for boys. What a monument is the Los Angeles public-school system to the leadership of Mrs. Dorsey, the woman who is being so highly honored to-day, whose portrait is being presented to the city to perpetuate the memory of her untiring devotion to service and the cause of education as the means of increasing the measure of human excellence in the world! It calls to mind the words used by President Campbell when conferring the degree of doctor of laws on Mrs. Dorsey last spring at the University of California:

"Susan Miller Dorsey, expert in the field of education; wise and vigorous administrator; far-seeing adjuster of a school system to the needs of a great and growing city; upholder of high standards; school superintendent of state-wide nation-wide repute."

When the portrait had been duly presented by a delegate of the teachers' organization and accepted by the board of governors of the museum, the painter himself unveiled it.

The little woman in black, who is the mother to ten thousand teachers and grandmother to a quarter million children, then gave a beautiful demonstration of her greatness in the benediction she pronounced at the close of the program. She said in part:

These great people have come here to honor education. The caps and gowns worn are not worn for any single person to-day. They are donned to do honor to all education. It is good to know that to-day many doctors in many institutions of learning now think it is as great to be able to understand and nurture the heart of a mere child as it is to measure a star.

As often as you look at this picture, see there reflected the light of the entire group of educators who have wrought valiantly for the youth of this city and state and nation. See in it the self-sacrificing labors of the school board members, the patience and courage of the teachers, and the willingness of all to cooperate in a great endeavor. See in this portrait the value you yourself place on education—your own interpretation of the great place education occupies in life. As oft as you look upon it believe in the dawn of a more promising day when children will be better born and bred, when the agencies which seek to thwart and weaken the worthy ambitions and yearnings of youth will be less powerful because education will do a more perfect work, releasing the spiritual forces and energies of mankind to an unheard-of degree. You teachers and helpers have made possible the worthy work of the Los Angeles public schools by your ungrudging effort. You have made it mandatory to march, march, march on. So this is your party to-day, in truth and reality. But, since you have seen fit to use my face for the picture, I can only thank you from the bottom of my heart and assure you your loving kindness shall not be forgotten.

And the event had become history. It was particularly significant and dear to Mrs. Dorsey, as it came just at the end of her ninth year of service as superintendent of public schools of Los Angeles and also practically on her seventy-second birthday and the day she has decided to retire from active headship of the schools. It was a fitting valedictory.

BURTON ELLSWORTH DAVIS

LOS ANGELES, CALIF.

DISCUSSION

EDUCATIONAL WASTE—A REPLY

IN SCHOOL AND SOCIETY for November 10, 1928, we find an article entitled "Educational Waste." It is not amiss to question the value of a highly condemnatory article dealing with the American public school system, especially when it contains little or no concrete suggestion for remedy. We can not subscribe to a wholesale criticism of the existing order when the critic raises no fundamental questions for discussion and when his meager suggestions for improvement are couched in vague generalities.

Many of the statements in the article can hardly be credited with a high degree of accuracy. We can take space for the analysis of only a few such statements. The opening sentence, "Education, as carried on in our public schools, is wasteful in that it is largely useless to those who partake of it," hardly conveys the facts to the reader. We shall by no means say that there is no waste in the public schools; it exists in some degree, always has and perhaps always will. We are hardly justified, though, in branding the American public school as a wasteful institution when we see the great good it has accomplished and is now doing. A better procedure would be to determine the points at which loss does occur and give definite suggestion for remedy.

Is it not true that administrators, supervisors and teachers are constantly alert for methods of conserving time, energy and money, thus practicing the greatest known economy? To say that public-school education "is largely useless to those who partake of it" is far from being in agreement with the best evidence thus far produced.

We can not agree that "The most the elementary school does is to teach children to read. This mothers could easily do, while children are growing up in the home, as a part of the children's play, and at no expense at all. That children should be taught to read at public expense is a disgrace to every parent that makes it necessary." To say that mothers could easily teach children to read as a part of the children's play while they are growing up in the home is to expose profound ignorance of the psychology of teaching reading. Reading is an exceedingly difficult and complex art. It requires a real master to produce a high degree of efficiency in the child. Furthermore, the assertion, that "The most the elementary school does is to teach children to read," indicates reckless dealing with facts. But even if it were true, the elementary school would still be a great boon to society. Howbeit, there is evidence on every hand that development in character, habit, ideals and knowledges in many phases of endeavor as a result of which the race has made great progress is a very vital outcome of the public school. Saying that it is a disgrace that children are taught reading at public expense is harking back to a philosophy which modern society knows has died a well-merited death. It points the way to illiteracy, superstition and a low social order.

The statement that "we teach a multitude of things hoping that sometime, somewhere, a few of them may prove useful," evinces little acquaintance with the aims of present-day education. The curriculum has been rather well purged of known useless things, and education is by no means a neglected and haphazard matter. There are definite ideas as to what may be looked for as just outcomes of the various subjects. To be sure, there are some unknown outcomes, some hoped-for outcomes, and some, as yet, unmeasurable ones. The pupil who has gone through this so-called wasteful public school is far happier and has a considerably better chance in life than the one denied this privilege.

We have decided respect for the "testers who worry the helpless children by measuring their respective amounts of progress in the various studies." Indeed, we have not found children worried by these tests. We have noted, instead, their keen delight at good objective testing. It is largely through the work of the tester that individual differences have been discovered, remedial measures applied and techniques devised which have greatly economized time, energy and money.

We admit the importance of knowing that a study is worth while, and the school will readily cast out any course that is proved valueless. Better evidence than the mere unsubstantiated opinion of an individual is required to abolish a study. We agree, also, that the "child should have experiences that profoundly modify his life in a practical way." One of the most valuable experiences of this type to be had is that of learning to read well. It is the efficient readers who count most in life. Of course the child should learn the practical manipulation of ordinary appliances about the house. However, daily routine experience in life in general, and about the home in particular, provides much valuable training of this kind. That "everything in or about the home should be mastered as to principle and mechanism" seems too visionary. Many of the principles of mechanisms in the home defy mastery by the child. Study of others is useless. We are users, rather than makers, of most of the complicated and expensive tools, appliances, etc., about the home, and will do well to leave their principles largely to specialists. The child, of course, must not be an ignoramus concerning the ordinary things about the house; his daily experiences at home and in school courses tend to preclude that.

A fundamental function of the school is to train the child to manipulate ideas, as well as mere physical things. It is attempting to fill this function in accordance with the best available advice. It is a well-known fact that the practical and manipulative abilities are readily acquired through experience when the intellectual background has been prepared, as the school aims to do. The big business of the school is not to turn out trained artisans. Rather, it tries to give such intellectual development and training as will enable the individual to adjust to the varied situations in life. Throughout the elementary and secondary period its chief objective is the making of adequate generalists rather than specialists. It should provide the tools for progress, rather than mere mechanical skill. These tools are found fundamentally in the subjects incorporated in the curriculum, rather than in the manipulation of appliances about the home. This physical activity would by no means guarantee progress if the child did not have the knowledge given by the school.

Unquestionably, "education should always contribute either to our ability to make a living or to our ability to enjoy living." There doubtless are still some courses or parts of courses which contribute little to either of these objectives. The schools err grievously in some particulars, but let us remember that they can improve no faster than society permits. The curricula should be "stripped of all useless rubbish." The teaching personnel is eager to determine what is useless and to eliminate it. When a vast public is to be reckoned with, it is not easy to cast out the useless in any of its institutions.

We heartily agree that "children too often take their education lightly," although we wish to remind our critic that this is not the wish or chiefly the fault of the schools. We plead for a remedy which will awaken the parents and the public to the importance of the school work.

If we should accept the idea that "the things taught to a child should be so necessary to him that he could not forget them" we should make some drastic reductions. Our curriculum would be encompassed in the two words "teach nothing."

The schools of to-day are more consciously and more effectively working to promote moral growth than did those of any past age. They are hampered by cases of poor native endowment and bad environment. Nevertheless, when we scan the pages of history we are soon convinced that the present generation is morally superior to any of its predecessors. The attitudes and behavior patterns which the schools have inculcated are largely responsible for the improvement.

The advancement made is surely worth the outlay of money entailed. The burden of our taxation is not for education, but for war, harmful luxuries and other useless things which cost us many times the amount spent for education. It would be the part of financial wisdom to increase, rather than decrease, our outlay of money for schools. It brings rewards in wealth, as well as in character, culture and happiness. The things our schools stand for and yield tremendously are character, culture, fair play, happiness, decency, etc.

T. H. SCHUTTE

DEPARTMENT OF EDUCATION AND PSYCHOLOGY,
WOMAN'S COLLEGE OF ALABAMA

THE CENSORSHIP OF STUDENT PUBLICATIONS

AT the Grand Convention of Pi Delta Epsilon, the national honorary collegiate journalism fraternity, held at Atlanta, Georgia, on December 6 to 8, 1928, the following resolutions were unanimously passed:

Resolved, that Pi Delta Epsilon go on record as taking an unfavorable stand concerning the publication of the types of "razz" or "scandal sheets" which bring the fraternity into public disrepute and into conflict with university or college officers.

By its action the fraternity disavows the type of "scandal sheet" that brings the producers thereof into disrepute and that in a few instances has brought the fraternity unfavorable notice. Pi Delta Epsilon exists for the upbuilding of college journalism. Its policy is constructive, not destructive. It advocates a high standard of journalistic ethics, and is not in sympathy with anything else.

At the same time the fraternity unanimously passed a resolution opposing censorship of college publications[1] in the following terms:

Resolved, that the 1929 Grand Convention go on record as viewing with disfavor any policy of suppression of the freedom of the college press.

Henry Grattan Doyle
The George Washington University

QUOTATIONS

PRESIDENT LITTLE AND THE UNIVERSITY OF MICHIGAN

President Little has stood boldly and courageously for certain policies which seemed to him to be right and true. Some of them were progressive conceptions in education—in some quarters they were considered even radical. But they expressed a high idealism in university administration. Difficulties came in an effort to work them out in practical terms. The president found himself at odds on some issues with the prevailing opinion of the Board of Regents, although the utmost personal friendliness exists between the president and individual members of the board. This is shown by the president's statement and by the regents' resolution. Unfortunately for the university, the regents were unable to endorse fully some of the methods President Little pursued in carrying out his ideas and President Little felt that the regents were not fully appreciative of certain policies which he felt were of significance in the development of his educational policies and plans for the university.

The president's letter makes specific reference to certain things which deserve further explanation. In mentioning "private donors, political interests, local interests and alumnae interests," the president had reference to certain particular questions which made an issue between him and the board.

It is reported that the gift to the university of a new legal research library by W. W. Cook, '80, '82*l*, was made with certain provisions which the president felt it was unwise to accept, as surrendering too much of the university's autonomy in purely educational matters. The regents, however, felt differently, and accepted the gift upon Mr. Cook's terms.

The president's mention of "political interests" has reference to the existing relationship between the university and the governor and the legislature, particularly the matter of the state tax survey which was proposed by the president in a letter to the governor last spring and which has been very strongly opposed in many quarters as being, in a sense, forced upon the state administration with only lukewarm support from the governor. It was this which led to the abandonment of the plan by the regents at their December meeting. President Little, however, felt very strongly that such a survey is desirable and could best be performed by an impartial body such as the university.

President Little's reference to "local" interests undoubtedly concerns the discussion which has arisen with a certain wing of public opinion in Ann Arbor over the proposed dormitory program. President Little has felt very strongly upon this subject and has insisted that the erection of a series of dormitory groups was one of the outstanding needs of the university. In this, the president has had the strong support of the best academic interests of the university and of the alumni. Opposition from rooming house keepers and some of the business interests of Ann Arbor has, however, been very strong, and it is very probable that the president feels that the board has not been as unanimous in its

[1] See School and Society for July 21, 1928, p. 78.

support of his whole program as he had hoped, though they have given approval of the plan for the erection of the first dormitory unit, with the land on which it is to be erected given by the Detroit alumni of the university.

President Little's final reference to "alumnae interests" brings up a discussion which has continued for some time over the eventual method of control over the new League Building. The president has insisted very strongly that the administration of the building should be in the hands of a committee representing the university in conjunction with the alumnae, of which committee one of the three advisers of women should be chairman. Certain of the alumnae, on the other hand, have felt that a representative of the alumnae organization should be made administrative head of the League Building.

* * * * *

The President's ideas and policies have met with hearty recognition and general approval from the alumni body. Wherever he has had an opportunity to set forth his policies before alumni gatherings—and he has had many occasions to do so—his ideas have met with cordial and enthusiastic response. He has worked in the closest accord with the Alumni Association, both in developing the Alumni Ten-Year Program and in setting forth his conception of an Alumni University, which attracted wide attention from our own alumni and from other universities. It is all part of President Little's educational thinking. He is committed to the belief that the educational responsibility of a university does not cease with the graduation of a student; rather he believes that, in so far as it is possible, some sort of constructive relationship should be preserved through all the years of the life of a college man or woman. He believes strongly in support for the university from the alumni, financially and in personal service; conversely he has stated many times that the university owes a certain educational obligation to the alumni. It was in the development of this idea that he secured the recent appropriation of $12,000 annually for the next two years toward the development of the educational side of the Alumni University through appointment of a number of Alumni Fellows.

President Little came to the university in the fall of 1925 as the successor of the late President Marion L. Burton. His appointment was the result of action by a joint committee of the faculty and regents. He was born in Brookline, Massachusetts, October 6, 1888, received his A.B. degree from Harvard in 1910 and his Doctor of Science in 1914. For some time he served as secretary for the Harvard Corporation and as assistant dean of Harvard College. Meanwhile he was continuing his scientific work in the field of biology, resigning in 1922 to become president of the University of Maine.

As a biologist, Dr. Little has been a strong advocate of race betterment programs and the science of eugenics, and his courageous statements of his views on controversial questions, such as a scientific consideration of the question of birth control, have led to criticism in some quarters.

Contrary to statements in some newspapers, President Little has no immediate plans for the future. His resignation has come as a result of a fundamental difference of opinion and a feeling on his part that the best interests of the university would be served by such an action. Throughout the whole discussion which preceded his action, President Little's first thought has been for the welfare of the institution.—*The Michigan Alumnus.*

REPORTS

THE RETIREMENT OF PROFESSORS[1]

SINCE the adoption of the amended statutes of 1890, a professor of Columbia University has had the privilege of retiring from active service at his own request on reaching the age of sixty-five, after which time and in which status he would receive a stated but greatly reduced measure of compensation. With the organization in 1905 of the Carnegie Foundation for the Ad-

[1] From the annual report of President Nicholas Murray Butler to the trustees of Columbia University.

vancement of Teaching to administer Mr. Carnegie's munificent gift of some $15,000,000 to make possible the establishment of a general system of retiring allowances for professors who were ready to withdraw from farther active service, Columbia University surrendered its independent system of retirement and gladly accepted the benefits offered by the Carnegie Foundation. It will surprise many to learn that from 1906 to 1928 Columbia University received from the Carnegie Foundation for the purpose of making allowances to retired officers or their widows no less than $1,132,474.79. At the present time the annual allowances received from the Carnegie Foundation amount to about $125,000. It is obvious, therefore, what great support Mr. Carnegie's gift has given to the work of Columbia University and to the scholars who are members of its academic family. Owing to conditions which need not be described here but which are fully set out in the annual reports of the president of the Carnegie Foundation, it became necessary for the trustees of that foundation, some thirteen years ago, to bring to an end the system of non-contributory allowances which had theretofore prevailed and to institute the system of contributory retiring allowances which is fully set forth in Section 68 of the Statutes of Columbia University. All officers appointed to full academic service since November 17, 1915, are protected by this provision of the statutes unless they shall have expressly declined to take advantage of it, in which case it must be supposed that they are better satisfied to make their own personal provision for disability or old age and prefer not to look to the university for any retiring or disability allowance whatsoever. There remain 235 officers of the university, 35 of whom are on the Barnard College Foundation and 37 on the Teachers College Foundation, to whom the provisions of the non-contributory system of the Carnegie Foundation as set out in Section 67 of the University Statutes still apply. Recent reports of the president of the Carnegie Foundation make it plain that that foundation may not be able much longer to continue the scale of retiring and disability allowances as these have hitherto existed. The maximum allowance of $4,000 has already been reduced to $3,600 and may perhaps be still farther reduced in the near future. The facts that these retiring allowances were made a function of the academic salary received by each individual teacher and that these salaries have been very greatly increased throughout the country during the past ten or fifteen years, appear to have brought about a condition in which the resources of the Carnegie Foundation, great as they are, will no longer be adequate to maintain the scale of retiring allowances as these have been established for some years past.

These facts bring Columbia University face to face with a very grave and important problem. The 235 officers to whom the provisions of Section 67 of the Statutes now apply simply can not be permitted to face disability or old age with so insufficient provision as the allowances of the Carnegie Foundation, if necessarily farther reduced, would provide. As salaries have increased in recent years it has been difficult enough for a retired officer to readjust the circumstances of his life to the retiring allowance which was in many cases less than one half, often only one third, of the compensation which he had received while in active service. Should these allowances be still farther reduced, it is plain that the gap between the allowance and the salary will be so wide that action by the university itself is imperative. Studies are now being made, which will in due time be submitted to the trustees, as to the manner in which this situation may best be met. At the moment, it would appear to be desirable to divide the officers protected by Section 67 of the Statutes into two groups—those who will become eligible for retirement within, say, ten or twelve years, and those who will not become eligible for retirement until a later date than that. For the first group it may be necessary for the trustees to make individual provision as each retirement comes about, taking full account of all the circumstances of each individual case as it arises. For the second group it may be desirable for the trustees to offer, in addition to the protection afforded by Section 67, the protection afforded by Section 68. Were that done, the academic officer in this group might look forward to the retiring allowance provided by the Carnegie Foundation in accordance with the provisions of Section 67, plus such additional allowance as, with his own cooperation, the university might be able to provide for him under the plan established by Section 68 of the Statutes for all officers appointed subsequent to November 17, 1915. Whatever happens, it may be taken for granted by every member of Columbia University that no one of the academic family will be permitted to suffer, so far as the university's resources can prevent, but that every energy will be bent to protect the academic career not only while it is at its point of most effective service but as it approaches its inevitable end.

There is a principle controlling the corporate attitude just outlined which is of utmost importance. There still exists and is widely accepted what may be not improperly described as the "hired man" theory of academic service. According to this very generally accepted theory, a member of an academic community is paid by the year, by the month or by the hour, to render a certain amount of service which is either explicitly defined or conventionally assumed. For example, less than fifty years ago every member of the faculty of Columbia College was expected to teach fifteen hours each week, just as a bricklayer is expected to work eight hours each day. Under the happier conditions that have developed since the university organization of 1890 became effective, Columbia has steadily grown away from that preposterous and undignified theory, although it must be recorded that progress in that respect has not infrequently been resisted with considerable ardor by members of the faculties themselves. An academic officer in the Columbia University of to-day is a member of a free society of scholars in which his duty and his ideals are identical, where he pursues that path of scholarship which appeals to his tastes and his capacities and which is his own free choice. His function as a member of this society of scholars is to promote and advance scholarship itself, to guide and stimulate youth, and to serve the public in a myriad different ways through his personal contacts, by his interpretations of scholarship, and by new discoveries in terms of life and its greatest satisfactions. In this conception of the academic life the "hired man" theory can have no possible place.

As a scholar advances in years he will naturally expect, and be expected, to reduce the amount of his visible and measurable labors, and to pass on to younger hands some of the more arduous occupations of the academic life. Unless, however, he is overtaken by actual mental or physical incapacity, or unless there be some other strong reason growing out of the interests and needs of scholarship itself for the final severance of his academic relationships, he should remain in the active service of this society of scholars, devoting his ripest years to those reflections, those researches and those publications for which the earlier years of labor have prepared him. It may well be that in the case of a university group restricted in number, this large and comforting policy could not be carried out without preventing, through lack of means, the appropriate advancement of scholars somewhat younger in years. Situations of that sort must be met as they arise with good judgment, with tact and with generosity.

These ripest and most experienced of scholars are in the truest sense the university's elder statesmen of highest distinction. Their service, so far as it is outwardly measurable, has been amply rendered through the years that have passed. Once the "hired man" theory be abandoned, then these older scholars are, first of all and most of all, entitled to be protected by the university to the uttermost as the marks of the passing years are made upon them.

EDUCATIONAL RESEARCH AND STATISTICS

THE STATUS OF HAZING IN AMERICAN COLLEGES

DURING the fall of 1927 there was a serious outbreak of hazing in the Louisiana Polytechnic Institute, with which institution the writer was then connected. So serious did the matter become that the president appointed a committee composed of faculty members and students to investigate the situation with reference to hazing in other colleges, and to work out some possible solution for our own problem.

This committee, of which the writer was chairman,[1] prepared a questionnaire which was sent to the deans of sixty-nine smaller colleges, scattered throughout the United States, as shown in Table I, column 1. This list of colleges was prepared by taking a random selection of all colleges, both state and private, whose enrolment was reported in the *World* "Almanac" for 1927 to be between 500 and 2,000, and adding to this all the colleges in the state of Louisiana. This addition accounts for the heavy representation which the south has in the total group.

A large portion of the material collected in this questionnaire was of immediate interest only, but certain parts seemed to be of such a nature as to demand general attention. It is the purpose of this paper to report these findings. They deal with two general phases of the problem: first, the extent and distribution of hazing in American colleges, and, secondly, the methods of control used.

TABLE I.—SHOWING DISTRIBUTION OF COLLEGES INCLUDED IN STUDY

	Colleges to which blanks were sent	Blanks returned		Colleges reporting no hazing		Colleges reporting hazing serious		Colleges reporting hazing not serious	
		No.	Per cent.	No.	Per cent.	No.	Per cent.	No.	Per cent.
North	15	10	67	1	10	0	0	9	90
South	24	23	96	1	5	13	56	9	39
West	15	10	67	1	10	2	20	7	70
East	15	13	87	2	15	2	15	9	70
Total	69	56	81	5	9	17	30	34	61

THE EXTENT OF HAZING

If we define hazing as "the subjection of freshmen to any practices of an abusive, derisive or ridiculous nature designed to identify them as a new and uninitiated group," then hazing is almost universal in American undergraduate colleges, for but few schools have no mark of distinction between freshmen and upperclassmen. Fifty-six of the sixty-nine blanks sent out were returned, and as shown in Table I, column 3, of this fifty-six, only five reported no hazing in any form. However, from the standpoint of the administration, hazing is probably of no concern except when it takes such violent form as to demand administrative intervention. Certain of the questions in the blank made it possible to set up an arbitrary point of distinction between hazing that was serious and hazing of a more or less harmless nature. These questions are:

(1) Is the hazing of freshmen prevalent in your college?

(2) Please list the forms which it takes.
(Serious forms, flogging, haircutting, etc.)
(Minor forms, freshman caps, pajama parades, etc.)

(3) Does hazing ever take such violent form as to demand the intervention of the administration?

(4) About how many times during the last three years have such cases arisen?

(5) What penalty or penalties were imposed upon the offenders?

On the basis of the information furnished in answer to these questions the fifty-one colleges that reported hazing were divided into two groups: first, those colleges where hazing has taken such violent form as to demand administrative intervention one or more times in the last three years and because of this intervention one or more students have been suspended from colleges, and, secondly, those colleges where the administration has not been compelled to interfere during the last three years. Making such a division of the colleges, we find that but one third have hazing that is of a serious nature.

[1] The other members of the committee were: Professor P. D. Nielson, Professor Eunice Nelson, Jack Bagwell, president of the senior class, and Byron Cann, president of the junior class.

TABLE II.—SHOWING GENERAL ADMINISTRATIVE POLICY REPORTED BY COLLEGES

	Guidance		Prohibition		*Laissez faire*		Total	
	No.	Per cent.	No.	Per cent.	No.	Per cent.	No.	Per cent.
Colleges where serious	3	18	12	70	2	12	17	100
Colleges not serious	17	50	3	9	14	41	34	100
Total	20	39	15	30	16	31	51	100

This group of colleges will hereafter be known as *colleges where hazing is serious,* and the remaining group as *colleges where hazing is not serious* (columns 4 and 5 of Table I), and certain comparisons will be made between these two groups.

The first striking difference noticed between the two groups is the surprising number of those *colleges where hazing is serious* that are located in the south. Columns 4 and 5 of Table I reveal the fact that 56 per cent. of the southern colleges have serious hazing, while none of the northern colleges, 20 per cent. of the western colleges and 15 per cent. of the eastern colleges have serious hazing.

THE METHOD OF CONTROL

The method of handling hazing employed by the two groups also reveals some interesting facts.

In reply to the question, "Is the general policy of the administration one of prohibition, guidance, or *laissez faire?*" we find, as shown in Table II, that when considering the total groups of colleges having hazing, the general policy is reported to be one of guidance in 39 per cent. of the colleges, prohibition in 30 per cent. and *laissez faire* in 31 per cent.; but when considering the two groups as separated above, we find that *colleges where hazing is not serious* report the policy of guidance in 50 per cent., prohibition in 9 per cent. and *laissez faire* in 41 per cent., while the *colleges where hazing is serious* report the policy of guidance in 18 per cent., prohibition in 70 per cent. and *laissez faire* in 12 per cent. of the cases. In other words, most of the colleges that report guidance or *laissez faire* as the policy (thirty-one of thirty-six, or 86 per cent., of them), have been classed as *colleges where hazing is not serious,* while most of the colleges that report prohibition as the general policy (twelve of fifteen, or 80 per cent., of them) have been classed as *colleges where hazing is serious.*

Further questions were asked concerning the handling of hazing as follows:

(6) Does the administration have any standing rules or regulations concerning hazing in general or particular forms of hazing?
(7) Does the college have any standing organized body to direct or control hazing or try offenders?
(8) Of whom is this composed?
(9) If there is no standing body whose duty it is to deal with hazing, by whom are cases which may arise handled?

The reports to the question concerning standing rules and regulations, which are summarized

TABLE III.—SHOWING COLLEGES HAVING STANDING RULES AND REGULATIONS CONCERNING HAZING

	Have rules and regulations		Do not have rules and regulations		Total	
	No.	Per cent.	No.	Per cent.	No.	Per cent.
Colleges where serious	13	76	4	24	17	100
Colleges where not serious*	8	26	23	74	31	100
Total	21	44	27	56	48	100

* Three of the *colleges where hazing is not serious* failed to answer this question.

TABLE IV.—SHOWING THE GROUPS CONTROLLING HAZING IN THE VARIOUS COLLEGES

	Student control		Administrative or faculty control		Adm. or faculty and student control		Total	
	No.	Per cent.	No.	Per cent.	No.	Per cent.	No.	Per cent.
Colleges where serious	3	18	11	64	3	18	17	100
Colleges where not serious*	16	55	10	34	3	11	29	100
Total	19	41	21	46	6	13	46	100

* Five of the *colleges where hazing is not serious* did not answer this question.

in Table III, show that standing rules and regulations are reported by 44 per cent. of the total group of colleges answering the questionnaire, but 76 per cent. of the group classed as *colleges where hazing is serious* report such rules and regulations, while 26 per cent. of the group classed as *colleges where hazing is not serious,* report them. In other words, most of the colleges that have standing rules and regulations (thirteen of twenty-one, or 61 per cent.) have been classed as *colleges where hazing is serious,* while most of the colleges that have no standing rules and regulations (twenty-three of twenty-seven, or 85 per cent. of them) have been classed as *colleges where hazing is not serious.*

The answers to questions 7, 8 and 9 above furnished a basis for determining the extent of student participation in the control of hazing. These data are summarized in Table IV. It will be seen that while 41 per cent. of the total group report student control, 46 per cent. administrative or faculty control, and 13 per cent. a cooperative control, the group of *colleges where hazing is serious* report student control in 18 per cent., administrative or faculty control in 64 per cent., and cooperative control in 18 per cent. of the cases; but the *colleges where hazing is not serious* report student control in 55 per cent., administrative or faculty control in 34 per cent., and cooperative control in 11 per cent. of the cases. Stated in another way, of the nineteen colleges reporting student control, three of them, or 16 per cent., are classed as *colleges where hazing is serious;* of the twenty-one colleges reporting faculty or administrative control, eleven of them, or 52 per cent., have been classed as *colleges where hazing is serious;* and of the six colleges reporting cooperative control, three of them, or 50 per cent., have been classed as *colleges where hazing is serious.*

To summarize, we have seen that serious hazing is chiefly confined to the south, that there is an intimate relation between the policy of prohibition and serious hazing, and between standing rules and regulations and serious hazing. We have also seen that where the policy is one of guidance or *laissez faire,* where there are no standing rules and regulations, and where the students have the control of hazing, there is apt to be no serious problem with reference to hazing.

In the interpretation of these results it is practically impossible to distinguish between cause and effect. Is hazing prevalent in the south because of the south, because of the ideals of the southern college and the nature of its student body, or is it but another indication of the slower educational development of the south? Is the policy of prohibition a causative factor in hazing or is the extent and nature of hazing the cause of prohibition, or are both results of some cause unknown? Is the absence of student participation in the handling of hazing a cause or is the control of hazing intrusted to students in those colleges where it is not serious, or is the method used indicative of a certain stage of development in the college? These and like questions are not answered by the data here presented, but the evidence would seem sufficient to justify giving student control with intelligent guidance a trial, since it appears that the policy of "authority from above" is not getting results.

VERNER MARTIN SIMS
UNIVERSITY OF ALABAMA

SCHOOL AND SOCIETY

EDITED BY J. McKEEN CATTELL

WITH WHICH IS COMBINED THE

EDUCATIONAL REVIEW

EDITED BY WILLIAM McANDREW

Volume XXIX   Saturday, February 16, 1929   Number 738

GOING STRAIGHT IN ATHLETICS[1]

By President GEORGE NORLIN

UNIVERSITY OF COLORADO

Shortly after Thanksgiving, according to the Associated Press, the students of a state university to the west of us met to discuss a proposition made by an outside group which was organized into a "Boosters Club" for the promotion of "bigger and better" football teams. This "Boosters Club" had proposed to raise a very considerable fund in order to supplement the salary of the coach and to supply "athletic scholarships."

There was nothing very extraordinary in this situation. Such proposals have been made in other educational centers and accepted by educational institutions apparently with gratitude, at any rate with no manifest reluctance thus to surrender largely the control of athletic policy to outside fans. But the extraordinary fact in this case was that the students voted unanimously to reject the proposition.

And yet what happened the other day at the University of Nevada is growing less extraordinary among students; and I know of nothing more interesting or more encouraging in the collegiate world of recent years than such protests among the students themselves against tendencies and practices which are obviously professionalizing college athletics and yet appear to be tolerated and winked at by educational authorities.

I do not suppose that such protestations among the students are the expression of any toplofty idealism. I suppose, rather, that they express simply a downright feeling on their part that the colleges should not be crooked, that they should, in the promotion of athletics as in all other things, be straight and above-board, and that above all they should not tolerate a situation where the college preaches one thing and permits groups within it or outside of it to practice another under the college flag.

We must all of us—students, faculties, alumni and governing boards—we must all of us face the fact that in our efforts to carry out an honest policy we are dealing with a very difficult problem, to some minds an impossible problem. The interest in intercollegiate contests is so tremendous; it organizes itself into forces that are so powerful; it expresses itself in storms of emotion which are so hard to stand up against, that some of us throw up our hands and let the winds carry us whither they list.

But to my mind the question is too vital to be dismissed in any such spirit of helplessness. To my mind—and I think that you will agree with me—a college or uni-

[1] Assembly address, January 8, 1929.

versity which allows itself to be dishonest merely because it is very difficult to go straight has lost its reason for existence. We in the colleges are expected, and rightly expected, in all that we do to have a sound influence upon the character of youth. But how can we do that and be crooked ourselves? I am using plain language, perhaps too brutally plain. None of us will, I suppose, admit that we are not straight. On the contrary, we talk unctuously about the ideals fostered by athletics—their good effect upon character, the discipline which they afford in self-control, in good sportsmanship, and so on; and we even set up, or we assent to, elaborate laws and rules to keep them clean. But when we passively permit the clamor of the fans, insistent upon a Roman spectacle, to speak to the coach and to the management in language more convincing than our own lip-service to ideals, saying to them, almost in so many words, "Get us a team; there are rules to be reckoned with, but rules or no rules, somehow, by hook or by crook, get us a championship!"—when we permit that, I ask, are we honestly on the job?

It may be, as a friend said to me the other day, that I am begging the question. It may be, as he put it, that men who are men of honor in all other matters, in business, in professional life and even in politics, have come to look upon bootlegging in athletics as honorable and praiseworthy. Well, if that is the case, why not be honest with ourselves and with the public? Why continue this manifest hypocrisy? "Hateful to me as the gates of Hell," said the most ancient of poets, "is the man who thinks one thing in his heart and says another with his lips." That was spoken three thousand years ago. Perhaps it is too old-fashioned for those who now cultivate cynicism as a pose, if not as a philosophy. But it is still the sentiment of the world at large, and I should be loath to think that it is too unsophisticated for the college men of this year of our Lord, 1929.

There are, I maintain, two ways, and only two, of being honest in athletics. One of these has been propounded by Hamilton Holt, president of Rollins College. Some of you may remember that not long ago he gave up the editorship of the *Independent Magazine* in order to devote the rest of his life to the work of building up an ideal small college in the south. Possessing a conscience undulled by long association with the devious ways of intercollegiate athletics, he grew quickly disgusted with the practices carried on under the cover of rules, standards and high pretensions, and proposed in a moment of impatience to drop all sham and pretense, to junk all rules of eligibility, and to go frankly into the open market and buy the best football material to be had for the money to uphold the name and spread the fame of the college. Such a course would at least be honest and above-board. It would also be fair to the athletes in that it would give them a lucrative career, instead of using them, and using them hard, for three or four years and then sending them out, as sometimes happens, with no future in athletics and with four years of such loose and casual contact with any educational process that they have advanced little, if at all, towards a trained and disciplined mentality.

Of course Hamilton Holt has not done and will not do what he threatened to do in a mood of exasperation. He would not in that case be the type of man to be the president of Rollins College; the emphasis which he is laying on building up a select faculty and adequate facilities for a liberal education would be out of place. On the contrary, he would be succeeded by a Connie Mack, D.D., LL.D., and the campus of Rollins College would be graced by a million-dollar stadium and a library which could be picked up at any Woolworth emporium.

The other way of being honest is perhaps more difficult, but it is not, I think, impossible. It is to diffuse throughout the college, its graduates and friends, its students, its athletic management and coaching staff—it is to diffuse, I say, throughout the institution an integrity, a conscience, which will be active and on the alert to make sure that any football team or any other team which represents the college in any intercollegiate sport is really representative of the college, that it is built up out of a student body which has been attracted to the college by its character, its quality and its reputation as an institution of learning; that it is bone of its bone and flesh of its flesh, and not something extraneous to the college; not something which has been brought into a quasi-relationship to it by emoluments, inducements or persuasions which have nothing to do with the drawing power of the college itself; in a word, something which is not foreign, but our own.

This honest way means, moreover, that athletics are made part and parcel of the educational process, both in respect to the athlete himself and to the student body as a whole.

First as to the athlete. The complaint is sometimes made that we in this university do not favor the athlete, that we do not, in appreciation of his prowess on the field, forgive him scholastic shortcomings or delinquencies, that in other words, we treat him like any other student and require that if he is to represent the university on a team he shall be representative of the university as a student in good standing. Perhaps the best comment I can offer in reply to that objection is the statement which was made by a graduate of our College of Engineering when on a visit here sometime ago. He had been a brilliant athlete—brilliant in football, base ball, basketball and track. He said that while a student here he had felt that he was not appreciated; he had resented that while he was doing so much for the prestige of the university in athletics he was required to do his work like any one else, but that *now* he was most grateful to the institution which had not permitted him to neglect his preparation and training for a successful career. That, you see, is another point of view; and to my mind there is nothing more reprehensible, more dishonest, more unjust to boys with good bodies and good brains than the practice in some high schools and some colleges of placing such over-emphasis upon athletic success that the student is made to feel that nothing else is important, until, after drifting along through his high-school or college course, with only the most casual and perfunctory attention to any mental training or discipline, he discovers at the end of his brief athletic career that other things are vastly important, that the best years of his life have been largely wasted, and that he has been allowed to fall into habits of mental lethargy and inertia which are serious handicaps in the battle of life.

Again, as to the student body in general—those who play the game from the grandstand. I have always felt that in our educational procedure we take too little account of the emotions and make too little appeal to them, and I think that there is a clear value in the pageant of enthusiasm which is staged around an intercollegiate game. Our hearts are quickened by the flag; we are carried out of ourselves into a unity of spirit; we feel as one man the "glory" of Colorado and we "hurrah for the Silver and the Gold." This seems to me to be a good thing to do. The highest of the emotions is loyalty to something outside of ourselves, and we do well to give expression to it now and again. But if we are to "holler our heads off" on such occasions, then it seems rather important that we should have something to "holler" about; in other words, if that pageant of enthusiasm is not to be a crude surrender to imbecile frenzy, then it seems to me rather important that it be staged about something which is our own, something which has been enlisted out of our own life, and not something which is imported from abroad. Mercenary armies have at times inspired men's fears and hopes, but they have never evoked a people's patriotism.

I have spoken now of two ways of being honest: one which would frankly professionalize college athletics and "make no bones" about doing so to the detriment of any educational program whatsoever; and the other which subordinates athletics to a principle, with a common conscience actively behind that principle, and makes them part and parcel of an educational process. Between these two courses I can see no middle course which is not devious, hypocritical and crooked.

I for one am grateful to the Rocky Mountain Athletic Conference for the work which it has done and for the influence which it has exerted, and I am glad that years ago I had a part in the forming of that organization. But rules and standards of eligibility are not enough. I have read somewhere that "the letter killeth and the spirit giveth life." It remains for each institution subscribing to the standards of that conference to determine whether its allegiance shall be of the letter or of the spirit. It is for each of us to determine—no conference can do it—whether we shall go straight.

THE SPIRIT OF TOLSTOY'S EXPERIMENTAL SCHOOL. II

By PAUL R. RADOSAVLJEVICH
NEW YORK UNIVERSITY

Is education for the individual or for society? Tolstoy analyzes this big question from the religious, philosophic, historical and experimental points of view and concludes in each case that it has failed to make a case. To religion alone does he grant the privilege, but religion has drifted from its moorings and is unable to do what it should. Tolstoy gives an analysis of the individual from different points of view. He concludes that in reading, in religious understanding, in composition and in every way, the individual proves the superiority of his own mind over the static and conventionalized standards of the group. He holds that there are inherent values in the individual which give him peculiar worth. Society is not the ultimate judge of its own value, nor of the value of its own situations. There is within the individual a spark of that divine consciousness which is in society but which rises above it.

Tolstoy is entirely against compulsory education, on the ground that by the very nature of it progress is impeded. Many arguments are given to support his contention. Perhaps he was correct. We must remember that he is talking in terms of the Russian mouzhik in relation to an imperial government. Causation is different. In one place in his educational articles (published in his periodical, *Yasnaya Polyana,* 1862) he admits the right in our United States of having a form of compulsory education, due to democratic evolution. Certainly in a country where the youth of to-day are to be responsible citizens of to-morrow, the country as a matter of self-protection must train its citizens, and for this reason we may go further and say that if the state demands these knowledges, skills and attitudes on the part of the embryo citizen, then education should not only be compulsory, but it should also be free. We have compulsory education, but have not yet developed freedom to its maximum. Many potential leaders are hampered because of this feature.

In his contention that the social demands should not form a criterion for the kind of education to be given, Tolstoy is what we term to-day anti-pragmatic. Whether he is right or wrong in this matter is, of course, of relative importance to us only as to our conception of his philosophy. Personally I believe Tolstoy is right, especially where social demands may not be in accord with ethical thought. Tolstoy, however, vacillates in some of these contentions, for he would teach only what the child actually needs, and what he actually needs is simply the result of the social system, the outcome of the customs of the community.

In trying to solve the eternal riddle, *How is progress measured?* Tolstoy presents an interesting contrast to some recent views, especially to our American pragmatic (or social) philosophy of education —the theories of Dewey, Kilpatrick, Finney, Bode and many others. Dewey sets up, as the standard of progress, the ideal of a world democracy. While he is denying the right of society to have any ideals beyond the present, he sets forth the fact that social progress demands democracy as a medium. This democracy is to be attained by the social education of the people, utilizing science. In opposition to such an educational gospel, Tolstoy sets up as his thesis the idea that "Progress is personal, and not social." There is something sublime in the calm, dispassionate way in which he weighs and considers the civilization of the present and finds it wanting. Tolstoy does not argue about little things, nor brag about material advances. One can almost hear his argument in the present-day terms: "Yes, we have electricity and aeroplanes and telephones and bathrooms, etc., but that is not the question; the real question is: Are men and women any happier, any more satisfied with life?" Tolstoy would ask progress to point out our own great men and compare them with Socrates, Plato or Aristotle. He could not accept the modern philosophy of Dewey and Havelock Ellis, who follow Protagoras's anthropomorphic dictum that man is the measure of all things, and who claim that science is nothing more than specialized common sense and who, moreover, confuse the wishbone (social) with the backbone (ethical) of humanity so beautifully expressed by the great Hebrew prophet, Isaiah—"A nation without vision must perish!" Tolstoy cries loudly, "The sole meaning of life is to serve humanity," and he goes even so far as to claim that art is "to establish brotherly union among men." Once he complained that Cain (esthetics) killed his brother Abel (ethics). If Tolstoy were alive to-day he would complain about our modern trouble when another Cain (social) is killing his old-fashioned brother (ethical).

After all, who has measured progress? Is it not the social classes which have most benefited by it? They have looked at their own well-being and called it good. How much better, or how much worse is the condition of the poor tenement dweller of the New York City East Side than that of even the Russian farmer of the days of Tolstoy? Is the law of "perfectability" written on his soul? Has progress made it possible for him to attain individual happiness? And Tolstoy would say, "Now we must educate all to save this wonderful democracy to preserve progress.'' He makes us view the whole thing from a different angle. Should education be compulsory for the bottom or the top of this present social structure? Certainly those who are so sure of their ground in laying out a method of world regeneration are taking a serious responsibility in risking everything on one method. Even Auguste Comte, the founder of sociology, suggested that we are governed more by the past than by the present, or to use his own words: ''We are governed more by the dead than by the living.''

Really, are we, you and I, better men than our grandfathers were? Are we closer to the infinite in our daily lives? Do we deal more justly with our neighbors? Do we take better advantage of our abilities and capacities to serve, or do we just use our powers for selfish ends?

Here is the crux of the question. The law of progress according to Tolstoy is found in the fact that we can learn all that is in the mind of the past generation, but they can not learn what is in ours. Have we anything to show them if they could? Wells is, perhaps, on the right track, far more so than Dewey, but he does not follow out his argument conclusively. In his ''Undying Fire'' Wells holds the measure of progress to be the degree of world understanding and social betterment attained, and these are to be secured through education based on a better teaching of history, which, of course, depends very much on the personality of the teacher. Wells is a rather poor philosopher; he seems to feel that there is a soul in the world, but he is not sure where to find it. Tolstoy, more logical than either Wells or Dewey, does not hesitate to look for the soul of things and finds that it is as strong in peasant as in lord, and as marked to-day as ever before. Its presence in the individual sets him off from the rest of society—makes him a man. Only as we give his soul freedom to develop according to its needs, and give it the mental and spiritual food which it needs, are we aiding progress in society.

But suppose we are able to find a measuring-rod for progress, then—*What are the means of education?* Here, too, we have an interesting contrast between Tolstoy and our great Dewey, who recently visited Soviet Russia. Dewey bases education and culture on science. Science rightly taught, he claims, ''is the agency of progress in action; ultimately and philosophically, science is the organ of general social progress.'' Dewey holds that knowledge within itself has moral values and that experience is the only ethical teacher. Morality is gained in moral action in social situations. Such knowledge gives culture. Science is as humanizing as any subject when it is taught humanistically. Thus in Dewey we have a direct line from knowledge to morality. In Tolstoy, on the other hand, we have a double line. On the one side we find the school and science. In this Tolstoy agrees with Dewey, but with this notable exception, ''Science is nothing in itself of value.'' But even here we might perhaps understand him to mean that science as extrinsic knowledge has nothing of value. On the other hand, and of predominant importance, Tolstoy places the ''teacher's relation to his students.'' The teacher must possess the personality that comes from love and understanding of his subject, and the pupil must desire help. There can be no social culture without freedom. The inherent consciousness of the pupil is the best judge of values and there must be freedom for it. To quote Tolstoy:

> Social education is based on pride of human reason. Culture is the free relation of people, having for its basis the need of one man to acquire knowledge and of the other to impart that which he has acquired. . . . The criterion of pedagogics is only liberty.

The fundamental difference between the two views is found in Tolstoy's faith in the divine quality of human personality. Here our American pragmatism as a philosophy is most weak. Here again, as in the question "Is education for the individual or for society?" we are back to the ultimate problem of the relation of the human-consciousness to the world-consciousness. And if we accept the conclusion of the first question then human personality is an individual expression of the larger right to freedom as the basis of any true culture, which Germans call *Bildung,* in contrast to *Unterricht* (instruction).

IV

Tolstoy is especially antagonistic to any standard method of teaching, believing that the teacher should employ the most natural means which present themselves out of a given situation, through which the pupil will best be able to grasp the subject. He is trying most earnestly to ward off formalism, pedanticism and especially that standardization which is so popular to-day. He found the old-fashioned curriculum based upon the *study of grammar.* This study appeared to him particularly senseless. The aim of learning grammatical rules was to speak the language correctly, but it is obviously possible to speak correctly without knowing the rules, and accordingly the value of learning them consists mainly in the mental exercise which can be obtained as easily in some other more useful way.

Tolstoy finds practice in *composition* by far the best way of studying language. In the first and second classes he left the choice of the subject to the children, who usually preferred stories from the Old Testament, which they wrote out eight weeks after they had heard them from Tolstoy. In the third class pupils tried compositions on a given subject such as "wheat," "pig," "pot," "table," etc., but to their surprise these subjects drove the children to tears, and even when Tolstoy helped them, and called their attention to the growing of the grain of wheat, its transformations and uses, they still worked reluctantly and made all kinds of errors in spelling, grammar and meaning. Tolstoy now changed his method of procedure and narrated some events to them; the children were immediately delighted, finding it much easier to recite an incident which they remembered than to describe a chair, house or wood. To Tolstoy these simple subjects seemed the easier, but the boy, as usual, looked at things from the opposite side, and was interested only in that which is complex and living. To describe a table requires really a high degree of philosophical efficiency, and the boy who cries because he has to write about a pot will express well a feeling of love or hate—either the meeting of Joseph with his brethren or a quarrel of his own with his comrades. Tolstoy gives two specimens of composition by a ten-year-old boy, Fedka, who is studying the third winter:

> "About grain:
>
> "Grain grows from the ground. At first it is green grain; when it grows up a little, there sprout from it ears and the women reap it. There is also grain like grass, that the cattle eat very well."

That was the end of it. He felt that it was not good and was aggrieved. About Tula he wrote the following without corrections:

> "About Tula:
>
> "When I was small I was five years old; then I heard the people went to some kind of Tula and I myself did not know what kind of a Tula it was. So I asked father: Dad! to what kind of a Tula do you travel, oh it must be fine? Father says: it is. So I say, Dad! take me with you, I will see Tula. Father says well all right, let the Sunday come; I will take you. I was happy begun to run and jump over the bench. After those days came Sunday. I just got up in the morning and father was already hitching the horses in the yard, I began to dress myself quickly. The moment I was dressed and went out into the yard, father had

already hitched the horses. I sat down in the sleigh, and I started. We travelled and travelled, and I made fourteen versts. I saw a tall church and I cried: father! see what a tall church. Father says; there is a smaller church but more butiful; I began to ask him, father, let us go there, I will pray God. Father went. When we came, they suddenly rang the bell. I was frightened and asked father what it was, whether they were beating drums. Father says: no, mass is beginning. Then we went to church to pray to God. When we were through praying, we went to the market. And so I walk, and walk and stumble all the time, I kept looking around me. So we came to the market, I saw they were selling white-breads and wanted to take without money. And father says to me, do not take or they will take your cap away. I say why will they take it, and father says, do not take without money, I say well give me ten kopeycks, I will buy me a small white-bread. Father gave me, I bought three white-breads and ate them up and I say: Father what fine white-breads. When we bought everything we went to the horses and gave them to drink, gave them hay, when they had eaten, we hitched up the horses and went home, went in to the hut and undressed myself and began to tell everybody how I was in Tula, and how father and I were in church, and prayed to God. Then I fell asleep and I see in my dream as though father was again going to Tula. I immediately awoke and I saw all were asleep I took and went to sleep."

Tolstoy does not hesitate to place Fedka above Goethe, and during such a happy moment of excitement he considers himself glad to understand and follow his Fedka, for he, Tolstoy, is "far from being able to guide or help" this child. The same talent, only in lesser degree, he found in other boys. His estimate of the artistic abilities of the peasant children in the way of authorship may seem a little exaggerated, but Tolstoy publishes the results and invites the assent of the public to his belief. He earnestly claims that we ought to learn from the peasant children rather than that they should learn to write from us adults. Children preferred writing compositions to any other exercise. Out of school, as soon as they chanced upon paper and pencil, they began to write stories. And they soon became critics as well, vexed when the story of a classmate was too long or disconnected, or when there were too many repetitions. They showed wonderful creative imagination, exhibited definite tastes of their own. Sometimes a pupil would refuse to read his composition, declaring that that of another pupil was better than his, and soon, when the essays were read anonymously the children would easily guess who the writer was. The subjects which the boys chose were either some peculiar event, their relations with some particular person, or tales that they had heard.

On the basis of all these experiences with his school children Tolstoy makes clever suggestions on the teaching of composition:

(1) Offer as large and varied a choice of themes as possible. Don't invent anything especially for the children, but offer those that seem most important, and most interesting to the teacher.

(2) Give the children stories written by the children. Use only children's models in compositions, because they are juster, more moral and more elegant than those written by adults.

(3) *Very important.* Never in looking through compositions make any remarks to the children about neatness, handwriting, spelling, structure of sentences or about logic.

(4) The difficulty of composition lies not in length nor in subject, nor in correct language, but in the mechanism of the work:

a. Choosing the number of thoughts and images.

b. Choosing the right words.

c. Remembering the right phrase and finding the right place for it.

d. Remembering what has been written so as not to repeat or omit, and finding a way to join the parts.

e. Then managing to think and write at the same time.

Here he indicates the following drill steps:

(1) Transfer the parts of the work gradually to the pupils.

(2) Choose what seems best and let the pupils choose.

(3) Indicate suitable places for the expressions.

(4) Look over the work to avoid repetitions.

(5) Do the writing and let the pupils clothe the thoughts and images.

(6) Then let them look over the writing.

(7) And finally let the children do the writing.

True to his Russian or Slavic nature Tolstoy loved and studied *music* seriously. Out of his experience he selects five points for guidance in music.

(1) To write sounds by means of figures is the most profitable method for children.

(2) To teach time separate from sound is best.

(3) Teach the art of singing from the first, and not mere dexterity in playing and singing.

(4) Nothing so harms musical instruction as a superficial knowledge of music.

(5) Teach the laws of music and not the false taste of the community.

Exceedingly modern in his psychology, especially in that of *reading,* Tolstoy recognizes the different methods of comprehension and would have instruction follow these lines. Text-books, according to him, usually begin with general ideas, those of grammar with adjectives, those of history with divisions of periods, those of geometry with definitions of space and of the mathematical point. But these general notions are the hardest to comprehend, and the children must begin with something tangible, related to their own common experiences. He found as much difficulty in *teaching geography* as history. The boys showed no interest at all in the fact that the earth revolves on its axis and passes around the sun. Just as Tolstoy had tried in history to begin with the pupil's own time, he now made the experiment of teaching geography by beginning in their own village. He was convinced that the children's interest in *history* was entirely dramatic—that is, artistic.

His ideas about art are also interesting. Unfortunately the works of *art,* literary, poetic, dramatic, pictorial and plastic, now produced are intended expressly for people of leisure, and are, therefore, useless to the people. Tolstoy regrets this deflection of art from the services of the masses. The attempt is to delight thousands and neglect the millions. This is a great evil.

Further, Tolstoy comments on the common, empty and stale paradox: that to understand the beautiful, preparation is necessary. Who said so? Why? What proves it? It is only a shift, a loop-hole to escape from the hopeless position of our art, produced for one class alone. Why are the beauty of the sun, of the human face, the sounds of folk-song, the beauty of deeds of love and sacrifice, accessible to every one, and why do they demand no preparation?

Plato, when asked whether the common people need *beaux arts,* answered no! Our educators, tired and confused, answer yes, but with certain limitations: for all to become artists would be bad for society. Art has its special servants, and some way should be left open for the entirely devoted and greatly gifted to escape from among the people, and devote themselves completely to the service of art. This is nearly always the way that the *élite* make it possible for each one "to become what he likes."

Tolstoy says this is all wrong. All are to enjoy art and this he regards as an axiom. The trouble lies with the direction that art has taken. The *beaux arts* are on the wrong track and are going the wrong way. What is said of music, poetry and art may be justly said of *literature.* Too many good things never reach the masses. They hear the hum of the telegraph wire but they do not use the telegraph. He is indignant at the suggestion that it is an error to allow the minds of peasants to develop "beyond their station." "Who will do the hard work," some people ask, "when everybody is either an artist or a philosopher?" According to Tolstoy the mind of the peasant is naturally like the mind of the landed proprietor, and each is entitled equally to have its craving for knowledge and mental exercise satisfied.

Tolstoy has something to say on *religion* in education. He does not like the presentation to the child of the idea that his God is a sort of personal, self-willed and dreadful evil being, a Jewish God, Jehovah of the Old Testament. God is neither a Jew, nor a Russian, nor an Englishman.* He believes that happiness depends neither upon the whims of a capricious God nor on liberation from eternal punishment, carried by some one else, nor in a blind belief in creeds and dogmas. Happiness comes from loving communion among men. We are here by God's will and it is well with us when we fulfil that will. God wills that we shall be happy; and for all to be happy there is but one means—that each should act toward others as he would wish that they should act towards him. God cares for us now and he will care for us in the end.

V

To conclude, Tolstoy is, no doubt, a great educational experimentalist. In his analysis of the ideals of education he is very much influenced by the political and social ideas of his time which had come to dominate his thinking. As a member of the aristocratic caste in a society dominated by caste distinctions and caste thinking, he, as an individual, had come to realize the futility of it all. His sensitive mind shrank from the consequences of this social structure to the masses; he came to realize the equality of these souls with his soul, and drew the economic analogy taken from understanding and not from knowledge. Accordingly at the basis of his educational philosophy we find three keys—*individualism, intellectual liberty* and a *religious sanction.* There is no doubt that Tolstoy's creative imagination, mental freedom and geometry of thinking are foundations of his pedagogy, too.

His school Tolstoy used only as a laboratory for experiments, refusing to accept without proof the most time-honored theories on education and culture. Before he established his own experimental school Tolstoy visited many European schools of all kinds. He became convinced that to consider the school as a disciplined company of juvenile soldiers, all obeying the same orders in the same way, is a blot on the face of modern Christian nations. He found that a certain degree of liberty, of disorder even, is necessary for the purpose of revealing the individuality of each child.

Tolstoy makes a sharp distinction between culture and education. Making his own résumé of that problem he arrived at the following conclusions:

(1) Culture is free, and therefore legal and just; education is compulsory, and therefore illegal and unjust; it can not be justified by reason, and consequently can not form the subject of pedagogy or science of education.

(2) Education, as a phenomenon, has its origin: (a) in the family, (b) in faith, (c) in the government, (d) in society.

*As is well known, Tolstoy has been very much against the anti-Semitic movement. He agreed with the noble spirit of Vladimir Solovyev's book—*Die juedische Frage ist eine christliche Frage.*

(3) The domestic, religious and governmental bases of education are natural and find their justification in necessity, but the *social education has no other foundation than the pride of human reason,* and thus bears the most baneful fruits, such as the universities and university culture.

From Tolstoy's experimentation and discussions we could sum up safely that the spirit of the Yasnaya Polyana School is this:

First, education is human activity having for its basis a desire for equality, and the constant tendency or urge to advance in knowledge.

Second, the pupil state of mind is the most important condition of successful education; and to secure good results freedom is indispensable.

Third, Tolstoy's general charge against day-schools, boarding-schools and universities is that at the base of them all lies the one principle: the right of one man, or a small group of men, to shape other people as they like.

Fourth, education as a deliberate moulding of people into certain forms is sterile, illegitimate and impossible.

Who knows, some day Tolstoy may be the educational leader of the world!

EDUCATIONAL EVENTS

BRITISH BOYS IN AMERICAN PREPARATORY SCHOOLS

MR. ALBERT HALSTEAD, the new Consul-General of the United States of America to Great Britain, speaking at a luncheon given by the English-Speaking Union on January 15, alluded to plans which are being made for sending British schoolboys to some of the preparatory schools of the United States to enable them to appreciate the life of that country. Dr. Archibald Fleming was in the chair. According to the report in the London *Times Educational Supplement* Mr. Halstead said:

Every institution and every activity that was calculated to diffuse a knowledge and a proper understanding of other peoples was an agency for promoting harmony in international relations and a valuable ally in the cause of peace. The peoples of the world desired to pursue their destinies without the anxiety of strained relations, or the horrible interruption arising from the tragedy and destructiveness of war. Among these organizations, the English-Speaking Union was performing a work that could not be too highly praised; it afforded opportunities of various kinds for the promotion of good-will and understanding. The women of the world, and particularly those of Great Britain and the United States, were having greater weight in international relations, and that meant a check upon the more aggressive character of men. The attitude of women was one of the influences which were cementing in bonds of friendship and sympathy the English-speaking peoples.

There was a plan in preparation, which would be in operation soon, to send British boys of the age of 14 to some of the great preparatory schools of the United States which were the nearest equivalent to the public schools of Great Britain. The American schools were St. Paul's; Philip's Academy, Andover; Philip's Academy, Exeter; St. Mark's School, the Kent School, the Hill School, the Hotchkiss School and the Loomis School. The plan was to send a limited number of boys, free of cost, to these schools, and they would be cared for during the holidays or, if desired, sent back to Great Britain. The boys would have an opportunity of learning, in the most formative period of their lives, something of the real life and tendencies of the United States, and understanding the real soul of that country, which was not fully appreciated. They would come back with ability to judge, when problems arose, what was the real United States. Like the American university and college graduates who had been enabled by the Cecil Rhodes endowment to study at British universities, they would return home with a sympathetic feeling for the country where they had studied, and they would be missionaries to preach the doctrines of tolerance and good-will. More of his own countrymen came to England than British subjects went to the United States; but the flow was not entirely in one direction, and the tendency to go to the United States for impartial study was certain to be of increasing benefit. They were all inclined, as were the ancients, particularly in youth, to regard those who were not of their own country as barbarians. That did not prevail as they grew older; but even men of the greatest experience found it difficult sometimes to understand the point of view of the people of other countries.

THE EXCHANGE OF LITERATURE BETWEEN PAN-AMERICAN COUNTRIES

The exchange of literature between Pan-American countries, together with the establishment of library schools in Latin-American universities, is urged by the Governing Board of the Pan-American Union, according to an announcement by the Union on February 7.

The establishment of library schools or chairs of library science in the several universities of the Latin-American countries; the establishment in Latin-America of associations of librarians and bibliographers; the translation and publication in Spanish, Portuguese and French of standard text-books on library science, and the translation and publication in Spanish, Portuguese and English of the best literary, scientific, bibliographic and historical productions by citizens of the American Republics was urged by the Governing Board of the Pan-American Union after hearing the report of its Permanent Committee on Bibliography.

The permanent committee of the Governing Board is composed of the Ambassador of Chile, Carlos G. Davila, the Minister of Panama, Ricardo J. Alfaro, and the Minister of Venezuela, Carlos F. Grisanti, and was appointed pursuant to the terms of a resolution on bibliographical cooperation adopted at the Sixth Pan-American Conference which met at Havana in 1928. The resolution approved at Havana proposes that an Inter-American Bibliographical Commission be convened by the Governing Board of the Pan-American Union, at which representatives of all the American Republics will be in attendance. At the April meeting of the board consideration will be given to the program of the proposed Bibliographic Conference, at which time it is probable that the date and place of meeting will also be fixed.

At the same time the board adopted a resolution fixing the meeting to be held in May as the time at which consideration will be given to the definite program of the Inter-American Conference on Agriculture, also provided for by resolution of the Sixth Pan-American Conference.

The Governing Board acted favorably on a communication received from the Rector of the University of Havana, Dr. Octavio Averhoff, suggesting the desirability of holding the Pan-American Conference of rectors, deans and educators at the same time as the International Congress of Universities which will meet at Havana on February 15, 1930. This conference will coincide with the bicentenary of the founding of the university. The Congress of Rectors, Deans and Educators was provided for by a resolution of the Sixth International Conference of American states, and will consider the establishment of an Inter-American Institute of Intellectual Cooperation.

AN INTER-AMERICAN EDUCATIONAL CONFERENCE

President Uel W. Lamkin, of the National Education Association of the United States, has issued invitations to the ministers of education in nineteen nations of the Western Hemisphere, requesting their participation in an informal Inter-American educational conference to be held at Atlanta, Georgia, from June 28 to July 4, in connection with the sixty-seventh annual convention of the National Education Association. Invitations were sent to Argentine, Bolivia, Brazil, Chile, Colombia, Costa Rica, Cuba, Dominican Republic, Ecuador, Guatemala, Haiti, Honduras, Nicaragua, Panama, Paraguay, Peru, Salvador, Uruguay and Venezuela.

Before sending the invitation President Lamkin was assured by representatives of a number of these countries, through Dr. Glen Levin Swiggett, of Washington, D. C., secretary of the movement for an Inter-American educational organization, that the various nations would look with favor on holding the preliminary conference in the United States and on holding the first formal meeting in one of the nations of the south. President Lamkin was reminded that the World Federation of Education Associations originated in a similar conference in San Francisco in 1923.

Mr. Lamkin expects each nation to send one or more representatives to Atlanta and he believes an organization of great significance will be formed. In commenting on the invitation he said, "The educators in these nations are on most cordial terms with each other. This organization will help to create a better understanding between the people themselves. I look upon this as a most important movement and one which will rapidly improve relationships. I am in favor of holding the first formal meeting of the proposed organization in one of the Southern Republics. It is a recognition of the kindly attitude of educators in those nations towards this country for the preliminary conference to be held at Atlanta."

THE ADMINISTRATION OF INDIAN SCHOOLS

THE alleged faulty administration of Indian schools and alleged mistreatment of children attending these schools were described to the Senate Committee on Indian Affairs February 6 by witnesses subpenaed in the committee's investigation of the Indian Bureau of the Department of the Interior, as reported in the *U. S. Daily*.

Conditions said to have existed on the Indian Reservation at Tuba City, Ariz., in the fall of 1927 were described to the committee by Eleanor B. Jones, formerly a nurse of the Public Health Service, detailed for work among the Indians.

About 300 Indian children were crowded into small dormitories where there was no heat, Miss Jones testified. The sick were not separated from the well, she asserted, and when she arrived there were epidemics of measles and whooping cough as well as tuberculosis and malnutrition. New children were constantly being brought in among those infected, the witness stated.

No effort was made to diagnose illnesses, according to Miss Jones, and "many children had been sick for weeks and weeks." There was a doctor for the school plant at Tuba City, she asserted, "but the doctor didn't do anything."

The Commissioner of Indian Affairs, Charles H. Burke, placed in the record letters from Miss Jones tendering her resignation, which showed, he said, that no complaint was made other than the fact there was no equipment for the field work she was employed to do.

Mrs. Julia C. Carroll, who was employed as matron from April 15 to August, 1923, at an Indian school at Genona, Nebr., told the committee that Samuel P. Davis, superintendent of the Genona School, took Indian boys out of school and put them to work on his own farms, where he used government machinery and commissary materials. Mr. Burke did not question Mrs. Carroll, other than say he would supply the committee with the record of the case, and stated that Mrs. Carroll was "not considered temperamentally qualified for her position."

Mrs. Ina M. Livermore, Veterans' Bureau employee, who had been an assistant matron at Genona in 1922, next took the stand and told the committee that the Indian boys had worked on Superintendent Davis's farm during school hours. One case in which it was alleged a girl had been beaten by Mr. Davis was outlined to the committee by Mrs. Livermore. The Indians at the school "did not get good food," she stated. Butter and milk were served only once a week, she said, although there were a large number of cows on the school farm.

INCREASES IN THE SALARIES OF NEW YORK CITY TEACHERS

THE New York City Board of Education has voted to allot $2,989,616 in salary increases to all teachers within the New York public school system who already have arrived at their maximum salaries, and at the same time established a new rule which practically will compel every teacher hereafter to take a course of study each year in order to qualify for an annual salary increment.

This was the solution accepted by the board for the puzzle of how to dispose of the $3,000,000 allocated for supermaximum salaries a year ago, which was not distributed because in July the supermaximum system was declared unconstitutional. Of this the $2,989,616 was actually appropriated, the rest to be held for emergencies. The salary increases go into effect as of February 1.

The resolution covering the new ruling read as follows:

WHEREAS, In the opinion of the board of superintendents, continuous improvement of the teacher in service, not only through increased experience but also through cultural or technical study, should be required throughout the entire span of the salary schedule, rather than at the end of a schedule, through supermaximal increments; and

Whereas, Section 888 of the state education law provides for salary and increment corresponding to years of service, unless service for the year immediately preceding has been declared by a majority vote of the board of superintendents to be unsatisfactory, after opportunity to be heard, therefore, be it

Resolved, That the Board of Superintendents hereby declares satisfactory service of teachers for the purpose of salary increments to be conditioned by reports from principals and district superintendents, by the number of days of actual teaching service within the salary year, and by the successful completion of a course of thirty hours of cultural or technical study approved by the Board of Superintendents for each salary year after permanent appointment, and continuing throughout the span of the salary schedule, under regulations to be determined hereafter by the Board of Superintendents and to become effective September 1, 1930.

The new definition of "satisfactory service" will not apply to teachers in their first three probationary years, but will begin to apply at the beginning of their fourth year.

Arthur S. Somers, chairman of the finance committee of the board, who presented the new salary schedule, announced that while the $3,000,000 already on hand would cover the increases this year, he felt confident that the Board of Estimate would accede to any increases in the budget of future years made necessary by the new rulings. According to Frederick D. Chambers, auditor of the board, $3,000,000 of state money will be available in 1930 when the new plan goes into effect.

The salary increases voted were divided as follows: Kindergarten to 6B grade teachers, an increase of $246, making a total salary of $3,390; 7A to 9B teachers, an increase of $230, making a total of $3,830; assistant teachers in high schools, an increase of $98, making a total of $4,500. Teachers in training schools did not share in the rise because the increase allowed to them a year ago was $872.

THE NEW JERSEY STATE EDUCATIONAL SURVEY

The survey staff of the New Jersey State Educational Commission, as well as the scope of its work, has been considerably enlarged in recent months. This was made possible by the increase of its appropriations from $25,000 to $50,000 during an October session of the legislature. The time of the making of the report was also postponed until the legislature convenes in 1930. The members of the staff as now constituted and their respective fields of work are as follows: Harlan Updegraff, formerly president of Cornell College and professor of school administration, University of Pennsylvania, director of the study; George F. Zook, president of the University of Akron, and L. E. Blauch, professor of secondary education, North Carolina College for Women, Greensboro, higher education; William C. Bagley, Teachers College, normal schools; Francis B. Haas, president of State Normal, Bloomsburg, Pennsylvania, and formerly Pennsylvania Superintendent of Public Instruction, state school administration; Julian E. Butterworth, professor of state school administration, New York State College of Agriculture, county and rural school administration; Arthur B. Moehlman, professor of school administration, University of Michigan, city school administration; Preston H. Smith, superintendent of schools, Bayonne, N. J., and Harl R. Douglass, professor of education, University of Oregon (visiting professor at the University of Pennsylvania), secondary education; J. J. Savitz, principal of Glassboro Normal School, Clifford J. Scott, superintendent of schools, East Orange, Francis M. Garver, professor of education, University of Pennsylvania, and Lois Coffey Mossman, associate professor, Teachers College, elementary education; F. G. Bonser, professor at Teachers College, special curriculum studies for pupils of lower mentality; Lewis A. Wilson, assistant commissioner, New York State Department of Education, vocational education; Edgar A. Doll, Vineland Training School, N. J., education of the feeble-minded; Owen D. Evans, professor at Girard College, Philadelphia, adult education; Harlan Updegraff and Carmon Ross, supervising principal, Doylestown, Pennsylvania, school finances.

The Survey Commission is composed of six members of the Legislature, the president of the State Board of Education, the commissioner of education, four appointees of the governor and three appointees of the commissioner of education. Senator Arthur N. Pierson, the author of a number of outstanding educational acts, is the chairman of the commission, and Charles H. Elliott, State Commissioner of Education, is its secretary. The offices of the commission are in the Trenton Trust Building, Trenton, New Jersey.

A COLLEGE COURSE ON THE PHOTOPLAY

THE Academy of Motion Picture Arts and Sciences of Hollywood, which unites in one body all branches of motion picture production, has joined with the University of Southern California in providing a college course, which deals with the photoplay as an art form and as a social institution. The academy has since its establishment in 1927 been actuated by an avowed desire to further develop the photoplay in art and social utility, and the university soon after announced that it would offer the degree of Bachelor of Science in Cinematography.

Those who are responsible for the content of the course include President R. B. von KleinSmid, of the University of Southern California; President Douglas Fairbanks, of the Academy of Motion Picture Arts and Sciences; Dr. Karl T. Waugh, of the college of liberal arts; William C. de Mille, vice-president of the academy; Professor Ray MacDonald, of the school of speech of the university; Milton Sills, chairman of the committee on college affairs of the academy; Dr. Emory S. Bogardus, chairman of the department of sociology of the University; Frank Woods, secretary of the academy, and members of the Committee on College Affairs of the Hollywood Academy, including Irving Thalberg, John W. Considine, Jr., Beulah Dix Flebbe, Edward J. Montagne, Chandler Sprague, Clara Beranger, Paul Sloane, J. A. Ball, Lotta Wood, Roy Pomeroy, Darryl Zanuck and Lester Cowan.

The lecturers include Ernst Lubitsch, Commodore J. Stuart Blackton, Benjamin Glazer, William Cameron Menzies, William de Mille, M. C. Levee, Clara Beranger, Frank Woods, Irving Thalberg, J. A. Ball, Edwin Schallert, Milton Sills and Douglas Fairbanks, of the academy; and President von KleinSmid, Dean Waugh, Dr. Bogardus and Dr. H. Wildon Carr, of the university.

Early history of the photoplay, scientific foundation, its growth and development, the silent photoplay, the modern photoplay with sound and voice, the story, the actor's art, pictorial beauty, principles of criticism, social utility of the photoplay, its relation to the esthetic culture of the world and the future of the photoplay are specific topics to be covered.

Observation and comment on current photoplays will be required of the students. Permanent reproduction by vitaphone and movietone will, it is planned, make the selected lectures available to all colleges. A library of a new literature, critical, analytical and allied to the screen art, will be developed.

THE INSTITUTE OF HUMAN RELATIONS OF YALE UNIVERSITY

YALE UNIVERSITY has received gifts and subsidies for the establishment of an Institute of Human Relations in which its resources for the scientific investigation of man's behavior from the physical and mental, the individual and social viewpoints will be concentrated. The institute is designed to bring together sociologists, biologists, psychologists and economists, who will combine with their colleagues in such applied fields as law, medicine and psychiatry to correlate knowledge of the mind and body and of individual and group conduct, and to study further the interrelations of the many factors influencing human actions.

An announcement made by President Angell states that all the departments of the natural and social sciences will cooperate, in so far as possible, in this plan, with the institute as the point of contact between them and as a center for their graduate and research work. Members of the institute will hold an appointment in a fundamental university department in order that its work may be articulated with that of the university as a whole. This will make possible a coordination of related activities dealing with man's welfare, and a concentration of knowledge and technique such as has never before been attempted in the solution of complex problems of human relations.

Of the total support, $1,500,000 has been given by the Rockefeller Foundation for a building. $100,000 a year has also been granted by the foundation for a period of ten years for the development of psychiatry, $50,000 to be used annually for the development of the educational program in this field and $50,000 for the care of patients. There is also available the income from $1,000,000, amounting to $50,000 a year, granted by the Commonwealth Fund in 1926 and continuing through 1931. This will be used as in the past for the work in mental hygiene. The income from $3,000,000, amounting to $150,000 a year, has been voted for ten years by the Laura Spelman Rockefeller Memorial for research in the social sciences and for the continuance of research in child development and in psychology.

Conduct of the institute will rest with the professors devoting their full time or the larger part of their time to its interests. The executive committee will be composed of the deans of the graduate, medical and law schools, one representative of the social sciences and one representative of the natural sciences.

Plans are now being drawn for a building which is to be on land already acquired in the immediate vicinity of the Yale School of Medicine and the New Haven Hospital. It will provide modern facilities for activities now inadequately housed and widely scattered, so that all may enjoy a constant exchange of ideas and facilities.

The Institute of Human Relations is, according to President Angell, a logical development of the best tendencies in modern education and research. It is designed to permit progress which can not well be made as long as sharp lines divide the various branches of science from one another in educational institutions.

THE REAL ESTATE LEASES OF COLUMBIA UNIVERSITY

WHAT was once considered a worthless parcel of land, a "white elephant" on the hands of the Columbia University trustees, becomes under the recent agreement, according to the *Columbia Alumni News,* a producer of $3,000,000 in revenue under the terms of the contract with Mr. John D. Rockefeller, Jr., which provide for a lease of twenty-four years dating from last October and for three renewals of twenty-one years each. According to the treasurer's report for last year, the 203 separate leaseholds, which have expired or which the university acquired, yielded only about $300,000 in rentals.

Concerning the increased revenue and its use by the university, President Butler had the following to say in his statement announcing the deal:

> In anticipation of an increased income from this property at about this time, the trustees of the university had already incurred debts and budget obligations which would absorb all of the increased income for some time to come. The greatly increased salary schedule for all academic officers, adopted in April last, the much greater cost of maintaining the work of the medical school at the new Medical Center, and repayment of the amounts borrowed to construct the costly research laboratories for the physical and chemical sciences which were completed last year, will require the use of the new income for several years.

The property, which for purposes of taxation has been valued at $30,000,000, and which real estate men say is worth much more, is part of a tract that came to Columbia University in 1814 as a gift from the State of New York, at which time Union College received a cash gift of $200,000, Hamilton College of $40,000, the College of Physicians and Surgeons of $30,000 and the Asbury Colored Church one of $4,000. The Reverend John M. Mason, of the Class of 1789, at that time President of Columbia, was roundly criticized for accepting so valueless a gift. Men of affairs claimed that the tract was hardly worth $6,000, and not the $80,000 at which the state legislature valued it. Five years later, the legislature "took pity" on Columbia, and, in an attempt to make amends, gave the college a gift of $10,000 in cash.

Prior to its gift to Columbia, the tract had been the site of the first botanical garden in North America. It was purchased at a price of $4,807.36 plus sixteen bushels of wheat payable each May from the City of New York in 1804 by Professor David Hosack, who in 1795 had become professor of botany at Columbia and later professor of materia medica at the College of Physicians and Surgeons of which he was one of the founders. He was one of the most prominent men in the city during his life time, although considered rather erratic. He developed the site as a botanical garden, having 2,000 rare plants growing two years later. This development, including the green house which he built on the site, cost him $100,000 in all. Unable to gain college or state aid in maintaining the gardens he finally sold the site to the state for $74,268.75 in 1810.

EDUCATIONAL NOTES AND NEWS

DR. CHARLES CURTIS HARRISON, formerly provost of the University of Pennsylvania, died in Philadelphia on February 12. He was eighty-four years old.

DR. ROBERT J. LEONARD, since 1925 professor of education and director of the school of education at Teachers College, Columbia University, was killed on February 9 when he fell from a window of his apartment on the ninth floor of Seth Low Hall. Dr. Leonard was suffering from an attack of influenza. He was forty-four years old.

THE degree of doctor of laws will be conferred on Mr. Frank Kellogg, secretary of state, by Georgetown University on February 18 in connection with the observance of the tenth anniversary of the founding of the institution's school of foreign service, when Mr. Kellogg will be the chief speaker.

DAVID W. HOPKINS, Republican, superintendent of schools of St. Joseph, Missouri, has been elected, by 2,000 majority, representative in Congress from the Fourth Missouri District in a special election.

AT the recent meeting at Great Falls of the Montana Society for the Study of Education, an "All-Montana" banquet was tendered to Miss May Trumper, retiring state superintendent. Mr. W. E. Maddock presided and addresses were made by Miss Elizabeth Ireland, the new state superintendent; Superintendent C. G. Manning, Professor E. A. Atkinson, Superintendent S. D. Largent and Miss Trumper. Principal Payne Templeton presented to Miss Trumper a life membership in the National Education Association and a platinum pin set with diamonds given by several hundred teachers of the state as a token of friendship and in appreciation of the twelve years of devoted and distinguished service she had rendered.

C. R. REED, formerly superintendent of schools of Bridgeport, Connecticut, who has been elected to succeed Superintendent W. F. Webster, of Minneapolis, has been formally released from his contract in Connecticut and will go to Minneapolis at the end of this school year to become acquainted with the administration of the Minneapolis school system, where he will formally take up his work on August 1.

THE REVEREND JOHN O. GOSS, district superintendent of the Methodist church in Kentucky, has been elected president of Union College, Kentucky.

DR. EVERETT L. AUSTIN, associate professor of rural education at the Indiana State Normal School, has been named dean of the school.

PROFESSOR FREDERICK J. E. WOODBRIDGE, Johnsonian professor of philosophy at Columbia University, has resigned as dean of the faculties of political science, philosophy and pure science and fine arts, his resignation to take effect on June 30. Dr. Howard Lee McBain, professor of constitutional law, has been appointed his successor.

EDWARD H. WARREN, Weld professor of law at Harvard Law School, after twenty-five years of teaching in the school, has resigned, his resignation effective on September 1. He was granted leave during the second half of the current year, and is now in England where he is taking up his residence.

DR. WALTER SCOTT ATHEARN, dean of Boston University's school of religious education and social service, has resigned, effective June 30. Dr. Athearn will pass the remainder of his academic year in Europe, Asia and Africa in educational research work in his capacity as chairman of the World Federation of Education Associations. He will sail from New York on March 22.

DR. CHESTER N. GREENOUGH, professor of English at Harvard University and formerly dean of Harvard College, has been selected as a master of one of the new "Houses" to be established at Harvard under the Harkness Fund.

Professor Chauncey Brewster Tinker, Sanford professor of English literature at Yale University, will give a course on the English painters of the seventeenth and eighteenth centuries, for the department of fine arts at Harvard during the second half of the academic year 1929–30. He will be on sabbatical leave from Yale University during the whole of that academic year.

Professor Henry W. Edgerton, who is at present a member of the faculty of law at the University of Chicago, has been appointed professor of law in the Cornell University Law School.

At Harvard University, Josef Redlich, professor of comparative public law, has been made Charles Stebbins Fairchild professor of comparative public law. Joshua Whatmough, assistant professor of comparative philology, who came to Harvard in 1926 from Cairo, Egypt, has been elected associate professor of comparative philology, and Leigh Hoadley, assistant professor of zoology since 1927, associate professor of zoology, both appointments to take effect on September 1.

Arthur S. Somers, member of the Board of Education of New York City and formerly president of the Brooklyn Chamber of Commerce, was nominated at a caucus on February 11 of Democratic assemblymen to succeed Robert W. Higbie, of Jamaica, L. I., as member of the State Board of Regents. The Republicans in the legislature have agreed to name Mr. Higbie for another term.

Dr. M. L. Brittain, president of the Georgia Institute of Technology, has become a member of the board of visitors for the U. S. Naval Academy at Annapolis.

The board of managers of the Ling Foundation of California, an organization devoted to the advancement of child health, recently awarded to Dr. William A. Howe, chief of the medical inspection bureau of the New York State Department of Education, a Ling medal for distinguished service in the promotion of child health. The medal will probably be presented to Dr. Howe at the next meeting of the American Association of School Physicians to be held in Minneapolis.

Professor Frank N. Bryant, head of the department of business mathematics, has been elected director of admissions and secretary of the board of admissions at Syracuse University, succeeding Dr. Eugene F. Bradford.

Miss Della Swartz has been named to membership on the New York State Industrial Board, by nomination of Governor Roosevelt, to take the place vacated by Frances Perkins, who has been made State Industrial Commissioner.

Elmer K. Sexton, for nearly thirty-five years a member of Newark's school system and an assistant superintendent of schools there for seventeen years, retired from active service on February 1.

W. J. Shirley has been elected superintendent of the city schools of Havre, Montana, to succeed Miss Elizabeth Ireland, who resigned to become state superintendent of public instruction. Mr. Shirley had been principal of the Havre high school since 1925.

Doña Concha Espina, the Spanish novelist, will visit America this spring as an "artistic envoy" from Spain. She has been invited to lecture at various universities. She has agreed to be at Middlebury College for the summer school and to lecture at Columbia University next autumn. She will speak in Spanish on the art and literature of Spain.

Five authorities on problems of national administration will give this year's series of Dodge lectures on the "Responsibilities of Citizenship" at Yale University. Robe Carl White, first assistant secretary of labor, opened the series on February 13 with an address on "Administrative Problems of Immigration." On succeeding Wednesdays, James M. Doran, United States prohibition commissioner, will speak on "Administrative Problems of Prohibition"; Dr. Raymond Moley, professor of government at Columbia, on "Administrative Problems of Criminal Justice"; William P. McCracken, assistant secretary of commerce for aeronautics, on "Administrative Problems of Commercial Aviation," and Dr. Oscar C. Merrill, executive secretary of the Federal Power

Commission, on "Administrative Problems of Super-Power."

THE dedication of the second unit of Conwell Hall, Temple University, Philadelphia, took place on Founder's Day on February 15. The address was given by Edward L. Katzenbach, president, New Jersey Bar Association, and honorary degrees were conferred as follows: Honorable John S. Fisher, governor of Pennsylvania; General W. W. Atterbury, president of the Pennsylvania Railroad; the Honorable Leon M. Conwell, mayor of Somerville, Massachusetts and editor of the Somerville *Journal*, and Frances Elliot Clark, educational director of the Victor Talking Machine Company.

The Daily Princetonian suggests that the proposed new university library should be dedicated to Woodrow Wilson. It says: "Of all the alumni who have gone out from Princeton in the 182 years of its history, there is none more widely known than Woodrow Wilson. Yet Princeton University, the institution in which he received his education and of which he was the chief member for a number of years, has no Wilson memorial."

A RECOMMENDATION that the executive committee of the Associated Academic Principals consider the erection of a tablet or other fitting memorial in the State Education Building or elsewhere to commemorate the record and life of Dr. Charles F. Wheelock, former assistant commissioner for secondary education and honorary president of the Associated Academic Principals, was made at the recent meeting of the association in Syracuse. Dr. Wheelock died on November 4. The resolution adopted by the association reads: "That we register our sorrow at the absence from this meeting, the first in over a quarter of a century, either in presence or in spirit, of that outstanding teacher, that rare personality, friend and counselor, that beloved and honored as well as 'honorary' president of this organization, Charles F. Wheelock, 'old timer' in and exemplar of ancient virtues, inspired prophet in modern faiths—beloved Chief! We hail that career and life, a contemplation of which at this realizing and recognizing hour of passing, inspires with renewed courage all who bear the name of 'teacher' and sheds a luster, as of gracious benediction, upon all who wear the purple badge of this, his favorite and favored organization."

A COMMITTEE of the American Association for the Advancement of Science has been formed for the purpose of drafting a resolution on the proposed simplified calendar. Members of the committee are: Professor A. E. Kennelly, of Harvard University, *chairman;* Dr. W. W. Campbell, president of the University of California; Dr. C. F. Marvin, chief of the U. S. Weather Bureau; Dr. A. R. Crook, chief of the State Museum Division of Illinois, and Gano Dunn, chairman of the National Research Council.

THE first number has been issued, dated February, of the *Journal of Adult Education,* a quarterly published by the American Association for Adult Education, 41 East 42d Street, New York City. The editors are Mary L. Ely and Morse A. Cartwright, of the association staff; the editorial board includes Alvin Saunders Johnson, *chairman;* Charles F. D. Belden, William Allan Neilson, Dorothy Canfield Fisher and Henry Suzzallo. The associate editors are: Ethel Richardson Allen, Olive Dame Campbell, John A. Lapp, Eduard C. Lindeman, Spencer Miller, Jr., Carroll R. Reed, James E. Russell, Hilda W. Smith, Kenyon L. Butterfield, Linda A. Eastman, Read Lewis, Everett Dean Martin, Harry Allen Overstreet, Leon J. Richardson, Elmer Scott and William C. Smith. Among the twelve articles in the current issue of the journal, which contains 112 pages, are "Breadwinning and Soulsaving," by Lawrence P. Jacks; "On Going on Learning," by James Harvey Robinson; "Liberating Liberty," by Everett Dean Martin; "Investigating the Curriculum," by Edward Lee Thorndike; "Vitality in Teaching," by Alvin Saunders Johnson, and a symposium "Is Adult Education a Fad?"

EDUCATIONAL organizations which have recently been admitted to membership in the World Federation are: Associación Pedagógica Universitaria, University of Havana, Cuba; the Maine Teachers' Association; Massachusetts Teachers' Federation; Minnesota Education Association; Missouri State Teachers' Association; South Dakota Education Association. The total membership of the World Federation now includes twenty full membership organizations and thirty associate organizations.

A BUILDING worth nearly $2,000,000 has been given by Mr. and Mrs. Frederick Brown to New York University. It is situated at the northwest corner of Washington Place and Greene St., New York City, and has been rented for about ten years by the university at a cost of $92,000.

EDWARD S. HARKNESS, of New York, has given $200,000 to the endowment fund for the College for Women of Western Reserve University. One half of the amount is given outright, the remainder to be turned over when the drive reaches its goal of $1,000,000.

BEQUESTS amounting to $959,350, alumnae gifts of $21,000 and a special donation of $7,000 by friends of Mount Holyoke College toward a new playshop laboratory, bring the total contributed to Mount Holyoke College by outside donors during the last twelve months to $987,550.

GROUP insurance totaling $3,566,000 is offered by the University of Chicago to its faculty members, officers of administration and employees. The university will bear more than half the cost of the premiums for all who participate. For faculty members the insurance will supplement the retiring allowances, and for all non-academic employees it will displace a death benefit system. The insurance will be issued by the Prudential Insurance Company of America.

ASSEMBLYMAN JAMES R. ROBINSON, of Ithaca, has introduced a bill in the Legislature providing $1,000,000 for the construction of a home economics building at Cornell University.

OF the $6,000,000 authorized by the congress for the rehabilitation of Porto Rican areas damaged by the hurricane of September 13 and 14, $2,000,000 is provided for rebuilding and repair of school houses and for reconstruction and repair of insular and rural municipal roads.

A BILL carrying an appropriation of $12,000,000 for the establishment of a national university, with an endowment fund of $60,000,000, as a memorial to George Washington, has been introduced in the House by Representative Guyer, Republican, of Kansas.

FREDERICK C. AUSTIN, a Chicago capitalist, turned over to Northwestern University on January 23 the F. C. Austin building at 111 West Jackson Boulevard, Chicago, valued at more than $3,000,000, the income from which will be used for the training of business executives. The building will be held as an endowment, President Walter Dill Scott said, in making the announcement, and the income used for scholarships to be awarded young men who show qualities believed to be essential for future business executives. The university, under the plan, assumes the responsibility for selecting the F. C. Austin scholars and for directing their training.

JAMES DALLAS BURRUS, first Negro to take a bachelor of arts degree in a college south of the Mason-Dixon line, and who died suddenly of a heart attack in a street-car on December 5, left approximately $100,000 to Fisk University at Nashville, Tennessee. He was eighty-two years old.

WILLIAM E. NICKERSON, a trustee of Boston University, has announced in a letter to President Marsh that he will follow up his recent gift of a 26-acre recreation field with still another gift of a duplex clubhouse that will be complete in every detail, and enable Boston University athletic teams to live side by side with visiting teams several days before meeting them on the field.

SPECIAL CORRESPONDENCE

A STUDENT LOAN FUND IN MISSISSIPPI

How the Feild Cooperative Association, Inc., has aided 1,440 Mississippi boys and girls during the last three years to continue their college training is a story well worth the telling.

Established in 1919 for charitable, educational and scientific purposes, and incorporated under the laws of Tennessee by Mr. Bernard B. Jones, the Feild Cooperative Association, Inc., did not establish its Student Loan Fund until August, 1925.

One million dollars was donated for this purpose. The entire capital is being used, the student borrowing the smallest amount possible and paying interest at the rate of 6 per cent. a year on the amount borrowed. From every section come boys and girls applying for a loan.

During the three years' operation, loans have been extended to 1,440 boys and girls in college, according to the records of the association. Of this number, 135 have repaid their loans in full, 480 are still in college and 825 loans are being paid.

This association seeks to prove that student character with group responsibility is a safe basis for financial credit without other forms of collateral. It is a project that strikes the heart of one of the problems of the colleges to-day.

There is a wide range of colleges represented through this loan and a variety of different lines of specialization of its members. During these three years 245 students attending Mississippi A. and M. College were aided by loans from this Permanent Student Loan Fund; 180 students from Mississippi College; 142 from M. S. C. W.; University of Mississippi, 129; Mississippi Woman's College, 89; State Teachers College, 86; Millsaps College, 81; Clarke Memorial College, 73; Draughon's Business College, 71; Blue Mountain College, 5; Delta State Teachers College, 30; Grenada College, 23; Whitworth College, 22; Hillman College, 21; Belhaven College, 15; Peabody College, 12; Tulane University, 11; Atlanta Southern Dental College, 8; University of Virginia, 8; College of William and Mary, 7; S. T. C. Harrisonburg, Va., 6; Vanderbilt University, 6; Columbia University, 5; L. S. U., 5; Loyola University, 5; University of Alabama, 5; Jonesboro College, 4; Baylor University, 3; Coyne Electrical College, 3; Hinds County Junior College, 3; Southern Business College, 3; Medical College of Virginia, 2; Southwestern University, 2; Tyler Commercial College, 2; University of Chicago, 2; University of Louisville, 2; University of Pennsylvania, 2; Virginia Polytechnic Institute, 2; Emory University, 2; Georgia Tech., 3; Mississippi Synodical College, 2; University of Texas, 2; University of Wisconsin, 2; Y. M. C. A. Graduate School, 2; Northwestern University, 2; one student at each of the following colleges: American College; Bowling Green Business College; Chicago School of Chiropractors; Chicago Tech.; Cincinnati Conservatory; Exeter College, Oxford, England; Howard College; Jefferson Medical College; Kellogg School of P. E.; Louisville Tech.; Michigan State College; Moody Bible Institute; Princeton University; Sophie Newcomb; State College of New Mexico; S. T. C. of Virginia; S. T. C. of Alabama; Utica Institute; University of Illinois; Yale University; the Johns Hopkins University, and one nurse in Memphis.

The line of work each of these students chose for specialization shows a great variety of interests. Of the 1,440 boys and girls helped, 554 secured a B.A. degree, 125 a two-year diploma and 119 a B.S. degree. One hundred and eleven students specialized in agriculture, 105 in commercial work, 74 in home economics, 55 in medicine, 48 in electrical engineering, 39 in civil engineering, 36 in law, 27 in ministerial work, 17 in dentistry, 14 in mechanical engineering and 13 in pharmacy. Fourteen received M.A. degrees. One specialized in chemistry, six in horticulture, three each in dairying, forestry, physical education, religious education, entomology and structural engineering; three received M.S. degrees; two, doctor of philosophy degrees. Two specialized in each of the following: architecture, plant pathology, railroad engineering and nursing; and one each in chiropractic work, metallurgy, sugar engineering, voice culture and library work.

The association owes much of its success to close personnel work with each student. Miss S. Frances Sale, secretary, is the one on whom the greatest responsibility falls. It is she who is responsible for the selection of borrowers and visiting of colleges; she meets the students and studies their problems, interests and needs. And clearly does she understand the student who is striving for an education, for she herself worked persistently for her master's degree and she appreciates more than another might the value of a college education.

"It is not always an easy matter to pick out the most deserving boy or girl," Miss Sale declared. "The Student Loan Fund will be permanent only so long as each borrower meets his obligations in full. One failure in whole or part would cause the impairment of the fund." Loans are extended to students only after the completion of at least one half of their college work. A copy of the record made and recommendations from members of the college faculty must be filed with an application for a loan.

Applications are accepted from students who need money in addition to such funds as can be furnished by their own and their family's effort, the secretary asserted; in no case will a loan be allowed to cover all funds necessary for a year in college. College records made in the classroom and on the campus are studied carefully, and student borrowers are encouraged at all times to put forth their best efforts to get the most from their opportunities.

Feild Cooperative Association, Inc., seeing the need of business training among young people, teaches all students to keep a cash book and render monthly statements of their personal accounts. Every student, at the end of each year and at the end of his college course, knows exactly what it has cost him to secure a college education. Students who have acquired the habit of keeping account of their personal expenses and who continue to keep their cash books after leaving college, pay debts promptly and save money, it was asserted. Prompt payment of a student loan establishes credit for the individual and greatly strengthens the ability of other members of the same family to secure loans when needed.

Miss Sale related several instances where loans have been or are being extended to three, four and five members of the same family. She told of one family, that of a minister with two sons and a daughter, who secured loans and are now holding good positions as teachers, while the younger daughter continues her course in college. Another incident was given where a boy who was a sophomore in college lost both parents and was left with two sisters fourteen and sixteen years old, and no property or money. He kept accounts, trained his sisters, economized and borrowed the needed funds to finish his college education, working during his spare time. He graduated in June of this year and now has a splendid position, his sisters are in high school and he is paying back his debt and hopes to educate his sisters.

A remarkably small percentage of the borrowers are allowing their payments to fall in arrears, it was asserted. Educators, legislators and other friends in the state have pledged full cooperation in the selection of the right students to whom loans may safely be extended.

After the establishment of the Permanent Loan Fund the association realized that college facilities in the state were inadequate to care for the large number of students enrolling in college. Feild Cooperative Association, Inc., does not limit its benefits to any one denomination or institution. Its services are for the promotion of higher education among the young people of Mississippi.

Gifts have been made in the state for endowment funds and buildings as follows: Belhaven College, $12,000; Blue Mountain College, $195,000; Grenada College, $14,000; George Peabody College, $125,000; Mississippi College, $20,000; M. S. C. W., $100,000; Millsaps College, $20,000; University of Mississippi, $12,000; Clarke Memorial College, $5,000, and Whitworth College, $10,000.

In addition to the above, a loan of $225,000 was made to the alumni of Mississippi to carry on its building program, and loans of $10,000 and $25,000 respectively to Clarke Memorial College and the alumni association of Blue Mountain College.

A gift of $35,000 was made to conduct an educational survey in the colleges, high schools and public schools of Mississippi, while $3,600 was allotted the state superintendent of education for the development of public music in the state. For the erection of a Cripple Adult's Hospital in Memphis the association donated $200,000.

Furnishing proper college facilities for the growing demands of its young people is the aim of this association. The Feild Cooperative Association, Inc., is interested in each young person, whether Jew or Gentile, Catholic or Protestant. Its work is for the promotion of the best opportunities which can be afforded the future citizens of Mississippi in order that the state may be placed in the forefront in the educational opportunities of its citizens.

JOSEPH E. GIBSON,
Superintendent of Schools
McCOMB, MISSISSIPPI

DISCUSSION

WOMEN IN COLLEGE LIBRARIES

THERE are in my mail to-day letters from three able, experienced women occupying subordinate but responsible positions in three medium-sized college libraries. All are college graduates. All have received the best library training the country affords. The three hold seven academic degrees. Their ages are thirty, thirty-six and forty-five. All have been continuously engaged in library work since graduating from library school. Two of them are assistant librarians; of these one has never had an active professional chief and has been practically the sole administrator for years. The third is the head of an important department. Each is happy in her present environment, and to my personal knowledge the work of all three is satisfactory to their librarians and college authorities.

In one case the college policy discriminates against women in the matter of salary. In another (where the nominal professor-librarianship is vacant) it seems that no woman will ever be made librarian, and the present assistant, having been practically librarian for years, very properly feels reluctant to continue in her present position under a new man who may or may not be a trained librarian. In the third case the writer knows that she is equal to an independent post, and seeks facts as to her chances for getting it, among college libraries.

These letters raise slightly different aspects of what is at bottom one large question. The writers seek facts and perspective as to the general outlook, rather than advice on individual situations. Undeniably for a generation men have been displacing women as librarians of college libraries, and this has been so noticeable within the last five years as fully to warrant misgiving and uncertainty among women who are ambitious and competent to fill such posts.

The following are some of the facts. Within my own experience, men have replaced women as librarians at Northwestern, Chicago, Kansas, Nebraska, Illinois, Iowa, New Hampshire, and within the past two years at Syracuse, Ohio, Delaware, Pomona. This list might easily be enlarged. I can recall instantly four college libraries where women under professorial librarians have carried the technical and internal administration of the library with such competence as to suggest their ability to run it outright but have been denied this opportunity in favor of men. A review of the most important college libraries now run by women shows that while women are holding their own in the women's colleges, in colleges for men or coeducational institutions they are represented, with very few exceptions, only in small, relatively unimportant institutions.

For years in library placement work I urged both public and college library authorities to take women who could be strongly recommended, instead of men, and on the ground that appeals most to trustees and presidents, that they would get more for their money. But beyond this argument, true as it is, there is the broader one of essential justice in rendering equal pay for equal work. Success in persuading library authorities that the best women are equal to important independent positions was not very encouraging. Those doing most library placement work in this country can cite numbers of cases where men not only of limited library experience but of no library experience or training have been chosen before women of unquestioned ability, professional training and pertinent experience. In the face of these facts, the writers of my three letters can scarcely be encouraged actively to seek new positions or to resign subordinate places with confidence that their experience and abilities will commend them to the independent posts they desire.

The main purpose of this letter is to draw the attention of appointing officers of colleges and universities to a neglected yet thoroughly competent and reasonably plentiful source of library personnel. I am also a bit curious as to the reasons for such consistent male preference. I have never heard one given. Refuge is always taken in the downright statement, "We must have a man," uttered as though that somehow settled the matter. It has always seemed surprising that the library should so long continue to be the sole academic exception to the educational policy of choosing for the head of specialized departments those with special training for and experience in the work they are called to do.

J. I. WYER

NEW YORK STATE LIBRARY,
JANUARY 17, 1929

THE DEFINITION OF INTELLIGENCE

NOTING with much interest and some perplexity the difficulty reported by Robert P. Carroll, of Teachers College, Syracuse University, in your issue of December 22, in arriving at a definition of "Intelligence," I make bold to offer one of my own, as follows:

Intelligence is nothing more, nor less, than *the totality of awareness of environment;* of interplaying activities and reactions, experiences and the memories of them; together with comparisons of and inferences from these, to the extent of which the organism may be capable. In its acquisition, possession and employment, man's physical senses, together with those finer sensibilities through which he may receive impressions of velocities and delicacy beyond the ken of organisms less complex, are the means by which That-Which-Looks-Out-of-Eyes gains acquaintance with That-Which-Is-Not-Himself. He who is defective in the possession and development, or ineffective in the use, of *any* of this equipment, whether by reason of congenital omission or of atrophy through disuse, is by just so much defective in *intelligence.*

Individuality in any particular instance—high or low in the scale of complexity, inherent quality, energy; and so of capacity for experience, memory and reflective power—is the margin by which the "pattern of interplay" is unique.

The individual entity of any kind does not *have* a mind; he *is* a mind, precisely to the extent of the complexity of his organization and his capacity for realizing his contacts and relationships. The *degree* of his intelligence is that of the efficiency and accuracy of perception, the dependability of memory, reflection and inference, and of the resulting *expertness of manipulation of the whole conscious being* in its relationships of all kinds, physical, mental, spiritual, with its neighbors in the universe.

This is *self-control,* and in its largest significance it is the whole and sufficient purpose of education.

To which, quoted from my own book, "College," I would now add that the acquisition of this self-control is not only the substance and purpose of education and so of intelligence; it is likewise the method.

JOHN PALMER GAVIT

QUOTATIONS

EDUCATION IN GREAT BRITAIN IN 1928

THE opening of a new year is by common consent the period of annual stock-taking, both in the individual and in the national sense. The present occasion may be regarded as of special interest, because it is just ten years since the clash of arms was silenced, and schemes of social reconstruction began to be taken in hand. And indeed, so far as education is concerned, the year which has just ended is better envisaged as the last of a series of years than as the mere passage of another twelve months. The year 1928 will not stand out in our educational history because of any decisive event that has taken place, whether in Parliament or elsewhere. It has rather been a time of comparatively quiet thought and discussion, a time of looking backwards and forwards, with a view to making as sure as possible that the next step in the development of national education shall be a wise one. It has also been a time of persistent, and sometimes severe, self-criticism. Our national faults may be many and serious, but it can scarcely be said that self-satisfaction is one of them.

Let us begin with the universities, for upon them ultimately depends, to a very considerable extent, the intellectual health of the rest of the educational system.

It is not consistent with our purpose to single out particular institutions for comment, and so we pass by the important constitutional changes that are taking place in the University of London—changes that have been duly noted in our columns during the year. More germane to our purpose is the kind of opportunities which the universities in general are affording to the youth of the country. One of the most important of recent criticisms relates to pass and honors degrees, and the allied question of specialization in study. It is said on high authority that the neglect of the "pass" student is becoming something of a scandal, and that the over-production of low-class honors students is in every sense a disadvantage. So far as the teaching profession is concerned, there is no doubt whatever that a person who neglects the humanities after leaving school, who ends a university career with a third class in (say) chemistry, and who then takes a year of training, is not well fitted for secondary-school teaching, and is far less suitable for primary-school teaching than is the product of the two-year training college. This problem of the pass degree, or, as we should prefer to say, the general degree, we take to be one of urgent importance. Are the universities —we refer, of course, especially to the younger universities—fully aware how much harm they may be doing by their neglect of that problem? The new type of school that is coming into existence needs better provision made for it than an army of third-class honors graduates.

We regard hopefully the coming changes summarized in the report of the Board's Committee on Universities and Training Colleges. It was, no doubt, high time that a department of state should cease to be responsible for the examination and certification of teachers of whatever grade. When Kay-Shuttleworth invented the teacher's "certificate examination" eighty years ago. there was no other way. That examination had become an anachronism, and the only fault we have to find with current changes is that they were thrust upon the universities and training colleges in too great a hurry. It is to be hoped that the universities thoroughly realize that for the first time they are now in a position to influence the education of the whole nation, and that the training colleges on their part realize the importance of resisting any tendency towards a too academic bias in the training of teachers of young children.

By a natural transition, we are thus brought to the problem of curricula and examination in secondary schools. The future historian of education, turning over the files of any educational journal for the year 1928, will be struck by the frequent and forcible utterances of prominent educators on these topics. The examinations, and therefore in effect the curricula, of secondary schools, are controlled by bodies in which the universities have a preponderating influence; and yet only a small percentage of secondary-school pupils ever proceed to a university. The danger of a too-strong academic bias in school education is obvious. That danger exists both in boys' and in girls' schools, though it is possibly at its greatest in the latter. At any rate, it is the headmistresses and assistant mistresses who are most emphatic upon the need of ampler recognition of those esthetic and practical activities by which the universities traditionally set small store, and in so doing ignore an important aspect of individual and national life. The manifesto of the Association of Headmistresses issued last March is clear on that point.

The indisposition of examining bodies to admit the claims of esthetic and practical subjects is partly due to the difficulty of adjusting these subjects to the existing machinery of examination. And we fear it must be admitted, that examination has become a species of machinery—a result which is inevitable when tens of thousands of pupils have to be dealt with by a few examining bodies. So we have the whole vast system of secondary-school examination very warmly debated, from every conceivable point of view, and never more so than in the year 1928, for have we not been reminded that the number of candidates for a first School Certificate is already 60,000, and will before long reach 100,000? As we remarked in our notice of the board's recent memorandum on examinations, the first-school examination seems to dominate the whole situation, including the program of the secondary school, the nature of the test for free places, and in its turn the work of the elementary school. No wonder there is a constant clamor for reform. But at present the secondary school is held fast in the grip of the external examiner.

So strong is the feeling in many quarters about the total influence of the first-school examination as a qualifying test for all pupils alike, that the proposal to invent a kindred test for the new type of school called "modern" in the Hadow Report, and for parallel arrangements for children over 11 years of age, has met with widespread suspicion and dislike. It is essential that the new type of school, like the central school, should be the subject of free experiment by teachers and administrators, and the best friends of external examinations can scarcely claim that their general influence is other than strictly conservative. To invent a new examination for the new schools would be to bind them in fetters from the start. The year 1928 has witnessed the early attempts to reorganize the elementary schools as junior and senior schools, in accordance with the findings of the report on the education of the adolescent. We are at the beginning of what will be seen, a few years hence, to have amounted to a slow revolution. The important thing in our judgment is that the revolution should be slow, and that every step taken in every area should be thoroughly well considered in all its bearings. A school system which represents the slow growth of sixty or seventy years had better not be drastically changed in a few months.

We can do no more than mention the efforts made in the course of the year 1928 to fix attention upon the provision of books in elementary schools, so that the "bookless school" shall be no more. Nor have we space to enlarge upon the new attempt to improve the relations between education and industry. We have gladly called attention in the course of the year to the progress of adult education, and to its need of more voluntary help. We view with satisfaction the declaration of the Association of Headmistresses in favor of the compulsory inspection of private schools, in order that the inefficient and the insanitary may be eliminated. And lastly we venture to express the hope that the nursery school, which has been proved to be as beneficial for the mothers as for the children of the poorest classes, but which has made little progress since it was given a place in the act of ten years ago, may soon be an established part of the national provision for the children of this country.

Such, we believe, are the problems, many and varied, which have chiefly been in the minds of educators during the year under review. There is no sufficient reason either for elation or for depression. We can only express the hope that when the time comes for summing up the educational progress of the year 1929, the mood of exultation may be better justified.—*The Journal of Education and School World, London.*

REPORTS

THE SIXTY EDUCATIONAL BOOKS OF 1928

The following list represents the titles of sixty books that have been carefully selected from the more than four hundred titles which were listed in the issue of School and Society for December 29, 1928.

The list, together with descriptive and evaluative notes, will appear also in the *Journal of the National Education Association* for March, 1929. This annual selected list has been prepared for several years for the American Library Association and the *Journal of the National Education Association.*

The bases of selection are: the careful examination of all the books; the careful consideration of all the printed reviews of the year's books; the scorings and comments gathered by correspondence with over one hundred educators in special fields through the United States.

It should be noted that this list is prepared, not so much for the readers of School and Society (which reaches a larger proportion of administrators, specialists and heads of research departments) as it is for the readers of the *Journal of the National Education Association,* a group composed more largely of classroom teachers and supervisors, including teachers in many rural schools. For this reason, the list does not include many of the more elaborate and technical contributions, even though these often contain the most important new material of the year. Nor does the list include those many books which, while having a bearing on education, are not written primarily for teachers—such as books for parents, books on general psychology, etc. The starred books are considered most useful for general use, and for college, normal school and public libraries.

Joseph L. Wheeler
The Enoch Pratt Free Library,
Baltimore, Maryland

PURPOSES, PRINCIPLES AND PHILOSOPHY OF EDUCATION

COBB, STANWOOD. The new leaven. 340 p. John Day Co. $2.50.

*FINNEY, R. L. A sociological philosophy of education. 563 p. Macmillan. $2.50.

GRIZZELL, E. D. Education: principles and practices. 428 p. Macmillan. $2.40.

HARRIS, P. E. Changing conceptions of school discipline. 384 p. Macmillan. $2.00.

KANDEL, I. L., *ed.* (Fourth) Educational yearbook of the International Institute of Teachers College, Columbia. 618 p. Teachers College, Columbia. $3.50.

SNEDDEN, DAVID. Educational sociology for beginners. 636 p. Macmillan. $3.50.

WASHBURNE, C., and STEARNS, M. M. Better schools. 342 p. John Day. $2.50.

ADMINISTRATION AND SUPERVISION

*AYER, F. C., and BARR, A. S. The organization of supervision. 397 p. Appleton. $2.25.

COUNTS, G. S. School and society in Chicago. 367 p. Harcourt, Brace. $2.50.

GIST, A. S. Administration of an elementary school. 308 p. Scribner's. $1.80.

LINDSAY, E. E. Problems in school administration with emphasis on fiscal and personnel phases. 544 p. Macmillan. $2.50.

*MORT, P. R. The individual pupil in the management of class and school. 383 p. American Book Co. $1.60.

NATIONAL EDUCATION ASSOCIATION. Department of Elementary School Principals. Seventh yearbook. The Elementary School Principalship. 638 p. The Association. $2.00.

NUTT, H. W. Current problems in the supervision of instruction. 538 p. Johnson Pub. Co. $2.00.

PIERCE, A. E. Deans and advisers of women and girls. 636 p. Professional Technical Press. $4.00.

*REEVES, CHARLES E., and GANDERS, HARRY S. School building management. 395 p. Teachers College, Columbia. $3.75.

CURRICULUM

*HARAP, HENRY. The technique of curriculum making. 315 p. Macmillan. $1.80.

NATIONAL EDUCATION ASSOCIATION. Department of Superintendence. Sixth yearbook. The development of the high school curriculum. 584 p. National Education Association. $2.00.

CONDUCT AND CHARACTER FORMATION

FISHBACK, E. H. Character education in the junior high school. 190 p. Heath. $1.24.

SYMONDS, P. M. The nature of conduct. 346 p. Macmillan. $2.00.

EDUCATIONAL PSYCHOLOGY

AVERILL, L. A. The hygiene of instruction. 386 p. Houghton Mifflin. $2.00.

HOLLINGWORTH, L. S. The psychology of the adolescent. 259 p. Appleton. $2.00.

NATIONAL SOCIETY FOR THE STUDY OF EDUCATION. Twenty-seventh yearbook: Nature and nurture. Part I. 465 p. Part II. 397 p. Public School Pub. Co. $1.75.

SANDIFORD, PETER. Educational psychology: an objective study. 406 p. Longmans Green. $3.50.

TESTS AND MEASUREMENTS

*DEARBORN, W. R. Intelligence tests. 336 p. Houghton Mifflin. $2.50.

HULL, C. L. Aptitude testing. 535 p. World Book Co. $2.68.

SMITH, H. L., and WRIGHT, W. W. Tests and measurements. 540 p. Silver, Burdett. $3.00.

EXCEPTIONAL CHILDREN

*GODDARD, H. H. School training of gifted children. 226 p. World Book Co. $2.00.

EDUCATIONAL RESEARCH

GOOD, C. V. How to do research in education. 298 p. Warwick & York. $2.50.

HOLZINGER, K. L. Statistical methods for students in education. 372 p. Ginn. $3.60.

TEACHERS AND TEACHING METHODS

*ALMACK, J. C., and LANG, A. R. The beginning teacher. 478 p. Houghton Mifflin Co. $2.40.

DORRIS, A. V. Visual instruction in the public schools. 481 p. Ginn. $2.64.

MAGUIRE, E. R. The group-study plan. 203 p. Scribner's. $1.80.

*RUGG, HAROLD, and SHUMAKER, ANN. The child-centered school. 359 p. World Book Co. $2.40.

STILLMAN, B. W. Training children to study. 247 p. Heath. $1.60.

THAYER, V. T. The passing of the recitation. 331 p. Heath. $2.00.

PRE-SCHOOL, KINDERGARTEN AND ELEMENTARY SCHOOLS

(See also Administration, Supervision, Reading, Tests, Social Studies, etc.)

JOHNSON, H. M. Children in the nursery school. 325 p. John Day. $3.00.

*LEWIS, M. H. An adventure with children. 250 p. Macmillan. $1.75.

*STORMZAND, M. J., and MCKEE, J. W. The progressive primary teacher. 352 p. Houghton Mifflin. $2.40.

WIECKING, A. M. Education through manual activities. 351 p. Ginn. $1.80.

JUNIOR HIGH SCHOOL

See the following titles in other sections: Fishback, E. H. Character education in the junior high school, Maguire, E. R. The group-study plan, Blackhurst, J. H. Principles and methods of junior high school mathematics.

SECONDARY EDUCATION

(See also Teaching, Psychology Tests, School Libraries, Extracurriculum, Health, etc.)

*FONTAINE, E. C. Ways to better teaching in the secondary school. 271 p. Ginn. $1.60.

*MONROE, W S., and WEBER, O. P. The high school. 511 p. Doubleday, Doran. $2.50.

WAPLES, DOUGLAS, and others. Problem exercises for high school teachers. 99 p. University of Chicago. $1.00.

READING, WRITING AND LANGUAGES

*GATES, A. I. New methods in primary reading. 236 p. Teachers College, Columbia. $2.25.

OPDYCKE, J. B. In the service of youth. 404 p. Pitman. $3.50.

YOAKAM, G. A. Reading and study. 502 p. Macmillan. $2.00.

MATHEMATICS

BLACKHURST, J. H. Principles and methods of junior high school mathematics. 355 p. Century. $2.50.

*NATIONAL COUNCIL OF TEACHERS OF MATHEMATICS. Third yearbook. 276 p. Teachers College, Columbia. $2.50.

SOCIAL STUDIES

*BRANOM, M. E. A teacher's geography. 252 p. Macmillan. $2.40.

*KELTY, M. C. Teaching American history in the middle grades of the elementary school. 748 p. Ginn. $2.40.

SCHOOL LIBRARIES

LOGASA, HANNA. The high school library: its function in education. 283 p. Appleton. $1.75.

VOCATIONAL

BROWN, C. M., and HALEY, A. H. The teaching of home economics. 395 p. Houghton Mifflin. $2.00.

EASTERN COMMERCIAL TEACHERS' ASSOCIATION. First yearbook. Foundation of commercial education. 423 p. The Association. $2.50.

HEALTH AND PHYSICAL EDUCATION

BENNETT, H. E. School posture and seating. 323 p. Ginn. $2.00.

LOWMAN, C. L., COLESTOCK, CLAIRE, and COOPER, HAZEL. Corrective physical education for groups. 521 p. A. S. Barnes. $4.50.

*MYERS, A. F., and BIRD, O. C. Health and physical education. 342 p. Doubleday, Doran. $1.50.

UNIVERSITY OF MICHIGAN. Dept. of Physical Education for Women. Physical education activities for high school girls. 322 p. Lea and Febiger. $3.50.

EXTRACURRICULAR

ROBERTS, A. C., and DRAPER, E. M. Extraclass and intramural activities in high schools. $2.40.

HIGHER EDUCATION

*HUDELSON, EARL, *ed.* Problems of college education. 449 p. Univ. of Minnesota Press. $3.00.

ADULT EDUCATION

*THORNDIKE, E. L., BREGMAN, E. O., TILTON, J. W., and WOODYARD, E. Adult Learning. 335 p. Macmillan. $2.25.

SOCIETIES AND MEETINGS

THE OHIO STATE EDUCATIONAL CONFERENCE

THE out-of-state speakers at the Ninth Annual Ohio State Educational Conference, April 4, 5, 6, 1929, are as follows:

Arthur J. Klein, U. S. Bureau of Education, Washington. "The Relation of the Adult Education Movement to Established Higher Educational Institutions." (Adult Education Section.)

Gerrit A. Beneker, Truro, Cape Cod, Mass. "Art and Education." (Art Section.) "Art and Industry." (Industrial and Vocational Education.)

Joseph Jastrow, New School for Social Research, New York City. (Attendance Supervisors, School Nurses and Visiting Teachers.) "Individual Differences in Relation to Personality." (Special Education.)

C. Stuart Gager, director, Brooklyn Botanic Garden, Brooklyn, New York. "Biology and the Public." (Biological Science.)

Edmund Prince Fowler, New York. "Prevention and Management of Deafness in the Schools." (City Superintendents.)

J. O. Malott, Bureau of Education, Washington, D. C. "An Appraisal of Commercial Education." (Commercial Education.)

C. L. Rhoade, county superintendent, LaPorte, Ind. "Evaluating Education in Terms of Rural Needs." (County Superintendents.)

J. E. Butterworth, Cornell University, Ithaca. "The Village and Consolidated Principalship in its Relation to the County Superintendency." (County Superintendents.) "Scientific Program Construction for Parent Teacher Associations." (Parent-Teacher Association.)

Paul T. Rankin, Detroit Public Schools. "Listening Ability—Its Importance, Development and Measurement." (Educational and Intelligence Tests.)

George R. Johnson, St. Louis Public Schools. "Administrative Problems of Testing in City Schools." (Educational and Intelligence Tests.) "Testing as a Function of Teaching." (Elementary Principals.)

Arthur I. Gates, Columbia University, New York. "Formal and Informal Testing of Educational Attainments." (Educational and Intelligence Tests.) "New Types of Printed Materials for Teaching Reading." (Village and Consolidated School Superintendents.)

B. R. Buckingham, Harvard University. "Getting Objective Data when Visiting a Classroom." (Elementary Principals.) (Kindergarten and Primary Teachers.)

A. Coleman, University of Chicago. "Achievement Testing." (Modern Language.)

E. H. Wilcox, University of Iowa. "Appreciation—A Chameleon in Music." (Music.)

M. Luckiesh, General Electric Company. "Artificial Light—Its Influence on Civilization." (Non-Biological Science).

Frank C. Whitmore, Northwestern University. (Non-Biological Science.)

E. H. Lindley, University of Kansas. "Why Stop Learning." (Parent-Teacher Association.)

Thomas D. Wood, Columbia University. (Physical Education.)

Esther Sherman, Detroit Public Schools. (Physical Education.)

Forrest L. Knapp, International Council of Religious Education, Chicago. "Principles of Modern Religious Education." (Religious Education.)

J. S. Mullan, sec'y Board of Education, Rochester, New York. "The Rochester Plan of Administering School Supplies." (School Business Officials.) "The Ideal Superintendent from the Standpoint of the Business Manager." (City Superintendents and School Business Officials.)

Olive A. Whildin, Supervisor of Hard of Hearing Classes, Baltimore, Maryland. "Teaching the Hard of Hearing Child." (Special Education.)

John W. Withers, New York University. "Are Our Programs of Teacher-Training Practical?" (Teacher Training.) "The Social Challenge to the High School Curriculum." (High School Principals.)

F. N. Freeman, Chicago University. "Does Education Affect the Child's Level of Intelligence?" (Elementary Teachers.)

Dhan Gopal Mukerji, Lecturer, New York. "The India of Kipling and the India of Gandhi." (English.) "The Spirit of the Jungle." (Kindergarten and Primary Teachers.)

A. P. Brigham, Colgate University. "Geography as a Cultural Factor in Education." (Geography.)

Mrs. Anna Garlin Spencer, Columbia University. "Parental Education for Parents and Teachers." (Home Economics.)

Arthur B. Mays, University of Illinois. "Changing Relationships in Industrial Arts and Vocational Education." (Industrial and Vocational Education.)

Rowena Harvey, South Side High School, Fort Wayne, Indiana. "High-School Publications, Bigger—But Better?" (Journalism.)

Douglas Waples, University of Chicago. "Evaluating Classroom Procedure by Means of Service Studies." (Junior High School Principals.)

Eugene Tavenner, Washington University, St. Louis, Mo. (Latin.)

E. R. Breslich, University of Chicago. "The Activities of the Class Period in Mathematics." (Mathematics.)

EDUCATIONAL RESEARCH AND STATISTICS

THE LONG-TIME EFFECT OF FRESHMAN COUNSELING

IN 1926 Lemon[1] made a study at the University of Iowa of the lowest decile of the freshman class as determined by the entrance qualifying examinations. He selected 106 students, practically the entire lower decile, and divided them into two very evenly weighted groups according to their scores on the tests. The examinations used that year consisted of the Iowa High School Content Examination, the Iowa Comprehension Test and the English Aptitude and English Training examinations of the Iowa Placement series. In addition, both groups were given the Thorndike Intelligence Examination, Part 1, Form D, and the experimental group was given fifteen other tests, most of them standardized. In the special standard tests, the experimental group obtained the results shown in Table I.

TABLE I

	Mean of the experimental group	National mean	Norm of group
Modified Woodworth emotional test	65.5	73.0	
Monroe silent reading comprehension test	29.6	36.0	11th grade
Monroe silent reading test	96.4	108.0	6th grade
Stanford revision vocabulary test	52.0	65.0	14th year
Mathematical test D348, Thorndike, Part 1	9.0	23.0	
Language test D12611, Thorndike, Part 1	26.0	34.0	
Whipple word-building test	17.0	21.6	
Whipple sentence-building test	4.6	6.6	
Pressey sentence-structure test	12.5	19.7	7th grade
Pressey capitalization test	18.8	23.4	7th grade
Pressey grammar test	12.8	23.3	7th grade
Pressey punctuation test	15.8	20.3	9th grade

The experiment as carried out depended upon a carefully planned program of coaching of the experimental group in order to determine the results of such procedure. The help given consisted of personal data questionnaires and interviews, remedial work on physical troubles such as bad eyes, tonsils, etc., training in methods of study, improvement of speed and comprehension in reading, development of imagination, memory and interest, and a careful planning of a personal daily program for each student of the group. This coaching was carried out throughout the year. The criteria for determining the success of the training was to be, according to Lemon:[2]

(1) The difference in the numbers of students from each group remaining in the university;

(2) The advantage in average grade points of the experimental over the control group; and

(3) The difference in the average numbers of delinquencies reported to the offices of the deans.

In comparing the groups for the first semester and the first year, the experimental group seems to have an advantage over the control group in having a greater number of students left in school, a higher grade point average and fewer delinquencies in scholarship. The data covering this point as summarized later will not follow exactly Lemon's data since many grades given as Fd., Cond. or Inc. (failed, conditioned or incomplete) have since been raised to passing grades, and several students dismissed from the university were reinstated, presumably upon probation, at the beginning of the fall term of 1926. Lemon gives a suggested program for freshman guidance which follows closely his own procedure with the exception of certain

[1] Allan Clark Lemon, "An Experimental Study of Guidance and Placement in the Lowest Decile of the Iowa Qualifying Examinations, 1925," University of Iowa Studies in Education, Iowa City, 1927.

[2] *Op. cit.*, p. 1.

suggested acts on the part of the university which could not be carried out at that time.

The most interesting thing about these two groups is their progress during the three years they have been in the university. In determining grade point averages, the University of Iowa follows the plan of giving four grade points for each semester unit carried with a grade of A, three for a B, two for a C, one for a D, none for an Inc., minus one for a Cond. and minus two for a Fd. Table II gives the attendance for each semester, together with the grade point averages and delinquencies reported.

TABLE II

RECORDS OF NUMBERS PRESENT AND SCHOLARSHIP FOR BOTH GROUPS

Sem.	No. present Exp.	No. present Con.	Av. Gr. Pts. Exp.	Av. Gr. Pts. Con.	Probation Exp.	Probation Con.	Dropped Exp.	Dropped Con.
1st	51	51	.57	.18				
2nd ...	40	26	1.09	1.12	11	5	7	16
3rd	34	19	.71	1.27	1	4		1
4th	26	19	1.16	1.43	7	2	6	
5th	19	14	1.73	1.61	2		1	1
6th	18	11	1.65	1.88			1	2
Total			1.02	.97	21	11	15	20

Unless they are encouraged, many students whose work is poor, though passing, in the beginning of their university work, drop out without waiting to see whether or not better choice of subjects and improved methods of study will help them. This is partially proved by the fact that the experimental group had twelve members with discouraging first semester grades of less than 1.50 (the university minimum for graduation) who yet had enough persistence to complete three years of work, while the control group furnished only five with this amount of persistence. Six of the experimental group received four, five or even six semester grades of this type, but only two of the control group have been able to surmount the discouragement of four semesters of bad work. The eighteen survivors of the experimental group have a total of seven probations and have survived 45 per cent. of their semesters with grade point averages of less than 1.50. The eleven remaining members of the control group have had three probations and have spent 25 per cent. of their time doing less than 1.50 work. The grade point average shows a steady rise for each succeeding semester for the control group, due partly to natural selection and elimination and partly to bettered study habits, but this even increase is not evident in the group where there was outside interference with the natural laws of selection. Less than 5 per cent. of these students from the lowest decile have done work with a passing grade point average of 2.00. To put it another way, only four students of the original 106 in both groups meet these conditions: (1) Are at present in the university; (2) Have a grade point average for the entire time of 2.00 (a grade of C), and (3) Are in a position to receive the bachelor degree next spring at the end of a four-year period.

Four experimental and five control members have transferred elsewhere. None did good work in the University of Iowa, one of each group having transferred after being dropped. The experimental group was in a little better shape when it left, as one had senior standing, two were sophomores and one was a freshman, with a total grade point average of .66, while the control group that left was composed of two sophomores and three freshmen, with a grade point average of .24. Most of the original 106 registered in the college of liberal arts, but a few have gone into commerce and several from each group enrolled in pharmacy, one of the experimental group graduating from that course last spring. Members of the experimental group have spent ten semesters in dentistry and medicine for a grade point average of 2.31, while seven semesters in dentistry with an average of 1.90 is the record of control group members.

Further evidence that the eleven remaining in the control group are products of natural selection to a higher degree than the others is shown by the first semester and total grades for the two groups (Table III). If the control survivors *are* a product of natural selection, we may infer that they were the best at the beginning, and compare them to the eleven best of the experimental group.

This shows in another way that the experimental group remaining consists partly of students who have been spurred on to unwonted effort, and stay in spite of poor work.

TABLE III

GRADE POINT AVERAGES FOR REMAINING STUDENTS IN THE TWO GROUPS

	Exp.	Con.	11 best exp.
Entire six semesters	1.46	1.71	1.82
First semester for same students	1.12	1.44	1.48

TABLE IV

FREQUENCIES OF VARIOUS GRADE POINT AVERAGES FOR THE FOUR CLASSES

	Fresh.		Soph.		Junior		Senior	
Gd. Pt. Av.	Exper.	Con.	Exper.	Con.	Exper.	Con.	Exper.	Con.
-2.00 to -.01	15	20	1	1				
.00 to .74	2	6	8	7	1			
.75 to 1.49	2	1	3	4	6	2	1	1
								*
1.50 to 2.24		2	2		4	4	5	3
2.25 to 2.99					1		1	2
3.00 up							1	
No. in classes	19	29	14	12	12	6	8	6

* This line indicates the 1.50 mark, the university requirement for graduation.

One indication of the interest taken in university work is the fact that the experimental group spent a total of eight and a half summers in school, and the control group seven, in an attempt to make up poor or missed work. The experimental summer average is 1.55, against 1.50 for the control. Also, the experimental and control groups have spent a total of 189 and 143 2/3 semesters, respectively, in the university, earning 2,206.1 and 1,601.7 hours, or an average of 12.33 and 11.72 hours per semester and 41.62 and 30.22 per student. The total number of hours earned to date regardless of the number of semesters spent and whether or not the student is enrolled at present, is shown for both groups by Table IV. The university regulations require a student to have twenty-four hours to be classed as a sophomore, fifty-six for a junior and eighty-eight for a senior, and this table shows the average grade earned by each group in each division, freshman, sophomore, junior and senior, basing the classifications upon the total hours earned to date. Seven experimental and eleven control students earned no hours at all and are classified as freshmen in Table IV.

Again the statistics seem to show a decided advantage in persistence on the part of the group which received the help during the time they were freshmen. There seems to be little difference in the groups in the last three years, but the significant fact is that ten more students dropped out of the control group than out of the experimental, before reaching sophomore standing. At the opening of the fall term in 1928, the enrolment is nineteen experimental and ten control, and the grade point average of the students now in school 1.45 and 1.87.

Lemon made a case study of each student in the experimental group, but in making a résumé of his conclusions with respect to the nineteen students still registered, no predominating factor stands out. Ages vary, the proportion between the sexes is unchanged, some were good in English or mathematics while others had considerable difficulty with the subjects, home life was splendid for some and mediocre or inferior for others. Several students mentioned as being hopeless did passing though poor work at a later time.

To summarize the results of this type procedure, at least in this instance, it may be said that the results with the experimental group were:

(1) A higher grade point average than would have otherwise been earned;

(2) Fewer students dropped for poor scholarship;

(3) Fewer students leaving the university because of discouragement over poor grades; and

(4) A more sincere effort on the part of the students to adjust themselves to university life.

What to do with the lowest group in the entering class of a large university is still a moot question, but one which will need to be settled eventually. It is possible that a study now going on at the University of Iowa and one to be made of Lemon's group at the end of their college life will throw more light on the subject.

P. W. HOLADAY

STATE UNIVERSITY OF IOWA

SCHOOL AND SOCIETY

EDITED BY J. McKEEN CATTELL
WITH WHICH IS COMBINED THE
EDUCATIONAL REVIEW
EDITED BY WILLIAM McANDREW

Volume XXIX | Saturday, February 23, 1929 | Number 739

PRESIDENT'S ADDRESS
ASSOCIATION OF URBAN UNIVERSITIES, 1928

By Dr. FREDERICK B. ROBINSON
PRESIDENT OF THE COLLEGE OF THE CITY OF NEW YORK

Probably the most beloved of professors who served the College of the City of New York was Adolph Werner, affectionately known as "The Golden-Hearted." One day, referring to the fact that Frankfurt was his native city, he said with a whimsical smile on his lips and a twinkle in his eye, reminiscent no doubt of some South German jingle, "I can not understand how any one could be born anywhere else than in Frankfurt." To the representatives of urban universities, I may say that it is difficult for me to conceive of a better place for a university to be born than in an American city. It is in the city that the throb and movement of life are most intense; it is from urban centers that the destiny of mankind is determined, and this is the beginning of the era of America's world leadership.

For ages, the culture life and the practical achievements of Europe converged in cities—in Athens, in Rome, in Florence, in Paris, Amsterdam, Berlin and London. To these cities came musicians, painters, sculptors, poets, philosophers, merchants, craftsmen, bankers, soldiers and divines enriching the current intellectual life, and from them princes and prime ministers directed the course of empire. They were and are focal points of life, ferments of civilization.

Up to the time when our parents went to college, America was primarily an agricultural country, paying financial tribute to creditor Europe and basking in such rays of scientific and artistic light as managed to find their way across the Atlantic. To be sure, there were some original achievements at home and steady growth, but the European lead was so great that the acknowledged standards of excellence were found abroad. The authoritative voice of architecture came from the Beaux Arts of Paris, surgery listened to Vienna, diplomacy was deferential to Downing Street, military men watched the German maneuvers, graduate students sought their Ph.D. degrees in German universities, and world exchange was in terms of pounds sterling. But during the last generation a gradual change took place; America grew from national childhood into vigorous youth. Steadily its cities increased in size and importance, its industrial life expanded and became more highly organized, its schools shifted the emphasis successively from the elementary to the grammar grades and from them to the high school, and during the last decade we have been pouring into the various activities of the nation more persons of secondary school training than do all the countries of Europe combined. And from our enrolment of nearly five million secondary students there came graduates to swell the number matriculated in colleges, universities and technical schools to the almost incredible total of a million. With great stirring in the social and industrial life of the country there has been unprecedented educational activity. America had been growing up rapidly for twenty-five years and after the World War we suddenly realized that she towered above all other nations in many respects.

But she is now only in her youth, with the promise of a great maturity that is yet to come. Her distinctive civilization and her major contributions to all time are yet to be made. It is my belief that through the outworkings of the democracy guaranteed in our federal and state constitutions, America will develop a degree of material prosperity, intellectual opportunity and liberty under law that will produce individuals of a very superior type. These people will adjust their economic affairs so as to produce a wide variety of goods that will be well distributed and enjoyed and on this industrial foundation they will build a culture life peculiarly vigorous, wholesome and free. They will have great mental capacity, creative initiative and breadth of spirit. They will be democracy's gift to the ages.

But, as I have said, America is now culturally young. It has power, speed and great promise, but it has yet to gain wisdom, control and poise. Our great cities are now assuming leadership, and the shaping of the national course of progress is more than anywhere else in the hands of the institutions of higher learning in these cities. Probably no one would seriously question the purpose of the universities. Their mission is to make a better humanity by constantly exerting influences which will make men more wholesome, better informed, more accurate in their thinking, more liberal and adaptable, more perfect in their performance, better able to live together in harmony and happier in the discharge of daily tasks and the engagements of life in its aspects of adventure and of service.

What is the college or university, and why can it shape human progress more advantageously where thousands are congregated like bees in a hive, with their daily deposits to make in many cells of industry, of professional practice, of music, the drama and the arts? These institutions of learning are aggregations of men who are the interpreters of life, who view humanity in relation to a long evolution of physical and mental character. They know of civilizations long since past. Among them are specialists who understand the motives of kings and princes who reigned in bygone days, who watched the rise of peoples, the conquest of nature and the development of social institutions and mechanical processes which are of importance to-day. Their standards of achievement and of taste were carefully formulated in the perspective of thousands of years. They are not easily to be thrown off their balance by things which seem new but which are mere imitations of thoughts and customs long since discarded by the race in its onward march. They know the old from the new.

Into their hands come the young men and women of the present generation to have their minds shaped, to have their standards set and their aspirations fired. While, to be sure, our faculties participate in active life, nevertheless they stand aside from life, meditate upon its shifting values, and reach conclusions more trustworthy than the snap judgment of one engaged in a swift-moving contest. It is their object to gather and to sift, to proportion and to interpret; and as a result they are both able not only to instruct students, but also to assist those in the world of action to cope with problems which currently present themselves. But even more, they with their researches reach out beyond those things clearly seen in the present and point the way to a better day. It is for them to see the sun rise on new realms of thought and spirit and to stimulate their fellow creatures to swing across the old land into the new, that they in their turn may view further horizons from still more distant realms.

The city is the place in which their work of observation, selection and instruction can best go on, because while they may have their intellectual resources and while they may have their lofty motives, they can not transfer these qualities except through instrumentalities and means that are practical. They must be where youth congregates. There is no place comparable with the city for the gathering of large bodies of young men and women. This has always been so. Where the parents live there come the greatest number of young to learn. Furthermore, the faculties of institutions in cities are stronger because of their contact with men who are engaged in the world's work. Research in the field of science is stimulated by actual problems and achievements in the arts and industries, for just as the scholar-scientist has something to say to the craftsman, so the machine shops, studios and industrial laboratories have inspiration for the seeker for new knowledge. There is, no doubt, such a thing as pure research and scholarship for scholarship only; but it is insignificant in quantity and in influence upon intellectual advance in comparison with research motivated by definite objectives related to life in its manifold activities, interests and methods of achievement. Of course the city university offers no obstacle to abstract scholarship, but it does afford many positive advantages to most researchers not only in science, but in the arts and social sciences. Faculties in city institutions are augmented by specialists who are part of the work of the world, and who come to the academic halls to tell of things that they have seen and done in that world. They tend to prevent the faculties from becoming academic and remote from reality while those who are professional scholars only tend to keep idealism alive in them.

In the city, life is rich. There has never been produced any art, music or drama except in response to demand and appreciation. It is all very well for the poet to say, "I sing because I wish to sing"; and for the artist to say, "I paint to please myself." It may be true that great artists disdain the criticism of those less sensitive than themselves, but the fact remains, quite apart from the element of economic necessity, that dramas are written so that people may be moved by them. Symphonies are composed and played in order that thousands may be stirred by their strains, and the artist paints in order that his canvases may hold the admiring and approving gaze of others. In the city is the largest concentrated demand for work, for play, for struggle and for high endeavor, and therefore in the city we find many-sided culture at its highest. The educator is endeavoring to draw all he can from life in order to give it to his students, that they in their turn may understand it more fully and play their parts more acceptably. He finds material at hand and also numerous quasi-formal educational agencies with which he can cooperate. He has the great museums, the art galleries, the Aeolian and Carnegie halls of music. He has the playhouses, the libraries and the zoological gardens. All lie ready at hand. The teacher of sociology does not have to draw imaginary pictures of poor relief; he can take his class to the rooms where relief is administered before their eyes. The medical schools have extensive clinics attached to them. The engineering schools, preparing men to take their places in industrial technology, have production plants in the city for observation and instruction. The whole city is a laboratory and life is the complex experiment to be observed.

The educator does not need to deal in mere shadows of knowledge; he can deal with life itself. Contrast this with the education of a boy in a rural institution in which professors remote from realities are trying to teach young men about a thing called life that is far removed, into which they must some day enter as timid novices. Even the social life in such institutions outside the classrooms tends to be artificial, and with values so distorted that thoughtful men and women smile at the solemnity with which silly customs are religiously observed. The city student is part of natural, real society and not of a small caricature. The line between living and learning in the city is not a sharp one, and that is as it should be for real education and for real life. While, to be sure, one might well wish to spend his childhood on a farm or away from the noise and bustle of a city in order that the body might get a good start, still his young manhood with its great intellectual awakening could best be stimulated and nourished in the eager, swift-moving life of the city.

The task of liberal education is to make men conscious of the great movement of humanity, to give them a broad picture of the whole human family, so that those who live to-day can be understood in the light of the past ages from which they came. It is the rôle of the educator to make his students intelligent members of this human family and to fire them with high resolve to contribute whatever they can to the betterment of life. Besides this broad conception and this fine resolve, the educator must also impart to the student mastery of the practical tools of intellectual and physical achievement which will enable him to bear himself well as a contributor to life's work. Here the pedagogue has the difficult task of balancing craftsmanship and speculation, specific competency and broad vision, practical achievement and high aspirations.

Before considering this problem it will be well to brush aside certain current sophistries. There are those who say that it is not well to produce specialists or persons superbly competent to perform particular tasks. They contend that in the industries our workmen degenerate into mere cogs, performing small tasks without any understanding whatever of the whole production process, that our professional men are so narrow that they are not aware of great movements of humanity, and even our scholars have lost in general culture because of concentration in particular fields of research. I myself do not believe all this. Indeed, I will go so far as to say that never before in America have people of all classes shown so much intelligent interest in current events, in political movements and in world affairs as now, during the so-called age of specialization. We can not here consider this general problem in detail nor take time to demonstrate the effect of specialization on efficiency of production, on time for leisure, on the lengthening of the period of compulsory schooling, on the elevation of the standard of living and on the culture life of the whole people. But confining our attention to specialization on the part of people of college and university level—to those who presumably would make contributions to the race heritage—I will say that the development of craftsmanship or perfection in the discharge of well-defined functions is one of the very best preparations for a broad understanding of the general problems of humanity and for the growth of the spirit.

Did the hours of toil in mathematics make Einstein less able to tread the paths of philosophy with Kant and sweep beyond the stars of our continent galaxy with a glorious vision of cosmic unity undreamed of even by Newton? It is from Pupin, specialist in electricity, that America now hears the most human lessons in citizenship and in spiritual growth. Who can doubt that young Moseley, as he painstakingly tabulated the effect of the bombardment of various elements with the cathode rays, had an inspiring glimpse of an orderly universe in which the same power "that shapes the stars and marks their ways upon the unknown deep" also arranged his atoms and even the subdivisions of those atoms in beautiful simplicity? We could multiply examples in modern life and from past ages to illustrate the thought that patient toil up steep and narrow paths of hard work and discipline leads to the heights from which the broadest and truest vistas are seen.

Was Leonardo da Vinci's technical skill a help or hindrance to his breadth? Was the consummate technician, Michael Angelo, bereft of inspiration? Was Rembrandt unable to add to the permanent art wealth of the world because he was the master craftsman when manipulating an etcher's plate? The careful musicianship of Bach, Brahms and Beethoven, developed through years of concentrated study and practice, lives in pure music that has ennobled the thoughts and feelings of thousands. Away with the absurd idea that special competency is inimical to broad culture!

Not only am I convinced that thoroughness in one or more fields of endeavor is the very best assurance that breadth of mind and spirit may be attained, but, on the other hand, I am persuaded that superficial acquaintance with a great number of things, unaccompanied by mastery of any, dooms the individual or group to circumscribed mediocrity, with no hope of intellectual adventure and discovery and with little likelihood of material or spiritual progress. There is no doubt in my mind that what American education and American life needs more than any other single thing is insistence upon thoroughness and honest craftsmanship. Our danger is not so much from specialization as from superficiality; not so much from delving for facts as from hasty generalization. Those concerned about greatness of soul need not fear a program of painstaking tests and checks nearly so much as the widespread indulgence in *non sequiturs*. America should not be skeptical of the prospects spread out before us by specialists and masters in the fields of science, arts and politics, but should rather beware of the seductions of attractive charlatans who have mastered nothing but the art of plausible persuasion. Indeed, America should learn the lesson that the most important thing for each individual is to do the task at hand painstakingly and well, and that in the integrity of skill and thought of that particular task will be found inspirations which will light the way to broader visions and greater achievements.

There is no royal road to learning, to skill, to fine character, or to that intellectual and spiritual freedom which marks the truly educated man. All must be faithful in a few small duties before independent mastery in great matters is granted unto them. It is because our lower schools and our homes have become soft and badly managed that we have laxity in business and in social life. Of course the schools can not be wholly responsible for what goes on in the world, but they can do much in the way of major reform.

Our schools contribute to superficiality because of two weaknesses. The first is a poorly organized or diffuse curriculum and the second is weak morale in the conduct of the work actually undertaken; the two are closely interwoven. The so-called "enriched curriculum" and "soft pedagogy" go hand in hand. Regardless of psychological methods which may or may not be best in the classrooms, the facts of life are such that human knowledge is all interrelated and some of it is basic or fundamental. If one is to ascend the intellectual ladder he can not skip any rung. Children must learn addition and subtraction accurately before they can serve as bookkeepers. They must learn all the operations of arithmetic well before they can truly comprehend algebra, geometry and trigonometry. The principle holds true in all lines of study. Our schools advance pupils through the grades on daily, monthly and term tests that do not measure actual achievement, and there is created the illusion of much progress when as a matter of fact there is relatively little real development. The seeds are sown in the elementary schools and much of the fruit is gathered in the high schools, so that in colleges the students have become skilful in "getting by." They want to seem to be rather than to be.

My plea is for reform that will eliminate this superficiality and temporary brightness which takes the place of solid achievement. The weakest link in the American educational chain is the high school. Its courses of study and its relationship to the grammar schools below and the institutions of higher learning above should be carefully examined and revised. The high school must demand certain basic achievement for entrance, otherwise secondary study is but a mockery.

I shall not attempt here to outline a secondary-school curriculum, but the point must be made that certain basic skills and knowledges must be obtained truly and thoroughly; and above all the individual must be trained to receive definite assignments and to persist in endeavor until they are carried out whether or not they may at the particular time be easy, pleasant or of supreme interest. No teacher would deny the advantage of arranging work so as to get as much interest, purpose and natural motive for effort behind each lesson or assignment as possible. But life is not always easy nor will it shape itself so that one can always choose to do only that which is of absorbing interest. The demands of life—practical life, artistic life, intellectual life and spiritual life—necessitate the development of individuals who will put duty above pleasure, judgment ahead of caprice and who will have character enough to hold themselves steadily to tasks which must be done for their ultimate importance or because of obligations that can not be shirked rather than because they are beguiling for the moment.

To you who are shaping urban colleges, I suggest a careful scrutiny of your curricula and methods of work. Let the courses of the early years be built only on the solid achievement of the high schools. Where the lower schools were weak, add elements of strength to your own courses. Then let progress be on the basis of real achievement. It wearies me to hear teachers of modern language say that their students can not read, write or speak the language but they have had cultural advantages of a literary character because of the courses pursued. Nonsense! No one can have even the remotest conception of the literary merit of a writer unless he is a master of the language in which the author wrote. I would desire above all things for our students of languages the fine cultivation that comes from converse with the great minds of other lands, but the real thing is based on linguistic mastery; not on sham, superficial patter, or the repetition of second-hand opinions.

We are faced with the problem of perfecting an educational program that will, at each level (that of elementary, secondary and higher intelligence) turn into our national life persons who will be both broad and capable. So far as material provision in the way of buildings and equipment is concerned, America stands foremost. It is also first in the extent to which it opens educational opportunity to the great majority of the people. But it needs more good teachers, especially in the high schools. These teachers must be prepared principally in urban institutions. Then it requires a carefully worked out curriculum, that will balance studies which will have a broadening effect with those which will impart basic knowledge and the tools of thought and achievement. Above all it must be genuine and thorough.

Modern life is so variegated and its kaleidoscope of ideas and happenings revolves so swiftly that our people need well-balanced mentality if they are not to look upon it like delighted though bewildered children at a ten-ring circus. Salvation lies in the serenity that comes from consciousness of trustworthy capacity. It is for us to send forth students who can view current happenings in proper perspective, participate effectively in chosen fields and be alive to nobler future possibilities. As I have said, the foundation for this security is honest capacity to be rather than the frivolous knack of seeming to be.

From such competency in thought and deed springs also morality. One who is intellectually honest will be ethical and dependable. He has the greatest spiritual possibilities.

A student of esthetics has said that there are in every work of art two elements, passion or vision on the one hand, and skill on the other. If the work be all emotion and no skill, one has the ineffective attempt at expression which is merely sentimental, transitory and often absurd. If the work is all technique with no great inspiration, the product is formal and cold. But if there be a just combination of mighty thought or feeling with mastery of the means of expression, then indeed the world is made richer by a work of art that will endure. Each man's life is a work of art. If he has great intelligence and nobility of character and also is capable, as a skilful technician, to make his spirit effective in word and deed, he achieves glory for himself and contributes to the permanent happiness of the race. At this period of the world's life, I know of no fulcrum upon which the educator may rest the lever of that influence by which he will lift men nearer to God than the urban university in America.

PROFESSIONAL TRAINING IN EDUCATION[1]

By Dr. MANUEL L. CARREON

PHILIPPINE ISLANDS BUREAU OF EDUCATION, MANILA

To begin with, I must express my hearty appreciation of the undeserved "historical" introduction by your class adviser and my personal congratulations. Nearly two years ago to-day I was invited to give one of the convocation addresses at your college. With the recommendations of the Educational Survey Commission then still fresh in our minds and the serious move on the part of both the government and the public-school officials to carry out

[1] Address before the Senior-Class Organization, College of Education, University of the Philippines, August 19, 1928.

these recommendations, particularly those referring to the strengthening of the "steering committee" of our public-school system, then making headway and finally culminating in the passage of the so-called educational leadership act, I chose to speak on the only related problem of the day, educational leadership.

Now that the educational leadership act is a law and has been operating for the last year or so, with our sincere wish and ardent hope that the steering personnel of our public schools become strengthened with the advent of new and more leaders in various lines of the teaching service, let us dedicate ourselves once more to the task of strengthening not the steering body but the rank and file of our teaching population—the teachers. I propose therefore to discuss before you the subject of professional training in education with special reference to teachers trained in the college of education, University of the Philippines, your institution.

In the Past

Years ago in the days of our elder brothers the young Filipino *aspirante* of the public schools was teaching his pupils while at the same time being taught partly how to teach but largely what to teach by his superiors, who were for the most part the pioneer American school teachers and administrators throughout the islands. In those days finishing one of the upper primary grades was perhaps sufficient qualification for the beginning *maestro*. A background of Spanish with perchance a modicum of teaching experience could have given the teacher-applicant a decided additional advantage over eligibles. Of this batch of early teachers we may still find in our midst a few still holding their own, toiling arduously with their younger brothers and sisters and trying to keep abreast of the ever-rising professional requirements of our public-school service. Some have gone on the retirement list, taking advantage of the teachers' pension law, or are devoting their time and energy to other fruitful occupational enterprises. A limited number perhaps have, in the words of the poet, joined the "innumerable caravan."

With the increased multiplicity of our social and individual needs came increased demands for classes of the higher grades and a corresponding necessity for teachers of better and higher qualifications and training. Graduates from the primary course, no longer acceptable, were superseded by graduates from a higher grade, preferably the seventh or the highest grade of the intermediate course.

But just as human wants and desires are never fully satisfied and perhaps will never be, so is the Filipino child's constant yearning for higher and better education and the consequent necessity for further teacher-training to cope with every new resulting situation. And so while primary graduation and later completion of the intermediate course were meeting adequately the needs of the early corps of teachers, these teachers had to make room for teachers of better qualifications of the later days. That is how it came to pass that intermediate graduates had to give way to the graduates of the first year, the second year, the third year or even the complete high-school course.

At Present

While the main emphasis in the early days was on the raising of general academic attainments there came a gradual shift of attention from general or academic to professional training, training in the theory and practice of teaching, methods of teaching different subjects, school supervision and administration, educational statistics and measurements and other courses in education and psychology offered in normal schools or teachers' colleges. The

Philippine Normal School began sending out professionally qualified teachers to the provinces at an early date. Soon after your college of education followed suit by paying special attention to the training of secondary teachers. Later on our provincial normal schools and provincial high schools offering normal courses had to supplement the yearly crop of graduates turned out by the Philippine Normal School. Private colleges of education joined, too, the institutions for training the vast army of teachers for the profession. And to-day we have colleges of education and normal schools, both public and private, destined to bring about the eventual and complete professionalization of our teaching staff from the teachers of the early primary grades to the instructors of the upper years of the secondary course. While in the days gone by the high-school graduate was already being acclaimed a conquering hero and as a commodity could command a high price on the school market, to-day we find many a high-school graduate unable to find a decent livelihood and fill a suitable place in the teaching profession, sometimes even after qualifying in an entrance eligibility test such as is usually given in nearly all provinces.

The Rising Tide of Professional Requirements

The bureau of education has since its organization driven home to the rank and file of our teachers the necessity for higher educational qualifications, especially professional training. On February 28, 1927, the director of education issued a circular prescribing in more or less definite terms the following qualifications of secondary teachers: (a) First preference to be given to graduates of colleges of education; (b) second preference to graduates of a four-year course in the college of liberal arts. There was, however, a stipulation that should the supply of qualified teachers under (a) and (b) not be sufficient to meet the demand, the employment of the following teachers might be permitted merely as a temporary measure: (a) Graduates of the college of agriculture and college of veterinary science for biology and physics only; (b) graduates of the college of engineering for mathematics and physics only; (c) graduates of other colleges depending upon special qualifications.

It was further stipulated that the services of these latter teachers should be dispensed with as soon as better trained teachers could be secured. The bureau promulgated these regulations as a step in the professionalization of our teaching force by eliminating as much as possible from the teaching service applicants trained primarily for occupational enterprises other than teaching. For to us, who are interested in elevating the prestige of our calling, an engineer, a veterinarian, a lawyer, a pharmacist or any other professional is as much a misfit in the profession of teaching as we, trained as teachers, are in any of their professions. In the same circular the director considered a teacher qualified to teach a secondary subject only if he has completed a minimum of twelve semestral units of work in that subject above the secondary level.

Proportion of Professionally Trained Teachers

In spite of this vigorous campaign we still find but a small proportion of professionally trained teachers in the different schools of the islands. In August, 1927, less than 2 per cent. of all Filipino teachers were graduates of colleges of education, 6 per cent. were graduates of the Philippine Normal School post-graduate course on the college level and a little over 8 per cent. were graduates of the provincial normal schools, normal courses offered in different provincial high schools and Philippine Normal School undergraduate course on the secondary level, making in all a total of less than 16 per cent. of our teachers who could claim the distinction of having gone through some form of professional instruction.

Professional Training of Supervisory Officials

According to similar statistical data collected in the general office, of the supervising teachers and principals employed in August, 1927, less than 2 per cent. were graduates of colleges of education, a little over 21 per cent. were graduates of the Philippine Normal School postgraduate course on the college level and nearly 16 per cent. were graduates of the Philippine Normal School undergraduate course on the secondary level and of the provincial normal courses, making a total of nearly 39 per cent. who had received some form of professional training. To the more ambitious and capable among you these figures offer many possible vacancies in prospect.

In order to push this professionalization campaign further, about a year after the issuance of the circular on the qualifications of secondary-school teachers, the director of education, on February 17, 1928, prescribed the following qualifications for supervising teachers and elementary-school principals:

(1) *For supervising teachers:*

(a) Graduation from the Philippine Normal School or college of education, with at least one year's experience as an elementary-school teacher besides one year's experience as principal of an elementary school; or

(b) Graduation from a provisional normal school and junior-teacher eligibility, with two years' experience as an elementary-school teacher and two years' experience as an elementary-school principal or with three years' experience as an elementary-school teacher and one year's experience as an elementary-school principal; or

(c) Graduation from a high school and junior-teacher eligibility, having completed at least six semestral courses in professional subjects in a normal school or their equivalent in a college of education and having had two years' experience as an elementary-school teacher and two years' experience as an elementary-school principal or three years' experience as an elementary-school teacher and one year's experience as an elementary-school principal.

(2) *For elementary-school principals:*

(a) Graduation from the Philippine Normal School with at least one year of (elementary classroom) teaching experience; or

(b) Graduation from a provincial normal school and junior-teacher eligibility, with at least two years of (elementary classroom) teaching experience; or

(c) Graduation from high school and junior-teacher eligibility, having completed at least six semestral courses in professional subjects in a normal school or their equivalent in a college of education and having had at least three years of teaching experience.

The director, in making these requirements, had in mind the availability of an increasing number of professionally trained graduates from the Philippine Normal School, different colleges of education, the provincial normal schools and the high schools offering normal courses.

Have our University Graduates Made Good?

I wonder if your faculty, the student body or the university authorities have ever stopped to raise the following question: "Have our college of education graduates made good?" From the testimonies of our field personnel—principals, supervisors and superintendents—the answer to this question is partly *yes* and partly *no.* *Yes,* because many have lived up to the expectations of our field administrators and measured up to the requirements of the bureau. Some have become not only efficient classroom teachers but good prospective timber for supervisory and administrative positions, to which a number have already been actually exalted.

The answer is also partly *no,* since the testimonies of our field personnel on the success of our university graduates are by no means unanimous. Listen to the following quotation from one of our most capable high-school principals: "Our experience with the eleven university graduates we have had has been on the whole disappointing. We have a new B. S. E. this year and we do not wish to assimilate any more." As an alumnus of the dear U. P. I hear these words ringing painfully in my ears. I indorse them to you to-day for your own personal satisfaction and consumption.

Perhaps we can not expect all success from all our university graduates and perhaps we should not, but the fact remains that your professional training in this institution is far from being beyond any unfavorable comment. It is fortunate that through the initiative of your dean, the faculty and the university authorities in general, entrance requirements in your institution have been constantly raised. There is, I understand, even a recommendation on the part of the dean of your college to make this college a graduate institution, a training school for strictly professional teachers, supervisors and administrators. The move is not only laudable but also in line with modern tendencies in the States. Recently Harvard, California and Stanford have professionalized the highest academic degree obtainable, the much coveted and often misrepresented Ph.D. These universities have substituted in place of this Ph.D. the degree to be known hereafter as the doctor of education, a strictly professional degree. At least two of these universities have also changed the master of arts degree to the master of education.

In the Future

I have tried to picture to you the professional status of our calling from the early inception of our public-school system to the present. There is no doubt that every indication points to ever-increasing professional requirements and qualifications. The bureau of education has tried its best to compensate amply deserving teachers by setting certain standard salary schedules and trying to follow these schedules as far as limited funds have permitted. The teaching profession in this country is bound to be completely professionalized. Our share is to assist in this great task of raising education from the level of the trades and still keeping it from turning out to be a mere missionary enterprise; in short, to make teaching, as it should be, a distinct profession, noble in its aims, attractive in its emoluments and patriotic in its accomplishments. My task and your task is to bring about the happy day when the mere *maestro* shall be raised to the pedestal of his fellow professionals and enjoy the prestige of his calling, the desired comforts of life and the satisfaction of patriotic service. Our joint task lies before us. As you leave this teacher-training institution, will you do your bit by contributing to this just cause, by striving with all your might to make good and become a successful teacher, a bulwark of the profession? I have great hopes that you will and you can. I have great hopes that your class can lead in this movement. Let not these hopes be in vain. As I began with congratulations for the inauguration of your organization, let me close with my best wishes for its success.

EDUCATIONAL EVENTS

THE GERMAN MINORITY IN UPPER SILESIAN SCHOOLS

THE disputed question of German minority schools in Upper Silesia has been settled, according to *The Christian Science Monitor,* by a mixed commission which, by the advice of Felix Calonder, president of the International Commission on Upper Silesia, has examined the matter.

By order of the Polish Governor of Polish Upper Silesia, six German minority schools had been closed, because in his opinion they did not answer to the requirements made for permission to establish German schools. It was proved that the native language of the majority of children frequenting these schools was Polish and not German, and they had been entered by their parents for the sake of certain material benefits, whereas the number of genuine German children was too small to warrant the opening of a school.

Mr. Calonder made a strong appeal to the parties interested to come to an understanding, and eventually the Polish government and the Volksbund (the Association of Germans in Upper Silesia) came to an agreement. Thus a matter has been successfully concluded that was already once before the forum of the League of Nations, and that would have again appeared at the coming session.

The provincial authority of Upper Silesia, wishing to show the greatest possible liberality in treating questions of minority schools, consented to open schools in Murcki and Czuchow, but did not allow the reopening of schools in Krzyzanowice, Wilcza Dolna and Brzozowice.

In Polish Upper Silesia 14 schools for the minority were closed during the present school year on account of a lack of sufficient numbers of children belonging to the minority. The "Volksbund" raised a dispute regarding six of these schools, and of these it has been granted two by agreement and one at the initiative of the authorities themselves. In return for these concessions the "Volksbund" has agreed to withdraw the complaint it had submitted to the League of Nations.

THE WORLD FEDERATION OF EDUCATION ASSOCIATIONS

A CONFERENCE of the World Federation of Education Associations will be held at Geneva from July 25 to August 4. More than five thousand participants are expected to be present, among whom will be a large contingent from the United States. The International Bureau of Education, 44 Rue des Maraichers, has issued a folder giving an account of the objects of the association.

The program of the 1929 conference is planned on an international scale; the work will be divided into sections. Besides the section meetings for reports and discussion on different branches of education, there will be several plenary sessions in which speakers of world-wide renown will be invited to address the conference on matters of international interest.

In addition, there will be practical exhibitions to illustrate the work of most of these sections. Evenings will be given over to meetings with messages from different countries, the cinema and visual education, the Swiss national fête and possibly a festival organized by M. Jaques-Dalcroze. Visits to the secretariat of the League of Nations and the International Labor Office will be planned, and the close cooperation of these two bodies in the general program will be of great value to all members of the conference.

Registrations for those wishing to attend the conference must be in at the International Bureau of Education before June 1. A committee on billeting will cooperate with the hotels, pensions, private families and the city of Geneva to see that every one is housed in the most comfortable manner possible. Dormitories will be set up to take care of those who wish to attend with the least expense.

A detailed program and full information may be had by applying directly to the International Bureau of Education, 44 Rue des Maraichers, Geneva, Switzerland.

EARNINGS OF CONTINUATION SCHOOL BOYS IN NEW YORK STATE

THE annual earning power of the employed boys, 14, 15 and 16 years of age, who are attending day continuation schools in the State of New York approximates $50,000,000. The annual earnings range from $150 to $1,300 and strike an average of $643.50. These findings are the result of a study of 75,000 employed boys in the continuation schools of the state, recently completed by the industrial education bureau of the State Education Department.

The annual earnings of more than half the number of boys reporting were $650, and this figure closely approximates the average of $643.50. The second largest group, approximately 20 per cent., consisted of boys who earned $900 a year. Four hundred dollars a year represented the yearly earnings of the third largest group, 12 per cent. Only a few boys earned over $1,000 a year, including 4 per cent. with earnings of $1,150. The high point was reached by 1.7 per cent. of the boys who reported annual earnings of $1,300.

Few boys were found unemployed. Of the 75,000 studied by the Industrial Education Bureau, 1½ per cent. were unemployed.

Commenting on the situation, Assistant Commissioner of Education Lewis A. Wilson said:

Due to a large number of factors such as schooling, age, ability, nature of the occupation, regularity of employment, industriousness, adaptiveness and other qualities, the wages of employed boys in continuation schools show a wide spread, but, in the aggregate, represent a large earning power. The boys constitute a class that for one reason or another leaves full-time school early, approximately one half only completing the eighth grade. As it costs the State of New York $103 a year to educate a boy in the public school the earnings of these boys in industry in one year, $48,262,500, is more than six times the $7,725,000 which it would cost the state if they were in attendance upon full-time school. Furthermore, some of their earnings indirectly contribute to the taxes, part of which go to the support of the public school in which other children continue their education into the higher grades. Thus, the continuation school boy contributes to the education of the more fortunate boys who can stay in school, while his own schooling, on account of circumstances, is limited to four hours a week.

These boys have a fine record for industriousness. They surpass to a marked extent the records of adults employed in our factories, mines and commercial establishments. An unemployment record of 1½ per cent. can scarcely be duplicated in any industry.

Of course each one of these 75,000 boys is entitled to attend a full-time public elementary or high school and to be educated at public expense until he completes the work of the high school or else attains the age of 21. Equal educational opportunity is guaranteed to every New York State child under the state constitution. The continuation school law was passed to carry out the constitutional guarantee. The continuation school is truly a democratic institution because it is compulsory and, being compulsory, it serves all children, rather than a favored few who might secure its advantages, were attendance to depend upon desire and ability to elect it.

NOMINATION OF OFFICERS OF THE AMERICAN LIBRARY ASSOCIATION

RESULTS of the election will be made public at the close of the fifty-first annual conference of the association at Washington, D. C., May 13–18. The slate is as follows:

President, Andrew Keogh, Yale University Library, New Haven, Conn.

First Vice-president, Everett R. Perry, Public Library, Los Angeles, Calif.

Second Vice-president, Jennie M. Flexner, Public Library, New York, N. Y.

Treasurer, Matthew S. Dudgeon, Public Library, Milwaukee, Wisconsin.

Trustee of the Endowment Fund, John W. O'Leary, Chicago Trust Company, Chicago, Illinois.

Members of the Executive Board, Linda A. Eastman, Public Library, Cleveland, Ohio; Judson T. Jennings, Public Library, Seattle, Washington.

Members of the Council, Robert J. Usher, Howard Memorial Library, New Orleans, La.; Charles H. Compton, Public Library, St. Louis, Missouri; Halsey W. Wilson, H. W. Wilson Co., 958 University Avenue, New York, N. Y.; Essae M. Culver, State Library Commission, Baton Rouge, La.; R. R. Bowker, The *Library Journal*, 62 W. 45th St., New York, N. Y.

The committee availed itself of the constitutional privilege to name "one or more persons for each office to be filled," and unanimously decided to submit a list of nominations for the official ballot comprising only one name for each office to be filled. Other nominations, if supported by any fifteen members and filed with the secretary at least two months before the next conference, will be included in the official ballot.

HOWARD UNIVERSITY

As a result of a definite law enacted by the congress authorizing federal aid to Howard University, the leading Negro institution of higher education in the United States, Secretary West held a conference in his office at the Interior Department on February 11 to consider plans to carry out provisions of the new statute.

One of its terms provides that the university shall be open at all times to an inspection by the Bureau of Education and that such an inspection shall be made at least once a year. A report is to be presented annually by the bureau to the congress making a full exhibit of its affairs. On account of the fact that Howard University is a privately controlled and supported institution, the adoption of a definite policy regarding the division of the support to be derived from federal and private sources is necessary.

While the federal government has been making appropriations of various sums annually to the institution since 1879, the status of these appropriations has been uncertain due to the fact that they were not actually authorized by a basic law. This has also affected to a large extent contributions for the university's support from private sources. The conference discussed plans for stabilizing future appropriations by the government under the new law with a view of assuring a fixed income to the institution. Segregation of federal funds for maintenance and new buildings was also considered. Another important subject under discussion was the promotion of medical and dental education and the training of teachers for the Negro race at the institution.

The outcome of the conference was a general agreement concerning the desirability of establishing a plan for a systematic program of support for the university through a considerable period of years. Inspections by the Bureau of Education are to be comprehensive in scope, including every phase of activity of the institution. The reports of the bureau to the congress may contain recommendations for a ten or twenty-year program of federal support and for the development of the various educational services offered by the university. A building program for the improvement of the physical plant may also be included in the bureau's recommendations.

The conference was attended by Secretary West, Assistant Secretary Edward C. Finney, Dr. Arthur J. Klein, chief of the division of higher education of the Bureau of Education; Senator Lawrence C. Phipps, of the Senate Committee on Education and Labor; Representative Louis C. Cramton, chairman of the subcommittee on appropriations for the Interior Department of the House Committee on Appropriations; Representatives Burton L. French and William W. Hastings, of the House Committee on Appropriations; President Mordecai W. Johnson, Secretary-Treasurer Emmett J. Scott, John R. Hawkins, Michel O. Dumas, C. H. Pope, Victor B. Deyber, members of the board of trustees of Howard University; President Edwin R. Embree, of the Julius Rosenwald Fund, and E. B. Fox, representing the Bureau of the Budget.

LEGISLATIVE APPROPRIATIONS FOR THE UNIVERSITY OF NORTH CAROLINA

THE University of North Carolina, according to its *Alumni Review,* requested of this year's Legislature $1,463,067 for 1929–30, and $1,270,868 for 1930–31 in maintenance. For permanent improvement requests for the biennium $1,823,000 was asked. The Budget Bureau's recommendation sliced the university requests heavily. In the maintenance request for 1929–30 the amount was cut from $1,463,067 to $848,100. For 1930–31 the request was sliced from $1,270,868 to $875,300. The amount recommended for maintenance in 1929–30 is lower by $31,900 than the amount appropriated for the current year. It is understood that earnings accruing from the university's service plants may increase this maintenance budget however, but only a nominal proportion of the amount requested.

The biggest slice came in the request for permanent improvements in the biennium. The request was $1,823,000; the recommendation by the Budget Bureau is $264,000. Principal items in the budget recommendation contemplate the expenditure of $100,000 for the water system, $44,000 for renovating the old library building for classroom use, and $50,000 for campus improvement. The cut does not allow any consideration for a much needed physical education building, teachers' college building, or medical building. Bynum gymnasium, erected in 1905 for a student body of three hundred, is not now large enough for the freshman class of 750, not to mention the student body of 2,700. This item is illustrative of conditions in other departments of the university for which appropriations were asked.

The Budget Bureau's recommendations are not final. At the midwinter meeting of the university board of trustees it was decided that the university should go before the joint senate and house committee on appropriations and ask for more money than was recommended by the bureau. The recommendations of the committee will go before the Legislature for final action.

According to the Budget Act of 1925, although the legislature appropriates money to the university, that appropriation can not be spent unless it is allotted to the institution by the Budget Bureau. Acting under the provisions of this act the bureau cut the university's maintenance appropriations off by $19,000 last year, and the recommendation to Governor Gardner is that $20,000 be lopped off the $880,000 appropriated to the institution for the current year, 1928–29. Governor Gardner has not acted on this recommendation.

THE DEPARTMENT OF EDUCATION OF YALE UNIVERSITY

MORE than three thousand public-school teachers in Connecticut have taken or are now taking professional courses in education offered by the department of education of Yale University. This number is approximately one third of the entire teaching force of the state. It is not merely the rank and file of the classroom teachers who thus seek professional improvement: those occupying the more responsible positions, principals, supervisors and superintendents are represented, in proportion to their numbers, even more strongly in the courses offered. Almost half of the superintendents in the state, more than half of the state supervising agents and almost two thirds of the principals in New Haven have taken courses offered by the department. Many take courses almost every year.

Most of the courses offered are designed primarily to assist the leaders, or would-be leaders, in the profession to deal more successfully with the numerous fundamental problems, such as school organization, courses of study, supervision, planning of the school plant and educational finances in all their bearings.

At the present time over six hundred Connecticut teachers, principals and superintendents are enrolled as students in the Yale Department of Education. They come from more than a third of all the towns and cities of the state. Nearly one fourth of them, a total of 143, are residents of New Haven and on the staff of the New Haven schools, but there are proportionately even larger numbers from several smaller towns. Meriden contributes sixty-one, or more than one fourth the number of its entire teaching staff; Plainfield thirty, about five sixths the number of its staff; Derby forty-five, nine tenths the number of its staff, and Putnam thirty-three, or practically its whole staff. Ten or more each come from such widely scattered places as Ansonia, Bloomfield, Bridgeport, Bristol, Hamden, Hartford, Milford, Stratford, Waterbury and West Haven.

Nearly half the entire Connecticut teacher enrolment are attending courses offered in New Haven. The department tries, so far as its force of instructors makes it practicable, to bring its work to as many as possible. To this end courses are offered at several centers outside New Haven. Just now ten such courses, enrolling nearly three hundred and fifty teacher-students, are being given in Bridgeport, Bristol, Derby, Hartford (two courses), Meriden, Plainfield, Putnam, Stratford and Waterbury. In recent years, courses have been given in nearly a score of other places, such as Ansonia, Branford, Danbury, Danielson, East Hartford, West Hartford, Fairfield, Milford, Norwalk, Seymour, Southington, New Britain, Groton, Shelton, Wallingford and Winsted.

EDUCATIONAL NOTES AND NEWS

THE Cleveland meeting of the Department of Superintendence of the National Education Association opens officially on Sunday, February 24. The meeting under the presidency of Frank D. Boynton, superintendent of the schools of Ithaca, New York, promises to be of special interest and importance. Details of the general program and of some of the other departments and organizations meeting at the same time have been printed in SCHOOL AND

SOCIETY, and it is hoped that an early issue will contain a full report of the meeting.

DR. WILLIAM JOHN COOPER was sworn in on February 11 as commissioner of the United States Bureau of Education. The ceremony took place in the office of Roy O. West, Secretary of the Interior, who was a witness, the oath being administered by W. B. Acker, chief clerk of the department. Dr. Cooper, who was appointed to the post of commissioner by President Coolidge on January 12, and promptly confirmed by the senate, is a native of California. He was graduated in 1906 from the University of California, where he specialized in Latin and history, which branches he taught in Stockton, California, for three years after graduation. He then became the head of the history department of the Berkeley Senior High School. He served successively as supervisor of social studies in the Oakland public schools, district superintendent of schools at Piedmont, superintendent of schools at Fresno and at San Diego. In 1927 he was made superintendent of public instruction for the State of California.

DR. WILLIAM WATTS FOLWELL, first president of the University of Minnesota, now president emeritus, celebrated his ninety-sixth birthday on February 15. Dr. Folwell is engaged in writing a history of Minnesota in five volumes.

VIERLING KERSEY has been appointed to succeed Dr. William John Cooper, who resigned as State Superintendent of Public Instruction in California to accept an appointment as United States Commissioner of Education. Both will lecture during the summer at the University of Southern California, Dr. Cooper on "Federal and State School Organization and Administration" and Mr. Kersey on "Education for Citizenship."

DR. RAY LYMAN WILBUR, president of Leland Stanford University, has accepted President-elect Hoover's invitation to take the interior portfolio in his cabinet. Dr. Wilbur has received a year's leave of absence from Leland Stanford University to undertake his work of reorganizing the Interior Department. Should additional time be needed, his leave will be extended.

ALUMNI of the University of Virginia have inaugurated a movement for the raising of a fund with which to purchase a gift for President Edwin A. Alderman, '82, in appreciation of his quarter of a century of service to that institution. He assumed the presidency of the University of Virginia on September 15, 1904, having previously served as administrative head of the University of North Carolina and of Tulane University.

A TESTIMONIAL dinner was offered on February 14 to Dr. W. H. P. Faunce, who retires at the end of the academic year from the presidency of Brown University. Mr. Charles Evans Hughes, Jr., presided at the dinner and the principal speaker was Dr. Harvey Nathaniel Davis, president of the Stevens Institute of Technology and alumni trustee of Brown University.

DR. JAMES P. KINARD, for many years connected with Winthrop College and more recently dean of that institution, has been elected acting president, to succeed the late Dr. D. B. Johnson.

PROFESSOR GRANT SHOWERMAN, of the department of classics at the University of Wisconsin, has been presented with the decoration of Cavaliere della Corona d'Italia in reward for services in the field of classical studies and Roman history.

THE honorary degree of doctor of laws has been conferred by the University of St. Andrews on Dr. Peter Comrie, rector of Leith Academy and president of the Education Institute of Scotland, which recently held its fifty-second annual congress at St. Andrews.

ELI KIRK PRICE, art connoisseur and patron, received at a meeting of the Philadelphia Forum on February 13 the eighth Philadelphia award, founded in 1921 by Edward W. Bok, given annually to the individual who in the opinion of the trustees has rendered the city the greatest service during the preceding year, the award consisting of a check for $10,000, a gold medal and a scroll outlining the achievement which merited the prize.

DR. FRIDTJOF NANSEN was the guest of honor at a dinner in New York City on February 18, under the auspices of the Universal Religious Peace Conference, which will hold sessions in Geneva next year. Dr. Nansen spoke on "How shall We Obtain World Peace?" Members of the committee in charge included Dr. John H. Finley, of the New York *Times;* President John Grier Hibben, of Princeton University; President Livingston Farrand, of Cornell University, and President Nicholas Murray Butler, of Columbia University.

DR. EDWARD CHANNING has retired from the McLean professorship of ancient and modern history at Harvard University. He has been on the Harvard teaching staff continuously since 1883, when he was appointed instructor in history.

DR. GEORGE FILLMORE SWAIN, since 1909 Gordon McKay professor of civil engineering at Harvard University, will retire on March 1, when he becomes professor emeritus.

DR. LUCIUS A. SHERMAN, since 1882 chairman of the department of English in the University of Nebraska, will retire at the end of the academic year. Dr. Sherman served as dean of the arts college from 1887 to 1901, and of the graduate school from 1901 to 1926, when he retired at his own request. He was offered and refused the chancellorship of the university in 1889. In June he becomes professor emeritus.

DR. W. M. CHILDS, first vice-chancellor of the University of Reading, and principal of University College, Reading, from 1903 to 1926, has tendered his resignation. The council of the university has accepted his resignation with much regret, and has placed on record its deep gratitude for the eminent services he has rendered to the University College and to the university since 1893, for his wise leadership and single-minded devotion as principal academic officer during a period of twenty-six years, and in particular for his courage and statesmanship in initiating and carrying into effect the policy of establishing a university in Reading." Dr. Childs hopes to remain in association with the department of modern history, in which he holds the position of honorary professor.

JOHN J. JACKSON, the director of education for Cardiff, Wales, will retire on May 31, and the recommendation of the subcommittee to the education committee appointed to consider what steps should be taken to fill the vacancy has been adopted, namely, that the post of director of education be offered to the present assistant director, Mr. Thomas McHowat, at a salary of £1,000 per annum, rising by annual increments of £50 to £1,200 per annum, and that the post of assistant director be abolished.

A. M. WOODWARD is retiring at the end of the present session from the directorship of the British School at Athens, which he has held since 1923 and has made memorable by his excavations at Sparta. Mr. H. G. G. Payne, research scholar of Christ Church, Oxford, has been appointed to succeed Mr. Woodward as director.

DR. ARTHUR S. PEARSE, of Duke University, has been appointed visiting professor of biology in Keio University, Tokyo, Japan, from February 1, 1929, to May 15, 1930, for the Rockefeller Foundation. He will then spend two months in research in Siam and India, and will return to this country by way of London about September 15.

DR. HERBERT E. HAWKES, dean of Columbia College, sailed on February 9 for Europe, to visit Italy, Egypt, Greece and Palestine. He expects to return to the university in April.

THE following telegram was sent recently by Secretary J. W. Crabtree, of the National Education Association, to Dr. William John Cooper, State Superintendent of Public Instruction in California, who has been appointed by President Coolidge to succeed Dr. John J. Tigert as United States Commissioner of Education: "On behalf of the officers and staff of the National Education Association, permit me to congratulate you on your appointment as United States Commissioner of Education. Your brilliant career as a teacher and educational administrator has won for you the respect of the whole profession. In your new post of leadership you may rely on our loyalty and cooperation."

DEAN WILLIAM F. RUSSELL, of Teachers College, has been appointed a member of two committees of Columbia University: the committee on honors for the one hundred and seventy-fifth anniversary celebration, and the advisory committee on educational policy.

Dr. Charles C. Hedges, assistant director of the Johns Hopkins Hospital, in charge of the out-patient department, has been appointed director of the Babies' and Children's Hospital of the Medical Center in New York City.

Dr. J. Q. Holsopple, formerly assistant professor of psychology at the Western Reserve University and psychologist at the Cleveland City Hospital, is now chief clinical psychologist at the State Department Institutions and Agencies of New Jersey, with offices at Trenton State Hospital.

Lecturers in the course at Harvard University on the theory and practice of government include A. Lawrence Lowell; Count Sforza, former Italian ambassador to Paris; Charles A. Beard, formerly of Columbia University; R. G. Hawtrey, assistant secretary to the Treasury, London, and Professor M. O. Hudson, of the law school.

Dr. Moises Saenz, acting secretary of education for the Republic of Mexico and brother of Aaron Saenz, formerly secretary of foreign relations for Mexico, will lecture during the summer at the University of California. Dr. Saenz is a Columbia University graduate. He will offer a course on education in Latin America and the United States.

Dr. Robert Hegner, professor of protozoology in the Johns Hopkins University School of Hygiene and Public Health, has been granted a year's leave of absence from May 1, 1929, to May 1, 1930, during which time he will serve as visiting professor of parasitology in the Graduate School of Sanitation and Public Health of the University of the Philippines at Manila. His address during this period will be University of the Philippines, Manila, P. I.

The following members of the faculty of Dartmouth College have been granted leaves for the current semester: Frank M. Anderson, professor of history; Rees H. Bowen, professor of sociology; Russel D. Kilbourne, professor of banking and finance; George D. Lord, professor of classical archeology; Arthur Fairbanks, professor of art; Nathaniel L. Goodrich, librarian of the college, and Frederick S. Page, assistant professor of botany.

It is reported in the daily press that a statement in regard to conditions at the Michigan State College, by Dr. Kenyon L. Butterfield, who was dismissed from the presidency last summer, has been released. Dr. Butterfield is said to recommend a legislative investigation.

M. W. Longman, for eight years superintendent at Muskegon, Michigan, has declined reelection and Mr. John A. Craig, principal of the senior high school, has been given a three-year contract at $6,000, $6,500 and $7,000. The teachers of Muskegon recently presented Superintendent Longman with a life membership in the National Education Association.

Dr. George W. Gerwig, secretary of the Pittsburgh, Pennsylvania, Board of Education, has resigned after thirty-seven years of service to the schools of the city.

Dr. Rufus M. Jones, president of the board of trustees of Bryn Mawr College, professor of philosophy at Haverford College and chairman of the American Friends Service for European Relief, spent the week of February 11 at Grinnell College, where he delivered a series of addresses on current religious problems before the fifteenth annual conference of ministers and laymen. These are the Gates lectures for 1929, and continue an annual series of addresses by distinguished educators, established in memory of Dr. George A. Gates, president of Grinnell College from 1887 to 1900.

Dr. Lowell Mason McAfee, former president of Park College and also of Parsons College at Fairfield, Iowa, died on February 12 at the age of sixty-eight years.

The death at the age of fifty-two years is announced of Loren M. Post, director of health education in the public schools of Detroit, Michigan.

The death is announced on January 30 at the age of seventy years of Mr. T. H. Berten

Shaw, who was for over forty years master in the City of London School.

At the annual meeting of the Educational Press Association of America, to be held on the morning of February 26 at the Hotel Statler, Cleveland, the following program will be presented: "Functions of Different Types of Educational Journals," by William F. Russell, dean of Teachers College, Columbia University, and editor of the *Teachers College Record,* the discussion to be opened by E. T. Cameron, executive secretary of the Michigan State Education Association and editor of the *Michigan Education Journal;* "The Policies of Typical Educational Journals as to Reviews," by James F. Hosic, professor of education, Teachers College, Columbia University, and editor of *Educational Method;* Reports of Committees: For the Committee on Standards, Joy Elmer Morgan, editor of the *Journal of the National Education Association;* For the Committee on the New Education Bill, Arthur H. Chamberlain, Pacific Building, San Francisco, California; For the Committee on Ethics and Business, J. Herbert Kelley, executive secretary of the Pennsylvania Education Association and editor of the *Pennsylvania School Journal.* After the election of officers and the transaction of miscellaneous business, luncheon will be served.

The U. S. Civil Service Commission announces open competitive examinations for teachers of secondary English and normal school demonstration teachers. Applications for these positions will be rated as received until further notice. The examinations are to fill vacancies in the Philippine service at 3,000 pesos to 3,200 pesos a year for teachers of secondary English, and 3,000 to 3,400 pesos a year for normal school demonstration teachers. The normal value of the Philippine peso equals 50 cents in United States currency. With the exception of a few demonstration teachers, married couples and single men will be given preference in making appointments. Women only will be admitted to the examination for normal school demonstration teachers. The Philippine school year begins in the early part of June and ends with the month of March. So far as possible, all appointments of teachers are made with a view to their arrival in Manila before the beginning of the school year, which requires that the appointees sail from San Francisco or Seattle during the first week in May. In this way the contract period of two years expires with the school year. Competitors will not be required to report for examination at any place, but will be rated on their physical ability and their education, training and experience.

Raising of a $250,000 fund, the income of which will be used to aid needy retired teachers, was voted as the major project for 1929 of the New York State Teachers' Association by the executive committee at a meeting just held. Immediate steps will be taken toward raising the fund by popular subscription.

Northwestern University will receive more than $8,000,000 for the use of the college of liberal arts by the will of Milton H. Wilson, one of the founders of Wilson Brothers, manufacturers and wholesalers of men's furnishings, who died on February 10. Mr. Wilson had been for many years a trustee of the university. Dr. Walter Dill Scott, president of the university, stated that the university would use the gift in carrying out plans for increase in teachers and building.

Yale University is the beneficiary of a bequest estimated at $3,000,000 in the will of Mrs. Ray Tompkins, of Elmira, N. Y., who died on January 22 in Cannes, France. Mr. Tompkins, a Yale football star, died on June 30, 1918, leaving to his widow the use of his estate and directing that if no provision was made otherwise it was to go at her demise to his alma mater. The combined bequests in Mrs. Tompkins's will, which disposed of her husband's $4,000,000 estate and her own of approximately $750,000, give to Yale a total amount of $3,000,000.

Mr. and Mrs. Percy S. Straus have made a gift of $1,000,000 to the unrestricted endowment of New York University. The donation is to be used as the Edith A. and Percy S. Straus Fund at the discretion of the university council. Mr. Straus is a member of the university council and is chairman of the Centennial Fund Committee.

Gifts of $2,000,000 from the General Education Board of New York and the Julius Rosenwald Fund of Chicago have been received by the Meharry Medical College, Nashville, for the establishment of an adequate school for the training of Negro physicians. A part of the project, to which alumni will contribute $200,000, will be a 120-bed hospital. There will be facilities for 200 students and departments of dentistry and pharmacy. The college was established in Nashville in 1876.

A gift of $200,000 from Charles Lathrop Pack, president of the American Tree Association of Washington, to Yale will establish a foundation for the advancement of applied forestry. Mr. Pack is the founder of the Charles Lathrop Pack Forestry Trust, a foundation through which aid has been extended to a number of schools and other agencies engaged in forestry work. As part of his educational work he has given three million forestry primers to schools throughout the country.

Mrs. Depew has given the income from $120,000 to George Washington University, to endow, as a memorial to the late Chauncey M. Depew, a department of public speaking.

DISCUSSION

THE TERM REPORT AS A COLLEGE TEACHING DEVICE

A critical examination of educational procedures and subject-matter is gradually extending from the elementary school through the high school to the college and the university. Higher education has been the last unit to come under the scrutiny of the educational investigator for reasons which need not be discussed here. That the college and university now more than ever before are being subjected to the techniques and principles discovered in connection with the lower units in our educational system is evidenced by the many experiments now in progress and the increasing literature in the field.

One aspect of college work of which a great deal is informally said is the method of teaching. It is accepted as a truism in many circles that the poorest teaching is done on the higher levels. This problem will eventually lead to controlled classroom experiments on the college plane. In absence of any such detailed investigation the college teacher must continue to hope that the particular procedure he is using is the best. Unsatisfactory as this method of deciding such an important matter is, we must rely upon opinion in the great majority of cases.

One step in advance is the collective opinion of well-informed and thinking men. To get such an opinion regarding one frequently used teaching procedure on the college level, that is, the term report, a personal letter was sent to twenty-five professors of education over the country. Twenty-one of these men replied almost immediately. These replies came from sixteen different states.

Before presenting the questions and replies let us be sure that we know what is meant by the term report. One gentleman thought that the marks sent to the office were referred to, and consequently found it difficult to answer the questions. The term report as a college teaching device refers to that procedure whereby an intensive study of some one problem or topic or group of related topics is made by the students; the results of such study are presented in writing or orally or both to the instructor or class.

The first question upon which an expression of opinion was sought was: What educative value may be expected to accrue to the student making such a study and report? The variety of replies precludes classification. Among those listed most frequently the following may be mentioned: "stimulates independent thinking," "provides training in independent study and organization of knowledge," "places responsibility upon the student," "provides a measure of the student's ability," "gives training in the technique of research" and finally, "assures the mastery of at least one bit of knowledge or part of the course."

The second and third questions sought to determine in which undergraduate courses the term report might be of greatest usefulness. The men replying are universal in their agreement that the teaching procedure under consideration can most advantageously be used in the social sciences and applied physical sciences, such as farm management. Mathematics, decorative arts, manual arts, natural sciences, foreign languages, "courses which call for specific knowledge and skills," were listed as subjects in which the term report could be used with only doubtful value.

The twenty-one men voted seven to one in favor of the written rather than the oral presentation of the results of the study. It should be noted, however, that ten of the twenty-one men thought both procedures should be used. The truth of the matter is probably that each form of presentation has a unique set of values to the individual and the class as a group.

The consensus of opinion was that only one report per term should be required; though five men thought that two should be used, and two men voted for three. The writer would agree with the nine in that only one intensive study should be required of the student per term. To require more is apt to vitiate the fundamental values listed under the first question. This one report should be written in the field and under the instructor selected by the student.

Nine men thought the term report should make up one fourth of the course. This is significant of the importance of this procedure. It should be remembered that the men were not selected because they favored the term report as a college teaching device, and the high percentage (84 per cent.) of replies precludes the possibility of a selective factor. One fourth of a term of twelve weeks would be, of course, three weeks, and of a semester of eighteen weeks, four and one half weeks devoted exclusively to the term report, or if not exclusively in time then that same ratio in the student's attention and energies.

Attention in this connection should be called to the replies to the last question: should the term report be emphasized more or less in college teaching? To this question eighteen of the twenty-one men replied "more." These two indices of emphasis, the time allotment and expression of favor toward increased emphasis, are possibly a reflection of the same spirit which has prompted Yale, Harvard, Dartmouth and other universities to institute honor courses or more independent work for superior students of the two upper classes. The thought suggests itself that the term report is a step in the same direction.

Another aspect of the term report covered by the questions was the defects or limitations. The fact that the term report requires a great deal of the instructor's time for conferences and reading was listed as the greatest drawback. The opinion is suggested that this is not a criticism of the term report, but of administrative details. Other possible defects listed were: "the students are prone to copy," "they lack interest," "topics are too broad," "materials unavailable" and "professors loaf on the job." No comment attacked the term report on fundamental psychological or educational grounds.

The prevailing opinion regarding the selection of topics was that the instructor should present a list of possible topics from which the student could select the one he preferred. It is suggested that the student be permitted to select a topic not on the list after a conference with the instructor. This a few superior students will do.

The characteristics upon which a mark was based were first, organization; second, originality, and third, manner of presentation.

It is fair to draw at least the tentative conclusion from the opinions herein reviewed that the term report is a valuable teaching tool on the college level and that it should receive more emphasis. From a theoretical point of view this teaching procedure holds great advantages. It provides first of all an agency for individualization; second, variation on the basis of dominant interest; and finally is in accord with the principle that the students learn only through their own self-activity and not by means of the lecturer's erudite philosophical speculation or entertaining capacity.

One final word ought to be added regarding the mechanics of handling the term report. Here indeed as with all methods of instruction is the crux of the matter. The educational return is always conditioned by the technique the teacher employs. No rules can be given, but as a concluding word the following suggestions are offered: (1) Present a list of live meaningful topics; (2) allow the student to select his own topic if possible—he will work best on that in which he is interested; (3) place at the students' command Reeder's "How to

Write a Thesis," or Monroe's bulletin "Reporting Educational Research"; (4) make a schedule of the dates on which the various steps of the work are due, for example, the subject selected by December 1, bibliography due by January 1, the tentative report due by January 15 and final typed report due by February 1; (5) give ample time for conferences, for perhaps the best teaching is done "in an office in the library where a chap can come to ask what to read, or chew over a theory."

ROBERT WENDELL FREDERICK
WILLIAM JEWELL COLLEGE

WHO TEACH FRESHMEN AND SOPHOMORES?

THE statement is often made that the bulk of instruction in the freshman and sophomore years of the universities of the country is given by young, inexperienced instructors, inadequately prepared for their work. That this criticism is not well founded as far as Stanford University is concerned is shown by a study of the final reports submitted at the registrar's office for the autumn quarter, 1927–28.

If physical education be omitted, 7,528 reports on students in lower-division courses were received for the autumn quarter, lower-division courses being taken as those numbered below 100 in the university register. While these courses are not restricted to lower division, *i.e.*, freshman and sophomore students, they are primarily intended for such and the registration in them of juniors and seniors is comparatively small.

The highest degree and the professional status of the instructor in charge of each of these courses were tabulated with the number of students under his instruction. It was found that over one half of the lower-division instruction was given by men who had received their doctor's degree, and that almost three fourths was given by men of professorial rank. It should be noted that the unit used was not the class, but the student instructed.

The distribution of students according to the highest degrees held by the instructors in charge of the various classes was as follows:

	per cent.
With the doctor's degree	58
With the master's degree only	20
With the bachelor's degree only	17
With no degree	7

The percentage of students taught by instructors of various university ranks was as follows:

	per cent.
By professors	49
By associate professors	13
By assistant professors	10
Total of professorial rank	72
By instructors	14
By teaching assistants	14

An analysis by departments showed that there were sixteen of the twenty-seven departments giving lower-division instruction in which all the classes were in charge of men of professorial rank, and five others in which over half of the students were under such men. There was only one department in which none of the lower-division instruction was given by men of professorial rank.

It would be interesting to have similar data published from other universities.

WALTER CROSBY EELLS
DEPARTMENT OF EDUCATION,
STANFORD UNIVERSITY

SPECIAL CORRESPONDENCE

A REVISED LIBERAL ARTS CURRICULUM

THE author recently published an article[1] in which he set forth a thesis concerning a liberal education. In that article the thesis is stated that the common characteristic of a liberal education in every age has been the development within the individual of the ability to deal masterfully with his environment. It is not intended to argue that thesis further in this article. It is the purpose of this article to tell

[1] "The Crisis in Liberal Education," SCHOOL AND SOCIETY, September 1, 1928.

how that thesis has been used as the basis for constructing an entirely new curriculum for Franklin College.

During the school year of 1927–28 the faculty of the college undertook to revise completely its requirements for the B.A. degree upon the basis of the thesis stated above. It is unnecessary to rehearse here all the details of that work; therefore, only the principles upon which the reorganization was done and the resulting requirements for the degree will be discussed here.

The thesis is stated in quite general terms. If a curriculum is to be built upon it, it must be made definite and concrete. If one is to be able to deal masterfully with contemporary life, specifically what is involved? What are the elements or factors in contemporary life which every individual, to be liberally educated, must master? This is an extraordinarily difficult question to answer in specific terms. But there are certain outstanding factors in modern life which even the casual observer can not overlook. In the first place, we are living in an economic society. Ours is an economic civilization. There is no escape from the economic factors in contemporary life. If this be true, then in terms of our thesis the liberally educated men or women of this age must know something of the fundamental principles that control and operate in our economic order. To be a master in any given sphere one must have the ability to understand the laws that operate in that sphere, and further must be able to organize these laws and direct them to serve his own chosen ends. If one can not do this, he has not yet become a master, but is still a slave to the operation of these laws. As a result, he is not in a position to furnish any intelligent leadership in a given field, and must depend upon others to do his thinking for him and to tell him how to conduct himself in the face of the principles operating in that particular field. This, certainly, should not be the position of the man who is liberally educated. How many economic slaves there are in contemporary life! It is safe to say that nine tenths of American citizens do not know how to vote intelligently upon any of the great economic issues that are presented to them for their decision. If this be true, it constitutes one of democracy's most vital problems. The United States is now rapidly assuming the economic leadership of the world. We are becoming the world's banker. We are changing rapidly from a debtor nation to a creditor nation. These facts demand a more intelligent citizenship in order that our financial and international policies may be wise policies. Franklin College, therefore, proposes to give an important place to the study of the economic organization of our society in its curriculum.

A *second* factor in our environment we may call the need for social adjustment. This factor involves all the problems of one's relationships to other individuals: his relationships to all the groups of which he may become a member, and all the problems of the relationships of group to group, state to state, nation to nation and race to race. It involves all the problems of individual and group behavior; furthermore, it involves all the problems of individual and social control—the problems of government. This, of course, involves the whole field of the social sciences—sociology, psychology, social psychology and political science. The slaves in these fields are legion. How few men are masters of their own conduct! Who is free from the enslaving influence of organized propaganda? How much hatred and jealousy and strife are there among the groups of contemporary life! How may these things be eliminated? How may we avoid the evils of "mob psychology"? How may we eliminate racial and national prejudice and hatred? It is in these fields that the need for masterful conduct is so great. It is here that the demand for leadership is so urgent. The liberally educated man or woman must meet the challenge of these problems.

A *third* factor in contemporary life is the necessity for proper adjustment to the natural universe in which we live. One needs an orientation in the natural universe. One must be the master of natural laws or else he will be mastered and controlled by them. In this is involved also all the laws of health and hygiene that relate to one's body.

A *fourth* factor of our environment is the necessity for discovering the spiritual values and aspects of life. Man has never been able to avoid attempts to interpret the meaning of life.

The search for the spiritual meaning of life is more earnest and sincere to-day, perhaps, than it has ever been. Man's great mastery of the natural universe and his development of unprecedented power has made the need for spiritual values all the more real. This is the field of philosophy and religion. It seems that no one could lay claim to liberal culture who was not familiar with these factors of life.

These four factors which have been mentioned do not by any means exhaust the list, but are only illustrative of the method to be employed in making the general thesis specific.

The new curriculum of Franklin College is based upon the following principles:

1. That a student should have a knowledge of four main fields:

A. The physical universe, which includes physics and chemistry as the basic physical sciences; astronomy and geology which present an observation of the inorganic universe; and the biological sciences.

B. The history of the race, which includes history, philosophy and religion.

C. The structure of society, which includes the fields of sociology, economics and political science.

D. The nature of the individual, which includes psychology, both individual and social; geography or human ecology and hygiene.

2. The second general principle is that it should give students a mastery of certain general mental tools, for example, mathematics, reflective thinking, oral and written English, and foreign language. Not all these tools are expected to be mastered by all students. The tool subjects are to be selected according to needs. This makes one of the important changes in the new curriculum in that mathematics and foreign language are not to be required of all students for graduation.

3. The third general principle is that it should give a mastery of some particular field. This involves the "major" concept of studies. Each student, especially in his last two years, will be expected to select some major field of interest and to devote a great deal of his time in the last two years under the guidance of his major professor to a comprehensive understanding of this field.

Some of the objectives related to this principle are: (1) to encourage in the student an attitude in which he views his college course more in terms of becoming intelligently conversant in fields in which he is interested and less in terms of required credit hours and credit points; (2) to offer the exceptional student an opportunity to work up to the limit of his capacity; (3) to arouse in the student an intellectual enthusiasm which he should carry with him into later life; to develop within him the ability to carry on his own intellectual development, and to give him a larger measure of responsibility for his own intellectual progress.

4. The fourth general principle is that it should give students an enlargement of life. This involves the whole field of the arts, which includes literature, music, architecture, sculpture and painting.

Upon the foregoing principles the following requirements for the freshman and sophomore years have been inaugurated:

FRESHMAN YEAR

First Semester		*Second Semester*	
English	3 hours	English, (*continued*)	3 hours
Orientation	3 hours	Hygiene	2 hours
Psychology or Bible	3 hours	Bible or psychology	3 hours
History, American or European	3 hours	History, (*continued*)	3 hours
Elective	3 hours	Elective	3 hours

Students who take psychology the first semester take Bible the second semester, and *vice versa*. The Bible course is a study of the life of Christ.

SOPHOMORE YEAR

First Semester		*Second Semester*	
Science	5 hours	Science (*con't.*)	5 hours
Sociology	3 hours	Sociology "	3 hours
Economics	3 hours	Economics "	3 hours
Elective	5 hours	Elective	5 hours

The year of science in the sophomore year is designed to follow the course of orientation taken in the freshman year. The object in this year is to have the student pursue a particular science with laboratory for a full year in order that he may become well acquainted with a given science and its methods and contributions to human problems. In addition to the requirements stated above, each student must have one full year's course in a survey of English literature. The English required in the freshman year is composition.

This program as outlined may be conspicuous for what it has left out as much as for what it has included. It will be noticed that no foreign language or mathematics is required of all students. This does not mean, of course, that there will be no students taking these courses, but they will take them either as electives or as prerequisites for other work. For example, a student majoring in pre-engineering work would be required by his "major" adviser to take the necessary prerequisite courses in mathematics. Likewise, students planning to enter graduate schools for higher degrees are strongly urged to take a foreign language. Some students who intend to teach the languages in secondary schools after graduation elect them. Virtually one fourth of the freshman class of the fall of 1928 elected a language.

For the last two years of the student's work he must select a major field of concentration and devote himself to an intelligent understanding of this field. His field of concentration having been chosen, his specific courses and work will be largely determined for him by his "major" professor.

Homer P. Rainey

Franklin College

QUOTATIONS

EDUCATION IN INDIA

Lord Lytton, president of this year's Conference of Educational Associations, opened the conference on December 31 at University College, London, with an address on "Some Aspects of the Problem of Education in India."

According to the report in the London *Times* he said that his experiences had been limited to one province, Bengal, of which he had been governor for five years—1922–27—and his remarks on education would require modification before they could be applied to other parts of India. The purpose of education, in the sense in which he used the word, was to understand life, to appreciate life, and to make the most of life. In short, it was the complete development of the individual. The first thing that struck him with regard to education in India was the immensity of the problem, the vast field which still remained to be developed. Popular education, as it was understood in this country, universal compulsory education in the schools, had not yet begun. Of the population of 350,000,000 only about 2 per cent. had reached the literary education that was represented by the capacity to read and write. School education in India was available only to those who were rich enough to pay for it, as it was in this country up to the middle of the last century. Further progress could not be made until the well-to-do section of the population was prepared to submit to the taxation necessary to provide schools for the very poor. There were missionary schools and colleges, of which he could not speak too highly, such was the zeal and devotion of the staffs, who carried on their work in their hospitals as well as in their schools, because they loved it and not because they were paid for it; but these schools could not take the place of a state system of education.

The complete neglect of women's education in India explained why the education of men had had so slight an influence upon the social life and customs and general thought of the country. Indians had been coming to our universities for two or three generations; others had been receiving some education in India. One would expect to see some effect of this, but it had been very slight. Why? Most of them had probably read Miss Mayo's "Mother India," which had created such a painful impression among its readers in the West and so much indignation in India. That book was necessarily highly controversial, and he was not going to discuss it. But there was one thing about it with which every one who knew India would, he thought, agree, and that was that the facts with which the book dealt, whether kindly or unkindly, whether accurately or inaccurately, were the strongest possible evidence of the need for education among Indian women. The early marriages which made it difficult for girls to remain at school long enough to receive anything more than the most superficial education, and the purdah system, which kept women secluded in their homes from a very early age, were obvious obstacles to the spread of education, but they were not insuperable obstacles. Whether these customs were desirable, whether they would survive or disappear when women became more educated, he did not know. But if they continued to prove an obstacle to women receiving any education they were indefensible, and the opposition to them would gain momentum year by year from the ever-increasing number of women who were beginning to become emancipated from them. If, however, purdah was held to be an essential feature in Hindu society in Northern India—it did not exist in the South—and if it was to continue in those parts of the country where it existed, it would be necessary for the orthodox section of the community who believed in it to devise an effective machinery for introducing education behind the purdah. Let them think of the opportunity which it afforded for reading. There was no reason why that should not be done. But it was a special problem, and required special attention.

It was really impossible to exaggerate the importance of providing education for women in India. There was nothing else which came anywhere near it in importance, or which would have such far-reaching and incalculable results. The influence of women in Indian homes was enormous—far greater than was the influence of women in the homes of this country. Not only was it supreme with the young children of India; it was almost equally supreme with the men of the household. We were apt to judge India by the men who came to this country and whom we met as students, as officials, or as visitors, and whose speeches and activities after they returned to their own country were reported in the newspapers. But those who lived in India knew that these men had hardly produced any effect upon their own homes, and still less upon the general social life and customs of their country. Those things were still what the women made them. Women's influence on the body politic was like that of the life blood in the human body. It was not seen; but there was not a feature, a limb, an organ, or an activity of the body which escaped its influence. It determined the health of the whole. Even so was the unseen but potent influence of women in the homes of India.

Then there was the important question of the medium of instruction. Was it realized that in India everything was taught in English? The conclusion had been come to in India in recent years that the use of English as a medium of instruction had imposed a great strain upon the minds of the students and detracted from the benefits which they were capable of deriving from their instruction. It would be realized what this meant if it were imagined that in this country we had all to learn everything we were taught—history, geography, mathematics, science—in, say, Japanese, and from English teachers whose command of the Japanese language was by no means perfect. It must also be imagined that hardly any books were available to us on technical subjects in the English language, and that for higher researches into any subject we were dependent upon Japanese books, or books in some other oriental language. He thought we should soon come to the conclusion that what we needed was to be taught elementary subjects in our own language and to be taught Japanese as a special subject by qualified teachers, so that we might be able to make use of technical books for our higher studies.

That was the conclusion which the authorities in India had come to with regard to English; and his last act as chancellor of Calcutta University was to sanction an amendment of the matriculation regulations, so as to make the vernacular the medium of instruction and examination, and at the same time to require a higher standard of English as a special subject. It would be some years before these regulations came into operation, as an entirely new set of text-books had to be prepared; but when that was done it would mean that all teachers of general subjects would have to know the vernacular language, and that there would be a great demand for competent teachers to teach English as a special subject.

REPORTS

RESIDENTIAL HOUSES AT HARVARD UNIVERSITY[1]

A FEELING has long been prevalent that the increase in numbers of the larger American colleges brings with it disadvantages. The personal contact of teacher and student becomes more difficult. Large communities tend to cliques based upon similarity of origin and upon wealth, a tendency that produced at Harvard the "Gold Coast," as the private dormitories on Mt. Auburn Street were called until they were bought by the university. Great masses of unorganized young men, not yet engaged in definite careers, are prone to super-

[1] From advance sheets of the annual report of President A. Lawrence Lowell to the Board of Overseers.

ficial currents of thought and interest, to the detriment of the personal intellectual progress that ought to dominate mature men seeking higher education. This drift of the American college has been the basis of much of the criticism leveled from outside, and of the dissatisfaction on the part of those intrusted with its management. It is the cause of the exaggerated importance of the secondary interests as compared with the primary object of education; of what Woodrow Wilson, when president of Princeton, called the overshadowing of the main tent by the side-shows. If this is less true of Harvard to-day than in the past, it is because of endeavors to make the intellectual life of the students more serious and more interesting. But the very fact that we have made some progress is a reason why we should be in a position to make a further advance in the same direction.

One of the first steps was an attempt to loosen the associations of origin, and give a chance to natural affinities, by the creation of the freshman halls, an effort supplemented at about the same time by Lothrop Withington, of the class of 1911, in bringing his classmates into the Yard for their senior year. This last has now served its purpose and may be replaced by a better plan. On the scholastic side progress took the form of requiring every student to concentrate his studies in some definite field selected by himself, while not wholly neglecting any of the great subjects of human thought. This was followed by the general examination and tutors in the student's field of concentration. That the system has stimulated effort and interest on the part of students can not now be doubted. It is, indeed, clearly shown by the result of the reading periods, which have been both another step in the path of developing self-education as the only enduring basis of intellectual growth, and a measure of the progress in this direction so far achieved.

Meanwhile, the question of dividing the college into residential groups was not left out of sight. For a long time it had been debated by people both inside and outside the faculties of American colleges.

The conception of an ultimate formation of residential groups has been kept in mind, the construction of new dormitories having been so planned that they might be useful in that connection.

Such was the situation when the anonymous benefactor, who had independently formed the opinion that a subdivision of large colleges into residential groups was of vital importance, came to Cambridge. He believed, as we did, that the division should not be based upon differences in the subjects studied or the career the members intended to enter; that, on the contrary, men interested in various fields of thought should be thrown together with a view of promoting a broad and humane culture. He indicated that if the university would commit itself to the whole project, to be carried out in such time and ways as seemed to it wise, he would give the amount necessary. Thereupon the faculty of arts and sciences passed unanimously the following vote:

> The faculty welcomes the idea of dividing the undergraduate body into social units of appropriate size and rejoices that means have been found to carry out this plan.

The estimates are now being prepared. It is proposed to build two such houses at once, adding the remainder as soon as the first have become established, and using for the purpose existing college dormitories. Naturally the details have not yet been worked out, but certain general principles would seem to flow from the object in view. The aim is to bring into contact a body of students with diverse interests who will by attrition provoke one another to think on many subjects, and will have a corporate spirit. For this purpose their number must be considerable without being so large as to subdivide itself into smaller self-sufficient groups. Until tested by trial it is impossible to be sure what the best number will prove to be, but taking the experience in the colleges of Oxford and Cambridge, and allowing for the differences between English and American youth, it has seemed that the right number will be between two and three hundred, varying somewhat with the conditions, but averaging not far from two hundred and fifty.

So far as subjects of concentration, pecuniary means and residence in different parts of the country are concerned, each house should be as nearly as possible a cross-section of the college.

The success of each house, and hence of the whole plan, will no doubt depend largely upon the selection of the students for membership. This is a human problem, not one of philosophy or physics. It can not be done well by rules, however apparently logical or rational, for it is largely a question of matching, or rather not mismatching, temperaments. Much discretion must be left to the authorities of the house, much voluntary choice to the students themselves, some influence to the upper classmen already members; and of course the plan requires for success that membership should be desired.

Certain misconceptions are sure to arise. One is that Harvard College is to be superseded or rivaled. This has no foundation. Save so far as tutors may reside, or have their conference rooms, in a house instead of in a lecture hall or administrative building, there will be no change whatever in the methods of teaching, which will remain wholly under the direction of the faculty of arts and sciences. The plan is expected to give an additional stimulus to scholarship and intellectual interest, but otherwise it is not an educational but a social one. The discipline of the dean's office and the administrative board for deficient scholarship will remain unimpaired.

To a few men the plan may not offer any benefits that they do not now enjoy. To far the greater number of undergraduates it should bring serious advantages, part of which would accrue to all large colleges, and part apply to special conditions here.

The plan makes possible more personal attention to the individual. This is an end for which all colleges are striving, and which is attained here when the student comes to the dean's office; but that means in most cases after he is in some trouble. For the young man who is liable to fall behind, or who is not developing his own natural gifts and qualities, foresight is better than cure. In that way the benefits of the small college may be combined with the rich offerings of a great university.

Then such a residential house, where members of the three upper classes live together, gives an opportunity for contact in cultured surroundings of younger with older undergraduates, and of both with instructors. This happens here now only to a limited extent; yet it is an extremely valuable factor in a true education. Strangers sometimes refer to the conversation about intellectual things among our college students, and so far as it exists it supplements and enhances formal instruction; but a house of this kind could not fail to promote it with all men not destitute of mental appetite.

A number of houses so formed would appeal to a quality which we have left far too much out of sight in educational discussion; that is the spirit of emulation, characteristic of youth in all its endeavors. The neglect of this quality explains in part the exaggerated interest in athletics which have been organized by the students themselves and therefore based on competition, as compared with academic studies, conducted by faculties and containing little spirit of emulation.

EDUCATIONAL RESEARCH AND STATISTICS

VARIABILITY OF INDIVIDUAL PERFORMANCE

A Preliminary Report

It is well known that an individual does not perform any kind of task equally well at all times. Baseball players have their good and bad days; a crack pitcher may pitch ten games in his best form and then go to pieces, so that for days, or even weeks, he is not allowed to pitch a game, and that for no apparent reasons. That is, he is variable in his performance. But this is not equally true of all players; some are known to be steady and consistent, while others are brilliant at their best and pretty bad at their worst.

A priori it seems highly probable that something of this sort is true of people in general, no matter what is the task to which they are set. All are variable as performers, but they differ in degree of variability.

Some interesting questions arise: How nearly uniform in their performance are the most consistent, and how greatly do the most inconsistent vary in this respect? How is this variability distributed in a population? The purpose of this paper is to report an investigation which leads to tentative answers to these questions. The investigation to be reported was suggested by an effort of one of the authors to standardize further a set of tests in arithmetic. To make clear the basis of the present study, a digression seems necessary. In 1924 "The Lennes Practice and Test Sheets" in arithmetic were published. These sheets contain thirty-two tests (in the first edition, on which this investigation is based, there were thirty-three) for each grade, to be given throughout the year, approximately one test each week, except in some odd weeks at the beginning and end of school terms; nearly all these tests are short six-minute tests. There is a record-card for each child on which all his test scores for the year are recorded. This record may be made either graphically or in numbers; in practice they were nearly all made graphically. Many thousands of these cards were collected from schools in various parts of the country. On looking them over, one is struck by the fact that consistency of performance differs greatly. On many, the majority of them, the record goes across the card in a fairly regular line; some of these show improvement and others the reverse, while many remain at about the same level; but the whole record moves in a comparatively regular fashion. Some are *highly* consistent and the record is very nearly represented by a straight line. At the other extreme there are records which zigzag from the upper to the lower edge of the card; the achievement for one week may be less than one half as great as that of the week preceding or following.

This fact suggested the following statistical study: "Assign to each record a number representing its degree of variability and study the resulting array of variabilities."

In this study scores of tests in the four fundamental operations on integers only are used, the other scores being omitted. Furthermore, the test scores have been segregated into groups so that one group contains scores in addition only, one group contains scores in subtraction, and so on. Pupils' variability in performing any one of these operations is the subject-matter of this study. This avoids the possibility that the variability that is studied may be due wholly or in part to the different proficiency of some in the different operations; that is, it is likely that some pupils will have relatively high scores in one operation when compared with their scores in one of the others.

The sheets in the Test and Practice sheets are numbered consecutively from one to ninety-six, thirty-three of these being tests and the rest practice work. In the sixth grade, for example, standard tests in the operations on integers occur as follows: Addition, sheets 3, 21, 42, 54, 66, 75; Subtraction, sheets 6, 24, 48, 72; Multiplication, sheets 9, 39, 45, 63, 83, 96; Division, sheets 12, 33, 51, 57, 69, 86. In this grade the remaining eleven tests contain operations in decimals and common fractions. The general distribution throughout the year of tests in the different operations is of this type in all the grades studied.

The study has been carried through for each of the grades from four to eight inclusive but a detailed report is given here on grade seven only.

Certain precautions were taken in selecting the records to be used: To avoid biased selection no record has been used unless the records for a whole class were available. Cards showing absences at one or more of the tests were usually rejected and all the others from that class were used. On looking over a set of cards giving the scores of a class it occasionally became evident that for some reason the scores for the class as a whole were very uneven; thus the scores for the first test might be unduly low or exceptionally high. This was also true, though much less frequently, of later tests. No doubt such discrepancies were due to general confusion or incorrect timing. In such cases the records for the whole class were rejected. The final set for grade seven consisted of 135 complete records.

The tests had been standardized with care, using the results obtained by investigators such as Courtis and others, supplemented by much less extensive tests carried out for the special purpose of standardizing this particular set. The plan was to have the tests at the beginning of the seventh grade a little below the standard for the sixth grade (there is some forgetting and slowing up during the summer vacation), and to have them rise at an even rate to reach standard for grade seven by the end of the year. To test this standardization for the scores used, the total of the 135 scores for each test was found. With perfect standardization and uniform average reaction on the part of the pupils, these sums should be equal. From this there was found to be some deviation, amounting in one or two extreme cases to nearly 15 per cent., the lowest total being used as the base. In all the scores studied (in all the grades) there is an interesting seasonal variation. There are three regions that show relatively high scores, the first occurring in the first two months of the school year, the second in January and February, and the third in the last part of the year. The two lows come before Christmas, and in March and early April. This seasonal variation appears persistently in all the grades and in each of the four operations studied for each grade. That is, there are twenty different sets of totals in each of which it appears, though of course in varying extent. It is very likely, therefore, that there is in reality such a seasonal variation in pupils' performance.

The raw scores were corrected by using a multiple for the scores in each test, so that the sums of the corrected scores, which were finally used, are practically equal.

In grade seven, in which there are six tests in addition, we find in these corrected scores records like the following:

SAMPLE SCORES

A	B						C	D	E	F
47	95	101	94	104	94	93	4	7	93	89
61	119	135	141	134	141	131	4	10	95	84
67	75	85	79	75	79	67	5	9	92	79
89	89	68	63	75	63	93	15	21	80	68
127	89	101	94	119	47	106	16	48	78	39
2	89	68	126	119	79	106	18	30	78	54
98	89	34	63	75	63	80	25	44	76	38
106	75	34	31	45	63	53	25	55	67	41
96	45	17	16	30	63	53	37	50	60	25
23	60	34	79	75	16	80	38	71	62	20
78	30	101	47	30	63	40	38	87	57	30

Column A gives serial numbers of pupils; columns B give the six consecutive scores in the addition tests; column C gives the pupils' average deviation in per cents. from their "trend"; column D gives extreme deviation in per cents. from trend; column E gives average score as per cents. of the highest; and column F gives lowest score as per cents. of the highest.

The "trend" was obtained by taking the average of the first three scores and of the last three and drawing a straight line through the resulting points.

These sample scores show typical variations, ranging from the least variable to some that are among the most highly variable.

Before giving the principal results that have been obtained, we will raise some questions: How are we to account for some of the variations that appear in the samples given? How are we to account for the score of 101 obtained by No. 78 in his second test? Did he cheat? There does not seem to be much chance for that in a six-minute test. Was extra time allowed? We only know that the pupils in the same class did not show any such variation in general; on the whole their scores on the second test were not noticeably higher than in the other tests. The score of 63 in the fifth test seems to show that "in a pinch" this pupil can do better than he usually does. But frankly we are puzzled. Why did No. 23 fall down so badly in his second and fifth tests? Is he one of that kind who have a poor day every so often? No. 106 shows interesting variations for which we do not know the reason, as does also No. 2. In any event, there is certainly great difference in variability between numbers 47, 61, and 67 on the one hand, and numbers 106, 23, and 78 on the other.

The following were computed for each record in each of the four operations:

(a) Each pupil's average deviation from trend as per cent. of the trend (Table I).

(b) Each pupil's extreme deviation from trend as per cent. of the trend (Table II).

(c) Each pupil's mean score as per cent. of his highest score (Table III).

(d) Each pupil's lowest score as per cent. of his highest score (Table IV).

(e) Total frequencies of scores where each score is expressed as per cent. of the pupil's highest score (Table V).

All percentages are given to the nearest whole per cent.

Which of these numbers is the best index of variability? Or is it possible that some combination of these would be a better index than any one of them? This problem will be faced again in our projected continuation of this study. It is perfectly clear that statistical analysis of our data beyond what has already been made might give information not yet obtained.

Using the average deviation from trend as a measure of variability we have the following arrays for the 135 pupils of grade seven:

TABLE I

Range in Per cents.	Frequencies			
	Add.	Sub.	Mult.	Div.
0– 5	6	15	11	11
6–10	28	11	31	9
11–15	40	28	33	31
16–20	27	18	21	26
21–25	17	17	14	16
26–30	6	14	6	13
31–35	1	7	10	6
36–40	4	10	4	6
41–45	0	4	1	4
46–50	3	4	0	3
51–55	0	2	1	0
56–60	1	0	0	2
61–65	2	1	1	3
66–70	0	1	0	2
Above 70	0	3	2	3

The first column shows the range of variation, and the next four columns show the number of scores which fall within each range in each operation. Thus in the addition score there are six records whose mean variation from trend is 5 per cent. or less, 28 records whose mean variation from trend are from 6 to 10 per cent., and so on.

The question arises: Are those who are variable in one operation also variable in the other operations? To answer this question correlations were computed for variabilities in pairs of subjects. These were all found to be positive, varying from twenty-five to thirty-four. That is, they show a slightly lower degree of correlation than parent and child show in physical traits.

The following table gives the frequencies of extreme variation from trend in each subject, expressed as per cents. of trend:

TABLE II

Range in Per cents.	Frequencies			
	Add.	Sub.	Mult.	Div.
0– 5	0	8	1	6
6–10	10	9	14	5
11–15	8	12	21	6
16–20	18	16	16	17
21–25	18	18	16	27
26–30	20	19	14	15
31–35	11	14	13	15
36–40	13	3	10	7
41–45	6	9	4	7
46–50	9	6	6	3
51–55	8	6	4	6
56–60	2	7	4	4
61–65	4	2	1	2
66–70	2	1	4	2
Above 70	6	5	7	13

The following table gives frequencies when each pupil's mean score is expressed as per cent. of his highest score:

TABLE III

Range	Frequencies			
	Add.	Subt.	Mult.	Div.
41– 45	0	1	0	1
46– 50	0	4	2	4
51– 55	2	2	3	1
56– 60	4	1	2	4
61– 65	10	7	4	5
66– 70	17	10	10	6
71– 75	18	19	19	23
76– 80	23	20	18	22
81– 85	33	31	26	27
86– 90	16	22	23	27
91– 95	8	14	22	4
96–100	2	4	6	9

From this table we see, for instance, if a test is taken at random from the least variable 20 per cent., the chance is even that the score in addition will be 86 per cent. or more of the pupil's highest score; while if a test is taken at random from the most variable 20 per cent., the chance is even that the score will be less than 69 per cent. of the pupil's highest score. If a test is taken at random from the most variable 10 per cent., the chance is even that the score will be less than 65 per cent. of the pupil's highest score.

The following table gives frequencies when each pupil's lowest score is expressed as per cents. of his highest score:

TABLE IV

Range in Per cents.	Frequencies			
	Add.	Sub.	Mult.	Div.
0– 5	1	1	3	12
6– 10	0	0	0	0
11– 15	2	1	1	0
16– 20	1	0	0	2
21– 25	4	0	5	3
26– 30	4	4	4	2
31– 35	6	3	5	5
36– 40	7	12	2	5
41– 45	11	10	3	7
46– 50	16	4	10	8
51– 55	11	15	13	17
56– 60	18	12	8	9
61– 65	16	13	14	9
66– 70	9	14	15	17
71– 75	11	20	11	23
76– 80	8	1	19	3
81– 85	7	6	11	5
86– 90	3	9	10	4
91– 95	0	5	1	1
96–100	0	5	0	3

From this table we see, for instance, that in addition, for the least variable 10 per cent. there is no score more than 79 per cent. below the pupil's highest score; while for the most variable 10 per cent., there is one chance in six that the score is below 34 per cent. of the pupil's highest score. For the least variable 20 per cent. there is no score below 71 per cent. of the pupil's highest score, while for the most variable 20 per cent. there is one chance in six that the score is below 41 per cent. of the pupil's highest score.

The following table shows the frequencies of all the scores in addition, when each score is expressed as per cents. of the pupil's highest score:

TABLE V

Range in Per cents.	0–5	6–10	11–15	16–20	21–25	26–30	
Frequencies	3	0	3	2	3	10	
R.	31–35	36–40	41–45	46–50	51–55	56–60	61–65
F.	9	10	23	21	31	53	44
R.	66–70	71–75	76–80	81–85	86–90	91–95	96–100
F.	44	89	65	81	84	67	168

The large number in the interval 96–100 is, of course, explained by the fact that each record (135 of them) contains at least one score listed at 100, namely, the highest score in the record. Of the total number of scores (810) 10 per cent. are below 51 per cent. of the pupil's highest score, 20 per cent. are below 60 per cent. of his highest score, 30 per cent. are below 70 per cent. of his highest score, 40 per cent. are below 75 per cent. of his highest score, and half of all the scores are below 81 per cent. of the pupil's highest score.

This investigation is subject to many qualifications. We do not know to what extent the time-limits set were enforced, and we do not know how far other conditions that are necessary for trustworthy results were observed. Our only checks on these are noted above. All the tests studied are short six-minute tests; longer tests might give different results. In a continuation of this investigation, which we expect to carry on during the coming school year, some of these defects will be remedied. For one thing we shall have eight fourteen-minute tests in some grades. A number of competent principals in different schools have undertaken to cooperate and to carry out our instructions faithfully. They have further undertaken to study individual cases of more than ordinary variability. To what extent is variability due to variation in health, to home disturbances, to changes in the pupil's social relations within the school? In general, to what extent is variability due to adventitious causes and to what extent is it due to the inherent qualities of the individual? These are questions on which we hope to get more definite light.

One reason for undertaking this rather laborious investigation, involving, as it will during the coming year, handling the records of some thirty thousand tests (about twenty tests for each of about one thousand five hundred pupils) is its obvious bearing on the general question of individual variability from time to time, and the distribution of such variability in a school population. When we know more about these matters, we shall have serious suggestions as to the validity of single tests of any kind.

N. J. LENNES
IRA B. FEE
MISSOULA, MONTANA

SCHOOL AND SOCIETY

EDITED BY J. McKEEN CATTELL

WITH WHICH IS COMBINED THE

EDUCATIONAL REVIEW

EDITED BY WILLIAM McANDREW

Volume XXIX | Saturday, March 2, 1929 | Number 740

EDUCATION: WHAT PROGRAM? WHAT PRICE?[1]

By Dr. FRANK D. BOYNTON

PRESIDENT, DEPARTMENT OF SUPERINTENDENCE, NATIONAL EDUCATION ASSOCIATION

It would be impossible for any one with a spark of imagination to stand unmoved before this assemblage. We are gathered here from the four corners of this great republic, adventurers in the continuously creative enterprise of developing and perfecting the American public school. Four days are to be devoted to the consideration of this fundamental proposition. If as a result we return to our classrooms and offices with a clearer vision of the meaning of our tasks, a firmer grasp upon the practical methods by which the end sought is to be attained, a renewed courage and determination to achieve, then this meeting will have served its purpose.

But before we enter upon the quest for the best practical means for securing these ends, let us look for a little at the thesis which we have chosen as the control theme for this convention, "How Can the Public Schools Better Serve Democracy, Increasingly Produce a Higher Type of Citizen?" In this one terse sentence we are calling public attention to the ultimate goal of American education, stating a major objective of the church and expressing the hope of good citizens everywhere.

Recognition of the value of the work of our public schools by great leaders is not lacking. President-elect Herbert Hoover says: "The progress of the race is upon the marching feet of healthy, instructed children," and that "if we were to suppress our educational system for a single generation the equipment would decay, the most of our people would die of starvation, and intellectually and spiritually we would slip back four thousand years in human progress." About a year ago, Roger Babson set down to the credit of the American public school system the following credit-results. Mr. Babson says:

> During the past twenty years the public schools have practically eliminated illiteracy and materially raised the general level of intelligence;
>
> They have supervised the health and safety of the nation's children to a much greater extent than ever before and to their great good;
>
> They have absorbed the great flood of immigration which inundated the country, and kept it American;
>
> Through courses in vocational education, they have prepared young people for specific trades and have increased the earning power of those thus educated;
>
> Our great advance in material prosperity can be ascribed in part to the higher educational levels

[1] Address delivered at first general session of Cleveland convention of the department of superintendence, National Education Association, February 25.

and thinking to which the work of the public schools has raised the masses.

Quotations of like import could be multiplied indefinitely. But the important thing to know is not that the service of the school is valuable, but how valuable it is. What measure of value can be applied to an institution that has practically banished illiteracy; looked after the physical well-being of 28,000,000 children; raised the level of living and thinking; increased the earning and purchasing power of the worker, thereby creating and building up a home market which consumes 90 per cent. of the product of farm and factory; and despite the flood of immigration kept the nation American? He is a brave man, or a fool, who ventures to place a money value upon such a service.

No considerable fraction of the public would deny the desirability of public education or the right of every child to some amount and some kind of education. The question is not "Shall we have public education at public expense?" That question is settled permanently. The question is rather "How much education and what kind shall we have and how much shall we pay for it? Are we trying to buy too much and too many kinds for too many people, and are we paying too much for what we are getting?" These are the questions the critics of the schools are asking. For it has become the fashion of late for certain speakers and writers on taxation and public expenditures to point an admonishing finger at the steadily rising cost of public education, questioning the value of much that has gone to enrich the curriculum, and leading the taxpayer to regard himself as the victim of ruthless exploitation at the hands of the professional educator.

But who is it that bewails the high cost of public education, declaring that we are trying to teach too many people too many things; whose heart is it that so yearns with sympathy for the overburdened taxpayer and who sees in the reduction of school costs the easiest road to his relief? Is it the working man living in a small rented home striving to support a large family on a small income and struggling against the approaching day when his older children must give up school and join the ranks of the wage-earners? Is it the less numerous middle-class worker, owning his modest home, whose children can look forward with a fair degree of assurance to attending the high school for a season? No, not these. They know that in education lies the hope of realizing for their children what circumstances have denied themselves; that through the American public school runs the straightest road to success and a more equal distribution of the world's wealth.

Who is it, then, that wishes to curtail the school budget and reduce the opportunities offered accordingly? It is that small but powerful and active class, made up in part of those who believe apparently that education, above the line of illiteracy, is the exclusive right of a few select souls and who claim it for their own by a sort of divine right bestowed by heredity and wealth, forgetting that they themselves and their prestige are the product of that democracy which they now desire to strangle; a class made up in part of these, and in part, also, of those gold-greedy go-getters who have always been willing to rob childhood of its birthright and to coin it into coupons, in order that, with unconscious irony, they may build monuments to themselves upon college campuses. These are our "conscientious" objectors to the school budget. But these enemies of universal education have been met before in the fight for free elementary, and again for free secondary schools and state universities and were defeated. Once more they are riding to a fall.

For see what has happened. The American public school is not something fixed, static, unchanging; it is a growth, reflecting the growth, the prosperity, the changing social, domestic and economic arrangements of the national life. More accurately and completely than any other institution it mirrors the national ideals and aspirations. The traveler in Europe on entering a town first sees the great cathedral; in America he sees the schoolhouse. It is ubiquitous and dominant. It gathers into itself an ever larger share of the life of our youth. Now it is reaching out for the adult also, offering him a share of its wealth.

At the time of the adoption of the constitution the average length of attendance upon school for the individual was 60 days; in 1920 it was 1,200 days, the highest average length of school life for a whole population ever attained by any nation. In 1775 the elementary curriculum consisted of the three R's with spelling and the Bible added. Fifty years later grammar, geography and bookkeeping had been added. Another twenty-five years and we had added history and begun the use of object lessons. By 1875 the "frills" of the previous fifty years had passed to the stage of "essentials," grammar, geography and history holding secure places in the program while new "frills" appeared in the form of civics, music, drawing and health education. By 1925, one hundred and fifty years after the beginning, the curriculum included not five but twenty-three subjects.

As it stands to-day, the program reflects and always has not so much the abstract theories of educators as to what constitutes correct educational procedure as it does the popular conception of what constitutes a satisfactory school. When the public school idea was first thought out, the home was the primary and authoritative institution and the most interesting. In large measure it was independent of all other institutions. The art of living out of paper bags and tin cans had not yet emerged. If the grocery boy overslept the family could still have breakfast. The railroad, the telephone, the factory, the department store and the bakery had not then made of the home a shell. The school when it came was merely a supplementary institution created by the home for the performance of certain of its own functions which it chose to delegate but for which it recognized its responsibility. Around the fireside the family gathered evenings; friends were entertained in the home and welcome. We had not learned then to rent halls for entertaining and to drive out to dinner in luxurious automobiles. The home designed the family clothes and made them; it did the canning and preserving; there was always something creative to be done there; and because of these things it was the most interesting and best-beloved place in the world—a place about which poets sang.

As our social and industrial organization has grown more complex the former activities of the home have been delegated one after another to other agencies, and the responsibilities which the home once bore have been definitely placed upon the shoulders of other institutions, principally the factory, the church and the school. The result has been the gradual transformation of the school from a place of merely training in the essentials of academic learning for the children of such parents as were rich enough to dispense with their labor, to great service stations, tax-supported and buttressed by child labor and compulsory attendance laws in every state in the nation, dedicated to the service of all the children of all the people. A service program, therefore, has been built up which accurately reflects the changes in our domestic, social and economic life. There is not a subject in the program but has found its place there as a result of either mandatory or permissive legislation or of pressure upon school officers by organized, active, persistent, local groups. Our present program, therefore, is the people's own, worked out and adopted in response to their demands. As it has been made, so it will be continuously remade—changing, developing, expanding to meet the needs of a changing social order.

This does not mean, however, that the schools will respond to the demands of every group that conceives the idea of furthering its own selfish interests or disseminating its pet propaganda by implanting its particular dogmas in the youthful mind. Our critics say that we are not teaching the children to read and write and spell correctly, but fail to show how this is to be done better by adding to our present program the items that they propose—instruction in aeronautics, in conservation of natural resources, in fire and accident prevention, in thrift and economy, in automobile driving and the theory of the gas engine, in music appreciation through radio broadcasting, in moral and religious education, in garment and dressmaking, in cherry and egg harvesting, in the advantages of private ownership and the failure of public ownership of public utilities (the glitter of whose gold has tripped some of the weaker brothers of the craft and tempted school board members), in the extended use of rubber in industry, in the best way to solve the liquor problem.

The schools should remain closed to all illegitimate demands seeking to further private or group interests; but it is obvious that if the public school is to serve the national life to the extent of its potentialities, it has a program of expansion ahead, and expansion to be achieved without loss to educational efficiency. But here is a danger to be guarded against, a danger frequently more apparent than real.

The educational efficiency of American schools, for example, has been criticized as being below that of Europe. Let the friends of American education remember that there is no European system that is not a class system based upon privilege. So severe is the cutting in the European schools at the fifth, eighth and twelfth grade levels as to indicate clearly the European belief that to the few belongs the right to be educated. Prussia has fewer than 9 per cent. of those of secondary school age in attendance upon these schools; England has fewer than 14 per cent.; while in the United States 52 per cent. of those of high-school age are in attendance upon secondary education. Thus we reverse the figures of Europe as we reverse its objectives; and our upper quarter, man for man, equals any European class in age, mental power and attainment. Europe's educational system has been unable during the centuries to get wooden shoes off the feet of the common people or thatch from the roofs of their homes or to reduce its standing armies which make it an armed camp in times of peace. When every European child stands equal to every other European child before the schoolmaster's desk, Europe will have taken the longest step toward international peace and good-will in its history, a step longer than has ever been suggested by her statesmen. The difference in the level of living in Europe and America is accurately measured by the system of education in each.

Expansion without the loss of educational efficiency has been achieved, and this policy must continue in order to meet the changes in our expanding national life. Never in the history of the world has any people been the beneficiary of a material prosperity so great and so widely diffused. More and more the burden of assisting in family support is being lifted from young shoulders. The old theory of the vicious circle with its underprivileged classes is being replaced by the newer philosophy of the never-ending spiral of expanding opportunities to the end that poverty, the last stand of vice and crime, like illiteracy, shall have its hold broken everywhere. Ever more the demand for universal free secondary and higher education grows insistent. "Maintained equality of opportunity" is a phrase made familiar to the ears of the people by the president-elect during the late campaign. This phrase means, he tells us,

> that there should be no child in America who has not been born and who does not live under sound conditions of health; who does not have full opportunity for education from the kindergarten to the university; who is not free from injurious labor; who does not have stimulation to ambition to the fullest of his or her capacities.

Continuing this thought, Mr. Hoover says:

> If we are to maintain America as the land of opportunity where every boy and girl may have the chance to climb to that position to which his ability and character entitle him, we shall need to be increasingly on our guard. If I could drive the full meaning and importance of maintained equality of opportunity into the very consciousness of the American people, I would feel I had made some contribution to American life. It is the most precious of our possessions that the windows of every home shall look out upon unlimited hope.

But, my brethren, do not be deceived. Greed of gain will contest every inch of the way to the realization of this goal.

The same industrial and economic changes that are gathering the children out of the shops and factories and pouring them into the schools are creating for their parents a growing margin of leisure whose proper use constitutes a major social problem. Already the more ambitious and intelligent elements of the population from whose shoulders the machine has lifted a portion of the age-old burden of drudgery, are turning to the public school with the demand that for them also, through provision for adult education and recreation, the way be opened to the more abundant life. Here is a new problem, calling for a new educational procedure and technique, a problem that must be met and solved if the added leisure is to be the blessing hoped for. Already the socially destructive forces are finding here an enlarged field for their operation. Already the schoolmen are fighting a public opinion set up for the moron. Birth control artists have furnished the information which makes sex indulgence for youth as safe as kissing; discredited judges are spewing the sewage of their courts through salacious magazines until our news stands groan under the weight of putrefaction which they contain; our theaters aim at a sex appeal so crass at times as to disgust the guilty; the press, civilization's greatest agent, is becoming the chief source of the criminal's information, where he finds himself daily featured upon the front page; our churches are clinging to man-made creeds hundreds of years old while their doors are closing rather than devoting themselves to interpreting the times to a befuddled and bewildered multitude. I am taking no delight in writing this paragraph nor am I shirking my share of the responsibility for the condition mentioned. What I am trying to do is to draw a picture of the conditions which schoolmen are called upon to combat; to indicate, if only roughly, the character of the defense upon which we must rely, namely, a greatly enlarged school program which shall call to its aid in ever larger measure the cultural resources which civilization has slowly built up for its defense and perpetuation—physical and health programs, science, technology, art, music, literature which records the march of the soul, the drama—and shall place them all freely at the service of the people; to cultivate a changed attitude toward the church and what is expected of the press; and to plead for the seeing eye and the understanding heart wherever the question of expenditure for school purposes is under discussion.

For rest assured the cost of maintaining the public school will be and should be a steadily mounting sum. Our population is rapidly increasing and the demands for an expanding program as herein set forth are discouraging indices to those looking for a reduction. Can the cost be borne? How are we spending our annual income estimated by federal authority to exceed ninety billions? According to federal authority we are spending out of each earned dollar 24½ cents for necessities; 22 cents for luxuries; 11 cents for investment; 8½ cents for crime; 4½ cents for government, local, state and national; waste 14 cents; miscellaneous 13½ cents; 1½ cents on education, and ¾ of a cent on religion and philanthropy. In 1927 we added fifteen hundred millionaires to our already handsome total, so we were told by the Treasury Department. Without taking any of the joy out of life is it not possible to double the amount expended for education and religion twice by a reduction of the waste and still be a long way from an economic breakdown from these two causes?

Like a dinner, a school program costs in proportion to the service. Recently in a city where the cost of schools was under criticism by the Tax Dodgers League the sum of $175,000 was voted for a snake house without arousing protest. We complain about and sometimes eliminate the cost of athletics from the school program and at the same time maintain municipal golf courses and tennis courts and swimming pools. Each state is under constitutional mandate to maintain a system of free public schools; but there is nothing in the constitution of any state requiring it to maintain a system of pleasure roads through its mountains, or a state fair, or fish hatcheries, or pleasure parks and camping sites for the sportsman tourist and the gentleman of leisure. I am offering no objection to these activities of the state. I approve them since they help the people to live larger and better lives, the objectives of our existence. But what I am objecting to is any curtailment in the expenditures for education, the most important the community, state and nation makes, excepting where it can be shown by the friends of American education to be a wise economy which can be effected without abridging educational opportunity for any one.

Upon the principle of the equal right of every individual to "life, liberty and the pursuit of happiness" this government was founded. This conception of the right of the individual to equality of opportunity, which does not mean the same opportunity necessarily, is unique and fundamental to our whole scheme of national life. To preserve this principle inviolate and to train each individual for such efficiency—civic, economic, moral, political—as his capacity makes possible, is the primary function of education in this great democracy we call America.

We live in proportion to our ability to respond to our environment. Education multiplies the points of contact with environment; trains man to interpret, to modify and, in a measure, to control environment; and leads him upward from savagery toward his Maker. Through education we have discarded the strong-back method of advancing civilization—the method which reared the pyramids and built the ancient temples. Through education we have lifted the burden from the sweating backs of men. Through education we have raised the standard of living; enlarged the circle of those who can eat white bread till it circumnavigates the globe; and have made the bathtub, once a luxury in the homes of the rich, a health necessity in the homes of the poor. Through education we erect our sky-scrapers, span rivers, bore through mountains, annihilate distance, reduce the ravages of disease and distribute more equally the blessings of prosperity. Through education we are bringing nearer a realization of the brotherhood of man and are welding the nations of earth into one great family. Through education our lamp of reason is lighted and set in the candlestick to give light to all the house. No longer is it hidden under the bushel of superstition and fear.

Each year the march of the nation's war heroes toward the setting sun increases apace. I wonder sometimes if on their westward march they pause for a moment to catch a glimpse of the New Grand Army of the Republic, an army whose line, marching in "fours" past a given point, would be paralleled by the children of the front ranks before the rear "fours" could pass the reviewing stand; an army marching against the citadels of ignorance and superstition and race hatred, upholding the traditions and defending the ideals of the republic they love, an army gathering every school day from hill and dale, from city and village, from the farm, the workshop, the mine, from industry and commerce, with the blood of the Occident and Orient coursing through its veins, speaking one language, loving one flag, destined in each of the forty-eight states of this great American league of nations to become citizens, not subjects, masters, not servants; an army trained to useful and intelligent citizenship and dedicated to the task of making a better to-day than yesterday, and a to-morrow better than either; an army whose proud accomplishments in the past and whose promise for the future lend glory to the wisdom and leadership of the nation's founders; an army whose high destiny lays upon every American citizen a sacred obligation to support to the limit of his power this stronghold of our democracy, this bulwark of our free institutions, the pride of the republic—the American public school.

EDUCATIONAL EVENTS

THE FIFTH INTERNATIONAL CONFERENCE OF THE NEW EDUCATION FELLOWSHIP

THE Fifth International Conference of The New Education Fellowship is to be held at Elsinore, Denmark, from August 8 to 21. The speakers include Professor Franz Cizek, Dr. O. Pfister, Dr. Maria Montessori, Dr. Ovide Decroley, Dr. Paul Dengler, Professor William Boyd, Dr. Adolphe Ferriere, Dr. Elizabeth Rotten, Miss Helen Parkhurst, Dr. Raup and Rabindranath Tagore.

The American delegation is being formed by the American Advisory Committee, of which Dr. William Kilpatrick, of Columbia University, is president, and Dr. Harold Rugg, of the Lincoln School, is chairman. The delegation is being limited so that it will not be disproportionate to those of other countries. To insure representation of the several American points of view the committee will review applications for membership.

Study groups are now being formed in different parts of the country for people wishing to make a comparative survey of the progressive movement at home and abroad. Outlines for study both for individual members of the delegation and for study groups have been set up under the direction of Dr. Thomas Alexander, of the International Institute of Teachers College, New York.

School visiting groups will be organized for delegates who wish to see European schools in operation preceding the conference. Each group will consist of eight or ten Americans under the leadership of a prominent educator. These expeditions will visit outstanding educational experiments in England, Scotland, Belgium, Holland, Germany, Czechoslovakia, Austria, Russia, Switzerland and Denmark.

Mrs. Marion Beaufait, 20 West 43d Street, New York, N. Y., is executive secretary for the American Advisory Committee.

A BRITISH BRANCH OF THE INTERNATIONAL SCHOOL OF VEDIC

THE International School of Vedic and Allied Research, which has as its object, as reported by the Institute of International Education, "a better understanding and appreciation of the cultures of the East—especially the Vedic culture and others allied to it—and of the West, as mutually complementary and as a vital and practical interest," held a meeting in New York recently at which it was decided to form a British branch of the school.

The school of which the headquarters are in New York consists of four departments, the first of which is concerned with educational exchanges and relations. It arranges for the training of scholars and students from India and other parts of the East in Western methods of study and research in the universities of Europe and America, and in such special subjects as have bearing upon Vedic and allied studies. It also sends Western students to important centers of learning in India, especially to Benares and Kashmir, where special facilities have been provided for resident study. The department arranges for courses of lectures at Western universities and assists in arranging for oriental studies in universities which are without them. Its ultimate aim is the establishment of an American university in India and an Indian university in Europe and one in America.

Another department is devoted to direct research, and is at present issuing a monograph urging the need for a newer presentation of Indian philosophy. The third department is concerned with Sumerian, Semitic, Hittite and other allied studies in relation to Aryan culture; and the fourth is concerned with archeological research.

The director of the school in New York is Pandit Jagadish Chandra Chatterji, formerly director of oriental research and archeology to the Kashmir government. J. G. Phelps Stokes is treasurer. Lord Ronaldshay has accepted the presidency of the London branch; Lord Meston will be treasurer; the Maharajah of Burdwan and Sir Charles Eliot will be vice-presidents, and Major Yeats-Brown and Dr. G. Margulies will be the honorable secretaries.

STATE LAWS RELATING TO COMPULSORY EDUCATION

ACCORDING to Bureau of Education Bulletin, 1928, No. 20, the first state to enact a compulsory education law was Massachusetts in 1852. Since that date each state and the District of Columbia have adopted laws requiring attendance at school; the last state to adopt such a law was Mississippi in 1918.

The average minimum age for compulsory attendance is 7.36. In 28 states, including the District of Columbia, the minimum age is 7; in 18 states it is 8; in 2 states it is 6, and in 1 state, Oregon, the minimum age is 9. There is also variance in the maximum age for compulsory education. Thirty-one states require attendance until 16; five states, until 17; five states, until 18; two states, until 15, and six states, until 14. The average maximum age for compulsory regular school attendance is 16, and the average number of years' attendance required is 8.65. Only one state, Ohio, requires 12 years regular school attendance. The average minimum term of required attendance annually is 7.23 months, though the length of term varies from 38 weeks, in Connecticut, to 3 months in Oklahoma; only one state, Alabama, has no minimum school term.

Part-time, continuation or evening-school education is also compulsory under varying conditions in 31 states for certain persons over 14 years. Compulsory attendance in schools of this character depends upon age, amount of education, necessity for employment during regular school hours for a competence and the maintenance of such schools within reasonable distance.

The minimum amount of education necessary to exempt children of compulsory age from school attendance varies: four states, New York, Nebraska, Nevada and Ohio, require completion of a four-year high-school course; thirty-nine states require completion of elementary-school course, and six states do not specify the amount necessary.

Attendance at school through the fifth grade is the average required throughout the United States for labor permits under present laws. Seventeen states require eighth-grade education for labor permits, while eight states require ability to read and write only, and seven other states appear to have no educational requirements. The ages at which labor permits are granted vary under certain conditions, from 12 to 14; the most usual is 14. Laws which require an eighth-grade education for labor permits appear to be operating satisfactorily.

The tendencies noted with regard to compulsory education are: (1) To lengthen the period of compulsory attendance by making it effective at an earlier and to a later age. (2) To increase the annual required school attendance. (3) To extend the compulsory provisions to include various handicapped children; also to provide parental schools for delinquents. (4) To require more education for exemption and for labor permits. (5) To require public relief to indigent children and subject them more to the attendance law.

THE CHILDREN'S MEDICAL CENTER AT THE UNIVERSITY OF CHICAGO

BUILDING permits have been issued to the University of Chicago that call attention to the full extent of the projected children's medical center. With facilities unexcelled in the United States and comparable to the famous children's medical center in Vienna, the project will represent an investment of $7,000,000, and is expected to be complete by June, 1930.

The latest buildings authorized, the Nancy Adele McElwee Memorial and the Gertrude Dunn Hicks Memorial Orthopedic Hospital, will be surgical units, east of and adjoining the present main hospital buildings. Made possible by the generosity of Mrs. Elizabeth McElwee and Mrs. Gertrude Dunn Hicks, each of whom contributed $300,000, the new structures will house the Home for Destitute Crippled Children. The Home, with an endowment of $1,000,000, has operated heretofore at Paulina Street and Maypole Avenue.

Of the other projected hospitals, the $500,000 Bobs Roberts Memorial Hospital, given by Colonel and Mrs. John Roberts, of Chicago, with a $500,000 endowment fund, in memory of their son, is already under construction west of and adjoining the present buildings, at Drexel Avenue and the Midway. The Charles Gilman Smith Contagious Disease Hospital, provided for in the will of the late Harriet G. Smith, also to be erected west of the present group, will add to facilities for treating children's diseases a unit for which there is inadequate provision in most cities.

The greatest single unit of the children's center will be the Chicago Lying-In Hospital, which now has assets exceeding $2,400,000, collected through the efforts of Mrs. Kellogg Fairbank. The new building, to be erected on the Midway between Maryland and Drexel Avenues, will have 140 beds for obstetrical cases, including an isolation pavilion with 20 beds for septic cases. There will be a separate laboratory for research and teaching, with a large gynecological library.

The Country Home for Convalescent Children, affiliated with the university last year, forms the final unit of the project. This institution, already in operation near West Chicago, has buildings worth $450,000 and an endowment of $1,200,000. Mrs. W. J. Chalmers is founder and chairman of the board.

THE SEVENTH ANNUAL INSTITUTE FOR REGISTRARS

THE Seventh Annual Institute for Registrars will be held at the University of Kentucky from April 1 to 6, 1929. Five courses will be offered, each course meeting daily. They are as follows:

"Principles of University and College Administration," by President Frank L. McVey.

"Problems of College Organization and Administration," by Floyd W. Reeves, professor of education in the University of Kentucky.

"A Course in Elementary Statistics for Registrars," by C. C. Ross, professor of educational psychology in the University of Kentucky.

"The Professional Functions of the Registrar," by the registrar of the University of Kentucky.

"The Technique of the Registrar's Office," by the officer of admissions and the recorder of the University of Kentucky.

The above courses are planned with a view to covering in a general way the field of administration in which the registrar is directly interested. All courses are planned so as to contribute to the professional functions of the registrar and to the technique of the registrar's office. Ample time will be given for discussion of problems presented by those in attendance.

The only expenses that will be incurred while in Lexington are living expenses. Everything possible will be done to make this a profitable investment for those attending. This is the annual contribution of the University of Kentucky to the development of the work of the registrar.

It is proposed to mail to members a program including a synopsis of each course.

Ezra L. Gillis,
Registrar

THE REORGANIZATION OF RUTGERS UNIVERSITY

Readjustment of regulations between the state and Rutgers University is recommended in a majority report submitted to the New Jersey legislature on February 12 by the special commission named last year to investigate the subject and reported by a staff correspondent of the New York *Herald Tribune*.

The majority would create a State Board of Regents to take over the activities, of which Rutgers forms the center, but which are actually maintained by the state. Instead of the present system, under which the state contributes about $2,000,000 a year to the university, the report recommends the imposition of a direct tax, the proceeds of which would be devoted to higher education.

Under this plan the free scholarships maintained by the state would be abolished. The commission, however, holds that lower tuition fees should be granted to residents of New Jersey than to those from other states.

The commission recommended that the name of Rutgers University be changed to indicate that it is operated as a state university. Colleges now operated in conjunction with the university would be reclassified and renamed. These activities include the New Jersey College for Women, the New Jersey College of Pharmacy, the university extension division and the State College of Agriculture, including the agricultural experiment stations at New Brunswick and Vineland.

Two plans discussed in the report, but rejected as impractical, were the establishment by the state of a new and independent institution under complete state control, similar to state universities in other states and the creation of a distinctive state university by a reorganization of the board of trustees of Rutgers.

The first proposal was rejected because of the tremendous cost involved for buildings and equipment, the gathering together of an adequate faculty and the building up of the morale and reputation of a new institution.

The second plan was disapproved, first upon the ground that it contemplates change of a private corporation into a public company.

The commission was unable to find any method by which this could be done legally. The trustees of Rutgers, operating under a perpetual charter, are charged with the obligation not only of carrying out the trust committed to them, but with the obligation of exercising their power of succession.

In addition, the commission said, it is evident that the state has entered into contractual obligations with respect to Rutgers, and these are further complicated by the agreements under which federal aid is afforded the university.

One of the difficulties which the commission believes would be met by imposing a direct tax is the conflict over the distribution of railroad taxes, a major portion of which are devoted by law to educational purposes. There are now three rival claimants for a share of these taxes. They are the public schools, the teachers' retirement fund and Rutgers College.

The funds now available for educational purposes are insufficient to meet these demands. The result has been that what is given to one must be taken from another. This the commission said has resulted in rivalry, jealousy and hard feelings.

A minority report, signed by J. Albert Dear, was presented. Mr. Dear argued that free college education should be afforded to every qualified boy and girl in the state by levying a special tax of one mill, which would produce an annual income of about $6,000,000. A reduction of approximately $2,000,000 in school taxes, Mr. Dear held, could be brought by devoting to primary, grammar and high schools the money heretofore diverted from the railroad tax to Rutgers. Mr. Dear submitted that the State Board of Education should be legally empowered as the only state body to receive and disburse all appropriations for higher education.

THE SUMMER SCHOOL OF THE UNIVERSITY OF SOUTHERN CALIFORNIA

Among fifty-five visiting professors from leading educational institutions of the country who are to augment the summer teaching staff of the University of California, the following have been named:

Dr. Thomas Nixon Carver, professor of political economy, Harvard University.

Dr. James A. James, dean of the Graduate School of Northwestern University.

Dr. Clyde W. Hill, professor of education at Yale University.

Dr. Harry K. Benson, head of the department of chemistry at the University of Washington, Seattle.

Dr. Henry C. Lancaster, professor of French, the Johns Hopkins University.

Dr. Oliver A. Ohmann, head of the division of psychology, Cleveland College of Western Reserve University.

Dr. David K. Brace, chairman of the department of physical education, University of Texas.

Dr. Carlos Castillo, University of Chicago.

Dr. Henry H. Goddard, professor of psychology, Ohio State University; author of the Kallikak Family, School Training for Defective Children, and School Training for Gifted Children.

Dr. Forest Chester Ensign, professor of the history and philosophy of education at the State University of Iowa.

Jessie M. Todd, of the art department of the University of Chicago.

THE MESSENGER LECTURES AT CORNELL UNIVERSITY

DR. EDWARD L. THORNDIKE, professor of educational psychology in Teachers College, Columbia University, will deliver the annual Messenger lectures in March. His subject is "The Nature and Evolution of Human Learning." He will give twelve lectures, beginning the series on March 5, and speaking on Tuesday, Wednesday and Thursday afternoons in the lecture room of the department of psychology.

Following are the topics of the several lectures:

March 5—"The Influence of the Frequency of Occurrence of a Situation."
" 6—"The Influence of the Frequency of Occurrence of a Connection; the Principle of Belonging."
" 7—"The Influence of the After-effects of a Connection."
" 12—"Explanations of the Influence of the After-effects of a Connection."
" 13—"New Experimental Data on the After-effects of a Connection."
" 14—"Identifiability, Availability, Trial and System."
" 19—"Other Facts Concerning Mental Connections, Conditioned Reflexes and Learning."
" 20—"Purposiveness and Learning; the Gestalt Theory and Learning."
" 21—"Insight and Analysis."
" 26—"Thinking and Reasoning."
" 27—"The Evolution of Learning in General."
" 28—"The Evolution of Learning in Recent Times; Future Possibilities."

The Messenger lectureship was founded in 1923 with a bequest of about $77,000 received under the will of Hiram J. Messenger, '80, actuary of the Travelers Insurance Company, who died in 1913. In his will he directed that the fund should provide for lectures on the evolution of civilization. The lecturers on this foundation have been James H. Breasted, Robert A. Millikan, Herbert J. C. Grierson and Thomas F. Tout.

EDUCATIONAL NOTES AND NEWS

PRESIDENT COOLIDGE delivered the anniversary address at the George Washington University, after which honorary degrees of doctor of laws were conferred on him and on Mrs. Coolidge. Dr. Cloyd H. Marvin, president of the university, in conferring the degree upon Mr. Coolidge, said: "Conservative leader during a period when thoughtful, firm action alone could hold the confidence of the people, proponent at the same time of a forward-looking social procedure, sponsoring scientific endeavors, espousing a program of economic responsibility, arousing in the nation a self-imposed feeling for cooperation and good-will, patron of education and of culture, respected leader of our people—the President of the United States of America." The citation for Mrs. Coolidge was: "Combining gift in exquisite taste and gracious kindliness with an uncommonly clear and understanding mind, you have touched life and it has reacted warm and true. You have unconsciously caused to be builded for yourself in the hearts of the people a temple of genuine friendship, loyal appreciation and true affection."

On the occasion of the installation of Dr. Edmund D. Soper as president of Ohio Wesleyan University on February 15, the degree of doctor of laws was conferred upon President William P. Few, Duke University; President Mervin G. Filler, Dickinson College; President G. Bromley Oxnam, DePauw University, and President Edward S. Parsons, Marietta College. Dr. Soper's address was entitled "Academic Freedom in a Christian College."

At the Founder's Week exercises, celebrating the forty-fourth anniversary of the founding of Rollins College, honorary degrees were conferred as follows: Mme. Marie Sundelius, doctor of music; Fred Stone, the actor, doctor of humanities; H. H. Westinghouse, the inventor, doctor of science; Robert Norwood, doctor of divinity; Mrs. John T. Fuller, the first woman legislator of Florida, Cornelius A. Pugsley, former member of congress, and E. W. Rollins, present head of the family that established the college, doctors of law.

Speakers at the inauguration on February 20 of Dr. J. L. Meader, as president of Russell Sage College, Troy, N. Y., included Dr. Frank P. Graves, State Commissioner of Education; William F. Russell, dean of Teachers College, Columbia University, and William Leland Thompson, of the New York State Board of Regents. The opening address was delivered by Miss Eliza Kellas, the first president of the college, who founded the school in 1916 at the request of Mrs. Russell Sage.

Princeton University has received from the class of '87 the sum of $200,000 to endow the chair of astronomy held by Professor Henry Norris Russell, a member of the class. The class has also presented a portrait of Professor Russell to the university. The university has also received a gift of $500,000 from the estate of the late James T. Walker, conditional on the raising of an additional $200,000 to be used to endow a chair in international finance in honor of Dr. Edwin Walker Kemmerer, now in China as head of an official mission to stabilize the country's finances.

Professor A. A. Michelson, of the University of Chicago, and Professor Robert A. Millikan, of the California Institute of Technology, received gold medals from the Society of Arts and Sciences, New York City, at a dinner at the Hotel Biltmore on February 22. Professor Michelson was introduced by Dr. Max Mason, of the Rockefeller Foundation, and Dr. Millikan by Dean Augustus Trowbridge, of Princeton University. The medals were presented by Mr. Walter Russell, president of the society.

A reception in honor of Dr. Edward T. Devine, who took up his work as executive officer of the Bellevue-Yorkville health demonstration on January 1, was given on February 20 by the house council of the New York City Health Center, comprising the heads and representatives of the various health and social welfare organizations that make up the demonstration. Dr. Devine was introduced by Health Commissioner Shirley W. Wynne, chairman of the governing board of the organization.

Dr. William M. Jardine, who before he became secretary of agriculture was president of the Kansas State Agricultural College at Manhattan, will retire from the cabinet on March 4. Dr. Jardine has accepted a position as counsel for the Federated Fruit and Vegetable Growers, with his offices in Washington, D. C.

Glenn Hughes, of the English and dramatic arts departments of the University of Washington, who is now on leave of absence traveling abroad on a Guggenheim fellowship, has been appointed professor at Scripps College, Claremont, California.

The retirement is announced of Dr. E. M. Fogel, who has taught German at the University of Pennsylvania for thirty-two years.

Dr. Harry A. Garfield, president of Williams College and chairman of the Institute of Politics, has returned after a two months' absence in Europe on behalf of the forthcoming session of the Institute of Politics in Williamstown.

President Paul D. Moody has returned to Middlebury College after a four months' leave of absence. President and Mrs. Moody during their stay abroad visited England, France, Switzerland, Italy and Spain.

Dr. Wilhelm Meyer-Lubke, professor at the University of Bonn, is Speyer visiting professor at the Johns Hopkins University from the end of February until early in May.

PROFESSOR GEORGE R. TYSON, of Ursinus College, will be visiting professor of education in the summer session of the University of Pennsylvania.

DR. CHARLES H. KEENE, professor of hygiene at the University of Buffalo, has been appointed director of the courses in physical education given in the Harvard Summer School for the summer of 1929, himself conducting two courses.

MISS HELEN PARKHURST, director of the Dalton Schools, Incorporated, New York City, will again direct during the summer quarter the demonstration school of the department of principles of education of the Ohio State University.

DR. P. F. VALENTINE, director of professional courses at the San Francisco State Teachers College, will lecture during the summer session of the University of North Dakota.

DR. FRANZ X. SCHAFFER, of the University of Vienna, will lecture on general geology during the coming summer at the University of California.

WILLIAM CHURCH OSBORN has been elected president of the board of directors of the Children's Aid Society of New York City.

GEORGE TRAUTMAN, assistant athletic director at the Ohio State University, has accepted the position of director of the bureau of conventions and publicity of the Columbus Chamber of Commerce.

MISS MARY PLUMMER, founder and director of the Pratt Institute Library School, has been appointed principal of the newly established library school of the New York Public Library.

MISS HELEN G. CUSHING, who has been catalogue librarian and first assistant in the Hamilton-Smith Library at the University of New Hampshire since September, 1919, sailed for France on February 16 to become cataloguer at the American Library in Paris.

WILLIAM LICHT, member of the firm of Licht and Wankelman, has been elected a member of the Cincinnati Board of Education to fill the vacancy caused by the death of John D. Sage.

RICHARD D. FAULKNER, for many years principal of the Horace Mann Junior High School, San Francisco, was recently honored by a program of special exercises on the occasion of the presentation of his portrait to the school as a gift of the faculty and student body.

F. H. BARBEE, assistant superintendent of schools, has been appointed superintendent of the St. Joseph, Missouri, schools to succeed David W. Hopkins, recently elected to Congress from the fourth district.

MISS KATHERINE HAMILTON, assistant superintendent of schools at St. Paul, Minn., has been given a five months' leave of absence, which she will devote to travel and study in European and Mediterranean places. Miss Hamilton expects to return to the United States in May.

DR. CARLOS DELGADO DE CARVALHO, of the Brazil Research School in Rio de Janeiro, Brazil, is in this country for the purpose of discussing with scholars and educators the possibility of organizing in Rio de Janeiro a summer session for North American students.

PROFESSOR ALBERT B. FAUST, of the department of Germanic languages at Cornell University, recently visited St. Louis, Mo., to confer with leaders of German-speaking societies and alumni of German universities on the proposed campaign for the Carl Schurz Memorial Foundation.

SIR HERBERT BROWN AMES, former financial director of the League of Nations, will visit the University of California on Thursday, March 7, and deliver a public address under the auspices of the League of Nations Association, California Branch.

THE REVEREND JAMES G. MCCLURE, D.D., president-emeritus of the Presbyterian Theological Seminary (formerly the McCormick Theological Seminary) in Chicago, will deliver the Bross lectures at Lake Forest University in May. Dr. McClure is writing a history of the seminary for its centennial in October, 1929.

SIR JOHN ADAMS, emeritus professor of education in the University of London and special lecturer at Harvard University, recently spoke at the Hughes High School of Cincinnati on

"The Difference of View Concerning Education Held by Americans and Englishmen."

The Rev. Dr. Harry E. Fosdick, of New York City, is to be the commencement day orator at Boston University on June 18.

Professor Carl Becker, of the department of history of Cornell University, was a speaker at the University of Iowa's ninth annual Conference of Teachers of History and Social Studies at Iowa City on February 1 and 2.

Dr. Walter Irenaeus Lowe, for many years a professor of history and at the time of his death a member of the faculty of Colgate University, died on February 22.

Dr. Foster Watson, emeritus professor of education in the University College of Wales, an authority on the history of education and translator of Spanish works on the subject, died on February 13. Dr. Watson was an honorary member of the Maine Historical Society. He wrote a "Bibliographical Account of English Books on Education, 1500–1600" for reports of the United States government, and was departmental editor of the "Cyclopedia of Education," New York.

DISCUSSION

COPYRIGHT LAW AMENDMENT PROPOSED

Although there has been an International Copyright Union since 1886, the United States has never adhered. A bill, known as H. R. 9586, was introduced into the House of Representatives in January, 1928, authorizing the president to effect and proclaim the adhesion of the United States to the convention creating an International Union for the Protection of Literary and Artistic Works organized in 1886 and revised in 1908 and 1914. The bill further gives to foreign authors, not domiciled in the United States, who are citizens or subjects of any country which is a member of the international convention, or authors whose works are first published in and enjoy copyright protection in convention countries, the same rights and remedies in the United States as citizens of the United States have under the copyright laws. It is further provided that such foreign authors shall not be subject to the performance of any formalities in order to secure copyrights, and that such authors shall not be required to comply with the provisions of the United States laws as to publication with notice of copyright, deposit of copies, registration of copyright or manufacture within the limits of the United States.

No effort is made to amend the copyright laws to relieve authors resident in the United States from the burdens of the formalities required by our copyright law with respect to notice, deposit, registration and manufacture within the United States. Obviously this gives foreigners a material advantage over United States citizens. This is done in an effort to procure, under the convention, foreign copyright protection for matter copyrighted within the United States by United States authors in a way and to an extent that can not be accomplished under the present law. The convention provides only for reciprocal rights, and our laws are not reciprocal now. It means in effect, however, that substantially everything published abroad will be immediately and automatically copyrighted in the United States, although no way is provided for residents of the United States to obtain notice that it is copyrighted.

The American Patent Law Association and the National Publishers' Association (periodicals) as well as the American Bar Association are opposed to such a law. Some individuals, however, notably book publishers and some composers, as well as the register of copyrights in the Library of Congress, are advocating the passage of the law on the ground that it is worth while giving protection to a foreigner without any formalities for the sake of getting foreign protection for our own authors, the theory being that we have ceased to be chiefly an importer of literary property, but are now giving to the world more than it gives us. Of course, a practical difficulty is that there is no convenient way of discovering whether any one is free to use or to copy matter appearing in a book or a picture, drawing or other artistic work. When the copyright protection expires such matter is free to any one, but if no notice of copyright is included in the book, etc., and there is no registration of the copyright, it is almost impossible to determine whether the matter is copyrighted and if the copyright has expired. Likewise it is almost impossible to determine who owns the copyrights and from whom authentic permission to use or to reproduce may be procured.

This bill or H. R. 15086, similarly authorizing adhesion to the Copyright Convention as revised at Rome, June 2, 1928, probably will be urged in the present session of Congress, and is of much interest to every one engaged in research and publication.

KARL FENNING
GEORGETOWN UNIVERSITY LAW SCHOOL

SPECIAL CORRESPONDENCE

THE WORK OF THE INTERNATIONAL BUREAU OF EDUCATION

IT is commonly said in the Assembly of the League of Nations that in order to establish peace throughout the world, moral disarmament is as necessary as a material disarmament. After the great upheaval following the last war, it seems to have been realized that education was perhaps the force most capable of creating a new spirit among men by developing in every individual a feeling of comprehension and sympathy towards other countries. The nations at war in 1914–1918 would not have fought so fiercely if they had known each other better. Indeed, the deficiency of international education was one of the causes of the world disaster.

Moreover, the traditional teaching of national history has too often accustomed the child to regard war as the only possible solution of political disputes, and it is for education to bring about a drastic change in this mental attitude and to uproot such a deep-laid prejudice.

Therefore, educators have a predominant part to play in the molding of a new world, and they have become more and more conscious of their possibilities and responsibilities at a time when the remarkable development of psychology and of all educational sciences is increasing and improving their means of action. That is why they have felt more keenly than ever the need for collaboration in order to find the best methods of creating a new type of man, who though firmly attached to the national soil, yet will possess a broad international and pacific culture. Of course, they do not contemplate a uniform pattern; their aim is not to standardize the different systems of teaching; they only want to hoard up the treasures of national experience and to coordinate progress and achievement.

For several years past, numerous educational associations have felt this need—such as The American School Citizenship League, the Ligue internationale pour l'éducation nouvelle and the World Federation of Education Associations—and have recommended the establishment of a central office which would act as a center of pedagogical information and of liaison between the educationists of all countries, at the same time favoring instruction on pacific lines in keeping with the ideal of the League of Nations. It is worth mentioning that the Peace Conference had actually before it a scheme proposed by the International Council of Women for the institution of a permanent bureau of education as an essential part of the League of Nations.

It was for Geneva to satisfy this general demand, not only because the seat of the League of Nations becomes more and more the favorite city of international institutions, but also because Geneva already possessed a first-class college of educational sciences, the J. J. Rousseau Institute, having manifold connections with foreign countries. So, two years ago, this institute inaugurated the International Bureau of Education, whose director is Dr. Pierre Bovet, the well-known educationist and professor in the University of Geneva. He is assisted by a council very international in character, since it consists of twenty-two members belonging to seventeen countries.

Though only two years old, the International Bureau of Education has evidenced its vitality, organizing several congresses, exhibitions and courses and extending its activity to sixty-seven countries, where it is in touch with 188 official correspondents and 500 members, many of whom are corporate members or large associations, national or international, and schools and colleges. It may be interesting for the readers of this paper to hear of the promising work already performed by the bureau and of the various services it might render educationists or mankind in general, and especially those who love peace.

The aim of the International Bureau of Education is to develop international relations in the field of education, so as to contribute to the general progress of education and to promote a spirit of peace. In order to carry out its program, the bureau keeps in close touch with the League of Nations, the International Labor Office, the boards of education in different countries and various associations interested in educational matters. In sympathy with the League of Nations ideal, the bureau preserves complete neutrality as regards the national, political, philosophical and religious standpoints. It seeks truth and truth only, in an objective spirit, and in whatever shape it may assume.

The activities of the bureau fall under three heads: information, scientific research and coordination. First of all, it is a central clearinghouse for all information concerning elementary and secondary education (both public and private), pedagogical psychology and professional orientation. Is it not of the utmost interest for all educationists to know that there exists in the world an impartial organization which is capable of providing them with reliable data based upon facts concerning such a method of teaching, such and such a system applied in a given country? Thanks to documents furnished by national educational bodies and others, to extensive correspondence, to interviews with experts and visitors from all over the world, the bureau is in a position to give valuable information upon the majority of countries and in all branches of education. It daily answers the most varied questions from all quarters of the globe: "How are morals taught in France?" a Belgian authority asks; "We want to build a secondary school for girls," a group of Algerian masters writes. "Can you send us plans of an up-to-date building?" Others inquire about the teaching of the arts in the Swiss schools, the working of the system of visiting teachers in the United States, the advantages of coeducation, etc. This kind of activity is more fruitful than one would think at first sight; is it not striking that the curriculum of a Turkish school has been entirely transformed, thanks to documents sent from Geneva?

The bureau publishes a *Quarterly Bulletin* in French and English and contemplates the editing of an international yearbook of education. In order to develop its information work, the bureau has established national centers in several countries, including Spain, Poland, Mexico and Czechoslovakia; these centers act as liaison agencies and contribute to the spreading of both national and foreign culture.

The bureau does not content itself with giving information; it also initiates or encourages experimental and statistical research in order to contribute to the solution of problems concerning child psychology, the science of education, methods of examination, etc. It has already made known the results of an inquiry on international school correspondence, carried on by the Junior Red Cross and the Bureau de correspondance scolaire international in Paris. The report which has been published has clearly evidenced the fact that this exchange of letters, albums and gifts of all kinds between school children of various countries, far from being a mere children's game, constitutes a wide and successful means of cooperation which brings the minds of young people into close contact, and transforms the "foreigner" into a friend. Is it not characteristic of a new spirit that in several countries the younger generation, thus rendered more amenable to foreign influences, is contributing to the pacific education of their parents?

The bureau is just now engaged in two other inquiries, one about the relations between parents and schools, the other about the international exchange of school children. The International Labor Office, paying due tribute to the impartial and scientific work achieved by the bureau, has entrusted it with an inquiry of the utmost social importance—that concerning the occupations of children in countries where they leave school before fourteen years of age, that is to say before they are allowed to work, and consequently are faced with dangerous material and moral problems.

When the bureau thinks that a question is especially preoccupying a great number of educators and is sufficiently mature for public discussion it convenes a conference, like the conference on bilingualism which met in April at Luxembourg to study the psychological and pedagogical difficulties arising when children are taught in a language not their mother tongue. Thus the bureau made a contribution, which was valuable because purely scientific, to the perplexing minorities question, examining it from a new view-point.

The field open to this sort of research is boundless, and many questions press to be studied by groups of educators representing different countries and different methods.

The third and perhaps the most important activity of the bureau is to act as a coordination center between the national and international institutions which deal in educational matters or work in associated fields. It has created international committees such as the Committee to Study Bilingualism and the International Commission on Teaching Material, which will deal particularly with self-correcting material and educative games and will undertake the compiling of an atlas of civilization. It is also through the efforts of the bureau that the World Federation of Education Associations will hold its 1929 conference in Geneva, bringing together hundreds of educators from all over the world.

Moreover, the bureau does not lose sight of the fact that the International Congress of Moral Education has entrusted it with the duty of carrying on its work. It tries to encourage the teaching of peace in agreement with ideals of justice and solidarity, and it was to emphasize this aspect of this activity that the bureau organized in Prague, April, 1927, a conference on "Peace through the School," attended by 450 educators from twenty countries. There were laid down the real foundations of education for peace, from the triple standpoint of psychology, teaching methods and education as a whole. This idea that education for peace ought not to be a secondary item of the school curriculum, but that it touches the whole subject of education, has been developed under its various aspects in the summer course for teachers given by the bureau during the past year on the following subject: "How to make the League of Nations Known and to Develop the Spirit of International Cooperation." This course brought to Geneva 161 teachers from many countries, including India, and was completed by a very successful exhibition of books and the various means used by international institutions to foster world friendship in the schools, and to make the child conscious of the unity of mankind.

Such, broadly sketched, is the work already carried out by the International Bureau of Education, and one can easily realize its far-reaching possibilities. The bureau stands ready to be a counselor and guide to those countries less advanced in matters of education, and it will do everything in its power to help them set up the institutions they need. Its work deserves the sympathy and encouragement of all those who believe that the world must have a new spirit to find a peaceful solution of the perplexing problems confronting mankind on all sides. Who can fail to recognize that education is the one power capable of marshaling all the resources of mind and heart for the promotion of justice and peace? "Ut per juvenes ascendat mundus"—this is the motto of the International Bureau of Education. Indeed the progress of mankind depends to a great extent upon the teaching given our younger generation in the schools of to-day. Humanity is striving hard to emerge from the era of war; the old diplomacy which found its support in armament must go, and the new diplomacy, teaching peace in the schools and finding its support in education, must take its place.

CONSTANCE MORLEY,
Assistant Secretary

QUOTATIONS

THE SALARIES OF UNIVERSITY PROFESSORS

A COMMITTEE of the Yale faculty has just issued through the Yale University Press a comprehensive and striking report called "Incomes and Living Costs of a University Faculty." The outstanding conclusion of the study is that the salary appropriate to full professorial rank is

$15,000 or $16,000. As everybody knows, professors are seldom paid more than half that sum, in many places not more than a third of it. If the Yale report is sound in its conclusions, the chief task of all who are concerned to keep the standards of university teaching high should be to secure an increase of income available for salaries.

The report is of great interest because it treats the problem of academic income and expenditure in detail, with entire candor and in the light of carefully ascertained facts; furthermore, it endeavors to establish permanent principles for dealing with the situation. Of these the most important is that a reasonable standard of living for a university professor is the standard maintained by men of comparable grade in other callings. This may be called (the phrase is ours) a competitive standard, in the sense that it is determined by the view that the universities are competing with other professions for men and must bid enough to secure good men. The report refuses to accept the idea that universities should rely on the advantages and satisfactions of the academic life to attract men into teaching at salaries markedly less than they could earn in other occupations. A second principle, not much less important, is that teachers should not be forced into extra work in order to maintain the standard of living found to be reasonable in their social and occupational class. The basic salary should be enough. If it could be attained, we assume that teachers might be required, or at least expected, to devote their entire time to instruction and scholarship. A third principle is that salaries should not be held down by expanding the program of instruction, thereby forcing the universities to secure more men instead of paying more to those already in service. Funds available for salaries do increase, and salaries could go up if faculties did not increase in proportion. In most departments new courses are less important than better teaching.

President Angell contributes an illuminating "Foreword" to the report. He remarks that there are two main questions to be considered in such a study: first, what college men must earn to live as they reasonably should, and whether they can earn this sum without resorting to extra work; and second, what standard of living should be attainable on an academic salary to keep the best men in college teaching. Obviously, these questions are closely related.

A university that pays a little more than other universities has not solved the problem of academic demand and supply. It may get the pick of the men available, but it has not done anything to assure a continuing number of good men, to say nothing of increasing the number. In the face of decreasing numbers of good applicants, all universities, including those that pay most, must eventually lower their standards. As the report says in conclusion, "the university will get the quality it pays for."

Professor Henderson and his colleagues on the committee are to be congratulated on this report. It sets a definite goal to be achieved and deals with the whole problem fairly, concisely and with breadth of outlook. The problem is admittedly difficult, especially when it comes to doing anything about it. This Yale study clears up much of the confusion as to what is really desirable to do.—*Harvard Alumni Bulletin.*

REPORTS

THE ORGANIZATION OF STANFORD UNIVERSITY[1]

The present period is one of change and development in the universities of America. The great increase in the number of those seeking higher education has compelled marked changes in procedure and in curriculum. It is evident that our universities must expect a period of readjustment in their relationships not only to preparatory institutions but also to their public responsibilities. Research, long one of the activities of the university, is now a part of the regular plan of many of the major business organizations of the country. More is being required all the time of university graduates in the way of training not only in the older professions but in the newer opportunities associated with modern trade and business.

At Stanford there is a growing emphasis both in the numbers applying and in the work done

[1] From the Annual Report of President Ray Lyman Wilbur to the board of trustees.

in the upper reaches of university instruction. With the striking development of the junior colleges in California and elsewhere there is less call for elementary work and more for advanced work. Since this movement is of comparatively recent origin and now getting into full stride, it is quite evident that the decade ahead will be one of utmost significance to the future of all of our American universities. Since Stanford is an institution of limited endowment, with a limited student group, it is vital that its plans for the future be made with unusual care. Three quarters of a million dollars of the present academic budget comes from tuition fees. It is imperative that this financial structure be maintained on a sound basis for the protection of our faculty and of our pension plans. Since there are already a number of institutions in the state competing with our Lower Division and offering, practically without tuition, the same work for which we demand about three hundred dollars per year, and since the number of these institutions is growing steadily, readjustment must be made in time and in accordance with the events occurring about us. Careful estimates indicate that there will be an increase in the population of California at the rate of about 200,000 a year, that there will be a marked increase in the number of high-school students and that within ten years the number of students doing work in junior colleges or in the lower divisions of state institutions will be in the neighborhood of 50,000. About 10 per cent. of the graduates of these institutions have been coming to Stanford. In all probability some such percentage will be maintained in the future. We can therefore look forward to a student body of approximately the present size made up of students selected from these extensions of the high schools in the state or from institutions offering similar work in other parts of the United States or the world.

By following out the plan for reducing the number of students admitted to the Lower Division and admitting larger numbers to the Upper Division, it seems likely that Stanford University can go through this period of financial adjustment without undue strain. It is interesting to note that, with the reduction in the number of new students admitted to the Lower Division for the academic year 1928–29, practically all of the men students applying, who reached the standard adopted by the committee on admission, were accepted.

The most difficult problem in adjusting the affairs of the university to the changes going on about it is that of the faculty. With appointments for three years for assistant professors, five years for associate professors and full professors up to the age of sixty-five, changes in teaching personnel and responsibility must take place slowly. Stanford University had added to its staff in recent years, as have most of the universities, men who are leaders in their particular fields and men whose primary interest is in the teaching of advanced students, professional students, or in research. It is practically impossible to interest the majority of the present faculty of the university in elementary teaching. This is natural since, in the presence of well-equipped laboratories, great libraries, and eager advanced students, attention is bound to be drawn away from elementary work.

The faculty of the ordinary junior college is made up of men who are primarily teachers. This makes their work much more vital and significant in the handling of students doing that elementary work, which comprises practically all of the curriculum of the lower-division or junior-college period. Our experience has shown that we need anticipate no slackening of our educational standards if our students are trained in such institutions instead of in our own departments.

During the year the comptroller was authorized, on behalf of the board, to enter into negotiations which could lead to leases for junior-college sites. One of these was to the Menlo School and Junior College and covered the Cedro Cottage grounds. The other, to a proposed Junior College District, included a tract of land near Mayfield.

While plans for these institutions are going forward slowly because of the many difficulties involved, within a few years we can anticipate the presence of a public junior college on one side of the campus and a private junior college on the other, both operated without expense to the university and both serving to give adequate preparation to a certain number of students who will enter Stanford.

EDUCATIONAL REVIEW

Edited by WILLIAM McANDREW

MATTERS OF MOMENT

DR. FRANK BOYNTON, as president of the Department of Superintendence of the National Education Association, in planning the program of the annual convention, sent out an exhortation to all the participants to "aim at a statesman-like consideration of the function of the public schools." "We must," he said, "produce a better type of citizenry." He formulated the convention theme in the shape of a question: "How can the public schools better serve the democracy?" The program of the Minneapolis meeting of the National Education Association as composed by the president, Miss Cornelia Adair, was similarly a series of political papers and addresses centering about the concept of education more as statesmanship than as scholarship. Superintendent Ward, of the public schools of Fort Wayne, Indiana, who had the largest share in presenting the annual expression of the superintendents' creed at the Cleveland meeting, began by a declaration that the sole and great purpose of the public schools is political, the perpetuity of the nation's purpose, the improvement of its institutions year by year toward the perfection visioned by its founders. That remarkably active Michigan State Teachers' Association which, in nine districts of the state, offers, each year, over a thousand papers, speeches and round tables, devoted recently a meeting in each city to a conference upon how the schools are promoting equality, respect for the rights of fellow beings to life, liberty and happiness, and how the classroom is training in the civic duties of union, justice, tranquillity, common defense and general welfare. I heard, at one of these meetings, Principal John Riemersma, of the high school of Holland, Michigan, called to the stand to answer questions as to the workings of the student self-government plan in the school of which he is the head. The lack of questioning from the audience, the necessity felt by the chairman to make all the inquiries himself, the apparent absence of self-government from all schools represented by the whole company other than Riemersma, were amazing. The Holland principal answered the interrogatories simply and fully. He said that the democratic organization has been running in the Holland High School many years; it is an essential part of the school service, more valuable than Latin, algebra or English. It makes school discipline more educative and character training more real. The chairman earnestly exhorted the school people present to mend their ways and by means of some organization like that of the quiet Riemersma to get their schools to doing that for which they were organized by the American statesmen who advocated education at public expense. I thought the program was direct, interesting, practical and convincing, and I believed that the number who would do any differently from what they had done before was zero. In Cincinnati I heard John Chewning, of Evansville, describe to a room full of superintendents the working of the self-government system in his city. Neither John nor I could imagine how any schoolman with any sense of duty toward the community paying the cost of the schools could continue to draw pay while neglecting the organization of the schools upon a basis that will make the preparation of citizens a paramount activity day by day. But during that meeting no repentant sinners came to the mourners' bench. No one before leaving the hall announced his intention to lead a better life.

How do you account for it?

Surprising slowness of orientation.—No sooner had the colonies united and cast off the British yoke than a wave of propaganda for schools as a function of government began to roll over the country. Noah Webster, statesman before he took up textbook making, Benjamin Rush, Franklin, Jefferson, Washington, Madison, Monroe, over a hundred others, eminent in their generation, spoke, wrote and pamphleteered, arguing that the principles underlying the establishment of the new union must be kept alive. The majority which had been won to them would soon pass away. The next and the succeeding generations must be trained to self-government. "Every man," said Madison, "is now a governor. We must educate our rulers." When these promoters at length got the majority of the people's representatives to tax non-parents for the education of other people's children, what had been a vision and a hope, that education would be a civic and not a scholastic function, a community benefit and not a preparation for personal advantage, seemed to have secured a solid foundation on which to build. The struggle for it achieved its practical victory in the last quarter of the nineteenth century when various courts decided that high schools and even universities might be made a charge on all citizens and be considered essential features of a self-governing state. It was America which carried this principle to the novel length not only of affording free education to all who sought it but of compelling every child to partake of it. Although the thinkers like Jefferson and Franklin, Webster and Rush, who went deeply into the problem of the preservation and perfection of democracy, insisted upon the thorough study of democracy as the most important feature of a public-school system, there was enough blind faith in the disciplinary power of a literary education to leave the studies laid down by the schoolmaster undisturbed. Educational statesmanship such as President Boynton is urging got no further than ordinary course of study scholarship. Horace Mann, legislator, protested against the delay. There was a wave of reform in the eighties bringing the institution of "civics" as a school study. Meade, Dole, Nordhoff wrote articles and made speeches to awaken school managers to the duty of training the coming citizen. William Ray, in the Hyde Park High School, Chicago, in 1886 put all his seniors through a whole year of daily lessons in American politics. As president of the Illinois High School Teachers Association he spread his gospel over every program. President Charles W. Eliot argued that the public schools are for public service and that the most important and universal need of this is honest government. It is a fundamental object of the public schools, he said. The real end of all education, so far as the development of character is concerned, is to cultivate a capacity for self-control or self-government, a habit of obeying the dictates of honor and duty. It is of the utmost importance to appeal steadily and almost exclusively to motives which should be operative in after life. We are best developed not by hearing or by reading about deeds but by doing them. Practice in self-government requires positive activity. It appeals steadily to motives in boys which well serve them when they become men. It is based on sound educational principles. These arguments of Harvard's great president were confirmed in detail by several experiments in public schools. Edwin Goldwasser, whose brilliant success as principal of a huge New York public school composed of children of the foreign born had attracted attention of newspaper editors and of writers for the magazines, published a notable article pricking a number of iridescent bubbles such as defenders of public schools are apt at blowing. Our school usages, he said, have the spirit of the monarchical days before the Revolution. Individual responsibility has little exercise. The rules, the laws, come down from above. When a child is subject to a monitor in whose selection he has had no voice, when he is expected to obey commands in the formulation of which he has had no part, he naturally attempts to evade the consequences of disobedience by influencing the officer personally. Real and true citizenship dissociates the personality of the governor from his official position. It is futile to rely on literature and history alone to cultivate the civic virtues. It trains the youngsters in hypocrisy. The finest formulation of the moral in a reading lesson often comes from the toughest and most dishonest young rascal in the class. Unless you make the essence of ethical teaching function in the conduct of your children you are getting nowhere in character building. School management isn't vital for a boy unless he is taking part in it with real responsibility. These ideas as developed by Goldwasser were confirmed by a number of schools in the metropolis. Principal Minnie Ledwith, Principal Oswald Schlockow, Principal Edward Maguire, the teachers' council of the Washington Irving High School, organized their children for self-government and have quietly maintained the project for more than twenty-five years. Mr. Maxwell, in the superintendent's annual report of eighteen years ago, described the plan, its officers, its court, its elections, its charter development, its making for loyal and devoted citizens. Lyman Beecher Stowe described the scheme with great detail and enthusiasm in the *Outlook* in 1908. Richard Welling, a well-known New York attorney, untiring wheel-horse in every campaign for good government since he graduated from Harvard, intimate of Roosevelt, Strong, Goddard, Jerome, Low, Waring, Mitchell and every New York fighter for a decent city, organized a "self-government committee" to coax the public schools into the service which their founders clearly promised would be tax-supported schools' main concern. John G. Agar and Robert L. Harrison, of the board of education, were members. So were Stephen Duggan, now wrapt up in international education; Samuel McCune Lindsay, Columbia's brilliant apostle of pure politics; George McAneny, tireless devotee of public service and of progressive schools; George Haven Putnam, glorious old war horse; Julia Richman, electric school reformer; Thomas Slicer, eminent divine; Stephen S. Wise, people's preacher, and others not so well known. Welling gave more time and did more work than all the others put together. The archives of our National Education Association show him addressing us on this theme at our meetings in 1903, 1911 and 1915. Major Meras, U. S. A., serving us at the Milwaukee meeting, was sure that the civic work of the schools is futile if it is mostly talking about patriotism and not doing things. At the same convention John Tildsley argued from American history and from present needs that the greatest failure of the public schools is honest-to-goodness direct training in the functions of citizenship. Walter Page and Edward Bok, the *Outlook*, the *Forum*, the *Saturday Evening Post*, the *Atlantic Monthly* have given wide publicity to the failure of the schools to achieve their fundamental purpose as trainers in politics. Miss Adair and Mr. Boynton devote the last two meetings of the National Association to consideration of this duty. Diogenes with a lantern walking through Michigan, a state with a high educational reputation, might find an institution other than the Holland High School doing its duty, but the Grand Rapids meeting failed to disclose any. How do you account for this?

What is bothering Richard Welling?—If you have read the book reviews in this magazine presented by a club of teachers calling themselves Hoi Bibliologoi you will recall that a surprising number of writers on present-day conditions—Horace Bridges, George Coe, Geoffrey Parsons, Walter Lippman, Charles Judd, Harold Rugg and others—are disappointed with the progress of democracy. The ease with which other constitutional governments than ours fall into the arms of dictators appalls us. We are living, Lawrence Hills, editor of the New York *Herald-Tribune,* tells us, in the era of the greatest test to which democratic government has ever been subjected. Parliaments have been discarded in some countries; in others there is continued agitation against the authority of legislatures. What is astonishing is the sloth of sincere advocates of democracy in making any approach to the solution of the problem of its repair. The fathers of our own republic created a system which has been the pattern used in the formation of younger nations, sometimes with grave deviations from the model. The principle of democracy is sound. The continuance of self-government depends on the success of realizing its principles. Mr. Hills reminds you of Lowell's reply to Guizot, who asked him how long the American republic was likely to last. Lowell believed that would be so long as the ideals of the founders were observed. Insomuch as "observed" means "practiced," Lowell, with the editor of the *Herald-Tribune,* must be added to Richard Welling's list of those who hold that the schools must make politics real.

To say the least, one might find every aspect of the whole matter presented at some time or other by this modest crusader during the forty years of his campaign. What are the real essentials of education at public expense or at the hands of an endowed school, he asked, in 1888. Not reading, writing, mathematics, or history, except in so far as they promote the general welfare. The best and most efficient training of the faculties which fails to imbue at the same time a desire to use them for the public good is a dishonest use of the money raised by taxation or donated by some benefactor. Citizenship was the aim and the justification in taxing everybody to educate all children. Citizenship is low because schools neglect it. Twenty-three years later he is saying that the indifference of Americans to their public affairs is alarming. We have come to the pass where apathy is regarded as an elemental fact of civic life. Writers, preachers, publicists, teachers, agree that this is the greatest asset of the political boss and the greatest obstacle to a decent democracy. Whoever looks into it comes to believe that the schools are mostly to blame. Inquire what they are doing for the responsibilities of citizenship; you will find them merely teaching the structure and functions of government. No one can hold that a knowledge of the machine is sufficient to insure its proper running. A perfect printing press may produce the most evil of books. The boss has an excellent knowledge of our form of government. See what he does with all his knowing! The tone of citizenship is low because you schoolmasters are not seriously attempting to perform your real duty. You have refined the teaching of grammar, but your civics are on the pattern of 1750. We have heard that any study well pursued will so discipline the mind as to make good citizens. You can't make a good farmer by teaching him thoroughly the principles of navigation. While you are hammering away on your ancient history the political boss is plowing and sowing and fertilizing. On election day your former pupils go blindly to the polls and help him gather to himself the crop that should be for the benefit of us all. Do you suppose, he asked in 1911, such spectacles as the vote-selling in Illinois, in Indiana, in Ohio, in Pennsylvania, in New York, could happen if the schoolmasters had done their whole duty by the coming citizen? You are leaving patriotism to the book, to the platform lecture, to the patriotic song, not to real loyalty, the inspiring of which is *your* job, the service *you* are paid for, the reason *you* are a public servant and not running a private school. In the midst of the sorrowful disclosures of the shame of corrupt government, when Lincoln Steffens and Ray

Stannard Baker were publishing their startling investigations, Welling's continual preachment was this: if the schools had done what they were made public institutions for these things could not be. For forty years he has clung to his faith in education as the cure of civic ills. From the first he has backed the junior republic at Freeville. Of the seventy-five "tough boys" who originally entered, he says, seventy are honest, self-controlled, industrious citizens, earning as much as $5,000 a year each. In all his straightforward accounts of the backwardness of the schools there is no note of discouragement from him. "Here," he says, "is what you men want. This is no mere device for the improvement of school discipline. Pupil cooperation in school-government is civic and moral training. Here is something which requires your best brains and your constant nurture. To organize the school city or state and expect the machinery of it to do the work is to let it be wrecked. Around the idea you will have to weave standards of the highest ethical significance. The dignity of citizenship, the sanctity of a promise, the responsibility of the public servant, the right of personal liberty, the value of initiative, the power of public opinion, the social injustice of wrong-doing—these phases of civic life are essential to the working of every plan of school self-government and they are the most respectable objectives any school for any purpose can have." It is remarkable how closely the conclusions of schoolmen experienced in promoting self-government plans in their own schools—the Tildsleys, the Rexfords, the Schlockows, the Ledwiths, the Zabriskies, the Goldwassers, the Maguires—parallel the theoretical considerations put forth by the amateur. Owen Johnson offered a prize for the best suggestion for social and civic organization of a college. Otto Bannard, banker; Henry Fairfield Osborn, scientist; Norman Hapgood, editor; acted as judges. The prize went to "Vittorino." Vittorino turned out to be Richard Welling. You would enjoy the disrobing act in which the doughty lawyer rips the formal robes from university practice and exposes the dummy underneath. You, the faculty, are the biggest joke in the college. You can't produce men by giving them the moral training of babes. Make every student a citizen and put on him the responsibility and duty to maintain the discipline of the school. He will learn more from passing a foolish law and setting it right than any prof-made law can teach him. You are disappointed with the honor system. Why shouldn't you be? You select one minor, petty offense and admit your inability to deal with it and so you say to the students, "Here, you do the spying yourselves." You have twisted the purpose of government into an aim of catching people doing wrong. You're in the silly season of man-training. Before your very eyes you have a big demonstration of what young men can do for themselves. You have a system of college athletics, student-managed, so prosperous that instead of employing these talents in a wider sphere you are beginning to be afraid that student activities are bigger than the interests of the professors.

Discipline by consent.—Almost thirty years after the beginning of his voluntary civic ministry, Welling was put in charge of several hundred naval reserve men in a post covering two hundred and fifty square miles of harbor and shore. He got his men together and said, "I presume you think I am going to keep after you and penalize every man I see coming late to drill, neglecting a button on your uniform, talking in the ranks, reading on duty, in fact doing your worst to make this a slack-run post and waiting for me to jump on you; doing your best to keep up the old antagonism between the commanding officer and the men, like the feeling between the school teacher and the naughty boys. I am going to do nothing of the sort. The fact is you, yourselves, want to belong to a post you are proud of. You can make it so most easily and speedily by electing a committee of your own number to see that the standards you set are realized." He nursed the plan along; he persuaded the committee to mitigate some of their too severe penalties. An *esprit de corps* that included the commander developed. His relation to the men was notably raised and dignified. They were no longer a lot of driven slaves but a company of self-respecting Americans—managing their common affairs. In telling us of this, Lieutenant Welling indulges his habitual and gentle laughter at the school and college discipline. "Our naval adventure in war time," he says, "was not an honor system, thank you. That sorry device starts off all wrong by admitting a warfare between governor and governed and is merely an agreement to abstain from a certain act of war in a single situation. It is as if students became willing to say, 'You stop watching me and I'll stop cheating, elsewhere I'll fret you with as much horseplay and silly pranks as heretofore.'" This war service must have given Welling a brimming cup of joy. He had seen his ideas bearing healthy fruit in big elementary and high schools in his own difficult city. He had urged the application of the doctrine in the higher institutions to which by long habit America looks for its civic leaders. And, now, he had seen it work with grown men so well as to bring an endorsement from the grand old sea-dog, Admiral Sims, who said, "I'm for the method you use. There is nothing better than what an inspecting admiral once designated as discipline by consent."

Why are we so shy?—I remember Welling at the Oakland meeting of our National Education Association thirteen years ago puzzled at the slowness of us. "Self-government in schools has worked successfully for over twenty years," he said, "but your prominent educators, Jeremiah Jenks, Dean Russell, Darwin Bardwell, Ella Cabot, seem to know little about it. The ideas are put into practice in but a small fraction of high schools though they have youth at the age when the social desires are most active. Demand for our literature on civic training is almost never from high schools. Why is the principle of self-government not more generally adopted by school men and women?"

What is your explanation of it? Francis Parker used to warn us that we are more prone to resist reform than are other professionals, omitting the ministers and lawyers. Albert Marble wrote a paper, "In the Rut," to show that Macaulay's characterization of universities as anchored in the onward-flowing stream of time applies to all teachers. Dr. Eliot called us fifty years behind in using what has been demonstrated to be essential. Professor Charters more generously says it takes ten years for an established truth to be adopted by public-school men. Private schools need never come around to it. A writer in the New York *World* records that we have been teaching hygiene to children for over fifty years, but in every school she visited there were some teachers with black and rotting teeth. Neglect of essentials, avoidance of perfectly obvious duties, are common enough everywhere and, unhappily for us, the community expects us to be behind the rest of the procession. If a question is unimportant whichever way it is answered it is called academic, that is, it is something fit for school, not for active affairs. If you are carrying on school without any effective attention to training children in the practice of democracy or representative government you are not lonesome and you have the answer of the complacent and the lazy: "It's not being done."

Lang says that along with our disinclination to invent improvements we have a curious aversion to copying any better thing some one else has devised. Wirt told me that most of the superintendents sent by their school boards to study the work-study-play schools in Gary came with the intent of finding things to bolster their pre-formed opposition to it. They filled their notebooks with reasons why it couldn't be adopted in their town. It is common knowledge that the political howlers who tried to drive Wirt's work out of New York admitted that if it hadn't had a foreign name attached to it they wouldn't have touched it. It is in New York, still, without the name. If a schoolman can persuade himself, said Bardeen, that he has invented something new, he'll push it until his successor is elected; and then, if there is any considerable mark of the earlier superintendent on it, the scheme is slaughtered with great ado. These reasons for omission of the service under consideration are not complimentary to us. You notice that Richard Welling does not suggest them. Neither do I. If we are slower than doctors to adopt improvements it's because there are more of us. If chemists, moving-picture producers and general manufacturers are speedier in scrapping old processes for new it's because an active competition puts more dollars into the pocket of the progressive. We have no competition and the amount of dollars added to his income by a progressive superintendent is negligible. Luckily for us, we have nothing but duty, and Mr. Welling and Miss Adair and Mr. Boynton urging us to remember that education is statesmanship, not scholarship.

Mr. Welling is astonished at our apathy but he does not seem to lose his temper with us. He assumes we are acting upon logical objections. He makes a canvass of every schoolman he meets. He'll stop even a wedding guest and ask him why not.

Now, these are the stated reasons why not.

Children aren't old enough to help govern one another. They need mothering. School is only a transferred home. Its atmosphere must be that of immediate and unquestioning obedience.

Welling doesn't answer. He does better. He quotes the Schlockows, Maguires, Goldwassers, Riemersmas, Chewnings, *et al.*, who have been using the plan for years. "Children *are* old enough; they get too much mothering now; unquestioning obedience is the political manipulator's best help. School must look forward, help children grow; don't keep them in the mental and moral swaddling clothes of infancy."

Objection two is that the scheme would take up too much time.

Answer by users of the plan: The maximum time is that of three teachers an hour a week in the largest schools. All other time is in assembly periods and is an excellent use of them. Furthermore, there is no school subject so vital among the justifiable purposes of tax-supported education as this. The objection reminds you of the complaint of a division head in the federal Department of War who, when the trouble with Spain precipitated a conflict, protested "everything was running all right here until you started a war."

Objection three: The machinery is so elaborate it kills the spirit.

Answer of the users: Don't make the machinery elaborate.

Objection four: It can not take care of serious cases, thievery, immorality, and so forth.

Answer: It has handled thievery, obscene speech, writing and markings. There are school offenses which may be best treated by adults. Every self-governing project should be frankly auxiliary. Final responsibility rests on the principal. He delegates what he thinks best.

Objection: It lessens the influence of principal and teacher.

Answer: Aha! Now you are getting warm. This is why George III opposed democracy; it lessened his royal influence. This is what makes pedagogues contemned: their love of power. Kill it.

Objection: The children don't take it seriously.

Answer: Not unless you do. But when a sincere headmaster respects the organization of his boys and girls it soon becomes as serious and practical as grammar, manual training, or any school activity.

Last objection: It has been tried many times and failed.

Last answer: This seems to be your strongest point and you know it is your weakest. It would have stopped the digging of the Panama Canal, the laying of the Atlantic cable, the navigation of the air, the cure of various diseases now under control, the success of every venture following much failure. The training of citizens is not a simple matter of machinery to be set going and left to itself. School cities and states, commission form of government, have, of course, danced gaily into some schools; they have attracted attention by their novelty; they have lost both; apathy has let them die. If we come to divest ourselves entirely of partiality we can say that the self-governing scheme may be harmful in school. It certainly may be harmful in the adult world, as witness the periodic scandals of it in New York, Chicago, Philadelphia, Baltimore and Cincinnati. So, too, the monarchical system, common as the type of school government, may be harmful. It was so when Henry VIII had his way with it, the brute! It seems so to many Americans when a dictator rules. But the thing that Welling is pushing in the concrete, and that presidents of the national association of teachers are promoting in general: direct training for politics, is so distinctly promised by American legislation, so unescapably required by accepting the funds of childless taxpayers, that we must feel ashamed of the neglect of civic training in our own schools and in the country at large.

Mine own eyes have seen.—I had the good fortune to be transferred to a school, the Washington Irving, New York, in which there was a group of teachers imbued with the ideas Richard Welling was spreading. These good people had a club. They read papers; they discussed. Instead of a principal's meeting presided over by him, the school developed the usage of putting school matters up to this club for discussion and recommendation. The club met Monday afternoons; any teacher could be a member. There were no dues. It elected a new chairman for every meeting. We had Edward Goldwasser lecture on school as a training-ground for citizenship.

One group of progressives advocated the self-governing plan. The majority of the teachers cheerfully voted it down. But when the innovators organized their own sections with student officers, had secretaries who called the roll and attended to the multitudinous details about which we are always protesting, and when the other instructors saw a class taken in hand by an elected officer and started at work pending the arrival of a delayed teacher, they, too, except a few hard-boiled ladies of the old school, adopted democracy. In time, by suggestion of teachers, the big company of over six thousand girls got itself into a well-ordered state with elected legislative, judicial and executive officers, entitled according to the work they did, and imitating the organization of the state government omitting many officers not needed in a school.

Mr. Goldwasser told us this student participation scheme would be harder. It wasn't for me or for any teacher on the staff. Our advance guard had been telling us we underestimate the brains and abilities of school children. What surprised me most was the better judgment of conduct by girls of fifteen than by teachers older than that. The punishment prescribed by a principal that had turned schoolgirl rowdies into popular heroes was now supplanted by a discussion by schoolgirl officers. The effect was astonishing. Along came the woman suffrage agitation with the possibility that these young women might have the duty of full citizenship put upon them. What had been started as a convenience in the management of a large school became a specific preparation for a civic obligation. It made government a personal concern. I recall that Mabel Skinner, who was one of the first to see the wide bearing of the device, used to break all of us of saying "the government," as if it were a thing apart. She made us always say, "the people organized as government," or "we, the government" or "our representatives," anything to get the realization that we are a republic. I recall that our history teachers almost revolutionized their instruction with their efforts to make it an aid to being a citizen, a voter, a public servant. Now, after twenty years of trial, the scheme is a part of the daily program of that school and is indispensable.

A rose to the living.—If Richard Welling were dead the tributes to his memory would not be so numerous or so well advertised as those for Mr. Tex Rickard, promoter of prize fights. I don't know that a subscription paper would be circulated collecting money with which to pay for putting R. W.'s statue in front of the Bureau of Education in Washington. So, I'll make his panegyric here, with the idea that his path of reading will not lead through these pages and I may be as frank as I choose.

TO RICHARD WELLING

HE GRASPED THE INTENT OF THE FOUNDERS OF PUBLIC SCHOOLS
HE MARVELED AT ITS NEGLECT
HE ORGANIZED GOOD CITIZENS TO REALIZE IT
HE ENCOURAGED PROGRESSIVE TEACHERS TO WORK FOR IT
HE GAVE OF HIS TIME AND LABOR AND EARNINGS TO FOSTER IT

WHAT?

THE PRACTICE OF REPRESENTATIVE GOVERNMENT IN SCHOOL
THE CULTIVATION OF CIVIC RESPONSIBILITY AND HONOR

WITH WHAT SUCCESS?
GOD KNOWS

What does the National Association of Superintendents mean?—I am past the time of life when I expect to see a proper thing, a desirable idea, a general need, such as this, taken up by everybody and pushed to success, unless there's big money in it. I have expected every year or so to see Welling give up the scheme because so many of us neglect it and chase after building surveys, project method or some more secondary concern. But there he stands like John Quincy Adams with his abolition proposals, or Susan B. Anthony with her plea for suffrage, or Andrew Carnegie with his prayer for peace. He might wish to break out into the sad old song:

Oh, Richard! Oh mon roi,
L'universe t'abandone

But he doesn't. Though the procession of once red-hot reformers goes passing on into voluntary ease and enjoyment, this happy warrior offers new bids for prize essays, new pleas for real civic teaching and practice. You really ought not to let him do your work, alone. You ought, as a pure matter of duty, to get the pupil practice in representative government started in your school and write Sir Richard the lion-hearted in his castle at 2 Wall St., New York, how you are coming on. For your president, Mr. Boynton, reminds you that citizenship, not scholarship, is the purpose of the public schools.

Our fathers risked and some of them gave their lives to set up an ideal which has cast its light into the farthest corners of the world. To keep it burning they especially conceived a new and different purpose of education. None are so particularly elected to realize their vision as we. None have more signally neglected the duty. No single class is more uninterested in politics than teachers are. Centuries of other aims have blinded them. Although and because this task requires the highest intelligence, the greatest patience, the irksome risk of wandering in new fields, the exercise of high courage, we must undertake it and persist.

A REVIEW OF BETTER BOOKS

By HOI BIBLIOLOGOI

FOR the thirty-third time the glimmers of light and leading, which are we, shone or flickered in the long *salle des notables* of the family Rose between lines of portraits of the worthies who have pushed their part of the world ahead: Socrates, Plato, Quintilian, Comenius, Locke, Franklin, Washington, Wilson, John Dewey and Frank Loesch. Books of many colors were ranged upon the narrow table. The bibliologoi chose what they thought they had a taste for. Father Rose distributed other volumes. For the remainder, lots were drawn. Whereupon, being invited, the members began the discourses.

Gains and near successes of the researchers: University of Illinois.—He whom we call our Energetic Euclid brought a sheaf of books on tests, measurements and research. He said:

"When you realize that between thirty and forty million copies of educational tests are now sold every year by the publishers you will wish to have in your professional library some volumes treating of this timely subject. May I begin with this live report on ten years of research?[1] Walter Monroe, the stable, well-balanced director of the research division of our state university, is the chief editor. When he began examining the bewildering mass of material that has been liberated since 1918 and noted its wild assumptions, he was ready to weep. Its shallowness, its dabbling, its lack of logic, its stopping short of definite conclusions, its apparent inferiority to studies in medicine and other sciences, its extravagant claims, its failure to use suspended judgment, disappointed him. But as he notes the growing critical attitude of researchers he cheers up. The day of high-pressure propaganda is passing; the dawn of patient, careful, temperate experiment and study is approaching. The net effect of the research movement justifies its continuance. Who wants to go back to the days when educational questions were decided by argument from general principles? Who wants to be working at a service which its leaders say can not be measured—must be done in a mist? When other fields have been illuminated, when farming, healing, electrical engineering, are supplanting guesses by scientific demonstration, we want more solid ground than the footing offered by the arm-chair theorists. You will find the history of the movement in this book an enlightening story. From James Rice's proposals forty years ago, from the experiments of Francis Galton and J. McKeen Cattell, to Thorndike, Binet, Simon, Ayres, the army tests, Pintner, Pressey, Buckingham, Terman, McCall, Strayer, Engelhardt, Scott, Rugg and others, the growth and refinement of measurements are traced with illuminating emphasis upon their value and defects. The University of Illinois bureau, alone, has printed nearly a hundred studies in this field. The list of books and articles on research and related materials from 1918 to 1927 includes 3,650 titles, one for every day in the year, except for the two twenty-ninth days of February, when some lady researcher was otherwise concerned. A topical index, beginning with 'abilities,' and ending with 'Zizendorf,' refers to each of these 3,650 discussions. 'Curriculum' has received the most attention by the writers of these ten years. Next come achievement tests, then intelligence, English, arithmetic, promotion, finance, extra-curriculars, junior high school, objectives, reading, high schools, rural education, surveys, salaries. You will pardon my enthusiasm if I express the opinion that this modest-looking gray volume, with its considerate bracing of stout linen on the hinge, deserves to rank in the front row of notable books of the year."

What youth is: Hollingworth.—Dr. Batwell will now be heard from:

"It has been a long time since any one has sent us a book on the adolescent. D. Appleton and Company now favor us, that's the proper word—benefit, aid, serve, entertain, edify and please us with Professor Leta Hollingworth's contribution[2] to our need of understanding American youth. The book is a good one for boys and girls; it is a good one for parents; it is especially valuable for us who are in the youth business and find it as necessary to keep informed of the best that has been issued as to the rearing of human livestock as does a guardian of other living creatures find it essential to

[1] Walter S. Monroe and others, "Ten Years of Educational Research." Press of the University of Illinois, Urbana. 367 pp. $1.00.

[2] Leta S. Hollingworth, "The Psychology of the Adolescent." D. Appleton and Co., N. Y. 259 pp. $1.50.

read his trade journals. Do you know when I look at you and realize that no owner of thoroughbreds would dream of letting you, with your rudimentary knowledge, undertake the rearing of his horses, I am amazed and astounded at the indifference with which the community intrusts to you these priceless human cubs and colts about which you know less than nothing, because what you do know isn't so. When I go to a teachers' convention and observe their cheerful stupidity about youth, I could weep. I am sustained only by the fact that parents know less than you do. Dr. Hollingworth wants you people to realize that you may be a great blessing to your country if you bring yourselves to understand these ambiguous years. She hints more gently than I have done—she is a lady—that you need to mend your ways of acting toward the changing child. What, then, have we here? Adolescence—what it is; what is happening physically, mentally, emotionally; how absurd and harmful the myth is that there is a magical change at puberty in disposition and intelligence; how the ceremonials of all races have celebrated the change of the child to a youth; what facts related to these ceremonials still are important in Chicago, in Carsapolis, on the farm. These are the preliminary subjects presented. You'll profit by the chapter on the second weaning, homesickness, the right and wrong kinds of mother and, especially, by the analysis of school failures. Vocational problems are especially pertinent for you. So is the chilling fear, such as you and I had when we looked into the dark prospects of earning our living. I pass over the sex problems which, of necessity, require extended consideration. They are, here, less hazy than usual. They are presented with dignity and without shame. Religion, doubt, adolescent philosophy, finding the self, stumbling-blocks, conflicts, companions, clothes, diaries, day-dreams, crimes, diseases and, at last, maturity, are the successive stages of the profitable and mind-expanding journey on which the able, interested and sympathetic guide conducts you. Years ago, the Appletons brought out the first big work on adolescence, the book by G. Stanley Hall. For a long time everybody quoted him. Now, the same house publishes this compact little volume on the same subject. I do not find G. Stanley even in the index. But wait, here is a satisfactory statement by the author, 'Students may miss extensive reference to Dr. Hall's voluminous pioneer volumes. The fact is, methods of study and social conditions have been so modified that such reference would seem of historic rather than of practical value to-day.' *Sic transit gloria Stanli.* He pushed educational science so far ahead with such a brave spirit that no one would rejoice more than he that it has left him so far behind."

Classroom discussions of courtship and marriage: Cooper.—The Doctor continued:

"Meanwhile Dr. John Cooper, of the Catholic University of America, issues his work on life problems[3] as course IV, in the series of outlines for colleges. Its emphasis is on the practical moral and religious life of the student, now, and in the near future. It is adapted to the senior year. The men are mildly interested in theoretical religion but keenly alive to its practical aspects. The Doctor gives headings for coming lessons and asks the students, later, to bring questions for answer and for discussion. Let the instructor select those that are vital. Plans are given for organizing this material. The matters presented in the volume include broad-mindedness, high motives, choosing life work, choosing a mate, courting, entering wedlock, playing the parent's part, leisure time, health, work and faith. Broad-mindedness doesn't mean freedom from truth. So long as the question had no conclusive answer men were perfectly free to hold that the earth was flat or not. Now we can't be broad-minded by holding that either answer may be right. A visitor was speaking to Pope Pius X in the harshest terms of non-Catholics. 'You can not,' said the pope, 'build religion on the ruins of charity.' Catholics must not be lacking in appreciation of those not of their religion. All men are brothers. Faith without love is faith without works, dead. In the choice of vocation, Dr. Cooper sets these criteria: The career for which one is best fitted, in which he can render best service to God and man, in which he may expect to be reasonably happy and content, is the one to be chosen. The imminent problem to those about to graduate, the selection of a wife or husband, is handled with a rare combination of delicacy and common sense. Falling in love is not the wild and blind process of the cheap novel. It is nearly always consequent on a studied and rational procedure,

[3] John M. Cooper, D.D., "Religious Outlines for Colleges." Course IV. Catholic Education Press, Washington. 207 pp. $1.25.

often on a more or less systematic search for a compatible companion to fall in love with. The questions for class discussion bearing on courtship and marriage, the weighing of looks, health, intelligence, education, domesticity, disposition, morals, tastes, situation, religion, are direct and essential. The Doctor quotes figures to show that in the opinion of college boys character is the first requisite of a wife; health, second; disposition, third, and wealth, last, in the ten desirabilities to be found. In the opinion of girls tested their preferences as to husbands are in this order: an intelligent, a moral, a healthy, a like-minded, a good-tempered, an educated, a religious, a wealthy, a domestic, a handsome, man. The Doctor's neat little book abounds in kindly, cheery, elevated, dignified and human ideas."

Putting value into May-day: Grover.—Our Martin of Tours reported:

"The time of out-door jollification will soon be here; the value of a reference book for various holidays is constant so far as the worker in a public school is concerned. So let me press upon your attention two works that were sent to the club in the last batch. Katherine Grover[4] has written a cheery account of the five years of campaigning to get the attention of the country focused, every May-day, on the health of children. The brochure starts with a cherishing of children and is signed, 'Herbert Hoover.' The book recounts the activities of the society devoted to getting the May-pole as a symbol of joy, health and beauty restored to a place in the activities of city and country. In every state of the Union the Child-Health Association is pinning daisies on lapels and singing, 'Ho for the May-pole, happy lads and lasses, better children for the nation, a better nation for the children.' How the different localities are celebrating May-day, children's health day, will interest and please you. Read the book."

A felicitous book of days: Hazeltine.—More from Martin:

"For every holiday Mary Hazeltine, principal of the library school, University of Wisconsin, has given us a surpassing aid.[5] The bright red volume is a calendar of days. Saint's days, movable feasts, birthdays of the great, anniversaries of events, are here in proper order. There are references to more than a thousand books, which have been analyzed to furnish additional material for those who wish. Customs, programs, exercises, pageants, costumes, flags, are here, with a marvelous index which only a modern library expert knows how to make. Being a Chicagoan, I think of LaSalle. There he is in the index with 'November 22' put after him. I turn to the page marked November 22 and here is my Robert Cavelier, sieur de LaSalle, 1643–1687, with library references telling me where I can find his exploits and his portrait. Alongside of him, for they belong to November 22, are St. Cecelia, Andreas Hofer and George Eliot. Now my lady Carolina, what's your birthday?"

"January 3, 1895," unblushingly responded our Lady of the South.

"Here you are," said Martin, opening his book. "Your patron saint is Genevieve, who is the guardian of Paris, the beautiful. You may get a good account of her in 'The Book of Golden Deeds,' Charlotte Yonge, p. 121; in Baring-Gould's 'Virgin Saints and Martyrs'; in Brewster's 'Saints of the Christian Church'; in eleven other books, most of which will be found in any good public library. On your birthday were also born Marcus Tullius Cicero and Lucretia Mott, and on it was fought the battle of Princeton. I'll not stop here, for I find in the index that your state, South Carolina, was born May 23, 1788, which day was later chosen as a good one to be born on by Margaret Fuller and James Buchanan Eads. Look, now, see how the book is made. First comes the chronological calendar, three hundred and sixty-six days, each with its events and personages and such supplementary matter as I have just demonstrated. When there is a big day, like the twelfth of February, come such things as quotations on Lincoln, typical speeches on him and by him, biographies, poems, program suggestions, stories to be read aloud, drama suitable for production on this day, memorials, portraits, statues. Following this full calendar come books about holidays, special days and seasons, holiday customs, programs and exercises, entertainments and parties, pageants, books about persons referred to in the calendar, how to make clippings and then—the marvelous indexes. A classified one in which

[4] Katherine Grover, "The Story of May-day." American Child-Health Association, 370 7th Ave., N. Y. 106 pp. 10 cents.

[5] Mary Emogene Hazeltine, "Anniversaries and Holidays." American Library Association, Chicago. 288 pp. $3.00.

men and anniversaries are sorted as actors, artists, architects, saints and scientists, teachers (thirty-two of us), soldiers (forty-seven) and, then, the general index of everything and everybody.

"Every librarian is asked for help for celebrations. Twenty-eight years ago the Wisconsin Library Commission began issuing bulletins of suggestions for holidays. The editions were soon exhausted. What we have now in this new book is the culmination of years of labor by the generous author, busied most of the time in training librarians and in giving university courses in bibliography. The number of people who helped is large. This, truly, is a monumental work. It has a unique chapter upon how to use it and what questions it will answer. Furthermore, it has blank spaces in which may be made appropriate entries as somebody rises into prominence. Charles Lindbergh is in, and Herbert Hoover, but as it went to press before the last nominating conventions we can add the name of that good American and true sportsman, Alfred E. Smith. Thompson is here. I turn to March 26 and find that he is dead and that his name was Ben—Big Ben, I imagine. He shone in physics, not in politics, and is better known as Count Rumford, inventor of a baking-powder and an acid phosphate. However, as Chicago is mentioned for the Fields, Eugene and Marshall, for Jane Addams, Cyrus McCormick, Professor Millikan, John Dewey, Theodore Thomas and Dwight L. Moody, and maybe for others, we shall survive."

Now children are trained for better use of their brains: Stillman.—Anna Abjornsen, the Viking, speaks:

"If either Frank McMurry or Boyd Bode would commend any one to me, I should consider such a one worth listening to. When both of them go to the length of writing commendatory introductions of a book, as they have in the case of Miss Stillman's work,[6] I expect something particularly good. I am not disappointed. Thinking, says the first-mentioned of these two indorsers, is more valuable than the facts imparted in school. The right way of thinking is in demand all the time. There is little need for most of the facts we get in a classroom. So most of them are soon forgotten. The time is at hand when examination on the methods of study will be the main test of the learner's progress. Not 'What do you know?' as Eddie McGuire says, but 'How do you find it out?' The ordinary curriculum is unfavorable to study. It scarcely allows it. Brother Bode chimes in with a remarkably persuasive plea for thinking rather than memorizing. The teacher who stimulates pupils to think should be at peace with all the world. She is a shining light in the murk. The work of the school tends constantly to rote. The assignments are merely so many tasks which, except for a few, have no interest or significance. For a long time failure to arouse genuine interest was attributed to the natural wickedness of children, something to be flogged out of them. Now we are coming to realize that the trouble is due to the stupidity of educators. Teachers, as a class, tended to misconceive the purposes of the schools. Results were naturally unsatisfactory. The school easily becomes an artificial thing. The learning in it differs from the learning outside. Albert Leonard has remarked that if he asks a boy in school about something that the boy 'hasn't had' in school no intelligent answer will forthcome. But if he takes the lad across the street and asks him, the boy will use his brains. Now, Miss Stillman, who has been using hers in the fifth, sixth and seventh grades of the Ethical Culture School, New York, begins by reminding us that a child who is merely told to study a lesson will make as poor a job of it as any one without instruction will make of playing a piece on the piano. We let children put emphasis on absorbing as much material as possible, not on understanding it. They learn to work for marks, not for mastery. If we are to produce citizens, and that's what schools are charged to the community for, we must train children to think. We can force children to take certain steps, but if the interest, the success, the satisfaction, are absent there will be small chance of their taking steps voluntarily after the pressure is removed. A child below the high school doesn't know how to go about school requirements. Leave him entirely alone and he is more likely to develop wasteful mind-habits than to get power. He flounders with trial and error experiences. With intent to show us the main point of training right mental control, Miss Stillman gives us chapters upon stimulating the questioning habit of mind, helping get food for thought, helping organize facts, teaching eco-

[6] Bessie W. Stillman, "Training Children to Study." D. C. Heath and Co., N. Y. 245 pp. $1.60.

nomical use of memory, making ideas function, self-expression. It seems to me the mere repretition of these chapter headings will show you what a lively little book this is. It is definite; it is comprehensive; it is bright."

History taught for mastery: Kelty.—Mr. Judd Post, the suburbanite who teaches social studies in a famous adjacent municipality and who, in our club, goes by the nicknames of Semaphore and Signpost, reported as follows:

"I see that Professor Henry C. Morrison's book on the mastery theory of teaching is beginning to show itself to be what this club proclaimed it when the volume appeared, an epoch-making work. The whole school system of Oak Park has been reorganized by Superintendent Hamilton on this plan. Now comes a book[7] by the very live lady who supervises history and the social studies in State Teachers College, Oshkosh. Miss Kelty tells us she is following, in general, Professor Morrison's technique applied to an organization of history material as influenced by Professor Tryon, of the University of Chicago. This is a masterly work for thoroughness and extent. The very liberal sprinkling of bits of startling common sense prevent it, large as it is, from getting dull. 'Don't interrupt to correct a child when talking.' 'Don't call your written exercise a test; tell the children you want to ask them several questions. They'll soon learn what is expected of them.' 'If you call on the best students at first, for the entire recitation a high standard of performance is set and all of the class gets a model for the whole term. Children learn more from one another than from an ordinary teacher.' 'Don't attempt drill before the children have enough to drill on.' 'Eliminating a child who makes mistakes, sending him to his seat, removes from the drill the person who needs it most.' 'Encourage the skipping over unfamiliar words on the first reading. Often the context will tell the meaning of such words.' 'There is little danger of having children dislike history through the reading of books that are easy; but there is great danger of causing children to form an aversion to the subject if the reading matter is too hard.' From these samples gleaned here and there from the pages, you well see that the lady Kelty has her eye on the children all through the course of her work of organizing elementary-school history on the mastery-unit basis. What is needed, she tells us, is to organize on social and economic lines the basic movements or forces working in American history. They must be given in simple narrative style. In this book the wholeness of history is observed. The narrative is continuous. The biographical element is subordinated to the progression of the idea or movement. Personages are selected from the lists recommended by William C. Bagley in his study of history texts and from reports of committees considering the social studies. Objective, informal tests are suggested for every story and provided for every subject unit. Special care has been taken to see that the tests measure comprehension rather than memory. Materials usually considered in separate civics courses are here treated as parts of historical movements, such as immigration, industry, labor unions and city problems. Now, as I said a moment ago, Miss Kelty is organizing the teaching of history on the basis of units to be mastered, not as matter to be 'covered' day by day till we are through the book. Only by organizing events into large movements, unified and coherent, can the piecemeal memorizing of unrelated facts be avoided. If you try to pick up a handful of loose beads they run through your fingers and escape. If they are on a string you can hold them. The hope in teaching unrelated events that you can bind them together afterwards by review has failed. Miss Kelty describes various methods of preserving unity. The details of getting complete mastery of essentials are made clear. The score-card used looks to me like a piece of good business. It gives the diagnostic element determining what to do next with each youngster. Children who fulfil the requirements of the score go on with the reading described in each lesson. Those who don't reach the score take seats in a compact group and study their cards to ascertain their failures. The teacher gives the explanation necessary to teach the point they missed. That strikes me as a very modern idea. It seems to assume that if the children fail on any point of the lesson the teacher, like the doctor trying, say, to quicken a heart beat, gives another portion of the tonic. Why not? It gets children much farther along than punishing them for what we assume is due to their own inattention or stupidity, when, if you look at it in another way, we have just as

[7] Mary G. Kelty, "Teaching American History in the Middle Grades of the Elementary School." Ginn & Co., N. Y. 748 pp. $2.40.

much reason to conclude that an unlearned point is an indication of more skilful teaching needed. With the particularity with which a work on medical practice would cover a typical case, Miss Kelty reviews the details of teaching for mastery. She illustrates the preparation, the presentation, the reteaching, the subpresentation, assimilation, drill, tests, organization, recitation, etc. These are technical terms. They mean definite procedures which are to be maintained as essential to success. A great many of us are impatient of formal steps. They seem unduly cramping. They prevent 'nishative.' But the lack of them, or of something, in the teaching of history has made it such a ramble that in order to enable her to get a basis for marking, many a teacher relies on memory of dates as a test of her children's history work. That is as bad as any formal procedure I ever heard of. Miss Kelty is taking a method that has been worked into a productive process in the Chicago University experimental school. It has been subjected to rigorous tests. It produces real learning that lasts to a higher degree than any class teaching yet found. You will enjoy my lady's enunciation of these procedures. The presentation is given by the teacher with the real story-telling attitude and not in the didactic manner of the lecturer. Teacher makes it as dramatic as the nature of the matter will permit, with life and motion and color. She does not stop to answer questions until she has finished. Then the children ask about what they did not understand or did not hear or about words they do not recognize. She must not wander off into elaborations. She must know her story thoroughly and not be bothered with her written notes of it. She has to hold the interest or she'll fail in getting concentrated attention. This must be secured by the story and not by admonitions. Then comes 'the presentation test.' It must closely follow the story. Miss Kelty's book is full of these. The teacher's score-cards of these tests show the points not mastered. She reteaches the presentation. Reading by the pupils gets 'the assimilation.' You begin to see how thorough and, at the same time, how interesting all this is. I can't reproduce the whole treatise for you. It blocks out the history in units: why men crossed the seas, why English people came to live in the New World, how the English colonies came to separate themselves from the mother country, and so on, until it ends with us as a world power. There are special chapters on drill lessons, dramatization, theme illustration by pupil drawings, picture study, etc. There are time charts for pupils to make locating men and measures in relation to other people and events. The author keeps the lessons within the comprehension of little children, even to avoiding throwing any shadow on the sunny optimism of infancy. 'All the people,' it says, 'who agree in their ideas come together and form a political party. They vote for one of their own men who thinks as they do. If there are enough of them they elect him and he runs the government as they think it should be run.' "

"I presume," said Polly the Politician, "the Signpost would want them given liberal doses of boss Quay and Tammany Hall such as he administers to his own youngsters in the finest school in the world."

"But I," retorted the Signpost, "teach night-school students, not innocent babes. Along with their Santa Claus and Prince Charming they have been fed the loveliness of human nature and the goodness of our institutions in the perfection that should obtain. It makes them idealists. By the time they get to me they are old enough to feel that these dreams of a perfect society ought to be realized. It is part of my duty as a history teacher to have them see the kind of political diseases that are to be cured. As Jethro said to Moses, we must teach them laws and ordinance and the work that they must do. They have been taught the perfection of American government. Therefore let them be shown what is yet needed to realize it."

Farming and football.—"While we are touching on the most important feature of American schools," continued the Semaphore, "let me enlist your applause for a creed of American teachers sounding the true note. Here is a doctrine presented in Los Angeles to a convention of a special group of instructors representing every state in the Union:

" 'I believe that education is primarily for the civic well-being of this democracy and not for individual benefit.

" 'I believe the main purpose of education in a democracy is to prepare all its people for the duties and responsibilities of citizenship.

" 'I believe the ordinary man needs educational service as much as the superior man, and that he is as much entitled to it,' and so on.

What kind of teachers do you think issue a political educational creed like this? Do you guess they are civics teachers, or history instructors, or apostles of the social studies? They are the teacher members of the American Vocational Association, representatives of the newest specialists among us. Wherever have you seen a statement of public-school objectives so essentially the real aims of the republic put forward as a basis of teaching?"

"Right here," promptly answered Anna the Argumentative. "The committee of Chicago teachers appointed by the Dever school board to revise the course of study built it directly and fundamentally on what our dear Signpost considers a California triumph. As a result of their preliminary conferences the Chicago "curricularii" fixed the basic principles for the entire course of study. They said the schools are paid for by all the people whether parents or childless. The schools were made a community service by the founders of the republic to train coming citizens to a knowledge of and a preservation and perfection of American principles and institutions. The purpose of public schools is identical with the aim of our civic union: equality, life, liberty, happiness, union, justice, tranquillity, defense and general welfare. Every course in every subject which our Chicago teachers outlined sprang from and depended on this fundamental doctrine, that school is a public, a civic, a political service."

"Fine! Splendid!" said the Signpost, "What became of it?"

"The year's work of thousands of live teachers went into the waste basket at the nod of the spineless puppet of the me'n'-America-first mayor."

"I ought to have known that," answered the Post. "Being reminded of it, I offer my bouquets to two groups, the Chicago curriculum committee and the vocational teachers of America. I have just read a lively book[8] by a vocational agricultural professor, of Colorado, who seems to me to know how to put his subject on the front row of important considerations and to keep it there by strong arguments. Long ago, he says, at the very beginning of its history, the United States put its faith in education as a preservative of the republic. Our fathers planned for peace and prosperity. They flavored almost every speech they made with reference to those desirable things. Accordingly, education must aim at prosperity as one of its important results. We must look to education to maintain a prosperous self-reliant and permanently productive agriculture. Vocational agriculture is completing its first decade of inclusion in schools below college grade. It is doubtful if, in all educational history, there was ever so great a progress in any instructional project in ten years as has marked this. The teachers concerned have been notably eager, alert and broad-minded. They are determined to maintain the amazing advance they have already made. This book gives a panorama of the opportunities of agricultural instruction. It proposes efficiency standards. All through it the idea that teaching and practicing agriculture is a social service prevails.

"Agriculture is our basic and most essential industry, but it is no longer dominant. The increase of urban populations will put us where our farms are not growing food enough to keep us alive unless the situation is clearly foreseen and mastered. The hit-or-miss method of farming, easy enough when land was free and labor plentiful, is gone forever. No one but a scientist and business man is going to be able to hold a decent position as farmer in the future. Already agriculture is giving its prizes to managerial ability. Sound business foresight in choice of crops, use of rainy days, reduction of operating costs and most of the usages of efficient factory management must be put into farming. A hundred years ago 90 per cent. of Americans were raising crops. Now, 25 per cent. of our people in gainful occupations are engaged in agriculture. Teachers of this vocation are in greater demand every year. They are training young men to get larger returns from the soil, greater production from labor, from live stock, and so forth, than the present farmers do.

"As a teacher of any public school subject you will find Professor Schmidt's interesting treatment of the purposes of education, the qualities needed in teaching, the use of real projects, the adaptation of teaching to the needs of the learner, drill in vocational teaching, productive ability, market demands, measurements of teaching, and so forth, well worth while. Here's an odd circumstance. What do you

[8] G. A. Schmidt, "Efficiency in Vocational Education in Agriculture." The Century Co., N. Y. 314 pp. $2.25.

think has been one of the serious impediments to agricultural teaching? Football! How so? A practice has grown up by which the principal of a high school, seeking a teacher of agriculture, specifies that he must also serve as athletic coach, both pursuits being *al fresco* occupations to a large extent. The children electing farming as a study have, in so many cases, been too few to occupy a teacher's full program that the thrifty school manager has combined two functions under one head. He's supposed to put the track in tractor."

Literature for healthy enjoyment: MacClintock.—The report of Polly was as follows:

"Porter MacClintock's talks on literature and children[9] have increased in popularity to the extent that a new edition is just out. He revises it to include the junior high school, to add readings and otherwise to enlarge it. Originally consisting of spontaneous and informal talks with teachers, the chapters retain the charm of natural conversation. What a mistake to turn literature into a load, a burden, a task! What's the use of making a baby tell in absurdly correct English that Henry Wadsworth Longfellow was born in Portland, Maine, in eighteen hundred and something, and so forth and so on. Let the little dear, uninterfered with, enjoy the swing and music of the verse, the loving appropriation and appreciation of the beautiful images and pictures. Literature is having a hard time in the schools. In addition to having its aroma smothered by formalism and fact the time allowed it has been cut by the introduction of other studies. Its attraction must be allowed to charm or the situation in Chicago, where a canvass shows thousands of fairly prosperous homes with no reading matter but the newspaper, will persist. We are glib in repeating that literature cultivates the imagination. Some children are so early crushed by the commonplaces of the adult world that they seem never to have a fancy. Some, especially in the period around the seventh year, live in a world of their own creation, moving in a maze of fantastic notions. They need to have abilities developed. They need to get useful and healthy notions and to put them together so as to satisfy taste and judgment. Now, literature is always seeking beauty of form. Emotion permeates, warms and colors speech and makes it literature. An outlook on life comes with it. The best thing we can do for a child in teaching this is to give him an innocent and permanent joy. One who reads the lists of works in courses of study sees numerous disastrous mistakes, heaped-up titles that various teachers have happened to like, all that the critics have praised, all whose titles sound as if they ought to be good, all that are concerned more or less remotely with things the children are studying, all that a generation of mistaken logic has suggested, all that a mature reader ought to have read in a lifetime, all that a blind interpretation of childhood and of literature has called suitable—a chaotic jumble. Literature is a fine art. A fine art is that which seeks to engage and refine the spirit, the emotions, the taste. Let the child see people expressing their best selves in deeds and words, transforming themselves and others, calling on him for sympathy, approval and condemnation. He finds here his heroes, his ideals, his models. Without tears he learns manners; without a sermon, morals. In a sense he sees life and sees it whole. The contact with a beautiful work of art should eventuate in a higher ideal, a pure and noble joy. This is the spirit with which Maestro MacClintock carries you through the choice of stories, poetry, drama, correlations and the lists of works he has found successful in the elementary grades."

Four teachers and the enjoyment of language: Scott, Congdon, Peet, Frazee.—Principal Manzer reported:

"The educational editor of the Houghton Mifflin Company says he enjoys the book reviews produced by this club more than those composed by the most experienced gentlemen who specialize in this field. He reminds me of Alexander the Great. That conqueror's table companions (trapezoi) were expressing their preferences for musical instruments. When the young world-beater came in they asked him his opinion. You remember he replied, 'The sweetest of music-makers is the voice of him who sings my praises.'

"Our Houghton Mifflin admirer knows we confine ourselves to works for teachers rather than undertaking to expose the excellences of text-books for pupils, nevertheless he sends us these three books designed to open the door to

[9] Porter Lander MacClintock, "Literature in the Elementary School." University of Chicago Press, Chicago. 332 pp. $1.85.

language use and appreciation.[10] What he has done is to harness Zenos Scott, superintendent of schools of Springfield, Massachusetts; Randolph Congdon, principal of the Potsdam State Normal School, New York; Harriet Peet, who used to teach with us here in Chicago but fell away from us and is in Harvard, researching; and Laura Frazee, assistant supervisor of primary grades, Baltimore; all to pull together and to drive as an even team along that old, never satisfactory road known as language study. As the 'guide' issued for this series is a teacher's book I shall take the liberty of giving you my opinion of it. I like it. I admire its emphasis on pupils' talk, conversation, its stress upon courtesy, its exercises aimed at naturalness and loss of self-consciousness, its modern tests, diagnoses and remedial work. The open-door idea these bright collaborators are working with is an intent to lead every child, no matter how endowed, so that he will develop himself in the use and enjoyment of language. These authors are persuaded that a child shall be childish enough and shall grow without dislikes into a refined and educated person. They have composed their course on the self-activity basis. The very first lesson invites and requires conversation. As you go farther you are introduced to pronunciation of hard words, use of capitals, grammatical necessities and refinements of various kinds of composition. The themes for reading, hearing, discussing and problem-solving are remarkably adapted to the interests of children of the ages involved. And, it seems to me, the authors are more concerned with worth-while ideas, citizenship, kindness, honesty and human virtues than is common in reading books not so enjoyable as these."

Teaching is not merely hearing: Monroe.—Then came Euclid II, to wit:

"Our Illinois Monroe, Walter, is beginning a teacher-training series to be done in collaboration with Messrs. de Voss, Weber and others, and to be published by Doubleday, Doran and Company. Educational psychology will be treated and various high-school and other problems. The editor of the series leads off with a solo[11] on the theme of how the teaching of us high schoolers can be so done that the pupils will learn. Both junior and senior high schools are considered. That we, ourselves, in using the book shall practice what we intend our students to do, there are numerous exhortations that the reader of this book get himself away from the passive habit and make himself work. You will be handicapped, says Walter, truly, if you fail to have clear concepts of the technical terms used. List them, write definitions, cite illustrations. He is in some doubt as to whether our predecessors did much more than assign lessons and hear them re-cited. He inquires, 'Do you feel that your high-school teachers specifically tried to direct your learning? If so, how? If not, why?' How was it with the Bibliologoi? As many of you as had little or no high-school teaching other than memorizing and repeating book stuff say 'I.'"

Everybody over forty and some under that age said it.

"There you are," said the Geometer, "you confirm the sad verdict of the author that 'recitation,' 'lesson-hearing,' has been the almost universal, wasteful usage of high schools. Even to-day, according to this book, the activities of many teachers do not extend much beyond. So the professor quietly but thoroughly takes up the exercises of learning, objectives, motives, habits, reading, making use of knowledge while acquiring it, patterns of conduct, class management, rewards and penalties, extra-curriculars, projects, measurements and plans. It is a stiffening book, not to be skimmed. It correlates and fits for use the results of many studies scattered through recent professional literature. I've had it for three months. I've read parts of it from day to day. If you will not carry this beyond our intimate circle I will tell you that I was a pretty good high-school teacher before and am a better one, now."

Examinations and the will of heaven: Orleans, Sealy.—More from the West Side Euclid:

"The World Book Company has adopted a pleasing ceremony of introducing its publications with a short and pithy observation written by some modest member of the staff whose de-

10 Scott, Congdon, Peet, Frazee, "Open-door Language Series." Houghton Mifflin Co., Boston. Books I, II, III and Teacher's Guide. Price not given, but may be surmised to be reasonable.

11 Walter S. Monroe, "Directing Learning in the High School." Doubleday, Doran & Co., N. Y. 567 pp. $1.60.

light in pleasing readers contents her or him with the obscurity of namelessness. This book on testing[12] has this pretty suggestion illuminating the copyright page: 'In other days there were ordeals by fire, by water, by battle, by examinations in academic subjects. But the will of heaven was not always truly divined. To take an examination was a highly chanceful proceeding. It is the purpose of the new tests to reveal the needs of the teacher as well as the needs of the student, to lighten burdens, to do good.'

"The authors prove to be an excellent team for work like this. Jacob Orleans served in the measurements bureau of the New York State Department of Education and had to work upon those continuously-bombarded things known as the regents' examinations. Glen Sealy is superintendent of a system of schools in Lewis County, New York.

"Now, say these gentlemen, the published standard tests are valuable but they don't fit all the needs of any school. Each educational unit should also have its own. Teachers make examinations but it is rare that the maker has had any training in proper construction. Let us show him how to make and use accurate and comprehensive tests and how to apply what is learned from them to the greatest advantage of the school. Why the tests? They are to tell me where I missed making my teaching effective, what my failures are, what I need to repair. They are for showing the school superintendent where the successes and failures of his school system are located. The book contains an apparently good series of usual examinations such as you and I are setting. By fair analysis it shows imperfections in them that any one except a hide-bound traditionalist will see are serious. The authors furnished a group of teachers with identical copies of papers written by pupils in answering these examination questions. Orleans and Sealy asked that the answers be scored. The same thing happened that Professor Eliot pointed out twenty-five years ago. Even in arithmetic, the least variable in true answers, there was a variation of 75 per cent. in the ratings of the same performance. Here's a good illustration: One question was, 'Why should the handkerchief be used to cover the nose and mouth when sneezing or coughing?' It was one of the several questions in the hygiene examination and was to score 12.5. The answer to be scored by all the teachers was: 'The handkerchief should be held over the mouth and nose because it helps the disease jerms from coming out.' Fifty-three teachers marked it. Six gave it perfect, 12.5; six gave it 0; the other forty-one markers scored it at different rates from 1 to 11. The impossibility of evading personal whims, hobbies or judgments in rating pupils, in judging essays or recitations, in appraising teachers, in promoting children, in giving prizes, in issuing certificates, on the basis of the usual type of tests, has been demonstrated over and again until not a college student or a school child or the parents of either, regard our ratings as of any account. What Messrs. Orleans and Sealy set out, here, to do is to suggest a scheme of testing which will materially decrease the unfair discrepancies in judging the abilities and learning of school children. The method of devising tests, the participation of all the teachers in the educational unit, the setting of the examinations, the tabulation of results, the class graphs changing day by day, the individual graph kept by each pupil, the use of results, a very generous assortment of tests in all the school subjects, constitute the body of the work. What gives it a particular value is the fact that it is not a treatise written in the library but an account of the team work done by the teachers of Lewis County. There are frequent pertinent suggestions of progressive usages found to be advantageous, like this: 'When the pupil puts his record on his graph get him to have a goal marked on it, also, toward which he aims to go during the next five months.'"

Everybody's fortune: Yard.—A discourse, or is it an address, by the young man who is called Old Locality:

"Ladies and Gentlemen, with your kind permission I shall now deliver a lecturette on my lands and parks. I own them in partnership with some odd hundred and twenty millions of other Americans. I am at the present moment an authority on this subject, having just studied a beautiful book[13] by Mr. Robert Sterling Yard, who confesses himself an amateur but whom I

[12] Orleans and Sealy, "Objective Testing." World Book Co., Yonkers-on-Hudson, N. Y. 373 pp. $2.20.

[13] Robert Sterling Yard, "Our Federal Lands." Charles Scribner's Sons, N. Y. 360 pp. $5.00.

pronounce a thorough, painstaking accurate and decidedly entertaining essayist. Following him, I divide my subject into forests, irrigated lands, parks, monuments and Indian reservations. I take the last first.

"Three hundred and fifty-five thousand red men own and occupy land set apart for them by us. They are scattered among twenty-four states, including New York, Michigan, Florida and the West. There is a persistent idea in many minds that the Indians are a degenerating and disappearing fragment of a once strong people, driven by force from their ancestral lands, decimated by centuries of persecution, wars and disease, undermined by liquor and drugs which we have sold them, impoverished by official oppression and private fraud. But if you take the trouble to count our conquered wards you find that not only are they steadily increasing in number, improving in health and education, but that they average the wealthiest people in the world. Besides individual holdings, which average $2,300 for every Indian, each has an interest in tribal property averaging nearly $3,000. Where they live and how, you may find described in a hundred and twenty-eight pages of interesting story, illustrated with remarkably well-taken photographs, in the fascinating book I hold in my hand.

"Next, Ladies and Gentlemen, behold our national forests. We owe them to a company of patriotic and scientific citizens who organized the American Forestry Association in 1891, only thirty-seven years ago, secured the act of Congress known as the Forest Reserve Law. It locked up such precious lumber that the attack of high financiers backing western senators seemed likely to brush President Grover Cleveland aside. But that first president for whom I cast my first vote justified my confidence in him and refused to be brushed. Then came President Roosevelt, without the assistance of my vote, and built up a conservation policy which is one of his best progressive services to us. I commend to you the perusal of the chapter on forests in this book. It uses enough statistics to let you feel you are getting solid fact; it selects and arranges events, description and argument so as to keep you alert and entertained.

"And now, my friends, I take up the reclamation service of our people. The growth of our population has now, for twenty-five years, constrained forward-looking men to see the eventual failure of our land, under its present style of cultivation, to feed the nation. Vast areas of fertile soil remain a desert from lack of water. For millions of years rivers like the Salt and the Verde had been only the flow of mountain waters to the distant sea. On each side of them so far as the eye could reach desert stretched in dreary solitude bearing only the useless sage and the prickly cactus. To-day the three hundred and seventy-five miles of former desert waste are unbroken green. The soothing hue of the alfalfa greets the eye. Wheat, oats, cotton, oranges, grape-fruit, a variety of lusciousness, make the mouth water. Where residence meant starvation, now a hundred and seven thousand Americans live, work, sing and go to school. My fellow countrymen, if you desire an hour of solid pleasure and profit I show you the way. Read Sterling Yard's narration in this book and look at his brilliant photographs. Reclamation! What an inspiring thought! In the west it is needed because of neglect by nature; in the east, by reason of abuse by man. New England, Virginia, the Carolinas, other old states, have exhausted and abandoned their farms. The most of the land is susceptible of being reclaimed. While water solves the problem in the west, fertilizer will, in the east.

"Next, I treat of the use of water-power. Although we have more than half of the known coal supply of the world and only 8 per cent. of the globe's population, our largest asset of power in the future will be that which can be had the cheapest. Up to the present time water-power has not averaged cheaper than steam. But the use of it saves coal. You see the implication involved. The money barons are after the waterfalls. Hence, as in Hetch Hetchy and Niagara, wonderful natural beauty is sacrificed. Boodle versus beauty. You are or should be interested in your coal, your oil, your other mineral resources which are yet in control of yourselves, organized as government. Let me suggest that you check up on your resources as described in the volume I hold in my hand.

"May I next speak of national monuments? The word in the technical sense in which Mr. Yard and I use it indicates not only a structure, as the obelisk at Bunker Hill, but any landmark, object or area which commemorates an event or preserves an antiquity or a striking work of nature, the artist artificer. Twenty-five years ago there began to be shipped from central Arizona gorgeously colored slabs of stone, coming by the carload to make mantels, table-tops and other embellishments for the homes and clubs of the rich. It was loot from the marvelous petrified forest. No law could stop the taking as the land was ordinary public domain. Lohn Lacey, of Iowa, and President Roosevelt in 1906 got an act passed to preserve such properties. I now own, in common with you, fifty-eight of these, according to the list Mr. Yard has made of my property. In our domain are the cliff-dwellings of New Mexico, natural bridges in Utah, caves in Oregon, in Wyoming, in New Mexico and in Nevada, mastodons and fossil plants, works of the mound-builders in Ohio and historic forts at Niagara and on the Atlantic seaboard. I have enjoyed few narratives more than Mr. Yard's descriptions of these possessions of mine. There is probably no other single object in the world so appalling in size and so exquisite in beauty as my Rainbow Bridge. It would easily span the Tribune Tower, stood upon the nearby group of sky-scrapers. The pile could slip under it with room to stack other buildings on before they touched the arch. Of red stone in a yellow desert, its modeling and proportions suggest the inspired art of man.

"Speaking of national monuments, there are many which by curious workings of a hasty law are not officially so named. Late in the movement of organizing national property came the act to create military parks. Chickamauga is one; Antietam is another. Our Lincoln monument in Springfield is not, under the federal act, a monument. It's a military park. Somebody persuaded Congress that Lincoln's birth was a military event; hence the designation of the structure commemorating his nativity.

"In conclusion, Ladies and Gentlemen, may I express the opinion that your perusal of the part of this book which covers our national park system will afford you much valuable pleasure? The movement originated in the desire to preserve for all time extraordinary beauty and majesty of native landscape in original, unmodified form. Yellowstone was the first to be secured. Its acquisition was an instance of patriotic generosity which ought to be put in the reading books designed to cultivate American virtues. About fifty years ago Christopher Hedges and a company of gentlemen adventurers of Montana, hearing wild tales of boiling fountains, of mountains roaring with internal fires and of other wondrous things, set out to explore the public domain in which the Yellowstone River rose. Such marvels there they found that, following custom, they resolved to take possession of the land under homestead laws and grow rich out of the admission fees and hotel charges to be gathered from sightseers. Hedges conceived the public-spirited project of making this wonderland the possession of all of us forever. His companions hailed the idea with enthusiasm. So was born our National Park system. What it comprises in its nineteen areas, what dangers confront it from money grabbers, from unbalanced local pride, from whizzing motorists, together with much of other engaging matter, you will find in 'Our Federal Lands,' by Robert Sterling Yard.

"To Robert be paid the compliment due a piece of work well done. He has given us a volume that should be in every public-school library, for it is a compendium of our common possessions presented in a style to engage young and old. You can, with much profit, use any chapter of it as an assignment for study and report in connection with civics, with history, with geography, with English composition, for it is all of these. Besides the general satisfaction of knowing about matters of general American interest, I am given by its perusal a fresh sense of pride in my country and gratitude for the work done by those officials who have seen the big significance of these movements. Especially grateful am I to Mr. Yard who has given me a delightful reading lesson. Ladies and gentlemen, I thank you for your kind attention."

By permission of the Paterfamilias the recorder folded his stenographic notebook and put it and his pencils in the gem of a mahogany case which Stephen of the cunning hand had made. The conversation centered upon whether a teacher should borrow money for a trip abroad before seeing America first. There was much animation around this point, and no conclusion, even though hot coffee and sandwiches revived the vigor of the debaters. When the lighted clock in the railway tower across the avenue said ten and a half, the chairs were stripped of their tapestries, the folding clothes-racks stored away, and hoi bibliologoi fell apart for the month.

SCHOOL AND SOCIETY

EDITED BY J. McKEEN CATTELL

WITH WHICH IS COMBINED THE

EDUCATIONAL REVIEW

EDITED BY WILLIAM McANDREW

Volume XXIX — Saturday, March 9, 1929 — Number 741

THE CLEVELAND MEETING OF THE DEPARTMENT OF SUPERINTENDENCE, NATIONAL EDUCATION ASSOCIATION[1]

By Professor W. CARSON RYAN, Jr.

SWARTHMORE COLLEGE

"Articulation" and pre-school education were the two topics emphasized at the 1929 meeting of the Department of Superintendence, National Education Association, held at Cleveland, Ohio, from February 24 to 28. Other subjects received a considerable amount of attention, notably school-financing, teacher-training, research and character education, but the two indicated emerged most definitely, not only in programs set apart especially for their consideration, but in other departments and affiliated organizations throughout the meeting.

Articulation of School Units

The actual title of the seventh yearbook of the department was "The Articulation of the Units of American Education." Under that title the commission headed by Superintendent Herbert S. Weet, of Rochester, presented accounts dealing with the articulation problem as a whole and articulation in relation to the elementary level—kindergarten and grades 1–6; in relation to the secondary school level—"junior high school through junior college"; at the professional and higher education level; in the field of teacher-training, and in the field of adult education. In presenting the yearbook Mr. Weet said:

> As this commission views its task there are three important fields with which it must concern itself. The first has to do with larger units of school organization, such as the elementary school, the junior high school, the senior high school, the college and university, the teacher training institutions, and finally the unit for adult education. That we have not as yet solved all the problems of coordinating these larger administrative units is a proposition that will be accepted without serious debate.
>
> The second field of work involves the smaller units of school organization such as the grades, or whatever other subdivisions may lie within any one of these larger administrative units. This field takes us at once into the whole subject of what is commonly understood as promotion.
>
> And, finally, in the third field the commission hopes to press back to those conditions which surround the pupil in his journey from one point of transition to the next and which so largely determine the nature of the problem at the transition point itself. The very working conditions as regards the curriculum, or the size and varying abilities in any given classroom, for example, may be such as to defeat all other attempts at proper coordination.

[1] For the address of the president of the department at the Cleveland meeting see School and Society for March 2, 1929.

Following Superintendent Weet's presentation of the work of the commission, Professor John Dewey attempted an analysis of the general principles of educational articulation. He pointed out there were two ways of approaching the problem of elimination of waste in the educative process of the schools—the administrative way, which takes the existing system as a going concern and inquires into the "breaks and the overlappings," and the "personal, psychological, moral" method, which starts from the side of personal growth of individual needs and capacities, and asks what school organization is best calculated to secure continuity and efficiency of development. He insisted that there was no necessary opposition between the two modes of approach—that they were, or should be, complementary, just as "when engineers in tunneling a mountain bore from opposite ends." On the one hand, an approach from the exclusively personal side will overlook certain administrative necessities; but, on the other hand, undue attention to the administrative side tends toward "rationalization" of the divisions that happen at a given time to be institutionalized.

In summing up this part of his paper Professor Dewey said:

It is recognized that adequate treatment of this fundamental problem—the mutually complementary character of the administrative and the moral psychological development of individuals—must wait upon command of greater knowledge of the actual process of normal growth than anybody now possesses. Nevertheless, reference to the latter is important, for it indicates, in the first place, the necessity of continued study of personal growth as an inherent factor in the problem of articulation from the administrative side. And, in the second place, it serves as a warning, a *caveat*. It cautions us against a too ready assumption that the present institutional division into separate units has necessary inherent value on account of corresponding "epochs" of personal development. It warns us against attaching too great value, decisive value, to matters of administrative habit and inertia. A complete examination of the question of articulation can be attained only when the experiences of classroom teachers in immediate contact with pupils are procured and utilized, as well as the experiences of administrators. . . .

The findings of experimental and progressive schools must also be included, not as models, but as providing data regarding processes of personal development under different conditions.

That selection and training of youth by higher educational institutions must be founded upon "a right assessment of qualities and abilities other than the merely intellectual," was the contention of President Edward C. Elliott, of Purdue University, who discussed the problems of articulation as seen by colleges and professional schools. He added: "The inevitable conclusion of the present trend is that in the not distant future the higher training afforded by our colleges, universities and technical schools will come to be regarded as the expected preparation of all those properly fitted for the responsibilities of complete American citizenship—in other words, the higher educational system of to-day is to be, indeed must be, amalgamated into the common school system of to-morrow."

In the eight discussion groups of Tuesday afternoon, February 26, the articulation theme was continued. Meeting jointly with the National Council of Childhood Education, some of the superintendents considered "the relation of creative education to the science of education." They heard Dr. Bessie Lee Gambrill, of Yale University, assert that "if creative education has discovered a method of freeing the powers of the child in ways that enrich his own life and that of his fellows, this discovery must be made available for all the children of the nation," and they also heard Professor Frank N. Freeman, of the University of Chicago, caution against excessive self-expression or self-activity as likely to develop "distorted personalities." Other discussion groups attacked the conventional articulation problem more specifically—the advantages and disadvantages of the 6–4–4 plan of organization, as set forth by William John Cooper, newly appointed United States commissioner of education; the six-year high school for the larger city and the smaller community; accrediting agencies and college entrance requirements, and economy of time in the reorganization of the educational units. Superintendent S. J. Slawson, of Johnstown, Pennsylvania, described a four-year junior college plan which sought to substitute for the traditional curricula of the freshman and sophomore years a content based on the needs of the community. Jesse H. Newlon, head of Lincoln School, Teachers College, Columbia University, was certain that as far as the secondary school and the college went articulation could not be achieved "while the secondary schools are bound hand and foot as regards the most vital part of the curriculum." Emery N. Ferriss, Cornell University, asserted that "organized guidance is destined to become one of the most dynamic forces operating in the direction of curriculum articulation." Henry C. Morrison, of the University of Chicago, reiterated his attempt to distinguish the secondary school from other units of the educational program by defining it in terms of function as "that period during which the pupil is capable of learning by study, but is not capable of setting his own problems, controlling his own time and advantageously pursuing specialized study," and pointed out that this definition is not a question of grades nor of years, but of development.

PRE-SCHOOL AND PARENTAL EDUCATION

Both meetings of the National Society for the Study of Education were given over to the twenty-eighth yearbook of the society, "Pre-school and Parental Education," the Saturday evening meeting discussing the organization and development of nursery schools and other forms of pre-school and parental education, while the Tuesday evening meeting considered "research and methods" in this new field. The report of the study was presented by Lois Hayden Meek, educational secretary of the American Association of University Women; Mrs. Helen T. Woolley, director of the Institute for Child Welfare Research, Teachers College, Columbia University, and Edna White, of the Merrill-Palmer School, Detroit. In introducing Miss Meek as chairman of the Yearbook Committee, Professor Koos pointed out that so far as the records seemed to show this was the first time in the history of the society that there had been three women on the program and a woman as chairman of the yearbook committee. All three of the women speakers agreed that pre-school education of the kind they had in mind (for children from a few months up to five years of age) was still too costly and too uncertain in its theories and techniques to be taken over as a regular part of the public educational program, but they looked forward to the time this form of education would definitely be a part of the public-school provision, not only for the sake of the children themselves, but also as part of the pre-parental education of junior and senior high-school boys and girls. Superintendent of Schools Carleton Washburne, of Winnetka, Illinois, the one administrative officer scheduled to discuss the yearbook, admitted that he had at first been opposed to the idea of pre-school education in connection with the school, but after having had a nursery school as part of his own public-school system had become heartily in favor of it. Professor Freeman, whose function it was to make a "critical evaluation," testified that the yearbook committee had done what seemed to him to be a very good piece of work, and his criticisms were confined to minor details.

That "the proper study of mankind is the child" was the statement with which

Professor Arnold Gesell, of the Yale Psycho-Clinic, began his description of research in child development at the Tuesday evening meeting. He reminded the audience that the kindergarten was already an important part of the public-school provision, and as a "frontier" institution would be of value in understanding the new movements for education and research with very young children. Miss Patty S. Hill, of Teachers College, enumerated the types of pre-school training described in the yearbook—home, day nursery, nursery school, kindergarten and Montessori school, and pointed out that the distinguishing characteristic of pre-school education was that it was first of all "a school of experience." Dr. Douglas Thom, of the Massachusetts State Department of Mental Diseases, emphasized the mental hygiene possibilities of pre-school and parental education. In his "critical evaluation" of the second part of the yearbook, Professor Edward A. Bott, of the University of Toronto, contrasted research in the field of child development and research in the natural sciences, pointing out that in studying child development it was never possible to disregard "the whole child." Professor William H. Kilpatrick carried out Professor Bott's dictum regarding the whole child, and paid tribute to the importance of the point of view in the yearbook as affecting not only pre-school and parental education, but the whole educational program. He asserted that mental hygiene should be a part of the preparation of all teachers.

Financing Education

Financing education was the main theme at the Monday morning session of the Department of Superintendence. Following President Boynton's address, Professor George D. Strayer, of Teachers College, launched into a vigorous and effective analysis of the school finance situation. Admitting the rising cost of education, he asserted that "a nation which is able to save fifteen per cent. of its income annually need not be anxious over the expenditure of a little over two and a half per cent. of its income for education." He pointed out, however, that the aid of both state and nation would in many cases be necessary to support local education in such a way that every child might have the chance to which he was entitled. Although there are throughout the United States some communities that are approaching adequate provision of education, side by side with these are "other schools and school systems that deny opportunity to the great majority of those who should profit from education."

Discussion of school finance was continued in the Monday afternoon discussion groups. Paul R. Mort called attention to the fact that the hold-over of an antiquated financing system has caused many states to attack the financing problem as distinctly a rural finance problem. "This is a serious error," he said. "The rural schools of the state can not be financed by a plan which does not take into consideration all communities, rural and urban." Superintendent L. P. Benezet, of Manchester, New Hampshire, analyzed in a somewhat novel fashion the increasing cost of the public schools to the taxpayer, showing among other things that the habit of some people of funding wealth in order to get a fixed but sure income has the effect of making such taxpayers peculiarly sensitive to even slight tax increases. He described the direct gains that a community obtained from public education, arguing that on the whole taxpayers were reasonably willing to pay if they were certain what they were receiving for their money. He pointed out that men who made a sufficient financial success in business were often quite ready, when they could afford it, to spend in tuition at a private school many times the amount of the *per capita* public-school cost.

Training of Teachers

Few recent meetings of the Department of Superintendence have given as much attention to teacher-training as did the Cleveland meeting. At the Wednesday morning session Superintendent E. C. Hartwell, of Buffalo, described the difficulties of teacher-training institutions in many states, which, he said, "annually fight a life-and-death battle for bare existence." Instead of being recognized as the most important institutions of the commonwealth, he said, they frequently rank far down in the list of state responsibilities, with "politics, indifference and low salaries" often combining to supply them with "a pathetically inferior administrative and teaching staff." Dr. Frank P. Graves, commissioner of education of New York State, argued for the right of the state to select with the greatest care the students to come to its normal schools and teachers' colleges and prepare for teaching.

Many other group meetings took teacher-training as a topic of discussion. Representatives of departments of education in landgrant colleges were told by Dr. William J. Cooper, U. S. commissioner of education, that the supposed oversupply of teachers in some parts of the country was really due to an excess of unprepared teachers—that recent Bureau of Education studies indicate that there is still a very real lack of qualified teachers in the United States. Miss Kate Wofford, of Laurens, South Carolina, said the biggest job the county superintendent of schools had was to give his teachers satisfactory in-service training; Professor Julian E. Butterworth, of Cornell University, put it up to training institutions to know more accurately what rural teachers really needed for their work, and A. G. Yawberg, county superintendent of Cuyahoga County, Ohio, emphasized the necessity for the type of teacher-training that would acquaint teachers with what is known as "creative teaching." Because normal schools and teachers' colleges tend to be far behind the best current practice, Carleton Washburne gave it as his opinion that "at no time has there been so great a need for training teachers in service as now." He said:

> To-day we need to train teachers to adapt their work to the wide differences that exist among individual children; to do active and worth while research in connection with their classroom problems; to look on the misbehaving child not as a culprit but as a patient; and to release each child's creative powers and train him in the best social use of those powers.

A still more fundamental attack upon the question of teacher-training was that of Ross L. Finney, of the University of Minnesota, who declared that present methods of "professional education of educators" were faulty in that they represented a false analogy between education and certain other professions, notably medicine and the law. If education was to do its real job it must, he believed, be rooted in an adequate study of what society is to become; it must emphasize the responsibility of educators for social guidance.

Character Education

Character education was the subject of most of the main addresses on Thursday, the final day of the convention. Dean W. F. Russell led off by explaining what impressions he had received from certain scientific investigations of character education that have just been completed. His conclusion was that character education was not merely important—it was "the outstanding end of our education. To the degree that we achieve it, we succeed; to the degree that it eludes our grasp, in that measure we fail. Once we learn to accomplish it, our major problems are solved." Dean Russell said that he had about decided that the schoolmasters of Eton and Rugby knew what they were doing when they "picked children from good homes and gave them 'schooling' inside the building and 'education' outside on the playing fields." America's task was to supplement the five-hour day, five-day-a-week type of schooling with something a little more like the twenty-four-hour day of the boarding school.

In one of his characteristic addresses, Dr. William C. Bagley repeated his denunciation of "soft pedagogy" and its place as one of the factors in current American problems of crime and divorce. Expressing faith in the new generation as at least as good as those that have gone before, and probably "more sane and wholesome," and specifically absolving leaders of the "progressive education" movement, he nevertheless argued that certain extreme examples of the freedom theory in education had much to do with the present situation.

Other Meetings

The printed official program of the Department of Superintendence at Cleveland included meetings of the following organizations: Department of Elementary School Principals; Department of Rural Education; Department of Secondary School Principals; Department of Vocational Education; American Educational Research Association; Municipal Normal School and Teachers College Section; National Association of Deans of Women; National Association of High School Inspectors and Supervisors; National Council of Childhood Education; National Council of Education; National Council of State Superintendents and Commissioners of Education; National Society for the Study of Education; National Society of College Teachers of Education. This list did not include, of course, various other associations meeting prior to the meeting or at the same time. Among important meetings just prior to the opening of the Department of Superintendence program were those of the National Vocational Guidance Association and the American Association of Teachers Colleges. The former organization held a meeting on Saturday, February 23, addressed by Randall J. Condon, William M. Davidson, Thomas E. Finegan, and Frank D. Boynton, which was well attended by the advance guard of superintendents. The teachers' colleges group had under consideration the statement of standards, about which so much of discussion and progress has centered in the past two or three years. Before the National Council of Education, Henry Lester Smith, of Indiana University, presented the preliminary results of a study of methods of teaching world-relationships, and John K. Norton, of the Research Division of the National Education Association, gave a thoughtful analysis of the proper functions of the council. The Department of Secondary School Principals authorized a committee, headed by Professor Charles H. Judd, of the University of Chicago, to cooperate with the U. S. Bureau of Education in the study of secondary education recently made possible by a special appropriation from congress. At a meeting of the Board of Directors of the National Illiteracy Crusade plans were adopted for a campaign this spring to have as many as possible of the million illiterate mothers in the United States taught to read and write before "Mothers' Day" in May. The International Relations Committee of the National Education Association held a meeting in anticipation of the Geneva meeting of the World Federation of Education Associations in July.

Election of Officers

The only nominee for the office of president of the Department of Superintendence was Superintendent Frank Cody, of Detroit. Other officers elected were: Second vice-president, Norman R. Crozier, Dallas, Texas; member of the executive committee, David E. Weglein, Baltimore,

Maryland. The retiring president, Frank D. Boynton, of Ithaca, N. Y., becomes first vice-president.

RESOLUTIONS

Resolutions were adopted as follows at the Thursday morning meeting:

1. *The Main Purpose of the Public Schools.*—Again we remind ourselves that our state systems of education were established in accord with the proposals of Washington, Franklin, Jefferson, and a long line of farseeing statesmen for the purpose of preserving and improving our political institutions. Again we recall that our wages are paid and our equipment provided by a tax on all the people whether or not they be parents. Thus reminded, we pledge ourselves anew to the direct teaching of the duties of citizenship in all the school grades. Not culture, not scholarship, not self-support, nor compliance with the entrance requirements of more advanced schools shall turn us from the duty of teaching our youth the needs of our civic life and from inspiring our citizens with a determination to improve it.

2. *Federal Department of Education.*—Again we commend to the Congress of the United States the establishment of a Department of Education not inferior in importance and dignity to the Department of Agriculture, or Commerce, or Labor, or War, or the Navy, and give to this department the standing and honor appropriate thereto. To consider that the levying of import duties, the operation of banking systems and of the postal service are more national and less local in scope than is education, is to deny to education the recognition which is its due. By national legislation we now seek to protect the republic against a flood of ill-prepared immigrants. It is no less a national matter to protect the nation as a whole against the ignorant fanaticism of improperly trained citizens growing up within our borders. The fundamental purposes of this nation, equal rights to life, liberty and happiness, equal duties to promote justice, domestic tranquillity, common defense and the general welfare are thwarted so long as the human product of a less fortunate state is free to carry his dangerous ignorance to any other state. We urge that a Department of Education be established as a means to secure a more perfect union.

3. *A Fair Chance for the Rural Districts.*—We renew our pledges to secure better support for rural schools through our advocacy of large units of financial support, to the end that the country child, and his parents, may fully enjoy that equality of educational opportunity which is our national boast.

4. *Extension of Public Schools.*—Convinced by the amazing increase in enrolments of the colleges and universities that our people are awake to the need of school training beyond the age of childhood, we commend the addition of junior colleges as an integral part of the public school system, and we advocate the establishment and generous support of one or more state universities in every commonwealth of the union.

5. *Fitness for Educational Service.*—If the nation's purpose is to be realized, and if the teaching profession is to profit through the improved technique developed by a notable increase of scientific educational research, a higher degree of professional skill than is now common will be required. We pledge ourselves to continued alertness in professional study; to more effective provision for the training of teachers in service; to demanding better preparation before the appointment of teachers, and to more drastic dismissals of those who fail to give adequate attention to improving their usefulness.

6. *War.*—We repeat our belief that war is an outworn barbarism which should be rejected by civilized nations. Education is life. It is inherently obligated to secure the use of intelligence and reason in the settlement of disputes. It proposes agreements in advance of difficulties so that settlements may be made without the destruction of life and property. We join with our fellow teachers overseas in devotion to the duty of training mankind to adjust disagreements without the shedding of blood.[1]

[1] In addition to the above resolution, there was printed in the official program of the department the following statement regarding the Pact of Paris:

"To the teachers of America.

"Your attention is called to the following Peace Pact signed by the leading powers of the world, whereby thinking men in control in the nations have agreed to bring their differences to the council table and to beat their swords into plowshares. Ours is distinctly a work of peace, preparing the boys and girls of this generation to promote international goodwill when they shall succeed to the control of affairs. Let us take advantage of this opportunity to teach to our children the spirit and the letter of this great Peace Pact which, perhaps more than any other one thing in the memory of men now living, will promote the principles of the Prince of Peace.

7. *Child Labor.*—We continue our indorsement of intelligent legislation aiming at the liberation of children from the stunting effects of severe labor. The main and great purpose of public education can not be realized unless all children are kept out of industry so long as their attendance upon school is more profitable to the nation than is their presence in factory, mine or store. We urge that adequate provision be made by the schools to assure equal opportunity to all children.

8. *American Education Week.*—Although every week of the school year is an education week, we believe that to concentrate the attention of the people upon the work and needs of the schools during a common period observed throughout the nation has proved a valuable project. We recommend a continuance of this observance as a period of demonstration of the purposes and work of the schools.

9. *Boy and Girl Scouts and Similar Organizations.*—We are convinced that the work of scout and similar organizations is strongly contributing to the training for character sought by the schools. We do therefore, in our several communities, continue to advocate provision for meeting places, aids to the instruction of adult leaders, and other helps which may be given by the school.

10. *Parent-Teacher Organizations.*—We compliment and commend the Parent-Teacher Associations for their increasing attention to the problems of public education. We shall encourage reasonable participation in their activities by public school workers and shall assure them of our cooperation in their efforts for the good of children.

11. *Other Supplementary Service.*—By sad experience, we know that too much dispersion of effort impairs the value of school service. Success in school work depends largely upon plans made well in advance of action. We pledge ourselves once more to persuade our communities to abstain from using or misusing the schools for the collection of money from children; for the celebration of the numerous special weeks and special days, and other similar interruptions other than those approved by school boards and superintendents at least a year in advance. We recommend that solicitors for replies to questionnaires be referred to the research division of the National Education Association, an obligation to which superintendents may consider themselves bound by the passage of this resolution.

12. *Economics.*—We urge upon every community an honest study of its school budget. We remind those whom we serve that the average emolument of physicians, lawyers, architects, of all those persons in charge of interests no more precious than those in our care, is higher than formerly and is not being reduced. We condemn the attacks made upon school cost by uninformed persons whose intentions are good, by informed persons whose intentions are bad and by paid objectors who are more concerned with their own fine salaries than with the good of the state. We believe that expenditure for public education is recognized by the best minds of the day as the most generally profitable investment the nation can make. We hold that failure to pay good wages for educational service is failing in securing the best results.

13. *Support of the Federal Bureau.*—We commend the Congress for its increasingly generous appropriations for the Bureau of Education pending the establishment of a Federal Department of Education.

14. *Propaganda.*—We reiterate our belief that the public schools shall offer no lodgement for literature of the propaganda type, nor any encouragement to speakers who have propaganda to spread through contacts with school children. We pledge ourselves to protect our schools against the insidious wiles of all agencies which seek to serve private ends through misuse of school publicity.

15. *Restricted Immigration.*—We endorse present legislation restricting the flood of an unassimilable immigration, whose only effect is to lower American standards of living, American wage rates and American ideals. We pledge our support to any legislation having for its object the maintenance of a thoroughly restricted immigration, and a close enforcement of such restrictions.

16. *Teachers' Retirement Funds.*—We affirm our belief that an equitable and actuarially sound teacher retirement system is essential to the best interest of the nation, and we therefore recommend a thorough study of such retirement programs by all persons interested in education.

17. *Appreciation.*—We desire to express to the good people of Cleveland, to its municipal administration, and especially to Superintendent R. G. Jones and his coworkers in the schools of this city our appreciation of their endeavors to make of this

---

"Article I—The High Contracting Parties solemnly declare, in the names of their respective peoples, that they condemn recourse to war for the solution of international controversies, and renounce it as an instrument of national policy in their relations with one another.

"Article II—The High Contracting Parties agree that the settlement or solution of all disputes or conflicts, of whatever nature or of whatever origin they may be, which may arise among them, shall never be sought except by pacific means."

convention a successful event, and to convey to all of them our heartiest thanks for their assistance.

18. *Our Own People.*—We record our satisfaction with the work of our officers, committees and permanent staff, who have conducted the business of the department with fidelity, intelligence and efficiency. Especially do we urge and commend the continuance of studies having for their object the elimination of waste in school procedure, the introduction of more successful methods of teaching, and the realization of the important aims embodied in these resolutions.

19. *Conclusion.*—Continuing in the public employ with intent to serve our country to the best of our ability; convinced that no line of national activity is of more importance, we pledge ourselves to the support of these resolutions and to a fearless, energetic conduct and defence of the public school system to the end that it may approach to the peerless consummation visioned by its founders.

Adopted this twenty-sixth day of February, 1929, by the Department of Superintendence, National Education Association, convening in Cleveland, Ohio.

THE UNITED STATES DEPARTMENT OF EDUCATION

ADDRESS ON BEING INTRODUCED TO THE DEPARTMENT OF SUPERINTENDENCE, CLEVELAND, OHIO, FEBRUARY 28, 1929

By WM. JOHN COOPER

UNITED STATES COMMISSIONER OF EDUCATION

MR. CHAIRMAN, President Lamkin, ladies and gentlemen of the convention: It is most gracious of Dr. Boynton to invite me to the platform of this great convention and to present me thus formally to my colleagues in education. He displayed toward me a rare quality of mercy, and perhaps toward you also, in suggesting that only a brief address would be expected on this occasion. I know that you do not expect from a commissioner who has been in office for less than three weeks and has had no opportunity to master routine and administrative detail to suggest even an outline of policies for the Bureau of Education. You rightly expect that policies will be developed as needs arise, and I am confident that in the development of such policies I shall enjoy the advice and counsel of many of you who are sitting in this audience to-day. It is not without significance to me, however, that this first formal introduction to my colleagues is to the Department of Superintendence of the National Education Association and that it occurs in the state of Ohio. For you will consider it in order, I am sure, if I recall to your minds some contributions of the state of Ohio and of this association to the establishment of the U. S. Bureau of Education. To do this in the short time allotted me I must pass directly to events immediately following the close of the Civil War and comment on those acts which actually accomplished the establishment of the Bureau of Education. This I do without in any way disparaging either the splendid vision of Henry Barnard or the heroic efforts of Barnard and his colleagues for more than twenty years before that time.

First, then, may I speak briefly of the contributions of Ohio as represented by three of her distinguished sons. The superintendent of schools of this very city in which we are now meeting, Andrew Jackson Rickoff, made an outstanding address before the National Education Association meeting at Harrisburg, Pa., in 1865, when he spoke to the topic "A National Bureau of Education."[1] In fighting for the endorsement of such a bureau on the floor

[1] National Teachers' Association: Journal of *Proceedings* and Lectures of the Annual Meeting held at Harrisburg, 1865, pp. 299–310.

of the convention Superintendent Rickoff moved an amendment to Hart's motion of approval. This amendment provided for a committee which should follow up the endorsement and make the association's approval known and felt in the halls of Congress.[2] It is worthy of note also that in Superintendent Rickoff's address are to be found outlined practically all the functions that the Bureau of Education has actually exercised since its establishment.

Next, may I remind you that the chairman of the committee which represented your organization, then called the National Association of School Superintendents, in its efforts to have a Bureau of Education established, was the Honorable E. E. White, commissioner of common schools of the state of Ohio. I would that there were time to read you merely the introduction to Commissioner White's report, since it constitutes an eloquent plea for universal education as a necessary prerequisite to universal liberty. So splendid is the argument that I wish to illustrate it by reading from it two brief paragraphs:[3]

When the exercise of sovereignty by the people is both universal and *for the welfare of all*, a democracy is the perfection of human government; but to the extent that such right is withheld from the people or is wrongfully exercised by them, just to that extent are democratic institutions imperfect and a failure. Hence the *capability* of the people to exercise sovereignty for the general welfare is a fundamental and vital condition of republican institutions. When such capability does not exist, the universal exercise of sovereignty is a condition of national weakness, if not of peril. I am thus led to inquire what this capability includes, and what are the essential conditions of its existence.

It clearly requires the necessary *intelligence* to determine what will best subserve the interests of all; and the degree of this intelligence must not only be sufficient for self-government on the part of individuals and individual communities, but the people, as a whole, must be able to weigh and decide upon questions which involve national interests. Hence the higher the civilization embodied, the wider the extent of territory embraced and the more various the pursuits and physical conditions of the people, the higher the degree of intelligence required for the right exercise of sovereignty.

But there is a third Ohio citizen whose interest was equally great and whose efforts actually accomplished the results desired. He was a distinguished educator, soldier and statesman, celebrated in our school histories as a martyred president, James A. Garfield, who introduced the bill "to establish a National Bureau of Education." He became chairman of the select committee of seven to which the bill was referred. He made an able and brilliant speech in its behalf on June 8, 1866,[4] and after an adverse vote on the measure secured a reconsideration of it and finally a favorable vote. During his speech on this bill Garfield paid splendid tribute not only to the educators of Ohio but to the public spirit of her taxpayers. He said in part:

Mr. Speaker, if I were called upon to-day to point to that in my own state of which I am most proud, I would not point to any of the flaming lines of her military record, to the heroic men and the brilliant officers she gave to the late contest; I would not point to any of her leading men of the past or the present; but I would point to her common schools; I would point to the honorable fact that in the great struggle of five years through which we have just passed she has expended $12,000,000 for the support of her public schools. I do not include in that amount the sums expended upon our higher institutions of learning. I would point to the fact that 52 per cent. of the taxation of Ohio for the last five years, aside from the war tax and the tax for the payment of her public debt, has been for the support of her schools. I would

[2] *Ibidem*, pp. 223–224.

[3] E. E. White, "National Bureau of Education," a paper read before the National Association of School Superintendents at Washington, D. C., February 7, 1866. In *Proceedings* of the National Education Association for 1901, p. 418.

[4] James A. Garfield, "Education—A National Interest." Speech of James A. Garfield, of Ohio, in the House of Representatives, June 8, 1866, on a bill "To establish a National Bureau of Education," etc. In *Proceedings* of the National Education Association for 1901, pp. 425–433.

point to the schools of Cincinnati, Cleveland, Toledo and other cities of the state, if I desired a stranger to see the glory of Ohio. I would point to the thirteen thousand schoolhouses and the seven hundred thousand pupils in the schools of Ohio. I would point to the $3,000,000 she has paid for schools during the last year alone. This, in my judgment, is the proper gauge by which to measure the progress and glory of states.[5]

Not only Ohio but also this great association assembled here to-day may take pride in the accomplishments of the Bureau of Education and a deep interest in its future success, since, according to the official records of the House of Representatives, yours is the immediate responsibility for the establishment of this bureau. From a report of the House Committee on Labor and Education to which was referred the report of the commissioner of education for 1867–68,[6] I read the following extract:

The Department of Education was established in pursuance of an act which passed this House on the 19th of June, 1866, by a vote of 80 yeas to 44 nays, and the Senate without a division, February 26th, 1867, and approved by the President March 2, 1867, as follows:

(Here follows the text of the act which created the bureau and which I omitted from this paper.)

To continue from the report:

The bill for the foregoing act was reported by a select committee of this House, appointed on a memorial of the National Association of State and City Superintendents of Public Schools, which met in Washington in February, 1866, and was unanimously of the opinion that the establishment of a national office "would greatly promote the interests of education by rendering needed assistance in the establishment of school systems where they do not now exist, and prove a potent means for improving and vitalizing existing systems."

The Bureau of Education is operated to-day under that very act the text of which I omitted above, slightly amended by later appropriation acts. That act as we are specifically told in the record grew directly out of "a memorial of the National Association of State and city superintendents of public schools."

If I may recall hurriedly the events of those few months they are these: The Washington meeting of the superintendents assembled February 7, 1866; Commissioner White's paper mentioned above was read on the same day. Three members of this body, E. E. White, of Ohio, Newton Bateman, of Illinois, and J. S. Adams, of Vermont, were appointed a committee to memorialize Congress on the subject. The memorial was promptly prepared dated February 10 and was presented in the House of Representatives by Congressman Garfield on February 18.

And now that you, the school administrators of America who are carrying on the work so well begun by the National Association of Superintendents of Public Schools, have formally received the eighth commissioner of education here in this state of Ohio, what more should the commissioner say? Perhaps it will suffice for him to state that he has the same faith in universal education as a prerequisite to universal liberty as did Superintendent Rickoff, that he is as anxious for the Bureau of Education to render service to the schools of America as was Commissioner E. E. White, that he has the same pride in the public school systems of the American states as James A. Garfield had in the public schools of Ohio. In fact your commissioner is the product of the public school system, elementary, secondary and collegiate, of one of the states of this union. For twenty-two years he has served public schools as teacher, supervisor and as administrator. For nearly a decade he has been sitting among you as a fellow city superintendent or as a fellow state superintendent. He now awaits your advice, your counsel and your instructions, for it is written: "Whosoever will be chief among you, let him be your servant."[7]

[5] *Ibidem*, p. 428.

[6] U. S. Congress. House of Representatives Committee on Labor and Education. Report 1869.

[7] Matt. xx: 27.

EDUCATIONAL EVENTS

THE INTERNATIONAL LIBRARY AND BIBLIOGRAPHICAL CONGRESS

THE first International Library and Bibliographical Congress will be held in Rome and Venice from June 15 to 30, Dr. Isak Collijn, Royal Library, Stockholm, Sweden, presiding. International schemes of classification, international cataloging rules, scholarships and fellowships, exchange of librarians, library relations and bibliography are among the subjects to be discussed.

According to the tentative program received from Dr. Vincenzo Fago, of the Ministry of Public Instruction in Italy, the delegates will arrive in Rome on June 13 and 14. The opening session will be held in Rome on June 15. From June 17 to 19 there will be sessions of the various sections. June 25 and 26 will be devoted to general assemblies, the making of resolutions and closing sessions, in Venice. From June 20 to 24 and from 27 to 30, there will be no sessions.

Special excursions will be arranged to give the delegates an opportunity to visit points of interest and the various exhibitions which are being planned especially for them. In Rome there will be an international exhibition of library work. In addition there will be local exhibitions of the history of ancient and modern Rome, of Italian books from Bodoni to the present time, and other special exhibitions in the great libraries of the city. Florence will offer an exhibition of Italian books from the invention of printing to the time of Bodoni, and, in the Biblioteca Medicea Laurenziana, an exhibition of miniatures. In Venice there will be an exhibition of bookbinding in the Biblioteca Nazionale Marciana. Special exhibitions will also be organized in other Italian cities.

To facilitate action, the Congress will be divided into twelve sections. Each section will have its own president and will discuss a different subject. Two Americans have been appointed as presidents of two of the sections—W. W. Bishop, librarian, University of Michigan Library, of the International Scholarships and Fellowship Section, and T. W. Koch, librarian, Northwestern University, of the Book Trade and Book Collecting Section.

On behalf of the international and local committee, Dr. Fago sends a welcome, not only to the official delegates, but also to all librarians and library workers, bibliographers, publishers, booksellers and book collectors in the United States and Canada. It is hoped that librarians traveling in Europe this summer will include the Congress in their itinerary. The committees have been assured of the hearty cooperation of the Italian government.

EDUCATION IN SOUTH AUSTRALIA

ACCORDING to *The Christian Science Monitor*, in 1928 South Australia spent £1,000,000 on education, and that amount will be increased substantially during 1929. A large part of this state is sparsely populated, but the government is determined that children in the outback districts shall not be handicapped by reason of long distances from the towns. No other educational system in Australia is so elastic in this respect. Special provision is made for the erection and maintenance of small one-teacher schools, and within recent months more than 2,000 additional boys and girls have been given instruction as well as accommodation.

About 800 of the state schools are each controlled by one teacher, and about 30 per cent. of these have an average attendance of less than 20 pupils. The expenditure per head of the population on education is £1 12s. 4d., and it is exceeded only by the amount of interest on loans per head, which is £2 3s. The cost of upkeep of roads and bridges is £1 5s. 9d. a head of the population, on police 8s. 3d. and legislature 2s. 6d.

The Education Department controls about 1,100 schools, with an enrolment of more than 90,000 children. Under its jurisdiction also are the Public Museum, Library and Art Gallery, School of Mines, School of Industries, Technological Museum and Observatory. Large grants are made by the departments to the university. A glance at the estimates for 1929 shows that a policy of further progress has been mapped out.

Apart from purely official activities, there are private enterprises which endeavor to meet the large need for teaching facilities in the far-away country areas. The Church of England Caravan Mission is a new venture. For the past five years some of the children in the rural districts, who have been unable to attend a Sunday school, have been taught by correspondence lessons under a scheme, now known throughout the Commonwealth, as the church mail bag school. It is felt that it is hard to get into personal touch with the children. A motor caravan has been purchased and is now being used as a missionary van for evangelistic activities among the women and children of the more isolated parts of the diocese.

NEW BUILDINGS AT PRINCETON UNIVERSITY

FIVE buildings are now being erected, or plans for their construction being drawn, with the total cost estimated at $3,100,000.

Among these is a new theater that has been made possible largely through the generosity of Thomas N. McCarter, Class of '88, of Newark, N. J., who pledged $250,000. The Princeton Triangle Club, which annually writes and produces an original play, contributed $100,000 that had accrued from its trips through the east and middle west, and the remainder was pledged by individual subscribers.

The exterior design of the building will harmonize with the surrounding buildings on the campus. Its seating capacity will be about 1,000, with stage machinery and galleries similar to those in modern New York theaters. Opening on the main lobby will be private offices for the Triangle Club managers and president, and in the basement it is planned to have a large clubroom with an informal rehearsal stage and shops where the sets, costumes and other incidentals will be stored.

The foundations have been laid for the Joline and 1903 dormitories which are being constructed on the southern side of the campus. As soon as better weather conditions prevail, work will go forward rapidly in the hope of having the buildings ready for occupancy in September, 1930. They will be constructed of Princeton stone and have rooms for 164 students.

The new Princeton chemistry building is practically finished and the equipment is rapidly being installed. Classes have already been held there, due to the cramped quarters of the department since the School of Science was burned last fall.

The Memorial Mathematics Building, to be erected in honor of the late Dr. H. B. Fine, made possible by a gift of Thomas D. Jones, of Chicago, is to be erected on the south side of the campus between Palmer Laboratory and the Class of 1903 dormitory, at an estimated cost of $400,000. Plans for this building will be drawn this spring and construction will begin soon after.

Plans for the construction of an addition to McCosh Hall soon will be ready, with work on the project expected to start before commencement. This building, which will form one side of a proposed quadrangle with McCosh Hall and the University Chapel, will contain class and preceptorial rooms and faculty offices. It will cost about $300,000.

PRESIDENT ANGELL ON YALE UNIVERSITY AFFAIRS

ANNOUNCEMENT that a new undergraduate dormitory in memory of John W. Sterling, '64, would soon be erected on the block front now occupied by the old gymnasium featured the address made by President James Rowland Angell to Yale's graduates who returned on February 22 for the annual observance of Alumni University Day. A gift to meet the cost of this dormitory, estimated at $2,000,000, has been promised by the trustees of the Sterling estate, President Angell stated, adding that the university felt it could rely on funds amounting at least to as much more, from sources to be announced later, for the erection of a new gymnasium and swimming-pool on another site.

President Angell, in his address, also told the alumni of the extent to which the university had been enabled to better conditions for the members of the faculty as a result of the success of the Endowment Fund Campaign. He said:

In October, 1925, when the campaign was inaugurated, the salary budgets in the four academic divisions of the university aggregated $1,106,005. As of October 1, 1927, the same salary budgets aggregated $1,239,070. As of July 1, 1929, they will aggregate $1,449,785, an increase of $343,780, the larger part of which has been made possible by the new endowment. It has already been possible to raise the salaries of over 300 members of the faculty by amounts ranging from $500 to $1,000 each, with a permanent upward change in the scale for all grades from instructor to professor in the divisions just mentioned. Instructors now begin at $1,800 instead of $1,500, and the $3,000 salary will be more often employed than heretofore. Assistant and associate professors of all grades are advanced $500 and the minimum professorial salary is advanced to $6,000, while a larger proportion of the professors have been moved into the higher brackets of the scale. As the remaining increments of the fund come in, we hope to be able to make still further advances.

President Angell closed his address with a résumé of the general situation at Yale, saying:

The implacable conservative must find the Yale of to-day a distressing place, for unquestionably change is in the air and for gentlemen of his kidney change is always inspired of the evil one. But for the man of progressive temper nothing could be more exhilarating than an intelligent apprehension of the great spiritual and intellectual forces that are moving all through our Yale community life. In literature, in art, in science, in the extraordinary group of our professional schools, students and faculty alike are turning with fresh enthusiasm and fresh creative insight to the tasks before them. Amid the stupendous up-rush of our majestic new buildings it is easy to forget this even more impressive flowering of vigorous intellectual achievement. But the former has meaning and enduring value only as it contributes to the enrichment of the moral, esthetic and intellectual resources of the university. To convince oneself that it is so contributing one need only visit any of a dozen new structures, such as the Gallery of Fine Arts, the Memorial Quadrangle, the Sterling Laboratory of Chemistry, the William L. Harkness Hall, or, indeed, the rising walls of the great Sterling Memorial Library. We are living in a time of profound and kaleidoscopic change, and that our Yale, like the Yale of the past, may faithfully serve her day and generation, she must to some extent adjust her policies and practices to fit the exigencies of the epoch. Ours it is to see that nothing is lost of her priceless heritage from the past, but ours also to see that her vision is not less fixed upon the golden future that she may surely fulfil the great destiny for which she was created.

THE AMERICAN UNIVERSITY CLUB OF NEW YORK

THE first invitations to a group of prospective members to become founder life members in a new university club for college and university graduates who have no clubs named for or representing their colleges in this city have been sent out by Hans P. Freece, executive secretary of the advisory board of the new club. At the same time plans for the organization were announced.

The club is to be known as the American University Club of New York, with executive offices for the present at 11 West Forty-second Street. The estimated cost is at least $5,000,000—40 per cent. to be financed by membership subscription and 60 per cent. by a bond issue. A site committee is picking a location, and construction is expected to be started before the end of the year.

It is planned to build a forty-story clubhouse in the mid-town district, which will be the largest university club in America. It will be completely equipped with lounges and library, dining-rooms, assembly halls and auditorium, sleeping rooms, gymnasium, swimming pool and roof solarium. The architect is expected to be Thomas Hastings, of Carrere and Hastings, who designed the New York Public Library and who is a member of the advisory board of the new club.

Each alumni unit of fifty members or more is to have separate quarters for meetings, as well as full access to the general clubrooms. For the first time groups of alumni will have a central location in which to meet. There will also be an out-of-town membership.

The advisory board of the club, in addition to Mr. Freece and Mr. Hastings, is composed of the Rev. Dr. S. Parkes Cadman, *chairman;* George W. Ochs Oakes, editor of *Current History;* Edwin W. Orvis, of Orvis Brothers and Company, brokers; Kirby Thomas, mining engineer; Senator Royal S. Copeland, Lee W. Maxwell, president of the Crowell Publishing Company, and Dr. Paul R. Stillman, dentist.

"There is only one other club like the one we contemplate in the country," according to a member of the board, "and that is a highly successful one in Chicago. As there are 161,000 alumni of colleges and universities here not affiliated with any New York university club, it will fill a distinct need. We have an initial capital of about $1,250,000. The membership will be limited to 1,500."

RURAL SCHOOLS IN NEW YORK STATE

THE New York *Times* reports that measures carrying additional state aid for the "little red schoolhouse" at a cost of $4,250,000 a year were reported on February 22 by the New York State Senate and Assembly education committees. They are sponsored by Senator Webb, of Dutchess, and Assemblyman Rice, of Cortland, both Republicans.

One of the bills would give to one-teacher school districts the difference between a four-mill tax upon the actual valuation of the taxable property in the district and $1,500. It also provides a minimum of $425 for every one-teacher district, and the sponsors said would make it possible for every one-teacher district in the state to furnish a $1,500 program. The proposal requires an additional yearly appropriation of $3,250,000.

The other measure would extend to school districts employing two, three and four teachers the so-called equalization quota which is now given by the state to districts employing five or more teachers. To carry out this plan another $1,000,000 appropriation is needful.

"These bills," said a statement made by the sponsors, "furnish a comprehensive plan for the apportionment of state funds upon the basis of wealth and the number of children to be educated, and should completely equalize both the tax rate and educational opportunity throughout the state, giving to the financially weak districts an abundance of state funds."

Much money is being wasted in the type of school which is being constructed in towns and the smaller cities, according to a report made by the special joint committee on taxation and retrenchment. The committee is headed by Senator Mastick, of Westchester, and Assemblyman Pratt, of St. Lawrence, is vice-chairman.

"Although in the state, the management of schools and school systems has been decentralized with the cities and school districts, the state government is still in a measure responsible for wastefulness in school construction," said a joint statement issued by Messrs. Mastick and Pratt.

The committee made a special study of school building construction in the smaller cities and in the new central rural districts where the state pays 25 per cent. of the cost of consolidated school construction. The report estimates that $80,000,000 will be spent in the state this year for new schools.

"In many communities state assistance in paying teachers' salaries, instead of relieving the local budget, has encouraged enlarged expenditures for building purposes and in some cases has been generally employed as an excuse for embarking on a costly building program," the report said.

After reviewing current practices in the construction of schools, the committee decided that the school building program is weighted on the side of expenditure rather than economy and that there is an inadequate check on expenditures.

As a result of such methods there is a variation in the design and cost of school buildings out of proportion to the needs of the districts.

"There exist all through the state," the report added, "school buildings containing waste space and otherwise so designed as to impose unnecessary costs on the taxpayer entirely apart from either esthetic or educational features."

The committee recommended that the state commissioner of education be required to work out a standard plan for determining the building needs of school districts. It also suggested an amendment to the education law, providing that the board of education of every district, before adopting any building design, shall hold a public hearing and submit the proposed design, together with the estimated cost.

PRESIDENT HOOVER ON EDUCATION AND PUBLIC HEALTH

IN his inaugural address, President Hoover said:

There is an equally important field of cooperation by the federal government with the multitude of agencies, state, municipal and private, in the systematic development of those processes which directly affect public health, recreation, education and the home. We have need further to perfect the means by which government can be adapted to human service.

Although education is primarily a responsibility of the states and local communities, and rightly so, yet the nation as a whole is vitally concerned in its development everywhere to the highest standards and to complete universality. Self-government can succeed only through an instructed electorate. Our objective is not simply to overcome illiteracy. The nation has marched far beyond that. The more complex the problems of the nation become, the greater is the need for more and more advanced instruction. Moreover, as our numbers increase and as our life expands with science and invention, we must discover more and more leaders for every walks in our national life.

We can not hope to succeed in directing this increasingly complex civilization unless we can draw all the talent of leadership from the whole people. One civilization after another has been wrecked upon the attempt to secure sufficient leadership from a single group or class. If we would prevent the growth of class distinctions and would constantly refresh our leadership with the ideals of our people, we must draw constantly from the general good. The full opportunity for every boy and girl to rise through the selective processes of education can alone secure to us this leadership.

In public health the discoveries of science have opened a new era. Many sections of our country and many groups of our citizens suffer from diseases the eradication of which are mere matters of administration and moderate expenditure. Public health service should be as fully organized and as universally incorporated into our governmental system as is our public education system to-day. The returns are a thousandfold in economic benefits, and infinitely more in reduction of suffering and promotion of human happiness.

President Hoover concluded his address with the words:

Ours is a land rich in resources; stimulating in its glorious beauty; filled with millions of happy homes; blessed with comfort and opportunity. In no nation are the institutions of progress more advanced. In no nation are the fruits of accomplishment more secure. In no nation is the government more worthy of respect. No country is more loved by its people.

I have an abiding faith in their capacity, integrity and high purpose. I have no fears for the future of our country. It is bright with hope.

In the presence of my countrymen, mindful of the solemnity of this occasion, knowing what the task means and the responsibility which it involves, I beg your tolerance, your aid and your cooperation. I ask the help of Almighty God in this service to my country to which you have called me.

EDUCATIONAL NOTES AND NEWS

CARROLL R. REED, superintendent of the schools of Bridgeport, Connecticut, formerly superintendent at Amherst, Rockford and Akron, has been elected superintendent of the Minneapolis schools. He succeeds Dr. W. F. Webster, who retires from active service.

DR. J. B. EDMONSON, director of the division of university inspection of high schools in Michigan, has been appointed dean of the school of education of the University of Michigan. He is succeeded in the work of high-school inspection by Dr. George E. Carrothers. This appointment was made on the recommendation of President Little with the unanimous endorsement of the university committee on accredited schools. Dr. Carrothers also succeeded Dr. Edmonson as chairman of the state committee for the North Central Association of Colleges and Secondary Schools.

H. W. ROCKWELL, president of the State Teachers College at Buffalo, was elected president of the American Association of Teachers Colleges at the Cleveland meeting held on February 22 and 23.

THE Columbia Alumni Club of Illinois arranged a luncheon on February 20 at the University Club to entertain Professor John Dewey, who was visiting in Chicago.

SIR ALFRED EWING will retire on September 30 from the principalship of the University of Edinburgh, which he has held since 1916. In recognition of his public service it is proposed that the freedom of the city be conferred on him.

THE honorary degree of doctor of science has been conferred by the University of Oxford on Dr. Oswald Veblen, professor of mathematics at Princeton University, who has been lecturing at Oxford.

EZRA T. FRANKLIN, president of Southwestern College, has been granted the honorary degree of doctor of divinity by Union College, Barbourville, Kentucky. Dr. Franklin served as president of Union College for thirteen years prior to his election to the presidency of Southwestern.

A PORTRAIT of James E. Rice, professor of poultry husbandry in the college of agriculture of Cornell University since 1907, was presented to the university on February 12 in a ceremony in the poultry building. The portrait, done by Professor Olaf M. Brauner, was presented by Dr. Gustave F. Heuser and was accepted on behalf of the university by Dean William A. Hammond. Dean Albert R. Mann presided. A scroll of all the donors was also presented by Dean Mann. The portrait has been hung in the poultry building.

ACCORDING to the *School Board Journal* Mr. Charles Riebsamen, of Titonka, in Kossuth county, Iowa, has completed fifty-one years as a member of the local school board, and claims a longer service than any other school-board member. Mr. Riebsamen became a member of the board in March, 1876, and served continuously until March, 1927, a term of fifty-one years.

PROFESSOR DANIEL C. KNOWLTON, of Yale University, will be among the visiting professors at the school of education of Boston University next month, on the cooperative program sponsored by the School of Education and the Massachusetts Elementary Principals' Association.

DR. E. A. TAYLOR, of Princeton University, is taking over some of the work of the English department of the University of Michigan during the leave of absence of Professor J. O. Campbell.

PROFESSOR WALTER R. SMITH, of the department of educational sociology of the University of Kansas, has been added to the list of thirty-three visiting lecturers who will assist in conducting courses this summer in the University of Wisconsin. He will conduct classes in the social philosophy of education and in educational sociology.

PROFESSOR KARL C. LEEBRICK, of the University of Hawaii, formerly professor of European history in the University of California, who is at present on leave of absence and is teaching in Syracuse University, will during the summer session lecture in connection with the Foundation for the Advancement of the Social Sciences at the University of Denver.

ALEXANDER B. TROWBRIDGE, for the past year director of the American Federation of Arts, has tendered his resignation to the board of directors. The appointment of Mr. Trowbridge, about a year ago, came at the time the federation announced a grant from the General Education Board. It was understood at that time, according to *Museum News*, that his services had been secured for a period of five years, during which time a general expansion of the organization was to have taken place.

PROFESSOR CHARLES N. WUNDER, head of the department of mathematics at the University of Mississippi, has been appointed the first dean of men at that university. He will continue as head of the department of mathematics.

DR. THOMAS ALEXANDER, of Teachers College, Columbia University, has been appointed an advisory editor to the John Day Company of New York to advise in the extension of its list of books for parents and teachers.

TRUE W. WHITE, manager of the Teachers' Exchange, Boston, was elected president of the National Association of Teachers' Agencies at the recent convention in Cleveland.

DR. HUGH CARTER, of the department of sociology of the University of Pennsylvania, has been on leave this year making a study of public poor relief in Pennsylvania since 1875. His results are to be published this spring. The study is under the general direction of Mr. Ralph G. Hurlin, of the Russell Sage Foundation, and is financed by the Commonwealth Fund and the Public Charities Association of Pennsylvania. Mr. Carter will again be on leave next year. He will be occupied with research for the committee on the cost of medical care. Mr. Harry H. Moore is the director of this committee.

PROFESSOR CHARLES W. FRENCH, head of the French language department at the college of business administration of Boston University, has been chosen representative of the National Federation of Modern Language Teachers at the World Federation of Education Associations at Geneva, Switzerland, to be held July 26 to August 4 this year.

DR. ESTON V. TUBBS, formerly head of the department of education of the Lewis Institute, Chicago, has been appointed director of the newly organized bureau of curriculum of the Chicago public schools.

MRS. SEYMOUR L. CROMWELL, of Mendham, N. J., has been confirmed by the New Jersey State Senate as a member of the State Board of Education. Mrs. Cromwell was first appointed a member of the board in 1921 by Governor Edward I. Edwards. She has been reappointed for another eight-year term by Governor Larson.

DR. ERNEST L. CRANDALL, director of lectures and visual instruction in the public schools of New York City, and Miss Agnes V. Birmingham, whose claim to the position of director of speech improvement was recently denied by the State Commissioner of Education, have been granted for the present term sabbatical leaves of absence by the Board of Education.

PRESIDENT EDWIN A. ALDERMAN, of the University of Virginia, will deliver the principal address at the ninety-first commencement of the Medical College of Virginia, Richmond, on May 28.

DWIGHT W. MORROW, United States Ambassador to Mexico, has accepted an invitation to be the Charter Day speaker at the University of California on March 23.

PROFESSOR CHARLES H. JUDD, of the University of Chicago, was the principal speaker at the annual dinner on February 9 of the Schoolmasters' Club of Cincinnati. Mr. McHenry Rhoads, state superintendent of Kentucky, spoke briefly on "Some Recent Tendencies in Education."

EDWARD J. MEHREN, vice-president of the McGraw-Hill Publishing Company, delivered the third of this year's series of Aldred lectures at the Massachusetts Institute of Technology on March 1. His subject was "Long-Time Guarantees of Prosperity."

THE Dowse lectures at Harvard University for the current year will be delivered on March 21 and 23 by Lawrence P. Jacks, principal of Manchester College, Oxford, and editor of *The Hibbert Journal.* The subjects are: "Religious Difficulties in Early Life" and "Sightseeing, Time-Thinking and Religion."

DR. ROVILLUS R. ROGERS, superintendent of the Jamestown, New York, public schools from 1890 to 1919, died at his home on February 27, in his eightieth year.

EDWARD HUNTINGTON DUTCHER, principal of Eastern High School, East Orange, New Jersey, for the last thirty-eight years, died suddenly on March 2 at the age of sixty-nine years.

DR. RAYMOND W. KIRKBRIDE, professor of French in the University of Delaware, died on March 1. Dr. Kirkbride was the originator of the foreign study plan at the university, and was forced by ill health two years ago to return from France, where he had been directing the activities of the foreign study group.

PROFESSOR RUDOLF WERTIME, since 1915 director of music at Wilson College, Chambersburg, Pennsylvania, died on February 25, at the age of fifty-two years.

DR. JOSEPH WELLS, formerly vice-chancellor of the University of Oxford, has died at the age of seventy-three years.

HENRY D. NEWSON, head of the educational department of Coward-McCann, Inc., died on March 2, at the age of seventy-five years. Formerly Mr. Newson had been in charge of the educational department of Harper Brothers, publishers. Later he established the H. D. Newson Company and originated the Aldine Series of school books. Since joining the Coward-McCann organization last July he had launched several publications. His death occurred just after his return from the meeting at Cleveland of the Department of Superintendence.

CHARLES JAY TAYLOR, professor in the college of fine arts in the Carnegie Institute of Technology at Pittsburgh, died on January 18.

THE death is announced of James G. Wilkinson, principal of Roosevelt School of New Rochelle, New York.

AT the recent annual meeting of the Chicago Botany Alumni held in New York City there was presented to the University of Chicago $25,000 to be known as the John M. Coulter Research Fellowship Fund. The sum for the fellowship had resulted from the contributions of 130 doctors and 75 other alumni and past students of the department of botany, of which Professor Coulter was for so many years the head. The interest only of this fund is to be used for an annual pre-doctorate fellowship, tenable in any branch of plant science at the department of botany of the University of Chicago. The presentation was made by Professor R. B. Wylie, of the State University of Iowa, and accepted by Dr. Max Mason, of the Rockefeller Foundation, formerly president of the University of Chicago. Dr. Coulter, who died in December, had been for fifty years a teacher and administrator, founder of the *Botanical Gazette,* president of Lake Forest College and Indiana University and president of the American Botanical Society and the American Association for the Advancement of Science. Retiring as professor emeritus from the University of Chicago in 1925, he was at the time of his death adviser of the Boyce Thompson Institute for Plant Research at Yonkers, New York.

The first number of *Social Science Abstracts,* to be published monthly under the auspices of the Social Science Research Council, will appear in March. The editor is F. Stuart Chapin, head of the department of sociology in the University of Minnesota. The committee in charge is composed of Dr. Isaiah Bowman, of the American Geographical Society, chairman; Davis R. Dewey, Massachusetts Institute of Technology; Ellsworth Faris, University of Chicago; Carlton J. H. Hayes, Columbia University; Frederic A. Ogg, University of Wisconsin; Frank A. Ross, Columbia University, and Clark Wissler, the American Museum of Natural History.

The League of Nations' Institute of Intellectual Cooperation will again publish a pamphlet giving full information concerning holiday courses to be given in Europe next summer. The pamphlet will contain information concerning where the courses will be held, subjects of instruction, fees, diplomas awarded, facilities for travel and residence, and the name of the person to whom inquiries may be addressed. It will contain programs of more than one hundred courses. The pamphlet can be obtained from the World Peace Foundation, 40 Mount Vernon Street, Boston, Massachusetts.

The 1929 meeting of the British Association for the Advancement of Science will be a combination of a scientific assembly and a scientific tour, in that it will be held in two widely separated cities, Capetown and Johannesburg, and the two-day railway journey northward will come as a break in the middle of the program. The visiting scientific men from Britain and other countries of the northern hemisphere will land in Capetown on the morning of July 22, and the meetings there will begin on the same day. Then, on July 28 and 29, sections of the association will start for Johannesburg by rail, arriving there on July 30 and 31. At Johannesburg the meetings will continue until August 3. In addition to the long but interesting train journey between the two meeting-places, there will be a number of systematic tours to points of scientific and scenic interest, including the famous gold fields and diamond mines. A third city, Pretoria, will participate in the scientific activities of the season. The Fifteenth International Geological Congress is to be held there from July 29 to August 7. The Pan-African Agricultural and Veterinary Congress will also meet in Pretoria. Since this city is only about an hour's run from Johannesburg, delegates to the British Association meeting will have no difficulty in attending such sessions as they wish to visit at Pretoria. The British Association for the Advancement of Science has held one previous meeting in South Africa. This took place in 1905.

It is reported that the Floating University, which has headquarters at 11 Broadway, has announced that a revised charter makes it possible to grant college degrees in connection with its work. These degrees, which the university will grant for the first time in the college year 1929–30, are bachelor of arts, master of arts and a new degree, bachelor of world affairs.

The senate of the University of London, England, has passed a statute exempting from its matriculation examination graduates of all the institutions on the list approved by the Association of American Universities.

A fund to provide scholarship grants for those preparing for library work has been set aside by the Carnegie Corporation of New York. According to the announcement, the minimum grant to be furnished by the fund will be $1,500 and will vary beyond that sum according to individual needs, even to renewal for a second year. The purpose is to enable persons who already have had experience in library work and have shown promise of capacity to contribute to the advancement of the library profession to pursue a year of study and research in library problems.

A gift of funds for the construction of a new library building at Woodstock College, the Jesuit seminary for higher studies at Woodstock, Maryland, has been made by Mr. and Mrs. Francis P. Garvan, of New York City. The library of the college is one of the most valuable collections of books in the United States, containing many manuscripts and rare volumes brought by Italian Jesuits from ancient European libraries in the middle of the last century. The building, which will cost approximately $200,000, is to be erected as an expression of the donor's admiration for Father John O'Rourke, veteran retreat master and missioner, who now is critically ill in St. Vincent's Hospital, New York.

Under the terms of the will of F. M. Hall, a Lincoln attorney, who died last summer, the University of Nebraska receives the collection of works of art which Mr. Hall had gathered over a number of years. The trustee is to hold the remainder of the bequest ($150,000) for the purpose of purchasing oil paintings, statuary and other works of art for the art gallery of the university, under the direction of the Board of Regents. The board may buy not to exceed $10,000 worth of such works in any one year. The purchases must have the written approval of at least two recognized expert judges of art. According to the will the purpose of this provision is to keep the collection at a high standard. It will be kept together and be known as "The Collction of Mr. and Mrs. Frank M. Hall."

The General Education Board has made a gift of $2,000,000 for a new medical and pediatrics laboratory and for a dispensary and service unit on the grounds of the New Haven Hospital, which is affiliated with the Yale School of Medicine, and A. E. Fitkin, of New York City, has added $100,000 to the gift of $1,000,000 which he made Yale University last year for the erection and endowment of the Raleigh Fitkin Memorial Pavilion for the hospital.

H. Rodney Sharp, an alumnus and trustee of the University of Delaware, has given $250,000 for an auditorium to be built this year for the university, in honor of Dr. Samuel C. Mitchell, of Richmond, Virginia, formerly president of the University of Delaware.

Raising of a $250,000 fund, the income of which will be used to aid needy retired teachers, was voted as the major project for 1929 of the New York State Teachers' Association by the executive committee at a meeting just held. Immediate steps will be taken toward raising the fund by popular subscription.

It was recently announced that a bequest of approximately $50,000 has been received by Barnard College from the estate of Miss Delphine Brown, who died in 1907. In her will she left the income of the bequest to two friends during their life time, with the provision that the principal should go to Barnard at their death.

Announcement was made at the recent semiannual meeting of the trustees of Illinois College at Jacksonville of the gift of $70,000 for the early construction of a new Men's Commons. The gift was made by Dr. and Mrs. George E. Baxter, of Chicago. President Rammelkamp, in view of his long service of twenty-seven years, has been voted a leave of absence for nine months beginning immediately after the Centennial Celebration of the College in October of 1929.

The University of the South at Sewanee has qualified for the final balance of the $300,000 gift from the General Education Board. This means that, at last, the university has passed the million-dollar mile-stone in permanent endowment, the culmination of an effort begun nine years ago. The income from this is being used for more adequate salaries for professors and to bridge the gap in operating expenses between what the students pay and what their education costs the university. The Sewanee Expansion

Fund calls for $2,000,000 additional, of which $442,000 has already been secured in cash or pledges. Part of the Expansion Fund is needed for further endowment, but the bulk of it is for new buildings and equipment. One million dollars will be used to build a new college unit. The present college has all the students it can accommodate; over 100 applicants were turned away this year. Sewanee has always held to the Oxford plan of a group of small colleges, linked into the university, where the individual student is not lost in the mass.

QUOTATIONS

ENGLISH RURAL SCHOOLS

THE report of the Board of Education's Departmental Committee on the training of rural teachers, of which an account appears on another page, is in effect a considered plea for more elasticity in the training of teachers and in the work which they are to be trained to do. One of its purposes is to secure for the teaching profession a great deal of good material which is at present lost to it, and will continue to be lost to it so long as secondary schools remain the sole avenue to teaching. When rural pupil teachers reach the training college there is plenty of testimony to their success. Their "slower, richer and wholly individual development" enables them often, in the end, to outstrip their fellow-students, and "they are too good a type, when trained, to be lost." It is well worth while, then, to have thought-out schemes by which this valuable material need no longer be stayed on the threshold of the teaching profession, but may be prepared under favorable conditions for admission to a training college.

A feature of the report, not surprising indeed but worth remarking, is that, in considering how to secure this good rural material for the teaching profession, it keeps steadily in mind the sort of work which such teachers should be asked to do if they return to the country to teach. The report, in fact, is rich in very interesting reflections on rural education. It urges very strongly that country schools should not be obliged to rely for their certificated staff upon teachers mainly trained and educated with other ends in view. Training for rural education should not be precisely the same as for urban education, and it is more than suggested that teachers who wish to go to rural schools should find opportunities at any stage of their career for the special studies that would fit them for the work. In old days, no doubt, rural education was looked down upon: village schools were poor and badly equipped, lodgings were hard to find, company was scarce and slow-witted. To-day conditions are changing, and with them the estimate of the rural teacher's importance in the village community. One of the witnesses before the committee spoke, as it were casually, about trained teachers "returning to the country as missionaries," and it is by no means only in school and during school hours that the properly trained teacher, as seen in the report, is to find play for the powers of knowledge and service which have been acquired and developed in the years of training. Ultimately, however, the very powers which are to make the teacher a valuable social force outside his school are the powers which are to make him a valuable educational force within it. For the report makes it very clear that rural education, seen now to be an essential factor in restoring the balance between town and country population, is to be deemed worthy of enlargement and adaptation to its important sphere in the national life. Biological science, for instance, is here stated to be necessary to a proper appreciation of the processes that belong to the various rural activities of a school. Gardening, housecraft, handicraft and other "semi-professional and practical" subjects have too much educational and cultural value to be taught by those who have only an obligatory smattering of knowledge about them, and something like reorganization of country schools is needed to make the teaching of them an essential constituent in rural education, and an organic part of the country school curriculum. Such are a few of the indications of the increased interest which education is taking in the rural teacher and the rural child, and the growing recognition of the national value of country life and country culture.—*London Times.*

DISCUSSION

INSTALMENT BUYING IN TRAVEL AND EDUCATION

THE expansion of instalment buying in the United States, the creation of million dollar corporations to finance the purchase of automobiles, radios, electric washing machines and the thousands of other modern creations that have been developed to make life less burdensome and more enjoyable, is based on sound arguments. Why wait years for the enjoyment of something that will contribute not only to the present but will add materially to the future? A man who objects to going into debt to buy his wife a washing machine is placing his pride and fear of debt above the physical well-being of his life partner. A student who fears to borrow to complete his education is depriving himself of increased earning power and enjoyment of life. A teacher who, handicapped by lack of funds, can not travel and enjoy the many courses offered during the summer months, is depriving himself and those who employ him of his best services, best and highest development.

In place of the old belief of abstinence and saving, economic thought is concerning itself with intelligent spending. Borrowing to earn is an accepted principle of business. This may well be brought into the realm of education and teacher preparation.

Travel authorities throughout the United States find that when teachers are approached on the subject of travel and attending foreign or domestic summer schools, they usually require several years before they can accumulate the amount necessary—years of saving, years of waiting with limited facilities before they can avail themselves of the golden opportunities offered by any one of the many summer schools in this country and thirty or more that flourish in Mexico, South America, Hawaii and Europe. It is a human failing that saving is exceedingly difficult when not compulsory. The average income of the teachers of the United States makes it possible for them to lay aside twenty to forty dollars a month if they were compelled to do so. But with the fleeting desires and demands of modern habits of living, it takes a determination above the average to save.

A teachers' savings and loan association in each city or community would do wonders in enabling educators to finish work for their degrees, to journey to different parts of the United States, to attend a lecture course in their particular field across the continent or in a distant city. The organization and workings of such an institution would be quite simple if placed in the hands of a capable committee headed by an able manager, who may or may not be salaried, depending on the amount of work demanded of him.

Taking an example of how such an organization would function, let us use the tours that are newest in the field of summer travel—the South American summer schools held for the first time last July in Rio de Janeiro, Brazil, and in Buenos Aires, Argentina. Inclusive costs of these tours range as low as $339 for a sixty-day tour from New York back to New York, including in this price ocean transportation, berth, meals and hotel accommodations while ashore, with three meals per day. Tips and conveyances are also provided, though it is difficult to see just how so much can be included for so little. In addition to this $339, the teacher going to South America would need $75 for the following expenditures:

Passports and visas, approximately...	$17
Gratuities on steamer	10 round trip
Tuition	30
Laundry, etc.	18

The teachers' savings and loan association would purchase the tour for the teacher. She would pay them one half or even one third its cost. Using one half for illustration, she would pay $168.50 before sailing next June, and would sign a note agreeing to pay the remaining $168.50 in ten equal instalments the following school year. Usually school teachers are exceptionally good credit risks, and, outside of death, illness or accident, there would be small risk attached to such a loan. The committee comprising the association would of course pass on each applicant, and their knowledge of the individual would determine whether or not the loan was to be granted. To guard against the aforementioned uncertainties of death or illness, a twelve-month limited insurance policy could be taken out for the teacher. In this policy the insurance company would agree to meet the monthly payments for the teacher in event of her death or incapacity. The type of persons applying for this insurance, their high moral qualifications and their intelligent care of themselves physically would eliminate much of the risk, thereby making the cost very low.

There would be two methods of financing the half of the cost that the teacher had not paid. In the illustration used, this sum was $168.50. However, this sum would be reduced by the commission paid by the steamship agency involved. Usually the commission is from 5 per cent. to 10 per cent. In this case it is 10 per cent., let us say, thus reducing the amount to be paid out by the association to $134.60. A savings system could be introduced within the association of teachers whereby the savings of the teachers could be invested in the organization at a fair rate of return. This money could then be used by the association to pay off the balance on the tour. Secondly, with such high character of risks and such abundant security as the names of the teachers, one or two endorsors, and the organization itself endorsing the teacher's note, it would not be difficult to find a finance company that would be willing to discount the notes. While the individual sum would be comparatively small, the total of ten, fifty or several hundred teachers' notes would make a respectable sum which even the largest organizations would be glad to handle.

All the costs of the association could be paid from the commissions on the tours sold to the teachers. But in case the money was borrowed for perhaps a trip to a domestic summer school where no commission is offered, the teacher could pay a certain small service charge covering the costs of administration. The entire carrying charge would not need to exceed 2 or 3 per cent. of the loan. The interest rate would be the going rate of interest.

Summing it all up, if the first suggestion were carried out, the teachers themselves supplying the savings to carry the plan through, we may assume that in a city of fifty to one hundred thousand, the sum of $15,000 could be raised. Then one hundred teachers could borrow $150 each at a cost to him of about $10.50, at an interest rate of 7 per cent. The commissions received for their travels (still using the South American example previously given) would amount to $3,390—more than enough to pay all expenses and still have a balance to add to the surplus or to increase the dividends the investors would receive. Of course, in this illustration, the entire 7 per cent. paid by the borrowing teacher would be or could be paid to the investors.

In the second case, discounting with a financial institution, the return above the tour commission would be dependent upon the arrangements made with the discounting house. If the discounting house agreed to charge interest only on the actual amount of money outstanding, while the agreement with the teacher caused her to pay the rate for the entire period of the loan, there would be a certain amount of profit accruing to the association, which could be used as a reserve fund, for scholarships or out and out profit to the members of the association.

The simplicity and the ease of operation of this method of financing teachers' study and travel should appeal to many communities where the local banks do not care to bother with individual loans of small amounts.

Through this method hundreds and thousands of our educators could take advantage of the marvelous opportunities being offered for self-improvement, and the communities themselves would benefit by having in their schools teachers who have been about, have experienced the beneficial results of travel, or who have been privileged to study in their favorite field under the direction of masters in the larger areas. The risk, the difficulties and the burdens imposed on the beneficiaries of such a plan are so slight that each group of teachers might seriously consider the possibilities of its application in their own community.

TOWNE NYLANDER

PALO ALTO, CALIF.

A NEW PLAN OF TEACHER EMPLOYMENT

THIS year one school system employed six new teachers. To get these six the superintendent had to consider 108 applications and write at least one letter to each applicant.

Last year the principalship of an important high school in a prosperous southern city became vacant. There were more than two hundred applicants for the position.

Professional ethics prevents a superintendent from visiting other school systems, picking out the capable teachers he wants, and enticing them away by the offer of higher salaries. He is forced to rely largely upon the commercial teachers' agencies for his supply of new teachers.

These teachers' agencies, instead of sending the superintendent the names of the two or three teachers on their files who are best qualified for the position, send name after name until the position is filled. This is natural, for every agency wishes one of its applicants to get the position. Their incomes depend upon it. The more applicants they place with a superintendent, provided these applicants meet the requirements of the new position fairly well, the more chance each agency has of placing one of its teachers. By the time several agencies send in their lists the total is appalling.

This system is unfair to the teachers, especially the best teachers. They pay the agency five per cent. of their first year's salary for its services. Yet the agency gives no teacher individual service. The teacher who best meets the requirements of the new position has her name sent in with the names of the good, bad and indifferent. Instead of having to compete with a few teachers of her own preparation and experience, she often has to compete with all the teachers who could possibly fill the place. The poor teacher and the indifferent teacher can often get as good testimonials as the good teacher. Many good-hearted principals and superintendents will write favorable testimonials for teachers either to get rid of them or more often to help them along. The results are disastrous to the superior teacher. She finds herself in competition with so many others, under the present system, that she often fails to get the promotion or the increased salary she deserves.

This system is unfair to the superintendent. Instead of having the applications of the two or three teachers best fitted for a position, he must read and digest the abstracts of from six to two hundred applicants with all the correspondence involved. The greater the number, the greater the uncertainty, because of the difficulty of comparing and weighing the merits of a large number of applications. Besides, the teachers who push themselves hardest and make the strongest applications are not always the best teachers. The agencies encourage these pushing tactics on the part of teachers. They advise applicants to continue writing to the superintendent and to school board members and to have their friends write for them. Often the best teachers, knowing their ability and the merits of their work, depend largely upon their professional records to get them a position. Many are too modest to advertise themselves. For this reason, unless they have friends to push for them, these teachers are at a disadvantage in competition with mediocre teachers who do not hesitate to use any means for their own advancement.

This system is unfair to the school boards, because the best teachers seldom change positions, unless there is some advance in salary. To this increase in salary is usually added the five per cent. agency dues. This makes the filling of a new position with good teachers more expensive than it should be.

Since we have no better system of employment, both teachers and superintendents must avail themselves of the only means at hand. It seems, however, that a much better system could be worked out. We suggest a state system.

We already have well-organized state departments of education. The purpose of state departments of education is to improve the schools of the state. Since the best way to improve schools is to train and employ the best teachers, these state departments can serve the schools in no better way than to act as employment agencies for teachers.

Let the teacher desiring a position in a state send in her school record, testimonials, references, the kind of position desired, etc., just as she now does to the commercial agency. From this record, the state can issue her the proper license. Her record can be filed. When a superintendent wishes to employ a teacher, he can write to the proper officer of the state department, stating the teaching qualifications desired for the position now open. This officer will go through his files and send the abstracts and testimonials of the one, two or three teachers who most nearly meet these requirements. The superintendent can study the records of these applicants and can enter into correspondence with one or all as he sees fit. If none seems suitable for the position, he can write to another state department of education in his section of the country and have them send abstracts of teachers available for the position.

The teacher can also file her application with as many state departments of education as she desires.

This system has another advantage. Most elementary teachers and many high-school teachers remain in the same state throughout their teaching careers. The commercial agencies usually cover many states. Under the new system, the teachers of a state will have better chances of employment in their own state. The school inspectors on their inspection trips can observe the work of teachers on the employment files, can obtain information about these teachers from superintendents and principals and from other sources and can add this information to the teachers' records at the state capitol. A teacher who has taught successfully for a period of years in a state will have such a strong record that her application for a position will have real weight. She will be able to get the full benefit of a fine record without having to push herself too hard.

The expenses of these state employment agencies can be met by charging a small percentage of the first year's salary, say one or two per cent. This will get the teacher real service at low cost and will in many cases save the extra three or four per cent. to the boards of education.

For the most important positions, the superintendencies and principalships in the larger towns and in the cities, the Bureau of Education at Washington might perform the same service. This would make available for important administrative positions the best men in the United States.

It is to be hoped that some enterprising state superintendent of education will have the necessary legislation passed and will develop a system of employing teachers that will be of real educational service to the schools of his state.

H. R. MAHLER

THOMASVILLE, GEORGIA

SPECIAL CORRESPONDENCE

MEETING THE NEW UNIVERSITY HALF WAY

FOR some years it has been evident that our universities are a part of our changing world. Whenever educators come together the new curricula, the new order of faculty and the new type of student are problems of discussion; but not many folk seem to be aware that the parents of this new student body are also a group to be assimilated into the spiritual life of the university which successfully meets the needs in the community in which it assumes leadership. The situation is particularly acute in urban universities. Thirty years ago most fathers were themselves graduates of the college to which they sent their sons. They knew, therefore, first hand, the ideals of the college. In many cases son came to college armed with a letter to one of father's favorite professors. Furthermore, the curriculum had changed so slightly from father's day that it was a comparatively simple matter to direct the student's course of study.

The situation is different to-day, especially in universities of the type of the University of Pittsburgh. Ninety per cent. of the students live at home in the city or within commuting distance; hence there are no dormitories under university management, and the common ideals which grow up subconsciously wherever people live together must be fostered in other ways. On the surface it would appear that young men and women who remain under the guidance of parents during college years should relieve the university of many problems in discipline. That may be true; but with the broader curricula, the increased and highly specialized faculty and the great increase of students, the contact between home and college so natural a generation or two ago has become practically impossible. In 1900 going to college meant following a course in arts, literature and pure science. To-day, the roll in college is diminished in favor of applied science. It is the parents of this new group of students who must be assimilated. Often the parents of these students have not been to college. Moreover, the professional courses attract many students who are foreign-born or who represent the first generation of education. The parents have the spirit of sacrifice. They are willing to give their sons opportunities, but they do not usually comprehend what it is they are giving. They take the university on faith. The burden of inspiration, sympathy and understanding must necessarily rest upon the university administrative officers and the faculty.

It is this situation which the University of Pittsburgh has faced squarely. For five years the University of Pittsburgh has been building up points of contact which are most gratifying in results. In November, 1924, Chancellor John G. Bowman invited the parents of all incoming freshmen to meet him and the university staff. The response to the first invitation was half-hearted. The drawing rooms of the Faculty Club, formerly a private dwelling, were quite ample enough to accommodate the guests who responded. Evidently those who came spread a favorable report. Last year it was necessary to use the spacious banquet hall and parlors of the Soldiers and Sailors' Memorial to receive the thousand parents who came, and this year fifteen hundred parents enjoyed this unique social gathering.

Although no details of decoration and appointment are spared to give the occasion a touch of festival, the purpose for which the parents have come is never forgotten. Young men from the campus honor societies meet the parents in the lower foyer. At the elevators on the reception floor, young ladies in their gayest party dresses greet the guests and take them to the receiving line to become acquainted with the chancellor, the dean of women, the dean of men and other officers. As the guests pass into the banquet hall, where they are to be seated during the chancellor's address of welcome, they are given programs with a chart explaining the placards placed about the room and in the balcony above. The music, the ferns and flowers, the charming arrangement for refreshment, make it quite evident that parents have not been called in to be lectured; moreover, the plainly written and conveniently placed placards spare the guests any awkwardness in meeting deans and instructors to whom they wish to speak. At the close of the chancellor's talk file clerks pass out student grade cards and parents talk to the instructors of their sons and daughters.

The results are gratifying to both faculty and parents. Many parents receive a new conception of college life and education. Many a freshman has changed his status because father and mother understand that a student must have time to study and a quiet and comfortable place in which to study. The faculty, on the other hand, get an angle on student difficulties mentioned in the informal talk of this social occasion that hours of conference in a dean's office would not unearth. To attempt to preserve the old intimate contacts is impossible. The new world in which our growing universities find themselves calls for a spiritual bond of new forging. Chancellor Bowman's reception to parents of freshmen is meeting that need at a vital point—the triangular contact between parents, faculty and students.

Ellen M. Geyer
University of Pittsburgh

REPORTS

THE AIMS OF OBERLIN COLLEGE[1]

The aims of Oberlin College with reference to its students are:

To train them in the methods of thinking and in the use of the main tools of thought;

To acquaint them with the main fields of human interest and to direct them in the acquisition of knowledge therein;

To guide them in the integration of knowledge;

To afford them intensive training, and to encourage creative activity, within a chosen field;

[1] Statement adopted by the faculty of the Oberlin College of Arts and Sciences.

To prepare them for further study or (within certain limits) for occupation after college;

To establish in them the habit of continuous scholarly growth;

To develop their power to enjoy, and to create, the beautiful;

To develop their physical and mental health;

To develop their social resourcefulness;

To develop their moral and religious life;

To prepare them for intelligent, effective, and loyal participation in the life of family, community, nation, and the international order.

The foregoing statement was prepared by the curriculum committee of Oberlin College as a chart for its own use in the process of revising and modernizing the curriculum.

It expresses, however, not merely the curricular purpose but the total purpose of the college with reference to its students, and has been approved by the college faculty.

Both committee and faculty regard it rather as a working chart than as a definitive formulation. It is, therefore, subject to revision and is published in the hope that it may suggest constructive criticism, which, whether private or public, will be welcomed and may be utilized in the actual process of curriculum building, which is now under way.

It is not claimed that Oberlin at the present time makes an adequate effort to achieve all these aims: they represent a program belonging to the immediate future.

It is not claimed or thought that the statement is strikingly new. It has, however, been worked over again and again, through several hours of interesting debate, and is believed to be a sound and more than ordinarily complete and thoughtful statement.

It is assumed throughout that success in respect to these several aims can be attained only with the active cooperation of the student.

The first five aims are to be achieved in the main through the regular course work of the college. In the case of these aims, fairly accurate measurement of the degree of success attained is possible and certification of success is therefore practicable. The conferring of the bachelor's degree upon a student will signify that in the types of educational experience represented by these five aims the student has, with the help of the faculty and in the opinion of the faculty, achieved a commendable degree of success.

Achievement of the remaining aims will be sought largely by other than curricular means; and success in these respects can not in general be closely measured and can not, therefore, be certified. These aims are none the less conscious and significant aims of the college.

We hope to attack the problem of training in thinking through direct practice in the field of logic as well as through the indirect practice to be had in all courses. By the main tools of thought we mean, in particular, English (written and oral), foreign language, mathematics and bibliography.

We hope so to plan each student's individual curriculum that it may in its generalizing phase include the gaining of a significant measure of ordered knowledge in each of several typically different fields.

The task of integration may be attempted in various ways: in part, very possibly—but not necessarily—by orientation courses.

Within the field of specialization we shall most heartily encourage a type of individual scholarly experimentation or investigation which may properly be called creative.

We send so high a proportion of our graduates into graduate or professional schools that specific preparation for this experience forms a part of our task. Our vocational preparation is limited to the fields of teaching and physical education.

We hope that the endeavor to establish in our students while they are with us the habit of a lifelong self-education may be fortified and made successful through careful study of the implications of this aim—in the field, for instance, of general reading.

Music and the other arts have long played a prominent rôle in Oberlin. We hope not only to maintain facilities for their ample enjoyment but definitely to encourage artistic composition and performance in music, in design and color, in literature and the drama.

By health we mean not merely freedom from disease but a positive glowing healthiness—athletic, typically, in its physical expression; and we accept as applicable to our own endeavor this statement of the National Child Health Council:

The aim of health training and instruction should be to assure healthful living by: (1) the formation and practice of habits essential to health, (2) the acquisition of knowledge necessary to health, and (3) the development of right attitudes and ideals with regard to health, both physical and mental.

Through life in residence halls and through association in varied outdoor and indoor activities we hope to give some guidance in the ways of good social comradeship.

Development of the moral and religious experience will be less a matter of indoctrination than of the general maintenance of high standards of thought and life within the college community. Our local policy entrusts to the churches of Oberlin a major share of the encouragement of religious life and growth in our students. In so far as the college acts in this field it seeks to combine open-mindedness and reverence.

The last of the stated aims recognizes the desirability of thoughtful preparation for the responsibilities and problems of family relationships, and for worthy citizenship in the larger human family.

ERNEST H. WILKINS

EDUCATIONAL RESEARCH AND STATISTICS

A TEN-MINUTE OBSERVATION IN THE LIBRARY

THERE is a sufficient amount of good literature designed to inform students on *how* to study, being attacked by dry-rot on library shelves, to cure all known study diseases of a pestilential nature, if the suggestions were accepted and if the attitudes and reactions of students toward them were as definitely positive as they are negative. When this material is read it seldom stimulates more than a *laissez faire* attitude on the part of many students. The evidence found in books is seldom as effective as concrete evidence seen in action in life situations.

There is a tendency for much of what is read in books to have a legendary effect, and therefore not to be considered as necessarily applicable to the reader.

A group of one hundred students, prospective teachers, after a discussion of study habits, made observations in the university library in order to get first-hand information on how students actually study, to determine what some of the prevailing difficulties are, and causes of distraction interfering with the study procedure of students as revealed by their behavior while at work.

The observation was made in the main reading room of the library. This room is equipped to accommodate comfortably five hundred students. It is designed and arranged to offer all possible inducements for effective study and to reduce distractions to the minimum. To illustrate, in examining the list of distractions given in the table (p. 337), it will be observed that the usual distraction of looking out the window does not occur, due to the fact that the bases of the windows are sufficiently high to eliminate distractions outside. The floors are concrete covered with heavy battleship linoleum, which reduces to a minimum the disturbance caused from walking in the room. The tables are too heavy and solid to be shoved. The chairs are new, heavy and strong, consequently there is no squeaking of chairs, which in many libraries is a source of distraction.

The observation was made by one hundred students, twenty-six boys and seventy-four girls, and extended over a period of two days. They were instructed to go to the library at their individual convenience, the library being open from eight in the morning until ten at night, sit down at a table as if to prepare a lesson. They were to select for observation some one who comes into the library and sits down at a table to work; the observation to begin the moment the student sits down, and continue for just ten minutes, by the watch. It was suggested that the observer select for observation some one whom he does not know, and to prevent being discovered as an observer, to select some

DISTRACTION TABLE

Distractions	Frequency of occurrence		Time in minutes		Percentage of time given to distraction		Percentage of total time given to distraction
	M.	F.	M.	F.	M.	F.	
(1) Conversation	32	29	61	54	32.45	25.59	29.0
(2) Aimlessly looking around	27	28	29	33	15.43	15.64	15.5
(3) Aimlessly leafing books	30	32	27	22	14.36	10.42	12.4
(4) Students walking by	25	20	23	15	12.23	7.10	9.5
(5) Use of vanity cases		16		33		15.64	8.2
(6) Attracted by certain individuals	18	13	16	10	8.53	4.73	6.5
(7) Day-dreaming	11	12	13	11	6.92	5.21	6.0
(8) Reading and writing letters	1	7	7	14	3.72	6.63	5.1
(9) Arranging hair and clothes	6	22	3	14	1.59	6.63	4.1
(10) Miscellaneous	11	9	9	6	4.78	2.37	3.6
	161	188	188	212			

one who comes in and sits down at a safe distance.

The student's behavior was to be closely observed and the results recorded under two headings: concentration and distraction. Under the heading concentration was recorded the number of minutes devoted to concentration. Under distraction was recorded the number of minutes devoted to distraction, the cause or nature of each distraction and the time duration in each case.

It is reasonable to expect that during the observation there may at times be elements in the behavior of certain individuals which would be difficult to classify. The observers were instructed to rely upon their best judgment in such cases. In any event such doubtful cases would be so rare as not to affect materially the results of the experiment.

The sex of those being observed was recorded in order to determine whether certain distractions were more prevalent with one sex than the other. It should be stated that those being observed were undergraduate students, since the work of the graduate students is carried on for the most part in the seminars.

It will be noticed that the observation was made of the first ten minutes of the student's work. The criticism may be offered that the first ten minutes is not the best ten minutes to observe in order to get the best results, and that the first ten minutes is not typical of the entire time spent in the library; that better results would be obtained if the second, third or fourth ten minutes had been selected to be observed. However, the observation of the first ten minutes does reveal how students go to work, which is an important factor in their study habits.

In tabulating the distractions, they were grouped under the ten headings as shown in the table.

(1) It will be observed that the most prevailing distraction is that of talking; not only the most prevailing but the most vicious in that a single case is likely to distract more students than any of the other distractions.

(2) The second distraction in the list, that of aimlessly looking around, is less damaging in that it is restricted to the individual so engaged. It is not likely to interfere with the concentration of other students.

(3) Aimlessly leafing through books is more distracting to students working in close proximity than is the act of aimlessly looking around, but less distracting than is talking.

(4) Walking in the library, of course, is unavoidable; however, it is the exceptional student who has not trained himself to tread softly.

(5) That the use of the vanity case merits perhaps a higher degree of tolerance than any of the other distractions is evidenced by the fact that in the specific cases where it is employed it serves a widely recognized need, and whatever distraction its employment may bring to others it apparently results from a sudden discovery of a strictly personal distraction.

(6) There sometimes develops, for various reasons, an attraction of one individual to another, usually of the opposite sex, but sometimes of the same sex, which often develops into a growing fascination to such an extent that undivided concentration to work becomes of an inferior quality. Highly pleasing personal appearance, striking combination of style, makeup or peculiar mannerisms may be causes for this kind of distraction.

(7) The distraction classed as day-dreaming, when properly characterized, usually consists in some kind of pleasant reveries in delusioned experiences of unsubstantial happiness or unfounded hopes. Such indulgences are not usually distracting to others.

(8) The library affords a very convenient place for reading and writing letters. This, again, seldom becomes a distraction to other students in the library. It serves as a distraction from studies only to those who employ the library for this purpose. This distraction is found to be more prevalent among the girls than among the boys. Boys, more than girls, prefer the privacy of their own rooms for their correspondence.

(9) Attention to personal appearance as evidenced by the amount of time devoted to adjusting the hair and clothes is practiced to a much greater extent among the girls than among the boys.

Of the one hundred students observed no one was reported with full ten minutes of concentration. Twelve, five girls and seven boys, were reported with nine minutes or over of undivided concentration, and in all of these cases the unnecessary waste of time was during the first minute. There were four cases, three girls and one boy, in which the entire ten minutes was recorded under distraction.

Fifty-three and eighty-five hundredths per cent. of the boys observed boys; 46.15 per cent. of the boys observed girls. Fifty-one and thirty-five hundredths per cent. of the girls observed girls; 48.65 per cent. of the girls observed boys.[1]

There were 161 cases of distraction recorded against the fifty boys observed, and 188 cases recorded against the fifty girls. Three items in the list of distractions are largely responsible for the total number of distractions being less for the boys than for the girls, the use of the vanity case, reading and writing letters, and arranging the hair and clothes. The table shows that for these three distractions the girls total forty-five cases while the total for the boys is seven cases.

The per cent. of the total time of the boys given to distraction is 37.6 per cent.; for the girls, 42.4 per cent. The per cent. of the total time of boys and girls combined given to distraction is 40 per cent.

In considering these modes of behavior from the standpoint of efficient study habits, it is evident that they are all positively detrimental to one's efficiency in concentration and study. A good antidote for one who is easily susceptible to distractions is to attack his work just a little more vigorously. By attacking work in this manner distractions are not so likely to occur, but when a distraction does occur under these conditions the worker becomes more highly conscious and can "snap out of it" with much greater ease. One's faith in the improvement of his study habits is just as strong as he cares to venture and no stronger. The secret of how to study is probably locked up in the *desire* to study. Student study habits have received less attention than any other phase of pupil activity. Schools in the past have been concerned more with the mere amount of learning than with the learning process itself. The successful teacher of to-day is concerned not so much with the pupil's mere learning as in his learning how to learn, and in seeing to it that he acquires efficient habits of study.

DENNIS C. TROTH
UNIVERSITY OF ILLINOIS

[1] Nothing was mentioned in the instructions that would in any way influence their selection.

SCHOOL AND SOCIETY

EDITED BY J. McKEEN CATTELL

WITH WHICH IS COMBINED THE

EDUCATIONAL REVIEW

EDITED BY WILLIAM McANDREW

Volume XXIX | Saturday, March 16, 1929 | Number 742

OUR CHIEF CONCERNS WITH THE FUTURE SCHOOL BUILDING PROGRAM

ADDRESS BEFORE THE DEPARTMENT OF SUPERINTENDENCE

By JOSEPH MARR GWINN

SUPERINTENDENT OF SCHOOLS, SAN FRANCISCO, CALIFORNIA

When President Boynton assigned me this duty and subject he did not advise how far in the future our concerns for the school building program should extend. The future is a long period and unknown.

As we, in the light and under the educational needs and demands of this good year, 1929, survey the school buildings of so recent a date as 1910, we see how inadequate and ill-suited these buildings are for use in the operation of a program of education adapted to the requirements of to-day. When we take cognizance of all the rapid and tremendous changes affecting education that are overwhelming us now with promises of still greater epoch-making discoveries both in the physical world and in the mental world, discoveries which will make the future even more unlike the present than to-day is unlike yesterday; when we read what the wisdom of to-day has to say about the stupidity of those who planned the schoolhouses of one or two decades ago, we might conclude that our chief concern with respect to the school-building programs of the future is that by that time we be quietly resting in some sound-proof urn so that our ashes be not disturbed by what the makers of school-building programs in 1950 will have to say about the criminal ignorance of school superintendents and school architects in 1929. If the dead past should bury its dead perhaps we should permit the unborn future to make its own school-building programs undisturbed by ancient and antiquated ideas and practices.

During the past several years there have been numerous school-building surveys and a large output of literature on the subject of school buildings. A survey of these surveys and a review of the literature impress one with the similarity as well as with the flagrancy of the errors and defects of the past school planning and with the need for facts and scientific methods as guides for future planning. The surveys reveal in practically all if not every instance that school buildings have not been built according to a program. Like Topsy, they just grew. The need of the hour, the push or pull of the politician, the plans of the past, the performance in neighboring school districts or other forces of opportunism, together with a large absence of proper conception of the meaning and purposes of education and future needs, have determined school buildings of the past. The surveys reveal that buildings within what is called a school system have been located, planned and built with little regard for relation to other buildings, the purposes of education, future trends of population and ability of the people to pay. As typical I quote from a survey of one of the great cities, omitting names: "No building program has been developed in X which prognosticates the need of X." I conclude, therefore, that our first concern for future school-building programs is that there be a program. School buildings should be provided, planned and erected according to a definitely formulated guiding policy, drawn in accordance with the best educational theory and practice, and calculated to meet the requirements of a progressive educational program suited to the present and yet capable of adjustment to future educational and population needs.

Under that conception of education, which made the teacher an imparter of knowledge and the pupil a receiver of instruction, a log might serve as a schoolhouse. Under the present-day conception of education quite a different schoolhouse is required. No longer a log where a single pupil sits, receives and recites, but a building with grounds and equipment, where children and teachers may live and move and have their being. It is a far cry from the log of Mark Hopkins to a modern school building, and yet universal education which is provided to-day is much more cheaply provided than it could be provided under the old log plan with one teacher for one pupil. Democracy's demand for universal education has been met through developing a school plant where both quality and quantity in education are possible. Education costs more to-day than it used to cost because we have more of it, much more of it. Economy in future school-building programs is to be served through providing buildings, grounds and equipment adapted to the needs of a modern program of education. A factory that turns out goods for which there is no market is an expensive factory. Better it were torn down and replaced by a factory of up-to-date type.

In the organization of a building program it is fundamental that the form of organization, the program of education and the objectives to be achieved by and for the children and adults attending the schools, and the methods and materials to be employed in attaining these objects, be the determining factors. The educational ideal with its expression in a form of organization, and a method of operation is the lodestar for makers of school programs.

One of the principal objective expressions of the educational ideal is found in the curriculum. It is imperative that the curriculum be the precursor of future building programs. Since the curriculum must respond to changes that will ever come it is evident that ways and means for intelligent and continuous curriculum construction and reconstruction must be provided.

The form of organization—how the pupils are to be grouped for administration, instruction and learning—must also be decided before a building program can be made. What years are to be accommodated in the various classes of buildings? This is one of the most pressing problems of the present. Shall the tenth year be added to the junior high school and the lower two years of the college added to the upper two years of the present high school, is a question typical of the problem of organization now confronting us. Economic and educational requirements will doubtless continue the group form of instruction, but demands for adjustments for individual needs will modify plans for grouping. Schemes for individualizing instruction in group organization will continue to modify building plans and sizes. At present, in order to provide many levels for groupings, larger schools are needed. It is to be hoped that this year's report of the committee on administrative units may guide the future in its form of organization of schools.

The list of the forces and facts that will influence future school-building programs is long. Economy is to be served through a proper recognition and balancing of these forces and facts.

Economic pressure may force curtailment of the movement to expand the school downward to include part of what is now the pre-school period, upward to include the junior college and outward to include adult and extension education of various forms. It may force larger numbers to be taught by one teacher, thereby necessitating classrooms, laboratories and shops of larger dimensions than are now approved; it may force the platoon and shift devices of operation to make two or three pupils receive education in the space where now one is educated and thereby reduce the number of school buildings required; it may force the continued use of antiquated and temporary buildings and in other ways greatly modify the form and extent of education in the future.

From a direction almost opposite to the economic force there are powerful social and psychological forces which would provide an expansion of education downward, upward and outward. They would make the school assume new and additional responsibilities once borne by the home, the church, vocation and by other agencies which are of recent development and due to changes in the social and economic orders. The necessity under educational, social and economic pressure to provide for feeding school children at the school has greatly modified school-building plans. The cafeteria and the kitchen occupy much space and clamor for more. The crowding of people into cities forces an expansion of playgrounds, gymnasiums and recreation rooms, and the end is not yet.

From the fields of educational research, experimentation and philosophy there are many forces acting from all sorts of directions. Some of these neutralize others; some support and some oppose the economic and social forces. Altogether they result in a variety of practices and theories which give little sure foundation for future building. Some researches find that large classes give better educational results than small classes, while some experimenters tell us that there must be individual instruction. If the first of these is right, then classrooms must be larger and fewer. If the latter is to be followed then classrooms would disappear. Some find that a unified course of study with one instructor is better for little children, while others adhere to a segmented curriculum with departmentalized instruction under a number of teachers. If one of these views is followed the instruction rooms would be quite alike; if the other be followed the instruction rooms would be widely differentiated.

Discoveries and inventions and their application to the structure and functions of society have modified, and will continue increasingly to modify, education and the means employed in its development. The electric train, the autobus and good roads, the airplane, the telephone, the radio and other means of rapid transportation and communication have greatly expanded the dimensions of neighborhoods, local communities and school districts. It is to be deplored that conservatism in education and the lack of social and economic television on the part of many have not permitted the one-room rural school to be replaced to any considerable extent by a many-room school building in a much larger school district with a school four or five times distant in miles yet much closer in time, safety and comfort than the one-room school only one or two miles away. Practically all other elements of economic and social living have been remade under the influence of rapid, safe and comfortable transportation and communication. The farmer takes his eggs to market thirty miles away; the doctor calls on his patient forty miles away more quickly than he did six miles away in the day of the gig and mud road. I can not believe that the anachronism of the small school district can much longer exist. Future building programs must be governed accordingly.

Recently the nursery school, the kindergarten and the university of the air are coming to us over shorter or longer wavelength and on the screen. Some we now call radio and visual education fanatics would have us almost believe that education by means of the radio may in the near future enable us to beat all the schoolhouses into loud speakers and silver screens and compress a million school teachers into a half dozen broadcasters. Each day schoolbuilding plans and specifications are changed in order to adapt the building better to education under the influence of the radio, the moving picture and other inventions.

Health with emphasis on physical development and well-being is a comparatively recent objective in education. The dependence of mental and moral growth upon the physical, and upon environment, has received increased recognition in recent years. These two have greatly influenced plans and recent programs for buildings. The school buildings of a few years back gave little heed to health, environment or the relations of the mental and moral to the physical. Because of the changed conceptions of education these older buildings are found quite defective by modern standards. Means of rapid transportation in cities and development of industries and business areas have caused shifts in population resulting in leaving some school buildings empty and overcrowding others.

A survey of the surveys of school buildings warn against the following mistakes common in the past:

Shifts and trends of population not taken into account; sites too small; schools not properly spaced or related to one another; many rooms unhygienic and ill-suited to purpose for which they are used because of lack of light, ventilation, size, location and structure; combustible materials used and improper planning with extreme fire and other hazards; inadequate storage accommodation; building placed in improper environment of noise, dirt and traffic; accommodations lacking now required in a modern program of education; location, size of site, and form of building making additions impossible; gloomy and depressing, unadorned and with drab coloring, narrow halls and squalid surroundings.

The extent to which the present school plant is utilized should be ascertained. The mistake of erecting new buildings or adding to old ones when the existing plant is entirely adequate is often made. Akin to this error is that of making buildings with classrooms too large for ordinary use or with more rooms than can be utilized.

A master's thesis by Gardner W. Spring, written at the University of California, shows that in thirty-eight California high schools the median percentage of time that classrooms are occupied is 69.96. The range of percentage of time used runs down as low as 39.45 per cent. In terms of per cent. of student stations used the median is 43.56 per cent. and the lower range 30.71 per cent. In terms of per cent. of standard sittings used, that is, the number actually using a room compared with the number that could use it if the standard number of seats for that size of room were in use, the median is 33.43 per cent. and the lower range 14.18 per cent. For the sake of economy a building should be as nearly 100 per cent. utilized as possible. The figures quoted show a low degree of utilization of classrooms. This means that money was spent for rooms that are only partially used. A smaller number would have sufficed.

It is evident that there are many forces and conditions which must be taken into consideration in shaping school building and educational programs. Time has not permitted my mentioning more than a few of them. The almost impossible is demanded of the schools. Dean William F. Russell, of Teachers College, Columbia University, in his recently issued annual report has expressed the situation clearly and forcefully. The dean said, "One of the most perplexing of the problems arises from the simultaneous impact upon the schools of three popular demands—that pupils be accommodated in greater numbers, that training of a better quality be offered and that there be greater economy in all public expenditures."

Education is met with the same demands as is commercial production—quantity production and quality improvement with cost reduction. These demands will have to be met by the makers of future school building programs. The schools will respond to these demands and in doing so will doubtless make changes in the grouping of students and the methods of teaching. There are numerous problems of organization, administration and method of teaching pressing for solution, or at least for more adequate expression in education. Shall the scheme of organization be 6-3-3, 6-3-3-2, 4-4-4-4, 6-4-4 or 5-3-4? Shall there be less of book learning and more of activity? Shall there be individual instruction or larger classes? Shall the demands of economy defeat those of democracy for an equal chance for all? Shall we pay as we go or borrow the money? It is evident that the future school building program is complex and difficult—a problem in the composition and resolution of many forces.

Nothing short of a thoroughgoing, complete building survey can provide boards of education a satisfactory solution of the difficult problems. The survey must show the past, present and probable future distribution of the school population, the appropriate locations and sizes of school sites and buildings. That a proper and adequate survey be made in preparation for building programs is certainly a chief concern.

A large concern for future school building programs is that a proper method of financing the building program be provided. School buildings cost money and the taxpaying public is entitled to as light a burden as is consistent with supplying educational needs.

There are three ways of paying for school buildings. The most common way is through bonds authorized by vote of the people and running for twenty to forty years. The second way, pay as you go, is to raise the tax rate high enough some year to provide the funds for the erection of a building. A third way, sometimes called the depreciation plan, is through an additional tax each year for several years in advance of the year in which the building is to be erected; the yearly payments to be placed on interest which, with the accumulated payments and interest at the end of the given period, produce an amount sufficient to pay for the building.

The actual tax cost, I refer to tax money only, of the same school building under these three methods is very different. Assuming twenty-year serial bonds at 5 per cent. and a twenty-year accumulative period at 5 per cent., the total tax cost of a $300,000 school building by the bonding plan is $481,454.60; by the pay as you go plan, $300,000, and by the depreciation plan, $181,454.60.

The difference in the actual tax cost to the public between the plan of paying in advance and of paying afterwards is the cost of the building, $300,000. On the face of it, it is apparent that anticipating future needs by ten or twenty years, and accumulating year by year to the end of the period is by far the cheapest way to provide schoolhouses. It is equally apparent that the most extravagant method of paying for school buildings is by bonding.

The depreciation plan requires foresight of a type rarely found and a willingness to sacrifice the present for the future equally rarely found. There is also the danger that the accumulating funds will not be wisely and honestly handled. Rapidly growing communities have enough to do to care for their present needs. For these and other reasons the depreciation plan of financing school buildings, while less than half as expensive as bonding in actual taxes, is seldom used. It is desirable as the rates of growth of our districts approach the normal for the country that the necessary legislation should be enacted and the practise established of saving year by year in advance for capital school outlays.

Between the pay as you go and the bonding plan it is evident that the first is better adapted to school districts of such size that each year there is need for a new school building. The assessed value of such a district must be great enough to provide sufficient funds from a tax within the legal limits to erect a building or buildings as required by growth or replacement. The pay as you go plan, in order to avoid wide fluctuations in the tax rate, must be followed up year after year. To do this requires a board of education of business ability and continuity of purpose, and with absolute control over its school building budget.

It is usually very much easier to gain the consent of the people for a bond issue than for an immediate greatly increased tax rate. Consequently bonding is frequently the only means possible for providing funds for school buildings. Districts with rapidly increasing school enrolment and districts with a small property assessment must resort to bonds because of their inability to secure a sufficient amount of money through current tax rates. In the interest of economy districts should issue bonds only when it is impossible to provide the necessary school buildings through the depreciation or the pay as you go methods.

The poet Burns says, "The best laid schemes of mice and men gang aft a-gley." So it is with school building programs. Boards of education and school superintendents with their experts may develop a perfect building program which will fail in whole or part when the people of the district through lack of understanding are opposed to it. It is essential that the people be informed and brought to the support of the building program. The program will run counter to local and selfish interests of many of the taxpayers, and counter to the political interests of many a politician. In almost any city there will be need for much expenditure of time and energy in educating the people of certain sections to the fact that educationally the city should be considered as one whole unit, and not an aggregate of competing neighborhoods. A sound educational program, a well-considered building program, an abundance of well-organized facts, with courage and perseverance, will win the way but with great difficulty.

One of our chief concerns with the future school building programs is to educate the people to the need and meaning of a modern program of education and the execution of a building program to make this type of education effective, and to save them from repeating the mistakes of the past.

Economy in future school building programs is not served through the continued use of old buildings ill suited to the purposes of education. It is economy in industry to build modern factories to replace the obsolete old ones. It is more important that the modern school have a modern building and equipment. We are concerned that the educational ideal expressed in the curriculum, method and form of organization of education has a full chance for expression in a proper school building. Economy in future school buildings is chiefly to be secured through wise and long-visioned planning. The population, together with educational, social and economic conditions past, present and future, must be surveyed. All that goes to make a thorough, scientific and continuous school building survey is prerequisite to wise spending, which is our greatest economy.

THE WORK OF THE ARTICULATION COMMISSION

STATEMENT BEFORE THE DEPARTMENT OF SUPERINTENDENCE

By HERBERT S. WEET
SUPERINTENDENT OF SCHOOLS, ROCHESTER, NEW YORK

THE purposes of this paper are to sketch the major fields in which this commission deems its work to lie; to review briefly what has been attempted up to the present time, and, finally, to indicate what the commission proposes and hopes to accomplish during the next two years, at the close of which the second yearbook to be prepared by this commission will be presented.

As this commission views its task there are three important fields with which it must concern itself. The first has to do with larger units of school organization such as the elementary school, the junior high school, the senior high school, the college and university, the teacher-training institutions and finally the unit for adult education. That we have not as yet solved all the problems of coordinating these larger administrative units is a proposition that will be accepted without serious debate. The second field of work involves the smaller units of school organization such as the grades, or whatever other subdivisions may lie within any one of these larger administrative units. This field takes us at once into the whole subject of what is commonly understood as promotion. And, finally, in the third field the commission hopes to press back to those conditions which surround the pupil in his journey from one point of transition to the next and which so largely determine the nature of the problem at the transition point itself. The very working conditions as regards the curriculum, or the size and varying abilities in any given classroom, for example, may be such as to defeat all other attempts at proper coordination. Each of these three fields will be commented upon in turn.

The presentation of the work in this first field, that deals with the larger administrative units, may well begin with a contrast. First of all we shall try to see conditions at the beginning of our educational journey in this country as they are set forth by Dr. Henry C. Morrison in his work on "The Practice of Teaching in the Secondary School."

In referring to elementary, secondary and higher educational institutions, Dr. Morrison declares that these three schools with which we are familiar have developed not by differentiation from a common institutional origin for the better service of a common purpose, but from three distinct schools, each of them in the beginning substantially unrelated to the others. The eight-grade elementary school as we know it is the indigenous common school organization and institutional purpose to American needs. The high school, on the other hand, comes down to us in direct descent from the academies which flourished in the northeastern states throughout the first three quarters of the nineteenth century.

The oldest of our existing institutions is the college, which early became essentially a preprofessional school. Each of these original schools had its own purpose and its own separate existence. The old common school was not ordinarily set to prepare for the academy, or later the free high school, nor was it the main business of the early high school or academy to prepare for college.

The above is the first picture in our contrast. It is essential that we keep it clearly before us in any attempt to appreciate or properly appraise the significance of this problem of articulation. In so far as we can bring to our minds these three institutions, each isolated from the others by time and locality and purpose, then to that extent we shall better understand the difficulties that have had to be faced and the progress that has already been made.

But there is another picture that is at least of equal importance. In this very city of Cleveland in which we are meeting, each individual child has to-day the opportunity to begin his career in public or tax-supported institutions on through the elementary school, the high school, the college and even the professional school. This is true in not a few of our larger city centers. In many of our states where the entire journey can not be made in tax-supported institutions within the local community, it can be made within the boundaries of the state through the state colleges and universities. And frequently in those states where these latter institutions are not found it is entirely practicable through state-supported scholarships for the individual to make the entire journey without tuition charges. Add to these benefits from tax-supported institutions the opportunities afforded by privately endowed colleges and universities, and the picture is one in striking contrast to the first picture presented. We have an American system of education at least in the sense of a wide-spread opportunity for a child to go from the beginning to the end of our formal educational institutions and thus go out into life equipped with the best that American education has to offer.

This, then, is the second picture in our contrast. Even the most casual reflection upon the changed conditions shown by these two pictures reveals a degree of progress that is both illuminating and encouraging. This appreciation of the progress made, however, will not blind us to the many important problems that still need attention.

Some years ago that distinguished educational leader who is next to address us at this morning's session focused the attention of school administrators upon this subject of articulation or coordination in such an effective and convincing manner that its influence has persisted during all these years. In referring to the conditions at the beginning of our educational journey in this country he set forth substantially a picture like the one of Dr. Morrison's that has just been presented. And then Dr. Dewey made this very significant statement:

> All organization is nothing but getting things into connection with one another, so that they work easily, flexibly and fully. Therefore, in speaking of this question may I call attention to the isolation of the various parts of the school system, to the lack of unity in the aims of education, to the lack of coherence in its studies and methods.

It is now thirty years ago since those words were written. Interestingly enough it is only about forty years ago, according to Morrison, that this effort to make the elementary school, the high school and the college pull together for a common educational purpose, began. He points out that down until nearly the end of the nineteenth century the number of pupils who passed on from the common school to the high school, and from the high school to the college was so small as to be almost negligible. But "the surpassing educational awakening which began to be evident about 1900 changed all this. Ordinary folks in ever-increasing numbers began to send their children to college. The easy-going ways which have answered for a century would no longer serve.'' And Morrison closes with this significant statement: ''Thus the history of educational administration since 1890 has been to a large extent a history of endless effort to make the elementary school, the high school and the college pull together for a common educational purpose.''

This, accordingly, is an occasion for sincere congratulation. Dr. Dewey, the man who more than any other awakened the educational world thirty years ago to the waste that was resulting from lack of coordination, is here this morning to discuss the same subject. He has lived and worked through thirty of the forty years that this effort at coordination to which Dr. Morrison refers has been under way. We appreciate his coming, and we shall listen with profound interest to his message.

To present as strikingly as possible the contrast with which we began, the most favored centers were selected for the second picture. But it would be a mistake for us to suppose that these favorable examples are representative of conditions in the country at large. Quite to the contrary. While in some places these larger administrative units have been brought into juxtaposition in such a way as to make for conditions favorable to continuity in educational progress, yet on the whole there are widely differing theories as to what the most desirable units are from the standpoint of this problem under consideration. I suggest that if any person doubts the accuracy of such statements he attempt to define in terms of current practice just what constitutes any one of these administrative units of school organization. Is the elementary school unit, for example, distinguished from the other units by the number of grades involved? Obviously not, for the number varies anywhere from five in some parts of the country to nine in other parts. Is it to be defined by the number of days of schooling provided by the elementary school? Clearly not, for five grades or years of elementary schooling in some states will provide only about half the amount that the same number of grades or years will provide in other states. By the same token the elementary school unit can not be defined in terms of common curriculum practice, or teacher-training, or any other one of these elements that are so closely linked with the elementary school. Equally pertinent questions may be asked with reference to the fields of secondary and higher education. The commission has accepted the definition of the elementary school unit adopted by the commission on the curriculum. This unit, accordingly, consists of the kindergarten and the first six grades. Its definition, however, is based rather upon present trends than upon present practice. In other words, there seem to be good grounds for believing that the development of the future will be and ought to be in the direction of the elementary school of six grades.

And there is no less uncertainty when we enter the field above and beyond this elementary school. What is the period of secondary education and what are the administrative units that are best adapted to an accomplishment of the things that secondary education should accomplish? Shall this secondary period, for example, accomplish all through the work from grades seven to fourteen, inclusive, thereby regarding the first two years of the arts college as coming essentially within the field of secondary education? Certainly this appears to be the direction in which we are moving. And if this is to be accepted as the period of secondary education, then how shall it be divided? Shall there be a separate junior high school unit consisting of grades seven, eight and nine, with a separate senior high school unit consisting of grades ten, eleven, twelve and then the junior college for the two remaining years or grades? If these are not to be regarded as separate administrative units, then what combination of these units shall be made? If we declare that the six-year high school, including grades seven to twelve, is more favorable from the standpoint of coordinating the different elements or providing favorable conditions for coordinating the different elements, are there losses in other directions that will more than offset the values from the articulation side?

These questions are broadly suggestive of the problems to be faced in the future work of coordinating these larger administrative units. Of the limitations that are inevitable because of local community conditions, we are all conscious. The most important of these have been discussed in the opening chapter of this seventh yearbook. There are, however, good grounds for believing that there is much that can and should be accomplished in the way of coordinating these units after even the most liberal allowance has been made for such limitations.

But while these points of transition from the elementary school to the high school, and from the high school to the college are matters of real concern, they are not the only, nor are they the most important points of transition involved in continuity of school progress. What shall be said, for example, about the transition from grade to grade, within any one of these administrative units?

This at once raises the whole question of promotion from within the unit itself. It is a subject to which the commission believes it necessary to give much attention in its studies of the next two years. It is entirely conceivable and in fact it is very probable that in many instances conditions may be quite as unfavorable for continuity of progress because of abruptness in the transition between any two of these smaller units of administration as they are at this changing point between any two of the larger administrative units of which we have been speaking. Just who, in the last analysis, determines whether a child shall or shall not be promoted? Upon what basis does the teacher, principal or superintendent determine that the pupil or class in any one grade is ready to proceed to the work of the next grade? Exactly what promotion records are kept? Are records simply in the form of non-promoted, or is there a record showing exactly the subject in which the pupil failed of promotion and a statement of the causes in each case? What use is made of such promotion records as are kept? These are simply suggestive of the many very important questions that merit careful and continuous study. It is unnecessary here to do more than suggest the important ramifications of the whole subject of the promotion of pupils. It is the second field with which the commission will concern itself and it hopes through the studies of the next two years to contribute something out of the varying experiences of the country with this matter that will be of real help.

But there is a third field of work that takes us directly into the fundamental issues involved in the whole subject. That field has to do with the curriculum and with the conditions that are essential to the fullest realization of what the curriculum is designed to accomplish. Certain type questions at once arise in this connection. Just what is American education to do for this individual who begins the journey in the kindergarten and continues it on through the professional school, or withdraws at some one of the stages in the journey? Of course the answer to this question determines the aims or objectives of education all along the way. If any one supposes for an instant that this question of objectives has been answered, let him simply attempt to formulate for common acceptance the purpose or purposes of American education as a whole, and the peculiar contribution that each of the administrative units involved in the process is supposed to make. In the yearbook just submitted the attempt has been made by the Committee on Elementary Education to formulate such objectives for the elementary school unit. In like manner the Committee on Secondary Education has submitted what it conceives to be the ten special functions or purposes of secondary education. In both cases whatever is submitted is wholly tentative in nature and the chief purpose has been to offer something definite that may continue to provoke discussion and clarify our thinking, to the end that during the next two years there may be developed with respect to these objectives a formulation that will meet with common acceptance and serve as a helpful guide. Out of all these efforts at coordination that have been made during the years there have gradually emerged more clearly defined notions as to what education in this country should accomplish and what the elementary school, and each of the other units, should contribute to this common purpose. Have we as yet gone sufficiently far to interpret the meaning of it all? This is a question upon which the commission hopes to throw some light. And then related to this are conditions that determine how effectively the curriculum and all other means of realizing these educational goals are to be used. The attendance of a pupil is one such condition. Failure to secure regular attendance is by common consent a very potent factor in preventing continuity of educational progress. Is it too much to say that all prospects of making the required transition from unit to unit have been forfeited by many a child through ill-health conditions that could with proper care and foresight have been remedied at the very beginning of the child's school career? Equally significant questions arise with reference to the training and attendance of teachers. Here, again, are we working as favorably as possible within the unavoidable limitations that exist? Is it possible to get further light upon the problem of the temporary supply or substitute teacher that will enable us in the necessary absence of the regular teacher to reduce the loss on the part of the pupil to the minimum? And what is to be said concerning this very important and much-discussed subject of homogeneous grouping? The whole history of the graded school from the days of Horace Mann down until the present time has been essentially an attempt so to group pupils as to enable them to go forward with a degree of progress commensurate with their industry and ability. No one, of course, supposes that the commission will in the next two years be able to answer these and similar questions to the satisfaction of all concerned, but if it can select out some of the fundamental ones and in a patient and judicial manner throw light upon them that will serve somewhat to guide in the days that lie ahead, its fondest ambitions will have been realized.

Having briefly sketched the major fields within which the work of this commission will lie and suggested certain illustrative problems in each field, it seems important to refer briefly to the controlling principle in accordance with which the commission must carry on its work. It is a highly controversial principle and because of this what I believe to be the attitude of the commission in the use of it should be frankly set forth. It is the principle of standardization. We are frequently told that standardization is dangerous to education. It happens here, as it so frequently happens elsewhere with generalizations of this kind, that a bill of particulars is required if fruitless discussion is to be avoided. There is a kind and degree of standardization that is dangerous to education. Back in 1923 the late President Eliot, of Harvard, pointed out a tendency to carry over into school procedure the standardization practices of industry, and entered his characteristic protest against the practice. With the dangers here there would be common agreement. If reports are true there is no industry in our country to-day in which the units involved are more closely and efficiently articulated than is the case with the Ford Motor Company. There is no uncertainty whatsoever as to what the finished product is to be. Every specification has been drawn with a nicety that baffles understanding. And if this be true of the finished product it is equally true of every step or unit of the process from the beginning to the end of the journey. Controls are so operated that flexibility is neither required nor allowed. In short, it is a well-high perfect example of industrial standardization.

We would all join in protest against any attempt to bring either this kind or degree of standardization into education. Children are not things of wood or metal or textiles. Social controls, varying abilities of children, and in fact practically every factor that grows out of the differences between human beings on the one side and inanimate materials on the other, strike out all attempts to draw analogies between industry and education in these matters. We would all, furthermore, join in equally emphatic protests against the attempts of standardizing agencies, either within or without the field of education, to force any kind or degree of standardization that would prevent the legitimate and essential exercise of that flexibility without which the educational process can not be effectively carried on.

But having said all this, we shall nevertheless not blind ourselves to the fact that in all this work we can not escape standardization if we would, nor would we escape it if we could. Nobody knows better than does the school administrator the Scylla and Charybdis between which we must steer in attempting to get all that standardization has to offer and at the same time prevent its possible deadening effects upon the processes themselves. A large part of his thought and time must be given to the task of establishing standards and then of so administering the affairs within his jurisdiction as to have such standards help and not hurt. With the administration of whatever standards may be established as a result of the work of this commission, the commission itself can have no concern. That naturally must be and should be the responsibility of each community or unit of administration. But this in no sense relieves the commission of the responsibility and the opportunity of seeking out and setting up such standards as in their best judgment will guide toward improved educational procedure.

The first part of the work of this commission is to sift out from the three fields here briefly sketched what may be considered the most important and far-reaching problems concerning which there is reason to suppose help can be given. In other words up until the present time the chief attention of the commission has been given to the nature and extent of articulation problems. The yearbook here presented is essentially an inquiry. The manner in which this inquiry has been carried on is clearly presented in this yearbook. The whole purpose of this meeting this morning is directed toward this same end of giving perspective with reference to problems. This afternoon some eight or nine round table discussions will be conducted, each upon some phase of this work.

In a very real sense, therefore, Part I of the work of this commission will be completed at the close of this day's session when the last of these round table conferences adjourns.

And then the commission will begin at once a study of such problems as are selected. This study will extend over a two-year period, and if present plans carry, the results of the studies thus made will be set forth in the yearbook of the department two years from now. A knowledge of present practices throughout this country is bound to be invaluable in this study. I can not do less than express in behalf of the commission gratitude for the cheerful and intelligent responses that have been given to the commission thus far, and I wish to make it as clear as possible here that nothing will be so genuinely welcomed by the commission as voluntary requests on the part of school systems of whatever size or kind to participate in this study. In like manner our schools of special education and the many laboratory schools that are in a position, as the public schools are not, to conduct experimental studies on important phases of this work have given and will continue to give invaluable aid to the commission. In so far as this commission can ascertain present trends, interpret their validity and point out such modifications as future improvement in school welfare requires, it will have accomplished its purpose. In this manner only will it contribute to the theme of this entire convention by pointing the way by which the schools can better serve democracy through increasingly producing a higher type of citizen.

EDUCATIONAL EVENTS

WOMEN STUDENTS IN LONDON MEDICAL SCHOOLS

ATTENTION is called in *Nature* to the circumstance that prior to the war all the medical schools of the University of London (with the exception of the London School of Medicine for Women) were restricted to men, but during the war seven of the schools admitted women in addition. These facilities for women were withdrawn a short time ago, except in the case of University College Hospital, which still admits a limited quota. The action of the authorities of the medical schools aroused considerable discussion, and a committee was appointed by the senate of the University of London "to consider the question of the limitations placed upon the medical education of women undergraduates." According to the report which is summarized in *Nature,* it is considered that the facilities in London for *pre-clinical* instruction of women are ample, and it is only the withdrawal of those for *clinical* instruction which has given rise to the present inquiry. The committee thinks that there is no valid argument against the provision of coeducation, but that coeducation to be successful must be voluntary. No countenance is therefore given to the suggestion which has been made that the university should enforce a policy of coeducation upon the medical (and other) schools by withdrawal of recognition or other means. Such a policy, to be logical, would have to be applied all round, and this would force men upon women's colleges, and men upon the London School of Medicine for Women. Nor does it seem desirable that coeducation should be universal in the medical schools of London, for such a policy might result that in some schools there would be only a very small number of women—possibly only one woman—which on various grounds is highly undesirable. The committee recommends, therefore, and the senate has given general approval, that its report be communicated to the schools in the faculty of medicine, and that the vice-chancellor be requested to invite them to consider the possibility of admitting a quota of women students in the future.

THE LLOYD MIFFLIN MEMORIAL HOME FOR PENNSYLVANIA TEACHERS

G. HAROLD ANTRIM, head of the department of English, Columbia High School, writes in the *Pennsylvania School Journal* that for some time the Pennsylvania State Education Association has been concerned with the question of acquiring a home for the Pennsylvania teachers who have either retired from active service or who are convalescing from illness that prevents, temporarily, their teaching. One of the results of the Reading convention was the appointment of a committee, headed by Superintendent Robert E. Laramy, Altoona, for the purpose of studying the situation and making a report at the next annual meeting of the association.

Through the public-spirited generosity of Dr. Houston Mifflin, retired surgeon and physician of Columbia, the association received, during the month of January, a handsome gift in the form of "Norwood," an estate near Columbia, that will serve aptly as a site for such a projected home. Dr. Mifflin is a brother of the late Lloyd Mifflin, talented Pennsylvania painter and poet. For years both Dr. Mifflin and Lloyd Mifflin were actively interested in the welfare of the public schools of Columbia and of the state at large. Of their many gifts to education, the deeding, outright, of this estate, which was the home of the painter-poet, to the association comes as a fitting and far-reaching climax.

The estate of "Norwood," just beyond the eastern limits of Columbia, consists of a tract of land containing twenty acres, with a spacious lawn, covered with trees of many species, at the front. The stone and frame house, erected in 1901 by Lloyd Mifflin on the site of the original cottage built by his father, J. Houston Mifflin, contains twelve large rooms. Adjacent to the house is the studio of the former artist. There are also a barn and a four-room tenant house on the grounds.

The gift includes, in addition to "Norwood," the adjoining property, consisting of six and one half acres of land, known as "Cloverton." On this tract of land are a large seventeen-room brick house and a four-room tenant house. Scattered throughout the two properties are several springs of soft water that furnish a constant supply of water to all the houses.

At a special meeting of the executive council of the association, held at Harrisburg on January 26, Dr. Mifflin's gift was formally accepted. During the year and before the next annual meeting at New Castle, the committee in charge of the project will study the situation and present proposed plans to the association at large.

Mr. Antrim says: "The teachers of Pennsylvania are indeed fortunate in having, in Dr. Mifflin, a friend so deeply interested in their future welfare. Too much can not be said in way of appreciation of his philanthropic act that has resulted in the association's acquiring such a beautiful site for its teachers' home, a home that will perpetuate the memory of both Lloyd Mifflin and Dr. Houston Mifflin, friends of education."

THE STANDARDIZATION OF HIGH SCHOOLS AND COLLEGES

A CONFERENCE of the officers of the national and regional associations interested in the standardization of high schools and colleges was held at Cleveland on February 27, 1929, in connection with the meeting of the Department of Superintendence.

Registrar Ira M. Smith, of the University of Michigan, representing the American Association of Collegiate Registrars, presented an account of the efforts of colleges and universities to inform high schools concerning the success of entering students. Mr. Smith recommended an effort to bring about uniformity in the reports returned by the colleges to the high schools.

Mr. Carl A. Jessen, specialist in secondary education of the Federal Bureau of Education, discussed plans for a nation-wide study of secondary education.

There was also a discussion of the possibility of extending the certificate privilege to high schools maintained for Americans in foreign lands. It was finally agreed to make a division of foreign territory as follows:

Schools in Europe to be assigned to the Association of Colleges and Secondary Schools of the Middle States and Maryland.

Schools in Cuba and South American countries to be assigned to the Association of Colleges and Secondary Schools of the Southern States.

Schools in Japan, China and the Far East to be assigned to the Northwest Association of Secondary and Higher Schools.

It was agreed that problems presented by the extension of the certificate privilege to Canadian schools should be referred to the North Central Association of Colleges and Secondary Schools.

The conference also endorsed the proposal to provide an annual bulletin which would include the names of all the accredited secondary schools and approved colleges of the United States. A committee was appointed to take up with the Federal Bureau of Education the question of publication of such a bulletin.

The conference voted to hold another session in 1930 and selected as officers: *Chairman,* Dean J. B. Edmonson, School of Education, University of Michigan, Ann Arbor; *Secretary,* Professor Joseph Roemer, University of Florida, Gainesville.

THE ALLEGANY SCHOOL OF NATURAL HISTORY

THE Allegany School of Natural History, conducted by the Buffalo Society of Natural Sciences, in cooperation with the New York State Museum, and affiliated with the University of Buffalo, which will be open for its third season, July 5 to August 24, in the Allegany State Park.

This school was established in 1927, to meet the need for well qualified teachers of natural history, which has developed with the increasing demand for instruction in the natural sciences, in public preserves, national, state, county and municipal, and in private camps and summer schools. The personnel of such centers of outdoor instruction now numbers many thousands, of whom a large proportion, teaching such sciences as zoology, botany, physiography and geology, requires wide and accurate knowledge and skill in leadership, to give their students all that they should receive from such summer sessions in the wilderness. Park officials, school directors and others responsible for the quality of such instruction are yearly seeking better talent for teachers of natural history.

The school is situated on a new lake made by damming Quaker Run, a tributary of the Allegheny River, which drains the southern part of Allegany State Park, in Cattaraugus County, in southwestern New York, seventy miles south of Buffalo. It is within a mile of the Pennsylvania line, across which is a larger public preserve, the Allegheny National Forest, containing virgin timber and large wild game. Allegany Park occupies a tract of sixty thousand acres, in the bend of the Allegheny River, where it enters New York from its source in Pennsylvania, and returns again into Pennsylvania on its way to the Ohio.

The Allegany School of Natural History is sponsored by the New York State Museum of the University of the State of New York, Dr. Charles C. Adams, director of the State Museum, having general supervision of the educational policy; by the Buffalo Society of Natural Sciences, of which Chauncey J. Hamlin, who brought about the establishment of the school, is president; and by the Allegany State Park Commission, which provided the site, created the lake nearby and built the cabins and other structures wherein it is housed. The school is provided with 40 cabins, each with two sleeping rooms.

The teaching staff will again be headed by Dr. Robert E. Coker, professor of zoology, University of North Carolina, who has been director since the school was established. Professor Allen C. Tester, of the University of Iowa, will again teach field geology; Mr. Aretas A. Saunders, of the Central High School, Bridgeport, Conn., will teach the natural history of birds, and Mr. William P. Alexander, field naturalist of the Buffalo Society of Natural Sciences, will again teach general nature study. A new member of the faculty will be Leslie A. Kenoyer, professor of biology, Western State Teachers College, Kalamazoo, Mich., who will teach field botany.

THE SCHOOL OF NURSING OF WESTERN RESERVE UNIVERSITY

THE School of Nursing of Western Reserve University, Cleveland, started five years ago as an experiment in education, received at that time five hundred thousand dollars, the gift of Mrs. Chester C. Bolton, who placed the sum in trust for it. On March 10 she turned the trust over to the university, having increased the principal to the sum of $1,500,000.

There are said to be only two endowed university schools of nursing in America, the Yale School and the Western Reserve School, though about a hundred university schools have some sort of university connection. The Yale School, also started five years ago, experimentally, recently received a million dollars from the Rockefeller Foundation.

In making the gift Mrs. Bolton recommends that any portion of the yearly income that may be spared from the budget of the school be spent for experimental work, which would be beneficial to nursing education. Accordingly, the school at once embarks upon a study of the cost of nursing education and nursing service—what it costs to care for patients and what it costs to educate nurses. Faculty of the school will make the study in cooperation with the university hospitals. Dr. May Ayres Burgess, of New York, director of the Committee on Grading Nursing Schools, will direct the study.

"The grading committee has discovered that we have a dangerous oversupply of low-grade nurses, many unemployed, and a dangerous shortage of high-grade nurses prepared for responsibility," says Dr. Burgess. Numbers of hospitals will probably have to be asked to stop running schools of nursing, or to raise the standard of their schools. At the present time there are no adequate data available on what it costs to nurse patients and what it costs to educate nurses.

"Hospitals will have to know what it will cost to shift from student service for patients to graduate nurse service for them; or from low-grade to high-grade students in terms of money."

THE PLAYGROUND AND RECREATION ASSOCIATION OF AMERICA

THE report of the Playground and Recreation Association of America has been issued, showing that requests for help on questions of recreation from 5,931 cities, towns and villages in practically every state were met by the correspondence and consultation bureau of the association. In addition, eighty-eight Canadian communities and thirty-two foreign cities sought the advice of the organization. The field secretaries gave direct service to 462 cities in forty-four states.

Adults throughout the United States are giving an increased amount of their spare time to dramatics. One thousand requests for advice and aid in this field were received in November alone. As one illustration of the rural interest in and talent for acting, the report cites the success of a group of mail carriers, housewives, storekeepers and teachers, of Redfield Grange, Oswego County, New York, who won first place for their presentation of the play, "Day by Day," by Paul Green, in a state contest at Cornell University. To serve the demand for training in games and music in rural districts, the association conducted institutes for 3,596 farm men and women, country ministers, teachers and home demonstration agents in twenty-one states last year. Forty states had requested the service.

One hundred and thirteen cities now employ part-time or year-round colored recreation workers. This is thirteen more than in 1927. Some of the most striking advances in community music have been made among Negroes. Numerous choruses of five hundred or more voices have achieved local triumphs in the singing of Negro spirituals and other music.

The National Physical Education Service, a department of the association, reports that thirty-five states, representing ninety per cent. of the population, now have physical and health education legislation, and twenty states, representing sixty per cent. of the population, have laws, manuals and state directors of physical education.

A manual on municipal and county parks in two volumes, a study of playground design and equipment, and publications on athletics and home play were among the principal publications issued by the association in 1928. New studies begun during the year were a two-year survey of the failures and successes of community music and one of girls' athletics.

HARVARD TEACHERS' ASSOCIATION

THE annual meeting of the Harvard Teachers' Association is being held in Cambridge on March 16. There are two sessions—one on Saturday morning at 10:30 in the Radcliffe Theater on Mason Street; the other a luncheon program in the main dining hall of the Commander Hotel on Garden Street.

The general topic for the meeting is "Education and its Relation to Modern Business."

At the morning meeting, where Mr. Walter F. Downey, headmaster of the English High School of Boston, presides, Professor Carl Frederick Taeusch, of the Graduate School of Business Administration, Harvard University, will discuss "Ethics and Business." Mr. A. Vere Shaw, of the firm of Shaw, Loomis and Sayles, Investment Counsel, will speak on "The Teacher's Personal Investment Problem." Opportunity for discussion of both of these papers will be given at the conclusion of Mr. Shaw's address.

At the luncheon program, where Dean Holmes, of the Graduate School of Education, is to be the toastmaster, there will be two speakers—Dr. William Trufant Foster, director of the Pollok Foundation for Economic Research, and Professor Frank William Taussig, Henry Lee professor of economics, Harvard University. Dr. Foster, working in collaboration with Mr. Waddill Catchings, has within the past few years been active in the production of books on economic questions. He will speak on some aspect of the questions raised by his books. Professor Taussig, long recognized as one of America's leading economists, is now collaborating with Professor C. S. Joslyn, of Harvard, in a study of the origins of business leaders. Professor Taussig is to discuss at the luncheon meeting some of the points that his investigation has disclosed.

The Harvard Teachers' Association was organized thirty-eight years ago "to promote the interchange of thought on educational questions" among teachers and school officers with Harvard connections. The suggestion for the founding of such an organization came from Professor Nathaniel S. Shaler, one of Harvard's most distinguished scientific men. Dr. Paul H. Hanus, however, was responsible for initiating the policies and directing for a long period the work of the association. For many years he held the office of secretary, being relieved later by Professor Henry W. Holmes and other members of the faculty of the Graduate School of Education. The secretaries, in cooperation with the executive committee, have been chiefly responsible for the programs annually provided.

The annual meeting, held on the third Saturday in March, consists of a morning and a luncheon program. An endeavor is always made to select for this meeting a topic that is both timely and permanently significant. The papers which are read are usually printed and distributed to members. The papers of the current meeting will probably be printed in SCHOOL AND SOCIETY.

EDUCATIONAL NOTES AND NEWS

DR. LOTUS D. COFFMAN, president of the University of Minnesota; Dr. Raymond M. Hughes, president of the Iowa State College; Dr. Frank LeRond McVey, president of the University of Kentucky, and Dr. Henry Suzzallo, of the Carnegie Foundation for the Advancement of Teaching, formerly president of the University of Washington, will lecture during the summer session of the University of Chicago.

A PORTRAIT, painted by C. S. Hopkinson, of Professor Edward Channing, who recently retired from the McLean chair of ancient and modern history at Harvard University, where he has taught for forty years, was presented to President A. Lawrence Lowell at a recent meeting in University Hall.

DR. CHARLES E. BEURY, president of Temple University, has been awarded for distinguished service in the field of education the 1929 gold medal offered yearly by the Philadelphia Kiwanis Club. The presentation was made by Richard J. Freeman, president of the club, after a eulogy of Dr. Beury had been delivered by Roland S. Morris, formerly ambassador to Japan.

AT the graduation ceremonial at the University of St. Andrews on June 28 the degree of doctor of laws will be conferred on Dr. T. Percy Nunn, principal of the London Day Training College and professor of education in the University of London; on Dr. A. E. Taylor, professor of moral philosophy in the University of Edinburgh, and on G. M. Trevelyan, fellow of Trinity College and regius professor of modern history in the University of Cambridge.

IN recognition of her work in promoting the health of school children of the community, the Ling medal has been awarded to Miss Barbara

Greenwood, supervisor of the nursery training department of the University of California at Los Angeles. The Ling Foundation, organized in 1927, has for its purpose the forwarding of child health work and to award those who have unselfishly worked in behalf of the health progress of the school children of southern California.

THE board of trustees of Monmouth College has determined that the most fitting tribute which can be given to Miss Alice Winbigler for the great service she has rendered to Monmouth College during a period of fifty years' continuous teaching is the establishment of a permanent endowment for an Alice Winbigler chair of mathematics in the college. It is proposed to raise the sum of $60,000. A retiring allowance of $1,500 each year, which will be approximately one half the income from this endowment, is to go to Miss Winbigler during her lifetime, after which the entire income will be used for the permanent support of the chair of mathematics.

THE Chancellor's medal of the University of Buffalo was conferred at the convocation exercises on February 22 on John J. Albright for his work in hydro development and as a patron of art.

PROFESSOR FRANK SCHLESINGER, director of the Yale University Observatory, has been awarded the Bruce medal of the Astronomical Society of the Pacific.

EDMOND S. MEANY, professor of history at the University of Washington, was recently honored by the French government with admission to the Legion of Honor, in recognition of "his distinguished services as an educator and historian."

IN recognition of their service to Italian art and culture in America, and particularly of the development of the Casa Italiana at Columbia University, King Victor Emmanuel of Italy has conferred upon Frank D. Fackenthal, secretary of Columbia University, and on James T. Grady, its director of public information, the rank of Cavaliere of the Order of the Crown of Italy.

DR. JOHN GARLAND POLLARD, formerly state attorney-general of Virginia and now professor at William and Mary College, has become a candidate for governor of Virginia.

THE resignation of Charles Francis Adams, Secretary of Navy in the Hoover cabinet, as treasurer of Harvard University has been accepted by the board of overseers. The board has announced as his successor Henry Lee Shattuck, class of 1901 and member of the Massachusetts Legislature. Mr. Shattuck's father and grandfather were prominent in the management of Harvard College. His father, F. C. Shattuck, who died last January, was a member of the class of 1863 and a professor in the Harvard Medical School. His grandfather, George O. Shattuck, graduated from Harvard in 1831 and later became dean of the medical school.

THE Alice Freeman fellowship of Wellesley College has been awarded to Deborah May Hickey, of Houston, Texas. The fellowship, amounting to about $1,600, will enable her to continue her study of mathematics in Germany. The Fanny Bullock Workman scholarship has been awarded to Miss Margaret Davidson, of Washington, who plans to continue her work at Cornell University. Miss Ruth Elvira Clark, associate professor of French, is the recipient of a fellowship given by Mrs. Frederick G. Atkinson, of Minneapolis, alumnae trustee of the college, to a member of the faculty, to carry on research that is already begun.

AT Harvard University lecturers have been appointed as follows: John Chin Hsung Wu, a member of the Ministry of Justice of the Republic of China; Robert Coleman Brown, assistant professor of law in Indiana University; and William Lewis Roberts, professor of law at the University of Kentucky and editor of the *Kentucky Law Journal*. Gustavus Hill Robinson, professor in the Boston University Law School, will hold the Judah Philip Benjamin Research Fellowship; James Jacques Robinson, professor of law at Indiana University, will hold the Brandeis fellowship. The Sidney Thompson Fairchild fellowship in the law of railroads and other public utilities will be held by Charles Lucien Baker Lowndes, professor of law at Georgetown University.

A CONTRIBUTION of $50,000 toward the endowment of the Alexander C. Humphreys chair of economics of engineering of Stevens Institute has been announced. Dr. William D. Ennis, director of research of the Technical Advisory Corporation of New York, has been elected the first incumbent of the chair. Though the endowment of the chair in memory of the late President Humphreys is only one fifth completed, the appointment of the occupant of the chair has been made possible by a special donation of the salary required for the first year, so that the income from the present endowment may be devoted to research. One half of this sum has been provided by Arthur Graham Glasgow, Stevens, '85, of London, England, formerly associated with President Humphreys in the firm of Humphreys and Glasgow.

SUPERINTENDENT ISAAC O. WINSLOW, Providence, R. I., for fifteen years head of the city school system, was recently elected superintendent emeritus. Superintendent Winslow will continue in charge of the Providence schools until his successor is named.

THE Children's Museum of Boston announces the appointment of Dana Rice as curator of exhibits. Mr. Rice has been instructor in fine arts at Dartmouth College, an assistant at the Pennsylvania Museum and museum assistant at the Rhode Island School of Design in Providence, Rhode Island.

PROFESSOR LEON J. RICHARDSON, professor of Latin and director of the extension division of the University of California, plans to attend the World Conference on Adult Education to be held at Cambridge, England, on August 22 to 29.

ARTHUR H. HILTON, headmaster of a country high school, has been selected by the government of Australia to make a study of the agricultural high schools of the United States, under the auspices of the Carnegie Foundation.

DR. DONALD YOUNG, of the department of sociology of the University of Pennsylvania, edited the November *Annals* of the American Academy of Political and Social Science. The issue is brought out as a separate volume, entitled "The American Negro." It is a symposium composed of nearly forty contributions from prominent authorities of both racial groups and deals with manifold aspects of the interracial problem.

A DIRECTORY of state-wide welfare organizations in Pennsylvania has been prepared by Mr. Jacob J. Blair, instructor in the department of sociology of the University of Pennsylvania, under the direction of Professor James H. S. Bossard, and under the active supervision of Mr. Arthur Dunham, secretary to the child welfare division of the Public Charities Association of Pennsylvania. The directory is being published by the Public Charities Association.

DR. GEORGE E. VINCENT, Yale, 1885, president of the Rockefeller Foundation, on March 11 delivered at Yale University the principal address entitled "Gentleman and Scholar" at the one hundred and forty-ninth annual banquet of the Yale Chapter of the Phi Beta Kappa Society, the second oldest chapter in the country. President Angell also spoke.

WALLACE B. DONHAM, dean of the school of business administration of Harvard University, and formerly vice-president of the Old Colony Trust Company, gave one of a series of five lectures at Northwestern University this month under the William A. Vawter Foundation on Business Ethics. The subject of Dean Donham's lecture was "Business Ethics: Its Rôle in Modern Life and Education."

PROFESSOR MARCUS WILSON JERNEGAN, professor of American history at the University of Chicago, is conducting a series of six lectures at New York University, on the general topic "The Political and Social Philosophy of New England Leaders in the Colonial Period: A Study of the Conflict of Conservative Thought—Political, Religious, Economical and Social—1620–1776."

DR. FRANK MASON COMSTOCK, dean of freshmen at Case School of Applied Science and head of the department of descriptive geometry and drawing for the last thirty-eight years, died suddenly on March 7 at the age of seventy-three years. Dr. Comstock was acting president in 1912.

Dr. Chauncey A. V. Pettibone, associate professor of physiological chemistry in the University of Minnesota, has died by suicide at Minneapolis. Dr. Pettibone had been in ill health.

The Reverend E. Earl Orwig, associate professor of the Bible at Lafayette College, died on March 12, at the age of thirty-seven years.

John Newton Tillman, Democratic representative in Congress from 1915 to 1929 and formerly president of the University of Arkansas, has died at the age of seventy years.

Dr. Allyn Abbott Young, professor of political economy at the University of London since 1927, formerly professor of economics at Harvard University, died on March 8, at the age of fifty-two years.

The Right Reverend George Henry Somerset Walpole, Bishop of Edinburgh, died on March 4, at the age of seventy-five years. Mr. Walpole, who was the father of Hugh Walpole, the novelist, was from 1889 to 1896 professor of dogmatic theology in the General Theological Seminary in New York.

Dr. William L. Mollison, a distinguished mathematician, died in London on March 11, at the age of seventy-seven years. He had been master of Clare College, Cambridge, since 1915.

Dr. Maurice Wakeman, of the Yale School of Medicine, died on March 2 aboard a steamship between the Azores and Southampton, England, after having contracted phlebitis while studying yellow fever in Lagos, Nigeria. Dr. Wakeman obtained leave in February, 1928, to study the chemical pathology of the disease which was indexed by the late Dr. Hideyo Noguchi. He sailed for Lagos as a member of the International Health Board of the Rockefeller Institute, three of whose members already have died. Six weeks ago Dr. Wakeman contracted the disease and his condition became so serious that it was decided that he must return to the United States. Dr. Wakeman was thirty-two years old. Dr. Wakeman's father is Dr. Alfred J. Wakeman, chemist of the Connecticut Agricultural Experiment Station; his brother, Dr. Edward Taylor Wakeman, clinical instructor in pediatrics in the Yale School of Medicine; and his sister, Mrs. Robert L. Calhoun, has received the medical degree from the Yale Medical School.

A public ceremony commemorating the relations of Carl Schurz with Columbia University, announced as part of the Carl Schurz Centenary, will be held at Columbia's Deutsches Haus, on Tuesday evening, March 19, under the auspices of the Institute of Arts and Sciences, the Germanistic Society of America and the Carl Schurz Centennial Committee. Charles Nagel, of St. Louis, secretary of commerce and labor in the Taft administration, will deliver the principal address. George McAneny, past president of the Borough of Manhattan, will speak for the centennial committee. Dr. F. J. E. Woodbridge, dean of the graduate faculties, will preside. Carl Schurz received the honorary degree of doctor of laws from Columbia in 1899. A Carl Schurz fellowship was established in his honor. The university also has a Carl Schurz Library Fund.

An unfortunate note was printed in the issue of this journal for March 2. A statement historically correct concerning the library school of the New York Public Library was made as of a current event. The library school of the New York Public Library became part of the School of Library Science of Columbia University in 1926.

As the result of a joint resolution presented to the Congress, the President will issue a proclamation calling upon the people of the United States to observe May 1 as Child Health Day.

The seventeenth annual convention of the American Association of Collegiate Registrars will be held in Seattle, April 16 to 18. E. B. Stevens, registrar at the University of Washington, is in charge of local arrangements. Present plans include excursions in the vicinity of Seattle and banquets at which the Pacific Coast registrars will act as hosts. The convention headquarters will be at the Olympic Hotel.

The United States Civil Service Commission announces the following open competitive examinations: Teacher of home economics, senior high school, $1,860; teacher of home economics, junior high school, $1,680; teacher of home economics, elementary, $1,560; applications must be on file with the Civil Service Commission at Washington, D. C., not later than April 9. An examination will also be held for principal in the normal training department in the Indian Field Service, for duty at Haskell Institute, Lawrence, Kansas. The entrance salary is $2,300 a year, less $240 a year for quarters, fuel and light. Higher-salaried positions are filled through promotion. For this position the Interior Department prefers unmarried women without dependents.

A THREE-MONTH campaign to raise $100,000 for the establishment of a World Education Foundation is being entered upon by the World Federation of Education Associations. It is hoped that 100,000 persons, professional teachers and others, will contribute $1.00 each toward the cause of international understanding through education.

THE Carnegie Corporation of New York has set aside a fund for scholarship grants to those preparing for library work. The amount available for the next school year is sufficient to provide for a limited number of appointments. The purpose of the grants is to enable persons who already have had experience in library work, and who have shown promise of capacity to contribute to the advancement of the library profession, to pursue a year of study and research in library problems. Their work will be done not necessarily in residence but invariably in connection with an educational institution recognized as appropriate for supervising the study, and the results will be expected to constitute a definite contribution to library science or to the professional equipment of the librarian. The stipend will be $1,500 or more and will vary according to the requirements of individual students. A report of the year's work will be required from each person receiving appointment. Applicants should write to the Advisory Group on Library Scholarship Grants, Carnegie Corporation, 522 Fifth Avenue, New York, from whom they can obtain full information.

FOR the first time the new Graduate Library School of the University of Chicago will offer summer quarter courses. Candidates for degrees in this school must have a bachelor's degree equivalent to that conferred by leading colleges, a year of training in an accredited library school, and a year of library experience. The Graduate Library School is an outgrowth of a movement on the part of the library profession for an institution devoted exclusively to research and to graduate study at the higher levels in the field of librarianship. The kinds of positions for which the school will give preparation include those of administrators of public, college and university libraries, teachers for library schools and training classes, teachers of library science in teachers' colleges and normal schools, and libraries of special collections such as law, history, medicine, science, mathematics and Americana. The summer quarter faculty will include James Christian Meinich Hanson, professor of bibliography, classification, and cataloguing, formerly acting director of the Harper Memorial Library; Douglas Waples, professor of educational method; Dr. Pierce Butler, of the Newberry Library, Chicago, and Henry Bartlett Van Hoesen, assistant librarian of Princeton University. Among the courses offered are those on "The Library and the Education of Adults," "Origin and Development of the Printed Book," "Bibliography" and "Individual Research."

DR. H. D. SHELDON, dean of the school of education of the University of Oregon, is reported to have announced that a non-sectarian school of religion at the University of Oregon will probably be opened next autumn. The school, of which Dr. Sheldon is acting chairman, will instruct in religion in a broad sense, and will aim to instil in the youth of the university a clearer conception and better understanding of religious faith.

THE superintendent of schools of Chicago has authorized the use of space in the Kinzie School, one of the older buildings of the north side, for a center where a group of health department and social service workers will serve as consultants with the educational staff of the surrounding schools.

THE New Jersey State Board of Education has passed a resolution in opposition to the present form of the bill in the legislature for the appointment of a Board of Regents to act in matters of higher education at Rutgers University or other institutions that may come under state control. One objection was to the provision that the Board of Regents determine the state's needs in connection with higher public education. "This board function and power might be claimed to include the state normal schools and particularly those at Trenton and Montclair, which are now of collegiate standard, and therefore institutions of public higher education."

A BILL has been introduced in the Maine senate to amend the law requiring the superintending school committee of every city to cause every child in the public schools to be given a physical examination once a year by requiring further that tests of hearing shall be made by apparatus adequate to detect even slight degrees of impairment of hearing.

ADEQUATE funds for the reconstruction of a State Normal School at Plattsburg, for the construction of a new building at the Potsdam State Normal School, and for the replacement of the present Normal School building at Geneseo will be requested of the Legislature as a result of action of the regents of the University of the State of New York.

DISCUSSION

WHO IS DISHONEST?

DURING the last five years a subsidized group of experts has been collecting statistics and announcing conclusions on the subject of honesty. In the aggregate, hundreds of school days have been occupied and thousands of children in school attendance have been subjected to these tests.

This is what usually happens. When a foundation wishes to expend money for social study of any kind, it expects its surveyors to domicile themselves in the public schools. The statistics would be more valuable if they reflected the thoughts and ideals of all classes and conditions of men and women, but it is so much easier to ask questions of children in regular school attendance. They can not escape the questions and they must answer.

It is difficult to see why school officials permit these intrusions. Parents send children to school that they may be educated, not that they may be subjected to tests whose sole purpose is to furnish the information which some scholar or some organization desires. No artificial test in honesty can in any way add to the child's education, while it must be admitted that it may be harmful to his personal ideals. However, regular school work and the educative process stop while school time and school organization are surrendered to the investigators. No one has tried to list the number of subsidized and individual workers who in this way approach the schools, but the total is large and no one can justify this expenditure of school effort. Only this month a student seeking for thesis material sent to all high-school classes in ancient history in a certain state questions which in subject-matter ranged from Determinism to the League of Nations and requested that a half-hour a day for four days be given to his tests. A number of acquiescent schools actually gathered for him this material.

Even more important in the tests of honesty is the ethical question involved. By deliberate planning, pupils are placed in situations where dishonesty is likely to be the result. May this fairly be done? The habits which we designate character are formed by the repetition of right actions and are weakened by irregular and unsocial responses. Two widely used tests are given as illustrations.

(1) *The over-change test.* The subject is sent on a purchasing errand. It is prearranged with the merchant to give him a certain amount of over-change. The test is what he will do with it.

(4) *The missent letter.* The subject receives a letter from a business firm enclosing twenty-five cents. The letter says that this amount is sent to balance his account with the firm, and requests that the receipt be sent back in the addressed and stamped envelope which is enclosed.

In other tests stealing, lying and boasting are suggested and the opportunity presented. These tests are frankly called by the testers the lying test, the stealing test, the peeping test, and the like.

Tests have been designed to answer these questions:

Can the subject be trusted not to cheat in a game?

Can the subject be trusted to refuse credit which is not due him?

Can the subject be trusted not to accept a tip for a trifling courtesy?

In all these cases the pupil is brought into an artificial situation and is secretly watched either directly or by some cunningly concealed checking device.

One test begins with this statement:

There are fifteen statements listed below and three questions under each. Check the *one* which you think you would do in each case. Read these carefully and be honest in your answers. Take all the time necessary. You need not sign your name to the paper.

The pupil accustomed to school conventions believes that when he is told he need not sign his name there is a guarantee that he may answer honestly and not be individually blamed. Yet entirely unknown to the pupils, several papers in each group, forty in all, were selected by means of a code marking. Twenty of the forty were pupils who were known to have been flagrantly dishonest during the year and who were generally problem pupils; twenty were considered as the most exemplary pupils in leadership and conduct.

It is difficult to defend unethical actions used in testing the ethical reactions of pupils. In fact, one of the strongest native characteristics of boyhood is contempt for one who does not play the game squarely.

In the test to which reference has been made, these are sample statements:

II. If, while you were playing, a street light was broken by some one in your crowd and you were asked about it, should you
1. Say you knew nothing about it?
2. Tell which one of the crowd threw the stone?
3. Take your share of the blame as one of the crowd?

V. As you go into a store you see very tempting candy on an open shelf. Should you
1. Take just a bite?
2. Not touch it even though you want it?
3. Take some for yourself and your friend?

VI. If you find a pocketbook containing money, should you
1. Take it to a lost and found office at once?
2. Take it home to think what to do?
3. Hide it and keep it for yourself?

It is evident that in this situation the proper answer depends somewhat upon accepted school conventions. This may be seen by translating into situations which adults face.

II. If, at a Rotary dinner, a careless member burned a cigarette hole in the table cloth, should you
1. Give his name to the proprietor?
2. Tell the proprietor that the contract with him included ordinary wreckage?
3. Pay the treasurer your share of the damage?

V. If, on a Sunday afternoon, you see fair apples under a roadside tree, should you
1. Take two or three as nature's gift?
2. Take a half-bushel and offer payment at the next farm house, if any one is at home?
3. Leave the apples untouched?

VI. If you find a spare automobile tire in the street before your house, should you
1. Advertise the find?
2. Scrutinize the lost columns?
3. Hold the tire until claimed?

Referring once again to these experiments, it is of interest to note that the pupils for whom the teachers hold thumbs down as scholastically dishonest scored in this honesty examination 9 per cent. higher than the teachers' lily white pets. Another interesting by-product is this conclusion: The children enrolled in sectarian schools, with regular formal religious instruction, in these tests deceive equally with those enrolled in public schools.

In general, in all these tests the fact has been ignored that honesty is not a single trait any more than is accuracy or good manners. There are scores of different honesties, and one who is entirely honest in many situations will deceive in certain others, if our standards are made the criterion. We all know that this is true for adults and it is equally true for children. An embezzler may guard his wife's reputation, his daughter's character, his friend's investments and his own spoken word with scrupulous care. In many situations, he is reliable; in one, at least, dishonest. A boy may be impudent to an irritating teacher. He may help a needy friend in an examination. He may deny that his slovenly mother is not immaculate—this, too, is dishonesty—but he may go long hungry before he will open another's dinner pail. He like others is honest in streaks.

One other device calls for criticism. It is called the improbable achievement technique. This is an illustration:

(1) *The puzzle peg.* This is a game of solitaire which may be bought in the toy stores. The problem is to jump all the pegs off the board except one and leave this one in the center hole. Any one who has tried this knows how very difficult it is. The time allowed is five minutes for the first trial and three for the second. Consequently, any child who claims to have solved it in the time allowed is cheating or else he is one of those very rare persons who by many hours of previous practice has learned the game so well as to do it in five minutes.

This technique is frequently used and is declared to be very satisfactory. It may use for a basis the curve of normal distribution, but it sets up a hypothetical time limit and then ranks as dishonest all who surpass this assumed standard. This is weighting the dice against the children with a vengeance. If they fail, they are dumb-bells. If they succeed, they are cheats.

E. W. BUTTERFIELD

CONCORD, N. H.

DORMITORY VALUES FOR STUDENTS

CONSIDERABLE attention has been given recently by college authorities to the way housing conditions affect the scholastic standing of students. In accord with this type of survey the recent grades of young women in Northern State Teachers College, Aberdeen, South Dakota, have been examined.

The "D" and "F" grades are the ones that have been considered. These are the two lowest grades given by our college. "D" is given by our college for achievement of poor quality, distinctly below the average, but still passing. "F" is given where the quality of work does not merit credit. The object of this survey was to find how "D" and "F" grades of the fall quarter of this school year were distributed among the following groups of women: those working for room and board in private homes, those doing light housekeeping and those living in dormitories.

The average distribution of "D" and "F" grades among all the young women students was 1.37 credit hours per young woman student. The young women doing light housekeeping averaged 1.74 credit hours; young women working for room and board in private homes averaged 1.81 credit hours; young women living in the dormitories averaged 1.33 credit hours. In other words, while the young women living in the dormitories made less than the average number of "D" and "F" grades made by all the women students, the women students working for room and board in private homes and those doing light housekeeping averaged considerably more low passing and failing grades.

To college authorities this is the natural result. Both the student working for room and board and the light-housekeeping student have to devote a number of hours per day to housework. That is not the case of the student housed in the dormitory.

Not only does scholarship suffer, but all too frequently other essential values to be derived while in college are diminished. The light-housekeeping girl very often goes home each week-end, so her social life and interests are not increased by college. Both the student working for room and board and the light-housekeeping student crowd out the values to be derived from extra-curricular activities and from making numerous friends. School authorities who are seeking employees are to-day anxious not only regarding the academic averages of candidates, but also how candidates will contribute to the life of the community.

Too many young students to-day are practicing false economy in their living. Let economies be more along the line of simple and inexpensive clothing, and let more of the recreation be the wholesome, varied recreation the college affords.

Stephen Leacock, of McGill University, insisted that the first need in establishing a college is to have halls of residence for the students. Learning to live with groups is a great preparation for life after college.

Presidents in many of our colleges and universities that have halls of residence have found that students housed in dormitories have higher academic averages than those living under other conditions.

There is no doubt that dormitories offer greater seclusion and quiet to the student if she really wishes to study. The life of the whole residence hall is centered around the idea of what is most conducive to the best interests of the student's life and comfort.

My advice as one deeply interested in young college women's getting the maximum returns for money and time spent in college is to live where conditions are most favorable to best academic and social conditions. Our recent survey agrees with numerous other ones—that the academic standing of students living in college halls of residence is higher than that of students living under other conditions.

ELLA LEE MOULTON,
Dean of Women
NORTHERN STATE TEACHERS COLLEGE

SPECIAL CORRESPONDENCE

STUDENT AMBASSADORS TO FRANCE

TWENTY-ONE American ambassadors, without college training or experience in public affairs, were about to embark on an important international mission. A casual observer on the pier in New York that morning early in last July would not have noticed anything very unusual or suggestive of ambassadorial dignity. He would have seen a crowd of keen, young American fellows, animated by an irrepressible spirit of enthusiasm and anticipation. From appearance it might have been the reunion of school friends after a good vacation. In reality, with the exception of a few small groups, they had never seen one another before that morning. They had come from many states from California to Maine, and they represented many schools from Chicago to Boston. To balance this geographical and institutional diversity they had several things in common. All were secondary school upperclassmen, or else had just been graduated, and every last one was intensely thrilled by the realization that he was not only going to spend the summer in Europe, but that he was also a part of a pioneer venture in promoting international relations.

At the end of eight days on board ship every one was thoroughly acquainted. It seemed as though they had known each other for years. The adult leaders, some of whom had lived on the continent, had in the meantime prepared the groundwork for the summer's plan by discussing the objectives of the expedition, explaining French customs and setting all to thinking in the same direction, so that definite group morale was established.

Every turn of the hundred and fifty mile motor ride up the Seine valley from Havre revealed so much of interest that the trip seemed but a fraction of the distance. The weather was so perfect that even the most confirmed grouch could have found no fault, except, perhaps, to complain that it was too good to last.

Finally, at the end of a winding, cobblestoned street of the village of Jouy-en-Josas the bus drew up before an impressive gateway in a great wall. A brass plate on one side was marked "Le Montcel." After the driver had made a cautious comparison of the width of the gateway with the breadth of his vehicle, the motor entered the grounds, climbing an immaculately swept and bordered driveway, winding under the trees, and stopped in front of a huge white stone building, the Château du Montcel, which seemed to have grown up out of the midst of lovely flower beds. A beautiful spot; and a place where the imagination could run riot! Part of the château was built in the thirteenth century, although it has been entirely remodeled and comfortably equipped with modern conveniences. Forty acres of eighteenth century landscaping of forest, lawns, flowers and streams stretched away from the château, up the hill and through the glens, the whole being surrounded by the usual high stone wall.

From Versailles, only three miles away, or from Paris, but ten miles distant, the French kings used to pass here to their favorite hunting-grounds nearby. Several other restored medieval châteaux looking down from the elevations about suggested the glamour of knighthood days. Le Montcel, once the residence of a wealthy titled family, now houses a private school for French boys during the winter months.

Here for the next six weeks the twenty-one American boys and ten French boys lived together and had the time of their lives. Forenoons between Monday and Friday were quite similar. Breakfast at eight was followed by two one-hour periods of required instruction. There was an intervening hour which could be spent optionally in a class in French harmonics or another in French literature or in reading, writing, light games, or just sitting about under the trees chatting together. During the instruction periods the American boys studied the French language and culture under French instructors. At the same time the French boys studied English and American history and life with the American instructors.

Afternoons were occupied in sports of both countries, each group teaching the other games not already familiar; in sightseeing trips to Paris by train; journeys in small groups by bicycle to Versailles, St. Cloud, Saint-Germain, Sèvres, the aviation fields and many other points; hikes over the hills, or in simply enjoying the allurements of Montcel. In the evenings there were dances, games, concerts or theater and opera parties to Paris. If an important point was to be visited on the morrow a French instructor would prepare the way by telling in French about its history, significance and spirit. Sometimes the whole assembly would hold a kind of council in which French boys would tell about French customs or current events in English, and the Americans would do the same in French. Occasionally the afternoon and evening were combined in a picnic supper taken to some delightful, memory-haunted spot within walking distance, followed by stories and songs and a homeward walk by moonlight.

Week-ends were reserved for the long excursions to the battlefields, Touraine, Fontainebleau, and other distant points. Motor buses were often used, but the combination train and bicycle trips were voted the most popular. All these experiences were shared by the French and Americans. As a result they learned to know one another quite well and formed many firm friendships.

August twenty-fifth, the day of leave-taking, came all too soon. Regretful good-byes were tempered for the Americans by the thought that there lay ahead four days of adventure in Switzerland, two more in London and then the homeward voyage.

What was it all about? In the autumn of 1927 several headmasters met in New York to wrestle anew with the problems and aims of education. No doubt every school in the land claims, or would like to claim, that it is giving its youth a liberal education. They understand it and try to achieve it in various ways. Everett Dean Martin says that a liberal education is "something that will broaden the interests and sympathies of people regardless of their daily occupation." Part of the aim of true education, according to G. Stanley Hall, is to "break down prejudices, religious, political, philosophical, literary and social." These headmasters believed that their real job was not limited to preparing young fellows to meet college entrance requirements, but that it also involved the broadening of sympathies, the breaking down of prejudices and, in this international age, the training for world citizenship. Believing that misunderstandings and wars between nations often arise through long-distance misjudgments, they sought to find ways in which American schools could develop contacts that would tend to promote cordial relations between countries, and at the same time advance the cause of education. Thus was born the "International Fellowship through Schoolboy Contacts" idea. For a number of reasons it was decided to try it first in France. The plan received an enthusiastic reception by the French educators, who gave full and immediate cooperation in setting up the program.

Invitations to join in the project and an outline of the plan were sent to a number of the leading schools. The following finally participated and sent representatives: Loomis Institute, Windsor, Conn.; Kent School, Kent,

Conn.; Tabor Academy, Marion, Mass.; Nichols School, Buffalo, N. Y.; Western Reserve Academy, Hudson, Ohio; Episcopal Academy, Philadelphia, Pa., and Winnetka School, Winnetka, Ill. Newton High School and Brookline High School, both in Massachusetts, each sent a delegate. The boys were selected as representing the best in character, scholarship, athletic spirit and citizenship in their respective schools. To be selected was justly considered a coveted honor. They paid their own expenses, except in some cases where they could not afford it, and where they were subsidized by benefactors interested in the experiment. All the necessary cost of the trip was put on a cooperative basis and was so well managed that it was very little more expensive than many summer camps in America. Last season's experience may make possible an even lower rate for following years.

The rather highly selective quality of the group was not only fundamental in the success of the venture but it was also a great satisfaction to the leaders. Everywhere they attracted favorable comment and aroused inquiry as to who these striking young fellows were. One English ship's captain remarked that he had never carried such a fine crowd of young gentlemen on any voyage!

In a similar way the French chose ten high-type boys from their lycées and colleges, which correspond to American high schools.

The American leaders in the project were: W. Huston Lillard, headmaster of Tabor; Roderick Beebe, of Tabor; Howard C. Rice, of Loomis; Maurice B. Makepeace, of Dartmouth College, and Raymond A. Mickel, of Western Reserve Academy. The French leaders were Paul Jeanrenaud, director of the school at Montcel; Charles Jeanrenaud, of Montcel; Lucien Broche, of the University of Paris; Laurent Gautier, of Paris; Joseph Harel, of Versailles, and Marcel Arland, of Montcel.

Time alone will demonstrate the full worth of the idea in promoting international understanding. That will be conditioned in part by the continuance of the plan. Before last summer was ended arrangements were made for continuing and enlarging the project, including its extension to other countries. Both sides were enthusiastic about carrying on. Judging from evidence now available, the initial season was successful even beyond the expectations of its promoters. In answer to inquiries recently sent out, the American boys were almost unanimous in asserting their increased understanding of the French people, their broadened appreciation of Old World history and culture and their deepened sympathies with certain French view-points as a result. These answers merely confirmed after five months what they had expressed in reports at the close of the summer. It is even more significant that fourteen of the American boys are carrying on correspondence with eight of their young friends in France.

The reactions on the other side may be summed up in statements from two of the French people.

> Before this summer my opinion of Americans had been formed from what I read in the newspapers, and from what I had seen of the tourists in Paris. I thought of them as being wealthy, extravagant, unrestrained, rather crude, always demanding things, and quite unappreciative of what we have learned to hold in great esteem. I frankly looked forward to the summer with somewhat mixed feelings. Now, I am happy to say that it has been most pleasant. My opinion of Americans has been completely revised in their favor.

Following is a letter from the father of one of the French boys:

> Jacques has just returned. He is very enthusiastic about his stay at Montcel which has given him the opportunity to appreciate your American young men.
>
> He continues to praise them. I believe sincerely that the end at which you aimed in bringing together all this youth in some ways of so different mentality, has been attained and that a common understanding of the mind and the characteristics of our two countries has been the result of these six weeks of close contact between our youth. Personally I appreciate the straightforwardness and ''spontaneity'' of the American boys with whom I have conversed.
>
> I hope this session is only a prelude and that in the years to come these boys will have again the joy of meeting each other either in France or America to create again a friendship for the very great good of our two nations so well adapted to understand each other.

RAYMOND A. MICKEL
WESTERN RESERVE ACADEMY

QUOTATIONS

THE CANADIAN NATIONAL COUNCIL OF EDUCATION

Only last month the Church Congress decided for the first time in its long history to venture overseas and to hold its annual meeting this year in Toronto. And now it is announced that the next meeting of the Canadian National Council of Education, to be held this April in British Columbia, will be an Imperial conference in a new sense. Not only will Australia and New Zealand be fully represented at Victoria and Vancouver, but the English Board of Education, in the persons of its permanent secretary and its chief inspector, will take an active part in the proceedings. This is excellent news, if it may be taken as evidence that the future of Canada and of the Mother Country is seen to depend very largely on closer cooperation in matters intellectual as well as material. The participation of Whitehall for the first time on such a scale in an education conference overseas should form a valuable precedent. But if the full benefit is to be obtained from mutual interchange of ideas, it will be necessary that our local authorities should also, so far as may be practicable, take part in the conference, and we understand that the Canadian Council is extending an invitation to them. Canada knows that at home national education is almost entirely decentralized. The work of the board is mainly advisory and, so far as the treasury concurs, financial; the practical conduct of the schools is in the hands of the local bodies, which are now given an opportunity of sharing ideas and experience in British Columbia. It will be welcome news if at all events the more important of them are able to accept it. Fortunately the special subject of the conference—"Education and Leisure"—is peculiarly suited to what should prove to be an international discussion. Vocational teaching is not so suited, for its methods must depend less on general principles than on local needs and conditions. In a sense, however, education in all nations and languages is, or should be, "education for leisure." If the hours not devoted to the business of earning a living are wisely spent, there follows well-being for nation and individual; if ill-spent, there will be crime, misery, discontent and all that is subversive of well-being, both for the citizen and for his country. Though in these difficult days of the crowded curriculum there is increasing danger lest knowledge come and wisdom linger, the old truth remains that "the wisdom of a learned man cometh by opportunity of leisure."—*The London Times.*

EDUCATIONAL RESEARCH AND STATISTICS

THE RELIABILITY OF RATING SCHEMES

Personality rating cards, blanks and forms of various kinds have been widely used and widely criticized. For a number of years the University of Chicago has been securing a large amount of information concerning each applicant for admission, and a part of this was in the form of a rating of the applicant on various points by one or more of the high-school instructors. These rating sheets are always given some consideration in determining what disposition should be made of an application, although they have always been used advisedly.

Two different forms for rating the student have been used. In the original form, the teacher was asked to indicate in which portion of his class a student ranked in certain traits including attitude toward school work, intellectual ability, leadership, purposefulness and social adaptability. This blank has been revised and is now in the form of a series of parallel lines representing certain personality qualities with descriptive terms placed at various points along each line—ranging from superior at the left to inferior at the right—with instructions to the teacher to place a check at the point on the line where, in his opinion, the student should rate. A typical example follows.

Intellectual Ability and Aptitude					
Alertness, cleverness, brightness, power to assimilate, faculty of adjustment to new situations.	Keen	Alert and clever	Learns readily	A slow learner	Dull

Two studies have been carried out, one on each type of rating sheet, to determine to what extent the blanks were reliable in predicting student success in the university.

In the first study, the entire membership of a freshman class was followed up. The ratings given them by high-school teachers were secured. Their scholastic records were tabulated, and the relation between this record and the previous rating noted. This relation is shown by Table I. This table indicates the percentage of the students given each rating whose scholastic records were satisfactory at the close of the first year in college. Seventy-one and nine-tenths per each composed of twenty-five students, were work.

TABLE I

PER CENT. OF FRESHMEN WHO MADE SATISFACTORY SCHOLASTIC RECORDS SHOWING THE RATINGS GIVEN THEM BY HIGH-SCHOOL TEACHERS

Rating	Per cent. of students in each rating who made satisfactory university records				
	1 (Highest)	2	3	4	5 (Lowest)
Scholastic ability	84.1	63.4	53.7	40.0	33.3
Attitude toward school work	79.9	68.4	48.3	42.9	28.6
Purposefulness	77.7	62.5	54.9	25.0	28.6
Leadership	81.6	71.3	64.7	74.4	53.8
Social adaptability	73.1	77.3	70.6	69.4	78.9

It will be noted that the highest rating under ability has denoted a group of students having a record much better than that of any of the other groups. This is also true, but to a smaller extent, of the highest ratings on "Attitude" and "Purposefulness." The ratings on "Leadership" and "Social Adaptability" are interesting in that there is so little variation in the percentages. They demonstrate quite clearly that teachers do think in filling out such blanks—since, if the tendency were to give the same rating right down the sheet, the same variation in percentages would appear under each point rated.

In the second study, three different groups, each composed of twenty-five students, were selected. The first was composed of freshmen who had made an average better than B for a full year of work. The second group was composed of freshmen who were failing scholastically. The third group was made up of applicants to whom admission had been refused because of low grades in high school and low scholastic aptitude test scores. Only students who had graduated from one of the large public high schools of Chicago or of the suburbs were included in any of the groups.

In each case, the rating line described above was divided into ten equal parts and a check in a given sector was given a value of from 1 to 10, depending on whether it was low or high. The averages of all the ratings of the three groups selected were next secured. These averages are presented in Table II.

TABLE II

AVERAGES OF RATINGS ON PERSONALITY POINTS OF THE MEMBERS OF THE THREE GROUPS STUDIED

Item rated	Average rating of		Group admission refused
	Superior group	Failing group	
Scholastic zeal	8.96	6.68	5.96
Intellectual ability	9.48	6.63	5.60
Initiative in study	8.88	6.83	6.12
Integrity	9.36	7.84	6.42
Leadership	7.40	6.68	6.04
Social adaptability	7.32	7.36	6.52

In reading Table II one must bear in mind that ten is the highest possible score and that these figures are averages. One or two low scores could draw a large number of very high ones down to a considerable extent. The median for the superior group was about 10 in the first four items rated.

Another point to consider is that 6 is at the mid-point for each line. In only two cases do the averages fall below this median. This fact becomes more impressive as one studies the individual cases—*i.e.*, that very few students are rated very low on any one point.

TABLE III

INDIVIDUAL RATINGS OF ALL MEMBERS OF THE THREE GROUPS ON THE POINTS OF SCHOLASTIC ZEAL AND INTELLECTUAL ABILITY AND APTITUDE

Scholastic zeal				Intellectual ability and aptitude			
	Number of each group rated:				Number of each group rated:		
Rating	Superior	Failing	Rejected	Rating	Superior	Failing	Rejected
10	12	......	......	10	15	......	......
9	6	......	1	9	2	......	......
8	2	5	......	8	6	10	3
7	4	10	6	7	......	3	1
6	1	7	9	6	1	4	10
5	......	3	8	5	1	7	8
4	......	......	1	4	......	1	1
3	......	......	......	3	......	......	1
2	......	......	......	2	......	......	1
1	......	......	......	1	......	......	......

Table III gives the individual ratings for all members of the three groups on the first two items of the rating scale. The central tendency in each group is quite clear, but the amount of overlapping is very noticeable. Another pertinent observation is that already noted, that there are very few really low ratings even in the poorest group. Whether there are no students in the high schools considered who should be rated so low, or whether such students realizing their weaknesses do not apply for admission to the University of Chicago, or whether teachers simply do not rate any students so far down the scale is a debatable point. The person using the scale must apparently assume that very few ratings of the lowest quarter will be made and can, if he wishes, draw an imaginary lower limit about one fourth of the way up. The fact should be emphasized again that the superior and failing groups are not those that had done well or poorly in high school or that the teachers expected would do well or poorly, but that these groups actually had performed as indicated in the university. These individuals now constitute successes and failures in the eyes of the college authorities. Table III emphasizes the fact that though such scales have value in general, in considering specific cases they can not be accepted as deciding factors unless other data agree with the ratings given.

Each applicant is asked to list five high-school teachers who are acquainted with his work. It is usual, when the rating by a teacher does not agree with other evidence or when there is a belief that further evidence would be of any value in making a decision on a case, to send directly to those four additional high-school teachers for additional ratings and statements regarding the student in question.

The difference between the ratings by various teachers of the same student was studied in ten cases. In each case, after the first rating was received, a letter had been sent directly to the other teachers asking them to send in an independent rating on the student. In about half the cases the various ratings agreed quite well. In only one was there very wide variation. In this one case the variation was clearly explainable by the rest of the student's record, since he rated high in general intelligence and performed in class in accordance with his desire to impress the teacher. In general, the statement seems justified that the agreement between ratings by different teachers was close enough to make the rating appear reliable enough for the plan to be continued.

The studies lead to the conclusion that such rating schemes, subjective as they are, are of value in judging applicants. Used as they are, in connection with general statements from other members of the high-school faculty, the student's school record and an autobiography, they aid in giving a complete picture of the prospective student. By recognizing the dangers and the weaknesses of any such plan, the officer of admissions can undoubtedly gain much valuable information from the teachers who have had a year or more of experience with the applicant.

GEORGE R. MOON

UNIVERSITY OF CHICAGO

SCHOOL AND SOCIETY

EDITED BY J. McKEEN CATTELL

WITH WHICH IS COMBINED THE

EDUCATIONAL REVIEW

EDITED BY WILLIAM McANDREW

Volume XXIX SATURDAY, MARCH 23, 1929 Number 743

THE COLLEGES OF CANADA[1]

By the Honorable VINCENT MASSEY

MINISTER FROM CANADA TO THE UNITED STATES

I AM happy to be with you here this evening for more than one reason. In the first place, my roots are firmly struck in academic soil, and although they have not been as well watered of late years as they should have been, they—to complete my horticultural metaphor—rejoice in the warm congenial collegiate atmosphere of an occasion such as this. Again, gentlemen, as a representative of another country, I am glad to be here because the realities of international affairs are nowhere better understood than in the realm of education. In the world of the mind there can be no disharmony between communities. The educational systems of two nations may differ widely, but it is the habit of educationists to regard themselves less as rivals than as allies in a common cause. What competition there may be between them is wholesome, for it is not in the realm of things material, but rather of ideas and ideals. In the sphere of the mind the asperities of life are softened. So it is with things of the heart. We are drawn together by whatever touches us most deeply. We have had recently a fine instance of this. No British subject in the last few weeks would fail to be touched by the vivid interest and genuine feeling which have been shown everywhere in your great country over the grave illness of our Sovereign. As one of His Majesty's representatives in the United States, I should like to say how deeply this attitude of friendly sympathy has been appreciated by the King's subjects in Canada who so fervently hope and pray for His Majesty's full restoration to health.

It is a pleasure to be here, ladies and gentlemen, because this is a meeting of the representatives of colleges in the true sense of the ancient word, and I am a sincere believer in the old-fashioned college. I am happy to realize that in so many places in your country it has maintained inviolate its old traditions of simplicity and thoroughness and idealism. In many cases in the modern world in which we live, the college through the generations has become surrounded with a vast fabric of professional and technical institutions, but whether it be isolated or part of a larger system, I believe it is not too much to say that the college, rightly conceived, is the dynamic of higher education.

The college has a peculiar significance to the people of, what for lack of a better name, we call the "English-speaking world." It is really part of the common

[1] Address before the Association of American Colleges, Chattanooga, Tenn., January 10, 1929.

heritage which we cherish. I may be wrong, but I believe that your colleges of liberal arts and the collegiate foundations of the old universities of England and the corresponding institutions in the British Dominions, possess certain common characteristics which are shared in full measure, at least, by no institutions elsewhere. What are these characteristics? There are probably three important ones. Our colleges are, for the most part, residential communities; secondly, they exist to teach the humanities and are essentially non-professional, and thirdly they endeavor to train the character as well as to educate the mind. This trinity of objects is, of course, common to secondary schools the world over, but in the realm of higher education, I believe these are the peculiar possessions of the American and British systems.

The genealogical tree of the college is interesting. I suppose we must regard as the original ancestor the group of poor scholars whom Walter de Merton formed into a permanent society at Oxford in 1264 when he commenced to devise statutes for their governance. My own college, Balliol, narrowly missed that honor by the excessive frugality of its founder. The picturesque story you probably know. John Balliol, the thirteenth century magnate, in his baronial operations had been none too delicate in his relations with certain churches in the diocese of Durham. The worthy bishop, justly incensed, ordered him, for the good of his soul, to make provision for the education of students at Oxford. This was shortly before the establishment of Merton. But John apparently set a modest valuation on his soul, because his endowment was meager—legend has it that it was the nominal sum of twopence. (I refrain from enlarging upon the fact that Balliol was a Scottish name.) However, for the honor of the family and for the glory of education, as we Balliol men modestly put it, John's wife, the Lady Dervorguilla, put the foundation on a permanent basis about twenty years later. Feminists have never made the most of the incident.

The English college encountered many vicissitudes through the centuries. Apart from the penury of the early generations, they had to cope in turn with the hostility of the monasteries, the menace of civil war and, not least, the lethargy of the eighteenth century. How the torch was carried across the Atlantic is a matter of commonplace knowledge. Education in this country and in Canada owes much to the tiny flame which was kept alive by devoted men who had been nourished in the ancient collegiate tradition. As a result of this effort, all over this continent there are institutions, new and old, rich and poor, whose simple aim and actual achievement have been to fulfil the aspirations of the founder of one of your oldest houses of learning which was created "that youth might be fitted for public employment both in church and state." The educational life of this country offers a fascinating study to the observer. As a visitor, I am subject to a constant thrill in learning at first hand something of your university systems, their schools for advanced specialized study, their courses of preparation for every profession which man can follow, the perfection of their organization, their capacity to give the multitude contact with knowledge. But in all this bewildering pattern there is no finer strand than that golden thread which represents the simple effort to produce the "good citizen." Such is the essential function of the college and this, I believe, must be the key to higher education, everywhere.

It was suggested to me that I should say something this evening about the colleges of my own country, their traditions, their problems and future development. You, however, are not unfamiliar with higher education in Canada. The natural interchange of teachers and students as well between our two countries makes possible a mutual knowledge of methods and ideals in our respective nations. Everywhere I go I find Canadians in the faculties of your universities. We are sorry to lose them but we are happy to feel, if they have left us, that they are playing some part in your great achievements. Many graduates of your universities are, of course, to be found in our faculties. In the student world, too, there is a reciprocal migration. Numbers of Canadians are taking advantage of certain courses offered by your universities. There is also a considerable movement to the north. I find that in one of our universities alone, and it is not the largest, nearly three hundred students from this country are at present pursuing their studies.

The score of universities and colleges in Canada which have the full right to grant degrees—we may perhaps thank the poverty of early years for the fact that we have not been led to dissipate our energies in a greater number—these institutions reflect varied traditions. The oldest are French. In Quebec two great universities and a group of secondary schools known as "classical colleges" maintain the best traditions of the ecclesiastical system of old France. There is much to be learned from these institutions. The torch of the classics is held high in their halls and—perhaps partly because of this fact—under no system is the use of one's own language as a spoken and written tongue more effectively taught.

In our English-speaking universities and colleges, the main influence, appropriately enough, is English and Scottish. Their personnel itself in the first half of the nineteenth century came principally from Great Britain and the models for the new foundations were British. The curricula and many of the forms of our academic life reveal English origins. On the other hand we must thank the Scot for much. For one thing, as the personification of self-reliance, it is probably due to him that it is the custom of our universities to leave the student to work out his own academic destiny without too much assistance. The product of the college, as the wise teacher knows, can sometimes be improved by judicious neglect. We are grateful for the Scottish strain in our colleges. Your system as well as ours owes much to the fact that the Scot, along with the many things which legend has it that he keeps, holds with commendable tenacity to a tradition of academic thoroughness.

Our universities, like yours, however, are open to constantly changing influences. The university is a curiously sensitive organism. Like Ulysses it can say "I am a part of all that I have met." The university can thus give the finest and most expressive reflection of the traditions of the community which it serves. It is often the very image and transcript of the forces which make up a nation. It is so with your colleges and universities. It is so with ours. On each side of our mutual border these foundations honestly express their respective civilizations which are fundamentally and perpetually friendly and yet are wholesomely different in their approach to common questions.

In the academic realm many of the questions with which we are confronted are identical. One of our mutual problems and probably the greatest is due to a virtue which all North Americans possess—an unquenchable enthusiasm for education. From this arises the vexed problem of numbers. The delicate mechanism of instruction is often threatened by the flood of those who wish to enjoy its benefits.

Professional and technical training can surmount the difficulty with relative ease. The acquisition of knowledge and imparting of technique—these functions can, of course, be organized by a scale commensurate with most demands without loss of power. But the peculiar task of the college—in which human relationships are all-important, in which the training of the individual mind and character is the objective—this function can be stultified by numbers. It is a truism to say that mass production is the negation of the collegiate ideal.

Some of us in Canada have been asking ourselves about the matter and method and aim of liberal education. Professional and graduate schools have, of course, clear objectives. They require no definition; but those courses which exist to impart to the student the gift of the humanities are subtler in their aim and more elusive in their substance. It often happens that we are so busy constructing curricula and devising tests and examinations that we momentarily forget the purpose of the superb mechanism which we have erected. And yet we well know the objective of liberal education when we stop to think about it, and we have only to remind ourselves that its over-organization can only result in its paralysis.

As I have said, our educational problems are in a large measure like yours. We are attempting, too, to solve some of them by similar methods. There is, however, one experiment which has proved successful in Canada of which it may interest you to hear. It is closely related to the problem to which I have alluded—how to keep liberal education from being submerged by the flood of those who seek it. About forty years ago the legislature of the Province of Ontario passed an act which provided for the association with the Provincial University of other colleges and universities which might wish to join forces with it under a scheme of "university federation." The plan, which has never been substantially changed, divides the instruction in the humanities between the university proper and an indefinite number of colleges, of which one is a "University College," a state-controlled body conducted by the university itself. Under the plan there was established a teaching faculty in the university proper in certain subjects including those requiring laboratory equipment. The federated colleges are required to provide their own instruction in the remainder of the field. Examinations are conducted and all degrees, except those in divinity, are conferred by the university alone.

The purpose of the plan of federation was originally to economize the financial and educational resources of competing foundations. The most difficult task of its authors was to safeguard the traditions and the corporate entity of federating institutions, and in particular to preserve their religious autonomy. The latter end was accomplished by giving constituent colleges the control of all subjects of instruction which might be religiously controversial. A due share in the academic government of the university as a whole is guaranteed to the colleges by giving them the right to elect an appropriate number of their members to the senate of the university, which body has supreme authority over all purely academic matters, as distinguished from those connected with finance, property and appointments. The latter are the concern of a board of governors. The colleges, however, retain their own administrative machinery and local independence in all matters not subject to university regulations. In short, the plan is a true federation.

Such, in very brief outline, is this system of university organization which I believe at the time of its inauguration was unique. Since the Enabling Act was passed in 1887, full advantage has been taken of its provisions. The first institution to enter federation with the University of Toronto was a Roman Catholic college possessing faculties in arts and divinity. A few years later, a long-established university of the Methodist Church (now merged in the United Church of Canada) became a constituent college of the university. Its example was followed a few years later by a university conducted by the Church of England and possessing old traditions. In addition to the four colleges of arts which are now grouped within the university, three divinity schools are enjoying the advantages of university federation. The plan has long since passed the experimental stage. It is regarded on all sides as a demonstrated success. Its example has been followed in many Canadian universities. There are, for instance, three Roman Catholic dioceses in Canada whose divinity schools have entered into relations with the local universities similar to those existing in Toronto.

The most striking achievement of this plan of university federation was, of course, to harmonize the jealously guarded rights of denominational colleges with their membership in a state-owned university in which no religious faith could occupy a privileged position. Another important result—the economy in personnel and equipment made possible by the scheme—requires no comment. But one of the greatest advantages of the federation was hardly foreseen by its authors. I refer to the fact that under the system the vast student body of what would otherwise be a great centralized university is divided into several homogeneous and manageable groups. Forty years ago there were many critics of this plan of university federation who, although they regarded the union of individual institutions with the Provincial University as undoubtedly wise, looked upon the perpetuation of these self-governing units in the larger community as a regrettable necessity. To-day I believe there is none who would not look on this very fact as one of the great virtues of this scheme. In certain respects, such a plan, it seems to me, represents one of the few cases in life where you can "eat your cake and have it too." The college as we know it under the arrangement I have tried to describe gives the undergraduate the intimacy of a smaller academic community, the close association with teacher and fellow student, the participation in a tradition local enough to be realizable and natural. On the other hand the student is privileged to enjoy in full measure the life and facilities of a great university—its libraries, its laboratories, its festivities and sports. Not the least of the advantages of such a plan is the healthy competition within the university between its colleges, in the realm of scholarship as well as in games. This consists not only in the rivalry between collegiate student bodies but in the competition between the college corporations themselves in the search for men for their teaching staffs, in the development of new methods and equipment, and all that might influence the standing of their undergraduates in the life and work of the university.

The experiment which I have just outlined is, of course, no longer novel. Schemes which resemble this are being tried in many places. I have been most interested in reading of a collegiate community which has been established within one of your great western universities. Lately, too, we have seen an announcement of the foundation of colleges within the bounds of one of your ancient universities in the east. In such plans I believe lie great possibilities. The idea of a college within a university is, after all, not really experimental. The principle has been in successful operation for centuries and is applicable "mutatis mutandis" wherever universities exist. It seems to me that if I were searching for a useful form which a gift to a large modern university anywhere might take, even after reviewing the many important objects which are the subject nowadays of such splendid benefactions, particularly in this country, I might, in the case of this imaginary university, be tempted to say to its head, "The modern university is often too vast to provide a coherent corporate existence for its undergraduates. Residential life as it prevails is frequently apt to emphasize only certain phases of human activity and to bear too little relation to the things which matter most. It is difficult, too, for the student to meet his instructors on those informal and unpremeditated occasions when their influence is greatest. As one attempt to meet these difficulties, I would found within this university a college for a limited number of men. They shall be subject to the same examinations and academic requirements as the others who are taking courses in liberal arts. Students, however, will be admitted to the college after meeting its own standards in scholarship and personality. The college will be housed in buildings which shall possess the beauty which is part of education. It will be given a name around which will cluster the traditions which will assist the growth of a corporate solidarity among its members. The most important equipment of the college will be men—a group of selected teachers with a vocation for their work, living as senior comrades of the undergraduates."

No one in theory or in practice can afford to neglect any part of the work of a university. In the academic world, of all places, proper proportions must be preserved. The greatest function of the university may well be the advancement of learning through research. Highly important, too, is its trusteeship of the learned professions. Of great usefulness is its transmission of knowledge to the community through popular media. The danger, it seems to me, however, is not that any of these will be neglected, but rather that humbler and less spectacular duties may relatively suffer. There is no greater function than teaching and, I would suggest, no greater peril to the modern university than that this, and all that the collegiate ideal represents, should be thought irrelevant. If a layman may be allowed to say so, this ideal is not only essential in itself but the importance of the teacher in his relation to all the functions of the university can hardly be overstated. Knowledge without character is, after all, useless, if not almost dangerous. Learning without a sense of balance and proportion becomes sterile. Society needs more knowledge—this is obvious—but it stands in need of something else, the ability to use what knowledge it has. Some one has said that the characteristic factor of a university is its library; that of a college its faculty. I do not think it too fanciful to suppose that the researches pursued within the library will bear a closer relation to human life when the scholar approaches them with some previous knowledge of human nature, with the feeling for proportion, perhaps too the common sense—I was going to say even the sense of humor—acquired from close association with a "human library," as a college has been well called. It is not, perhaps, without significance that both *Universitas* and *Collegium* meant associations of men in the pursuit of learning. The emphasis was on the men and not upon the books.

However, gentlemen, I must not ride my hobby past the point of discretion. I have been encouraged to speak of the collegiate ideal to-night, because I have the honor of meeting here some of the most distinguished trustees of that ideal. To you, ladies and gentlemen, representing the colleges of the United States, I am happy to bring the greetings of the colleges of Canada, not as a perfunctory message of good-will, but as a salutation cordial and sincere, between members of a great fraternity in which common ideals are highest and mutual understanding deepest—the salutation from teacher to teacher.

STATISTICS OF REGISTRATION IN CANADIAN UNIVERSITIES

By Professor RAYMOND WALTERS

DEAN OF SWARTHMORE COLLEGE

The enrolment of full-time students in Canadian universities is continuing at about the same rate as during the past five years, according to a statistical study made by the present writer of the twenty universities of the Dominion of Canada. For fifteen of these institutions which supplied earlier figures, it is found that the increase in full-time registration was 4.6 per cent. greater on January 1, 1929, than on January 1, 1928, and that the 1928 registration was 24 per cent. greater than five years earlier, January 1, 1923.

As was shown in a report in School and Society of December 15, 1928, the increase of full-time students in 215 approved colleges and universities of the United States this academic year over last was 2 per cent., as compared with 25 per cent. for the preceding five-year period.

All but three of the Canadian universities have more students than last year. In accounting for their continuing gains the registrars ascribe it to "the growth and prosperity of Canada" and to "improved local facilities."

The full-time enrolment of the twenty universities of Canada this year is approximately 26,500. Table I gives figures in detail for students and teachers; for two universities which could not supply statistics at this early date there are inserted the 1926 figures as printed in the latest "Survey of Education in Canada," published by the Dominion Bureau of Statistics (December, 1928).

The Canadian registrars were asked to report their enrolments on the same basis as that followed for colleges and universities of the United States in the annual School and Society article. The definitions of terms, as here used, were endorsed by the American Association of Collegiate Registrars in 1922. The full-time regular student is defined as a student who has completed a four-year high-school course and is devoting his full time (twelve hours a week or more) to study during the collegiate year. The student whose main time and attention are given to some other employment and who takes college and university courses in late afternoon, evening and Saturday classes is listed as a part-time student. The grand total figures for 1929 include full-time regular students, part-time students and summer-school students of 1928 but do not include extension and correspondence students, who are, however, recorded in Table I.

Table II lists the twenty universities in order of size.

Various details of interest are as follows: The five universities having the largest number of undergraduates in liberal arts courses are: Toronto, 2,602; Manitoba, 1,377; Montreal (1926), 1,365; Laval (1926), 1,343; British Columbia, 1,253.

Among schools of engineering or applied sciences in these universities the five largest are: Toronto, 555; Queen's, 307; McGill, 270; British Columbia, 263; Manitoba, 233.

The largest medical schools are: Toronto, 746; McGill, 476; Queen's, 315; Manitoba, 272; Laval (1926), 245.

In commerce and business courses, Toronto has an enrolment of 275; McGill, 225, and Queen's, 168.

The largest enrolments in other fields are reported as follows: agriculture, Manitoba, 146; dentistry, Toronto, 251; education, Toronto, 256.

The five largest summer schools of 1928 were: Manitoba, 751; Queen's, 492; British Columbia, 401; Saskatchewan, 392; Ottawa, 275.

The following paragraphs explain statistics presented in Table I and give additional information:

The 58 students at Acadia University (Wolfville, N. S.) listed under other courses are in household economics. The increase in full-time enrolment from 293 in 1922–23 to 510 in 1927–28 was due, the registrar writes, "to erection of new buildings, providing better equipment, and appointment of many additional members of the faculty, the average being now one teacher to

TABLE I. CANADIAN UNIVERSITIES

	Acadia	Alberta	Bishop's	British Columbia	Dalhousie	Laval	Manitoba	McGill
College men	156	229	95	1,253	474	1,343	817	594
College women	108	254	30				560	388
Engineering	46	204	....	263	58	....	233	270
Law	....	27	....	....	42	88	54	82
Medicine	....	165	....	....	127	245	272	476
Non-Prof. Graduate	13	40	....	39	8	....	12	154
Agriculture	....	78	....	56	....	51	146	62
Architecture	....	1	....	....	....	....	32	27
Art	40	....	....	....	....	....	....	....
Commerce	....	68	....	....	46	62	....	225
Dentistry	....	54	....	....	37	....	....	40
Divinity	37	6	30	....	....	368	....	....
Education	40	....	....	61	....	....	....	....
Forestry	....	....	....	....	....	22	....	....
Journalism	4	....	....	....	....	....	....	....
Music	30	....	....	....	4	406	....	31
Pharmacy	....	24	....	....	10	10	59	22
Other courses	58	81	....	47	5	241	204	190
Deduct duplicates	20	....	....	....	....	100	1	6
Total	512	1,231	155	1,719	814	2,736*	2,388	2,555
Part-time	....	61	....	171	55	....	37	320
Summer session	....	87	....	401	....	....	751	193
Deduct duplicates	....	6	....	....	....	....	145	....
Gd. tot., Jan. 1, '29	512	1,373	155	2,291	869	2,736*	3,031	3,068
Gd. tot., Jan. 1, '28	510	1,440	153	2,386	823	....	2,928	2,958
Gd. tot., Jan. 1, '23	293	1,183	74	1,559	753	....	2,055	....
Exten. courses	....	81	....	....	....	....	316	966
Teaching staff	46	143	13	94	126	540*	258	473
Administrative staff	19	13	2	10	19	9*	13	35

every eleven students. The enrolment of 1928–29 is about the same as in 1927–28, due to less advertising and higher standards of admission. The aim is to keep attendance down to approximately 500 in the future."

In the figures of the University of Alberta (Edmonton, Alberta) for other courses, 64 are nursing students. The 1922–23 full-time enrolment was 1,067; that of 1927–28 was 1,336.

The full-time enrolment of the University of Bishop's College (Lennoxville, Que.) was 74 in 1922–23 and 153 in 1927–28.

The 47 students given under other courses for the University of British Columbia (Vancouver, B. C.) are in nursing. The 1922–23 full-time numbers were 1,194 and in 1927–28 they were 1,741—a little higher than this year.

Five students in "fisheries" are included in Table I under other courses for Dalhousie University (Halifax, N. S.) The 1922–23 full-time

TABLE I. CANADIAN UNIVERSITIES—(*Concluded*)

McMaster	Montreal	Mount Allison	New Brunswick	Ottawa	Queen's	St. Dunstan's	St. Francis Xavier	St. Joseph's	Saskatchewan	Toronto	Western Ontario
178	1,365	200	92	185	513	75	230	70	491	1,378	462
96		83	64	......	367		36	......	299	1,224	250
......	128	49	75	......	307	44	18	......	143	555	......
......	147	......	7	......	......	......	......	......	32	......	......
......	212	......	......	......	315	......	......	......	26	746	136
4	......	......	......	......	......	......	7	......	36	371	12
......	88	......	......	......	......	......	......	......	158	......	......
......	......	......	......	......	......	......	......	......	......	44	......
......	......	......	......	......	......	......	......	......	......	......	......
......	107	......	......	125	168	38	......	......	46	275	......
......	133	......	......	......	......	......	......	......	......	251	......
64	295	......	......	150	13	......	......	1	......	......	......
......	......	......	......	25	......	......	......	......	48	256	......
......	......	......	59	......	......	......	......	......	......	66	......
......	......	......	......	......	......	......	......	......	......	......	......
......	......	......	......	......	......	......	......	......	......	26	......
......	97	......	......	......	......	......	......	......	77	......	......
......	479	......	......	......	......	71	......	279	37	272	6
......	......	......	......	......	175	......	7	......	......	345	......
342	3,051*	332	297	485	1,508	184	284	350	1,393	5,119	866
56	2,364*	56	......	1,840	22	......	......	......	118	547	170
......	......	180	15	275	492	......	......	......	392	169	98
......	......	......	......	......	5	......	......	......	......	70	74
398	5,415*	568	312	2,600	2,017	184	284	350	1,903	5,765	1,060
379	......	......	233	2,200	1,991	164	250	364	1,620	5,209	950
321	......	......	136	......	1,557	231	364	349	1,112	4,705	610
......	......	......	......	830	1,269	......	......	......	......	2,607	......
21	875*	26	18	198*	108	15	19	32*	80	637	202
5	32*	5	......	6*	......	2	9	......	25	76	18

* Figures for 1926, Dominion Bureau of Statistics.

attendance was 687; in 1927–28 it was 772.

Reporting that their current statistics are "not yet available," the secretary of Laval University (Quebec, Que.) gives the 1922–23 full-time attendance as 2,005 and the 1927–28 attendance as 5,563.

The 204 students listed under other courses for the University of Manitoba (Winnipeg, Man.) are taking home economics. The 1922–23 enrolment was 1,976 full-time students, with 2,247 in 1927–28.

The McGill University (Montreal, Que.) report shows a total of 190 students under other courses, made up as follows: Household science, 53; graduate nurses, 50; physical education, 40; social workers, 29; library school, 18. The summer school at McGill is in French only.

The 1922–23 full-time enrolment at McMaster

TABLE II. CANADIAN UNIVERSITIES

University	Regular Students Full-Time	Rank	All Resident Students	Rank
Toronto	5,119	1	5,765	1
Montreal	3,051*	2	5,415*	2
Laval	2,736*	3	2,736*	5
McGill	2,555	4	3,068	3
Manitoba	2,388	5	3,031	4
British Columbia	1,719	6	2,291	7
Queen's	1,508	7	2,017	8
Saskatchewan	1,393	8	1,903	9
Alberta	1,231	9	1,373	10
West Ontario	866	10	1,060	11
Dalhousie	814	11	869	12
Acadia	512	12	512	14
Ottawa	485	13	2,600	6
St. Joseph's	350	14	350	16
McMaster	342	15	398	15
Mt. Allison	332	16	568	13
New Brunswick	297	17	312	17
St. F. Xavier	284	18	284	18
St. Dunstan's	184	19	184	19
Bishop's	155	20	155	20

* 1926, Dominion Bureau of Statistics.

University (Toronto, Ont.) was 247; in 1927–28, it was 323. The university plans to move to larger quarters at Hamilton. A faculty committee "is considering the whole matter of curriculum. We expect to expand somewhat along the science lines."

The 479 students listed under other courses in the 1926 statistics of the University of Montreal (Montreal, Que.) include 356 in household science, 93 in pure science, 17 in veterinary medicine, and 11 in social service and two not differentiated. The figures of the present year are not yet available.

At Mount Allison University (Sackville, N. B.) there was an increase in full-time students from 195 in 1922–23 to 253 in 1927–28. The 1928 summer school had 57 more students than in 1927.

The 1922–23 full-time enrolment of the University of New Brunswick (Fredericton, N. B.) is reported as 135; in 1927–28 it was 229.

In addition to the 485 full-time students doing work of university rank, the University of Ottawa (Ottawa, Ont.) reports 600 in high school courses, 310 in high school and arts, 45 extra-mural and 15 extension and also "830 students in affiliated institutions, not registered for examinations at the university." The grand total for 1928–29 is given as 2,600 as compared with 2,200 in 1927–28.

There are 1,269 extension students at Queen's University (Kingston, Ont.) taking work in banking, accounting and extra-mural arts. The 1922–23 full-time enrolment was 1,164; in 1927–28 it was 1,484.

A decrease and an increase in the full-time enrolment of the University of St. Dunstan's (Charlottentown, P. E. I.) are shown in the report: 1922–23, 231 students; 1927–28, 164 students; 1928–29, 184 students.

The 1922–23 full-time students at the University of St. Francis Xavier (Antigonish, N. S.) numbered 214; the 1927–28 total was 250.

The enrolment at the University of St. Joseph's College (St. Joseph, N. B.) was 349 in 1922–23; in 1927–28 it was 364; this year it is 350.

A large increase is revealed in the comparative figures of the University of Saskatchewan (Saskatoon, Sask.), where the full-time enrolment was 743 in 1922–23, 1,068 in 1927–28 and 1,393 this year. The 37 students listed under other courses in Table I are in household science.

The largest university in Canada—the University of Toronto (Toronto, Ont.)—has this year reached its highest total, with 5,119 full-time students, as compared with 4,961 last year and 4,408 in 1922–23. In Table I, the 272 undergraduates listed under other courses are divided as follows: Household science, 166; social service, 38; public health nursing, 34; library school, 34. The 555 listed under engineering include 130 students in chemical engineering. No students are listed under the heading law in Table I. "Admission to the bar in Ontario is controlled by the Law Society of Upper Canada, which conducts a law school at Osgoode Hall, Toronto. Any of the students in law courses at the university are taking this work in certain of the honor courses in the faculty of arts. . . . Instruction in the fine arts is given in the Ontario College of Art, which is associated with the University of Toronto, but has not the status of a department. Courses in divinity are given in the various theological departments of the federated colleges: Victoria, Trinity, St. Michael's, Knox and Wycliffe. No divinity enrolments are reported in the university statistics here."

The growth of the University of Western Ontario (London, Ont.) is indicated in these full-time figures: 1922–23, 478 students; 1927–28, 802 students; 1928–29, 866 students.

As is pointed out in the 1926 survey, published by the Dominion Bureau of Statistics, about 1,000 students from the United States are enrolled in Canadian universities and colleges, and about 1,200 Canadians are in higher institutions in the United States.

The report shows that the total expenditures of Canadian universities in 1926 was $10,435,-055. "Of the income almost exactly the same amounts were received from investments and tuition fees. Almost half the total income was contributed by governments and municipalities."

In 1926 the Canadian universities conferred 4,829 degrees, 3,432 upon men and 1,397 upon women. Bachelor's degrees were granted to 2,343 men and 895 women; master's degrees to 209 men and 61 women; doctor's degrees to 531 men and 18 women.

EDUCATIONAL EVENTS

THE HEALTH OF SCHOOL CHILDREN IN GREAT BRITAIN

SIR GEORGE NEWMAN'S annual report for 1927 on the Health of the School Child has been issued. It contains a full account of the medical work of the British Board of Education, of which he is chief medical officer. According to the summary in the London *Times,* the number of children in the three age groups medically inspected was 1,823,775, in addition to 861,964 "ailing" children outside the prescribed age groups. The number of routine children found to be suffering from physical impairment or some particular defect or disease was 374,855, or 20.6 per cent. The principal morbid conditions of school life in 1927 (including all "special" and routine children found to have defects) were: Eye defects, 252,091; enlarged tonsils and adenoids, 162,533; defects of ear and hearing, 47,476; malnutrition, 24,049; deformities, 22,771; tuberculosis, 12,901; heart disease, 5,509. In addition, there were 818,413 cases of minor ailments. At all school ages something like 18.22 per cent. of the children required medical treatment, and these did not include dental disease, uncleanliness and disorders of the mind.

The number of children under 15 years who died during the year in England and Wales was 82,968, and the principal causes of death were: Disease of the respiratory system, 26 per cent.; prematurity and congenital conditions, 24 per cent.; certain infectious diseases, 15 per cent.; diarrhea and digestive disease, 9 per cent.; tuberculosis, 6 per cent.; all other causes, 20 per cent.

While a fair measure of success had attended the efforts of the school medical service in the treatment of children, their "inability to prevent much of this disease and the acceptance of 83,000 deaths of children under 15 years of age must be counted as our failure. Yet it is not complete failure, for that figure of 83,000, large though it be, means that we saved in 1927 as many as 30,000 lives as compared with six years ago (1921), when the nation lost no fewer than 112,900 children's lives."

A chapter of the report is devoted to a comparative study of the health of the secondary school child, which states that the survey "leads us to the general conclusion that their health as a whole compares favorably with that of public elementary school children. With the exception of minor conditions of subnormality, rightly or wrongly attributed to overstrain, all other specific medical defects are of less common occurrence in the secondary scholar."

With certain reservations, it is stated that "as compared with the secondary school child in 1920 there are signs of slight improvement. If, however, we compare the condition of the secondary school child with the elementary school child the differences which were obvious in 1920 are tending to disappear, and on the whole this is probably due to the greater relative improvement in the last few years in the condition of the elementary school child. He is improving physically at a greater rate than the secondary school child."

STUDENT DISORDERS IN SPAIN

According to a special cable to the New York *Times*, under date of March 16, student disorders continue in Madrid and in other university towns of Spain and the directorate has announced drastic measures to suppress the disturbances and punish those held responsible for them.

The University of Madrid will be closed until October, 1930, thus sharing the fate of the Artillery School at Segovia. The students of the Special Engineers' School, also implicated in the riots, will have a year's study added to their requirements toward graduation, and a month's extra work will be exacted from students in all of the provincial universities with the exception of those at Valencia, Zaragosa, Barcelona, Granada and Laguna, which did not join in the movement of protest.

All members of the board of directors of the University of Madrid will be required to resign, as well as the directors of the Special Engineers' School. These boards will be reorganized by the government.

On March 16 nearly all the members of the faculty of the University of Madrid signed a petition of protest in which the government was declared responsible for the outbreak of disorders.

More than a thousand participants in the student manifestations have been arrested, including sons of well-known families, professors and journalists. As the jails have been filled to overflowing, many of the rioters have been temporarily held at police stations and barracks. At the University of Salamanca the students have destroyed a tablet commemorative of General Primo de Rivera's being made a doctor honoris causa and a similar tablet to the Minister of the Interior has been effaced at the University of Santiago.

EDUCATIONAL FEATURES OF NATIONAL PARKS

A committee was appointed a year ago by the Secretary of the Interior for a study of educational problems in the national parks consisting of Harold C. Bryant, Hermon C. Bumpus, Vernon Kellogg, John C. Merriam, Frank A. Oastler. A summary of their report presented to Secretary Wilbur states that national parks must be clearly of importance to the nation as a whole. Their support and maintenance from federal funds can be justified only on that basis. Where the special characteristics are of less than national significance parks should be supported by local interests.

The distinctive or essential characters of national parks lie in the inspirational influence and educational value of the exceptional natural features which constitute the reason for existence of these parks. Outdoor recreation is recognized as an important factor in national park administration, but it is not the primary purpose, and can also be enjoyed through abundant opportunities furnished elsewhere.

The primary function of national park administration concerns the use of the parks for their inspirational and educational values. The educational program in national parks should relate itself primarily to the essential features of the parks. Since the greatest possibilities for education arise through inspirational sources, these exceptional opportunities should be developed as fully as possible.

It should be the primary object of the educational work to make possible the maximum of understanding and appreciation of the greater characteristic park features by the visitor, together with the stimulation of his thinking. Educational work should be reduced to the lowest limit which will give the visitor opportunity to discover the things of major interest, and to inform himself fully concerning them if he so desires.

The specific subjects toward which education in national parks should be directed comprise major problems of physical, geological, biological and historical science represented there. The program should also include consideration of the beauty and meaning of nature in the esthetic and spiritual sense, as illustrated in every expression of the outstanding phenomena represented.

There should be an advisory body of five to seven of the ablest men conversant with national parks, appointed by the Secretary of the Interior, on nomination by the director of national parks, to serve without salary, whose duty it shall be to advise him on matters pertinent to educational policy and development in national parks.

There should be a division of education coordinate with other divisions of the national park service directed by a man with the best of scientific and educational qualifications who shall administer the educational program in the parks.

NATIONAL MUSIC WEEK

THE sixth annual observance of National Music Week sponsored by the National Music Week Committee, 45 West 45th St., New York, N. Y., will take place from May 5 to 11. As applied to the schools, Music Week may be made a medium of linking the schools and homes, children and parents, to the advantage of public school music. Under this plan, not only the schools but the parent-teacher associations, music clubs, women's clubs and other groups may profitably support the plan. The program is as follows:

1. *Parents' music days* in the schools, with special programs and visits to music classes in operation. Suggestions for these are found in the leaflet, "Special Activities for Schools during National Music Week," one copy of which as well as other leaflets can be obtained from the committee.

2. *Discussions or debates* on phases of school music, before parent-teacher associations or clubs. The purpose is to bring out the truth regarding the values of public school music and the advantages of advanced methods of training, thus creating among the parents a more informed attitude toward school music. The superintendent, principal, supervisor of music, or other teacher may suggest the topics and take an active part in discussions. Ideas as to subjects will be furnished by the committee, as will pamphlets for preparing discussions, such as "The Value of Musical Training to Children in Schools of America," "Music and the Sacred Seven" and "A Letter to the Parent-Teacher Associations of Kentucky."

3. *Home guidance* of children's music training on the part of parents through a more intelligent understanding of it. These activities will be supplemented by the use of such material as "Pre-School Music—A Guide to Parents."

4. *School ensembles for home music,* with formation of small choral and instrumental groups to take part in family music hours. See "Home Night in National Music Week."

5. *American history through music,* with eras in that history illustrated by study and assembly singing of traditional American songs, presenting of chronological programs of American music and musical quiz games on American subjects. Source material: "Stories of America's Songs," "America's Music in Review," "American Music that Americans Should Know," "What's What in America's Music" and "Quiz Yourself on Music."

6. *Massed concerts* of bands, orchestras or piano ensembles—an effective demonstration of school music work. Source material: "Massed Band Concerts," "Piano Ensemble Concerts," "State and National School Orchestra Contests."

7. *Groups of simpler instruments,* suitable for enabling a large proportion of the student body to use these as stepping-stones to the regular orchestral or band instruments. Source material: "Fretted Instrument Orchestras," "Harmonica Bands for Boys and Girls," "Simplified Course in Ukulele Playing" and "Toy Symphony."

RURAL JUNIOR HIGH-SCHOOL BUILDINGS

RURAL junior high schools are growing in favor in all parts of the United States, but serious limitations are imposed on them because of failure to provide essential building space and material equipment through which the desirable special activities as media of instruction are made possible.

According to a bulletin of the Bureau of Education issued in 1928, there are 131 junior high schools represented in a study made of buildings and equipment of rural junior high schools.

The committee which made the study point out eight qualities as essential to any modern high-school buildings—comprehensiveness, convenience, flexibility, safety, healthfulness, expansiveness, economy and efficiency and esthetic fitness.

Of the 131 rural junior high schools, 11 are housed in separate buildings; 14 in buildings with elementary schools; 46 in buildings with senior high schools; 58 in general buildings for all schools of district, and 2 not specified. Only 10 of the 11 separate buildings were erected with special reference to junior high-school work, and the first one of these was erected in 1916.

As to the materials used in the construction of these buildings, 59 per cent. of all schools reporting this item were brick; 6.7 per cent.

brick and concrete; 3.8 per cent. concrete and stone; 16.1 per cent. frame; 2.9 per cent. stone; 9.5 per cent. concrete and brick, and 2 per cent. concrete.

The one-story type of building is generally regarded as most satisfactory for junior-high-school work; however, of those reporting only 18 were one-story; 62, two-story; 21, three-story and 1 contained 4 stories.

On account of the health program, the gymnasium is considered an essential feature of the junior high school. About 60 per cent. of those considered in this study are provided with gymnasiums.

Seventy-nine per cent. of them are provided with auditoriums, with varying seating capacity, 50 per cent. having a seating capacity of less than 300.

The study is said to show that the buildings of the rural junior high schools must be regarded as inadequate. Ordinary classrooms with provision for mass assembly and for physical education characterize the great majority of the schools. A bare majority make some provision for cooking and for a general science laboratory. Not more than one school in three can be regarded as having adequate housing provisions.

THE SCHOOL BUILDING PROGRAM OF NEW YORK CITY

"Now we will go to work and wipe out short-time in two years," Associate Superintendent William A. Boylan, in charge of the building program of the Board of Education, said to the representative of the New York *Times,* in outlining construction plans based upon the appropriation of $46,150,000 made by the Board of Estimate. The sum was the school system's share in the appropriation of $156,552,450 for civic improvements.

Superintendent Boylan explained that the disposal of the $46,150,000 was still in a tentative stage, but that plans were taking shape rapidly. Some of the money appropriated will be used as early as April for new buildings.

The construction of about seventy-five new structures, independent schools or additions to old buildings, has been made possible by the large sums put at the disposal of the Board of Education. The board asked about $11,000,000 more than it received, but its requests included demands for equipment, while the Board of Estimate's assignments provide for construction alone. In other words, with every new building going up, separate appropriations will have to be made for equipment.

Two purposes will be served by the construction funds. In the first place, it is intended to provide school facilities in overcrowded districts where the old schools are rapidly becoming inadequate. Second, it is necessary to push school construction in the newly opened sections and growing developments, particularly in Queens.

Short or part-time attendance is a problem of the crowded districts and will be solved by the buildings projected. "We now have 30,737 students on part-time in the high schools and more than 38,000 in the elementary schools," Mr. Boylan said. "The former figure represents an increase of 8,000 during the past year, the latter a decrease of 11,445."

The buildings in the $46,150,000 program will be started in 1929 but can not be expected to bring relief during the same year. But by the end of 1930 we expect that the additional buildings will have solved this pressing problem.

Mr. Boylan said that the cuts made by the Board of Estimate affected high schools, training schools and continuation schools more than elementary and junior high schools. This will necessitate a restudy of the needs of the first group with a view to selecting the most pressing and erecting the most urgently needed buildings.

THE F. C. AUSTIN SCHOLARSHIP FOUNDATION AT NORTHWESTERN UNIVERSITY

A formal announcement of the F. C. Austin scholarship foundation at Northwestern University for the training of business executives has been issued by the university and is now being mailed to high schools. This foundation was created recently by Mr. F. C. Austin, of Chicago, by a gift to the university of more than $3,000,000, the income from which is to be used exclusively for scholarships.

Only five scholars will be assigned for the year 1929–30, and the five recipients will be expected to become freshmen in Northwestern University next September. Scholarships will be awarded, the announcement says, "to male persons of the Caucasian race, without reference to nationality, religion or wealth, for the purpose of fitting the recipients to attain proficiency in business and industrial pursuits, having especially in mind the fitting such persons for executive positions in large business and industrial enterprises."

Applicants will be examined in such qualifications as scholarship, leadership, character and health, and those will be selected who in the judgment of the university have the greatest potential capacity for proficiency in business, this proficiency to be measured "by terms of public service rather than the accumulation of private fortunes." Each recipient of a scholarship will be known as an F. C. Austin scholar.

"This title," says the announcement, "is a distinction that may be permanent but may be terminated at the discretion of the university. Uniform treatment is not promised or anticipated. The university will, however, grant to each scholar the financial assistance deemed most beneficial for him. The amount may vary from the cost of tuition to $1,500 dollars a year and may be in the form of a loan or a direct grant. No scholar will be compelled to abandon his desire for adequate training because of lack of funds. This training may necessitate study and travel abroad, and study at institutions in America other than Northwestern."

The director of personnel at the university will be the chief adviser of the F. C. Austin scholars. At the completion of the period of formal training he will assist them in obtaining favorable positions for practical experience. The university expects to continue its cooperation with each scholar permanently. As soon as sufficient number of F. C. Austin scholars are in residence at Northwestern, dormitories will be constructed for their exclusive use.

"The F. C. Austin scholars, as alumni, will be expected to cooperate in the administration of the foundation and in the selection of their successors," the announcement says. "It is planned that these alumni shall meet annually in quarters especially provided for such meetings, and that they shall confer upon matters of mutual interest, or upon the promotion of the foundation and of the scholars."

EDUCATIONAL NOTES AND NEWS

THE installation of Dr. James M. Kieran as president of Hunter College, New York City, will take place on March 26. Among the speakers at the ceremony will be Mayor Walker, Joseph V. McKee, president of the Board of Aldermen; Dr. John H. Finley, of the New York *Times;* the Rev. Francis P. Duffy, Dr. George S. Davis, the retiring president; Mrs. Maxwell Hall Elliott, president of the Alumnae Association and a trustee, and Dr. Kieran. A luncheon for Dr. and Mrs. Kieran at the Hotel Madison will follow.

MEMBERS of the teaching staff of the graduate school of education of Harvard University recently presented to Professor Henry W. Holmes, dean of the school, a gold watch suitably engraved.

DR. JAMES E. RUSSELL, dean emeritus of Teachers College, Columbia University, is spending February and March at the University of Hawaii in Honolulu in the capacity of visiting professor. He is giving a series of lectures on "Types of Public Education."

DR. RAYMOND WEEKS has retired from the faculty of Columbia University, where he has been professor of Romance languages since 1910.

DR. NED H. DEARBORN, director of the teacher training division of the New York State Education Department, has presented his resignation effective on August 31.

THE resignation is announced of Dr. William Alfred Millis, for twenty-one years president of Hanover College at Hanover, Indiana.

THE resignation on account of ill health is announced of General William H. Cocke as superintendent of the Virginia Military Institute at Richmond.

DR. SAMUEL T. ARNOLD, associate professor of chemistry at Brown University, has been appointed acting dean during the absence of Dean Otis E. Randall, who has leave of absence.

On the occasion of the dedication of the new building of Temple University, Philadelphia, on February 15, the degree of doctor of music was conferred on Dr. Frances E. Clark in recognition of her work in bringing music to the schools.

Professor William C. Bagley has accepted a place on the committee of the National Society for the Study of Education which is to prepare a yearbook on "The Textbook."

A local branch of the Italy America Association has been formed at the University of California at Los Angeles, with Dr. Ernest C. Moore as president.

The Board of Trustees of Teachers College, Columbia University, has elected Miss Mercy Hayes, of Detroit, a permanent member of the board. Miss Hayes has served four years as alumni trustee.

Dr. Sao-Ke Alfred Sze, '01, Chinese minister, has been elected an honorary member of the governing board of the council of Cornell University in recognition of his many years of distinguished service in the activities of that organization.

The department of sociology and anthropology at the University of Chicago has been dissolved and reconstituted as two separate departments. The department of sociology will be under the chairmanship of Dr. Ellsworth Faris, while the chairman for anthropology is Dr. Fay-Cooper Cole.

At the University of Oxford, Mr. David Nichol Smith, fellow of Merton College, has been elected Merton professor of English literature in succession to Mr. G. S. Gordon, president of Magdalen College, who recently resigned.

Dr. Thomas Harrison Reed, professor of political science at the University of Michigan, will lecture in the department of government of Harvard University during the second half of 1929–30. Dr. James Blaine Hedges, associate professor of American history at Clark University, will lecture throughout the year 1929–30. Dr. Ernest Stacey Griffith, associate professor in the school of citizenship at Syracuse University, will lecture in the department of government. Charles Augustus Whittemore, member of the firm of Blackall, Clapp and Whittemore and lecturer at Harvard University in alternate years, will lecture during 1929–30 on "Mechanical Plant of Buildings in the School of Architecture."

Fred E. Smith, deputy state superintendent of South Dakota, has been appointed superintendent of the schools of Windsor, Connecticut.

F. H. Barbee, assistant superintendent of schools at Kansas City, Missouri, has left for St. Joseph, where he has been appointed superintendent.

Dr. L. P. Jacks, principal of Manchester College, Oxford, and editor of *The Hibbert Journal* for more than a quarter of a century, has made a six-weeks' tour in America, speaking on adult education.

Professor Harry H. Love, of the department of plant breeding of Cornell University, has been granted sabbatical leave to engage in work at Nanking University.

Dr. Andrew J. Bigney, professor of botany and biology at Evansville College, will be granted leave of absence from the summer school faculty in order to conduct two courses in botany at the summer session of the University of Southern California.

The Grey University College at Bloemfontein, the chief town in the Orange Free State, has instituted a course leading to a degree in astronomy, the first in the Union. Professor Jan Paraskevopoulos, of the Harvard Observatory, and M. E. Jessup, of the University of Michigan, will conduct the course.

Professor Louis Cazamian, of the Sorbonne, is lecturing at Columbia University during the present term on the modern development of English and French literature. He will be in New York until the middle of May, when he will go to the University of California, at Berkeley, for the summer session.

Dr. J. E. W. Wallin, who recently finished a mental hygiene survey for the Ohio State Department of Education, will conduct a survey during the next month of provisions for physically, mentally and morally handicapped children in the city of Baltimore. He will offer courses of instruction in the summer school of the University of Virginia on handicapped children and in clinical and abnormal psychology.

PRESIDENT GEORGE F. ZOOK, of the University of Akron, will give a course of lectures on "College and University Administration," at Teachers College, Columbia University, during the coming summer. President Zook has given a similar course of lectures at Teachers College the past two summers, and for three summers at the Ohio State University.

PROFESSOR CORA M. WINCHELL, of Teachers College, Columbia University, is giving an extension course under the University of Rochester on ten Saturdays during the spring session. The course is entitled "Methods of Curriculum Reorganization in Household Arts," and is a response to the needs of the teachers in home economics in Rochester, who are revising the curriculum.

DEAN EMERITUS JOSEPH KENNEDY and Governor George F. Shafer gave the principal addresses on the Founders' Day program at the University of North Dakota on February 22.

AT the invitation of Sigma Xi and the departments of mathematics and physics, Professor J. H. Van Vleck, of the University of Minnesota, delivered two lectures at Iowa State College on March 7. The subjects were "Modern Physics and Molecular Structure" and "The New Quantum Theory."

CHARLES E. HUGHES, former Secretary of State, lectured at Yale University on March 15 and 16 on "Pan-American Peace Plans."

DEAN ROSCOE POUND, dean of the Harvard Law School, will be the 1929 Charter Day speaker at the University of California on March 23.

THE REVEREND HOWARD ALLEN BRIDGMAN, of Shirley, Massachusetts, headmaster of the Bridgman School and for many years editor of *The Congregationalist,* died on March 13 at the age of sixty-eight years.

DR. ALEX HILL, formerly master of Downing College, Cambridge, and later principal of University College, Southampton, died on February 27 at the age of seventy-three years. Dr. Hill was vice-chancellor of the University of Cambridge in 1897 and 1898.

MRS. CALVIN COOLIDGE on March 13 turned over to the Clarke School for the Deaf the $2,000,000 endowment fund which has been raised by friends and admirers of Mr. and Mrs. Coolidge, and is known as the Coolidge Fund. The ceremony was held in the chapel of Gardner Green Hubbard Hall. Miss Caroline A. Yale, eighty-year-old principal emeritus of the school, was present at the ceremonies to accept the gift on behalf of the school. Dr. Irving F. Wood, president of the board of trustees and professor of Biblical literature at Smith College, in introducing Mrs. Coolidge, said that the campaign for a large fund for the school and for research in the problems of the deaf had its inception in June, 1927. Later the Coolidges permitted their names to be used in connection with it, and much of the fund was raised as a tribute to them.

IT is announced that the University of Texas will receive approximately $1,000,000 and the heirs of W. J. McDonald, Texas banker, the remainder of an estate valued at about $1,350,000 under a compromise agreement in the district court.

THE dean of the University of Oregon Medical School, Dr. Richard B. Dillehunt, announces that the Rockefeller Foundation has given $400,000 to the medical school, $300,000 of which will be used to construct a new clinic building on Marquam Hill, Portland, and the remainder for equipment.

OF the $2,000,000 required to erect and equip the new building of the Neurological Institute of New York at the Medical Center, $1,800,000 has been raised. The trustees of the institute have authorized the raising of $2,000,000 additional for research. The building was dedicated on March 15 in the presence of distinguished neurologists from New York and other cities, officers of the institute and of Columbia University, officials of city and state, leaders in philanthropy and representatives of medicine and allied sciences. The speakers included Robert Thorne, president of the institute; General William Barclay Parsons, chairman of the board of trustees at Columbia University; Commissioner Frederick W. Parsons, of the State Department of Mental Hygiene, and Dr. Frederick Tilney, professor of neurology and neuro-anatomy in the Columbia Medical School.

THE University of Chicago has received a gift of $400,000 from the son and daughter of the late John P. Wilson, a Chicago lawyer, for the endowment fund of the law school.

THE alumni and directors of the University of Akron, Ohio, have raised $175,000 toward the building fund of the proposed new university to be located three and a half miles from the center of the city.

DR. AND MRS. D. W. SMOUSE, of Los Angeles, California, formerly of Des Moines, Iowa, have made a gift of $250,000 to the independent school district of Des Moines for erecting a school building especially designed and equipped for crippled and otherwise handicapped children of the city.

THE University of Wisconsin has completed the quota necessary to endow a room in the American dormitory at the Cité Universitaire, the international student center of the University of Paris. The university proposes to allow full credit for work done in Paris during the junior year.

THE trustees of Phillips Academy, Andover, have asked the Massachusetts Legislature's Committee on Education to report favorably on a bill which would authorize them to hold real and personal estate without limit. Under the present law, their limit of expansion is fixed at $12,000,000. Andover's holdings have almost reached this figure already, and the school is planning a program of development which will involve from fifteen to twenty millions more.

FORMATION of an educational trust, believed to be the first of its kind, was made known following the filing of an incorporation certificate at Albany by the National City Foundation. This organization will assist men and women employed by the National City Bank, New York City, and affiliated corporations to obtain more practical and cultural education than their means or circumstances would otherwise make possible. Directors and executives of the bank have contributed funds for the foundation and it will begin its work with an amount representing the income from more than $2,000,000. According to an official statement, "The foundation's funds are derived from personal contributions from executives and directors, and this circumstance frees it from the limitations that have surrounded other endeavors. Large amounts of money are bequeathed every year to educational institutions, but the benefits of these bequests go solely to those with time and funds. The National City Foundation will offer opportunities heretofore not available to the bank's employees and this offer is not conditional upon their having time or funds. The bank will see that they have the opportunity and the funds will be provided by the foundation."

UNDER the will of Elizabeth B. Frasch, the widow of Herman Frasch, formerly chemist to the Standard Oil Company, the income from $1,000,000 is given to three institutions for research in agricultural chemistry. The awards were made by the United States Trust Company under the advice of the American Chemical Society, and the beneficiaries are the Boyce Thompson Institute, Yonkers, which will receive $20,000 annually; the University of Missouri, which will receive $12,000 annually, and the University of Wisconsin, $8,000 annually. By the terms of the will the income was to be used for "research in the field of agricultural chemistry, with the hope of attaining results which shall be of practical benefit to the agricultural development of the United States."

LEHIGH UNIVERSITY made the laying of the corner-stone of an addition to its library, built at a cost of $580,000, a feature of its alumni home-coming on February 22. The new building will have a floor capacity of five times that of the old and will have stacks and other shelving for 500,000 volumes and a reading room to seat between 350 and 400 readers. Eleven seminars, a treasure room with large vault, a browsing room and an art gallery are features of the new building. Addresses were given by President C. R. Richards, Mr. Walter R. Okeson, Professor H. S. Leach, the librarian, and Mr. Paul M. Paine, librarian of Syracuse Public Library and a graduate of Lehigh.

BY the will of Mrs. Jule Hopwood, of New York and Cleveland, her residuary estate is left to the University of Michigan for the founding of "the Avery Hopwood and Jule Hopwood prizes," to be given annually to students in the rhetoric department for the best creative literary work. The estate is said to be worth over $150,000.

A LEGACY of $100,000 has been left to Willamette University by Eric Hauser, of Portland, former contractor and hotel owner.

GEORGE BOSCH, of Sydney, New South Wales, has given £250,000 to the University of Sydney.

NEW MEXICO has received $200,000 from John D. Rockefeller, Jr., for the establishment of an anthropological laboratory at Santa Fe, with $70,000 additional toward maintaining it for the next five years.

THE Essex Institute at Salem enters into possession of the George L. Ames home on Pleasant Street between Pickman and Spring Streets, due to the death of Minerva Lane, who under the will of Mr. Ames was the beneficiary during her life. Other real estate disposed of in the will also goes to the institute.

EX-VICE-PRESIDENT CHARLES G. DAWES has given $20,000 to the Lawrenceville School toward the cost of rebuilding the Dawes house recently destroyed by fire. This contribution, together with others already received, makes the total amount available $80,000.

THE alumni and other friends of the Polytechnic Institute of Brooklyn who are interested in the future of that institution, have established what is known as the "Living Endowment Fund." This method of financial aid has been tried by several colleges, with results highly satisfactory, both in raising funds and in stimulating interest in the college. The fund operates in this way: the donor, instead of making a gift in one lump sum, pledges himself to give each year a sum representing the interest, figured at five per cent., that would be earned on the corresponding capital sum. The response of the alumni and other friends has been so immediate and hearty as to give assurance of the entire success of the plan when it shall have been fully developed. The income from the "Living Endowment Fund" will be used for various essential purposes—increasing the salaries of the teaching staff, increasing and improving the equipment, developing the graduate school and giving aid to deserving students.

A GIFT of $150,000 for a new building and equipment for Santiago College, Santiago, Chile, as a means of "kindlier mutual understanding, making toward peace and security between the Latin-Americans and ourselves," has been made by Mr. and Mrs. M. C. Migel, according to an announcement made public by Dr. Ralph E. Diffendorfer, corresponding secretary of the Board of Foreign Missions of the Methodist Episcopal Church. The gift is made conditional on the securing of a like amount for the college by the Board of Foreign Missions. Mr. Migel is a New York City business man who in his early career established himself in Santiago, Chile. Mrs. Migel is a graduate of Santiago College and is now president of the board of trustees of the college, which has been incorporated by the Regents of the State of New York.

IT was recently stated in the British parliament that the British government has decided to offer to the University of Cambridge a grant of £50,000, subject to the provision of funds by parliament. It is believed "that the highest national, as well as Imperial and international, interests demand that the scheme made possible by the benefaction of the International Education Board of the Rockefeller Foundation should be fully carried into effect for the advancement of agriculture and of the fundamental sciences on which agriculture depends."

THE sanitary code of New York requires a medical examination of each school child on his entering school. The *Journal* of the American Medical Association states that the health department gives each child a form card on admission and a letter explaining to his parents the requirement and urging them to have the examination made promptly by their family physician. If no report is received from the parents in a reasonable time, the health department takes steps to have the child examined by the school physician. The health commissioner requests physicians to assist his department in this work by returning reports of their examinations promptly and by urging parents to have the necessary corrective work done before the child gets in the upper grades. It is the constant aim of the department of health not to undertake any medical work that can and will be done satisfactorily by the family physician. Section 200 of the sanitary code states that a health certificate prepared in accordance with the regulations of the department of health and signed by a physician licensed to practice in New York shall be furnished by each pupil at the time of his admission to public school or other free school supported in whole or in part by direct taxation.

PLANS are being made for a field trip which will be conducted by Professor Frederick J. Breeze, head of the department of science at Ball Teachers College, Muncie, Indiana, from July 20 to August 24, during the second summer term. The itinerary will include the Colorado Rockies, the high plateaus of Utah, Zion National Park, Bryce Canyon and the Grand Canyon in Arizona. This will be the seventh trip conducted by Professor Breeze; three trips have been made to New York, and three trips have been to various points in the West. Travel this summer will be made by motor coach, and a distance of 4,200 miles will be covered.

THE trip to be taken by the Princeton Summer School of Geology this summer will cover 11,000 miles in Canada and the northeastern part of the United States. The party is limited to twenty-three undergraduates of eastern universities, and will leave on June 22, returning on August 5.

TWENTY-FIVE college students at Beloit College are gaining actual teaching experience at the Burr Training School, connected with the college department of education. There are forty-eight pupils in the two grades, and college students who expect to teach are thus securing teaching experience as well as training in club work and special activities. The plan of Great Britain, allowing for more individualization, which is unique in American training schools, is being inaugurated slowly.

DISCUSSION

SCHOLARSHIP OF APPLICANTS FOR TEACHING POSITIONS

THE article, "Haint Eney Place," in a recent issue of SCHOOL AND SOCIETY, decried the ignorance of the president of a school board who had been elected to lead those who were responsible for the selection of teachers. It is very unfortunate that this difficult task is still a part of a school director's duty in some sections of the United States. In most communities, however, the educational executive selects the teachers and recommends their election to the school board. As one of this group, the writer is greatly pleased to learn that at least one college graduate who is entering the teaching profession has high ideals of scholarship for those who are connected with the public schools.

For several years, however, the writer has felt that the quality of scholarship exhibited by many of the applicants for teaching positions has been very poor. An examination of the following two samples of letters of application will convince any one of the justice of this criticism.

Sample No. 1. (Exact copy with personal items changed.)

Glendale, Pa.
March 1st. 1928.

Supt. of Schools,
Ingram, Pa.
Dear Sir:

I wish to be
considered as an ap-
plicant for position
in the Latin, English,
or French departments
of your High School.
Will graduate
from Glendale College
in June.

Have had a
summer of nine weeks
at Millvale Normal and
one of six weeks at the
University of Harrisburg.

I will have complet-
ed twenty six semester
hours of English, eighteen
semester hours of French

and twenty semester hours
of Latin, including
teachers course in all
three.

Also will have completed the requirements
of the Penn. State Board
of Education and received
a college provisional
certificate by June.

If there are any
vacancies in your High
School will you please
send me application
blank.

Very truly yours
Mary Jones.

Sample No. 2. (Same changes as in the other.)

Sharon Pa.
2146 Mackin Street

Mr. M A Steiner

My dear Sir Could you
assist me in finding a
teaching position do you
happen to know of vacany any
where Could teach economics
History Business Law or Finance
mathematics Could coach or
be assistant coach Will be glad
to come for personal application
available at once answer

(Second page of letter)
to James B Graber
2146 Mackin Street
Sharon
Pa

Will be glad to go any where
will appreciate very much
any assistance you may be able
to give me in finding a position

Exact copies of the first sample followed by six questions were prepared and presented to tenth-grade pupils. The last question was, "What mark do you think you should receive on this letter as a tenth-grade pupil?" About two thirds of the class gave the letter the lowest passing mark used in their school and three of the forty-one pupils marked it unsatisfactory. How does it happen that colleges will graduate such students, much less qualify them for teachers of English? If they are graduated from college why should any state department certify them for teaching?

An analysis of the possible causes of poor scholarship is not very difficult. Part of the blame must be placed upon the high school. In many high schools it is possible for boys and girls to acquire sufficient credits to enter college without mastering the fundamentals of English or of any other subject. "Educators," high-school principals, will claim that universal high-school education has forced them to lower the standards of scholarship. This may be true to a certain extent, but why should intelligent and capable high-school pupils have every feeling of mastery and of scholarship crushed by the "piffling and twaddling" work done in many high schools? This language is used to describe much of the teaching actually observed by the writer in some of the most widely known high schools of this country. Colleges have become so alarmed at the product of the modern high school that many are excluding from admission the lower two thirds of all graduating classes. If the average quality of scholarship is so low, it must seriously handicap the efforts of the best students. Many eager students, especially among the boys, lose every incentive or desire to study, because so many high-school teachers fail to encourage and to stimulate high ideals of scholarship.

With an inferior quality of freshmen entering college, does the college meet its obligation to society by graduating and recommending for teaching those who are unfit? The writer's experience in taking college courses has been quite extensive, but this has not strengthened his faith in the wisdom of permitting any college graduate to teach any subject in which he has secured a total of twelve credits, a requirement in Pennsylvania. Regardless of how little a freshman may know at the time of entrance and regardless of how little he may learn in college, there are many college professors who do not have the courage to fail more than a very few of their students. Perhaps this is the reason why the writer has observed college graduates teach that a quantity in algebra with a zero exponent was equal to zero; that an introductory "there" always required a singular verb; that the clause in the sentence, "The man *to whom you spoke* was my father," was a substantive clause the object of the preposition, "to." Many other examples could be cited, but many supervisors have had similar experiences. It is not a lack of definite learning that is so serious, but it is the poor quality of scholarship that such teachers have acquired in their high school and college life. A real student would not make such mistakes, for he would master the situation by careful thought and study. Surely this should be one of the outcomes of real schooling. If the teacher has not acquired a desire for and a skill in studying, what can be expected from his pupils?

When the elementary and the high school begin to be satisfied with an inferior quality of work it affects not only the immediate product of the schools but the scholarship of those who return to the schools as teachers. For this reason the deterioration in scholarship is much more rapid. With the wide-spread use of tests, there is no excuse for any school system to be ignorant of the quality of work done. A much more serious indictment, however, can be made against those schools which have discovered very unsatisfactory conditions without making any serious or organized attempt to remedy them. Most schoolmen realize that the standards for many tests are too low, although almost 50 per cent. of the schools do not attain even these which are based upon the average throughout the country. Medians, moreover, do not tell the whole story, for there is always a hopeless 50 per cent. below these medians that are crying out for attention. Mastery of nothing and a superficial impression of everything seem to be the aim of some school systems. Educational leaders must take cognizance of the situation, for no one can predict the result when the patient and ignorant taxpayer becomes dissatisfied with the results of the schools which he supports. If the public schools desire to function more effectively in American democracy, it will be necessary to improve the scholarship of beginning teachers as well as the amount of schooling, which has already been increased.

The standard of scholarship for entrance into the teaching profession can be raised by the proper selection of those who desire to enter teacher-training institutions and by the successful elimination of poor students who may have gained admission. Not every high-school graduate should be permitted to select teaching for his life work. Selection should be based upon many factors, of which scholarship must be one. This should be determined by the interest manifested in study and learning during the individual's public school life and by various tests of achievement and ability. After admission to teacher-training courses, those who show any lack of mastery in their special courses or in their professional courses must be eliminated. Unless these training institutions will accept this responsibility, final aptitude and achievement tests must be administered by the state as it now does to graduates of other professional schools.

M. A. STEINER

THE SO-CALLED HINDU-ARABIC NUMERALS

NOTWITHSTANDING the perennial interest in the history of our common numerals, very little is yet definitely known as regards their origin. It may therefore be desirable to note here a few somewhat striking statements relating thereto which appeared in a recent article, published in the *Zeitschrift für Mathematischen und Naturwissenschaftlichen Unterricht aller Schulgattungen,* 1928, by J. Tropfke, who is now commonly regarded as one of the foremost writers on the history of elementary mathematics. These statements are the more worth noting here because they seem to represent a slight change of view on the part of their author since the appearance of the second edition of his favorably known "Geschichte der Elementar-Mathematik" in seven volumes, 1921–24. A free translation of one of these statements follows:

> How difficult is it for the historian to re-tie the threads from the disappearance of Hellenism to the time of the Moslems. The investigator is forced to the conviction that what was accomplished by the Hindus, the Persians, and the Arabs, is mythical. What was really accomplished in this period seems to have its origin in the Greek intellect, such as our positional system with nine digits and zero . . . but these assertions based on feeling can not as yet be proved scientifically.

From this statement it is clear that its author was inclined at the time of writing it to favor the theory that our common numerals, including the zero, had their origin in Greece. It is to be observed that he does not claim that the evidences tending to support a European origin of these numerals are as yet sufficient to justify a definite conclusion, but they show that the common term Hindu-Arabic numerals is apt to convey the impression that we know more about their origin than is actually the case at the present time.

While we know as yet very little about the origin of our common numerals it is a healthy sign of progress along this line that so many writers no longer accept the view that their Hindu origin is an established historical fact. On the contrary, in the article to which we referred above J. Tropfke remarks that the earliest known positional number with digits appeared in Egypt in 873, and presents a mixture of the forms used by the eastern and the western Arabs. The western forms spread later in Spain and became the prototype of our numerals. A large number of Arabian manuscripts and Egyptian papyri have not as yet been carefully studied, and hence there is hope that we may soon know much more about the history of our common numerals. For the present it is interesting to note that some of the leading investigators along this line are inclined to favor the view that our already great debt to early Greek civilization may be enhanced in the future by establishing the origin of our common numerals in their midst.

G. A. MILLER
UNIVERSITY OF ILLINOIS

QUOTATIONS

TENDENCIES IN THIS YEAR'S SCHOOL LEGISLATION

IN the states where the legislature is in session at this time, the educational forces are also ready to advocate programs for reforms. These programs include a variety of innovations and changes in the school laws of the several states. In the main, they aim at a better diffusion of educational opportunity and a more equitable distribution of the tax burden.

The measures proposed bear in mind the incongruities in the several school units in the state, namely, the difference between the rich and the poor school districts, and contemplate a method of state support that will equalize between the two. The legislator who is confronted with these measures soon realizes that education, like everything else, costs considerably more than it did a decade or two ago.

The laws that were deemed satisfactory two decades ago are badly out of tune with present-day needs. The expansion and momentum which America's popular system of education has experienced has also emphasized the financial inequalities which afflict the school units. The school child has grown. Larger clothes are needed.

The solution must be found in more liberal state aid and an equitable distribution of that aid between the several school units. One of the basic considerations which enters here is that of establishing the county as the unit of administration and thus bringing the several districts under some unified form of control. Such control brings to the surface the weak districts and enables the administrators to designate the remedy.

The legislative trend promises also to secure greater financial independence for the city boards of education. Many of these are subjected to city council control on matters of finance far beyond the bounds of reason and common sense. The forces that contend against greater financial freedom for boards of education are inclined to resist a change of laws. A modern city council is better equipped to influence state legislation than is the average board of education. It holds to its prerogatives with a peculiar tenacity.

The several state educational organizations are better equipped with definite legislative programs than they ever have been before and will go forward to their task with considerable energy and preparedness.

Underlying much of the school legislation is found the question of taxation. A more liberal school aid means more taxation which in many instances will reduce the whole program to new sources of revenue or a heavier burden upon present sources. The educator who champions greater school aid will also have to come prepared to suggest where and how that aid is to be secured.—*The School Board Journal.*

SCHOOLS AND POLITICS

Hard experiences often breed bitter proposals. To circumvent the high-handed methods of political expedience occasionally employed in the appointment and removal of the State Superintendent of Public Instruction, Pennsylvanians are offered for consideration the doubtful alternative of the removal of this office to the farthest boundary possible from the electorate.

At the recent meeting of the Pennsylvania State Education Association in Reading the excellent president of the association suggested a possible solution for this rarely-occurring political trick. This suggestion was that the State Superintendent of Public Instruction be appointed by the State Council of Education, this body in turn to be selected by the Supreme Court of the state. Very fortunately such a process requires constitutional sanction.

If our theory of the superiority of democratic government is sound there is the gravest cause for alarm in the increasing advocacy of government by appointment. This is particularly so since provision is rarely made for obligatory supervision of the activities of these appointive bodies, or for their rejuvenation by changes in personnel through removals, other than by the hand of Providence.

The practical remedy for taking the position of state superintendent out of politics is in the hands of the local school authorities throughout the state. Let them so thoroughly purge their own administrations of political practices as to convince the public mind that the instrument they are unwilling to use must be denied to others as a weapon. Once persuade the people that the school administrators are sincere and able in the execution of such an undertaking and there will be massed back of the schools a weight of public opinion which the most politically-minded governor would not dare ignore in making appointments to the highest educational position in the state.

This program demands conviction, courage and consistency for its accomplishment. Have Pennsylvania school authorities these qualities and the will to exercise them?—*The Pittsburgh School Bulletin.*

BOOKS AND LITERATURE

INDUSTRIAL ARTS EDUCATION

Policies in Industrial Arts Education. Wm. E. Warner, Ph.D. Ohio State University Press, Columbus. 1928. $1.00.

The Training and Experience of 480 Industrial Arts Teachers. Fred Strickler, Ph.D. Lincoln School Studies. Bureau of Publications, Teachers College, Columbia University, New York City. 1928. $1.00.

Scientific research studies for almost every subject have become relatively common in recent years, but in industrial arts education real beginnings have just been made. The two studies here reviewed not only compare well with research studies in other fields, but they also are highly valuable in practical significance. Both are timely studies, providing a wealth of material of interest and value for teachers and administrators and for those training teachers of industrial arts.

Professor Warner develops a state-wide policy for the training of industrial arts teachers in Ohio, based upon five methods of inquiry, namely: (1) a study of trends in the United States since 1876; (2) a study of comparable teacher-training institutions in Ohio and elsewhere in 1927; (3) a study of the statements of industrial arts objectives by a jury of fifty-eight specialists in industrial arts education; (4) a study of the recommendations made by the 480 experienced industrial arts teachers of Dr. Strickler's study, and (5) an interpretative analysis of the views of leaders in the field concerning the preparation of teachers. In the application of the policies derived, certain program essentials for the training of teachers are suggested in three divisions, technical, professional and academic, together with some minor essentials not falling within these three groupings.

The need for the study and the situation to which it contributes are well presented in the following statement:

Departments in institutions where industrial arts teachers are prepared have the problems of what courses to offer, what shops or laboratories to equip, what kinds of students to admit for preparation, what methods to use in preparing the students to teach, what kinds of teachers to produce, what changes to make in departmental programs, what courses to require, what kind of staff to employ, what research to do if any, what should constitute a fair teaching load, and many other similar problems. What are the answers to these questions?

The investigation brings out the materials and lays the foundation on a scientific basis for deriving policies believed to be sound for the training of teachers in Ohio and for developing teacher-training programs based upon these policies. Out of the study emerge satisfactory answers to many of the questions which enter into the general problem. While the findings are applied to conditions in Ohio, this does not limit their usefulness for institutions in other states.

One illustration of policy relating to the qualifications of the teaching staff of institutions training industrial arts teachers shows what variability the investigation uncovers. School "X" has a staff of nine teachers, six of whom have the bachelor's degree, two the master's degree and one the doctor's degree. School "Y" has a staff of nineteen teachers, of whom only one has even the bachelor's degree.

The activities in industrial arts courses reported by 294 shop and drawing teachers in schools of Ohio outside of Cleveland totaled sixty-three in 1927. Fourteen of these are reported by only one teacher each, while not a single one of the sixty-three is reported by more than 179 of the 294 teachers. After all that has been said and written about vocational guidance in connection with the study of the industries, only 6 per cent. of these teachers reported the study of industrial occupations. Throughout the study the wide variety of practice impresses the reader with what seems to be a general absence of policy in both the teaching of industrial arts and the training of industrial arts teachers. Yet the writer finds, by taking account of all that his several forms of investigation reveal, certain definite trends and sufficient positive evidences of unified purpose in all the seeming diversity to furnish the basis for constructive and progressive policies that are reasonable and consistent with present conditions. The study is stimulating and suggestive, and it does not require the vision of a prophet to see that it has inherent possibilities for stirring up a great deal of wholesome thought about the work and the training of teachers for it.

The investigation by Dr. Strickler includes a very searching account of the training and experience of 480 industrial arts teachers and supervisors from thirty-seven states. Of these, twenty-two are supervisors and twenty-nine are college teachers. To find what differences in time of training revealed, the men were grouped into those receiving their training before 1910; those between 1910 and 1920, and those since 1920. Each one of these 480 teachers had the patience and the interest to fill an inquiry blank containing 433 topics, and the items checked made a total of 117,776 which were tabulated and analyzed. Each person checked whether he had had the given topic in his own training and whether he would now include it in courses for training teachers.

Space permits the inclusion here of but two or three items illustrating the results from the inquiry. For the period 1910–20 there was an increase of 15 per cent. in professional training over the period before 1910. There is a striking parallelism between what teachers themselves had and what they would recommend. As the writer says, "On the average, industrial arts teachers think as they were taught in spite of their experience and their dissatisfaction with certain elements of their training." While supervisors recommend about 8 per cent. more professional training than they themselves had, the whole group of 480 recommend only 2 per cent. more than they received. The results show that there has been an increasing emphasis upon professional training during the period covered by the study. On the whole, the greatest expressed need is for more training in the subject-matter which bears a close relationship to the problems of everyday teaching.

Only 59.8 per cent. of the 480 have had four years of high-school training, while 22.4 per cent. have had no high-school training at all. One hundred seventy of the 480 had but one year or less of professional training, and 320, two thirds, have no college degree. May not this be one item of "inside information" as to why industrial arts has not often met with favor as a college entrance subject? Of course, as the study brings out, "It is a misconception to think that industrial arts teachers have studied only shop subjects." Most of those trained in the more recent periods have had from one to four years of work beyond high school. Each of the 480 indicates the subjects which he studied which have been of most value and which have been of least value in his work.

Excluding the supervisors and college teachers, because of the incompleteness of their replies about books in their personal libraries, the 429 teachers reported 912 different book titles. The highest number of times any one book was reported was sixty-six. The next highest was reported forty-eight times. Reported only twice were 123 different books, and only once were 609. Is there no really good book on industrial arts? It would seem so, since only sixty-six teachers of 429 have the book most often listed. The names and frequencies of mention of all the eighty-nine books listed five or more times are given in the study. Books on woodwork lead the list—446 of the 912, with thirty-one different titles. To quote,

> Books on education, psychology and philosophy are rarely found in the libraries of industrial arts teachers. In these turbulent days of curriculum revision, we do not find a single book on curriculum making listed by the 429 teachers. . . . Many questions arise. Are present books inadequate to meet the needs of industrial arts teachers? Is there a need for new kinds of books, or better books?

Turning to magazines, fifty-seven of an industrial arts or educational interest are listed. The mean number for the 429 teachers is 2.59 magazines per man. One hundred per cent. of the supervisors take both the *Industrial Arts Magazine* and the *Industrial Education Magazine*. Of the teachers, 280 subscribe to the *Industrial Arts Magazine*. The list of the magazines and the frequency of subscription to each are given in full in the study.

One year or more of trade experience has been had by 184 of the 480 men. Over 50 per cent. of all trained before 1920 have had a year or more of trade experience. The report on salaries is interesting, and a thorough analysis is made of the factors which seem to determine salaries. The average salary of teachers of one year's experience is $1,600 and for teachers of twenty years' experience is $2,500. The range represented for all is very wide—from $720 to $5,700 a year. The evidence from this study is that salaries are not influenced by trade experience. The frequent assertion that trade workers receive more annual income than industrial arts teachers is not sustained by this study. Trade workers would have to work forty-seven weeks a year to earn amounts equal to teachers' salaries, basing comparisons upon salaries reported and trade wages for 1927 and the preceding years covered by this study. The amount of trade experience of industrial arts teachers is in inverse ratio to their professional training.

The foregoing are but random samplings of the content of the compact pages of these two studies, illustrating the range of interests and the wealth of findings which they include. They illustrate both the need and the possibility of research work to bring out the conditions, the facts and the means for placing industrial arts on a sound basis as an educational subject. We may deplore some things that are revealed by research, but the only way to make progress is to get the facts and then face them squarely. Both of these studies are constructive in that they point clearly the way to higher standards in the preparation of teachers. As Dr. Strickler states,

> People believe what they are taught. . . . This places the burden of progress upon the shoulders of the teacher-training group. . . . Institutions for the preparation of industrial arts teachers must therefore carry the added load of a search for facts if improved teaching in the public schools is to result.

It is devoutly to be hoped that these studies will be followed by others which will help to place industrial arts on a plane of larger usefulness and larger recognition for the educational values which the work represents when properly developed.

The two monographs are inexpensive, they are presented in a form that is easily readable and full of interest and they are constructively helpful and stimulating. To call attention to them is fulfilling a duty to the cause and placing an opportunity before every teacher and supervisor of industrial arts.

F. G. BONSER

TEACHERS COLLEGE,
COLUMBIA UNIVERSITY

REPORTS

ACTIVITIES OF THE COMMONWEALTH FUND

APPROPRIATIONS amounting to $2,083,621.80 were made by the Commonwealth Fund last year in furthering a wide range of public health, mental hygiene, child welfare and educational activities, according to its tenth annual report. Eight major enterprises administered by the fund through its several divisions and committees received $1,675,191.45 during the fiscal year ending September 30, 1928, while the remainder, $408,430.35, was distributed among forty outside organizations, hospitals and universities in the form of grants for special purposes.

The fellowships for British graduate students in American universities, one of the principal projects of the fund, received appropriations totaling $198,150 for the year. There are now fifty-one fellows studying at seventeen colleges and universities, making eighty-five in all who have spent or are spending a two-year period of study and travel in this country since 1925, when the fellowship program was established. Commenting on the three years of experience in this undertaking, Barry C. Smith, general director of the fund, says,

> It is clear, even after so brief a period, that through these fellowships a high type of British youth is eagerly accepting the opportunity not only for scholarly attainment, but also for securing a knowledge and understanding of American people and of American life which can not fail to increase, however gradually, the good feeling between the two nations.

Modern fifty-bed hospitals have been awarded to five communities since the beginning of the fund's rural hospital program, for which $358,438 was appropriated during the year. The first of these was opened in Farmville, Virginia, in November, 1927. The institutions in Glasgow, Kentucky, and Farmington, Maine, will be completed this spring, and those in Beloit, Kansas, and Wauseon, Ohio, will probably be opened before the end of 1929. The report says:

> The rural hospital program is an experiment in social organization involving much more than a building project; it is an effort to attack from a fresh angle the difficult problem of medical and public-health service in small towns and the open country, and to change community standards in respect to the care of the sick, the prevention of disease and the protection of health.

Typical of the general program is the work now going on in the district of nine Virginia counties served by the Farmville Hospital. The state health department has organized this territory into a single unit with a district health officer, under whose leadership a comprehensive health service is being gradually developed. Two medical institutes have been held, with clinical demonstrations and lectures on chosen topics. Ten local physicians have been awarded fellowships for brief post-graduate courses at well-known medical centers. The hospital itself is proving its usefulness to the community and has been operated under the direction of the local board of trustees on a gratifyingly high standard. As with all hospitals constructed under the fund's cooperative program, a third of the cost of the building and equipment and the entire expense of administration has been assumed by the local community.

Experience in carrying on for the past six years a program for the development of child-guidance clinics and visiting-teacher service in the public schools has brought the conviction that the greatest present need in this field is the adequate training of sufficient personnel. The fund's chief contribution toward meeting this need has been the Institute for Child Guidance, opened in New York City on July 1, 1927, and now in its second year of operation as a clinic and training center. The student group now includes seven psychiatrists, five psychologists and forty-four psychiatric social workers, who are specializing in work with children. Continued support has also been given to the Division on Community Clinics of the National Committee for Mental Hygiene, which has assisted in the organization of thirteen clinics, including a new one in Charleston, S. C., and a state clinical service in Virginia; and to the National Committee on Visiting Teachers, under whose auspices training centers have been established in New York and Chicago, ten scholarships have been awarded, and eleven summer courses in the theory and practice of visiting-teacher work have been given at various universities. Appropriations covering all forms of mental hygiene work for a period of nineteen months totaled $568,779.45.

For several years the fund has assisted in a program for the development of child-guidance clinic work in England. A period of careful study of plans and many visits by prominent professional workers to study American methods in this field resulted in a decision by the Child Guidance Council of Great Britain to establish a special service and training clinic in London for this field of activity. Official approval has been obtained from the London County Council making possible close working relationship with the London school system. This clinic will be opened in the spring of 1929 under the auspices of the council, of which Sir Humphry Rolleston is chairman. During the past year the council has sent five social workers on Commonwealth Fund fellowships to this country for training along mental hygiene lines, and has fostered observational trips by a number of persons.

The program of five-year demonstrations of child-health work which the fund undertook in four American communities is drawing to a close. The work in Fargo, North Dakota, was completed at the end of 1927 and full reports of the results have been published during the past year. The demonstrations in Rutherford County, Tennessee, and in Athens and Clarke County, Georgia, ended in December, 1928. The work in Marion County, Oregon, is entering upon its final year. Local appropriations and arrangements for carrying on all essential activities at their own expense have been made in these communities. In Rutherford County, particularly, the report finds "an outstanding example of the possibilities in public health created in a rural community by an awakened public conscience." The total appropriations for the child-health program last year were $229,587.84.

On July 1, 1929, the fund expects to complete the program of child welfare and public-health work in Austria, which it took over in 1921. The various child-health stations will be continued by the Austrian authorities, a new emphasis is being placed upon the adequate training of personnel and the whole program promises to be successful beyond the hopes that were entertained when the work was begun.

The death of Dean Hall, of the University of Chicago Law School, has made necessary a reorganization of the fund's Legal Research Committee. George Welwood Murray, one of the directors of the fund, has become chairman, and two new members, Dean Young B. Smith, of Columbia University Law School, and Dean Henry M. Bates, of the University of Michigan Law School, have been added to the committee. The outstanding accomplishment of the year has been the publication, under the auspices of the committee, of Professor Ernst Freund's notable book, "Administrative Powers over Persons and Property."

Among the forty-three special grants made by the fund for public health, mental hygiene and miscellaneous welfare projects during the year the following may be noted: $22,500 to the American Public Health Association for the study of public-health programs in rural areas; $117,000 for fellowships in psychiatry at the Boston Psychopathic Hospital, the Henry Phipps Psychiatric Clinic at Baltimore and the University of Colorado Medical School; $16,500 to the National Conference of Catholic Charities for a study of child-caring homes; $12,500 to the Boy Scouts of America for a study of the effects of scout work in a number of American cities; $7,500 to the New York Tuberculosis and Health Association for cardiac research, and $10,000 to the American Forestry Association for a program of education looking toward the conservation of forest resources in three southern states.

EDUCATIONAL RESEARCH AND STATISTICS

SEX DIFFERENCES IN HISTORY RETENTION

ON hand are data which show the extent of sex differences in remembering history. These were derived from testing pupils as follows: Grade VI A,[1] twenty-eight boys and girls; Grade VII B, twenty-three boys and girls, and Grade VII A, forty-four boys and girls. Each group was equated on the bases of (1) initial history test scores, (2) interest and effort and (3) ability to pass the Pressey-Richards test of "Understanding of American History." These groups were equated on interest and effort and ability to pass the standard history test because, in the light of the author's dissertation,[2] these were the two factors which gave the highest prediction for history retention.

The history tests were based on the information outlined in the history course of study in the City of Baltimore. They were given at four-month intervals. On the tests for each of the grades there were forty true-false, ten completion, twenty multiple-choice and a choice of three out of four modified-essay questions.

In preparing these retention history tests many facts had to be kept in mind. Among these was the necessity of keeping a well-balanced choice of the topics called for in the history course of study. Attention was given to the vocabulary used and to the securing of varying degrees of difficulty in the questions, though not in any regular sequence.[3]

Grade VI A—The Father of the English navy was ————.
Why did the German barbarians succeed in conquering the Romans?

Grade VII B—The people liked the Constitution because it had a Bill of Rights when adopted in 1788.
The "———— of ————" states "that all men are created equal."

Grade VII A—For a long time the Barbary pirates preyed on the commerce of Christian nations.
Tariff is (a) a veto; (b) a debate; (c) an amendment; (d) money paid on imported goods.

In order to secure adequate records for the children's interest and effort, the history teachers of the particular classes were called upon to supply the marks, which are composite scores of the pupils' attention, contributions and activities connected with history.

Table I shows the means and Q's for the three equated groups of boys and girls.

TABLE I

GROUPS OF BOYS AND GIRLS EQUATED ON THE BASES OF THE INITIAL HISTORY TEST (T_o), INTEREST AND EFFORT (IE), AND ABILITY TO PASS THE PRESSEY-RICHARDS TEST, "THE UNDERSTANDING OF AMERICAN HISTORY" (HIS)

Grade	Number of pupils		T_o	IE	His
VI A	28 Boys	M*	53.61	74.54	26.75
		Q	5.88	7.50	4.38
VII B	23 Boys	M	56.39	69.96	26.57
		Q	12.25	14.75	5.80
VII A	44 Boys	M	60.93	74.70	24.36
		Q	8.08	10.17	5.50
VI A	28 Girls	M*	53.55	75.04	26.18
		Q	5.67	7.62	4.00
VII B	23 Girls	M	56.48	70.35	24.65
		Q	11.94	14.90	5.05
VII A	44 Girls	M	60.45	75.27	23.63
		Q	8.00	9.03	4.59

* M = Mean.

The sex differences in history retention for the three groups of pupils, 190 cases in all, are given in tabulated form in Table II. The group of twenty-eight VI A boys slightly surpassed the mean for the twenty-eight VI A girls by 1.28, 1.29 and 3.11 points for the four, eight and twelve-month intervals, respectively. For the same intervals, as well as the sixteen-month lapse, the twenty-three VII B boys went beyond the mean of the twenty-three VII B girls by 1.30, 2.66, 1.18 and 1.05 points. On the four, eight and twelve-month intervals, the mean of the history scores for the forty-four VII A boys excelled that of the forty-four VII A girls by 1.61, 2.30 and 1.32 points, respectively.

[1] The A division of a grade is the higher section while the B division is the lower section.

[2] S. J. Bassett, "Retention of History in the Sixth, Seventh and Eighth Grades with Special Reference to the Factors that Influence Retention." The Johns Hopkins University Studies in Education, No. 12, pp. 118, 1928.

[3] The tests were criticized by specialists in history and education, given to 187 try-out cases, and revised by the writer in the light of the evidence thus secured. Dr. Fowler D. Brooks, of the Johns Hopkins University, directed the study.

TABLE II

INFLUENCE OF SEX ON RETENTION OF HISTORY SHOWN BY MEANS AND Q DIFFERENCES FOR GROUPS OF BOYS AND GIRLS ALIKE IN HISTORY KNOWLEDGE ON INITIAL TEST, INTEREST AND EFFORT, AND ABILITY ON PRESSEY-RICHARDS' TEST, "THE UNDERSTANDING OF AMERICAN HISTORY."

Grade	Number of pupils	Intervals of time between retention tests 0 mo.	4 mo.	8 mo.	12 mo.	16 mo.
VI A	28 Boys Mean	53.61	46.21	43.68	42.18	
	28 Girls "	53.55	44.93	42.39	39.07	
	Difference in Mean	– 0.06	– 1.28	– 1.29	– 3.11	
	Q Difference				1.746	
VII B	23 Boys Mean	56.39	46.91	44.70	39.44	37.22
	23 Girls "	56.48	45.61	42.04	38.26	36.17
	Difference in Mean	+ 0.09	– 1.30	– 2.66	– 1.18	– 1.05
	Q Difference				2.386	
VII A	44 Boys Mean	60.93	54.95	50.98	48.68	
	44 Girls "	60.45	53.34	48.68	47.36	
	Difference in Mean	– 0.48	– 1.61	– 2.30	– 1.32	
	Q Difference				1.392	

Another interesting element in the sex differences of history retention was revealed by the Q of the difference for the group of boys and girls for the twelve-month interval, where it was 1.75, 2.39 and 1.39 respectively. Hence the differences between the means of the boys and girls are real ones and not merely due to chance.

These findings are in keeping with those of preceding investigations. E. W. Cober writes of the sex differences in the recollection of once familiar facts in history and geography, "It is remarkable how much better the results are for the boys than the girls in the various schools tested. In schools where both sexes attend, the results show a higher percentage of correct answers for the boys."[4] D. H. Eikenberry found that college men are superior to college women in the retention of high-school history.[5]

Going a step further and analyzing the VII B questions, we found that the boys were superior to the girls in the retention of history information relating to war and fighting. For example, Burgoyne's surrender to General Gates illustrates the type of question which the boys revealed the greater ability to retain. Another outstanding difference between the boys and girls was evidenced in a multiple-choice question that required a knowledge of the location of the national capital, Washington, which the boys retained better than the girls. However, a completion question relating to the colonial home life was remembered better by the girls than the boys.

SUMMARY OF CONCLUSIONS

(1) Boys are slightly superior to girls in history retention. The boys maintain this superiority for all the retests after various lapses of time.

(2) Boys show greater retentiveness for knowledge relative to war and fighting or to some geographical place.

(3) Girls are superior to boys in retaining history which treats of domestic conditions and home life.

(4) Lastly, the sex differences in retention of history in the sixth and seventh grades are of significance to educational and psychological procedure, for provision should be made for these differences if the pupils are to derive the greatest benefit from their instruction.

SARAH JANET BASSETT

[4] E. W. Cober, "A Study of High School Pupils with a View of Determining the Extent of Recollection of Once Familiar Facts." University of Pennsylvania Thesis, p. 46, 1912.

[5] D. H. Eikenberry, "Permanence of High School Learning," *Journal of Educational Psychology*, 14: 463–81, November, 1923.

SCHOOL AND SOCIETY

EDITED BY J. McKEEN CATTELL
WITH WHICH IS COMBINED THE

EDUCATIONAL REVIEW

EDITED BY WILLIAM McANDREW

Volume XXIX — Saturday, March 30, 1929 — Number 744

GENERAL PRINCIPLES OF EDUCATIONAL ARTICULATION[1]

By Professor JOHN DEWEY
COLUMBIA UNIVERSITY

There are two ways of approaching the problem of elimination of waste in the educative processes of the schools. One is the administrative. This takes the existing system as a going concern, and inquires into the breaks and overlappings that make for maladjustment and inefficient expenditure of time and energy on the part of both pupil and teacher—useless and therefore harmful mental motions, harmful and not merely useless because they set up bad habits. The other may be called personal, psychological or moral. By these adjectives is meant that the method starts from the side of personal growth of individual needs and capacities, and asks what school organization is best calculated to secure continuity and efficiency of development. It sets out from the side of pupils and asks how the successive stages of the school system should be arranged so that there shall be a minimum of blocks, arrests, sudden switches and gaps, futile repetitions and duplications, as the children and youth pass from one state to another, from kindergarten to elementary, from this to high school, from the latter to college, etc.

This statement of two modes of approach does not imply that there is a necessary opposition between the two. They should be complementary. What is common to both is that each looks at the educational system as a whole and views each part with respect to what it does in making education really a whole, and not merely a juxtaposition of mechanically separated parts. Each avenue of approach is equally concerned to eliminate isolations and render the function of each part effective with respect to the others. There is no more necessary opposition between the two than there is when engineers in tunneling a mountain bore from opposite ends. Before they start work, the tunnel must be considered as a single thing and the work done from either end must be thought out and undertaken with reference to examination of the entire project. But a preliminary intellectual survey of the whole is necessary to make the two modes of approach meet at a center.

When the consideration of the problem is undertaken from either side without regard to the considerations which necessarily exist at the other side, there are dangers and evils that can not be avoided.

[1] Address before the general session, Department of Superintendence, Cleveland, February 26, 1929.

Thus an approach from the exclusively personal side will overlook certain administrative necessities that seem to be inherent in the situation. An important consideration here is pointed out in the general introductory report of the commission. The area of the region drawn upon and the different numbers of children and youth who go to school in the elementary and higher grades must be considered. Younger children as a rule must be in buildings nearer their own homes, and because of their greater number there must be a certain amount of physical segregation from older pupils. Moreover, for the older pupils there must be a greater variety of courses, differentiation of teachers and amount of equipment. These facts demand a large number of pupils in the high school and this in turn demands that they be drawn from a wide area. Hence consideration from the personal development side must take into account administrative necessities.

Consideration of the latter must, however, be checked at every point by taking into account the conditions that make for effective mental and moral growth of individuals as individuals. Undue attention to the administrative side tends toward "rationalization" of the divisions that happen at a given time to be institutionalized. Reasons are found which justify their continued existence as more or less independent units. Then the problem of articulation becomes an external one, that of smoothing transitions from one to another and getting rid of the more obvious sources of friction. This is a gain as far as it goes, but it does not go far enough to touch the basic matter of securing adequate and complete personal growth. In consequence of this external approach, there will be a tendency to assume that mental and moral growth is marked by "epochs" which correspond, at least roughly, to the isolated units of the school system. The fact that interests and capacities change with age is undeniable; that the boy and girl of sixteen differ markedly from those of twelve, and those of the latter age from those of eight and the latter, in turn, from those of five and six is too evident to escape notice. But the underlying problem is whether the changes occur gradually and almost insensibly or by sharply marked off leaps which correspond to the conventional institutional school divisions. This is a question which must be investigated and the answer found by independent study of the facts of development in individuals. The need of this independent inquiry as a check and test is the more acute because the divisions that exist among school units react upon personal development. Hence it is in consequence easy to assume that changes in personal growth are inherent, when in fact they may be the relatively artificial products of the existing school divisions and in so far abnormal and undesirable.

For this reason the study of the best methods of articulation can not be complete without a comparative study of schools in which division into units is minimized; that is, so-called unified schools in which children of different ages, from primary to high school, are found together and wherein there is no administrative break between junior and senior years in the high schools. Only by such a comparative study can the elements, if any, that are artificial and conventional in the schools where units are emphasized be detected. This statement does not contradict what was said earlier about the problems of area of distribution and the need of increased variety of courses and equipment in higher grades. For, in the first place, cities vary greatly in population and there may be median range of size to which the unified school is well adapted. In the second place, the results of comparative inquiry would throw light upon the methods of organization to be adopted in the schools of towns of such a large size that the unified system can not be literally adopted. For there is a question of limits, and educators can work in either of two directions, toward opposite poles—either to that of independent units, or to the maximum possible of relative unification of the assembling of pupils—without carrying either principle to its logical extreme. This consideration seems to me to be fundamental in the whole problem of articulation. Mere convenience of administration should not be permitted to override it.

It is recognized that *adequate* treatment of the fundamental problem here—the mutually complementary character of the administrative and the moral psychological development of individuals—must wait upon command of greater knowledge of the actual process of normal growth than anybody now possesses. Nevertheless, reference to the latter is important, for it indicates, in the first place, the necessity of continued study of personal growth as an inherent factor in the problem of articulation from the administrative side. And in the second place, it serves a warning, a caveat. It cautions us against a too ready assumption that the present institutional division into separate units has necessary inherent value on account of corresponding "epochs" of personal development. It warns us against attaching too great value, decisive value, to matters of administrative habit and inertia. A complete examination of the question of articulation can be attained only when the experiences of classroom teachers in immediate contact with pupils are procured and utilized, as well as the experiences of administrators. This statement does not signify that principals and superintendents in their reports do not take advantage of the experiences gained in actual classroom work, much less that there is any antagonism between the point of view of classroom teachers and of administrators. It is, however, a reminder that specialized experience always creates a one-sided emphasis, in habits of thought as well as of outward action, and always needs to be checked. There is much evidence in the various reports of the extent to which conference and exchange of reports and information already obtain as necessary methods of avoiding unduly sharp breaks in subject-matter and methods and harmful repetitions. What I am pleading for is a more direct obtaining of data on the whole subject of continuity of personal development from classroom teachers, and a *direct* inclusion of such reports in the gathering and interpretation of material along with those of superintendents and supervisors and principals. The findings of experimental and progressive schools must also be included, not as models, but as providing data regarding processes of personal development under different conditions.

Conceding that we have not *adequate* knowledge of the course of mental development in individuals, I propose now to consider the bearing of what is available in this respect upon the general problem of articulation. I begin with a statement which is so general that it can hardly arouse dissent. The ideal is that the achievements at any one period of growth be the tools, the agencies and instrumentalities, of further growth. The statement is not one that refers simply to the transition from one unit to another. It is of constant application. That is, whatever the pupils gain at any period, whether in skill or knowledge, should be promptly funded into something actively employed in gaining new skill and knowledge.[2] A new

[2] This principle is recognized in the almost unanimous denial that there is a period of "imita-

level of intellectual achievement should mark off each successive month and week of school life, and not be thought of as occurring only in the transition from one unit to another. The bearing of this principle upon the specific problems of articulation which the various reports of the commission bring out may be postponed until another basic principle has been stated.

The idea of ripening, maturing, is evidently fundamental in the question of individual growth. Now what needs to be especially borne in mind with reference to maturing is that it is plural, that is, various powers and interests mature at very different rates. Maturing is a continuous process; the mature fruit may appear, as with fruits on a tree, only at some later stage, even if we assume, which it is probably wrong to do, that there is any such completely matured fruit in the case of a human being as in a plant. But the normal maturing as a process goes on all the time; if it does not there is something the matter with conditions. Arrest of growth and incapacities to cope with subject-matter and inabilities to respond to methods employed at a later period are all of them always signs of something wrong. They need to be studied as symptoms and be diagnosed with a view to constructive remedies.

Since maturing is a continuous process and also a plural one, it is not a uniform four-abreast thing. One has only to observe a baby to note how one ability ripens before another, the ability to fixate objects with the eye, to grasp, to sit up, to creep, to walk, to talk, etc., and how each operation as it matures is utilized as a factor in bringing about some maturing of another ability and adaptation. No parent ever makes the mistake of overlooking this plural nature of maturing. When we come to schooling, however, I wonder if there is not too much of a tendency to assume an equal, uniform, four-abreast maturing, and if that does not underlie the conception of "epochs" of growth which correspond to various units of the school system. If the assumption is not made in a positive form, it is made in a negative way, that is, by overlooking the specific needs and capacities that are ripening, or that may ripen, during each year and month of school life. It is this neglect which is responsible for the idea that each stage is merely preparation for some later stage, particularly that the aim of the early years of the elementary school is chiefly the purpose of gaining social tools to be independently employed and enjoyed later on.

I am always surprised and disturbed when I find persons who insist that the high school must not be dominated by the idea of college preparation ready to assume as a matter of course that the first two or three primary years must have as their main purpose the securing of "social tools" for later use, instead of being devoted to gaining those experiences which are appropriate to the powers that are ripening at the time. I must express my profound dissent from the position taken in the general introduction that sets up a dualism between the actual experience of children in the early years and the requirements imposed and dictated by the needs of later school years.

At this point, the two principles laid down cease to be innocuous generalities. The way to get possession and command of a tool for later use is by having the experiences proper to the immediate time—experiences which awaken new needs and

tion," or receptivity, and one of application, or active initiation and use, on the part of those reporting in the second chapter of the general report. There is very general agreement that acquiring and applications of what is used as tools must go on hand in hand from the start and be continued all the way through, the difference being at most one of emphasis.

opportunities and which, just because they are achievements, matured developments, form the natural agencies or tools for later activities. Any theory which sets out by denying that this is possible so misstates the problem of articulation that its "solution" is bound to be defective. Unless powers as they ripen are put to immediate use in acquiring new knowledge and skill, tools are not shaped for later use. The real problem is not one of early maturing for a fruitage to come in a later unit. It is, from the side of earlier years, the problem of discovering those particular needs, interests and capacities which are ripening, not attempting a premature introduction and forcing of others; and then of finding that use and application of them which passes insensibly into the ripening of other more complex tendencies. From the side of later years, it is the same problem, with the added factor of adjusting subject-matter and methods so that the powers already relatively ripened shall be used in developing new powers that are showing themselves. Only in this way can the maximum of continuous growth be secured and an internal rather than mechanical articulation be secured.

The point and force of the two principles laid down is found in their concrete application. I propose, accordingly, to consider some phases of isolation and waste, of non-articulation, in their light.

In the first place, they suggest that reasonable integration within the school can not be secured by limiting the problem to what goes on in the school. The fundamental problem of articulation takes us outside the school to articulation of its activities with the out-of-school experience of the pupils. It is for this reason, of course, that the problem of curriculum is so fundamental; to articulate successive phases of subject-matter with one another there must be an articulation of the curriculum with the broadening range of experiences had at home, in the neighborhood and community. This principle applies at the beginning and all the way through. I remember hearing an intelligent parent complain that kindergarten teachers seemed to assume that children came to them blanks, and treated them as if everything had to begin afresh, thereby boring children with things they could already do and were familiar with, and failing to utilize the capital they had already acquired. This complaint was made over thirty years ago; doubtless cause for it no longer exists. But it is typical of what is meant by the present point. Except for highly specialized matters, the ripening of powers does not go on exclusively nor mainly in school. This fact gives great significance to matters contained in the various reports which at first sight are remote from the question of school articulation; matters of health, nutrition, regularity of attendance, home life, reading and occupations out of school, economic status of parents and children, as well as the general changing demands of a rapidly changing civilization. But it extends to the whole matter of utilizing in school the experiences gained in school.

More specific points are involved in the application of the two principles. One of these is the principle of alternate concentration and remission of work in special lines. While great improvements have taken place, there is still an undue tendency to a uniformed four-abreast treatment of the subjects that make up the school program. Certain studies tend to appear in every month and in every year of a school program. There is need for flexible experimentation in periods of intensive concentration upon such things as reading and number work in the elementary grades, followed by periods of relaxation in which achievements gained are capitalized in concentration upon other studies. The same principle applies to history, geography, nature study and science. Each might be made for a time the relative center with subordination of other factors. The effect would be to disclose better than does the uniform method special aptitudes and weaknesses, and would, I think, greatly minimize the breaks that now come with change of pupils to a new year and new unit.

Other difficulties in the present situation arise, I believe, from the isolation that comes from the confining of teachers to single years. The pupils are the only ones who come into direct contact with the whole process. Artificial breaks, sudden introduction of new demands and new methods of discipline, teaching of new kinds of subjects, duplications and need of review of subjects already supposedly mastered are the result. They are in large measure due, I think, to the isolation of the teacher resulting from too exclusive confinement to a single year. Articulation is secured only as at each stage of the school system, pupils' activities are directed in reference to a continuing wholeness of growth. One year is too short a span in which to survey the process of growth. Much has been done, as appears from the reports in exchange of records and data, and in joint committees to form the curriculum; unified supervision helps. But these things do not cover the whole situation. There are administrative difficulties attending transfers of teachers from one grade to another, or in having a teacher give instruction during the same year in more than one grade. But I do not believe that, without a greater use of these methods, teachers can get that real appreciation of continuity of school movement which will enable them to secure articulation from within.

One aspect of this matter involved the question of having younger children in contact with more than one teacher. I recognize the objections that are so clearly pointed out in the section of chapter II of the report dealing with departmentalization in the elementary grades. But these objections have to be offset not only against the point already made regarding the need of intimate acquaintance on the part of the teacher with children at different stages of development, but against the evils of the conditioning of a child to the habits and methods of a single person, and against the fact, frequently noted, of the friction that arises when the pupils enter a unit in which departmental teaching does exist. It does not follow, because departmental teaching can easily be overdone in the early grades, that children may not profitably get used to more than one teacher even in the first grade. It is a concrete question of proportioning. Nor does it follow that in high schools teaching should be rigidly departmentalized. We need a little more "give" at both ends. Still less does it follow that departmentalized teaching in high schools should be confined to a teacher having many sections of algebra or geometry or physiography in only one year of the school. Genuine correlation or integration and genuine continuity of articulation may depend upon a teacher having more than one topic and in teaching a subject through more than one year. As Ella Flagg Young used to remind teachers many years ago, what often passes for departmentalization is in reality only a subdivision of labor such as obtains in a factory where each worker is confined to making a part of a shoe, which part is then passed on to the next worker.

A point frequently mentioned in the reports is connected with the last two. Attention is called to the difficulties arising from the fact that teachers in training often specialize on some one phase or unit, to the neglect of knowledge of the system as a whole. It would seem to follow that all teachers in training should have at least one thorough course to familiarize them with the system in its entirety, with special reference to the place, in the whole, of that part of the system for which they are specially preparing. If this were a regular procedure, it is possible that the reluctance of teachers to change from one grade or one unit to another might give way to desire for a broader experience. In connection with the training of teachers there are so many problems relevant to the issue of articulation that it is possible to select only one.

Graduate schools of universities are in a large measure training schools for teachers in colleges and in an increasing degree in high schools. Through instruction given to those in colleges who go out to teach in high schools there is, in any case, a reaction into high-school teaching. These conditions account in large measure for the gaps and maladjustments frequently referred to in articulation of senior high schools with the junior, and in general of high schools with upper elementary grades. I allude, of course, to the distinction often drawn between greater attention to development of pupils on one side and to subject-matter as such on the other. I must content myself with calling attention to the problem; no survey of the causes of bad articulation is complete that does not take into account the influence, direct and indirect, of the training of future teachers in graduate schools of universities. It is a phase of the old question of the isolation of normal schools from colleges with the greater emphasis of one upon method and of the other upon subject-matter. Although the problem is not as acute as it used to be, since there has been reapproachment from both sides, it is still a factor not to be neglected.

Time permits only of these few selected illustrations of some of the meanings contained in the two general principles when they are applied. I conclude by recurring to the original statement of the problem: that of coordinating the administrative approach with the psychological-moral approach through personal development. It makes a great difference how we take up the problem of articulation. If we accept too readily any existing distribution of units as even relatively fixed, I am skeptical of any solutions being found which do more than eliminate some of the more striking cases of external friction. It is a natural trait of the human mind to "rationalize" what exists—that is, to find adventitious reasons that justify what is found. We should, it seems to me, view the problem of articulation as one of *differentiation.* The metaphor of organic growth is helpful if not pressed too literally. The problem of coordinated physiological growth is not one of coordinating bones, muscles, lungs and stomach, etc., together: not until mal-coordinations have been established does the latter problem arise. There is gradual differentiation of different organs and functions, each cooperating with the others.

Analogy fails with educational process of growth because the former takes place so largely intrinsically, requiring from without only provision of normal conditions. In education there is no such inherent internal development; direction by means of provision of suitable environment, both of things and personal associations, is relatively more important. But the problem of such external guidance may still be conceived as one of bringing about differentiation in a consecutive way. The meaning of this general statement can be only briefly illustrated. For this purpose I select once more a portion of the introduction of the commission which in its implications appears to diverge from the principle. I refer to the contrast which is set forth between the earlier years and later with reference to docility of a passive type and personal independence and individualistic initiation in the latter, and the conclusions about legitimate separation of units drawn from the alleged fact. The statements seem to overlook several facts, such as that well known to parents, the fact called "contrary suggestion" in very early years: the fact that development in the school years comes through activities, and also the adoption of the method of socialized activities in the kindergarten. Receptivity and assertive activity are *constant* functions. What differs with different stages of growth is the range of exercise and the fields in which they are exercised. Because a child of six or seven can not assume the same active responsibilities that he can when he is eight or nine does not mean that some field for its exercise is not available at the earlier age nor that it is not an indispensable factor in normal development. The problem is to find the particular ripening activities which are operative. To generalize wholesale from the regions in which the capacity does not exist, and infer from them that the willingness of children to accept what is put over on them "dictates" certain subject-matters at that period is to fail to prepare pupils for greater independence in other fields later, and thus puts a premium upon excessive "individualism" later. The problem is one of constant differentiation of powers of independent action through prior utilization of those which already exist. A normal differentiation will create in pupils a willingness to recognize later on their need of guidance and receptivity in respects in which they are not developed to the point of independence, and thus reduce an abrupt and undesirable "individualism."

The example is taken from a limited field, but it applies throughout. At each stage the pupil, whether in elementary grades, junior high school or college, has a certain region of experience in which he is relatively at home and has certain tendencies which are relatively mature. Attention to these things as the agencies to be connected with in securing new powers of independent and responsible action in wider fields of experience gives the key to a continuous process of differentiation which will place the problem of articulation in its proper light.

I can not conclude this exposition, at once too fragmentary and too general, without acknowledging my great indebtedness to the studies embodied in the report of the commission. Much more important than any personal indebtedness is the evidence afforded that the educators of the country are alive to their responsibility. In our American system of diffused control, in the absence of any central directive body, our sole guarantee of constant improvement is the method of cooperative voluntary inquiry and mutual conference. The report of the commission is a notable contribution to the accomplishment of this task in a problem of fundamental importance in the advancement of education. We all owe them thanks for the alertness and thoroughness with which the task has been performed.

FEDERAL AID TO EDUCATION[1]

By Dr. FRANK W. BALLOU
SUPERINTENDENT OF SCHOOLS, WASHINGTON, D. C.

FEDERAL aid to education may be either professional or financial or both. Federal aid to education is provided by the Departments of Agriculture, Interior and Labor, and by the Federal Board for Vocational Education.

[1] Address given at the Cleveland meeting of the Department of Superintendence, February 25, 1929.

I select for discussion federal aid to education as illustrated by the Bureau of Education of the Department of the Interior, and the kind of federal aid provided by the Federal Board for Vocational Education.

Bureau of Education. The U. S. Bureau of Education serves public education through the studies of education which it makes from year to year in the several states and cities, and through its investigation of numerous educational problems. The results of the work of the bureau are distributed to the nation as professional information. The bureau exercises no administrative or supervisory control over education throughout the nation.

As an example of the work of the U. S. Bureau of Education, attention is called to the provision in the appropriations for the Department of the Interior for 1930, for a study of the organization, administration, finance and work of secondary schools at a total not to exceed $225,000. Of this amount, $50,000 is available for the first year, and it is expected that $100,000 will be available for the second year and $75,000 for the third year of this study.

The total appropriations for the work of the U. S. Bureau of Education, exclusive of education and medical relief of the natives of Alaska and the reindeer industry, have increased from $305,745 in 1920 to $346,960 in 1930.

Federal Board for Vocational Education. While the U. S. Bureau of Education is a bureau in the Department of the Interior, the Federal Board for Vocational Education is an independent establishment created by an act of Congress and independent of the executive departments of the national government.

The Federal Board for Vocational Education expends federal money appropriated by the national government on the basis of fifty-fifty subsidies; that is, a dollar of money from the federal treasury is distributed by the Federal Board for Vocational Education to the states and local communities on the basis of a corresponding dollar having been appropriated by the state for the same purpose.

In contrast with the lack of authority of the Bureau of Education, the Federal Board for Vocational Education sets up standards in accordance with which federal money will be distributed to the states for vocational agriculture, vocational trade and industrial education, trade and industrial part-time continuation school education, vocational home economics education and vocational teacher training.

By means of distribution of federal money in the aid of vocational education, the Federal Board for Vocational Education is setting up standards of vocational education for the states and the subdivisions thereof. For example, of the $25,715,760 expended for vocational education in 1928, only $6,821,451 was federal money. The balance of the total was divided as follows: $7,028,986 was state money and $11,865,321 was local money. In so far, therefore, as the Federal Board for Vocational Education determines the standards of vocational education as a basis for the allowance of federal aid, in just so far is the Federal Board for Vocational Education controlling not only the education provided by the $6,800,000 of federal money, but also the education provided by the much larger sum of nearly $19,000,000 of state and local money. In other words, by means of the distribution of what was supposed to be a fifty-fifty subsidy from the federal government, the board is determining, to some extent at least, the vocational education purchased by an expenditure of nearly $26,000,000.

Attention is further invited to the fact that many states are appropriating for vocational education a sum far in excess of the amount originally contemplated in the establishment of the fifty-fifty subsidy plan. While the establishment of the Federal Board for Vocational Education and the plan for fifty-fifty subsidies in 1928 was for the purpose of encouraging the states and the local communities to develop opportunities for vocational education, the question may be seriously considered whether many of the states are in need of encouragement at this time, or whether they are not looking upon the appropriation from the federal treasury for vocational education primarily as a means of being relieved of what might be considered their proper financial responsibility for their local educational program.

Time does not permit of a discussion of the apparent undesirability of continuing the separation of so-called vocational education from other kinds of education. Neither is this the appropriate occasion for discussing the comparative merits of an independent establishment such as the federal board and an executive department of the government as proper agencies for the administration of federal funds. Another principle involved in the question of federal subsidies is indicated in the following statement of Ex-President Coolidge, which superintendents of the nation would do well to ponder:

> There are always those who are willing to surrender local self-government and turn over their affairs to some national authority in exchange for a payment of money out of the federal treasury. Whenever they find that some abuse in their neighborhood needs correction, instead of applying a remedy themselves they seek to have a tribunal sent on from Washington to discharge their duties for them, regardless of the fact that in accepting such supervision they are bartering away their freedom.

EDUCATIONAL EVENTS

NEW UNIVERSITIES OF INDIA

A BULLETIN of the Bureau of Education states that India has made more important and far-reaching changes in the realm of higher education since 1920 than any other country. The Governor-General of India, some ten years ago, appointed a commission to make a thorough inquiry into the affairs of the University of Calcutta and its affiliated colleges and to recommend any changes of constitution, administration and educational policy which it deemed desirable. The thirteen-volume report rendered in 1919 constitutes a most valuable résumé of the conditions of education throughout all India, and indicates the lines of progress which it must take in the future.

The commission was confronted by two very difficult problems—the medium of instruction, and the education of women. For the former, the general aim is that the educated classes of India shall be bilingual; and for the latter, the development of an enlightened public opinion that will recognize the supreme importance of the rapid development of women's education, and will be ready to spend time, thought and money in bringing it about.

As a result of the report of the commission, several universities were established as follows:

The University of Dacca (Bengal) was founded in 1921 to create a new type of teaching. It was the residential university in India as opposed to the then affiliating type. It was to meet the desire of Mussulmans of eastern Bengal to stimulate educational progress in their community. It was to relieve the congestion at the University of Calcutta. Special attention is given to Islamic studies, but the university is open to all students without distinction of race, sex, creed or class.

The University of Rangoon, founded December, 1920, includes University College and Judson College. The grounds comprise an estate of about 458 acres of fine ground on the outskirts of Rangoon. Both colleges have opened new departments in biology, education, medicine and university extension. Both have instituted courses in forestry, engineering, geography and geology.

The University of Delhi became on May 1, 1922, a teaching and residential institution formed from three constituent colleges formerly affiliated with the University of the Punjab.

Aligahr Muslim University in 1920, the University of Allahabad, in 1922, and the Nagpur University, established in 1923, all became residential teaching institutions.

Agra University was established by Act VII of 1926 empowering it to affiliate colleges in the United Provinces, and to supplement the instruction in affiliated colleges by instituting teaching posts at selected centers. Women who have carried on private study are eligible for degrees and other academic distinctions.

The Andhra University at Bezwada was created by an act of 1926. The university area consists of 12 districts, and the colleges within these districts were previously affiliated with Madras University, but are now affiliated with the new institution. The purposes of the university are, among other things, to promote the development of the study of Telugu, Kanarese, Urdu and Oriya and their use as media of instruction and examination; to maintain colleges and hostels; to erect, equip, and maintain laboratories and libraries, and to provide funds for the maintenance of a publication bureau, an employment bureau, students' unions and university extension boards. Every student must reside in a hostel or under such conditions as may be prescribed.

PARIS CLUB FOR WOMEN STUDENTS

THE "Foyer international des étudiantes" was dedicated recently at ceremonies presided over by M. Cavalier, director of higher instruction. The *Journal* of the Medical Association reports that Madame Whitney-Hoff, who donated the site, was accompanied by Mlle. Watson, director of the club. The building is located at 93, Boulevard St. Michel, diagonally opposite the Parc du Luxembourg. A large hall or entry, decorated with green marble, leads to the assembly room, which is contiguous to the dining-room. The various installations or arrangements of the club are conceived in a manner to assure the maximum of comfort without making the upkeep too expensive. In the subbasement and the basement, both of large dimensions, are installed the heating apparatus, the coal bins, the transformers, the incinerators, the general storerooms, a model kitchen and the hydrotherapeutic equipment. On the main floor, next to the assembly room, is a large cafeteria, in which from 400 to 500 persons may be served. On the mezzanine floor are the administration offices and seven large *salons* for the use of the women students. The upper stories contain 100 rooms, some with two beds, thus assuring a total of 120 beds. There are several bathrooms on each of these floors. In addition, there are the infirmary, the rest room, the library, the terraces where tea is served and a solarium. The club will accommodate a hundred or more boarders, while many other students will be able to belong to the club and profit by the advantages offered them: study halls, recreation and rest rooms and medical care. The representative of the minister inspected carefully all features of the institution, whereupon he congratulated the organizers on the success of their undertaking. Madame Whitney-Hoff thanked the French government for its support of the enterprise, also the many individuals who had lent their aid, and closed her speech with a eulogy of "those persons who devote their whole lives to the service of humanity."

THE INTER-AMERICAN EDUCATIONAL FEDERATION

INVITATIONS have been dispatched by Uel W. Lamkin, president of the National Education Association, to the Ministers of Education of 20 Latin-American countries requesting their participation in an informal conference to be held at Atlanta, Ga., in connection with the sixty-seventh annual convention of the National Education Association. At this meeting it is proposed to organize an Inter-American Federation of Education Associations as a practical and dependable channel for the development of an all-American understanding.

The Washington correspondent of *The Christian Science Monitor* reports that, in advancing their plan, American educational leaders believe that through the cultural interrelation that would result if their ideas were realized, a sound foundation would be laid for a permanent and lasting understanding between the nations of the American continents. By contacts and cooperation between the educators of the American republics, they believe a means can be found to work out practically the good-will policy that President Hoover promulgated when he undertook his Latin-American tour. The movement has been under way for some time and much work in pressing its realization has been accomplished under the direction of Dr. Glen Levin Swiggett, organizer of the Second Pan-American Scientific Congress.

The Atlanta meeting, an informal gathering, will enable personal exchanges between the educational representatives of the various governments and at the same time allow them the opportunity of observing the work of the National Education Association convention. The real organization conference of the federation is planned for 1930, to be held in a Latin-American capital still to be selected.

Invitations have been sent by President Lamkin to Argentina, Bolivia, Brazil, Chile, Colombia, Costa Rica, Cuba, Dominican Republic, Ecuador, Guatemala, Haiti, Honduras, Mexico, Nicaragua, Panama, Paraguay, Peru, Salvador, Uruguay and Venezuela. Cuba has already officially signified its intention of being represented. Before sending the invitations, President Lamkin was assured by representatives of a number of the countries, through Dr. Swiggett, that the various nations would look with favor on holding the preliminary conference in the United States, with the first formal meeting later on in one of the southern countries.

Cooperating with Dr. Swiggett in advancing the conference idea are Moises Saenz, of Mexico, brother of Aaron Saenz, a Mexican cabinet officer; Ramiro Guerra, Cuba; Mario de Breto, Brazil, and Ernesto Nelson, Argentina, all educational leaders in their countries.

COMMUNICABLE DISEASES AMONG CHILDREN

PRACTICAL measures for preventing outbreaks of communicable diseases in schools concern both parents and teachers and affect the welfare of the children. For this reason all concerned should understand these measures and the basis on which they have developed.

Dr. Harold B. Wood reviews in *Hygeia* for April some of the most important modern methods for preventing the spread of diseases among school children.

Teachers and parents must report all cases of contagious disease to the health authorities. Only by rapid work can these outbreaks be suppressed. The health officers must know of them immediately in order that they may know what schools are involved, may hunt up and control the spreaders and determine what measures should be applied to help the community as a whole.

Schools are frequently closed during an epidemic, but health officials have concluded that the usual effect of closing the schools is to disseminate the infection. Better results are obtained by keeping the children under intelligent observation with individual examinations for early symptoms of the disease.

Fumigation is an outworn process, Dr. Wood emphasizes. It was advocated in the days before it was known that contagious diseases are caused by germs. Only objects that have been recently infected can spread disease. Public drinking cups and towels are therefore dangerous. But the destruction of school books and other valuable property that have been handled by children with contagious diseases will not accomplish anything. They should be laid aside till the end of the quarantine period and then returned to the child. To rely on sprinkling a disinfectant on the floor or burning some substance in the schoolroom and neglect examination of the children is dangerous.

It is cheaper and easier to immunize children before disease breaks out. That is their best protection. They can be definitely immunized against smallpox, typhoid and diphtheria and with less satisfaction against measles, scarlet fever and whooping cough. Immunization should be regarded as a preventive, however, and not a means of checking an established outbreak.

Dr. Wood points out that the community that promotes successful annual campaigns to have the children, including those of preschool age, completely protected by immunization against diphtheria and smallpox and also against scarlet fever and typhoid, will be accomplishing an outstanding benefit in safeguarding the lives of its little ones.

GREENWICH HOUSE AND COLUMBIA UNIVERSITY

THE trustees of Columbia University have approved a proposal of the Board of Managers of Greenwich House to be affiliated with the university's social, educational and research work.

The agreement, which leaves the community center independent financially and in management, is the final step in a long informal association between the two. It is said to offer stability to Greenwich House and also provide the university with a practical opportunity for participation in a broad and diverse field of social effort.

The plan involves appointment by the university of four representatives to the Greenwich House board of managers. It provides for the acquisition of the property and funds of the Cooperative Social Settlement Society of the City of New York—the legal name of Greenwich House—if at any time in the future, through movements of the population or changed social conditions, the center should outlive its usefulness in its present form.

Greenwich House conducts a Health Center, including baby and preschool clinics, a Music School at 44 Barrow Street, workshops at 16 Jones Street, where boys are taught by the apprenticeship method the techniques of woodcarving, stonecutting, drawing and modeling; a pottery department, a recreation center for clubs, athletics, plays and dances, and domestic science training for girls.

The incorporators of the society were Felix Adler, R. Fulton Cutting, Eugene A. Philbin, Harry C. Potter, Jacob Riis, Carl Schurz and Mary Kingsbury Simkhovitch. Mrs. Simkhovitch, who is the director of the house and the wife of Professor Vladimir Simkhovitch, of Columbia University, says:

> The house is a general information center for the neighborhood and its personal service is fundamental to all its activities.
>
> The settlement movement began under the aegis of the university, with the purpose of sharing the culture available for one group with the unprivileged. Since that time vast economic changes have taken place. To-day in America we are broadening our conception of education to meet social changes. The growing emphasis on both child-study and adult education makes it especially appropriate to bring together in cooperative efforts educational centers of different types.

THE TROJAN AIR COLLEGE

Lectures on art appreciation, psychology, economics, business law, real estate, journalism, foreign trade, political institutions, chemistry and commercial aviation are being broadcast from the Radio-Correspondence Education Division of the University of Southern California, KEJK, beginning on March 18, when the Trojan Air College officially opened.

Supplementing correspondence courses for which college credit is granted, the University of Southern California has extended its educational service to an indefinite area by inaugurating the most modern method of teaching, by means of radio.

Courses which grant college credit are scheduled for KEJK broadcast as follows:

Monday:
- 4:00 P. M., Semitic and Oriental History
- 4:30 P. M., Secondary Education
- 5:00 P. M., Management of Secondary Schools and Classroom Methods

Tuesday:
- 4:00 P. M., Contemporary Political Institutions of South America
- 4:30 P. M., Journalism—Supervision of High School Publications
- 5:00 P. M., School Organization and Administration

Wednesday:
- 11:00 A. M., Short Story Writing
- 4:00 P. M., Modern European Literature
- 4:30 P. M., Public Education in the United States
- 5:00 P. M., Fundamentals of Economics

Thursday:
- 4:00 P. M., Constitutional History
- 4:30 P. M., Psychology and the Professions
- 5:00 P. M., Growth and Development of the Child
- 9:30 P. M., Business Law

Friday:
- 9:30 P. M., Commercial Aviation

While these lectures are of interest to the general public, reference will be made to correspondence work in the form of mimeographed outlines in the hands of those interested in university credit.

In addition, college lectures not granting college credit began on the 18th instant over KEJK, including foreign trade, business English, and a dramatic review listed as "Broadway Successes and Failures," Friday mornings at 11:00 A. M.

THE JUNIOR HIGH-SCHOOL CONFERENCE AT NEW YORK UNIVERSITY

THE fifth annual junior high-school conference was held at New York University on March 22 and March 23, under the auspices of the school of education of the university according to a report made by Dr. Philip W. L. Cox, professor of secondary education, chairman of the Junior High School Conference Committee for 1929.

At this conference representatives of the State Departments of Education of New York, Connecticut, New Jersey and Pennsylvania, the city and village school organizations of the metropolitan area and of the department of secondary school education of the School of Education of New York University, discussed problems of a practical nature relating to the operation and the improvement of the operation of the junior high school system.

All the sessions of the conference were held in the School of Commerce, Accounts and Finance building at the Washington Square Center of the university.

At the general session at 8 o'clock on March 22, at which Dean John W. Withers, of the School of Education presided, Miss Margaret M. Alltucker, assistant director of the research division of the National Education Association, addressed the delegates on "Articulation Problems of the Junior High School." Joseph K. Van Denburg, of the Board of Examiners of the Board of Education, of the City of New York, spoke on "Some Definite Convictions regarding Articulation."

Benjamin Veit, district superintendent in charge of junior high schools, of the New York City Board of Education, presided at the general session on Saturday morning.

George Wheeler, associate superintendent of schools of Philadelphia, addressed the conference on "The Junior High School as influenced by Other Administrative Units." Professor Philip W. L. Cox, chairman of the Conference and professor of secondary education at New York University, spoke on "A Way Out."

At the Friday evening general session the orchestra of Junior High School No. 61 of the Borough of the Bronx furnished the music. The student orchestra from the Bayonne (N. J.) Junior High School rendered the musical program at the session on Saturday morning.

Round table discussions of the topics presented at both general sessions of the conference followed the formal programs both on Friday evening and on Saturday morning.

THE INSTITUTE OF SOCIAL SCIENCES AT BOWDOIN COLLEGE

To give both student body and the public at large an opportunity to view the arts and natural sciences in their relationship to present-day affairs, Bowdoin College has announced an Institute of Social Sciences to be held from April 29 to May 11.

This is the fourth project of this type that the college has sponsored, and is expected to exceed in scope its forerunners, its list of speakers being drawn from leaders in fields of political science, economics, sociology and history, who will emphasize the place of political and social institutions in present-day society.

The program falls into four groups: Present-day international relations, political, social and economic; internal economic problems, including recent trends in business, labor problems and the problems of the consumer; constitutional and legal questions, particularly social influence upon the American Constitution, and the present status of the civil and commercial law; social problems, including population, crime and civil liberties.

As it stands at present, the list of those who will address the institute include: James T. Shotwell, director of the division of economics and history, Carnegie Endowment for International Peace; T. R. Powell, professor of law, Harvard Law School; H. Parker Willis, editor-in-chief of the *New York Journal of Commerce;* Whiting Williams, author and consultant; Stuart Chase, writer and economist; Clarence C. Little, president of the University of Michigan, resigned; Miss Sarah Wambaugh, recent adviser to the Peruvian government for the Tacna-Arica plebiscite; Roscoe Pound, dean of Harvard Law School; George W. Kirchwey, lawyer and criminologist, and Arthur Garfield Hays, lawyer, active in many cases involving civil liberties.

EDUCATIONAL NOTES AND NEWS

DR. HERMAN G. JAMES, dean of the college of arts and sciences and dean of the graduate college of the University of Nebraska, has been elected president of the University of South Dakota, Vermillion.

DR. CHARLES S. HOWE, for twenty-six years president of the Case School of Applied Science, has resigned, his resignation to take effect in August. He will be succeeded by Dr. William Elgin Wickenden, of New York City, director of investigation for the Society for the Promotion of Engineering Education.

THE installation of Colonel Frank Parker Day, who was recently elected president of Union College, Schenectady, N. Y., will take place on May 4.

DR. HARRY WOODBURN CHASE, president of the University of North Carolina, is reported to have declined an invitation to become head of the Social Science Research Council, which has headquarters in New York City.

DR. L. A. SHERMAN, dean and chairman of the department of English at the University of Nebraska, who is now in his forty-seventh year of active service, has been granted sabbatical leave from the close of the present school year until September 1, 1930, when he will retire. Dr. Sherman is now eighty-one years old. In accepting his resignation, to become effective at the close of his sabbatical leave, the regents moved to create him an emeritus dean and professor of English, effective on September 1, 1930.

PROFESSOR FRED W. TAYLOR, of the economics department of the University of Michigan, has become professor emeritus after a teaching service of fifty years, thirty-seven of which were at the University of Michigan.

PRESIDENT EMERITUS WILLIAM FAIRFIELD WARREN, of Boston University, celebrated his ninety-sixth birthday on March 13.

THE degree of doctor of literature will be conferred by the University of Edinburgh at its spring convocation on Dr. Harold William Thompson, of the New York State College for Teachers.

ACCORDING to press despatches, Dr. Max Meyer, since 1900 professor of experimental psychology, and Dr. Harmon O. DeGraff, have been summarily dismissed from the faculty of the University of Missouri, owing, it is said, to having assisted students in a course in sociology to prepare and distribute among the students a questionnaire on sex problems.

DR. EDWARD L. THORNDIKE and Dr. William A. McCall, professors of education in Teachers College, Columbia University, have leave of absence for the coming academic year. Among visiting professors are Dr. Ellwood P. Cubberley, dean of the school of education of Stanford University; Dr. Henry Suzzallo, formerly president of the University of Washington, and Ernest Horn, professor of education at the University of Iowa and director of the university elementary school.

DR. PERCIVAL R. COLE, of the University of Sydney, Australia, who is lecturing on comparative education, has been appointed Carnegie visiting professor of international relations at the University of Hawaii. Dr. Cole will go from Honolulu to Seattle in June to fill a lecture engagement at the University of Washington and will then return to the summer session at the University of Hawaii, beginning on July 2.

THE University of Chicago has announced the following foreign professors as members of the faculty for the coming summer quarter: P. W. Bryan, lecturer on geography, University College, Leicester, England; Karl Bühler, professor of psychology, University of Vienna; Baker Fairley, professor of German, University College, University of Toronto; George Bagshawe Harrison, lecturer, King's College, University of London (Frederic Ives Carpenter visiting professor of English); Werner Heisenberg, professor of theoretical physics, University of Leipzig; Theodore H. Robinson, professor of Old Testament, University College, Cardiff, Wales; Garnett Gladwin Sedgewick, head of the department of English, University of British Columbia; Charles Edward Spearman, professor of psychology, University of London, and George Struve, professor of astronomy, University of Berlin.

THE following appointments are announced at Tufts College: Professor George S. Miller was advanced to a full professorship of history and government; Professor Kirtley F. Mather, of Harvard University, was appointed exchange professor in geology; Albert H. Imlah was made assistant professor in history; Laurence W. Chidester, assistant in the department of music; Albert E. Irving, graduate teaching fellow of history, replacing R. F. F. Tyner, and Robert L. Nichols, instructor in geology.

FRANCIS T. SPAULDING has been appointed associate professor of education in the graduate school of education of Harvard University. He has been an assistant professor since 1926.

DR. LLOYD M. SHORT, at present associate professor of political science and public law in the University of Missouri, has been made assistant dean of the graduate school and professor of political science and public law. Dr. Frank Fletcher Stephens, at present assistant dean of the faculty of arts and science and professor of American history, has been made dean of underclassmen in the college of arts and science and professor of American history.

PAUL J. WEAVER, who has been professor and director of music at the University of North Carolina since 1919, has been elected professor of music in the college of arts and sciences of Cornell University. He will take charge of instruction in the theory and history of music and organize choral singing.

PROFESSOR CARL N. SCHMALZ and Professor Robert L. Masson, of the school of business administration of the University of Michigan, have resigned to accept similar positions at Harvard University.

PROFESSOR N. A. BENGTSON, of the department of geology and geography of the University of Nebraska, was elected president of the National Council of Geography Teachers at its recent annual meeting.

THEODORE WESLEY KOCH, librarian of Northwestern University, is one of the two Americans who have been selected as sectional heads for the first International Library and Bibliographical Congress, to be held in Rome and Venice in June.

AT the meeting of the executive committee of the Association of American Colleges held in the office of the executive secretary in New York City on March 8, Mr. Archie M. Palmer, assistant director of the Institute of International Education, was elected associate secretary of the association. Mr. Palmer will enter upon his work on August 1, and will be concerned more particularly with the "Research Department," the need for which was set forth by the executive secretary in his annual report at Chattanooga.

DR. JOSEPH MAYER, head of the department of economics and sociology at Tufts College, has been granted leave of absence during the next college year.

DR. ROBERT E. PARK, professor of sociology at the University of Chicago, has leave of absence to attend the Social Science Conference in Batavia, and will spend the balance of the year in the Orient.

SIDNEY I. SNOW, of the Philadelphia *Public Ledger,* will take over spring quarter classes at the University of Washington in news writing, newspaper administration and specialized reporting.

COURSES in Latin-American history, culture and diplomatic relations are to be offered during the summer quarter of the University of Virginia by Victor A. Belaunde, formerly of the University of Lima, Peru, now professor of history in the University of Miami, Florida.

AN administrative board of religious and social work has been named by Columbia University to serve for three years from July 1. Its chairman is Chaplain Raymond C. Knox. Other members are: Dean Frederick J. E. Woodbridge, Dean Herbert E. Hawkes, Dean William F. Russell, Professor Wilhelm A. Braun, Professor William E. Weld and Professor Herbert W. Schneider.

DR. OSCAR M. VOORHEES, of New York, national secretary of the United Chapters of Phi Beta Kappa, presided at the installation of Epsilon of California Chapter of the national honorary scholastic society at the University of

Southern California on March 14. Dr. Henry Suzzallo, of the Carnegie Foundation, was the principal speaker.

THE annual dinner of the Alumni Association of the Harvard Graduate School of Education took place in Cleveland on February 27, in connection with the meeting of the Department of Superintendence. Dean Holmes presented at the dinner the new plan of instruction recently adopted by the faculty of education, emphasizing the requirement of two years of study for the degree of master of education. The following officers were elected for 1929: *President,* Thomas C. McCracken, dean of the college of education, Ohio University, Athens; *first vice-president,* Frank A. Scott, superintendent of schools, Belmont, Mass.; *second vice-president,* Ruth A. Merrill, assistant dean of Radcliffe College. The secretary-treasurer of the association is Henry L. Gerry, Teachers College of the City of Boston.

PROFESSOR T. N. CARVER, David A. Wells professor of political economy and chairman of the department of history, government and economics at Harvard University, will deliver a series of lectures on sociology at the University of Illinois from April 8 to 12.

SHIROSHI NASU, of the University of Tokio, and Corado Gini, of the Royal Statistical Institute, Rome, will be the principal speakers at the sixth summer institute conducted at the University of Chicago under the Norman Wait Harris Foundation. Organized for the purpose of "promoting a better understanding on the part of American citizens of other peoples of the world," the institute has sponsored lectures and round-table discussions on pressing international problems during the first term of the summer quarter at the university for the past five years. This year's institute is announced for June 17–28, with "Population and Migration" as the central theme.

MARK SULLIVAN, the journalist and author, gave the Bromley lectures at Yale University on March 26 and 27 on "Journalism and the Historian." The Bromley lectureship was founded in 1900 in memory of Isaac H. Bromley, B.A., Yale 1853, for many years an editorial writer on the New York *Tribune.*

FRIENDS, colleagues and former pupils of Professor Archibald Cary Coolidge, of Harvard University, teacher, historian, diplomat and former director of the Harvard College Library, have planned to collect $6,500, most of which has already been subscribed, to erect a memorial tablet in his honor. The memorial, in the form of a bas relief of Professor Coolidge, will be erected in the passageway of the Widener Library leading to his former office.

THERE was unveiled on March 12 in the library of the International Labor Office, Geneva, a bronze bust of Robert Owen, the pioneer of international social progress, a gift to the International Labor Office by the people of his native country, Wales. The presentation was made by Mr. David Davies, M.P., at the head of a delegation representing the Welsh League of Nations Union.

WILLIAM CAREY POLAND, professor emeritus in art at Brown University, died on March 19 at the age of eighty-three years.

THE death is announced on March 22 at the age of ninety-two years of Miss Helen L. Mellen, who was librarian at Tufts College for a period of twenty-seven years.

PROFESSOR HERBERT VAUGHAN ABBOTT, for more than twenty years a member of the Smith College faculty, a son of the late Dr. Lyman Abbott, former editor of *The Outlook,* died on March 25 at the age of sixty-four years.

THE death is announced of Dr. Frank Comstock, head of the department of descriptive geometry and drawing and dean of freshmen at the Case School of Applied Science, on March 7 at the age of seventy-four years.

MISS SARA MICHEL, one of those who introduced the Froebel educational system into the United States, and who devoted half a century to kindergarten teaching, died on March 18. For ten years Miss Michel taught in the kindergarten of Dr. Felix Adler's Workingman's School. Then, after seventeen years on the east side with the New York Kindergarten Association, she established her own Froebel kindergarten.

MRS. ANNA BOWMAN BLAKE DODD, widow of Edward William Dodd and an authority on

French history, has bequeathed the residue of her $200,000 estate to the American Academy of Arts and Letters, which also receives many art objects, including a portrait of herself, done in black and white by Sargent. Mrs. Dodd creates two prize funds, one, amounting to $30,000, to be set apart from the residuary estate for annual or biennial prizes for the best books or essays on travel by Americans. The other is a $10,000 trust fund, out of which $1,000 is to be awarded each year to the most efficient and diligent stenographer in the employ of the Farmers Loan and Trust Company for a three months' vacation in Europe.

THE New York State Publishers Association, Post-Standard Building, Syracuse, N. Y., cooperating with the school of journalism of the University of Missouri, has issued an appeal, signed by J. D. Barnum, Frank Gannett and Victor Ridder, asking for support of a school of journalism in connection with Yenching University at Peking, China. The creation of the fund, to which $36,500 has already been contributed, is urged by Vernon Nash and is said to be sponsored by publishers throughout the United States.

MRS. ANNIE KILBURN KILMER, mother of the poet, Joyce Kilmer, who was killed in France, has presented a scholarship fund to be known as the Joyce Kilmer English prize to Rutgers Preparatory School of New Brunswick, N. J. The prize of $500 will be awarded annually to the best writer of English poetry or prose.

ALFRED I. DU PONT, who a few months ago offered to finance the building of a public school in Brandywine Springs, Delaware, to the extent of $100,000, has added $50,000 to the gift so as to have a larger school. This school will replace four smaller ones. Henry J. Krebs, of Newport, Delaware, manufacturer, who recently built a $150,000 school and presented it to the people of that town, has made an additional gift of five acres of land to the school grounds, making in all thirteen acres.

ONE hundred and fifty members of the advisory body of the Schubert Centennial Committee have voted to reorganize as the Council of the Columbia Award for the Advancement of Music. Otto H. Kahn, of New York City, is to be chairman. The award is offered for outstanding service in the cause of music by an individual or group. It is of the value of $5,000 and will be offered for a period of ten years. The scope of the award is international.

THE tuition fee at Barnard College has been raised from three hundred and forty to four hundred dollars. Simultaneously with the decision to raise the tuition fee, the trustees have established additional scholarships to aid students of marked ability coming from families of limited income.

THE first number of *The Journal of Modern History,* a new quarterly intended to cover the range of European history and its expansion from the Renaissance to the close of the World War, has been issued by the University of Chicago Press. Established at the request of the American Historical Association, this journal becomes the fifteenth in the series of learned periodicals being published currently by the university. Articles dealing with intellectual history and the history of the arts and sciences will come within the scope of the publication, as well as the more familiar political, religious, economic and social aspects of history. "Historical revisions," showing how traditional views have been modified by historical research, will be a leading feature. The *Journal* will also publish documents of importance not easily available and will have departments for bibliographical surveys and reviews of historical publications. Dr. Bernadotte E. Schmitt, professor of modern history at the university, is the managing editor, and Louis R. Gottschalk, associate professor of history, is assistant editor. Other members of the board of editors include representatives of Western Reserve University, Columbia, California, Wisconsin, Harvard, Texas, Miami and Cornell.

THE House of Representatives and the Senate passed as a part of the appropriation bill the following provision: For all expenses, including personal services in the District of Columbia and elsewhere, purchase and rental of equipment, purchase of supplies, traveling expenses, printing and all other incidental expenses not included in the foregoing, to enable the Secretary of the Interior, through the Bureau of Education, at a total cost of not to exceed $225,000, to make a study of the organization, administration, financing and work of secondary schools and of their articulation with elementary and higher education, $50,000: *Provided,* That specialists and experts for temporary service in this investigation may be employed at rates to be fixed by the Secretary of the Interior to correspond to those established by the Classification Act of 1923, as amended, and without reference to the Civil Service Act of January 16, 1883. The plan of expenditure which is contemplated in this action is the use of $50,000 during the year 1929–30, $100,000 during the year 1930–31, and $75,000 during the year 1931–32. The initiative in recommending this appropriation was taken by the North Central Association of Colleges and Secondary Schools. The other regional accrediting associations, the American Council on Education and the National Education Association at its Minneapolis meeting indorsed the request.

DISCUSSION

FURTHER COMMENT ON FOREIGN LANGUAGE VALUES

SOME time ago, apropos of an article of mine in SCHOOL AND SOCIETY, Professor E. A. Kirkpatrick presented some extremely interesting views on foreign language instruction, written from the standpoint of the psychologist, which deserve the careful attention of language teachers.[1]

Summarized briefly, the issues raised by Professor Kirkpatrick are: (1) the extent to which the ten objectives listed by me can be realized; (2) the extent to which mastery in any one phase of foreign language learning can be imparted in the schools; (3) the amount of "carry over" from one language process to other language processes; (4) the validity of our present arrangement of language courses.

My purpose in mentioning the first ten objectives formulated by the Committee on Modern Foreign Language Study was, as Professor Kirkpatrick will recollect, simply to emphasize the fact that the ability to read the foreign language with ease and enjoyment is still the major aim of modern language teaching despite impressions to the contrary created by some of the educational experts.

To what extent "those who study languages get any or all of the ten possible benefits from language study" it is probably impossible to estimate with mathematical precision in all cases. The non-factual objectives, such as appreciation of foreign literature and understanding of the ideals of foreign nations, do not lend themselves readily to statistical accounting. In the case of the ability to read and to write several statistical appraisals have been made. My own belief, based on years of observation, is that all students profit appreciably in all the ten lines indicated, the exact degree of profit depending on the personal, environmental and instructional factors that are responsible for differences of progress in every subject.

That language teachers "are attempting the impractical when they try to give all the ten possible benefits at once in a two or three year course," most language teachers will, I imagine, deny. They do not consider it impractical to try to inculcate ideas about foreign civilizations, literature and art, to dwell on habits of correct articulation, to encourage improvement in English, and the like. How well or how badly they fare is not the only criterion by which their efforts are to be judged. The effort itself is as important as the results so long as language instruction maintains a respectable cultural status and differs from the teaching of the mechanics of typewriting, shorthand or automobile driving.

Whether or not mastery in any line of foreign language work can be achieved in the schools is hardly a fair question to raise. The only kind of mastery that can be obtained in the schools in any subject consisting of something more than mechanical or manual operations is a partial and relative mastery. That sort of mastery is gained as effectively in the foreign languages

[1] In "Further Revaluation of Language Studies Needed," SCHOOL AND SOCIETY, June 26, 1926. The article unfortunately escaped my attention until recently.

as the mastery of mathematics, history, economics, etc., given in the same length of time and under similar classroom conditions. When school administrators and educational experts discriminate against the foreign languages on the ground that mastery is unattainable in the time to which they themselves are chiefly instrumental in limiting the language course, they are yielding to other dictates than those of the reason.

Though I can not presume to controvert the psychological fact regarding the "carry over" presented by the distinguished psychologist whose discussion I am commenting upon, I feel justified, nevertheless, as an experienced language teacher, in offering some of my views.

Professor Kirkpatrick appears to feel that grammar is of but negligible value in the art of using any language and has, therefore, little or no right to a place in the practical teaching of a language. Some of my colleagues take the same stand, moved perhaps by the desire to overcome the objections of educational experts to language teaching or by the anxiety to live up to our much-advertised national ideal of efficiency.

The truth is that grammar, as we actually handle it in our elementary language courses, is not taught for its own sake or with the object of developing grammarians, but as a short-cut, a norm and a necessary part of the equipment of any well-educated person. As a short-cut, the grammar that we teach performs much the same function as the slide-rule; as a norm, it affords the sureness of operation that comes from authorized knowledge; and in both instances it has tangible "carry over" value. Any temporary interference with spontaneity is more than compensated by the assurance that results from having a guaranteed standard upon which to rely, and the temporary interference disappears with adequate use. As an example of the value of the grammar taught in foreign language classes for general educational purposes, I may say that many English teachers look upon it as their strongest ally in the curriculum.

If psychological testing has proved absolutely that "the net amount of real 'carry over' of habit proper from one process to the other is close to zero," then in language work we must look for some other factor that carries over something positive from one process to another and from one language to another. To my mind, that "something" exists, and those who are persuaded that knowing one modern language facilitates the knowing of another are not far wrong. Possibly that "something" is knowledge in the form of a nucleus of usable facts. Possibly it is the power that comes from increased linguistic consciousness. Dr. Arnold Gesell recently reported that experiments with infant twin girls have convinced him that learning depends not only upon practice but also upon maturity of the nervous system. A parallel inference may be drawn in language work if we substitute increased linguistic consciousness for nervous maturity.

As a language teacher who has had abundant opportunities for observation, I am strongly of the belief that translation from English into the foreign language and a sure command of important grammatical principles markedly improve oral facility, though I can not as yet express the same opinion about the effect of translation from the foreign language into English upon oral fluency. Similarly, though I am doubtful about the "carry over" from mathematics or chemistry to the foreign languages, I believe that a knowledge of one foreign language helps appreciably in the knowledge and handling of another.

To me it seems entirely reasonable to assume that the habit of making the proper grammatical agreements, of watching the personal endings of verbs, of paying attention to stress and written accentuation, of observing the order of words in sentences, and of bearing in mind other like factors common to all the modern foreign languages usually studied in our schools carries over from one language to another. In addition, the vocabulary and the fundamental phonetic values carry over to a considerable extent, especially in the Romance languages. If, then, I am not entirely at fault, the acquisition of any foreign language has a broader significance than the acquisition of that particular language. In other words, there is point to the contention that study of one modern language promotes facility in other modern languages.

With Professor Kirkpatrick's suggestion as to the need of some kind of reorganization of our foreign language work I am in hearty sympathy. My personal preference is for a bipartite arrangement allowing students, if they so wish, to pursue either practical work or literary work exclusively. But I should deplore, both as unnecessary and as an educational mistake, the elimination of cultural instruction from either of these two phases.

J. Warshaw
University of Missouri

TRAINING ON COLLEGE NEWSPAPERS

Training on college newspapers is given to many men who later enter active newspaper work. Every year sees the improvement of existing campus newspapers as well as the launching of new publications.

The improvement in the student newspaper has been marked even though gradual over the past fifteen or twenty years. Standards of news writing, editing and editorial writing have improved, often with the active help and encouragement of faculty members teaching English or journalism. In several schools of journalism, the department has a daily newspaper for the use of the students as a laboratory. Actual experience under conditions nearly like those to be found on the usual daily is given the students working on such campus papers.

Improvements have not been limited to the writing and editing departments, but the papers have grown in size and financial prosperity with increased business efficiency and the realization on the part of merchants that the successful college press is an important advertising medium. The publication of college newspapers has grown to be an enormous business—to an extent that few persons realize. When it is known that there are more than four hundred papers published at least once a week, with an average of more than twenty-five students per paper taking an active part in preparing the material, one begins to realize that this extra-curricular activity has grown into an enormous business.

To-day there are thirty-two college daily papers in the country, about half of which use the telegraph service of some nationally known news-gathering organization. In physical appearance these papers are very much like regular dailies. They range in size from four to thirty-two pages, carrying the usual material of interest to their readers. In some cases these papers, being the only paper in the small town where the college is located, serve the townspeople with the news of the world. All of the work of local news-gathering, copy-reading, editing, editorial writing is done by students.

About thirty-five other college papers are published either twice or three times a week. In every case these papers limit their field to the activities of the campus. As varied an experience is given staff members on these papers as is given to those working on dailies. More than three hundred colleges have weekly newspapers which give training to students in the work of news-writing and editing. Nearly a hundred more small colleges have newspapers appearing less often than once a week, but more often than monthly. This does not take into account the many other student publications, such as the year-book, comic, literary, departmental and pictorial magazines that give some experience in publication matters.

As was to be expected, the college paper has taken the daily paper as its model and has written its news stories, its headlines, its editorials, and has adapted its make-up to that of the regular dailies. Many of the same problems that newspaper executives have to face are also faced by the student editors. Even the problem of the press-agent occurs, for with the many organizations on the campus, "hand-outs" have to be prepared and stunts resorted to in order to attract attention. In short, the campus forms a miniature world for the youthful news-getters and editors.

With the increase in size and the improvement in quality of the newspapers, the exacting of more time from the students holding responsible positions resulted. This took time from studies or from outside activities. With the increased prosperity of the papers many were able to pay some executive members of the staff a certain percentage of the profits each year. In other cases, the men petitioned the faculty for academic credit for work on the paper and in a few instances were granted this request. To a certain extent, the granting of academic credit and surely the giving of financial compensation takes away the amateur qualities of working on the student publication, the idea under which athletics are presumably conducted.

In an endeavor to find out to what extent staff members receive compensation, a survey was made and answers received from 230 papers. Academic credit for work on the staff is the exception rather than the rule, according to the reports received, for only six dailies, eight semi-weeklies and forty-eight weeklies reported that staff members received classroom credit. In some places, notably schools of journalism, students are required to do a certain amount of laboratory work on the paper.

When it comes to the question of receiving actual money for work on the staff, either business or editorial, it appears to be the rule rather than the exception that certain members, at least the editor-in-chief and business manager, receive a certain definite sum or percentage of the profits. Twenty-four of the twenty-five dailies that reported give financial compensation to the editor-in-chief and business manager, while seven divide the profits among members of the entire board. Some compensation is given to staff members of twenty-four out of twenty-seven semi-weeklies that reported. Compensation is received by staff members of 106 weekly papers. In some of these cases the business manager is the only one to receive compensation.

The amount of money that the staff members receive varies to a remarkable degree. In 40 per cent. of the cases the amounts given are based on the percentage of the profits that the paper has made during the school year. In the other papers where definite sums are given, the amounts vary from $100 to $800 a year for heads of staffs of papers publishing daily. The salaries of heads of semi-weeklies range between $25 and $300 a year. On the average, the amount paid is $100 a year for each issue a week. For example, a majority of heads of weeklies get $100 a year; many heads of publications appearing twice a week receive $200 a year, and several heads of dailies publishing five times a week receive $500 a year.

Conditions have changed and no longer does experience warrant the following story, which was often told as typical of the attitude of editors.

"The candidate who was applying for a position as a reporter cited as experience the fact that he had been editor of his college paper. The city editor promptly retorted that he wouldn't hold that against him." To-day, editors are willing to recognize the fact that some experience in newspaper work is obtained as staff member of the college paper.

ROBERT H. MCNEIL
VIRGINIA POLYTECHNIC INSTITUTE

SPECIAL CORRESPONDENCE

COOPERATION BETWEEN THE HIGH SCHOOLS OF MICHIGAN AND THE UNIVERSITY OF MICHIGAN

THE University of Michigan has the distinction of being the first higher institution in America to establish the certificate plan of admission. This plan was introduced in 1871 by Acting President Henry S. Frieze.

Since that date the university has actively sought to maintain a friendly, sympathetic and helpful relationship with the high schools. The principals of the high schools have fully reciprocated. A free interchange of ideas between the secondary school principals and the university authorities brings the problems of each group before all for discussion and solution.

The most frequently suggested method of improving the relations between high schools and colleges is cooperation.

The schoolmen of Michigan are entirely in harmony with the policies and practices of the University of Michigan. The university authorities understand the problems of the high schools but do not interfere with their management, which is far better than interference without understanding. One of the important agencies for bringing about this close cooperation is the Michigan Schoolmasters' Club. This organization was first established on Saturday afternoon, February 27, 1886, when a committee of teachers, of which Professor John Dewey, now of Columbia University, was a member, presented Articles of Association and stated that the aim of the association was to be as follows:

We unite in forming the Michigan Schoolmasters' Club and aim to secure an opportunity to discuss matters that pertain to our common work with particular reference to high-school and collegiate training. In doing this we do not wish to antagonize any existing organization, but simply to obtain a larger opportunity to discuss such topics as are necessarily and properly left untouched by associations that now exist.

Through the Schoolmasters' Club the relations existing between the university, the colleges and the secondary schools have been wholesome and beneficial to all concerned.

The office of president is filled in rotation from the university, the small colleges, the normal schools, the superintendents, the principals and the classroom teachers. This, of course, provides and insures varied contacts and points of view at successive annual meetings.

One of the latest methods adopted to bring about a better mutual understanding is the plan of inviting high-school principals and teachers to visit the university classes to learn by first-hand impressions the problems which confront the freshmen when they come to the university and to consider ways and means for effecting a better correlation between high-school and university work.

The following is an excerpt from the letter of President Clarence Cook Little, dated April 8, 1927, addressed to the principals of the high schools of Michigan and to the members of the high-school faculties.

In the last week of April many of you, we cordially hope, will attend the meetings of the Michigan Schoolmasters' Club and other educational organizations in Ann Arbor. I write to extend a welcome to all who may attend and in particular to urge you, on that occasion, to visit university classes, especially those in freshman subjects.

This suggestion comes in the first instance from the executive committee of the Michigan Schoolmasters' Club, and appeals to me very strongly, as I hope it will likewise to you. The university is at this time giving its most serious attention to bringing about a more intelligent selection of its students and helping them over the difficulties of the critical transition from high school to college. In what we have thus far done we have received, and acknowledge with hearty gratitude, extremely valuable cooperation from the high-school principals and teachers of the state. This cooperation we are eager to retain. The problem is after all a mutual one; our students come from your classes. We believe, therefore, that such contacts as those suggested, between the university instructors and the high-school teachers, in university classrooms, will be of interest and value to both of us. It will permit you to see at first hand what situations your former students are called upon to face in college; and we hope that we may receive from you any observations, impressions or advice bearing upon the closer articulation of the work of the secondary schools and the freshman year in the university.

In response to this invitation in April, 1927, about one hundred and twenty-five principals and teachers visited freshman classes in the university and later attended a conference with university officials to discuss problems of mutual interest.

In April, 1928, President Little wrote to the high schools again extending the invitation to visit university classes. The following is taken from his letter of April 2, 1928:

The officers and faculty of the University of Michigan recall pleasantly the events of a year ago, when for the first time an invitation was extended to the high-school principals and teachers, in attendance upon the meetings of the Michigan Schoolmasters' Club, to visit university classes, especially in freshman subjects. This letter is written as a cordial renewal of the invitation for 1928.

We all felt that the institution of such a visiting day or visiting days last year was a real help, both to the schoolmen and the university teachers. It allowed the former to become better acquainted with the conditions which their own pupils, in whom they have naturally a deep interest, face when they come to the university, and it permitted the university teachers to meet and talk with those who are yearly sending the bulk of the students in their classes to them. At a time when the university is heartily desirous of bringing about more perfect adjustment for every individual student who enters, an ambition in which we are well aware the schoolmen of the state likewise share, this arrangement is particularly desirable. We shall especially appreciate it if we may receive any suggestions whatever which occur to you after having made your visit to the university.

The number responding to this invitation was even greater than the preceding year, and the subsequent conference with university teachers was profitable to a greater extent perhaps than the year before.

At this conference there was a general discussion of the problems involved (a) from the point of view of the university instructor and (b) from the point of view of the high-school instructor. The following topics were also discussed:

(1) Evidence of lack of articulation between work in the high school and corresponding work in the university.
(2) What additional information should the university furnish to assist the high school in directing students in their preparation for college?
(3) Advisability of revision of freshman work to include general orientation courses.
(4) Freshman week at the University of Michigan.
(5) University of Michigan admission blank.

The experiences of these two years have definitely proven the value of such conferences, which undoubtedly will be continued from year to year concurrent with the annual meetings of the Michigan Schoolmasters' Club.

In addition to class visitation by high-school principals and teachers with subsequent conferences and discussions, another plan has been started intended to bring about a closer relationship between the high schools and the university.

In this year's freshman class we have a total of 1,291 students entering from 583 high schools in forty-one states and the District of Columbia—a really cosmopolitan university with freshmen from Maine to California. The closer contacts we can have with the students and with the principals the better able the university will be properly to perform its share of the work in the educational process.

Suggestions received from Mr. Frank Cody, superintendent of schools of Detroit, and Professor J. B. Edmonson, dean of the university, led to the adoption of a plan whereby high-school principals are invited to Ann Arbor about the middle of the first semester each year to confer with freshmen who have recently been graduated from their high schools. It is hoped that this plan will soon be developed to include the principals of all the high schools from which students are admitted.

In 1927 the university invited the principals of Detroit, Highland Park and Hamtramck to come to Ann Arbor on December 8, for principal-student conferences. All the freshmen concerned received special letters of invitation to call at the registrar's office for the conferences. Twenty-six principals and teachers came to Ann Arbor and conferred with over one hundred and fifty freshmen.

Mid-semester reports were placed in the hands of the principals and also a special interview memorandum blank. These conferences were intended to bring about a closer cooperation between the high-school principals and the university and to facilitate the process of admission to the university with advantages to the student, the high school and the university.

The initial effort in 1927 was so successful that the invitation list was expanded in 1928 to include thirty-two high schools and over four hundred students. The thirty-two high schools sent forty-five principals and teachers for the interviews on Thursday, December 6, 1928. The students responded most admirably to the invitations issued by the university to confer with their former high-school teachers. This plan provided a medium of contact between the high-school alumni and their former principals.

In addition to this contact it also provided a method for high-school principals to acquire first-hand information relative to the problems of the university students and to understand from personal observation how to properly advise prospective university students while they are completing their preparatory courses in the high school.

Such conferences also bring to light points on which the university is at fault so that mistakes caused by misunderstanding may be rectified.

These class visitations and conferences of freshmen with their principals will serve to furnish bases to guide pupils in the selection of proper courses in the high school as prerequisites for college courses.

Such visits will also suggest to the high-school teachers the aims, content and methods best adapted to serve the purposes of college courses, and to indicate to the university professors the type and extent of preparation for college courses reasonably to be expected in the high-school work.

In general the plan enables the high-school teachers to detect faults in their own educational system and to become more familiar with university methods; to permit the student to discuss his own problems and seek advice and to allow university educators to become more familiar with preparatory-school methods.

A better understanding of all the problems by each group of educators will aid in the satisfactory solution of mutual problems.

Was it worth while? Let the principals answer. One said: "It did me good to see my old students, and I feel, too, that they were glad to know that the high school and the university were cooperating for their best interests."

Another principal said: "The visit was a really profitable one to me. I was glad to find that the boys who thought certain teachers too severe in the high school had now changed their opinion completely. I found other reactions that I am sure will be of value to us."

Another remarked: "The visit was very profitable to me because I learned where we can help our people, who are now in school and who expect to go to college, in some respects."

IRA M. SMITH

UNIVERSITY OF MICHIGAN

NATIONAL COUNCIL OF ADMINISTRATIVE WOMEN IN EDUCATION

THE National Council of Administrative Women in Education has completed a two-year program under the leadership of Miss Caroline S. Woodruff, Castleton, Vermont, *president; vice-president,* Mrs. Susan M. Dorsey, Los Angeles; *secretary,* Miss Edna E. Hood, Kenosha, Wisconsin; *treasurer,* Miss Evelyn Butler, Indianapolis, Indiana; *auditor,* Miss Isabel Eckles, Santa Fe, New Mexico, and the following five directors: Miss Minnie J. Nielson, Valley City, North Dakota; Miss Florence M. Hale, Augusta, Maine; Miss Lida Lee Tall, Towson, Maryland; Miss Eva G. Pinkston, Dallas, Texas, and Miss Lillian Weyl, Kansas City, Missouri.

The activities of the council for these two years have centered around achievement and recognition of achievement among women in administrative positions.

Several concrete things have been accomplished and several definite procedures have been established, among which are:

(1) The Ella Flagg Young Award for outstanding achievement in public school service. This takes the form of a gold medal designed and made at Tiffany's in New York City. The awarding of the first medal was a conspicuous feature of the banquet program at the Hotel Statler on the evening of Monday, February 25, when the presentation was made by Miss Mary McSkimmon, chairman of the Committee on Award for Outstanding Achievement. It was awarded to Mrs. Susan M. Dorsey for her conspicuous service as superintendent of the Los Angeles public schools. It was received by Mrs. Helen Watson Pierce, who came on from Los Angeles for this special purpose in place of Mrs. Dorsey, who was unable to be present. This medal will be awarded each year to one chosen by the committee made up of Miss Mary McSkimmon, Brookline, Massachusetts, *chairman;* Dr. Charl O. Williams, Washington, D. C.; Miss Florence M. Hale, Augusta, Maine; Mrs. Josephine Corliss Preston, Olympia, Washington; Miss E. Ruth Pyrtle, Lincoln, Nebraska, and Miss Margaret Maguire, Philadelphia, Pennsylvania.

(2) A life membership to the National Education Association will be awarded each year to one chosen for conspicuous service in a particular field of public education—the first one to be awarded at Atlanta in July and thereafter it too becomes an annual event. The committee on award consists of: Mrs. Susan M. Dorsey, Los Angeles, California; Miss Cornelia Adair, Richmond, Virginia, and Miss Olive M. Jones, New York City.

(3) Professor Katherine Lee Bates was elected the first honorary life member of this organization in recognition of her song, "America, the Beautiful," that has had wide use in public schools.

The council is arranging for a dinner at Geneva to be given to the visiting women delegates representing all the countries in attendance upon the great Conference of World Federation of Education Associations in August of this year.

Miss Caroline S. Woodruff will be succeeded as president by Miss Olive M. Jones, of New York University; Miss Evelyn Butler, treasurer, by Miss Jennie Scolley, assistant superintendent of schools, Holyoke, Massachusetts, and Miss Eva Pinkston and Miss Lillian Weyl, directors, by Miss Evelyn Butler, dean of women, Butler College, Indianapolis, Indiana, and Miss Agnes Samuelson, state commissioner of education, Des Moines, Iowa. E. E. H.

QUOTATIONS

HUNTER COLLEGE

A CONTRIBUTOR to the March *Atlantic Monthly* complains that men do not have equal opportunities with women and adds: "It is improbable that women will ever give them to us." It might be said in answer that such a fate would be only just retribution to men for withholding opportunities from women during so large a part of the history of the human race. Even in America, higher educational advantages were a long time coming to women. Women's colleges, supported by private endowments, are not even yet having their fair share by the side of men's colleges of the same type. On the other hand, where, as in the western and southern state universities, women are on the same educational footing as men, they are usually so much more eager for a higher education than men, except in professional or "practical" subjects, that they seem to be putting men at a disadvantage. A prominent eastern university president, returning from a trip across the continent a few years ago, predicted that in a few years women would come to be the sole exponents of culture in America.

Even New York, which has surpassed all other cities of the world in providing higher education for its young men, was slow in offering anything beyond elementary training to young women. When, a quarter of a century after the founding of the Free Academy, the institution which is now called Hunter College, in honor of its founder, was established, it was solely for the training of teachers. Nearly another quarter of a century passed before it came into the status of a college of liberal arts and science. Under President George S. Davis, who has just retired after twenty years of efficient administration, it came to take its place among the foremost colleges for women. To-day, as President Kieran formally assumes the duties of the office which he has for some months filled as acting president, it is with the prospect that Hunter College, as an institution both for liberal culture and for training of teachers for the city's schools, will have buildings and equipment comparable with those for men.

With President Robinson at the College of the City of New York and President Kieran at Hunter College, the city has now at the head of its two higher educational institutions men whose training has been had largely under its own public tuition, from the elementary school to the baccalaureate degree. Both colleges will soon be brought under the control of one central higher educational board. This gives double assurance that equal opportunities will be offered to men and women. The people of this city have reason to be proud of what is being done out of their own public treasury for the higher education of their youth. President Kieran, who has been for twenty-five years professor of education in Hunter College and for several years its dean, may be relied upon to carry forward its sound policies in the direction in which they have been moving.—*The New York Times*.

EDUCATIONAL RESEARCH AND STATISTICS

RECIPIENTS OF MOTHERS' PENSIONS

THE stigma of charity is declining in at least one field. Pity for the helpless mother left with young children prompted search for a method that would not carry the taint of charity. As a solution of this problem the mothers' pensions, or, as better called, mothers' compensation, were evolved. The plan was first operated in Kansas City, Missouri, in 1911. By 1925, forty-two of the forty-eight states had adopted some form of mothers' pensions. This movement came as a result of the White House conference on the care of dependent children which was held in Washington, D. C., in January, 1909. The following resolutions adopted by this conference set forth clearly the basis of this movement:

> Home life is the highest and finest product of civilization. It is the great molding force of mind and character. Children should not be deprived of it, except for urgent and compelling reasons. Children of parents of worthy character suffering from temporary misfortune and children of efficient and deserving mothers who are without the support of the normal breadwinner, should as a rule be kept with the parents, such aid being given as may be necessary to maintain suitable homes for the rearing of the children. This aid should be given by such methods and from such sources as may be determined by the general relief policy of each community. Except in unusual circumstances, the home should not be broken up for reasons of poverty, but only for considerations of inefficiency or immorality.

The theory of the movement is that the children should be kept with their mothers in order that they may have the proper physical, mental and moral training which only a normal home can give. Before the enactment of laws providing for mothers' pensions, these children were placed in many charitable and state institutions. The public was supporting them in a careless, indifferent way. The mothers' pensions pay the mother a part of what it would cost to care for the children in institutions. In this way the mothers care for their own children, and normal homes are theirs—an impossibility in any institution—and the loving care and affection of their natural mother are bestowed upon them. Dr. Edith Abbott says that no other form of social legislature has been so popular in the United States.

In most states the mothers' pensions are administered by the juvenile court. The trend of administration is indicated by the more general provisions in a number of states. Colorado includes a parent or parents who because of poverty are unable to provide properly for a dependent child; a few states include relatives other than parents or guardians having custody of the child. Wisconsin provides for grants to grandparents or persons having the custody of a dependent child; Minnesota to grandparents and stepmothers; Florida to a female relative or guardian upon whom the child is dependent. In four states the law is applicable to "mothers who are needy," to dependent mothers or mothers with dependent children. In North Dakota any woman who has had one or more children dependent upon her for support is eligible for a grant. Unmarried mothers are specifically included in Michigan and Nebraska. A beginning of maternity benefits is found in Colorado and Missouri (outside of Kansas City and St. Louis), where aid may be granted under the law during certain periods before and after childbirth, and in Pennsylvania where aid may be given for an unborn child of the mother who has other children entitling her to assistance under the act.

It is not the purpose of this discussion to prove or disprove the value of mothers' pensions. Its primary purpose is to state the facts in general and then pay special attention to the data obtained in the local study. In all legislation or reformative movements pertaining to children there is always a danger of emotionalism and irrationality preventing unbiased rationality. If social work or sociology is a science we must subject its problems to careful analysis. This study endeavors to do that.

Before the attention of the reader is called to the local data, it will be interesting to make extracts from the Nebraska law quoted in part:

> If the parent or parents of such dependent or neglected child are poor and unable to care for said child, but are otherwise proper guardians and it is for the welfare of such child to remain at home, the court may enter an order finding such facts and fixing the amount of money necessary to enable the parent or parents to properly care for such child, and thereupon it shall be the duty of the county board, through its county agent or otherwise, to pay to such parent or parents, at such times as said order may designate, the amount so specified for the care of such dependent or neglected child until the further order of the court.

The law also provides that the maximum amount per child shall be $10.00 per month, and the maximum amount per family must be $50.00 per month.

The Nebraska law is administered by the juvenile courts. It became effective in 1915. In making this study in Douglas County it was decided that a five-year period should be selected, and all cases handled during that period should be studied. The period selected was from January 1, 1921, to December 31, 1926. Some of the cases studied were new cases, opened or renewed from previous years as well as carried over from the preceding years. At the time of the study the law provided for the child until he reached the age of fourteen, but recently the age limit has been increased to sixteen. During this five-year period 356 cases of different mothers or families were handled by the court. To these aid was given, ranging from nine to fifty dollars per month, at some time during the period.

Homes of the right kind that are kept intact by mothers' pensions are training schools for wholesome citizenship. This is shown by the fact that only 8.1 per cent. of the 356 homes studied had contributed any children to the juvenile court.

The Nebraska law requires that the recipients of mothers' pensions be residents of the respective counties in which they apply for aid. Of the 356 cases, the average number of years resident in Douglas County was eleven years and two months.

Since the percentage of foreign born is rather high in Omaha, this item has to be reckoned with in every sociological study in the city. In this study of this phase of dependency nearly 40 per cent. of the cases studied were foreign born, as compared to 18.6 per cent. of the population as a whole. This 40 per cent. is distributed among many different nationalities. The following table shows the distribution and also shows that the Italians and the Polish received far more of the mothers' pensions in proportion to their percentage of population than any other foreign-born people.

Nationality	Number Father	Number Mother	Per cent. Father	Per cent. Mother	Per cent. of population
American	154	152	44.1	43.3	76.0
Colored	63	62	18.1	17.3	5.38
Polish	21	23	6.3	6.3	1.24
Italian	20	19	5.7	5.9	1.6
German	20	17	5.7	5.4	2.23
Swedish	8	16	2.5	4.8	1.93
Bohemian	10	5	2.8	1.4	2.3
English	5	5	1.4	1.4	.75
Jewish	5	5	1.4	1.4	
Irish	6	5	1.7	1.4	1.0
Danish	6	3	1.7	.8	1.5
Hungarian	4	3	1.1	.8	.27
Others	22	20	6.5	5.6	6.5

Poverty and pauperism have very little connection with religious affiliation. Yet it is interesting to note the general distribution of the recipients of mothers' pensions as to Protestants, Catholics and Jews. In this study it was found that 230, or 64.6 per cent., of the families were listed as Protestant; 108, or 30.3 per cent., as Catholics; 10, or 2.8 per cent., were Jews, and 8, or 2 per cent., were not connected with any religious faith. The chief reason for the high percentage of Protestants is the lack of organized private outdoor relief. The Catholics and Jews have highly developed methods of administering private outdoor relief among their own people.

Mother's pensions remain in force until the children reach the maximum age limit as prescribed by law, unless some condition arises in which the pension is no longer absolutely necessary as determined by the court. It is then discontinued for the time being but may be renewed if necessary at some later date. Many of the 356 cases studied had been discontinued some time during the period but had been renewed. In a few cases this had happened several times. There were thirty-two cases in which the pensions had been finally discontinued. The reasons given were as follows: twenty remarried; three were found to be immoral; four left the county; one family was broken up and the children distributed among relatives; one family failed to pay its bills; one family of which the husband had deserted was reunited when the husband returned; one family inherited some money and became self-supporting. The court tries to keep a careful check of all pensioners at all times lest any one receive aid unworthily. In this way the public is protected.

Conditions found in these homes were appalling. They present pictures of dire need and human distress. In states where the fund is provided for widows only the social conditions are more uniform. But in Nebraska the aid is given to others as well as to widows as previously shown. We found in this study that 164 cases, or 46.5 per cent., were widows. Fifty-three, or 15.05 per cent., received aid because the husband and father was afflicted in some way so that he could not make a living. Twenty-two and four tenths per cent. were mothers whose husbands had deserted them. In these cases the deserters should be forced to care for their families if there is any possible way whereby they can be apprehended. Ninety-three were wives of prisoners. Only 1.9 per cent. were separated from their husbands, but were not divorced. In most of these cases divorce suits were pending in the courts. Only 31, or 19 per cent., of the husbands who died left any life insurance. Even where they did most of the policies were so small that the burial and doctors' expenses took most of it. Yet the policy helped; in the more than 80 per cent. of cases where the husband left no material aid, we see the mother and her little flock left helpless in the hands of society.

The most vivid picture of the home conditions can be given the reader by taking a few remarks here and there from the pages of the research workers' note-books. Each sentence represents a brief description of conditions; one may read between the lines. "Father is disabled with cancer." "Husband deserted. Returned once but deserted again." "The mother drinks and smokes." "Husband is in jail because he would not pay alimony, and a girl is in the state reform school." "Only outside income the mother has is 85 cents per day she makes selling flowers." "Husband committed suicide by drowning." "Husband is in jail." "Husband became suddenly insane." "Both parents dead, children cared for by aunt." "Husband has dropsy." "Husband unable to work for the past year." "Husband bought stolen goods, was afraid of the law, so he left town with another woman." "Mother has two illegitimate children." Many other remarks showed conditions in these homes, sad, but considerably improved since they had been receiving the pensions and were under supervision. All these conditions have to be dealt with by the administration of the pension fund. They make it imperative that trained social workers should always be on the staff. Dexter says: "Without trained social service mothers' pensions are at the best but a negative good; with service supplementing the money, the possibilities of mothers' aid are almost limitless."

In some instances the children work outside of school hours. Yet the supplemented income in this way did not help much, as only nineteen children under fourteen years of age reported doing anything to supplement the family income. One hundred and fifty-four, or 43 per cent, of the mothers reported working away from home. Their average weekly wage was $10.65. These ranged from eight to fifteen dollars, with most of them near the lower figure. The type of work and distribution were as follows: factory, 26; maid, 19; waitress, 12; clerk, 12; day labor, 41; laundress, 17; seamstress, 3; janitress, 8; stenographer, 8; usherette, 1; bootlegging, 2; keeping boarding house, 5.

Two hundred and seven mothers, or 58.1 per cent., were paying rent on an average of $15.28 per month. Only 54, or 15.2 per cent., were buying a home. They were paying on an average of $19.33 per month payment. Twenty, or 5.6 per cent., were living in a house with some one else, usually a relative. Thirty-nine, or 10.9 per cent., stated that they owned their homes. In most cases these were very poor houses and located in very poor communities. Yet nearly all were paid for.

The amount of pension to the family differed in all cases, as financial conditions, income from other sources, age and number of children are vital factors that are considered carefully in each case. The amount allowed by the law in Nebraska is not sufficient under the present high cost of living. This form of relief is the most economical of all. Institutional care of children is expensive. It costs nearly six times as much to care for a child in an institution as it does by means of the mothers' aid. It has been shown that it costs an average of $5.00 per month to keep one child by the mothers' pension. The self-respect and independence created and perpetuated by this means can never be adequately estimated.

Following are the distribution of amounts of pensions per month and the number of mothers receiving aid: $9.00, 1; $10.00, 71; $15.00, 60; $20,00, 110; $25.00, 46; $30.00, 33; $35.00, 14; $40.00, 16; $45.00, 1; $50.00, 4.

Two thirds of the recipients receive a monthly allowance of $20.00 or less. One hundred and ninety-one, or 53 per cent., of the 356 cases had received aid from some other private or public relief agency before they applied for the mothers' pension.

The number and ages of the children for whom the mother drew aid are as follows:

Age	Number of children	Percentage
1 year or less	150	10.5
2	83	5.8
3	90	6.3
4	92	6.4
5	84	5.9
6	110	7.7
7	99	6.9
8	96	6.6
9	92	6.4
10	101	7.09
11	71	4.9
12	77	5.4
13	50	3.5
	1,208	
14	53	3.7
Over 14	159	11.1
Ages not given	16	1.1
	228	
	1,436	

Calculating on the basis of the number of children under fourteen years of age, we found that the average family receiving aid averaged 3.4 children. The table shows that over one half of the children were under eight years of age. The fact that the largest number were one year or less shows the reason why most of the mothers can not supplement the fund with out-of-the-home labor.

The ages of the children determine largely the duration of the pension. Many of the cases were intermittent, but the data are based on the total time in force during this period. For example, a pension may have been paid a family for seven months during 1921, discontinued for a year, renewed for two years, and so on. In such a case a family may have received the fund a total of three or four years during the five-year period. Or the pension may have been in force several years before the study was made. The total time and the number of cases are as follows: 6 months or less, 78; 1 year, 49; 2 years, 75; 3 years, 53; 4 years, 28; 5 years, 15; 6 years, 14; 7 years, 16; 8 years, 10; 9 years, 6; 10 years and over, 11; no report, 1.

This shows that the pension is a long-drawn-out process of relief-giving, but a temporary relief. Yet, in some cases, the pension in varying amounts was continuous for ten years and over. This would be true in cases which were recipients of pensions in 1915 or 1916 with children of very young age. But in two thirds of the cases pensions were granted for only three years or less. Two hundred and ninety-eight, or 83 per cent., received pensions for five years or less, the greatest number being for six months or less—78, or 21.8 per cent.

The two main criticisms of the existing mothers' aid systems in the United States are: (1) that there is too much delay in getting the pension started; and (2) either that the amounts given are insufficient or that the appropriations made by the legislatures are not adequate to cover all cases.

GENERAL RECOMMENDATIONS

(1) Amount per child should be at least $15.00 per month.

(2) Maximum amount per family should be at least $75.00 per month.

(3) The social and moral welfare of the children should always be considered.

(4) Trained social workers should always apply modern case-work methods to the study of each family.

(5) Careful oversight should be constantly maintained over each case receiving aid.

(6) Instruction on budgeting and spending should be given every recipient of mothers' pensions.

(7) Provisions for temporary aid should be made while the regular judicial "red tape" is carried through and applicant is being considered.

(8) More Americanization classes for foreign-born mothers.

(9) Stricter laws dealing with deserting husbands and fathers, and enforcement of same.

T. EARL SULLENGER
UNIVERSITY OF OMAHA

SCHOOL AND SOCIETY

EDITED BY J. McKEEN CATTELL

WITH WHICH IS COMBINED THE

EDUCATIONAL REVIEW

EDITED BY WILLIAM McANDREW

Volume XXIX | SATURDAY, APRIL 6, 1929 | Number 745

LITERATURE BY INFECTION

By Sir JOHN ADAMS

THE gentlemen of Port Royal supply one example the more of that tendency to anticipate that writers on education methods find so exasperating. For myself, as soon as I have an idea on the subject that I think is new, I find my way to the shelves in my library where Plato and Aristotle live, and in their pages I am all but certain to find my brand new idea sketched out in some form or other. It is very offensive. But in this case of the good Port-Royalist gentlemen, there need be no resentment, but rather a gentle satisfaction that a certain new idea turns out to be really old.

These wise gentlemen in their all too brief period in the sun—their schools kept open door from 1637 to 1661—freed literature from the bonds of grammar. Not that they neglected grammar: they merely kept it in its proper place. They depended on literature rather than on mere linguistics to produce good effects on the character of their pupils. While their contemporaries thought that the intricacies of Latin grammar supplied the best whetstone of wit, these genial gentlemen relied upon literature itself, and set it free from the trammels that enslaved it in the ordinary schools of their time.

In this they are at one with certain progressive educators of to-day, who maintain that even at the earliest stages literature should be freed from the swaddling bands of mere grammar and verbal criticism. Last October one of those important persons known in Great Britain as H. M. I. S. (which, being interpreted, runs His Majesty's Inspector of Schools) delivered an address to the teachers of Glasgow, in which he claimed that as usually taught English literature is made up of two parts that he named the Grind and the Graces. Then he proceeded to make the startling suggestion that the best plan of dealing with the situation is to eliminate the grind altogether and concentrate on the graces.

When the scandalized teachers were inclined to protest that the proposal was absurd if not indeed actually indecent, the inspector proceeded to elaborate his thesis and to maintain that not only was grammar teaching not essential to the work of the teacher of literature at the early stages, but that there was no need for *teaching* of any kind in treating literature at the beginning. He did not go quite so far as in her enthusiasm Dr. Montessori goes, when she declines to call her professional followers teachers, and insists upon labeling them simply *directresses.* Our inspector admits that there is a place for teaching—for example, grammar must be taught—

but the literature hour is not the occasion for this teaching. Literature has to be communicated or instilled, rather than taught. It is a matter of experiencing rather than of learning.

In his enthusiasm the inspector went the length of using a truly formidable simile, and said that literature was communicated in the way that a disease is spread. He went the whole length and mentioned a specific disease that has a certain standing in school circles. He said that children should pick up literature just as they do measles.

He did not refer to a saying that is popular in America where we are apt to speak of a person being exposed to education even though it does not take on. It is obvious that in this phrase there is the underlying idea of infection: so that this ingenious inspector like the rest of us has the harrowing experience of being anticipated. But though the Americans had it first, our inspector put the idea boldly, and said in plain words what the exposure theory only suggests.

Now the measles warning is much more needed in Britain than it is in America. When it comes to a discrimination between Grind and Graces in American schools the Graces have the habit of coming out on top. The tendency in Britain is rather the other way, as is well illustrated in this very matter under discussion. Last century in Britain literature was largely taught by means of text-books that certainly did not err by favoring the Graces. The situation is indicated by a series of Shakespeare texts that was very popular in the schools. It was known as the Clarendon Press Series. In point of fact the books were literally bursting with good qualities. The editing was scholarly in the highest degree, and if any one wants to rub up his knowledge of any of the plays he can not do better than use the Clarendon series. But this assumes that the play is known already, and that what is wanted is a critical treatment of it.

The radical objection to the series for school purposes was to be found in the "Notes." In themselves they were excellent: the trouble was that there were far too many of them. Sometimes it was a matter of thirty pages of well-printed text that got completely lost among the three hundred pages of small-print notes. The proportion between the text and the notes naturally produced a false perspective in the minds of the pupils. In the hands of the capable teacher "The play's the thing," but in those scholarly days the pupils knew that in reality "The Notes were the thing." If ever one of the Gestalt psychologists finds a difficulty in getting an example of the thing his philosophy abhors, let him turn to an English annotated nineteenth century edition of a play of Shakespeare. In biological science we know that in order legally to dissect we must first kill; and what is true about animals is equally true about books.

Truth to tell, the teaching of literature should not be compared to anatomy but to physiology. It deals with something living, something to which Henri Bergson's favorite adjective *palpitating* may be justly applied. The Grind side may be attended to in the way of ordinary teaching. There we have facts to be communicated, judgments made, conclusions drawn. We are in the region of the cognitive, and the ordinary laws of didactic teaching may be legitimately and effectively applied. But when we deal with the Graces we are in the affective realm, and the process is one of direct application. The figure of infection is definitely in place. We have to "put over" the state of mind we ourselves are experiencing. It is a matter of personality.

Dr. F. H. Hayward, whose book on "Appreciation" has not made on the American teaching public the impression it should, is the apostle of training young people to see the beauty of literature and art, and has much that is helpful to say on this subject. But when it has been all carefully analyzed, the outcome of the whole is reducible to the old *faber fabricando*—we become a workman by working, a speaker by speaking, a smith by smithing. So in teaching to appreciate, the secret of the process is to appreciate. Unless the teacher himself has the reactions to poem or story that he wishes to rouse in his pupils, he labors in vain to produce the desired effect. But once the appropriate state of mind has been induced in the teacher, all that remains is to expose the pupils to his influence. There is no need for actual teaching.

What may be called the finger-post criticism is here of no avail. No amount of "note the beauty of this passage" appeal, will have the least effect in rousing the desired reaction. All that such injunctions can accomplish is a cognitive state, in which the pupil is aware that the passage in question is included among those that it is customary to regard with respect and to praise on appropriate occasions. But he is unaffected himself by the appeal. He is immune. The more pessimistic among teachers of literature are inclined to seize upon this term, and maintain that quite a large proportion of the pupils in an ordinary class are really immune to the infection that we are considering. Now it has to be confessed in all honesty that there are junior human beings who appear to be immune to the infection that an enthusiastic and sincere teacher brings to bear upon his class. But their number is small. It is almost ridiculous to suggest a percentage, but I should be inclined to mention 3 per cent. as a reasonable limit. This guess is based upon the fact that in many of the human qualities that have been analyzed quantitatively, somewhere round about 3 per cent. is found to be a common figure that represents the minority who are entirely destitute of the quality in question.

It is not to be inferred that the remaining 97 per cent. of an ordinary class will respond to the same extent to the teacher's infection. As with measles and other disreputable states that are communicable, individuals vary in the intensity with which they react to esthetic literary stimulus. There is indeed a certain percentage of the pupils who if the literary presentation were made in the "finger post" method would actually respond by a *contrary* reaction. All those pupils with whom Dr. Keatinge, of Oxford, makes such play under the name of "contrariants" naturally take up an antagonistic attitude towards matter that their teacher praises. But when the infection is applied gently, naturally and honestly, not only does no antagonism arise, but a curious collective force is set up to strengthen the state of mind initiated by the personality of the teacher.

Too often the collective reactions of the class are things to be opposed by the teacher: so it is indeed pleasant to trace here one of the cases in which it works on his side. Once he has set up the attitude he desires towards a piece of literature, he gets all manner of unexpected support from the interactions developed among his pupils. To be sure this support may be altogether undeserved, for it is quite possible to get the class all agog about something that is not worth while. Take, for example, the following extract from a sermon to children. I have not the text by me, but it was preached by a reputable American clergyman, and the passage runs somewhat as follows:

> And away down in 81st Street a poor woman was sewing by the light of a guttering candle, and as she sewed she wept. What she worked at looked like a little night-gown: but ah me! It was something sadder still! For her little baby had died and she was making a little shroud. Can we wonder that the tears fell down?

Many years ago I made the experiment of reading this passage (along with the context just before and immediately after the part quoted above) to a class of divinity students to whom I was lecturing. Naturally I read it with the pathetic stop out, and the young men were furious with themselves for being so completely deceived by my tone that they did not notice the ridiculous blunder of the clergyman who had represented a little night-gown as something desperately sad, only less sad in fact, than a little shroud.

I was probably justified in my trick, for it had as its end the warning of these clergymen-about-to-be. In any case it conveys a lesson to those who propose to treat literature on the infection plan. Fortunately in writing for teachers one is freed from the necessity of elaborating moral issues. The teacher is *ex hypothesi* a good moral citizen, and not given to use his powers for bad ends. In any case experiments like the above demonstrate that infection can be communicated on the literary plane, and that even without sincerity. This in no way lowers the value of sincerity in the process of genuine literary infection: if it can be conveyed by mere histrionic display how much more effectively it will be carried over when backed by genuine appreciation of the passage read.

The assumption is that the teacher selects material of high quality that is all the same within the comprehension of the pupils, so far as the subject-matter is concerned. It has to be noted that the meaning of almost any passage is beyond the full comprehension of children. Even ''Mary had a little lamb'' conveys a somewhat different meaning to an adult and to a child. In the higher regions of literature there are degrees of comprehension, depending on the background against which a given passage is presented. Let us not forget the moral of the incident about Browning's ''Childe Roland to the Dark Tower Came.'' Asked by a bewildered admirer what the poem exactly meant, the poet is reported to have replied that it meant to every man just as much as he could put into it.

Accordingly, when the teacher puts his whole soul into the reading of a passage, and contrives to infect his pupils with the general tone of the whole, it does not follow that they understand it in quite the same way as he. Their appreciation and his coincide so far as they go, though his may include much that lack of experience may deny to them. It is not a matter of mere knowledge, but of tone and background. The danger of ordinary expository teaching, especially when worked along the lines of linguistic and historical notes, is that the passage may lose its real character. It can not be too often repeated to teachers of English that the passages they expound were originally written to be read, not to be expounded, and that in the process of exposition they may be made to change their character entirely. A teacher who understands and enjoys ''L'Allegro,'' by merely reading it aloud and enjoying it as he goes along may do far more to make the appeal Milton intended than if he analyzed it for the class in the most perfect way, and gave the detailed meaning of every word in the text.

This matter of the meaning of the words is one of the most pernicious bogeys in the teaching of literature. Teachers are liable to a great temptation here: they are inclined to make the word the unit of thought. In point of fact children are far more frequently thrown out of gear by a peculiar twist of a sentence than by the presence of an unfamiliar word. An unknown word here and there does no great harm. Note what Jean Paul Richter, dealing with children, says in his ''Levana'':

Do not be afraid of not being understood even for whole sentences. Your look and your accent, and the instinct that devines before understanding, illumines the half, and these and time together the other half; also remember that they *understand* your language before they can learn to speak it, just as we do in the case of Greek, or any other foreign language.

We must not forget that in our ordinary intercourse with our pupils we are continually using words that the pupils do not quite understand. Even if we could perfect the classification of the Lewis Terman vocabularies for the different school ages, and could, for example, make a complete list of the 7,200 words that make up the vocabulary of our twelve-year-old pupils, we could not guarantee that in our teaching we would keep rigidly to this list. Nor is it desirable that we should. If we could keep exactly to the words with which the pupil is familiar, we would cut off all possibility of extending the pupil's vocabulary. It is because we are continually using words outside the pupil's range that we compel him, without using any other force than that of circumstances, to add steadily from day to day fresh material to his extending list of usable words.

Using lists of words and learning their dictionary meaning is a part of the study of literature, but it belongs to the Grind section, and has little to do with the Graces. We teachers ourselves in our learning of a foreign language may work either by Grind or by Graces. If we take the first way we begin by learning lists of words and then go on to reading the language, making a point of looking up in the dictionary every word that we do not know. If we follow the Graces we plunge into the foreign language reading straight away after acquiring a minimum vocabulary. We select the most interesting type of article or story, generally finding a play the easiest form for our purpose. Paying no attention to the dictionary, except in the few desperate cases where we can make no sense at all out of a passage, we plough through the new country buoyed up by the interest of what we are reading, and knowing that we are picking up a vocabulary as we go along. We are really absorbing the new language by infection, and if our consciences will allow us to carry on we will ultimately make a conquest of the language, as a matter of reading at any rate, though we will need to go through another process to acquire a speaking acquaintance with it. If we wish to go on to the writing of the language we have to fall back on the Grind process, for at this stage the infection plan rather breaks down.

All this, however, need not discourage us in the use of the infection plan with our pupils, for as responsible guides for them we can arrange that the grind part of English literature shall be attended to at other school periods than those at which we are infecting our pupils with the virus of literature. The conscience of the most high-toned moralist among teachers need give him no trouble so long as he can assure himself that his infection plan demands not an abandonment of the Grind aspect, but merely a redistribution of time devoted to Grind and Graces respectively.

The infection plan is really a process of direct influence brought to bear upon the pupils, that force being the teacher's personality. Very likely some sensitive reader may complain: "Now why couldn't you have said that at first?" Such readers have probably been repelled by the implied reference to disease. But good has probably been done by using the title at the head of this article. Teachers are a little bored with the continual reference in a glowing way to the value and use of personality. The term has lost its tang: whereas the infection figure by its very grimness attracts attention. At any rate it has enabled the H. M. I. S. referred to above so to stimulate the teachers of the schools of Glasgow that they have given the plan a year's trial, beginning in August, 1928, and ending with June, 1929. It takes a good deal to get those hard-headed Scots to adopt a plan that puts Graces before Grind, but in their severe way they will give the Graces every chance, and we outsiders will wait with interest for the report that no doubt will make its appearance in due course. In the meantime it may be that some of the enterprising American teachers will make the experiment on their own account. Many of them have already tried it out in the higher grades: the problem remains to discover how far down in the school life literary infection may be profitably carried.

EDUCATIONAL EVENTS

SCHOOL ATTENDANCE IN LONDON

A DECREASE in the number of children attending London elementary schools in the last two years and a slightly more than corresponding increase in the number of students at continuation schools are mentioned by Mr. G. H. Gater, the education officer of the London County Council, in his annual report for 1927, which is accompanied by statistics for 1928–29. According to the abstract in the London *Times,* Mr. Gater says: "In round figures the statistics recorded [for 1927] show that, owing to the fall in the child population and the migration of families to new housing estates outside the County of London, there was a decrease in the elementary school rolls of 11,600 children, and of 109 teachers, as compared with the rolls for 1926. On the other hand, there was an increase of 11,700 students at continuation schools."

Last year the total number of persons educated wholly or in part by the London County Council was nearly 1,000 more than in 1927. This was due to the expansion of continued education. A decrease of 30,341 in children up to 14 years of age was more than offset by increases in adolescents of 13,742, and in adults of 17,537—a total of 31,279. Those educated in London during 1928 numbered 910,109, comprising 642,460 children, 134,566 adolescents and 133,083 adults. The number of children in the special schools for the mentally and physically defective is decreasing.

The total cost of education for 1928 was £13,126,666. This was £362,071 more than in 1927, owing to new liability imposed on the council for teachers' superannuation.

The *Times* states that Mr. Gater describes how after several years' hard work an area of 60 rods, entirely occupied by street refuse, has been transformed into a beautiful garden by East London schoolboys. The garden is surrounded by docks, factories, a railway terminus and old houses. Work was begun in 1923, and in May, 1924, potatoes, cabbages and other common garden crops were planted. The garden is now maturing and provides a pleasant background, making outdoor life for the subnormal children seem really worth while. Twenty-eight boys attended an open-air class, "camping out in blankets," during the winter, with definite physical benefit. The boys showed no wish to return to the classrooms, and the only time last winter when the class vacated its shelter (always open on two sides and closed only by canvas sheets on the other two) was when it was "washed out" by heavy rain.

ORGANIZATION AND ADMINISTRATION OF RURAL JUNIOR HIGH SCHOOLS

WHILE the junior high school as a distinct educational unit is as yet practically confined to urban areas, the junior-high-school idea has spread generally to rural communities.

According to Bureau of Education Bulletin, 1928, No. 28, there are in the United States 2,368 secondary schools which include the junior-high-school grades. Of these schools, 99 are 5- or 6-years undivided type secondary schools. That is, they make no effort in any way to organize the school into separate junior and senior units. The total of segregated junior high schools is 880, and there are, in addition, 1,389 schools where the junior and senior units are recognized as distinct but associated in a single institution.

The junior high schools in rural districts occur most frequently in the consolidated school districts which are most conveniently served by one school centrally located, and they number 1,181. Of these, 173 are completely segregated junior high schools in rural areas. The additional schools, 1,008, termed rural junior high schools, exhibit various degrees of distinctness in organization and administration, ranging from nothing more than a term applied to grades 7 and 8, which have been partially departmentalized, to a rather complete educational entity with distinct curriculum, social organization, teaching and administrative staffs.

An enrolment of more than 150 pupils in the rural junior high school is comparatively rare. The prevailing type enrolls fewer than 100 pupils in the junior unit.

Junior high schools are giving an important place in organization and administrative practice to provisions which seek to overcome the faults of mass instruction by permitting pupils to advance through the grades at a rate which is normal to their abilities to learn. These practices concern themselves with bases of admission to junior high school, pupil classification and bases of promotion.

Completion of six elementary grades is a recognized basis of admission in 94.8 per cent. of all schools. Other bases of admission are relatively infrequent. Use of mental age, chronological age and educational age as one of two or more bases of admission are reported in approximately the same frequencies.

The effort to group pupils into homogeneous ability groups for purposes of instruction has received wide attention in educational literature and in actual practice. In rural junior high schools this effort has been made in 48.9 per cent. of the schools. The most frequent basis used is a composite of several factors. Grouping on the basis of teachers' estimates or marks alone is practiced by 17.7 per cent. of the schools.

Grouping by ability affords a possibility of varying requirements for promotion.

Particular interest attaches to the extent to which the junior high schools have substituted subject for grade promotion and a composite of several measures of ability for teachers' estimates or marks.

In view of the number of schools that report variable programs, grouping and other promotion practices looking to flexibility of progress, it is of interest to note that 87 of these rural junior high schools report a practice of not allowing graduation in less than the normal time required for completion of the course.

THE BROOKLYN BOTANIC GARDEN AND THE SCHOOLS

The report of Dr. C. Stuart Gager, director of the Brooklyn Botanic Garden, which was recently issued shows that during 1928 more than 3,800 teachers were supplied with living plants, plant parts and other study material in quantity sufficient for the instruction of more than 156,000 pupils last year. Personal conferences were held with 1,000 teachers concerning problems of biology and nature-study teaching. The garden distributed 560,000 packets of seeds to 177,000 pupils for planting in school and home gardens. Teachers brought more than 54,000 pupils to the Botanic Garden for instruction in the plantations, conservatories and classrooms.

In the study of bacteria more than 3,200 petri dishes with sterilized culture media were given to school children. Members of the garden staff gave sixty-seven addresses, lectures and talks, which were attended by more than 31,000 children.

More than 800 requests came from schools for nature material, according to Miss Ellen Eddy Shaw, curator of elementary instruction. This figure included requests from schools which were supplied with 18,000 living plants for class work and for purposes of decoration and about 30,000 seedling plants which were raised by children's classes at the garden for use in school and home gardens.

The three greenhouses given over to instruction, out of which annually thousands of plants go to schools and to classes for instruction purposes, are maintained almost entirely by the department of elementary instruction of the garden and by school children.

Dr. Gager, in summarizing the garden's work with children in the annual report, points out that the garden does not confine its work with children to cooperation with the schools. The total attendance at popular courses of instruction organized independently of the schools in the plantations, children's greenhouses, conservatories, children's gardens, classrooms and laboratories is now approximately 50,000 a year.

MEETING OF DEANS OF MEN

THE annual convention of the National Association of Deans and Advisers of Men will be held in Washington, D. C., under the auspices of the George Washington University, April 11, 12 and 13.

An outstanding event on the program of the three-day session will be an address by the Honorable Ray Lyman Wilbur, secretary of the interior and president of Stanford University.

Other speakers on the program are Dean Thomas Arkle Clark, of the University of Illinois; Dr. George B. Culver, of Stanford University; Dr. David Allan Robertson, of the American Council on Education; Dr. Ben D. Wood, of Columbia University; President Cloyd Heck Marvin, of the George Washington University; Dean James W. Armstrong, of Northwestern University; Dean S. H. Goodnight, of the University of Wisconsin; Dean Henry Grattan Doyle, of the George Washington University; Dr. J. A. Park, of Ohio State University; Dean R. Rienow, of the University of Iowa, and Dean Stanley Coulter, formerly of Purdue University.

Dean Henry Grattan Doyle, of the George Washington University, is chairman of the local committee on arrangements. The meeting will be attended by deans and advisers of men from colleges and universities throughout the country.

The program includes a banquet at the Cosmos Club, a pilgrimage to Mt. Vernon, a sightseeing tour of Washington and vicinity, and a reception by the president, trustees and faculties of the George Washington University, followed by a concert by the George Washington Glee Club and a dance. The ladies of the George Washington faculty are making plans for the entertainment of the visiting delegates.

Some of the problems to be discussed at the conference are: Scholarship, student conduct, fraternities, initiations and "hell week," student housing, intercollegiate athletics, attendance, student loan funds, orientation courses and the duties of the office of dean of men.

THE SUMMER SESSION OF THE NEW YORK STATE COLLEGE FOR TEACHERS

THE coming summer session at the New York State College for Teachers at Buffalo will witness an experiment in cooperation between student body and institution which gives evidence of the desire on the part of elementary school teachers for professional improvement.

To expand and improve the summer session offerings of the college, last summer's student body, about 1,000 in number, pledged itself, and by implication, the registrants in the session of 1929, to raise a special extension fund to be used to supplement the regular summer budget provided from state appropriations. With this fund the institution has been able to add to its summer faculty ten leaders in educational theory and practice who will offer advanced instruction in a number of elementary school fields. The courses added to the regular summer offerings are designed particularly for advanced students, normal school graduates desirous of earning credit toward the bachelor's degree and teachers of experience preparing for supervisory and administrative positions.

This group of ten visiting professors includes: Dr. Albert Edward Winship, editor of the *Journal of Education;* Dr. Leo J. Brueckner, professor of elementary education at the University of Minnesota; Dr. Philip W. L. Cox, professor of secondary education at New York University; Dr. J. Cayce Morrison, assistant commissioner for elementary education in New York State; Dr. Carleton Washburne, superintendent of schools, Winnetka, Illinois; Miss Etta Anchester, supervisor of kindergarten-primary teaching at Chicago Teachers College; Mr. Barrett Stout, professor of elementary school music at the Kirksville State Teachers College; Dr. Edgar A. Dawson, professor of history and political science at Hunter College; Miss Evelyn Holston, supervisor of elementary school subjects at Springfield, Mass., and Mr. Mendel E. Branom, head of the department of geography at the Harris Teachers College, St. Louis.

In addition, seventeen courses of an advanced nature and thirty-four courses belonging mainly in the second and third years of the standard normal curriculum will be offered by the regular members of the college faculty and visiting professors from other colleges and normal schools.

Special features of the summer session include a course in home hygiene and care of the sick under American Red Cross auspices, a course in teaching English to immigrants and curricula for dental hygiene teachers and school nurses.

A portion of the special fund contributed voluntarily by the students will be set aside for a program of special lectures and recreational activities. This feature will be directed by Dr. George B. Neumann, professor of sociology at the State College.

COURSES IN EDUCATION AT THE UNIVERSITY OF MICHIGAN

Four weeks' double-period courses in education will be offered for the first time at the summer session of the University of Michigan. Twelve different courses designed for teachers and administrators will be given on the four weeks' plan, either from June 24 to July 19, or from July 22 to August 16. One half the normal eight-semester-hour load may thus be carried by students attending the first four weeks or the last four weeks of the session.

In these twelve courses the departure from the eight weeks basis was made to meet the demand of a considerable number of teachers and school administrators who feel the need of vacation and rest, but who still have the desire and the time for a briefer period of study. The titles of several of the courses will indicate the interests of the students likely to take advantage of this new arrangement: "The Construction of the Elementary School Curriculum," "The Teaching of Science in the Junior and Senior High School," "Special Problems in the Teaching of Physics," "Administrative Work for Deans of Girls in High Schools," "The Administration and Supervision of Vocational Education," "The Constitutional and Legal Basis of Public School Administration," "The Planning of School Buildings."

The session is also inaugurating non-credit courses, especially designed for the superintendent and the principal who desire lectures and round table discussions dealing with problems of the public schools. These non-credit courses, given on six week-ends, have been arranged beginning on Friday and Saturday, June 28 and 29. Leaders in the field of education and educational administration, both members of the university summer session faculty and others, will direct various phases of the work.

The above courses are in addition to upwards of one hundred courses offered by the school of education as a part of the full eight weeks' session.

The following appointments to the faculty have been made from other institutions for the coming session: Frederick S. Breed, University of Chicago; Claude C. Crawford, University of Southern California; Wren J. Grinstead, University of Pennsylvania; Charles W. Hamilton, director of commercial education, Elizabeth, New Jersey; Chester O. Mathews, Ohio Wesleyan University; Arlee Nuser, State Teachers College, Fresno, California; William M. Proctor, Stanford University; Luther T. Purdom, University of Missouri; Joseph Roemer, University of Florida; Paul R. Spencer, George Peabody College, Nashville, Tennessee; William W. Theisen, assistant superintendent of schools, Milwaukee, Wisconsin; Agnes E. Wells, dean of women, Indiana University; Arthur D. Wright, Dartmouth College; Wendell W. Wright, Indiana University.

RESOLUTIONS ON THE DEATH OF DR. BALDWIN

In the death of Dr. Bird T. Baldwin, on May 12, 1928, the National Society for the Study of Education has suffered a great loss. He was elected to active membership at the Washington meeting in February, 1908, and was continuously and helpfully active in the work of the society for the past twenty years. He was a welcome speaker in the meetings of the society and an important contributor to its yearbooks. He made notable contributions to the yearbooks entitled "Standards and Tests for the Measurement of Efficiency of Schools and School Systems," "The Education of Gifted Children" and "Nature and Nurture." In the months immediately preceding his last illness, he gave his inspiration and help to the preparation of the current yearbook on preschool and parental education.

The members of this society were constantly impressed by his warm interest in the work of the society; his unselfish encouragement of the work of others; his public address; his charm of manner in friendly and informal discussion; his unusual thoughtfulness and consideration for those with whom he worked; his generous giving of himself to assist in worthy causes; his earnest belief in the ideals and methods of science in the study of education, and his devotion to the welfare of young children. Therefore, be it

Resolved: That the National Society for the Study of Education direct its secretary to transmit to Dr. Baldwin's nearest relatives, as a token of appreciation of his services to education and of the personal esteem in which he was held by his fellow members in this organization, this memorial statement; and be it further

Resolved: That a copy of the statement and resolutions be published as a part of the minutes of the annual meeting of this society and in the columns of School and Society.

EDUCATIONAL NOTES AND NEWS

Dr. Brander Matthews, emeritus professor of dramatic literature at Columbia University, died on March 31 at the age of seventy-seven years. Professor Matthews, who held the chair at Columbia University for thirty-two years, was distinguished as an author and critic.

Dr. Robert M. Wenley, since 1896 head of the department of philosophy in the University of Michigan, died suddenly on March 30 in his sixty-eighth year. Dr. Wenley returned to Ann Arbor last September after spending two years in London as director of the American University Union.

President George F. Zook, of the University of Akron, has declined the presidency of the University of Louisville, which has been offered him at an annual salary of $15,000.

Dr. Max Meyer, professor of experimental psychology at the University of Missouri from 1900 until the recent difficulties in regard to a student questionnaire, was unanimously elected president of the Southern Society for Philosophy and Psychology at the meeting held at the University of Kentucky on March 30.

The Ohio State University *Monthly* states that a statue is to be erected in honor of Dr. W. O. Thompson, for twenty-six years president of Ohio State University and now president emeritus. It is to be of heroic size and will be erected at a central point on the campus. It will be executed by Professor Erwin Frey, sculptor in the department of fine arts, and will constitute the combined memorial from four recent Ohio State classes.

Wilberforce Eames, the bibliographer, librarian of the Lenox Library of New York City until its consolidation with the New York Public Library and librarian of the Bibliographical Society from its origin until 1909, has had conferred on him one of the gold medals of the British Bibliographical Society. The medal, instituted by the society from funds given by Mr. E. F. Bosanquet, has been made at the Royal Mint from designs by Mr. Langford Jones, the obverse (based on a miniature in a manuscript of Mielot's "Les Miracles de Nostre Dame," 1456) showing an author at work, the reverse (based on a title-cut in "La Fauconnerie de F. Ian des Franchieres" printed at Poitiers in 1567) an early printing house with pressman and compositor at work.

Professor Lawrence Pumpelly, chairman of the department of Romance languages at Cornell University, has been made a Knight of the Legion of Honor of France in recognition of his many years of service to the interests of France as a teacher of Romance languages and as an aide and interpreter during the World War.

Dr. George W. Andrews, professor of organ in the Oberlin Conservatory of Music, has completed fifty years' connection with the Oberlin Musical Union, twenty years as organist and thirty years as director. He will retire from active connection with the union at the conclusion of the spring concert, when the union sings "St. Francis of Assisi," by Gabriel Pierne.

Dr. Leonard W. Richardson has retired as professor of Latin in the New York State College for Teachers at Albany. He had been a member of the faculty for nearly thirty-five years.

Frank H. Wood has submitted his resignation as director of the school building and grounds division of the New York State Education Department, a position which he has held for fourteen years, to take effect on April 30. Mr. Wood leaves the department after forty-six years of service to the schools of the state, thirty-three years having been spent in the Department of Public Instruction and the State Education Department.

HOMER B. VANDERBLUE, professor of business economics in the graduate school of business administration of Harvard University, has resigned.

PROFESSOR EUNICE MORGAN SCHENCK, head of the department of French at Bryn Mawr College, has been appointed to the newly established position of dean of the graduate school. For the past three years Dr. Schenck has directed the graduate school, acting as the president's representative.

PROFESSOR ALFRED FRANCIS PŘIBRAM, of the faculty of Anglo-Saxon history at the University of Vienna, has been appointed to fill the chair of history at the University of Oxford, recently endowed by Henry Ford.

DR. ROY MALCOLM, head of the department of political science at the University of Southern California, will be a visiting professor at the University of Washington this summer.

DR. G. B. HARRISON, of the English department of King's College, London, has accepted the invitation of the University of Chicago to be the first holder of the Frederic Ives Carpenter Visiting Chair of English.

JAMES E. PIXLEE, athletic director at Westminster College, at Fulton, Missouri, has been appointed athletic director of George Washington University.

DR. SAMUEL EDWIN WEBER, superintendent at Charleston, West Virginia, has been appointed associate superintendent of schools of Pittsburgh, Pennsylvania, at a salary of $10,000.

DR. OLIVER C. LOCKHART, head of the department of economics and finance at the University of Buffalo, has been granted leave of absence to accompany Professor E. W. Kemmerer as a member of the Commission of Financial Advisers to the Government of China.

PROFESSOR LAUDER W. JONES, who holds the Hepburn chair of chemistry at Princeton University, has left for France, where he will take up his new work as European director of the division of natural sciences of the Rockefeller Foundation. Dr. Jones succeeds in this work Dean Augustus Trowbridge, dean of the Princeton Graduate School, who was abroad several years.

THE Honorable Ray Lyman Wilbur, secretary of the interior and president of Stanford University (on leave), will be the speaker at the commencement exercises of Goucher College on June 3.

DR. L. P. JACKS, principal of Manchester College, Oxford, and editor of *The Hibbert Journal,* will speak on April 25 at 8:30 in the evening at the New York Academy of Medicine on "The Education of Adults."

PRESIDENT ERNEST HATCH WILKINS, of Oberlin College, is conducting a seminar course at the University of Chicago on Mondays during April and May in the department of Romance languages and literature. The subject of the course is "The Chronology of the Letters of Petrarch." President Wilkins was formerly a member of that faculty.

DR. FRED W. MALONEY, director of public health in the Atlantic City public schools, will give three courses at the summer session of Columbia University. These will be on physical education and the organization of athletics for the entire city, the organization of medical service, and health work in a representative city.

PROFESSOR H. E. SLAUGHT, of the University of Chicago, delivered a lecture on "How Men Learned to Count" at Lehigh University on March 11, at Lafayette College on March 12, at Haverford College on March 13, at Swarthmore College on March 14 and at Rutgers University on March 15.

KATHARINE LEE BATES, professor emeritus of English at Wellesley College, died on March 28 at the age of seventy years. Dr. Bates was appointed instructor at Wellesley in 1885, she became associate professor in 1888, full professor in 1891, retiring with the title of professor emeritus in 1925.

The Ohio College Association Committee on Intelligence Tests for Entrance, under the chairmanship of Professor H. A. Toops, is planning a five-year research program looking into the causes of college failure and success.

The seventeenth annual convention of the American Association of Collegiate Registrars will be held on April 16 to 18 and the Conference on the Reorganization of the Lower Division on April 18 and 19 at Seattle, Washington. Dean Charles E. Friley, president of the association, is in charge of the program and Registrar E. B. Stevens, of the University of Washington, is chairman of the committee in charge of local arrangements.

The fourth Canadian National Conference on Education will be held at Vancouver during the second week in April. The discussions will center around adult education, and representatives from all parts of the British Empire will be present, as well as delegates from Italy and Czechoslovakia.

A gift of $1,000,000 from Edward S. Harkness as a personal tribute to the late Cleveland H. Dodge has been announced by the Near East College Association. Mr. Dodge started the $15,000,000 campaign for an endowment for Robert College, American University of Beirut, Constantinople Woman's College, the International College of Smyrna, American College of Sofia and Athens College, Greece. Mr. Harkness's latest gift is conditional upon the completion of the educational fund by July 1, the closing date set for the campaign by the late Mr. Dodge. Others have pledged $530,000 conditionally. A total of $2,500,000 remains to be raised within the next three months.

An anonymous gift of $450,000 has been made to the Johns Hopkins University for the erection and endowment of a building for the new institute for the study of law.

The General Education Board has made a gift of $80,000 to Howard University for salary increases.

John Spencer Camp, of Hartford, Connecticut, has given $100,000 to Wesleyan University to endow a chair of music, which will be named in honor of the donor.

The late W. J. McDonald, of Paris, Texas, who died about three years ago, left the bulk of his estate to the University of Texas for an observatory. The will was contested by relatives, who have now come to a settlement by which the university receives approximately $1,000,000.

The Board of Education of Chicago has appropriated $20,000,000 for the construction of sixteen new public schools.

Senator Arthur N. Pierson, of New Jersey, has proposed legislation to recover nearly $700,000 of funds, originally raised for the schools, but diverted to other uses. The bill would direct the comptroller and the treasurer to withhold all further distribution of moneys received from the railroad tax to special funds such as the highway extension fund, the soldiers' bonus sinking fund, and the state institution construction fund, for the benefit of the school fund.

A fund is being collected for a Spanish residence to be established at Barnard College, Columbia University, to provide headquarters for Latin-American students and American students who wish to live in a Spanish atmosphere. The "casita," as the residence will be called, will be built on Claremont Avenue. In it will be guest rooms for distinguished visitors from Spanish-speaking countries, an extensive Spanish library and clubrooms. It will be designed like a typical Spanish house, built around an inner courtyard and patio and will be furnished throughout with Spanish furniture.

Ten reappointments and ten new appointments to scholarships in fine arts by the Carnegie Corporation of New York have been announced. The selections were made by the advisory group for the foundation from a list of 111 applications. The stipend ranges from $1,200 to $2,000. The scholarships were established to increase the number of qualified college and university teachers in the arts.

Back numbers of the *National Geographic Magazine* have been made available by the National Geographic Society for use in schools. This service has been offered at the request of many educators. With the cooperation of its membership the society has collected a limited number of copies of sets which will be delivered to the schools upon requisition by the superintendent or principal. It is desired that these sets be allotted to schools in rural areas or villages where library facilities are limited. The recipient is required to pay only the cost of handling and carriage.

IT is planned to erect in New York City a motion-picture house especially for children on a site already selected in Fifty-third Street, near Lexington Avenue. Instruction in aviation, geology, zoology, astronomy, botany and anthropology will be given in the theater, supplementing these courses in the schools. Travel pictures will be given, current events will be taught by a careful selection from the best news reels, while an introduction into the best literature will be given by approved screen versions of important literary works. The movement, it was said, will also include the showing of the best amateur and experimental motion-picture work in Europe and America.

DISCUSSION

NATIONAL AND STATE STATISTICS ON HIGH-SCHOOL EDUCATION

DURING recent years one of the leading arguments in the agitation for a federal department of education has been the need for research and the dissemination of the results on a nationwide basis. The efforts of the present Bureau of Education and of the state departments of education in collecting and distributing information are commended by many educators and writers, although all are free to admit that the work is not carried on as extensively as it should be. Certain writers have pointed out the inadequacy of the statistical reports published under the present system. Possibly a greater realization of the shortcomings of the current reports is the first step necessary for improvement.

As a part of a recent study,[1] the writer had occasion to attempt a comparison of certain statistics on high-school education published by the U. S. Bureau of Education and by the state departments of education of the various states. Since the materials which were desired for the study did not seem to be readily available a more complete analysis of the figures presented in the reports was essayed. The study disclosed amazing discrepancies between the several reports published by the Bureau of Education itself and between reports published by the Bureau of Education and by the states. The comparison of the state reports showed a lack of comparability which would discourage any careful worker from attempting to make state-to-state comparisons on the basis of the figures presented in the reports.

[1] O. L. Troxel, "State Control of Secondary Education," Warwick & York.

A comparison of the figures presented in two bulletins of the Bureau of Education,[2] giving figures for the high schools of the various states for the same year, shows only nineteen states in which the total enrolments in high schools differed by as little as 10 per cent. as given in the two places. A comparison in similar bulletins of figures for 1925–26[3] shows only twenty-one states in which the figures given in the two bulletins differ by as little as 10 per cent. For four states the differences are above 50 per cent., ranging as high as 70 per cent. in two states.

For twelve additional states the differences are 20 per cent. or greater. The discrepancies, whatever their cause may be, place a serious limitation on the use of these figures for any careful work.

Turning to the reports published by state departments of education, we find difficulties which, while they do not give us cause to question the accuracy of the figures, nevertheless prevent their use for purposes of comparisons. Of seventy-nine items for which reports were given or which were reported in a separate way, concerning high schools, in the forty-eight states, there is *not a single item* for which material is available in the reports for all states, and statistics are available for *only five*

[2] Statistical Survey of Education 1921–22, U. S. Bureau of Education Bulletins 1924, No. 38, pp. 22–23; Statistics of Public High Schools 1921–22, U. S. Bureau of Education Bulletin 1924, No. 7, pp. 21–22.

[3] Statistical Survey of Education 1925–26, U. S. Bureau of Education Bulletin 1928, No. 12, p. 13; Statistics of Public High Schools 1925–26, U. S. Bureau of Education Bulletin 1927, No. 33, p. 28.

items for as many as half the states. These materials are collected and reported in such a variety of ways that one never has any feeling of assurance that the statistics for any two states are comparable. The manner of reporting is also such that comparative figures, except for state or county totals or averages, can not be computed for any one item for more than a fourth of the states.

In some of the states only partial statistics are included in the reports. In other items there are great differences in the detail of the report. In many, the explanation of just what an item includes is lacking.

It is a surprising thing that from the reports of some states, it is difficult to figure the total high-school enrolment, and in one state, Arkansas, it was impossible to compute the enrolment because no figures whatever were given for high schools. Enrolment, average daily attendance, number of graduates, school census and number of teachers, are the only items available in the reports for as many as half of the states.

Two remedies are suggested for the condition which exists. We should have either a federal agency empowered to collect and publish data on high schools and with authority to compel the submission of full reports, or a united effort on the part of state officials to collect and publish comparable statistics on at least a minimum number of important items. If the states do not find it possible or convenient to collect reports on a comparable basis for their own purposes, they might cooperate with the Bureau of Education in securing for the bureau complete statistics for the schools of their state. This might be done by having the state department send out to the schools the forms prepared by the bureau at the same time the state forms are sent out. The state department could then require the submission of the bureau reports along with its own. This would insure for the Bureau of Education reports as accurate and complete as could be secured.

College of Education, O. L. Troxel
Municipal University of Wichita

SPECIAL CORRESPONDENCE

THE GENEVA CONFERENCE

There are fifty educational organizations in the world whose slogan just at present is "Geneva, 1929," and there are approximately five thousand individual teachers whose thoughts are turned toward Geneva waiting for vacation time to come, when the Third Biennial Conference of the World Federation of Education Associations will be held from July 25 to August 3 in the cosmopolitan Swiss city whose name has become synonymous with international cooperative endeavor.

"International Understanding and Good-will Through Education" is to be the theme of the meeting. The general program will deal with the subject from a variety of standpoints and will include many of the most eminent educators in the leading countries of the world. This general subject will be constantly in the minds of the chairmen in preparing the programs for the various sections into which the Conference will be divided.

The National Education Association has approved Thos. Cook & Son, 585 Fifth Avenue, New York City, to conduct trips of delegates from their organization and of other visitors to the conference, and the National Education Association is urging that members of that association arrange their tours through the travel bureau. In a similar way the American Federation of Teachers has approved the Travel Bureau of the National Union of Teachers, arrangements with which can be made through Captain Anderson, care Canadian Pacific Railway Company, New York City, or through Miss E. L. Spence, care Canadian Pacific Railway Company, Montreal, Canada. In addition, the World Federation has arranged with three other bureaus to conduct approved trips of visitors, namely, Walter H. Woods Company, 80 Boylston Street, Boston, Massachusetts; Temple Tours, Incorporated, Boston, Massachusetts, and International Travel Club, Terminal Tower Building, Cleveland, Ohio.

All indications at the present time point to a splendid attendance from teachers all over the world. Several Asiatic countries, including China and Japan, are preparing to send delegations. India has already appointed a delegation of more than twenty educational leaders.

The International Bureau of Education is making special arrangements by which probably every country of continental Europe will be represented. Moreover, it seems certain that the British Isles, Canada and the United States will send large delegations. The meeting is especially convenient for teachers from the United States who may be spending the summer in Europe. All such teachers should plan to include the conference in their itinerary. The opportunity of visiting the fine old city of Geneva, of hearing many of the most eminent educators of the world, and especially of forming friendships with teachers of other lands, is one that no teacher can afford to neglect. Those who attend will experience a benefit and an enjoyment not soon to be forgotten.

C. H. Williams,
Secretary, World Federation of Educational Associations

PLANS OF THE NATIONAL SOCIETY FOR THE STUDY OF EDUCATION FOR THE SUBVENTION OF RESEARCH

At the meeting of the board of directors held at Rochester, New York, in November, 1928, it was voted to increase the investments of the society in interest-bearing securities by $2,000 or more annually until a permanent fund of approximately $20,000 is accumulated, the income of which (approximately $1,000 annually) shall thereafter be employed, under direction of the board, for the stimulation and subvention of investigations in the field of education.

This permanent fund will presumably be established in five or six years. However, in order that this undertaking of the society may not be delayed, the board of directors also voted that, pending the completion of the fund, the society announce its willingness to consider the support of such proposals for educational research as meet the approval of the board, and that provisionally the sum of $2,000 be allocated to this purpose.

The investigations contemplated under this new development of the society's activities are conceived of as carried on independently of the activities of the society's various yearbook committees, though it is assumed that the investigations will often emerge from, or lead to, the production of yearbooks.

Members of the National Society for the Study of Education and others interested are urged to submit proposals for research or constructive suggestions for the general organization and development of this phase of the society's work. Communications should reach the secretary, at Danvers, Massachusetts, before May 1, if they are to be considered at the next regular meeting of the board of directors, to be held May 11–12, 1929.

Guy M. Whipple,
Secretary

QUOTATIONS

VENTILATION OF SCHOOLROOMS

The New York State Commission on Ventilation reported six years ago that it had found less respiratory disease in schools with old-fashioned window ventilation than in the more modern buildings mechanically ventilated. Many states already had outlawed the older method, and the engineers had some justifiable pride in the devices they had made to insure what seemed to be ideal atmospheric conditions for the indoor life. The engineers proposed that future investigations should take into account a conformation to a "rating schedule" of the various physical measurements of the atmosphere rather than the morbidity rate among those who breathe it. The public health investigators, however, insisted that the health of the school child is the final criterion of success, though it is desirable to understand what are the physical conditions that promote his health. Further studies have been undertaken with additional precautions to avoid sources of error. Thus Mr. Duffield reported to the annual meeting of the American Society of Heating and Ventilating Engineers last year the results of a survey in Syracuse wherein careful allowance had been made for varying characteristics in different school populations. He found that American children are liable to be kept at home with a cold more than are the children of Italian parents. Yet, when all due corrections were made, the conclusion of the 1923 report was amply confirmed. Another report has been published of a survey made by an engineer of the U. S. Public Health Service in New Haven. Once again window ventilation is in the ascendant. Three schools provided with mechanical ventilation and automatic temperature control have an average rate of total absence of 6 per cent. of pupil sessions as compared with 3.9 per cent. of pupil sessions for the naturally ventilated group. Whether longer or shorter absences are taken into account, the mechanical ventilation comes out second best. Nor can the difference be explained as due to higher temperatures in one group than in the other, for the temperatures found in all schools were closely alike. There remain possible differences in air motion and humidity which it was not found practicable to measure in this investigation. Such measurements should certainly be made in future research as well as temperature measurements at different points in the rooms. The present advantage of window ventilation must depend on physical factors; conditions which, when they are thoroughly understood, will be imitated in artificial ventilation and may even be improved on. The need for further research is urgent. School buildings are not alone in containing expensive ventilating systems that may subsequently need to be modified or replaced.—*The Journal of the American Medical Association.*

REPORTS

SOCIAL SCIENCE RESEARCH COUNCIL FELLOWS

FELLOWS of the Social Science Research Council for 1929–30 have been elected as follows:

Baldwin, Frances Elizabeth, Ph.D. (Johns Hopkins), professor of history and political science, Hood College. Project: "A Study of the English Constitution in the Tudor Period." Study in England.

Black, Jean Phyllis, Ph.D. (University of Rome, Italy), instructor in history, College of St. Catherine. Project: "Lord Palmerston's Italian Policy during the Years 1846–1849." Study in Italy, England, France and Austria.

Branch, E. Douglas, Ph.D. (State University of Iowa), research associate, State Historical Society of Iowa; honorary associate, department of history, State University of Iowa. Project: "The Life of Ramsay Crooks: more exactly, a general history of the American Fur Company." Study in New York, St. Louis, Detroit and St. Paul.

Brown, Esther Lucile, Ph.D. (June, 1929, University of New Hampshire), assistant professor of sociology, University of New Hampshire. Project: "Lycanthropy—the Loup Garou." Study in Canada and France.

Hamilton, Earl Jefferson, Ph.D. (Harvard), assistant professor of economics, Duke University. Project: "Money, Prices, and Wages in Castile, 1500–1660, especially as affected by the influx of treasure from the Hispanic Colonies of the New World; and American Gold and Silver Production, 1557–1660." Study in Spain, especially Castile.

Heinberg, John Gilbert, Ph.D. (Brookings Graduate School of Economics), assistant professor of political science, University of Missouri. Project: "An Intensive Study of the Personnel of French Cabinets since the Establishment of the Third Republic." Study in Paris.

Hoover, Calvin Bryce, Ph.D. (Wisconsin), professor of economics, Duke University. Project: "The Banking System of the Union of Socialist Soviet Republics; with special reference to the problems of a 'managed currency.'" Study in Russia and the United States.

Johnson, Edgar A. J., Ph.D. (February, 1929, Harvard), instructor and tutor, Harvard University. Project: "A Study of British Mercantilism of the Eighteenth Century to Ascertain the Relation between the Theory of Mercantilism and the Commercial Policy of the Selected Period." Study in London.

La Monte, John L., Ph.D. (February, 1929, Nebraska), instructor in history, University of Nebraska. Project: "A Study of the Life and Work of Foulque Plantagenet, Count of Anjou and King of Jerusalem; with special reference to the feudal and princely institutions of France and Syria of that period." Study in France and probably also in Venice and Rome.

Lattimore, Owen. Project: "An Anthropological Study in Manchuria" (to be worked out in consultation with a committee consisting of Professors R. B. Dixon, L. Warner and A. M. Tozzer). Study at Harvard and in China.

Leighly, John Barger, Ph.D. (California), assistant professor of geography, University of California. Project: "The Plans and Modes of Occupation of the Land in the Commercial Towns on the East Side of the Baltic, in their Historical Development." Study in Germany, the Baltic States and Finland.

Lesser, Alexander, Ph.D. (June, 1929, Columbia). Project: "An Inquiry into the Possibility of Law in Social Phenomena; with special reference to the social organization of primitive peoples." Study in New York City and Southwestern United States.

Lewinson, Paul, Ph.D. (Brookings Graduate School), instructor in history, Ohio State University. Project: "The Recent History of Negro Suffrage and of White Local Politics in the South, and their Interaction, together with Some Evaluation of the Possible Contribution to the General Theory of Race Relationships Arising from the Problem of Negro Suffrage." Study in Southern United States.

Lumpkin, Katherine Du Pre, Ph.D. (Wisconsin), instructor in sociology and economics, Mount Holyoke College. Project: "A Study of Social Situation as Related to Conduct Problem Children in Dependent Families." Study in New York City.

Ratner, Joseph, Ph.D. (Columbia), lecturer in philosophy, Columbia University. Project: "A Study of Methods in the Social Sciences." Study in the United States.

Rauber, Earle Le Roy, Ph.D. (August, 1929, Chicago), student and research assistant, University of Chicago. Project: "(1) Electrification Program and Labor Legislation in Actual Practice in Czechoslovakia, Austria and Russia; (2) Labor Legislation as Manifested in Practice as Compared with Paper Programs." Study in Prague, Vienna and Moscow.

Schaupp, Zora, Ph.D. (Bryn Mawr), instructor in philosophy and psychology, University of Nebraska. Project: "Infant School Education in Europe; with a special study of the Beacon Hill experiment of Mr. and Mrs. Bertrand Russell." Study in England, Russia and Germany.

Schiller, A. Arthur, J.D. Candidate (Columbia), research assistant in social science and lecturer in law, Columbia University. Project: "The Libellary Procedure of the Fifth and Sixth Centuries A. D.: A Study of the Legal and Papyrological Materials Dealing with the Post-Classical Imperial Legal Procedure of the Roman Empire." Study in Germany, Austria, France or Italy.

Simkins, Francis Butler, Ph.D. (Columbia), associate professor of history, State Teachers' College of Virginia. Project: "South Carolina during the Period of Reconstruction, 1865–1877: A Study of the Political, Agricultural, Industrial, Religious, Educational and Social Changes in a Typical Southern State." Study in South Carolina, Washington, D. C., and New York City.

Smith, Richard Joyce, LL.B. (Yale Law School), instructor, Yale Law School. Project: "A Study of the Method of Regulating Public Utility companies in Great Britain; with particular attention directed to the control of the power industry." Study in Great Britain, principally England and Scotland.

Sward, Keith, Ph.D. (Summer, 1929, Minnesota), teaching assistant in psychology, University of Minnesota. Project: "An Experimental Study of Leadership." Study in Palo Alto, California.

Turner, William Donald, Ph.D. (June, 1929, Harvard), instructor in psychology, Tufts College, Harvard University. Project: "Socialization of Emotional Expressions in Infants and Young Children." Study in Vienna.

Vandenbosch, Amry, Ph.D. (Chicago), associate professor of political science, University of Kentucky. Project: "Dutch Colonial Policy and Administration." Study in London, the Netherlands and the Dutch East Indies.

Wirth, Louis, Ph.D. (Chicago), assistant professor in sociology, Tulane University. Project: "Segregated Areas and Local Communities in German Cities: A Comparative Study in Methods of Social Research as Affected by Recent Developments in Human Ecology and Social Psychology." Study in Germany.

Reappointment of Old Fellows:

Gower, Charlotte Day, Ph.D. (Chicago), Social Science Research Council Fellow 1928–29. Project: "An Ethnological and Sociological Study of a Typical Sicilian Village Community as a Contribution to the Background of the Problem of the Sicilian Immigrant to the United States." Study half in Sicily and half in Chicago.

Hohman, Elmo P., Ph.D. (Harvard), Social Science Research Council Fellow 1928–29. Project: "A Comparative Study of American and European Seagoing Labor in the Twentieth Century; with special reference to the operation of the LaFollette Seamen's Act." Study at Geneva and Far East maritime centers.

Pollock, James K., Jr., Ph.D. (Harvard), Social Science Research Council Fellow 1927–28. Project: "The Use of Money in English, French and German Elections." Study in England.

SOCIETIES AND MEETINGS

SCHOOLMEN'S WEEK AT THE UNIVERSITY OF PENNSYLVANIA

About five thousand persons, representing public and private schools of all grades in Pennsylvania, New Jersey and Delaware, attended the sixteenth annual meeting of Schoolmen's Week, held from March 13 to 16 at the University of Pennsylvania, in connection with the Southeastern Convention District of the Pennsylvania State Education Association.

A feature of the program was eleven demonstration lessons, which were very largely attended. Among the topics presented in papers and addresses during the four days of the convention were: Teacher tenure in Pennsylvania; teacher-training programs; recent tendencies in primary education; individual instruction in the elementary and junior high schools; pupil failures in the high school; ability levels in the high school; high-school supervision; guidance programs; athletics in secondary schools; consolidation and transportation; state school finances; demonstrations by the psychology department of the University of Pennsylvania.

Among the visiting speakers were the following: President W. W. Atwood, of Clark University; Professor H. Theodore Becker, of the University of Hamburg, Germany; Dr. E. F. Bradford, Cornell University; Professor O. G. Brim, Ohio State University; Professor W. W. Charters, Ohio State University; Professor Charles H. Judd, University of Chicago; Dr. I. L. Kandel, International Institute, Teachers College, Columbia University; State Superintendent John A. H. Keith, Pennsylvania Department of Public Instruction; Professor J. R. McGaughy, Teachers College; Professor H. C. Morrison, University of Chicago; Professor Paul Mort, Teachers College; Professor L. C. Mossman, Teachers College; Chief Justice Harry Olson, Municipal Court, Chicago; Superintendent Frank G. Pickell, Montclair, N. J.; Dr. Frederick R. Rogers, New York State Department of Education; Superintendent Carleton Washburne, Winnetka, Illinois; Superintendent David E. Weglein, Baltimore.

The committee in charge of Schoolmen's Week is constituted as follows: Representing the University of Pennsylvania: Professor Arthur J. Jones, *chairman;* Professor LeRoy A. King, *secretary;* Professors H. T. Collings, J. P. W. Crawford, John Dolman and Francis M. Garver. Representing the state: Milton C. Cooper, district superintendent, Philadelphia; Robert M. Steele, principal, Southwestern State Normal School, California; A. M. Kulp, superintendent of schools, Montgomery County; A. P. Diffendafer, superintendent of schools, Nanticoke; E. H. Snow, principal, Lower Merion Township Junior High School; Emma C. Dowling, primary supervisor, Reading. Representing the Southeastern Convention District of the Pennsylvania State Education Association: Albert L. Rowland, superintendent of schools, Cheltenham Township, *president;* W. Carson Ryan, professor of education, Swarthmore College, *vice-president;* Carmon Ross, superintendent of schools, Doylestown, *secretary;* Charles R. Foster, president, Pennsylvania State Education Association, *ex officio;* J. Herbert Kelley, executive secretary, Pennsylvania State Education Association, *ex officio.*

R. W.

EDUCATIONAL RESEARCH AND STATISTICS

WHAT PROFESSIONAL MAGAZINES DO PROSPECTIVE EDUCATORS READ?

Our national professional magazines are the most reliable barometers of educational progress. Educational growth and improvement is exhibited in educational periodicals long before it becomes solidified in text-books. Doubtless all educators will agree that it is essential for them to read several professional journals if they expect to keep up to date.

But should not interest in educational periodicals and familiarity with them be gained long before the busy superintendent, principal or teacher is plunged into the varied and exacting demands of his position? Should not the leading journals then be tried and trusted friends—

not strangers? That acquaintance with the principal educational magazines should begin with the first professional course in education is the firm conviction of the writer.

The course in "Introduction to the Study of Education" as given in the School of Education at Stanford University is required of all candidates for any form of California teachers' recommendations and of all major students if without teaching experience. It is normally taken by juniors but by a considerable number of seniors as well, and by a few graduate students. For the past two years, while this course has been conducted by the writer, one definite requirement has been the reading of periodical articles. During the eleven weeks of the course each member of the class is required to read twenty-two articles from at least six different current educational periodicals, and at the close of the term to hand in a list of these articles with a single sentence summary or characterization of each. A mimeographed list of forty of the leading periodicals available in the education library is furnished and the different magazines are briefly characterized. No restriction is placed on choice of magazines nor is any guidance offered in the selection of articles, the object being to encourage independent browsing and sampling and a general acquaintance with a large number of different journals. The prospective teacher or administrator who forms an acquaintance with the leading educational periodicals in his student days is much more likely to use them all through his course and to continue his reading of them when he enters active professional work.

It is interesting and significant to see the relative frequency with which members of this year's class chose articles from the different periodicals. This may be taken as one measure of the relative interest, value and usefulness of the journals in later active professional life. A classification of over 2,500 articles thus freely chosen for reading by 115 members of the class is given below for the twenty-eight journals in which twenty or more articles were reported. In addition some forty other journals were reported with less than twenty articles each.

Numbers 3, 12, 16 and 20 are largely local journals, but the others are all national in scope

Name of journal	Number of articles reported
1. School and Society	290
2. *School Review*	223
3. *Sierra Educational News* (State Journal)	202
4. *Educational Review*	180
5. *Journal of the National Education Association*	169
6. *Journal of Education* (Boston)	110
7. *School Life*	100
8. *Education*	98
9. *American Educational Digest*	90
10. *American School Board Journal*	86
11. *Teachers College Record*	79
12. *California Quarterly of Secondary Education*	72
13. *Journal of Educational Research*	70
14. *Progressive Education*	58
15. *The Nation's Schools*	56
16. *The High School*	48
17. *Education-Outlook*	42
18. *Elementary School Journal*	41
19. *American Childhood*	37
20. *Teachers Journal of Northern California*	31
21. *Journal of Educational Psychology*	28
22. *English Journal*	28
23. *Playground*	26
24. *Industrial Arts Magazine*	24
25. *Journal of Geography*	24
26. *Journal of Educational Method*	23
27. *Primary Education-Popular Educator*	22
28. *School Science and Mathematics*	20

and circulation. They comprise a substantial but highly differentiated educational diet.

It will be of interest to compare this list with two others which have been compiled from entirely different standpoints, and to note similarities and differences in the three lists.

In 1917 all members of the National Society for the Study of Education and of the National Society of College Teachers of Education were asked to give the names of from one to five educational journals which it would be desirable to have in the public library. Replies were received from 253 members, who recommended the following, in the order named. Only the first ten on the list are given here. Twenty-seven were named altogether.[1]

[1] School and Society, 6: 433 (October 13, 1917).

1.	School and Society	221
2.	*School Review*	179
3.	*Educational Review*	156
4.	*Elementary School Journal*	108
5.	*Educational Administration and Supervision*	73
6.	*American School Board Journal*	67
7.	*Journal of Education*	57
8.	*Journal of Educational Psychology*	55
9.	*Education*	46
10.	*Teachers College Record*	42

The second study was reported in 1927 by J. L. LaPoe,[2] of Ohio State University. Three hundred and eighty-one senior high school principals, representing all the states, indicated which ones of ten designated educational journals were most read by them. The number indicating the reading of the different journals, in order, follows:

1.	*State Journal of Education* (various ones)	279
2.	*School Review*	275
3.	*American School Board Journal*	245
4.	*Educational Review*	152
5.	School and Society	135
6.	*Teachers College Record*	111
7.	*Educational Administration and Supervision*	109
8.	*Journal of Educational Research*	101
9.	*Journal of Education*	96
10.	*Education*	87

Both the dates and the purposes of these three lists vary, yet there is a striking similarity between them as far as the first ten on each list are concerned. Six journals are common to the first ten in all three lists: School and Society, *School Review, Educational Review, Journal of Education, Education* and *American School Board Journal. Teachers College Record, Educational Administration and Supervision* and a state journal (*Sierra News*) are common to two lists. Some of the periodicals were not in existence when the 1917 library list was compiled.

School Review consistently occupies second place on all three lists. School and Society was most frequently recommended for library purposes (even though yet in its infancy in 1917), and was most frequently read by the class in "Introduction to Education," but did not rank so high with high-school principals. Now that it has so recently been combined with the *"Atlantic Monthly* of educational journalism," the *Educational Review,* which stood third or fourth on all three lists, its eminence in the educational periodical field may be considered greater than ever.

No effort was made to secure comments from the class regarding the value of the assignment, but a number volunteered them in connection with their written reports. Two or three sample ones may be of interest.

I feel that this reading has been very beneficial. I value not only the subject-matter read, but the introduction to the magazines.

I would like to take the opportunity to say here that I obtained a fund of information from these periodical readings. It has brought to my mind the fact that educators are doing a great work and that they have many difficult problems to solve every day.

It seems rather unconsciously I have developed the habit of dropping into the education library during spare minutes before class or even spending an hour there. I have also developed likes and dislikes for different magazines and naturally pick the ones I find the most interesting. I am writing this little comment so that the designer of the course with its twenty-two articles will know that there is a possibility of such a requirement arousing an interest in subjects that before had never been noticed.

The class, however, were asked to express their opinion of the value of the periodical reading assignment in comparison with a dozen other elements of the course, with the following results:

Characterization	Number of Students
Greatest value of all	5
Very great value	22
Considerable value	43
Some value	24
Slight value	11
No value	2

Walter Crosby Eells
Stanford University

[2] J. L. LaPoe, "The Senior High School Principals' Professional Magazines," *Educational Research Bulletin,* Ohio State University, 6: 259 (September 14, 1927). Also reprinted in *School Review,* February, 1928, Vol. 36, p. 86.

EDUCATIONAL REVIEW

Edited by WILLIAM McANDREW

NOTES ON AN EDUCATIONAL PILGRIMAGE TO ANTIOCH

WHEN occasional good fortune has permitted your so-called humble servant to get outside the ring of routine, school-board meetings and leisurely self-seekers who "don't want to take up your valuable time" and do take it whether valuable or not, I have spent a day or more in the schools of Omaha or Binghamton or close to the work of Frank Rexford or Richard Welling.

These educational pilgrimages have been recorded in the pages of this magazine. It is a precarious business. The ideas of a man responsible for any organization of school service suffer by translation. But so far no libel suits have been filed for any injury done by printing the notes of my promenades through the premises of John Beveridge, Daniel Kelley or Frank Boynton. Here follows an attempt to show how Antioch, the shrine of Horace Mann, looks to me. Nobody officially connected with that unique development at Yellow Springs knows I have turned my camera upon it. My enthusiasm for it is great, but I have tempered it below the warmth of those who know more about the project than I.

Realizing your idea before you die.—If you had not been yourself you surely would have enjoyed being Ezra Cornell at the time he put his brains and money into an educational system organized on a new basis. Or, if you had had the power of being who, other than you, you wished to be, you would have had a happy time in the person of Charles Pratt, who poured his wealth into an educational scheme of his own. The persuasive presidents of existing institutions demonstrated that their colleges were most worthy of benefactions, but the modest and quiet Brooklynite founded a new kind of school to supply a need he, himself, had discovered. He personally nursed his plan into a going concern renowned for design and service. It would be a delight to play the rôle of a John D. Rockefeller and back an educational inventor like William Rainey Harper until a University of Chicago should demonstrate the vitality and worth of a new scheme and fresh ideals. Those three benefactors had wealth enough to perform their brilliant tasks without going hungry or depriving their families of three good meals a day. Let their good works outweigh my American envy that they had more dollars than I. Let me play my accordion and sing the praises of an educational pioneer who had no millions to support his adventure but who gave up a career of money-making and threw himself into the giant's task of building a school project with little, at first, to back him other than his own pluck, brains and faith.

He's wary of generalizing.—The first time I met Arthur Morgan he upset me neatly and gently. I was arguing for better payment for teachers. America doesn't really honor education, I said, or it would put its respect into the form our countrymen most value, the almighty dollar. Better-paid teaching would insure the prosperity we have gained through abundant natural resources which are already less generous than they were. Ptolemy knew how to build up a country. He brought the best teachers of the world to

Egypt and rewarded them with palaces, gardens and good living. His realm, when teachers were substantially honored, yielded its increase. Greece made Plato, Aristotle and its teachers rich. It ruled the intelligence of the world. Whenever the teacher is held in the highest regard the nation is great.

"Like China," remarked the genial constructor of dams.

An engineer's idea of college.—Morgan's career has been in the field of applied science. You could show him how a dike should be built diagonally across a piece of terrain and at once he would tell you how an embankment of that sort below Arles cheerfully gave way before the next spring freshet of the Rhone. Building levees, sluices, spillways, bridges, he had working under his direction a thousand college or university graduates, mostly from engineering schools. He has said he wondered that their schooling had left them so one-sided. They needed more than their profession. They lacked health or books or friends or civic pride or a philosophy of life. Except for seeing technical ability their professors had been almost blind. The boys from the liberal arts colleges had fared better, but even these had been given a more or less accidental accumulation of studies which had had merely value enough to survive. The idea of aiding a young man or woman to form a working plan of a whole life did not appear as a controlling element of college policy. Versatility had been preferred to proportion. To put a city like Dayton in a condition of safety from flood requires a definite line of thought involving a completely defined objective, a survey of obstacles, a consideration of means, a knowledge of failures and successes in projects having some similarity to the problem, an estimate of costs for various plans, the time element, and other complexities which are stored away in the mental pigeonholes of the efficient executive. By the method of the engineer, Morgan's mind at various periods attacked the problem of education. You may remember, a dozen years ago, an article or two on schooling in which his views as those of a man in the bustle of the workaday world flashed with a bright freshness as different as stimulating. He had a vision of a teaching that would base its methods on the intent of delivering purposeful, well-rounded men and women fitted for the life of our own country and our own time. Instead of being satisfied with passing over its counter such portions of an old and revered curriculum as could be retailed in four years the college was conceived by him as an organization controlled by the changing demands of life and by the nature of the student, not by the respectability of ancient studies. The schools, said our engineer, have never realized more than a small portion of what, even with their present staffs and equipment, they can do. Higher education is out of balance. It doesn't see life whole. Most of the technical schools give nearly their whole attention to professional efficiency. The colleges overlook practical economic life. The classroom and laboratory are too narrow. The graduate needs broad, direct contact with affairs. The country has a wide-spread discontent with its colleges, not because they have deteriorated but because men and women demand more value and higher standards than they themselves obtained in their education. Intuitively the people who support the college expect it to provide opportunity for the enlarging of life. They conceive it as an institution in which incompleteness may be repaired and provincialism may be cast off, where interest and outlook may expand. For this, fathers and mothers economize, sisters teach school, to make opportunity for younger members of the family to get the blessings of the higher education. In the minds of the average American the purpose of the college has been imagined to be the best of life, nothing less.

Religio pedagogica.—It is a ticklish thing to undertake an exposition of the educational doctrines of living men. Some undue emphasis here, some missing of the point there, may throw the picture out of symmetry. I have no charter to proclaim the gospel of Arthur Morgan. But he has been for a dozen years in the field some of us have occupied for fifty. What an ordinary schoolman has observed of him and thinks of him is fair grist for the editorial mill, provided one's ink is free of acid. Admiration for his adventure, respect for his theories, conviction that his service ranks in the front row of needed demonstrations in our time are responsible for this attempt to epitomize the man and his work.

I see in Morgan a vision of the new freedom which requires no ridicule of the best that was in the clean hearts of our grandmothers. His goal of liberty is freedom from poverty and sickness, freedom from ignorance and fear, freedom from hindrance in the work we long to do. And he quotes Washington that "freedom is not licentiousness." His idea is what you desire for yourself and your children. It is attainable. It is achieved through a plan of life. You can not make a success if you leave your life to chance. Leaving one's monthly bills to luck is disaster. A common mistake of letting fortune decide the future is a reason why failure is common. After much agitation by the banks and the magazines sensible people are learning to run their finances on a budget. Foresight properly organized brings freedom from worry over monthly bills. It could be the function of a college to determine what are the important things in the well-rounded life and adjust training to give students the mastery of these. Mere drill and regimentation fail to do this. They do develop skill in their narrow grooves, but they dwarf the creative spirit. American elementary and secondary education are under this menace. Rigid discipline brings such quick returns that it blinds the schoolman to the loss of creative power.

One might compile a religion of an engineer from some of the bits of doctrine Morgan has enunciated:

> To serve buyer and seller is sound business and true. To profit the seller only, to cater to ignorance, credulity or frailty is dishonor.
>
> Who makes or sells or serves must do his best for human well-being.
>
> Great accomplishments require men to work together without conflict. Many a graduate has failed from lack of training in that ability.
>
> The college man's lack of success in business or industry comes not so much from lack of knowledge as from poor development of important traits of character and personality.
>
> The elements of a well-rounded life include health, work, society, religion, economy, beauty, proportion and a well-grounded knowledge of history, literature, philosophy and science, all bound together by a purpose in life.

Faculty epic.—To sit upon the shore and discourse on the proper captaining of ships is not without its benefit. When suddenly and unexpectedly, nine years ago, the little old college of Antioch, founded in 1853, called Morgan to Yellow Springs, he left his bridges behind him and accepted the risky adventure of putting the new wine of his educational policy into the bottle of an existing organization. Antioch, long before Morgan, had the distinction of killing Horace Mann, its first president. Famous, fearless, full of progressive plans, the virile statesman educator crossed from stately Massachusetts to a boyish and boisterous Ohio to be smothered under board dominion and worried into his grave by an imperial college janitor. One trace of superstition would have kept most men of new ideas far from the waters of Yellow Springs.

Teaching the student his business.—But whatever barricades against novelty any safety-first trustee or professor may have thought himself in duty bound to raise have not appeared. A faculty, gratified at the opportunity of teamwork in a new scheme alterable at any point of failure to work, formulates and subscribes to a doctrine of education based on present purposes, not tradition. It worked fairly well when first attempted, but amazingly better after eight years of trial.

The principles of higher education which this group of teachers has outlined and developed into a working program have engaged the interest of the country at large.

The old and recurring dictum of Comenius, that education is life, gets striking emphasis at Antioch College.

Freedom, creation and size.—Like Osborn, like Lindeman, like Kilpatrick, like Rugg, like the cheerful and lively tribe of the Deweyites, these Antiochans invoke the creative spirit. "To preserve this, which thrives in freedom, is the large task of education. It can not come from slovenliness of thought. That is the accompaniment of lack of discipline. Creative freedom is a temper of life not engendered by administrative devices too prone to repression. Creation comes from finding one's work and doing it in the spirit of a freeman."

There seems to be none of the common American craze for size in the Antioch spirit. "It is a small college, yet there are those who love it." One of the issues of the *Antioch Notes* confesses it without tears: "The big universities, with great resources, will educate most of our youth who go to college. Large size in a school makes exploration and adventure difficult. We wish to be a help to the great universities. We are free to do what men in them would like to do but can't." How Dean McConn will clap his hands at that.

So much for a few gleams of theory from the men of Antioch. There have been similar expoundings of educational theory from Emerson's time to ours. If a declaration of principles were the most of Antioch we would have a mere voice crying in the wilderness of college discussion. The most significant thing is the theory working out its program.

They begin with a course of two hours a week called "College Aims." It is an introduction to self-directed methods of study. The president and other men and women of the faculty acquaint the freshman with the college purposes and standards in study, cooperative work, social life, extra-curricular activities and recreational reading. They aim to lead him to inquire what are the fundamental aims which every human being must satisfy if he would live a complete life. They introduce him to the principles which the masters of living have evolved from experiences in satisfying the needs of body, mind and spirit. You and I went up to college with a belief that a power over these was to be given to us. But, if you are at all near to my age, your first dose of college medicine was a bewildering mess of unrelated subjects, administered by instructors who knew little of what their colleagues were doing to you. If there was any theory at all behind the process it was that of the old school of doctoring, that medicines injected would do their work. No college professor gave me any hints on why the prescribed courses were given me. No one offered me any instruction on how to study. It was a common usage to refer to us young cubs as "men." We were only high-school boys—material which might have been helped to grow into men. My entrance into that estate was hindered and delayed by my four years in college. My companions who got into life earlier were mostly ahead of me on commencement day. Most of them have kept ahead ever since. Far be it from me to invite reprimand for throwing mud at my dear old Alma Grandmater. But she didn't much look after me. She had gathered a congeries of subjects. She had assembled a company of scholars who had mastered the assorted knowledges. These men cut off their daily pieces of them and ordered, "Swallow this." At intervals they examined some of our imperfectly chewed cuds and put figures in a class book. The Antiochers have awakened to the damage of such a procedure. "We are more concerned," they say, "with students than with studies. We train our youth to understand themselves and to find their dominant life interests, to make a choice, to learn their excellences and deficiencies, to stand on their own feet, to perfect their talents for the benefit of the world." The course seems to us of the old school revolutionary. These Yellow Springs professors assume to equip all their foster-children with a substantial introduction to every main field of human concern.

What they study.—In carrying out his program each student has science all through his course, including mathematics, chemistry, physics, astronomy, physiography, geography, geology and psychology. Each person studies for four years social science, history, economics and government; for a year, philosophy; for two years, English, literature and physical education. Each takes courses in personal finance; each gets a look at art and esthetics. Every student chooses some dominant interest for his specialty and must devote to it not less than a third of the college course. These "fields of concentration" are art or biology or business management or chemistry, or education or economics or engineering, or English or language or geology or history, or politics or sociology or home-management or mathematics or health or physics, or psychology. Those are the specialties to-day. To-morrow they may be different; for, every year, the faculty reexamines the course to determine its contents and proportions and its proper claims upon the student's time, in order to adapt the studies to those who take them and to the work that men and women will do.

Was any such examination made of the work passed out to us? Not so that the ripples reached the part of the pond where we were floundering. The assignments by our professor of Greek, every working day, required from three to four hours of preparation by the average student. In addition we had five days' work in Latin, seven in different kinds of mathematics, two in a dismal monotony called English literature. Five greedy eaters of the time and strength of youth—*edaces temporis rerumque*—were our taskmasters. I think they permanently injured what I call my mind. God rest 'em; they're all now in the better world where all eyes are opened and things are seen as they are.

Mental dyspepsia.—Recognizing the fact that we are all different from the average, the Antioch faculty leaves us from a quarter to a third of our college time to fill with our own choice of studies. But so serious a decision can not be left to our youth and inexperience without the counsel of those who are skilled in these matters. Accordingly, at Antioch, the business of counseling, advising and guiding is no less important than the assignment of tasks. I am sorry no collegiate officer but one ever gave me any suggestion for a wise choice of electives. He was the professor of mathematics. In our required work in trigonometry and loci he found me too weak to get a passing mark. "You seem to have worked very hard," he said. "The trouble is probably due to imperfectly developed mathematical centers in your brain. They need exercise. Elect the sophomore mathematics and we'll count the first year's work as passed." I did. At the end of the year I was passed on, under exactly the same conditions; and, a year later, ditto; getting lower and further into a mathematical morass. At last the professor gave me the opportunity to get a credit by "mathematical reading." I copied the greater part of a huge tome into a set of notebooks with as much understanding of the contents as you have of the language of the Martians. I have certificates of proficiency in trigonometry, analytical geometry, loci of equations, conic sections, differential calculus, integral calculus and quaternions. My instructors knew what these subjects were. My professors knew as much of them when I quit as when I began, for I took nothing away. My teachers made no diagnosis of my cerebral condition. If they had they would have learned that it takes more time for my cells to function than the collegiate drivers allowed. I could digest a logarithm if you would give me time. But by crowding chunk after chunk of mathematics down me these well-meaning but ignorant practitioners produced a mathematical dyspepsia. As I run over my notes of those days I find that sixteen out of a hundred of my classmates felt themselves similarly injured. Possibly twice as many were in as bad a state but hesitated to admit it. We were not brilliant; we were not speedy, but we worked uncommon hard. I venture into these personalities that you may be warned of my peculiar enthusiasm for a college management that is adventuring into a service so untried in my day and so badly needed by me.

A "close-up" view of the world's work.—The knights of Sir Arthur's table round, accordingly, attempt to adjust the program of the college to the different personalities which come under its influence. But the guardians there realize that no college can maintain on its small campus a veritable condition of real life. Therefore the plan of alternating work in college and out in the field is an essential feature of their program.

Most of us have made approaches toward this. We took our high-school seniors to the rolling mills forty years ago. It was a pleasant picnic. Professor Davis worked engineering students on the Ann Arbor railroad in 1882. Dean Schneider introduced an alternating out-and-in system into the industrial courses of the University of Cincinnati and, at the invitation of Mayor John Purroy Mitchel, showed the city of New York how to work it in the public high schools. At Antioch the faculty says it is not seeking by this program primarily to develop technical skill but to secure those elements of all-round education and personal growth which can not be secured in the inevitable isolation of the college. For this reason they consider it no advantage for a student to get and hold one outside employment throughout his whole college membership. They want you to change your job when longer continuance means diminishing educational discipline. Railroads, factories, stores, offices, farms, newspapers, hospitals, laboratories and other works somewhere between the Rocky Mountains and the eastern coast employ one half the students at a time. Two people fill the same position at alternating periods. The men hire out for accounting, advertising, farming, architecture, art, building, engineering, journalism, manufacture, publishing, printing, research, selling, teaching, etc. The women do this and social service, home management, library work, and other things. All learn responsibility. They are allowed two weeks to find whether the placement is what they want. Then they must stick and do their best for a year unless the faculty finds good reason for remission of the particular task. A student learns how the world does its work, what men's hopes and motives are and what the share of the student is to be. This helps one choose his calling. Maybe you had your line picked out when you entered college and have happily pursued the work you were fitted to perform. The most of us fell into whatever hole was in sight and have dug around inside with little prospect of any other. Three quarters of the Antiochites change their vocational objectives after they have been taught what work is like. First choice is first guess, little else. From the very general program taken by each student when he begins the faculty outlines a gradual convergence to each person's special aptitude and interest. In selection of a calling the continued counsel and evaluation by professors of personnel is helping you reach an intelligent choice. How accurately does it work? The college records show half the graduates remaining with an institution in which they tried themselves while in college. They get paid for the outside work they do. This cuts the cost of a college education down one half. Being of Scottish ancestry I am by this feature led to throw my tam into the air and shout for Antioch. But the management reproves me: "Self-support during college years is not the aim of the part-time program. It is educational and preparatory rather than remunerative. Yet upperclass students frequently entirely support themselves." 'Rah for the upper-class students! Arthur Morgan well said that the experience of a large measure of earning while learning gives a degree of self-dependence and self-respect and a measure of values that are of no small account in a useful education. He said that young men who could start with an assurance of between three and four hundred dollars a year for the first half of the college course commonly earn the remainder of expenses needed to carry them through the whole program. A young woman may require $100 a year more. Observers have this to say of the outwork feature, that it does away with the common distress of earning an education in a standard college. There the hard-pressed boys have to work at odd jobs and carry a full-time program, often with the loss of health, scholarship and social experience. At Antioch everybody works. The program is based on it. Self-support is not an extra burden. The normal college life of study and social recreation is not upset.

This arrangement of in-and-out activity makes the college course six years long. It puts you farther on at the end of six years than four years in school and two years wondering why the world is so slow to recognize your value.

Some particulars.—Besides the employment in outside work what fills these six years? Liberal studies, vocational studies, bodily exercise and health, community service, comprise the activities. I have in front of me 109 pages listing what these are.

I find our old familiar acquaintances, Latin, Greek and modern languages. I find English and American speech and literature, journalism, advertising, "art through the ages," drawing and painting, genetics and eugenics, personal accounts, business finance, income tax, industrial civilization and its problems, business research, factory and store methods, lumber study, all the sciences usually found in a college course, education and teaching, measurements, junior high school, vocational guidance, engineering mechanical, engineering civil, engineering hydraulic, engineering electrical, theory of coaching athletics and sports, social and folk dancing, boxing, wrestling, swimming, first aid, physiology of sex, household economics, child care and training, lunchroom management, nineteen courses in mathematics, mental hygiene (I wish my professors had taken it), fourteen classes in psychology and philosophy including President Morgan in "life aims," twelve in social sciences including labor relations, public business and government. There are twenty-two offerings in history, politics, civilization and law. My catalog lists eighty-two professors, associates, instructors, directors and administrative officials, 691 students. The dormitories house 650.

I find in this family young folks from Oklahoma, Delaware, New England, Minnesota, Missouri, Pennsylvania, Illinois, California, Michigan, Montana, New York, Nebraska, Arkansas, Washington, Iowa, Oregon, New Jersey, Alabama, North Dakota, Georgia, Indiana, Florida, Wyoming, Idaho, New Mexico, West Virginia, Arizona, Ontario, Alberta, Saskatchewan, British Columbia, Mexico, Ireland, Trinidad, Ceylon and China.

Turning on the searchlight.—The administration in accordance with its emphasis on self-direction puts out some pretty frank announcements to would-be students. In effect these communications say that the institution has to devote its none too lavish resources to such youth as will make the most of them. "Don't come unless you want work and responsibility. You must have evidenced more than the average intelligence, seriousness of purpose and sound morality of a representative high-school group. We are undertaking to deliver to the country all-round men and women able to perform the part of high-class citizens skilled in their callings, determined to advance the progress of society." You have to show the certificate of the National Life Extension Institute or of an experienced physician that your lungs and liver, blood, etc., are up to the detailed standard required upon the college list of specifications. You have to study the bulletins sent you that the plan and purpose of the college is apprehended, you have to send a photograph of yourself without a hat on. You will do well to get a personal interview at Antioch or with some representative of the college in your vicinity. You have to write an autobiography telling why you want to go to college and why to this particular one. A dozen intimate inquiries are made the basis of the different paragraphs you write. When you get through you will have pointed a searchlight into pretty nearly every important room in your mental mansion. Why not? Here is a school committed to the method of diagnosis, appraisal, specific prescriptions for special needs, self-development. It begins at the beginning, as soon as you put yourself within its radius. An admission board at once considers the applicant's school record, the psychological test, the physical diagnosis and the recommendations of referees. There is no waiting list. You are accepted or rejected at once. You have time to apply elsewhere. Throughout the year acceptances are made so that the quota for September is filled before the college opens. The discipline and life of this college, so thoroughly in earnest, must cater to some extensive demand, for Antioch has, under its new organization on unusually virile lines, more applications from high-class workers than it can accommodate—twice over.

When you make your pilgrimage to Yellow Springs you will find more to surprise you than this itinerary through its program can suggest. A delightful auto-bus ride from Springfield, Ohio, takes you, ten miles, through a smiling land. The trip from Dayton is twice as far. The campus, groomed for seventy-six years, comprises 250 acres of hill and dale, woods, streams and ivy-covered halls. You'll be delighted with it. You will not find the perfection of philosophers in the lively young persons you see coming and going. They are as noisy as you would wish. If you take the chance to talk with any one of them picked at random you will find he has a clearer idea of what the whole thing is about than you can hear enunciated on an ordinary campus. Take, for instance, the Antioch Autonomous Plan of Study. Call it that and no doubt the boy will "kid" about it. But ask the junior as to its details: the abandonment of the formal class exercise, each student "going on his own," the personal consultation with the professor, informal groups conferring with and asking questions of the instructor. You will find the "autonomous plan," in spite of its scholastic name, a scheme that works. The experimenters after a trial of it put it to a vote of the students: shall we keep it or go back to the usual lectures and quizzes? The vote to go on was in the ratio of ninety-five out of every hundred. So, here in Ohio, is the scheme that Wilson set his heart upon in Princeton and failed, that Burton and Little dreamed of in Michigan, and didn't get. You could easily calculate that it means ten times more work for the professor to inaugurate it but the Antioch adventurers see in it ten times more worth for the beneficiaries. You'll find the "activities" dear to the heart of young America—the publications, the theatricals, the glee clubs, the orchestra, the band, societies of various sorts and the sometime Frankenstein—athletics. Nearly every one is in them, but, says the Morgan, "It does not dictate to the college."

"Is this in accordance with your fundamental principles of symmetry, harmony, proportion, all-roundness, isomorphism which I have so heartily admired in your concept of education?"

"You never heard me drown it in such pedantry," replies the head Antiochian. "Athletics is a part and not the chief business of college. For health, for spirits, for recreation, the masters welcomed sports into the curriculum. When the farmer spends more time in chasing squirrels than in cultivation, what you want me to call 'isometry' is gone. Athletics is for health. Beware the overdose. I called on a friend in a sanitarium. I told the doctor this man had been the outstanding athlete in his class. 'O yes,' the doctor said, 'this town is full of tubercular athletes. Overathleticism is one of the commonest records of our patients.' So, college men are dying before their time, from lack of proportion."

I get the idea that Antioch athletics is not for most of the students mere vocal exercises on the side of an intercollegiate game, but that enough fun is obtained from contests between their own teams. It satisfies your reason to see a college using sports for refreshment in order that one may do better the larger tasks. In my dear old school the athletic teams get so tired by their play they can't do their work.

Statistics, smoke and shoes.—These Antiochish professors appear to be open-minded on the health question. They went at some problems with the true scientific spirit. They studied the habits of the men that were falling behind. Out of those dropped from the rolls for poor work 88 per cent. were smokers. Taking the hundred lowest grade students they found eighty-three of them smokers. Martin O'Shea has similar but more thorough details for Wisconsin. The Yellow Springs scientist says, "My son, there is a valuable branch of statistics that deals with probabilities. Your expectancy of success is lowered by smoke, 95 per cent. Bodily health and mental vigor are largely autonomous. You can preserve yours. You want to leave tobacco alone." If I remember correctly Helvetius gave the world a large boost by insisting that our abilities may be considered practically boundless. Henry Morrison has come out for that by believing that any average person can learn anything if he starts early enough and sticks to it for a sufficient length of time. My Antiochissimi are saying, "Get rid of your inhibitions—tobacco is one—and believe you will make good. Then the coefficient of success becomes what will seem to be very large." They say in Yellow Springs that bad teaching has given vogue to a fallacy that many persons are found unable to learn. An instance is a belief that a woman can not master mathematics. She can, if she doesn't smoke. Speaking of women. Here is another bit of scientific method in this remarkable school. The professor of physique noted that faulty posture in girls is due to badly designed shoes. She made a study of woman's foot and its coverings. Scores of experimental lasts were made; hundreds of trial shoes were worn. The researchers aimed to design shoes not only sound from a health standpoint but of such unquestioned beauty as to be attractive to the woman who takes pride in being well dressed. They have put the "Antioch Shoe" on the market: a union of foot hygiene and structural beauty. Now is your chance to think something bright about the understanding.

The bigness of the experiment.—I draw near the boundary of the area allotted me by this magazine. I should like to tell you of the nursery school among the trees, flower gardens and playgrounds, adjoining the college campus. It is another recognition of the need of preparing in college for the main issues of life. Besides the service rendered these babies and their parents the Nursery School takes the task of preparing students for intelligent care of their own children and affords an opportunity to train women as managers of similar schools elsewhere. One interesting theory of Antioch is that a mother may be able in her own home to maintain a nursery for her own and a little group of children of her neighbors. Such a service would extend from ten to twelve and from one to three o'clock. Her little ones and those of her friends will be better trained by this means than if they were without contact with other children under guidance. I should like to tell you of the Antioch school conducted by the department of household economics. It covers the elementary grades. It puts into practice the ideals I have outlined as pertaining to the college: joy of living, guided freedom, creative work, recreation, cooperative government, citizenship by practice and the perpetual attention to health and growth. For high-school grades the college works with the regular secondary school system of the town, contributes money towards support and helps with service and advice by students and professors.

These, then, are the notes of a little pilgrimage to Antioch. To make them seem scholarly I ought to add a bibliology. See "College," Gavit; "The American College," Kirkpatrick; *Atlantic Monthly,* March and May, 1922; *Century,* October, 1923; *Pictorial Review,* January, 1924; *Collier's,* June 3, 1922. For Mr. Morgan's discussions of the principles of education, see "A Budget for Your Life," *Woman's Home Companion,* March, 1927; "An Adventure in Education," printed by the Antioch College Press. For official expositions by the faculty try "At Antioch," "Information for Prospective Students," "General Catalog," all issued by the college at Yellow Springs, Ohio.

From Ellery Sedgwick, of the *Atlantic;* from General Kiefer, former speaker of the House of Representatives; from Henry Dennison, of the Dennison Manufacturing Company; from William Mayo, chief engineer of the Ford industries; from Dave Morris, New York attorney and railroad executive; from Mrs. Jessie Armstrong, of Erie, solid American citizen; from other writers, thinkers, doers, who, if known to you, have your confidence, I get the assurance that my fervor for this reasoned, tried, progressive movement in the upbringing of men and women is justified. A big adventure, expensive of energy and money, and worth its cost, still needing endowment if it is to extend its service to double its present enrolment (for this year it turned away as many applicants as it took), needs the help of those who have the American faith that intelligent education is the hope and safety of the nation. Morgan has made a big sacrifice and done a prodigious service. His colleagues are carrying heavy loads. All of them are putting to work ideals which have brightened the pages of writers on education since the long line of lovers of their fellow man have turned their thoughts to the great problems of life and mind. To keep this Antioch enlightenment spreading will seem to you, no more urged to it by any appeal of its promoters than I have been, one of the worth-while privileges of living in these interesting times.

A REVIEW OF BETTER BOOKS

By HOI BIBLIOLOGOI

Here is a patchwork of history, philosophy, geography, the longing for learning, the appetite for arguing, the tests and questions of our calling and other pieces offered for your good pleasure by amateurs who are of Chicago and glad of it.

WE are a club of Abou-ben-Adhems (and Adhemesses) organized in December, 1924, by Professor John Rose for the encouragement of professional reading by teachers working in the public schools. These are the archives of the thirty-fourth meeting. We want to be recorded as lovers of our fellow men (and women) who we believe will be advantaged as more teachers read the literature of their profession. A physician who, in practice, continues the study of the writings upon his art is, according to the universal belief of practitioners, a public benefactor as well as a self-satisfier. This was the theme of the introductory remarks of our founder, Papa Rose, when the score of participants whom duty and the hospitality of him and Lady Alice has kept together these five profitable years, gathered in the Rosegarten, high up in the former hospital, now an apartment house, on the boulevard that looks out over the harbor.

"You have grown in grace," said our paterfamilias. "By persistence you have really formed the habit and acquired the taste of professional reading. In this you are part of a promising advance throughout the world. The number of educational magazines grows. The output of books increases. The quality improves. That the estimable SCHOOL AND SOCIETY magazine continues to print your book talk, amateurish though our offerings often are, is a sign that there are in other cities good souls who had rather hear of the profit their fellow teachers get from the volumes issued by the publishers than to observe a critical reviewer matching his own erudition against that of the author. Commendations continue to come in by mail. Here is a fresh consignment of letters I shall lay upon the table for your encouragement."

"All from authors?" asked Anna.

"Oh, no," replied the chief, "some are from publishers."

The matter of an out-of-door meeting was discussed. The General had an invitation from a college mate to visit Geneva Lake. William Wirt, of Gary, would like the club to use the Dunes Club's house and grounds. Martin of Tours had a map showing available groves north of the city. The club failed to make up its mind.

National high and low spirits, lassitudes, energies, indifferences and enthusiasms: Guérard.—Peter the Reader contributed somewhat in this wise:

"I want to knit my teaching into a lasting fabric for as many youth as is possible. I am always short of books on history. So many are too similar in organization to the texts used in the class. Here is one[1] to enrich the reference library. It is a fascinating exposition of the classical age in France from Francis I through the days of Napoleon. It covers the thrilling sixteenth, seventeenth and eighteenth centuries. The impelling spirit of the period shows itself as rationalism, a development of reason; as absolutism, the advance from loosely connected feudal powers, and as classicism, a love of rule, of law, of discipline as opposed to individualism. The age ended with an outburst of Roman ideals in Napoleon, with his code, his conquest and his copies of columns and triumphal arches. The revolution and the empire brought the climax of this ideal.

"Professor Guérard seems to me safely to resist the temptation besetting one who gets overactive in collecting 'trends.' One gets too fascinated with the hope of reducing a multiplicity of events to a simple system. Not so, this writer. Over and again he cites the formulas of different historians who have succumbed to the enthusiasm of translating their theories into the happenings of the time. Like the scientist who will refuse to venture out of the field of probabilities so long as contradictory facts lie unresolved into their causes, Guérard leaves no important movement out of his consideration. No exception is glozed over. He brings into clear light the events which are

[1] Albert Léon Guérard, ''The Life and Death of An Ideal.'' Charles Scribner's Sons, N. Y. 391 pp. $4.50.

not in accordance with the idea of rationalism, absolutism and classicism. His whole work is so flavored with the good-humored caution not to be too sure of anything, that its reading is a good medicine for autocrats such as the censorious are likely to accuse us teachers of being. His style is animated. His comparisons are with familiar American examples: our Bryans, our Wilsons, our Tennessees.

"Professor Guérard's presentation of the Renaissance, illuminated by a wealth of particulars, will correct your high-school notion of that movement. The expulsion of a few learned monks from Constantinople can not seriously be considered the cause of it. The 'rediscovery' of antiquity wasn't the reason. The progress of the human mind would have gone on without the 'rediscovery.' The revival of classical learning was by no means merely incidental to the progress of the sixteenth century; but neither was it essential. The sixteenth century is a continuation of the fifteenth. But there was an important difference. That difference was a revival of optimism. Nations, like men and women, have periods of high and low spirits. In the eighteen nineties, that is, within the memory of all here present except the ladies, God bless 'em, France was permeated with a spirit of self-depreciation and haunted with the idea of decadence. Anthropologists, moralists, journalists united in proclaiming the racial decay of their own people and seeking 'the causes of Anglo-Saxon superiority.' The hopeless inferiority of the French in the colonial field was taken for granted; it was admitted that their political life could be nothing but a succession of malodorous scandals. There was a spirit of lassitude and despair like that which hung over Chicago for the year preceding the sixth of last November. In France poets adopted decadence as their watchword. Renan, Anatole France, Jules Lemaître infected the atmosphere with an ironical Nihilism. Then, in the first decade of the twentieth century, long before the World War, the whole company of writers and public men are singing 'the awakening of French pride,' 'France herself again.' A confidence asserted itself which gave France her amazing attitude throughout the Great Ordeal and carried her, unaided, through the greater trial of the reconstruction period. Why was this? No new manuscript had been brought from Constantinople. Classical studies had received rather a sharp blow in 1902. The fact is the country had been suffering from the blues. Without the aid of any drug or surgical operation or systematic diet her robust constitution enabled France to recover. The history of the world records several such depressions and elevations in national spirits. One of the sure ways to misunderstand history is to select some one circumstance and credit it with the complex changes which occurred coeval with it or subsequently. Accordingly, Professor Guérard finds the fifteenth century to have all the elements of greatness of the sixteenth except confidence and joy. The Dance of Death was a favorite theme. Villon and the other poets sing of fears and regrets; they exhale an acrid, pungent odor. But along comes Rabelais. He is the apostle of the joy of living. He makes a merry tale of giants, robustious youth gamboling on a young earth. His heroes go through the world with gigantic appetites for all good things, all experience, all knowledge. The spirit of great adventure gets into swing. It marks this marvelous sixteenth century.

"I hope I give you some idea of the spirit and animation of the book. You shall find yourself in it tracing the moving force behind French civilization. You will realize how the people lived, how the industries flourished and languished, how the seigneurs in their walled towns lost their power as nationality, union under its symbol, the king, supplanted feudalism. What manner of men and women were the kings, the queens, the cardinals, the mistresses, the soldiers, the writers, the philosophers? Dr. Guérard knows how to make you acquainted with people. He will cause you to feel yourself a participant in the big events which march through his pages. I could not designate for you any more engaging matter, more entertainingly handled, than his sprightly chapter on the philosophy of the eighteenth century. It was a time of a hundred Bernard Shaws and H. G. Wellses. His interpretation of the French Revolution will give you a new idea. It will satisfy you much more than your schoolbook account. To attribute it to a peculiar psychology of the French mind is to meddle with a pseudoscience, for in their long history the French had shown exactly the reverse of a revolutionary temperament. For eight hundred years they had faithfully served the same dynasty. They had been obstinately loyal under most tragic circumstances: when their king was a child, when he was a prisoner, when he was a wastrel, when he was a madman. They had remained attached to institutions of slow change. England, on the contrary, had given glaring examples of religious instability and political fickleness. It was English-speaking people on both sides of the Atlantic that had first revealed a radical turn of mind and had shattered the majesty that doth hedge a king. The popular, dramatic and picturesque theory is that the revolution broke out because conditions became bad beyond human endurance. Dickens worked it up in 'The Tale of Two Cities.' But why was it that the revolution burst in France whilst conditions were as bad, and in most cases considerably worse, in other countries of the continent? Why was it that the poorest peasantry in the West took up arms in defense of the ancient régime? There is no such thing as 'the energy of despair.' Despair depresses. A pessimistic nation will sullenly accept its ills. It will even cling to them. A sudden suffering may lash a country into fury. A prolonged oppression degrades men into dumb acquiescence. A riot may be an expression of mad resentment; a revolution is an act of faith, a proof of intense vitality. So does Dr. Guérard go, one by one, through the glib and easy ways in which the great overturn has been explained for us. I was taught that the philosophers, the Encyclopedists, Voltaire, Rousseau, caused the revolution. Hear our author: 'Philosophy' did not destroy anything except abuses. It expressed itself in rational terms; it appealed to principles instead of arguing solely from precedents. For this insistence on definiteness and reason Montesquieu, Voltaire and Rousseau can not be exclusively responsible. The germs of this growth existed long before. Back of them we find Boileau, voicing the creed of classicism that reason should be loved and served. We find Descartes refusing to accept anything as true unless it appealed to his mind clearly to be such. Earlier still, we find the constant efforts of Frenchmen to reduce to intelligibility the chaos of customs. The eighteenth century is accused of inventing the dangerous doctrine of general human rights. But if we go back to the Middle Ages we read in a charter of 1147, 'A decree of divine Providence has ordained that all men, being of the same origin, be endowed at their birth with a sort of natural liberty. It belongs to Our Royal Majesty to raise them again to it.' Or we might find in the famous Ordinance of Louis X in 1315, 'As, according to the law of nature every man should be born free, we, considering that our realm is called the kingdom of the Franks, "the Free," and that there should be reality in accordance with the name, have ordered, etc. . . .' The Rights of Man, natural liberty, natural equality, were commonplaces of ancient standing long before the revolution. The social philosophy of the revolutionary time was based on English doctrines and English examples on the island and on the western continent.

"None of the explanations of the French Revolution carries convictions. The French are not a revolutionary people; their sufferings were not growing intolerable, they were becoming less. The 'philosophers were not preaching disloyalty; their ideal was not mob rule but the correction of abuses by the firm government of a despot.' These striking assertions Dr. Guérard elaborates by adequate specific facts cited from a wide field of events. He carries you through the main cause of the outbreak: the uncompromising attitude of the privilege holders.

"So proceeds the enlightening comment through the career of the supreme classicist: Napoleon. The author is clear of the influence of the myth by which so many biographers of Bonaparte have been led into romance. Guérard is no less entertaining in his treatment than dear old Jacob S. C. Abbot, who charmed our grandfathers, fifty years ago, with the best-selling 'Life of Napoleon.' But your entertainment in Guérard's work is not impaired by a suspicion that you are being drugged. I think it was Gibbon, of 'The Decline and Fall,' who called Tacitus the first of historians who applied the science of philosophy to the study of facts. Guérard warns us of the danger of presuming that there is yet a 'science' of human deeds. But his book makes every reader think. His narratives make the long string of events, instead of a bare chronicle, a living, growing unity. I must not dim any luster of the late lamented Tacitus. But Mr. Guérard has more creative thought to the page than the old Roman got into a whole chapter. I commend 'The Life and Death of an Ideal' for the high-school library."

A brainy man's geography: Branom.—This was the short report of our Euclidean member who has been under the weather for several months and was welcomed back with applause.

"Mendel Branom is head of the department of geography in Harris Teachers College, St. Louis. He is a man who intends geography study to exercise the brain to a much greater degree than comes from learning names and locations. I have read a book by him on the project method. He has four or five up-to-date works on the teaching of his subject and now gives us a definite treatise[2] based on interpretative activity rather than on the old recitation of descriptions. Few teachers have a geography content adequate to give a grasp of the instructional values of this school subject. Here they are, two hundred and sixty-four large pages of them, covering the field from New York State around the world and back again with Zanzibar for cloves, Norway for nitrates, and the dangerous dingo of Australia. One after another the countries and cities of the world are taken as integrating centers, an introductory exercise blocked out to warm the proper cranial centers of the young Americans; then come 'discovery,' 'problem' and 'endeavor.' The first seven chapters in which Mr. Branom elucidates these steps and the value of each process must convert every reader of them to the belief that geometry, or any favorite subject with nuts to crack, is in danger of falling behind the new geography which is saturated with human interest and capable of contributing through knowledge and sympathy to an ultimate peace of the world. Branom is not afraid of the children as too many of us appear to be. He gives them stiff questions to investigate: How has the presence of Niagara affected the development of Buffalo and of Oswego? How the rainfall of the Great Plains has influenced human occupations there. Why the Mohawk River has its sources in the plains of Ontario. Why Illinois has hot summers and cold winters. Why iron ore is concentrated near the head of Lake Superior. Your teachers of geography must master it on a college level and related to the human values that ought to be acquired by the children who study it. This is a fine book for a lazy principal. He can't read a page of it without using his brains and feeling inspired to get into the procession."

Any child's ability runs constant for at least two years: Keys.—Our Geometer continued:

"My next is an interesting detailed study[3] made by Dr. Noel Keys, associate professor of education of the University of California, who set out to find remedies for some of the deficiencies in ordinary tests. He found that Eugene Nifenecker, director of the New York City research bureau, had on hand the records of tests given three times at intervals of eighteen months to ten thousand children as they passed up through the grades. I find the tables, the calculations, the provisions for correcting errors decidedly interesting. I wish you would let me go into them in detail. I suggest that you do this for yourselves by studying the book. Dr. Keys inquired whether the rating of John and Mary as given just before promotion to-morrow and always more or less of a guess could be trued up by using the results of previous tests of the ordinary group variety. The experiment involving the study of the records of these New York children brings the doctor to the conclusion that John's rating to determine what he is to do next year will be much more nearly a just one if you average any test you give him to-day with any score made on any parallel form of test given at any time within the past two years. The ten or a dozen other conclusions which a study of this kind brings you can readily imagine. Then turn to this study and find out how nearly right your guesses are."

A solid little book on making history stick: Barnes.—Now, these are some of the words of Luther the Literary:

"Another help for getting American history study out of its patchy collection of memorized material into a result that is a competent knowledge of our origin, progress and destiny, comes from Detroit. Charles Barnes is supervisor of social studies there. He has produced a little

[2] Mendel E. Branom, "A Teachers' Geography." The Macmillan Co., N. Y. 252 pp. $2.40.

[3] Noel Keys, "The Improvement of Measuring." Press of Teachers College, N. Y. 81 pp. $1.50.

handbook[4] to aid high-school students to get from books the real history contained therein which some perverse bedevilment keeps from being got at unless it is pointed out. Brother Barnes develops his work according to the laboratory plan. He directs the study, point by point, saving time and giving a coherence to each unit. He trains the readers to use books, to keep notes and to be better understood by their teachers. He, too, adopts the usage developed by our experimenters, providing for introductory survey, unit outlines, presentation, assignment, discussion, questioning, etc. 'Do you think we should belong to the League of Nations? Why, or why not?' 'Should there be a general debt cancellation? Why? Why not?' And so on, making you get some sort of defensible opinion on navy reduction, Volstead acts, budgets, suffrage, farm-relief, treaties, expansion, tariff, civil war, Mexican ditto, the others, the obstacles we have overcome, the hindrances to our destiny we have yet to remove. The book is well sprinkled with page references to history texts now on the market. It's a decidedly high-class piece of work, as valuable as a road map to a tourist in a country of many highways."

Whether debating is immoral: Baird.—The General had this to say:

"Craig Baird is professor of speech in the University of Iowa. Ginn and Company have sent the club his timely book on public discussion.[5] I have ventured the opinion in this presence before that discussion is an indispensable necessity to progress. I can think of no civic advance that has come to any democracy unless there had been previous presentation and defense of argument. I am reminded by Professor Baird that school and college debating has expanded to include committee conferences, hearings, business talks and open forum exercises. His book goes beyond the old-time debate for exhibition purposes or contest. He discards extended excerpts from classical models because he finds that the present-day student won't pay any attention to them. He takes his examples—good, for imitation; bad, for warning—from Senator Borah, William Jennings Bryan, R. S. Childs, Charles W. Eliot, Newell Dwight Hillis, David Starr Jordan, Otto H. Kahn, Walter Lippman, Roscoe Pound, Woodrow Wilson and other moderns of note. There is a growing belief that debating is unmoral. Professor Baird does not dodge the attack. He quotes Colonel Roosevelt's well-known condemnation of the current school practice. Roosevelt's autobiography stresses the need of school and college graduates with ardent convictions on the side of right, not young men who can make a good argument for either right or wrong. School debating, according to the colonel's idea, encourages precisely the wrong attitude among those who take part in it. It doesn't instil sincerity. On the contrary, its result is to make the debaters feel that their convictions have nothing to do with their arguments. My own experience in school and college debating has given me the same notion. Professor Baird's defense doesn't seem to me very strong. He agrees that any one who debates with facility on either side, pretending to believe in a cause, is laying a foundation of moral weakness. But, he says, a beginner in debate probably has few settled convictions on problems that are given. With a good conscience he may take either side. Conclusions are only tentative. Fresh thought overnight may wreck one's case and lead to a revision of judgment. Somehow this argument of Dr. Baird seems to lack the moral sturdiness that I should like to have flavor my school. The professor also answers the growing opposition to competition in school exercises. He says you may say that the teams are more intent on winning than establishing the truth. Are we to renounce, then, he asks, the whole principle of competition? We recognize and encourage it in the economic world and in scholastic circles. Not I, professor. To my mind competition is a curse to the competitors. It is selfish, covetous, illiberal, ungenerous, un-Christian. The fact cited by the author that university systems of awarding honors both in America and in England are based upon the theory of competition makes no dent on my cortex whatsoever. Prizes, medals, honors, personal glory, victory seem to me undesirable survivals of a barbaric age to supplant which a band of patriots, pledged to equality, not to superiority, established the Constitution of these United States

[4] Charles C. Barnes, "Directive-Study Sheets in American History." Houghton, Mifflin Co., Boston. 116 pp. 30 cents.

[5] A. Craig Baird, "Public Discussion and Debate." Ginn & Co., Boston. 370 pp. $2.00.

of America with no yelling for distinction, for superiority or for America first. There, now that I have radiated these waves of my own conviction, let me give Professor Baird high praise for his very complete and able presentation of a notable series of aids to argumentative and persuasive speaking. The ability to think while standing on one's feet, the power to present the essentials of a proposition effectively, to give courteous attention to opposition and courteously to answer it, are abilities which the graduates of public schools, future participants in community service, ought to have. The clear and effective manner in which the author directs such training is excellent. The newer forms of debating are made clear. The dishonest practices of appropriating arguments without giving credit to the authors, or of coaching debaters so that the ideas used are almost entirely those of the English teacher, are properly reprimanded. The hints on gathering material, note-taking, analyzing the proposition, making the brief, weighing the evidence, refuting and rebutting the arguments, perfecting delivery and edifying the audience, are given in a masterly manner. I shall use the book with our boys and girls."

"I thought we heard you say you were opposed to debating," observed Carolina.

"No," responded the General, "we use it but we always have the debaters assigned to defend causes in which they believe. We never have a decision announced or applause vented."

"I should think they would be pretty tame affairs," ventured the Viking Maid.

"Well, we are not wild men, my dear," said the General.

"Wasn't it Dr. Holmes who said that a debate puts the fool on an equality with the wise man, and both know it?" asked Peter the Reader.

"He didn't say it loud enough for Chicago to hear," observed Polly the Political. "Even our dead-in-earnest Woman's City Club advertises 'debates' on school questions and gets answers from some of those invited that put the club in the class of Dr. Holmes' wise men."

"Our neighborhood Parent-Teachers Association," said Martin of Tours, "had Charles Spain, of Detroit, engaged to address it on the platoon school. When he learned they had a well-advertised opponent of platoons scheduled to turn the meeting into a debate, the Detroiter canceled the assignment. He said he had a picture to exhibit and describe but no criminal to defend."

The rag-tag of school service in a glow of light: Lindeman.—Principal Philip Manzer said, in part:

"Once I heard that grand old man of Michigan, Woodbridge Ferris, schoolmaster, governor, senator, now a radiant memory, talk on American education. 'We're only playing with it,' was the main text of his discourse. No psychologist, no statesman, no ordinary man who gives the matter any real thought, would dream of considering public education a service, merely or even principally, for children and youth. We learn best when we know what we want. We can't know it until we have experience. Governor Ferris thought the Danes, with their wholesale provision, at public expense, for the continued dispersal of useful and refining knowledge, are putting the proper theory into effect. If you have read, in the *New Republic,* John Dewey's reminiscences of his recent visit to Leningrad and Moscow you will recall that he thinks the Russians' wholesale establishment of community centers for everybody, especially for the grown-ups, is a pretty good thing for us to imitate, here. Chicago is decidedly behind many American cities in this regard. The school people in charge of the adult service are singularly alert and well prepared. The idea hasn't the hold on the board of education that it has in Boston, New York or Wilmington. The appropriations are not enough. The entertainment features are starved, the heat and light are often begrudged, the pay of instructors is too small. Meantime there is in America a remarkable growth of the appetite for general as well as special education for the common citizen. The correspondence schools are making good money supplying the need of those who will pay. The public libraries report demands they can not fill for solid works in history, science and general knowledge. The troops abroad surprised the welfare agencies by neglecting the fiction books and asking for thoroughgoing instruction.

"This club has been edified by many accounts of recent essays on the training of people beyond the school age. Those treatises were composed by professional educators. The volume[6] I hold in my hand is altogether different. It might be described as the experiences of one of the victims. Not that its author, Eduard Lindeman, satirizes, complains or reproves those responsible for current adult teaching; he does something more serviceable. He presents what an intelligent citizen who had not the opportunity to get in regular course the offerings of the public school system might conceive to be the proper spirit and service of education for the mature man.

"'Adult education,' says our author, 'presumes that the creative spark may be kept alive throughout life and, moreover, that it may be rekindled in those adults who are willing to devote a portion of their energies to the process of becoming intelligent.' I find Mr. Lindeman's book one that gives me, as I get the various sober imports of it, a good jolt. Perusal of it puts into the night-school work I have to supervise a dignity and importance much more, I'm afraid, than I have been giving it. Most of us have a traditional and indolent disregard for the teaching offered those of man's estate by our city school boards. It came last; it ranks last. No school report puts it on the front page. Entrance to its teaching positions is less guarded. Hour for hour it is the most valuable work we do. Officially it is the rag-tag of the system. Lindeman sees in it a golden opportunity. I fear much of the provision for it is leaden.

"'Now,' says our author, 'it may be that democracy, reared on metaphysical foundations, must decay more or less completely before we find our way. The dictator may be the true prophet of our time who says that liberalism, popular government, parliamentary representation have fulfilled their functions. At any rate the liberal has lost his effectiveness; parliaments have ceased to function or they serve badly and democracy is fast becoming a word and a delusion. I do not regard these as signals of despair. The fact that our political, economic and social structures and processes are disintegrating makes experiment feasible. We have once more reached one of those historical periods which seem like a dead-end because the shell of old institutions and habits, although crumbling, still possesses sufficient resiliency to prevent the new from bursting forth. In like periods of the past thinkers worked out imaginary Utopias. It set activity toward new goals, to redirect ideals. If we do not utilize our present difficulties as opportunities for adventurous challenges to the future we shall deserve to be recorded a generation of people who possessed many things but lacked courage and vision for high ventures.'

"Now, here are some of the observations which one reads every day in serious essays. Mr. Lindeman, in expressing calmly enough his opinions, is in tune with a note we hear much and which concerns us deeply. Education conceived as preparation for life misses the mark. Youth educated in terms of adult ideas and allowed to think of learning as a process that stops when adult life begins will make no better use of their intelligence than the elders who retain that system. Education becomes, not a joyous enterprise, but something endured for the sake of the amusements which have been annexed. There can be no joy in the standardized regimen of education. Those who have taken it, promptly turn their faces away from it when it is over. Once the belief was current that if education were free to all, intelligence would be used to manage the affairs of the world. We have made certain levels of learning compulsory. The result has been disappointing. The spirit and meaning of education can not be enhanced by giving the same dose to more people. The growing doctrine that education is life is supplanting the static concepts which relegate the learning process to the period of youth. The whole of life is learning; education can have no ending. This is the spirit of what we are latterly calling adult education—not because it is restricted to men and women but because it continues to the end of adulthood. More accurately defined it begins where vocational training leaves off. If the good life, the life interfused with meaning and with joy, is to come it will be something wider and higher than what is got by being taught how more effectively to run a machine. Adult education will aim to teach us how to make profitable use of leisure. There is an amazing diversity in the variety of experiences which are

[6] Eduard Lindeman, "The Meaning of Adult Education." The New Republic, N. Y. 219 pp. $1.00.

enjoyable and recreational. But they tend to become standardized and stereotyped. This is a denial of the very essence of recreation. No compulsion should tend to make you pretend to enjoy the same pleasures that fascinate me. Adult education must be alert to discover what has meaning and joy for particular students; to uncover hobbies, pursuits which may seem ludicrous but which to the doer bring peculiar satisfactions. Indeed adult education will have justified itself if it does nothing other than to make adults happier in their leisure hours. Grown-ups among us are pathetic because they don't know how to achieve pure delight for its own sake. They play for stakes. The majority of collegians expect their training to enable them to make more money.

"If these ideas, gathered here and there from Mr. Lindeman's book, give you the trend of it I may hurry to my conclusion by advising you to read and profit by his comments upon our present state, our silly art collections, our absurd sales of first editions, our wicked hypocrisy in the matter of civic participation, and a lot of stupidities very near home. We heard debates, as a school exercise, considered here to-night. You'll, maybe, agree with my writer that debates follow rules which are of no value to discussion. The debater selects his conclusion in advance and proceeds to gather facts and opinions to prove his case. His aim is victory, not enlightenment. He represents what Overstreet calls 'militarism in the intellectual life.' Purposeless conversation may have too little point, but debate has too much. What Mr. Lindeman has issued is a smooth-running, unirritating analysis of education as is, and a clear, high-aiming, attainable scheme for adult schooling as it ought to be. Creative freedom, individuality, artistry, adventure, joy, are the main essences of it. He speaks for those who have faith in intelligence, for those who appreciate, for those who seek a dynamic for collective enterprise, and he concludes in terms of method. It's a strong book."

Testing made attractive: Levine and Marks.—The Stevedore delivered himself of something like the following:

"When I saw the name of Louis Marks on one of the books laid on the table for our selection I chose his volume for review because, when I spent a summer in Teachers College, New York, I met him. Our instructor had given us some assignments that sent me to the headquarters of the New York public schools. A student who knew the ropes told me to go to Louis Marks, 'He's an examiner; but he's still human.' I found this cheerful official in a compact little cell with stacks of answer-papers around him. I didn't lie to him by saying I didn't want to take up his valuable time because I did want to take it up. If it hadn't been valuable I wouldn't have wanted it. But I did tell him I feared I might be a trouble to him. He said, pushing his papers to one side, 'You're not a trouble; you're a relief.' The book[7] I have is by him and Dr. Albert Levine. Mr. Marks's name comes second, so I may be in this instance giving him too much credit, but I do not think I could overpraise the work of either author. Coming into a field which already has so many volumes this book brings a freshness and interest that is altogether delightful. I leave it to you if the very first paragraph is not a brilliant opening:

"'There is a passion for both abstract and concrete. Man is as eager to plumb the depths of the soul as to measure the hair's breadth. He evolves the broadest philosophy and the most delicate scales. The history of the testing movement is woven with the strands of philosophy, metaphysics, psychology, physics and mathematics. The fabric isn't even in its texture; coarseness and fineness alternate. This must be expected when you consider the mobility of mind and the rigidity of arithmetic. Yet a quantitative organization of data has been secured.' This is a true and temperate summary of the measuring movement.

"In thirty-seven entertaining pages these authors condense the immense literature of testing into an engaging story. It is what those of us who can not be specialists want to possess, a simple account of the development of teaching into a science by the contributions of Itard, Seguin, Galton, Cattell, Binet, Simon, Goddard, Terman, Pintner, Spearman, Hillegas, Rice, Ayres, Thorndike, Woody, McCall and others. We are yet unsteady in our knowledge of the movement. Educators will hail with acclaim

[7] Albert J. Levine and Louis Marks, "Testing Intelligence and Achievement." The Macmillan Co., N. Y. 399 pp. $2.00.

the publication of an investigation whose findings have been discredited but of whose repudiation the applauder is in ignorance. No inconsiderable number of school folks are in the state of mind regarding tests and measurements as was a voter in the first ward toward the candidates on the ticket. On his ballot the clerks found written across the face, 'to hell with the whole of 'em.' Our tests are being retested and refined. The inadequacy of the IQ is becoming apparent. The surprise of finding a high mentality in a child with low achievement leads to the discovery of an AQ and a combination called the EQ, educational quotient. In our Chicago, observers counting the number of children, minute by minute, who are using their minds in the classroom have calculated a teacher's AHQ, attention-holding quotient.

"Levine and Marks give us a bright, illuminative chapter upon personality. We teachers have always been estimating dispositions, personal qualities, character. As I read these pages I am amazed at the crudeness of my amateur judgment of such a vital factor. I learn the complexity of character and the remarkable thought and experiment put upon means of getting a fair and equitable estimate of an equipment so important as personality. I fear that my crude conclusions as to the kind of boy young Smith must be are absurdly partial and unfairly damaging. Happily, Smith's other teachers may and often do consider him a high-class boy.

"You will be entertained and helped by finding the effects of reprimand, discouragement and fault-finding treated with a serious quotation from observers and authorities. There may develop a science of school success, a program of praise. Scolding has been measured and its damage reduced to a mathematical formula. Here is a summary of many experiences good for teachers to use toward children; principals, toward teachers; superintendent, toward principals; school board, toward superintendent; public, toward school board: 'maintain an atmosphere of success. Encourage by judicious praise and abstention from censure. Extravagant compliment is better than tepid commendation. 'That's fine,' 'Very good indeed' help the world along."

"If it is really good," sniffed the Signpost, our suburban member.

"That's the usage in Detroit," said Carolina. "I spent a day in the platoon schools and met a woman member of the board of education."

"It's true of Omaha," said Martin of Tours, who has relatives in Beveridgeville.

"And most of all in Cincinnati since the revolution," remarked the General.

"Along that line," continued the reviewer, "my book has some pertinent observations upon the hate-arithmetic attitude and its trail of damage through the schools. The feeling is entirely eradicable by a policy of seeing that the habit of getting sums done right is followed in school. Achievement, success, victory, persistence, personal power and confidence come soon when there is the proper direction.

"So, here is this book—a compact and rapid survey of a new and essential addition to educational practice. The charts of published tests available are alone worth the price of the volume. The treatment of diagnosis is superb. The studies of deceit, lying, stealing, schoolhouse sins, are tremendously important. No more usable, instructive, simple, thorough book for us every-day teachers has appeared in a long time. That it is the work of members of the public-school system of the metropolis ought to make New York teachers proud. I give it no tepid compliment. 'It's fine.' 'Very good indeed.' "

The questionable questionnaire: Koos.—The report of Dr. Batwell, in somewhat condensed form, is herewith submitted.

"Whenever Leonard Koos[8] comes with a book into our circle he is received with welcome. We have acknowledged with gratitude his broad and accurate studies of high schools, senior and junior. His latest volume is a solid little manual on a matter which has assumed wide importance in education but which, until Dr. Koos addressed himself to it, has been treated only in school periodicals. With a courage and industry which we may justifiably term Koosifactual, the author has digested something like a total of 20,000 pages of educational literature appertaining to the questionnaire. Research must lean so heavily upon inquiry by the method of written canvass, numerous and ill-considered questionings have engendered so much irritation, that a thorough survey of the situation, cau-

[8] Leonard V. Koos, "The Questionnaire in Education." The Macmillan Co., N. Y. 178 pp. $1.25.

tion, advice and encouragement to researchers and to us who furnish much of their material are remarkably timely and valuable. I hereby make, second and carry a motion that the thanks of investigators and of school administrators are hereby tendered to the industrious and progressive professor of secondary education in the University of Minnesota for this service to educational improvement. It is unanimous.

"He begins with some peppery refusals of solicited schoolmen to answer the questionnaire. It looks to me as though they put as much time and nerve into their refusals as would have got the wanted work done. Dr. Koos says nothing about the courtesy of these replies. He couldn't. There isn't any. He does lament that brilliant executives like Ernest Butterfield and well-known periodicals like the *Educational Review* abet the condemnation of the method by such allusions as 'the fast-growing band of questionnairicides.' But, scientist as he is, our author does not score or slap these critics. He studies the reasons for their negations and with a concise but comprehensive exposure of his data, he comes to a conclusion, which must impress every decent schoolman, that we can not advance without using the circulated inquiry as one of the methods of getting a foundation for our building. Without research we talk through our hats. I mean no slangy triviality when I say this. Educational propositions without a wide collection of facts examined and digested are as if the proposer held a hollow and non-transparent covering in front of his face. Dr. Koos calls his book a critique and a manual. His examination of the thousands of questionnaires already issued is graphic and interesting. The manual feature is a set of salutary suggestions to senders and receivers of question lists. 'Make it as easy as you can'; 'don't ask what is beyond the intelligence of the recipient to answer,' are some of the recurring suggestions he gives to the researchers. Here is a tip-top one: 'Try it on a few dogs first.' The author says that one of his questions was 'In your science teaching do you precede or accompany or follow the development of the principle by the practical illustrations?' When he came to tabulate the replies he found that a large proportion of the respondents answered, 'yes.' After the celebration of a peace jubilee in the separate schools of New York City, Superintendent Ettinger issued a questionnaire to gather material for his report to the board of education. One of the inquiries was, 'Where were your outdoor exercises held?' A principal of a Staten Island school replied, 'Indoors.'

"For those receiving questionnaires the author collects much good advice, including hints from Edwin Boring: 'If you can answer in a few minutes, do it as a matter of courtesy; don't answer an unknown person unless he has a scientific reputation or is introduced by some one in whom you have confidence; don't answer at all unless you can be accurate; don't answer if the questioner can get his facts from a library or a bureau; don't consider a stamped envelope or thanks in advance any claim on you.'

"I wonder whether I might venture a suggestion. It is that the establishment of a bureau of research and information as instituted by President Thomas Churchill, of the public schools of the City of New York, ought to be followed by every large city. Under Albert Shiels and, thereafter, Burdette Buckingham and Eugene Nifenecker, this bureau considered one of its duties the answering of all questionnaires. The recipient has only to turn the blank over to the experts in his own school system. The National Education Association has a similar bureau. Any school system can join it. It will answer all questionnaires transmitted by its subscribers. Whatever I thought before, Dr. Koos's solid and courteous little book has convinced me that the help to educational advance secured by the questionnaire method of gathering facts is too valuable and necessary to be impaired by our selfishness, indifference or laziness. 'Am I my brother's keeper?' is no answer for any one in our business."

Carolina and the Lady Alice had been slipping out of the circle several times during the past quarter of an hour. A tantalizing aroma of coffee floated into the studio. A crook of our lady's finger took Steevie and Philip away from us and then the procession burst upon us with great pomp, bearing food and drink and napery. Soon erudite discourse gave way to badinage such as is rife among familiars. The viands vanished in their appointed ways and, two by two, the Bibliologoi wended.

SCHOOL AND SOCIETY

EDITED BY J. McKEEN CATTELL

WITH WHICH IS COMBINED THE

EDUCATIONAL REVIEW

EDITED BY WILLIAM McANDREW

Volume XXIX — SATURDAY, APRIL 13, 1929 — Number 746

SHALL WE JOIN THE LADIES?[1]

By President WILLIAM ALLAN NEILSON

SMITH COLLEGE

As a text for this sermon I am going to take a remark we used to hear, in the older days, quite often: "Gentlemen, shall we join the ladies?" It is a good symbolic phrase to suggest the relation in society of the sexes in the generation in which I have grown up.

It is nearly thirty years since I left Pennsylvania, and I don't know what has happened to social life in Philadelphia in that time. What I am going to describe is more or less valid, for it is what I remember. Philadelphia may have departed from it long ago. What I am going to recall to those of you whose memories go back to the end of the nineteenth century was the prevailing procedure on a social occasion like a dinner, when the ladies withdrew and the gentlemen remained to talk politics, to talk shop, to talk sport, to talk that other kind of talk which they euphemistically called humor—these and other things from which the ladies were excluded. The ladies were not supposed to know much about politics. They were supposed to be totally ignorant of business and other professional "shop." They were babes in the matter of sport, and the "humor" was not for their ears.

And then, after half an hour or more over the cigars and what were then the liqueurs, some one said, "Gentlemen, shall we join the ladies?" And the ladies were supposed to have occupied themselves in the drawing-room in domestic discussions, in talk over Jack's measles and Jane's cold, and the comparison of symptoms and illnesses, in notes on fashion, in gossip about their neighbors. These trivialities were supposed to be what occupied the minds of women. These were the things from which the men saved themselves.

That was the atmosphere into which they plunged as they came out of the dining-room; and the two sets of conversations, and the separation between them, suggest pretty well what, at least in the days of your fathers, was taken for granted with regard to the minds of women and the minds of men. The assumptions that underlay that procedure were assumptions dealing with the supposed lack of capacity of women to understand those profound things the men talked over by themselves; and, further, a desire to shield the innocence of the feebler sex through ignorance.

[1] Address at a dinner given to the presidents of the seven colleges by the Philadelphia alumnae of the seven colleges, and their friends. The seven colleges which are cooperating in a joint effort to increase their endowments are: Barnard, Bryn Mawr, Mount Holyoke, Radcliffe, Smith, Vassar, Wellesley.

Thank God we have learned a way of shielding the innocence of our women by something other than ignorance.

What the women's colleges have done and are doing is to bring home, first to them and then to the men of our country, the fact that women as much as men are capable of looking truth in the face, that there is no guardian of women's virtue that can be relied upon better than truth. That seems to be a truism, but it is one that is not yet accepted.

No man in the position of any one of us who are at the heads of colleges can fail to be aware of the constant resistance to what seems to you, perhaps, as I utter it, an axiomatic statement. Not to tell women, to keep them ignorant, to suppose that they are ignorant—these are still the ways in the minds of a great many of our countrymen to preserve the womanliness of woman.

They are, of course, very foolish men who think that—not only because the method is profoundly false but because they are shutting their eyes to the facts. The sophisticated people of the present day are not you of my age and older—the sophisticated people are the people below the age of twenty-two; it is they who are shielding you, my venerable friends. It is they who are worried about shocking you. The cat is out of the bag—all the cats are out of all the bags—and what we have got to do is to see that knowledge is complete, that ways of thinking are made familiar, that thinking is trained to be accurate and precise, not stifled.

This change, which has largely come about and is coming about more and more every day, is due to a great variety of causes; but if you think for a moment what it is that the modern educated woman does and thinks about, you will see how preposterous it is to try to return to the point of view when the gentlemen joined the ladies. Science has come into the house, and the modern mother has to know about it before she arranges your diet; and you are all benefiting in your digestions, day by day, from the fact that the modern leader of the house is a person who knows something about what people ought to know who supply you with your daily food.

The greatest advance in medicine in our time is the change of emphasis from cure to prevention, the growth of preventive medicine. And the people who administer preventive medicine are women—it is they who arrange the life of the household and who care for the children so that they don't get ill. It is they who cultivate, so far as we have yet succeeded in cultivating, good habits of life. The progress that may have been made mainly by men in scientific discovery, in the field of medicine—these new facts that they have discovered, are mainly applied by women, and by women who have had their minds cultivated enough to understand these results and to make use of them.

Perhaps more than anywhere they have turned the results of modern research to purpose in the training of their children. It is extraordinary to reflect on the enormous change in a short time in this matter of discipline of the household. For as long as we know, in the history of the family, the most vicious kinds of training have been administered to children. Parents have let themselves behave toward their children in a criminal fashion. I remember a domestic incident in my own family. A little girl remarked, "Father is tired tonight. He is educating us." The irritations of the parent were constantly—with more or less unconscious hypocrisy—made the basis for the administration of discipline. Modern psychology, which has got a lot of things to be said against it, at least is beginning to do this: it is opening the eyes of the parents to the facts with regard to their own moods; it is taking the veil away from the petty tyrannies that have dominated the family life. And the women are the people who have learned that; and in the course of a generation they may teach it to their husbands.

Art has come into the household. We have got away from the antimacassar age. Think back, will you, please, thirty-five years only and remember what our interior decoration was like, and compare it with the average well-to-do house to-day; and then ask yourselves, "Who is responsible for the atmosphere of beauty that surrounds our children to-day—is it the man, or the woman? Who is it that determines the cultural atmosphere of the household? Who is it that is responsible for most of the pictures on the walls? Who is it that is responsible for the music? Who is it that is responsible for most of the books that lie on the table?" Not the busy American man of affairs. He may have a den where there are some kinds of intellectual effort or intellectual activity to which he occasionally retires, but that part of it that has profited the family life is the woman's doing; and woman is able to do it because she is better educated than she was.

And when you come to talk about her, think of one other thing: one need not say at this moment in this country (November 2) that she knows nothing about politics. In politics she has arrived. She has arrived this summer more than before. The political parties are all guessing because of this great new registration made up largely of women. Woman has arrived in the political field. We know that she is thinking; and the fact that she is thinking is the fact that troubles the politicians. They had hoped that she would not think. They had hoped that she would follow as the men had followed; that she would be duped as the men had been duped; that she would have stuck by her traditions, by family influence, as the men had stuck; and it is not happening. Families are splitting; nobody knows, when he goes into a household, whether both ends of the table are going to vote the same way or not. Politics in America is being shot through, as never before, by thinking; and it is largely because the women are thinking, and because the talk can come from both ends of the table.

They have gone in, as has been said, to many professions, but I am not going to elaborate that. They come, as always, into teaching; but the difference between the modern college-trained woman as a teacher and the older teachers is very clear. I don't want to be misunderstood—for hundreds of years there have been successions of wonderful women teachers, making the most of their small stock in trade often, but born teachers. To these we owe much and make acknowledgment. But there were many others who were pitiful, and more and more their places are being taken by women who have some idea of scholarship and some idea of method.

The effect of all this used to be looked forward to with apprehension, lest it should destroy the womanly influence of woman. All of us seven presidents have read of the controversies that arose in our various localities at the time our respective institutions were founded. Much of it is fantastic to-day; but everywhere, whether in Massachusetts or New York or Pennsylvania, you found these new institutions surrounded by croakers who told us that the physique of women was going to be endangered, that their nervous systems were going to be wrecked, and that they were going to lose their womanly influence.

To-day every time a mother finds that her daughter is not accepted for college she begins to say the colleges are getting to be made up of "blue stockings." Well, that is not the color of the stockings in my college. If anybody tells you that the present generation of college girls is a generation of grinds, of queer girls, of intellectual monstrosities, come to one of our campuses for an hour and you won't need any other answer. It is perfectly clear that now a woman goes to college without sacrificing any part of her charm, any part of her social value. To say otherwise is merely to echo something thoroughly outworn and to shut one's eyes wilfully to facts that stare any one in the face.

I don't mean to exaggerate the intellectual discipline our girls get in the colleges, but it is enough to make them see much of what used to be regarded as femininity as funny; and the development of a sense of humor in women, through the colleges, is something that so far as I know has never been stressed.

There are times when I confess I get despondent about the lack of serious scholarship. One always sets up impossible ideals, and one confuses the failure to achieve them with a sluggish mentality; and then suddenly one comes face to face with a bit of undergraduate satire, and one realizes that there, really, are the brains of the nation. The undergraduate's power of penetrating sham, whether in her teachers or her parents or her contemporaries, is appalling. She is going to bring into our life the most healthful of breezes—as she has blown away, to a large extent, all those silly matters of affectation and false sentiment which before were supposed to be the marks of her sex. And undoubtedly that is going to have its effect, and *is* having its effect on men.

Men can not overawe women as they used to, and one of the reasons why we find it hard to get a good endowment for women's colleges is that many men do not like women to stand up to them and measure them as they are; they prefer to be on a pedestal; they prefer to be the possessors of a great deal of wonderful esoteric information. They don't have much, of course; we know it is mainly bluff—but it won't work any more, and they don't like it. So the thing to do, of course, is to be grudging to the women's colleges.

Now, I don't mean to say that this change in regard to science and politics and general intelligence is all due to women's colleges, but I do claim there has been no other one force so potent in this direction as have been these institutions.

You remember, again to go back to the days of our youth—remember I am speaking to the men here and not to the alumnae—you remember there used to be institutions called "finishing schools." They called themselves "finishing schools," but did not say what it was they finished. These were institutions which were confined entirely to women. Men never were finished. The curriculum of the finishing school had to do mainly with what were frankly regarded as the non-essentials of human life. Where is the finishing school to-day? What institution calls itself by that name? It has been killed, and killed by the women's colleges, partly because the schools have been preparing for them, and partly because the institutions preparing girls for college have forced up the education of those girls who didn't go to college; and for the tens of thousands of those who have gone to college there are hundreds of thousands of girls whose education has been made more worth while on account of the leaven of college preparation.

If these things are half as strong as I have put them, what is the reason for the difference of treatment between the men's colleges and the women's colleges? Because it is not solely, as Mr. Lamont has pointed out, that the men's colleges have had a longer time to accumulate; it is not solely that these larger endowments are partly devoted to the professional schools, museums, and the like, far beyond the burden that women's colleges are called upon to bear; the main reason is that the rate of accumulation is so inferior in the women's colleges to what it is in the men's.

I belong to an institution which is neighbored, half a dozen miles away, by a man's college of the same type; and we have gone through the same period of strenuous campaign during these last eight years. That college is less than half the size of mine, and the millions come in about twice as quickly—of course, because the men have the money. But these very men have got, I think, most of their wives out of my college. They send their daughters to my college, and they profess to love these daughters—they do dote on these daughters; and yet when there is a campaign for Amherst and a campaign for Smith, Amherst gets hundreds and we get tens. Why?

There is one right that women haven't yet received, and that is not, so far as I know, in the program of any women's party—the right of a woman to dispose by gift or bequest of her share of the common fortune she and her husband have accumulated. Men are not willing to accept the implications of that last sentence. They do say sentimental things about the partnership. They call their wives their partners; both put all they have into that partnership, and at the end there is an accumulation; but what has the woman to say about that accumulation? Nothing at all. Usually she does not know how much there is of it. She is not supposed to understand. But for my purpose she does not need to know these things—she only needs to have her rights as a partner recognized in the disposal of these fruits of the partnership. These are not now recognized in anything like a proportionate measure, and that is the root of our trouble.

And, as is noted in the article which has been referred to several times to-night, not only are the men self-regarding, negligent of the rights of their partners in this matter, but the women themselves, to a most irritating degree—women, of course, of the pre-college-woman generation—when they happen through the accident of widowhood to be left in charge of that fortune, go and give it to their husband's college, or their son's college—not their daughter's or to any woman's college at all.

Well, we do think that it is not fair; and it is not fair because the woman's rights are as great as the man's in matters of the development of mind and character. At bottom you have no faith in what I am saying about the importance of the education of women; and what we are doing here to-night, and what we are doing in all the activities with which this particular committee is associated, is to try to develop that faith. We are not passing the hat, we are not aiming at a campaign—we are trying to correct a state of mind, to evoke faith.

I have abundant opportunity to observe the degree to which American fathers worship their daughters. What is it that they worship in their daughters? Something apparently that leads them to be satisfied with giving them motors and fur coats and candies—all kinds of things to have a good time; but when it comes to be a matter of giving them opportunity for the development of their minds, of receiving that intellectual discipline which will have much to do with their characters, they lose interest.

There was once a father of the church who debated whether women had souls. I think that was about fifteen hundred years ago. But Saint Jerome, or whoever it was, has many descendants among the men of our generation. They really are not quite sure whether women have souls or not; they know they have sensations and bodies and certain kinds of charm; but they are not really thoroughly convinced that they have minds and that these minds have a claim upon the educational resources of the country equal to that of their brothers.

We have, of course, gone to the foundations with our story, and the kind of answer that we are apt to get from the people in these institutions who regard themselves as authorities on the education of the country is something like this: "We read these figures that Mr. Lamont read to you, and say there are lots of good second-class colleges that haven't as much money as you have."

I say, "Precisely. I know there are lots of second-class colleges—but who was talking about second-class colleges?"

We are not here to-night talking about second-class colleges. We are talking about first-class colleges, and our claim is that we want first-class treatment; and if in this and that respect we are not able to tackle all the experiments and accomplish all the results that we should like, some of which are achieved in the men's colleges, it is mainly because we are expected to do first-class work with second-class resources.

The challenge which I bring you to-night is a challenge to make the women's colleges take their place in the front rank, not to remain as well off as many second-class men's colleges. The second-class men's colleges are second class largely because they have deserved to be so. We are conceited enough about our achievements and our organization now to say that with the talent that has been given us we have done wonders; and I say that not egotistically, because I am comparatively a newcomer in the field; but I think of what the women's colleges for the last fifty years have done, and I know their achievements have not come by chance.

To you alumnae I say what Mr. MacCracken has written here, "Don't apologize for yourselves." Miss Park tells me that the Philadelphia alumnae are apt to be shrinking—to hide their light under a bushel. Perhaps it takes courage to be an educated woman in Philadelphia. I don't know! But take courage. Stand up to the men. Don't let them assume that either your brain or your training is second class—for they are not. And demand their rights for your institutions.

Gentlemen, shall the ladies join us?

THE PARENT-TEACHER MOVEMENT—ITS PLACE IN EDUCATION

By SELDEN CARLYLE ADAMS

DIVISION OF PUBLICATIONS, NATIONAL EDUCATION ASSOCIATION

FROM the very beginning of man's existence, the family has been the center of human life. All we have learned about the relations that ought to exist between people we have learned from the relations of members of the family toward each other. Our highest conceptions of ethics and religion have been patterned after the conceptions of love, truth and obedience to authority which have forever been present in the family. The ancient Hebrew prophet sought to interpret to the primitive human mind the bond of contact between man and God by apotheosizing the contact between the father and his children in the earthly family. That ancient prophet had mastered a fundamental educational principle of which we sometimes lose sight in modern teaching. He knew that great truths must be taught by relating them to the intimate experience of the learner.

Great social truths that have been accepted by whole communities and nations had their inception in the family. The precarious conditions under which the primitive family lived resulted in a spirit of cooperation and mutual helpfulness, substituted for competition and strife. As groups of families later banded together in tribes, all members of a given tribe learned to give and receive the tribe's mutual benefits. And so the principle has advanced with civilization by expressing itself in communities, cities, states, nations and groups of nations.

Although the family has been the source of all ethical ideals, all social relationships, all government and all business, it has not remained static through the years of social and political development. It has continued to perform its fundamental functions, preserving the normal relations between men and women, giving birth to children and providing for the care of those children through the early years of life. The function of the family has constantly diminished in scope. Even to-day it performs certain other duties beyond those mentioned. On the other hand, there are now circumstances under which specific families are unable to meet the third-named obligation to childhood.

The primitive mother who taught her babe in the shelter of the forest was an educational system unto herself. Her curriculum consisted in the lessons in the methods which enabled her to protect him from wild beasts, to find food, and to keep his body warm and comfortable. He learned his lesson of social relationships from contact with other members of his own family. Community problems did not concern him.

But to-day no mother can work out her family problems independently. Her baby is supplied with milk that comes from the farm many miles away. She depends on the dairy and the railroad to bring it to her. Rental rates affect the choice of a community in which to live. Family life must be related to the life of the entire community.

Every one knows that civilization is becoming complex, *but few people regret it.* I have no sympathy with the tendency toward pessimism on the part of intelligent and educated people. The very fact that one is equipped with a better than average supply of knowledge and information in the fields of science and history should indicate conclusively to him that for every great social and economic problem that arises there is to be found a solution. Family life must inevitably change with the change in civilization. The family is not growing less important as a social institution. Its function is merely *changing.*

Chapman and Counts, in their book on "The Principles of Education," state that the family is "no longer the stable institution of a few generations ago." After citing the rapid increase of divorce in this and other countries, the authors continue:

> Owing to the operation of a wide variety of forces, some of which go to the heart of the Great Society, the essentially patriarchal family of a hundred years ago is rapidly passing away, and is apparently being replaced by an institution with less centralization of authority. In the social mind there has been a gradual reappraisal of the relative values to be assigned to the several functions performed by the family. This reappraisal has tended to recognize the personal rights within the family group.

What are some of the social changes that affect the family life?

Because living has become more complicated it has become necessary for individuals to have a wider fund of information before beginning any important work. Such a condition inevitably prolongs the period of education. Aristotle at the age of seventeen was mingling among the philosophers of Athens. The accumulated information of the world at that period was so little that long years of preparation were not necessary. Men could begin at an early age actually to discover new truths.

At the age of twenty Galileo discovered the law of the pendulum, and when he was twenty-seven he was professor in the University of Padua, lecturing to such great throngs that he often had to move from the university hall to the open air. But in Galileo's day people thought the sun moved around the earth. To-day a man at twenty-seven is hardly ready to enter upon his life work if he is engaged in professional study.

Herbert Spencer refused to go to Cambridge because he did not care to study subjects that would be distasteful to him, and now his works on education are standards. But in this generation the professional or scientific world will not listen to the man who has not received years of organized training in the university or college before he begins to produce thoughts.

What has this to do with the family? It simply means that family life must be postponed until after men and women have completed their academic training.

Every problem in life is a challenge to education. This problem of extended training is now receiving attention among the leaders of the teaching profession. There is a tendency on the part of many to urge that the secondary school unit be rearranged to shorten the period required for preparation for specialized or professional study.

But the average citizen of the United States goes to school only through the seventh grade. Most families, therefore, are established by men and women who are not hampered by the necessity for postponing marriage because of academic training. The question there is an economic one, often the result of the desire for luxury. The modern tendency is for the young family to begin its life on the same economic plane now enjoyed by the parents who have achieved their present status after long years of accumulation.

The educational problem here is that rising from the situation in which both father and mother are employed. Such a situation must, of necessity, throw a greater responsibility on the school.

Other problems growing out of the increasing complexity of civilization, which more directly affect children, are those concerned with fatigue and with vocational adjustment.

Because little children to-day do so many things which their parents did not do when they were young, fatigue becomes a serious problem. The school helps to meet the problem by a wise regulation of the study hours, properly interspersed with recreation periods. Efforts must be made to reduce the prevalence of noise on the city streets. Few factors are so deadly to the adequate nervous adjustment of the young child as unnecessary noises in the city.

The problem of fatigue places on the family a new type of responsibility. Fatigue or nervous tension gave little concern to the primitive mother.

The problem of vocational adjustment is one of the greatest in the whole field of education. There are thousands of occupations open to men and women to-day. For most of them there is no standard system of preparatory training. Most people enter them accidentally. All who are in touch with educational movements know of the tragedies in the lives of men and women who, too late, discover that they have entered the wrong field of endeavor. Life no longer is a joy—it merely consists in making a living. Vocational adjustment meant nothing to primitive life. The changing civilization has brought this new problem to the front.

How has education met the challenge of the changing civilization?

The new education has realized that its great function is guided growth or adjustment to environment. The major objective is no longer merely that of imparting information. Children are now taught how to take their part in the community—to meet situations as they arise. Subject-matter is provided as a tool for meeting such situations.

The objectives of education are known to every parent-teacher audience. One of the greatest of the many contributions made to the parent-teacher movement by Joy Elmer Morgan has been his constant emphasis in the past few years on those seven cardinal principles first formulated by the Committee on the Reorganization of Secondary Education, which reported to the National Education Association in 1918. Education is meeting the challenge of the changing world by providing a curriculum which concerns itself with making children physically and mentally sound; preparing them for worthy home membership; providing them with an appreciation of the tools, techniques and spirit of learning; instilling in them the loftiest ideals of faithful citizenship; guiding them into the path of vocational and economic effectiveness; equipping them for the wise use of leisure; and so directing the whole process that the development of noble character will be the self-improvement goal of every boy and girl.

The school has entered civilization to help to solve its increasing problems. As families came together in groups there arose the need for equipping individuals to recognize community responsibilities. It was found that children taught within the home did not learn to meet problems that might arise after they left the shelter of that home. As new knowledge was discovered the mother or the individual tutor became less efficient. People began to realize that there is value in cooperating in schooling just as in industry. They learned that a group of children gain more from a trained teacher in a well-equipped school than they do under the teaching of a parent who lacks teaching ability.

Miss Cornelia Adair, when she was president of the National Education Association, delivered an address to a parent-teacher group in Washington. In that address she compared the trend of thought and common practices among men to the swinging of a pendulum. She said:

> We are constantly passing from one extreme to another. The swinging of the pendulum has taken the major responsibility of education from the home and has placed it in the school. But we know that a pendulum never remains long at one extreme as it describes its arc. It either comes to the normal point of rest or is kept swinging by some stimulus. In the case of the school that stimulus is the support which the public gives to education. Some of us are looking ahead to the time when a large amount of the responsibility in training children will revert to the home.

Education is a cooperative enterprise. When the home turned over to the trained school teacher the major tasks of education it did not assume the right to relinquish all of its own responsibilities in the matter. Children live twenty-four hours a day. Of those hours not more than six or seven are spent in the school. The childhood or youthful mistakes that result in tragedies seldom take place in the classroom. It is true that school conditions do sometimes wreck the life of a boy or girl, but the real danger hours are those which come after the school has closed its doors for the evening—the hours over which the school has no legal control.

Let us think of the positive or constructive side of the matter. The school has a program of adjustment and character building. It is a program which is intended to apply to the whole life of the pupil, through his school years and after he graduates. It is a program whose results are intended to influence his leisure as well as his working hours. If effectively carried out it will enable him to share his responsibility in his home life as well as in his community life. All lessons are vitalized through practice. The home, therefore, becomes the field of practice to the child who will some day maintain his own home and family life.

That is the field of education to which the parent-teacher movement has made such important contributions. It has brought the family and the home back as vital factors in the educational process. It has given to the trained educator the courage that comes from the knowledge of intelligent and earnest cooperation in a gigantic task.

The home, through the sponsorship of the parent-teacher movement, makes four definite contributions to the field of education.

First, upon the home has begun to rest the responsibility for assuring the mental and physical health of every child before he enters the school. If the National Congress of Parents and Teachers performed no other task, its existence would be justified by its conduct of the annual summer roundup of children in which an effort is made to see that no child is forced to enter school in the fall with any remediable physical defect. The pre-school examination should soon extend to the realm of mental health, an extremely vital factor in the school success of the child and especially of the student in the higher grades.

Dr. Smiley Blanton says, "Psychiatrists who work with children realize that fully three fourths of the behavior problems they deal with are due to unwise training in the home."

Parents have done the best they could, with limited knowledge. To-day the parent-teacher movement appears as a light on the horizon bringing a release from suffering through which millions of innocent children have passed because of the inability of their parents to appreciate the fact that many emotional difficulties which have always been considered quite normal are really the beginnings of serious mental maladjustments.

The family's second auxiliary educational duty is that of imparting to the child those basic life truths which need to be learned before he starts to school and which can be made much more effective in the familiar shelter and quiet of his own home than in the more public atmosphere of the classroom. The family may well expect the school to give the child the sense of self-discovery and of community freedom, and to find, in the light of the child's comparison with others, those points in which he is different from the average or normal child. But the school, in return, has a right to expect the child to come to it with a foundation of truth and information on which to build.

Mrs. Helen Thompson Woolley has said, "The education of the child in the home is more fundamental than that which takes place in the school." Mrs. Woolley has suggested several basic lessons which may well be taught in the family circle. Among them are respect for authority, the value of property, the qualities of leadership, cooperation and a love for the past which does not "quench the spirit of independent thought."

The question of social hygiene ought to be mentioned at this point. Great forward steps have been taken in the last two or three years in social hygiene instruction in the school. But the advantage which comes to the child who receives that instruction from intelligent parents can not be overlooked. It is so ably set forth in Mrs. Edith E. Read Mumford's book, "The Dawn of Character in the Child" (Chapter 10). Some one has recently suggested that attention to sex hygiene should begin in the first grade of the elementary school. If it can be ably taught by a teacher to a class of first-grade children, why can it not be begun by a mother with her four- or five-year-old child? The basic attitude which the child receives is so important that no time should be lost in assuring its correctness.

The parent's third auxiliary educational responsibility is that of creating a proper attitude toward the school in the mind of the child who is just entering the kindergarten or primary grade. The time-worn belief that children dislike school is rapidly passing away. It could be completely eliminated in a very short time if adults would cease to persist in reminding children that they ought to "hate to go to school."

There is a fourth phase of the educational process to which the parent-teacher movement has given splendid encouragement. Case work in psychiatry, psychology, education and social service began with adults. The early experimenters in the field of nervous maladjustment sought to enable disoriented men and women to regain their proper place in society. The social case worker endeavored to correct the evils which brought suffering and misery to families and to place the parents of such families in employment which would permit them to become again productive members of the community.

But here, just as in medicine, we have learned the relative value of prevention over cure. Later the case workers concentrated on adolescents. More recently they have begun to adjust little children before they become old enough to fall into unfortunate social situations. But to-day the great emphasis is on parental education.

If every social worker in America devoted his attention to the direct mental and physical treatment and adjustment of preschool children the task would never be accomplished. In the first place, there never could be enough case workers. If there were enough case workers, they would be wasting much energy because new children are being born every day. The emphasis then must be parental and pre-natal education. That, I believe, is the great field ahead of the parent-teacher movement. Such training does not begin with young mothers and fathers whose first babies have just been born. It begins back in the high school when boys and girls are forming the fundamental habits of adult life. It is too difficult to reach them with adequate instruction after they leave the classroom.

Dr. Kilpatrick has said, "Child life is too sacred to be spoiled through parental blundering. Mother love is not sufficient to child training. Love needs intelligence to guide its care." And Miriam Van Waters supports him by writing, "Nature gives parents affection. They know nothing of the child's inner growth, his struggles, conflicts and goals."

We must be freed from the old superstition that, with the birth of a baby, there comes to both parents all the knowledge they will require in regulating that life committed to their care. It is almost a miracle, through the ages in which that belief has been held, that children have become adjusted at all. Most of them who were successful men and women became so in spite of parental influence. But that does not tell the story of the failures that were due to parental ignorance.

The fourth auxiliary educational task sponsored by the parent-teacher movement, then, is parental and pre-natal education.

These four points we have just covered are actual educational tasks, augmenting the work done by the classroom teacher and the school administrator and supervisor. The family, under the guidance of the parent-teacher movement, has still another contribution to make to education.

One of the greatest essentials to every school system is the intelligent support of the public; and to the school administrator and teacher the most tangible representative of the public is the parent-teacher association. We have reached the day of professional administration in education. It is generally conceded that the trained superintendent of schools knows more about school management than any one else in his community. But the enlightened superintendent of schools realizes that the owners of the school system—the tax-paying people of the district—will continue their support only so far as they believe his administration is effective; and he also knows that unless they know certain basic facts about schools they can not measure the effectiveness of his work.

Professor Arthur B. Moehlman, of the University of Michigan, in his most valuable book on "Public School Relations," suggests seven points on which parents should be informed with reference to public education. Those seven points are: (1) instruction, (2) finance, (3) buildings, (4) teachers, (5) sanitation, (6) health, (7) administration.

The logical channel through which the parent may become informed on these seven points is the parent-teacher association to which he belongs. The fact that *teachers* are members of the parent-teacher associations means much in the adequate presentation of those important facts.

After reviewing these contributions of the parent-teacher movement to education, it becomes evident that this great body of a million and a quarter men and women is not only *beneficial* to the school but has become absolutely indispensable. There may have been a time when such an organization was not needed. But it is one of the new institutions which our changing world has demanded.

EDUCATIONAL EVENTS

THE BRITISH NATIONAL UNION OF TEACHERS

THE National Union of Teachers at its concluding session at Llandudno, Wales on April 4, according to a wireless report received by *The Christian Science Monitor*, unanimously adopted a resolution demanding legislation immediately raising the school-leaving age from 14 to 15 years.

The mover of the resolution, W. Merrick, of Salford, alleged that Lord Eustace Percy, Minister of Education, opposed the raising of the age before 1933 on the grounds of lack of school buildings and the inconvenience it would cause the local authorities. Every time the school age question was raised, he said, short-sighted employers predicted disaster to industry. Mr. Merrick also submitted that the cost of keeping children at school until fifteen years of age would be counterbalanced by the saving on unemployment, to the benefit of older workers and on traffic centers and continuation schools.

A. E. Baxter, London, another member of the executive, stressed the unemployment aspect of the question, pointing out that the schools were sending into the labor market every year 500,000 children and all but 20,000 obtained employment.

Miss W. J. Walmsley, Birmingham, contended that the most dangerous tendency in national education was widespread—the sacrifice of infants' departments in schemes of amalgamation. In Birmingham children were being educated in masses, reaching in some cases 720. Educationists must condemn this mass production. She charged that during the past eight years 1,100 primary departments had been deprived of teachers by amalgamation.

H. J. Jackson, Nottingham, who seconded, said an "economy" practice of some of the local education authorities was to employ uncertificated teachers. Cooks, waiters, nursemaids were trained and so, he said, should be the teachers in infants' schools.

Two further resolutions upheld the child's right to improved schools, one charging that the sanitary accommodation in many elementary schools of the poor districts and rural areas were "gravely deficient." Another resolution welcomed the activities of the National Playing Fields Association, demanding:

(1) That every new school shall be equipped with an adequate playing field.

(2) That in congested areas centralized playing fields shall be provided for groups of schools.

(3) That in rural areas the needs of village schools shall not be overlooked.

(4) That in housing and town-planning schemes adequate provision for open spaces shall form an essential part of such schemes.

The conference before adjournment passed without debate resolutions demanding a time limit for the existence of classes of more than 40 children, calling for more nursery schools and advocating a maximum 38-hour week for workers under sixteen years of age.

NEW YORK STATE NORMAL SCHOOL BUILDINGS

Adequate funds for the reconstruction of a state normal school at Plattsburg, recently destroyed by fire, for the construction of a new building at the Potsdam State Normal School, and for the replacement of the present normal school building at Geneseo are to be requested of the Legislature by the State Education Department as the result of action taken on February 22, at the meeting of the Board of Regents of The University of the State of New York.

The building at Plattsburg is a total loss. It housed approximately 400 students, about half of whom are preparing to become elementary school teachers. The department proposes to transfer the commercial course to the State College for Teachers at Albany but believes that there is a need for a normal school in the Plattsburg section for the preparation of city, village and rural elementary school teachers.

The school at Potsdam consists of four parts, including a modern main building and two annexes, the Stowell and Cook annexes. The former comprised about one third of the total available space of the school plant. The State architect's office at the invitation of the Commissioner of Education recently inspected this building and condemned it for further use. Temporary quarters are being used therefore for about one third of the 700 students registered at the school.

The Geneseo State Normal School is regarded as by far the poorest normal school building in the State. From the standpoint of lighting, ventilation, heating and fire hazard, the department recommends that the building be replaced at a very early date. The portion of the building used as a practice school is held to be the worst part of the structure.

STATISTICS OF NEGRO ELEMENTARY AND SECONDARY EDUCATION

Negro elementary and secondary education in public and private schools has made more progress in the past nine years than in any like period of our history.

According to Bureau of Education Bulletin, No. 19, 2,218,312 negro pupils were reported in public schools in 18 southern states in 1926. Of this number 1,055,674 were boys and 1,162,638 were girls. The average daily attendance was 1,563,975.

To instruct these children 47,594 teachers were employed, 38,942 women and 8,652 men. While the large majority of colored schools reporting were public, there were 168 private schools with 3,722 teachers and 61,509 pupils.

The libraries of the private secondary and higher schools for negroes in 1925–26 contained 630,892 bound volumes; the grounds and buildings were valued at $41,044,777 as against $17,323,108 in 1916.

In the 425 public high schools for colored pupils only, there were 2,566 teachers, and 98,705 colored pupils were enrolled in these and in other schools attended by colored pupils. The teacher-training institutions for negro students numbered 29, located in 17 southern states and Pennsylvania.

The increasing growth of schools has made a corresponding demand for more and better trained teachers. This demand has caused increases in salaries, which, however, do not yet equal the average of $1,277 paid both colored and white teachers throughout the United States.

ACCREDITED SCHOOLS OF THE MIDDLE STATES AND MARYLAND

The next list of Accredited Secondary Schools of the Association of Colleges and Secondary Schools of the Middle States and Maryland will be published January 1, 1930. Schools which have not been accredited and which desire to be considered for inclusion on this list must apply to the Commission on Secondary Schools before September 15, 1929. Application blanks have been sent to all schools in the territory whose names do not appear on the present list. The territory includes New York, New Jersey, Pennsylvania, Delaware, Maryland, the District of Columbia and the Panama Canal Zone. Schools having the following types of grade organization are considered: Grades 7–12, 9–12, 10–12.

The standards for secondary schools adopted by the association furnish the principal basis for consideration of schools, but all available facts are taken into consideration. A school that has applied but that has not been approved is advised of its shortcomings, and the information it submits is retained on file in the office of the commission until new evidence is presented which warrants the approval of the school for inclusion on the list. The commission holds as confidential all information regarding each school and gives no publicity to any unfavorable action or to any contact that it may have with the school. The efficiency of a school is the fundamental requisite for accrediting.

As a means of establishing local contacts and facilitating the work of accrediting, the commission has established a system of state committees to act in an advisory capacity. Each state committee consists of a public secondary school principal, a private secondary school headmaster, a representative of the State Department of Education in charge of secondary schools, a registrar or director of admissions in a higher institution, a professor of secondary education in a higher institution, the resident member or members of the commission and the chairman of the commission. These state committees meet early in October of each year to examine the information submitted by schools in their respective states applying for inclusion on the list, and recommendations to the commission are made. The commission meets in November and takes final action on the application of each school.

Heretofore, the cost of accrediting was defrayed by a subvention of the Carnegie Foundation, but the work of the Commission on Secondary Schools will now be conducted on a self-supporting basis. All schools which meet the standards for secondary schools and are placed on the list of accredited secondary schools will be required to pay a fee of $15.00. If the commission finds that the report of a visitor is necessary before taking action, the school will be required to pay the visitor's fee of $20.00 and his traveling expenses.

Inclusion on the list of Accredited Secondary Schools of the association and membership in the association are entirely independent. A member school is entitled to have its faculty attend the annual meeting, to participate in its sessions and to receive copies of the *Proceedings* and other publications. Such membership may be secured by application to the secretary, Dr. George William McClelland, University of Pennsylvania, Philadelphia, Pennsylvania. Inquiries concerning accrediting should be addressed to E. D. Grizzell, chairman of commission on secondary schools, Bennett Hall, University of Pennsylvania, Philadelphia, Pennsylvania.

THE SUMMER SESSION OF THE UNIVERSITY OF OREGON

WITH a faculty drawn from all parts of the country, and with a "floating university" trip to Alaska as a feature of the post-session, early indications are that a new record in enrolment in the University of Oregon summer sessions both in Eugene and in Portland will be set.

The sessions open June 24 and close August 2. Post-session at Eugene lasts from August 5 to August 30. The cruise, which will accommodate 165 students, sails from August 7 to 21, with two weeks' study following on the campus of the university.

The faculty for the sessions will consist of more than one hundred members, with thirty of these being recruited from outside Oregon. Among the visiting faculty men will be Dr. Joseph Schafer, state superintendent of the Wisconsin State Historical Society; Frank Chapman Sharp, professor of history at the University of Wisconsin; Arthur E. Nilsson, professor of economics at Yale University; Ulysses Grant Weatherly, professor of sociology at the University of Indiana, and Dr. Grace

M. Fernald, professor of education at the University of California.

Outstanding faculty men from the university who will offer courses either in Portland or Eugene include Olof Larsell, professor of anatomy; Thomas H. Gentle, professor of education; Alfred L. Lomax, professor of business administration; Nowland B. Zane, professor of art; David E. Faville, dean of the school of business administration; O. F. Stafford, head of the department of chemistry; Mrs. Otillie Seybolt, in charge of drama; H. D. Sheldon, dean of the school of education; Eric W. Allen, dean of the school of journalism; John J. Landsbury, dean of the school of music, and Edmund S. Conklin, head of the department of psychology.

The summer school of athletic coaching is to be extended to Portland this year. Coaching of track, basket-ball, football and women's sports will be offered. William Hayward, track coach; William J. Reinhart, baseball and basket-ball coach; John J. McEwan, football coach, and Robert Krohn, supervisor of physical education of the Portland schools, will compose the faculty.

The faculty for the summer cruise to Alaska, which will be taken on the S. S. *Queen*, of the Admiral line, includes Dr. J. Duncan Spaeth, professor of English at Princeton; Dr. Warren D. Smith, professor of geology at Oregon; Albert R. Sweetser, professor of botany, and Professor Nowland B. Zane, professor of art.

THE HOME STUDY DEPARTMENT OF COLUMBIA UNIVERSITY

THIRTY thousand students, large numbers of whom are holders of college and professional school degrees, have been enrolled in the home study department of Columbia University since this department was organized under the authority of the trustees in 1919.

Practically all the states of the Union and many foreign countries are represented, which characterized encouragement of learning through home study as a service to the state.

The present home study registration is 15,000, including more than 6,000 women. The North Atlantic States furnish the largest group, New York leading, with Pennsylvania second, Connecticut third and Massachusetts fourth. Nearly 2,000 residents of New York State, and a somewhat smaller number from New York City, study at home under the guidance of Columbia instructors.

Among the South Atlantic States, Virginia, North Carolina, Maryland and the District of Columbia have the largest group. In the South Central States, Texas, Louisiana and Alabama lead. In the North Central States, students are most numerous in Michigan, Ohio, Illinois, Indiana and Missouri. California leads the Western States, with Washington second and Oregon third.

Of the foreign countries, Canada is first, with Cuba second. Australia, Brazil, Ceylon, China, Denmark, Dominican Republic, Ecuador, Germany, Great Britain, Haiti, Honduras, India, Japan, Jamaica, Madagascar, Mexico, Norway and Peru also have quotas.

English is the most popular field of study, with mathematics second, history third, banking fourth, psychology fifth, French sixth, Latin seventh and art eighth. Courses in chemistry and chemical engineering, Greek, German, Spanish, physical geography, scouting, Biblical literature, biology, botany, actuarial mathematics, law, economics, statistics, drafting and government also attract large numbers of students.

THE HARVARD CHEMICAL LABORATORIES

THE formal opening of the new Mallinckrodt and Converse Memorial Laboratories of Chemistry at Harvard University, erected at a cost of $2,000,000, was held at 4 o'clock on the afternoon of April 8 with a reception for the donors. President A. Lawrence Lowell, Professor Arthur B. Lamb, director of the laboratories; Professor Gregory P. Baxter, chairman of the division of chemistry, and Dean Wallace B. Donham, of the Harvard Graduate School of Business Administration, executive chairman of the committee appointed by the corporation to raise funds, were the speakers. Of the more than sixty donors who made the new buildings and their equipment possible, some twenty were present. In addition, members of the overseers committee to visit the department of chemistry, members of the department and a few invited guests attended.

In the evening a dinner was given at the Algonquin Club for the donors and the visiting committee. Mr. Edward Mallinckrodt, son of the donor of the new Mallinckrodt laboratory, served as toastmaster, and Professor Lawrence J. Henderson, of the Harvard department of chemistry, and Dr. C. M. A. Stine, director of research for the du Pont Company, spoke.

The original gift, which formed the nucleus of the building fund, was made in 1923 by Edward Mallinckrodt, Sr., president of the Mallinckrodt Chemical Company, of St. Louis, who gave the sum of $500,000 "toward the construction of a new chemical laboratory." Mr. Mallinckrodt died during 1928, before the completion of the building. His son, Edward Mallinckrodt, Jr., Harvard, '00, represented the Mallinckrodt family at the reception. The Converse Memorial Laboratory, to be devoted largely to research, is the gift of the family of the late Edmund C. Converse, president of the Bankers Trust Company of New York City. Mrs. Edmund C. Converse, one of the donors of this memorial to her husband, represented the Converse family.

The Mallinckrodt Laboratory will house practically all the undergraduate courses in chemistry and enable the department to abandon Boylston Hall, which for years has been inadequate for modern needs. Quantitative analysis will be carried on in the Horsford Laboratory. Physical chemistry, electrochemistry and photochemistry are placed on the first floor. Industrial chemistry is provided for in the Bradley Laboratory, given by Robert S. Bradley, '76, president of the American Agricultural Chemical Company, in memory of his son, Robert Stow Bradley, Jr., '07.

Laboratories of all sorts, three lecture halls, one of them equipped with facilities for motion pictures, a library located in the Converse Laboratory and the most up-to-date equipment are provided. In addition, the sum of $1,000,000, raised by a committee of which Bishop William Lawrence was chairman and Dean W. B. Donham was executive chairman, will provide for the endowment of the laboratories. The firm of Coolidge, Shepley, Bulfinch and Abbott were the architects.

DR. HERBERT PUTNAM AND THE LIBRARY OF CONGRESS

DR. HERBERT PUTNAM has completed three decades of services as head of the Library of Congress and his associates in the library have presented him with a volume of essays commemorating the event. Sixty-one contributors are represented in this volume, which bears the title "Essays Offered to Herbert Putnam by his Colleagues and Friends on his Thirtieth Anniversary as Librarian of Congress, April 5, 1929." The volume is published by the Yale University Press, under the editorship of Dr. William Warner Bishop, librarian of the University of Michigan, and Dr. Andrew Keogh, librarian of Yale University.

Dr. Bishop made the presentation. Senator Simeon Fess, chairman of the joint committee on the library, author of the first essay, takes up the library as a whole. Senator Burton, of Ohio, and Senator Gillett, of Massachusetts, follow each with an essay on Mr. Putnam. Charles F. D. Belden, librarian of the Boston Public Library, contributes an essay on "The Library Service of Herbert Putnam in Boston." Other contributors include Jean Jules Jusserand, formerly ambassador of France to the United States; Sir Frederick K. Kenyon, director of the British Museum; Dr. Hugo A. Kruess, general director of the Prussian State Library; M. Pierre Roland-Marcel, administrator general of the National Library of France; T. P. Sevensma, librarian of the League of Nations, and Monsignor Eugene Tisserant, of the Library of the Vatican.

The volume contains five portraits of Dr. Putnam. One is from the album of the class of 1883 at Harvard College, and three are dated respectively 1898, 1900 and 1912. The frontispiece is a reproduction of a photograph by Miss Laura Gilpin of a portrait bust of Dr. Putnam executed in 1923 by his daughter, Miss Brenda Putnam.

EDUCATIONAL NOTES AND NEWS

THE fiftieth anniversary of the birth of Professor Albert Einstein will be celebrated at the Metropolitan Opera House on the evening of April 16, under the auspices of the Jewish National Fund and the Zionist Organization of America. The principal address will be made by the Honorable Ray Lyman Wilbur, secretary of the interior and president on leave of Stanford University.

LEO W. BREUER, graduate of the University of Washington, has been appointed commissioner of education for the Territory of Alaska. He succeeds Lester D. Henderson, who has held the post since its creation ten years ago.

THE formal inauguration of Dr. Mervin G. Filler as president of Dickinson College will be held on April 26.

FOR the fourth consecutive election in Baldwin, Kansas, the citizens have elected a member of the faculty of Baker University to office. At the city election held on April 1, Professor E. J. Cragoe was reelected mayor by a nearly unanimous vote.

THE King of Italy has conferred the decoration of Officer of the Crown of Italy upon Dr. Raymond Pearl, director of the Institute for Biological Research of the Johns Hopkins University.

THE Roumanian legation has conferred the decoration of the Order of the Commander of the Crown of Roumania on Dr. Arthur I. Andrews, professor of history at the University of Vermont, in recognition of his writings as a historian on Roumanian subjects. Dr. Andrews in engaged in research work at Harvard University.

THE King of Denmark has conferred the Danish Gold Medal of Merit upon Miss Björksten, the Finnish authority on gymnastics for women. Miss Björksten has for a number of years held a course for Scandinavian women teachers of gymnastics, alternately in the different Scandinavian countries; last year it was in Finland, this year it will be at Sigtema in Sweden.

A BANQUET in honor of Señor Moises Saenz, of the Mexican Ministry of Education, is being prepared by the committee on cultural relations with Latin-America. It will be held at the Boston City Club on April 15. Many educators and leaders in public life are expected to hear Señor Saenz and his companion speaker, Ernest Gruening. Willis J. Abbot will preside.

THE full Board of Curators of the University of Missouri on April 7 upheld the dismissal of Dr. Harmon O. DeGraff, assistant professor of sociology, for his part in the circulation of a sex questionnaire among students. It granted reinstatement to Dr. Max F. Meyer, professor of psychology, who, however, was ordered suspended for one year. A statement issued at the conclusion of the hearing said that Dr. Meyer was to be reinstated because "of his long service to the university and our conviction that the offense for which he was suspended will not be repeated." The full board held with its executive board that "the promiscuous circulation" of the questionnaire "by every tenet of sound sense and common decency should have been suppressed," and that the investigation "by its very nature tends to create the condition which it is alleged to correct."

DR. LEICESTER H. HOLLAND, of Philadelphia, has been appointed chief of the division of prints of the Library of Congress, a position that will carry with it the incumbency of the chair of fine arts established under a grant for the purpose by the Carnegie Corporation. Dr. Holland was in 1925 and 1926 engaged in teaching at Vassar College. Since then he has been bringing his work on the Erechtheum to a conclusion and will assume his post at the Library of Congress in September.

WILLARD P. LEWIS, a graduate of Wesleyan University and of the New York State Library School, after ten years as librarian of the University of New Hampshire, has resigned to become librarian of the new Olin Memorial Library at Wesleyan University, commencing on July 1. Dr. William J. James, for thirty-eight years librarian of Wesleyan University, becomes librarian emeritus.

ADRIAN O. MORSE, dean of men at the University of New Hampshire, who has been in Washington, D. C., on leave, serving as secretary to William M. Jardine, Secretary of Agriculture in the Coolidge cabinet, has taken up his work as executive secretary at the Pennsylvania State College. Norman Alexander, associate professor of economics in the University of New Hampshire, will become dean of men in September, succeeding Dean Morse.

DR. WALTER M. W. SPLAWN, who is now referee in the office of the war claims arbiter and was formerly president of the University of

Texas, has been appointed dean of the graduate school and the school of the political sciences of the American University, Washington. He will take up his work next September. In making the announcement, Chancellor Clark stated that Dr. Splawn will also become professor of economics. He will fill a newly created position which combines two formerly held by Dr. Edward T. Devine, dean of the graduate school, who resigned to return to New York City, and by the late Dr. Albert H. Putney, director of the school of the political sciences.

Dr. G. E. Condra, head of the conservation and survey division of the University of Nebraska, has been appointed dean.

Miss Miriam F. Carpenter, for the last nine years registrar, adviser of women and secretary of the committee on admissions with charge of the appointment office in the graduate school of education at Harvard University, will succeed Miss Emma M. Denkinger as dean of Wheaton College.

Professor Ernest C. Marriner, chairman of the executive committee and librarian at Colby College, has been elected to fill the newly created office of dean of men.

Ralph Bunche, instructor in political science at Howard University, has been granted leave of absence to accept an Ozias Goodwin memorial fellowship at Harvard University for graduate work in government. As a student at the University of California, Mr. Bunche won highest honors, graduating valedictorian in a class of six hundred and sixty-five.

Dr. A. G. Black, associate professor of agricultural economics at the University of Minnesota, will become head of the department of agricultural economics at the Iowa State College at Ames.

A Beloit College graduate will return to his alma mater next year to be head of the department of art. He is Phillip Barrows Whitehead, Ph.D., now teaching at the University of Vermont. Simultaneously with this announcement it was reported that specifications for the college's new $125,000 art hall have been completed and that the contract will be let on April 18th.

William R. Moody, son of Dwight L. Moody, the evangelist, has resigned as president of the Northfield Seminary for girls and the Mount Hermon School for boys, after twenty-nine years' service.

Erik Barnouw, of New York City, and Gerard P. Van Arkle, of Haddonfield, N. J., Princeton University seniors, have won the Zilph Hayes Palmer scholarship for one year's travel and study abroad. Awards of $2,500 each are given each year to two members of the senior class who, in the opinion of the committee, will best fulfill the purpose of the scholarship, "to afford their recipients an opportunity to broaden themselves by travel, by study and by life among foreign peoples."

Officers of the Ontario Educational Association were elected at the recent Toronto meeting as follows: *Honorary president*, F. C. Ashbury; *President*, J. T. Jenkins; *Vice-president*, R. N. McKenzie; *Secretary-treasurer*, R. B. Young.

John A. Craig, principal of the senior high school at Muskegon, Michigan, has been appointed successor to Superintendent M. W. Long, who has served for eight years and has declined reelection.

It is reported that the Baltimore School Board has retained Dr. George D. Strayer, of Teachers College, Columbia University, as adviser in the expenditure of the new school loan.

Dr. C. B. Cornell, of the Colorado State Teachers College at Greeley, recently received an invitation from Mr. Donald W. McKay, superintendent of schools at Raton, New Mexico, to make a survey of the school buildings there in order to assist them in preparing material to present to the public in behalf of a building campaign. Dr. Cornell visited all the school buildings and is preparing a report to present to the board of education.

Professor McQuilken DeGrange, of Dartmouth College, sailed for France on March 29 to be a member of the jury which passed on the thesis of M. Charles Mollon, a candidate for the D.és'L. degree, at the Université de Claremont on April 13. Professor DeGrange is returning to America at once, sailing on April 16. This is believed to be the first time that a member of an American faculty has been invited to cross the seas to serve as a member of such a jury at a French university. Professor DeGrange is one of the few Americans who possess the Doctorat d'Etat degree from a French university. This degree was granted to him at Claremont in 1923.

DR. C. E. MARTIN, dean of the social science faculty and head of the political science department at the University of Washington, is *en route* for Honolulu, where he will teach at the University of Hawaii. His place has been taken by Professor William George, a former member of the political science department, who has been at the University of Hawaii for the past year.

DR. FRED MORROW FLING, professor of European history in the University of Nebraska, has been granted leave of absence for the coming academic year to continue his historical work in Europe. Dr. Fling has served on the faculty of the university for more than thirty-seven years.

DR. VERNON L. PARRINGTON, professor of English at the University of Washington, sailed for Europe on April 6 to spend the summer in research work in the British Museum and other European libraries. Professor Parrington, it will be remembered, last year received a Pulitzer prize for his book on "Main Currents in American Thought."

DR. CYRUS ADLER, president of the Dropsie College, Philadelphia, and of the Jewish Theological Seminary, New York, arrived in Jerusalem on April 3. Dr. Adler and his family spent the Passover week in Jerusalem with Mr. and Mrs. Felix M. Warburg.

DR. ALBERT PINKEVITCH, president of the Second State University of Moscow, is visiting the United States.

PROFESSOR T. Y. WANG, of the Northeastern University, Mukden, and his associate, N. C. Piliangyeh, are making a tour of investigation to study European school systems, industrial plants and public park developments. Berlin, Cologne and Leipzig are included in the itinerary. According to Professor Wang, Manchuria expects in the near future to improve its schools and universities along European lines.

AT the recent meeting at Toronto of the Ontario Educational Association, the premier of the province, the Honorable G. Howard Ferguson, delivered an address on "The Necessity of Some Improvement in the Rural Educational System of Ontario."

DR. ADOLF DEISSMANN, of the University of Berlin, will deliver the Haskell lectures in the graduate school of theology of Oberlin College from April 10 to 19.

DR. ANDRÉ MORIZE, professor of French literature at Harvard University, is offering a course of five lectures at the University of Cincinnati.

PROFESSOR HARLOW SHAPLEY, director of the Harvard College Observatory, has been appointed, for this year, Henry Todd lecturer at the Massachusetts State Normal Schools and the Massachusetts School of Art. His subject will be "The Galaxy of Galaxies." This lectureship, named in honor of the donor of the fund which maintains it, was established in 1926 by the Massachusetts Department of Education, and the lecture is given every year at each of the ten normal schools maintained by the State of Massachusetts. The lecturers preceding Dr. Shapley have been: 1926, Dr. Edward H. Griggs, on "The Influence of the Parent and the Teacher in Character Training and Development"; 1927, Dorothy Canfield Fisher, on "Creative Reading," and in 1928, Dr. Charles H. Judd, on "Social Inheritance."

DR. LAWRENCE PEARSALL JACKS, principal and professor of philosophy at Manchester College, Oxford, who is on a tour of this country under the auspices of the American Association for Adult Education and of the Carnegie Corporation, New York, was recently the guest of a group of Boston educators at luncheon at the Union Club. Dr. Jacks addressed the gathering on "Education for Leisure," which was followed by a discussion. Dean Willard L. Sperry, of the Harvard Theological School, presided. Guests at the luncheon included Dean Henry W. Holmes, of the Graduate School of Education at Harvard University. President William Allan Neilson, of Smith College, presided at a dinner at which Dr. Jacks spoke on "The Animating Idea of Adult Education."

THE first group of lectures in schools of journalism by the Don Mellett Memorial Foundation will be given at the University of Missouri during journalism week, May 8, by Marlen E. Pew, editor of *Editor and Publisher,* New York. A group of American newspaper men have contributed several thousand dollars for this memorial in honor of Mellett, former editor and publisher of the *Canton Daily News,* Ohio, who was murdered in July, 1926. His murder followed a campaign against vice elements conducted by Mellett through the *Daily News.*

A BRONZE memorial which will perpetuate the memory of Dr. Dudley Allen Sargent, professor of physical education at Harvard University, founder of the Sargent School in Cambridge, has been received at the school as a gift from the alumnae association. The memorial was designed by Dr. R. Tait McKenzie, head of the department of physical education at the University of Pennsylvania. It bears the inscription: "Dudley Allen Sargent—to keep in memory his life work." Figures of three girls and a boy at play complete the design. The bronze will be erected on the flag pole of the Sargent Camp at Peterboro, New Hampshire.

DR. LAURA HORNER CARNELL, associate president of Temple University, died on March 23, in her sixty-second year. Dr. Carnell joined the faculty of Temple University in 1895, later becoming professor of the history of art. She became dean in 1905 and following the death of Dr. Conwell in 1925, when Dr. Beury was elected president of the university, she became associate president. Dr. Carnell had been a member of the Philadelphia Board of Public Education since October, 1923, and was active in civic affairs.

THE American Association of College News Bureaus will hold its annual meeting at Nashville, Tennessee, from April 11 to 13.

A THREE weeks' institute in the principles and practices of progressive education will be conducted by the Progressive Education Association at Pennsylvania State College from July 1 to 19. It is open to teachers, principals, superintendents and others interested in the newer attitude toward childhood and in better schools. The courses carry college credit. Topics for the sessions are: "The Principles of Progressive Education," "The Progressive School in Practice," "Development through Expression." The instructors and lecturers are: Dr. W. Carson Ryan, Jr., Swarthmore College; Mr. Morton Snyder, Rye, New York, Country Day School; Mr. Stanwood Cobb, Chevy Chase Country Day School, Washington, D. C.; Miss Rachel Erwin, Winbrook School, White Plains, New York; Dr. Otis W. Caldwell, Teachers College, New York; Dr. Robert D. Leigh, Bennington, Vt., College for Women, and Mr. Hughes Mearns, New York University. The Progressive Education Association has its headquarters at 10 Jackson Place, Washington, D. C.

SCHOOL AND SOCIETY has received from Principal J. A. Berger, of the Gresham School of Economics, London, an announcement of the summer school to be held from July 22 to August 23, with courses prepared exclusively for citizens of the United States and of Canada. Students must be in attendance at an approved college or university. The subjects will be the English banking system; public finances of the United Kingdom; European markets; joint stock companies and corporations; foreign exchange. Two scholarships are offered for candidates writing theses rated highest. Applications for admission should be addressed to the principal of the Gresham School, 66–67 St. Paul's Churchyard, London, E. C. 4, England.

THE governing board of the Pan-American Union has approved the draft of the program of the Pan-American Congress of Rectors, Deans and Educators, as well as the basis of organization of the Inter-American Institute of Intellectual Cooperation which will be submitted for the consideration of the congress. The congress will meet at Havana, Cuba, in February, 1930, at the time of the celebration of the bi-centenary of the founding of the University of Havana. At the same time, the governing board approved the program of the Inter-American Bibliographic Conference which was provided for by resolution of the sixth International Conference of American States. The date and place of the meeting of this conference will be determined by the governing board at a later date.

BEQUESTS amounting to about $700,000 to Princeton University, the University of Pennsylvania, the Presbyterian Hospital and Bryn Mawr Presbyterian Church are made in the will of Harold A. Freeman, a business man of Philadelphia.

A GIFT of $300,000 has been made to the Hill School, in Pottstown, Pennsylvania, by Mrs. Alexander Hamilton Rice for a general science building as a memorial to her son, Harry Elkins Widener. In addition to the usual scientific facilities the building will provide small private laboratories for the use of gifted students.

PLANS for a fine arts center at Washington University, St. Louis, include a new building for the school of architecture and a museum of art, architecture and archeology.

To organize and develop its work of training young men and women in all branches of social work, the school of sociology and social service of Fordham University will begin an intensive campaign for an endowment fund with a concert in the Metropolitan Opera House on April 15. The campaign will continue for the week of April 15 only. The objective is an endowment of $500,000, with the immediate objective of $125,000. The sum of $25,000 already is in the endowment fund, and an anonymous friend of the school has promised to donate $50,000 if the school has raised $150,000 by June 15. Patrick Cardinal Hayes has contributed $10,000 and has promised an additional $5,000.

IN order to bring about better relations and closer trade contacts between Great Britain and the dominions there has been established a professorship of empire at the London School of Economics. It will be known as the chair of Imperial Economic Relations, and the Empire Marketing Board, whose work is now said to be receiving wide attention, has made a grant in support of the chair of £2,000 a year for five years.

THE bill to readjust the territorial distribution of scholarships bequeathed by the late Cecil Rhodes for the benefit of American and British dominion students at Oxford has passed the committee stage of the House of Lords and is now unopposed. Unanimity regarding the bill has been reached by the trustees accepting the contention put forward on behalf of Jamaica and Bermuda that the three scholarships accorded these islands should be guaranteed against reduction as already provided for those which concern the United States, Canada, Newfoundland, Australia, New Zealand, South Africa and Rhodesia.

THE German minister of education, Dr. Becker, has agreed to the request of a number of directors of Berlin-Charlottenberg higher schools to place English foremost in foreign language instruction. Hitherto French has taken precedence of modern languages in the curriculum.

DISCUSSION

PERSONALITY VS. METHODS

IN my study of education the fact which has impressed itself most firmly in my mind is the lack of a technique for developing the personality of the prospective teacher before she enters the classroom. We have courses in classroom procedure, psychology of learning, etc., but nowhere have I heard of a course in "personality development." If we analyze this problem we find that after many years of experience in the classroom the teacher has managed to develop proper traits or else had a natural-born personality which made her a success. We might point out the latter type as the teacher of whom people in referring to her say, "She is a born teacher." But—what of the other kind? Shall we place teachers in the classroom trained to the minute in teaching methods and armed with psychological facts if they have not the personality to make them successful and to change them from a teacher skilled in methods but lacking in human traits to one who can make learning interesting to the students? We strive in our modern methods to interest the pupils, to eliminate the old formal plan of learning and, so far, all efforts have been directed in developing methods. I believe that we should go farther back if we are to gain the interest of the pupils and that in doing so we must develop the personality of the prospective teachers in the training school at the same time that classroom procedure is studied.

An article by Dr. Caswell Ellis, of Cleveland College, seems to bear me out in this idea when he made known the results of an experiment which he had made. At his direction a professor experimented with a dozen different systems of education, teaching one subject, one year, in six different ways. In one class he used the lecture method, in another the quiz, in the third the individual research, and so on. At the end of the year a check up was made and the conclusion was that all classes had fared alike. The system made no difference. "The important factor in a classroom is the personality of the teacher. If she can fire her class with enthusiasm for a subject, if she can make study a lively activity, she will be successful in turning out a finished product."

We find no two teachers using the same methods with the same results. Often a method successful with one is unsuccessful with another. Here we find a teacher who can accomplish unheard-of things with a class and yet another teacher in the same building with the same class can do very little. Granted, even, that two teachers have had the same preparation and experience, we find the same results to be true. Can we blame methods?

To my mind the answer lies in the personality of the teacher. Has she looked to herself to solve her problem, since she has received no training in personality development, or does she vainly try one method after another, seeking to develop interest and to stimulate her pupils to active thinking? The keynote of a successful teacher lies in her personality. Shelley could kindle the spirit of revolution in thousands who would have been bored with the same fiery doctrines in the abstract and cold pages of Godwin, from whom he derived his ideas of "political justice." A genuinely enthusiastic personality kindles its own fire in the hearts of others and makes them appreciate as no mere formal analysis could the vital and moving aspect of things. Good teaching has been defined as communication by contagion, and the teachers whom students usually testify to have influenced them most are not those who doled out flat prescribed wisdom, but those whose own informed ardor for their subject-matter communicated to the student a warm sense of its own significance.

For the aforementioned reasons I believe that we stress formal and informal methods so much that personality development is ignored. For that reason the inexperienced teacher is apt to depend too much on problematical methods. Since we all recognize the importance of personality and since no specified training in personal development has been given to us, let us see what can be done to fill the gap.

Begin by analyzing your personality to find what you have and what you lack. It is then and then only that you should concern yourself with a method suitable to the subject and to your personality. The logical question that now arises is, "How can I examine my own personality?" This might be partially solved by watching other successful teachers. From my experience I would suggest that you ask yourself the following questions.

(1) Have I a good sense of humor?
(2) Am I sincere in the attitude I have toward my school work or do I put on a "false front"?
(3) Am I "hard-boiled" in my attitude toward the pupils?
(4) Do I magnify the importance of subject-matter to the exclusion of minor yet influential small things.
(5) Am I always seeking to improve myself?
(6) Do I like my work?

These are a few questions which a teacher might well ask herself in the attempt to develop the proper personality traits for teaching success.

Let us look to the near future when courses in personality development will be instituted in the training school unencumbered with psychological facts and classroom methods.

James A. Boyd

OUR EYE-MINDED GIRLS

We have gotten used to the expression "hand-minded," describing those people whose minds are not adapted to the abstractions of ordinary academic work in education. Some of these pupils are mentally of low grade, but some are as intelligent, in anything else but the academic work, as the natural scholars. In the human relations they are often as good and as valuable as anybody, as members of a family and as citizens. In some matters, as in the use and construction of tools and machinery, they are singularly adept and quick-witted. "Hand-minded" is sometimes used as a euphemism for moron, but that is a slander on the true "hand-minded" boy. There are differences of kind as well as differences of degree in intelligence. The true "hand-minded" are typically boys who know all about automobiles, aeroplanes and all sorts of other instruments and tools.

There is another group of students, not scholarly in the narrow sense and not "hand-minded" in either sense. These are people who are "eye-minded." They are mostly girls. They automatically forget algebra and Latin, but they know how things look, and can learn whether this looks well or that looks ugly. They are the natural designers, interior decorators, illustrators, window-dressers, dress-designers, of the world. They are not born scholars, not because they are not intelligent, for they are, but because their intelligence is of another kind; they are eye-minded.

Just as we have machine shops and trade schools in our public-school systems for the hand-minded boys, we have an art department especially for the eye-minded (and for art appreciation and for so much of eye-mindedness as belongs to each of us). We ought to expand and develop it into a school of design on the same plane as our trade schools for the fuller development of this large group of pupils. Their most valuable faculties are not yet generally given scope for want of a larger and more varied program, and because the pupils waste too much time on things they never can learn anyhow.

Albert W. Barker

Public Schools,
Wilmington, Delaware

SPECIAL CORRESPONDENCE

A BOOK LIST WITH PERSONALITY

As the crystallization of twenty years' work in interesting boys and girls in good books, the Montclair junior high schools are just issuing in a new and novel form their revised list of books for home reading. Mechanically the lists are of the loose-leaf variety, clipped into hand-decorated covers, five by seven and one half inches, which is a convenient size to slip into a boy's pocket.

With these covers and printed lists issued from the school press every month, there are blank pages on which the student is to paste pictures illustrative of the books read, and there are printed forms on which the pupil is to record simply his own reactions to the same books. In this way each pupil will produce a book which is essentially his own and interesting enough to be kept long after he has left school.

For many years the students have been required to read from four to ten books each year from a list of books carefully chosen as representative of the books of rather more than passing value. The tendency of boys and girls if left unguided is to limit their reading to one kind of book—possibly a series, telling how Mary Jones goes to school, Mary Jones goes to camp, Mary Jones goes to college, Mary Jones goes to Canada, or, perhaps, Tom Smith wins the baseball game, Tom Smith wins the football game, Tom Smith goes to camp. They leave untouched the great wealth of equally interesting books of adventure and travel and sport written by masters. Some publishers have recently put out fascinating illustrated catalogues that stimulate the interest of the favored few into whose hands they fall. But to make an ordinary book list put out by a school a vital factor in a boy's interest is a problem solved more or less in the ratio of the teacher's love for books.

The Montclair junior high schools are issuing a new and different type of book list in the belief that a list can be so published that it will mechanically have power to interest a boy at other times than when discussing it perfunctorily in class, and in the belief that a book list can and ought to reflect the personality of the owner. The list is being issued in sections, and parts of it will be contributed by the owner himself. When, therefore, Sam Blake's list is completed three years hence, it will be quite different from Frank White's list.

Usually when a book is made the cover is put on last. Our list starts with a heavy, perforated cover which is a scrumptious affair—for to what child is a thing made by himself *not* scrumptious! "Books and My Adventures among Them" is the title now being used on these covers. The pupils of the five junior high schools compete for the honor of designing a special cover to be used in their own building. These designs are printed in outline in the print-shops, but the painting is done by the individual owner. It *then* and *thus* becomes "*my* cover for *my* book list."

Topics under which books are listed appeal to junior high-school boys and girls—"Tales of Adventure," "Mysteries and Surprises," "Humor," "Myths, Legends, and Romance in the Days of Old," "History Told in Fiction," "Real People," "Travel and Exploration" and "Interesting Occupations and Careers That Thrill." Lists on new subjects are added each month. The most personal addition to the list is a page of remembrance added for each book read. On this page are recorded notes needed to help one recall the book when he wants to recommend it to a friend or to make a report on it to the book club—more commonly known as the English class. From this many interesting projects develop, such as the printing of each school's favorite poems. The public library cooperates closely, sending the schools frequent communications about its new books.

From time to time we expect to drop off books of temporary interest. Thus our list will always be up-to-date in so far as our own printing department can function rapidly, for after the initial distribution of parts the printing will be done in our own shops.

Children have not only generally expressed their appreciation for new book lists to their teacher but have in a number of cases, either individually or by groups, written notes of appreciation to the committee of extra-curricular reading. These notes contain interesting comments, of which the following are typical:

We are greatly indebted to you for the exceedingly neat and convenient way in which the book lists are arranged.

We feel that we have a greater amount of freedom in choosing books to read because the books are not listed by certain grades.

It is so much better, when you find a book you like, to read it without fear of its being for another grade.

The loose-leaf idea is a great improvement.

These lists contain books by modern authors. These books are read more.

Loose leafs are more useful for we can add more books.

I like the idea of not grouping the books by grades.

It is with a feeling of real pleasure that I look over our book lists to find a book to read.

We have a vision that this list will become a treasury of one's own reactions to literature—a book list with personality.

The present book list is the outcome of eighteen years' work with outside reading for boys and girls. The first one was a typewritten affair made in 1910. Since then it has been published in book form four times, each time after a very thorough revision following the frank criticism of the boys and girls, the suggestions of new members on the committee, the suggestions of our own town librarians and of certain nationally famous librarians, the recommendations of magazine discussions of best books, and the help of a rare friend of the school, Mr. Dallet Fuguet, who had time to spend looking up in New York the best editions of folk-lore and historical material. The radical change in form is an attempt to meet a changed condition in our schools. The committee is indebted to the "enthusiastic inspiration of a member of the board of education, Frederic G. Melcher, editor of the *Publishers' Weekly* and founder of the John Newbery prize given each year for the best children's book published that year, and to the far-sighted educational policy of Superintendent Pickell."

In each junior high school there is a librarian who helps the pupil select the book suited to his age and interests, and helps him over what too often is a bugbear, the first few descriptive pages of a book. This condition seemed to call for no book list or else one of an entirely new type, which we hope we have now supplied.

The preparation of a list like this means many days of labor spent in looking up other lists, in reading reviews and comments on books not yet on the list, in finding out what books publishers recommend, what librarians think of the books recommended, into what grades teachers think a book should go, how boys and girls respond to it, and in doubtful cases in reading the book oneself, in looking up the exact name of the author, in deciding whether the book is fiction or non-fiction, and in making an orderly, alphabetical list for the printer. This has taken us not only to our Montclair Public Library, to the New York Public Library, to the Boston Public Library, but also to the library section and sessions of the National Education Association.

But the more we have worked over this list the more we believe that it is an excellent list for Montclair. In fact we think the list is so good that we advocate putting on *pressure* to induce boys and girls to read the listed books and not to wander far afield until they have read several of these. Pressure! ! Shades of modern education! Pressure? Yes, pressure!

We believe that a boy or girl loves what he knows. For fear that we may make one boy hate a book may we not commit the more grievous crime of letting ten boys think they hate worth-while things? Come now! Let's give good literature a sporting chance!

After all, isn't putting on pressure a matter of skill? Some time ago a very interesting article on "Nagging" appeared in the New York *Times Magazine*. After telling many experiences, the writer concluded that it was right and salutary and even beneficent to nag, provided the nagger was skilful in inventing new and interesting ways to nag. We believe that this matter of getting boys and girls to read the right books is exactly the question of inventing new and interesting ways to "bring the ever-changing supply of young readers into contact with really worth-while books."

Our book list is proving to be a new and interesting method of attack, a method which does not seem to the boys and girls one of nagging but rather one that will add enjoyment to the pleasure of reading.

Ellen M. Cushman

Hillside Junior High School,
Montclair, New Jersey

SEMINAR FOR PERSONNEL WORKERS

Keeping up to date with new developments in his own and related fields is a major problem of the typical vocational counselor and personnel worker. The many details of the daily tasks and the tremendous demands upon his time and energy leave little opportunity for reading and study while literature and experimentation are increasing by leaps and bounds.

In response to demand from workers in the field who had completed their professional training, who had something to offer others and who wanted to keep in touch with latest developments, the department of personnel administration of the School of Education, New York University, is including in its training program for personnel service in education a rather unique course.

Two years ago a seminar was established, meeting once a week on Monday evenings, open only to experienced counselors and personnel workers in education and industry. Each member of the group selects some phase of the personnel field in which he is particularly interested and becomes responsible to the group for reviews and reports on all the new material appearing on this phase of the subject. During the current academic year, one meeting each month has been conducted by a specialist in some related field. Present and former graduate students in the department have taken advantage of these special opportunities to keep in touch with what is going on. Attendance at the monthly talks, which is limited by the capacity of the room available for the meetings, has varied from sixty to eighty. Speakers for 1928–29 include:

Professor Robert A. Kissack, director of the department of art education, New York University, "Art in Industry; Its Significance for the Personnel Worker in Education and Industry."

Meyer Bloomfield, one of the founders of the vocational guidance movement, and now private consultant in business personnel practices, "Modern Personnel Work in Education and Industry and their Interrelation."

Noel Sargent, industrial secretary of the National Association of Manufacturers, "The Educational Program of the National Association of Manufacturers."

Dr. Edgar A. Doll, director of research of the Training School at Vineland, New Jersey, "The Contribution of Clinical Psychology to an Understanding of Personnel Principles and Practices."

Dr. Hugh Hartshorne, director of character education inquiry, Teachers College, Columbia University, "The Scientific Approach to the Study of Personality."

Dr. Lawson G. Lowrey, director of the Institute of Child Guidance, New York City, "The Contribution of Mental Hygiene to Personnel Work in Education and Industry."

D. H. T.

QUOTATIONS

THE LONDON SCHOOLS

THE London County Council has authorized an education scheme for the triennium 1930–1933 which will take seriously in hand, as suggested in the Board of Education Circular 1397, the elimination of large classes, the problem of "black list" schools, and the establishment of senior schools for children over eleven years. It is strange that there still should be "black list" schools in London. It is to be presumed that these schools, including schools that are rendered almost untenable by the roar of traffic, will vanish at a very early date. No doubt the council's own inspectors have reported upon these black spots in the London educational system. It is difficult for the Board of Education to press upon poorer authorities the duty of abolishing "black list" schools when those authorities can point to breaches of the law on the part of the richest authority in the country. To what extent bad accommodation is affecting the health of London children it is difficult to say, but it is good news that Miss Adler, on the reception of the report of the Special Services Sub-Committee, has raised the question of the health of young workers as dealt with in the annual report of Sir George Newman. Another and not less important health question was also raised by Miss Adler, the inspection and medical treatment of pupils in evening institutes. These institutes give the opportunity of following up to some extent the last medical reports on school-leavers. The question of health is also to be associated with crowded classes, and as the London authority in the past has been very active in the matter, it is good to know that in the coming triennium the subject is again to be specially dealt with. Smaller classes will make for efficiency in every direction.

Of another kind is the effort to be made to extend the operation of the Consultative Committee's report on the Education of the Adolescent in respect to the establishment of senior schools for pupils over the age of eleven. The London Education Committee has been moving experimentally in this direction for more than four years, and after the issue of the Consultative Committee's report the number of experimental groups was extended in May, 1927, to twenty-four. There will be after Easter altogether twenty-four—there are now eighteen—groups of reorganized schools. Though the reports on these groups have individually all been favorable, yet the degree of success has varied, and the Education Committee is still moving in the direction with what is described as "considerable caution," with too much caution many educationists, who have no doubt as to the necessity of making a break at the age of eleven, will think. However, in the next triennium a larger field is to be surveyed and the number of experimental areas is to be doubled, and there will be forty-eight groups—not more—of elementary schools organized on the basis of a complete educational break from primary school work to (presumably) secondary school work at the age of eleven plus. It is difficult to justify the half-hearted acceptance of an accepted principle, and it is open to the criticism that it is financial and not educational considerations that are preventing London from giving a lead on a great scale to the principles laid down in the Hadow Report. London, however, has never moved rapidly in educational methods in all its long history except in the famous departure in the direction of higher elementary education which culminated in the Cockerton case. It is to be hoped that higher elementary education is not to be the goal of the new senior schools. All higher education must be secondary in spirit.—*London Times Educational Supplement.*

EDUCATIONAL RESEARCH AND STATISTICS

INITIAL PERFORMANCE AS A BASIS FOR PREDICTING ULTIMATE ACHIEVEMENT

From the behavior of a subject in the beginning stages of the learning process can one foretell with any confidence his relative standing in the later phases? Where a new act is to be mastered, is it possible to detect the eventually competent person at the outset as well as at the finish? This question is often answered in the affirmative by industrial and educational executives, and many of our practical judgments on individual ability postulate the correctness of such a view.

Recent work in mental testing, however, suggests that initial accomplishment is disproportionately affected by chance variables and that an adequate measure of skill can be derived only from a prolonged series of measurements. Hence, most experimenters permit a few preparatory trials before taking any critical records.

It was thought possible to approach this problem in at least one narrow function by an adaptation of a suggestive device first used in a different connection by Bair.[1] The material is designed primarily to measure the speed of verbalization in the following four aspects: (1) the repetition of the alphabet as rapidly as possible *forward, i.e.,* A-B-C; (2) the interception of the letter "n" between each pair of the letters, *i.e.,* $A_nB_nC_n$; (3) the repetition of the alphabet as rapidly as possible *backward, i.e.,* Z-Y-X; and (4) the repetition of the alphabet backward intercepting "n" between each pair of the letters, *i.e.,* $Z_nY_nX_n$.

The data were obtained from fifty members of a class in educational psychology by means of an individual experiment ostensibly designed for the analysis of practice curves. The students worked in pairs, one partner giving directions to the other and measuring the time for each repetition in *seconds.* Twenty trials were made of each of the four series listed above, records being taken *twice daily.* The high reliability of the measures (see Table II below) argues against the presence of any motives inimical to objectivity.

[1] J. H. Bair, "The Practice Curve," Psy. Rev. Mon., No. 19, 1902.

The data were first treated by finding the total average time in seconds for all twenty trials in each series; the initial average time from the first *three* trials, and the final average time for the last three trials. (Throughout this discussion the number of each series corresponds to the order above described.) The next step consisted in finding the correlation between the initial and final averages in every series with the results shown in Table I.

TABLE I

Series	Pearson r between initial and final means	Probable error (N = 50)
I	.78	.03
II	.43	.08
III	.64	.05
IV	.56	.06

The average correlation here is approximately .60, which, to the writer at least, is surprisingly high. On the strength of these values it would appear that even in such a restricted capacity as reversed alphabetization most subjects adhere to the level of achievement they have struck at the start.

If, as seems likely, the man who is excellent at the beginning of practice will be good at the end, and *pari passu* for the poor subject, we are naturally led to inquire if the competent subject in one series will also distinguish himself in the others. A solution to this subsidiary problem may be sought in the intercorrelations of the total averages for the four distinct learning processes.

TABLE II

Series	I	II	III	IV
I	*.91 (.02)**			
II	.76 (.04)	*.86 (.03)*		
III	.30 (.09)	.43 (.08)	*.99 (.005)*	
IV	.36 (.08)	.50 (.07)	.93 (.01)	*.97 (.009)*

*Probable errors in parentheses. N = 50.

The figures lying along the italicized diagonal indicate the reliability of each series obtained by matching the measures of the odd and the even trials. It will be observed that the intercorrelations are all moderately positive and that the greater the degree of external similarity between any two series the greater will be their intercorrelation; *e.g.*, series III (saying Z-Y-X) is concomitant to the extent of .93 with series IV (saying $Z_nY_nX_n$). One may interpret this as attributable to the high degree of overlap between the different neuromuscular patterns involved, or as evidence for the action of a general factor, according to one's theoretical predilections.

Another question which might be raised in this connection would be: Do the initial or final intercorrelations deviate more from the total average correlations of Table II? The logic demanded in answering this is simple enough, although the calculations are laborious. Table III gives the necessary information. (The *first* decimals represent the *initial intercorrelations* and the *ones in parentheses* stand for the *final intercorrelations.* P.E. values are omitted, but may readily be estimated from preceding figures.)

TABLE III. (N = 50)

Series	I	II	III	IV
I	——			
II	.31 (.53)	——		
III	.16 (.38)	.67 (.45)	——	
IV	.03 (.42)	.44 (.52)	.83 (.92)	——

In all but one case the final intercorrelations are higher than the initial. To find which deviated more from the total average intercorrelations, the algebraic mean differences in points between it and the initial and final intercorrelations were obtained for each series. The mean differences are .22 and .07, respectively, showing that the final intercorrelations approach more closely the values of the total average intercorrelations.

It is of some interest to note how this investigation confirms a conclusion earlier reached by Hollingworth[2] to the effect that "the intercorrelation coefficients become greater the longer the practice is continued." Another dictum of modern psychology here illustrated is best expressed by a quotation from a related experiment of Wells:[3]

> A high initial efficiency may carry with it as much or more prospect of improvement under special practice than a low one. It is not because the favored individual has had more of the general experience enabling him to meet the experimental situation better, but because he possessed the native ability to profit more by such experience, general or special, past or future. Not practice, but *practiceability*, is responsible for the superior position of such an individual; and in broader aspect, not education, but educability.

SUMMARY

(1) The rate of learning for four different types of alphabetization was secured from fifty subjects with the purpose of discovering the nature of the relation between their early and later scores.

(2) The average reliability of the four tests obtained by the matching of alternate items was approximately .93.

(3) Correlating the means of the first three and last three trials of each individual's record resulted in coefficients of moderate size. Despite the relatively large probable errors, the consistency of the values justifies the assertion that the size of the initial score provides a reasonably good prediction of the final score, at least within the limits of the twenty trials here taken. It is impossible to say whether this situation would be altered by an extension of the trials; nor do we know whether the same state of affairs would be found with other material.

(4) Speed of verbalization appears to be a common factor, since its presence in one task parallels its presence in another. The degree of correspondence increases with the apparent similarity of the tasks.

(5) Intercorrelations between the various series based on data derived from the end of the practice curves deviate less from those secured from the composite averages than the intercorrelations obtained from initial performances.

GEORGE W. HARTMANN

PENNSYLVANIA STATE COLLEGE

[2] H. L. Hollingworth, "Correlation of Abilities as Affected by Practice," *J. Ed. Psy.*, 4: 405–414. 1913.

[3] F. L. Wells, "Relation of Practice to Individual Differences," *Am. J. Psy.*, 23: 75–99. 1912.

SCHOOL AND SOCIETY

EDITED BY J. McKEEN CATTELL

WITH WHICH IS COMBINED THE

EDUCATIONAL REVIEW

EDITED BY WILLIAM McANDREW

Volume XXIX | Saturday, April 20, 1929 | Number 747

THE NURSERY SCHOOL AND CHILD DEVELOPMENT[1]

By Professor R. S. WOODWORTH

DEPARTMENT OF PSYCHOLOGY, COLUMBIA UNIVERSITY

We find ourselves in the enviable position of participating in the beginnings of what may prove to be one of the great forward movements of modern times. Many indications point to the importance of the first few years of the child's life in shaping his later behavior as an individual, and thus controlling the destiny of society. Now we are to focus the sciences of health, growth and behavior upon the young child. That period between babyhood and school life, which has been relatively neglected by science and organized education, is to come into its own. We are to have people professionally concerned with the young child, trained to apply to him what science we already possess, to discover much more about him and to record what they discover, so that the bits of knowledge that every child has drilled into the minds of his parents shall not, as hitherto, be dissipated as that child disappears from the scene. With an institution, however cosy and informal, devoted to his interests, and with wide-awake persons whose chosen profession it is to observe and labor for his good, knowledge is bound to accumulate, and better and better use will be made of those formative years. Instead of remaining the neglected years, they may turn out to be the high point of the educational system—the period during which wise and restrained effort by adults can accomplish the most for the budding individual.

[1] Paper read at the dedication of the Nursery School, Vassar College, February 7, 1928.

Some sort of a school for children of from two to five years was probably first conceived in the hope of improving the physical condition of children from poverty-stricken homes. These little children, now coming every day under the eyes of the doctor or nurse, could be better guarded against disease and have better attention in the way of nutrition and the correction of physical defects, and thus the baby school would turn back to the home or to the nation a generation of sturdier youngsters, better equipped to withstand the strain of the regular school years and to grow up into healthy and vigorous adults. Such a use for the nursery school has by no means been outgrown with improvement in the general economic condition of the people, for the advance in the sciences of nutrition and health has more than kept pace with the economic advance. Even more to-day than a century ago, there is much that the mother of a family can not be presumed to know or to be able to do for the best health of her little child. Even children from well-to-do homes often profit in their general health by attendance at a good nursery school.

The nursery school is a help to the mother in other obvious ways. Having the child out of her care for a portion of the day sets free some of her time for occupations which may be very important to herself and to her family, and she is left in a less strained condition to associate with her child when he does come home. Relieving her of part of her responsibility still leaves plenty with her, and leaves her fresher to carry out her part, often with helpful advice from the school in doing her part. There is no doubt that the child in the home is becoming an increasing burden as the standards of what should be done for the child continually rise, competing as they inevitably do with the multifarious other demands laid upon the home by modern civilization. The declining birth-rate, especially among the more ambitious people, is to a large degree a reflex of this increasing burden. As children become more expensive, they become scarcer, and as they become scarcer, they become more valuable articles. We can not afford to lose them through infant mortality, or to waste them by unskilful bringing up. The nursery school tends to offset the declining birth-rate in two ways: by salvaging children who would otherwise be total or partial losses, and by making it feasible for many a desirable home to afford another child or two.

The nursery school helps the child in other ways than by watching over his physical condition; it is an agency of mental hygiene as well. Useful habits and much useful routine are taken on more readily in the school than in the home—partly because of the influence of the group upon the individual child, and partly because of the presence in the school of adults who know what to do and have the time to do it. Tantrums that seem unavoidable at home often disappear after a time in the school. The helpless dependence of the child is overcome. The domineering, selfish child, often spoiled in the home, learns some of the give-and-take of social life. The absence of excessive emotional demands and reactions, which often fall to the lot of the child in the home, is a godsend to him. Thus, in many ways, good emotional development and social adjustment are fostered by a sojourn in the nursery school.

Again, what we loosely designate as "motor development," including the skilful manipulation of tools and other objects, as well as posture and locomotion, is likely to proceed faster in the nursery school than at home. The school has a greater variety of suitable equipment for instructive play of this sort, and the fear of the child's possibly hurting himself is not such an inhibitor of active play as it is apt to be in many homes. Little manual operations, such as buttoning and lacing, which the child has done for him at home, he learns rather early to do for himself in the school. He makes relatively rapid progress in mastery of what is sometimes called the sociophysical environment, the world of specially made or selected objects, to be manipulated in definite ways for definite uses, with which we have so fully surrounded ourselves that we may scarcely ever come in contact with strictly natural objects. But the child does also have a better chance of forming the acquaintance of strictly natural objects, such as growing things, in the nursery school than in the city home at least. Also, his introduction to music and the rudiments of decorative art is likely to be more instructively managed in the school than at home. His vocabulary develops rapidly, he learns to talk freely to other children and even before a group. He participates in group games and activities and in projects that require time, as well as cooperation, for their completion. The addition of the nursery school environment to that of the home gives the child a better start in many directions. When the nursery school has become more thoroughly established, it may be in a position to call the attention of the grade school to several loose ends where the good start afforded by the nursery school is not followed up. It may even be, if we can keep the nursery school true to its own line and free from the domination of the existing schools, that important educational reforms in the schools higher up will result from following up the ideas of the nursery school.

I was singing the praises of the nursery school, in much this strain, to a man of my acquaintance, when I got a rather startling reaction, which, however inadequate to the true state of the case, does contain some food for thought. I should state that this man is not a bachelor or child-hater. Quite the contrary, he is the proud father of several children, both boys and girls, and much interested in his children's activities, especially during the period of life corresponding to the nursery school.

"Nursery school!" he said. "I don't like the sound of those words. Do you mean to say they are substituting a school for the nursery, and making the kiddies go to school? I call that a shame! My own idea of progress is to keep the children out of school a year or two longer rather than to send them promptly at the stroke of six years. But to pack them off to school at the age of two—it is heartless, incredible. Let them play. Let them have their freedom. They will learn more of the fundamentals of living, by themselves, than your schoolmarm can ever teach them, and be healthier and sounder into the bargain.

"Are you too old to remember," he went on, "how you felt as a young boy? Didn't you hate school? At least, weren't you relieved when school was out? Weren't you tickled to death when vacation came? I say, school should be out all day for the little child, and vacation should last the year around.

"You say the ordinary school subjects are not taught in the nursery school. Well, what is taught then that the children couldn't and wouldn't learn out of school? I suppose you want to standardize and socialize the kids, make them into little machines all just alike, ready to wiggle this way or that way as the schoolmarm pulls the strings. Now I respect the schoolmarm," he admitted, "but she is not like the kid's mother, or older sister, or playmate. She has too much of a certain background behind her to make a fit companion, day in day out, for a little child."

"Well," I said, "this schoolmarm is extra nice, and she doesn't act the same as a grade teacher. She is a specialist in young children. And we have another sort of child specialist there with her, the doctor, or else the nurse with the doctor within easy reach."

"The doctor," he cried. "Is it a nursery hospital rather than a nursery school? Worse yet! Of course, if this is a school for sick children, you may as well call it a hospital. But if the children are well, why should you have doctors and nurses flitting and fussing about? These children, if free, with only a good home to keep track of them, and the family physician ready in case of need, would be so healthy they wouldn't know there was such a thing as health. You will be making little hypochondriacs of them. A fine environment you are creating for the poor children. Who else is there in your set-up?

"Oh, you have a psychologist, and he, or she, tests the children from time to time. What is this, a school for the feebleminded? Otherwise I can't see what good your testing is going to do, unless it be an advantage for a child to know his IQ. I heard of one who told his grade teacher that she couldn't expect him to do much in school, as his IQ was only 85. But I think he was better than the other one who asked the teacher to button his coat for him, 'because, you see, I have a very high IQ, almost 150, and my mother says I am to save my strength for intellectual pursuits, and not bother with mere manual trifles.' I think the normal child should know as little about intelligence as about health, and I would keep the psychologist far, far away from him. Have you any other scientific experts monkeying with these children?

"Ah, a psychiatrist, to be sure. The children are all potential nuts, I suppose, and had better all be treated as nuts till one is sure. Your psychiatrist, I suppose, is the one who quizzes the little boy and cajoles him into saying that he wants to see his mamma in her bath, and that he hates his daddy because daddy kisses mamma. His idea of early education is to start by explaining just where babies come from, and to follow along with as much sex information as the child will listen to. He certainly is a great addition to your staff of experts, only I think he would better begin on the staff. Anybody else?

"What! A nutrition expert and a good cook? Now that isn't so bad. I've noticed that sometimes the kids didn't seem to get just what was best for them, and didn't relish what was supposed to be best for them. If your nutrition expert and your good cook could get each child to eat just what he needed, if your children were provided with a good nap, if the rest of the time they were free to play around, out of doors a good share of the time, if your schoolmarm were so well camouflaged that no one would know her for a schoolmarm, and if your medical and psychological experts were kept way, way off in the distance—and if your children didn't have to waste very much of their precious day on your precious nursery school—why then the thing might not be so bad after all."

So I advised him to visit a nursery school some day, in the hope that his picture of what "might not be so bad" would be found to be the true picture. But it seemed to me that his first horror-stricken reaction, naïve as it was, unscientific and unmodern, yet embodied a wholesome warning to all adults who earnestly set about to do something for the little child. We adults exaggerate our own importance to the child. We are apt to assume that we need to map out and supervise everything the child should do. Supervised play, educational games, pictures and stories, strike us as the *summum bonum* for the child, whereas often they strike him quite differently. To the educationist, no environment could be finer than that of a first-class school, just as to the doctor, no place short of heaven is so ideal as a really good hospital. There is perhaps no danger that the nursery school will, by degrees, approximate to the perfect hospital, but there is more danger that it will be assimilated to the first-class school. It has happened before. For that reason, even the name of "nursery school" contains a danger, which we might avoid, perhaps, by choosing this for our motto: "When is a school not a school? Of course, when it's a nursery school." I believe we should add, as corollaries to this main proposition, the following: "When is a teacher not a teacher? When she's a nursery school teacher," and "When is a doctor not a doctor? When he or she's a nursery school doctor." Seriously, both the medical and the educational professions, if they are to cooperate in building up a suitable environment for the young child, must each adapt itself to the other, while both "let the little child lead them." The result, if successful, is bound to be a new adaptation, unlike anything we have seen—not a hospital and not a school and not wholly like a home nursery, either—nor a mere mixture of the three, but a new creation, the lines of which are suggested by observation of the child himself.

It is significant that these two great professions, the medical and the educational, are joining their efforts on approximately an equal footing in the creation of the nursery school. Hitherto, the medical profession has viewed the school mostly from outside, and with a good deal of skepticism. From the physician's point of view, the school has been loading the pupils with a mass of knowledge, some of it useful no doubt, and has been drilling them in certain forms of skill which may come into play later on, but has given very little thought to the stamina of the young people as they leave school and enter life. Where the teacher looks for achievement, the physician insists upon condition. With the young child, every one will admit that condition is as important as achievement. Therefore it is a guarantee against one-sidedness, and an augury of success, that the nursery school is enlisting the doctor right along with the teacher, where he can not simply guard the flock against contagious disease and malnutrition, but bring his point of view to bear upon the whole situation.

When talking with my friend who was so dubious about the nursery school, I did not venture to acquaint him with the nursery school as a place for research on the young child. I imagined he would be up in arms at once against the idea of "experimenting on the children." But there is an immense need for fresh knowledge of the child from two to five years of age, fresh knowledge as to nutrition, physical growth, mental growth, the emotions and motivation, and many related topics. And it is fortunate that we can experiment on young children in certain ways. There are limits, naturally, to what we are willing to try in the way of experimentation. We can not deprive the child of what we believe is for his good, nor apply any condition which we suppose will be harmful, in order to watch the results. But we can administer to a group of children something which we have good reason to believe will be for their good, and watch how this works. We can compare the children so treated with a control group which has not received this treatment, but is getting just ordinary treatment, and see whether there is any noteworthy difference between the two groups. For example, suspecting that attendance on the nursery school is itself a benefit to the child, we can take a group of children into the nursery school for a year, and compare their achievement and condition at the end of the year with that of a comparable group who have not been to nursery school, in order to see whether the school has actually made any difference. Such check-ups have been projected, and will be very valuable if properly carried out. Still better, in the course of time we shall be able to follow up our nursery school graduates into later school life and even beyond, and compare their careers with those of a comparable group of children who have not enjoyed the supposed advantages of the nursery school. This sort of experiment can be varied in a hundred ways; and there are numerous other forms of experiment, test and observation which can quite safely and properly be made on young children, and which will gradually build up a scientific foundation for much more adequate handling of the child than we now can even imagine. At least, such is our reasonable hope. Only through research can we know what we need to know in order to do our best for the children.

We may expect the experience and experiments of the nursery school, in the course of time, to throw much light on what is perhaps the biggest scientific and practical problem in child development, the problem of how far heredity and how far environment are responsible for the adult condition and achievement of the individual. Put in just that way, the question is rather absurd, as it seems to imply that development or behavior may sometimes be the outcome of heredity alone, and sometimes of environment alone, whereas, as a matter of fact, every reaction of an organism obviously depends on the environment, while also it depends on the organism and ultimately on the original constitution of the organism. To ask whether heredity or environment is responsible for certain behavior is like asking whether it is the engine or the gas that makes the car go. But it is not absurd to ask whether the *differences* between different organisms are due to heredity or to environment, any more than it would be absurd to inquire whether the different performance of two automobiles was due to differences in the motor or to the different gas used. We find one child in school speaking English easily and correctly, and another very brokenly; but if we discover that the first child comes from a home where English is spoken fluently and the other from a home that employs some other language, we conclude that the difference is to be set down to environment rather than to heredity. Here, on the other hand, we find two boys from the same home, brought up together, but one very musical and the other not musical at all; and we conclude that the difference must probably be due to differences in the genes composing each boy's native constitution. So the fact that heredity and environment operate conjointly in all development and behavior does not by any means set aside the very important question whether individual differences are due to heredity or environment—differences in intelligence, for example, or in muscular strength, or in many other traits of great importance to the individual and to society.

No, the question is not absurd, but the answer is by no means clear as yet. The opinions of authorities go very wide asunder. Every one agrees, no doubt, that as between different cultural groups, there are differences of purely cultural origin. Whether all apparently ''racial'' differences are really of cultural, and so of environmental origin, is indeed a question on which there is great disagreement and little evidence. But we are concerned more especially with the differences between individuals within the same culture, the differences between the children in our schools, or between us as adults. Some would say that, since the cultural environment is alike for all within the group, the individual differences must be due to heredity. Thus the intelligence quotient, remaining as it does approximately constant for the same individual from the age of three, four or five to maturity, represents for these authorities a native factor, an original endowment of the individual which characterizes his behavior and achievements (of a certain broad type) throughout his life. Other authorities—if any one can really be called an authority on such a debatable question—point to subtle environmental differences existing within the same community, and even within the same family, and believe such factors to control the career of the individual. Especially the first few years of life are held to be important as regards environment. If the IQ remains constant from the age of five up, that, they say, is because the propensities of the individual are fixed by the social environment of the first five years. And propensities may be fixed in very subtle ways. If the older of two boys in a family is applauded for his musical performances and so likes them and practices them, while the younger boy is ridiculed when he makes his feeble efforts to imitate his brother, and so comes to hate and avoid music, the appearance of one musical and one non-musical child in the same family may be a matter of environment after all. The environment needs to be studied with much attention to subtle detail.

No one has expressed the environmentalist point of view so outspokenly as John B. Watson, in his book called "Behaviorism." Perhaps you are all familiar with this striking passage,[2] which certainly has a pregnant meaning for us who are interested in the nursery school:

> Give me a dozen healthy infants, well-formed, and my own specified world to bring them up in and I'll guarantee to take any one at random and train him to become any kind of specialist I might select—doctor, lawyer, artist, merchant-chief and, yes, even beggar-man and thief, regardless of his talents, penchants, tendencies, abilities, vocations and race of his ancestors. I am going beyond my facts and I admit it, but so have the advocates of the contrary been doing it for many thousands of years. Please note that when this experiment is made I am to be allowed to specify the way the children are to be brought up and the type of world they have to live in.

From our point of view, it is a pity that Dr. Watson has not published the specifications of environment and bringing up which he believes would determine the traits of the individual. If such specifications could be made available, the nursery school could make good use of them. I strongly suspect, however, that the above passage is to be taken as a pious wish rather than as a scientific conclusion, for the author goes on to admit that he has an axe to grind, that he wishes by his emphatic statement to clear away presuppositions and assumptions (as to the importance of heredity) "that are blocking us in our efforts to spend millions of dollars and years of patient research on infant psychology . . . because then, and only then, can we build up a real psychology of mankind." Need for much further research on the problem, rather than a conclusion that any one can assert, represents the true state of the matter. We do not by any means know how much we can accomplish by working with the young child; and, even if we were somehow assured that we could accomplish everything if we only went about it aright, we should have only the vaguest idea of how to go about it.

Nor would I leave the impression that we have at present no real evidence of the importance of heredity in making one individual different from another. Even very young children, of nursery school age, differ one from another in tested intelligence. And children of professional men, tested at ages from one to four years, show a distinctly higher IQ, on the average, than do the children of skilled workmen, as these latter children, in turn, give a distinctly higher average than do the children of laborers. In fact, the differences in intelligence, according to the occupation of the fathers, come out about the same at this early age as they do in older children.[3] If, then, it is early environment that fixes the IQ of the child, the environment that does the work must be early indeed.

Foster children, adopted at birth, are very important children from a scientific point of view, because their environment does not correspond to their heredity. They are usually adopted into rather superior homes, while their own parents, as far as can be learned (these babies being usually the children of unmarried mothers), would average only fair in intelli-

[2] "Behaviorism," p. 82. New York, 1925.

[3] Florence L. Goodenough, "The Kuhlman-Binet Tests for Children of Preschool Age," pp. 45–49. 1928.

gence and occupational status. Judging from their heredity, we should predict an average IQ of perhaps 100 for these children, but judging from their foster-home environment, we should predict for them an average IQ of about 115. Now how do foster children turn out? They turn out encouragingly well, on the whole, but they do not measure up to the level of their foster homes. Two recent studies, one in Chicago[4] and the other in California,[5] carried out by investigators with differing prepossessions in regard to this question of heredity and environment, agree in finding an average IQ for foster children, adopted at birth, of slightly over 100. The Chicago study gave an average IQ of 104, and the California study of 107. The result lies between what would be predicted from heredity alone and what would be predicted from environment alone, but rather nearer to what would be predicted on the basis of heredity.

The probability is that the nursery school, when through preliminary research it gets well into its stride, will be able permanently to raise the physical, intellectual, emotional and practical level of its children, but that, in thus raising the general level, it will not, after all, abolish individual differences. It may even increase such differences. That is, we may find that while all children profit by the motor opportunities of the nursery school and there get a start which enables them always to keep ahead of where they would have been without the nursery school, still the children who were more gifted in a motor way derived the most benefit from the school, got an especially good start and maintained their lead into adult life—and that the same could be said regarding artistic activities, intelligence and sociability. After all, it is not so important to make all men equal as to make them all better; and a good deal could even be argued in favor of the thesis that, if time allowed for making only a few better, these few might well be the ones who already promised to be the best.

[4] Freeman, Holzinger and Mitchell, in Twenty-seventh Yearbook of the National Society for the Study of Education, 1928, pp. 102–217.

[5] Burke, same Yearbook, pp. 219–316.

EDUCATIONAL EVENTS

THE GENEVA SCHOOL OF INTERNATIONAL STUDIES

THE Geneva School of International Studies will open for its sixth session on July 8, the work being conducted as heretofore in the Conservatory of Music of the city of Geneva. A preliminary list of the lecturers for the coming season is now ready and may be had on application at the New York office, 218 Madison Avenue. Such men as J. M. Keynes, author of "The Economic Consequences of the Peace"; Viscount Cecil, Professor Gilbert Murray, Dr. Christian Lange, Louis Eisenmann, professor of central European history at the Sorbonne; J. L. Brierly, professor of international law at Oxford, and many others, have undertaken to give single lectures, or in most cases short courses of lectures, at the coming session. On the basis of their background and ability, students will be assigned to the "preparatory course," the work of which is grouped into four two-week periods, the advanced course, composed of students of graduate rank, who are required to attend the whole period of eight weeks, and Professor Zimmern's seminar, consisting of a carefully selected group of twenty students.

Last summer the enrolment of the school comprised 316 students, representing thirty different nationalities, about a third of whom were Americans. For the sake of those desiring academic credit in the United States, the school is affiliated with the University of Buffalo. In September, after the close of the school proper, Professor Zimmern, the director, gives an additional lecture course on the daily work of the Assembly of the League of Nations. The scope of the institution is not confined to the study of international politics, but includes all departments of international relations, such as sociology, economics and even literature, art and music. The advisory committee, the membership of which has been made public, is as follows: J. L. Brierly, professor of international law at Oxford; Sir Arthur Salter, head of the economic and financial section of the League of Nations; Sir John Fisher Williams, British legal adviser to the Reparations Commission; David Hunter Miller, American legal adviser to the Peace Commission, author of "The Making of the Covenant"; Charles P. Howland, chairman of the Greek Refuge Settlement Commission, 1925–26.

FOREIGN STUDENTS IN GREAT BRITAIN

The Universities Bureau of the British Empire has issued a pamphlet containing lists of students from other countries in the universities and university colleges of Great Britain and Ireland in the current session. According to an abstract in *Nature,* the names of the students are grouped, separately for each institution, under the names of the countries to which they belong, and there is a table showing the total number of students from each of the countries named. The grand total of these numbers is 5,170. The countries contributing most to this total are: India and Burma 1,575, South Africa and Rhodesia 574, United States of America 556, Egypt 382, Australia and New Zealand 336, Canada and Newfoundland 203, Germany 157, West Indies 128, Ceylon 121, China 93. Of the Indian students more than half are in the London colleges, and of the remainder Oxford and Cambridge have 181, the modern English provincial universities 288, Edinburgh 133 and Glasgow 99. Of the 574 South Africans, 222 are in the London colleges (123 in the medical schools), 163 at Oxford and Cambridge, 100 at Edinburgh. Oxford has 168 students from the United States, including 96 Rhodes scholars, Cambridge 64, London 136 and Edinburgh 127. The Egyptian students are chiefly in the modern English provincial universities (162), especially Birmingham (55), in London (131) and also in Edinburgh (55). Australians and New Zealanders congregate chiefly in Oxford and Cambridge (157), London medical schools (64) and Edinburgh (37); Canadians in the London colleges (77), Oxford and Cambridge (74) and Edinburgh (35). German students have been coming to England in rapidly increasing numbers in the past four years; they are chiefly in London (94), especially the School of Economics (40), and the modern English provincial universities. A comparison with similar pamphlets published two years and four years ago discloses some interesting increases: grand totals—4,385, 4,596, 5,170; India, Burma and Ceylon, 1,199, 1,361, 1,696; Germany, 34, 93, 157; and decreases—South Africa, 747, 624, 574; Siam, 79, 62, 37.

THE RHODES TRUST

We learn from the London *Times* that concessions on the part of the Rhodes Trustees led to the settlement on March 27 of the opposition by Jamaica and Bermuda to the bill promoted by the trustees, when it was further considered by a Select Committee of the House of Lords, presided over by Lord Chelmsford.

The bill is designed to give the trustees greater freedom in the administration of the trust in order that the ideals and desires of the testator may be more effectively realized. It is proposed to vary the terms of the American scholarships, so that, instead of two scholarships being allocated to each state irrespective of size or population, there shall be the same total number of scholarships (96), but with the United States divided into eight regions of six states each, each having four scholarships a year.

Another proposal was that instead of Jamaica and Bermuda having three scholarships each as provided in the will of Cecil Rhodes, all the British colonies and islands in the western Atlantic, except Canada and Newfoundland, should be included in the territory to compete for these scholarships. This proposal was resisted by the Governors of Jamaica and Bermuda on behalf of the populations of those islands as being an interference with the definite dispositions of the testator and an alteration of his will. For the trustees it was argued that there was difficulty in getting a succession of the right type of men in a sparse population like that of these islands.

Mr. Tyldesley Jones, K.C., for the opposition, contended that these scholarships were definitely allocated and provided for by Rhodes in his will; that there was no precedent for Parliament altering a testator's will except with the consent of all the beneficiaries, and that to do so in this case would be substituting the will of the trustees for that of Rhodes.

Evidence was given by Mr. Henniker Heaton that the scholastic achievements at Oxford in the past of Rhodes scholars from Jamaica and Bermuda were equal to many and better than some from other parts of the empire, with whose allocation it was not proposed to interfere.

Mr. H. P. Macmillan, K.C., for the trustees, said that they were quite prepared to amend the bill so that the petitioners would be in the same position as they were before, and would confer with them as to the best method of future procedure.

The chairman expressed the satisfaction of the committee that the matter had been thus amicably settled and the bill was passed for third reading.

AMERICAN EDUCATION WEEK

THE National Education Association has announced the program for the ninth annual observance of American Education Week from November 11–17, under the joint auspices of the association and of the American Legion.

Secretary J. W. Crabtree, of the National Education Association, said, "American Education Week is observed each year during the week including Armistice Day. It begins on Monday and ends on Sunday. It is the purpose of American Education Week to acquaint the public with the aims, achievements and needs of the schools. The program is built around the seven cardinal objectives of education, formulated in 1918 by a committee of the National Education Association."

The program has been worked out by the officials of the American Legion and of the National Education Association. Dan Sowers, national director of the National Americanism Commission of the American Legion, and Joy Elmer Morgan, director of the division of publications of the National Education Association, served as a committee to formulate the week's schedule, which is as follows:

Monday, November 11—Armistice Day—Education for Citizenship.

Tuesday, November 12—Home and School Day—Education for Worthy Home Membership.

Wednesday, November 13—Know Your School Day—Mastery of the Tools, Technics and Spirit of Learning.

Thursday, November 14—School Opportunity Day—Education for Vocational and Economic Effectiveness.

Friday, November 15—Health Day—Education for Sound Health.

Saturday, November 16—Community Day—Education for the Wise Use of Leisure.

Sunday, November 17—For God and Country Day—Education for Ethical Character.

SAVINGS OF NEW YORK STATE CONTINUATION SCHOOL BOYS

SAVINGS in excess of $5,000,000 a year is the proud record set by the employed boys of the state, 14 to 17 years of age, in attendance upon day continuation schools. Some of the boys save nothing, but approximately 75 per cent. lay aside each week savings which range in amount from 50 cents or less to $6.00 or over. The annual earnings of this group exceeded $48,000,000, 10 per cent. of which was saved. These figures are based on a study of 65,000 employed boys who are attending continuation schools of the state, recently completed by the Industrial Education Bureau of the State Education Department.

One dollar a week was the favorite sum saved and 24 per cent. reported themselves as saving this amount. Some 16 per cent. of the boys were able to save double this amount and reported savings of $2.00 a week. Combining the two groups we have over one third of the boys having savings of $2.00 or less, a proportion that more than offsets the 26 per cent. who reported themselves as not saving anything from the weekly pay envelop.

It was impossible for some boys to save $1.00 a week so they contented themselves with savings of 50 cents or less. This group with 10 per cent. ranked third in numerical importance.

Five dollars a week saved was the record of over 8½ per cent. of the boys, followed by $3.00 for 6.7 per cent. A small but earnest group, 4.7 per cent., completed the list with reported savings of $6.00 or over each week. This was the high-water mark for saving.

"The tendency of the employed boy, who is attending continuation school, to save something, no matter how small, is encouraging, especially in view of the fact that the movies, jazz, baseball and other commercial amusements make such a strong appeal for spending money," said Dr. L. A. Wilson, Assistant Commissioner for Vocational and Extension Education of the State Education Department.

Roughly, three out of four of these boys are practicing saving and while the amounts saved by some are not very large it represents a tendency that will grow into a habit, provided it is given sufficient encouragement by those who are interested in working boys. The banks, the schools and many individuals are now encouraging the school boy in habits of thrift by providing attractive ways of saving. The fruit of their efforts is already being shown.

THE UNIVERSITY OF PENNSYLVANIA AND VALLEY FORGE

The trustees of the University of Pennsylvania have unanimously ratified a subcommittee report recommending a five-year optional acceptance of a 175-acre tract of land at Valley Forge for the extension of the university's activities along new lines.

The tract, known as Cressbrook Farm, was offered to the university three years ago by Henry N. Woolman, a member of the board of trustees and president of the General Alumni Society. Although there had been some agitation for the removal of the entire undergraduate school to Valley Forge, no department of the university will be moved to the site now or in the immediate future.

If, within five years, money is found available for the erection of university buildings, they should be for two departments only, namely, for a new College of Liberal Arts, entirely separate and distinct from the present undergraduate college department, and for a School of American History and Government.

The possibility of the erection of two such suburban schools depends entirely upon the acquisition of funds from a source and in a manner which shall not interfere with any of the needs of the present university. That possibility, according to the report, is predicated upon the conviction that all of the graduate and professional schools, and certain of the undergraduate schools closely allied with them, remain in West Philadelphia.

In the language of the report, the Valley Forge site, with its reputed inspirational qualities, will make "a place at which the university will rise to its greatest heights in the field of liberal education of the undergraduates" and "may involve the development on that site of a college complete in all its aspects in addition to the college at West Philadelphia."

If at the end of five years no definite work had been started upon the Woolman tract, or if by that time there were not an endowment fund of at least $1,000,000 for the beginning of such work, the farm land would be reconveyed to Mr. Woolman.

The report recommends further the purchase, with money preempted from the University of Pennsylvania endowment fund, of an additional tract of 150 acres adjoining the Woolman site. The additional land, which is bisected by the Valley Creek, which runs directly between Mount Joy and Mount Misery, scenes of the Continental Army's encampment in 1777–78, could be acquired for $175,000.

To carry on the recommendations of the trustees, a general Valley Forge committee has been formed, with former Senator George Wharton Pepper as chairman.

FURTHER GIFT OF MR. HARKNESS TO COLUMBIA UNIVERSITY

Edward S. Harkness has given to Columbia University $2,000,000 for the immediate construction of a residence hall at the new Medical Center, Broadway and 168th Street, for medical students and junior unmarried hospital officers. The plans are being prepared by James Gamble Rogers, the architect of the Medical Center. It is hoped that the hall, which in general will be uniform in style and type with the buildings of the Medical Center, will be ready for occupancy in October, 1930.

The building will stand on property which the university has acquired for the purpose, adjacent on the north. This property includes approximately twenty-one city lots and has a frontage on Riverside Drive beginning at the north line of 168th Street and extending to the north line of 170th Street, a distance of about

450 feet. The frontage on Haven Avenue is approximately 300 feet. Because of the grades, not all the property is available for development.

Mr. Harkness already has made several generous gifts to the Medical Center. The property at 168th Street upon which the new College of Physicians and Surgeons of Columbia University, the Presbyterian Hospital and associated hospitals have been erected, was given by him and his mother and this real estate was valued at $4,000,000. In addition he gave $1,500,000 for the erection of a pavilion at the center, contributed $1,000,000 to the College of Physicians and Surgeons, and $150,000 to the Neurological Institute for its building at the Medical Center.

His numerous gifts to other universities have included $11,392,000 to finance the plan of dividing Harvard College into small residential groups, $1,000,000 for the establishment of a dramatic department at Yale, $1,250,000 for the building and endowment fund of Union Theological Seminary, $1,000,000 to the Medical Center of Western Reserve University and very recently $1,000,000 to the Near East College Association.

THE NEW DEGREES IN EDUCATION AT THE JOHNS HOPKINS UNIVERSITY

PRESIDENT FRANK J. GOODNOW announces that on April 8 the trustees of the Johns Hopkins University, acting upon the recommendation of the academic council, created the new school of higher studies in education and established the two new degrees of master of education and doctor of education. By this action, the graduate work in the department of education becomes, in part, a university unit parallel to the school of higher studies of the faculty of philosophy. In taking this action the trustees of the university express their recognition of the distinctive position of public and private schools in present-day life, of the institutional need for the specific training of school officers and teachers, and of a more intensive and systematic study of educational problems.

The trustees also created an advisory board of the school of higher studies in education which consists of the president of the university and Professors Edward F. Buchner, Florence E. Bamberger, Fowler D. Brooks, David E. Weglein, George E. Barnett, Neil E. Gordon, J. Buford Johnson, H. Carrington Lancaster and Kemp Malone. This board has charge of the arrangements for the instruction of advanced students and of the examinations for the degrees of doctor of education and master of education.

Students admitted to the new school must be graduates from an approved college, or, in exceptional cases, have completed two preliminary years in collegiate work. Candidacy for either of the degrees is restricted to teachers and school officials with at least three years of approved experience as teachers, supervisors or administrators.

The formal requirements for the degree of master of education include a minimum residence of two academic years in the case of college graduates and of three academic years in the case of other students, the satisfactory completion of not less than ten courses of two hours per week for a year, and the preparation of an approved essay. College graduates accepted as candidates have the privilege of completing the residence requirements for this degree by attendance at not less than eight sessions of the summer courses.

In the case of candidates for the degree of doctor of education these requirements include residence of not less than three academic years in the case of college graduates and not less than four academic years in the case of other students, and one year of residence—preferably the last—in this university, the satisfactory completion of such courses in addition to those required for the degree of master of education as may be specified by the department of education, the passing of required examinations and of an oral examination before the advisory board, and the preparation and publication of a dissertation. There are no formal requirements as to foreign languages, but each candidate shall be expected to have a knowledge of such foreign languages as are necessary to carry on his researches, these being determined by the department of education.

The trustees continued the present arrangement whereby students in education so desiring may become candidates for the degrees of doctor of philosophy and master of arts under the board of university studies, in accordance with its regulations.

EDUCATIONAL NOTES AND NEWS

DR. GEORGE A. WORKS, dean of the graduate library school of the University of Chicago, has been appointed president of the Connecticut Agricultural College at Storrs. He succeeds Professor Charles B. Gentry, who has been acting president since the retirement of Dr. Charles L. Beach in July, 1928. Dr. Gentry will remain as a member of the faculty. Before his election as acting president he was dean of the division of teacher training and head of the department of education.

CHARLES J. RHOADS, a Philadelphia banker, president of the Indian Rights Association, has been invited by Mr. Hoover to succeed Charles H. Burke, who resigned several weeks ago as head of the Indian Bureau.

MAJOR ENOCH BARTON CAREY has presented his resignation as president of St. John's College, Annapolis, to become effective at the end of the present scholastic year.

THE complete list of officers of the Department of Superintendence of the National Education Association for 1929–30 is: *President,* Frank Cody, superintendent of schools, Detroit, Michigan; *First Vice-president,* Frank D. Boynton, superintendent of schools, Ithaca, New York; *Second Vice-president,* Norman R. Crozier, superintendent of schools, Dallas, Texas; *Executive Committee,* E. E. Lewis, professor of school administration, Ohio State University, Columbus, Ohio; Frank M. Underwood, district superintendent of schools, St. Louis, Missouri; Paul C. Stetson, superintendent of schools, Dayton, Ohio, and David E. Weglein, superintendent of schools, Baltimore, Maryland.

SEVEN new names will be inscribed in the Hall of Fame at New York University on May 9. Those honored are William Cullen Bryant, poet and editor; Nathaniel Hawthorne, author; Henry Wadsworth Longfellow, poet; James Madison, fourth President of the United States; Henry Clay, southern orator and statesman; Francis Parkman, historian, and Emma Willard, pioneer in woman's education.

DR. KARL C. LEEBRICK, professor of political science and history at the University of Hawaii, has accepted the deanship of the College of Liberal Arts of Syracuse University. He has been teaching in the school of citizenship and public affairs at Syracuse University during the past year, while on leave from the University of Hawaii. A cable from Hawaii has released him from his position there.

PROFESSOR MARJORIE NICOLSON, of the department of English at Smith College, has been appointed acting dean for the coming year. The college has been without a dean since the resignation last year of Mrs. Frances F. Park.

DR. J. O. CREAGER, dean of the college of education of the University of Arkansas, is returning to the college of education of New York University in July to resume the professorship of education he held there two years ago.

DR. JOHN ARTHUR THOMSON, regius professor of natural history at the University of Aberdeen, will join the staff of the University of California at Los Angeles next year as visiting professor of biology.

DR. WILBUR WILLIS SWINGLE, director of the department of zoology at the University of Iowa, has been appointed professor in the department of biology at Princeton University.

PROFESSOR JOHN READ, dean of the law school of Dalhousie University, Nova Scotia, and a former Rhodes scholar, has been appointed legal adviser to the Canadian Department of External Affairs.

DR. F. K. RICHTMYER, professor of physics at Cornell University, has been selected consulting editor of the International Series in Physics to be produced by the McGraw-Hill Book Company. Dean Dexter S. Kimball, of the Cornell College of Engineering, is the consulting editor for the Industrial Management Series.

LAIDLAW BROTHERS, publishers, Chicago and New York, announce that Mr. Edward E. Keener has accepted the position of editor in their educational department. Mr. Keener was director of research in the Chicago public schools during the administration of Superintendents Mortensen and McAndrew. Mr. Keener went to Chicago from Richmond, Indiana, where he was in charge of the department of research. He took up the work of his new position on April 1.

THE suit of Professor David S. Muzzey, of Columbia University, against J. J. Gorman, former congressman, has been set for hearing on June 4. The suit is an outgrowth of the anti-British crusade of Mayor Thompson, of Chicago, during which Mr. Gorman reported that Professor Muzzey's history texts were pro-British.

S. D. LARGENT, for thirty-one years superintendent of the schools of Great Falls, Montana, will retire at the close of the school year. He will be succeeded by Mr. Irving W. Smith.

GUY WHITEHEAD, formerly assistant superintendent of schools at Louisville, Ky., has been elected superintendent of schools at Lexington, succeeding the late M. A. Cassidy. Mr. Whitehead will assume his new duties next September.

WILLIAM W. TRITT has been promoted from the principalship of the Belmont High School to be assistant superintendent of the Los Angeles public schools.

The School Board Journal notes the following appointments as superintendents of schools. Mr. C. A. Beaver succeeds Henry Bullesfield, at Yankton, South Dakota; Mr. John R. Hall, principal of the high school at Weston, West Virginia, succeeds Mr. A. D. Horton, who has gone to Ridgefield, Connecticut, and Mr. F. H. Barbee, of Kansas City, has been elected superintendent at St. Joseph, Missouri.

PROFESSOR SARAH HINCKS, of the department of English of Smith College, has been elected principal of Shady Hill Country Day School, Chestnut Hill, Pennsylvania.

THE resignation of Adeline B. Zachert, as supervisor of school libraries in the library extension division of the New York State Education Department, became effective on April 1. She leaves the department to become field secretary of the World Peace Foundation.

MORE than 500 members of the teaching and administrative staffs of Hunter College attended a recent dinner at the Hotel Biltmore in honor of Dr. James M. Kieran, the new president of the college, and Mrs. Kieran. Dr. Harry P. Swift, chairman of the board of trustees; Mrs. Maxwell Hall Elliott, president of the associate alumnae; Dr. Blanche Colton Williams, head of the English department, and Dr. Kieran spoke. Dr. Lewis D. Hill, dean of studies, was the toastmaster.

A LUNCHEON in honor of Charles Herr, assistant secretary of the New York City Board of Education, given to mark the completion of thirty years of service with the New York City school system, was held on March 13 at the Hotel Commodore. Several hundred employees of the Board of Education, teachers and friends were present. George J. Ryan, president of the board; William J. O'Shea, superintendent of schools; Harold J. Campbell, associate superintendent; Frederick D. Chambers, auditor; Eugene C. Gibney, director of extension activities; Gustave Straubenmiller, associate superintendent; C. C. Mollenhauer, member of the board; Joseph Miller, secretary, and William E. Grady, toastmaster, were at the speakers' table.

DR. FREDERIC C. WOODWARD, acting president of the University of Chicago, will give the commencement address at the seventy-first annual commencement at Northwestern University on June 17. Dr. Frederick C. Eiselen, president of Garrett Biblical Institute, will deliver the baccalaureate sermon.

DR. GEORGE E. VINCENT, president of the Rockefeller Foundation, will be one of the speakers at the annual luncheon of the Westchester County Children's Association, to be held in the Hotel Commodore, New York, on April 24. Mrs. Caroll Dunham, the president, will preside.

THE new chapter of Phi Beta Kappa was installed at the State College of Washington on April 6. Norman F. Coleman, president of Reed College, delivered the address.

DR. WILLIAM B. MUNRO, of Harvard University; Professor Edwin A. Cottrell, of Stanford University (former mayor of Palo Alto and a member of the executive council of the National Municipal League), and Samuel May, professor of political science at the University of California at Berkeley, will lecture this summer in a short summer course announced by the division of public administration of the University of California at Los Angeles.

DR. CHARLES GROSVENOR OSGOOD, since 1913 professor of English and chairman of the department at Princeton University, an authority on the poet Spenser, is to conduct the final examination in the honors course in English literature and culture of the sixteenth century at the University of Maine. The examination will be conducted orally, each student answering questions for fifteen or twenty minutes. The entire class will be present for all the examinations and Professor Osgood has consented to the presence of a few members of the faculty as visitors.

FOLLOWING an address by Dr. F. J. Kelly, the new president of the University of Idaho, an unofficial faculty meeting of state college teachers was held to consider means of improving college teaching. A committee was appointed to outline some projects for experiment, and it is hoped that the results of the studies will arouse interest in the subject of better teaching.

CHARLES ALEXANDER MCMURRY, since 1915 professor of elementary education at George Peabody College, Nashville, Tennessee, died on March 24 at the age of seventy-two years.

JOHN RAYMOND CRAWFORD, professor of Latin and head of the department of Latin and Greek at Lafayette College since 1919, has died by suicide. Dr. Crawford was in his forty-third year.

DR. JOHN MASON TYLER, professor emeritus of biology at Amherst College, died on April 12 at the age of seventy-eight years.

DR. ROVILLUS R. ROGERS, for thirty-eight years identified with the Jamestown, N. Y., public schools—nine years as principal of the high school and twenty-nine years as superintendent of schools—died on February 26 in his home in Jamestown. He was seventy-nine years old. He retired from the superintendency in 1919.

THE Association of Deans and Advisers of Men concluded its three-day conference on April 13 with the election of the following officers for the ensuing year: *President,* James W. Armstrong, dean of men, Northwestern University; *Vice-president,* G. E. Ripley, dean of men, University of Arkansas, and *Secretary-treasurer,* V. I. Moore, dean of men, University of Texas. The conference, which was held under the auspices of the George Washington University, was the eleventh annual meeting of the association. Seventy-eight members were in attendance. The Eastern Association of Deans and Advisers of Men, affiliated with the national association, was organized during the conference. The following officers were elected: *President,* Henry Grattan Doyle, dean of men, the George Washington University; *Vice-president,* Harry F. Stone, dean of men, West Virginia University, and *Secretary-treasurer,* Kenneth O. Mason, dean of freshmen, Brown University.

THE Seventeenth School and College Conference for Colorado was held at the University of Colorado on March 28 and 29. There was an attendance of 450, about 100 more than ever before. The central theme was "Good Teaching" and in both general and section meetings the programs dealt with some phase of this subject. President M. F. Coolbaugh, of the School of Mines; President Richard Aspinall, of Western State College; President Ira Richardson, of Adams State Normal School; Superintendent John C. Unger, Hugo; Harry M. Barrett, University of Colorado; Linah Swanzey, Pueblo; Suzanne Lovelace, Boulder; R. R. Russell, Montrose, were Colorado speakers on the general program. Dr. Henry Suzzallo spoke on: "The Fundamental Spirit of American Education, A High School for Everybody," and "Our Methods of Professional Progress," the last address being given before the Colorado Schoolmasters Club and those attending the conference. Katherine L. Craig, state superintendent; President George Norlin, University of Colorado, and Chancellor Frederick M. Hunter, University of Denver, presided at the general sessions. The sections were: *Superintendents,* President, A. J. Foster, superintendent, Brighton; *High School,* President, Wilbur M. Heaton, principal, Pueblo; *Elementary School,* President, Myrta Pantall, principal, Sterling, and *School Directors,* President, R. B. Spencer, Fort Morgan.

THE daily papers report that H. Wallace Caldwell, president of the Chicago Board of

Education, reports that, without legislative relief, the schools will be unable to reopen next September. The board has authorized the issuance of a pamphlet to inform parents of the situation, described as desperate. Announcement was made at the meeting that all Chicago public school playgrounds must be closed on May 15 because of lack of funds and within a few months the free text-book fund also will have been depleted, so that free issuance of text-books will be discontinued.

The Carnegie Foundation for the Advancement of Teaching has announced a further reduction in its retiring allowances, the exact character of which has not been made public. According to a widely printed Associated Press dispatch Mr. Monell Sayre, executive vice-president of the Protestant Episcopal Church pension fund and former pension expert of the Carnegie Foundation, charged in an address at Columbus, Ohio, on March 12, that "extraordinary ineptitude" of the management has brought the foundation to a state of virtual bankruptcy. Dr. Henry Smith Pritchett, president of the foundation, is reported to have replied, "It always has been made clear in our rules that adjustments were to be expected when any large increases in salaries made the drain upon our resources too great. We have made these readjustments in the past and now are forced to do so again, but such changes by no means indicate bankruptcy. The foundation will fulfill its obligations and pay out many millions of dollars in pensions in the coming years."

By the will of the late Brander Matthews, for thirty-three years a member of the faculty of Columbia University, the university receives half the residuary estate for the maintenance and enlargement of the Brander Matthews Dramatic Museum, a collection of model stage sets depicting the history of the drama from ancient Greece to the present, which is now housed in the Hall of Philosophy at Columbia University. Other bequests to the university include the testator's books, manuscripts, letters, correspondence, a portrait of himself by E. E. Simmons and three red marble reproductions of the columns in the Roman Forum. Professor Matthews asked that the portrait and reproductions be used in the Men's Faculty Club.

Gifts made to the Bishop Charles Henry Brent Memorial Foundation at Hobart College, Geneva, New York, planned to commemorate the services of Bishop Brent as chancellor and president of the board of trustees from 1918 to the time of his death in Lausanne, now amount to more than $100,000, according to an announcement made by the Reverend Dr. Murray Bartlett, president of the college. The foundation is a part of a $2,000,000 building and endowment fund which was initiated largely by Bishop Brent before his departure for Europe last fall, and in which he had planned an active part on his return to this country. The plans for enlargement include a new science hall, an extension to the library and a new gymnasium for the William Smith College for women. They also include endowment of professorships in art, education, government, history, ancient and modern languages, philosophy, psychology and science.

Lucius N. Littauer, of New York City and Gloversville, has given $50,000 to Albany Medical College to build up a cooperative system between it and hospitals in the city for the advancement of medical education. Mr. Littauer's gift also provides for the establishment of two research fellowships in pathology and one in physiology at the college, in memory of his mother, Mrs. Harriet Sporborg Littauer. The gift to the college was made through the Lucius N. Littauer Foundation, which Mr. Littauer recently established with an initial endowment of $1,000,000.

Salmon O. Levinson, Chicago, has made a gift of $55,000 to the University of Idaho for the establishment of a "William Edgar Borah Outlawry of War Foundation." The endowment is offered to perpetuate "the great contribution of William Edgar Borah to the cause of world peace and democracy."

The contest in the courts of the will of the late W. J. McDonald, of Paris, Texas, who left in 1926 almost his entire estate to found an astronomical observatory in connection with the University of Texas, has been settled by a compromise. In place of the $1,200,000 originally bequeathed, a little less than $900,000 is secured to the observatory by the compromise. The Board of Regents of the university have full power to use this fund at once or later to advance astronomical knowledge in any way that they may deem wise. It being known that Mr. McDonald at times contemplated the accumulation of this fund over a number of years before the actual establishment of the observatory, the regents will proceed with plans very slowly and in accordance with advice from leading astronomers.

A PROVISIONAL gift of $675,000 to Swarthmore College toward an endowment fund of $2,750,000, has been made by the General Education Board, on condition that a total of $2,000,000 be added to the general endowment of the college for the support of honors work and for the improvement of academic standards throughout the entire student body. The additional $750,000 is to be used for the improvement of the college plant and for the endowment of athletics, making it possible for every student to compete in athletic contests without depending on gate receipts for finances.

ANNOUNCEMENT has been made that at the recent meeting of the trustees of Dartmouth College plans were approved for an impressive new and commodious plant for the Amos Tuck School of Administration and Finance, and that authorization has been given for the immediate erection of the buildings projected at a cost of from $750,000 to $1,000,000. They will consist of a central structure for lectures, recitations, conference rooms and offices, and two flanking residential buildings with living quarters for 100 men. A refectory, likewise, will be attached.

WORK has begun on the Hall of Philosophy of the University of Southern California, which is to cost $285,000 and be a memorial to the late Colonel Seeley Wintersmith Mudd, a Los Angeles mining engineer. The building will be devoted exclusively to the offices, classrooms, lecture halls and library of the Department of Philosophy. Rising above the two-story structure will be a tower, 140 feet high, which will contain a clock and chimes. Within the building, which will be of the North Italian Romanesque type, will be a series of professors' offices and studies, each of which will open on a common, walled garden; three major classrooms and a lecture hall seating around 400 persons, and available for public assemblies and social gatherings; two large seminar rooms and a library with stack-room space for ultimately 100,000 volumes. The main library room will be two stories in height, 114 feet long and 36 feet wide, and will be finished in manner suggestive of one of the great halls of an old-world university. Individual study and book-storage rooms will be provided in the tower. The building, which is an anonymous gift to the university, will commemorate the services to philosophy of Colonel Mudd, who late in life developed a profound interest in philosophy and made a number of substantial gifts to the philosophical library of the university.

DISCUSSION

STUDENT RATING OF COLLEGE TEACHING

AN article by Mr. George S. Wykoff "On the Improvement of Teaching"[1] contains some statements which have made me question the wisdom of furthering the "student-criticism-of-instructor" method. He states that "these rating sheets do not seem to go quite far enough. There is a tendency in most cases, for the student to use too high a figure, and there is little opportunity for concrete destructive and constructive criticisms."

Mr. Wykoff seems to assume that good teaching can be gotten from the criticism—chiefly destructive—of content and methods by the students *in cursu*. He suggests that a stenographer make a digest of these reports and that "copies of this digest should be sent to the head of the department and to the instructor concerned, so that both will know the strength and weakness of the course and teacher and can work together on plans for improvement." Destructive criticism seems to be very popular to-day. We are witnessing the heyday of the iconoclasts.

It seems rather generally agreed that the function of the college is to teach, but we seem to be devoting all our energies to measurement; first, of the student from kindergarten to Ph.D., and now we want to devise a method to measure the teacher. After that, our next

[1] SCHOOL AND SOCIETY, January 12, 1929.

step should be to measure the measurer—or should we begin here?

It is a difficult thing to rate teachers' efficiency. There are certain localities in which there are so many efficiency experts that their own efficiency is impaired by getting in the way of each other or by overstepping their respective bailiwicks. I have consulted journals and individuals available here and I can find no standard for rating teaching ability which has been generally adopted. Excerpts from two recent considerations of the subject may be of interest.

> A review of these data should be sufficient to convince any one that the problem of predicting teaching success for the purpose of selection, and the problem of judging the results of teaching, on which selection is dependent, are far from solved. . . . It may be there is no such fact as general teaching success: "this concept, as now understood, may undergo a radical change."[2]
>
> A reliable method of measuring teaching efficiency would make it possible to promote men for success in teaching. Success in research is objectively demonstrable by the recognition won from learned societies. Who is so successful a teacher has remained a matter of personal judgment.[3]

I am sure the report of committee B of the A. A. U. P. with Mr. Hardin Craig as chairman will do much toward correlating the existing systems.[4] What seems to be one of the most sensible schemes of teacher rating is that of President Wilkins, of Oberlin, which goes hand in glove with the system of advances in salary as passed by the board of trustees of that institution on December 7, 1927. In this scheme the alumni and faculty are considered as well as the students in attendance.[5]

Evidence or opinion, to be of weight, must show that the person offering it is competent to judge the subject and that he is unbiased and unprejudiced. Student opinion used by H. H. Remmers[6] may be open to question since Wykoff, of the same institution, questions this same opinion as shown in the first paragraph of this article. I consider the student's opinion as no absolute criterion of the teacher or material, because he may be either incapable of judging or prejudiced about the result or both. With apologies for a personal reference, I remember a college teacher whom I disliked in every respect, whom I called an ass on every occasion, about whom I haven't changed my mind now; but I have changed my mind about the value of his method and material. He got results. My favorite was and is a wretched teacher but a jolly good fellow. I look askance at the power of judgment of students who, after a year of high-school biology, show that "90 per cent. believe that stars are five-pointed in shape, 85 per cent. believe that a whale is a fish, 60 per cent. believe that a bat is a bird, 80 per cent. believe that sponges are plants, 65 per cent. state that corals are plant formations, 70 per cent. say that bacteria are animals."[7] I think student opinion prejudiced because I think that human nature in the student is no different from human nature in general and it seems to be the long-established tendency of the race to follow the line of least resistance, other factors being equal. If the student is biased he thus becomes judge and party at the same time.

If students are to be the sole judges of the material and method, why examine them at all? Why have them examine us? They will pass on us favorably by seeking our product; unfavorably, by avoiding us. If they decide what we shall give and demand of them they will choose according to their present ability, thus defeating the purposes of education or development.

> Wenn man wollte
> Was man sollte,
> Könnt' man alles,
> Was man wollte.

The learning process is not absolutely natural, for if it were, we could dispense with teachers

[2] Ernest Walter Tiegs, Ph.D., "An Evaluation of Some Techniques of Teacher Selection," Public School Pub. Co., Bloomington, Ill. pp. 74, 77.

[3] Moss, Loman and Hunt, "Impersonal Measurement of Teaching," *Educational Record*, January, 1929. p. 50.

[4] Bulletin of the A. A. U. P., February, 1928. Since this was written Dr. Craig's report has appeared in the Bulletin of the A. A. U. P., March, 1929.

[5] *Ibid.*, April, 1928.

[6] School and Society, December 15, 1928.

[7] *Ibid.*, January 5, 1929.

and allow the child to evolve. We have "Spanish Without Tears," we talk of "Natural Method," "Rhythmic Method," etc., but when it comes to subjects in which results count, we see a tremendous amount of effort to overcome certain things and develop others; *e.g.*, football, instrumental and vocal music, plastic arts, technical science or any field in which technique plays a part.

The institutions of higher learning have not adopted generally activities programs and the system of gradual transition in subjects through natural interest of the student. Even the junior college of this type is considered an innovation and has definite ends other than the A.B.[8] The Meiklejohn theory is a noble experiment.

So long as we have our present "credit" system, I question the wisdom of granting students the power to dictate what they shall receive. If we are going to adopt the European systems with reference to the student body, we shall certainly have to establish some indication of attainment such as a state's examination or a college "finishing" examination board. But we are still debating whether European systems are suitable to American conditions. We must first determine our objectives and then adapt our means. Johns Hopkins, Stanford and Columbia are making experiments in the separation of strictly university work and preparation for the same. In graduate work, the credit system can be easily abolished. There are numerous junior and senior high schools. But are these arrangements suited to American needs throughout the country, east, west, north, south; to city as well as rural districts?

Doesn't it seem that we need more education courses on how to *teach* and practice in teaching and fewer on curriculum building, school administration, measurements, etc.? I assume that the bulk of those taking education courses will be teachers and not principals, superintendents or administrators, and what the teacher wants to know is what to say and how to act when she first stands before Johnny and above all how she is going to "handle" Johnny's mother when occasion arises. Are we drifting away from teachers and becoming directors and testers? What was the matter with the product of our old system of education? Times have changed, it is true. We have new material, new methods, new classes of students, but human nature seems to be about the only constant in this age of shifting ideas and ideals. After all, are we not dealing primarily with human nature, taking it for granted that the facts of the subject have become part and parcel of the teacher?

MERLE I. PROTZMAN
GEORGE WASHINGTON UNIVERSITY

[8] Marion Coats, "A New Type of Junior College," *Journal* of the N. E. A., January, 1929; and "The Junior College as the Next Step in Progressive Education" in "The Changing College" (reprints from *Progressive Education*, October, November, December, 1927).

SPECIAL CORRESPONDENCE

THE MERGER OF INDUSTRY AND EDUCATION IN SOVIET RUSSIA

THE student of Soviet education is struck by the rapid, almost kaleidoscopic changes in organization and method which are taking place in the Soviet schools. This is particularly true of the secondary and higher technical educational institutions, which are faced with the titanic task of supplying trained workers for the rapidly changing industrial and agricultural situation of the Soviet Union.

Soviet education had naturally to adjust itself to the radical changes which the revolution has wrought in the economic and social structure of the country. In the economic field the revolution struck hard at the urban industrial enterprises. It practically extinguished the small private undertakings, and the large plants and factories were nationalized and reorganized into government trusts or government-controlled cooperatives. The process of centralization and enlargement of industry continues, following more and more the model of the gigantic industrial combines of America's big business. By this process, it is believed, the country will eventually reach the socialist goal.

But while the revolution is eliminating the small, urban, private industries and replacing them by large government trusts, its effect upon agricultural production was the reverse. The agrarian revolution destroyed practically all large scale production of agricultural products. The land was taken from the large landowners and was distributed in small holdings among the poor peasants and landless farm laborers. This reform, though inevitable, however proved disastrous to the economics of the country, for it was the large landowner who produced for export and for the city markets, whereas the small peasant chiefly produces for his own use. In addition to this, this primitive method of cultivation did not give him half of the yield that the large scale scientific farm did. Thus, while the cultivated area at present is 95 per cent. of the pre-revolutionary area, it yields from 200 to 300 million pouds[1] less grain than the same area did before the revolution, and as a result half as much grain gets on the consumers' market for an ever-increasing city population. Thus little remains for foreign export, and yet the future of this much desired industrial development of the country depends chiefly upon grain export, in return for which Soviet industry receives its machinery and raw material, particularly cotton, rubber and the like.

To escape this disastrous situation the government decided to go into large scale grain production, and for this purpose organized a new grain-producing trust, "the Zernotrest," which is to produce within the next five years up to 100 million pouds of grain for export purposes. To accomplish this much machinery and a scientifically trained personnel is needed. In mobilizing its present resources it was discovered that of large agricultural machinery there was only enough to produce five million pouds. The same shortage exists in a trained and experienced personnel to run and repair this machinery. Thus altogether unexpectedly the Soviet school system was faced with a new and tremendous problem of technical education and training, and is calling for serious readjustments to meet the emergency.

There is at present a great deal of large scale planning and figuring being done in the Soviet Union. This work is entrusted to a special institution called the Gosplan State Planning Commission, in which are engaged experts for every branch of industry, agriculture, finance, organization, etc. These experts were charged to produce a five-year plan for the expansion of the industry of agriculture. It must calculate the amount of capital, industrial equipment, raw material and personnel needed to carry out the plan. Its calculation showed what an enormous army of skilled workers and technical leaders are needed which the school must produce at the end of the fifth year of the plan. There are wanted:

Workers of high qualification	82,400
Workers of more than average qualification	123,600
Workers of average qualification	1,752,300

At the same time it was shown that the existing school system can at its best prepare:

Workers of high qualification	43,400
Workers of more than average qualification	55,200
Workers of average qualification	1,262,300

The terms "high," "more than average" and "average" mean respectively: engineers, technicians and skilled workers.

The disproportion between supply and demand is evident. Thus the problem is to find new means to bridge this gap, otherwise the whole gigantic scheme of industrial and agricultural reconstruction will break down.

One may ask, is this plan for rapid industrial and agricultural development artificial or is it dictated by natural demands of growth? Unquestionably the latter is true. The revolution has awakened the masses, who continually make new demands and relentlessly push toward a higher standard of living. The revolution has released tremendous creative forces which formerly lay dormant. The growing literacy of the population indicates this. It is only during the last decade that Russia seriously began to develop the education of the people, which fact is best illustrated by the following data:

The census of 1897 shows for the territory of present Soviet Russia 33.7 per cent. literacy among the male and 11.7 per cent. among the female population; in 1920 it was 34.6 per cent. for males and 25.8 per cent. for females; in 1926 it increased to 58.2 per cent. for the male and 34.4 per cent. for the female population.

[1] A poud equals 36.11 English pounds, 16.38 kg.

The school census for all grades of education showed, in 1914, 8,200,000 persons; in 1925–26 it was 12,800,000, and during this school year, 1928–29, it is estimated that it will reach 15,700,000. This means almost doubling the number within fifteen years, and registers an increase of 22.7 per cent. during the last three years.

These figures of course mean little unless the quality and grade of education shows a corresponding improvement. So far less than one third of those who completed the elementary grades (three to four years) continued to attend the secondary grade or special schools.

Particularly alarming is the dropping out of children in the rural districts even from the elementary grades. The subsequent table shows the percentage leaving school at the end of the second and third year in city and rural schools:

	1926–27		1927–28	
Schools	2nd grade	3rd grade	2nd grade	3rd grade
City	3.6	6.6	3.5	6.0
Rural	32.5	47.7	32.5	45.0

It was shown that those leaving are almost exclusively the children of the poorest peasants and workers—a class which the Soviet government wishes particularly to help and use in its reconstruction plans.

To overcome the shortage of trained, skilled workers and to obtain a competent technical leadership, the government decided in spite of its strained finances to invest heavily in education and improve its quality from the bottom upward. This is best seen from the recent report of the Gosplan, showing the increase in the cost of education per pupil in the various grades of schools, not including cost of new buildings.

Cost per Pupil	1927–28	1928–29
Elementary grades	26.11 rbls.	33.42 rbls.
Secondary schools	80.32 "	94.43 "
Apprentice shop-schools	84.70 "	92.90 "
Industrial secondary schools	154.20 "	179.30 "
Professional high schools	262.20 "	374.70 "
Workers faculties	364.50 "	429.20 "
Higher schools, universities (average)	422.16 "	564.30 "
Among these technical higher schools	——	741.90 "

The actual amounts appropriated for educational purposes from the central and local state budgets are shown to be: 1927–28, from the central, 142 million roubles; from the local, 332 million. In 1928–29, from the central, 184 million roubles; from the local, 457 million roubles.

These amounts are equal to 19 per cent. of the total state budget, but they do not include the large expenditures for various educational and cultural work carried on through labor, party and other voluntary organizations. Taking these, the total expenditure of the Soviet Union is estimated to amount up to 1.5 milliard roubles—about 750 millions of dollars.

A glance at the facts presented shows that the chief concern of Soviet education is to improve the technical efficiency of the population. The clamor for a qualified and technical leadership is responsible for this. It is the industrial worker and the engineer who are to revolutionize the country and turn the Utopia of Socialism into a reality. Inspired by this goal, school and industry have made their alliance in Soviet Russia. The government ownership of practically all mills and factories makes this alliance workable. Recent legislation shows what importance the government attaches to this alliance. According to the act of July 27, 1928, by the central government, eleven of the more important higher and special technical schools[2] were transferred from the supervision and support of the Commissariat of Education to the Supreme Council of National Economy, which is a department of the Soviet government directing all the larger and more important industrial enterprises of the Soviet Union.

The act of July 27 provides also for the transfer of the Moscow Institute of Transport Engineering and the Leningrad Institute of Means of Communication to the Commissariat of Transport. These two departments of state

[2] These are: (1) The Moscow Higher Technical School, (2) The Moscow Mining Academy, (3) The Moscow Textile Institute, (4) The Moscow Chemical and Mechanical Mendelyev Institute, (5) The Leningrad Technological Institute, (6) The Stalin Mining Institute, (7) The State Electro-Machinebuilding Institute, (8) The Moscow Building Technicum, (9) The Moscow Chemical and Mechanical Technicum, (10) The Grozny Naphta Technicum, (11) The Moscow Textile Technicum.

have large financial resources which will permit them to equip these schools with modern laboratories and provide more abundantly for the needs of professors and students than the Commissariat of Education with its relatively meager means was able to do. All industry is to participate in the support of technical education. A law provides for a special tax to be levied upon all government industrial enterprises, amounting to 3 per cent. of their annual profits. These funds will not only greatly improve the technical schools in equipment, but will benefit the teachers and the students as well. The former have received, beginning with October 1, an increase of 30 per cent. in salary, and the latter receive stipends large enough to provide for their full support.

The merging of education and industry will naturally call for a thorough revision of the curricula of these schools and also to a degree change the organization of industry itself. For example, it is planned that each student is to have from ten to twelve months, instead of from three to four months as at present, of continuous practical work in the given industry for which he is specializing. Considering that there are already this year 20,800 students in the industrial high schools and about 80,000 in the higher technical schools, this army invading industry will call for considerable readjustment in the organization of the labor supply of these industries. Whether these plans will prove workable time will show. Meanwhile one can not but welcome these experiments in higher technical education. Industrial and educational leaders of the whole world will follow this experiment with great interest; once more Soviet Russia is becoming a world laboratory for testing an important and interesting educational scheme.

J. F. Hecker

Moscow, Russia

QUOTATIONS

MILITARY SCHOOLING

The Association of Military Schools and Colleges meets in Washington, D. C., during the week of March 17, with much favorable attention from the War Department and with representation from a wide-spread constituency. The discussions at the meeting will cover an impressive list of educational problems and are frankly inclusive of the fundamental question as to whether military schooling, taken as a whole, is or is not of value.

To the individual boy, military discipline at school may be of decided value; but everything depends on the circumstances of the case, including the boy and the management of the school. Military schools admit that there are some boys who ought not to be subjected to the strictness of a military régime; and there are any number of ways in which one military school differs from another in the application of military forms to the uprisings and the down sittings of its pupils. Uniforms, exact terms of respect, great promptness, mass action, and a sternly fixed schedule may be just the things that will stimulate Henry and just the things that will stifle Charles. No one, however, can observe a military school without realizing that the military mode of life is an extremely handy and efficient way of dealing with young humans in large groups; that companies and platoons are natural units in which to move boys in a crowd; captaincies, and lieutenancies, and "non-com." posts natural honors to seek; military forms of authority, inspection, control, action, punishment, and reward very acceptable and simple in their application to boys *en masse* at school. They are not fool-proof, these military ways of doing things; but they are, in combination, a fashion of living that is not irksome to most boys, that keeps the lazy on their toes and the vagrant in line, and adds something to the color and tone of schooling.

Whether military features help a school to perform its purely instructional function is somewhat doubtful. There are military schools with good records in the College Board examinations, but none, so far as we know, that stand with the top group of comparable non-military "prep." schools. This may be an accident, or the effect of many causes, or in some part the direct result of the military discipline, which favors regimentation and rote-learning rather than initiative and originality. Clearly, there is no impossibility in the combination of military life and highly effective preparation for college; but the military schools may have a problem to face in not letting the atmosphere of military snap and rigor become the mental atmosphere of their classrooms and studies.

What military schools have most to fear, however, is the burden of actual military instruction. Military discipline, as a mode of life, is one thing. It is easily learned and can be kept at concert pitch by the right methods. It may help some boys to study; it may hinder some; on the whole, it is not strictly compatible with the emotional attitudes most needed for study, but it can be so handled as not to obstruct study. The science of modern warfare is quite distinct from military discipline. It is a complicated subject, which calls for theoretical study and practical application in a variety of forms. And whereas military discipline need not carry any very direct reference to war, military science assumes war, talks war, means war. Military discipline is not in the least bloodthirsty; but the principles of combat can hardly be taught without envisaging human destruction. Granting that the science of warfare must still be taught and that we want some young Americans to learn it, do we want any school preparatory to college to carry the subject? Is it too mature and too sternly realistic to serve as an addition to a schoolboy's curriculum? This, as we view it, is the most serious problem now before the military schools.—*Harvard Alumni Bulletin.*

SAUCE FOR THE GANDER

The school board of Monroe County, Tennessee, has adopted a regulation under which only unmarried men and women are eligible to teach in the public-school system. Five married men and nineteen married women have been dismissed in accordance with the rule. The men are victims of a movement which started out to exclude married women from the teaching staff. When this proposal came up for action the four male members of the county board divided, two for and two against, in the discussion that followed. The woman who completes the personnel of the board argued that if married women were declared ineligible as teachers, married men should be also. The advocates of the rule accepted her argument, and the double prohibition was adopted by a vote of three ayes and two noes.

To exclude married women from teaching staffs was for a long time a favorite sport of school committees. Opposition to them was supported by declaration that their home duties, the care of their children and other outside interests impaired their usefulness in the schoolroom. These erroneous notions were widely held, and many communities have been more or less excited over them. Common sense has made headway; generally to-day marriage is not considered cause for the dismissal of a woman teacher. Probably the Monroe County rule will have a short life. Inclusion of married men in the banned class emphasizes the absurdity of barring married women. The feminine fifth of the county school board made a flank attack on a ridiculous prejudice that may bear worthwhile fruit of enlightenment.—*New York Sun.*

SOCIETIES AND MEETINGS

SPRING MEETING OF THE NEW ENGLAND ASSOCIATION OF COLLEGES AND SECONDARY SCHOOLS

The New England Association of Colleges and Secondary Schools held its spring meeting at Yale University on April 13, with representatives in attendance from member institutions in all parts of the section, but most largely from southern New England. The program included the morning session, a luncheon with addresses, and a round table conference on the junior college in the afternoon. The entire meeting was in charge of President Mabel H. Cummings and Secretary Walter B. Jacobs.

Dr. William John Cooper, United States commissioner of education, in an address at the morning session, made five suggestions, following an analysis of the present situation as to secondary and higher education in this country. He advocated first:

> more studies to ascertain what legitimate demands various callings may make upon educational institutions. We all realize the value of

studies already made in some of the professional fields, especially in medicine and law. Pharmacy is ready to submit its case. Engineering is not likely to be far behind in asking for increased standards of admission to its ranks. It may be that we shall find the motive of trade-regulation behind some demands for higher standards, but let us study the situation anyway.

Commissioner Cooper's second suggestion was to determine "What should constitute the course of study" in providing "the advantages of a liberal education to an ever-increasing percentage of our population." He praised the experiments in controlled study authorized by the North Central Association at Stephens College, Columbia, Missouri, at Joliet, Illinois, and at Kansas City, Missouri, and urged the New England Association and other regional associations to similar undertakings.

That the whole field of academic degrees should receive fresh consideration was the third point presented by Commissioner Cooper. He expressed his opinion that "the growth of the junior college will force the degree problem to the front."

As his fourth point Commissioner Cooper said he believes "the senior college in arts should become more and more preparatory to the work of the graduate school." He referred to honors courses and to "the recent experiments of Harvard and Yale for improving the standards of work."

Fifth—"I should like to see all diplomas and degrees given as marks of mastery of certain fields at different educational levels. This means, of course, doing away with free election of courses. It certainly means preventing the piling up of units merely to graduate." Commissioner Cooper suggested definite fixed levels of performance for the bachelor's, master's, doctor's degrees in arts, science, music, medicine, law, education, dentistry, pharmacy, etc.

Could we agree upon some such general platform, our standardizing agencies could then be occupied less with units, courses, etc., and more with defining fields and determining qualities of work for high school level, junior college level, senior college level, etc. . . . Such definitions of fields of study and standardization of levels of work constitute no small assignment. If, however, the regional associations working in conjunction with the Association of American Universities could perform these services, American scholarship would profit much.

Dr. Katharine M. Denworth, president of Bradford Academy and Junior College, set forth "Objectives of the Junior College" in an address in which she disavowed, at the outset, any claim to speak officially for the junior college movement. She discussed the situation in New England and made a plea to the association to go slowly in putting into effect standardizing regulations which may defeat the main work of the junior college. "Don't cabin, crib, confine the junior college so that you restrict it to two years that simply duplicate the two lower years of the liberal arts college." Dr. Denworth listed this as one objective of the junior college. A second objective she gave as the pre-professional function—preparing for medicine, law, engineering, theology, dentistry. But most important she regarded as the objective of "taking care of the young people between the age of sixteen and twenty who do not intend to go on with further formal education. Why should they be cut off from the chance to profit by two years of college work?"

The junior college has a peculiar opportunity in the field of education for women, Dr. Denworth said. It may very profitably afford training for home-making in the broad sense of that term: a knowledge of heredity, the development of children; what Vassar designates as euthenics.

In the course of her address Dr. Denworth sketched the rapid development of the junior college throughout the country and listed and described "the three main types: The lower division of a university; the public junior college; and the private junior college."

Professor Chester N. Greenough, of Harvard, was the third speaker at the morning session. He told of the new house plan at Harvard by which the students in the three upper classes of the college are to have their living quarters in six separate houses, each containing about 250 undergraduates and six resident tutors. For this purpose Harvard has received from Mr. E. S. Harkness a gift of more than eleven million dollars. The plan has already been reported in SCHOOL AND

Society. Professor Greenough discussed the general details of selection and operation which are expected to prove "a biological growth" rather than a mechanical thing. The great purpose of the houses, he said, will be to help in carrying out Harvard's instruction through the general examination and tutorial system.

At the luncheon of the association, President Angell came in to extend greetings in behalf of Yale and these were more formally presented by Professor R. N. Corwin. Other luncheon speakers were Dr. Horace D. Taft, Dean Frank W. Nicholson and Professor F. A. Pottle.

The afternoon discussion on the junior college was opened by President E. E. Cortright, of the Junior College of Connecticut.

Raymond Walters

Swarthmore College

EDUCATIONAL RESEARCH AND STATISTICS

A CRITICAL REVIEW OF BOOK REVIEWS

The Problem

Presumably, the review of a book in an educational periodical is intended to provide readers with a description and evaluation by a competent person who has taken time to read the book with some care. But many readers probably have wondered if the reviews they read are trustworthy, especially in the matter of evaluation. Hence it seems worth while to analyze a number of book reviews for the purpose of ascertaining their significant characteristics.

Book Reviews Examined

An examination was made of the reviews of one hundred books in the field of education published between 1922 and 1925 for which three or more reviews were recorded in the files of the Bureau of Educational Research at the University of Illinois.[1] The books selected were, in general, text-books for courses in education. The total number of reviews studied was 548, an average of a little more than five reviews per book. This number does not include all the published reviews of the one hundred books selected, as the card files at the bureau do not cover all educational periodicals; moreover, some reviews for certain books included have been printed since the list was collected in the fall of 1927.

[1] Since 1921, the Bureau of Educational Research has made a practice of recording the reviews of all educational books that appear in the periodicals received, which include all of the more important ones and a number of minor ones.

Table I shows the number of books for which the various numbers of reviews were found. It is to be read as follows: Of the one hundred books considered in this study, twelve were reviewed three times each, twenty-four were reviewed four times each, etc. It is perhaps significant that some books are reviewed more often than others. Examination of the list did not seem to indicate that the frequency with which a book is reviewed is, in all cases, an index of its importance. The varying policies of publishers in submitting review copies, and some other factors, probably are more potent than the merit of the book in determining the frequency with which it is reviewed.

Table I. Frequency with which Books were Reviewed

Number of books	Number of reviews
12	3
24	4
26	5
13	6
12	7
6	8
1	9
3	10
1	11
1	12
1	14
100	

Periodicals in which the Books were Reviewed

The 548 reviews examined in this study were located in forty-six different educational periodicals. These are listed in Table II and in the

TABLE II. SOURCES AND CHARACTERISTICS OF REVIEWS

Periodicals	Number of reviews	Favorable	Unfavorable	Doubtful	Approximate number of words in reviews		
					Max.	Min.	Ave.
Journal of Educational Research	73	53	7	13	1,200	140	580
Elementary School Journal	64	47	5	12	1,200	180	540
School Review	50	40	5	5	1,000	250	615
Journal of Educational Psychology	49	38	1	10	1,600	90	420
Educational Administration and Supervision	40	34	4	2	1,550	100	640
Chicago Schools Journal	29	23		6	800	60	200
Educational Review	25	20	1	4	2,150	90	540
Educational Measurement Review	20	17		3	600	110	260
SCHOOL AND SOCIETY	19	9	1	9	880	80	380
Bulletin of the New York Society for the Scientific Study of Education	18	15		3	1,375	65	365
Pedagogical Seminary	17	9	1	7	975	60	250
Mental Hygiene	15	13	1	1	6,000	250	1,400†
Journal of Educational Method	13	10		3	300	75	200
High School Journal	12	12			775	190	425
Peabody Journal of Education	11	8		3	450	100	200
Journal of Applied Psychology	10	10			800	120	580
Other periodicals*	83	76	1	6	1,400	60	340
Total	548	434	27	87	6,000	60	445

* The other periodicals and the number of reviews in each are as follows: *News Letter* (8), *American Schoolmaster* (6), *American Education* (5), *Bulletin of High Points* (5), *Education* (5), *The High School* (5), *High School Quarterly* (5), *Baltimore Bulletin of Education* (4), *Educational Review* (China) (4), *Sierra Educational News* (4), *American School Board Journal* (3), *Historical Outlook* (3), *Normal Instructor and Primary Plans* (3), *University of Pittsburgh School of Education Journal* (3), *High School Teacher* (2), *Ohio State Educational Research Bulletin* (2), *Schooling* (2), *Virginia Journal of Education* (2), *Catholic School Interests* (1), *Detroit Educational Bulletin* (1), *Educational Digest* (1), *English Journal* (1), *Journal of American Statistical Association* (1), *Journal of Education* (1), *Kentucky High School Quarterly* (1), *Educational Research Bulletin of Pasadena City Schools* (1), *Journal of Delinquency* (1), *Pennsylvania School Journal* (1), *School Life* (1), *School Topics* (1).

† See footnote 3.

footnote accompanying the table. The number of reviews per periodical ranged from one, in each of twelve periodicals, to seventy-three, in the *Journal of Educational Research*. However, over half of the total number of reviews appeared in five periodicals: the *Journal of Educational Research*, the *Elementary School Journal*, the *School Review*, the *Journal of Educational Psychology* and *Educational Administration and Supervision*. Of the fifty-one books which were reviewed five to seven times, each book was reviewed in one or more of the five periodicals just mentioned. These books were not confined to any one division of education, but included volumes on administration and supervision, methods of teaching, psychology, educational measurements, etc. Of the six books for which ten or more reviews were found,[2] the *Journal of Educational Research* and the *Journal of Educational Psychology* reviewed all, the *School Review* reviewed five, and the *Elementary School Journal* reviewed four. These facts lead to the conclusion that most of the noteworthy books in any field of education will be reviewed in one or more of the following educational periodicals: *Journal of Educational Research, Elementary School Journal, School Review, Journal of Educational Psychology* or *Educational Administration and Supervision.*

METHOD OF SCORING REVIEWS

After a number of reviews were given a preliminary examination, a list was made of the characteristics of books commonly mentioned in reviews. This list consisted of descriptive items, such as mechanical features and description of content; and evaluative items, such as general statements with and without evidence and specific criticisms. (See Tables III and IV for the complete list of items.) Each of the 548 reviews was scored according to this list as follows: After the approximate number of words was calculated, the review was read twice; once, rapidly, in order that a general impression might be obtained of the favorable or unfavorable attitude of the reviewer, the quality of his writing, etc.; and again, more carefully, in order that a tabulation might be made of items in the list which were given attention in the review. An attempt was made to make the scoring as highly objective as possible, but, in the case of certain items, the scorer was required to use personal judgment. For instance, with regard to "general statements with evidence," the scorer was compelled to decide whether or not evidence was cited for the statements made. Such statements as "This book is a real contribution to the literature of the field," are frequently encountered at the end of a mediocre description which may or may not be considered to justify the conclusion.

LENGTH OF REVIEWS

The 548 reviews studied varied in length from 60 to 6,000 words, the average length being 445 words. The average length of the reviews in each of the twenty-three periodicals that contained ten or more reviews, as shown in Table II, ranged from 200 (in the *Chicago Schools Journal,* the *Journal of Educational Method* and the *Peabody Journal of Education*) to 1,400 (in *Mental Hygiene*).[3] There is little difference in length between the reviews of the books most frequently reviewed (eight to fourteen each) and those least frequently reviewed (three each), the average of the former being 412 words, and of the latter, 425 words.

TABLE III. DESCRIPTIVE ITEMS IN BOOK REVIEWS

Items	Reviews including each item: Number	Per cent.*
A. Mechanical features		
1. Number of pages	469	85
2. Illustrations, tables, diagrams, etc.	90	16
3. Other characteristics (binding, size of type, quality of paper, etc.)	11	2
B. Description of content		
1. Table of contents or other material quoted	283	51
2. Purpose of book stated	441	80
3. Intended audience designated	384	70
4. Comparison with existing books or authors	75	14
5. Special features (biographical notes, bibliographies, problems or questions for study, summaries, appendix, index, glossary of terms)	325	59

* The base used in computing the per cent. was 548, the number of reviews analyzed.

[2] The six books having the greatest number of reviews were the following:

Otis, "Statistical Method in Education"—14 reviews.

Monroe, "An Introduction to the Theory of Education"—12 reviews.

Ruch, "Improvement of the Written Examination"—11 reviews.

Caldwell and Courtis, "Then and Now in Education"—10 reviews.

Pintner, "Intelligence Testing"—10 reviews.

Rugg, "A Primer of Graphics and Statistics"—10 reviews.

[3] This very high average is due to the inclusion of one unusual review of 6,000 words.

Description of Book

A. Mechanical Features

Table III shows the number and per cent. of reviews that include each item having to do with description of the book. Practically every book review examined gave the name of the book, its author and publisher, and the date of publication. Eighty-five per cent. of the reviews also gave the number of pages of the book reviewed. In most cases, the foregoing items were listed separately from the review proper, either in a preceding paragraph or in a footnote. Only 16 per cent. of the reviews mentioned the presence of illustrations, tables or diagrams, but of course these features do not appear in all books. Only 2 per cent. described other mechanical features of the book, such as binding, size of type or quality of paper. Although at first thought these items appear insignificant, each of them may be of vital importance to a teacher who wishes to select the text that will be most usable for the students concerned. A poorly bound book with flimsy leaves and very fine print would be less desirable than another book lacking these flaws but having practically the same type of content.

B. Description of Content

Table III shows that a large percentage of the reviews examined stated the purpose of the book and the intended audience, but that only approximately one half of them contained any quotations from the book reviewed. In many instances, reviews would be improved if the table of contents or the headings of the main divisions of the book were quoted in order to give a general notion of the author's treatment and organization of his subject. Other quoted material, if carefully selected, may enable the reader to discern the writer's purpose, point of view and quality of writing more accurately than if he depends entirely upon the reviewer's opinions.

Another desirable way of providing the reader with a means of forming a definite opinion about a book is to compare it with existing books, either one written previously by the same author, or books in the same field written by other authors. The fact that only 14 per cent. of the reviews studied contained such comparisons indicates that this is a phase of reviewing which has not yet been generally recognized.

Over half of the reviews (59 per cent.) mentioned the presence or absence of one or more special features: biographical notes, bibliographies, problems or questions for study, summaries, appendix, index or glossary of terms. In most of these cases, attention was called to the presence of the feature rather than to its absence. In a few instances, however, the reviewer noted the absence of an index.

In addition to the items included in Table III, a fairly large per cent. (41) of the reviews included an introductory discussion by the reviewer. This generally consisted of a brief survey of the status of the particular field to which the book applied, a statement of the number of books available on the subject or an explanation of the need for such a book as the one reviewed. In general, such introductory material is valuable in providing a setting for the book for the benefit of those unfamiliar with the field, but its inclusion means that the actual reviews were shorter than indicated in Table II.

In some instances the reviewer described the method in which the subject-matter of the book was presented. This was given only in the case of books composed of unusual material, such as articles by different authors, case studies or questions and answers. As the majority of books consisted purely of exposition, their reviewers made no mention of the type of presentation.

Evaluation of the Book

Table IV shows, for each evaluative item listed, the total number and per cent. of reviews mentioning each item, the number giving criticisms that were favorable, unfavorable or doubtful, the latter classification including those reviews which were non-committal and those that gave both favorable and unfavorable criticisms.

As previously stated, the personal judgment of the scorer was necessarily called upon in determining whether or not evidence was cited for the general statements regarding the value of the book. In the main, quotations or definite

TABLE IV. EVALUATIVE ITEMS IN BOOK REVIEWS

Items	Reviews including each item				
	Favorable	Unfavorable	Doubtful	Total number	Per cent.
A. General evaluation without evidence	107	4	9	120	21
B. General evaluation with evidence	242	20	26	288	52
C. Specific criticisms					
1. Point of view of author	95			95	17
2. Form (spelling, punctuation, bibliographical references)	10	10	5	25	4
3. Quality of writing	189	20	2	211	38
4. Scholarliness of author	199	2	2	203	37
5. Appropriateness of title	36	4	1	41	8
6. Adaptation to intended audience	38	9	2	49	6
7. Appropriateness of content (adequacy, accuracy of statements, interpretation of facts or data, utilization of available material, documentation)	173	78	54	305	53
8. Organization	49	11	2	62	11
9. Special features (biographical notes, bibliographies, problems or questions for study, summaries, index, appendix, glossary of terms)	52	8		60	9
10. Others' opinions of book quoted	8			8	2

statements in regard to specific characteristics of the book were treated as evidence. According to this criterion, slightly over half of the reviewers furnished evidence for their evaluations of the books concerned. Not all of the reviews, however, contained such general statements; only 408 of the total 548 did so. It is enlightening to note that of the 408 reviews, 349 (64 per cent.) were definitely favorable, and only 24 (4 per cent.) were definitely unfavorable. In case no general statements regarding the value of the book were made, the review was classified as favorable, unfavorable or doubtful, according to the criticism of specific factors.

In regard to critical statements about specific features of books, it may be observed from Table IV that no single feature was noted in as many as 50 per cent. of the reviews, although one or more of the items under "appropriateness of content" were discussed in 53 per cent. of the reviews. The scholarliness of the author and the quality of his writing were criticized more frequently than any other specific features of the book, but even these were mentioned in only 37 and 38 per cent., respectively, of the reviews. Critical evaluation of form, appropriateness of title, adaptation to intended audience, and of the special features of the book (biographical notes, problems or questions for study, etc.) appears to be negligible. One interesting means of evaluating the book is by quoting the opinions that other writers or well-known critics have expressed about the book.

Only eight of the 548 reviews included this type of criticism, and, as is to be expected, all expressed favorable opinions.

Of the 100 books dealt with in this study, twelve were reviewed only three times each in the educational periodicals received at the Bureau of Educational Research. Of the thirty-six reviews for these books, twenty-seven, or 75 per cent., were definitely favorable, while the remaining nine were either unfavorable or doubtful. For the thirteen books having the greatest number of reviews (from eight to fourteen each), there were 123 reviews, 108, or 96 per cent., of which were favorable. This suggests that the books attracting the most attention in general receive somewhat more favorable criticism than do those which are reviewed less often. Although this is to be expected, the per cent. of favorable reviews for both extremes is undoubtedly too high. The fact that 75 per cent. of the reviews for the thirty-six books reviewed three times each point out only praiseworthy factors makes one wonder why more reviewers have not proclaimed the merits of these apparently valuable books.

Evaluation of the Reviews

In the judgment of the scorer, most of the reviews were stereotyped; that is, they were "just like all the rest," neither particularly good nor extremely poor. Almost 70 per cent. were considered inadequate in that several important questions which an interested reader should ask about the book were left unanswered. A few, on the other hand, were of such length, usually due to an excess of quoted material, that they became tedious. About seventy of the reviews were noted for giving a particularly good description of content, while nearly half that number contained extremely meager or poor descriptions. Five reviews were regarded as exceptionally good, either because of being remarkably well written or because of unusual treatment. An example of the latter is furnished by one reviewer, who, deciding that "book-reviewers have as much right to objective methods as have other classes of the population," selected thirteen samples from the book concerned—"samples intended to represent its best quality, its poorest quality and a number of qualities between. These samples were ranked by nine men. . . . The ranks were from 1 to 13, 1 being high. These men also indicated which samples seemed good enough to occupy space in an educational psychology."

Conclusions

Book reviews in general may be criticized upon at least two grounds: they are inadequate and they are non-critical. Their inadequacy lies in their failure to give sufficient information about the book. Too many reviews consist of only a few general statements describing the nature of the content and make no reference to many specific details that should be mentioned. In addition to a general description of the content, reviews commonly mention such items as purpose of the book, intended audience and the number of pages. Except for the latter item, mechanical features, such as binding, size of type, quality of paper and illustrative material, are rarely mentioned. Very few reviews compare the book reviewed, or its author, with others. Only a small per cent. quote a table of contents, and no more than half include any other quoted material. Special features, such as bibliographical material, problems or questions for study, summaries, etc., are seldom mentioned.

A more serious fault with the present-day book review is the lack of critical evaluation. The vast majority of reviewers point out the good qualities of books, or, very frequently, make general statements in praise of them, to the utter neglect of any deficiencies. The usual method of evaluation appears to consist merely of stating that the book makes a contribution to its field. It appears justifiable to say that reviews are failing to render a needed service to their readers. Teachers could select their textbooks more intelligently if reviewers would distinguish between valuable books and those of doubtful merit. And perhaps some amateur writers would be discouraged from rushing into print, if reviewers had the courage, or took the pains, to criticize in a meaningful rather than in a stereotyped manner.

Walter S. Monroe,
Mabel R. Hull

Bureau of Educational Research,
University of Illinois

SCHOOL AND SOCIETY

EDITED BY J. McKEEN CATTELL

WITH WHICH IS COMBINED THE

EDUCATIONAL REVIEW

EDITED BY WILLIAM McANDREW

Volume XXIX | Saturday, April 27, 1929 | Number 748

COMMEMORATION DAY ADDRESS

By President FRANK J. GOODNOW

THE JOHNS HOPKINS UNIVERSITY

The last twenty-five years are memorable years. They are memorable, not so much because probably the most destructive and wide-spread war was fought during this period, but rather because of the great advances that have been made in our knowledge and because of the wide-spread application of that knowledge to the conduct of every-day life. During this period, great strides have been made in the practical application of science. The use of the internal combustion engine, both in transportation and industry, dates from the beginning of the present century. During that time we may notice also very great extension in the use of the telephone and the beginnings of the science and art of aviation. The discovery and application of wireless communication, which has resulted in the present almost universal use of the radio, are also to be placed in this last quarter of a century.

The internal combustion engine, the telephone, the aeroplane and the radio have done much to change the situation in which we live and are destined with probably increasing force to modify our life.

The applications of our scientific knowledge have not, however, been confined to the fields of industry and transportation. The progress which has been made in the treatment of disease and in preventive medicine has been probably just as marked. The "rule of thumb" methods of diagnosis which were common not much more than a quarter of a century ago have given place to exact and precise methods which have made it possible for the physician to recognize more easily and with greater certainty than was formerly the case the conditions which he is called upon to treat. The measures which have been adopted with the idea of preventing the development and spread of disease have been based upon more exact scientific knowledge of the causes of diseases and have consequently gained in effectiveness.

The last quarter of a century is notable, however, not merely for the applications of science. Our knowledge of fundamental scientific truth has been as well greatly increased, and our attitude towards nature has been greatly changed. Those of us who received our education in the latter part of the nineteenth century have been called upon to revise our views with regard to almost all the sciences. The discoveries which have been made with regard to the constitution of the atom and the cell have modified in a fundamental way our views with regard to the operations that are going on in the universe.

The last twenty-five years, furthermore, have been characterized also by a great increase of our knowledge of the facts of the past. Probably in the last twenty-five years more has been done in the excavation of places connected with ancient civilizations than had been done ever before. Egypt, Mesopotamia, Palestine, Greece and Rome have been studied, and successfully, with the result of connecting more closely the present conditions of Western Europe with those which preceded them in Asia, from which so much of the impetus towards the development of our modern life has come. These excavations have been, it is true, primarily connected with places which throw light on those civilizations to which the races of Western Europe are indebted. There is unquestionably a great field for work of this sort elsewhere which will throw such light on the development of other civilizations. But even here the beginnings have already been made, and we are gradually being placed in a position which enables us to obtain more comprehensive and accurate ideas as to the origins and development of the social life of humanity in general.

The great advances of the last twenty-five years which have been so briefly and incompletely outlined have imposed a new and heavy burden upon the institutions of higher education to whose work in the past these advances have been at least in some measure due. The old idea which was so prevalent in this country that the duty of the university was primarily to teach what is known has been supplemented by the conviction that the university must as well contribute to the discovery of truth and as a result must foster investigation and research.

In addition to this extra burden which universities among other institutions have been obliged in greater and greater measure to assume is to be added the burden imposed upon them as teaching bodies because of the great increase in the number of students who have clamored for the opportunities of a higher education.

It has been thought by some that the great increase in the number of university and college students in the United States has been caused in no small measure by the occurrence during this period of the great war. It has been believed that this increase was due mainly to the appreciation of the advantages of higher education which was manifested by those who in this country entered the armies of the United States and found themselves lacking in the knowledge and experience that might have been gained in college. The increase in the number of university and college students which was noticeable immediately subsequent to the close of the war was attributed also in part to the fact that many young men who otherwise would have gone to college had been obliged to delay their college training in order to take up arms in defense of the principles for which this country stood in that great conflict.

It is probably true that both these causes did have an appreciable effect upon the influx of new students into American institutions of higher education, but I believe that the primary cause for this increased burden is a deeper one. For a number of years prior to the war there had been, throughout the country almost everywhere, a marked development in our institutions of secondary education. The high-school population throughout the country increased at a rate altogether out of proportion with the increase in our population. It is a well-known fact that a reasonably definite percentage of high-school graduates desire to continue their studies in college and university.

The increased burdens of college and university, due to the recognized necessity of the pursuit of truth and of teaching this greatly increased number of students have had as a result a great increase in the budgets of all these institutions. The increased budgets have had to be met in the case of privately endowed institutions by a great increase in their endowments, and in the case of state institutions by an appeal to the state for an increase in the funds allotted by it to higher education.

The Johns Hopkins University has during the last twenty-five years, like all other universities, been affected by the tendencies and movements which I have outlined. In 1903 the total number of its students was 715; in 1928 this number had increased to 5,175. In 1903 its balance sheet showed that it possessed property, including plant and endowment, amounting to $5,640,000. In 1928 its balance sheet shows assets equal to $34,947,000. In 1903 it expended for all its activities the sum of $277,000. In 1928 its annual budget was $2,111,000.

The contrasting of these figures produces an impression of marked material progress. But, if we compare the material progress which the Johns Hopkins University has made in this last quarter of a century with the progress which has been made by some other institutions in this country, the impression which we can hardly fail to receive is one of disappointment. It is to be remembered that it is only during the last twenty-five years that the habit of giving largely to universities has been acquired. Indeed, it has been said that during that period the universities and colleges have acquired 75 per cent. of their present assets. Comparatively speaking, we at Johns Hopkins probably have not received all that we should. Such good fortune as we have had certainly is therefore nothing for us to boast about. We all realize, and no one more keenly than one who has been in a position to survey all our activities and to appreciate all our needs, that never were these activities more dependent on effective support and never have our needs been greater if consideration is given to the burdens which we are compelled to shoulder.

The changes in the conditions of human life which have been incident to the last quarter of a century of human development have been responsible further for a great change in the purposes of American colleges and universities. I think it was Herbert Spencer who once said that "The history of education is the history of the adaptation of knowledge to need." The change of purpose which has been mentioned is due to the change in our intellectual life and to the necessity of meeting present-day needs.

In a recent interesting address made by President Glenn Frank, of the University of Wisconsin, attention is called to the fact that while instruction in professional and technical branches in this country has been followed by a large measure of success, "liberal education is the ugly duckling of the American school system." He says:

> Everybody pays lip-service to liberal education, but nobody will admit responsibility for the results we are getting. Uneasily aware of the nation-wide breakdown of the liberal educational process, each of us seeks to shift responsibility to other shoulders. The grade schools blame the parents, the high schools blame the grade schools, the colleges blame the high schools and the professional schools blame the colleges. At every point of transfer from one education unit to another there is an orgy of criticism of the liberal educational results of the group that had the students last. Almost every educational conference, when it touches the issue of liberal education, degenerates—if I may resort to classical phraseology—into a high carnival of passing the buck.

I personally have sometimes thought that this problem of providing a liberal education is due somewhat to the impossibility of securing any such result merely by seeking to obtain it. Like happiness, which eludes the grasp of one who pursues it as an end, and would seem to be really incident to a well-ordered life where the desire to perform one's daily duties as effectively as possible is the primary end, the attainment of a liberal education would seem to be possible only as an incident to the broad-minded and thorough study of some particular subject or group of subjects, the mastery of which is the end always kept in view by the student. Furthermore, a liberal education is dependent, as indeed is all education, upon the individual work of the student. If he is sincerely interested in some particular subject, he soon finds that to understand even that subject he must have considerable knowledge of its various ramifications. The pursuit of a liberal education through imposing upon the student the necessity of studying superficially a large number of more or less unrelated subjects, will be, in all probability, almost futile.

Dr. Abraham Flexner, in an address delivered before Vanderbilt University a year or two ago, says that the lack of interest which is noticeable in many students upon whom is forced a curriculum such as I have described, produces something in the nature of an intellectual vacuum, and as nature abhors a vacuum, all sorts of side interests develop, among which may be mentioned the almost frenzied interest which the mass of students who are supposed to be pursuing a liberal education manifest in athletics.

How true this is it is difficult to say, but it is noticeable that professional and technical students, particularly where they have some degree of maturity, do not seem to care for these outside activities, which, as an Australian professor once remarked, are, as he thought, significantly dubbed "student activities" in the colleges of the United States.

There is no question but that the existing situation so far as concerns liberal education is very well recognized at the present time. Various attempts have been and are being made to remedy conditions. Almost all these attempts are characterized by the endeavor to provide a curriculum in which the students' interests are centered on comparatively few subjects.

Several years ago on such an occasion as this and in this place, I proposed that the Johns Hopkins University should make an attempt of the sort which has been described. Inasmuch as educational bodies do not always move with the rapidity which is supposed to be characteristic of modern life, the plan which was then proposed was not adopted until two years had elapsed from the time of making the proposal. Even then the plan was adopted rather as an ultimate goal towards which we should strive to attain than as a plan to be immediately realized. Although we have adopted the plan then proposed, we have had only a little over two years' experience as to its operation. We have, furthermore, because of financial and educational reasons, been unable to put the plan into complete operation.

At the present time what we are doing is to offer the earnest and capable student, at the end of his first two years in college, the opportunity to specialize in some branch of knowledge in which he is interested, and have, with this end in view, roughly speaking, consolidated the last two years of college with our former graduate department. We have not had enough experience to enable us to reach a conclusion of any very great value with regard to the success of this plan. In the first year that the plan went into operation, nineteen students, three of whom came from other institutions, entered under the new plan. Three of the nineteen were subsequently advised to drop the work, so that sixteen were in attendance at the end of the year. Fourteen of these returned last year. During the past year, thirty-two students with two years' preparation entered under the new plan. Six came from outside institutions. Two of the thirty-two were subsequently advised to drop the work, so that at the end of the year we had forty-four new-plan students. This current year is the third year during which the plan has been in operation. At the beginning of this year thirty-three students entered under the new plan, nine of whom came from other institutions. There are, therefore, at the present time, about seventy students who entered under the new plan, and it is to be noticed that the number coming from other institutions is slowly increasing.

Another fact with regard to the operation of the new plan is to be noticed. Some of the students who enter drop out either voluntarily or upon the advice of the instructor with whom they are studying. It is evidently therefore the case that the new plan will not suit all students who desire to enter under it. Some prefer the curriculum which is intended to give the so-called "liberal education." A few would seem to be unable to do the work. But generally the students who enter under the new plan stay with us, and the testimony of the faculty is that this large majority are doing well.

The Hopkins plan is our contribution to the solution of one of the problems with which higher education is confronted as a result of the changes of the last quarter of a century.

So much for the development of the university in the past twenty-five years and for the problems which it will have to face in the near future.

I am glad to say that I have a number of interesting announcements to make on this occasion.

It will be remembered that several years ago it was found that our School of Medicine had somewhat outgrown the facilities which are offered by the hospital for the purposes of medical instruction. The few years preceding had been characterized by the development of a number of medical specialties which added greatly to the work which the hospital was doing and which also were of great service to those who came to the School of Medicine with the desire of studying along special lines. The department of pediatrics had been greatly strengthened by the establishment of the Harriet Lane Home for Children; a department of psychiatry had been made possible through the generosity of Mr. Henry Phipps; a well-equipped urological institute had been constructed owing to the generosity of Mr. James Buchanan Brady, and Mrs. Wortham James had made provision for a women's clinic. But the hospital wards for internal medicine and surgery which form the backbone of general medical instruction were small and the beds available for instruction were not sufficient in number to take care of the increased number of students in the School of Medicine.

A program which has become known to us as the hospital and medical school expansion program was drawn up, which was primarily directed toward the enlargement of the medical and surgical clinics. It was, however, recognized at the time of the drafting of this program, that some more adequate provision would also have to be made for housing the nurses in the hospital and for enlarging the service and heating plants. The heating plant was also intended to provide for heating the building of the School of Hygiene and Public Health, and, in order that we might have a unified heating system, to take care as well of the buildings of the School of Medicine. Application for aid was made to the General Education Board. The board made us an appropriation which, with the interest on the balances that have remained unexpended, has amounted to nearly four million dollars. The Carnegie Corporation also gave us two million dollars for the purpose of constructing and endowing a much more adequate dispensary than was in existence at the time of the gift.

While the buildings which we were enabled to erect as a result of these gifts were in process of construction, the plan for the establishment of an ophthalmological institute took shape. We were very fortunate in being able to secure the services of Dr. Wilmer as the ophthalmologist of the hospital and professor of ophthalmology in the School of Medicine, and, with the aid of the William Holland Wilmer Foundation as well as of the General Education Board, to construct the building necessary for the carrying out of the work. This building I am glad to announce has been completed. It is expected that this building will be formally opened in the autumn of this year with appropriate exercises. Its formal opening will mark a step in the history of American medicine. For the Wilmer Ophthalmological Institute is the most serious attempt to provide for the study and cure of the diseases of the eye which has been made in this country.

In addition to the Wilmer Clinic, which was not a part of the original expansion program, we have also, thanks to the generosity of the General Education Board and Mr. Edward S. Harkness, of New York, been able both to construct and endow the new medical library which is named after our honored colleague, Dr. Welch. This will house the three libraries of the hospital, the School of Medicine and the School of Hygiene and Public Health, as well as the work of the new department for the study of the history of medicine, which we also owe to the generosity of the General Education Board and which is under the charge of Dr. Welch.

We have, in addition to the completion of the Wilmer Institute and the Welch Medical Library, been able out of the funds given to the hospital and the university to complete the new nurses' home, to reconstruct and equip the service building of the hospital and to begin the construction of a wing to the physiological building which is primarily to house the work of Dr. Mansfield Clark, our new professor of physiological chemistry. We have also completed the new dispensary which has been in operation for about a year, and have started the diagnostic clinic for people of moderate means, which was one of the purposes that the Carnegie Corporation had in mind in their gift to us.

We have had enough money remaining from the gift of the General Education Board to the general expansion program to reconstruct the wards of the hospital devoted to internal medicine and surgery. It had not, however, been possible for us to enter upon the construction of these buildings because we did not have sufficient money to enable us to operate them when built.

I am very glad to be able to announce on this occasion that a donor who desires to remain anonymous has only recently promised us a gift of $3,000,000 in order to give us sufficient money to operate the medical and surgical clinics when constructed.

This munificent gift thus offers us the possibility of completing the hospital and medical school expansion program and puts us in a position in which we can offer much more satisfactory instruction to the students who come to us to be trained for the practice of medicine. We shall also be able to add 165 public beds to the existing accommodations and thus make quite an addition to Baltimore's hospital facilities.

I would not have you think, however, that the completion of this expansion program, which will be an accomplished fact in the near future, puts the hospital in such a shape that no further efforts for its endowment are necessary. All these gifts which I have mentioned have provided the opportunity of doing more work than otherwise would have been possible. At the same time the general endowment of the hospital still remains inadequate, and it is with the greatest difficulty that the budget of that institution can be balanced. The work of the Women's Auxiliary has been of the greatest service in helping to balance this budget, and I sincerely trust that our recent good fortune will not have the effect of causing those ladies who have so generously given of their time to remit in any way their efforts, and also that those who have in the past so generously contributed to our yearly budget will not feel that we have no use at the present time for what they can continue still to give us.

Some of you may be surprised that at the commemoration exercises of the university the president of the university should make an announcement which would seem to concern primarily the hospital. The reason is, of course, that the School of Medicine is as dependent upon the hospital as any scientific department in the university is dependent upon its own laboratory. It is because of this fact that in a number of cases the large funds which have been given for the expansion program have been given either to the hospital and the university jointly or to the university alone. The university has, indeed, at the present time very large funds invested in buildings and plant administered by the hospital. Those funds have been so invested because of the intimate relation that must exist between its medical work and the hospital.

Those of you who are interested in the history of the two institutions which Johns Hopkins founded fifty years ago will remember that in his letter to the original hospital trustees he said, "It is my wish and purpose that the 'hospital' shall ultimately form a part of the Medical School of the University." While, from a strictly legal point of view this wish and purpose of his have never been effectuated, at the same time from most practical points of view the hospital is a part of the Medical School, and it is owing in large measure to the cordial relations which have always existed between the trustees of what are legally two separate corporations that the School of Medicine has had the success which may justly be accredited to it.

I have also to report a gift of $60,000, from Mr. Francis P. Garvan, for cancer research. This money will be used in connection with Dr. Bloodgood's work on cancer.

Finally I have to report a gift of $10,000, from Dr. Emanuel Libman, to be used to establish in the department of the history of medicine a lectureship which is to be named the Hideyo Noguchi lectureship, in honor of Dr. Noguchi, whose work in connection with the Rockefeller Institute of Medical Research is so well known, and whose tragic death in the carrying on of medical research has so recently occurred.

As this is probably the last time that I shall have the opportunity of addressing this audience I wish in closing what appears always on our program as "Announcements by the President" to express to my colleagues of the different faculties my appreciation of their kindness and patience towards me during the past fifteen years and to voice the hope that every success possible may follow their efforts in the future.

I wish also to express to the citizens of Baltimore my thanks for the treatment which I have received at their hands. I am afraid at times they have regarded me as an importunate beggar, but whether they have or not, they have not, by their behavior, made the process of begging a difficult one. Their support has made possible what the last twenty-five years have brought forth. I bespeak for both the university and the hospital a continuation of that generosity without which our future progress will be very difficult.

THE IMPORTANCE OF THE NURSERY SCHOOL IN MORAL EDUCATION

By HARRIET GRUBE and S. R. ELLIS

RIPON COLLEGE

BECAUSE science reveals that the mental development of an individual begins at birth we are beginning to realize the necessity for early education. No longer are we satisfied to begin education at the traditional age of five or six years. Knowing that some natural tendencies are to be cultivated and encouraged, some to be modified and changed, while still others are to be checked and entirely inhibited, we are coming to a realization that education should begin at the cradle and proceed hand in hand with experience. An atmosphere created solely for the child, in which he is the center of interest, where his individual differences are carefully studied and catered to, should certainly yield good results in both mental and moral training. Of course this assumes that the teachers who study and teach the children are mentally and morally equal to the task of administering an efficient nursery school.

A history of the preschool with its activities and equipment may serve to both introduce and defend the institution. The first nursery school was established by Oberlin at Walbach, France, in 1774. In England the movement was begun by Robert Owen, who set up a school at New Lanark in 1816. The school was originally established for an aid to the children of the factory workers, but finally degenerated into an ordinary free kindergarten with formal instruction. In 1908 the British Board of Education recommended the establishment of nursery schools and in 1918 the "Education Act" established such schools all over England for children from two to five years of age. These schools provide for cleanliness and physical care, aim to remedy defects, recommend proper nutrition and create an atmosphere of freedom and affection. Great stress is laid upon habit formation and conduct controls.

The nursery school in America was first the result of a fusion of Sunday schools, nurseries, infant schools, day nurseries and kindergartens and arose primarily to provide experimental work.

The pragmatic educational philosophy of John Dewey, developed in 1899 to 1913, has had much influence in furthering preschool education. Dewey believed that "education is life itself," emphasizing learning by doing or motor activity. He declared that the school should serve as a reproduction of adult life on the child's plane with the proper social aspects included. The child should be encouraged in creative and productive activities. Fisher, in America, also began work following the design of Madame Montessori, thus encouraging initiative by providing material which is largely self-administrative and providing a motive for effective learning.

One of the recent outstanding projects in this realm of education is the nursery school established in September, 1921, by the Iowa Child Welfare Research Bureau. A laboratory was opened, which provided for three groups of children, those from two to three years of age, from three to four, and from four to five. The first two groups are of the most interest since the third group follows much the same course as the formal instruction of the average kindergarten.

The school has the nominal tuition fee of eleven dollars a year, which makes it possible for the children of average families to attend. The school is held in a house which is arranged with much beauty and comfort. There are three experimental rooms and a large assembly room, all built in proper proportions. In the laboratory rooms physical and mental measurements are taken, while the large group room is equipped to provide games and motor activities. The room is equipped with swinging lattice gates, which open from the wall to form tiny stalls which provide the room for individual and project work. Chairs and tables, a sand table, blackboards, phonograph, doll house, dolls, housekeeping equipment, scissors, blocks, soap-bubble materials, lacing cards, sewing cards, paper-weaving materials, beads, pencils and crayons and modeling clay complete the equipment. Outside the playground is furnished with small swings, a teeter and a chute for sliding into the sand pit.

Tests and measurements of the physical and mental status of the child are taken each month on or about the day the child was born. The Stanford-Binet tests are used. The standard test given to the three-year-old group follows:

(1) Points to parts of the body.
(2) Names familiar objects.
(3) From pictures, enumeration of objects.
(4) Gives sex.
(5) Gives last name.
(6) Repeats six or seven syllables.

The four-year-old test provides:

(1) Compares lines.
(2) Discrimination of forms.
(3) Counts four pennies.
(4) Copies squares.
(5) First degree comprehension.
(6) Repeats four digits.

Experiments in motor control are performed through the Wallen "Peg-board," Montessori "tower," squares, cubes, and so forth. Usually children are peculiarly inapt in motor controls and only exceptional pupils are successful in this experiment. Although these facts can not be relied upon as a criteria of the child's intelligence, yet they furnish valuable data for studies in individual differences and pave the way for character building.

The program of the nursery school begins usually by teaching the child the day of the month or week, either by using a song or a rhyme. Then the children sing with the phonograph, usually some Mother Goose rhyme or a song they have learned at home. Musical training enters here, for a sense of rhythm is developed through such singing. Learning to skip or march in time to music also increases the child's sense of coordination in activities. When the phonograph is playing the children are often made to sit quietly listening to the music. This furthers an appreciation of music and at the same time stimulates those essential qualities of restful relaxation so necessary in the well-developed moral character.

Esthetic experience is provided by the beauty of the room. The teacher points to a picture or a beautiful object, calls the attention of the pupil to it and the child is then asked to talk about it.

The program next provides for projects in handicraft. The children construct houses of blocks, sew cards, play ball, mold clay and make attractive things to decorate the room. Individuality is encouraged and the children usually work alone.

After interest in the games decreases the children are sent to the lavatory to wash and then they bring tiny chairs to the lunch room, where they receive small bottles of milk for their lunch. For the hour and a half period which remains after lunch the time is usually devoted to story telling, nature talks or excursions. Contrary to current opinion, it is quite difficult to tell stories to the small child, since they must be told in very simple words and must have some direct relation to the objects of their experience in order to hold the interest.

The nursery school thus provides for the development of motor control through elements of dancing, skipping and marching; it aids in giving the child poise through the development of motor control and in overcoming natural shyness by associating with other children in an atmosphere of freedom and affection in the schoolroom. The building of percepts and concepts is begun by acquainting the child with the ordinary objects of life. Esthetic impulses are created by interest in the beauties of environment. Proper habits and character traits are promoted while bad habits and qualities of weak personalities are inhibited. An early acquisition of group consciousness is gained through association with other children, and the child learns to recognize the rights of other children; thus attitudes of selfishness are curbed.

Often children are much better off in a nursery school than in the home, since the equipment and arrangement are frequently more suitable than in the average home where conditions are usually for the convenience of adults. The child has, also, the exclusive attention of trained expert teachers, and the environment is designed to bring out the intellectual and moral traits which might otherwise lie dormant. In the average home the child does not learn to treat his playmates as fellow beings, but in the nursery school he becomes conscious of the give and take of group play, thus realizing that his playmates are persons like himself.

The nursery school movement is becoming more important, better known and increasingly more effective. With keener appreciation of children's needs, with less and less prejudice on the part of parents, with improved scientific methods the movement is bound to succeed.

(1) The preschool child should be the center of our attention as a recently recognized educational problem.

(2) Nursery schools are effective educational agencies and should be affiliated with our great American school system.

(3) A moral education program is incomplete without the cooperation of parents and teachers who are willing to begin character training when experience begins.

EDUCATIONAL EVENTS

THE ESTABLISHMENT OF A NATIONAL EDUCATION BOARD IN PORTUGAL

A DECREE has been signed in Portugal establishing a Board, or "Junta," of National Education. This Junta's chief aims, according to a report in *The Christian Science Monitor*, are to collect the necessary elements for a scholastic revival in Portugal, which is still suffering in this respect from the material consequences of the war. This measure is particularly necessary for the development of the higher educational courses, and has been generally welcomed, both by the public opinion and in the press, as a step leading to the recovery of intellectual strength, the lack of which in latter years may be said to have contributed to the slow material progress of Portugal.

According to the determinations of this decree, the Junta has, among others, the following functions:

To help all culture in the sciences, independently of the official institutions for instruction and investigation already in existence; to improve the professional staffs in the higher colleges; to perfect and bring to the front men of average intelligence; to send competent persons to educational and cultural centers in other countries for the purpose of establishing relations with such circles for the benefit of the intellectual progress of the Portuguese nation. It will also create missions for instructive ends, subsidize the publication of works of a scientific nature and so on.

The Junta is composed of twenty-one members, including professors from the three universities of Portugal—Coimbra, Lisbon and Oporto—of non-university professors, members of scientific corporations, men of letters and others.

CHILD WELFARE IN THE IRISH FREE STATE

THE *British Medical Journal* reports that with the object of promoting certain amendments of the Children's Act, 1908, a deputation composed of members of various organizations recently visited the Ministry of Local Government, where it was received by the secretary in the unavoidable absence of the minister. The amendments suggested were as follows: (1) That effect should be given to the recommendation of the report of the Poor Law Commission—namely, that the law should be strengthened in the direction of prevention by the introduction of affiliation orders. (2) That homes with attached maternity and probationary departments should be established to accommodate the mother and child for as many months, up to a year, as might be considered necessary; that it should not be lawful for the owner of any private house or nursing home to take a maternity case for profit unless it has first been licensed by the local authority; the premises must be open for inspection and a register be kept of the names and addresses of the mothers of all children born in such home, and the names and addresses of all persons into whose care such children are given when leaving. (3) That any person acting as agent in putting a child under the age of 7 out to be nursed should be equally liable with the person who receives the infant. The person acting as agent must forward to the local authority a receipt stating the amount received for placing the infant, and the person who receives the child may be required to attend before a divisional magistrate or district justice to satisfy the justice whether any fee has been given, and that the transaction was for the benefit of the child. (4) That no child should be sent to any person for maintenance for reward unless and until the local authority for the district gives a certificate that the person who is to have charge of such an infant is a fit and proper person, and that the premises are suitable in every respect. (5) That any offender against the children's act may be prosecuted within, say, twelve months after the committal of such offence or continuing offence, notwithstanding the provisions of any act or acts to the contrary. There was agreement as to the necessity for additional safeguards, but the discussion revealed certain difficulties which more stringent regulations or changes in the substance of the law would create. The deputation undertook to give the matter further consideration and to prepare a supplementary memorandum.

SURVIVAL RATES OF PUPILS ENTERING THE PUBLIC SCHOOLS

Frank M. Phillips, chief of the Division of Statistics of the U. S. Bureau of Education, has made a study of the survival rates of students entering the public schools throughout the country. He states that a study made by the bureau in 1918 shows that of every 1,000 pupils reaching the fifth grade at that time, 634 reached the eighth grade, 342 entered the high school and 139 were graduated. Since then the number enrolled in the early grades has decreased slightly, while the number in the upper grades has increased considerably. In 1918 the public high schools enrolled 1,933,821 pupils, and in 1926 they enrolled 3,757,466, not counting junior high school pupils below the ninth grade, or nearly twice as many. The 1918 rates are, therefore, no longer applicable.

In making survival rates for 1926 it is observed that a larger number of children are enrolled in each of the first five elementary grades, allowing for duplicates, than there are six-year-olds, or seven-year-olds. Without correcting for repeaters, or for those enrolled in private schools, it is assumed that practically all children attend school until after they enter the fifth grade.

Making allowance for duplication, it is now estimated that of an original 1,000 entering the public schools for the first time, 957 reach the sixth grade, 795 reach the seventh grade, and 720 reach the eighth grade. No data are available concerning the number of pupils who complete the work of the eighth grade.

Of the original 1,000, the number entering the first year of the high school is 605, while 432 reach the second year, 321 reach the third year, 262 reach the fourth year and 247 are finally graduated from high school.

After making an adjustment for those communities that have but seven years of elementary school work instead of eight, the length of public school life to-day is just a little short of the completion of the first year of high school.

It is not possible to show survival rates by years beyond the high school at this time, but, excluding preparatory students, the colleges, universities, professional schools and teachers' colleges enrolled 338,759 students in 1918, and 945,079 in 1926. First and professional degrees were granted to 37,915 college students in 1918, and 96,956 in 1926, with 32,500 continuing with graduate work.

Of the original 1,000 in 1918, the number entering college was 72, and the number graduated was 23. A conservative estimate for 1926 would indicate that 177 of the original 1,000 entered college, and 48 were graduated. These data do not include 143,808 students in summer schools in colleges in 1918 and 209,454 in 1926, nor 138,074 enrolled in normal schools in 1918, and 116,248 in 1926, nor those in private business colleges, nor in other types of schools not mentioned herein.

THE PITTSBURGH SURVEY

At the suggestion of William M. Davidson, superintendent of the Pittsburgh public schools, the board of education in 1928 appointed a group of school administrators to scrutinize the plans and policies of the board and the educational practice and procedure of the superintendent and his staff. The survey committee consisted of Thomas E. Finegan, chairman, former state superintendent of public instruction, but now with Eastman Teaching Films, Rochester, N. Y.; H. S. West, superintendent of schools, Rochester, N. Y., and John W. Withers, dean of the school of education, New York University.

According to the report in the *Pennsylvania School Journal,* the committee found the whole school organization moving along in harmony and with a fine spirit of cooperation for effective work with abundant evidence that the public has complete confidence in the management of the school interests of the city. Instead of bringing a staff of surveyors to Pittsburgh, the committee utilized the staff of the superintendent's office, the school principals and the entire teaching force. They made a complete study of the city school system by the city's own teaching and supervisory staff of 3,100 members.

In teaching load in the elementary school, the report gives an efficiency rating of 99.5 per cent. with 39.8 pupils to a teacher. In the junior high school the average number of pupils per teacher is 27, in the senior high school, 23. There is a satisfactory balance between the financial economy factor, on the one hand, and right working conditions, on the other, in the organization and administration of the junior and senior high schools. The committee found that the elementary schools were used to 96.5 per cent. of their capacity, and pronounced this an "eminently satisfactory condition." There is also a satisfactory relation between the capacity and use of all of the high schools.

The committee gives high praise to the members of the board of education for their service to the city. It states that the progress made in the school system since its reorganization in 1911 has been phenomenal, and that no city in the country has a record of greater achievement. This progress is attributed to the sound policies adopted by the board, and the wise and sympathetic manner in which Dr. Davidson has executed them. The Court of Common Pleas is commended for the type of men and women which it has appointed to membership on the board.

The committee approves the general program of studies in the elementary schools, the junior high schools and the senior high schools. The committee specifically states that this part of the organization of the Pittsburgh schools "conforms to the best thought and practice of the country."

One of the principal recommendations of the commission is that there should be a much closer affiliation between the Frick Training School and the School of Education of the University of Pittsburgh. The commission points out that the new training school building, the administration building, the Carnegie Library, the Schenley High School, the present university buildings, and the "Cathedral of Learning" now in the process of construction, all within two blocks of each other on Pittsburgh's civic center, should be merged into one enterprise for the training of teachers.

CHILD HEALTH DAY IN NEW YORK CITY

The health records of 1,000,000 public school children in New York City will be examined by teachers on May 1, designated by President Hoover as National Child Health Day, in an effort to correct physical defects.

Dr. William J. O'Shea, superintendent of schools, has sent a circular to district superintendents and principals, asking that records made last November on School Health Day be checked, so that neglected ills might be traced and parents and guardians urged to remove dental, nasal or visual defects of pupils. The circular says:

> Principals are advised to instruct their teachers to inspect the physical examination records of all pupils on Wednesday, May 1, and to make note of those children who have failed to have corrected the defects of vision, hearing, nasal breathing, nutrition, teeth, etc. This follow-up will enable the present class teachers to familiarize themselves with the names of children suffering from physical defects, and to urge them to remove physical defects wherever present.
>
> Immediate steps should be taken by teachers to seat children with defective vision and hearing near the front of the room and to insist on the correction of dental defects. An effort should be made to stimulate an interest in the importance of proper diet, fresh air, sunshine, exercise, rest and sleep.
>
> To facilitate a satisfactory follow-up of the teachers' findings of uncorrected physical defects, principals are further advised to consult with parents, school medical inspectors and school nurses.
>
> In the event that principals find that the school medical inspectors and school nurses have not yet confirmed the teachers' findings of physical de-

fects found on School Health Day, held last November, they are directed to forward this information to Dr. A. K. Aldinger, Director of Health Education.

APPROPRIATION FOR THE STUDY OF LANGUAGES AND LITERATURE AT HARVARD UNIVERSITY

THE General Education Board has appropriated the sum of $250,000 to be used over a period of five years for the pursuit of studies of the humanities at Harvard University. Inasmuch as special provision has been made for history and fine arts, the term "humanities" is restricted to ancient and modern languages and literatures. The committee in charge of the awards for the year 1928–29 has recommended the following assignments:

THE DIVISION OF ANCIENT LANGUAGES; for "Harvard Studies in Classical Philology."

THE DIVISION OF MODERN LANGUAGES; for "Harvard Studies and Notes in Philology and Literature."

EDWARD KENNARD RAND, professor of Latin; for a survey of the manuscripts of Tours and work on Horace, Virgil and Ovid.

RICHMOND LAURIN HAWKINS, associate professor of French; for publication of unpublished letters existent in America from Frenchmen of the seventeenth, eighteenth and nineteenth centuries.

CHESTER NOYES GREENOUGH, professor of English; for one research assistant and two cataloguers for a bibliography of English prose fiction.

JOHN LIVINGSTON LOWES, professor of English; for an edition of the Gutch Memorandum Book in the British Museum, and for work on Chaucer and Coleridge, including the help of a research assistant.

JEREMIAH DENIS MATTHIAS FORD, Smith professor of the French and Spanish languages; for clerical work in compiling a bibliography of Spanish-American and Portuguese-American literature; for photostats used in a Grammar of Early French; for clerical assistance in a study of Don Quixote; for the publication of letters of John III of Portugal.

FRANK STANTON CAWLEY, assistant professor of German; for the publication of an Icelandic Saga.

WALTER SILZ, assistant professor of German; for typewriting and other expense entailed by publication of work on the German Romanticists.

NEW BUILDINGS OF THE AMERICAN MUSEUM OF NATURAL HISTORY

THE American Museum of Natural History of New York City has received gifts and appropriations amounting to $5,000,000, which will be used to provide three new buildings. They will be known as South Oceanic Hall, Roosevelt Memorial and African Hall.

At a recent meeting of the Board of Estimate, presided over by Mayor Walker, it was agreed to appropriate $2,400,000. In announcing the appropriation, the mayor pointed out again that the city stood ready to match with like sums any private subscriptions for enlargement of the museum.

Of the city's appropriation, $750,000 will match a sum of like amount given by Harry Payne Whitney toward the new Oceanic Hall. That portion of the city's donation will be provided from the sale of serial bonds.

The announcement came after George R. Sherwood, director of the museum, had appeared before the Board of Estimate and Dr. Henry Fairfield Osborn, president of the institution, had conferred with Mayor Walker and other members of the board.

Matching an appropriation of the state of $1,200,000, a similar sum of the city's gift will be used for the foundation and the first two stories of the building named in honor of President Roosevelt. The remaining $400,000 will build a heating and power plant to serve African Hall and the Roosevelt Building.

The cost of African Hall will be about $3,050,000. In addition to the Whitney gift of $750,000, donations amounting to $866,000 from other sources had been obtained, which will be used in the building of the Roosevelt Memorial and African Hall.

The mayor, the comptroller and the president of the Park Board are members *ex officio* of the board of trustees of the museum. It has thirty members and is self-perpetuating. The first and second vice-presidents of the board are George F. Baker and J. P. Morgan.

THE CHILDREN'S FUND OF MICHIGAN

SENATOR JAMES COUZENS, of Michigan, has created a trust fund of $10,000,000 "to be used to promote the health, welfare, happiness and development of the children of Michigan primarily, and elsewhere in the world."

The corporation administering it, which is headed by Dr. Hugo A. Freund, Mr. Couzens's personal physician, will be known as the Children's Fund of Michigan, and a clause in the trust instrument stipulates that the principal and income must be disbursed in its entirety inside of twenty-five years.

Judge Arthur Lacy, personal counsel and a trustee of the fund, states that Senator Couzens "is opposed to holding a large fund of this kind in perpetuity. He wants the coming generation of children to get the entire benefit and prepare itself to assume a similar responsibility to the succeeding generation. He desires to aid personally in making this fund do as much good as possible and to see the result."

It is also provided that where expenditures fall below the stipulated amount the unexpended portion must be spent the succeeding year.

Dr. Freund has issued a statement in which he says that it is too early to state all the lines of activity that are contemplated. Mental hygiene and child guidance clinics will be encouraged. Plans for properly supervised group recreation will be assisted; dietetic, hygienic, nutritional and other subjects bearing upon the health of children will be investigated whenever and wherever the indication for their study arises. For the present no research in the pure sciences will be attempted, nor will any edifice be erected to serve as a center for the many activities. This fund is for the purpose of assisting and developing these agencies and institutions that are already established, or creating new projects for the welfare of children and supplementing the work already begun in well-established organizations.

The trustees include former Judge Arthur J. Lacy, Senator Couzens, Dr. Freund, Frank Couzens, the Senator's son; McPherson Browning, president of the Detroit and Security Trust Company; William J. Norton, executive secretary of the Detroit Community Fund, and Clarence E. Wilcox, Detroit attorney.

EDUCATIONAL NOTES AND NEWS

THE degree of doctor of laws will be conferred by the University of Edinburgh on Dr. Abbott Lawrence Lowell, president of Harvard University.

A PORTRAIT of Dr. Elmer Ellsworth Brown, chancellor of New York University, was presented by the alumni of the school of education of the university to Dr. William J. Cooper, U. S. Commissioner of Education, at the second annual luncheon of the graduates held on April 20 at the Hotel Pennsylvania. The portrait will be hung in the Federal Bureau of Education Building in Washington as part of the collection of portraits of commissioners of education. Dr. Brown was commissioner of education from 1906 to 1911. The portrait was painted by Robert A. Kissack, professor of art education at the university.

DR. EDWIN A. ALDERMAN, president of the University of Virginia, was the guest of honor of New York alumni on April 17 at a dinner at the Hotel Brevoort in celebration of Dr. Alderman's twenty-fifth anniversary as head of the university. Dr. Fielding Lewis Taylor, president of the alumni association, presided.

APRIL 8 marked the twenty-fifth anniversary of the election of G. E. Maxwell as president of the Winona State Teachers College. In appreciation of his service a program was given in which the resident director and representatives of the elementary school, the alumni, the faculty and the students took part. During Mr. Maxwell's term of service, the original building of the college has been replaced by five modern buildings and the institution has grown from a normal school with undifferentiated programs into a teachers college with a program specialized so as to prepare teachers for many phases of public education.

PROFESSOR MILTON C. DEL MANZO has been appointed provost of Teachers College, Columbia University, with a seat in the faculties of education and practical arts. He will continue to hold his present offices as professor of education and associate in the International Institute. Professor Paul R. Mort, of the education department, has been appointed director of the school of education to succeed Dr. Robert J. Leonard.

DEAN ROBERT WILLIAMS, of Albion College, has been appointed acting president of Ohio Northern University, the appointment to take effect at the end of the present school year. He will become president in 1931 on the retirement of Dr. Albert E. Smith, now president of the university.

AN honorary doctorate has been conferred on Dr. Abraham Flexner by the medical faculty of the University of Berlin.

DR. WALTER C. BINGHAM, of the Personnel Research Federation, New York City, and Professor M. S. Vitales, of the University of Pennsylvania, have been elected honorary correspondents of the British National Institute of Industrial Psychology.

DR. JULIUS KLEIN, formerly assistant professor of American history and economics at Harvard University, now director of the Bureau of Foreign and Domestic Commerce, has been appointed assistant secretary of commerce.

DR. KENYON L. BUTTERFIELD, formerly president of the Michigan State College, has been appointed a special representative of the Carnegie Corporation to make a study of the needs of rural education in South Africa.

DR. BELMONT FARLEY, a member of the faculty of the Western State Teachers College, Kalamazoo, Michigan, has been appointed an assistant director of the division of publications of the National Education Association. Dr. Farley will go to Washington to assume his new work in June.

W. I. NICHOLS, assistant dean in charge of freshmen at Harvard University, will resign in September to enter the publishing business in New York City.

AT Wesleyan University, Wilbert Snow has been promoted to a professorship in English and Mr. T. A. Langley to an assistant professorship in psychology.

DR. J. A. ESTEY, for over fourteen years a member of the department of history and economics at Purdue University, has been named head of the department to succeed the late Dr. Thomas F. Moran.

DR. GUSTAV KAFKA, professor of psychology in the University at Dresden, has accepted an invitation to become visiting professor of psychology at the Johns Hopkins University for the winter semester of 1929–30.

SIX foreign psychologists, Professors Robert H. Thouless, Wolfgang Köhler, James Drever, L. Wynn Jones, F. Roels and F. Aveling will give a series of lectures in the Universities of Michigan, Wisconsin, Minnesota, Iowa, Missouri and Pittsburgh during the coming summer session. Each visitor will spend one week in each of the institutions, thus covering the circuit in six weeks. The lectures will center about the subject, "Points of View in Psychology." These men are coming to this country primarily for the purpose of attending the International Congress of Psychology in September.

MR. I. A. RICHARDS, of the University of Cambridge, has been invited by the Tsing Hua National University at Peking to be visiting professor in the department of foreign languages and literature for one year. Mr. Richards is a fellow of Magdalene College and lecturer in the faculty of English in the university.

PHILIP W. L. COX, professor of secondary education at New York University, will teach at the summer session of the State Teachers College at Buffalo, N. Y., this year.

DR. C. O. MATHEWS, associate professor of education, Ohio Wesleyan University, Delaware, will give two courses in measurements at the University of Michigan this summer. One will be "Introduction to Measurements," and the other "Individual and Group Mental Tests."

VISITING professors at the summer session of the University of Southern California include: in education, Dr. William J. Cooper, U. S. Commissioner of Education; Dr. Norman Fenton, director of research of the California Bureau of Juvenile Research; Dr. Harlan C. Hines, Eastern Montana Normal School; Dr. Clyde M. Hill, Yale University, and Vierling Kersey, California State superintendent of public instruction; in economics, Dr. Thomas Nixon Carver, Harvard University; in Spanish, Dr. Carlos Castillo, University of Chicago; in psychology, Dr. Henry H. Goddard, Ohio State University; in history, Dr. James A. James, dean of the graduate school, Northwestern University, and Dr. Edward L. Hardy, president of the State Teachers College at San Diego.

Professor Frederic A. Ogg, chairman of the department of political science at the University of Wisconsin and editor of the *American Political Science Review,* is on leave of absence during the current semester and is engaged in research and editorial work in Washington and New York City. The Macmillan Company is publishing a new book by him dealing with English government and politics.

Professor Grant Showerman, of the University of Wisconsin, will again direct the seventh summer session of the American Academy in Rome, School of Classical Studies, which will open on July 8 and end on August 16. The enrolment consists of graduates of American colleges and universities, and is limited to fifty.

Professor Albert L. Cru is personally in charge of the Paris group of Teachers College, Columbia University, this year and will remain until the final examination at the Sorbonne in mid-June. During Professor Cru's absence his courses on Civilization, *Explication de Textes* and Methods are given by Mr. D. P. Girard.

Professor J. C. Lyons, of the Romance Languages department of the University of North Carolina, will be in charge of a student tour through France, during the coming summer, to be held under the auspices of the university extension division. The itinerary includes a three-week period of residence in the summer resort of Bagnères-de-Bigorre in the Pyrenees Mountains. All the points of greatest interest in western and southern France will be visited. A week will be spent in Paris, and visits to the larger cities of Switzerland, Belgium and England will be made.

William Cassius Cook has become State superintendent of West Virginia, in succession to Mr. George M. Ford.

Dr. Landis Tanger, superintendent of schools at Reading, Pennsylvania, will become principal of the Millersville State Teachers College on September 1, succeeding Dr. Charles H. Gordinier, who plans to retire.

E. S. Russell, formerly superintendent of the public schools at Simsbury, Connecticut, has been appointed director of the New Haven Teacher-training School. Mr. Paul D. Collier, of Texas, succeeds Mr. Russell at Simsbury.

John R. Williams, of Painesville, Ohio, has been elected president of the North Eastern Ohio Teachers Association.

At the annual meeting of the American Scandinavian Foundation the following fellowships were announced: For study *in Sweden,* Dale Allen White, Yale University, for the study of architecture, and Frederick Tylberg, associate professor of European history in the University of North Dakota, for the study of history; *in Norway,* Dorothy Wyckoff, Bryn Mawr College, for the study of geology, and Joseph Auslander, an honorary fellowship for the study of Norwegian poetry; *in Denmark,* Harold Herbert Nielsen, University of Michigan, for the study of physics, John Randolph Huffman, Yale University, for the study of physical chemistry, and Alexander Haggerty Krappe, University of Chicago, an honorary fellowship for the study of medieval literature.

Dr. Albert Bushnell Hart, professor emeritus of history and of government at Harvard University, will give the Founders' Day address at Franklin and Marshall College, Lancaster, Pennsylvania, on May 10. Founders' Day will mark the beginning of Lancaster's two hundredth anniversary celebration, which will continue for about three months.

Dr. Ray Lyman Wilbur, secretary of the Department of the Interior, was the guest of honor and principal speaker at the reunion of the alumni of the Wharton School of Finance and Commerce of the University of Pennsylvania on April 25. Other speakers included Dr. Emory R. Johnson, dean of the Wharton School, and Dr. James T. Young, professor of public administration.

Dr. Henry Noble MacCracken, president of Vassar College, will address the Parents and Teachers Association of the Ethical Culture Schools of New York City, at the annual dinner on the evening of April 30 which will be held at the Engineering Societies Building, on "The American Conception of a Higher Education."

Dean Robert M. Hutchins, of the Yale University School of Law, will give the commencement address at Lafayette College on June 7.

The Rev. Everett C. Herrick, president of Newton Theological Seminary, will deliver the baccalaureate sermon at the University of Maine in June.

Dr. William Westley Guth, president of Goucher College, Baltimore, died on April 19 at the age of fifty-eight years.

Christie Creelman, who for sixteen years was president of the Ontario Agricultural College at Guelph, retiring from this office six years ago owing to ill health, died on April 18, in his sixtieth year.

Dr. Arthur S. Loevenhart, professor of pharmacology and toxicology at the University of Wisconsin, died on April 20 in his fiftieth year.

The Edward W. Stitt Memorial Association will establish a memorial research fund in the school of education of the College of the City of New York as a memorial to the late associate superintendent. The fund now amounts to $4,737. Its administration will be placed in the hands of a committee of three, consisting of the president of the College of the City of New York, the dean of the school of education and the president of the association, who at present is Dr. Joseph H. Wade. Professor Paul Klapper, dean of the school of education, will select among the active post-graduate students several teachers in the New York City school system who have chosen for research problems of special value to current educational practice. The income of the fund will enable the college to publish the results of these studies. From the fund a sufficient amount will be retained by the committee to defray the expenses of placing a bronze tablet in memory of Dr. Stitt in the Edward W. Stitt Junior High School, which is in course of construction.

Speakers at the recent three-day conference of the New York Society for the Experimental Study of Education at which more than one hundred and fifty students of education of the Middle Atlantic states were present included U. S. Commissioner of Education Wm. John Cooper; Cameron Beck, personnel director of the New York Stock Exchange; Dr. Ned H. Dearborn, director of teacher training of the New York State Department of Education, and Dr. Charles H. Elliott, commissioner of education for the State of New Jersey. Dr. Ambrose L. Suhrie, of New York University, was chairman of the conference.

St. Lawrence University has received a gift of $100,000 from the F. L. Carlisle Company, New York, to be paid over a period of five years in annual installments of $20,000.

DISCUSSION

AN ANALYSIS OF THE BETA HYPOTHESIS OF LEARNING

A short time after the appearance of Knight Dunlap's article, "A Revision of the Fundamental Law of Habit Formation,"[1] a college professor of mathematics approached me with a rather vigorous challenge that the law of exercise had been shown to be unsound. He had been reading Thorndike for some time, but had failed to see that the three laws of learning as given in this author's writings are really not three laws, but three divisions of one law. He seemed to have failed to grasp the psychologist's extensive discussion of the law of effect in connection with the law of frequency. Neither did he fully grasp Dunlap's point on catharsis relative to his experiment in writing "the" incorrectly in order to break himself of the habit of writing it "hte." I refer to his interpretation because it seems to be too typical of the conclusions drawn by many educationists from the simple experiment made by Dunlap.

There is a great tendency, even on the part of some teachers of psychology, to present the laws of learning as being independent of one another. This is done in spite of Thorndike's insistence that in learning, exercise alone is not sufficient. Dunlap, also, obviously failed

[1] *Science*, April 6, 1928.

to grasp the idea of the unity of the laws. He says, "But running through all our disquisitions on learning has been the implication that repetition itself, aside from other factors, has a positive effect." This remark is made regardless of Thorndike's position which he stated clearly more than ten years ago. Gates also points out the fact that exercise is not sufficient in itself but must have some specific purpose connected with it in order to be the most effective.[2] He says,

> An investigator once asked a large number of students whether the four on their watches was a IV or a IIII. Of 200 students whose watches carried a IIII, 179 declared it was IV. These students no doubt saw the IIII hundreds of times, but with this exercise there was no definite purpose to remember specifically the kind of marks on their watches.

It is a well-known fact that a great deal of exercise in the various high-school subjects may take place with little or no apparent results. In a somewhat perfunctory way pupils may go through the process of hunting up certain words in the vocabulary and writing out their home work in Latin, for example, and in so doing learn almost nothing about their lessons. A similar kind of thing may happen in spelling. Pupils may write or repeat the words of a lesson primarily with the purpose of satisfying the present demands of the teacher. Under such circumstances the mere exercise or response does not necessarily produce a positive effect toward making a correct reproduction probable. Readiness and set influence purpose; purpose largely determines the effect; effect influences the speed of learning and the permanence of retention.

In "A Note on the Beta Hypothesis of Learning"[3] Holscopple and Vanouse say, "Dunlap cites as an instance leading to his revision of the law of frequency his correction of a typewriting error by voluntarily practising the word as incorrectly written." It would seem that these writers also have overestimated the value of Dunlap's brief experiment. Furthermore, they describe the conduct of a more extensive experiment that they did and from which they obtained similar results. These experiments, however, instead of showing the necessity of revising the law of frequency, rather tend to emphasize more clearly the importance of the two divisions of the law of effect: satisfiers and annoyers. They also show that purposeful exercise is really very effective.

Dunlap was doubtless annoyed by the waste of time in repeatedly writing "hte" and also by the fact that he was writing the word incorrectly. Moreover, in writing the word in this way he was developing greater resistance to this form and consciously increasing a greater tendency for the correct form. The same facts held true apparently relative to the second experiment, for the experimenters say, "The instructions, which were usually considered 'funny' or 'mysterious,' were repeated, and the practice supervised to see that the student wrote just what he was asked to write and nothing more." Knowing that they were writing a word incorrectly the students doubtless were building up greater resistance to this form and were thinking more and more about the correct spelling of the word. In spite of the technique employed the law of recency was functioning. Also, an annoyer was doubtless connected with this kind of work, so that a release from the apparently futile and a return to the more important gave an effective satisfier to the correct response.

Furthermore, the novelty of the experiment was not without effect. A short while ago my small boy had some trouble in learning to spell Massachusetts. After he had made several unsuccessful attempts to get the word straightened out in his mind I wrote it MassachUSetts, and had him copy this several times. The difficulty soon disappeared, at least temporarily. The novelty of capital letters in the midst of the word and perhaps some association with the US helped to clear up the matter. It is a well-known fact that a new method of presentation often attracts attention and increases interest. If Dunlap had written "the" tHe, that is, with a capital in the middle, a few times he might have cleared up his difficulty even more quickly that he did.

The theory of catharsis might have some application here, but it is difficult to see just how a strong tendency to write "hte" would originate.

2 A. I. Gates, "Psychology for Students of Education," page 267.

3 SCHOOL AND SOCIETY, 29: 15, January 5, 1929.

It might possibly result from writing large numbers of words in which *h* precedes *t;* such as, night, light, right, slight, sight, etc. Then, if, as is generally supposed, a response releases stored-up energy, the tendency might be overcome temporarily by giving expression to it. It would seem, however, that such a method would apply only to the narrower mental functions, not to be broader, more complicated ones. Furthermore, the idea of catharsis is weakened somewhat by the fact that all who tried the experiments were conscious of the fact that they were writing the words incorrectly. If writing a word incorrectly gave expression to some mysterious, unaccountable tendency to do the wrong thing, and thereby gave relief, it would not be necessary for an individual to be reminded emphatically of what he was doing. Neither would continuous repetition for a stated time be necessary. A very few reactions, whether conscious or unconscious, should be sufficient.

In many of the practical situations of life it might be well to point out some of the things that should not be done in order to show more clearly and effectively what should be done. For example, in teaching one to drive an automobile it would be well to explain why one should not step on the starter while the car is in gear. To explain the danger would certainly stimulate a normal person to see that the car was out of gear before using the starter. In giving courses in electricity, medicine, surgery, etc., it is, of course, advisable to explain clearly and emphatically many things that should not be done, but positively to give students exercise in doing things in the wrong way would seem to have few, if any, real advantages.

For further illustration, no one would think of trying to teach a child how to drive nails by having him pull them out; of endeavoring to teach a child to keep clean by encouraging him to go dirty; of attempting to develop within him a feeling of real patriotism by teaching him to hate his country's flag.

Those who conducted the experiments referred to relative to the Beta hypothesis of learning have brought out an important point in methods but the results as presented do not reveal any fallacy in the laws of learning. They show chiefly the effects of a novel type of motivation.

ROBERT P. CARROLL

TEACHERS COLLEGE,
SYRACUSE UNIVERSITY

PROFESSIONAL IMPROVEMENT AND SALARIES

A QUESTION which has been considered by many boards of education during the past few years and which is receiving considerable attention at the present time is whether increases in teachers' salaries should be conditioned by professional improvement requirements.

Various plans have been advanced and in some cases adopted in attempts to base salary differences on merit. Many of these plans have involved teacher-rating schemes, but it is pretty generally conceded that up to the present time there has been no satisfactory plan for rating teachers. Teacher rating is lacking in objectivity, validity and reliability. The methods of teacher rating involve too much personal judgment and too wide a range of standards. The following is a case in point, and is not uncommon. A certain teacher was given a "C" rating for three consecutive years, but when transferred to a different school in the same system was given a rating of "A" for each of the next two years. Teacher rating is invalid in that it does not measure the thing it attempts to measure, the degree of excellence of the teaching. For instance, there is no known way of measuring the effect of a "strong personality" or a "pleasing voice" on teaching ability because there is no standard by which to determine what constitutes a "strong personality" or a "pleasing voice." A "strong personality" means one thing to one person using the teacher-rating sheet and an entirely different thing to another person using the same rating sheet. It is plain that teacher rating is unreliable because it has been demonstrated that rerating of the same teachers by the same people, using the same rating plan, or an equivalent form of the same plan, produces widely different results.

The failure of teacher-rating procedures to prove satisfactory to boards of education, superintendents and teachers is one of the reasons why professional improvement of teachers has been given a prominent place in the consideration of salary schedules.

Professional improvement of teachers in service is of great educational and financial value to the school system. Many superintendents and teachers, too, believe that a half year of training after a teacher has had some teaching experience is equal to a full year of training prior to teaching experience. The proponents of the plan of definitely recognizing professional improvement of teachers while in service take the position that it is so valuable that it should be required of all teachers so far as possible, and that the only way it can be successfully demanded of all teachers is to make the annual salary increases in some way dependent upon a certain amount of professional training beyond the amount which the individual teacher has when she enters the service of the school system, or to make the annual salary increases, beyond a certain maximum, dependent upon professional training in service. Possession of the master's degree usually exempts the teacher from these requirements.

The last-mentioned plan involves a salary schedule having a minimum, a first maximum and a final maximum salary. In most cases it defines professional improvement as the taking with passing credit of educational courses which carry credit toward a college degree. In some cases it requires that the courses shall be in the particular field in which the teacher is working, that is, in the field of elementary education for the elementary teacher, etc. In some cases the requirement goes so far as not to recognize, for purposes of meeting the salary schedule requirements, courses in the history of education if taken by primary-grade teachers.

It is a well-established fact that in many school systems the great majority of teachers are professionally minded and that for those teachers rules and regulations regarding salary increases are not necessary in order to insure a proper amount of professional improvement. But an argument in favor of the requirements is that if no requirements exist there will be some teachers who will not improve themselves professionally but will nevertheless receive all the advantages of automatic salary increases which the more professionally minded teachers receive. A common argument is that it is necessary for the welfare of the school system and in justice to the other teachers that this group of teachers be compelled to improve themselves professionally in order to benefit by the salary increases.

The whole plan of basing salary increases upon the taking of professional improvement courses, however it may vary in details in different localities, is subject to serious objections. How about the coercion and restriction of the large group of teachers who would and do pursue educational courses regardless of salary increases? How much real professional improvement results from a course taken under compulsion, and under the threat of punishment by loss of a salary increase unless it is taken in accordance with superimposed restrictions which limit the teacher's freedom of choice? There is every reason to believe that Thorndike's laws of learning[1] apply in this situation just as much as they do in a fifth grade, and probably more so because the mature mind resents interference and authoritative dictation more than the child mind does. Certainly there is no great degree of spontaneous and enthusiastic "readiness" in the situation. The teacher's application to the task of learning will very likely be leveled at the passing requirement. The "effect" will consist of as much resentment as satisfaction. The result will be measurable only in terms of points of credit and of requirements satisfied. The amount of *professional* improvement is liable to be negative.

What about the effect of such procedure upon the originality, initiative and professional self-respect of the teacher? The dean of an eastern university has stated that many teachers who take courses to meet the requirements of salary schedules deliberately seek easy courses having the largest number of points, and that their main purpose is to meet the requirements with the least amount of work possible.

What about the effect of the compulsory professional improvement plan upon educational democracy, group-directed cooperation and inspirational leadership in the school system? Educational administration and supervision through the application of rules and regulations and superimposed authority never have produced good results, and there is no very good

[1] Readiness, exercise and effect.

reason in the evidence at hand to expect that they will do so in the case of professional improvement of teachers.

It is doubtful whether the acquiring of a certain number of points of credit through coercion represents professional *improvement,* but even if the taking of professional courses while in service does represent professional improvement, compulsion is not necessary. Common sense, as well as an understanding of the laws of learning, tells us that, other things being equal, a person will do better the thing he wants to do, and over which he exercises freedom of choice, than he will do something else. He will also do better the thing he wants to do if coercion is absent. In Massachusetts the per cent. of teachers who took professional courses in service in 1927 was greater in a city in which there were no school board requirements than in any other Massachusetts city. In Revere 271 teachers (91 per cent.) took professional improvement courses, and most of those who did not were young teachers in their first year of teaching. These courses were sponsored by the Principals Club and the Teachers Club. Enrolment was entirely voluntary. No salary increases were involved. The only coercion was the coercion of individual and group pride in achievement.

W. C. McGinnis

SPECIAL CORRESPONDENCE

SOME EDUCATIONAL MOVEMENTS IN MEXICO

Recent years have seen a decided movement forward in popular education in Mexico, particularly in the rural districts. It is in these sections of Mexico that the federal government has sought to supplement the educational activities of the states. The problems of rural education, always somewhat more difficult of solution than those of the cities, are here made especially difficult by the frequent lack of adequate communications and by the variety of population. In several sections the so-called "indigenous races"—that is to say, the original population, largely untouched by Spanish influence, and with little or no admixture of European blood—present a very definite difficulty in the educational program. In some states there are a number of these tribes, each speaking its own language. It is in these sections that the federal government has sought to found schools, teaching not only children but adults, and offering, in addition to the elements of a literary education, those vocational subjects most useful to the people in their present situation. While this program of rural education was to some extent projected during the days of the Madero government, it has been carried into effect in the administration of President Calles, recently ended. The new government announces its purpose of carrying forward these educational activities, and plans are under way for the founding of five hundred new rural schools by the federal government in the near future.

The establishment of open-air schools for certain classes of children, especially the physically weak, is not an altogether new thing, but what amounts practically to a new departure in educational work has been initiated during the administration of President Calles in the establishment of open-air schools for all the children of certain school districts in the City of Mexico. These schools are of advantage particularly for the children of the more congested districts. One factor of importance, of course, is the unusual climate of Mexico City, which makes it possible for children to study in the open air, without any considerable discomfort, at all seasons of the year. Just a few days before the close of President Calles's administration, he, in company with various other persons prominent in the educational life of the nation, was present at the opening of the ninth open-air school in the City of Mexico. All these schools were founded during his administration. The school is admirably equipped, the grounds and buildings are beautifully arranged, and contain room for about four hundred pupils.

The present educational plans for the nation, as recently announced, include the use of the theater as a practical means of instruction. Particularly in the rural sections, it is planned to teach hygiene, care of the home and related subjects by means of plays prepared specifically for this purpose. The people of the rural sections will take part in the presentation of these plays, being thus active learners of the lessons it is desired to teach.

The Union Theological Seminary of Mexico recently closed the twelfth year of its work, graduating nine young men, who will at once go out to take their places as pastors in the Evangelical churches of the country. The seminary, as its name indicates, is a cooperative enterprise, carried on by seven Protestant denominations in Mexico. The cooperating bodies are the two Methodist churches, the two Presbyterian, the Disciples, the Congregational and the Friends. During its history the seminary has graduated forty-three young men, nearly all of whom are now in the ministry or in other forms of religious or educational work. Many other students have attended for a limited time. In common with similar institutions in other countries, the seminary is an expression of the conviction that a closer measure of cooperation is desirable as between the educational agencies of the several churches.

Milton C. Davis

Evangelical Seminary of Mexico,
Mexico City

A CONFERENCE ON THE HISTORY OF THE TRANS-MISSISSIPPI WEST

A conference on the history of the Trans-Mississippi West—the first of its kind to be held—will be sponsored by the University of Colorado, from June 18 to 21.

Matters concerning the history of the part of the United States that lies west of the Mississippi River will be discussed at the three-day conference, which will be conducted in the form of round table discussions in the morning sessions and the reading and discussion of papers in the afternoons. Leading historians of the west will participate in the conference.

The idea of such a meeting originated with Dean F. B. R. Hellems, of the College of Arts and Sciences, who submitted it to Professor James F. Willard, head of the department of history. Dr. Willard has conducted all arrangements for speakers and subjects, assisted by Professor Colin B. Goodykoontz.

The conference has as its purpose the stimulation of interest in the history of the Trans-Mississippi West, and the exchange of ideas and points of view regarding such a field. Dr. Willard has secured as leaders of round table discussions and writers of papers men who are outstanding in their lines, historians who are authorities on the topics assigned them.

Outstanding among the guests will be Frederick Jackson Turner, late of Harvard, now retired. It was Dr. Turner who, with a paper on "The Significance of the Frontier," published in the report of the American Historical Association for 1893, started interest in a movement which was to revolutionize the history of the west—and which, incidentally, started the movement which results in this conference.

Dr. Turner will preside at one of the meetings, and be present at all of them. As the dean of historians who have written on the Trans-Mississippi West, he is the author of "The Frontier in American History," "The Rise of the New West," and other books and papers. He was with the University of Wisconsin before going to Harvard.

A public address by Professor Herbert E. Bolton, of the University of California, on the evening of June 20, is one of the high spots of the conference. He will talk on "Defensive Spanish Expansion and the Significance of the Borderlands."

Round table discussions will be held each morning. Topics, with the men who will lead them, are:

"The Problems of Adequate Historical Collections," to be led by Dr. Solon J. Buck, superintendent of the Minnesota Historical Society.

"The Industrial Revolution and the Great Plains," Professor W. P. Webb, University of Texas.

"The West in Foreign Relations," Professor Eugene C. Barker, University of Texas.

"Geographic Influences," Professor Carl Sauer, University of California.

"Finance and the Frontier," Professor Frederick L. Paxson, University of Wisconsin.

"The Problems of an Agricultural Survey for a Western State," Dr. Joseph Schafer, superintendent of the Wisconsin State Historical Society.

"Western Missions," papers by Professor Colin B. Goodykoontz, University of Colorado; Professor G. J. Garraghan, S. J., St. Louis University, and Professor Archer B. Hulbert, Colorado College.

Afternoon sessions will include reading of papers on topics relating to the following major subjects:

"Western Transportation," papers by Professor Louis Pelzer, University of Iowa; Dr. LeRoy Hafen, historian and curator of the Colorado State Historical Society, and Professor John C. Parish, University of California at Los Angeles.

"The West in American Literature," papers by Professor Lucy L. Hazard, Mills College, Oakland, California, and others.

About fifty persons are expected to attend the conference, including fifteen historians who will take active part in the program, fifteen or twenty guests from other schools and possibly twenty history teachers and advanced students attending summer school.

University of Colorado A. T. W.

QUOTATIONS

PROGRESSIVE EDUCATION IN SPAIN

It has often happened that a great human activity may be carried on in comparative obscurity and yet perform an invaluable service to the people of the area in which it works. Such is the accomplishment of the *Junta para Ampliación de Estudios* of Madrid. The *Junta* is made up of the most distinguished scholars of Spain in all fields of scholarship whose sole interest is in learning and its advancement. Its president is the great biologist, Santiago Ramón y Cajal, and its chief administrator is that educational genius, José Castillejo, who has done so much for the cause of educational progress in Spain. One member of the body is Doña María de Maeztu, the very soul of the movement in favor of higher education for women in Spain. She presides over a splendid institution, the International Institute for Girls in Spain, which houses a fine body of young women, some of them from the highest families of the country. Señorita de Maeztu is hopeful in the near future to transform her school to a college on the model of the women's colleges in the United States.

This splendid body of scholars is really the hope of higher education in Spain. With most inadequate resources it began twenty years ago to train a small body of young men in modern methods of scientific research in natural sciences and the humanities and it accomplished so much that when five years later the attention of the International Education Board was drawn to its work, the board gladly made an allotment of funds for the establishment of excellent laboratories in biology, chemistry and physics in the outskirts of Madrid. To these laboratories a carefully selected group of enthusiastic research students has been drawn who live in dormitories attached to the laboratories. Although a government organization, the *Junta* is a self-governing body, made up of centers devoted to higher investigation for post-university students. These centers are under the direction of the best university professors, and the most able students pursue their investigations there. The *Junta* sends students to study abroad, and conducts various educational centers, such as the *Residencias de Estudiantes,* and a model secondary school, the Instituto-Escuela. The young scholars trained in these research centers in increasing numbers are occupying the chairs in the universities. The Spanish university is thus gradually being regenerated, and time and continuity in these efforts will in all probability put it on a plane with the universities of western and central Europe. Few enterprises could be more gratifying to believers in the cooperative effort of private individuals to accomplish a great purpose than the *Junta.* It is a pleasure to mention that an organization was formed several years ago to develop closer cultural relations between Spain and the United States, *viz.,* the Instituto de las Españas which is the sister organization to the *Junta* in Madrid. The instituto has already done a splendid piece of work in developing an interest in Spanish culture in the United States. The *Junta* selects a distinguished scholar each year to lecture at our institutions of higher education under the auspices of the instituto. The instituto also publishes annually two or more volumes dealing with subjects of Spanish interest and has as its organ the *Revista de Estudios Hispánicos.* Information about the activities of the instituto and membership in it will be gladly furnished by the Institute of International Education.—*Stephen P. Duggan, in The News Bulletin of the Institute of International Education.*

REPORTS

FOREIGN HOLIDAY COURSES

The following summary of various holiday courses to be offered in Europe during the coming summer is given in the *London Times Educational Supplement*.

Courses are to be held at the Sorbonne, including a six-weeks' course in French language and literature from July 1 to August 10; an advanced course in French literature, including a study of "The French Contemporary Novel," "French Contemporary Drama," and a course in style. From July 29 to August 10 there will be afternoon lectures on French politics and administration, the rôle of sociology in contemporary French thought, France after the war, and the educational problems of modern France. On Saturdays there will be all-day excursions to Chartres, Chantilly, Senlis, Fontainebleau, Chateau-Thierry and other places. From August 12 to August 21 those who wish can join a conducted tour through Touraine to Saint-Malo and Dinard, returning to Paris by way of Bayeux, Caen, Lisieux and Rouen. Full particulars can be had from M. Henri Goy, Bureau des Renseignements, Sorbonne, Paris. The "Cours de Civilisation-française" for foreign students will as usual continue throughout the year; students can enter at the beginning of any month. October will be devoted to the study of French civilization after the war.

The Guild of the British Institute in Paris (6, rue de la Sorbonne) announces holiday courses to be held from July 1 to July 27, and from August 2 to August 28. Instruction in French is given every morning followed by a lecture, the students being divided into two grades according to their knowledge of the language. The afternoons are free. Thursdays are given up to excursions. The lecturers will treat the following subjects: French drama during the last 25 years; contemporary French poetry and fiction; "La vie mondaine pendant un siècle français"; "La France d'aujourd'hui"; the literary geography of France. Excursions will be arranged if desired to Reims, Port-Royal, Soissons, Compiegne, Fontainebleau, Maintenon, Rambouillet and other places within easy reach of Paris. No courses are arranged for September, but students can have private lessons if they wish. The regular courses of the institute will recommence on October 11. The guild of the institute undertakes to place students in French families.

The holiday courses at the University of Lausanne begin on July 11, and will be held in three series, from July 11 to July 24, from July 25 to August 7 and from August 8 to August 21. In addition to classes in French language, literature and phonetics, there will be lectures on French-Swiss literature of to-day, and on contemporary Swiss politics and administration. Every Wednesday morning there will be lantern lectures, concerts and recitals, and a visit to some point of interest in Lausanne. Two series of excursions have been arranged; one for those who are not alpinists and do not wish to climb and others for those who wish to make acquaintance with the heights. For the former there will be excursions to the Rhone Valley, the Gruyère and the Alps of Vaud and Valais, Fribourg and Berne; the more active can join parties and climb the Dents Blanches de Champéry, the Dents du Midi and the Grand Muveran, the Diablerets, the Tour Sallière, the Pointe d'Orny, or the Aiguille du Tour. From August 21 to August 25 a visit has been arranged to Zermatt. A second course, in most respects similar to the first, is being arranged to take place from September 2 to October 12.

The University of Strasbourg will hold a holiday course from July 1 to the end of September in its Institute of Modern French Studies, an organization of the Faculty of Letters intended to promote the knowledge of the French language, of the history, literature and art of France, and of contemporary French civilization. Particulars can be had from the Bureau des Renseignements pour les Étudiants étrangers, Université de Strasbourg, France, with a list of houses offering accommodation for students, including the Foyer Universitaire, a foundation of the university. The Faculty of

Letters will also organize during the holidays a course of practical and literary German.

A holiday course for foreign students is being arranged at Saint-Servan-sur-Mer, near Saint-Malo, by the University of Rennes, under the auspices of the Alliance Française. This will include an elementary course for beginners, as well as intermediate and advanced courses, conversation classes and lectures which are open to all students capable of following them. The courses are divided into three fortnights: July 18 to July 31, August 1 to August 15 and August 16 to August 31, each of which can be taken separately if desired. The lecturers in the advanced course include M. Wolf, formerly reader in French in the University of Cambridge and now of the University of Rennes, M. Rebillon, of the University of Rennes, who will lecture on the history and geography of Brittany, and others. Application for further information should be made to M. Louis, professeur au Collège de Saint-Servan-sur-Mer.

The Royal Italian University for Foreigners at Perugia, founded by the Italian government in 1925 to make Italy better known to foreign students, will be open for a summer session from July to October, and offers courses in the history of Italian institutions, Italian literature, the history of art, Italian history, Italian thought throughout the centuries and other subjects. An elementary course leads up to a certificate of proficiency in the Italian language and an advanced course to a diploma qualifying the holder to teach Italian abroad. Foreigners are admitted to the courses without any formalities as to previous studies and are entitled to special privileges in regard to accommodation, railroad fares and passports, besides being given free entrance to picture galleries and museums. The opening ceremony of the summer session will be held on June 30, when the Minister of Education will give an inaugural address. Excursions will be organized to Assisi and other places in the neighborhood. Detailed information can be had from the Regia Università Italiana per Stranieri, Palazzo Gallenga, Perugia, Italy.

The Spanish Ministry of Public instruction announces summer courses for foreign students to be held in Madrid from July 11 to August 7. Lectures will be given on grammar, phonetics, literature, history, art and geography, and students will be grouped into classes of not more than ten for practical work. Special courses are offered on the Spanish novel, Spanish life and customs, contemporary literature, popular music and commercial Spanish. Visits will be arranged to the principal art collections and museums of Madrid and to the Royal Palace, and excursions to Toledo, Segovia and other places of interest in the neighborhood. Foreign students can also take an autumn course from October 7 to December 14, or a winter course from January 7 to March 20. Particulars can be had from the Secretario de los Cursos para extranjeros, Centro de Estudios Históricos, Almagro 26, Madrid.

The Touraine Institute for the Study of the French Language will hold vacation courses from July to September for the study of the French language and of the region in which Touraine is situated. Inquiries may be made of M. le Directeur de l'Institut de Touraine, 1, rue de la Grandière, Tours.

SOCIETIES AND MEETINGS

THE SPRING MEETING OF THE COLLEGE ENTRANCE EXAMINATION BOARD

Examinations in English, in two different aspects, received a large share of the time and thought of the College Entrance Examination Board at its spring meeting, held on April 10 at Columbia University. The first action taken was to authorize experimentally an examination in English for foreign students to be conducted in April, 1930, at about twenty centers in foreign countries. The purpose is to ascertain the command of English of candidates for carrying on work in American colleges and universities, in accordance with petitions presented to the board by the American Association of Collegiate Registrars and other bodies.

As authorized by Professor Adam Leroy Jones, chairman of the committee, the new examination will include the following:

1. One-paragraph passages averaging about 150 words. (*a*) Narrative English of distinct simplicity. (*b*) Historical, topical or journalistic English with greater difficulties in vocabulary and structure. (*c*) A passage of some critical weight on a matter of specific social import, of about 100 words. (*d*) A passage of scientific prose, of about 100 words.

2. A passage of three to four hundred words of some difficulty, dealing with debatable or conditioned ideas.

Questions on the above passages are to be directed at the student's understanding of their substance.

3. (*a*) Transcription of a passage from dictation. (*b*) A dictated long passage to be reproduced in substance in writing.

4. An oral test to determine fluency, responsiveness, rapidity, articulation, enunciation, command of construction, of connectives, usable vocabulary and the use of idiom.

5. A composition of 250 to 300 words to be written within a period of one and one half hours, the subject to be selected from a list of topics.

* * *

Grades should be given not only in percentages but also in terms of relative numerical standing and percentiles for all the applicants from the country in question. It seems to the committee that this would be particularly important with regard to students whose language differs radically from English, as does Chinese or Japanese.

It was agreed that a foreign student coming to the United States for research or advanced work does not need to be as proficient in speaking English as a student starting upon undergraduate courses. As with the comprehensive examinations of the board, the papers written by foreign candidates will be sent to the colleges and universities they desire to enter. The fee is to be $10.00.

The second important matter relating to English was the decision of the board to appoint a commission to reconsider "the principles that underlie the setting and reading of the comprehensive examination in English." This action was in consequence of an application to the board by the School and College Conference on English, a body composed of representatives of Bryn Mawr, Mount Holyoke, Smith, Vassar and Wellesley Colleges, of ten private schools and of ten public high schools. In reporting for the board's committee on examination ratings, Dr. Wilson Farrand emphasized that a careful study of the reading and marking of the comprehensive examination in English given in June, 1928, had been made by a committee of the following experienced readers: Mr. A. W. Leonard, Phillips Academy, Andover, *chairman;* Professor H. W. Herrington, Syracuse University, and Professor Alice D. Snyder, Vassar College. This committee approved the paper "on grounds of fairness, inclusiveness, opportunity offered to brilliant students," but concluded that it would be wise to consider "the whole question of the framing of the examination papers and the conduct of the reading in order that both may conform more closely to changing conditions in the teaching of English."

Upon motion of Professor A. N. Corwin, chairman of the committee of review, Secretary Thomas A. Fiske was instructed to take up with the Modern Language Association and sectional associations the desirability of revising the present requirements in modern foreign languages, particularly as to the lists of books recommended for reading.

The board passed certain changes in the constitution and by-laws, as recommended by the executive committee. Professor H. W. Tyler, chairman, explained that the main purpose of the amendments was condensation. Under the new provisions the board voted to receive five representatives of the New England Association of Colleges and Secondary Schools, five representatives of the Association of Colleges and Secondary Schools of the Middle States and Maryland, and one representative of the North Central Association of Colleges and Secondary Schools.

The Scholastic Aptitude Test of the board is being returned to its former date of Saturday morning in the examination schedule for 1930, according to the report of the committee on examination schedule, of which President Ellen F. Pendleton is chairman. Secretary Fiske told of the conflict of the Wednesday date this year with the New York Regents' examinations. Out of this statement there grew a long discussion of the unfortunate general conflict of the college board and regents schedules, which both parties concerned lament but for which there has thus far seemed no solution. Upon motion of Dean Howes and Professor Babbitt, the board passed a resolution expressing its earnest hope that some arrangement may be possible whereby the dates will not conflict.

Secretary Fiske distributed specimen copies of the new style of answer book to be used next June whereby the anonymity of the candidate and his school will be preserved while the readers are marking the answers.

The meeting was in charge of Chairman Henry A. Pennypacker.

RAYMOND WALTERS

SWARTHMORE COLLEGE

EDUCATIONAL RESEARCH AND STATISTICS

A STUDY OF PARENT, TEACHER AND STUDENT COOPERATION IN HIGH SCHOOL

THE following study of school and home relations was made in a high school located in an exclusive suburb of a large metropolitan city. The facts themselves are probably of little actual value except for the institution concerned, but the method of procedure and the accompanying results are offered here as a suggestion which might be adopted elsewhere. The writer does not presume to infer that similar studies have not been made in other places but wishes to add this as one more contribution to the many attempts at increasing understanding between the homes from which come American adolescent boys and girls and the schools which are so very important in influencing those plastic years between childhood and adulthood.

The community with which this present study is concerned is a purely residential district and is free from the conditions of a manufacturing environment. The inhabitants are engaged largely in big business projects in the nearby city and so find this a congenial place for living. They give much attention to landscaping and pride themselves on the great beauty of the place. This attention is not confined to general improvement but is also directed to the artistic treatment of the home. Herein are provided most things that money can buy. Moreover, since the home routine is largely in the hands of competent and well-trained servants, the young folks of the community are practically freed from all such responsibility.

As might be expected, much emphasis is placed on purely social activities. The social rank of these people is in keeping with their financial status. Their social program is quite extensive and very well planned. It includes not only functions which are especially adapted to the older members of the community but also those specifically arranged for the younger set. Interestingly enough, the high school plays a minor rôle in the social program; the church has a larger influence in directing the trend of the social life. However, the major social influences are very definitely other community organizations. The folks have learned to use their leisure in many ways. Their interests carry them to the enjoyment of the best talent of the stage, music, art and science. Although to the outsider this group may seem to represent a rather exclusive individualism, yet it also exhibits a very desirable interest in civic problems.

This brief description of the community gives the reader a picture of the social and economic background of the majority of the students who constitute the personnel of the high school. The boys and girls are allowed much initiative in their homes, which also leads to a very definite individualism. Their attitude is for the most part healthy and desirable. The students are responsive to real challenge, are interested in the best and are willing to give and take on most issues. Mentally they are above the average, and with the extra leisure time at their command should make excellent student material. However, much of this ability and opportunity is not directed to study but is used for social dissipation.

All these factors have combined to put the high school at the time of this study in an unstable condition. There seemed to be little school spirit, due largely to the lack of any unified effort towards school activities. Year after year, many of the students have left the school, not because of a lack of confidence in its academic status but rather because attendance at a private school seemed to be a little more "exclusive." It might be noted here that the teaching corps of the high school is on a very high intellectual level. A large proportion of the faculty hold higher degrees or are working toward them.

In an attempt to offset the existing situation and to bring about better understanding and cooperation among the students, parents and teachers, appropriate questionaries were submitted to the members of each of the three groups for their consideration. A brief presentation of the data follows.

Student Questionary and Results

This questionary was presented to 548 students with directions that they read each question carefully, grasp its meaning and then answer it honestly.

Assignments

	Results Yes	No
Do you write your daily assignments in each class?	411	137
Do you understand your assignment?	428	78
Do you prepare first the subject you like best?	220	328
Do you consult the teacher if you do not understand the assignment?	109	429
Do you think your lesson assignments too long?	329	219

		Minutes	
How many minutes do you think that you need to spend in the preparation of each subject?	Language	25	30*
	Mathematics	50	45
	History	25	30
	Commercial	30	40
	Science	45	50
	English	25	30

* How much time do you spend on each subject?

Home Work

What time of the day do you do the most of your studying?	Study hall	85
	Afternoon	165
	Evening	298
Where do you study at home?	Room—Alone	398
	Room—Others	135
How much help do you obtain in your lesson preparation?	None	259
	Little	277
	Much	12
From whom do you obtain this help?	Parents	75
	Teachers	28
	Pupils	6

	Yes	No
Do your parents see or hear your homework?	159	359

Reactions to Conditions

	Yes	No
Do you have difficulty in understanding meaning of questions put to you in class?	176	372
Do you realize that your home work is not always fully and properly prepared?	384	164
Have you ever been shown the proper way to study your lessons?	390	158
Do you consider high-school education worth while?	548	0

Why do you think that you are not getting a higher mark?

Unable to hear well	0	Unable to see well	2
Long lessons	30	Lack of attention	60
Dislike of teacher	18	Confusion in class	20
Dislike of subject	30	Laziness	181
Unable to grasp subject	44	Sickness or absence	4
Outside school work	8	Sports, etc.	0

If your marks are not satisfactory what do you do about it?

Consult teacher	92	Forget about it	23
Become discouraged	29	Whine about it	2
Work harder	182	Criticize unjustly	12

Teachers' Questionary and Data

The following questions were given to the twenty-three teachers of the junior and senior high school, and the indicated results were obtained.

Assignment

When do you make assignments?	Beginning of period	14
	Middle	4
	End	5

	Yes	No
If your assignment is at the end are you always justified in so doing?	14	6
Have you ever experimented in your own class as to the logical time for the assignment?	13	10
Is your assignment clear and definite?	16	7
Do you provide for individual differences?	13	10
Do you require assignments to be written?	18	5
Do you keep a daily record of all assignments?	18	3
Do you indicate the high lights and pitfalls?	19	1

How much time do you expect pupils to put on assignments? .... 25–45 min.

Discipline

	Yes	No
Do you waste time haranguing your class?	1	17
Do you send pupils out of class?	1	15
Do you believe in harsh, coercive measures as primary functions of good discipline?	1	19
Is your recitation hampered by lack of discipline?	1	19
Do you endeavor to use indirect control?	19	1
Do you use group reaction as a disciplinary force?	12	9

Which type of difficult pupils is most common to your class?

Haughty	0	Rebellious	0
Irresponsible	20	Vicious	0
Stubborn	2	Self-complacent	12
Quick-tempered	0		

Examination and Marks

Are your marks based on:

Uniformity	6	Impartiality	17
Precision	5	Purpose of the course	13
Objectivity	10		

What form of exams do you favor?

True-false	6	Frequent ten-minute tests	11
Oral	5		
Written lessons	10	Combination of tests	11

How much do you rate your exams?

1/3 of grade 23

Which of the following characteristics of a mark do you stress?

Written tests	8	Daily rating	19
		Teacher's judgment	9

Do you include the following in your marks?

Effort	23	Attendance	8
Interest	18	Punctuality	5
Conduct	11		

Do you recognize the normal curve of distribution as a marking scale? .... Yes, 23

Home Work

	Yes	No
Do the boys do their home work?	15	4
Do the girls do their home work?	17	6
Do you check whether or not the pupils do it?	17	3
Are you available for afternoon make-up work?	19	1
Do you believe that extra drill after school accomplishes its purpose?	9	14
Do you coerce pupils to do their home work?	18	2
Do you insist upon neatness, form and legibility in written home work?	20	3

Personal Relations

What personal elements do you allow to enter into your relationships with students?

The answers included:

Sympathy	Encouragement
Love	Inspiration
Friendship	Interest
Square deal	Praise

	Yes	No
Is the respect of your students worth winning?	20	0
Do you endeavor to function as a real counselor?	22	1

Recitation

Which of the characteristics of a recitation do you stress?

Strict attention	21	Individual answer	23
Clear enunciation	11	Confidence	7
Audible tones	18	Courtesy	19
Correct posture	19	Initiative	20

Which type of recitation do you use most?

Question and answer	18	Socialized	8
		Project	6
Supervised study	8	Formal	2

Which of the following factors do you consider stifles responses most?

Lack of preparation	16	Sarcasm and ridicule	12
Lack of praise	1	Lack of recognition	2
Lack of self-reliance	6		

Do your responses indicate that:

Lesson was well planned	8	Assignments had been made correctly	13
		Teacher did not monopolize time	5

	Yes	No
Do you allow unsolicited answers?	0	17
Do you have a definite goal in each recitation which you attempt to attain?	22	1

Administrative Attitude

Do you realize that failure to have reports in on time slows up administrative efficiency?	23	0
Are you always willing to serve on committees and do other extra-curricular requirements?	22	1
Do you endeavor to acquaint yourself with the machinery of administration?	22	1

Do you think that the teacher's sole duty lies in the classroom?	0	23
Do you believe the statement, "Every teacher should be a good administrator?"	15	4

How much time per week do you spend on extra classroom activities?

Range 1 to 15 hours

PARENTS' QUESTIONARY AND DATA

To the parents was sent the following questionary, to which were received 253 replies as indicated below.

To parents of pupils of Memorial High School: We are making a very serious attempt to improve the scholarship in the high school. As a working basis, a questionary has been submitted to the pupils and teachers. In order to obtain all the evidence desired we earnestly request your cooperation in answering the following:

	Min.	No.	Min.	No.
How many minutes does your child spend on the average each school day in home study?	0	10	90	57
	30	48	120	46
	60	77	150	14

	Yes	No
Does your child study alone?	112	140
Do you occasionally see his prepared homework?	208	44
Do you understand that a red mark on a report card means a failure?	197	0
What reasons does your child give if he fails in a subject? None	164	
Does your child attend any of the following on school nights?		
Motion pictures	81	140
Dances, parties	11	210
Clubs	8	213
Other amusements	14	207

Does this happen, occasionally 221; often 0.

There are four legal excuses recognized by the state for absence from school:
(1) Personal sickness.
(2) Sickness in the family requiring the services of the child for a day or two until other help may be secured.
(3) Weather conditions that make it unsafe for the child to be out.
(4) Impassable roads.

Do you permit your child to be absent from school for other reasons?	2	246

CONCLUSIONS

It will be readily recognized that these facts have no absolute value, and possibly little relative value. However, the study had a profound influence upon the student body, as it brought to a focus of attention that type of thinking which is so vital to a successful attitude. It is the writer's belief that a study of this kind is well worth while in any community because of the attention which is focused upon the various school problems. It is his further belief that any effort which will cause one to take stock is usually productive for all concerned.

A detailed analysis might have been given but the writer will content himself with a brief statement of possible outcomes.

Outcomes for parents:
(1) It focused attention of the parents upon the study habits of the student.
(2) It brought to the parents' attention the school law pertaining to absence in a way which was most forceful yet indirect.
(3) It gave the parents suggestions for methods of checking up on the study of their boy or girl.

Outcomes for teachers:
(1) It caused a valuable introspection on the part of each faculty member.
(2) It developed valuable discussion on the part of the faculty upon the questions involved in the questionary.
(3) It placed before them a definite program which was suggestive of desirable attitudes and practices.
(4) It enabled each to compare his methods and practices with those of the group as a whole.
(5) It gave a wealth of material for discussion in faculty meetings.

Outcomes for students:
(1) It presented to the students the idea that the school was interested in them.
(2) It helped the student to feel that the school was for him and thereby increased his devotion and loyalty for it.
(3) It brought to the student ways and means through the medium of suggestion.
(4) It helped the student better to understand teacher attitudes, student-teacher relationships and student-student responsibility.

L. D. CROW

INSTITUTE OF EDUCATION,
NEW YORK UNIVERSITY

SCHOOL AND SOCIETY

EDITED BY J. McKEEN CATTELL

WITH WHICH IS COMBINED THE

EDUCATIONAL REVIEW

EDITED BY WILLIAM McANDREW

Volume XXIX | SATURDAY, MAY 4, 1929 | Number 749

WHAT A TEACHER SHOULD EXPECT FROM THE SCHOOL[1]

By FRANK PIERREPONT GRAVES

PRESIDENT OF THE UNIVERSITY OF THE STATE OF NEW YORK AND STATE COMMISSIONER OF EDUCATION

"No man is so unhappy as one who has had his dreams come true," declared Robert Louis Stevenson. If one may judge by the vast number of unsolved problems and the sad state of teacher training depicted by some of the preceding speakers this morning, we are none of us in imminent danger of being plunged into the depths of woe from such a cause. Moreover the list of complaints uttered might have been indefinitely extended, had these Jeremiahs chosen to consult the detailed analysis made in the last chapter of the teacher-training section of the Seventh Yearbook just issued by this department. It is rather appalling to find that there is so much that is wrong in teacher training and so many things about which we know so little. But Stevenson again tells us that "to travel hopefully is better than to arrive," and we may well rejoice that there are still so many imperfections in the training of teachers to challenge our best efforts and keep us from falling into smug complacency. To quote van Dyke: "It is resistance that puts us on our mettle; it is the conquest of reluctant stuff that educates the worker."

[1] Address before a general session, Department of Superintendence, Cleveland, February 27, 1929.

Hence by way of a post-mortem, which I have been requested to perform upon the operations of the previous doctors before proceeding to my own bit of diagnosis, let us examine some of the outstanding problems in the preparation of teachers—elementary and secondary, rural and urban. In this investigation let us first tackle our difficulties at the source. Selection of the raw material out of which teachers are to be made has never been altogether countenanced or given sufficient attention. We have in the past tended to act as if educational institutions supported by public moneys must of necessity be open to all who desire to enroll. The principle of selection in terms of fitness for the teaching profession has either not dawned upon us or not been widely approved. Possibly the main reason for this is that we have as yet established no thoroughly tested prognosis of fitness. We agree in general that scholastic achievement, mental ability, physical fitness, character, personality, interest and aptitude are all important factors in making a selection of students, but we widely dissent as to the relative values of these qualifications, and no one can tell with certainty whether each factor plays an equally important part in teaching service of the different types. Happily, many leaders in teacher training are at length making pioneer studies in this field, but such efforts should not be limited to the specialists. The public school people should help, especially as they are more affected than the teacher-training institutions, and they should endeavor to do this not through mere recrimination and guesswork, but fair-minded and constructive coöperation in scientific investigations.

After the students have been selected, the next question we have to consider is the choice of a faculty to train them. This morning we have witnessed the usual assertions as to the relative importance of university degrees and public school experience. If teacher trainers unduly stress the one and school administrators the other, that is simply because the professors are themselves likely to be short in experience and the superintendents in degrees and education, and it is difficult to understand the value of that which you do not yourself possess. It is, of course, easy to find a doctor of philosophy who knows no more about public education than he unconsciously absorbed as a pupil in the elementary and high schools, but it is also not difficult to discover public school people who have little knowledge beyond the subject-matter they are inflicting upon others by means of apprenticeship instruction. Heaven deliver us from both the pure theorist and the pure empiric! We should insist upon an even balance between the two types of qualifications. We need valuable experience and sound scholarship alike in those who are to become our teachers of teachers.

Closely related to this problem of the qualifications necessary for teacher training is one which all the speakers have touched upon in discussing the curriculum. It has reasonably been urged that graduates of teacher-training institutions should possess a mastery of the subject-matter they are required to teach in the public schools, but by what token is it to be assumed that because a man has attained the doctorate in philosophy he will be so stupid as not to realize this?

On the other hand, control of the materials to be taught should never lead the teacher trainer into a mere review of subject-matter and similar barrenness of procedure, such as has often occurred when the training instructor was without college education. The teacher's knowledge must be far wider than mere attainments in the field of knowledge to be taught his pupils. Teacher training falls far short of its obligations if it stops with the required content and necessary teaching skill. The crying need in our training work to-day is for the development of judgment and the determination of why this or that should be taught and this or that method be used. Nothing short of a miracle will enable the instructor to develop this power in the embryonic teacher when he has not himself been trained beyond the subject-matter of the course and has not acquired habits of honest inquiry through university training, even if taking this training should involve him in the pernicious act of receiving an advanced degree.

Thus far we have dealt with the pre-service education of the teacher in the training institution, but the in-service education that he should receive after graduation is of fully as much importance. The teacher-training institutions have hitherto concerned themselves almost entirely with the pre-service education, and the public systems with that in service, but I have been gratified to note the firm belief expressed in the addresses this morning that the public schools and teacher-training institutions both have direct obligations for pre-service and in-service education alike, and that there must be an increasing amount of coordination in defining these obligations and meeting them honestly and effectively. As the schoolboy declared in an examination: "Parallel lines are the same distance apart all the way and do not meet unless you bend them." The obligations of the public school and of the training school certainly are parallel from the point of view of ends sought, and it appears at times as if some bending on either side might be wholesome and welcome.

This brings me naturally to the contribution I am personally expected to make to this discussion—"What Should a Teacher Expect in the Way of Help, Guidance and Professional Stimulus from the School Engaging His Services?" In other words, what sort of opportunity should be granted him in service? In the first place, it should be recognized that his preparation in the teacher-training school was merely the beginning of his education as a teacher. The ordinary course of preparation can not give sufficient time for a complete acquaintance with all the problems of any given type of school service. Even if the arrangement and length of the course provide for fairly adequate training in the theory and methods of the field, there still remains the necessity for acquiring skill in understanding children and using materials and methods effectively in terms of individual needs. Skill is developed by even the most gifted teacher only after long and intelligent application of theory, and the school system has no right to expect maximum performance from the new graduate of a teacher-training institution. This means that the school authorities should always assume the obligation of providing special instruction for the novitiate. The kind and amount of assistance of this sort through supervisors, principals or master teachers will vary from one school to another, but in different forms these opportunities are now being afforded by many wise superintendents throughout the first year or two of the teacher's work. I regret to say that many cities answer this need of their teachers by demanding two years of experience outside before permitting the graduate to teach in their systems, but such cities have shirked their plain duty in the matter. Moreover, this is clearly a case of the old principle that, if you want a thing well done, you would better do it yourself.

A second point to be noted in connection with in-service training is that the new teacher, unless a local resident, is relatively unfamiliar with the character of the community. All American communities would seem to be more or less peculiar; most of them more. The smaller the place the more likely it is to be set in its ways; but each local group, large or small, represents some distinctive customs and habits to which the new teacher must adjust himself, if he is to succeed with his work there. The metropolis of New York has a score of idiosyncrasies—social, economic, political, racial and religious—which the state commissioner of education fails to appreciate fully after eight long years of adjusting. The new teacher will always find it difficult for six months or more to keep off the spiritual corns of the community. The earlier he can be acquainted with the sociological, industrial, commercial and theological mind-sets of the group, the greater will be his advantage in making his work effective. It should be the business of the school officials to recognize this and help the newcomers in the teaching force to understand and adapt themselves to the peculiarities of the locality before there is bitter disappointment, if not actual shipwreck.

Thirdly, the teacher should be constantly impressed in service with the fact that the idealism with which he has been indoctrinated in the teacher-training institution is, after all, the real objective of the public school in which he is working, even when the superintendent seems to be arriving at it in devious ways. A direct effort must be made to keep him from becoming cynical and distrustful, when things occur that he does not understand. The beginning teacher will often be unable to appreciate the ultimate aims of the superintendent and school system because of diverting episodes. No practical school man would for a moment deny that members of the community or even members of the local boards of education are guilty at times of assuming an attitude not in accord with the best professional standards, and it is those occasional lapses that often force the school leaders into a false position. But this is very far from justifying the conclusion that no superintendent can succeed unless he is a truckler and an unmitigated liar, as the new teacher, who does not fully understand the situation, is likely to hold. The teacher should be taught better. If such skepticism as to the ideals of the school is allowed to flourish, it may become an extraordinarily dangerous factor in upsetting the *esprit de corps* of the entire system. The administrator should make it part of the in-service training of teachers to guard against this cynicism in his teachers by explaining his policies and methods to them in season and out.

But a point of more importance to training in service than any I have yet mentioned is that the teacher should be given working conditions that will stimulate him to continued and uninterrupted growth. There are many things connected with our systems of certification and our educational standards for teachers that tend to breed complacency and a feeling of contentment and so seriously retard professional development. We all know many instances of people who hold permanent teachers' certificates who feel that there is little more to be accomplished. It has been said many times that the most important duty of the school superintendent is the selection of teachers. I think it could be said with equal justification that ranking close to the selection of teachers is the duty of providing a constant stimulus for professional improvement. Altogether too often we find that stimulus coming in the way of a salary increment or a financial bonus. Consequently we find summer sessions enrolling many teachers who are primarily concerned in securing a given number of credits, the record of which they may present the following September to the superintendent of schools. In so far as this incentive is in operation it is deplorable. The kind of stimulation which in the long run will constitute a strong and enduring structure is the encouragement in terms of professional idealism which compels the teacher to struggle everlastingly for that equipment which will enable him to do effectively the important work before him. This will come best through a clear understanding on his part of what that work is, its obligations, its opportunities and its privileges.

In this brief review of the case, one can scarcely do more than deal in general statements. If the points made are substantiated by the every-day experiences of school men, then it is safe to conclude that the thesis earlier stated is entirely sound; namely, that public school people and teacher-training people are, after all, carrying in a large measure the same obligations. We must recognize that the public school has a right to expect certain results from the institutions engaged in teacher training. It is equally true that the teacher-training schools have a right to expect intelligent and therefore sympathetic understanding of their problems from the public schools. And it is true above all that graduates of our teacher-training institutions have a right to expect help, both from the institutions which have given them the initial preparation, and from the school system which they serve.

STUDENT TOURIST THIRD CLASS

By Professor H. R. BRUSH
UNIVERSITY OF CALIFORNIA AT LOS ANGELES

It is a matter of common knowledge that immigration restrictions have forced transatlantic steamship lines to find a substitute for the former profitable steerage section. There was conceived the notion of a "white collar steerage" with regular staterooms, steward service and more deck room at a round-trip rate approximately $100 less than the second-class minimum. The accommodations are clean and comfortable enough for persons not disposed to be too exacting or unduly fastidious. The idea was to catch the business of students, teachers and others desirous of visiting Europe as cheaply as possible. Some lines reserve the entire third-class space on certain sailings for students and teachers, and at least one line has demanded that prospective passengers give evidence of belonging to supposedly cultured groups. The development has gone so far that some steamers carry only tourist third class.

The new arrangement has proved astonishingly popular. One tourist bureau announces that its business in this class trebled in 1928 that of 1927. One of the distinguishing features noticed last summer by travelers was the great number of young people, mostly college students and young teachers, who were making the trip. The greater part of these were traveling in groups of some size under leaders who were to accompany them on the Continent. I was in charge of such a party, which included my daughter, my niece and a number of my daughter's sorority sisters. On the steamer on which we had passage the steamship company attempted arrangements for entertainment, instruction and supervision by providing a host and hostess who acted in a semiofficial capacity.

Any new proposition is likely to develop points of weakness and various criticisms must be expected. In August and September of last year some of the metropolitan newspapers contained hectic interviews, given by persons who had made the return trip in tourist third and who voiced their horror at what they claimed to have seen and heard. I came back with my group the last of August, and the day after my arrival in New York I read a lurid account of our ship, its officers and our companions. From the recital one might easily presume that our tourist third class was a sort of combination of Long John Silver's group of carousing pirates and a thoroughgoing Australian aboriginal corroboree. Not only were there extreme statements of a direct nature but also frequent subtle suggestions that would lead a reader of vivid imagination to believe that American college men and women are totally devoid of self-restraint. Attention was focused on the young people; one was left to assume that the elder element was a model of propriety.

Some one has remarked that there are two kinds of hypocrisy: (1) that which makes us out better than we are; (2) that which makes us out worse than we are. I believe that these criticisms of the tourist third must be placed in the latter group. Our particular ship was one of those most severely condemned and it may therefore be permissible to tell my own observations. There were between seven and eight hundred passengers in the tourist third. Probably about a dozen men were consistently "pickled" from Boulogne to New York, and perhaps as many as eight girls were silly fools who tried to follow their bad example. The bar adjoined the dining saloon, and in the evening this carousing element would stay close to the base of supplies until sufficient liquid cargo had been taken aboard, after which there was commonly adjournment to the deck.

Practically any evening one could see various "petting parties" up on the boat deck. This undesirable modern development is, however, not a peculiarity of ocean steamers. I saw nothing but what one may see in the average home town nowadays. In fact, there were practical restraints not found in sedans parked by the roadside. The ship's lights burned on the decks, the officers were about and after midnight the stragglers received fairly urgent invitations to go below.

Some of the "illuminated" would come down between decks, any time from midnight to two in the morning, sing songs and talk maudlin stuff. A couple of times I called to them from my stateroom and once I got up and went out to enforce my objections. I saw no cases of young men going into girls' staterooms, as alleged, at that time of night. Four of the girls whose behavior was most subject to criticism occupied a stateroom next to that of my daughter. Her comment was to the effect that, while men came there during the day, she recalled no case where a man and girl were in the room alone.

Reduced to plain matters of fact, then, the situation on this steamer was that approximately 3 per cent. of the passenger list was composed of young people who did not know how to use the liberty they had, who were boisterous, bad-mannered and generally offensive to the rest of us. The rest of the passengers, young and old, behaved themselves and were frank in their expressions of disgust at the actions of this small group of revelers. And one can understand that the disgusting actions of a few can make such a strong impression on some critical individuals that totally unfair generalizations will result.

The newspaper interviews and magazine accounts—an article of a critical nature has recently appeared in an important monthly—might easily be ignored as being of but passing moment were it not for the discredit that is cast upon an enterprise that has much to commend it. There is no dispute about the educational value of a European tour. Nor is there good reason to deny the success of the student third-class arrangement in affording cheap transportation to those who might not otherwise be enabled to make the trip. We shall all agree that some way should be found to check misbehavior on the part of even the few. Of course, the problem is complicated by the fact that, in recent years, older people are acting with considerably more unconventionality. And we are also reaping the result of that educationalist sentimentality that has set up the Rabelaisian "Do what you want to" as a motto for youth. I have confidence in our youth, but they need to be safeguarded against themselves and aided in preserving their poise. Parents must be made to understand that it is hardly a safe plan to send immature boys and girls to Europe for study or travel unless arrangements are made to look after them. Such competent agencies exist.

The suggestion is made that the parents should accompany them, but that is not always possible. And I do not know that a parent is always a guarantee. I regret to say that the most disgusting case of foolishness on the part of American college girls that came under my observation last summer happened on the boat from Naples to Capri. Two girls carried on a sickening flirtation with a couple of army lieutenants—and their mothers were present and seemed to think it amusing. It has been urged that guides and instructors are not intended to exercise control. I believe this objection is not valid. I had a college group with me and had no hesitancy, either in making suggestions or in seeing that they were carried out. I rarely had need for the suggestions.

Tourist bureaus will have to exercise more care in picking leaders. Not every person who negotiates for a group leadership is qualified by character or personality for undertaking such responsibility. In the long run, it will be to the interest of the bureaus to pick leaders of ability and pay them for their services, making the charge part of the cost of the tour. Moreover, the steamship lines will have to formulate a more definite policy, since many groups are traveling under independent leaders who have no connection with a responsible agency. The host and hostess in the student third class, if general leadership be secured in that way, must be people chosen with great care. On our outward trip last year the host was a former officer of the A. E. F. and the hostess was his wife. The man had the instinct for tactful command and his wife had both force and common sense. They were both on the job; tendencies to obstreperousness were quietly checked. On the return voyage, the host was a young fellow, pleasant enough, but without much personality or physical impressiveness. The hostess, although a dean of women in one of our larger state universities, did not seem to grasp her responsibility. She retired early and let matters take their course.

In addition, the few who were inclined to cast restraint aside came to feel that the ship's officers were not greatly concerned. The captain of a ship has very definite legal powers. If, after warning the two or three evident ringleaders, they had been put for a short time to sober up in the place that all vessels provide for such purposes, if there had been evident a prompt disposition to back up the host and hostess, much trouble would have been avoided. It will, therefore, be to the distinct advantage of the steamship company to secure competent hosts and hostesses, remunerate them properly, expect them to be on the job and back them up in it.

It is regrettable to see a storm of criticism against an enterprise that is, in the main, praiseworthy. Such a type of criticism will hardly effect reform. It may be that a letter addressed to the principal tourist bureaus and to the steamship companies by the American Council on Education or by Dr. Duggan's committee will result in some definite policy and in concerted action. Travel is too important a part of education to be abandoned because of the foolishness of a few individuals.

EDUCATIONAL EVENTS

THE SPANISH UNIVERSITIES

THE London *Times* correspondent at Madrid writes that a royal decree closing the University of Oviedo has been published in the *Gazette*, which also announced the removal of the chancellor and the vice-chancellor, and their substitution by two government nominees. During the year and a half in which Oviedo University will remain closed, the students must go to other universities for examination, and the professors are forbidden to hold any meetings.

A long *communiqué* declares that weakness on the part of the university authorities and, possibly, connivance between professors and students, had led to the creation of an intolerable center of rebellion, which, besides wasting time, was creating a bad precedent. Similar symptoms, it adds, are noticeable at Barcelona, where the same action may have to be taken.

The *communiqué* goes on to say that the government will not hesitate to order the closing of all the universities should this be necessary to prevent the spread of a political movement of a revolutionary character, in which the students are unconscious participants. Reduction in the number of universities, it says, can do no harm to Spain, because lawyers and doctors are far too numerous in the nation. Moreover, declares the *communiqué*, it is well known that many lawyers and doctors, after having received their diplomas, have to begin an intensive course of study. "In these intangible centers of culture, which claim so many privileges and merits, it is difficult for a serious student to obtain a solid education." Professors are often late in arriving to deliver their short lectures; they delegate their functions to incompetent persons or waste time in incoherent or picturesque conversations. Long vacations, political dabblings and other amenities of Spain's traditional university idiosyncrasies are also noticed.

FELLOWSHIPS FOR STUDY IN FRANCE

SEVEN American Field Service fellowships have been awarded for the coming academic year by the Institute of International Education. The fellowships, which carry a stipend of $1,400, are awarded for advanced study in France. The fellowships announced are as follows:

MORRIS GARNSEY, graduate student at Clark University; B.A. Drury College, will study under Professor Rist at the University of Paris.

RAYMOND HOEKSTRA, graduate student at the University of Michigan; A.B. Calvin College, M.A. Michigan, will study the philosophy of Spinoza under Professor Leon Brunschvicg at the University of Paris.

ERIC P. JACKSON, associate professor of geography and geology at Hillsdale College, graduate student at the University of Chicago; A.B. Brown, M.A. Clark, will work at L'Institut de Géographie Alpine of the University of Grenoble with Professor Raoul Blanchard.

FRANK MONAGHAN, assistant editor of the "Dictionary of American Biography"; B.A., M.A. Cornell, will complete a study on American social history as recorded by French travelers.

William Rogers Quynn, instructor in French at Amherst College; B.A., M.A. Virginia, also studied at Columbia University and Johns Hopkins University, will complete a thesis on "Guez de Balzac" and will study with Professors Bédier, Hazard and Chamard at the University of Paris.

Paul C. Snodgress, assistant in Romance languages at the University of Illinois, graduate student at the University of Illinois; A.B., A.M. Little Rock College, LL.B. Arkansas Law School, will prepare critical studies in the later modern period of French literature.

William Troy, Jr., instructor in English at New York University, graduate student at Columbia University; A.B. Yale, will study comparative literature with special emphasis on the interrelationships in thought and form between modern French and modern American literature.

Fellowships have been renewed for a second year to the following named fellows elected last year:

William T. Bandy, Jr., assistant in French at the University of Illinois; B.A., M.A. Vanderbilt, is working under the direction of Professor Baldensperger at the University of Paris for the doctorat de l'Université de Paris on "L'Evolution de la Critique Baudelairienne."

Milton Lowenstein, graduate student at New York University; A.B. Columbia, also studied at the University of Paris and the Fontainebleau School of Fine Arts, will complete a treatise on monastic Romanesque architecture of the twelfth and thirteenth centuries.

Application blanks for the next award and information about these fellowships will be ready for distribution in October, 1929, and may be obtained from Archie M. Palmer, assistant director, Institute of International Education, 2 West 45th Street, New York, N. Y.

PROJECT OF THE YALE INSTITUTE OF HUMAN RELATIONS

Under the direction of Dr. William Healy and Dr. Augusta F. Bronner, of Boston, who have recently been appointed research associates in the Yale Institute of Human Relations, an intensive study will be made at Yale University during the next few years of a selected group of families.

For comparative purposes, studies will be conducted simultaneously in New Haven and Boston. In both places families of children who have come in contact with the juvenile courts will be chosen. Faculty members and graduate students in the Institute of Human Relations, the Yale School of Law, the School of Medicine and the social science section of the Graduate School will assist in the collection of data. Complete physiological, psychological, psychiatric and social examinations will be made. At the same time other investigations of the institute may deal with economic and community factors, so that the net result will be a complete picture of a group of functioning individuals in a known environment.

Assistance to the families involved will be one of the purposes of the inquiry. Cooperation of local agencies will be enlisted so that an adjustment may be effected wherever there are found problems of sickness, unemployment, legal entanglements, or lack of educational and recreational opportunities. Since no publicity is to be given to findings concerning individuals, there will be no danger of embarrassing those who are to be studied.

This investigation is among the first in which experts in many fields have combined in an actual and thoroughgoing study of a small group of families to discover the effect of environmental influences upon the development of the child. It is seen to be important by members of the Institute of Human Relations not only as a means of increasing the understanding of human behavior, but also because it may affect directly the treatment of delinquents, it will have an influence upon education, particularly in legal and medical fields, and it may point the way for further and broader studies of human interrelationships.

THE AMERICAN ASSOCIATION OF SCHOOL PHYSICIANS

The American Association of School Physicians has been organized, says a statement from the U. S. Bureau of Education, as a result of the recent growth in school health work.

This organization came as an outgrowth of two conferences, the first of which was held at Buffalo, N. Y., in October, 1926; and the second, in Cincinnati, Ohio, October, 1927. The first annual meeting of the American Association of School Physicians was held in Chicago on October 15, 1928, and was largely attended by school physicians from 27 states, the District of Columbia and Canada. The membership numbered 324 in November, 1928.

Among the subjects discussed were: Education qualifications for school physicians; a study of medical inspection and health service in normal schools and teacher-training colleges; correction of remediable health defects; the teacher's health condition and attitude a factor in her professional rating; health examinations; a standard group Snellen test for school children, and the present status of student health service, its extent and scope.

A study was recently made of 100 strictly teacher-training institutions. City normal, state normal schools and teachers colleges were selected at random from the *Educational Directory* issued by the Bureau of Education, as representative of various sections of the United States. From this selection it was possible to make a reliable study of 50 schools. These were scattered over the United States and located in 33 different states. To this number were added schools available to various members of the committee, making possible a study of 65 different schools.

Some of the findings of this study were: 1. Seventy-six per cent. of these teacher-training institutions require a health examination of students on entrance; only 12 per cent. do not require it. Six per cent. of them give a partial examination, and with 6 per cent. it is optional. 2. The examinations of 62 per cent. of the students in these teacher-training institutions were made by the college physician; 12 per cent. by the local physicians; 2 per cent. by family physicians; 4 per cent. by the physical department of the institutions, and 20 per cent. did not state who made the examination.

This association advocates very strongly the employment of a school nurse, and the provision of a room designated as a Health Room, where the nurse reports at an appointed time, and where the children, parents and teachers come to talk over with her their many problems and difficulties.

CONFERENCE OF ENGLISH TEACHERS AT NORTHWESTERN UNIVERSITY

LAST year Northwestern University invited college teachers of English in neighboring institutions to a conference where problems faced by all of them might be discussed. The response was so spontaneous and the meetings of the conference so helpful that those who attended were unanimous in hoping that the conference might become an annual event.

The second Conference of College Teachers of English, on invitation of the department of English, was held on March 29 and 30.

Those in attendance at the conference were greeted by Dean Raymond A. Kent, of the college of liberal arts, and by Dean James A. James, of the graduate school. Dean Kent commended the group for the interest shown in the professional problems which they were seeking to solve and for their devotion to their tasks evinced by their being at such a conference during a vacation.

The first session was devoted to a discussion of encouraging and maintaining the students' effective and personal interest in English beyond the range of the classroom. The discussion dealt with two aspects, indicated by these questions: Wholly aside from "assigned readings," what can be done to stimulate taste in and for reading? Apart from courses in composition, what can be done to lead students to write for pleasure and to maintain high standards in their writing?

The second session, on Friday afternoon, had for its subject the superior student. What is being done at present to aid his development, and what can and should be done to enable him to get as much out of his college work in English as his ability will permit?

On Friday evening, the university was host at a dinner. The speakers on this occasion were Professor E. H. Lewis, who discussed the exceptional student, and Professor J. H. Harrison, who talked about making English vital.

At the third session, on Saturday morning, the general topic was the program of study for the Master of Arts degree in English. What should this degree represent? What should the content and the aim of the first year of graduate training be?

Those attending the conference voiced at its conclusion their conviction of its great value to them and their hope that a third conference will be held next year.

THE SUMMER SESSION OF THE UNIVERSITY OF MICHIGAN

ALL schools and colleges of the University of Michigan will offer courses in the 1929 summer session. In addition, there will be the work given at the Biological Station on Douglas Lake in Northern Michigan, at the Field Station for Geology and Geography in Kentucky, and at the new camps for surveying and for the School of Forestry and Conservation in Wyoming and the Upper Peninsula of Michigan, respectively.

The regular session of eight weeks begins on June 24. In the Law School the session is eleven weeks in length, from June 18 to August 29. There will also be a number of four weeks' courses in the school of education, and a six weeks' session for the division of hygiene, public health and physical education. Six Public Health Institutes on six successive week-ends, beginning June 28, will again be given.

On the faculty of about 350 members, 49 are professors from other institutions, including the following American universities—Stanford, Southern California, Montana, Kansas, Missouri, Illinois, Wisconsin, Indiana, De Pauw, Ohio State, Ohio Wesleyan, Pennsylvania, George Washington, Virginia, North Carolina, Duke, Florida, the Johns Hopkins, Princeton, Wesleyan, Yale and Harvard. Six British university professors and two from continental European institutions will also teach during the session.

The extra-curricular program announces thirty public lectures, most of them by members of the teaching staff, and a series of eight excursions, the latter including the Ford Industries and the Ford Airport with its laboratories. Professor Chester M. Wallace, of the School of Drama, Carnegie Institute of Technology, will direct the Michigan Repertory Theater's seven weeks' program of plays. These public performances, plus many private laboratory presentations, will offer workshop opportunities for all students enrolled in the courses in dramatic art.

THE PRESIDENCY OF THE UNIVERSITY OF CHICAGO

Appointment of Robert Maynard Hutchins, dean of the Law School of Yale University, as president of the University of Chicago is announced by Harold H. Swift, president of the board of trustees. He succeeds Dr. Max Mason, who resigned in June of last year and is now director of the division of natural sciences of the Rockefeller Foundation. He will assume office at the university on July 1.

University of Chicago history is repeating itself in the selection of Mr. Hutchins as president, for its first head, William Rainey Harper, also a Yale graduate and faculty member, was but thirty-four years old when he was chosen president of the nascent institution. When he was but thirty years of age, Dr. Harper had been offered, but declined, the presidency of the old University of Chicago.

In accepting the appointment, President Hutchins said: "Because of its geographical position, its tradition of freedom and enterprise, the excellence of its faculty and the spirit of cooperation that exists between its members and the board of trustees, I regard the University of Chicago as the great educational opportunity in the United States. The University of Chicago is known in the educational world as a pioneer. The genuine spirit of academic freedom and unfettered investigation which have characterized its efforts have contributed greatly to its remarkable progress and the outstanding position it has achieved in its 37 years of existence. In my association with the university, I have found an able and enthusiastic group of investigators and teachers engaged in inspiring and valuable effort, and I welcome the opportunity to cooperate in the progress they are making."

Mr. Hutchins comes of old New England ancestry and of a family that is active in education. His father, William James Hutchins, graduate of Yale and of the Union and Oberlin Theological Seminaries, is president of Berea College, Kentucky. His mother, Anna Laura Murch Hutchins, is a graduate of Mt. Holyoke College. A younger brother, Francis S. Hutchins, 26 years old, is head of "Yale-in-China," and an older brother, William, is a master in the Westminster School, Simsbury, Conn.

Mr. Hutchins was born in Brooklyn, January 17, 1899. He studied at Oberlin Academy, graduating in 1915, and then went to Oberlin College for two years, entering the ambulance service of the United States in 1917. He served with the ambulance corps until 1919, and was with the Italian army in 1918–19. The Italian government decorated him with the Croce de Guerra for bravery under fire. Entering Yale after leaving the service in 1919, he received his A.B. degree in 1921.

In 1923 he was appointed secretary of Yale University, succeeding Anson Phelps Stokes, and in 1924 he continued his study of law during the summer. He graduated from the Law School in 1925 with an LL.B. degree, *magna cum laude,* and was elected to the Order of the Coif because of his scholastic record. After graduation, he taught in the Law School, becoming a full-time professor in 1926, but retaining the secretaryship of the university. When Dean Thomas W. Swan, of the Law School, was appointed to the Circuit Court of Appeals, Mr. Hutchins was made acting dean, and afterward was appointed dean.

EDUCATIONAL NOTES AND NEWS

DR. MERVIN GRANT FILLER was installed as the eighteenth president of Dickinson College, Carlisle, Pennsylvania, on April 26. Dr. Josiah Penniman, of the University of Pennsylvania, was among the speakers.

DR. FRANK PARKER DAY will be installed as the thirteenth president of Union College, Schenectady, N. Y., on May 4. He succeeds Dr. Charles A. Richmond, who has been president since 1909.

THE request of Professor Gonzalez Lodge to be retired from active service after February 1, 1930, has been granted by the trustees of Teachers College, Columbia University. Professor Lodge will become emeritus professor of Latin and Greek.

DEAN FREDERICK J. E. WOODBRIDGE, of the graduate faculties, has been serving as acting president of Columbia University since Dr. Butler's illness early in March.

DR. RAY LYMAN WILBUR, Secretary of the Department of the Interior and president on leave of Stanford University, will be the Howard University commencement speaker on June 7.

ROBERT M. HUTCHINS, dean of the school of law of Yale University and president-elect of the University of Chicago, will give the commencement address at Lafayette College on June 7.

DR. W. T. FOSTER, director of the Pollak Foundation of Economic Research since 1920, author of "The Road to Plenty," will give the commencement address at the University of Colorado on June 10. Dr. Foster was formerly president of Reed College, Portland, Oregon.

THE National Academy of Sciences at its annual meeting held in Washington on April 22, 23 and 24 elected new members as follows: Dr. Roger Adams, professor of organic chemistry at the University of Illinois; Irving W. Bailey, associate professor of botany, Bussey Institution, Harvard University; Dr. A. F. Blakeslee, botanist at the Carnegie Institution's station for experimental evolution at Cold Spring Harbor; Dr. James B. Conant, associate professor of chemistry, Harvard University; Dr. Bergen Davis, professor of physics at Columbia University; Dr. C. J. Davisson, physicist at the Bell Telephone Laboratories, New York; Dr. Joel H. Hildebrand, professor of chemistry at the University of California; William Hovgaard, professor of naval design at the Massachusetts Institute of Technology; Dr. Albert W. Hull, research physicist at the General Electric Company's Research Laboratory at Schenectady; Frank Leverett, geologist of the U. S. Geological Survey and lecturer in glacial geology at the University of Michigan; Dr. Paul W. Merrill, astronomer at the Mt. Wilson Observatory, Pasadena; Dr. David H. Tennent, professor of zoology at Bryn Mawr College; Dr. George H. Whipple, dean of the School of Medicine and Dentistry and professor of pathology at the University of Rochester, N. Y., and Dr. Clark Wissler, curator of ethnology at the American Museum of Natural History, New York, and professor of anthropology in the institute of psychology at Yale University.

DEAN VIRGINIA C. GILDERSLEEVE, of Barnard College, Columbia University, has been elected president of the Association to Aid Research by Women.

THE degree of doctor of laws will be conferred on Dr. William S. Thayer, professor emeritus of medicine at the Johns Hopkins University, by McGill University on May 29.

MILTON B. MEDARY, JR., of Philadelphia, has received the gold medal of the American Institute of Architects, awarded for distinction in the fine arts.

THE freedom of the city of Edinburgh has been presented to Sir Alfred Ewing, principal and vice-chancellor of the university.

G. H. A. WILSON, treasurer of the University of Cambridge, has been elected master of Clare College in succession to the late Dr. W. L. Mollison.

MRS. LEAH MANNING, head mistress of an open-air school in Cambridge, has been elected vice-president of the British National Union of Teachers, with automatic succession to the presidency next year.

AT the meeting of the trustees of Teachers College on April 18 Miss Anna E. Richardson, field worker for the American Home Economics Association, Washington, D. C., was elected alumni trustee for the term ending March 1, 1931. The resignation of Mr. B. T. Babbitt Hyde, a member of this board since 1895, was reluctantly accepted. Mr. and Mrs. Hyde expect to make their home in New Mexico, where they have been during the past two years.

JUDGE H. WALTON MITCHELL, for twenty-seven years a member of the board of trustees of Pennsylvania State College, has presented his resignation.

CHARLES E. CLARK, Lines professor of law in the Yale Law School, has been appointed dean of the school, to succeed Dean Robert M. Hutchins, who has been elected president of the University of Chicago.

AT a recent meeting in Chicago, Dr. John L. Seaton, president of Albion College, was reelected for a term of four years to the presidency of the University Senate of the Methodist Episcopal Church. The senate is the standardizing agency of the church and has the distinction of being the oldest body of this character in the United States.

MARY A. ROKAHR, for the past nine years state home demonstration leader and management specialist at the University of Wyoming, has recently been appointed by the office of cooperative extension work of the extension service of the U. S. Department of Agriculture as the first federal extension specialist in home management to give time exclusively to this phase of extension work.

DR. GEORGE S. AMSDEN, director of the psychopathic department of the Albany Hospital since 1924, has been appointed professor of psychiatry in the New York Post-Graduate Medical School and Hospital.

THE *Journal of Education* reports that William McNeeley, superintendent of schools of Robertson County, Tennessee, for ten years, has been reelected for the sixth two-year term with no opposing candidate. This is the fifty-second year of his educational service.

SUPERINTENDENT HARRY D. KIES will at the end of the present year leave Mankato, Minnesota, where he went after an extended service in the Iowa State Department of Education.

DR. WILLIAM DAVIDSON, superintendent of the Pittsburgh schools, has a three-months' leave of absence to attend the International Conference on World Education in Geneva.

DR. GRAYSON N. KEFAUVER, now assistant professor of secondary education at the University of Minnesota, has accepted an associate professorship at Teachers College, Columbia University, and will join the staff there in the fall. A native of Maryland, Dr. Kefauver took his bachelor's degree from the University of Arizona and his doctorate from the University of Minnesota.

E. W. JACOBSEN, principal of the Roosevelt High School, Oakland, California, has accepted a half-time position with the department of secondary education at Teachers College, Columbia University. Mr. Jacobsen will offer courses in the administration of secondary schools, which have been given previously by Professor Franklin W. Johnson, who becomes president of Colby College.

AT Yale University, John Shaw Boyce, of the U. S. Bureau of Plant Industry, has been appointed professor of forest pathology. John M. S. Allison, associate professor of history, has been promoted to a professorship of history; and Chester R. Longwell, associate professor of geology, becomes Henry Barnard Davis professor of geology.

THREE new professors and three visiting lecturers will go to Harvard University in September. William L. Crum, professor of statistics at Stanford Business School, will become professor of economics. Major Walter S. Sturgill, who completes his course this year at the Army War College in Washington as professor of military science and tactics, will replace Major L. A. Craig. Johannes A. C. F. Auer, professor of church history and philosophy at Tufts College, will be assistant professor of church history; Otis J. Todd, associate professor of the classics, University of British Columbia, will be lecturer in Greek and Latin; Arthur M. Wilson, instructor in history at Grinnell College, is visiting instructor in history, under the exchange agreement between Grinnell and Harvard. Dr. Tibor Rado, since 1926 privat-dozent at the University of Szeged, Hungary, will be in residence for the first half of the year as lecturer in mathematics.

APPOINTMENTS in philosophy include Glenn R. Morrow, of the University of Missouri, to become associate professor in the University of Illinois, and Arthur E. Murphy, Cornell University, to become associate professor in the University of Chicago. Professor Glanville Terrell, of the University of Kentucky, will become professor emeritus at the end of the year.

PROFESSOR from abroad who will lecture during the spring quarter at the University of Chicago are Dr. Werner Heisenberg, professor of theoretical physics of the University of Leipzig; Professor Paul Haensel, until this year lecturer in economics and dean of the faculties at the University of Moscow, Russia, and Professor C. Delisle Burns, of London, Stevenson lecturer in citizenship at the University of Glasgow, who will teach in the department of philosophy.

VISITING professors who will lecture during the summer session of the University of California include Dr. Hermann Weyl, research professor in mathematical physics at Princeton University, and professor of mathematics at the Technische Hochschule, Zurich, and Alexander M. Drummond, professor of public speaking and head of the department at Cornell University.

DR. JOSEPH RALSTON HAYDEN, professor of political science in the University of Michigan, will lecture in the University of California summer session at Berkeley from July 1 to August 10.

DEAN THOMAS W. GRAHAM, of the graduate school of theology of Oberlin College, will be the commencement speaker at Illinois College on June 12. The baccalaureate speaker on the preceding Sunday will be Dr. Ozora S. Davis, president of the Chicago Theological Seminary.

THE annual lecture of the Alfred Ernest Stearns Foundation at Phillips Academy, Andover, was given on May 3 by Professor Paul Shorey, of the University of Chicago, on the subject: "How Modern Were the Ancients?"

PROFESSOR JAMES HENRY BREASTED, director of the Oriental institute of the University of Chicago, is now at Bryn Mawr College initiating the series of lectures under the Mary Flexner Lectureship Foundation, established by Bernard Flexner, of New York. Professor Breasted is conducting graduate and undergraduate group conferences, and will give a series of lectures on "The New Crusade."

PRESIDENT ALBERT BRITT, of Knox College, will deliver the annual address before the Illinois State Historical Society at Springfield on May 9.

COMMISSIONER WILLIAM JOHN COOPER, of the U. S. Bureau of Education, attended the meeting of the Massachusetts Superintendents on April 15, 16, and 17, and made addresses on "Responsibility of the Superintendent for an Educational Program," "What Shall Become of the Rural School?" and "The School Supervisor."

MRS. JOSEPHINE CORLISS PRESTON, who recently retired as superintendent of public instruction for the state of Washington, an office that she had held for sixteen years, lectured on May 6 before the graduate school of education of Harvard University on "Twenty-five Years of School Administration."

Theodore Salisbury Woolsey, professor emeritus of international law at Yale University since 1911, died on April 24 at the age of seventy-seven years.

Garrett Masselink, president of Ferris Institute at Big Rapids, Michigan, died on April 20 at the age of fifty-six years.

James D. Sullivan, formerly director of the attendance division of the New York State Education Department, has died at the age of seventy-six years.

Dr. John William Harshberger, professor of botany at the University of Pennsylvania, died on April 23, at the age of sixty years. He graduated from the university in 1892 and had taught there since that year.

Dr. Frank Goodrich, professor emeritus of Williams College, died on April 29 in New York, where he had been a resident since his retirement five years ago. He was born in 1856 at Dryden, New York, and graduated from Yale University in 1880. After studying for several years at the universities of Berlin, Heidelberg and Halle, he served as an instructor in German at Yale University and then at Williams College. Later he was appointed professor of European history, continuing in that position until his retirement.

Professor Inez Whipple Wilder, who had taught in the department of zoology of Smith College since 1902, died on April 29, within a few weeks after giving up teaching. After the death of her husband, Professor Harris H. Wilder, who founded the department, Mrs. Wilder succeeded him as its chairman. For nearly thirty years she had collaborated with him in departmental administration, in teaching and in research. Mrs. Wilder was born in 1871 and was a graduate of Brown University.

Dean F. B. R. Hellems, of the college of arts and sciences of the University of Colorado, died on April 19. He became ill in November in the closing days of a year as acting president of the university. He had been dean of the college of arts and sciences since 1899. Dean Hellems was the author of articles appearing in *The Dial, The Atlantic Monthly, Harper's, The Forum, Asia, Poet Lore* and School and Society. Professor T. D. A. Cockerell writes of Dr. Hellems: "The students of the university have lost their best friend. For a quarter of a century I have seen him at work administering justice, diffusing wisdom and developing among us those ideals of decency and courtesy which have done so much to make the university an influence for good throughout the state. He loved the students as a father, and had an extraordinary capacity for interesting himself in every one of them. Many a time I have had occasion to speak to him about some student in my classes, and after offering my information or opinion, found he knew much more about that student than I did. He was always ready to help with wise counsel, and no one will ever know how much he spent of his own resources to assist those he considered worthy. On the other hand, he was not afraid to be just, and yet the feeling about him was such that he had warm supporters among those he had punished. In an age of narrow specialization he was broad in his outlook, a genuine philosopher in the old sense. We shall not see another like him, nor will it be possible, now that the university has grown so large, for any man to take his place as a builder of traditions. But those traditions remain with us, to be cherished and developed with the growth of the institution. Like knights of olden time, we are pledged to their defense, and to the overthrow of low standards, whether of scholarship or of personal conduct. What he did, he did by incessant labor and ceaseless vigilance, and we, his heirs, can not keep our inheritance by other means."

The second annual lecture under the auspices of Delta Omega, the honorary public health society, was delivered at the Massachusetts Institute of Technology on April 12, by Dr. George T. Palmer. Dr. Palmer spoke on the school health program of the American Child Health Association, of which he is director of research. Members of the Gamma Chapter at the Massachusetts Institute of Technology and of the Beta Chapter at the Harvard School of Public Health, as well as many others interested, were present. Following the lecture, a dinner of the Delta Omega Society was held with Dr. Palmer and Dr. James A. Tobey, of New York, national secretary of the society, as the principal speakers. Professor S. C. Prescott presided.

THE South African meeting of the British Association for the Advancement of Science will be held at Capetown from July 23 or 24 to July 26, and after that at Johannesburg. Dr. C. W. Kimmins is president of the section of education and will give an address on "Modern Movements in Education."

THE fourth triennial Canadian National Conference on Education opened at Victoria on April 6, the Governor-General, Lord Willingdon, welcoming delegates from nine countries. These delegates included Sir Rabindranath Tagore (India); Sir Aubrey Symonds, secretary to the Board of Education, Great Britain; Sir Charles Robertson, University of Birmingham; Sir Archibald Strong, Australia; Dr. Bruno Roselli, Italy; Comte Fleury, France; Dr. Mosbach, Germany, and Professor Matousek, Czechoslovakia. A ten-day conference was held at Vancouver beginning on April 8 with a debate on education and leisure. Discussions followed on the influence exerted by literature, the cinema, music, the drama, wireless and organized recreation on contemporary education.

NEARLY 3,000 teachers of the schools of England and Wales attended the fifty-ninth annual conference of the National Union of Teachers which opened at Llandudno on March 30. It is twenty-four years since the conference met in Llandudno. In 1905 the membership was 57,586; to-day it is 131,044. Mr. C. W. Cowen, of Sheffield, was installed as president at the first session, and gave his presidential address. At the public reception of the conference the speakers included Mr. Lloyd George, Mr. J. Cheetham, the chairman of the Llandudno Council; Lord Mostyn, Major Owen, M.P., the Archbishop of Wales, the Rev. W. Phillips, the Rev. Canon Francis Thompson, and Alderman William George, the chairman of the Carnarvon Education Committee.

DISCUSSION

RELATION OF LABORATORY TO FIELD METHODS IN ECOLOGICAL AND ECONOMIC STUDIES

THE demands of branches of governmental research and of certain types of large industries have placed upon our schools and colleges the necessity for training a group of biologists of a new type.

Toward the close of the nineteenth century and running well over into the twentieth century there flourished in our institutions of learning a group of enthusiastic biologists who were somewhat obsessed with the idea that they could place living organisms in their laboratories and analyze their bodies, their functions and their relations to environment, in much the same way that the chemist analyzed minerals. There were many hasty conclusions and many failures, with the result that in the past there has been a lot of contention between those biologists who have attempted to use the laboratory as a means for analyzing and interpreting the behavior of organisms living out of doors and those biologists who have gone into the field and made observations of the organisms in their natural habitats. The field man has complained, with frequent justification, that the unnatural environment and the methods of the laboratory gave results which in no manner could be applied to the field, and that, therefore, the work led nowhere and was a waste of time. The conclusion was also frequently reached that it was impossible to analyze the activities of our lower organisms.

A careful review of most of the results turned out in the laboratories of these earlier workers will disclose the fact that much of their endeavor fell short because of two weaknesses: (1) the inability of the experimenter to comprehend and control the multifactored environment in which his animals were placed, and (2) the inadequacy of apparatus and technique. The second weakness was undoubtedly the result of the first, since the construction of suitable apparatus and the control of environmental factors depend primarily upon the insight of the experimenter into the relative values of these factors. It can very frequently be found that an experimenter working with light was apparently so engrossed with light alone that he completely ignored the fact that his sources of light were likewise sources of heat. His results were probably the double effect of these two stimuli. Also, experiments were many times repeated in the laboratory with apparently definite results, but when another worker attempted them or when the field man would use them for his purposes they failed utterly. The first results may have been correct for a given humidity or for a given barometric pressure but not for another.

Factors found important under one condition must not be considered as always being so, for frequently an effect is the result of a peculiar combination of environmental influences. For instance, it has been shown that fourth instar larvae of the Mexican bean beetle will pupate and emerge under conditions of atmospheric humidity varying from 0 per cent. to 100 per cent. and under rates of evaporation varying over a wide range, providing the temperature is not excessive. It has been further shown that larvae, pupae and adults can be killed in large percentages upon three-hour exposures to high summer temperatures (98° F.+) if the relative humidity is very high or very low, while the mortality is very low at these same temperatures if the humidity is near 70 per cent. of saturation. In this case it is a *temperature-humidity-time* combination that is important and not any one of these factors alone.

Chapman has shown[1] that it is possible to predict population or degree of infestation in stored grains by accurately taking into account the conditions of humidity, temperature and food supply under which the insects must live. This problem is relatively easy since the natural environment is somewhat of a constant and the insect is adapted to what corresponds closely to laboratory conditions, but it is an excellent place to begin studies of this sort.

The laboratory is being freely resorted to by many leading ecologists (*i.e.*, Shelford, *Biol. Bull.*, vol. 25, 1913) in the solution of their problems and by the various branches of governmental research, such as the Bureau of Entomology and Bureau of Plant Industry, with the result that it is safe to say that in the next decade there will be made available a great mass of valuable information upon the physiological relationships of both plants and animals.

In reality there is no difference between laboratory and field conditions in dealing with the fundamental problems of animal life and behavior. If properly controlled methods are used and sufficient variety of conditions and combinations of factors are employed, a very large part of the natural environment can be reproduced and results studied and analyzed in the laboratory in greater detail and with far greater accuracy than in the field. The great weakness of the laboratory man of the past has been in not controlling or measuring *all* phases of environment, and in not knowing enough of the natural field conditions so as to be able to correlate the two in any significant manner. This has brought just criticism and, unfortunately, a lack of respect for his work from those who should by all means have been his coworkers. Fortunately the field men are now recognizing the necessity for this type of work when properly carried out, and many of the important problems of the future will be in the hands of those who have enough training and experience in both methods to make the necessary correlations.

D. F. MILLER
OHIO STATE UNIVERSITY

[1] *Ecology*, 9: 2, 1928.

SPECIAL CORRESPONDENCE

THE NEW GENERAL CURRICULUM IN THE COLLEGE OF LIBERAL ARTS AND SCIENCES AT THE UNIVERSITY OF ILLINOIS

THE board of trustees of the University of Illinois has recently approved a new curriculum of the College of Liberal Arts and Sciences which represents the first major change in the general requirements for the A.B. degree since that college was formed by the union of the older College of Liberal Arts with the College of Science in 1913. Certain features of the new plan may prove of general interest, although no radical innovations are introduced.

The committee of the faculty charged with the duty of framing a new curriculum commenced its task by considering the general aims of the college. While not attempting to add to the numerous definitions of a liberal education, the committee prepared to arrange its minimum requirements to insure:

(*a*) A reasonable facility with language characteristic of the educated man or woman, including the ability to write the mother tongue and to read at least one foreign language, ancient or modern.

(*b*) A diversified background, to be completed before the senior year, of elementary instruction in the traditional fields of the arts (including the social or humane sciences) and the sciences.

(*c*) A concentration of interest after the freshman year in some one selected subject buttressed by work in one or two closely allied fields of learning.

(*d*) A growth in maturity by requiring that during the last two years a certain minimum of credit be obtained in courses not open to freshmen or sophomores.

(*e*) A liberal opportunity to select preprofessional courses offered by other colleges and schools of the university.

The total number of hours necessary for the A.B. degree is 130, including courses in physical education, hygiene and military science and tactics (for male students) which are required of all registered in the undergraduate colleges during the freshman and sophomore years.

Six hours of rhetoric are also a university requirement. Now, however, incoming students with exceptional preparation may be excused from the formal course work in rhetoric by demonstrating their ability through "proficiency examinations" offered during the first two weeks of each semester.

The requirement in foreign languages is now established as a reading knowledge of some language taught in the university, equivalent to that obtainable after four semester courses (sixteen hours) when the language is begun in college. If a student desires to satisfy this requirement by taking formal courses, his high-school credits are evaluated on the basis of one semester for each high-school unit. He has, however, the option of taking a "proficiency examination" as in rhetoric. The student who anticipates postgraduate studies is advised to acquire a reading knowledge of French and of German.

The requirement of a diversified background of elementary studies replaces the existing set of "group" requirements which arose as an aftermath of the period of free electives. These "groups" were of the greatest efficacy in promoting faculty debate, but from a practical standpoint presented serious difficulties in arranging the program of the more mature students, especially those transferring from other institutions. Accordingly they are abandoned and instead the student is required to present at least fifteen hours selected from the offerings of three different departments on the arts side of the college and a similar number selected from at least three different departments on the science side. There is a further requirement that one of the courses included in the arts group be in English or foreign literature or in the history of philosophy. This, it is hoped, will result in some acquaintance with first-rate authors and with the university library. Similarly on the science side, one of the courses offered must include at least four clock hours per week in the laboratory to insure some familiarity with natural phenomena and the scientific method.

The requirement in the major subject is twenty hours, supported by twenty hours in not more than two allied fields as defined by the several departments, all exclusive of work taken in the freshman year.

A minimum of thirty hours in courses not open to freshmen and sophomores is required in the hope that it may effect a partial segregation of upperclassmen and associate them with graduate students rather than with underclassmen. In this connection a maximum limit hitherto imposed of forty hours in any one department has now been removed.

A maximum limit of thirty-six hours has been set to courses outside of the arts and science group. This is large enough to take care of seniors graduating after a year *in absentia* at the College of Law or of Medicine, and to other students who have not made up their minds as to their future life work it offers an opportunity of sampling the wares of the professional schools.

Supplemented by an elaborate system of "class advisers" for underclassmen and "major advisers" for upperclassmen, it is believed that this curriculum will insure the minimum requirements proposed by the college while affording an opportunity for every qualified student to obtain instruction in the fields which he finds most interesting or profitable, so far as the facilities of the university permit.

WALDO SHUMWAY,
Assistant Dean
UNIVERSITY OF ILLINOIS

QUOTATIONS

CARNEGIE PENSIONS

IT is bad enough to be reminded from time to time that corporations are not supposed to have souls, but when a corporation that is not operated for profit calmly announces that it does not any longer propose to keep faith in the beneficent social enterprise in which it has long been engaged, the reminder seems to be rubbed in with peculiar harshness and brutality. When, in addition, it appears that the corporation in question has been run on a low plane of intelligence, and that policies which would have done discredit to an amateur in merchandising or finance have produced their natural fruit in virtual bankruptcy, the most sympathetic critic may well wonder whether the boasted efficiency of American business possesses, after all, the high virtues that have been claimed for it.

The recent announcement by the Carnegie Foundation for the Advancement of Teaching that the pensions which it has been paying, or which it has expressed its intention to pay, to retired teachers in American and Canadian colleges and universities would, after May 1, be materially reduced came as a rude shock to the more than 800 actual beneficiaries of the fund which the foundation administers, and to the approximately 3,400 teachers now in service who will become eligible to pensions in due course. The reason for the proposed reduction is the depletion of the income of the foundation to a point where drastic retrenchment is necessary. The reduction, it appears, is to take two forms. The maximum allowances of $2,400 a year to professors who retire at the age of sixty-five, and of $3,600 to those retiring at seventy, are to be cut down severely in the case of future pensionables, while a less severe reduction is to be applied to the minimum allowance of $1,000 a year. At Smith College, for example, according to President Neilson, the maximum pension under the new scheme for a professor who retires at sixty-eight will be only $1,280. The 800-odd professors who are now receiving allowances under the non-contributory plan that was in force until November, 1915, when the non-contributory list was closed, will also have their pensions reduced, but outright payments, not exceeding $500 a year in any case, will, it is said, be made by the Carnegie Corporation, a different organization from the foundation, to make up some of the difference between the former pension and the new one.

* * * * *

The rude debacle of which the professors have been made the victims suggests two or three observations. The first relates to the character of the intellectual performance which has brought the Carnegie Foundation to its present pass. The calculations upon which a pension organization should be expected, under ordinary circumstances, to base its plans of payment are akin to those of any life insurance company in so far as they deal with the expectation of life in the class of persons who are eligible as beneficiaries. To these calculations are to be added, where the benefits are to be restricted to a definite class or group, an estimate of the probable number of beneficiaries to be provided for over a series of years. It does not seem that it would have been a crushing intellectual feat for the foundation, with every facility for obtaining information and expert advice, to have met these elementary requirements. Yet as early as 1909, only four years after the Carnegie gift was made, Professor J. McKeen Cattell made public a calculation which showed that "a complete pension system for academic teachers might require two hundred times the income of the foundation" as it then stood. Granting, for the sake of argument, that Professor Cattell's scheme proposed the inclusion of a far larger number of academic teachers than the foundation was disposed to regard as eligible, it is nevertheless apparent that the calculations, if any, upon which the foundation relied were wide of the mark. In 1916 a commission which the foundation felt compelled to appoint, after the American Association of University Professors had eviscerated one of its proposed changes of plan, reported that prospective pensions called at that time for more than four times the income of the foundation for 1917. No one supposes that the foundation intended to land itself in such a dilemma, but its intellectual treatment of the situation was stupid.

In a statement given out on April 11, Dr. Henry S. Pritchett, president of the foundation, was quoted as saying, in substance, that "the foundation had always given notice that higher salaries would necessitate pension changes." Dr. Pritchett offers a poor justification for the procedure which the foundation has followed. If a material increase in average salaries was reasonably to be expected, common business prudence dictated that the foundation, unless it was able to foresee commensurate additions to its funds, should not launch a pension scale to which it could not adhere. Yet to-day, with more than three times the annual income with which it began, the foundation is compelled to make a further drastic cut in its retiring allowances because salaries have risen, and this notwithstanding that a large part of its prospective obligations were shifted to another organization years ago.

It would seem only natural to assume, further, that a corporation charged with the administration of a fund intended to make academic life more attractive should not only have done its best to cut its coat according to the cloth, but should also have had some reasonably consistent theory of the principle upon which it was acting. At this point the foundation has backed and filled deplorably. At the outset, apparently, a professorial pension was regarded, as it should be regarded, as a kind of deferred salary payment, an honorable retiring allowance designed to make good, in some measure at least, the income which the professor could not be expected to insure from savings. By 1916, however, the pension had become a "very gracious and noble charity," a sop from the rich to relieve the necessities of the poor. Now, we are told, the non-contributory pension represents a giving of something for nothing, an anti-social largesse which the foundation should not be expected to defend. Whether, because salaries have increased, Dr. Pritchett assumes that a saving which was impracticable before has become practicable now is not clear, but any one who knows the actual conditions of academic life in this country knows that the rise in salaries which has driven the foundation into virtual bankruptcy has taken place only within a very few years, that only a small percentage of teachers of professorial rank enjoy the maximum salary in any institution, and that the salary increase has been accompanied by a portentous rise in living costs.

There remains the serious question of moral obligation. It is true that pension agreements are not, as a rule, enforceable legal contracts as against all contingencies, and the foundation undoubtedly has the law on its side in arbitrarily cutting down the scale of payments to which it has hitherto adhered; but when an agreement has been regularly made on definitely stated terms, and the beneficiaries of the agreement have fulfilled the requirements that have been set up, a moral obligation has been created which the controlling party may not disregard without doing violence to good faith. It is the good faith of the Carnegie Foundation that has been impugned, as it was a dozen or more years ago when the American Association of University Professors challenged another repudiation of the pension assurances. "The foundation's record," a *Nation* reviewer wrote on August 2, 1919, "is full of evasion, shuffling, misstatement, omission of important and damaging points, assumption of a lofty superiority, and all the attendant qualities of the autocratic psychology." To that all but overwhelming condemnation is now to be added the odium of conduct which the American professoriate will assuredly regard as dishonorable.—*William MacDonald in The Nation.*

REPORTS

REQUIREMENTS FOR GRADUATE STUDY AT HARVARD UNIVERSITY

Several proposals for the reorganization of graduate study at Harvard mark the annual report to President Lowell of Dean Clifford H. Moore, of the faculty of arts and sciences. He recommends a reconsideration of the basis for the award of master's degrees and suggests the need for differentiating between candidates unequally prepared for advanced study. Graduate study at Harvard is said to have become an increasing problem with more than 900 students resident in the Graduate School during each year since 1926 as compared with 406 in 1907–08 and as few as 541 in 1920–21.

Dean Moore says:

The teaching of graduate students is confessedly the easiest in the whole range of instruction, in that graduate students are with rare exceptions eager to learn, and therefore determined to extract instruction from a learned man, even if he should prove reluctant to impart it. Historically our graduate schools have grown out of our colleges as extensions or projections into the higher intellectual atmosphere; and in some cases perhaps they still retain too long from this projection some methods that can be improved—that is, there may be danger of keeping competent graduate students too long in leading strings fitted for undergraduates.

Not that the break between college and the graduate school in methods of instruction can be too sharply made, for under present conditions at least it will probably long remain true that many students, properly classed as graduate students, will nevertheless require instruction identical with or very similar to that suited to the more advanced undergraduates. The danger lies in letting the abler men work in a way which does not demand the exercise of their full powers and which fails to develop their independence. The students in our graduate school vary widely in native ability and intellectual experience; but there is always a considerable proportion of men among them who are equipped to begin to learn for themselves, under due guidance—that is, to engage in research, so-called—and who can not profitably work as many of their fellows must do.

In the year under review, of the 946 men listed in the catalogue as Graduate Students of Arts and Sciences, 239 were graduates of Harvard College, and of this last number 138 had graduated with honors. Such men, with the abler men who come from other colleges, at entrance into the Graduate School form an élite body intellectually; in most cases they are prepared to begin promptly to make researches in their chosen field; and, in fact, they are already encouraged to do this in some departments and by certain teachers in most. Naturally there will be many gaps in the knowledge of even the best students which they will have to fill before they are equipped for the doctorate; but it certainly will be worth while to encourage them to try their wings for sustained flights even in their first year of residence. Some will prove unequal to long flights; but most may from the start profit by their opportunity.

Convenience and tradition have operated for a long time to continue the practice of counting graduate work for the master's degree by courses; but this method has now become distinctly out of date since the habit of giving the bachelor's degree on knowledge of a subject, tested in a general examination, has for most departments put an end to the successful scoring of courses as the sole method of proving fitness to graduate. Therefore the plan proposed by the department of economics and approved by the faculty, whereby the master's degree can be won by men working in that department only by examination on the subject, is a welcome change, and one which may well be considered by all departments. It surely is anomalous to demand a general examination for the lower degree and to allow marks of B in four courses to be the warrant for the higher. In fact, the whole system of counting by courses in the graduate school appears antiquated in view of the developments in education here during the past ten years.

In this connection the further question may well be raised whether it is necessary or desirable to continue longer to fix two years as the minimum period of advanced study in which a candidate can secure his doctor's degree. In practice a much longer time is taken by most students, so that the danger is that men will spend too many years under tutelage rather than too few.

Therefore, it would appear wise to consider whether the several divisions should not be empowered to decide when a man is ready to face the examinations for the doctorate regardless of time of residence; the divisions would then invite a candidate to present himself when the professors thought that he was ripe for the test, the mechanical counting by courses in residence would have no excuse for being, and the divisions would be freed from the work of examining men who in their judgment are not yet prepared.

All this has a bearing on instruction in the graduate school. If the best prepared and ablest men can at entrance be set to work independently in considerable measure and if the mechanical counting by courses can be abandoned, there will probably be fewer graduate students in lecture courses and a larger number in those courses in which research is directed. This will not reduce the burden of teaching; indeed it will have the contrary effect; but the change will be stimulating to teacher and pupil alike.

EDUCATIONAL RESEARCH AND STATISTICS

WHAT A FRESHMAN WANTS TO KNOW

IN the current academic interest of various colleges and universities regarding the orientation of the entering student, the focus of attention seems to be on what shall be taught the freshman during the period at the opening of the college year known as "freshman week." Usually each department or administrator involved writes a section of the handbook which is given the entering lumber for the academic sawmill and by which it is supposedly shaped into the finished product.

Unfortunately for the freshman, the prejudices of the makers of the manual and of the program for the orientation week are apt to enter into their actions, and the freshman is still wondering, after the festivities are over, just what it is all about.

In a study of this matter by the writer and Miss Alice King in 1927, a questionnaire was given to 125 college students in which this question was asked: "If you were compiling a manual for freshman week, what items would you include which you would have liked to know when you entered college? Please be specific."

Sixty per cent. of the 125 students were second-quarter freshmen, with the remainder about equally divided among the second- and third-year classes. Sixty-six were from a large university and fifty-nine from a small, rather rigid denominational college.

In addition to the questionnaire, the university newspaper which had carried a question and answer column was consulted, and the psychological clinic reports were investigated as to types of questions asked. The files of the paper offered no new questions, and the queries of the maladjusted students in the clinic served to reinforce the results of this survey.

The questions asked by the students in the returns of the questionnaire may be seen in the following table. Most students listed several or more matters which had puzzled them at the beginning of the freshman year.

In regard to the last item, the smaller college group were the only ones who were so perplexed (and they had experienced three months of daily chapel!). On all the other items, however, the two groups varied so consistently that it was not considered necessary to divide the result.

Desired information concerning	*No.*	*Percentage*
Entrance requirements and procedure, schedules	14	3.17
Fraternities and sororities	69	15.6
Requirements, rushing, pledging, initiation, standards, relative ranks		
Living quarters, room and board	8	1.8
Class attendance, cuts	12	2.7
Health service, hygiene	2	.45
Employment	6	1.3
Extra-curricular Total	—	6.25
Activities open to non-fraternity men and freshmen	2	.45
Open to freshmen	5	1.13
Dramatics and glee clubs	4	.90
Athletics, eligibility	4	.90
Campus organization YM-YW	2	.45
Classification and teaching staff Total	—	13.09
Special abilities in special subjects	30	6.81
Relation between professor and student	10	2.27
Introductions, etc. Faculty not known	12	2.7
Partiality of faculty	6	1.3
Campus publications, objects, nature, prices	2	.45
Text-books, use of, how to obtain, etc.	4	.90
Vocational guidance	8	1.8
Library, use, rules, etc.	25	5.67
Point-hour system explanation, grading system explanation	25	5.67
Majors and minors	8	1.8
Honorary fraternities, significance and requirements	11	2.49
Departmental and campus clubs	23	5.22
Location of buildings, classrooms, etc.	16	3.63
Friends, selection, etc.	20	4.54
Dates, etc.	4	.90
Parking problem	1	.22
Time budget	27	6.12
Financial budget	6	1.3
Advisers	18	4.08
Campus conduct and class attitude	11	2.49
Traditions and ideals	29	6.58
Religious ideals (peculiar to the small college only)	16	3.63
Total	440	100.00

The leading items about which the students were perplexed, as will be seen from the above table, were: (1) fraternities and sororities and (2) faculty ability and relationships—two matters which are usually omitted from the existing handbooks.

It is most evident that existing handbooks do not suit the student's needs to the fullest extent. One student aptly says that a handbook would not dare to tell the students what they want to know about the faculty, and rightly so. We have included several pages of student comments which seem particularly pertinent. Some of the questions may be answered easily, but others will require a bit of thought before printing in a handbook for general consumption.

The following student responses are included chiefly to "see oursilves as ithers see us" and are listed without further comment:

A. The thing that most perplexed me when I first entered college was to whom should I go for information concerning courses—major-minor—the greatest possibilities for the future in graduating with such and such degrees, etc. And I have not yet found any one on the campus who can give me the kind of information I desire. My own college office is very *unsatisfactory,* as are others in other colleges of the university.

B. The freshman should be told that the responsibility of graduating is entirely up to him.

C. Elimination of professors who have reached a certain age and replacement by younger men because old men become partial and are ruled by their emotions. Younger profs. understand the conditions that determine the life of the students.

D. Homesickness is an ailment characteristic of all freshmen, but they should win new friends, broaden their cultural status, and homesickness will be a thing of the past.

E. This is an experiment I have tried—please do not repeat. (I might want to do it again.) A theme written for one class in English was handed in and returned with some correction and a grade of "A." The same theme handed to another Prof. also in English and for the same purpose received a grade of "C+." Why the difference in the faculty grading in the same department?

F. I do not believe a handbook would aid a student. It would not be frank and sincere, nor answer the fundamental questions of sex, religion, social relationships, etc. A handbook which did answer these questions would offend the stiff-necked teaching staff and directors of this giant machine we call the university. No, don't help a student to become individual—keep him just a cog, a bolt, a nut.

G. Why should a student agree with each instructor to the very limit of every fact in order to make a grade?

H. Some points on etiquette—many need 'em!

I. When will the university get to the point where students may choose what they intend to use and what they are fitted for? (Some of us would choose sensible courses at that!) Why not give us a chance?

J. Why don't they try to make the heavy requirements—the necessary evils—interesting? It's sad to hear a junior say, "I haven't had a thing I wanted yet"—I often hear myself talking out loud.

K. Why don't they rule out more of the freshmen—why clutter up the classes with dumb-bells?

L. I think the handbook should warn the freshmen in book buying. Some instructors have classes pay five dollars for a book for the course. The course could have been completed with as much advantage without the book; one can get just as much out of the lectures. This has happened to me time and time again. Now I don't buy books until I'm sure that I really need them.

M. Why is it that certain students get through courses merely through the fact that they belong to the same fraternity or sorority as the instructor?

N. If a student does not pass the freshman intelligence test, is he allowed to enter the university or is he barred from any certain college?

O. To help choose an instructor who will best bring out the points in certain courses. There is a difference in ability in instructors and there should be a list classifying the instructors as to their special abilities in a certain subject.

P. To whom should a student go with regard to difficulties which arise? Not to the dean—he's never in. His faculty adviser—try and find him; the secretary of his college—he feels and lets one see that he feels that his time is being wasted. What can one do?

Q. Rules and regulations made clear to the freshman. Traditional customs and new plans as to traditions, etc. A complete outline of student-government methods of election. A history of the university; status of a freshman; a handbook for every freshman.

The writer queries: Why not ask our present sophomores concerning the questions that puzzled them as entering freshmen before proceeding with the elaboration of our freshman week plans?

LESTER RAINES
THE OHIO STATE UNIVERSITY

EDUCATIONAL REVIEW

Edited by WILLIAM McANDREW

AN EDUCATIONAL PILGRIMAGE TO ATLANTA

Here are some considerations bearing on the rewards of thinking of education in higher terms than those of school-board politics, of superintendents' peculiarities, of principals as persons, and of parents who think themselves the whole community. Teachers have to put up with as many petty annoyances as doctors do, or clergymen, or traffic officers, or saleswomen, or farmers. To keep us from wizening there are pleasant cures available.

Bouquets for Michigan teachers.—"Professor" Pearce is at the head of the schools of Michigan. That state came into the Union with an uncommon regard for public education. Michigan worked out a scheme of it extending from classes for little children up through a university and set a model followed by every commonwealth reaching statehood after her. She put a mark of respect upon her schoolmen from the first. She failed to adopt the New England title, "master," or the Scottish "dominie" or the later New York correctly translatable term, "doctor." "Professor" became the word for the husky young chaps who taught the children of the early forties. It has held through all these years as much of deference, admiration and respect as the Wolverines ever put into "Squire," "Judge," "Reverend" and the set of military titles still in vogue. "Professor" Pearce, therefore, he is, and state superintendent of public instruction, in charge of all the other professors from Ann Arbor to Zilwaukee. Recently I heard him and Professor Sexton, superintendent of the schools of Lansing, addressing a convention of the public-school teachers of the state. Professor Sexton ran through an interesting set of experiences creditable to teachers and to the citizens of the commonwealth as showing how precious the reputation of school people should be to all of us. "I don't know all the towns of Michigan," he said, "but I know sample ones in various parts, and I read newspapers of state-wide influence. I can't think of a single city, town or rural community in this state where the teacher is otherwise than highly respected. The Rotary, the Kiwanis, the Lions and other clubs show honor to the men. The churches, the literary and social societies go after the women. Our calling brings a presumption of respect. Its opportunities for friendships and affectionate regard of the people best worth knowing in any city are not surpassed by those of workers in any other occupation known to me. Do you know of any exception to this assertion? If you do, I wish you would let me know the locality, for I don't want to be making wild statements merely for the sake of being cheerful and complimentary."

Professor Pearce, in following, was led into commenting upon the same cheery theme. His conclusions were that the type of pioneers from New York and northern Ohio, who made up the first Michigan population, brought with them a well-defined regard for schools and teachers which the later immigrants from Germany, Holland, Scotland, Scandinavia and Upper Canada did not fail to strengthen. "But," said the state superintendent, "the main reason for the high regard shown our teachers comes from themselves." He enlarged upon the notable activity they show in improving their knowledge and their skill. The third normal school in America was established in Ypsilanti. The University of Michigan organized a department fifty years ago for the training of teachers and superintendents. The thousands of teachers in service who attend Michigan summer schools in education are considered by its state superintendent an evidence of professional improvement not equaled by physicians, clergymen or those engaged in any of the high-class services to the public. Superintendent Pearce went into details as to the effect of organization upon the development of any profession. Students of world progress notice three main signs of the advancement of any profession: organization, skill and character.

Organization brings skill, character and respect.—Civilized mankind has reached a high degree of respect for the medical profession. Those who write upon this theme are sure that the physician respects himself and his calling, and, in turn, is more highly regarded than at any other epoch of the world. Organization has been largely responsible. The doctors set up their medical associations; they assemble to hear papers upon new experiments; they hold clinics at which expert practitioners demonstrate effective means of repairing the human frame. Thus, organization increases skill, skill brings self-confidence, self-respect and the regard of the public. The doctors make codes of ethics and subscribe to them. Their associations emphasize the necessity of high-grade character in their members. If one of their number falls below the standard they eject him from their guild.

Among the lawyers the same influences are at work. The practitioner is admitted to a company jealous of its respectability. The Bar Association hears addresses upon the improvement of public service; it issues protests against the debasement of law by corrupt politicians; it has its strict rules for professional honor; it casts out unworthy members. Organization, skill and character count high among the lawyers.

The engineers, the pharmacists, the opticians, the dentists, the artists, the clergymen, promote respect through organization, skill and character.

Becoming more respectable.—Reading of life and manners in the days of not so many generations ago, one is impressed by the lower regard for many of the occupations of men. Skill was distinctly lower than now. The physician could enter practice after a short and narrow experience in the office of a preceptor. The lawyer polished up the handle of the big front door, hung around the courts, and read the two or three books recommended by his master. Schools and societies of engineering were almost unknown. The ordinary seller of goods held a low place, indeed. A hundred and fifty years ago a committee of the British parliament bewailed the degeneration of the times because England was in danger of becoming a nation of shopkeepers. The occupation of high regard was that of the commander of troops or of warships. Now, with us, the merchant and the manufacturer hold themselves in high respect and command deference from society. These men have organized. They hold numerous conventions. They hear addresses and reports; they see demonstrations covering the details of merchandising, of guarding costs, of saving waste. Business is becoming a science. The business man has developed skill. His societies frame ethical codes for the conduct of their members. We find no one in our country ashamed to be in trade. On the contrary, when one of our former schoolboys comes to see us and we ask what he is doing, he radiates a proper pride when he lets us know he is "a business man." He is in a company composed of men of character. Within the memory of persons still alive the ethics of the storekeeper was lower than now. *"Caveat emptor"* was a business motto: "It is the buyer's lookout to see that I don't cheat him," "Business is business." Association has substituted new mottoes: "The customer is always right," "Better lose on a sale than displease a buyer," "Unless the service is worth what is paid for it, the transaction fails." Organization has brought skill, character, and respect to the business man.

A great union.—By this line of thought State Superintendent Pearce brings himself to congratulate teachers on the really marvelous organization they have set up in America, a national association of 200,000 workers devoted to the maintenance of skill, high character and public service. It is responsible in no small degree for the high respect which Professor Sexton declares is given to Michigan teachers. I imagine that a questionnaire sent to every state would result in showing that the support of teachers' organizations is as heartily given by schoolmen as is the case in Michigan. I have heard it with my own ears from Cooper in California, Meredith in Connecticut, Blair in Illinois, Miss Samuelson in Iowa, Thomas in Maine, Smith in Massachusetts, Miss Trumper in Montana, Butterfield in New Hampshire, Graves in New York, Miss Palmer in North Dakota, Keith in Pennsylvania, Ranger in Rhode Island, Marrs in Texas, Dempsey in Vermont, Mrs. Preston in Washington and Callahan in Wisconsin. I can remember when some superintendents hesitated to urge upon us with real fervor our duty to enroll. They thought it unseemly to suggest the sacrifice of any part of a teacher's hard-earned salary. They were influenced by the objection of small minds that teachers were being asked to contribute to the glory of the men higher up, who took all the offices and exploited the rank and file. The association was alleged to be in the control of a "ring." There were complaints that it featured the same ambitious speakers over and over and was used by them to build their reputations. If we can borrow the optimist's motto that all things work together for good, we may rejoice that the superintendents now have a big division of their own and that the main section of the association belongs to everybody. We may elect man or woman, class teacher or college president, to any office up to the top. In the forty years that I have known it, the organization has moved into a policy that parallels the highest motives to be found in any association, be it of clergymen, physicians or any group of devoted public servants.

What's the big idea?—The reasons for supporting the National Education Association are now the most exalted that animate the best impulses that are in any of us. When we get away from the pettiness, the *Kleinlichkeit*, that we inherited from an ancient period and look at education unhampered by local considerations, we soon realize that its aims are indeed of the very highest kind of inspiring impulses that guide such natures as every decent man or woman wants to acquire. The supreme aspirations that make life worth living—progress, civilization, culture, betterment, service—are so universally conceived to be the mission of education that one has only to think over these things with some natural seriousness to begin to realize what a really fine thing it is to be a teacher. The sneers directed against words like these are curious and interesting. In the memory of men not yet a hundred years old, contumely, disdain, and scorn have been poured by the snobs of pen and ink upon abolitionists, Republicans, ministers, prohibitionists, peacemakers, purity advocates, League of Nations, woman suffrage, suppression of lotteries and upon the public-school system. You need not be very old to be able to note a marvelous diminution of contempt for all of these. To be in a profession, or employment or business, or pursuit, or whatever you prefer to call it, that is moving ahead as ours is will bring satisfaction to you whenever you think it over broadly and adequately.

How's your philosophy?—A number of contributors to this magazine have lately been urging that we need in our present educational thought more philosophy. We have been testing, counting, measuring, so much that these writers fear we are losing sight of the large and soul-expanding ideals which it is the mission of philosophy to give.

Very well, let's philosophize. What you get out of our own James and Durant, the French Bergson, and the English Wells is the conclusion that there is an urge ahead and a pull behind. There are forces seeking to improve, to build up, to refine and to beautify; there are powers active in impairment, destruction, disordering and hurting. Your grandfather called them God and devil. You can name them what you please. You need no eminent authority to argue you into believing they exist. You can meet them on the streets of your own town on the way from home to school. The men who made education a public service of the states of the American Union justified making everybody contribute for teachers' wages on the ground that we shall be dedicated to the positive, constructive, progressive, refining, bettering forces of the world. If the spirit of God is in these things and has to fight and struggle against the powers of evil, then by taking employment as public-school teachers we have elected to play the rôle of God's helpers. No matter how cleverly any brilliant magazine writer may sneer at this, the conclusion is unescapable. The schools were not organized give us a living nor to give any one "an education," but as the American nation's deliberate intent to encourage religion, morality, and that knowledge which is necessary to good government and to the happiness of mankind. The National Congress said so and by precise words incorporated the idea into a law which has stood unrepealed these hundred and forty-two years.

Why are you teaching?—The satisfactions we feel at alliance with the positive and constructive influences of the world are enlarged by knowing that the performance of a great duty is involved. We get encouragement from recalling that Washington, Franklin, Jefferson, Adams and the revered builders of the nation put upon us what they called a matter of primary importance. We get a proper pride from remembering that Lincoln, Garfield, Roosevelt, Wilson, Coolidge and Hoover have concluded that no public service is so important. We hear with approval our own fellows adopting similar declarations, as when our Cleveland convention prints on the front of its program Frank Boynton's statement of our creed—that every child born in or adopted by this republic has by virtue of that fact the right to the development, by education, of whatever talent he may have as far as his ability and ambition may permit. We consider it proper that the participants of that convention should repeat in unison a prayer of the teachers of Colorado, "rejoicing in life, grateful for the chance to serve, anxious to learn new things, to behold new visions, to attempt worthier tasks, determined to help." Now comes the president of the National Association, Uel Lamkin, and tells us that not only are all the theories of education of the sort to make us proud of them, but the achievements of teachers are distinctly commendable and, now, not inferior to those of any profession. Twenty-eight million young lives are being guided by us. Our own training keeps getting better. We are being taught the real problems of childhood. Our teaching grows more vital. We are paying attention to the men and women who missed education in their earlier years. We are rapidly moving toward the goal of a fair start for every child. For those reasons, Dr. Lamkin urges us all to join the National Association and thus to keep the procession moving ahead. The college presidents are impressed by our advance. I notice that Dr. Upham takes for the subject of his inaugural address, when inducted into the presidency of Miami University, the improvement in skill that has come to teaching. The development of your knowledge of methods and technics, your application of scientific knowledge and procedure to your problems, are marvelous. So says the college president.

The Associated Press goes to your secretary, Professor Crabtree, because of the importance of your service, and asks him for a statement. The people, says the secretary, are not going back on the schools but are more confident in them than ever. Clubs and associations are cooperating amazingly. Citizens understand teachers and teachers, citizens, better. The lawyers and doctors now place the teaching profession on a par with their own. Our ethics are higher than before. We won't apply for positions to the disparagement of those occupying them. We won't jump our contracts. We have a higher respect for the work we do than ever. So says our national secretary.

William Bagley's cheerful reconnaissance.—If any doubting Thomas objects that some of these statements were made to teachers and purposely play up the pleasant side I can give him William Bagley's picture of American teaching as shown by him to the foreign students at Columbia University. It is one of those circumstantial presentations of an observer who keeps his feet on the ground. "The rising of the teacher's status," Dr. Bagley told his young listeners from all over the world, "is the most recent and the most far-reaching fact in American educational history. A patronizing attitude of thinly veiled contempt, common the world over, was a very serious handicap to the service in America. It kept morale at a low point. Those who remained as teachers acquired an inferiority complex of large dimensions. They openly regretted they had not gone into other work. They advised their students not to teach. This notion has been one of the most serious obstacles to the development of a real profession of teaching in our country. To-day many of the old handicaps are gone. Fifteen years ago the average teacher had no more than a high-school training. To-day sixty per cent. of our teachers have had at least two years preparation beyond high school. In several states the proportion of better prepared is nearly one hundred per cent. The enrolment in normal schools and teachers' colleges has doubled in five years. In public esteem the teacher's calling has made significant advances. High school enrolment has trebled in fifteen years; college registration has doubled in ten years. The inferiority complex is certainly giving place to a sense of professional pride and dignity, tempered, as may it be always, by a keen sense of the complexities of the teaching problem and a recognition of the serious responsibility upon us. Teachers within the last ten years have increased their membership in the National Education Association so that it has grown from 10,000 to 200,000. It rests with teachers to decide where our profession will advance and how it will do it. We are getting toward a real democracy, breaking down distinction between elementary-school teachers and those of older students." These are some of the gains enumerated by Dr. Bagley.

Not done yet.—If now you turn to the survey by Dr. Ross Finney you will get a conception of the magnitude of problems yet to be solved. We have the prospect of so much yet to do that the satisfaction of knowing how greatly we shall be needed and wanted will not wane. We can congratulate ourselves with the classical truth that it is better to travel hopefully than to arrive. There is plenty yet to do.

The testimony establishes the gain in character, skill, self-respect and public regard achieved parallel to the strengthening of our voluntary association. It points plainly to my duty as teacher actively to support our great organization. One need not argue for the personal advantage one gets from meeting the bright and agreeable people that will assemble at the meeting in Atlanta. A large proportion of those in attendance will be teachers of the South. In charm of personality, in hospitality, in professional spirit, they rank so high that every visitor from other parts of the country gets a distinct inspiration from meeting them. The sociability and liveliness of the sessions are tonic in their effect. One leaves with a distinct feeling of greater satisfaction at being a teacher. A big convention washes away pettiness that comes to any practitioner from too much confinement in one locality. These personal benefits are worth while, but they do not give the satisfaction that can come to every participant who will keep alive the larger motive of duty toward what the most eminent of Americans have called the greatest of public services. I should go to Atlanta because I want to push a great cause, nothing less than the hope of the world. Mr. Hoover is the latest to call it that. I should go with intent to become a more valuable pusher in a great movement. I should intend that the service in my own town should be better from my having attended the meetings. No matter how remote or unimportant my district may seem to be, it is for it and all others like it that the programs are organized. The association meetings are a concentrated summer school. I can get much from them if I go about it as I set my own pupils about any important study.

Making the best of it.—It is a good plan, before leaving home, to obligate ourselves in some way that will compel us when we reach Atlanta to get out of the meetings that which they are intended to give. If we should engage, with intent to benefit our own system, to present to teachers' meetings at home next fall "forward-looking suggestions from the Atlanta meeting," this would make our attendance more worth while for everybody. If every school board would aim at this advantage and should designate and pay teachers to render this service the money would be well spent. But if no official offer of this sort comes to us, it is well worth while for us to offer this service ourselves before leaving home. I know it. I have sometimes been bound to report conventions for an educational magazine. On such occasions I have had to use what I call my mind. I have been obliged to select my sessions with care, to take my notebook and pencil along, to be laughed at for working so busily while so many of the others were sitting easy in their chairs as one might indolently warm himself in front of a good fire. They had the easier time, but I got the more benefit. It stands to reason that if you go to a meeting with no sense of real responsibility the pearls cast upon the audience by the choicest educators of the world will mostly slip through your mental fingers and, when school opens in the fall, your memory of Atlanta will be a jumble of pretty women, handsome men, hot waffles, beautiful gardens, and a few strains of sweet songs. These are delightful recollections to have but they are much more enjoyable if they go along with some of the carefully worked out conclusions that the speakers have laboriously and skilfully prepared for you. The old junketing days of the association are over. It is no longer a merry picnic with the main attraction made up of pageantry, music, and bright shows. It is an assemblage of "professors," you and the rest of us, seeking to mark the progress of a great calling and to push it ahead some notches more. It represents a tremendous amount of work by a multitude of industrious people giving you their best.

If the speaker does more work than his audience the affair is out of kilter. Everybody, if he thinks about it, knows this to be true.

Don't be laughed out of it.—Get your notebook, then—good size and stiff covers. Take it to the meetings. Don't be ashamed to have it on your lap. Get the drift of the speaker's argument. Write your analysis of it. You'll find that your enjoyment of the meeting is enhanced tenfold. Who says so? William James, his brother, Henry, David Grayson, Nathaniel Hawthorne, Ralph Waldo Emerson, David Belasco, Bernard Shaw, H. G. Wells, Lawrence Abbott and B. C. Pythagoras. The mortal remains of some of them may be buried, but what they said about taking notes lives on and is especially applicable to you and to me listening to an address at an educational meeting. Note-taking in such circumstances is a real exercise in courage, because your timid and lazy friends and especially the book men, who are neither timid nor lazy, but hardened to conventions, will laugh at you. That great traveler, Augustus Hare, remarked what you get from an important place depends on what you take with you. Take a notebook. You think I am making Atlanta a task. You are right.

Here, then, is a sum of the whole matter. Your National Education Association, following the track of the learned professions, business and industry, has, through organization, advanced the character, skill, confidence and reputation of teachers. You are obligated to push these benefits further. You do it by attending the Atlanta meeting and reporting its high points to your brother and sister professionals back home. It adds to your satisfaction in life and enables you to aid us in getting nearer that far-off divine event toward which the whole creation moves.

A REVIEW OF PROFESSIONAL BOOKS

By HOI BIBLIOLOGOI

WITH everybody present and on time our club came to order without being called to it and heard some informal reports upon the progress of professional reading. Principal Philip Manzer told us that since November some eighteen teachers in his school had been meeting with him from three o'clock until half past four following a program similar to those of the Bibliologoi, except that only one contributor reports at each meeting. "It was a little constrained at first," he said. "Although nearly all the teachers have worked with me for several years they seemed nervous when undertaking to discuss the contents of a book. I knew there would be a strong inclination to read papers. So I made it a prime agreement that we wouldn't. A thing that bothered me a good deal was the tendency of the reciters to look at me most of the time and to expect me to ask the questions and to lead the discussions. We obviated that by electing a moderator, a different one for each meeting. She, whoever she is, keeps the affair from getting stiff and formal. I have said they mustn't have any hesitation about staying away from meetings. We'll call any session a success that has as many as two present. The interest has been remarkable."

"I guess I made myself too much of a manager," said the Viking Maid. "I've been the chairman right along. My folks elected me. I wanted to make the thing go and knew I could. Next year I'll adopt the idea of a new moderator for every session."

The General, Dr. Batwell, and Old Locality all reported their branch Bibliologois as running well. Euclid and the Stevedore told of theirs only just begun. Polly, the political, informed us that Anna, the arguer, and Luther, the literary, had joined with her and a group of teachers getting ready for the principals' examination and that their program consists of weekly discussion of chapters of Henry Morrison.

A Sympathetic Scientist Succoring Schools Sociologically: Snedden. Martin of Tours began the reviewing. He spoke as follows: "Dr. Snedden has a new book.[1] I like it. I like his American view of the office of public education. It is a precaution taken by the people, organized as government, to provide that the people's affairs shall be conducted so as to supply an enlightened public opinion. It would be easy for a professor of education in the college of teachers at Columbia University to be so saturated with the lore of methods and principles as to lose sight of the fact that when our educational pioneers made all people, whether parents or not, pay for the schooling of children the logic of that act is the assumption that the public schools are to benefit everybody, not merely or chiefly the families which have children. 'The teacher needs to have,' says Dr. Snedden, 'a substantial range of appreciations of the societies and social conditions, past, present, and of the not distant future in the service of which education has developed and must continue better to serve. Heretofore these appreciations have been derived largely from the history of education or from the study of its principles and philosophy.' It is not enough. Education under our American laws, education from its development out of our Revolution, education from the nature of its obligatory support, is, with us, a political, a civic, a social service. Therefore the social sciences must be drawn upon to give teachers the necessary backgrounds for interpreting the purpose of public schools and for improving processes and means with more adequate aims.

"Dr. Snedden is fully aware of the unsatisfactory condition of public school service. He reminds us that of the 750,000 teachers in America, forty-two per cent. of the 635,000 women are under twenty-five years of age; twenty-two per cent. of the men are under twenty-five. With immature personalities in such numbers attempting the very difficult problems of developing better citizens the hopelessness of the situation is aggravated by a yearly turn-over of 100,000 persons. This great horde, often with little supervision, is unequal to the task as conceived by students of education. When one sees what a complex and delicate task the training of a human disposition is and that, for the most part, it is entrusted to half-baked youngsters who say they are attempting it only for a short time until something better turns up, we realize how easy it is for a writer to revile, abuse, denounce and cover with contempt the whole tribe of teachers. We have a past history, centuries old, wherein we were the butts of ridicule, from Horace to Shakespeare to Dickens, to the time of men yet living.

"One of our fellow townsmen, the brilliant Edward Yeomans, Chicago manufacturer, advertised us by articles in *The Atlantic Monthly* and then in a book, 'Shackled Youth.' As I remember his widely published picture it was of us as part of the mass of those immersed in antediluvian thought, often with intelligence of the monkey grade, going about our tasks with deadly complacency, knowing nothing of our responsibilities, unable to understand any explanations of them because we have no faculties with which to understand. Mr. Yeomans, by means of that little book, pumped such a stream of muddy water over us as to make him applauded by the always available crowd of people who like to see something dirtied. Because of the remarkable difference in his attitude and that of Dr. Snedden I revert to Mr. Yeoman's diatribes. In the midst of really beautiful pas-

[1] David Snedden, ''Educational Sociology for Beginners,'' The Macmillan Co., New York. 636 pp. $3.50.

sages upon the joy of life and while giving delightful details of his realization of it in New England during his summers and in California in his winters, he has his fling at us as putting the shadows of a prison-house around the growing boy. I remember he asked whether children are stimulated in school to continue their intellectual interests. With astounding assurance, as if he were familiar with the schools of his own Chicago or of New England or of California, he answers as readily as a sworn witness, 'Not at all.' Too many of us who have no right to teach are teaching was the conclusion of this brilliant writer who confesses that standing outside the school he looks upon it with perennial sadness because it 'evidently is not functioning in such a way as to justify any more hope for increased happiness.' 'Outside'—that explains him.

"Now, Dr. Snedden is not standing outside the school as Mr. Yeomans says himself to be. Perhaps that is why the Snedden book is permeated by a calm assurance that the American school and the American teacher are progressing toward all the things that Mr. Yeomans, from the outside, proclaims us too stupid to see. 'Education,' says our Snedden, 'is rapidly becoming a science, a great field of human work in which the most useful findings of many sciences are increasingly applied.' Our Chicago author remarks if Americans had sense enough they could get on without schools. 'They are not essentials. Something happened to make them seem so. The man with a book put it over the man who had none. He finally got himself intrusted with the education of other people's children.' On the other hand, our Teachers College author thinks the facts so well known to all his readers that he merely hints at the recorded truths that our schools were not instituted by teachers who got themselves intrusted with other people's children. Snedden assumes that we know that schools were proposed by Franklin and Washington and Jefferson and Madison and Monroe and Webster and Clinton and Mann and Lincoln and a long line of Americans who were not schoolmasters but statesmen. He knows that the citizens, not the teachers, of the New England towns introduced schools and that associations of workingmen in Pennsylvania petitioned for public education before the Revolution. Whereas Mr. Yeomans remarks 'the less necessary you make schools the better.' Dr. Snedden notes that America is fonder of her children than is any other nation in the world and is making the schooling of them more and more necessary, to the amazing extent of 600 per cent. increase in high schools alone in the past ten years.

"The professor conceives that for many purposes it is useful to divide us into two more or less interlocking groups: the policy makers and those who carry out their intent. Superintendents, supervisors, principals and researchers are clearly, he says, of the first class, as are progressive teachers who make themselves worth appointment in curriculum revision. The essence of this kind of work is scientific. Educational sociology, still in its infancy, is naturally not yet secure, even though it is one of the fastest in development among the social sciences. It is handicapped by the fact that teaching is in the hands of so large a proportion of young girls. Stenography is the only pursuit that has a larger percentage of them. Dr. Snedden, in his chapter, 'Who are the policy makers?' seems to have had his eye on our town. Readers in other localities will think him looking at them. He gives a pen sketch of what may be considered a typical situation. 'Miss B. D. is twenty-one years old. She graduated from a near-by teachers college. She is healthy, attractive, and very sociable, almost excessively fond of good times, dress and the refined male and female companionship of her own age and type. Her intelligence quotient is at the high point of the third or at the low point of the fourth quarter for all adults. She is disposed to work hard and faithfully as a teacher and shows no ability to work through the larger problems of education which were frequently called to her attention in the training school. She has no intention to teach more than four or five years. In spirit and training she is fitted to serve as a fairly good executant of educational programs set by her official superiors.' Hold that picture in your mind and set beside it Dr. Snedden's portrait of 'Superintendent E. M.'

"'He graduated from a good college, served five years as a high-school teacher, seven years as principal of elementary and of high schools, gave two and a half years to study for his doctor's degree, six years as principal of a large high school, and ten years as superintendent. Obviously he ranks in the upper twenty per cent. of all the men who graduated thirty years ago. He writes a good paper and makes a well-received address. He is keenly interested in educational progress.

"'The school board is ready to authorize reconstruction of the whole curriculum. The superintendent recommends that members of the local system, a few educators from abroad and a few well-equipped laymen cooperate in the work. How much should Miss B. D. and those like her,' asks Dr. Snedden, 'be looked to for help in policy making?' And then he gives this suggestion to those bewildered school boards who are hypnotized by the slogan 'democracy in education.' 'The great majority of teachers are not to inaugurate or even to reconstruct educational policies, but rather to give effect to them. It would seem no less absurd to expect most teachers to decide what courses should be given as to look to a young engineer to say into what region a new railway should be built, or a young interne to make basic policies for the hospital, or a young lieutenant to serve on the board of strategy.'

"Dr. Snedden's persuasive logic as to why the coming teacher should study the social sciences seems to me not only sound but as outlining a procedure which requires immediate adoption. Examine the courses in our training schools: the history of education, the philosophy of teaching, general psychology. They might be useful to an intending researcher or curriculum-maker, but the mass of the young women taking the courses certainly will have very little to do with the determination of educational policies. But they should be helped toward becoming adept in working with the social groups, the school classes, that custom and economy require. They should, in their training schools, have learned well what are the local and community adjustments which they should make and maintain toward children, parents, gossips, and school authorities.

"Accordingly, Dr. Snedden addresses himself to these beginners in the study of education. He seems to me to have a real affection for them. He has no condescending or patronizing air. He is an appreciator. He says he wants us to appreciate the social world which schools of all kinds should serve. He carries us into the visible and invisible relationships and how they serve humanity. He treats of American races and their possible decay, of family life, of getting and using wealth, of politics, of democratic hopes and gains, of our national culture, aspirations and prospects, of religion, of our social diseases, and considers the question of what progress we are making. He goes into our status as professionals, our life outside of school, and of the sociological foundations of the different things we teach and do.

"It is a progressive book in a new field. It conceives our service in a large and complimentary spirit restrained by a healthy caution but inspired by a vigorous faith."

The Road out of the Ruts: Park. Principal Manzer speaks of other enthusiasms and of his own.

"You people are an interesting study in group psychology. Have you ever noticed that the praise of the books reviewed by you always grows warmer as the evening advances? Perhaps there is a subconscious feeling of competition in you as in the bally-hoo men at the fair. Perhaps you have an instinctive urge to convince us that the book you selected from the pile was better than the others because you are a better judge of books, or perhaps the memory of the delicious collations the gracious Lady Alice has given us here moves us to sing our best for our supper. At any rate any one reading the accounts of our meetings might think we had discovered the best that man has printed."

"We have," said Anna the arguer, "I mull over half-a-dozen books and give you only one or two of the best."

"I've often wondered," said Polly the political, "what Papa Rose does with the discards which we bring back unreviewed."

"That's simple," said the paterfamilias. "I wait a meeting or two and then put 'em on the table again. If nobody takes them, I assign 'em to Peter the Reader. If he doesn't find them worth reviewing they must be pretty poor, so I give them to dentists for the tables in their waiting rooms."

"What I was about to say," continued Philip, "is that my enthusiasm for my book[2] has an entirely different source. The subject is not as interesting to me as it ought to be. The master advised me to take the book. It has gained my admiration. It has warmed me to ardor. Why? Because its author, Maxwell Park, a student of the fundamentals of education, a teacher of teachers, an author with experience, has condensed into eighty-four pages the very essence of a broad, a concrete, a searching, a gripping theory and practice of present-day education. I applaud him with all the fervor of one who has experienced a real thrill. Park's book, I think, is a discovery.

"What does he do? He carries into teacher-training and professional study the big principles of self-activity, individual adjustment, discussion, and diagnostic testing, such as the advance of education has been securing for the teaching of children. Park accepts the repeated dictum worked out convincingly by Wm. H. Burnham that the method of life's progress is the attack upon problems and tasks. I can imagine the author asking himself what are the present needful things for teachers to know and do. Can I choose a small workable library that will give a clear and concise view of these things? A five-foot shelf is too long for the purpose. I must have something comparable to the courses offered in the training schools, say, a three-hour course for one term. I'll make my library half a dozen books best suited for beginners. Here is what he chooses:

Bagley and Keith: "Introduction to Teaching." Macmillan.

Cubberley: "Introduction to Education." Houghton, Mifflin.

Dearborn: "Introduction to Teaching." Appleton.

Frasier and Armentrout: "Introduction to Education." Scott, Foresman.

Henmiller: "A First Book in Education." Century.

Judd: "Introduction to Scientific Study of Education." Ginn.

The author gives you thirty-seven more readings that you may find valuable. But on his snug little six he concentrates, so that they completely cover the points he (and I) considers essential.

"For the first time in my experience I find an authority (besides myself) who recognizes the wasteful futility of the common usage of professional reading. A principal will earnestly and enthusiastically urge his teachers to read. In the vast majority of cases I have observed the reading is improperly done in that the lady or gentleman undertakes the whole book as a task. We in this book-reviewers' club read in that way. For reviewing, it's about the only thing we can do. But for professional study it is comparable to devouring a month's ration of victuals at a single sitting. 'Don't read too much' is a necessary caution. A teacher, in service, should be persuaded to read a short piece, to ruminate on it, that is, to chew it well, to use it in the classroom practice. Only so is it digested and made a part of one's organism. Now, a prime feature of Maxwell Park's little manual is that it requires this very thing. You can't do anything with his book in any other way. He must be a fascinating teacher, for he makes the progress through the fundamentals of teaching intensely personal and interesting. Like old Admiral Fisk and Von Moltke, before that, like the masters of work, Park begins with a distinct array of objectives. I can imagine him ever since he made up his mind to produce this book, jotting down, in his classroom, in his walks, in his reading, after conversation, what our occupation needs to give it the respectability of a profession. I can picture him sifting and classifying his notes, rejecting what the brevity he intends for his book will not admit. He gives a striking outline of the aims of his work. In them are the saving of the time and energy of pupil and teacher in reaching a concept of the things that make a teacher a professional. 'I wish,' says Mr. Park, 'to get a student to establish his aims, to know what thinkers are saying education is for, to form a judgment on their proposals, not to swallow whole what he reads, but to develop a constructively critical attitude.' Accordingly, the book asks the intending teachers some four hundred questions and leaves the blank space under each one for the answer. 'What do you think are the needed steps for professional growth?' 'What does Mr. Bagley think about it?' 'Mr. Judd?' 'Mr. Dearborn?'

[2] Maxwell G. Park, "A Problem Outline in Introduction to Teaching." The Century Co., New York, 84 pp.

'What do you think, now, after getting their view?' 'You, you, you, are the person I am after. It is you who are going to teach. It is your ideals that are going to guide you, not Bagley's, Judd's, nor Dearborn's until whatever of them you have tried and selected becomes a part of yourself.'

"Mr. Park fights against the transitory nature of ideas obtained from easy reading and from listening to speakers at teachers' institutes. His book develops in you the habit of note-making, outlining, organizing and summarizing the results of study. When you have finished the course you have here a work of your own. All Mr. Park's matter will then be in the nature of secondary contributions to your own book. I hope in subsequent printings he will give the volume a shape approaching that of an ordinary book, say eight and one half by five inches. Then you can stand it on an ordinary bookshelf along with your library of six other authors, besides yourself, on education. I agree with a writer in School and Society that a need of our age is solid, well-bound, lasting, handy-shaped notebooks, diaries, and souvenir volumes conducive to retention rather than final discard because they don't fit anywhere.

"As I have already suggested, this book is planned to make the user think his own thoughts, fortified by the judgment of men of experience and sane view. 'I wish,' says the author, 'to develop initiative and responsibility in educational procedures.' He might have called it 'getting out of grooves.' Although it seems primarily intended for beginning teachers in the early terms of a training school, I should think it a prime basis for the classes of principals, superintendents and coaches for promotional examinations for higher certificates conducted in every live educational system. Mr. Park repeatedly sets the stage for group discussion by classes. He gives them live topics to talk about, current theories and practices, pressing problems.

"Observe a few samples: 'Note some of the attractive aspects of teaching.' 'Name and rank as to importance, means of professional growth.' 'Give your idea of your proper attitude and effort toward it.' Remember he wants you to write your conclusions permanently with ink directly in the place provided for them. Recall that he gives you book and page of your daily half-dozen authorities who, in advance of you, have thought upon these same questions. 'Illustrate what is meant by the professional ethics of your position.' Along with this he gives the Cortland Teachers' Oath, framed by Principal De Groat. I remember him. I met him at a National Education convention when he was a high-school inspector of the New York State Department of Education. He was one of the most cheery, solid, business-like, modest, dead-in-earnest participants in the discussions I heard. Here is his oath for the teachers who come out of his state normal school: 'I now publicly declare my faith. I will always by my practice set forth the life that I would have lived by those whom it is my duty to influence. I will exalt truth and honor, despise meanness and deceit. I will pity and encourage the weak and inspire the strong. I will be charitable. I will be loyal to my superior officers and to my associates. I will be courageous, temperate, persevering, patriotic, and true. I will treat the children intrusted to me as I would have others treat my brothers and sisters. I solemnly engage to direct my efforts toward making each day's work better than that of the days before.'

"Park's book is staunchly in earnest. No palaver, no sob-stuff about the hard work of the teacher. He conceives it to be as important and difficult and fascinating as that of a hospital nurse or a family doctor. 'Write here,' he says, 'what your duty is in finding the individual difficulty of the failing child in your arithmetic class.' 'Explain what you mean regarding your duty to train desirable habits of conduct.' 'How will you develop altruistic leadership motives?' 'List a few of the most worth-while out-of-school professional or semi-professional activities in which you should engage.' 'How would you use a teacher-self-rating scale?' (He submits a sample.) 'Why is it unsafe to teach children the most frequently accepted notions and practices of present-day books and of adults?' 'Why should you be an active member of the local, state and national education associations?' And so on, runs the most solid, personal, thorough self-analysis of us, as teachers, to be found in print. Here is a conception of education that dispenses with the old wishy-washy, apologetic tone for 'the noble army of teachers' and presents the service as the nation's big business, no pastime, no stop-gap, but a profession, a career, full of the possibilities of high skill, attractiveness, and satisfaction.

"Among the forty-eight men and women with whom I have the honor to work in the school of which I am the able or too unworthy principal, depending on how I feel at the time, are six and sometimes eight teachers who cherish a laudable ambition of getting a certificate and a school to manage. I am recommending each to get Mr. Park's remarkable course and to use it as self-culture. I commend it to each of you as stimulant, tonic, and food."

He is worth a Nobel prize. This was the contribution of Polly the political.

"Here is a book[3] that increases my pride in my profession and my satisfaction at being a teacher because one of our number, William Carr, instructor in school administration, Stanford University, tackles a world problem and handles it with such comprehension, capacity and sane judgment as to put his treatise in the front rank of the best discussions of the supremely important problems of peace and war. We teachers, says Mr. Carr, are certainly agreed that the fundamental justification of making everybody contribute the cost of educating children is that they may be prepared in the fine art of getting along with other people. The social, civic, political, aim of public schools is very prominent in educational thought at present. We don't seem to have come very far into the training for world-citizenship. We all seem to agree that such training is a preponderant obligation upon the schools. We pass good, honest resolutions to this effect in our educational conventions but when Mr. James Glass, or Mr. George Counts, or Professor Leonard Koos make their surveys of what is actually done in the classrooms they tell us that it is very little, indeed, of this sort. Dr. Frederick, in SCHOOL AND SOCIETY, gives surprising facts brought out in his investigation of the results of civic teaching, or lack of it, upon high-school students. Fifty-nine per cent. believed that no patriotic American would admit that any country is superior to the United States in any important respect. Thirty-eight per cent. held that we ought to conquer, annex and develop Mexico. Forty-eight per cent. said the offices of the League of Nations are in France. In general, the high-school students lacked sympathy, ideals of friendship, understanding, and tolerance for other nations. Mr. Carr reluctantly concludes from what information is available that civic training practically neglects all but a narrow and inadequate aspect of the duty of the citizen trained at public expense for the preservation and improvement of civic ideals. Teachers outside of resolution-passing meetings are not living up to their professed beliefs. In some communities it is difficult and dangerous for a teacher to present any but an unpatriotic patriotism, that of the self-centered, America-first, domineering type. It is a pseudo-patriotism that actually harms the nation morally and materially. In certain localities one stands in danger of being called traitor if he denounces it. The hysterical charges against a former superintendent of Chicago schools illustrate this tendency. There are many instances in which schools have encouraged international hatred.

"Mr. Carr seems to me to realize the difficult situation of the teachers and to give credit to the prevailing sentiment of them toward sanity, progress and departure from the barbarity which is war. He knows that when we are given a chance to help in making courses of study we put in lessons on the promotion of good will between the nations as we did here in Chicago. He knows that we have hostile boards of education to contend with who order such matter suppressed as did our Chicago board. But Mr. Carr does us the honor to recognize that courage and righteousness are existent and necessary characteristics of a public-school teacher, and his book, without anything of the manner of the preacher or exhorter, is calculated to reach and strengthen the best impulses of our profession.

"The calmness of his style is a remarkable element of strength. You may take, for example, his chapter on the fighting instinct. If I didn't belittle the intent and effect of his treatment I would say these pages are nothing short of delicious. With a cheerful nerve, he

[3] William G. Carr, "Education for Citizenship." Stanford University Press, California. 225 pp. $2.50.

calls out William James, Walter Cannon and William McDougall, and gives their arguments for pugnacity plenty of light. With his keen scalpel he dissects their reasonings, throws away the portions which you see have no bearing upon any conclusion, and, as you look for what is left, you find there is nothing. Fighting has been called an instinct. Your writer gets for you the authoritative definitions of instinct. He puts fighting alongside this definition and that one. It doesn't match, anywhere. This whole chapter, quite apart from its moral significance, is an example of reasoning so well done and withal so entertaining that it is worth transferring bodily to a school text-book on composition, or rhetoric, or debating, or logic. I've read it three times already. Like a piece of good music, it stands repetition.

"The entire book has a rare combination of vigor and modesty. You are not pushed by it into any conviction the author has. You are given an elevated conception of your business as a public-school worker. You are reminded of what world-citizenship has come to mean by changes in your own day. You are retold the objectives of education, the essential facts of psychology. You are lured into a discussion of physical-training, military drill, geography, history and literature, all flavored with a refreshing simplicity and pleasing manners. Try his analysis of the personnel of wars. You come to the conclusion that wars are really fought by those who would have voted against going to war if all the facts in the dispute could have been placed before them without exaggeration or appeal to passion. When we examine any war we find that its strongest support was not an instinct but propaganda. Propaganda is a kind of education. There you are! War is caused by the people who expect to gain by it. They educate the community into war. What are we doing? Oh, following a tradition which assumes that the classroom and teacher are remote from the world. How did Germany get so remarkable a war spirit? By making militarism a part of the education of the whole people, old and young. How is a sane conception of life to be secured in the world? By the guidance of reason. By the making of its teachings the preponderating, day-by-day, work of the classroom. What is necessary? Organization, teacher-training, school-board action, a program, a philosophy of life and progress.

"Not only has Mr. Carr put into a short and vivacious essay a complete treatment of the large subject, but he has listed what he considers the best two hundred books bearing on the subject suitable for teachers and for school children. I am prepared to argue with any one that the book should be given a Nobel Prize."

How teachers behave when children misbehave: Wickham. The Viking Maid said this:

"The Commonwealth Fund gives us a remarkable study[4] of misconduct, alleged and real, by school children. The investigator is a former Chicagoan of the staff of our Institute for Juvenile Research who, after experience as public-school teacher and principal, took up studies in child guidance in Cleveland, St. Paul, and New York. He is now one of the psychologists of the New York Institute for Child Guidance. Our judgment as to what constitutes misbehavior is mostly unscientific and unsound. Our customary opinions on it are more and more called in question as a calm and scientific observation is employed. We are having more opportunities of getting a consistent knowledge of child life and child needs. Consideration and treatment of problems are being scrutinized and reformed. The relation of behavior disorders to adult action is coming to be seen as a surprising situation, not very highly creditable to us. Our own attitude needs careful scrutiny. When we are dissatisfied with a child's behavior we assume there's something wrong with him. How do we know the trouble is not with us? Nobody is more concerned with children than we teachers. We are in the youth business. Child-study has been recognized as an essential for us. Now, says Mr. Wickham, it is desirable that we have more teacher study. Accordingly he asks, what are the things you think are chiefly back of the conduct of children? If I measure the responses of enough teachers I will have a measurement of the attitude of the American school. Most of the text-books on school discipline treat of faults which are those considered important by the individual author. Mr. Wickham gets teachers of Cleveland and

[4] E. K. Wickham, "Children's Behavior and Teachers' Attitudes." The Commonwealth Fund. 578 Madison Ave., New York. 247 pp. $2.00.

of Minneapolis to list behavior problems for him. He subjects his many hundred responses to analysis and tabulation. Disorderliness in the classroom is reported existent in 100 per cent. of their pupils by some teachers while others report hardly any as observable. One teacher reports 92 per cent. of her children as dishonest. Others say there are no instances of untruthfulness in any of their children. Some call attention to the wilful disobedience in a large number of their boys and girls. Many other teachers record that they never have observed it in a single child. You learn that over two thirds of school children cheat and that none of them do: that all whisper contrary to rules and that only one does so. You are saying everybody knows that the personal equation throws all opinions out of gear. You are recalling the experiment of having papers rated by different expert teachers until the same set of answers gets scores of from 0 to 100. You are wondering why the wise Wickham bothers to go any farther into an investigation which, at the start, discloses such a lack of solid foundation on which to build any conclusion. But it is this very mushiness which is the object of Mr. Wickham's study, which is so important that the hard-headed trustees of the Commonwealth Fund vote the money necessary to carry on the survey.

"From the tables and charts which list and compare the fifty faults of pupils you discover that the conduct which is interpretable as lack of respect for our authority is that which we rate as most reprehensible. We develop an appetite for admiration, praise, agreement. We feed our conceit, our egoism, our love for authority. We want a declaration accepted from us because we say it. That's natural enough, says Mr. Wickham. It is the adult manifestation toward children. Vanity is the most sensitive spot. By such an attitude we get more immediate compliance with our plan of the hour and do more lasting damage to the child than by any other known method. Our main consideration seems to be to cover the course of study. Any behavior that interferes with our doing it seems to us most serious. Mr. Wickham is not at all sarcastic or unkind about this. He notes the difficulty of our acting otherwise with the weight of tradition all about us. He gives the tables showing that we rate whispering, inattention, disorder in class, interrupting, acting 'smart,' impertinence, at the head of our lists. Shyness, suspicion, temper outbursts, cowardice, etc., we put among the least important. He notes that teachers prefer the less active, more complaint behavior of girls to the more aggressive, independent attitude of boys. I see you shaking your heads at this. You have only to look at his tables to note that, by their own weighting, desirable conduct, as conceived by public school teachers, takes on the distinguishing characteristics of girl behavior. In place of the Spartan concept of public education as the culture of men there does seem, from this study, basis for a not uncommon charge that American schools tend to baby and sissify the boys. The question of sex behavior and the tendency of school managers to preserve ignorance of it has an interesting side-light in a footnote: permission for aid of teachers in the New York City schools was granted on condition that all items relating to sex problems or even suggesting sex would be eliminated. Thus may we see how the matters which are intricately bound up with the questions of morality are forbidden to be mentioned in the study of conduct engaging the teachers in our largest school system.

"Mr. Wickham took his conduct tables to thirty mental hygieists of the Child-Guidance clinics of Cleveland, Philadelphia and Newark. They took the fifty misdemeanors which he had found regarded by teachers as serious enough to record. The hygieists gave their separate ratings of the importance of these faults as conditioning the child's future usefulness to society. The contrast is astonishing. Unsocialness, suspicion, depression, resentfulness, fear, cruelty, discouragement, super-criticism of others, cowardice, shyness, temper tantrums, nervousness, now jump to the top of the list. Down go whispering, interrupting, disorderliness in class, tardiness and disobedience to the bottom. I see a smile or two. I don't want to be disagreeable but, my much respected friends, the time is coming and is near at hand when the minority of teachers to whom we say pooh-pooh on account of their repudiation of the old-school attitude will stand where the believers in antiseptic medicine, the slavery-abolitionists, and the demonstrators of mosquito-carried malaria have come to. You can't forever go contrary to the facts brought out by the scientists studying behavior. This book is no promulgation of a writer's opinion. It is a survey of what teachers think, what they do, how they punish, what the clinical students find, what the sociologists teach as to life requirements, what the teachers misinterpret, what reeducation of us, as teachers, is necessary. It is a calm, unexaggerated, sympathetic, forward-looking treatment of a very vital issue."

A Brave Little Book: Eldridge and Clark. Then came Carolina with this:

"Seba Eldridge is associate professor of sociology in the University of Kansas. Carroll Clark was high-school principal and afterwards superintendent of schools in Wakefield in the same commonwealth. The two have put their experience together to produce a high-school textbook[5] aiming to realize the main function of public education: enlightenment of public opinion. What is needed, say these authors, is a more realistic presentation of crucial problems to solve which public schools are maintained by the taxation of all citizens, parents and childless. 'We would,' our two Kansas friends declare, 'concentrate the attention of the school on fundamental and persistent problems; we would make them intelligible and interesting to high-school youth; we would be thorough, we would show both sides of these controversial questions; we would not settle them for the student; we would push him into thinking about his duty as a citizen concretely and with intent to serve the nation which is spending its resources to train him for this original American purpose.' After a thorough and most profitable reading of this book in detail I wish to be recorded as testifying that the authors have done what they proposed. I think it would be extremely difficult to find a text so remarkably consecutive. Paragraph after paragraph grows out of its predecessor with a remarkable continuity of development. The process reminds me of a healthy plant that blossoms and produces its seeds. Immediately you see them springing up and performing their function in turn.

"Our authors, like charity, begin at home. Listen to the order of discussion: family, women, population, national resources, the country, the city, better living, health, work, play, leisure, art, education, morals, charity, crime, politics, our American ideals, you as a citizen. What impresses me about the presentation of these social questions is the vividness with which the actual perplexing situations are presented. Here is an intimate story of the life of a typical American family, your own or your neighbor's, its disappointments and successes, black sheep, divorce, unmarried mother, public-spirited father, creditable children, value to the town. With a thoroughness which is notable, with a fairness which is refreshing, with a frankness which is tonic, the authors give a clear picture of each problem, a scholarly abstract of solutions that are currently proposed, an honest résumé of objections urged against the offered remedies, and a straight-from-the-shoulder declaration that you, boy, girl, teacher, can't side-step these problems. They are fundamentally within the field of your duty. They are what the logic of public support for schools requires you to consider. The absence of the flag waving and hurrah-boys' boast of our having the best government and the best people in the world is a singularly strong point of the work. The study of democracy belongs to the field of social science. Science is the product of the search for truth. A propaganda for patriotism can do only damage if it is made up of lies about the Revolution or the war of 1812 or the Mexican conflict or the activities of the French or Germans.

"So this brave little book takes up all the public questions supposed to be loaded with dynamite, marriage and divorce, labor and capital, democratic, republican and socialistic politics, and all, and says these are the things that belong in school. To know about them is the duty of the citizen. To make a knowing citizen is what a school is for. With remarkable skill the touchy themes are so presented that you can not, for your life, tell on which side either of the authors is. You think possibly they hold opposing views and have written their work as an exercise in debate. This impartial quality gives the book its singular strength. No one but a bigot who wishes only the views of his own party known can oppose the book's adoption for any public school.

(*To be concluded*)

[5] Seba Eldridge and Carroll D. Clark, "Major Problems of Democracy." The Century Co., New York. 585 pp. $1.80.

SCHOOL AND SOCIETY

EDITED BY J. McKEEN CATTELL
WITH WHICH IS COMBINED THE

EDUCATIONAL REVIEW

EDITED BY WILLIAM McANDREW

Volume XXIX | Saturday, May 11, 1929 | Number 750

THE RELIGIOUS CURRICULUM OF THE ROMAN CATHOLIC ELEMENTARY SCHOOLS

By ROBERT E. O'BRIEN

The Roman Catholic parochial schools are in theory and practice religious schools. One hundred twelve pastors stated that the aim of the parochial school was to unite "religion with the study of secular subjects so that the child would become a good Christian as well as a good scholar." Interviews with 311 superiors and teachers revealed that without exception the teaching communities defined their task in terms of "other worldly salvation." The religious element in the parochial school curriculum may be discovered in many of the practices operating: in the mass before school, in the prescribed course of study, in the esthetic setting of the classrooms and in the dress of the teachers. These items will be discussed here in sufficient detail to show that the parochial schools exist primarily to provide instruction in religion to the end that the pupils may become loyal Catholics.

Mass before school. Eighty-five out of 214 elementary schools maintained in Chicago by the Roman Catholic Church had mass each day before school. Pupils and teachers attend these services voluntarily and go directly from the church to the school. This "seven-thirty" or "eight o'clock" mass is intended for children only; often adults are requested not to attend.

Nearly two thirds of the parochial schools of Chicago do not have mass before school except during one of the festal seasons of the church year. The reason most frequently given for the failure to hold mass in these churches is the distance of the church from the homes of the pupils. In 46 parishes, teachers estimated that 50 per cent. of their pupils had to leave home at seven A. M. to reach the school by eight-thirty. To require these children to leave home three quarters of an hour earlier would be too great a hardship. Some of the teaching orders believe that mass before school imposes a heavy burden on both pupils and teachers and that it serves no worth-while pedagogical ends; consequently this practice is discouraged in schools controlled by these orders.

One school where mass had been discontinued was governed by a superior who vigorously defended its abolishment. When asked for her view-point she exclaimed, "What's the use of it anyhow? There's C——— [a young man who recently had confessed to a brutal murder]. He attended here until he graduated and never missed a single mass. Now look at him!

Why the boys say he attended mass the morning after the murder. Just think of it! The morning after the murder! No, sir! We have no more masses for children. They are just a plain waste of time." This vigorous superior, who was in charge of one of the best schools visited, felt that mass served no real purpose; so she was instrumental in its abolishment.

Mass before school is not an instruction period but a worship service; nevertheless one of its religious values is training in worship. Children learn the ritual of the church from teachers who are scrupulously careful to see that every part is correctly observed. Even little children, too young to know the prayers, knew when to kneel. These services were serious and solemn and the pupils were always quiet and well behaved. The solemn service, the large room, the candles at the altar, the vested priest and the pictures, statues and stained-glass windows impressed the children and developed a feeling of awe and reverence.

Attendance at mass before school is wholly voluntary. Children are not regarded as tardy at school if late or absent because of this service. The aid of the truant officer is not invoked to secure attendance at mass. Nevertheless strong pressure is brought by pastors and teachers to secure the attendance of all the pupils. Special privileges and awards are not given for punctuality and regularity as in the school itself. The efforts of the pastors and teachers to secure a good attendance at this mass is usually confined to personal calls on the parents. On the whole the attendance at mass before school is good. The record for both punctuality and regularity in schools having mass was higher in all grades than in schools not holding this service.

Instruction preceding first communion and confirmation. Instruction preceding first communion and confirmation is doctrinal and ritualistic in character. This is usually administered by the priests, and the Baltimore catechism is the standard but not the sole text used for this purpose. First communion is usually administered at the age of seven and is preceded by intensive doctrinal instruction on such subjects as "God, our Heavenly Father; Mary our Mother; Heaven; sacrament of penance; Holy Eucharist, etc."[1] Ritualistic instruction is limited to teaching the pupil how to enter and act in the church. Such instruction includes items like "taking holy water" or the simple genuflection. Each child is taught how to receive the holy wafer and to say the proper prayers. Teachers illustrate and enforce the doctrinal and ritualistic instruction with stories from the Bible and the lives of the saints. Especial attention is paid to teaching each child the act of confession. Priests sometimes alleged that children from the public schools, lacking this instruction, did not make proper confessions, tending to confess the other person's sins rather than their own.

Confirmation is held in some parishes once every year, in others once in two or even three years, depending on the number to be confirmed. Instruction in ritual and doctrine is much more thorough than preceding first communion. Confirmation makes the child a member of the church, entitled to all its rights and privileges. The period preceding this sacrament is devoted to a study of the sacraments, the sacramentals, the ritual and the obligations and privileges of a member of the church. The "Course of Study for Religion" prescribes that since confirmation permits the pupil to assist in the administration of the sacraments, he should be instructed in the manner in which they are prepared and how to assist in them. The "Baltimore Catechism Number II" is memorized verbatim preced-

[1] "Course of Study for Religion," page 3.

ing confirmation. Much of the recitation is devoted to explanations of the questions and answers in the words of the pupil.

The course of study for religion. The prescribed course of study for the parochial schools of Chicago provides for definite instruction in religion in all grades. Before the child has opened his primer in the first grade, he is taught to say a simple prayer or aspiration such as "My Jesus, I love you" or "My God, I believe in you, I hope in you, I love you." These aspirations and ejaculatory prayers are part of the day's program in every grade. A typical aspiration used in the seventh grade is "Blessed be the Holy and Immaculate Conception of the Most Blessed Virgin Mary, Mother of God." Frequently pupils, when called on to recite, use such ejaculations as "Dear heart of Mary, guide and direct me." Others are supposed to be used in moments of temptation. A careful distinction is made between *learning* a prayer and the *use* of the prayer in worship.

Much time is spent in the memorization of prayers, the creed and certain great hymns. The second grade is expected to memorize and sing

Mother at your feet is kneeling.
Why do bells for Christmas ring?
Guardian angel from Heaven so bright.

Hymns for the fourth grade include "Come Holy Ghost." Often third-grade children sing in Latin "Adeste Fidelis" and "Tantum Ergo."

First- and second-grade pupils learn short verses designed to teach certain doctrines. The following is an example of an attempt to develop in first-grade pupils a sense of angelic relationships based on the theory of angel guardians:

Angel of God, My Guardian dear,
To whom His love commends me here;
Ever this day be at my side
To light and guard, to rule and guide.

As aids to worship and as a means of showing proper Catholic loyalty and respect certain forms are taught. In the first grade pupils learn to make the sign of the cross, to bow at the "Holy Name of Jesus" and at the *Gloria Patri.* Likewise they learn to take the sacraments and to give thanksgiving for them. Every pupil has a rosary and learns its use. They are taught to show respect in passing a church or in meeting a priest. After first communion the children are taught how to behave on their first visits to the holy sacrament: "What to do, what to say, what to tell Our Lord, and what to ask Him." Even first-grade pupils learn to say "My Lord and my God" at the elevation of the host during mass.

The aim of teaching "Bible history" appears to be to show how God at different times and in a miraculous manner intervened in human affairs and aided his worshipers. Much emphasis is laid in the upper grades on "types" of the Old Testament. Characters like Abel, Noah, Melchisedec, Isaac and most of the patriarchs are said to be "types" of Christ. The paschal lamb, the manna and the showbread are called "types" of the eucharist. By this method teachers try to show that the Old Testament foreshadows and predicts the Catholic faith.

Church history is taught in most schools in the fifth grade. The aim is "To give the child some definite knowledge of the working of the church and of the faith that is in him."[2] The dogmas concerning the church are carefully studied. Instructions are given to pay particular attention to the church's nature, composition, discipline, indeflectibility, infallibility and marks, and to the conditions for entering the church. Detailed examples of lessons on subjects such as "The marks of the

[2] "Course of Study for Religion," page 17.

church'' are given for the use of teachers.[3] Every effort is made to develop Catholic loyalties even at the expense of tolerance. The Archdiocesan School Board instructs teachers to

> instill in the minds of children a feeling of pride that they belong to the Old Church that was established by Christ and His Apostles. Let them know that most of the Protestant Churches were founded by disgruntled and fallen-away Catholics who could not live up to the teachings of the Church. The Catholic Church requires more of her members than any other religion but she has more to offer than any other. We do not teach that all Protestants go to Hell. If they live up to their religion and are in good faith they will be saved. But they have not the aids that a Catholic has and very few of them live up to the teachings of their church.[4]

Indoctrination begins in the first grade. The catechism is used extensively. Although the ''Course of Study for Religion'' recommends that the Baltimore catechisms be followed closely, nine other catechisms were found in use. The more important doctrines such as dogmas regarding Christ are carefully outlined for the use of teachers. Bible stories are used to illustrate and prove the doctrines of the church. Thus stories of the wedding feast at Cana and Jesus' sympathy for Mary and Martha at the tomb of Lazarus are used to make clear to the child that Christ had both a human and a divine nature. The prevalent method of teaching is for the pupil to memorize the daily lesson in the catechism, then in class the teacher tests the memorization. After this is done the lesson is discussed and questions are asked. The aim is to clear up every doubt and misunderstanding in the minds of the pupils. Besides the catechism the Archdiocesan School Board recommends the use of Conway's ''Question Box'' and Loyola's ''Spiritual Exercises.''

The esthetic setting of the classrooms. Every Roman Catholic elementary school in Chicago is equipped with religious statues, pictures and inscriptions on plaques. The mean number of religious pictures per school was 73. Some of these were old, but almost all were neat and artistic. It is hard to estimate the religious inspiration derived from these pictures. Even the aspirations or prayers printed on the blackboard are usually ornamented with Old English capitals and with colored scroll work and leaves. Cutouts from religious magazines and catalogues were often used by schools that owned few religious pictures. One of these cutouts used most frequently was a series of illustrations showing the different positions assumed by the priests during mass with explanatory sentences attached under each illustration.

Statues are found in all parochial schools in Chicago. These are almost always on display in the halls and, if the parish can afford enough of them, in the rooms. These vary from approximately one half life-size to life-size. Provision is made before most of the statues, especially before those of Christ and the Virgin, for the burning of candles. These candles are on sale in the office of the superior and pupils very frequently purchase them and burn a candle for their spiritual benefit.

Twenty-two of the 214 schools had stained-glass windows in the halls. While these greatly reduced the amount of sunlight, the effect was not unlike that of a church. The illusion was further heightened by the flickering candles burning in front of the statues, showing that some one had recently worshipped there. The pupils passing in uniform, and frequently stopping to pray, lend an atmosphere of worship to the building.

Schoolrooms are always equipped with receptacles for holy water, placed on the door post at a height that may be reached by all the children. As they enter the room to begin the day's work, or as they leave

[3] *Ibid.*, page 18–19.

[4] *Ibid.*, page 19.

it, they pass before the receptacle and solemnly cross themselves with holy water. In cases of danger such as a thunder storm the pupils file by the container and cross themselves. The holy water is contained in a sponge which is placed in the receptacle to prevent too rapid evaporation.

Sand tables were in use from the first to the fourth grades in 188 out of 214 schools. In these the children made replicas of certain shrines. The Grotto of Lourdes was a favorite subject during the year 1926–27. In this grotto the children placed a small image of the Virgin in the act of stating, "I am the Immaculate Conception." Such replicas were not regarded by the pupils as mere handwork. Candles were sometimes burned in front of them and other acts of reverence and respect performed.

All pastors and teachers interviewed expressed an opinion that the teacher's garb was one of the most influential factors in producing a religious atmosphere in the schoolroom. Certainly the unique dress of the sisters impresses the pupils that their teachers are different from other people. One of the first questions children ask when they start in school, according to a number of superiors, was why the teachers dressed as they did. The answer was given that these people had consecrated their lives to the service of God and of the church, and on that account they wore peculiar clothing. Thus the child is constantly reminded of the fact that he is attending a religious school. The one outstanding objection of the sisters to the use of lay teachers was that they could not "teach religion as well as we for they do not wear the habit which is part of our religion."

The aim stated in the "Course of Study for Religion" and which was evident in the parochial schools was to develop loyalty to the Roman Catholic Church in the pupils. The pictures, the statues, the acts of worship in the schoolrooms, the children's mass, the garb of the teachers, the frequent visits of the priests, the prayers and aspirations, in addition to the regular doctrinal and ritualistic instruction, all remind the child of the church.

The result of these activities can not be measured. However, they must have a powerful influence on the pupil, for among the Protestant children enrolled conversions are frequent. It should be stated that these Protestant children are not required to take any of the religious studies that are taught to the Catholic children. One school reported 136 conversions during the year out of 627 Protestant children enrolled. One hundred twenty-six other schools, not situated so that they enrolled as large a number of Protestant children, stated that a total of 587 Protestant children had been converted during the school year 1926–27. On the whole the evidence would lead one to conclude that the parochial schools are effective agencies for developing loyalty to the church and for the winning of new converts among Protestant children enrolled as pupils.

COURSES IN PARENT-TEACHER WORK

By FLORENCE V. WATKINS

EXECUTIVE SECRETARY OF THE NATIONAL CONGRESS OF PARENTS AND TEACHERS

PERHAPS one of the most far-reaching and significant developments in the work of the National Congress of Parents and Teachers is the growth of credit courses in universities, colleges and normal schools on the "Educational Aspects of the Parent-Teacher Movement." Columbia University, New York City, was the first to introduce such a course during its summer session seven years ago. The executive secretary of the congress gave the course, which has been repeated each year since its initiation. This is not a course in parental education, as some suppose, but in educational administration. Many educators have failed to realize the valuable contribution which parents can make to education; have failed to use this vast reservoir of potential support for the new movements in education when once the public is taken into the confidence of the school leaders. It is primarily to bring about a solution of such problems that this course was organized. On the other hand, many parents do not realize how vital is their need to understand and appreciate the school and how necessary it is that the children sent to school have five or six years of the best possible education at home before the public schools receive them. This is the second reason for the course.

While primarily the accredited course in education is for those students who are working for advanced standing, parents and others interested in the work of parent-teacher groups are welcomed to the class upon payment of the registration fees.

During the past seven years there has been an average registration of seventy-two students for the course at Columbia, from an average of twenty-five different states and several foreign countries each year.

In 1924 the president of the Georgia State Congress of Parents and Teachers secured the cooperation of the University of Georgia, and credit courses were established at that institution. Similar courses have been given each summer since that time. The average registration has been between thirty-five and forty, with many visitors.

In 1925 a credit course was given at the University of Pennsylvania, and in 1926 at the University of Tennessee, which has been repeated each year. In the same year Florida offered a similar course which also has been repeated each year. In 1926 the University of Virginia had its first six weeks' credit course. The following year a three weeks' course was given. In 1928, the six weeks' course was repeated.

In the past two or three years other colleges and universities have been sensing the need for parent-teacher courses for teachers and school administrators and have held short credit or non-credit courses. In 1928 the following institutions offered credit courses: Alabama College for Women; Northern Arizona State Teachers College; State Teachers College, Little Rock, Arkansas; University of Florida; University of Georgia; Georgia Normal College; University of Mississippi; University of Nebraska; State Teachers College, Peru, Nebraska; Columbia University; North Carolina College for Women; Wittenberg College; Cleveland College; University of Tennessee; University of Virginia; Marshall College, and Winthrop College. Non-credit courses were offered at: University of Hawaii; Albion State Normal School; Southern Illinois State Normal University; Indiana University; Central State Teachers College; University of North Carolina, and State Teachers College, Valley City, N. D. These courses were all given by parent-teacher workers or duly qualified instructors sent by the National Congress of Parents and Teachers.

In some states members of the college faculty have conducted parent-teacher courses. This is most desirable, provided the one teaching the course really knows the parent-teacher field and has had some first-hand experience with the best organized of such groups.

Some one asks, "What is given in these parent-teacher courses?" The one given at Columbia University is, probably, typical. During the course at Columbia, known as S133K, consideration is given to the fundamental significance of the parent-teacher movement, its place in education and its development here and in foreign countries; the organization, objects and parental education program of the National Congress of Parents and Teachers; its relation to other educational, social and welfare agencies; its relation to state and local parent-teacher groups; the organization of a state branch, its function and its relation to the national congress and to the local groups within its borders; the organization, conduct and special function of districts, and county and city councils.

As many educators are interested in the work of local associations but are unacquainted with approved methods of organizing and developing them, the course acquaints its members with plans for organizing and conducting the different types of parent-teacher associations and the legitimate fields of work and appropriate activities for each; the preschool association and study group in which parents are helped to solve their practical problems in training the baby and the toddler; the grade-school association, in which teachers and parents consider together all aspects of the relations which should exist between the home and the school, the home and the community, the school and the community; the high-school association, in which parents and teachers study together and work out solutions of the problems which the adolescent boy and girl face in home, school and community relations; the college association, with an organization which enables it to be of value to the college authorities, to the parents in far-away homes, and to the young man or woman facing for the first time the complicated problems of college life in a new town or city.

An exhibit of the many varieties of published helps furnished by the national congress and its state branches, and of the literature of the national cooperating organizations, and a poster and chart display are open to students in education, to superintendents, principals, teachers and parents.

In addition to the regular work done in class periods, assigned readings, group studies and reports are required. The groups work out such projects as: Appropriate activities for each type of association; typical rural one-room-school program; causes of failure in parent-teacher associations and how these may be remedied; how to interest foreign-born parents in the work of the parent-teacher association; qualifications for leadership; best plans for publicity for parent-teacher projects; the object, function and field of church-school parent-teacher associations; surveys needed before determining the year's parent-teacher association program; a year's program for a preschool, grade-school, high-school and college association and for a church group on the seven objectives in education. This course is open to students in education and to parent-teacher workers. Students with experience in the above field who wish more extended work with reference to teaching the subject take a second advanced course.

This advanced course is planned for students who have had at least two years' experience in local parent-teacher associations, who have had or are taking the more elementary course and who may desire to prepare for teaching parent-teacher courses in normal schools, colleges or universities. As this course is designed primarily to prepare instructors of parent-teacher courses, the projects considered are related to the teaching of courses on the educational aspects of the parent-teacher movement. Students are required to work out several projects, to do assigned reading, to give reports, etc. Such texts are used as Mason's "Parents and Teachers," the "National Handbook," "The Publicity Primer" and various national leaflets. Projects include the preparation of outlines for use in two, three and six weeks' parent-teacher courses, a syllabus to accompany the outlines, and outlines for conducting round tables for parent-teacher groups on each of the seven objectives in education. The course is open to students of education. The demand for instructors in state normal schools, colleges and universities to conduct parent-teacher courses has become so great that the National Congress of Parents and Teachers was unable to supply the number needed this past year.

What is the outlook for the future for parent-teacher courses? Thus far none of the larger institutions has introduced a parent-teacher course during the regular scholastic year. At Wittenberg College, in Ohio, an extension course has been given for the past three years on parent-teacher work, and this year a course is being given at Cleveland College. It is hoped that before another college year opens, Columbia and several state colleges will present courses during the scholastic year of the same grade as others in education.

Because of the changes taking place in education, in the revisions of the curriculum, in extra-curricular activities, etc., it becomes increasingly necessary for teachers and school officials to have the active support of the school clientele for these changes. A college course should be designed to train those taking it to make the best use of this great unutilized parent power, with a minimum of friction and a maximum of result. Educators are increasingly realizing the need for close cooperation between home and school, and school and home and community, but have not found an effective way of securing it. Those who are working for their college degrees would greatly appreciate courses which would help them solve the problem. So far as discovered, the parent-teacher association is the channel through which such cooperation is best secured. For thirty years and more, the National Congress of Parents and Teachers has been experimenting and developing the best methods of securing home and school cooperation. Through its efforts, educators have learned to "take the public into their confidence" through the parent-teacher association where they have the opportunity of explaining the newer movements in education and demonstrating their value to both parents and teachers. Through this group work parents have been made to realize the responsibility resting upon them to "back up" the school program. Parents are, moreover, learning what a responsibility they have during the preschool years to train their children so that they will be a school asset and not a liability when school days come. When in a college course parents and educators together make a careful study of parent-teacher cooperation, they will go back into their respective communities to insist upon the best for the children in all the homes and schools. What an educational revolution will come quietly and peacefully and enthusiastically when parents and teachers and communities and churches join forces for child welfare. It is the duty of the colleges and universities and normal schools to show the way through the parent-teacher courses.

EDUCATIONAL EVENTS

THE BRITISH PRIME MINISTER ON EDUCATION

MR. BALDWIN, as the leader of the Conservative Party, has opened the party's general election campaign with an address in which he referred to education. According to the London *Times Educational Supplement,* he said:

There is another record which I think will bear the most intense scrutiny. That is our education record, which bears comparison with that of any previous period in the history of this country. We have more than fulfilled every pledge that we have made but we are only halfway through the work of reform to which our minister of education and the government have set their hands. But by what we have done we have proved our will to go farther. We have shown that we believe in education. We have shown that we know what the country wants, and we are going forward.

I renew here all the previous pledges we have taken, and we shall put forward a rather more detailed statement on education before the election takes place. But what we are aiming at is a full course of higher education for all children, in schools adequately equipped for the purpose and adequately staffed, and we want to see the linking completed of those schools not only with the universities, but with the technical colleges, so that a connected education can be pursued right through from childhood to manhood. A new conception of technical education is now being worked out, and worked out in close consultation with commerce and industry, which are now fully aware of what it means to the welfare of the country. These things will probably have to be embodied in a new Education Act; but that is the direction in which we are moving, full of hope and full of faith. Incidentally, we have treated the non-provided schools as equal partners with the State and with the local authorities, and we have given them increased assistance from public funds. We have sought to remove any disabilities from which their pupils may suffer. We shall continue to base our future policy on the principle of equal partnership and impartial justice to all types of school, and on equal opportunities for all children in all types of school.

We have also given the teachers security both in their remuneration and in their professional prospects—a security they have never before had. They got that in the national settlement, which is universally applied. It is our policy to maintain that security for them unimpaired, and to embody it, as the new reforms are more fully worked out, in a permanent settlement in harmony with new conditions which will protect teachers from the uncertainties to which they are still exposed under the existing agreements. Our conception of education is not a bureaucratic one. We regard the State and the local authorities as the agents of the parents, and we believe in the teaching freedom of the individual schools.

After a reference to the subject of maternity, the Prime Minister continued:

That brings me naturally to child welfare. I was very much impressed one day in the winter when I went down to Deptford to see that wonderful child's school of Miss MacMillan, and I am quite sure that the next advance to be made by the State is in the care of the children from the ages of 1 to 5. I have no time to develop the reasons, but I think the mere statement of the subject to any one who has any familiarity with our social conditions will carry conviction. But on that subject there is not yet in the country a great deal of experience, and all I can say at the moment is that one of our first acts when we come in will be to form a strong committee of inquiry into this whole subject to advise us what would be the best way of treating it, and after that I hope that we shall be in a position to go forward. I think, too, the time has come when the various children's Acts should all be consolidated. That has become a very serious business, and is one which I think should be done.

CHILDREN'S LABOR IN ECUADOR

A SUMMARY has been issued by the International Labor Office of the League of Nations, and summarized in the New York *Times,* of a law for the regulation of the labor of young children in Ecuador that became effective on January 1.

Under this law no child under 14 years old may be employed. The labor inspectorate, or the police where there is no labor inspectorate, may, however, permit the employment of children between 12 and 14 years old who have completed the minimum school course prescribed by law and who are compelled by their own need, or that of their parents, guardians, brothers or sisters, to work.

The employers of children or young persons under 18 years old who have not completed their primary education must allow them two hours daily in which to attend school. In places where twenty or more children are employed, if there is no school in the neighborhood, the employer must provide a primary school at his own cost.

Children under 12 years old may not be hired out for wages as domestic servants by their parents or guardians unless such children are obliged to work in order to provide means for their own support or education; in such cases the employer must provide for the education of the child.

The employment of children or young persons under 18 years old for more than eight hours daily or forty-eight hours weekly is strictly prohibited.

Night work is forbidden for young persons under 16 years old unless employed in domestic service; by night work is meant work between the hours of 7 P. M. and 6 A. M.

No boy under 12 years old, and no girl under 16 years old, may be employed on his or her own account or on account of another person in any trade carried on in the streets or public places.

Young persons under 16 years old may not be employed in the dangerous or unhealthy trades or occupations specified in the act, to be more particularly prescribed by a special regulation. Further, notwithstanding the provisions relating to night work and dangerous and unhealthy occupations, the employment of young persons between 16 and 18 years old in work prejudicial to morals or physical development may be forbidden by the competent minister on the recommendation of the labor inspector.

In the case of illness or accident to a young person under 16 years, if it arises out of a breach of the provisions of the act, or if the young person concerned was employed contrary to the provisions of the act, such illness or accident will be presumed to be due to the fault of the employer.

INDEX OF TEACHERS' SALARIES

DR. HAROLD F. CLARK, of Teachers College, Columbia University, in cooperation with the research division of the National Education Association has issued the table given below, giving an index of teachers' salaries:

Column 2 is the index of wages received by teachers in the United States. The average wage in 1926 is given the value 100. On this basis the wages of teachers in April, 1929, were 109.2.

Column 3 is the index of the cost of living for teachers in the United States. The cost in 1926 of the typical items purchased by a teacher is given the value 100. On this basis the cost of living of teachers in April, 1929, was 97.0.

Column 4 is the index of real wages, that is, the purchasing power of teachers' wages in the

1 Month	Wages in dollars 1926 = 100 2 Index	Index of the cost of living 1926 = 100 3 Index	Index of real wages 4 Index
1929			
April	109.2	97.0*	112.6*
March	109.2	97.2*	112.3*
February	109.2	97.1	112.5
January	109.2	97.3	112.2
1928			
December	109.2	96.9	112.7
November	109.2	97.3	112.2
October	109.2	97.9	111.5
September	109.2	99.7	109.8
August	106.5	98.8	107.8
July	106.5	98.2	108.4
June	106.5	97.2	109.5
May	106.5	97.8	108.8
April	106.5	96.8	110.0
March	106.5	95.6	111.4

* Not final.

United States. The indices of this column are obtained by dividing column 2 by column 3. The index of real wages rises either from an increase in wages in dollars or from a decrease in cost of living. In April, 1929, this index stood at 112.6.

SELECTION OF ABLE HIGH-SCHOOL STUDENTS BY MR. EDISON

Mr. Charles Edison, son of the inventor and president of the Thomas A. Edison Industries, announced on April 29 that his father had offered a free college scholarship, consisting of tuition fees for four years, to the high-school or preparatory school student who gives the best answers to one of his questionnaires. The announcement expresses the inventor's hope that the winner of the prize might become his successor. The elder Mr. Edison is now at his winter home in Florida.

"As the weight of advancing years falls on the great inventor's shoulders he is seeking a youth of unusual capabilities who perhaps will have the genius to carry on the great work he has so well started," the announcement reads in part. Mr. Edison wants to bring "this unusual opportunity and this unusual youth together," according to the statement.

The governor of each state and the commissioners of the District of Columbia will be asked to designate one male student who is the best representative of American manhood and possesses the highest ability in scientific subjects during the school year 1928–1929. The choice of winners in each state is left to the governors.

Each of the forty-nine winners will receive a free trip at Mr. Edison's expense to the Edison Laboratories, where they will be entertained. Each will receive an Edison radio-phonograph. The visiting students will receive questionnaires personally prepared by Mr. Edison, and the one submitting the best replies will win the scholarship. He will be permitted to select his own technical school.

The names of state designees must be in Mr. Edison's hands by July 1. He will return from Florida about June 15 and begin work at once on the questionnaire. The visit of the state winners to the laboratories will be made early in August.

PRIZES FOR ESSAYS ON HIGHWAY SAFETY

Offering as principal awards a trip to Washington to the winning pupil and the successful teacher who submit the best papers in their respective competitions, the Highway Education Board announces the eighth annual safety essay and lesson contests open to elementary school pupils and elementary school teachers of the nation.

The successful pupil also will receive a gold medal, a check for fifteen dollars and a gold watch, while the teacher, upon her arrival at Washington, will be presented with a check for $500.

Contestants from every state in the Union, and from Alaska, the Philippines, Hawaii, Porto Rico and the Canal Zone are expected to strive for the many prizes, aggregating $6,500, offered for the best essays and the best lessons written in this annual competition. The contests in each state are conducted with the aid and cooperation of the state departments of education, and other educational authorities. The prizes are given by the National Automobile Chamber of Commerce.

In the pupils' contest, 442 medals and a like number of cash prizes are offered as state awards. To the first national winner is given a visit to the nation's capital and a gold watch, while pupils whose papers rank second and third to the national winner also receive gold watches, appropriately engraved, of slightly less intrinsic value than that given the winner. National winners are chosen by a process of elimination from those whose essays have ranked first in their respective states.

Awards to teachers, according to the rules, are less numerous but more substantial. For the best lesson, the board offers the visit to Washington, of four or five days' duration, and a check for $500. Second and third national awards in the lesson contest are $300 and $200, respectively.

THE HECKSCHER FOUNDATION FOR CHILDREN

The gift of a new fund of $4,000,000 to expand the work of the Heckscher Foundation for Children by the establishment of day nurseries, dental clinics and playgrounds in the congested areas of Manhattan, Brooklyn and the Bronx and a summer camp nearby has been announced by Mr. August Heckscher, real estate owner and operator. The new fund, according to Mr. Heckscher, will "carry the service of the Heckscher Foundation to the children" and marks the end, for the present, of the donor's efforts to find a solution of the housing problem and the concentration of his efforts on child welfare in the city.

"When it recently became evident to me after three years of intensive effort," said Mr. Heckscher in announcing the gift, "that the housing problem in our congested cities will not be solved or even seriously considered at this time, the question arose how best to assist in other directions and do something radically helpful for childhood and for overburdened motherhood."

Next to decent homes for the under-privileged, Mr. Heckscher found the "crying needs in this ant-heap of ours" to be day nurseries, dental clinics, playgrounds, "be they ever so modest, but locally available for the smaller children," and summer camps. Six units containing some or all of these features are to be established as soon as the localities in greatest need are determined and adequate sites can be secured. An amendment to the foundation's charter, widening the scope of its activities, was passed at the last session of the legislature.

For the present the income only of the fund will be used to purchase sites and build and equip the welfare units. As further needs develop it was indicated by Mr. Heckscher that the donation might be increased and that contributions from others might be used to swell the fund. City-owned land that might be utilized for playground purposes would be welcomed, Mr. Heckscher said, to be leased and equipped by the foundation.

Plots of ground in sections in which there are inadequate welfare and settlement facilities, approximately 100 x 100 feet, are being sought for the establishment of the new units. Low structures covering a quarter of the area will be built, leaving the remainder for playgrounds. The work will be designed primarily to aid the small child by providing him with a place for healthy exercise, dental service free or at negligible cost and nurseries in which mothers, on going to work, may leave their children "freed from the obsession that they may be harmed."

Purchase of a site for a summer camp, 200 acres in extent, is now being considered. This camp, near the city, will be fully equipped and will have segregated quarters for boys and girls. Announcement of the location will be made in the near future.

"We have uptown at the Foundation Building, Fifth Avenue and 104th Street, a magnificent plant for the most diversified service," Mr. Heckscher said. "Our mistake was to spend too much money in one locality. The children should not be forced to come to us—we should go to them. In other words, our work from now on ought to be more and more decentralized."

The new program will be administered however by the trustees of the Heckscher Foundation for Children, it was announced by E. C. Stuckless, treasurer of the foundation and member of the finance committee. The foundation has previously been given $5,000,000 by Mr. Heckscher.

THE INSTALLATION OF PRESIDENT DAY

AT the installation of Dr. Frank Parker Day on May 4 as the thirteenth president of Union College, more than fifty colleges participated and the audience numbered about 2,000.

In connection with the inauguration there was a luncheon at which men representing other colleges, industrial organizations, governments and the alumni and student bodies spoke. Following the luncheon the conference on honors courses took place. On the evening of May 4 Phi Beta Kappa and Sigma Xi societies held a joint meeting, at which President James R. Angell, of Yale University, made the principal address.

Dr. Richmond opened the inaugural ceremonies and Dr. George Alexander, '66, president of the board of trustees and pastor of the First Presbyterian Church of New York City, officially inducted Dr. Day into office. Dr. Day's inaugural address was on Eliphalet Nott, president of Union College from 1804 to 1866. The address of welcome to the newly installed president was made by President Frank Aydelotte, of Swarthmore College.

Dr. Franklin H. Giddings, a graduate of Union in the class of '77, professor of sociology in Columbia University, was the toastmaster at the inaugural luncheon. The other speakers were: Dean Alfred C. Hanford, of Harvard University, representing the American colleges; Colonel Ralston, representing the Canadian colleges; Gerard Swope, president of the General Electric Company, representing local industries; Dr. E. Z. Hawkes, '87, of Newark, representing the alumni, and Frank Zierer, '29, of Rochester, representing the students.

At the exercises the honorary doctorate of laws was conferred on the retiring president, Dr. Charles Alexander Richmond. The citation by Dr. Day reads in part as follows:

CHARLES ALEXANDER RICHMOND, Bachelor of Arts in the class of 1883 at Princeton University and of the Princeton Theological Seminary in the class of 1888; Master of Arts, Doctor of Divinity, Doctor of Laws, Phi Beta Kappa, ordained minister of the Presbyterian Church. You have been many things, lecturer, musician, poet, fisherman, author of political and educational pamphlets, contributor to magazines, composer of children's songs. . . . The bright particular star in your crown is your conduct of Union College and Union University from 1909 to 1928. You found the college small and poor, you made it large and comfortable. . . . My only grudge against you is that I must forever stand in the shadow of a great predecessor. Union College is your great debtor and no honorary degree was ever more truly won. *Honoris causa*, I admit you to the degree of Doctor of Laws and direct that your name be enrolled among our honorary alumni.

EDUCATIONAL NOTES AND NEWS

THE Wyoming State Board of Education has elected George E. Brown, for the last thirteen years city superintendent of the schools of Greeley, Colorado, commissioner of education to fill the vacancy caused by the resignation of Lewis C. Tidball, who had served as commissioner for eight years.

DR. RONALD A. KENT, dean of liberal arts at Northwestern University, has been elected president of Louisville University, Kentucky. He succeeds the late George Colvin. Dr. John L. Patterson, chancellor emeritus, has been acting president.

DR. CLARENCE A. BARBOUR, president-elect of Brown University, succeeding Dr. William H. P. Faunce, who retires in June, attended the meeting of the board of fellows on May 2.

J. F. REES, professor of commerce at Birmingham University, has been appointed principal of the University College of South Wales and Monmouthshire, Cardiff, in succession to Dr. A. H. Trow, who retires at the end of the present term.

AT the charter-day exercises of the University of California the degree of doctor of laws was conferred on Dr. Roscoe Pound, dean of the Harvard Law School, and on Dr. L. O. Howard, of the bureau of entomology of the U. S. Department of Agriculture.

DR. WILLIAM H. WELCH, now professor of the history of medicine and director of the new medical library at the Johns Hopkins University, was guest of honor at a dinner celebrating his seventy-ninth birthday on April 8.

A LUNCHEON in honor of Dean John W. Withers was given on May 4 by the New York University School of Education Graduate Club. Dr. Elmer Ellsworth Brown, chancellor of the university, was the principal speaker.

A PORTRAIT of President Paul W. Horn, of the Texas Technological College, will be given to the school by the senior class of 1929. Formal presentation of the painting will be made on May 25.

DR. CYRIL NORWOOD, headmaster of Harrow School, has been elected a member of the Athenaeum Club, London, under the provision which empowers the annual election by the committee of a certain number of persons of distinguished eminence in science, literature, the arts or for public service.

AT Yale University Professor Edgar Stevenson Furniss, chairman of the department of economics, sociology and government, has been appointed associate dean of the graduate school, and Loomis Havemeyer, registrar of the Sheffield Scientific School and assistant professor of anthropology, has been appointed assistant dean of the Sheffield Scientific School.

APPOINTMENTS at the University of Chicago are Dr. Karl S. Lashley, now of the Institute of Juvenile Research, Chicago, this year president of the American Psychological Association, professor in the department of psychology; Floyd W. Reeves, of the University of Kentucky, professor of education; Harold Shepherd, of Stanford University, visiting professor in the law school; John Mann Beal, head of the department of botany at Mississippi State College, associate professor of botany; Dr. Russell M. Wilder, of the Mayo Clinic, professor and chairman of the department of medicine; Reuben G. Gustafson, of the University of Denver, visiting associate professor in the department of physiological chemistry; Francis W. Jacob, of the University of Idaho, and Sheldon Tefft, of the University of Nebraska, visiting associate professors in the law school; Arthur E. Murphy, of Cornell University, associate professor of philosophy; Clarence E. Ridley, of the National Institute of Public Administration, associate professor of political science; Harrison A. Dobbs, associate professor of social economy in the Graduate School of Social Service Administration, and Dr. Franklin C. McLean, director of the University Clinics.

AT the University of Virginia, Dr. Bruce Williams, professor of political science in Cornell University, has been recalled to fill the chair of political science. Dr. Walter A. Montgomery, professor of ancient languages in the College of William and Mary since 1920, has been elected professor of Latin. The newly created position of athletic director has been filled by the appointment of James Glenn Driver.

EUGENE F. SAVAGE has been appointed professor of art in the College of the City of New York to succeed Professor Leigh Hunt, who reached the age of retirement last year.

MRS. JESSIE TRUBE WORDEN, who from 1908 to 1920 was principal and owner of Miss Trube's School at Dobbs Ferry, N. Y., and who at present is assistant professor of primary education at Ball State Teachers College, Muncie, Indiana, has been appointed director of Forest Hall, one of the residence halls for women at the college.

DR. EDITH ELLEN WARE, head of the department of history at Russell Sage College, at Troy, N. Y., has been appointed dean of the Spence School in New York City.

FRANCIS RICHARD DALE, headmaster of Plymouth College, has been appointed to the headmastership of the City of London School, which will become vacant at the end of the summer term by the resignation of Dr. Arthur Chilton, who has served for nearly twenty-four years.

THE Social Science Research Council has elected the following members under the recently created classification of members-at-large: Professor Henry M. Bates, dean of the law school of the University of Michigan; Dr. Adolf Meyer, professor of psychiatry and director of the Henry Phipps Psychiatric Clinic of the Johns Hopkins University; Dr. C.-E. A. Winslow, chairman of the graduate school and professor of public health at Yale University, and Professor Robert S. Woodworth, department of psychology, Columbia University.

Four new councilors have been elected to the National Industrial Conference Board, according to an announcement made by Magnus W. Alexander, president of the board. They are: Ex-president Coolidge; Dr. Frank Goodnow, president of the Johns Hopkins University; Dr. Michael I. Pupin, professor at Columbia University, and Paul M. Warburg, chairman of the International Acceptance Corporation.

Dr. Robert Francis Seybolt, professor of the history of education at the University of Illinois, has been elected an honorary associate member of the New York Historical Society, in recognition of his work in American history.

Dean Herbert E. Hawkes, of Columbia University, has returned to his work at the university, after a prolonged stay abroad.

At a recent meeting of the trustees of Wells College, a leave of absence with full salary for two years was granted to Miss Frances H. Relf, professor of history. She is the editor of Lord Elsing's Diary, which is being published by the Royal Historical Society, and is now engaged with Professor Notestein, of Yale, in collecting, editing and preparing for publication several diaries covering the sessions of Parliament in the early seventeenth century. It is for the purpose of permitting this work to be brought to a satisfactory conclusion that the leave was granted.

Newton D. Baker, secretary of war under President Wilson, will be the commencement speaker at Mount Holyoke College on June 11.

Dr. George F. Zook, president of the University of Akron, will deliver the commencement addresses at Saint Louis University School of Medicine on June 4, and at the College of Saint Teresa at Winona, Minnesota, on June 11.

Dr. Ulrich Bonnell Phillips, professor of American history at the University of Michigan, has been awarded the foreign traveling fellowship of the Albert Kahn Foundation. The holder of the fellowship, which has an annual value of $5,000, must spend a year in travel, familiarizing himself with different peoples, countries and civilizations, and must make a formal report on his return.

Dr. Charlotte Bühler, privatdozentin in the University of Vienna, will give advanced courses next fall at Barnard College on "Child Psychology" and "Twentieth Century Psychology in Europe."

John A. Mandel, professor of chemistry at New York University and Bellevue Hospital Medical College, died on May 5 in his sixty-third year.

Edward Nourse, for twenty-nine years professor of Biblical theology in Hartford Theological Seminary, died on May 1 at the age of sixty-eight years.

In order to develop a closer educational relation among nations of the Western Hemisphere, President Uel W. Lamkin, of the National Education Association, has invited the ministers of education of nineteen South and Central American countries to attend the Inter-American Conference to be held at Atlanta, Georgia, in connection with the National Education Association convention from June 28 to July 4.

The first assembly of the Pan-American Geographical and Historical Institute will convene at Mexico City in the month of August. The institute was created by resolution of the Sixth International Conference of American States which met at Havana, Cuba, in 1928, and by resolution of the Governing Board of the Pan-American Union, Mexico City was selected as the seat of the institute. Its purpose is to serve as the center for coordination, distribution and publication of geographic and historic studies and as a means of cooperation between the geographical and historical institutes of the American continent. The government of Mexico has extended invitations to all the governments of the American republics to appoint delegates to the meeting.

Portraits of six trustees of the Peekskill Military Academy and of two principals were presented to the academy on May 5 by Mr. Chester D. Pugsley, a trustee, in a ceremony in which Dr. James Rowland Angell, president of Yale University, and Dr. John Grier Hibben, president of Princeton University, participated. The trustees whose pictures were hung in the auditorium of the academy were Chauncey M. Depew, Charles Alexander Robinson, General Henry Tureman Allen, James Bishop Ford, Cornelius A. Pugsley, Bishop Lincoln Ferris and Chester D. Pugsley. The principals were Charles Alexander Robinson, who now holds that office, and John Calvin Bucher. The address by General Allen made a plea for the reduction of military armaments and condemned war as "worse than hell." He said: "The League of Nations, the World Court and similar movements culminating in the Kellogg Treaty and the Gibson offer should convince all who have regarded war as inevitable to adopt a saner attitude. We are now on the sure road to universal peace. It is to be hoped that America will lead in driving home this wholesome influence toward better international relations and to put war as an instrument of international policy definitely outside the pale of the law."

IN a recent address before the annual meeting of the American Council of Education which took place in Washington on May 3, the Secretary of the Interior, Dr. Ray Lyman Wilbur, said, in regard to the proposed Federal Department of Education, that "the place of the national government is not that of supplying large amounts for carrying on the administrative functions of education in the communities, but to develop methods, ideals and procedure, and to present them, to be taken on their merits. The national government, too, can give widespread information on procedure, can report on what actually is going on in different parts of the country and in the world, and can unify, to some extent, the objects of those in the field of education, in so far as unification is desirable. There is a distinct place for this sort of thing in the administrative side of the national government, but it should not be recognized as an administrative position with large funds at its disposal. A Department of Education similar to the other departments of the government is not required."

IN 1928, through cooperation of the National Academy of Sciences, the National Park Service invited a number of leading scientific men of the country to visit the Grand Canyon in order to study the educational problem of the Canyon. The program initiated through invitation of Mr. Stephen T. Mather for 1928 will be continued. In the period from May 22 to June 1, Dr. Douglas Johnson, professor of physiography at Columbia University, will be present at the Canyon and will confer with National Park officials and with visitors especially interested in the significance of the Canyon. It is planned that from time to time brief talks will be given by Dr. Johnson at the station recently established at Yavapi Point through cooperation of the American Association of Museums and the National Academy of Sciences.

YALE UNIVERSITY LAW SCHOOL receives $35,000 for the purchase of books dealing with international law, under the will of Professor Theodore Salisbury Woolsey. Professor Woolsey, who taught international law at Yale for more than thirty years, also left his library to Yale, and $5,000 to the City of New Haven for the beautification of the municipal parks.

THREE fellowships in fine arts, two with an income of $2,000 each and one with an income of $1,000, to be known as the Shady Hill Research Fellowships in the Fine Arts, have been established at Harvard University. They are open to any American or European, man or woman, and will be awarded annually to scholars of proved ability—students, instructors or others—to pursue advanced study in any part of the world in the history, principles or methods of the fine arts. The university has also received an endowment of $75,000 to provide a permanent fund known as the Charles W. Holtzer Fellowship Fund, to be used to bring young Germans to continue at Harvard preliminary training begun in Germany. Among the other gifts the George G. Wheelock Holiday Fund, given by Mr. William H. Wheelock, is the most unusual, for it will enable a few boys, who could not otherwise make the trip, to return home for the holidays.

A GIFT of $250,000 to the Hill School at Pottstown, Pennsylvania, has been made by Mr. Edward S. Harkness on condition that a further $1,750,000 be raised. This is the second large gift that the Hill School has received within three weeks. The first was a gift of $300,000 from Mrs. Alexander Hamilton Rice, Philadelphia.

MILTON S. HERSHEY, of Hershey, Pennsylvania, has given $200,000 for a building to house industrial training shops for school children.

The building will be a unit of the Hershey Industrial School for Boys, to which Mr. Hershey has turned over his personal fortune of more than $60,000,000 as an endowment fund. It also will be used by pupils of the Hershey High School.

AN Associated Press dispatch reports that a gift of $1,000,000 has been made by Mrs. Justine B. Ward, of Dobbs Ferry, New York, for the establishment in Washington, D. C., of a foundation for the propagation of Gregorian and classic polyphony, and the preparation of teachers through normal and advanced courses leading up to a degree of B.A. and M.A. Nicola A. Montani, who is editor of *The Catholic Choirmaster,* has announced that the school will teach all subjects dealing with technical and cultural equipment, including sight reading, vocal training, choir conducting and liturgy.

JULIUS ROSENWALD, of Chicago, has pledged $250,000 toward the Endowment Fund for the American University of Beirut, Syria. The pledge was made on condition that the total endowment of $4,500,000 is raised by July 1. That amount represents the share allocated to that institution in the $15,000,000 fund being raised for the six American schools in the Near East. The pledge was made on the basis of the statement that the trustees of Beirut will create a temporary fund, into which at least $3,000,000 of university funds will be placed.

THE sum of $300,000 is offered by the General Education Board to Morehouse College, an institution for Negroes at Atlanta, Georgia, on condition that an equal amount is raised by the college. The present endowment is $320,000.

HALF the residuary estate and the residence in New York City of the late William Burhans Isham will be held in trust for the use during her lifetime of Mrs. Hannah Collins Isham, and will then revert to Princeton University. The bequest is expected ultimately to amount to several hundred thousand dollars.

THE scholarship committee of the Harvard Club of New York will provide at least three scholarships of $400 each at Harvard College to be awarded annually to students in the graduating class of public or private schools in New York City. The scholarships will meet the full tuition fee of the first year and in exceptional cases the amount may be increased at the discretion of the committee. Holders of these scholarships are not to be barred from holding a Pulitzer scholarship at the same time.

THE board of trustees of Teachers College, Columbia University, have formally approved the plan of cooperation between the Jewish Theological Seminary of America and Teachers College, thereby allowing students in the seminary to qualify through Teachers College for the degree of bachelor of science of Columbia University with a major subject in religious education.

DR. F. B. MUMFORD, dean and director of the college of agriculture of the University of Missouri, announces that the degree of B.S. in rural public welfare has been established by the faculty.

THE State Senate of Tennessee has passed a bill requiring that the Bible be read in public schools. The bill permits the teacher or students to select passages from the Bible to be read without comment each day.

ARRANGEMENT whereby the Central School of Hygiene and Physical Education, New York City, will act as a department of physical education and hygiene for the Russell Sage College of Troy, has been made by President J. Laurence Meader. Under the agreement, Russell Sage College, beginning with the opening of the fall term, will offer professional training in hygiene and physical education. At the same time, students of the college will have less specialized courses in literature and the arts and sciences. The aim of the curricular expansion is to provide technical training of vocational merit without forfeiting general studies in liberal arts. Miss Helen McKinstry, present director of the school, will serve as director of the newly created department of the college. Classes of the department will be held at the school in New York until the completion of the new buildings in process of construction at Troy.

GOVERNOR ROOSEVELT, of New York State, has signed the Downing and Moffat bills relating to the New York City teachers' retirement system. Under the Downing measure all teachers are brought under the retirement system, and to the retirement board is given authority to appoint medical examiners, assistant medical examiners and additional employees as it may deem necessary. The Moffat bill provides for the payment to a teacher's estate of the accumulated deductions and in addition 6 per cent. of his average salary multiplied by the number of years of city service prior to this law; five per cent. of his average salary multiplied by the number of years of city service subsequent to this law. It is provided, however, that the city service under the first plan shall not exceed thirty-five years and twenty years under the second plan.

THE number of days each year during which school must be in session has been increased from 180 to 190 by recent action of the New York State Legislature. Compulsory attendance upon part-time instruction by employed minors, 14 to 17 years of age, except graduates of 4-year high schools, is required in cities having a population of 20,000 or more, and in districts where there are 200 or more such employed minors. Exceptions are made for children mentally or physically defective. The penalty against parents for permitting their children to violate attendance requirements was increased from $5 or 5 days' imprisonment to $10 or 10 days' imprisonment for a first offense.

THE Geological and Natural History survey of Wisconsin has prepared a collection comprising 39 rock and mineral specimens designed for use in high schools and other institutions in which general science, elementary geology, physical geography or geography of Wisconsin is taught. In order to insure that this expensive collection will be preserved in good order, a box has been made which permits the specimens to be displayed for class use in convenient form. It is sent out for about the cost of the box—$10.

FOLLOWING a plan inaugurated at Teachers College in 1928, Teachers College, Columbia University, and George Peabody College for Teachers at Nashville, Tennessee, will offer courses in safety education during the summer session of 1929. These courses, which are under the auspices of the Education Division of the National Safety Council, will give two points of credit to undergraduate and graduate teachers enrolled. The instruction will be in charge of Herbert J. Stack, 1928–1929 Fellow in Safety Education in Columbia University.

THE Section on Diseases of Children will be represented for the second time in the Scientific Exhibit at the Portland meeting of the American Medical Association. The exhibit proposed for this session is on the same topics as last year, in view of the fact that last year's exhibit was so favorably received. The topics are: (*a*) The Effects of Vitamins as Applied to Infant Feeding, and (*b*) Milk and Its Modifications. It is the purpose to make the exhibit of interest and value to the profession at large, as well as to the members of the section.

THE first regional educational conference to be held in East Africa assembled at Dar-es-Salaam on March 4, under the chairmanship of the director of education of Tanganyika. Official delegates were sent by the Union of South Africa, Bechuanaland, Basutoland, Swaziland, Southern Rhodesia, Northern Rhodesia, Nyasaland, Kenya, Uganda and Zanzibar. The conference was held in accordance with the policy of the British government to hold regional conferences of technical officers in different parts of the Empire. The delegates were welcomed by Mr. Jardine, the acting governor.

IT is reported that Augusto Turati, secretary of the Fascist Party in Italy, has addressed a circular to the secretaries of the Fascist university groups, informing them that he has placed himself at the head of Italian universities. There had been hitherto some hesitation, and in some cases even mild opposition among university professors, to join entirely with the Fascist movement and to make Fascist theories their only basis of instruction.

THE council of the University of Melbourne has adopted the report of the committee appointed to consider the advisability of appointing a paid vice-chancellor. The committee has recommended that the sum of £2,000 should be provided to include salary, contribution to provident fund, and hospitality allowance, that the vice-chancellor be a full-time officer and should represent the university in dealing with outside bodies, and that he should be the chief administrative officer of the university. His tenure of office, the council decided, would be limited to a period of five years. It was decided to ask the committee to lay the proposal before the Premier and to ask for the necessary funds to carry it into effect.

THE International Bureau of Education has received from Madame Stokowska, a life-member, a gift of $1,000 for the express purpose of undertaking an inquiry on the books for children particularly characteristic of various countries. The object of this inquiry is to prepare, for July, 1929, at Geneva, an exposition of children's books, together with an analytical catalogue and a report (published in English and French) which will give the editors a clear picture of the best books existing in other countries and thus stimulate translations. Mlle. Blanche Weber, graduate of the University of Geneva, possessing valuable experience with books, will take charge of the inquiry. The bureau has also had the good fortune to obtain the collaboration of Miss Jasmine Britton, director of the City School Library of Los Angeles, who is just starting on a tour of Europe to study children's literature.

DISCUSSION

A BAS EUGENICS

CERTAIN modern eugeneticists worry because the intellectual classes do not breed fast enough. It seems that college graduates and Phi Beta Kappas are in danger of being swamped by fecund mortals who range from idiots to average school teachers. This breeding bogey has frequently been vilified by public speakers until the stuffing within the poor fellow's garments has almost reached the ignition point. Along with this straw man, eugenics has also in its philanderings produced that unlovely offspring—birth control. The two slogans of modern engeneticists are "the prevention of the breeding of the unfit" and "birth control." Can not something more positive and inspiring than the Kallikak family and Dr. Swope's clinic be given the leading eugenetical rôles?

It is of course desirable to improve racial stocks by wise selection. Nature has always been eliminating the unfit and rewarding the fit; not in every individual instance, to be sure, but in a by-and-large way. The human race has long practiced careful selection. As families grew into clans, tribes, nations and leagues, it became increasingly difficult for young people to mate as they pleased. They were advised by parents, prohibited by potentates and priests, influenced by pride and forced in various ways to respect the opinions of others in the matter of choosing mates. If some bold spirit chose outside his own level, clan or caste, there was trouble—and man does not like trouble! Not all the selections brought about by the customs and prejudices of society have been good. There is no doubt that selection as a tool for mating can be improved.

The greatest satisfactions and the greatest sorrows that a normal man or woman can experience perhaps come with the rearing of children. But love is blind, man is fickle and woman is many things; so there are many maladjusted marriages. However, it is yet to be demonstrated that matings by eugenics boards will decrease the number of divorces. In some states laws are being passed which provide for the sterilization of the mentally defective and of vicious criminals. Even though such measures nullify "the God-given rights of individuals," they probably benefit society if administered properly. Yet such tamperings with the biological machinery of the world should be undertaken with great caution. Normal personalities long to raise children, and such longing, for physiological, psychological and ethical reasons, should be satisfied.

There is not, and never has been, room in the world for many extraordinary personalities. The world must always be made up largely of average people who work under the direction of the specially endowed. If a thousand Napoleons or a thousand Carrie Nations should appear in one generation, the world might become a rather disagreeable place. The present attainments of civilization would not have been possible without cooperation, recognition of superior ability or fitness and delegation of authority. The bright men and women direct, exploit and care for their less able fellows. Each man has a level and usually finds it. Darwin would never have been a happy, contented truck driver; Pasteur would have led a sorrowful life as a sheep herder. These were born to be intellectual leaders and mankind generally admitted it.

Now, about breeding. The extraordinary people in the world can not be very numerous because there is barely enough room for them, now and ever. There are parts of the earth where they have practically unlimited opportunities for producing offspring and the average level of the population has not become unusually high in such localities. For example, in Venezuela in 1918 the president, though unmarried, had already fathered over a hundred children, and was still producing. This president is a keen, capable patriot who has done much for his country and is generally recognized as a great man. His productiveness in children is typical of many of the prominent men in Latin countries. Custom in Latin America has long given the exceptional, wealthy and powerful men unusual opportunities for producing offspring; yet Venezuela has not, after several hundred years, given the world a race of supermen. In Nigeria the writer was fortunate in being able to come in contact with two great dignitaries of the Yoruba nation, which numbers several million people. The Orni of Ife was a local chief who possessed unusual ability and personality. He supported about sixty wives and, though comparatively young, possessed something over a hundred children. In the same country, the Alafin of all the Yorubas was an elected king holding the highest political office in his nation. He had more than seven hundred wives and uncounted children. The Orni and the Alafin both enjoyed the privilege of being able to buy (all wives are bought in Nigeria) any woman they chose from the whole nation. Other chiefs, according to their degree, have the same privilege. Yet, in Nigeria, as in Venezuela, the excessive breeding of the high-class people has not produced an unusual race. The Yorubas are generally admitted to be inferior to the Hausas, who live in adjacent territories to the north, and among whom great men are limited to four wives each by Koranic law. These are serious arguments. The eugeneticists take themselves seriously. Why not I?

Birth control should be judged by its motive. If it is used to permit selfish pleasure and as an escape from offspring in order to enjoy idle ease, it is of course evil. If it permits a great personality to carry out a life work which might otherwise be impossible, it may be good. The writer feels that it will make little difference with the human race. If the selfish produce few or no offspring, society will profit. If the capable work for the world instead of rearing children, civilization will progress. There always seem to be enough people to take charge of human institutions.

Personally, I hope it will be a long time before eugenics boards, even if composed wholly of Ph.D.s, sit in judgment as to who is to breed and how. The Spartans attacked the eugenics menace directly by butchering their weaklings. Let us rejoice that civilization has become so decadent that Steinmetz, dwarfed and hunchbacked, was able to finish his career, and that Stevenson, though horribly tuberculous, was permitted to write as long as he could.

Like all young things, is not eugenics a little callow? Is it not perhaps a little too ready to proceed with control and propaganda? Should it wait patiently for maturity and knowledge?

Perhaps, after all, natural checks will keep the human race more or less adjusted to available food and space. As time goes on man will doubtless resort less to robbery and war and more to business and arbitration. He will learn to make his living politely, but let us hope he will never be relieved from the necessity for making it. Civilization rewards self-control. If a man lives in a society, self-control is his best tool for attaining success. Any one who does more than merely live from day to day must have a plan for his life and this means that he must make continual sacrifice and continually keep from doing things that he yearns to do. Self-control in breeding, in eating, in spending, in talking, and many other things is an every-day matter to every one who succeeds in modern civilized society. Why are eugeneticists so excited about their particular control child?

A. S. PEARSE

DUKE UNIVERSITY

SPECIAL CORRESPONDENCE

THE AMERICAN LIBRARY IN PARIS

THERE have been a number of staff changes recently at the American Library in Paris, due partly to the fact that some of the former members of the staff have been compelled to return to the United States and partly to the reorganization and expansion of one of the departments. The library is especially fortunate in that it has applications on file from trained librarians from the principal libraries of the United States, and is therefore able to fill all vacancies with experienced and thoroughly capable people.

Miss Helen Grant Cushing has arrived to assume charge of the cataloging department. She is a graduate of the New York State Library School and comes to the American Library in Paris from the library of the University of New Hampshire, where she was catalog librarian and instructor in cataloging and classification. She will have as assistant Miss Jean Fuller, who comes from the Enoch Pratt Free Library at Baltimore, Maryland, where she had had five years' experience. Another new assistant for the same department is Miss Helen A. Kirwin, a Simmons College graduate, who comes from the New York Public Library to devote her time to the cataloging of the books of the international reference department.

Miss Phyllis Wedd, who has been the library's accountant for some years, has just left for a visit to the United States, and her place has been taken by Miss Mary Moser, formerly of the extension department. To replace Miss Moser, Miss Mary Washburn has just arrived from the United States. Miss Washburn is also a graduate of the Simmons College Library School, and has been reference librarian at the University of New Hampshire since 1924.

The staff of the reference service on international affairs has been completely reorganized, and Mr. Kenneth W. Colegrove, of the department of political science at Northwestern University, will arrive early in June to assume charge of this department of the library. He has been given a year's leave of absence to undertake this work. Pending his arrival, Mr. Marcus E. Ravage is acting as editor of the *European Economic and Political Survey,* one of the publications of the department. Mr. Ravage is a well-known writer, a contributor to many magazines and the author of a number of books dealing with European conditions.

For librarian of the international reference department, the library has secured Mrs. Natalie Friedheim, a graduate of the library school of the New York Public Library, where she afterwards had several years' experience in the economics department, going from there to the Foreign Policy Association in New York, whose library she organized and administered for a period of two years. Her assistant is Miss Denise Montel, a graduate of Simmons College, and more recently assistant librarian of the International Institute of Agriculture at Rome. It is planned to develop the collection of material dealing with current affairs in Europe as rapidly as possible and to make it of the utmost possible value to students of current European economics and politics. The department is fortunate in having secured the services of Professor Norman Dwight Harris, lately head of the department of political science at Northwestern University, in an advisory capacity, and some announcements concerning its future program will soon be made.

BURTON STEVENSON,
Director

THE AMERICAN LIBRARY IN PARIS

QUOTATIONS

UNION COLLEGE

THE record and inaugural address of Dr. Frank Parker Day, the new president of Union College, give promise that the college which President Eliphalet Nott made "a rival of Harvard and Yale" in his day, and which President Charles Alexander Richmond found "small and poor" but lifted again, is to go forward to an even more important place in American education. The personality of this latest successor of Dr. Nott, who was not only a great preacher and teacher but a student of the physical sciences and an inventor, notably of the first stove for burning anthracite coal, is compelling. A

Rhodes scholar for New Brunswick, Canada, where he had his early education, he brings to his new office a broad and deep culture and a first-hand acquaintance with European and Canadian methods as well as a teaching and administrative experience in a variety of American institutions. To all this is added a gallant record during the war.

In engaging to take as many leaves as possible from Eliphalet Nott's book he is harking back to what Professor Franklin Giddings, one of the most distinguished sons of Union, calls the "old breed" of education, which sent men forth from college with the reading and thinking habit. As he says in his "Mighty Medicine";

> Within their limitations the breed and the education were fine. The breed did not believe and it did not hypocritically proclaim that colleges were for hewers of wood and drawers of water. It did not attempt to distribute erudition by encouraging the guzzling of unfermented erudition. The old breed was proud and it had standards.

The new breed of education, to which President Day was committed both by what he said himself and by what President Aydelotte, of Swarthmore College, and others said in welcoming him, must preserve the quality of the old breed, but its knowledge must be comprehensive and its sympathies broad. If quality is sacrificed to quantity by substituting lecture mass production and "authoritative didacticism" for the intimate method of teaching in small groups, it will mean, to use President Aydelotte's phrase, "intellectual suicide for democracy." If it be said, to turn again to Dr. Giddings, that democracies dislike intellectual aristocracies as deeply as those of birth and wealth, the answer is that they do, but that unless democracies cease to distrust intellectual aristocracies and learn to walk respectfully and at the same time self-respectingly with them, "the days of democracy and of civilization are numbered." In consistency with this view those of high intelligence must be provided with means and incentives to go to the very limits of their powers.

Union College has a unique opportunity to develop such a breed of education and such a breed of liberally educated men, and to send them not only into the traditional professions, but into such practical occupations as are carried on at its very doors on a vast scale, and thus to assist in liberalizing them. For this historic institution the trustees have seemingly found a leader who meets the requirements of the definition of the ideal college president: one who knows the frontiers of knowledge and moves forward with them, who also knows the background of human values, unchanged by time.—*The New York Times.*

EDUCATION BECOMES NEWS

Canada has just presented to the world a conference on education that should have delighted newspaper editors from one end of North America to the other. It furnished magnificent copy for the press. If editors have heretofore hesitated about giving front-page space to an education conference, this meeting in Vancouver should have dissolved every doubt. The Canadian National Council of Education conducted a notable assembly of educationists—not professional educators, but men and women of industry and business, writers, philosophers, leaders in many fields. As far as the reports show, not an academic moment was permitted in the nine-day conference. Here was discussion of education on a broad, universal basis. No one talked of education as a mere classroom enterprise. The meeting was of those who believe that school and college are but a beginning, that study and thought enrichment by the adult should be a continuing unfoldment, and that adult education is an integral part of the great educational process. Hence, this conference dealt perforce with the great educational influences—the radio, the motion picture, the popular magazines—and concerning these plain talk was employed, to the end that undesirable conditions might be rooted out.

A result of the conference, therefore, was the setting up of four commissions: to work for government control of radio for the sake of more worth-while programs; to purify motion pictures; to exclude undesirable magazines published in the United States, and to establish a good Canadian magazine for children. There was no mistaking what the delegates wanted. And they were confident that clear-visioned people in the United States would agree with their desire to rule out undesirable influences of such major consequence.

This council of education, acting as a clearing house for some of the best thought of the world, wants to arouse a keener appreciation of the educational problems common to the whole of Canada. But in so doing it is bound to help other countries to get a more definite sense of the needs of modern life, of how to restore a finer sense of leisure, and a greater sanity in the use of modern inventions.

Speakers from nine countries in addressing the conference were united in the point that there are no national boundaries in education. For education is a bond that can bring the whole world together on a friendly basis, say German, Englishman, Japanese and East Indian alike. The message from the Orient is that there must be a fusion of the ideals of the east and the west through education if political clashes are to be averted.

Physical education must be taken out of the hands of those who see it as mere exercise of the body; Canada and all nations must be allowed to develop their own national individuality free of the obtrusive practices of neighboring countries, and magazines which are filled with salacious material, murder, robbery and crimes of every sort, must not be permitted to cross national borders, declares the Canadian National Council of Education.—*The Christian Science Monitor*.

SOCIETIES AND MEETINGS

THE AMERICAN ASSOCIATION OF COLLEGIATE REGISTRARS

THE American Association of Collegiate Registrars helds its seventeenth annual convention in Seattle, on April 16, 17 and 18. This was the first meeting of the association to be held in the far west, and was attended by 118 delegates from twenty-eight states and two Canadian provinces.

Dean Charles E. Friley, of the Agricultural and Mechanical College of Texas, president of the association, presided at the opening meeting. The invocation was given by the Reverend Harry L. Meyer, University Congregational Church, Seattle, and the address of welcome by David Thomson, dean of faculties of the University of Washington.

Among many splendid addresses the following are noteworthy: "The Organization and Administration of the Registrar's Office in the Large University," by R. M. West, registrar, University of Minnesota; "Recent Developments in Recording Systems," by W. S. Hoffman, registrar, Pennsylvania State College; "The Efficient Registrar," by Ezra L. Gillis, registrar, University of Kentucky.

A complimentary luncheon was given Tuesday noon by the Pacific Coast Registrars' Association at which Dean J. R. Jewell, of Oregon State College, gave a summary of some of the progressive movements in higher education in the western states.

The banquet on Tuesday evening was presided over by Worrall Wilson, toastmaster, and addresses were delivered by Judge George Donworth on "A Layman's View of Present Tendencies in Higher Education" and by Nathan Eckstein on "What the Public Expects of Higher Education." President Leonard C. Klinck, of the University of British Columbia, gave a brief survey of the development of higher education in Canada.

The delegates were the guests of the University of Washington at luncheon on Wednesday. Dr. M. Lyle Spencer, president of the University of Washington, gave an address at this luncheon on "The Function of the Registrar in Administration." During the afternoon sectional meetings were held to discuss problems of admission and registration. Later in the afternoon the visitors were the guests of the local registrar's staff on a boat trip which took them through Lake Washington, Lake Union and the government locks to Elliott Bay dock.

The evening session was devoted to the problems of the new registrar and was under the leadership of Ezra Gillis, of the University of Kentucky. Modern tendencies in the registrar's office were discussed, including the conference method of office management and the use of the permanent record card in making transcripts by the photographic method.

On Thursday the convention joined with the Lower Division Conference for the morning session. In the afternoon a business meeting was held at which the following officers were elected for the coming year: *President,* E. J. Grant, Columbia University; *first vice-president,* E. B. Lemon, Oregon State College; *second vice-president,* Emma E. Deters, University of Buffalo; *third vice-president,* Elida Yakeley, Michigan Agricultural and Mechanical College; *secretary,* C. P. Steimle, Michigan State Normal College, and *treasurer,* Alan Bright, Carnegie Institute of Technology.

On April 18 and 19, 1929, there was held at the University of Washington, Seattle, a conference on the reorganization of the first two years of college work. The first session of this conference was held jointly with the American Association of Collegiate Registrars. At this session Professor Herman V. Tartar, of the University of Washington, presented a report of the faculty committee on lower division work of the University of Washington, and I. M. Smith, registrar of the University of Michigan, presented plans for University College of that university. Both of these plans emphasized the importance of better articulation between secondary schools and universities and also improved personnel service for lower division college students.

The second session was devoted to financial problems involved in different plans for reorganization. Walter Morgan, assistant state superintendent of public instruction of California, presented a detailed report on financial aspects of the junior college in California in which he emphasized three important points in the development of California's junior colleges: first, the vast areas to be served in that state; second, the density of the population in those areas, and third, the high property evaluation within those areas. Professor August Dvorak, of the University of Washington, discussed the cost of reorganizing the first two years of the four-year college. He pointed out the possibility of reorganizing these years without an increased expenditure, but he placed more emphasis upon the present high cost of maladjustment within the lower division.

At the third session Professor George W. Knight, of Ohio State University, emphasized briefly the origin of the earlier attempts to meet the needs of lower division students. At the same session E. L. Rea, registrar of Riverside Junior College, Riverside, California, and Dean W. T. Boyce, of Fullerton District Junior College, Fullerton, California, discussed the scope of junior college education and the differentiated treatment of students, some of whom are planning to continue their training in higher institutions while others regard the junior college as a finishing school.

The fourth session was devoted to discussions of improvement of instruction involved in plans for reorganization. Dean H. S. Rogers, of the college of engineering, Oregon State College, discussed the improvement of instruction through better teaching procedures, and President F. J. Kelly, of the University of Idaho, discussed the improvement of instruction through better organization and articulation of courses and topics. Both speakers emphasized the integrity of the learning process and the fact that our common separation of method, content and pupil activity for purposes of discussion is somewhat artificial. They contended also that good junior college procedures are also good secondary school procedures and *vice versa.* President Kelly discussed Idaho's new plan for the lower division work in which better articulation of high school and college is effected by allowing no duplication of course in the two institutions.

At the closing session President Kelly described the attempts which are being made at Idaho and Minnesota for improved personnel administration. At the same session, Professor Herbert E. Cory, of the University of Washington, in discussing orientation courses in the lower division, showed the advantages and the disadvantages of having such courses offered by one broadly trained man and by a group of specialists.

This conference was attended by representatives from many of the leading universities of America. Plans are being made to continue conferences of this nature in collaboration with the American Association of Collegiate Registrars. The proceedings of the conference are being prepared for publication. Persons desiring copies should write to Dean W. L. Uhl, of the University of Washington.

EDUCATIONAL RESEARCH AND STATISTICS

A TECHNIQUE FOR ANALYZING THE SUPPLY AND DEMAND OF EDUCATIONAL WORKERS[1]

THIS study is concerned with the development of a technique for analyzing supply and demand of educational workers in reference to institutions which train such workers. The technique is applicable to any such institutions provided certain types of information are available. First, it is necessary that there be available information concerning the nature of the institution's output of educational workers. Second, it is necessary that there be available information concerning the nature of the vacancies which are reported to the institution during the school year. The technique consists chiefly in an analysis and comparison of these two types of information. The result is a body of objective information concerning the relation of the supply of educational workers to the demand for such workers in reference to the institution in question. By repeating the analysis from year to year it is possible to establish the reliability of the procedure.

The data used in this study are derived from the files of the Board of Vocational Guidance and Placement of the University of Chicago. The two terms "supply" and "demand" will be used throughout this study and are therefore defined at the outset. The term "demand" refers to such requests for educational workers as were received by the Board of Vocational Guidance and Placement during the school year 1926–27. The term "supply" refers to those individuals who were registered with the Board of Vocational Guidance and Placement during the school year 1926–27 as candidates for educational positions. Subsequent discussion in this paper will be concerned with an analysis and evaluation of these two bodies of data as reflecting the relation obtaining between supply and demand of educational workers at the University of Chicago.

A partial analysis of the data described above is presented in Table I. In the first column there are listed four different types of educational work. These are self-explanatory except

TABLE I

COMPARISON OF SUPPLY AND DEMAND WITH RESPECT TO TYPES OF WORK

Type of work	Supply	Per cent. of total	Demand	Per cent. of total	Supply and demand ratio per cent.
Non-teaching	165	10.1	302	13.9	54.6
Teaching single subjects	1181	72.5	1521	69.9	77.6
Teaching two subjects	204	12.5	310	14.2	65.8
Teaching three subjects	79	4.9	44	2.0	179.5
Total	**1629**	**100.0**	**2177**	**100.0**	**74.8***

*Ratio of total supply to total demand.

perhaps the first. Positions involving duties other than teaching, such as executive positions, librarian, supervisor, etc., are included under the first type, "Non-teaching." In the next column there appears the per cent. which each of these numbers is of the total. In the fourth and fifth columns the same information is given for the demand. In the last column there appears an index of the relation of supply to demand.

Before Table I can be properly interpreted, it is necessary that the index referred to above be explained. It has already been said that this index expresses the relation of ratio of supply to demand. For convenience this index is expressed in terms of percentage. Whenever this index is one hundred, then the supply is equal to the demand. Whenever the ratio is larger than one hundred, the meaning is that the supply is greater than the demand. Also, whenever the ratio is less than one hundred, the supply is less than the demand. Thus, for example, in the case of non-teaching the ratio of the supply to the demand is 54.6 per cent., which means that here the supply is less than the demand. In the case of the teaching of three subjects, however, the supply is larger than the demand as expressed by the index 179.5 per cent.

It should be noted that the index used to express the relation between supply and demand

[1] Taken from an unpublished study made at the University of Chicago under the direction of Professor Frank N. Freeman.

depends for its reliability upon the number of cases upon which it is based. For this reason the per cent. which each of the numbers representing supply and demand is of their respective totals is indicated in columns four and five. Succeeding tables will be constructed similar to Table I and will be subject to the interpretation suggested above.

A more detailed analysis of the data presented in Table I appears in Table II. Here is

TABLE II

SUPPLY AND DEMAND WITH REFERENCE TO VARIOUS SUBJECTS

Subject	Supply	Per cent. of total	Demand	Per cent. of total	Supply and demand ratio per cent.
English	288	18.2	314	14.7	91.7
French	74	4.7	102	4.8	72.5
German	26	1.6	36	1.7	72.2
Spanish	36	2.3	58	2.7	62.0
Latin	51	3.2	72	3.4	70.8
Other languages	19	.6	36	1.7	52.8
Mathematics	144	9.1	136	6.4	105.9
Chemistry	53	3.4	78	3.6	67.9
Physics	53	3.4	74	3.5	71.6
Science	14	.9	94	4.4	14.9
Biology	84	5.3	98	4.6	85.7
History	188	11.9	126	5.9	149.2
Social studies	53	3.4	57	2.7	93.0
Economics	48	3.0	75	3.5	64.0
Psychology	26	1.6	57	2.7	45.6
Philosophy	14	.9	19	.9	73.7
Sociology	31	2.0	58	2.7	53.5
Home economics	99	6.3	124	5.8	79.8
Education	88	5.6	114	5.3	77.1
Religion	35	2.1	14	.7	250.0
Commercial	21	1.3	56	2.6	37.5
Physical education	8	.5	67	3.1	11.9
Manual arts	8	.5	28	1.3	28.6
Fine arts	85	5.4	98	4.6	86.7
Kindergarten-primary	31	2.0	89	4.2	34.8
Elementary	12	.8	61	2.8	19.7
Total	1589	100.0	2141	100.3	74.2*

* Ratio of total supply to total demand.

shown the nature and relation of supply and demand of educational workers with reference to the school subjects. In the first column are listed the various school subjects. In the second and fourth columns there are given the numbers representing supply and demand with reference to these various subjects. In the last column there is given the ratio of supply to demand, the interpretation of which has been discussed above. Attention should be called to the fact that in Table I the total of supply for teaching is 1464, whereas in Table II it is 1589. This is explained by the fact that those prepared in two subjects are included twice in Table II. Those prepared to teach three subjects are not included in Table II since in the original study they were treated separately. The explanation of the totals for demand with reference to Tables I and II is the same.

In connection with Table I it is stated that the reliability of the index used to express the relation of supply to demand was dependent upon the size of the totals upon which it is based. The same is true for Table II, and for this reason, columns three and five show the per cent. which each of the numbers representing supply and demand is of their respective totals.

It will be noted that there are twenty-six subjects listed in Table II. The average per cent. for each is therefore approximately four. This suggests that one way to evaluate the information in Table II is by considering those subjects which are above average in point of supply and demand. The subjects which are above average in point of demand are as follows: English, mathematics, history, home economics, education, French, biology, fine arts, science and kindergarten-primary. These same subjects are also above average in point of supply with the exception of science and kindergarten-primary.

Having established that English, French, mathematics, biology, history, home economics, education and fine arts are above average in both supply and demand, it is now important to determine how these subjects are related with reference to supply and demand. It will be noted from the totals at the bottom of Table II that when the total supply is compared with the total demand the ratio is 74.2 per cent. In other words the supply is approximately three fourths of the demand as these terms are here defined. When the ratio of supply to demand for the subjects mentioned above as being above average in point of supply and demand is considered, we find it to be higher, with the exception of French, home economics and education, where it is about the same as in the totals. For biology and fine arts it is about ten points higher. Mathematics, English and history are all more than sixteen points higher. Mathematics is 31.7 points higher and history 75 points.

The fact that the ratio of supply and demand is much higher in the case of English, mathematics and history than it is in the case of the other subjects for which the ratio is reliable, suggests that in these cases placement will be difficult. Students trained to teach these subjects will find it difficult to secure positions.

TABLE III

SUPPLY AND DEMAND IN RELATED FIELDS

Group	Supply	Per cent. of total	Demand	Per cent. of total	Supply and demand ratio per cent.
Language	435	30.6	529	27.2	82.2
Science	296	20.8	421	21.6	70.3
Social	444	31.1	481	24.7	92.3
Miscellaneous	250	17.5	516	26.5	48.5
Total	1425	100.0	1947	100.0	73.2*

* Supply and demand ratio for totals.

In Table III there appears a comparison of supply and demand in related fields. In this table the individual subjects have been grouped under the headings language, science, social and miscellaneous. The supply and demand ratio for the totals is 73.2 per cent. For science it is slightly less, but for language and social it is ten and twenty points higher respectively.

SUMMARY

The purpose of this study has been to illustrate a technique for the analysis of supply and demand in educational workers in reference to higher education. Information to illustrate the procedure has been taken from the files of the Board of Vocational Guidance and Placement of the University of Chicago. The procedure consists chiefly in comparing data which represent an institution's yearly output of educational workers with data which represent the vacancies reported to the institution during the same period. The relation between supply and demand has been shown for types of work, individual subjects and related subject fields. It is evident that other comparisons are possible. It has been suggested that the reliability of the results depends upon the size of the numbers involved. Further indication as to reliability can be achieved by making the analysis perennial.

ALBERT GRANT

THE VOCATION BUREAU,
CINCINNATI PUBLIC SCHOOLS

W. H. COWLEY

BOARD OF VOCATIONAL
GUIDANCE AND PLACEMENT,
UNIVERSITY OF CHICAGO

EDUCATIONAL REVIEW

Edited by WILLIAM McANDREW

A REVIEW OF PROFESSIONAL BOOKS

By HOI BIBLIOLOGOI

(*Continued from page 594*)

We're not giving the community fair value. Glueck. Old Locality's report was short:

"Eleanor Glueck, research assistant, Milton Fund Project, Harvard University, makes a thorough reconnaissance of the wider use of school buildings and offers a summary in the form of a book[1] indispensable to school boards,

[1] Eleanor T. Glueck, "The Community Use of Schools." The Williams and Wilkins Company, Baltimore. 222 pp. $3.00.

superintendents, and persons forwarding social service. The schoolhouse is the logical center of the precinct. It is the proper place for deliberation, discussion and civic education. The main purpose leading to its erection and maintenance is not merely to advantage children and their parents by enabling families to have their youngsters trained for their personal benefit. The whole community pays. The whole community should receive wide service from its schools. The school is the proper polling place. It is the true center for voters' leagues, for party rallies, speeches, and instruction. Politics is the main business for public schools. The school is the place for the public libraries, art exhibits, drama, music, festivals, health training, employment agencies, recreation, sociability. Quoting this declaration of Edward Ward, the father of community center in America, Miss Glueck, who uses the results of the most complete survey of these activities ever made, illustrates by the existent usages of various cities and rural communities the working of each line of service. She covers the laws and rules of different states and localities, the kind of buildings needed, costs, methods of financing, control by boards, and by community organization. All her demonstrations are of centers actually operating. She got her information from 6,353 school superintendents and from a multitude of reports, books and articles upon her subject. She hopes to aid in definite recognition by school boards and all concerned that community use of school buildings is no outside or extra affair but an essential part of the American educational project. Dean Holmes, of the Harvard University Graduate School of Education, in a note on Dr. Glueck's work, asserts that it is apparent that the community use of schools will grow and will develop wisely on the fundamental ideas I just reviewed. 'No one now supposes,' he says, 'that public education can be limited to childhood and youth, nor are we any longer restricted in our ideas that public funds may not be properly expended upon the affairs that heretofore were left to the initiative of separate groups.' He urges getting school boards informed upon the definite facts collected in Dr. Glueck's study.

"I am impressed by the strength of the arguments collected from various sources. There is a large place for social activity that has been created by the abolition of the saloon, and by the increase of free time due to the shortening hours of labor. Unless our decent people make available the right kind of refreshment for the idle hours, which are increasing so prodigiously, the deterioration of our national character seems to me inevitable. Dr. Glueck's figures show that in those states which have, by law, compelled school boards to give the buildings for this kind of service, the community activities are the most numerous. But only 5 per cent. of the buildings are employed in this way. In the larger cities the administrative red tape, the discouraging attitude of school boards, the tendency to standardize and boss the work and play stifle initiative and enthusiasm and hold back the advantages that are possible. Unless those who are served have a voice and control, paternalism takes the spontaneity and democracy out of the affair and puts it into the class of the debilitating amusements the Roman emperors used to beggar their subjects with: free shows and food. But the movement is coming along. More and more local clubs are becoming accustomed to use the schools. The Parent-Teachers organization is one of the strongest aids to this community service. More school boards are paying the cost of heating and lighting and encouraging the people to say what they want. But, too generally, is the whole thing considered an 'outside' movement. Wider enlightenment is necessary. This book is so reasonable, so circumstantial, so persuasive, that its wide distribution is bound to help along this very important move."

We are now our own critics: Grizzell.

"Time was," said Peter the Reader, "when the chief critics of the schoolmaster, reviling him for being behind the times, were the laymen. The Montaignes, the Rousseaus, the Spencers, the Manns. Now we are our own appraisers. Here comes Dr. Grizzell,[2] professor

[2] Emit Duncan Grizzell, "Education: Principles and Practices." The Macmillan Co., New York. 428 pp. $2.40.

in the school of education, University of Pennsylvania, who tells us, in the gentle Philadelphian manner, that the old curriculum survives regardless of the fact that much of it is outgrown by the developments of a rapidly changing world. People regard the curriculum as sacred because it is old. To consider it a collection of subjects or knowledges is the common and the debilitating error of the past. The true curriculum is the exercises and experiences which develop habits, skills, attitudes, ideals and powers. The status of teaching with us is unsatisfactory, to say the least. To get scientific procedures instead of traditional practice is our difficult duty. The recitation, recitation of the text-book—question and answer, reproduction of memorized statements—is so common as almost to stifle education. An outstanding weakness is the dependence of the children on the teacher at the expense of independent thinking.

In setting out in a general outline the essential principles and the prevailing practices among us, Dr. Grizzell accompanies his diagnoses of our diseases by clear statements of what the corresponding healthy states are and how we may bring ourselves from worse to better. His approach to his subject seems to be historical and comparative, so that we may view our system of education in its full setting of origins and tendencies. For six years the main topics in this book constituted the substance of his course for teachers as given by him in the university. Then, he had the manuscript mimeographed and used by other instructors. It was revised and used again.

"The present volume has been tested in the field of discussion, controversy and experience. It cites and applies the work of late researchers: Morrison, Judd, Koos, Thorndike, Colvin, Bagley, Kilpatrick, Cubberley, Bobbitt, Baldwin, Inglis—all the best-known moderns—and develops the school as an institution for social, civic, political service. It confesses the critical weakness of public education at the hands of unqualified, untrained school boards; argues that the carefully trained superintendent can't render efficient service under political control, and closes with three ringing chapters on the reorganization needed in our school system to enable it to use the knowledge of educational processes possessed by its progressive practitioners."

A science book nearly self-operating: Menge. Next was the General:

"I have noticed an interesting thing about children and animal life. Both boys and girls seem generally born with a strong interest in it. They revel in zoological gardens, museums, and in making collections for their own cabinets. They come to high school as potential John Burroughses or Muirs. Something kills the interest of most of them. In my own case I feel sure it was the dullness of the science classes. Emerson remarked this in contempt for the scientist's 'pride of classification': 'He has dried all the plants in his herbal and he himself has lost sap and humor. The boy, gathering shells on the beach, has a saner view,'—something like that. There was a science teacher in the Hyde Park high school, here, in Chicago, who maintained boyish enthusiasm in botany and zoology. In physiology he hurried over bones and anatomy and illustrated functions with fascinating apparatus of his own devising. His botany and geology picnics were a delight as various excited pupils would come running to him with their finds. His name was Fred Stevens. He came from Eaton Rapids. I wonder what has become of him. Edward Menge's book[3] reminds me of Stevens. It awakens in me the youthful enthusiasm of long ago. He begins it with a charming quotation of 1465 on the planting of trees. He undertakes a complete biology for high-school use, treating it as a general introduction to the method of science. He argues, rightly, as it seems to me, that biology is more suited for this purpose than are the colder sciences—geology, astronomy, physics, etc. The natural interest of the young is thus made use of. You notice a new and valuable feature here, a vocabulary at the head of each chapter. The interesting derivation of the words used is given along with their meanings in simple terms. The work enters directly into a remarkable discussion of the

[3] Edward J. Menge, ''The Laws of Living Things.'' Bruce Publishing Co., Milwaukee. 530 pp. $1.72.

scientific manner of thought and work. It is a straight little talk on the psychology of the scientist. It is sure to prove interesting and valuable to pupil and teacher. It is followed by a section, just as valuable, 'how to study,' giving in simple language advice not only for getting the most satisfaction out of this book but for obtaining from school what it is maintained for and what a really large number of boys and girls expect and wish to secure.

"With a typical vertebrate, the perch, a selection which seems to me a great gain over the traditional approach by means of the clam, Dr. Menge launches us upon the great expanse of living structure and function. His exposition of digestion, circulation, respiration, nervous and muscular systems, in man and beast, follows immediately, with enough on the bones to hold the organism together. Whenever the subject requires allusion to chemistry, physics, or other sciences, a simple but complete excursion into those fields is conducted. Industry and commerce are shown in connections that need them. Hygiene, the remarkable gain over malaria and other parasitic diseases, are emphasized when needed. The book is a remarkably well-done presentation of science to beginners in that it avoids the error of baby talk. It is exact. It doesn't say, 'Men have found that mosquitoes carry malaria,' but it tells who found that out and how it was done. So, through the most valuable facts concerning plants, animals, and man, these chapters run, admirably illustrated with beautiful drawings. It is the work of a master teacher. Experience is evident in the style of thorough preparation of the reader at the entrance upon new conceptions and in the recurrent allusions to important matters earlier considered. I have never seen a biology book so easy to use as this. It almost runs itself."

The principal's office and the abnormal child: Wallin. Dr. Batwell's report:

"The presence of handicapped children in so many rooms of the public schools, the rapid advance in devising more adequate service for them, warrant my calling your attention to the work of Dr. Wallin,[4] professor of clinical psychology and director of the psycho-educational clinic for subnormal and delinquent children, Miami University, Columbus, Ohio. It is not hammock reading. No good handbook is. It is packed with facts from the author's wide clinical experience and extensive acquaintance with the literature of the field. I should think it as necessary a part of the clinician's office as Webster or the Medical Dictionary. Do you want accurate knowledge concerning your own and others' disturbances of perception, attention, memory, association, ideation, speech, language, reading, movement, emotion, and character? Do you want insight into intricate or unusual mental mechanisms, submerged complexes, alexia, amusia, aphemia, hysteria, compulsion neurosis, introversion, or any other mental vagaries? Do you want these and more explained in lucid phrase by one who has inspected, observed, tested, measured, I.Q.'d, and psychographed 7,000 abnormals? If so, read 'Clinical and Abnormal Psychology.' The book was prepared as a systematic text in clinical psychology, the first in its field, particularly for students in psychology and education, and for would-be psychological and medical clinicians. But its message should also reach the intelligent layman, and the special teacher and social worker who want to get back of the psychologist's recommendations, and find out what he is really talking about when he sends them the technical results of his expert examinations. Here they will find an outline of the inside workings of the clinic. They will find its aims and methods discussed and evaluated. If they read with a serious purpose, the psychologist's suggestions will become live and meaningful for them.

"Do you want to know how to organize special instruction for mentally deficient, retarded, delinquent, crippled, speech-defective, deaf and blind children? Do you want to acquire definite ideas regarding the objectives, methods, guiding principles and conditions of successful special class work? Do you want to know what mental

[4] J. E. Wallace Wallin, "The Education of Handicapped Children." 394 pp. $2.25. "Clinical and Abnormal Psychology," same author. xxii + 649 pp. $3.00.

deficiency is, what causes it, what its types and forms are, and what its consequences are to the individual, the family, and the state? Do you want to learn all this from one who has spent almost two decades organizing and assisting in the organization of special classes in scores of cities, large and small, in training special class teachers in many states, in familiarizing himself with the best that has been written, and in making voluminous contributions? If so, read Wallin and then resolve to become a practical idealist, even in the humdrum of schoolmastering education, and make your class a model of what every special-class teacher and school administrator should know about special classes. If you reach only three-quarter perfection measured by the ideals of this practical book, you will have earned double promotion, if not double salary, and the other rewards which, I hope, will eventually come to the 'good and faithful servants' of Eros, if not of Demos."

Chicago English: Camenisch. From Luther the Literary:

"When I was at the meetings of the elementary school principals of the National Education Association in Boston, last year, I heard a New England schoolman say that Chicago has made a name for itself in the teaching of English. He mentioned Wilber Hatfield and *The English Journal,* James Hosic, whom New York stole from us, Professors Gray and Lyman of the University, all of whom seemed to be held in high honor in Boston. Think of that! Our gangsters and politicians have invited so much ridicule for our city; our Anglophobia has been so widely advertised, that a compliment from the seat of American culture for our English is worth recording. I am now elected to present a justification[5] for a continuance of our repute. See what Miss Camenisch has done. She has devised a book of tests of the essentials of good English, and so arranged it that every pupil must get everything that any member of the class does. Instead of the old plan of recitation by which a boy would get a thirtieth or fortieth of the questions given out, he and everybody get them all. What are they? Sentence recognition, grammar and usage, punctuation, capitals, abbreviations, possessives, letter forms, all the particulars covered in a standard work. The drills in the mechanics of English are individualized. There are simple diagnostic tests and check sheets. They enable you to know what pupils need bracing up in commas and who is weak with capitals. There is a generous assortment of practice tests which teachers have found needed for the most frequent errors made by a large number of children. The sentences are natural and appeal to pupils' interests; they introduce one limited problem at a time. The person taking the test works on the page assigned to him, crosses out any error and writes the correct form over it. The tan-colored book is then given him and with its aid he corrects his own work. By a very simple scheme of numbering, pupil and teacher have a quick and comprehensive check on what each child especially needs. I commend this book to you as a remarkable saver of teacher's time and effort. If you have lost as many golden hours as I have marking mistakes on dead papers only to find the same errors cheerfully bobbing up in the same pupil's work, you will bless Sophia Camenisch for devising this simple and workable scheme for having corrections made by the children, now, while the matter is warm and while you are present. This is the practice the great William H. Maxwell advocated when he came out here to address us on the teaching of English. No more dismal papers to take home and correct when we ought to be refreshing ourselves for meeting our children to-morrow! 'Self-teaching,' said the famous Marcel in 'The Study of Languages,' 'is the work that makes men great.' Here you have it, reduced to a workable and interesting scheme. Let us sing a hymn to St. Sophia, our lady who slays the dragon of drudgery."

In came the crackers and six kinds of cheese which Lady Alice had brought from Katwyk on the Northern Ocean. There were fizzlely water, cakes, coffee and cocoa. Much pleasant talk and cheery au revoirs.

[5] Sophia C. Camenisch, "Chicago Practice Tests for Mastery." The English Journal Co., 6705 Yale Ave., Chicago. Two vols. 50c. for the set.

SCHOOL AND SOCIETY

EDITED BY J. McKEEN CATTELL

WITH WHICH IS COMBINED THE

EDUCATIONAL REVIEW

EDITED BY WILLIAM McANDREW

Volume XXIX | Saturday, May 18, 1929 | Number 751

ELIPHALET NOTT[1]

By Dr. FRANK PARKER DAY

PRESIDENT OF UNION COLLEGE

As soon as I came to Union College I began to hear of Eliphalet Nott, great president of bygone days. His clarion name took a hold upon my imagination; it rang like a war cry, the yell of a Highland Clan charging across a moor with flashing claymores, or the resounding name of some fierce prophet of Israel; the surname Nott suggested a hard, stern, tough-minded man but the euphonious Christian name Eliphalet, that he might have been a poet, a dreamer, a great lover.

Day by day as I labored to learn, talked with professors and walked the campus with those who loved Union College, I heard many quaint stories of this grand old man, and realized soon that he was the genius of the place. I knew that I was being inspected during that initial period by trustees, alumni, faculty, students, but little by little I began to feel that there was some one watching me more important than all these, a watcher who sat unseen in the corner of my office, who of dark nights stood beneath shadowing trees, and who trailed me home when the long day's work was done. I became obsessed with the idea, that there was only one person that I really need please and satisfy, and that was Eliphalet Nott, grand old president, who in his old age thought that he owned Union College, and who did own it, if the work of art is ever the possession of the creator.

During the first initial weeks of my apprenticeship, I lived alone in a room of the president's house, then in a sad state of rehabilitation; paper torn from the walls, rooms littered with lumber, shavings, paint-pots and stepladders. At night it was an eerie place, a man might easily have been murdered there. Eliphalet Nott had built the house, died there, and been carried out from its portals. Entering at night I always dashed swiftly for the electric light switch, fearful lest I might see him lurking in the shadows of the big stairway. One night I came there tired after a day of much advice; I had been advised to speak in chapel, I had been advised not to speak in chapel; I had been advised to continue the traditions and teach like the other executives, I had been advised to avoid teaching and stick to executive work; I had been advised to coordinate some of the departments, I had been advised to keep hands off, and mind my own business. As I entered Eliphalet's house that night my head buzzed with advices like a hive filled with angry bees. I got to sleep quickly, but

[1] Inaugural address of the president of Union College and the chancellor of Union University, May 4, 1929.

after midnight there resounded throughout the empty house terrific clanking of the radiators; I woke with a start and sprang out of bed with the conviction that Eliphalet Nott had come for me. So strong was the obsession that half awake I called out: "Do not come to-night, good old man, with more advice, I have had all that I can bear to-day," and a line of one of Shakespeare's sonnets ran drowsily through my brain:

Give not a windy night a rainy morrow—

Fully awake I laughed at my fears, locked the door and got back into bed, but before I slept again I had determined to write my inaugural address on Eliphalet Nott. Perhaps that was the midnight advice the old man wished to give; perhaps it was the best way to lay his shade.

And I am glad now that I began to read his sermons, temperance lectures, commencement addresses, diaries, notes on the margin of books, for since his life is so bound up with the college, I could have learned its history in no better way.

Let me give a few salient facts of his life. Eliphalet Nott was born in Ashford, Connecticut, on the twenty-fifth day of June, 1773. His father, a luckless man, after having wandered from venture to venture was, at the time of Eliphalet's birth, trying to make a living by farming sixty acres of rough stony stubborn soil. They were miserably poor. The house was low and in ill repair; the countryside desolate and woebegone. Seldom had a babe been born amid circumstances less conducive to development into greatness. His great asset was a mother of intelligence and high character. At the age of three a zealous biographer informs us he could read, and at four had read through the Bible. This seems to have been the common penance of great men in childhood. His early schooling consisted of the Bible and the sermon, for as his mother's health failed when he was very young, little Eliphalet was sent to church with paper and pencil, to note down text and points, so that he might report all on his return home. His verbal memory through his whole life was amazing, and was perhaps due to this early concentration on what must have often been dull and longwinded. For a year at the age of eight he studied in the home of his brother Samuel, a rising minister; but the discipline was too severe, there were too many whippings, and at nine little Eliphalet returned home to help his father on the farm. There he felt that the whole of life was slipping by him and that he would never escape the rocky fields of Ashford. One incident reveals the working of his childish mind and his desire to escape. One day, as the little farm hand, aged ten, was hoeing potatoes in the stony fields, Dr. Palmer, the physician of the district, drove up to his father's door. Moved by a frantic impulse, the little boy threw down his hoe, and ran to the fence crying: "Won't you make a doctor of me?" "Not yet, my little man, not yet," replied the good-natured doctor, "but if you study hard, I will make a doctor of you some day." But that was not to be his way of escape.

At the age of fifteen his mother died and the tie that bound him to home was broken. Again at the age of sixteen he became an inmate of his brother Samuel's home, alternating three hours of study with three hours of farm work, for Samuel, to eke out his slender stipend as a parson, took pupils and ran a farm. There for five years young Eliphalet studied classics, the elements of mathematics and religion, industriously but none too happily. Writing in 1860 he says of those days: "If I was not whipped more than three times a week when at Franklin, and this in addition to warnings and daily admonitions, I considered myself peculiarly fortunate—and I formed a resolution, that if I ever lived to be a man, I would not be like other men in regard to the treatment of children."

He began his teaching in the country school around Franklin, but it was doubtless with sighs of relief that he escaped the ægis of the puritanical Samuel and became in 1794 the principal of Plainfield Academy. He had now stepped out upon the highroad towards success.

He was a successful teacher in Plainfield, successful too as a lover for there he won the promise of Sarah Maria Benedict, daughter of Joel Benedict, pastor of the Congregational Church.

Always he labored over his books, for we find him in May, 1795, boldly presenting himself to the faculty of Brown University demanding examination and a degree. He was advised to study the courses of the senior year throughout the summer; he did so and in September passed the examinations with distinction. He had never spent a day in college as an undergraduate. The faculty of Brown was nonplussed; here was a man with the substance of an education, without the form; some unusual action must be taken; they compromised by giving Eliphalet Nott the honorary degree of M.A.

In 1796 the missionary society of Connecticut asked him to undertake mission work in the west of New York State, at that time a savage frontier land. He accepted without hesitation work to his liking, for he was by nature an adventurous pioneer. He married Miss Benedict on July 4, 1796, and incredible as it may sound, left his bride next day at her father's house, to set out for what was then the Wild West. Through Hartford, Springfield and Albany he pressed, through the forest westward, by trails known only to Indians and woodsmen, gnawing a smoked herring without bread for his supper, his horse cropping the scant herbage of forest glades, till he came one day to a high hill overlooking the tiny settlement of Cherry Valley, and found his heart cheered by the sight of cultivated fields. That spot he knew by a strange instinct would be for a time his home. Westward he pressed to frontier posts, till he had fulfilled his mission, then returned to Cherry Valley to become pastor of an infant church, to send for his wife, and establish a home and school in the beautiful valley he never ceased to love.

After two happy peaceful years, he was called to the First Presbyterian Church in Albany and accepted the call. On his way thither, he put up for the night in Schenectady at an inn that once stood on the corner of Union and Ferry Streets, and hearing that a religious service was to be conducted near at hand, by the Reverend John Blair Smith, president of Union College, he went there, and met and conversed with President Smith. Does chance govern us, or some strange destiny shape our ends? Had his horse cast a shoe he might not have met President Smith. Albany and Schenectady were then far apart. This trivial meeting forms his first known connection with or interest in Union College and may well have been the initial cause of his future great presidency.

His ministry in Albany was effective; he became widely known for presence and oratory. A writer of his day commenting on his preaching says: "His ambition was to make men wiser and better, rather than to promote sectarian interests." During those years that he labored in Albany to build up Sunday-schools, church and charitable organizations there is evidence, however, that his primary interest was in education. Here is a rather extraordinary extract from a letter he wrote in March, 1803:

"The alarm of an intruder breaking into my house, called me from my pillow, this morning, somewhat earlier than usual. By this means I am furnished with a leisure hour: that hour I devote to an object in which we both feel an interest—I mean an academy." Think of it, Eliphalet Nott rising before daybreak to chase out a burglar, and grasping at the hour thus stolen from dawn to write a treatise on education! And what an excellent treatise it is.

In 1803 we find that his congregation express their approbation of his services by raising his salary, and that the young men of his church present him at New Year's with a cask of wine, which he does not spurn.

1804 is a sad and fateful year for him. In that year he loses his young and beautiful wife, and his family is scattered, then comes the death of his friend Alexander Hamilton, and the consequent famous sermon from a heart full of fierce indignation against the savage custom of duelling. In the same year came the offer of the presidency of Union College.

Long he debated with himself; he could not believe himself worthy; he consulted friends and brother Samuel. From the latter he received a tart elderly-brother letter. Young Eliphalet must not be too uppish but must be kept in his place.

"God puts up and puts down whomsoever he pleases," writes brother Samuel. "Some think you will do right others wrong in leaving Albany. They say the college does not stand in the right place. Your sermon on the death of General Hamilton was the best of anything I have seen, though that I think was not without fault. There is one fault you have fallen into in your sermonizing—that partakes strongly of profanity. I mean your frequent interjections: 'O my God,' 'Good God!' with other similar exclamations, far too common to stand the test of criticism, though perhaps, not ill calculated to render you popular in your part of the country."

Eventually he accepted the presidency of Union College, writing humbly to a friend: "I am willing to go and to be wherever my Master directs." He directed the affairs of Union College from 1804 till his death in 1866; he found it small and insignificant, he left it famous. Briefly shall I touch upon what he did for the college as I must have time to speak of his educational ideas.

Dissatisfied with the cramped quarters of the down-town buildings he looked about for new grounds. One evening he stood upon this hill and decided, "Here will I build a college." He had the seer's eye that could visualize the ideal. In one of his letters he tells us what the land looked like on the evening of his vision: "It was rough, full of shaggy ravines and heavily wooded." With little or no money he bought on the security of his own name 250 acres, part of which the college now stands on. With rare foresight he engaged the services of Jacques Ramée, distinguished engineer and landscape artist, to make a plan of college buildings and of development of grounds; his eloquence and personality won money from stubborn legislatures and persuaded them to grant him the privilege of conducting state lotteries for the support of the college. In this he was no niggard for he plead at the same time the cause of Hamilton College and the College of Physicians and Surgeons. With his own hands he helped lay the bricks of North and South College; by a skilful process of irrigation he washed sand hills into unsightly hollows. Besides attending to all these physical things, he remade the curriculum, he taught many hours daily, he built up a good faculty, he was the master, the beginning and end of everything, in his aim of creating a perfect school. Writing rather boastfully to his brother about 1812 he thus describes Union College:

> Our college under the new system is increasing fast in numbers, and perhaps it would not be extravagant to say in respectability. Some of our professors are men of the highest standing, and the system we have adopted can not fail to excite attention and command the approbation of the public. Our students like those of the Moravian

Schools are to be entirely separated from the great world. The president is to lodge in college, and board in common with the family, as are all the other officers of the faculty. Each class belongs to the family of the officer who instructs them; and in our dining hall is preserved all the decorum, ceremony and politeness of refined life. Not the least disorder is allowed in or about the edifice. From prayers, from church, from recitation, such a thing as absence is unknown. The week is completely filled up with collegiate, the Sabbath with religious exercises. On the latter day, no student ever goes from the yard except to church and even then he walks with his professor in procession, sits with him, and with him returns. Perhaps no college has ever furnished such complete security to the manners and morals of youth, or a course more likely to insure a thorough education. Strangers visit us with interest, and leave us, astonished at the order, punctuality and diligence which prevail. By the new arrangement, board has been reduced from $2.50 to $1.45 per week, and we expect still further reductions. An establishment of this kind for boys in the country is new, and I flatter myself that it will be attended with the most extensive and salutary consequences. I say extensive, for I suppose, other parents feel a solicitude similar to what I feel, and I should not hesitate to send a son to the ends of the United States, to place him in that state of security, and in enjoyment of those advantages, which our youth enjoy.

He was a true pastor to his flock, whose hands knew how to hold the sheep hook, guide, philosopher and friend of talented but wayward boys: trained in the narrow school of his time he felt the necessity of making Union undenominational; with a background of Greek, Latin and theology, the rising star of science swam into his ken when it was scarce above the horizon, in the face of a board that fiercely opposed his introduction of scientific studies he became the trustee, and later president of Rensselaer Polytechnic Institute, that great scientific foundation, while remaining president of Union; he studied heat, and invented stoves for heating students' rooms, so cunningly strong and heavy, that they could neither be carried away, nor broken by being hurled down stairs; he took out numberless patents, and from his invention of the base burning stove for the consumption of anthracite coal, fortunes have been made; he was the friend and adviser of Robert Fulton; in the office of the Mohawk Bank hangs his portrait as one of the directors. Students flocked to him and hung upon his words with reverence. Wayland, his disciple who afterwards became president of Brown, said in his old age:

"I think him the ablest man I have ever known intimately." Seward, another of his boys, piqued at not having received the Republican nomination for President of the United States, balked at accepting the Secretary of State-ship under his rival, Lincoln. It was old Eliphalet Nott who went to Seward and persuaded him to accept a position in the cabinet. Under his régime Union was the rival of Harvard and Yale, and because of a stamp he set upon the boys, an inclination of mind, an idealistic goal, Union men became judges, bishops, governors of states, generals, and one president of the republic.

What could this old man not do, and what did he not accomplish? Yet in his old age we find him writing: "I have always been hurried through life, and yet have brought little to pass." This amazing humility from the lips of inventor, famous preacher, beloved leader, financial genius, builder of colleges, shaper of statesmen, reminds one of Shakespeare's famous sonnet in which he sighs regretfully,

Desiring this man's art and that man's scope.

Certainly humility is the hall-mark of genius and "Whosoever exalteth himself shall be abased; and he that humbleth himself shall be exalted."

Through what a big period his useful life stretched; I have talked with two old Union alumni who were his students, one is in this audience to-day, yet he was 16 when George Washington became president, and in 1804, when Eliphalet Nott came to Union, Napoleon Bonaparte, only four years his senior, had just made himself Emperor of France, and disposer of thrones. The French Revolution seems far back in time, yet Eliphalet Nott in talking with a doubting student said: "Once during the French Revolution I too was troubled with such thoughts." Legends of his chariot, his three-cornered hat, his shrewdness in outwitting mischievous boys, his odd mannerisms have grown round his sweet memory thick as the leaves of vines that clothe stone-work of some noble structure. Of all the legends one seems to me most touching. He was buried in the Union plot of Vale Cemetery on a bitter day of February, the snow driven in fierce wind-swirls. When the mourners had left the cemetery one remained gazing down upon the grave; it was "Mose," colored servant, valet, man-of-all work, picturesque charioteer, the slave whom Eliphalet Nott had redeemed, "Mose," who thought his dead master the greatest man in all the world.

His ideas on education like all great ideas were simple. He was one of the first advocates of free schools as an absolute necessity for a republic; he saw before almost any one else the necessity of reforming curricula and of introducing modern languages and science. Soon after his appointment he writes triumphantly to brother Samuel, "A professor is coming from France with some chemical apparatus for us." He strove hard to educate himself in the sciences, yet never ceased to love the classics, or to believe in their value as civilizing forces in the minds of men.

"Young man," he said to Tayler Lewis, newly appointed professor of Greek at Union College,

> you are of Greek, it is a noble study, and may it ever retain its place in our colleges. I care less for Greek than you do, and less for books generally as a means of educational discipline. But a college must have a wide curriculum to be varied or enlarged as circumstances may demand. All kinds of men and minds are needed. Make the boys as fond of Greek as you can. If you can infuse into their minds a love of the old literature, and of the old philosophy, that is the very purpose for which we have called you here. Go on, ride your hobby, but do it becomingly; do not rail, as you are inclined to do, at the practical, the utilitarian, the scientific, but make as much as you please of your department, and I will give you all the aid in my power.

But the important thing he believed in was the necessity of developing the minds of those who associated with him, of teaching them logical thinking, analysis and correct deductive and inductive reasoning. At this he labored and it was by this simple plan that he was able to send from his classroom so many men of distinction. This giant in strength, this great, great personality scorned all methods of teaching except the intimate one. The college was comparatively small and he taught every man in college. He was mature, he had ripened, his mind was mellow; he talked to students as if they were men, not foolish children, and revealed to them all his knowledge of men and affairs. He took as his text-book some treatise on philosophy or criticism; Kame's "Elements of Criticism" was his favorite, and from that as a starting point, he encouraged argument on politics, religion, ethics, life. His was the Socratic method; he had infinite patience. He drew out ideas rather than poured on facts, he encouraged a point of view, he elaborated the text with examples from life; he had read widely, he had dared to live, he had something to impart, he encouraged students to work their brains.

Laughingly he once said, "A good book of hard riddles would make a first class text-book." In other words, the text-book for him was but the suggestion point from which mental operations started. In the margin of Kame's "Criticism" in the preserved diaries of those who were his students we find his elaborations of the text.

He interlarded his lesson with much worldly wisdom. One day in class the discussion was of mobs, and of mob psychology, though perhaps they called it by some other name in his day, and after getting opinions from his students he summed up by saying:

> Man seldom acts from pure reason. In a small class now a few students might be very rational; but where the class is twenty there is less reason, and if there were 1,000 here there would be no reason at all. In dealing with a mob or crowd you must always endeavor to get the name of an individual and deal with him. I remember one night, when after a fight between the rougher townsfolk and the students, a threatening mob gathered before the Blue Gate. I went out to disperse them but was greeted with yells and angry hoots, and at first could do little with them. Then I heard one member of the mob address his fellow by name as Yaup Ostrander. I had never heard of this person before, nor knew not who he was, but I called out boldly, 'Yaup Ostrander, Yaup Ostrander, I will call on you in the morning and settle this disagreement.' Yaup Ostrander replied civilly and the mob dispersed because its spirit had been broken by the selection of an individual. Next morning I hunted up Yaup Ostrander, found him a low ignorant fellow and dealt with him summarily.

In lighter vein he would say to his students: "Young gentlemen, always choose the proper time and place for what you have to do; never ask a man for money before breakfast."

His extraordinary sympathy, humanity and largeness of religious view appealed to the hearts of young men. Think of this from a sermon in his eighty-first year by one who had been whipped into a set and narrow school of theology by brother Samuel.

> You will find the teachings of Greece fundamentally the same as those of Palestine. The same loving gardener that planted the Rose of Sharon and the Lily of the Valley, nurtured those flowers that bloomed in the Vale of Tempe and Ida and Olympus no less than Carmel and Tabor testify of God.

We can do no better in the conduct of Union College than to take as many leaves as possible from Eliphalet Nott's book. We must reduce to a minimum the large lecture system, and return as far as possible to this intimate method of teaching in small groups. With that thought in mind, we hope in the near future to begin the honors system of education, a conference on which will be held in the chapel this afternoon. Every one knows that the handing out of facts by the teacher and their notation and reception by students does not constitute the process of education. A true teacher should have a point of view, a rich thoughtful conception of life, and a gentle patience to listen to youthful conceptions and piece together fragments that are sound and good. In a radio speech a few Sundays ago, I read part of Tennyson's "Ulysses" to illustrate a point; a few days later I got a letter from a very intelligent old lady in Vermont, who wrote: "How can you expect young men to comprehend Ulysses, when they have never been avoyaging? They could perhaps understand a little of his first vôyages but for his last they have no experience to check against or compare." When I came back from the war and re-read Chaucer and Shakespeare, I was astonished to find how much better I understood both, than when I had formerly taught them. I hope I shall not hurt the feeling of any young instructors present when I express what I have been leading up to, namely, that a good teacher should have some experience in living, and that young men from the graduate schools who wish to make teaching their profession would do well to mix in the affairs of life for some years before beginning to teach. It takes a good while to assimilate what we have learned and to get rid of waste. True, Eliphalet Nott was president and teacher at thirty-one, but what an apprenticeship in living he had served. The teacher who will inspire the student must be himself a student, who feels the years too short to encompass his own field of knowledge.

Union College has been voyaging for almost 150 years. Her history has been fifty years of wonderful swift sailing, fifty years in the doldrums with much flapping of sail and idly kicking tiller, then two great master mariners Raymond and Richmond who stared with eyes undimmed toward the pilot stars, and set the ship's course for the unattainable Happy Isles. Union College would go on triumphantly had I never existed, but since I do exist and the trustees have thought me worthy to put at the helm, I too stare for pilot stars and dream of happy voyaging, lucky trafficking, and treasure-trove.

I dream of physical things, a fenced campus, beautiful park-like place, more playing fields, an outdoor rink, many tennis courts, athletic facilities for every student, a new electrical laboratory, of the pasture set out with clumps of trees as Jacques Ramée planned it, a better library, refurbished dormitories, a splendid student body that wants to learn, a well-paid happy faculty. I dream of spiritual things, of something without price; something that cannot be bought with money, a spirit that will permeate us all, teachers and students, that will give us belief and enthusiasm to put every ounce of strength into our work, belief and enthusiasm similar to that which led people in the Middle Ages to go crusading to the Holy Land and build sky-climbing cathedrals.

Thanks to the generosity of our alumni and friends, who believe in the college, and to our fairy Godfather, the treasurer, most of the physical things can be done and that speedily; for the spiritual ideal, we must work, hope and trust.

I suppose I should be expected to announce a policy, but I remember the remark of a wise viceroy of India, "Policies are pitfalls that fools dig so that they may fall into them." If I have any policy it is simply this, I shall work to the limit of my capacity for the college, and take it for granted that every one in the employ of the college will do the same.

If after the manner of the fairy stories, I could have one wish granted, it is, that the mantle of old Eliphalet Nott might fall upon my shoulders to-day, so that in the conduct of Union College, I might have something of his courage, humanity and charity, something of his idealism that inspired Union men to serve the state with honor and devotion. He is the genius of the place, he loved the college as no one else could love it and if we believe in immortality, he treads this campus daily to see how we are doing, and walks and ponders o' nights in the glade beneath his favorite elm.

EDUCATIONAL EVENTS

EDUCATIONAL ESTIMATES OF THE LONDON COUNTY COUNCIL

At a recent meeting of the London County Council, Sir John Gilbert, chairman of the education committee, in submitting the education estimates, said that the year was the last of the three years' program. The capital estimates were for £850,000, as against £1,000,000 last year—a decrease of £150,000. The maintenance estimates amounted to £11,344,205, against £11,412,320 last year. The estimates of other committees for educational work were £1,716,691, that the maintenance figures reached the total of £13,080,896, against £13,126,666, or a decrease of £45,770. There had been a decrease in the number of children in the elementary schools. Last year the roll was 531,350. For the coming year the figures were estimated at 513,000—a decrease of 18,350. There was an increase in the numbers in the central schools. Last year the roll was 22,650, and for the coming year the figures would be 24,000, a substantial increase of 1,350. There had been a saving in cleaning the schools owing to the oiling system, the actual saving in two years being £20,000.

The cost per child in London in 1913–14 was £7 5s., as against the cost for England and Wales of £4 15s. 2d. In 1926–27 the cost of a child in the council's schools was £15 12s. 4d., as against £11 16s. 8d. in the schools of England and Wales. Whereas, in 1913–14, the cost in London was 63 per cent. above the cost outside, to-day it was only 24 per cent. above the cost outside. That seemed to show that the provinces were making developments such as were initiated in London years ago. The actual rate this year would be 2s. 2¾d. in the pound. Of the total cost the Board of Education would bear £6,123,215. The balance would come from the rates.

In the last 21 years the development had been most impressive. There were no central schools in 1908. The system as such did not exist. To-day there were 80. In the maintained secondary schools in 1908 there were 20,000 pupils. There were now 32,000. In the old days only 37 per cent. of the scholarship children remained until the fifth year. Now 78 per cent. of the children remained in the schools until the fifth year. Technical education and continuation education showed a similar impressive progress. In 1908 there were 44,000 students in technical schools. To-day there were 66,000. In 1908 there was only medical inspection for vision; there was no medical treatment. In 1908 the children inspected numbered 35,000. In the estimates he was submitting provision was made for the medical inspection of 357,000 children, and for the reinspection of 187,000. Provision was also made for the medical treatment of 289,000 in hospitals and clinics.

THE RHODES HOUSE AT THE UNIVERSITY OF OXFORD

A WIRELESS dispatch to the New York *Times* reports that on May 10 Viscount Grey, of Fallodon, chancellor of Oxford University, formally accepted Rhodes House, the new building erected by the Rhodes trustees as a permanent memorial to Cecil Rhodes and as suitable headquarters for the Rhodes Trust.

One wing of the new building will contain the residence and offices of the Oxford secretary, who at present is F. A. Wylie. Another wing and a stackroom in the basement are to contain a library of the literature and history of the English-speaking peoples, which will be administered as a part of Oxford's great Bodleian Library. The main hall and some of the common rooms will be available for lectures and other general university purposes, but the building will not be a clubhouse nor will Rhodes scholars have special privileges in it.

Over the bronze entrance door of the great hall is a carved ship of state with the British lion depicted on one side and the American eagle on the other. Under the ship is written "De Goode Hoop"—the name of the ship of the first Dutch Governor of the Cape Colony.

According to the account in the *Times,* Lord Grey expressed satisfaction that the new library would relieve some of the congestion from which the Bodleian Library and the British Museum were suffering. "It will contain a collection," he said, "dealing with past history and present progress from which those whose ambition it is to serve the British commonwealth of nations or the great American republic will be able to draw inspiration and get information. The collection under this roof must do something to further the spirit of enterprise and patriotism which Cecil Rhodes had so much at heart."

Sir Otto Beit, senior Rhodes trustee, expressed the hope that the building would survive through the centuries "with Oxford's medieval and Renaissance structures as an example of the architecture of the twentieth century" and added that Rhodes House was certain to play a big part in Oxford life and help to maintain Oxford as the most beautiful university town in England.

A round chamber, done in marble, which will serve as a memorial to the Rhodes scholars who have earned the gratitude of their countries, is at the entrance of Rhodes House. In the center of the floor lies a round slab of gray granite taken from a spot near the grave of Mr. Rhodes in South Africa, and executed in brass upon this stone is the symbol of the South African natives for the fire or life spirit.

In the small dome in the roof are symbols representing the dominions which compose the British Empire. Upon the walls will be carved the names of Rhodes scholars who have deserved well of their country, whether it be a dominion of the British Empire, Germany or the United States. The empire builder desired above all that those who benefited by his scholarships should devote themselves to public service.

At the entrance of the building, the names and countries of all Rhodes scholars who lost their lives in the war have been carved. From the front chamber, one enters a pillared hall in which will be placed a statue of Mr. Rhodes and busts of leading trustees under his will. Immediately adjoining is a great hall with seasoned oak beams overhead in which will be given the banquets of the Rhodes Trust.

GUIDANCE COUNSELORS AND BUREAUS IN NEW YORK STATE

THE question of finding a job for the boy or girl who has completed his or her education will be less perplexing for parents to answer because of the recent passage of a law which provides for the creation of vocational guidance officers and bureaus in the public schools of New York State.

According to the provisions of the law which has been analyzed by the industrial bureau of the State Education Department, school authorities in each district "may employ one or more qualified persons for the purpose of providing vocational and educational guidance for minors." The service as well as the qualifications of persons employed for this work are subject to the approval of the commissioner of education.

The law provides that in the large communities where a guidance staff is necessary, a bureau of vocational guidance may be established "to provide information and counsel for pupils regarding educational and occupational opportunities; to assemble and maintain cumulative records of pupils; to provide employment and follow-up service for minors; to conduct research studies of pupils and the local educational and occupational opportunities."

Part of the work of the bureaus will be to cooperate with the schools in establishing counseling services in order to advise pupils regarding their plans for education and the choice of a vocation. The bureaus will also prove an efficient aid to the schools in providing a placement service for minors who have completed their education and are ready to enter industry.

A final provision of the law calls for the appointment by the State Education Department of a supervisor of vocational and educational guidance, who is to cooperate with school authorities in the development of a program of guidance along educational and vocational lines and in studies and investigations dealing with these subjects. He is also to prepare a report on vocational training and educational opportunities in the state and make yearly revisions of this information for the purposes of accuracy.

TROUBLES AT DES MOINES

THE entire faculty, including the president, and all employees of Des Moines University, a Baptist fundamentalist institution directed by the Baptist Bible Union of North America, was dismissed on May 11 by vote of the board of trustees. The action, announced by Dr. T. T. Shields, of Toronto, president of the board and also head of the Bible Union, was taken after the board had reinstated Dr. Shields, after his recent suspension in controversy as to the administration of the school.

Dr. Shields left Des Moines under police protection, being hustled aboard an eastbound train as students swarmed about the railroad station seeking him. A few hours before, the board had ended a lengthy session during which they listened to and found to be without foundation charges of alleged indiscretions on the part of Dr. Shields and Miss Edith Rebman, secretary of the board. According to the press reports Dr. Shields and members of the board, together with Miss Rebman, had hidden in a closet during a student bombardment of the structure with eggs and stones. "It was only a miracle that we were saved," Miss Rebman is reported to have said. "The students would have torn him [Dr. Shields] limb from limb if they had found him."

Then on May 13, according to the Associated Press, the university, ordered closed "until further orders" by the board of trustees following the student riots, was reopened by issuance of an injunction restraining invocation of the order of the board.

Dr. Harry C. Wayman, dismissed president of the university, was notified of issuance of the injunction by telephone and without waiting for formal serving of the District Court's order summoned the students to return to their classes. Earlier in the day, Dr. Wayman, who, with the remainder of the faculty, had been released by the trustees, said he would carry out to the letter the order of the trustees suspending all classes and lectures in the university until further notice from the trustee board.

Among much else the following is printed in the New York *Times:*

In the summer of 1928, when the board was casting about for a president, Dr. Shields said attention was called to Dr. Wayman, of William Jewell College, Missouri, who was reported to have secured the dismissal of three professors on account of their modernist tendencies. The board believed he was a "solid man" for Des Moines.

"Some time after his appointment, but before his inauguration as president," Dr. Shields said, "an open letter written by Louis M. Hale, of Springfield, Mo., a former member of the trustee board of William Jewell, came to our attention. Hale contended Wayman resigned from William Jewell because he was using three degrees to which he was not entitled, including one from Oxford. As I had taken a strong stand against bogus degrees, I told Dr. Wayman we would have to sift the matter to the bottom."

"You will ruin me," Dr. Shields quoted Wayman as saying.

"Man need not be afraid of the truth," Dr. Shields said he replied.

"But they have the goods on me," Dr. Wayman replied, according to Dr. Shields.

After some correspondence with the William Jewell trustees and alumni, Dr. Shields said that they finally advised him to let the matter of Dr. Wayman's degrees drop, "as it would only do harm to all concerned."

Dr. J. W. Million, former president of the university, is quoted as saying:

The trouble dates back to the time when the university was taken over by the Baptist Union of North America early in 1927. It was formerly operated under the State Baptist Convention of Iowa, but got into financial straits when funds allotted to it from a national financial campaign by the Baptist Church failed to materialize fully.

Efforts to meet a budget made out in anticipation of those funds failed and the Bible Union offered to take over the institution with all its debts. That was agreed to. The acid test for the instructors was the requirement of the new board that they be unquestioned fundamentalists. They were required to sign a pledge to fundamentalism before they could teach. I think all the faculty were fundamentalists, but the members of the board were ultra-fundamentalists. Dr. Shields was so radical a fundamentalist that he kept people on the ground to keep him informed.

APPOINTMENTS AT YALE UNIVERSITY

FORTY-ONE appointments to the faculty of Yale University have been announced. The list includes four visiting professors, three associate professors, nine assistant professors, two research associates, two research assistants, eighteen instructors and three lecturers.

The visiting professors are Carl Sumner Knopf, M.A., B.D., professor of Old Testament at the University of Southern California, who becomes visiting professor of Old Testament at Yale; Harold J. Laski, professor of political science at the University of London, who has been appointed visiting professor of law; Morris Raphael Cohen, Ph.D., professor of philosophy at the College of the City of New York, who becomes visiting professor of philosophy, and Roger Sherman Foster, LL.B., assistant professor of law at Harvard University, who has been appointed visiting professor of law.

The associate professors are Dr. Hilrie Shelton Smith, associate professor of religious education in the Divinity School and director of field work; Harold Edwin Himwich, M.D., who is promoted to be associate professor of physiology, and Winthrop Morgan Phelps, M.D., who is promoted to be associate professor of orthopedics. Professor Smith has been professor of religious education in Teachers College, Columbia University, and for five years was director of the department of leadership training of the International Council of Religious Education. He received the Ph.D. degree at Yale in 1923.

Those who have been appointed assistant professors are Carl Hermann Kraeling, Columbia University, 1918, Ph.D., 1927, New Testament criticism and interpretation; William Gershom Downs, D.D.S., Vanderbilt, 1922, Ph.D., Pennsylvania, 1929, pathology; Ashley Webster Oughterson, M.D., Harvard, 1924, surgery;

Edgar VanNorman Emery, graduate of medicine, Toronto, 1911; Carl George Deuber, B.S., Missouri, 1921, Ph.D., 1925, plant physiology, (promotion); Hempstead Castle, B.A., Cornell, 1921, Ph.D., Yale, 1927, botany (promotion); Clark Hopkins, B.A., Yale, 1917, Ph.D., Wisconsin, 1927, classics (promotion), and Hugo Kortschak, violin-playing (promotion). Stuart Holmes Clement, B.A., Yale, 1917, assistant in the department of personnel study, has been promoted to be assistant director of the department.

Three lectures are included in the list of appointments, Alfred Benjamin Butts, Ph.D., in government; Philip Birkenstock Brill, in industrial management, and Behrend Mehrtens, B.D., in the history and polity of the Lutheran Church. Frank Gildea, M.D., has been appointed research assistant in the institute of human relations, and Olive Moore, B.S., in visual education.

APPOINTMENTS AND PROMOTIONS AT COLUMBIA UNIVERSITY

New appointments at Columbia University (including St. Stephen's College, Annandale, now a part of the Columbia educational system), have been made by the trustees as follows:

Francis R. Flournoy, associate professor of history; Joseph E. Harry, Hoffman professor of Greek; Vasil Obreshkove, associate professor of biology; C. Theodore Sottery, assistant professor of chemistry; Edward N. Voorhees, associate professor of English; Stanley F. Brown, assistant professor of chemistry; Carl Garabedian, associate professor of mathematics; Joseph D. Eby, assistant professor of dentistry; Bern B. Gallaudet, associate professor of anatomy; Albert R. Lamb, professor of clinical medicine; Armin K. Lobeck, professor of geology; Douglas B. Maggs, associate professor of law; Douglas M. Whitaker, assistant professor of zoology, and Oskar Wintersteiner, assistant professor of biological chemistry.

Forty-seven members of the university teaching staff received promotion, effective on July 1. Following is the list with the new ranking:

Walter P. Anderton, assistant professor of clinical medicine; Jacob J. Beaver, assistant professor of chemistry; Adolf A. Berle, Jr., associate professor of law; Adolph Berger, William Carr professor of oral surgery; David C. Bull, assistant professor of surgery; Wendell T. Bush, professor of philosophy; Cornelia L. Carey, assistant professor of botany; Lester R. Cahn, assistant professor of dentistry; Mary L. Caldwell, assistant professor of chemistry; William Crawford, associate professor of dentistry; George Draper, associate professor of clinical medicine; Herbert O. Elftman, assistant professor of zoology; Earl T. Engle, associate professor of anatomy; Harold A. Fales, professor of chemistry; Hermon W. Farwell, professor of physics; Frederick B. Flinn, associate professor of physiology in industrial hygiene; Ross Golden, associate professor of medicine; W. Cabell Greet, assistant professor of English; Louis P. Hammett, associate professor of chemistry; Franklin M. Hanger, Jr., assistant professor of medicine; Thomas H. Harrington, professor of engineering; Leland Hinsie, clinical professor of psychiatry; Houghton B. Holliday, assistant professor of dentistry and superintendent of clinics; Albert C. Jacobs, associate professor of law; Clinton W. Keyes, associate professor of Greek and Latin; Minor W. Latham, assistant professor of English; Robert B. McGraw, clinical professor of psychiatry; Richard P. McKeon, assistant professor of philosophy; Michael G. Mulinos, assistant professor of pharmacology; Gardner Murphy, assistant professor of psychology; S. Butler Murray, Jr., professor of fine arts; Robert von Nardroff, assistant professor of physics; John E. Orchard, associate professor of economic geography; Howard W. Potter, clinical professor of psychiatry; Blanche Prenez, assistant professor of French; Willard L. Severinghaus, associate professor of physics; Mary M. Shaver, assistant professor of bibliography; Martin deF. Smith, assistant professor of clinical medicine; Paul Smith, assistant professor of mathematics; Russell G. Smith, assistant professor of sociology; T. Clinton Taylor, associate professor of chemistry; William D. Tracy, professor of dentistry; Sam F. Trelease, professor of botany; Clifford L. Treleaven, assistant professor of physics; Harold W. Webb, professor of physics; Lincoln T. Work, assistant professor of chemical engineering, and J. Enrique Zanetti, professor of chemistry.

FELLOWSHIPS OF THE AMERICAN-SCANDINAVIAN FOUNDATION

Awards of nine university fellowships and one industrial fellowship for advanced study in

Sweden, Norway and Denmark have been announced by the American-Scandinavian Foundation.

Simultaneously it was announced that two new university fellowships have been donated to the foundation by William H. Todd, of the Todd Shipbuilding Corporation, and G. Hilmer Lundbeck, resident director of the Swedish-American Line, respectively. The Todd fellowship was awarded to Leonard Schneider, of the Hobbs-Greenland Expedition, for the study of weather conditions in the north preparatory to establishing weather forecasting stations.

The four fellowships providing for study in Sweden were awarded to Frederick Tilberg, assistant professor of European history at the University of North Dakota, to study history; Dale A. White, of Yale University, to study advanced architectural design; Alden Bruce Hatch, of Yale University, to study forestry, and Oren Reed, an industrial fellow, to study engineering.

Miss Dorothy Wyckoff, of Bryn Mawr College, and Joseph Auslander, of Harvard University, received fellowships for studies in Norway. Miss Wyckoff will study geology and Mr. Auslander comparative lyric poetry.

Awards for studies in Denmark went to Harold Herborg Nielsen, of the University of Michigan, physics; John Randolph Huffman, of Yale University, physical chemistry; Alexander Haggarty Krappe, medieval literature.

THE AMERICAN LIBRARY ASSOCIATION

ANNOUNCEMENT of the election of the following officers was made at the Fourth General Session, May 18, of the American Library Association at the fifty-first annual conference at Washington, D. C.

President: Andrew Keogh, librarian, Yale University Library.

First Vice-president: Everett R. Perry, librarian, Public Library, Los Angeles, California.

Second Vice-president: Jennie M. Flexner, Public Library, New York, N. Y.

Treasurer: Matthew S. Dudgeon, librarian, Public Library, Milwaukee.

Trustee of Endowment Fund: John W. O'Leary, president, Chicago Trust Company.

Members of the Executive Board: Linda A. Eastman, librarian, Public Library, Cleveland, Ohio; Judson T. Jennings, librarian, Public Library, Seattle, Washington.

The following members were elected to the council:

Robert J. Usher, librarian, Howard Memorial Library, New Orleans, Louisiana.

Charles H. Compton, assistant librarian, Public Library, St. Louis, Missouri.

Halsey W. Wilson, H. W. Wilson Co., 958 University Avenue, New York, N. Y.

Essae M. Culver, executive secretary, State Library Commission, Baton Rouge, Louisiana.

R. R. Bowker, editor, *The Library Journal*, 62 W. 45th Street, New York, N. Y.

EDUCATIONAL NOTES AND NEWS

THE sixtieth annual convention of the Department of Superintendence of the National Education Association will be held in Atlantic City, N. J., from February 23 to 27, 1930, according to an announcement made through the association's Washington headquarters by Frank Cody, superintendent of the Detroit Public Schools and president of the department. With the meeting of the Department of Superintendence there will be fourteen other departments and allied groups holding sessions in Atlantic City at the same time.

CHANCELLOR THOMAS E. BENNER has been notified that he has been discharged by action of the trustees of the University of Porto Rico. According to press reports Juan B. Huyke, commissioner of education and acting president of the trustees, said that President Antonio R. Barcelo, who is also president of the senate, told the trustees that either Benner or he must resign. The vote was said to have been four to three in favor of dismissal. Professor Benner was inaugurated as chancellor on March 13, 1925, on the twenty-second anniversary of the founding of the university. He is a native of Massachusetts, a graduate of Harvard University with advanced degrees in education, and went to Porto Rico from the Alabama Polytechnic Institute. He had been superintendent of schools in Massachusetts.

PATRICK T. CAMPBELL, who has been a member of the faculty of the Boston Public Latin School for thirty-two years, has been elected assistant superintendent of the Boston schools. He succeeds Mr. A. L. Rafter, who has reached the age of retirement.

SUPERINTENDENT J. H. BEVERIDGE, of Omaha, Nebraska, has been made an honorary member of the newly established Ohio University chapter of Phi Beta Kappa. Mr. Beveridge will be visiting professor on the staff of the college of education of the University of Cincinnati for the summer session this year.

ARTHUR I. ANDREWS, professor of history at the University of Vermont, has received the decoration of the Order of the Commander of the Crown of Rumania, in recognition of his writings on Rumanian history.

THE John Newbery medal, given annually by the Children's Librarians' Section of the American Library Association for the most distinguished children's book of the past year, was awarded this year to Professor Eric P. Kelly, of Dartmouth College, for his book "The Trumpeter of Krakow." Carrie E. Scott, chairman of the section, presented the medal at the fifty-first annual conference of the association in Washington on May 16.

THE honorary doctorate of laws was on May 8 conferred by the University of Paris on Professor Albert Einstein. This degree is said to be the first to be awarded since the war to a citizen of Germany.

THE honorary doctorate of science was conferred on Dr. Simon Flexner, director of the laboratories of the Rockefeller Institute for Medical Research, on the occasion of the dedication on May 11 of the new laboratory of anatomy and physiological chemistry of the University of Pennsylvania. Dr. Flexner, who was professor of pathology at the University of Pennsylvania from 1899 to 1903, made the principal address.

PROFESSOR ARTHUR G. CANFIELD, head of the department of Romance languages at the University of Michigan, who retires from active work at the close of the academic year, was given a dinner on April 23 by members of the faculties.

THE retirement from the faculties of Columbia University is announced of Harold Jacoby, Rutherfurd professor of astronomy; George L. Meylan, professor of physical education, and Henry L. Moore, professor of political economy.

PROFESSOR CLARENCE I. LEWIS, of Harvard University, has been appointed visiting professor of philosophy at Columbia University.

DR. CHARLES H. GORDINIER will retire from the principalship of the Millersville Normal School, Pennsylvania, in September. He will join the faculty of Beckley College at Harrisburg.

EUGENE S. FARLEY, an instructor in the University of Pennsylvania, has been appointed to the newly established position of head of the department of reference and research of the schools of Newark, New Jersey.

DR. E. J. ASHBAUGH, assistant director of the bureau of educational research of the Ohio State University, has been appointed dean of the school of education of Miami University, the appointment to become effective on September 1. He will succeed Dean H. C. Minnich. Dr. Ashbaugh was chief of the bureau of educational research and service of the University of Iowa from 1914 to 1921, and has been assistant director of the bureau at the Ohio State University for eight years.

ERNEST C. WITHAM, director of research of the schools of Wilmington, Delaware, has been appointed associate professor of education at Rutgers University.

WILLIAM CULLEN FRENCH, of New York University, has been appointed professor of elementary education in the school of education of the George Washington University. Mr. French has done graduate work at the University of Chicago and New York University and has had extensive experience in public-school work in Oklahoma.

MME. MARIE DE PIERPONT, for eleven years an instructor in French at the Rensselaer Polytechnic Institute, has been appointed head of the department of foreign languages to succeed her husband, Professor Arthur de Pierpont, who has resigned on account of ill health after serving for thirty-three years.

AMONG the new appointments for 1929–30 to the faculty of Oberlin College are the following: Carl E. Howe, assistant professor of physics, after three years of research and teaching at the University of Chicago; Dr. Paul P. Rogers, assistant professor of Spanish, who goes from an assistant professorship at the University of Missouri, having taught previously at Cornell, Acadia University and the University of Cincinnati; Glenn E. McLaughlin, acting assistant professor of economics, who is completing work for his doctorate at Harvard University; Dr. Wendell S. Niederhauser, acting assistant professor of chemistry, at present an instructor at Brown University, and Miss Anna L. Hughitt, assistant professor in the physical education department, since 1913 a member of the faculty of the department of physical education at the University of Illinois.

HENRI GUY, rector of the University of Grenoble, will be the exchange professor from France to Harvard University during the first half-year 1929–30. Professor Guy was exchange professor during the first half of 1921. At that time he was dean at the University of Toulouse.

DR. RICHARD C. CABOT, professor of clinical medicine and of social ethics at Harvard University, has been elected a vice-president of the Massachusetts Schoolmasters' Club.

HAROLD C. WASHBURN, who has been since 1926 headmaster of the Cincinnati Country Day School, Cincinnati, has been made assistant to the director-general of the Brooks-Bright Foundation, 342 Madison Avenue, New York City.

DR. AUGUSTUS O. THOMAS, Maine State Commissioner of Education and president of the World Federation of Education Associations, will sail on July 6 for Geneva, Switzerland, to preside over the deliberations of the World Federation of Education Associations, which will meet from July 25 to August 3. It is expected to have an attendance of 5,000 educators from practically every country and every province throughout the world. Dr. Thomas expects that there will be 1,000 teachers from the United States, while about 500 Canadian teachers are planning to be present.

PROFESSOR JAMES F. HOSIC, of Teachers College, Columbia University, recently spent three weeks in Mexico City for the purpose of making a survey of the American School for the American School Foundation. His report to the board of trustees bore particularly upon the revision of the curriculum and the improvement of methods of instruction.

DR. CHARLES W. COULTER, head of the department of sociology at Ohio Wesleyan University, has been appointed by the Carnegie Corporation as visiting professor to make a survey of the poor white situation in South Africa. He will sail at the end of the college semester and will remain in Africa until February, 1930.

PROFESSOR THOMAS ALEXANDER, of Teachers College, Columbia University, has sailed for Germany, where he will accompany a group of thirty students in a six weeks' school visitation. Professor Alexander will direct the studies of several students who are doing field work in Germany, and will assist in organizing at Mainz a conference on American education for German teachers. He will also be a delegate of the National Education Association to the World Federation of Education Associations meeting in Geneva.

DR. JOSEPH EDWARD RAYCROFT, professor and head of the department of hygiene at Princeton University, has accepted an invitation to conduct classes in the University of California summer session to be held in Los Angeles from July 1 to August 10.

DR. CHRISTIAN A. RUCKMICK has been appointed visiting professor of psychology in the summer session of the Ohio State University, beginning on June 19. He will give a course of lectures in advanced psychology.

DR. WALTON B. MCDANIEL, professor of Latin at the University of Pennsylvania, will be a member this year of the faculty of the University of Chicago during the summer quarter.

DR. R. P. RAUP, professor of the philosophy of education in Teachers College, Columbia University, New York City, delivered a lecture on May 8, on "The Psychological Basis of the Project Method," in the Library of the Central Hall, Westminster, London, under the auspices of the New Educational Fellowship.

PROFESSOR WILLIAM H. KILPATRICK'S "Education for a Changing Civilization" has recently been published in Japanese, having been translated by Mr. M. Nishimoto, of the Women's College at Nara, Japan. Mr. Nishimoto, who was once a student in Teachers College, previously translated Dr. Kilpatrick's "Foundations of Method" into Japanese.

PRESIDENT GEORGE F. ZOOK, of the University of Akron, has accepted an invitation to deliver the commencement address at St. Louis University on Tuesday, June 4.

DR. CHARLES H. JUDD, director of the School of Education of the University of Chicago, will deliver the commencement address on Friday evening, June 14, for the graduating classes of the Central Y. M. C. A. Schools of Chicago, in the auditorium of the Second Presbyterian Church.

A MEETING in memory of Mr. Frederick T. Gates was held at the Rockefeller Institute for Medical Research on May 15, at which the speakers were Mr. John D. Rockefeller, Jr., Dr. William H. Welch and Dr. Simon Flexner.

As a memorial to the late Alfred Dodge Cole, formerly professor of physics at the Ohio State University, it is planned to collect a fund of $50,000 to establish a library of physics as part of the university's Mendenhall Laboratory of Physics. Professor Cole's collection of scientific books has been given to the laboratory. The project is in charge of a committee of which Dr. Michael Pupin, Dr. Robert A. Millikan and Charles F. Kettering are members.

FRANK A. DOUGLAS, for thirty-two years superintendent of the Winthrop, Massachusetts, public schools, died in Cleveland, on April 25. A correspondent writes: "At the time of his retirement in 1927, Mr. Douglas was one of the oldest superintendents in the matter of continuous service in any one community in the Commonwealth of Massachusetts. He went to Winthrop in 1891 as principal of a grammar school. After serving in this capacity four years he was elected superintendent of schools and was the first full-time superintendent of schools employed in Winthrop. He saw the schools grow from small numbers to a student body of 3,300 with 120 teachers. Nearly all the school buildings now used were erected during his administration. He was widely and affectionately known by thousands of boys and girls who passed under his supervision as 'Pa Douglas.' Funeral services were held in Winthrop on April 28, and were attended by a great many of his former pupils and friends."

THE annual meeting of the American Association for Adult Education will be held at the University of North Carolina from May 20 to 23, inclusive. The program includes fifty speakers, among whom are Dean James E. Russell, president of the association; Dr. Frederick P. Keppel, president of the Carnegie Corporation of New York; Everett Martin, director of the People's Institute of New York; Arthur Cartwright, executive director of the association; Dr. William John Cooper, United States Commissioner of Education; Robert I. Rees, vice-president of the American Telephone and Telegraph Company; Dean Chester D. Snell, of the University of Wisconsin, and Dr. Harry W. Chase, president of the University of North Carolina. There will be eighteen section meetings with public sessions on Monday and Tuesday nights.

THE Sargent School of Physical Education, Cambridge, has been transferred to Boston University by Dr. Ledyard Sargent, president and owner, and will become a part of the Boston University school of education, under the direction of Dean Arthur H. Wilde.

ANNOUNCEMENT is made at the University of Virginia, that the anonymous gift of a trust fund of $6,000,000 for scholarships and fellowships made last year to the university was a bequest of the late Philip Francis du Pont, who was a student at the university from 1897 to 1900. The university will receive a much larger sum in case there are no direct heirs.

BY the will of Mrs. Sarah Wey Tomkins, late trustee of Wells College, the sum of $500,000 is bequeathed to the college.

THE University of Denver has received gifts amounting to $200,000 from Paul T. Mayo for the salary endowment fund. The fund is to be spent in eight years at the rate of $25,000 per year, and will provide substantial salary raises for all faculty members.

F. M. KIRBY, of Wilkes-Barre, Pennsylvania, has given $100,000 toward the fund of $2,000,000 which is being raised for Hobart College and William Smith College.

A FUND of $100,000, the gift of Mr. Herbert E. Miles, of Los Angeles, will be used for the promotion of research in educational problems and in the humanistic studies at Lawrence College at Appleton, Wisconsin.

HENRY J. FULLER, of New York, has donated $100,000 toward a $250,000 new building program for St. Johnsbury Academy. His father, Dr. Henry Fuller, was principal of the academy thirty years ago.

GROUND was broken for a new Men's Commons on the campus of Illinois College at Jacksonville, Illinois, on April 19. The proposed new building is a gift from Dr. and Mrs. George E. Baxter, of Chicago, and will cost about $75,000.

THE General Education Board of the Rockefeller Foundation of New York has made a conditional gift of $400,000 to Harvard University to construct a physics laboratory. The gift is offered subject to the raising by the university of an additional $600,000.

PLANS have been made for the erection of a hotel costing $500,000 for the practical training of students taking the hotel management course at Cornell University. The scheme is sponsored by the United Hotels Company of America, which controls a chain of hotels. It is said that the hotel will contain 200 rooms ideally suited for practical training for studying hotel management at the university. Financing has been completed and negotiations for a site are under way.

THE International Federation of University Women and the American Association of University Women plan to raise $1,000,000 for a scholarship and fellowship fund by 1934, to be used in reducing the inequalities of opportunity from which women scholars suffer under present conditions. The Illinois Association has pledged itself to raise $30,000, to be known as the Marion Talbot Fellowship Fund, in regard to which the secretary of the state division writes as follows: "In doing this we honor one of the founders of our organization; we place Illinois in line with the other four states of the Northeast Central Section, each of which has agreed to raise a similar amount, and we give ourselves the opportunity of blessing the world in all the creative work which holders of the fellowships shall do in years to come."

A PLEDGE of $3,500 has been received from the American Association for Adult Education for the support of research in reading-habits of adults, under the direction of Mr. Douglas Waples, professor in the graduate library school of the University of Chicago.

AT its annual meeting on May 2, the board of trustees of Lafayette College adopted a plan which provides for the retirement and the insurance of the faculty of the college. The pension plan provides that a retirement fund be established for the teachers of the college which will permit them to retire at the age of seventy. Full professors will receive $2,500 a year, and associate professors $2,000 a year. Although the recipients will be relieved of all teaching work these pensions will be known as service salaries, so that the retired professors can engage in some congenial work for the college in other capacities. According to the insurance plan which was also adopted, members of the faculty will pay $7.50 per thousand dollars of insurance and the college will pay the difference between that and the rate charged by the insurance company. Full professors and associate professors will take out $7,000 of insurance; assistant professors $5,000; instructors $3,000, and members of the clerical staff $1,000.

MRS. ELISE STERN has made the first gift of $40,000 to provide playgrounds for children in Paris, a project which has been approved by the municipality which has set aside sites. It is expected that Mrs. Stern's contribution will be the foundation of a fund to which all the citizens of Paris will be encouraged to subscribe.

THE number of veterinary students in Germany has increased largely this year. The number of students in forestry, commercial and agricultural colleges ranking as universities, dropped sharply. The number of foreign students decreased to 6,500, and about half of these come from lost German territory and from Switzerland and Austria. The number of women students increases constantly and now has reached 10.4 per cent. of the total enrolment in the highest institutions of learning. The ratio of students has jumped from 136 to 155 for every 100,000 inhabitants. Luebeck heads the list with 193.5 students for every 100,000 inhabitants, while Bremen stands at the bottom with 86.9. All the universities, without a single exception, report a large increase in enrolment. Berlin for the first time has more than 10,000 academic citizens, as students in Germany are known, the exact number being 10,907.

THERE has recently been completed in Berlin a municipal open-air river bathing establishment on the Spree, at the eastern suburb of Lichtenberg, which contains a large swimming bath equipped with every requirement for water sports, a special swimming pool for school children, a paddling pool for small children and a stretch of sandy beach. A novel feature of this establishment is that, although in the open air, the water is warm, being drawn from neighboring electricity works. The cost of admission for adults is 25 pfennigs and for children 10 pfennigs. The use of the swimming pool by school children in parties under supervision is free.

DISCUSSION

A PROBLEM FOR COOPERATIVE RESEARCH—THE HIGH-SCHOOL DROP-OUTS

IN meetings of national organizations such as the North Central Association, the National Education Association, the Department of Superintendence and even the National Educational Research Association, one hears many proposals for cooperative research, but relatively few of these ever get beyond the proposal stage. Probably fewer proposals are offered and still less of cooperative research is accomplished in local or sectional groups unless it is within single school systems. In other words, very little cooperative research is actually carried to completion. One can not assume that this situation is chargeable to a lack of interest in research activities, for apparently there are other and more relevant explanations.

Three reasons seem to be especially significant in explaining the restricted amount of cooperative research. First, it may be expected that a considerable portion of those who are engaged in or who might be engaged in educational research projects prefer to work on their own special problems; in other words, variety of interests may be a more dominant factor with them than is unity of interests. Second, there is doubtless a disposition on the part of many individuals to assume that research activities presuppose or demand a high degree of technical knowledge, statistical training and experience in research technique, so that as a consequence many who would gladly participate hesitate to do so due to feelings of modesty with reference to their preparation for the work.

A third factor which may in the long run be more determinative than the two which have been mentioned is the necessity for a unifying and directive agency to give continuity and unity to the work of the various participants in a common cooperative venture. Probably it is a recognition of these restrictions and difficulties pertaining to cooperative research that accounts for my being invited to prepare this brief outline of a proposed cooperative investigation. It is appropriate at this time to state that the practicability of cooperative research in this state has been clearly demonstrated by the various cooperative studies which have already been completed under my direction. One of the most recent of these, which extended over a six-year period, was reported in part in the September, 1928, issue of the *Journal of Educational Research.* Much of the credit for its completion belongs to the sixty school systems which cooperated over this six-year period.

I am proposing at this time to investigate the problem of high-school drop-outs in view of the fact that much attention has already been given to studies concerning students while they remain in high school, and little attention to the drop-out students, subsequent to their dropping out. In addition to the fact that few schools have any follow-up program of guidance, counsel or direction for these drop-out students, no other agency is directly and consistently charged with helping them to capitalize their opportunities, to escape blind-alley occupations and to secure a reasonable amount of wholesome recreation in connection with their work.

Records should be available in usable form in any high-school office to furnish much of the preliminary information needed in a study of the drop-out students. One should be able to find from these records in what year or semester of high-school work a student dropped out, what grades he had made in his school work, what was his record with reference to health, industry, economic or home conditions, and the variety of his special interests. These facts reported separately for boys and girls should cover the drop-out students over a period of several years. Likewise, complete school records will disclose the reasons given by students for leaving high school, and the type of occupation or employment, if any, to which they went directly.

Starting with these facts, which the school records should provide, one might trace each of these students from his first employment to subsequent types of employment, noting the number of jobs held, the time spent in each kind of employment, the time out of employment, the pay received in each type of work and the specific character of the work required in each position. It should be possible also to analyze the opportunities for vocational, educational or social advancement of the student in the various types of work. In this connection an analysis of the preparation which students had received in school for the type of work which they were later called upon to do and the kind of training which the school might have provided in preparation for their later employment would doubtless be of much direct value to both the school and its students. The need for certain types of continuation instruction may also be disclosed. To trace those drop-outs who have moved or who have changed their names by marriage will probably constitute one of the chief difficulties in this study.

If a high school seriously assumes the responsibility of training its students for their later occupations, that responsibility will certainly apply in a pertinent way to the drop-out students, since in most high schools they constitute a majority of all students who enter the high school and since their schooling is probably ended when they leave the high school. Relatively few high schools graduate more than 50 per cent. of the students who enter as freshmen, and the percentage in many high schools is far below 50 per cent. Any acceptable program of vocational guidance, school counseling or specific preparation for vocational occupations must involve an adequate knowledge of what happens to high-school students who go into various industrial or commercial employments, especially if the employment continues over a period of years. Again, if the statement may be repeated, this need is more serious because of the fact that no other agency than the school is at present assuming more than a partial responsibility for constructive follow-up work.

When data of the several types indicated have been collected by the schools participating in a study such as is outlined here, tabulations of the data may be made for each school, employing a uniform plan of tabulation. The data from the several schools may then be assembled by a competent agency to provide composite tabulations inclusive of the several schools. This central agency should be responsible for suggesting specific and uniform procedure to be employed in collecting the various items of information concerning each high-school drop-out and for suggesting a uniform mode of tabulating these items. The procedure outlined should give assurance of unity in the study and comparability of the facts collected. The composite tabulations may provide the basis for a profitable period of discussion, criticism and suggestion when the persons participating in the study have been assembled for such a purpose. Extensions, modifications or divisions of the study may follow the discussion, and the final report should then be a contribution in which the various participants may feel the pride of cooperative achievement.

F. P. OBRIEN,
Director
SCHOOL SERVICE AND RESEARCH BUREAU,
UNIVERSITY OF KANSAS

THE STATUS OF VALEDICTORIANS AND SALUTATORIANS IN AMERICAN COLLEGES

ON March 25, 1929, a brief questionnaire was sent to the deans of one hundred American colleges, asking for information concerning the status and method of selection of valedictorians and salutatorians of senior classes. The colleges addressed are representative institutions from all parts of the United States.

Replies were received from eighty-seven colleges. It is quite evident from these replies that the traditional practice of choosing a valedictorian and a salutatorian to represent the senior class in commencement exercises has been abandoned by most of the colleges. Of the eighty-six colleges replying, twenty-three report that it is their practice to select a valedictorian, and fifteen of these select both a valedictorian and salutatorian. Ten of the colleges have the valedictorian and salutatorian speak at the commencement program, and five have them speak at the senior class day exercises. In sixteen of the colleges the valedictorian and salutatorian are selected on the basis of scholastic standing only; in three, they are selected on the basis of scholastic standing and character, while two colleges report that scholastic standing, participation in extra-curricular activities, character and intelligence quotient are considered in their selection.

While the questionnaire did not ask for information concerning the recognition of high scholarship, several replies included this information. Colleges have substituted for this old practice the plan of giving recognition to high achievement by using the terms *summa cum laude, magna cum laude* and *cum laude*.

R. D. Wellons

Tusculum College

SPECIAL CORRESPONDENCE

FOREIGN VACATION STUDY

An item of particular interest to students and faculty members of our American colleges and universities who find themselves faced with the long vacation period between the end of one academic year and the beginning of the next is the almost unprecedented reception and development of the summer school idea in foreign lands. The stimulus provided during the World War for the utilization of our educational plants during the summer vacation period has extended abroad, and we find in practically every country facilities provided for the pursuit of summer courses, many of them organized on the American plan.

The summer sessions in French universities, so well known during past years, will again be held during July and August, and in some instances will be continued through September. As an introduction to their study in France the junior-year-abroad groups of the University of Delaware and Smith College go to Nancy and Grenoble, respectively, both smaller university cities, for an intensive preliminary training in speaking and following courses in French before proceeding to Paris for the opening of the university in November. Both these provincial universities are centers for American summer groups. The Universities of Besançon, Clermont, Dijon, Lille, Paris (the Sorbonne), Poitiers, Rennes, Strasbourg and Toulouse and the Alliance Française and the British Institute in Paris will also conduct summer sessions this year.

Summer schools in French universities are organized primarily for foreign students who wish to obtain a knowledge of the French language and to attend lectures in French on French history, French literature and French civilization. At the University of Strasbourg courses and lectures of the same nature will be given both in French and in German. In all university towns, hospitality committees organize various forms of recreation to provide students with profitable diversion from study and at the same time to afford them an opportunity to profit from their sojourn in France by acquiring a knowledge of French habits, customs and character. These committees endeavor to bring the students into contact with the residents of the towns, and plan excursions for the week-ends. There are no entrance requirements for these summer courses. Students may register or withdraw at any time during the session.

In Germany the Universities of Berlin, Hamburg, Heidelberg, Jena, Marburg and Munich will this year be in session during the summer months. These universities offer courses in German language, literature, history and civilization, with lectures in many other fields.

The University of Leipzig is arranging a "Leipzig University Week" to be held from June 23 to July 9. There will be lectures and discussion groups, also conducted tours and excursions for consideration of the industry and culture of Leipzig and its environs. The University of Göttingen is arranging a series of lectures on "The Eternal Problem; Theology and an Outlook on Life" from July 6 to 20.

At the University of Berlin there is a special institute, the Deutsches Institut für Ausländer, offering graded instruction in the language, coupled with courses in the cultural and intellectual life of Germany designed exclusively for foreigners. This institute gives instruction all the year round. The special summer courses for American students have been carried on with marked success for a number of years by the institute. They will be given this year from July 11 to August 21.

The Austro-American Institute of Education has arranged to conduct this year its third summer school at the University of Vienna from July 17 to August 13. There will be courses in the German language and lectures given in English on European civilization, art, music, literature, education, political economy, sociology and welfare work by distinguished professors. Special courses are conducted in education, individual psychology, teaching of art and music.

In response to requests which have been brought to their notice during the last few years the board of extra-mural studies of the University of Cambridge has decided to arrange during the summer vacation of 1929 courses of study specially suited to the needs of students from English-speaking countries overseas. This summer session will be held for four weeks, beginning on July 23 and closing on August 20. It is designed primarily for college and university graduates, teachers and persons of similar standing. There will be two principal subjects of study, "History of Great Britain and Europe in Recent Times" and "English Literature," each of which will be treated in a course of lectures given in the mornings. There will be a number of lectures upon matters of general interest, probably held in the evening and given by different persons, on subjects such as English architecture, English music and education in England. There will also be opportunities for excursions to places of interest in the neighborhood.

It is proposed to hold a summer meeting at Oxford for three weeks, beginning about July 30. The main subject of study will be "England and English Literature in the Stuart Period."

The University of Geneva will again conduct summer courses for foreigners in French language and literature from July 6 to October 19, while from July 15 to August 15 a course in botany for advanced students will be given.

The Geneva School of International Studies will be open on July 8, closing with the assembly. The school presents four groups of courses: a seminar course open to advanced students; a coordination course open to American graduate students; a contact course open to students and others interested in international relations, and special courses arranged for teachers dealing with international aspects of educational problems. During the session of the assembly there will be a daily commentary by Professor Zimmern and an evening meeting consisting of a lecture by an assembly delegate followed by discussion.

The International Bureau of Education in Geneva will offer a course from July 25 to August 4 on "How to Make the League of Nations Known and to Develop the Spirit of International Cooperation." The Universities of Lausanne and Neuchâtel will have summer courses covering French language, grammar and phonetics. Lectures will also be given on French literature, history and art.

The University of Rome and the Royal Italian University for Foreigners at Perugia, as well as the Italian universities at Florence, Milan and Venice, will offer summer courses in Italian language, history, history of art and literature. There will be a summer music school for foreigners at Capri during July and August under the direction of Maestro Ottorino Respighi, courses being offered in composition, piano, singing, violin, cello, harp and opera singing, and in the Italian language.

The University of Madrid will again offer courses in Spanish language and literature this summer. There will also be lectures on Spanish geography, art, history, music, life and customs.

The tenth annual summer school of Spanish arranged by the University of Liverpool will be held at Santander on the north coast of Spain from August 3 to 30. At Burgos, Spain, the University of Toulouse will offer a course in Spanish from August 3 to September 15 at which there will be given practical exercises and courses and lectures on modern Spain by teachers of Spanish. The University of Zarazossa will hold a summer course at Jaca in Aragón from June 1 to July 31.

Vacation courses for foreigners will be held at the University of Coimbra, Portugal, from July 20 to August 30. These will include both elementary and advanced courses in Portuguese, Spanish, French, Italian, English and German languages and literatures conducted by distinguished professors from those countries. Lectures and conferences on the history and geography of Portugal and Brazil will be given, as well as a series of social evenings, visits and excursions.

The University of Debrecen in Hungary will hold vacation courses for foreigners in July. Lectures will be given on Hungarian subjects (partly in foreign languages) and different language courses.

A summer course is given each year at the Academy of International Law at The Hague during July and August, the lectures being in French. Courses are offered in historical development of international law; principles of public and private international law; international administrative law; commercial and economic international law; penal international law, and the law of war.

There will be a vacation course in August at Copenhagen including practical exercises in the Danish language and lectures on Denmark.

The National University of Mexico will hold its summer session from July 2 to August 17 with courses in the Spanish language and lectures on Mexican history, art, literature and civilization. The University of Porto Rico will again offer courses during the summer.

The first summer school in South America will be held this year at Rio de Janeiro. It will be under the supervision of the Brazil Research Institute, and the leading scholars and scientists of Brazil will give the lectures. There will be courses on the physical geography and topography of Brazil, the political and social development of the Brazilian people, the present economic and industrial status of Brazil, the historical evolution of Brazil and tropical biology as observed in Brazil.

Those interested in securing detailed information regarding the various summer courses to be held in Europe in 1929 can procure a bulletin entitled "Holiday Courses in Europe," compiled by the League of Nations Institute of Intellectual Cooperation, by addressing the World Peace Foundation, 40 Mount Vernon Street, Boston. The Institute of International Education at 2 West 45th Street, New York, N. Y., has the programs for the various courses and accepts registration for the sessions at Cambridge, Vienna, Berlin and Rio de Janeiro.

Archie M. Palmer,
Assistant Director
Institute of International Education

QUOTATIONS

EDUCATIONAL BROADCASTING IN ENGLAND

Already we have heard much concerning the powerful influence which broadcasting must have upon what we now accept as civilization. Its effect in helping to break down national and geographical barriers, and its consequent destruction of the suspicions, hatreds, meannesses and intolerances which ignorance breeds among peoples living within narrow circles, can not yet be fully estimated. That effect is a result of a broad and informal educational influence. It is an effect which is inevitable just because broadcasting can not be other than an educational influence. If that be the case at present, it is clear that, when the possibilities of broadcasting as a formal and deliberately organized means of education are considered, there can be no doubt that an instrument of incalculable value will be shaped for the service of mankind.

The British Broadcasting Corporation is to be congratulated upon the steps it has taken towards linking its activities with the educational system of Great Britain. From its early days it has striven untiringly towards that end.

The history of those steps may be briefly described. It began with a committee of inquiry into broadcasting and adult education under Sir Henry Hadow. Then followed an interim committee to deal with that specific problem. Finally, a central council for broadcasting adult education was set up under Lord Justice Sankey. That council is composed of representatives of the most important national interests, and it is now completing admirable organization which will use wireless in the great service of adult education. Meanwhile, the famous Kent experiment in the use of wireless to broadcast to schools having been successfully completed, the B. B. C. has just set up a central council for school broadcasting under the chairmanship of the Right Honorable H. A. L. Fisher, which is composed of similar national interests to the council we have described above. This council is proceeding to deal with the specific problem of broadcasting to schools.

The building of such excellent machinery can not, of course, be productive of anything but good. If, then, at the very moment when we whole-heartedly welcome it, we also make one or two suggestions for its use, we feel sure that we shall be acquitted of any desire to make querulous and carping criticism at too early a stage. The B. B. C. is, however, a very modern part of modern life, and we would be sorry if it missed the special opportunities it has of taking care that its educational activities follow, and get the best out of, the changes which are taking place in the structure of our civilization. That does not mean that it should wholly ignore tradition or indulge in a crude stamping upon our special—almost sanctified—academic traditions. It means the frank recognition of new values which the changes we have mentioned are presenting us.

For our present purposes we have in mind the work of adult education rather than the work of our primary and secondary schools; and we direct attention to what we have called new values because, in a paper on the relation of broadcasting to further education, read recently to the Association of Technical Institutions, we see a tendency to make the old distinction between what is called cultural and what is called vocational education. "I have often wished," said Mr. Siepmann, the author of the paper, "that it were possible to introduce into the technical colleges more subjects representative of the cultural *as opposed* to vocational interests" (our italics). Later he suggested that by "correlating cultural and vocational aims, and by the establishment of a broader basis of instruction, and an attempt to give to the life and work of your institutes a social as well as academic significance," a recruitment of disinterested students would take place. Finally, he is "inclined to think that the technical subject [for the purpose of a broadcast talk] is less appropriate than the cultural," and suggested that, while the B. B. C. will go carefully and sympathetically into the matter, there is no "immediate possibility of the extensive adaptation of our programs to your needs."

If Mr. Siepmann thinks that those needs include broadcast talks on engineering or chemistry or building, we are sure he does not yet understand the tone and spirit of the modern technical institution. If he thinks that the curriculum of the same institution does not include subjects which he himself would regard as "cultural as opposed to vocational," he is very much mistaken. His errors are, however, common ones and arise out of the words "technical education." Much misunderstanding might be removed if Lord Eustace Percy's phrase "education for industry and commerce" were used. It is a term which may be neither entirely satisfactory nor descriptive, but it would help to do away with much of the false distinction between cultural and vocational education—the new phrase under which the ancient and arid controversies over, and distinctions between, science and art, tend to be revived.

If education is to help in the solution of our problems, we must realize that to treat academic matters apart from social and industrial matters is to fail in all of them. What are usually known as academic or cultural subjects are only a part of education. In themselves they can not support life as we know it. The spiritual values on which we set so great a store are dependent on what are, at first sight, merely material things. But the two can not be separated. Education for industry and commerce can be, and is, used to make men and women realize social relationships. Through the grouped course methods of technical institutions, students are shown how one subject is akin to others, how it has value not merely in its own utilitarian content, but also in kinship with others which are at first apparently independent and unconnected.

The process is producing a culture which is wider and nobler than our older notions, a culture which is neither lonely nor snobbish, a culture which does not stop short at pleasant abstractions, but is forging a link between the many sides of our world and humanizing industry no less than making it efficient. Those who know technical institutions know that they are places where is taught not only the art of earning a living, but also the sacred art of living itself.

We hope, then, that the B. B. C.'s new educational machinery will not hold too fast to all the parts of academic tradition; that it will realize the vital need for education to march with our changing conditions; that it will be thorough in its examination of phrases like "cultural and vocational and technical subjects"; and that it will regard the changes to which we have referred not as tending to a blind and formless industrialism, but as the outward forms of the newer values which science has made available for us.—*Nature.*

SOCIETIES AND MEETINGS

THE THIRD WESTFIELD CONFERENCE FOR YOUNG TEACHERS

THE Massachusetts State Normal School at Westfield held its third annual conference for young teachers on April 10, 11 and 12, 1929. The general plan of the first two annual conferences was followed. The members of the graduating class were sent out to the schools of the graduates of the class of 1928, where they spent Monday and Tuesday, April 8 and 9, in observing the work of the schoolrooms to which they had been assigned. For the remainder of the week they acted as substitutes while the young teachers returned to Westfield for a three-day conference on the problems which had arisen during their first year of teaching. There were in all ninety-four young teachers in attendance—seventy-two graduates of the class of 1928 who were in teaching positions, seven graduates of the school who were unplaced, five graduates of previous classes who had been unable to attend previous conferences and ten graduates of other normal schools and colleges.

This year an individual schedule was made up for each young teacher, and the group discussions were limited in size to fifteen persons. Most of the groups had no more than ten young teachers taking part in the discussions. Each teacher had been asked to send to the school information concerning the problems which had impelled her to register for the conference groups, and this information was assembled for each group and was given in advance of the conference to those who had been invited to act as group leaders. More than five hundred problems were thus brought up and dealt with in the group discussions. The titles of the conference groups and the number of sections of each group were as follows:

Conference group	Number of sections
Reading, general	2
Reading, beginning	3
Art, general	3
Penmanship	2
Physical education, classroom	2
Physical education, playground	1
Health education	2
Social studies, general	1
Geography	1
History	1
Language	1
Nature study and general science	3
Literature	1
Spelling	1
Rural school seat work	4
Rural school program	1
Retarded children, lack of English	2
Retarded children, mentally deficient	2
Retarded children, repeaters	1
Discipline, special cases	2
Discipline, general	2
Clubs	1
Projects	2
Testing	1
Blackboard drawing	6

For each young teacher in attendance the fourteen-hour program of the conference was distributed as follows: six hours devoted to discussions on the specific problems listed above; two hours devoted to observation of demonstration teaching by the master teachers of the training school; two hours devoted to discussion of the problems brought out by the demonstration lessons taught by the master teachers of the training school; two hours devoted to general demonstrations of blackboard drawing; one hour of general practice of blackboard drawing, and one hour of general assembly at the conclusion of the conference.

The feature demonstration of the conference was blackboard drawing, conducted by Mr. DeMerritte A. Hiscoe, teacher, and the Misses Kilgore and Durant, students, of the State Normal School at Lowell.

The leaders in the 1929 conference were as follows: Dr. Charles Russell, director; the entire faculty of the normal school and normal training school; Viola E. Bettinger, teacher in the Mundale rural school of Westfield; Rosa M. Bowker, principal of the William Street school of Springfield; Helen T. Brophy, teacher in the public schools of Amherst; DeMerritte A. Hiscoe, teacher, and the Misses Kilgore and Durant, students, of the State Normal School at Lowell; Mrs. Mabel W. Hull, principal of the Court Street school of Westfield; Elizabeth M. Jenkins, director of rural education and correspondence courses of the State Normal School at North Adams; Mary T. Leary, supervisor in the elementary schools of Chicopee; Ellen E. Morrissey, teacher in the public schools of Springfield; Alma Porter, assistant director of physical education in Massachusetts; Mary O. Pottenger, supervisor of elementary schools in Springfield, and Jennie T. Scolley, assistant superintendent of schools in Holyoke.

Charles Russell
Massachusetts State Normal School,
Westfield

EDUCATIONAL RESEARCH AND STATISTICS

TENURE IN PRESENT POSITIONS AND TRAINING OF CITY SCHOOL SUPERINTENDENTS

The median tenure of superintendents of city schools in their present positions is seven years. Is there any relationship between size of city and tenure in office of the superintendent of schools? The occasional dismissal of a superintendent of schools on political or other grounds causes this question to arise frequently.

Until recently data relative to this point were not available. The list of members in the 1929 yearbook of the Department of Superintendence of the National Education Association includes 1,679 city superintendents of schools. Each member of the department was asked to list his college degrees and to state the year when he entered upon his present position. The great majority complied with this request, and this information relative to each member is included in the 1929 yearbook.

These data relative to tenure in present positions are summarized in Table I. This table shows that the median length of time that 1,371 city superintendents of schools have been in their present positions is seven years, or since 1922. For cities above 5,000 in population, the median tenure of superintendents of schools in present positions is eight years, or since 1921. According to Table I, 1921 is the median year of entrance on present positions for superintendents of schools in cities of four population groups above 5,000. In cities less than 5,000 in population, the superintendent of schools holds his position a much shorter time. For 320 superintendents of schools in cities with a population of 2,500 to 5,000, the median length of service in present position is six years, or since 1923. For 209 superintendents of schools in villages of less than 2,500 population, the median length of service in present position is five years, or since 1924.

One city school superintendent has held his present position for fifty years. Of the 1,371 city superintendents of schools listed as members of the Department of Superintendence and for whom year of entrance on present position

TABLE I

YEAR WHEN 1,679 CITY SCHOOL SUPERINTENDENTS ENTERED ON THEIR PRESENT POSITIONS

Year of entrance on present position	Population of city in which superintendent is located						Total
	Over 100,000	30,000–100,000	10,000–30,000	5,000–10,000	2,500–5,000	Under 2,500	
1879	—	1	—	—	—	—	1
1882	—	1	—	—	—	—	1
1885	—	—	1	—	—	—	1
1891	—	—	2	—	—	—	2
1892	—	—	—	1	—	—	1
1893	—	1	1	—	—	—	2
1894	—	—	—	1	—	—	1
1895	—	2	2	—	—	—	4
1896	—	1	2	—	1	—	4
1897	—	—	1	2	—	—	3
1899	1	—	—	1	1	—	3
1900	—	1	3	1	—	—	5
1902	1	1	1	1	—	—	4
1903	—	—	2	1	4	—	7
1904	—	1	1	1	2	—	5
1905	—	—	4	4	—	2	10
1906	1	3	2	4	3	1	14
1907	—	—	9	4	—	—	13
1908	1	2	2	5	4	—	14
1909	—	1	6	1	4	2	14
1910	—	2	5	5	4	—	16
1911	1	3	4	4	3	—	15
1912	2	5	6	6	5	—	24
1913	2	2	13	4	1	1	23
1914	2	6	8	5	3	2	26
1915	1	1	5	3	5	—	15
1916	1	4	9	5	4	4	27
1917	1	5	9	15	7	4	41
1918	3	6	12	14	12	3	50
1919	3	7	9	22	16	6	63
1920	3	7	22	26	22	16	96
1921	7	10	21	23	20	9	90
1922	5	12	27	20	21	19	104
1923	6	10	28	24	38	20	126
1924	2	8	23	31	27	32	123
1925	5	8	21	34	36	29	133
1926	1	14	24	26	31	29	125
1927	3	5	19	23	34	23	107
1928	4	6	8	21	10	7	56
1929	—	—	—	—	2	—	2
Not Given	10	33	67	66	62	70	308
Total	66	169	379	404	382	279	1679
Median*	1921	1921	1921	1921	1923	1924	1922

* Median year of entrance on present position of those superintendents for whom data were given in the 1929 yearbook of the Department of Superintendence.

Read table thus: Of 66 superintendents of schools in cities of over 100,000 population, none entered upon their present positions in 1879; one of this group entered on his present position in 1899. The median year of entrance was 1921. Similarly, read data for superintendents of schools in other sized cities.

is given in the 1929 yearbook, Edward C. Glass holds the record of longest service in his present position. He has been superintendent of schools of Lynchburg, Va., since 1879.

The names of the five members of the Department of Superintendence oldest in point of service in their present positions in cities of six population groups are given in Table II. This table shows that among the superintendents of schools who have been longest in their present positions are: Lawton Bryan Evans, who has been superintendent of schools in Augusta,

Ga., for forty-seven years, or since 1882; Louis J. Rundlett, who has been superintendent of schools in Concord, N. H., for forty-four years, or since 1885; W. H. Kirk, superintendent of schools in East Cleveland, Ohio, for thirty-eight years, or since 1891; Samuel D. Largent, superintendent of schools of Great Falls, Mont., for thirty-eight years, or since 1891, and Frank L. Miller, superintendent of schools of Harvey, Ill., for thirty-seven years, or since 1892.

These long periods of service appear all the more remarkable when one considers that Nathan Bishop, the first full-time professional superintendent of city schools in America, did not begin his service in Providence, R. I., until 1839. Previous to that time others had borne the title of superintendent of schools, but, according to the U. S. Bureau of Education,[1] they were laymen who gave only part of their time to the work, after the manner of the acting school visitors of New England.

Of fifty-eight superintendents of schools in cities over 100,000 in population, twenty-three, or 40 per cent., have doctors' degrees. Table III lists the academic degrees held by 1,679 city school superintendents who are members of the Department of Superintendence. This table shows that in cities of over 30,000 population,

[1] See: *School Life*, Vol. XII, No. 4, December, 1926, p. 70.

TABLE II.

THE FIVE CITY SUPERINTENDENTS OF SCHOOLS WHO HAVE HELD PRESENT POSITIONS LONGEST IN CITIES OF SIX POPULATION GROUPS

Name	Year of entrance on present position	Superintendent of schools of		Population of city (1920 Census)
		City	State	
Frank H. Beede	1899	New Haven	Conn.	162,537
M. E. Pearson	1902	Kansas City	Kan.	108,851
John R. Wilson	1906	Paterson	N. J.	135,875
Allen P. Keith	1908	New Bedford	Mass.	121,217
Herbert S. Weet	1911	Rochester	N. Y.	295,750
Edward C. Glass	1879	Lynchburg	Va.	30,070
Lawton Bryan Evans	1882	Augusta	Ga.	52,548
Charles B. Boyer	1893	Atlantic City	N. J.	50,707
William G. Coburn	1895	Battle Creek	Mich.	36,164
S. E. Shull	1895	Perth Amboy	N. J.	41,707
Louis J. Rundlett	1885	Concord	N. H.	22,167
W. H. Kirk	1891	East Cleveland	Ohio	27,292
Samuel D. Largent	1891	Great Falls	Mont.	24,121
Fred A. Verplanck	1893	South Manchester	Conn.	18,370*
Frank Evans	1895	Spartanburg	S. C.	22,638
C. W. Shumway	1895	Vancouver	Wash.	12,637
Frank L. Miller	1892	Harvey	Ill.	9,216
W. H. Keister	1894	Harrisonburg	Va.	5,875
W. M. Peirce	1897	Ridgway	Pa.	6,037
W. Scott Ward	1897	Athol	Mass.	9,792
Ernest P. Clarke	1899	St. Joseph	Mich.	7,251
J. R. Houston	1896	Aurora	Ind.	4,299
George W. Hanna	1899	Valley City	N. D.	4,686
E. N. Cassaday	1903	Brookfield	Ill.	3,589
Arthur B. Rowell	1903	Glencoe	Ill.	3,381
James M. Stevens	1903	Ocean City	N. J.	2,512
J. W. Wyandt	1903	Bryan	Ohio	4,252
C. F. Martin	1905	Owingsville	Ky.	Under 2,500
John L. Chapman	1905	Central Village	Conn.	
W. W. Lackey	1906	Midland	Texas	
Olney J. Silverwood	1909	Ellsworth	Kan.	
William E. Wenner	1909	Ashtabula Harbor	Ohio	

* Population of Manchester, Conn.

TABLE III

Academic Degrees Held by 1,679 City School Superintendents

Academic degree	Population of city in which superintendent of schools is located						Total
	Over 100,000	30,000–100,000	10,000–30,000	5,000–10,000	2,500–5,000	Below 2,500	
Ph.D.	4	7	5	5	2	2	25
Pd.D. or Ed.D.	8	10	4	3	....	....	25
LL.D.	10	7	3	....	1	....	21
Litt.D.	1	1	2	....	....	....	4
J.D.	....	....	....	1	1	....	2
Total with doctors' degrees	23	25	14	9	4	2	77
M.A.	20	69	146	156	119	83	593
M.S.	....	....	3	3	6	4	16
Pd.M. or Ed.M.	....	4	6	9	4	6	29
M.L.	....	1	....	....	....	....	1
Ph.M.	....	3	6	6	1	1	17
Total with masters' degrees	20	77	161	174	130	94	656
B.A.	5	21	80	84	116	67	373
B.S.	5	6	27	37	34	34	143
Ed.B. or Pd.B.	....	3	....	2	4	1	10
Ph.B.	3	3	14	16	18	5	59
Litt.B. or B.L.	....	1	4	1	1	1	8
LL.B.	1	....	1	4	....	1	7
B.D.	....	....	....	1	....	....	1
Total with bachelors' degrees	14	34	126	145	173	109	601
Diploma	1	1	5	4	8	6	25
Not given	8	32	73	72	67	68	320
Grand total	66	169	379	404	382	279	1679
Per cent. with doctors' degrees	40	18	5	3	1	1	6
Per cent. with masters' degrees	34	56	53	52	41	44	48
Per cent. with bachelors' degrees	24	25	41	44	55	52	44
Per cent. with diplomas	2	1	1	1	3	3	2

Read table thus: Out of 66 superintendents of schools in cities over 100,000 in population the academic degrees held by 8 were not given in the 1929 yearbook of the Department of Superintendence. Of the remaining 58, 23, or 40 per cent., have doctors' degrees (4 have Ph.D. degrees; 8, Pd.D. or Ed.D. degrees; 10, LL.D. degrees, and one has a Litt.D. degree); 20, or 34 per cent., have masters' degrees; 14, or 24 per cent., have bachelors' degrees, and one, or 2 per cent., holds a normal-school diploma.

superintendents of schools have much higher academic degrees than do those in the smaller cities.

Seventeen superintendents of schools in cities over 30,000 in population have been honored with LL.D. degrees; and twenty-nine have earned the Ph.D. or Ed.D. or Pd.D. degree.

Of 1,359 superintendents of schools in cities ranging in population from less than 2,500 to over 100,000, only twenty-five, or 2 per cent., hold a normal-school diploma; the rest are all college graduates, and 733, or 54 per cent., hold either a master's or doctor's degree.

Margaret M. Alltucker

Research Division,
National Education Association

SCHOOL AND SOCIETY

EDITED BY J. McKEEN CATTELL

WITH WHICH IS COMBINED THE

EDUCATIONAL REVIEW

EDITED BY WILLIAM McANDREW

Volume XXIX | Saturday, May 25, 1929 | Number 752

INSTITUTIONAL RESOURCES AVAILABLE FOR COLLEGIATE EDUCATIONAL RESEARCH[1]

By Professor M. E. HAGGERTY

DEAN OF THE COLLEGE OF EDUCATION, UNIVERSITY OF MINNESOTA

The purpose of this discussion is to sketch briefly the institutional resources available for research in college education. In approaching the subject it seems desirable to clarify a matter about which much confusion prevails concerning research in general—a confusion that has made for laxity of thought and fantastic practice in the whole field of so-called educational research. Reference is to the widely held distinction between practical research and other research, the useful results of which are remote and unforeseeable. Among persons engaged in the promotion of social institutions the view prevails that practical men should be interested only in the first type. All investigations must be conceived in a manner to produce results that will immediately modify practice. In quarters where this notion is strongly held there is short shrift for the man who would take a long view of research activities, who is willing to work for years without assurance that his findings will materially change conditions, and even with the hazard that they may never do more than add to knowledge. The epithet that is usually hurled at such a student is that he is theoretical, and those who prefer this charge usually do it with that air of superiority which damns the so-called theorist as one who may be neglected with impunity, or even thwarted in his efforts at investigation.

In a comprehensive view of human progress as well as in a synthesis of the motives that actuate men to engage in research, this apparent distinction between practical and theoretical is largely illusory. The history of science is replete with illustration that what is dubbed theoretical at one time proves later to have the most practical bearings upon human affairs, and the story of man's upward striving toward civilization carries no clearer lesson than is contained in the repeatedly demonstrated value of theoretical science. Conversely, the effort to modify practice frequently leads to the unraveling of highly theoretical considerations.

A brief analysis of the basic interests upon which substantial research endeavors are founded will explicate this point a bit. The practice of research, which has as-

[1] Paper read at the Cleveland meeting of the National Society of College Teachers of Education in discussion of the 1929 year-book on "Current Educational Readjustments in Higher Institutions," on February 26, 1929.

sumed so large a place in current intellectual life, finds its actuating motive in either of two impulses, both of which played a large rôle in human endeavor long before the present century, the century which has seen these native impulses of men institutionalized into organized agencies in modern civilization. These two impulses may be loosely described as *the desire to know the truth,* and *the impulse to do good.* Evidences of the working of these two forces lay a trail across the whole endeavor of mankind to evolve the structure of society and the world of knowledge. More often than not they are both present in any research activity of major importance, although frequently individual workers are possessed of one largely to the exclusion of the other. This individual, and often temporary, detachment makes easy the false distinction which we have noted and allows the partial and often harmful emphasis upon one or the other aspect of a process that is essentially integral in character. Let a man commit his energies to the search for truth, and his passion may drive him to indifference to the immediate welfare of individuals, or the situation from which his modicum of new truth is to be derived. Thus, in the biologist's effort to derive new knowledge about life, even when he is attempting to discover the means of its perpetuation, the worker may risk or even destroy the very life which he seeks to understand. Knowledge of life appears, at the time, more important than life itself.

The individual whose impelling aim is to discover truth, and who, thus, detachedly seeks to illuminate with understanding some small point of the vast universe, is sometimes mistakenly called a *pure* scientist. The error in such description inheres in the fact that the singleness of purpose and the detachment from relationships which the phrase "pure science" implies is almost never an accurate description of the experimenter's mental processes, and its use leads to many pseudo-scientific assumptions and practices. It is only justified because it is possible, at times, for a man to abstract his intellectual processes from many relationships which are their usual accompaniments. Under such conditions his ideas assume an unwonted simplicity and clarity that, by contrast with their ordinary occurrence, makes them seem pure and refined.

Though the term is always relative, endeavors in the field of so-called pure science are characterized by a neglect of the immediate consequences of new ideas in terms of human welfare. Changes in human institutions or modes of living may be recognized as a remote and necessary outcome of new truth, but such use of ideas is relegated to a later activity or, indeed, to other persons. For the time, and even for the individual, the truth is its own justification for pursuit and is sought in a wholesome indifference to the impulse to do good.

Quite at the opposite pole of endeavor is the individual whose effort is directed, as he thinks, to making improvements in himself, in the conditions of his living or in the wider sphere of institutions affecting other lives. Without effort to expand or verify his knowledge, or to add to it through research, he works industriously to realize conditions the value of which he already accepts. *To do good to people* affords for him a wholly absorbing drive to action. It is out of this impulse that the school itself has arisen, and its development on this continent is an eloquent testimony to the strength that lies in this spring to action. Here we have a body of workers, millions of them, equipped with whatever skills have been derived from racial experience and imbued with an extra-personal outlook upon life, giving themselves to the business of education. They desire to do their work in better ways, but, for the most part, effort at educational improvement has merely sought to systematize experience, regularize tradition and, through logical analysis, to forward its techniques.

The worthiness of our efforts at human betterment can not be denied, but the miscarriage of many of them because of the lack of knowledge is a common experience in many fields. Evidence multiplies in abundance that the intent to do good is frequently made in ill-advised ways to fruitless ends, and is dogged with miscarriages and abortions that squander material resources, defeat the ends of social adjustment and limit the desirable fruition of human personality on a scale that is not merely wasteful, but even fraught with disastrous issue. The history of medical practice trails after it tragic illustrations of this fact, but medicine by no means stands unique in this respect. Politics and religion, as well as education, have equally vulnerable records. One need only remind oneself of the oft-told sentimental tale of the "three R's," the alphabetic method of teaching reading, or the failure of the modern school in character education, to understand the point as applied to education. No clearer inference may be garnered from fifteen years of school surveying than that teachers and school administrators are the victims of a pervasive illusion concerning the detailed outcomes of school practices, and it is increasingly clear that the college can claim no immunity in this respect.

So flagrant are the evidences of misdirected effort in many matters of vital moment that modern society has seen fit to develop in certain fields a social machinery for the examination of accepted knowledge and for its extension. It has, if not created, at least institutionalized the desire to know the truth, in behalf of an ultimate purpose of doing good. Witness the foundations for medical research and the gradual but wide-spread development of research activities in colleges and universities, and even in the government service.

Within a quarter of a century the ideal of scholarly research has so affected both our lives and our thinking that the term research has become the symbol of something very much to be desired. Many organizations have adopted it almost as a slogan, with little or no comprehension of its import. In cases where the term is something more than a merely laudatory phrase, it implies an effort to discover new facts that may be used to aid or redirect human activities. The dominating purpose remains the desire to do good, but new knowledge is sought as the handmaiden of conduct and not, in any sense, for its own sake. The halo of service enshrouds both the processes and the results of its quest.

With the praiseworthy motive of men to make research a means of more effective action, one can but have the greatest sympathy, but certain evils are inherent in this gospel of practicality which are very great and which account for much of the aridity and crassness of current research activities in the whole field of education. The miscalled "practical man" has little understanding of and less patience with the very small minority of persons who raise perplexing questions about the validity of his practices. So absorbed is he with *doing good* that deliberate *inquiry about truth* seems either irrelevant to his tasks or so remote in its contingency upon his business in life that he feels free to ignore endeavors in research, if he does not also hold them in scorn and make them seem ridiculous in discussion.

There is, for example, a wide-spread insistence that the schools should be available only for investigations that promise immediately useful changes in school practice as contrasted with studies whose contingency is more remote. The writer has been told on numerous occasions that he might use the schools for an investigation if the administration could be promised some results that would be useful to the schools. He has, also, seen school superintendents and principals refuse to modify the day's routine in behalf of an important experiment because no forehand guarantee could be given that the children to be studied would profit by it, thus assuming an adequacy and perfection in prevailing practice which any thoughtful student of education may well doubt. This attitude, arising from the desire, so aggressively cherished by this generation, for doing good to people, and, particularly, to children and youth, in effect stunts growth in that knowledge upon which genuine improvement depends, and frustrates its own purpose, masking in ignorance a faith in works that is essentially illusory. It accounts for the fact that many of the bureaus of research established in the schools have done so little to further a knowledge of educational matters. All too often they have been merely convenient administrative agencies for the handling of school bookkeeping.

Education might well learn a lesson in this respect from certain other areas of human interest. It could profitably go to school both to medicine and to industry where, also, the pressure for improvement of practice is extremely great. In the latter field, where the practical ideal flourishes unabashed, men have found it necessary to support theoretical studies lest industry be engulfed in ruthless ignorance, and in medicine society has taken a genuinely long view, realizing that demands for immediately usable knowledge may frustrate and make abortive the very search for improved practice which research seeks to further.

Education, and I speak now in particular of college education, needs to take the long view; it needs something more than the platitudinous reiteration of traditional concepts, something more than a description of present working plans, something more than its laudation as the sesame to individual success and achievement, and as a safeguard of democratic society. More than anything else just now it needs illumination. It needs that form of intellectualization which we have come to describe as scientific description and understanding. Many traditional concepts need to be riven asunder and explicated by the methods of experimental investigation. Educational beliefs must be subjected to verifiable facts which in some cases will eat them away as acid devours a copper plate. The necessity is upon age-old institutions to justify their continuance in a changing and in some aspects an essentially new world. Similarly, newly conceived educational projects may not ask for confidence upon the ground of their novelty, but upon the factual evidence that they represent an advance upon traditional practice. *The will to service* must be based upon effectual knowledge. In order *to do good* intelligently we must learn the truth in abundance and in great detail.

All this is but another way of saying that college education must develop a program of disinterested research. Let the fundamental aim remain its desire to render service to oncoming generations of adolescent youth, the situation should be clearly recognized that it is in desperate need of new knowledge in order to do this in the best way, and the very institution that *seeks to do good* must provide the social machinery by which its processes can be continuously corrected and readjusted in the light of knowledge. The institution which absorbs all its energy in the immediate endeavor to serve its present student body is both short-sighted and in the long run ineffective, and is in the way of denying to its future clientele the best of service it might give.

Nor must research be conceived in a manner too immediate to service, despite the feeling of administrators and of teachers that only practically useful research is justified in the school situation. Plentiful illustration in the field of physical phenomena could be given that the studies which are most practical in the long run have seemed at the time of making remote from the field of real need. Like illustration can be given in the field of education. More than a quarter of a century was spent by psychologists in the experimental analysis and measurement of individual differences before intelligence tests that are generally usable in school practice were achieved. Except for the cataclysm of the World War the time might have been even longer. In the early stages of investigation the current usefulness of such tests could have been conceived by but a few, if any, of the laboratory workers, and little assurance could the experimentalists have given to educational Babbitts that they were not wasting precious energy and resources in their efforts. Much of the early work was done in laboratories. It was necessary to emerge from the laboratory upon the schools. This was done, and many children, both in Europe and in America, were subjected to tasks that had little resemblance to ordinary school work. Despite the fact that this was done in many places and by many workers, there is not, I think, on record, an adequately described and authenticated case of a single child who was made less efficient in school or life. Certainly there is no available evidence that all this experimental work increased one whit the misdirection of guidance and control to which our educational efforts are continuously liable. Many cases can be cited of children who were helped. All this is true despite the emotional outbursts of the highly nervous "anti-determinists" and their kind. All honor is due to the psychologists, the teachers and school administrators who joined in this lengthened program of research. Millions of children in the schools to-day, and other millions yet to come, as well as school workers everywhere bear them a debt of gratitude that can only be discharged by a like devotion to as yet undiscovered truth. Those who may not share in this gratitude are they who insist that the schools may not be used for experimental purposes.

Whatever import these considerations bear is to the effect that colleges must not merely set before themselves the task of continuous investigation of their own problems, but the program of collegiate educational research should be conceived with such ample perspective that it will envisage fundamental as well as surface problems. Colleges and organizations of colleges should frankly face the fact that much of present practice is clouded and hampered by ignorance, not the grosser ignorance which is easily detected, but a delicate and often cleverly defended ignorance of matters and issues that concern forces too refined for ordinary sophistication to observe. The resolution of such ignorance requires a courageous and aggressive program of experimental investigation, and colleges are abundantly justified in reserving and diverting to such endeavors a portion of present energies, for, whatever their obligations to the present generation of students may be, they must also meet even greater demands on the part of those who are yet to come. It is the simplest wisdom to prepare for future certainties.

The type of research which any institution should undertake is to be determined by many considerations, but it may be said that the whole compass of college education is in need of examination. Roughly, the special problems may be grouped under the four heads of student personnel, curriculum, instruction and administration. Let a problem arise in any one of these fields, however, and its thoroughgoing investigation will almost inevitably lead into the others. One can not go far in a study of student personnel without raising questions about the curriculum, about the methods of teaching and about some phases of institutional administration. Similarly, if one starts to examine the plan of college administration, then the relation of administrative machinery to the character and purposes of students, the scope and content of the curriculum and the techniques of college instruction are certain to intrude themselves and affect inferences and conclusions.

To be sure, one may not in each case pursue a problem into all its contingencies, but an overview of the whole field of study will always be useful in determining the significance of a particular problem, in determining the character of the investigation to be made, the means to be employed and numerous other matters about which practical decisions must be made. A useful purpose may then be served by a descriptive overview of the field of college investigation with illustrative examples in particular fields. Such an overview has been given in the second chapter of the year-book and may be assumed in this discussion.

With this prospectus of the fields of investigation in mind, let us inquire as to the resources available in our college institutions for the prosecution of useful studies. What do the colleges now have as capital in beginning a program of collegiate educational research? The first item of importance to be noted is that every college has a plant in which all the basic problems to be studied exist. Even the smallest college has its student body, its curriculum, its methods of instruction, its staff, its buildings, its means of support, or the lack of it, its problems of control and direction, its alumni and its interested public. Wherever a college student treads, there arise all the basic educational problems. While certain problems are intensified and complicated in the larger institutions, it is also true that the smaller colleges fairly reek with issues about which little authenticated information is available, and college practices prevail for which there is little or no factual support. It is also true that many of these matters are more easily studied in the smaller and simpler environment. The simplification of experimental conditions is an ever-present drive in controlled investigation, and in some respects the smaller college would seem made to order for the scholarly study of college problems.

Let us note, therefore, as our basic institutional resource for the investigation of college education, the existence of the plant from which the problems of college education arise. In this respect the development of research in the college has an obvious advantage over such endeavors in the elementary and secondary school. When college professors of education have sought to examine the problems of the lower schools, they have had to go outside the college walls, to make contacts with an alien administration, or barring this, to establish, at great expense, laboratory schools on the campus. Diversely, in the study of the college problem the whole machine—the investigator and the thing to be investigated—are under one organization and within the narrow geographical limits of a single campus.

The second resource for the study of college problems is the presence in the institution of men and women trained in methods of scientific investigation. We may be dealing here with a less universally present factor than in the matter just discussed, but the probabilities are that most colleges are richer in this respect than they may at first think. Experience testifies that, once the idea of investigating college problems arises, aid will be forthcoming from unexpected sources. College presidents and deans are continuously plagued by unsolved problems, and in some cases they have been able to save the time from routine performance to search for the facts upon which wise decisions may be made and constructive educational policies developed. It is quite probable that more of them could do so if the importance of such a line of action should become clear to them. Much depends upon just this clear understanding of the importance of collegiate educational research.

Much, also, depends upon the resolute will of the administrative officer to defend his own intellectual alertness in regard to the understanding of his own problems. The spirit of the dean who said, "I'll be damned if I'll surrender to routine; I am going to study my job as well as perform it," is widely needed, and evidence increases to show that that spirit is growing. An administrative officer with this outlook will add his own mite to needed knowledge, but he will also do something of vastly greater moment. He will make his institution habitable by scholarly students of educational problems, and will generate in his faculty a sympathy with educational research. He is likely, further, to find that some members of his staff in the strictly academic fields also decline the "damnation of routine," and themselves set about the examination of their own practices with a consequently increased intellectualization of the tasks which they daily perform, possibly with an enlargement of professional knowledge.

Two reasons prevail for the encouragement of a responsive interest on the part of the academic faculty in educational research. In the first place the faculty is the responsible, and, in the end, the only effective agent in the improvement of college education. They who are only students of education can, at the best, do little but produce new facts and frequently they can do this only with the cooperation of academic teachers. The latter alone are in a position to make new facts useful in college improvement.

The second reason is even more important, namely, that many of the methods of research useful in the study of education have had their origin and their greatest development in strictly academic fields. Education has done less than some suppose in the creation of new scientific methods, but has levied extensively upon the devices and methods of other fields of investigation. This point may be emphasized by an outline of the currently used methods of educational research prepared by the writer with the assistance of his colleague, Dr. W. C. Olson. This outline is as follows:

METHODS USEFUL IN EDUCATIONAL RESEARCH

1. Documentary
   a. Historical
   b. Legal
   c. Analysis of current literature
   d. Text-book analysis
   e. Institutional records and reports
   f. State records and reports
   g. Federal records and reports
   h. Catalogs
   i. Courses of study
2. Questionnaire
   a. Fact
   b. Opinion
   c. Simple information
   d. Variable verbal response
   e. Yes or No
   f. Checking
   g. Ranking
   h. Rating
   i. Weighting
3. Rating scales
   a. Graphic (cross on the line)
   b. Order of merit ranking
   c. Man to man comparison

d. Scale sample comparison
e. Range of values
f. Score card
g. Others ____________

4. Personal interview
a. Prepared questions
b. Unstandardized
c. Trained interviewers
d. Untrained interviewers

5. Description and analysis based on
a. Uncontrolled observation
b. Controlled observation
c. Stenographic reports
d. Verbal analyses

6. Survey
a. Population
b. Buildings
c. Finances
d. Organization and administration
e. Teaching staff
f. Pupil progress
g. Curriculum
h. Educational results
i. Others ____________

7. Case method
a. Individual history
(1) Health
(2) Social
(3) Educational
(4) Economic
b. Individual examinations
(1) Medical
(2) Psychiatric
(3) Educational
(4) Psychological
(5) Family history

8. Experimental
a. Laboratory
b. Classroom
c. One group
d. Equivalent groups
e. Rotation groups
f. Learning
g. Physiological
h. Psychophysical
i. ____________

9. Bases for equation of groups
a. Random selection
b. General intelligence
c. Status in experimental trait
d. Socio-economic status
e. Marks in ____________
f. Educational tests ____________
g. ____________
h. ____________

10. Mathematical formulas.

The manner in which these methods shoot across the intellectual interests of a college faculty is fairly clear from the mere listing of them. Our Minnesota experience has given us copious illustration of their pervasive character. At one time or another during a five-year period we have had the assistance of men and women from many teaching fields, who have enriched our understanding, not merely of the problems to be studied, but also with clear perceptions of the applicability of methods which they knew better than did we. The individual departments will be given later, but it should here be stressed that inquiring minds are not confined to any college or university department.

To be sure, some members of a college faculty are more closely in touch with methods useful in educational research than others are likely to be. Among these we may place first the psychologists. The content of currently taught psychology is largely a development of studies made during the past thirty years. It still bears the marks of the experimental method upon it, often the crudities and partiality of a rapidly changing body of knowledge, but, also, it is redolent with the spirit of investigation. Among the more than seven hundred psychologists listed in the 1928 Year Book of the American Psychological Association more than half indicate an interest in education. Two hundred and six are teaching courses in education and educational psychology, and 238 name these and related matters as their fields of research. If we couple this evidence of interest with the obvious pertinency of the methods of psychology to the study of educational matters, it would appear that here exists a resource widely distributed among colleges for an attack upon the problems of college education, although it would be excessive to claim that all psychologists are assets in this endeavor.

It would be gracious to speak with equal enthusiasm about the possible services of the sociologists, since it is obvious that many of the problems of college education are essentially social in character. Many of these estimable colleagues of ours, however, are still terribly distressed about the aims of education and spend a large portion of their energies in a verbal reanalysis of old concepts and more or less futile attempts at a resynthesis of accumulating knowledge that results in little but a plaguing addition to the articles and books we must read. The importance of clear understanding about the objectives of college education can not be denied, and any of us may at times find it helpful to attempt a redefinition of our aims with a view of improved practice or the redirection of educational research. Each of us must occasionally perform this process for the preservation of his own intellectual integrity. The occasional master mind, the kind that occurs once in a generation or so, may do it helpfully for all of us. It may be recognized, however, that real progress in the clarification of these aims results, not from verbal and dialectical processes, but from the accumulation of factual knowledge and from the inexorable contingencies of economic and spiritual forces that move forward as indifferent to the verbalists as is the flooding stream to the chirping of birds along its banks. The sociologists have no monopoly on verbalism, nor do all sociologists employ themselves in this manner, but the scientific method needs to make great inroads upon educational sociology if its widest possible usefulness is to become a reality.

There is ample ground for belief that the situation is changing. Within the field of sociology itself there is rapidly growing up a genuine interest in the scholarly investigation of social problems by the methods of science. The number of persons so interested is steadily growing, with many recruits among the more recently trained men, and the body of literature from this source is increasing in volume and quality. The usefulness of an investigator who is sensitive to the social aspects of college education and equipped with the technical training for social research is undoubted. It is a pleasure to acknowledge in this connection the cooperation which we have received on numerous educational studies at Minnesota from Professor Stuart Chapin, and, in particular, his leadership in the study of the extra-curricular activities of college students.

One would like to say in this connection that the educationists on the college faculty are an unfailing source of aid in the study of college education. Unfortunately, this seems not to be the universal situation. In fact, in some cases, sober judgment ranges them on the side of liabilities rather than elsewhere. The causes for this condition vary. Lack of ability and effective training, coupled with unwarranted presumption of competency on the part of teachers of education, as well as prejudice among academic teachers play their part. Wherever the educationists have met rigid standards of high scholarship, have proved themselves good teachers and have been wise in service and cooperation the way is opened for all the skill which they may offer in the study and control of the college problem. In many places they have become, as they should be, the leaders in such endeavor.

Since this discussion is addressed to instructors in education, it will not be out of place to utter a useful caution. In the first place, the speaker believes that educationists can best approach the college problem by the way of research rather than by way of didactics. From the view-point of sound educational knowledge the college is a relatively new field. Most of the serious study bearing upon its problems is a product of the last decade, and is antedated by a generation of research in elementary education and to a somewhat less extent by investigation in the secondary field. The material available for instruction in college education is small, partial in character and relatively unorganized. To assume otherwise is presumption and insincerity. Because of this fact the educationist is on insecure ground in essaying that his knowledge of college matters exceeds to any great extent that of good academic teachers who have garnered from rich experience a fund of principles and useful traditions. Until college teachers of education learn to improve their own classroom performances, they may well sit in humility at the feet of master teachers in academic fields, one or more of whom almost every college numbers among its present staff. The immediate import of educational inadequacy is that teachers of education should go slowly in offering courses in college education. It is a doubtful measure of progress that more than twenty-five college departments are now attempting to do just this thing, whereas but a few have a staff trained and equipped for this purpose. Let us have intelligent investigation, as extensive and thoroughgoing as possible, but let us maintain a scholarly conscience in the realm of didactics.

One resource available in the larger institutions is the presence of graduate students—some in education, others in subject-matter fields. Increasing social pressure is certain to impinge upon our graduate schools to recognize the need of professional equipment on the part of college teachers, and the right of graduate students to professional training during the graduate years. One need only cite the recent action of the Association of American Colleges in requesting graduate schools to recognize a situation that is hastening upon them, and the tendency of state authorities to make professional training a requirement for teaching in public junior colleges in support of this statement. The graduate schools in whose faculties the teachers of education have their place must be prepared to guide graduate students both into the available knowledge and, even more important, into the attitude and technical competency to study their teaching and related problems. It is ancillary to this fact that some graduate students may become the most effective agents of a research program.

Quite as important as any technical equipment on the part of individuals is the matter of morale in the college situation. The improvement of college education is based upon the presence of a spirit of good-will among those responsible for such improvement. This means that the academic staff and the teachers of education must enter into a relation of genuine cooperation in the study of college problems. The disgraceful hostility of these two groups in American colleges must be overcome in behalf of the overwhelming problems which they face in common. It is the part of educationists to meet the present unhappy situation with an honest recognition of their own limitations, a genuinely scientific conscience, a desire to be of service and an epidermis impervious to the cynical jibes and ignorances of some of their academic colleagues.

One of the means which we at Minnesota have found most useful in meeting our local situation has been the cooperative investigation. It would not be true to say that, in beginning this program, we anticipated all the helpful relationships which have grown out of our efforts. In the earlier stages, the persons most concerned were largely administrative officers who were facing, in common, certain perplexing problems and who associated themselves and a small group of instructors, with the president's encouragement, into a committee on educational research. As projects developed out of the discussions of this committee, it was possible to enlist the aid of individual instructors in the work of subcommittees. As these committees have been formed they have usually contained one or two men from education and from three to ten instructors from other departments of the university, the majority always lying with the non-education faculties. The individuals have been drawn from the professional groups as well as from the liberal arts college. The names of these departments will give a vivid picture of how widely interest has been distributed. They are as follows:

Administration	Municipal and Sanitary Engineering
Agriculture	Nervous and Mental Diseases
Anatomy	Nutrition
Biochemistry	Obstetrics and Gynecology
Botany	Pathology
Business	Pediatrics
Chemical Engineering	Physical Education
Chemistry	Physics
Civil Engineering	Physiology
Dentistry	Physiological Chemistry
Economics	Plant Pathology
Educational Administration	Political Science
Educational Psychology	Psychology
Elementary Education	Romance Languages
Engineering	Secondary Education
English	Sociology
History	Speech
Home Economics	Surgery
Journalism	University Health Service
Law	Zoology
Library	
Marketing	
Mathematics	
Mechanics	

The list of projects will give an idea of the area over which our activities have ranged. They are:

1. Student Personnel
2. The Efficiency of Instruction in Classes of Different Sizes
3. An Analysis of the Marking Systems in Vogue at the University of Minnesota
4. The Educational Value of Extra-Curricular Activities of University Students
5. Alumni Contacts
6. The Mental Hygiene of College Students
7. Dissemination of Research Information
8. Vocational Guidance for Women
9. Training for Out-Door Leadership
10. The College Teaching of Science
    a. Laboratory Instruction in Human Anatomy
    b. The Value of Laboratory Instruction in Human Physiology
    c. The Value of Laboratory Instruction in College Physics—Mechanics
    d. The Effect of Class Size in College Physics—Heat
    e. Some Determinants of Achievement in College Physics—Magnetism and Electricity
    f. A Study of Prognosis in College Physics
    g. A Study of Prognosis in Human Anatomy
    h. Laboratory Instruction in College Chemistry
    i. The Value of Prerequisite Courses in College Botany
11. The College Teaching of the Social Sciences
12. The Reading Problems of College Students
13. Comparative Scholastic Standing of Athletes
14. Prerequisite Courses
15. Student Self-Appraisal
16. Cooperation in the Land-Grant College Survey
17. The Characteristics of Superior College Teachers
18. Instruction in Clinical Medicine

The spirit of the committee's work has been one of inquiry. Here is an important problem needing investigation; the best possible scientific techniques should be used in its solution; new methods must be invented if necessary, and the study carried through to a point making it worthy of publication as a valuable contribution to our knowledge of college education.

It remains to recognize the vital importance of an attitude on the part of the administration favorable to the promotion of institutional research. The president of an institution, together with the deans, can open the way for the study of educational problems in any college. If they do not direct it, they can appreciate it and encourage it. They can support it with money—and even a little money makes a great difference in some cases—and they can utilize research findings in the practical business of administration. Barring the generous encouragement and support which our committee has continuously received from President Coffman, the projects we have conceived would have languished or been still-born. What he has done for Minnesota certain other presidents and deans have done for their institutions. Proper mention should be made of Jessup, at Iowa, Hawkes, at Columbia, Angell, at Yale, Aydelotte, at Swarthmore, Hall, at Oregon, Morgan, at Antioch, Elliott, at Purdue, Frank, at Wisconsin, Scott, at Northwestern, Randall, at Brown, to which list could be added a score or more of additional names, some of whose services have been equally conspicuous with the work of those named.

In view of the institutional resources available for collegiate educational research we may well caution ourselves against the foundationists with which, in these days, we are so easily infected. The educational foundations with their vast resources intrigue us into expecting outside aid in our projects. No doubt exists that these agencies, with their power to grant subsidies of substantial proportions to favored projects, can powerfully further investigations, where other desirable conditions prevail. It is earnestly to be hoped that they will do just this thing, do it generously and distributively. But an inquiring mind is as much to be desired as money, and where this is present the colleges will find that they have some resources within themselves—resources much greater than they may at first believe. In this matter of research, as in many others, the colleges will do well to harken to the ancient tale of the farmer and quail.

THE FUTURE OF THE BUREAU OF EDUCATION[1]

By J. W. CRABTREE

SECRETARY OF THE NATIONAL EDUCATION ASSOCIATION

The opportunities and responsibilities which lie immediately ahead of you are the problems also of the National Education Association and of the Bureau of Education. The president of the National Education Association is building the program for the Atlanta convention around this thought—"Education for a New World." Many new problems have, within a decade, taken on major importance.

One of them is the problem of character training. The new set of conditions which give us essentially a new world has removed the fireside and the hearthstone from the home life. These new conditions have decreased the waking hours of children in the home almost to the vanishing point. Can you help the home give more time and attention to young people than it is now giving? Can the Bureau of Education and the National Education Association impress more strongly upon teachers and school authorities the imperative need of their assuming greater responsibility in character training than ever before?

The parents of America, the teachers, all citizens interested in the welfare of children, are looking to our great national organizations for information and for guidance. Let us try to meet our responsibility as to character training on the part of the youth of the nation as the largest and most fundamental problem of our civilization.

Your association is reaching out and enlisting the organized support of parents and teachers in every community in the land. The National Education Association represents the entire profession of teaching in its membership.

[1] An address before the annual convention of the National Congress of Parents and Teachers, Washington, D. C., May 6, 1929. Preprinted from the *Journal* of the National Education Association, June, 1929.

The Bureau of Education, under the leadership of a new Commissioner of Education, looks ahead to growth and increased efficiency.

It is most encouraging to note the fact that the new secretary of the Department of the Interior advocates the enlargement of the Bureau of Education. It is high time that the government should open its eyes to its own responsibility in the matter of education. This is an advanced step for the Department of the Interior to take. Other secretaries have not realized the importance of this particular bureau. They have allowed it to run along for a half century with its duties limited and its opportunities restricted.

Your work and ours has, undoubtedly, helped to awaken this new interest. As long as the friends of education were satisfied with a bureau and as long as they limited their efforts to its improvement, very little gain was made. But when they decided on a Department of Education as an ideal and united to reach the goal, the bureau began to take on new importance. Whatever the new secretary gets for the bureau will be due to the feeling over the United States that the government owes as much attention to education as to commerce, labor or agriculture. The most effective help that can be given Secretary Wilbur for the enlarged bureau is to increase the efforts for a Department of Education.

Are you aware of the low salaries paid to research specialists in the bureau? Are you aware of the fact that the city librarian in the District of Columbia receives a much higher salary than the National Commissioner of Education?

There is a great opportunity for not only enlarging the bureau but for increasing its efficiency and prestige. The first step for Secretary Wilbur to take is to place Dr. Cooper's position in a higher salary classification and to pay adequate salaries for experts in research and for leadership in the various educational activities. We have one of the greatest leaders in the United States at the head of the bureau. Let us all join him and Secretary Wilbur in urging the enlargement of the bureau and in increasing its efficiency even to the point of converting it into a department with the name "commissioner" changed to "secretary."

In behalf of the president and officers, I bring you greetings of the National Education Association. We honor ourselves in honoring the founders of the National Congress of Parents and Teachers. No leaders of the last generation excelled them in vision, insight and high purpose. They have laid the foundations of an organization which has come to have a large place in the life of the nation. Their service has magnified the home, it has dignified parenthood, it has honored teachers and teaching. Your congress has taken as its permanent platform the seven cardinal objectives of education. It has worked for worthy legislation. It has enriched and strengthened community life. It has dedicated itself to the great principle that every child shall have a fair start and that the human values shall stand first in the life of our people. It has been my privilege to know personally the founders of this association, their successors and the devoted headquarters staff which shares with us our beautiful building in the nation's capital.

EDUCATIONAL EVENTS

THE CARNEGIE UNITED KINGDOM TRUST

THE London *Times* states that the report of the Carnegie United Kingdom Trust upon its activities during 1928 again records a full year of practical work and various experiments, but, like previous reports, insists more upon the value of spreading the ideas by which the trust is inspired than upon the immediate beneficial results of the grants.

It is an entirely wrong view, says the report, that "Trust funds are merely a bank at which any deserving body may legitimately present its demands," or that the trustees are failing in their duty, or are guilty of inconsistency, if they decline to help in 1928 an enterprise similar to one which Mr. Carnegie or they themselves assisted in 1908 or 1918: "It is not sound policy for the trustees to undertake permanent responsibility for the maintenance of institutions or movements which they decide to help; they must give, liberally but cautiously, what is required for the adequate launching and testing of new enterprises, keeping their resources ready at all times for yet newer movements."

The playing fields policy is the outstanding recent experiment pointed to in the report. The response to the offer made by the National Playing Fields Association and the trustees is described as having abundantly justified the belief that the provision of playing fields on a national scale was in a real sense a "new need." Grants to the number of 123 were made by the trustees during 1928. In nearly every case trust grants were supplemented by National Playing Fields Association grants, and the total sum from the two bodies was approximately £50,000, of which the trustees gave, roughly, £33,000. Apart from gifts of land from private donors, this means that the country is richer in playing fields by well over 3,000 acres.

The borough library policy has evoked such a response that by the end of 1927 the allocation for 1928 was exhausted and the allocation for 1929 encroached upon to the extent of about one third. The results proved so satisfactory that the trustees set aside the largest available supplementary allocation, so that the library committee entered upon 1928 with £8,000 a year to spend in 1928, 1929 and 1930. The increased supply of books, the increase of free access and other changes led to substantial increases in issues (50 per cent. being not uncommon), and generally to an improvement in the local status of the library service. Cooperation between the smaller boroughs and the county service has in many cases broken down the old cramping limits of library areas, to the great advantage of residents in both types of area.

In regard to the rural community councils, the trustees have, after consultation with the National Council of Social Service, reconsidered their previous decision against undertaking responsibility for the establishment of new councils. This followed upon the statement of the Minister of Agriculture, who expressed the hope that the trustees would set aside a further allocation to encourage the formation of further councils, and promised that the government would continue to give all the help which lay in the power of the departments concerned. The radical difficulty is the problem of maintaining the councils after the grant period expires. The fifteen councils already established are steadily increasing their revenue from public and private sources, but the problem can not be regarded as solved. The minister is to be asked if he will state more definitely the extent to which government assistance might be expected.

The trustees have assisted adult education rather more definitely during the past year. The most important new grant was a three-year subsidy to the Workers' Educational Association to enable that body to strengthen its organization at the national and district headquarters.

A CUBAN PHYSICAL TRAINING INSTITUTE

REGULATIONS have recently been published for the National Physical Training Institute at Habana, which was provided for last year by a decree of June 30. The new school, which has been placed under the direction of the Department of Public Instruction and Fine Arts, will help to solve one of the problems with which school authorities have been struggling—that of providing adequately prepared teachers for physical education in the public schools throughout the country. It is expected that one hundred students will be graduated every other year with the diploma of "Teacher of Physical Education," and these teachers will be placed throughout the island.

Training in the two-year course, which includes both theoretical and practical studies, is based on the "natural method" of physical education as popularized in France by Professor Georges Herbert. Several Cuban students were sent to France by the Cuban government to familiarize themselves with the system, and on their return they will be granted the diploma, which will enable them to teach in the schools of their own country.

To enroll in the institute, the students must be from seventeen to thirty-two years of age and must meet certain physical, moral and educational requirements. The entrance examination covers questions on the primary school subjects (a six-year course), while exemption may be claimed upon the ground of possessing an elementary or secondary-school diploma or one from an institution of higher education. The hundred best-qualified applicants will be accepted every two years.

Final examinations covering the work of each year must be passed before the pupil can receive his diploma. Both theoretical and practical in character, the examinations are written and oral, including also drills open to the public in which the student alternately takes part and directs.

In order to train the present physical education teachers as quickly as possible in the use of the "natural method" the Department of Public Instruction and Fine Arts has arranged for short vacation courses to be held through July and August open to a certain group of normal school graduates and to teachers of calisthenics in the secondary schools. Financial assistance will be given to those coming from outside of the capital in the way of traveling and living expenses. Upon successful completion of this intensive summer course, the physical training teachers will be granted the diploma.

AWARDS OF COMMONWEALTH FUND FELLOWSHIPS

Commonwealth Fund fellowships have been awarded to thirty honors students of British and Colonial universities.

These fellowships were established in 1925 by the Commonwealth Fund of New York, of which Edward S. Harkness is president, in the thought that additional facilities for British university graduates to study and travel in the United States would foster the development of understanding and good-will between this country and Great Britain. This year the number of fellowship awards has been increased from twenty-three to thirty, including three for men in the British Colonial Service. This is the fifth annual award. Including the present appointees, 115 British students have received these fellowships. The following list groups the new fellows under the American universities to which they are coming and indicates the British or Colonial universities from which they have been graduated and their special topics of study in this country:

California: Vernon Siegfried Forbes, Christ's College, Cambridge, geology. Alexander Harvey, Armstrong College, Durham, physics.

California Institute of Technology: John Watson Maccoll, Glasgow; Imperial College of Science, London, aerodynamics. Harry V. Warren, University of British Columbia; Queens College, Oxford, geology. Richard van der Riet Woolley, University of Cape Town; Gonville and Caius College, Cambridge, astronomy.

Chicago: Eric Ashby, Imperial College of Science, London, botany. Gwendoline Hilda Faulkner, Edinburgh; Aberdeen; Bedford College, London, zoology.

Columbia: Walter Robson Humphries, Aberdeen, education. Andrew Forrester Skinner, St. Andrews, education.

Cornell: Reginald Clifford Hinton, London School of Economics and Political Science, economics.

Harvard: Frank Ongley Darvall, University College, London; University of Reading, history. Thomas Penberthy Fry, University of Queensland; Magdalen College, Oxford, law. William Gerald Humphrey, Queen's College, Oxford, chemistry. Edward T. C. Spooner, Clare College, Cambridge, medicine.

Johns Hopkins: Nora Mallinson, Girton College, Cambridge, history.

Massachusetts Institute of Technology: Denis Morrell Robinson, King's College, London, electrical engineering.

Michigan: James Norman Goodier, Downing College, Cambridge, engineering.

Princeton: Montefiore Barak, Canterbury College, New Zealand; Hertford College, Oxford, physical chemistry. Harry Julius Emeleus, Imperial College of Science, London, chemistry. Reginald Iceton James, Corpus Christi College, Oxford, history. John Henry C. Whitehead, Balliol College, Oxford, mathematics.

Stanford: Beatrice Mary I. White, King's College, London, bibliography.

Wisconsin: Andrew James Watters, St. Andrews, chemistry.

Yale: Geoffrey Crowther, Clare College, Cambridge, economics. William L. S. Fleming, Trinity Hall, Cambridge, geology. Leslie Alfred Lickfold, Trinity Hall, Cambridge, music. Herbert Lavallin Puxley, Brasenose College, Oxford, economics.

The three colonial service fellowships were awarded as follows:

Eric Jean Bradshaw, of Trinity College, Dublin, now in the India Civil Service, will study oil engineering at the University of California.

Richard Mitchelson Campbell, of Victoria University College, New Zealand, now in the New Zealand Civil Service, will study agricultural economics at Cornell University.

Alexander Herbert Crane, of Adelaide University, now in the Australian Forestry Service, will study forestry at Yale University.

GRANTS OF THE AMERICAN COUNCIL OF LEARNED SOCIETIES

AWARDS of grants in aid of research to seventeen American scholars are announced by the American Council of Learned Societies. Those to whom the grants have been made are pursuing investigations in the fields of history, art and archeology, philology and literature, folklore, medieval and Byzantine studies.

In historical research Frederick E. Brasch, chief of the Smithsonian Division of the Library of Congress, is making a study of the history of astronomy in Colonial America. Viola F. Barnes, associate professor of history in Mount Holyoke College, is conducting researches in the British archives on England's new policy after 1763 and its effect on the colonial empire of Great Britain. Edgar B. Graves, associate professor of history in Hamilton College, is working in the Public Record Office of London, and in the archepiscopal archives of York and Lincoln on problems connected with the State of Praemunire in 1353.

Three of the grants are to aid in the preparation of historical works. They go to George D. Hadzsits, professor of Latin in the University of Pennsylvania, for assistance in preparing for the press his book on the "History of Roman Religion to Augustus"; to Roy F. Nichols, assistant professor of history in the University of Pennsylvania, for securing photostat copies of letters of Franklin Pierce, in private possession, for use in writing a "Biography of Franklin Pierce," and to Gertrude E. Smith, assistant professor of Greek in the University of Chicago, for assistance in preparing for publication her book on "Administration of Justice from Homer to Demosthenes."

In the field of art and archeology a grant has been made to Henry Roy W. Smith, assistant professor of Latin in the University of California, for photographs in a study of Calabrian and Lucanian vase-painting.

In philology and literature grants go to: Leroy C. Barret, professor of Latin in Trinity College, Hartford, for purchase of a photo-zinc copy of a manuscript of the Atharva Veda Paippalada in the library of the Bombay Branch of the Royal Asiatic Society; Ruby Davis, professor of English, Earlham College, Richmond, Indiana, for purchase of photostats and for travel in Europe in connection with a study of the sources of Bede; James Hutton, instructor in classics in Cornell University, for research in London relating to the influence of Greek anthology on modern literature since the Renaissance; Lawrence M. Price, associate professor of German in the University of California, for travel in Germany incidental to the completion of his study on the reception of English literature in Germany and to the completion of his bibliography of English belletristic works in German translation in the eighteenth century; Evan T. Sage, professor of Latin in the University of Pittsburgh, for expenses of photographing and collating the various manuscripts of the Satiricon of Petronius in an effort to establish a definitive edition; Cony Sturgis, professor of Spanish, Oberlin College, for his study of the romantic novel in Spanish literature between 1830 and 1850.

In the field of folklore, a grant goes to Stith Thompson, associate professor of English in Indiana University, for secretarial assistance in the completion of his classification and bibliography of motifs in folk tales, ballads, traditions, myths and fables.

In medieval studies grants go to Roy J. Deferrari, professor of Greek and Latin in the Catholic University of America, for the purchase of texts to be used in compiling a concordance to the works of Prudentius, and to William Jerome Wilson, professor in the department of language and literature, State Normal School, Cheney, Washington, for expenses in continuing his work on an edition of the astrological and alchemical hermetica.

In Byzantine studies, a grant goes to Clarence George Lowe, professor of classics in the University of Nebraska, for purchase of facsimiles and transcriptions of manuscript materials relating to Theodorus Metochites.

CARNEGIE SCHOLARSHIPS FOR LIBRARIANS

To attract young men and women to the library profession, and to encourage persons already engaged in library work, the Carnegie Corporation of New York has established a series of scholarship grants for graduate study in library problems. Eight librarians have been recommended to receive the awards for 1929–30. The stipend under the first grants will be uniformly $1,500, but the amount may vary in future to meet requirements of individual students. The successful librarians, who will all pursue their studies in this country, were chosen from among 190 applicants for the awards. They are:

H. Elaine Boylan, reference librarian and assistant secretary of the Oklahoma Library Commission; Marion Patch, classifier, University of Michigan Library; Rose B. Phelps, instructor in the Library School of the University of Illinois; Marie Tremaine, reference assistant at the Toronto Public Library, and Nell Unger, librarian at the Reed College Library, Portland, Oregon, all of whom will pursue graduate study in the School of Library Service, Columbia University. Miss Boylan will specialize in study of library extension agencies. Miriam D. Tomkins, head of the department of adult education of the Milwaukee Public Library, and Leon Carnovsky, assistant to the librarian of Washington University Library, St. Louis, Mo., will pursue studies of adult reading interests and in adult education, respectively, in the Graduate Library School, University of Chicago. Katherine P. Carnes, librarian of Wesleyan College, Macon, Ga., will study college library problems in the department of library science at the University of Michigan. Margrothe D. Brandt, student in the Graduate Library School, University of Chicago; Mary Rebecca Lingenfelter, cataloguer, Penniman Library of Education, University of Pennsylvania; Ruth C. Coombs, director of circulation, Providence Public Library; Grace O. Kelley, supervising cataloguer and classifier, John Crerar Library; Leonida I. Sansone, Italian librarian at the Aguilar Branch, New York Public Library, and Edith Wirt, head of foreign literature division, Cleveland Public Library, were named as alternates.

THE WORLD'S FAIR AT CHICAGO

AT a recent conference to consider the scientific and educational exhibits there were present Dr. Frederick C. Woodward, acting president of the University of Chicago; Dean K. C. Babcock, of the school of arts and sciences, University of Illinois; the Reverend Robert M. Kelley, S.J., president of Loyola University; William J. Bogan, superintendent of the public schools of Chicago; Dean Henry C. Morrison, of the experimental school of the University of Chicago; Dr. Lotus D. Coffman, president of the University of Minnesota; Dean Charles W. Judd, of the department of education of the University of Chicago, and Walter Dill Scott, president of Northwestern University. Representing the World's Fair were Mrs. Rufus C. Dawes, trustee and wife of the president of the board; Dr. Allen D. Albert, assistant to the president, and Dr. William A. Pusey, who filled a dual capacity as trustee and guest member of the conference, he being also a member of the National Research Council committee cooperating with the trustees of the fair.

Following a conference of several hours, the following resolution was addressed to the committee of the National Research Council:

That the proposed World's Fair of 1933 offers an extraordinary opportunity for the interpretation of the service rendered by the educational systems of America; of the social consequences of universal free education; of experiments in educational methods, and of the development of a body of scientifically established principles which provide the only adequate basis for progress in education.

That the special committee of the National Research Council should be so enlarged as adequately to represent not only the natural sciences, but the social sciences and education, in the formulation of plans, supervision of exhibits, and the presentation of programs.

Previous great expositions have consisted of competitive exhibits, alike in steel, textiles, education and everything else. The sponsors of the Chicago World's Fair announce that "the old idea will be discarded; that the fair will exemplify the principle of 'strength in union,' by collective exhibits. The relationship of iron, steel, cement and the like to modern life will each be displayed in collective exhibits, tracing the progress of industry from infancy to the present time."

Dr. Frank Baldwin Jewett, vice-president of the American Telephone and Telegraph Company, is chairman of the committee of the National Research Council. Associated with him are Dr. Max Mason, formerly president of the University of Chicago and director of the division of natural science of the Rockefeller Foundation; Dr. William A. Pusey, professor emeritus of the College of Physicians and Surgeons of the University of Illinois and former president of the American Medical Association; Dr. Simon Flexner, medical head of the Rockefeller Institute for Medical Research; Gano Dunn, vice-president in charge of engineering and construction for J. G. White and Company, New York; Dr. Michael I. Pupin, professor of electromechanics, Columbia University, and Dr. Vernon L. Kellogg, secretary of the National Research Council.

THE SARGENT SCHOOL AND BOSTON UNIVERSITY

As reported in last week's SCHOOL AND SOCIETY, the Sargent School for Physical Education founded in 1881 by the late Dr. Dudley Allen Sargent, and since his death in 1924 carried on by his son has been transferred to Boston University.

Mr. Ledyard W. Sargent and his wife, Mrs. Etta Sargent, have donated the school in its entirety to the university. The following statement in regard to the school has been made by President Daniel L. Marsh:

When the Sargent family gave their school of physical education to Boston University last week it was an event of the first importance for physical education in New England. Not only was the gift a large and generous one, but it was most unusual.

Great endowments have been created in our American universities for the classics and for other academic studies, but physical education has been neglected. Until recently the colleges have been unwilling to recognize the importance of the education of the body in connection with the education of the mind and even now they often allow scant credit for it.

Boston University in receiving this gift of the Sargents will maintain the essential character of the work started by Dr. Dudley A. Sargent and continued by Mr. Ledyard Sargent and his wife. It recognizes the large contribution made to physical education by this school and will make sure that all that is sound in the past history of the school shall be retained. Mr. and Mrs. Sargent will serve with three other experts on an advisory board which the university is appointing to counsel with Dean Wilde of the School of Education.

The university will at once place the curriculum of the Sargent department of the School of Education on a collegiate basis. While the present three-year course will be retained for those who have entered under it, a four-year degree course will be developed. This will include all the substantial parts of the physical course and also courses in academic studies and in general education.

Mr. and Mrs. Sargent were the guests of honor at a dinner of the faculty of the school of education of the university on May 22.

THE SUMMER SESSION OF COLUMBIA UNIVERSITY

NON-RESIDENT lecturers at the summer session of Teachers College, Columbia University, include:

Thyrsa W. Amos, dean of women, University of Pittsburgh; Raymond N. Ball, treasurer, University of Rochester; Earl W. Barnhart, chief, commercial education service, Washington; Francis F. Bradshaw, dean of students, University of North Carolina; John Seiler Brubacker, Yale University; Wilbert Lester Carr, professor of Latin, University of Michigan; Morse A. Cartwright, executive director, American Association for Adult Education; Herbert E. Hawkes, dean of Columbia College; Lillian Hethershaw, Drake University; Louis B. Hopkins, president, Wabash College; Vernon Jones, Clark University; John A. H. Keith, superintendent of public instruction, State of Pennsylvania; Truman Lee Kelley, Leland Stanford University; John G. Kirk, director of commercial education, Philadelphia Public Schools; Edgar W. Knight, University of North Carolina; Leonard V. Koos, University of Minnesota; Charles T. Loram, member of Commission of Native Affairs, Cape Town, Cape Province, South Africa; John K. Norton, director of research, National Education Association, Washington; Osmond T. Robert, Smith College; Charles Russell, principal, Massachusetts State Normal, Westfield, Mass.; Zenos Scott, superintendent of schools, Springfield, Mass.; William E. Sealock, dean of the college of education, University of Nebraska; Alexander J. Stoddard, superintendent of schools, Schenectady, N. Y., newly elected superintendent of schools of Providence, Rhode Island; Charles H. Stone, North Carolina College for Women; Raymond Walters, dean of Swarthmore College; Florence V. Watkins, executive secretary, National Congress of Parents and Teachers, Washington; Frederic Lyman Wells, Boston Psychopathic Hospital; John C. Wright, director, Federal Board for Vocational Education, Washington, and George F. Zook, president, Akron University.

EDUCATIONAL NOTES AND NEWS

SIR THOMAS HENRY HOLLAND, rector of the Imperial College of Science and Technology, London, has been appointed principal of the University of Edinburgh in succession to Sir Alfred Ewing. Sir Thomas, who is a Canadian by birth and sixty-one years of age, was formerly professor of geology and mineralogy at Manchester. Sir Robert Falconer, president of the University of Toronto, had declined an offer of the principalship at Edinburgh.

DR. WILLIAM WALLACE CAMPBELL, president of the University of California for the last six years, has announced his resignation, effective on July 1, 1930, when he will have reached the age of retirement. Dr. Campbell has been director of the Lick Observatory since 1901.

A DINNER in honor of Dr. Charles S. Howe, who is retiring from the presidency of the Case School of Applied Science after a service to the school of forty years, of which twenty-six have been in the presidency, will be given by the alumni, faculty and students on May 31. Dr. William E. Wilkenden, president-elect, will take part in the celebration.

THE Educational Society of Baltimore, Mayor Broening and Dr. David Weglein, superintendent of public instruction, have given a testimonial dinner to Dr. Frank J. Goodnow, president of the Johns Hopkins University, in acknowledgment of the progress made by the university during his administration. The establishment of the College for Teachers was especially emphasized. Dr. Goodnow offered his resignation in January last year, to take effect when his successor should be chosen.

DR. ALEXANDER GUERRY, headmaster of the Baylor School at Chattanooga, Tennessee, a private institution, has been nominated for president of the University of Chattanooga, to succeed Dr. Arlo Ayres Brown. The election will take place at the annual meeting of the trustees on June 5.

LANDIS TANGER, superintendent of schools of Reading, Pennsylvania, has been elected principal of the State Teachers College at Millersville. Dr. Tanger succeeds Charles H. Gordinier, who expects to retire this summer and who may later work in connection with Beckley College, Harrisburg. Mr. Tanger will be succeeded in the superintendency by Amanda E. Stout, who is now assistant superintendent, having been connected for forty-seven years with the school system at Reading as teacher and supervisor. Miss Stout expects to retire in July, 1930, serving for one year only for which she will receive a salary of $7,200.

AT the meeting of the Cincinnati Board of Education on May 13, Dr. Randall J. Condon, superintendent of the Cincinnati schools since January 1, 1913, announced his retirement at the close of his present contract on August 31. At the same meeting, Edward D. Roberts, who has been associated with Dr. Condon throughout his service in Cincinnati, during the last two years as associate superintendent, was elected superintendent.

A. J. STODDARD, formerly superintendent of schools at Schenectady, N. Y., has been elected superintendent of schools at Providence, R. I., to succeed Mr. Isaac O. Winslow. Mr. Stoddard goes to Providence on a three-year contract, effective on August 15, at a salary of $10,000, $11,000 and $12,000, respectively.

GEORGE J. RYAN has been elected for the eighth consecutive term president of the Board of Education of New York City.

DR. CHARLES E. PRALL, who has served for the past year as research professor of education in the University of Arkansas, has been appointed dean of the college of education of the university to succeed Dr. J. O. Creager, who will return to New York University next year. Dr. H. M. Hosford, of the department of mathematics of Southern Methodist University, has been appointed head of the department of mathematics to succeed Dr. George W. Droke, who will become emeritus professor on the first of next July, after serving in the institution for forty-seven years.

THEODORE KRATT has been appointed dean of the new School of Fine Arts at Miami University, Oxford, Ohio. Mr. Kratt has been head of the department of music at the University of Idaho since 1927. He was connected with the Chicago Musical College for five years previous to that time.

PROFESSOR FRANCIS W. COKEN, for eighteen years a member of the faculty of the Ohio State University, has accepted the new graduate professorship of government at Yale University.

DR. ROSCOE POUND, dean of the Harvard Law School, and Dr. Ada L. Comstock, president of Radcliffe College, have been appointed by President Hoover members of the National Law Enforcement Commission to study the failures of law enforcement and shortcomings of judicial procedure. President Comstock is the only member of the commission who is not a lawyer.

Justice Edward R. Finch, of the Appellate Division of the Supreme Court, was elected head of the New York Chapter of Phi Beta Kappa at the annual meeting on May 9.

Walter W. Head, president of the State Bank of Chicago, has been for the fourth time reelected president of the Boy Scouts of America.

A committee headed by Dr. Jacob H. Hollander, professor of political economy at the Johns Hopkins University, has been appointed by Mayor Broening, of Baltimore, to determine the "current wage scale" to be paid mechanics and others employed in municipal work.

Arthur W. Packard will succeed Mr. Archie Palmer as assistant director of the Institute of International Education, of which Dr. Stephen P. Duggan is the director.

Dr. Benjamin C. Gruenberg, liaison officer of the American Social Hygiene Association, has joined the editorial staff of the Viking Press, New York City.

President Daniel L. Marsh, of Boston University, has been appointed by the National Education Association a delegate to the meeting of the World Federation of Education Associations, which meets at Geneva, Switzerland, from July 25 to August 4.

Miss Neva Boyd, assistant professor of sociology at Northwestern University, will leave on June 6 for Poland, where she will spend the summer lecturing on adult education in the School of Social Work at Warsaw.

Dr. C. C. Ellis, vice-president and professor of education in Juniata College, Huntingdon, Pennsylvania, has returned from a vacation trip to Europe and the Near East. He had been granted a leave of absence for the spring semester.

Governor Franklin D. Roosevelt, of New York, will be the orator at the anniversary meeting of the Harvard Chapter of Phi Beta Kappa on June 17. Assistant Professor Robert Silliman Hillyer will be the poet. The president of the society, Dr. William Sydney Thayer, of Baltimore, will preside. The public is invited to the literary exercises, and all members of the fraternity will be welcome both at these exercises and at the dinner.

President Frank L. McVey, president of the University of Kentucky, has accepted an invitation to deliver the commencement address at the University of Nebraska on June 8.

Dr. Charles Horton Cooley, professor of sociology at the University of Michigan and for thirty-seven years a member of the faculty, died on May 8, at the age of sixty-five years.

Professor William Austin Bassett, director of the division of municipal and industrial research at the Massachusetts Institute of Technology, died on May 19. He was fifty-four years old.

Alvin W. Miller, principal of the Central High School at Washington, D. C., died on May 19.

Secretary Wilbur, of the Department of the Interior, announced on May 17 that he had asked the President to appoint an advisory committee on education to work out a program to be recommended to Congress which would permit the federal government to render the greatest possible degree of service in the field of education. He believes that that committee should be made up of representatives of the great educational organizations and of others interested in this field and that it should meet in Washington for a consideration of all phases of the subject. A plan will be developed which will permit the government to render through education the greatest possible service without disturbing local self-government. Another problem which the committee would be asked to study would be that of bringing together all the educational forces in the national government which are now in existence, under an assistant secretary or under-secretary of one of the departments.

Congress has authorized the United States Bureau of Education to make a study of the organization, administration, financing and work of secondary schools and their articulation with elementary and higher education. The survey will cost approximately $225,000, of which $50,-000 will be available during the fiscal year 1930.

Plans for the survey will not be actively undertaken until the beginning of the fiscal year on July 14.

AN increase of $100 a year in their salary has been granted to the women teachers of the Cambridge, Massachusetts, high schools, the masters of the elementary schools and the directors of music, arts and physical education. At the same time an increase of fifty dollars a year in salary was granted to master's assistants in the elementary schools. No increase was granted to the teachers in the elementary schools. The women high-school teachers had asked for an increase of $600.

THE first move to remodel the Lloyd Mifflin Memorial Home as a haven for retired teachers of the State of Pennsylvania was taken at a meeting held at Lancaster, Pennsylvania, of committees of the State Education Association. The home will be composed of two groups of buildings now on the Mifflin estate. They are the gift of Dr. Houston Mifflin as a memorial to his brother, Lloyd Mifflin. Included in the gift were paintings and art objects, some of which will be sold to help pay the cost of remodeling. Members of the Pennsylvania State Education Association, which has an enrolment of 58,000, will be asked to contribute a nominal amount to complete the fund.

THE new Burris School, a demonstration school, which has been built at Ball State Teachers College, Muncie, Ind., at a cost of $238,000, is about ready for occupancy. Bids are now open for a new north wing, which is to be added to this structure at a cost of $60,000. The building is named in honor of Benjamin J. Burris, late president of the college. A south wing will be built in the near future. The school will be opened in September, and the north wing will be ready in October.

THE Nature Training School of the Coordinating Council on Nature Activities will be held from June 1 to 29 at Gardner Lake, Connecticut. The purpose of this school is to provide opportunities for men and women to gain practical information and approved methods for nature service. The leaders of the various courses offered are men and women known to be qualified to give the best in their chosen field of activity. Classes will be offered in tree study and forestry, birds, insects, stars, plant ecology and physiography, Indian trails and gardens, music interpretation and photography, outdoor sketching and nature education. Registration should be sent to the Coordinating Council on Nature Activities, The American Museum of Natural History, New York City.

IT is announced that Northwestern University and Armour Institute of Technology, "by mutual consent," have abandoned the plan, which has been under consideration for the last four years, to merge the two institutions.

MURRAY GUGGENHEIM, whose family is of Alsatian origin, has made a donation of $100,000 to the University of Paris, while a group of Alsatians have subscribed $40,000. The donors of these sums asked in exchange that 75 out of 200 rooms in a building which the National Foundation is about to erect in the Cité Universitaire shall be reserved for students from the Haut et Bas Rhin and from the neighborhood of Belfort. The building in question will be the first to be dedicated exclusively to the use of students from the provinces, although these make up over 50 per cent. of the strength of the University of Paris.

THE University of Southern California will celebrate its fiftieth anniversary in June. Invitations are being extended to institutions of higher learning to send delegates. The celebration will include announcements of endowments, the dedication of new buildings and the laying of corner-stones for still newer buildings projected. There will be educational conferences, participated in by some of the country's most eminent scholars. The plans include the publication of a series of monographs contributed by members of the Southern California faculty, and a special volume will contain the proceedings of the celebration. Ten special committees have been constituted to head special phases of the fiftieth anniversary celebration, in addition to an honorary faculty committee, comprising those who have served the University of Southern California for a quarter of a century or longer.

THE budget announced by Columbia University for the coming year shows an increase of about $2,000,000 over the budget for 1928. Educational administration and instruction for the year will require $9,027,501, and upkeep of buildings and grounds $1,034,061. Other figures are: For the university libraries, $465,211; for the administration of the business of the corporation, $237,872; for annuities, $48,206; for taxes and other like charges, $59,215; for interest on the corporate debt, $461,151; for the redemption fund on account of the principal of the loan of 1919, $100,000; for the amortization of the loan of 1925, $47,500. Units of Columbia's educational system have likewise appropriated sums for the maintenance of their separate corporations, which money will be disbursed directly by them and not through the treasurer of Columbia. These budgets are: Teachers College, $3,312,361; Barnard College, $473,965; College of Pharmacy, $228,314, and St. Stephen's College, $195,632. The estimated deficiency for the year ending June 30, 1930, is $618,267.

The Harvard University Press has issued the sixth edition of the Official Guide to Harvard University, the first revision in twelve years. The present issue was edited by Mr. Stewart Mitchell, instructor in history and tutor in the division of history, government and economics. It is illustrated with more than fifty pictures, among them a reproduction of the famous Paul Revere engraving of Harvard in 1775. These illustrations and a historical map, showing the gradual acquisition of what is now the college yard, add interest and utility to the edition. The guide contains an account of the founding of the university, its constitution and departments, and the position in the university of the faculty of arts and sciences and of other faculties. There is an historical sketch of the college yard from its earliest beginnings to the present time. The visitor will find the description of the fence and the various gates and the history of the grounds and buildings very useful.

The Institute of Euthenics at Vassar College, Poughkeepsie, N. Y., which will last from June 24 to August 3, is offering several courses intended primarily for teachers. The institute represents an attempt to bring together and correlate the resources of modern science which bear upon the problems of living. Two demonstration schools are included, composed of children of members of the institute. The Nursery School, directed by Dr. Smiley Blanton, professor of child study, and Miss Dorothy Cannon, director of the Cannon School, New Haven, will be used as a laboratory to familiarize members with the most approved methods of child care as applied to the pre-school child. The school for children from four and a half to seven years old will be in charge of a group of teachers from The City and Country School, New York City, who will demonstrate the technic of helping them to become acquainted with their world through play. Vassar College will grant credit in certain courses to qualified registrants. Besides the work in education, psychology, child guidance, speech training and mental hygiene, the curriculum will include instruction in nutrition, religious adjustment, consumption of wealth, crafts, horticulture, household technology and food preparation.

The department of education in the graduate school of the University of Illinois is offering a large number of courses for students who are candidates for the master's degree in education, at the summer session to be held in Urbana from June 17 to August 10. Among the so-called strictly graduate courses, that is, courses to which undergraduates are not admitted, are included educational theory, educational administration, high school administration, methods of teaching, curriculum construction, supervision of secondary education, supervision of elementary education, educational measurements, educational research, advanced educational psychology, high school curricula, source problems of the junior high school division of secondary education, analysis and evaluation of high-school texts, studies in secondary education, problems in the teaching of English in the secondary school, psychology of the elementary school subjects, psychology of the high school subjects, public school finance, supervised study and public school business administration.

The Collège de France, founded by François the first in 1530, will celebrate its four hundredth anniversary next year. A large attendance of delegates from French and foreign universities is expected.

DISCUSSION

PERIOD EDUCATION IN EREWHON

In a former paper[1] in School and Society I gave an account of a most interesting meeting with Professor Egsin, Erewhonian,[2] at which he told me a good deal, as much as time then allowed, about educational practices in his country. Much more recently, a singularly fortunate and wholly unexpected meeting with Professor Egsin, far from the entrance to his homeland but within the range of air travel, as perfected, gave me a further opportunity to learn of educational ways in his unique society. You may be sure I embraced the opportunity, for what I had learned in the former interview served to quicken interest.

A chance reference in his first few words became the clue to as interesting a disclosure of exotic experience as one might ever hope to become acquainted with; he alluded to "period education," a phrase which adumbrated a misty epoch in Erewhonian culture, evidently long since displaced, but still redolent of a grandeur and an impressive decadence. "Period education" at once exercised a fascination on me, even as a solid black walnut antique appeals to the heart. What might "period education" be?

Reversing a rather common method of narration, let me begin at the close rather than at the beginning, in trying to give an understandable account of what he said; perhaps thus a reader if he has to break off early in the recital may carry away a fairly good sense of the more striking facts.

Late in the decades of period education, according to the historically precise and amusedly reminiscent Professor Egsin, the Erewhonians woke up with a start to realize that the entire population above high school age was ranking as university graduates. Old and young, that is, down to secondary school age, rich and poor, although there was not much poverty in Erewhon, and all sorts and conditions were annually accessioned to the ranks of university graduates, and with no regard to essential intellectual condition; this kept on till the population became homogeneous, academically speaking, all acquiring degrees.

This culmination did not come about in a trice; before it, various stages. It was not by sudden bound that Erewhon's university system achieved the result described. The final stage was an end phenomenon, before which lay a train of occurrences. Little by little, it seems, graduation requirements had been leveled and popularized until it became as easy as falling off a log to become a university man in Erewhon. The astonishing apogee of academic decline was reached when students, so-called, were able to demand credentials of graduation on proof—of what? You will be amazed to know: students were graduated, in the closing days of period education, on proof that they had made the rounds of the campus and had gazed upon the magnificent buildings *even if they had not been inside.* From one resplendent structure to another students might be seen making their way, in their hands the course of study, an itinerary with names of buildings starred and double-starred and listed in varying sequences; a certain massive pile might, for example, be twentieth on the itinerary curriculum of one student and be tenth in the log of another. It was amusing, said Egsin, that students meeting on their peripatetic way should occasionally dispute the relative merits of programs which differed only in the order of visitation of buildings whose interiors neither student would see.

But before this absurd degeneracy of requirements students had been held to stricter demands; they had been called upon to produce proctors' certificates showing that the undergraduate had some knowledge of the interiors of the ornate and eternal structures identified with higher education in the period education of which Professor Egsin gave account. No student who had failed to see the inside of a building whose name was starred on his program might hope for graduation, much less for honors. The human element, as the reader may divine, had now disappeared on the instructional side, though a skeleton personnel manned the administrative offices, to see that forms were complied with; Egsin, said, as I recall it, that some sort of automatic device was in use for the final proceedings of graduation, campus mileage records going into an adding machine, or something like that. The proctor's certificates and the mileage slips were evidently of a

[1] "Diplomas in Erewhon," School and Society, Sept. 22, 1928.

[2] Butler, Samuel, "Erewhon, or Over the Range."

relatively reputable stage, compared with the time, later, when only the mileage slips were taken into account. The reader will no doubt experience a sense of wonder when asked to believe that Erewhon developed a system of higher education of this character, that in any part of the known world such declension from a university of books and men should have taken place. Many of us, when we think of seats of learning, have before our minds books and professors, libraries and lectures; if we indulge in the old imagery of the log and Mark Hopkins, we are not likely to think of the log to the exclusion of M. H. The log is rather casual, as it were. Of course Egsin made no defense of the *reductio ad absurdum;* he laughed with anatomical completeness time after time during his description of the unique decadence of period education.

"But how," I asked, "did things ever get to going that way?"

Egsin explained after the similitude of land elevations, on a high slope, of a manner to decide the direction of flow of the first trickle of water which should afterwards become a mighty river; it is conceivable that slight variations of surface at the beginning should have far-reaching effects on the course of waters. It seems that at a seemingly innocent stage in the evolution (more properly devolution) of Erewhonian higher education the nice balance between personnel and plant, between psychology and architecture, was lost, and, one thing leading on to another ("such dependency of thing on thing"), finally there was little left to do but to let the perverse motive work itself out to the total supremacy of bricks and mortar, pillar and pilaster, of the closing days of period education. The acceptance of buildings as synonymous with culture had become so general that there was nothing to do but wait. Thought had become superficial, and the materialism of the times seemed to crave impressive monuments of objectivity; so, with increasing disregard of the human factors in higher education, the Erewhonians plunged forward to the world's crowning default.

I do not intend to relate here how it was that Erewhon managed to emerge from the dead center of period education, though Egsin gave some account of that; it is a pretty tale, but a tale by itself. Our conversation seemed to come perilously near to disaster from threatened change of view-point, for when he was talking ancient Erewhon my mind was shuttling back and forth between that time and mine. Egsin noticed my distress. "Oh, it's nothing," I said. "I was just thinking of some disquieting factors in modern education, not Erewhon. But," I added, "nothing to worry about; everything will come out all right with us."

"You should pray to your gods," said Egsin earnestly, "that you may escape the full folly of period education in Erewhon."

After this it was but a short time until the delightful Egsin took off. And surely the strange Erewhon could boast of few scholars of finer blend of feeling and thought, or with fairer division of attention among significant matters.

ARLAND D. WEEKS

NORTH DAKOTA
AGRICULTURAL COLLEGE

JUNIOR COLLEGE GRADUATES IN THE UNIVERSITIES

THOSE who maintain that the junior colleges have proved their ability to prepare students for advanced university work rest their argument upon the high scholarship record made by junior college graduates at Stanford University.

The Stanford report, recently published, shows three things:

(1) That the junior college transfers have a ''markedly superior'' intelligence rating compared with the Stanford juniors, indicating that they are a more carefully selected group;

(2) that despite this much higher intelligence score (80.5 measured by the Thorndike test compared with 72.3 for the four-year men and 69.1 for the four-year women) the scholarship record of the junior college graduates during their first quarter in residence falls below that of the native Stanford juniors, and

(3) that the junior college transfers, though they overtake the native Stanford students in their second quarter, do not reach their own full stride until the last quarter of their senior year, whereas the four-year students have found their natural pace by the time they enter the upper division.

The junior college, as at present organized, has undertaken a double purpose: (1) to meet the need for a people's vocational college and

(2) to supplant the lower division of the universities. Whether these divergent aims can be successfully combined in one institution seems highly doubtful. The Stanford statistics suggest that the lower division training given by the junior colleges is not so thorough as that offered by the universities—at least for a restricted group of superior students. The experience of the University of California, which receives the graduates from the same junior colleges in larger numbers and with less rigid selection, has not been made public.

G. M. Okerlund

University of Washington

QUOTATIONS

TWENTY YEARS OF PRESIDENT LOWELL

It is just twenty years ago that, on May 19, 1909, Mr. Lowell took his place at the plain old table in the plain, but sunny and pleasant, room in University Hall which we know and which, we may hope, many generations will continue to know as the President's Office. He entered upon his work with the purpose of maintaining and enhancing the "superlative" quality (to use his own term) which he believed ought to attach to Harvard University. In particular he was confident that among the undergraduates of Harvard College respect for good scholarship and the ambition to be a good scholar needed to be, and could be, stirred. By organizing the social conditions of freshmen, which seemed possible only through the construction of the Freshman Halls, by the appointment of a new type of regent, by a wise choice of a professor of hygiene, and the careful selection of all the officers who come in contact with students, by steady support of and participation in the chapel services, by never-ceasing and sympathetic interest in every aspect, including the sports, of undergraduate life, by many ideas put in practice, culminating in the long-considered plan of the houses, he has endeavored to make Harvard College conform to the definite ideal which he has pictured in his imagination. In the reorganization of studies which has been put into effect his thought has led the way, by virtue of his clear vision of the goal he had in view, and with the constantly increasing confidence and support of the Faculty of Arts and Sciences. To the college degree of bachelor he has felt that a certain sacredness belongs; and in that purpose, at the very outset of his administration and under his leadership, the new rules for the choice of studies were made by the faculty and these followed by a better plan of admission to college, by gradually attained success in making significant and attractive the college honor degrees, and by the institution of the "general examinations" for the bachelor's degree. This last institution has been, indeed, the central spring of the new system in the college; on it depended the development of the staff of tutors, and the advantages, now proved to be without attendant hazard, of the "reading period" are but one illustration of the new spirit which has been made to permeate a large section of undergraduate life and thought. These improvements in Harvard are no longer precarious; they have assured permanance, and will lend themselves effectively to the adjustments which the changing conditions of the future will require, for they proceed from a living ideal which has struck its roots deep.

Unremitting concern for the opportunities of fruitful work by the faculty, for the maintenance of the dignity and pleasantness of the professor's life, for the reputation of Harvard in the world at large has been manifest, and Mr. Lowell and Mrs. Lowell have won for their own persons not only the respect but the gratitude and affection of their colleagues—not least of all because pains have been taken to recognize that the president of a college is but the color-sergeant, that the efficient force consists of those who teach.

In these twenty years the professional schools and scientific establishments and the museums and the public interest in music have not lacked their due share of the president's attention. Great gifts of money, beyond the dreams of earlier generations, have attested public confidence in the type and the aims which we share with others of the great universities, notably with Yale and Princeton. New buildings have been built, or are substantially provided for, which fairly complete the physical frame of this university. All this is well known, and need not here be rehearsed.

On this anniversary, sir, and in the name of this Society of Scholars, we thank you—and Mrs. Lowell—that with this unstinted devotion and sacrifice and with the single-minded practice of public spirit you have given us—yourselves.—*Harvard Alumni Bulletin.*

PRESIDENT CHASE AND THE UNIVERSITY OF NORTH CAROLINA

The decision of Dr. Chase to remain as president of the university affords a sigh of relief. Ever since it was learned that he was seriously considering the attractive offer to become head of the Social Science Research Council, which carried a salary double his present, university folks have feared his loss. He announced this month his decision to stay in the South, and as head of North Carolina University.

The president has not issued any statement which explains his decision. Just what influenced the decision is for us mere conjecture. Dr. Chase's statement that several factors were involved is clear.

The financial temptation to accept the offer was not as great, perhaps, as might be impulsively thought. To us a significant thing about the offer is that it illustrates the position of the university in its efforts to retain and acquire faculty men of quality and ability. Dr. Chase decides to stay in North Carolina at $10,000 annually rather than accept a $20,000 offer in New York. Other faculty men have had offers of similar kind; some have gone—others have remained. But the university can not expect to maintain its leadership and quality faculty without considering increased faculty salaries and retirement allowances; we are in competition with the better institutions in the country.

From a personal standpoint President Chase is still a young man. He is not yet fifty. He is active, and can enjoy the active requirements as chief executive of the university. He can feel, and justly so, that in the last decade considerable progress was made in the university because of his leadership. He can have the satisfaction of seeing his efforts bearing fruit, and continuing the process. He is in public life, is an outstanding figure in the changing South and enjoys a position of prestige. He is heading a program which is building for North Carolina a state institution which will in time be a great national university in the South. He has faith in the progressive element of North Carolina, faith that the state will respond to the hopes and aspirations for distinction and finesse.

The last decade, though marked off as a unit, does not constitute an isolated period of endeavor or of accomplishments. The seeds sown in the past decade will mature in the next, and the next. President Chase wants to see the job further along, his physical self permitting. There is a future for the South—and for North Carolina—and the university president is in the midst of the fight to make of that future a civilization embracing cultural and educational qualities as well as material expansion.

That is the attitude which we like to take of the Chase decision. It is an attitude which calls North Carolina and university alumni everywhere to the task of building a finer university. A rededication to service and leadership—that's the significance of the Chase decision.—*The Alumni Review.*

REPORTS

THE BRITISH BOARD OF EDUCATION

The report of the Board of Education, with statistics of public education in England and Wales for 1928, has been issued. According to a summary in a recent issue of the London *Times* the board emphasizes the necessity of viewing the reorganization of schools, the reduction of the size of classes and the replacement and repair of defective school premises as parts of the same problem, and as a result of the steps taken throughout the country to deal with this problem the number of classes containing more than fifty pupils fell from 20,201 on March 31, 1927, to 16,686 on March

31, 1928, while during the year under review 277 schools were removed from the "black list" and plans were approved which will result in the replacement or satisfactory reconstruction of 349 further schools. Of the total number of schools on the "black list," about 1,000, or 35 per cent., have now been dealt with, or plans have been approved which will secure their removal from the lists.

In secondary education the year has been one of continued expansion. The number of schools recognized by the board, the number of pupils, the number of free places, the number of entrants and the number of successful candidates in the approved examinations, and the amount of advanced work all show a marked increase. Plans for approximately 10,000 new secondary school places have been approved during the year.

The year has been notable for the inception of a program of inquiries specially directed to education for commerce and industry. These inquiries take the form, on the one hand, of regional inquiries, such as the board have already undertaken in Yorkshire and which they have now undertaken in the Midlands, into the general organization of education for commerce and industry in the main industrial areas, and, on the other hand, of inquiries into education for particular branches of industry and commerce. Their object is to focus the requirements of industry and the various types of training designed to meet these requirements. The special subjects which have been selected for the first inquiries on these lines are education for salesmanship and education for the engineering group of industries. The success of this program will depend almost entirely upon the amount of cooperation which the board are able to secure from the representatives of commerce and industry. Advisory committees for these two inquiries have therefore been set up under the chairmanship of Mr. F. W. Goodenough and Sir Dugald Clerk, respectively.

The report devotes much attention to two circulars issued by the board to local education authorities last year on the subject of the school-leaving age and reorganization, which followed upon the representation of the Association of Education Committees, that the age of compulsory school attendance should be raised to fifteen in 1933, in accordance with the recommendation of the Consultative Committee on the Education of the Adolescent.

It is not possible to make any statistical estimate of the progress achieved, but during the twelve months ended March 31, 1928, there was a net increase of sixty-nine in the number of departments classified as senior, while the number of children in these departments increased by 11,069. This increase presents a genuine advance.

These figures take no account of the departments, such as many in rural areas, which, in addition to providing organized courses of instruction for pupils over eleven, also provide for children under that age. There is, however, no doubt that in rural areas considerable progress is being made with the concentration of the older children in groups sufficiently large to permit of a substantial measure of classification and greatly improved facilities for practical instruction. Evidence of the increased activity during the period is afforded by the fact that no less than 742 departments were affected by reorganization schemes during the year ended March 31, 1928, as compared with 550 in the previous year.

While the total number of children on the books of public elementary schools was substantially the same on March 31, 1928, as in the two preceding years, wide variations occurred in particular age groups. The fall in the birth-rate which followed the peak period 1919–20 is beginning to affect the number of infants in the schools. While the number of children aged five to eight on March 31, 1927, showed an increase over the previous year of about 186,000, the number on March 31, 1928, showed a fall of about 34,000.

The number of children over eleven on March 31, 1928, showed a decrease of nearly 90,000, which followed a decrease of about 60,000 in the previous year, and these decreases must be expected to continue until the effect of the high birth-rate immediately after the war begins to be felt. The number of children in voluntary attendance on March 31, 1928, was 54,227, which compares with 51,107 in the previous year, an increase of about 6 per cent.

SOCIETIES AND MEETINGS

THE ATLANTA MEETING OF THE NATIONAL EDUCATION ASSOCIATION[1]

President Lamkin is arranging to present a list of distinguished speakers at the sixty-seventh convention of the association, which meets in Atlanta, Georgia, from June 28 to July 4. The theme of the meeting will be "Education for a New World."

At the closing session on the morning of Independence Day, July 4, the speaker will be Arthur M. Hyde, Secretary of Agriculture of the United States. This session will be the inspirational climax of the convention week.

Among the outstanding people, both in and out of the teaching profession, to appear on the program, will be Lorado Taft, the Chicago sculptor, who will tell of the part to be played by art in developing the future citizen. "Education for the Vocations" will be presented by William Green, president of the American Federation of Labor, and J. C. Wright, director of the Federal Board for Vocational Education.

Prophecies for the future of teacher training in America will be discussed by Dean William F. Russell, Teachers College, Columbia University; Dean Shelton Phelps, George Peabody College for Teachers, Nashville, Tennessee; President W. P. Morgan, Western Illinois State Teachers College, and president of the North Central Association of Colleges and Secondary Schools.

"International Aspects of Education" will be presented by A. O. Thomas, president of the World Federation of Education Associations, and Madame Castellani, of Italy.

Among the other speakers who are to have prominent places on the program are Dean Walter Williams, school of journalism, University of Missouri, and president of the Press Conference of the World, whose subject is "As a Reporter Sees the New World"; William J. Bogan, superintendent of schools, Chicago; M. R. Trabue, University of North Carolina; Principal Robert R. Moton, Tuskegee Institute, Alabama; Lucy Gage, assistant professor of elementary education at George Peabody College, and Dean Anna P. MacVay, of Wadleigh High School, New York City, who will speak on "Vergil, Prophet of the New World." An outline of the program follows:

Friday, June 28. The opening session of the convention will be held at 7:30 P. M., in the Atlanta Auditorium. The speakers will be William John Cooper, United States Commissioner of Education, and Bishop Francis J. McConnell, president of the Federal Council of Churches of Christ in America. Registration will open at 8 A. M., Friday.

Saturday, June 29. In the morning there will be a general session. At 12 o'clock members of the state delegations will meet in their respective state headquarters to elect members of the board of directors of the National Education Association. At 2 o'clock delegates and others attending the convention will be guests of the citizens of Atlanta at a barbecue. At night there will be a program of negro music arranged by N. C. Newbold, chairman of the Committee to Cooperate with the National Association of Teachers in Colored Schools. The program will be given by students from Tuskegee Institute, Fiske University, Morehouse College and the Georgia College for Negroes.

Sunday, June 30. In the morning, churches throughout Georgia will give attention to the convention theme. Three hundred educators have been invited to occupy pulpits in the state on this day. In the afternoon at 4 o'clock there will be a vesper service with an address by a religious leader of national prominence.

Monday, July 1. The representative Assembly will hold its first session at 9 o'clock. At the same time there will be a meeting for those who are not delegates. Reports which will be presented before the Representative Assembly will include that of the Committees on Necrology, Ethics of the Profession, Retirement Allowances, and International Relations, and a preliminary report of the Committee on Appointment of Delegates and Kindred Questions. On Monday afternoon there will be meetings of the departments of the association.

Tuesday, July 2. On Tuesday morning there will be an open meeting of the Representative Assembly for all people attending the convention. At this session there will be reports of the special Committee of Ten by its chairman, Superintendent E. C. Broome, of Philadelphia; the Legislative Commission, and the Committee

[1] Preprinted from the *Journal* of the National Education Association, June, 1929.

on the Economic Status of the Teacher. There will be brief addresses by Howard R. Driggs, of New York University, and Principal Robert R. Moton, of Tuskegee. On Tuesday afternoon, departments will continue their meetings and at night there will be an outdoor pageant.

Wednesday, July 3. The third session of the Representative Assembly will hear the completed report of the Committee on Appointment of Delegates and Kindred Questions presented by A. L. Threlkeld, superintendent of schools, Denver, and the annual reports of the Secretary, Treasurer, Board of Trustees, Budget Committee and Board of Directors. The election of officers will be held on Wednesday. Simultaneously with the session of the Representative Assembly there will be a general session in one of the downtown churches. There will be department meetings in the afternoon and another general session at night.

Thursday, July 4. The closing session of the convention will be held on the morning of Independence Day. The speaker will be the Secretary of Agriculture of the United States, Arthur M. Hyde. Before adjournment at noon President Lamkin will introduce the new president of the National Education Association. Many delegates will leave on Thursday afternoon for New York, where they will sail on Saturday, July 6, for Europe to attend the conference of the World Federation of Education Associations at Geneva, Switzerland.

EDUCATIONAL RESEARCH AND STATISTICS

THE RELIABILITY OF SELF-SCORED MEASURES

APPROXIMATELY a year ago the writer reported in this journal[1] a study of the reliability of self-scored measures. An opportunity was presented during the past summer to repeat the experiment with another group and to make additional observations especially in relation to the mental level of the subjects who were unreliable.

The subjects were the members of a summer-school course in which it was possible to give a number of tests for the purpose of demonstration and incidentally determine the mental ability of the subjects. The group numbered fifty-six women and three men, ranged in age from twenty to fifty years, and had scholastic attainments ranging from the completion of the eighth grade to the master's degree.

The technique used to check the reliability of self-scored measures was similar to that of the previously reported experiment in which the subjects scored their own papers, except that the subjects were allowed only one half the time generally allowed for the completion of the test. The test used was the Ohio Literacy, which is a five-minute test of literacy requiring the subject to draw a line under the word "no" or the word "yes" indicating the answers to the questions. The usual instructions were given the subjects and time was called at the end of two and one half minutes. The papers were then collected and while the subjects were taking the Morgan test the literacy tests were removed from the room without their knowledge and the responses copied exactly by a group of trained workers. That is, all responses were copied and all blank items were indicated. This done they were returned to the room while the subjects were still busily engaged in the other test. At the conclusion of the Morgan test the class was told that they would be given an opportunity to score their own papers for the purpose of demonstrating a method of scoring tests. The literacy test papers were then returned to them and they were told, "I will read the correct answers to you. Please check the items that are incorrect. After your papers are marked I will show you how to compute the 'rights minus wrongs' score." The correct answers were then read very slowly. This was done in order to avoid confusion and also to give those who wished to change their papers a chance to do so. The papers were handed in at the end of the lecture hour. It is to be observed that no word of caution was given which would cause them not to change their responses nor were they urged to do so. In other words, in all respects this was a natural situation.

In making the study as to the reliability of this method of allowing the subject to score his

[1] SCHOOL AND SOCIETY, November 19, 1927.

own paper we did not take into account the inaccuracies of computing the final scores but only the changes that had been made by the individual. The test sheets were compared with the records of the initial responses. Two types of changes were possible: (1) erasing or otherwise eradicating an incorrect response in order to mark it correct, or, (2) the filling in of those that had been left blank. The results are shown in the following table.

TABLE SHOWING PERCENTAGE OF CHANGES

Number taking the test	59	100 per cent.
Number of papers unchanged	39	66 " "
Number of papers changed	20	34 " "

The degree of reliability is somewhat lower than the previously reported study when the

TEST RESULTS AS COMPARED TO RELIABILITY IN SCORING

x—indicates change in score.
o—indicates no change in score.

Morgan Test

Age score	Raw score							
11.8	60– 64	o						
12.4	65– 69							
12.9	70– 74							
13.5	75– 79	o						
14.0	80– 84	o	x					
14.6	85– 89							
15.1	90– 94	o	o					
15.7	95– 99							
16.2	100–104	o	o	o	x			
16.8	105–109	o	x					
17.3	110–114	o	o	o	o	x	x	x
17.9	115–119	o	o	o				
18.4	120–124	o	o	o	o	o	x	
19.	125–129	o	o	o	o	x	x	x
	130–134	o	o	o	x			
	135–139	o	o	x				
	140–144	o	o	x	x	x	x	
	145–149	o	o	o	x			
	150–154	x						
	155–159	o	x					
	160–164	o						
	165–169							
	170–174	o						
	175–179	x						
	180–184	o						

Median raw score 125

Number of changes below the median	7	12 per cent. of total
Number of changes above the median	13	22 per cent. of total

percentages of papers changed in the two groups reported were 29.5 and 24.5. In the previous experiment, however, one of the sections appeared in the experiment both times and the second time four individuals who had been unreliable the first time failed to change their scores. Had these four not had the opportunity to profit or repent the total number of papers changed in the group of fifty-three would have been seventeen instead of thirteen and the percentage would have risen from 24.5 to 32, which is quite comparable to the percentage of 34 found in this last experiment.

In an effort to determine "what manner of people are these" that change their scores or who are not reliable when the opportunity is given to score their own papers the Morgan test was used. The results are shown in the accompanying table.

The foregoing data clearly show that in this group of fifty-nine subjects there was a distinct tendency for the brighter ones in the group to change their scores when given the opportunity to do so. (It must be remembered that they were not given the opportunity to score their own Morgan tests!) This is shown by the fact that while seven cases who changed their score, being 12 per cent. of the total number, were below the median score, thirteen, or 22 per cent., approximately twice as many, were above the median.

The present study seems to warrant the conclusion that it is a characteristic trait for at least one in every four, if not one in every three, individuals to take advantage of the opportunity to present themselves in an inaccurate manner. It is certainly a fairly conclusive indictment of the practice of self-scoring and further leads us to conclude that the brighter individual is more than likely to be the offender.

LLOYD N. YEPSEN

THE TRAINING SCHOOL AT
VINELAND, NEW JERSEY

SCHOOL AND SOCIETY

EDITED BY J. McKEEN CATTELL

WITH WHICH IS COMBINED THE

EDUCATIONAL REVIEW

EDITED BY WILLIAM McANDREW

Volume XXIX | SATURDAY, JUNE 1, 1929 | Number 753

THE STATE AND THE STATE UNIVERSITY[1]

By Dr. MELVIN A. BRANNON

CHANCELLOR OF THE UNIVERSITY OF MONTANA

THE state and the state university have the relationship of an organism and one of its important organs. The state is a social institution composed of people who function politically for the welfare of citizens and for the protection of their economic, social, cultural and political possessions. The state university is an institution organized by the state and charged with the responsibility of directing higher education. It is specifically commissioned to develop and improve the advanced training of youth in social-mindedness, in accurate and sustained thinking and in dependable behavior in all human relations.

The political functions of the state and the educational functions of the state university have become highly differentiated and multiplied in this high-powered and intensively industrialized age. The state has become engaged in far-reaching programs of good health, highway building, exploitation and conservation of natural resources, regulation of business, elementary, secondary and higher education, and extension of activities in the legislative, judicial and executive branches of government. The state university has amplified highly diversified courses of study, multiplied professional schools, admitted armies of students, engaged in extensive projects of adult education and conducted intensive research in the natural sciences, medicine, engineering and many other subjects for the purpose of extending the bounds of knowledge.

The extensive and intensive activities undertaken by the state and the state university are in part responses made to requests and mandates of society and in part self-initiated and self-imposed. The benefits derived from this enlarged public service of the state and its state university have not been uniformly satisfactory to that mythical person "the average citizen." He has developed frequently the antithetic attitude of demanding on the one hand ever-increasing service from the state and the state university and on the other a reduction of financial support. His slogan is "More Service, Less Taxation." This state of mind is due to political illiteracy, to emotional desires to enjoy luxuries far above the economic level of the antithetic individual, and perhaps most of all to his inability to evaluate correctly the significance and cost of the functions which he accepts casually and even demands from the state and the state university. This antithetic and prejudiced attitude of mind is a definite condition and not a theory. It can be changed and corrected somewhat by

[1] Address of the president of the National Association of State Universities.

three types of service which the state university alone can render: first, adult education in the fundamentals of government and higher education; second, determination of causes and cures of huge wastages endured apathetically by an uninformed public; and third, development of inclusive fiscal policies by the state.

Very few people to-day have a clear idea of the structure and functions of the state and the state university. From their viewpoint the state is a mythical agent which possesses the power to make people virtuous and economically independent by means of legislation. The more laws enacted, the more individual responsibility passed on "to George," the better will be the social and economic status of every citizen. They regard the state as a mythical Santa Claus who bestows liberal gifts and pays for them from mythical wealth. They view the state university as the place where social salvation is provided by fraternities, and physical insurance and entertainment are provided by proxy vested in the "Great God Football." High scholarship and intellectual development do not bulk large with many "patrons" of state universities. They believe that "exposure" to learning is all that is necessary to have it "take." Under these circumstances the indubitable reaction of society to increasing costs of state and state university functions is one of active resistance. The uninformed and the unthinking citizen does not know and does not admit that his failure to receive benefits from highly organized state and state university service is largely subjective. Because this is true there is a growing and an imperative need of extended and continuous adult education relative to the structure and functions of the state and the state university. This is the most important kind of extension work that a state university can perform.

The average citizen's subjective difficulty and his slogan "More Service, Less Taxation" do not explain all of the adverse criticism and increasing resistance to the adequate financial support of the state and the state university. Even intelligent publicity regarding greatly increased service rendered by the state and the state university in response to the demands of society may not alter greatly the growing opposition to increasing taxation. There is an imperative need for intensive investigation of the economic problems which burden society to-day. Suppose that research should be undertaken which would show the causes and cures of great wastage in economic power in both state and nation, is it not reasonable that the public, *i.e.*, the average citizen, and the operator in big business would register appreciation in providing increased economic power for the research agency? Surely the beneficiaries of great savings would share their benefits with their benefactors. I believe it is the high function of the state university to examine minutely the huge wastes now accepted by society apathetically and to point the way to scientific savings. This is an inherent responsibility of the state university. Moreover, it is one of the logical solutions of its financial problems.

In a discussion of state universities in 1921 President Kinley said:

> Properly regarded, a state university with its teaching, extension and research work, constitutes a division of the state, using that word in the sense of the people organized for the performance of political, economic, and other activities that have to do with their life as a group. We have provided in a legal and constitutional theory for a legislative arm of the government, for a judicial arm, and for an executive arm. Nowhere in our system is there any provision for what I may call the developmental arm or agency of the state. Such an agency is one whose work is to search out the paths the people must follow in order to progress; to discover how the culture of the people, using that phrase to include the totality of their life activities, may be improved; to find new truths and new ways which will make it possible for the people at large to attain a

higher life, economically, socially, intellectually, culturally. The state university is, therefore, the fourth division or arm of the state, organized by the state although it is not categorically so recognized. It is fundamental to all the rest, so far as concerns the necessity of depending on positive legislation for the crystallization of progress. We must look to the state university as the agency which will open up new worlds of truth on which to base legislation (Transactions and Proceedings, Nat. Assn. State Universities, 29: 108–109).

The suggestion that the state university function as the fourth arm of the state, particularly in regard to research, is sagacious and appealing. The causes of growing taxation, the devices for alleviating those causes, and the technique for securing more adequate returns from the expenditures of public revenues demand the efficient, continuous service of highly trained and technical research workers. All these problems are complex and critical. Their solution is necessary not only for the well-being of society but also for the release of adequate revenues required for the support of the state and the state university. We have definitely reached the limit of the procedure expressed by the slogan "More Service, Less Taxation."

There is an old dictum that the two most certain things in the world are death and taxation. No way has been discovered whereby either may be escaped. Scientific research has, however, during the last two decades, pushed the life curve upward many years. During the same decades comparatively little has been done to develop a just and scientific program of taxation. The situation has been made more serious, of course, by the colossal costs of the World War and by the release of mechanical power equivalent to 175 slaves for every man, woman and child in America. The release of this mechanical energy has produced a congestion of population in great industrial centers. It has caused the concentration of enormous wealth in the hands of a few. During these recent years there has been an increase in population as well as in wealth. One would suppose that the distribution of the tax burden among more and more people would cause a lowering of costs to the individual. This is not true. Taxes have advanced in greater proportion than has the population. Moreover, it is reckoned by tax experts of this country that the distribution of the taxes has been shifted from those of great wealth, those who have the ability to pay, to the great middle classes. In many industrial centers the average man is forced to work one fourth of his time to pay his taxes, directly and indirectly, and when he has paid for the housing, the clothing and feeding of his family an inadequate amount is left for the purchase of education, for the comforts which the family enjoy and the accumulation of revenues for his non-producing years. Speaking on this subject Dr. Wilbur C. Abbot, of Harvard University, has asserted that:

The danger exists not only in the field of economics but in that of politics. That danger is greater because it is more insidious. Much of our recent taxation has three great evils ingeniously combined into one system. It is not merely excessive. It has led to ridiculous and pernicious extravagance in so-called public works and public service by the ignorant and incompetent or, still more, the self-seeking activities of local, state, and even national legislators. It has done much to increase the cost of life, to establish the vicious circle of higher wages to meet higher prices, and higher prices to meet higher wages. Worse still, it bears most heavily upon the class of relatively fixed and moderate income. It does not touch those below that scale, and in no inconsiderable degree it is evaded by men of large wealth, anxious and able to escape the punitive, even confiscatory taxes laid on them. Through the popular device of non-taxable securities, established in most instances by the very local and state authorities which increase the borrowings, the expenditure and consequently the taxes, of their communities, the burden is shifted from the shoulders of great holdings to those of the farmer, the small business man, the professional elements and the householders. The result, unless this movement is checked, will undoubtedly be the creation of another kind of "proletarian dictatorship"—the great fortunes, the officeholders, the "privileged," and between them and the non-taxpaying masses the taxpaying middle class will be crushed out of existence. Such are the fears of many men alarmed by the present trend of events in the economic as well as the political world.

Service to remedy these serious economic, social and political ills may be rendered by the state university in connection with the study of present great public wastages and in the formation of an inclusive fiscal policy for the state. The determination of causes and cures of the huge wastes complacently endured by society will require long and intensive investigation by research workers. The wastes may be classified under three heads—first, those concerned with duplication, inefficiency and unscientific administration in states and state universities; second, those concerned with preventable diseases, reproduction of the unfit, and crime control; third, those associated with scientific methods of taxation and the allocation of state and federal revenues to the various state agencies in proportion to their relative value. Continuous and intensive research is superlatively needed in these three groups of subjects. Inasmuch as the state work is done largely by elective officers, whose tenure is subject to political turnover, it is obvious that continuity of service is rarely possible. On the other hand, state universities emphasize and secure continuity of service. Consequently, it is logical that difficult research work should be delegated to highly trained economists, sociologists and statistical engineers in state universities. In this way only can adequate information, acid-proof, be obtained, analyzed and made available for the public. The average taxpayer has slight understanding of such terms as "economic power," "cost and importance of public service," "efficiency, and real economy in social and political operations" and kindred economic measurements. Research and the interpretation of research in these and other public matters are essential for the enlightenment and guidance of society. The research relative to duplication, inefficiency and unscientific administration in government probably should be done largely by state and federal commissions. The efficiency problems of state universities must be solved largely by the president and a group of economic, educational and statistical specialists selected to function with his business officers, his advisers and himself.

Much research concerned with preventable diseases has been done already by universities and commissions of specialists. The U. S. Department of Commerce, boards of health and specialists in epidemiology have made exhaustive studies relative to preventable diseases. Herbert Hoover, when commissioner of commerce and labor, reported that preventable diseases caused an annual loss in the United States of $1,000,000,000. He made it clear that this huge wastage might be prevented if all citizens could be properly educated in positive health programs and persuaded to live them. This huge annual loss of $1,000,000,000 should be avoided for the release of productive energy in our economic and social relations.

The control of the reproduction of the unfit demands intensive research in eugenics, sociology and political science. Monumental work has already been done in these subjects by university specialists. Society, however, has been apathetic and complacent in regard to this great and growing burden of taxation. It is estimated that there are 10,000,000 feeble-minded persons in America. A very large percentage of them are free to reproduce themselves without let or hindrance. In some of the older states it is estimated that nearly one half of the public revenues is now used to care for the defectives and the delinquents. To these millions spent by the older commonwealths must be added many millions more spent by younger states of the Union; and the tide of cost is ever rising. Unless an early solution of this problem is reached we shall have a reversal of a sound economic program. Society will be taxed more heavily for the lowest than for the highest classes.

The wastages incident to the growing crime wave in America accent the need of far-reaching research in sociology, political science and their application to government. It has been estimated that the annual cost of crime in this country is not far from $10,000,000,000, covering loot of about $3,500,000,000 and $6,500,000,000 as police, insurance, prosecuting and prison charges, together with the economic loss in man power. Accepting these figures as reasonably correct, the cost of crime to each inhabitant of the United States is $83 a year. Charles R. Holden, president of the Chicago Crime Commission, made this remarkable statement regarding the activities of the underworld in that city:

> Chicago could afford to pay its 30,000 crooks not less than $20,000 a year each to retire from business or go elsewhere. If we could do that, the expenditure of $600,000,000 would be no greater than the cost of crime to Chicago under present conditions.

The wastages due to mismanagement and wasteful operation of publicly supported institutions, preventable diseases, reproduction of the unfit, and crime are so great that they threaten the perpetuity of the nation—even as rich and powerful as the United States is.

Adult education in citizenship, government and the services of higher education is important; research in the causes and cure of wastages in connection with administration of state and state universities, preventable diseases, reproduction of defectives and the control of crime has tremendous importance and value. Basic, however, is the research requisite for the formation of a scientific, inclusive fiscal policy for the state and the state university. The term "inclusive fiscal policy" signifies, first, a correct evaluation of all state activities; second, a determination of the economic power of the state; third, the equitable allocation of that power to the proportional needs of the various state activities. To be specific, an inclusive fiscal policy for any state requires primarily a careful evaluation of the needs of the governmental activities performed by the legislative, judicial and executive branches of the state government, and a sharp and scientific measure of the needs of the departments concerned with public health, highway construction, conservation and development of natural resources, elementary, secondary and higher education, and such other activities as the people elect. It requires next exact research to determine the real economic power of the commonwealth. This economic power is, of course, measured by two major factors: (a) the accumulated wealth, and (b) the annual income of the state. It requires finally additional exact research to determine the equitable allocation of the taxes assessed against the state's economic power to the various state activities. Thus far there have been developed no precision units for measuring the exact value of definite state services. Many of them at present lie entirely within the field of approximation. Moreover, the relative values change from year to year and they are different in different states. Because these are facts it would be a distinctive service if the state university would do the research work concerned with developing an inclusive fiscal policy for the commonwealth, and clearly interpret its findings to the public and particularly to the governor and the members of the legislature.

During the past year the University of Montana, under the able leadership of President Charles H. Clapp, of the state university unit, has conducted a statistical survey of twelve western and Rocky Mountain states. Efforts were made to determine the extent to which each of the twelve states had developed its various state activities, how it had taxed its economic power and how it had allocated its revenues to the various activities of the state. It was discovered that not one of these twelve western and Rocky Mountain states had developed an *inclusive fiscal policy.* This means that not a single state had made a searching survey, first of the value and relative importance of each of its state activities, such as departments in the general state government, public health, charities, corrections and pensions, agriculture and conservation, highways, public schools, higher education, and miscellaneous activities. Not a single state had adopted a scientific method of taxation based upon a study of its economic power, measured in terms of accumulated wealth and current income. Consequently no one of the states was assessing taxes on the fundamental basis of ability or power to pay. Moreover, not a single state had made scientific investigations of the difficult problem of allocating state revenues to respective state activities in proportion to their importance and value to the state. True, so-called budget commissions are operating in most of these states, but their functions seem to be confined to recording the requests of the competing directors of the various state activities.

The negative exhibit relative to the development of an inclusive fiscal policy in our twelve northwestern and Rocky Mountain states led to a nation-wide inquiry. Extended correspondence from New York to California revealed the fact that no state had developed an inclusive fiscal policy. The nearest approach seems to have been made by Pennsylvania. In that state, under the directorship of Governor Pinchot, there was developed an efficient budget commission with Dr. Clyde L. King, of the Wharton School of Finance and Commerce of the University of Pennsylvania, acting as secretary of the commonwealth and the budget officer. This budget commission prepared for Governor Pinchot and the state legislature of Pennsylvania a remarkable and voluminous report. The commission proposed estimated expenditures from all sources for the biennium 1925–27 of $211,154,000. The Pennsylvania budget project is worthy of the careful study of all state and state university administrators. I had been referred to Dr. King's work as a result of correspondence with President Jessup. I found that although Pennsylvania does not have an inclusive fiscal policy as I have defined it its procedure is a marked step in advance. You will be interested in Dr. King's response to my inquiry.

In actual practice each state executive came to the budget officer to present his own claims. As a matter of actual working out within the Pinchot cabinet, the department of welfare came to know and understand the needs of the department of agriculture, and so with all the members of the cabinet. And it became quite possible so to present the needs of one department to another department head that all became satisfied in their own minds that under all circumstances the best possible had been done for each department. This was peculiarly true under a Pinchot cabinet united by his high standards and fine personality, but I think it would usually work out in some such fashion. The responsibility rested directly with the department head on the one hand, and the budget officer acting for the governor on the other.

I do not think that competition is particularly harmful. I wanted department heads to state vigorously and completely their exact needs so that I could go as far as possible in reaching those needs, and at the same time I have known one department to say to the budget officer that the needs of another department were sufficiently recognized so that the department would be ready to acquiesce in smaller sums in that department, and I believe that that type of cooperation can be gotten under certain types of governor-personalities, while with other types, of course, it can not be gotten. And hence in final analyses, the responsibility must rest with each agency on the one hand, and the governor on the other.

It may be Utopian to propose that the state university function in the research work requisite for the formation of an inclusive fiscal policy in the state. That is a matter for each state university to determine for itself. It is obvious, of course, that the same inclusive fiscal policy will not be suitable for all states. Indeed, it will be necessary to vary it in any one state from biennium to biennium. It would also be necessary to develop a technique for presenting in a wholly non-partisan and judicial manner the results of such research, first to the people of the commonwealth and then to the governor and to the legislature. If the work is done in the proper way and the correct technique is employed, the project seems to me entirely feasible and highly desirable. Some of my respondents definitely questioned whether an inclusive fiscal policy would be effective with any governor and with any legislature. No one can answer that question in the abstract; but if the state university does the research work in the three fundamentals of determining: first, the relative value of different state activities; second, correct and fair methods of assessing the economic power of the state; and third, procedure for allocating the economic power of the state to each state activity; and if the results of such research are presented to a survey commission, the personnel of which is chosen by the leading industrial, professional, economic and social organizations within the state, it is quite certain that the governor and the legislature would welcome and utilize such service surveys.

The problem of adequately financing state universities can not be solved always by the use of state resources alone. The theory of American democracy rests upon the ideal that educational opportunities shall be equalized for all children within the state and within the nation. Unhappily this theory is largely ignored by most of the states and by the federal government. In recent years one notable effort was made by the federal government to equalize educational opportunities among the different states. The legislation relative to agricultural extension, the so-called Smith-Lever law, provided for a larger distribution of federal aid to the southern states than to the more highly economically developed northern states. Clearly, this was a move in the right direction, if democracy rests upon the idea that educational opportunity should be equalized in every commonwealth of the nation. Indeed, it may well be urged that the federal government should make larger contributions to certain states in order to equalize opportunities for higher education. The land-grant colleges and the agricultural experiment stations receive approximately the same amounts from the federal government in every state which has these educational units. In commonwealths where the state university is separated from the land-grant college it is sometimes a question whether the aid of the federal government to land-grant colleges does not exaggerate rather than diminish the inequalities of higher educational opportunities. Those of you who are presidents of separate state universities definitely raise the question at times whether the federal government ought not to increase its efforts to equalize higher educational opportunities and grant aid to projects that belong legitimately to the state university.

Apropos of this discussion, it is interesting to recall certain statements which President Coolidge made in his budget address to Congress on December 7, 1927. Speaking on the subject of federal aid to the states, he said:

> I am including in this budget an estimate of $1,108,000 for the promotion of the welfare and hygiene of maternity and infancy. I refer to this estimate for two reasons. The first is that the authorization for this appropriation expires with the fiscal year 1929. The second is that it

marks the termination of federal contribution to a project which is for state control and administration. The extension for two years of the provisions of the act for the promotion of the welfare and hygiene of maternity and infancy was approved with the understanding that its administration during these two added years would be with a view to the discontinuance of federal aid thereafter. Six years of experience under the able administration that has characterized the government's policy warrants this permanent withdrawal of federal aid, assured that the states are now or should be able to carry on this work without aid or interference from the federal government.

This opens up the whole subject of state aid, which despite frequent warnings continues strongly intrenched in federal operations. While the amount of money taken annually from the federal treasury for subsidies to states is not inconsiderable, the dangers inherent in the policy are of far greater importance. To relieve the states of their just obligations by resort to the federal treasury in the final result is hurtful rather than helpful to the state, and unfair to the payers of national taxes. To tempt the states by federal subsidies to sacrifice their vested rights is not a wholesome practice no matter how worthy the object to be attained. Federal interference in state functions can never be justified as a permanent continuing policy even if, which is doubtful, such interference is warranted by emergent conditions as a temporary expedient. As shown in the maternity and infancy act, when once the government engages in such an enterprise it is almost impossible to terminate its connection therewith. We should not only decidedly refuse to countenance additional federal participation in state-aid projects, but should make careful study of all our activities of that character with a view to curtailing them.

President Coolidge spoke as a Jeffersonian Democrat and not as a Hamiltonian Republican. Clearly, he did not take into consideration two interesting phenomena, one economic, the other political. In economics it is recognized that the great additions to our national wealth have come through the wise and able direction of machinecraft in the elaboration of raw into manufactured materials. Through these industrial activities the value of raw materials has been augmented tens and hundreds of times. Consequently great industrial centers have become the centers of immense wealth and very dominant political control. The phenomenal growth of Detroit and other manufacturing centers is convincing evidence of this fact. This great accumulation of wealth in manufacturing centers has been further stimulated through the consolidation of great banking interests. Judge Brandeis, of the U. S. Supreme Court, in his book "Other People's Money and How the Banks Use It," showed the amazing concentration and centralization of economic power. He made clear that many banking industries and railroad interests were controlled by two closely associated New York banks and pointed out that one great financial institution held more than seventy directorates in nearly five hundred of the largest corporations in America. This was a situation set up in a book written more than ten years ago, and does not adequately represent the enormous centralization of wealth in the United States to-day. Only recently, according to press reports, two Chicago banks were consolidated with the resulting capital of over a billion dollars. President Coolidge in his budget address may or may not have had these economic facts in mind. The political phenomenon which President Coolidge ignored is the impotency of the state, with its constitutional limitations and its limiting sovereignty, to control and direct huge economic resources which are interstate in function. Such control and direction can be exercised only by a centralized political power free from the limitation of state boundaries and state rights. Research in the fields of economics and politics should be undertaken in two phenomena—centralization of enormous wealth in industrial centers which receive raw materials from distant states, and the release of great corporations from taxes in many states by reason of state boundaries.

Taxation in states and in the nation has followed very much the same type of development that Topsy claimed for her biological history. It has "just growed" and it has grown without symmetry. Without question there has been and there is excessive taxation in the interest of officialdom in states and in the nation. This should cease. Possessors of great wealth have escaped taxation by the use of tax-exempt securities and the use of the archaic system of taxing personal property. This is in no sense an indictment of great wealth. It merely accents the need of research in social and political affairs, state and national, comparable in quality and quantity with that used in our twentieth century industry. The federal government with its centralized power is the only agency which may function as collector of excess profits and distribute them to the various communities and commonwealths which lack the resources necessary for social, educational and political equality.

The constitution of this association declares that the purpose of this association shall be the consideration of questions relating to the promotion of higher education in all its forms in the universities of the several states of the Union and the discussion and prosecution of such questions and plans as may tend to make more efficient in their work the institutions included in the membership of the association.

Might it not be in harmony with the purpose of the constitution of the association, with the record of its past achievements and with the numerous requests for organized, continuous working programs to establish a council on research? Such a council could correlate and encourage the work of research specialists in our state university departments of economics, sociology and political sciences. It could render great assistance, first, in searching for the cause and cure of the present huge economic and social wastages; second, in the development of an inclusive fiscal policy for the state; and third, in securing better cooperation from the federal government in the effort to equalize opportunities for higher education in each state and in the nation.

EDUCATIONAL EVENTS

OVERSTUDY IN FRENCH SCHOOLS

THE Paris correspondent of the *Journal* of the American Medical Association writes that Dr. Dufestel, head physician of the schools of the city of Paris and of the department of the Seine, recently made statements that attracted considerable attention, on the dangers of overstudy among young pupils, owing to the overloading of the curriculum. Statistics show that great harm to the general health often results from overstudy, at an age when neither bodily nor mental development has been completed. By multiplying the number of subjects in the curriculum, the number of teachers claiming a large part of a pupil's time has been increased. Now-a-days, a child often spends more than eight hours at school, and, in addition, has home work to do, which further increases the duration of his intellectual toil. The eight-hour law, which legislation has imposed on adult workmen, should be, for even greater reasons, applied to the child.

Dr. Dufestel thinks that four hours a day is a sufficiently long study period, and that the rest of the time at school should be devoted to games, physical training and sports. Medical examination of those children who are subjected to overstudy brings out, every year, a considerable proportion of weakly subjects, many being anemic with a poorly developed chest, while from 30 to 40 per cent. may be regarded as being in a pretuberculous state. These facts are known, and an endeavor is made to remedy the evil by creating open-air schools. These have given excellent results. In addition, numerous philanthropic societies organize vacation outings at the seashore, in summer, extending over from three to four weeks. The children return considerably improved in health, and showing good gains in height and weight. But these results are not maintained for more than two or three months. A better solution, according to Dr. Dufestel, would be to reduce the number of class hours; that is to say, the number of hours spent in the classrooms, by ceasing to overload the curriculum and by giving fuller recognition to the logical law of pedagogy that the attendance at school has not as its basis the idea of teaching a child everything, but to develop his brain, through appropriate training, to a point where he can learn readily when he quits the public school and begins to acquire the special knowledge needed for the career to which he plans to devote himself.

THE EYESIGHT OF LONDON CHILDREN

The National Society for the Prevention of Blindness gives a report of the School Medical Officer of London, England, for 1927, indicating that during 1927 there were 193,876 children in the elementary schools medically inspected. It was found "that 51.1 per cent. of the boys and 52.9 per cent. of the girls at the age of eight years failed to pass the test for normal vision; the corresponding figures for 1926 were 51.9 per cent. and 54.7 per cent. for boys and girls, respectively. Among 12-year-old children, 43.2 per cent. of boys and 46.6 per cent. of girls failed, corresponding with 42.2 per cent. and 46.3 per cent. in the previous year.

While a larger proportion of the children attain normal vision at the age of 12 years than at the age of 8, the number with severe defect increases between those years. At age 8, among boys, 17.7 per cent. have severe defect, which is increased to 20.4 per cent. at age 12; among girls, 18.4 per cent. at the earlier age with severe defect increased to 21.5 per cent. at age 12. Owing to increased attention to sight saving in the schools, the prohibition of sewing in poor light and modification of the curriculum in favor of those with poor sight, the much severer incidence of visual defect upon girls than boys is no longer so marked as it was before school medical inspection became general.

Dr. McVail reports that the total number of children now being taught under sight-saving conditions is thirty-seven (thirty-two girls and five boys). All are inspected at school every six months, and although a much longer time must elapse before any definite opinion can be formed as to the results of secondary school education on the eyes of myopes, the scheme has so far been successful. In most cases the myopia has, within the year, remained practically stationary, and in no case has there been any significant increase. Even under sight-saving conditions some children head their forms and the social benefits derived are equally desirable for children whether their aim is scholastic or non-scholastic. The main difficulty has so far been concerned with home occupation. No home lessons are allowed, but some children, mostly of high ability, admit to reading at home. Myopic children in secondary schools are not the only offenders in using their eyes for close work when unsupervised, and attention is not infrequently drawn to children in ordinary myope classes who read or do crossword puzzles at home, though the temptation is greater among the more intelligent.

THE WORLD CONGRESS ON LIBRARIES AND BIBLIOGRAPHIES

The Christian Science Monitor states that following a decision taken by the International Committee of Librarians, which met in Edinburgh in September of last year, the first World Congress on Libraries and Bibliographies will be held in Rome during the second half of June.

In addition to about 100 official delegates representing 32 states, Rome expects to welcome several thousand librarians and book lovers from all parts of the world, attracted to Italy by the half-fare railway rates offered by the Italian government to participants in the congress, and by the exhibitions and other ceremonies to be held in different parts of Italy in connection with this congress.

The main object of the congress is to determine the most suitable means, from an international standpoint, for following more closely the progress made in culture in different countries.

The official delegates and other participants in the congress will visit the principal libraries, public and private, of Italy as well as of the leading universities. Several Italian cities are planning special exhibitions to attract the librarians and their friends.

In Venice, for instance, the librarians will see a special exhibition of 100 of Italy's best specimens of book binding; in the library of Monte Cassino they will examine the great number of priceless manuscripts that have been in possession of the monks since the middle ages; at Bologna they will visit one of the most renowned musical libraries in the world, and in Florence they will be shown several libraries, rich with old books and manuscripts and rare first editions.

EDUCATIONAL MEASURES BEFORE THE MASSACHUSETTS LEGISLATURE

THE Ways and Means Committee has reported to the House of Representatives resolves for an investigation of the adequacy of the teachers' annuity fund and of the need of increasing educational requirements. The former was voted in place of a bill filed on petition of John F. Scully for the Massachusetts Teachers' Federation. The resolve reads as follows:

Resolved, The department of education on behalf of the teachers' retirement board is hereby directed to investigate the adequacy of the teachers' annuity fund for teachers retired under Section 10, Chapter 32 of the General Laws, and to make such recommendations as may be necessary to provide for past and future deficits in said fund; also the necessary changes in the teachers' retirement law so that the pensions of teachers retiring in the future shall be substantially the same amount as the anticipated pensions which they have been encouraged to expect under the actuarial tables which have been previously used.

Said department shall report the results of its investigation, including the sum necessary, if any, to make up the deficits in the annuity fund as of December 31, 1929, and drafts of legislation to carry into effect its recommendations relative to deficits and future retirement allowances for teachers by filing said report, on or before December 15 in the current year, with the clerk of the House of Representatives.

The resolve in place of the bill for part-time attendance in public schools of employed minors between the age of fourteen and sixteen years reads as follows:

Resolved, That an unpaid special commission, to consist of seven persons to be appointed by the governor, including persons familiar with the labor, industrial and educational conditions and needs of the Commonwealth, is hereby established to study the general question of increasing the educational requirements of the Commonwealth, including the subject-matter of so much of the address of His Excellency the Governor, printed as current Senate document number one, as relates thereto, and of current House documents numbers two hundred and sixty-six and twelve hundred and sixty-three. Said commission in the course of its study shall consider the effect of any legislation recommended by it upon the textile and other basic industries of the Commonwealth, the opportunities for children under sixteen years of age in part-time employment and the extent to which they are now employed, the ability of parents to maintain their children while attending school for any recommended increased period and the cost to the Commonwealth and to the cities and towns thereof of carrying out any recommendations. Said commission may call upon the Department of Education, other departments, commissions and officers of the Commonwealth and of the several counties and municipalities for such information as may be needed in the course of its study.

A FORENSIC HONOR SOCIETY

ROY NEWTON, instructor in psychology and coach of debating at Ferris Institute, Big Rapids, Michigan, was elected national president of Phi Rho Pi, national honorary forensic society for junior colleges, at the first national convention held at Grand Rapids, Michigan, on May 4. Other officers elected were R. R. Pfeiffer, debate coach at Crane Junior College of Chicago, vice-president; Rolland Shackson, debate coach at Grand Rapids Junior College, national secretary-treasurer; Joseph Sherry, student at Grand Rapids Junior College, national student representative.

Phi Rho Pi was founded in 1928 by Professor Rolland Shackson, of Grand Rapids Junior College. Its purpose is to promote the interests of debating, oratory, extemporaneous speaking and other forensic activity in the junior colleges of the United States, by affording a means of fellowship and cooperation among them, and by rewarding their deserving candidates with badges of distinction, graduated according to achievement. Phi Rho Pi is neither a secret society nor a social fraternity, but strictly an honor society, and is thus unaffected by anti-fraternity legislation. Merit alone determines membership.

By May 12, 1929, nine chapters had been established and charters granted. They are distributed geographically as follows: two in Michigan, two in Illinois, one in Kansas, one in Minnesota, one in West Virginia, one in Texas and one in California.

THE HARVARD COUNCIL ON HISPANO-AMERICAN STUDIES

There has recently been established at Harvard University the Harvard Council on Hispano-American Studies. It has on it representatives not only of Harvard, to which belong Professors Whittem and Rivera as well as the director of the council, but also of Boston University (Professor Waxman), of Stanford University (Professor Coester), of the University of California (Professor Torres-Rioseco), of George Washington University (Professor Doyle), and of the University of North Carolina (Professor Leavitt).

All members of the council have been for some time in immediate contact with issues concerning the literature of the Hispano-American lands, and several of them have already published the results of research that they have made. The council as a whole is now proceeding to prepare a complete bibliography of the literature of the New World in both Spanish and Portuguese. While *belles-lettres* is the prime consideration, it is the intention of the council to include also all possible items of the domain of political and economic history and of the fine arts; in fact it is hoped to make a complete record of printed books and articles and of manuscripts that concern the life of Hispanic America since the early days of discovery and colonization.

The headquarters of the council will be at Harvard University, but it has been deemed wise to divide the work among the members of the council in the following way. Professor Coester holds himself responsible for items concerning the Argentine, Uruguay and Paraguay; Professor Leavitt will deal with Peru, Bolivia and Colombia; Professor Doyle will care for Central America; Professor Torres-Rioseco will account for Chile and Mexico; Professor Waxman has the Spanish West Indies and Venezuela as his province; Professor Ford, Professor Whittem and Professor Rivera will gather information regarding Cuba, Ecuador, Porto Rico and Brazil.

It is the hope of the council that all persons in this country interested in the history of Hispano-American culture will lend their support to this enterprise by contributing to it all items of information in their control and by calling the purposes of the council to the attention of useful agencies in Hispanic America.

THE BUREAU OF PUBLIC PERSONNEL ADMINISTRATION

Affiliation of the Bureau of Public Personnel Administration, a national organization representing civil service commissioners of the United States and Canada, with the University of Chicago is announced. The affiliation is said to be in furtherance of the university's plan to make its resources in the social sciences and its force of investigators available for the betterment of government.

Other steps in this program recently announced have been the establishment of a center for research in crime, headed by Chief August Vollmer, of Berkeley, California, and affiliation with the International City Managers' Association. All three projects will be closely related with the university's local community research committee, which has been using the City of Chicago as a research "laboratory" for the past three years.

The Bureau of Public Personnel Administration was founded in 1922, and for some years operated as a unit of the Institute for Government Research in Washington. In 1926 it became an independent organization, and in 1928 it was made the official secretariat for the Civil Service Assembly, the national organization representing the civil service commissioners of the United States and Canada. Organization of the bureau followed recognition of the need for competent personnel in the public service, and the necessity for scientific methods of determining personnel standards.

The bureau has drafted, at the request of legislative bodies, civic agencies and other organizations, suggestions for legislation which would provide the authority and machinery necessary for effective personnel administration. The bureau, however, does no lobbying, nor does it attempt to push legislation. Tests have also been developed for the selection of qualified employees for various classes of positions, such as policemen, firemen, food inspectors, playground supervisors, plumbers, electricians and other skilled trades. Numerous classification and compensation studies of positions intended to provide the basic machinery for a scientific treatment of personnel problems involving tests and other means of recruiting employees, service ratings and salary adjustments have been made.

Control of the bureau is vested in a board of trustees, who at present are William G. Rice, chairman, commissioner of the New York State Civil Service Commission; Charles P. Messick, chief examiner and secretary, New Jersey State Civil Service Commission, and Oliver C. Short, state employment commissioner, Baltimore, Maryland. Support of the bureau comes partly from public appropriations and partly from private contributions. The director of the bureau is Fred Telford, a graduate of the University of Chicago and the American University, Washington, D. C. Mr. Telford will continue to direct the work, and has also been appointed lecturer in political science at the University of Chicago.

THE DEPARTMENT OF PHILOSOPHY AT THE UNIVERSITY OF SOUTHERN CALIFORNIA

THE corner-stone of the Seeley Wintersmith Mudd Memorial Hall of Philosophy, which is being erected at the University of Southern California as a memorial to Colonel Mudd, Los Angeles mining engineer and patron of philosophy, was laid on May 16 in the presence of representatives of several hundred persons, including representatives from California universities and the American Philosophical Association. At a convocation following the laying of the corner-stone addresses were made by Dr. Robert A. Millikan, president of the American Association for the Advancement of Science, whose topic was "Three Elements in Human Progress," and by Dr. Ralph Tyler Flewelling, chairman of the philosophy faculty of the University of Southern California, who spoke on "Why a School of Philosophy?"

Announcement was made at the convocation of the elevation of the department of philosophy to the rank of a school in which special attention will be paid to graduate work in philosophy. Twenty-four persons who have been active in the advancement of the university's work in philosophy were named as honorary founders and fellows. The permanent appointment of Dr. F. C. S. Schiller, of Corpus Christi College, Oxford University, as professor of philosophy was announced. Dr. Schiller will divide his academic year between Oxford and Southern California.

In his convocation address Dr. Millikan cited as three great ideas that have been of stupendous influence in human progress the idea of the Golden Rule, which he considered the sum and substance of Christianity; the law of causation, which forms the basis of all modern scientific progress, and the idea of evolution of growth, without which there can be no interpretation of history or scientific or ethical progress.

Edmund Howard Hollands, professor of philosophy at the University of Kansas since 1913, has been named visiting professor of philosophy at the school of philosophy for 1929–30. He will succeed Dr. Joseph Alexander Leighton, head of the department of philosophy of the Ohio State University, who has been visiting professor for the past year. He will lecture on the history of religion and the history of philosophy and will conduct the seminars in metaphysics and ethics.

THE DEPARTMENT OF SUPERVISORS AT ATLANTA

THE newly created Department of Supervisors and Directors of Instruction of the National Education Association will hold its first summer meeting in Atlanta on July 1 and 2. Two half-day sessions are planned. At the first, the more general problems of supervisors will be discussed by representatives from city, county and state departments of education; at the second, problems peculiar to supervision of particular subjects of instruction will come under consideration. The program in full is as follows:

Monday, July 1, 2:00 P. M.

OUTSTANDING PROBLEMS OF SUPERVISORS

Greetings:

Mary A. S. Mugan, president of the department.

Purposes and Aims of the Department:

J. Cayce Morrison, assistant commissioner for elementary education, State Department of Education, Albany, New York.

Problems of Supervisors:

As Seen by the Principal

Mary McSkimmon, principal of the Pierce School, Brookline, Massachusetts.

As Seen by the Director of Research

Harold H. Bixler, director of research, Atlanta, Georgia.

As Seen by the Organizer of School and Community Relations

Danylu Belser, director of school and community organization, State Department of Education, Alabama.

As Seen by the Supervisor of Rural Schools

Hattie S. Parrott, State Supervisor of Rural Schools, North Carolina.

Tuesday, July 2, 2:00 P. M.

PROBLEMS OF THE SUPERVISORS OF THE SPECIAL SUBJECTS

Introductory Address:

James F. Hosic, professor of education, Teachers College, Columbia University.

The Supervisor of Art Education:

Minnie S. Martin, supervisor of art education, North Carolina.

The Supervisor of Handwriting:

Luella Chapman, director of handwriting, State Teachers College, Buffalo, New York.

The Supervisor of Music:

W. P. Twaddell, supervisor of music, Durham, North Carolina.

The officers of the Department of Supervisors are: *President,* Mary A. S. Mugan, assistant superintendent of schools, Fall River, Massachusetts; *First Vice-president,* A. S. Barr, associate professor of education, University of Wisconsin, Madison, Wisconsin; *Second Vice-president,* I. Jewell Simpson, assistant state superintendent of schools, Baltimore, Maryland; *Secretary-Treasurer,* James F. Hosic, professor of education, Teachers College, Columbia University.

EDUCATIONAL NOTES AND NEWS

PROFESSOR PAUL SHOREY, head of the Greek Department at the University of Chicago for the past thirty-two years, has been elected an associate member of the Belgian Royal Academy of Science and Letters.

AMONG the honorary degrees to be conferred at commencement by Fordham University is the doctorate of laws on Harold G. Campbell, associate superintendent of schools of New York City.

DEAN ROBERT WILLIAMS, of Albion College, who will become president of Ohio Northern University next year, and Dr. W. W. Whitehouse, who will succeed him as dean of Albion, were recently honor guests at a dinner sponsored by the Y. M. C. A. and the Y. W. C. A. of the college.

DR. HANS FROELICHER, professor of art criticism and head of the German department at Goucher College, will serve as acting president of the college until a successor for the late Dr. Guth can be named. Dr. Froelicher has been connected with Goucher College for forty-one years.

DR. E. T. FRANKLIN will be installed as president of Southwestern College on June 4, preceding the forty-first annual commencement. The address at the inaugural luncheon will be given by Dr. Charles Abram Ellwood, head of the department of education at the University of Missouri. Bishop Ernest Lynn Waldorf will give the charge to the president, who will respond with his inaugural address, "Purposeful Education a Discipline." Other speakers are: Dr. Ernest Hiram Lindley, chancellor of the University of Kansas, and Dr. Wallace Bruce Fleming, president of Baker University.

DR. G. H. VANDE BOGART, dean of Hibbing Junior College, has accepted the presidency of Northern Montana School, Havre, Montana. This is a two-year college established by the Montana legislature at its recent session.

DR. E. J. KLEMME, president of Intermountain Union College for the past five years, has presented his resignation to the trustees. Before he became president at Intermountain, Dr. Klemme was head of the department of psychology at the State Normal College at Ellensburg, Washington, for eight years, after which he was head of the department of extension service at the State Normal College at Bellingham, Washington.

AT Clarkson Memorial College, John Alexander Ross, Jr., professor of mechanical engineering, has been made dean of administration, and Frederick Charles Wilson, professor of civil and sanitary engineering, has been made dean of the college of engineering. They will take charge of the routine affairs of college administration so that President Rowe may have more time officially to represent the college.

J. PAUL LEONARD, who recently took his doctor's degree at Teachers College, Columbia University, writing on "The Use of Practice Exercises in the Teaching of Capitalization and Punctuation," has been elected assistant professor of secondary education at William and Mary College.

GROVER C. HOOKER, professor of education at Millsaps College, Jackson, Mississippi, has been appointed acting assistant professor of education at Stanford University for the academic year 1929–30. For the past three years Professor Hooker has been head of the education work at Millsaps College and has had some years of experience as a city school superintendent. Clark W. Hetherington, a Stanford graduate, has been appointed professor of physical education and hygiene. Mr. Hetherington taught for a time at Stanford in the department of physical education and served for several years as director of physical education in the school of education in New York University. At one time he was director of physical education in the State Department of Education in California.

VISITING professors who will conduct classes during summer school at the University of Washington include Dr. Luther L. Bernard, professor of sociology, University of North Carolina; Dr. Frederick Eby, professor of education, University of Texas; Dr. Arthur J. Jones, professor of education, University of Pennsylvania; Dr. Roy Malcolm, professor of political science, University of Southern California; Dr. W. S. Miller, professor of education, University of Minnesota; Dr. Clifford R. Shaw, associate professor of sociology, Institute for Juvenile Research, Chicago; Dr. C. E. Ragsdale and Dr. M. H. Willing, professors of education, University of Wisconsin, and Dr. Frank Joseph Klingberg, professor of history, University of California at Los Angeles.

MISS ROSE K. BRANDT, formerly rural school supervisor for Montana, but for the past two years doing graduate work at Columbia University, has been appointed to the department of elementary education in the Bureau of Indian Affairs, Department of the Interior, Washington, D. C. Her initial salary will be $4,600.

DR. HELEN P. LANGNER, Richmond, Virginia, has been appointed director of the child guidance clinic of Indiana University, Indianapolis, which will be maintained by the Indianapolis Foundation under a bequest by Delavan Smith for two years. Dr. Langner, a graduate of Yale University in 1922, was for five years with the Manhattan State Hospital, then was with the National Committee for Mental Hygiene and director of the mental hygiene clinic of the State Department of Public Welfare at Richmond.

FREDERICK WOOD, professor of mathematics at Hamline University, has been appointed dean of men to succeed Miron A. Morrill. Mr. Morrill will leave Hamline to become director of publicity for the cooperating staff of the world service commission of the Methodist Episcopal Church, with headquarters in Chicago.

JANE L. JONES, dean of the academic department of the Katharine Gibbs School of Boston, has been appointed dean of women at St. Lawrence University.

DR. PAUL S. MILLER, professor of secondary education at New York University, has been appointed principal of the Stockton and East Orange, New Jersey, high schools. He will take the place of Edward H. Dutcher, who died recently.

HUBERT S. UPJOHN, who has served as acting county superintendent of schools for Los Angeles since the death of Mark Keppel, has been elected county superintendent.

EDGAR G. JOHNSTON, for the past two years associate in the department of secondary education at Teachers College, Columbia University, has been elected principal of the University High School at the University of Michigan with the rank of assistant professor. Mr. Johnston is now completing his dissertation on "Point Systems for Guiding, Stimulating and Limiting Participation of Pupils in Extra-curricular Activities."

Matthew P. Gaffney, formerly principal of the Roger Ascham Academy, White Plains, and now superintendent of schools at Aberdeen, South Dakota, has been elected principal of the new high school at Great Neck, Long Island.

H. J. Loper, formerly superintendent of schools at Oxford, Mich., has been appointed principal of the Lincoln Junior High School at Pontiac.

H. Wallace Caldwell has been reelected president of the Chicago Board of Education and Walter H. Brandenburg, vice-president.

Appointments by the managing committee of the American School of Classical Studies at Athens to fellowships in the school for 1929–30 have been announced by Professor E. D. Perry, secretary, as follows: *Fellow of the school:* Miss Marian Elizabeth Allen Guptill, A.B., Smith College, 1926, with highest honors and special honors in classics; A.M., University of Chicago, 1928; student at the American Academy in Rome as Veltin Traveling Fellow, 1926–27; now a graduate student at the Johns Hopkins University as Smith Students Aid Society Fellow. *Fellow of the institute:* Henry Ess Askew, A.B., *magna cum laude,* Harvard University, 1928; Charles Eliot Norton Fellow at the American School of Classical Studies at Athens, 1928–29. *Fellow in archeology:* Miss Lucy T. Shoe, A.B., Bryn Mawr College, 1927; A.M., 1928; now a graduate student at Bryn Mawr College.

Professor L. A. Pechstein, dean of the college of education of the University of Cincinnati since 1922, has been granted sabbatical leave of absence for 1929–30.

Professor O. P. J. Oxley, of Natal Technical College, Durban, South Africa, is at present in the United States on a Carnegie fellowship studying art education.

President William Mather Lewis, of Lafayette College, will give the commencement address on June 18 at St. Stephen's College of Columbia University.

Professor Edward Scribner Ames, of the department of philosophy of the University of Chicago, will be the commencement speaker at Rockford College on June 10.

United States Senator Joseph T. Robinson, Democratic nominee for vice-president of the United States in 1928 and an alumnus of the University of Arkansas, will deliver the commencement address at the university on June 3 next.

The Reverend Norbert C. Hoff, president of Mount St. Charles College, Helena, Montana, will deliver the baccalaureate address at Notre Dame University on June 2, the commencement oration at St. Ambrose College, Davenport, Iowa, on June 5, and the baccalaureate address at the University of Washington on June 16.

Dr. David A. Robertson, assistant director of the American Council on Education, addressed the American Library Association at its annual meeting in Washington, D. C., on May 14 in the afternoon on "A College Library List" and in the evening on "The Library of Congress Classification as an Aid to Instruction and Research."

Dr. Truman Lee Kelley, professor of education and psychology at Stanford University, gave a series of lectures at Ohio University at Athens, on May 15, 16 and 17, on "The Application of Measurement and Statistics to Educational Problems." Ohio University is the home of Dean T. C. McCracken, national president of Kappa Delta Pi, and also of Dean of Women Irma E. Voigt, one of the charter members. Dr. Kelley, who, with Dr. Bagley as faculty adviser, was the founder of the chapter, was present at the final initiation and banquet held on the evening of May 14, and gave an address on "Kappa Delta Pi's Early History."

Dr. Virgil E. Dickson, assistant superintendent of the Berkeley public schools and director of the bureau of research, has been invited to represent America in a symposium on "Testing and its Place in Education" at the Fifth World Conference on Progressive Education, which is to be held at Elsinore, Denmark, from August 8 to 21.

Lord Justice Sankey, president of the British Institute of Adult Education, delivered the first Haldane Memorial lecture at Birkbeck College on May 14. Lord Haldane was president of the college from 1919 until his death last August, and the governors have instituted an annual lecture in his memory. Lord Justice

Sankey took for his subject "Lord Haldane's Life and the Adult Education Movement."

DR. ALEXANDER HOWARD MACKAY, who for thirty-five years was superintendent of education for the Province of Nova Scotia, died on May 5 on the eighty-first anniversary of his birth. Dr. MacKay had served as president and vice-president of the Dominion Education Association and president of the World's Education Congress in Chicago and the Nova Scotia Institute of Science and as an officer of many other organizations.

THE Progressive Education Association of the United States will hold a Progressive Education Institute at Pennsylvania State College from July 1 to 19, open to teachers, principals, superintendents and all others interested. Speakers have been secured from several prominent eastern schools and the courses carry college credit.

THE eleventh International Congress of Secondary Education will open on July 18 at The Hague, thus enabling its delegates to proceed to the Geneva Conference of the World Federation of Education Associations. Coeducation will be the principal topic of discussion.

THE University of Minnesota has invited the various agencies of the State of Minnesota engaged in adult education to a series of conferences or informal meetings on this subject at the university on June 13 and 14. The agencies interested in this field are the State Department of Education, the Minnesota Education Association, the State Federation of Women's Clubs, the Parent-Teachers Association, the State Library Association, City Librarians, U. S. Bureau of Education, the State Department of Health, Y. M. C. A., Y. W. C. A., State Medical and Editorial Association, League of Women Voters, American Association of University Women, St. Paul Institute, Dunwoody Institute, City Boards of Education, State Conference of Social Workers, American Institute of Banking, Teachers Colleges and the Endowed Colleges.

THE American Association of University Professors will hold their next annual meeting at Duke University and the University of North Carolina, from December 28 to 30, in conjunction with the American Historical Association. This decision was taken at a recent meeting of the council. It will be the first time that the Association of University Professors has met south of Washington. The program will include reports on academic freedom cases, on university ethics in connection with public utilities propaganda, on migration and interchange of graduate students, on sabbatical years, teaching load, pensions and insurance, student health and library service. The association has more than 7,000 members representing nearly three hundred colleges and universities in the United States and Canada. Its object is "to facilitate a more effective cooperation among teachers and investigators in universities and colleges for the promotion of the interests of higher education and research and in general to increase the usefulness and advance the standards and ideals of the profession." It has recently established national headquarters in Washington, D. C.

AT the close of the fourth annual meeting of the American Association for Adult Education its officers were reelected. These are: James E. Russell, dean emeritus, Teachers College, Columbia, *president;* E. W. Richards, director, extension division, University of California, *vice-president;* Margaret E. Murton, National Board of Y. W. C. A., *secretary;* John P. Puelicher, American Bankers Association, *treasurer.*

TEACHERS COLLEGE, Columbia University, is offering in the summer session of 1929 two courses on the parent-teacher movement. The first course deals with educational aspects and the second with projects and methods for advanced teaching. This year each course will be six weeks in length with two points of credit or four points for the two courses. The courses are of graduate grade, and, in the case of students matriculated in Teachers College, may be credited towards the master's and doctor's degrees, as well as towards the degree of bachelor of science. The work will be of especial interest to those connected with city systems of schools, to county supervisors and others interested in bringing about a closer cooperation of the homes and schools of the community.

AT its annual Conference on Secondary Education, held on May 11 by the college of education of the University of Cincinnati, visiting speakers were Dr. Francis T. Spaulding, of Harvard University, and Dr. B. P. Fowler, of Tower Hill School. The former spoke on the topic "What the Senior High School has a Right to Expect of the Junior High School"; the latter addressed the audience on "Are the Principles of Progressive Education Suitable for the Secondary Schools?" This conference is one of several Saturday conferences presented annually by the college of education of the University of Cincinnati.

A limited number of scholarships have been offered by the Carnegie Endowment for International Peace, for American men and women for study in the Institute of Art and Archeology of the University of Paris during the 1929 summer session. Each scholarship will carry a stipend of $400, which will cover traveling, living and tuition expenses for the seven weeks of the summer session. The courses at the institute are designed primarily to meet the needs of the following persons: (a) University and college students who expect to specialize in art with a view to becoming teachers of art, curators of museums, architects, art workers and writers; (b) teachers of art and curators of museums who would like the opportunity of taking advanced instruction, acquiring new points of view and studying directly the art treasures of Paris and France; (c) students or teachers of French or of history particularly interested in art. Further information about these opportunities and about the courses offered at the summer session may be obtained from the Institute of International Education, 2 West 45th Street, New York.

The city of Glasgow and the school authorities have organized for the second time, in May and June, an extensive education exhibition, which shows the many branches of education activity in Glasgow: work of the pupils (from the kindergarten to the end of secondary and technical schools), model classes and laboratories with demonstrations given by the pupils, extra-curricular activities, such as clubs, school newspapers, etc., instruction for the subnormal and crippled, physical training, education in the arts (concerts, dramatics), aid for needy children and adult education.

DISCUSSION

WHO IS PRACTICAL IN EDUCATION?

It is easy to say of the other person, "He is not practical," or "His work is very impractical." This is a criticism with which teachers and students of education sometimes assail the work of one another. The most proficient experimentalists and the most experienced schoolmen in the field are not free from such indictments—or from accusing their coworkers for that matter. Why is it so easy to charge others with being abstract, theoretical, vague and wasteful? Does specialization in education lead to narrowness? Are investigations and administrative labors so self-absorbing as to detach men from the important professional activities carried on elsewhere? What lies back of this all too prevalent comment that the educational practices of others are of little value?

Perhaps men with intellectual hobbies and professional specialties are incapable through preoccupation of seeing the worthwhileness of the enterprises of others. Are they so wrapped up in their own pursuits that they fail to note the projects of others except with passing superciliousness? Making a creditable contribution in one sphere of scholarship seems to isolate and disable a student for any clear understanding of achievement in other divisions of interest. Educational wildcatting, moreover, makes skeptical attitudes easy. There are sufficient failures among the experiments in these times to warrant a moderate amount of suspicion; but solicitation and support are indispensable to progress. Overevaluation of one's own achievement, on the other hand, is a serious form of professional sinning and a pretty certain confession of being impractical. Failure to keep up in a general way with the whole field of education in its onward movements is another blunder and a sure self-revealing conviction of impracticalness.

History unfolds for us a story of changing view-points concerning the practical. Skills and techniques that we would call antiquated once had a vital function to perform in the life of the people. Stone cutting and weapon making were formerly essential to survival, and individuals had to master these arts. Ability to speak fervently in public was once not only desirable, but absolutely indispensable to political success. Familiarity with the Latin language was formerly not only an evidence of culture, but downright necessary for social, professional and commercial leadership. Passing time is not alone in giving different pictures of the practical; geographical location is another significant factor of differentiation. Community conditions, institutional needs and personal capacities are also agents in helping us answer the question, "What is practical?" It is, therefore, necessary to be familiar with the total situation to be able to say fairly, "Who is practical in education?"

Experts in statistical procedure may say that no good can be derived from the study of the history of education, and specialists in the field of experimental psychology may claim that the study of sociology is unscientific and futile. Those engaged in standardizing the measurement of subject-matter attainments may see no value in the philosophy of education, and the apostles of a liberal education may fail to understand and appreciate the claims of those who advocate specific procedures for certain types of instruction. Only the most thorough students and widely experienced educators are in any position to admonish and negatively criticize the work of others, and even then there are certain subjective factors of great weight that are never fully revealed.

The professional educator, especially, needs a broad and rich background. An extensive acquaintance with subject-matter of many kinds, a sympathetic attitude toward the numerous academic fields, intimate familiarity with the principles and theories that underlie the various practices in our schools, a considerable degree of experience with the concrete problems of administration and supervision, profound scholarship in both general and professional history, ability to employ some of the more commonly used techniques of research, etc.—these are some of the qualifications essential if one is to be privileged to condemn others as impractical. The office slave performing his administrative duties faithfully must not be blind to the merit of the library researcher engrossed in his source materials and encyclopedic cross references. The statistician computing his correlations must look up occasionally and smile approval at the conscientious efforts of the enthusiastic classroom instructor. The director of the activities of a large institution needs to note little detailed excellences made possible by the painstaking service of a humble subordinate. Writers of books and department heads preparing their voluminous reports are not infrequently misled into vague abstractions and faulty generalizations. It is not what we do that makes us practical so much as how well we do it. There are all sorts of duties to be done by all sorts of persons. Heredity, individual equipment and local circumstance all contribute to the varieties of assignments that schoolmen and women are requested to execute, and the way the work is done should be the measure of practicalness. No one has a monopoly on the practical; there are opportunities for all. No particular type of genuine service is more practical than the other types of service. Making most of the positions we are in and helping others to do their work better by means of our own efficiency—this is what it means to be practical. Coordination of function for the improvement of the general service—each person employed performing his work in a most proficient manner.

Three different groups of teachers were asked to list the features of their professional service that they deemed most practical and of greatest value to their communities. There were over two hundred teachers all told, and their reactions listed in order of frequency are as follows:

Relating class work with out-of-school life.
Stimulating individual pupils to greater achievement.
Cultivating social attitudes in children.
Creating a sincere and lasting interest in learning.
Employing system and routine effectively.
Instruction presented on the pupil level.
Developing worthy habits in boys and girls.
Procedures guided by clear, universally sanctioned aims.
Keeping up to date.

Giving all children a square deal.
Training children to think accurately and discriminatingly.
Refusing to teach any subjects except those best known and liked best.
Individualizing instruction appropriately.
Watching sharply to improve health and hygiene of pupils.
Orienting youths in the ways of the world.

Education must always be practical to be profitable. To use common sense and to make repeated applications to life, whatever our school work may be—this is what it means to be practical in education. Writers, lecturers, philosophers, laboratory observers, kindergarten instructors, building principals, college professors and all the rest have equal opportunity and every incentive to success. To give our best in the cause of that which is just—this is what it means to be practical in education. Administration, instruction, the formulation of theories, the manipulation of statistics, the distribution of supplies—these are all essential services and equally practical when equally well performed.

CARROLL D. CHAMPLIN
PENNSYLVANIA STATE COLLEGE

THE EARLIEST RECORDED OBJECTIVE TEST?

PRESENT-DAY developments in objective testing make this passage from the Old Testament assume new interest.

> And the Gileadites took the passages of Jordan before the Ephraimites: and it was so, that when those Ephraimites which were escaped said, Let me go over; that the men of Gilead said unto him, Art thou an Ephraimite? If he said, Nay; Then said they unto him, Say now Shibboleth: and he said Sibboleth: for he could not frame to pronounce it right. Then they took him, and slew him at the passages of Jordan: and there fell at that time of the Ephraimites forty and two thousand. *Judges,* 12: 5–7.

The validity of the Gileadite's test was determined by the attestation of fact—the Ephraimites 'could not frame to pronounce' *Shibboleth.* The pronunciation *Sibboleth* was in all probability a case of dialectical variation among tribes of the same nation and speaking the same language. The number of cases, 42,000, certainly was large enough to establish reliability. Might this not be the earliest objective test on record?

NORMA V. SCHEIDEMANN

SPECIAL CORRESPONDENCE

THE PRELIMINARY COURSE ON "HOW TO STUDY" FOR FRESHMEN ENTERING COLLEGE

FOR the third successive summer the University of Buffalo has offered a three weeks' course in the *techniques of study* for all entering freshmen who have not done well in high school but who wish to take a college course. The first summer it was required only of those from the lowest two fifths of their high-school graduating class, but for the past two summers it has been required also of those from the middle fifth of the smaller high schools of the state, unless these applicants had received high scores in the intelligence tests. The methods and preliminary results of this experiment are reported in a previous article.[1] It might be of interest, however, to point out some additional drills and changes in emphasis, with a more up-to-date evaluation of the results.

What effect has this preliminary course had on the enrolment in college? Before the course was instigated, about 20 per cent. of the entering freshmen came from the lower sections of their high-school classes, and would now be required to take the course. The percentage has steadily decreased, so that this year only 12 per cent. of the incoming freshmen are from the lower scholastic divisions. This is partly due, I believe, to the fee charged for those taking the course, partly to the strenuous nature of the course and partly to the general attitude of the registrar's office tending to discourage these "poor risks" from attempting a college course.

The students who have taken this course are unanimous in the opinion that it is the most arduous toil that has ever been required of them as students. From nine o'clock until four-thirty they had to apply themselves to lectures, drills or examinations. And there was a good deal of home-work in addition.

[1] *The Personnel Journal,* 6: 182–91. 1927.

On the basis of unsigned reports from students at the end of the course and from comments given later to the personnel office, we are able to classify the various aspects of the course in the approximate order of their value from the student's point of view.

(1) Practice in taking notes from lectures stands out as the most valuable drill in the experience of the past two years. Twelve lectures an hour in length were delivered, eight of these on the various techniques of study by those administering the course and four by other speakers on more general topics. At the end of each lecture all the notes were collected, carefully graded and marked, and the next day each student was interviewed on this basis, usually by the person delivering the lecture. The notes were all discussed with each one, as to their logic, their completeness, their accuracy and form. All were urged to adopt the outline method in order to avoid the danger of becoming mere recorders. By a fairly objective device of scoring notes, it was possible to show marked improvement in note-taking over the three weeks' period. Many of these students had never taken notes before, and only a few had given attention to the effectiveness of their notes.

(2) Next in value came the drills in writing English themes, followed by individual conferences with expert college instructors in this subject. These themes were usually written under pressure of time, before the instructor, and were then read aloud to the student later, with particular attention given to correct sentences and to clarity.

(3) The content of the lectures was considered next in importance by these students. The most frequently mentioned as valuable were the lectures on purpose, habits, memory and attentiveness. Comments were made to the effect that such lectures gave them new insights, concrete suggestions to try out in their studying. As one man put it, it made studying for the first time "something to get excited about."

(4) For drills in rapid reading, newspaper clippings were passed to each student at least once a day, and record was made of the time required for reading these by each student. The comprehension, or ability to answer questions on the printed matter, was also checked, so that mere skimming over the pages without understanding could be detected.

(5) For training in assimilating the content of books, required assignments were given from three books on study, and additional assignments from which selection was optional were suggested. For example, those intending to study medicine later were advised to read and report on "Arrowsmith," by Sinclair Lewis.

(6) Problems in mathematics were also of value to those planning for a mathematics or science major. There was a partial review of the main concepts of intermediate algebra, but particular stress was placed on the methods of solving and checking simple problems.

(7) To acquire practice in using library reference books, a number of assignments were given to look up information in twenty miscellaneous common reference books. Various dictionaries, encyclopedias, almanacs, etc., were discussed, and finally the students were examined as to their ability to trace the best source of information for a number of unfamiliar subjects.

(8) Oral ten-minute reports were required on outside reading. The form and the content of what was discussed were both critically examined later. This drill proved of first importance to two, but was considered of minor importance by the others.

(9) Experiments were tried out in memorizing lists of foreign words. There were demonstrations, rather than drills, in the use of a set of cards for building up vocabularies. To several students this was enlightening.

(10) A good deal of time was spent on drill in taking notes from difficult and abstract mimeographed excerpts from text-books. It surprised us that it was not considered of greater value. Our surmise is that it is so different from the usual habit of studying from books—underscoring or the mere passive surveying of the page—that it was felt to be distasteful and unnecessary. However, two out of forty students did feel that it was the single most important drill that was given.

Taken altogether, the results of this preliminary course justify its continuation as a regular procedure. The proportion of individuals surviving the freshman year with an average of C or better is doubled; that is, increased from 25 per cent. to 50 per cent. of the total number. And the number of those who failed entirely and dropped out of college is reduced from about 40 per cent. to 15 per cent.

It is possible now to determine the value of the "how to study" course for each of the subjects in the college curriculum. Those who had taken this course were compared, subject for subject, with the other students admitted who were not from the upper two fifths of the better high schools. The marks were recorded for each subject as E or F for failing, D for barely passing, and C grade or above. For purposes of direct comparison the proportion of those grades in each group was put on a percentage basis. The following table will indicate how the two groups compared.

Subject studied	Lower two fifths of High School (How to study group) 72 cases			Middle fifth of High School 90 cases		
	Per cent. receiving			Per cent. receiving		
	F	D	C or above	F	D	C or above
English compos. (taken by all)	16	48	35	21	40	39
Modern foreign languages	31	42	27	43	39	18
Mathematics	19	24	57	21	27	52
History	32	36	32	9	37	54
General science (no lab.)	33	31	36	30	36	34
Lab. science (Chem., Biol.)	21	36	43	18	34	47
Economics	15	37	48	34	45	21
Average from all marks	24	37	39	25	35	40

The conclusions from this comparison are:

(1) The "how to study" group seems to average as highly as those from the middle fifth of the larger high schools and the upper two fifths of the smaller schools of the state.

(2) There is a decided tendency for the "how to study" group to benefit particularly in those courses which are drill subjects. That is, they are relatively better in the foreign languages, in English composition and in mathematics. Their superiority in English composition can be largely explained on the basis of the excellent training received in writing compositions under a college teacher in this subject, and it is important to note that this same teacher did not have any of these freshmen in regular class work. But the improvement in capacity to handle foreign languages and mathematics can hardly be explained in terms of such a definite transfer of training. There were various suggestions given as to methods of memorizing lists of words, short cuts in mathematics and a good deal of drill in the speeding up of the simpler processes of adding, percentage problems, etc.

(3) The relative advantage of the "how to study" group in economics is a clearer example, we believe, of practice in definitely sticking to tasks, as almost nothing was said about the subject-matter of economics during the three weeks' course. In the economics courses a text was followed closely, and accurate note-taking during classroom lectures was also quite important.

(4) It is quite significant, we believe, that there was the least benefit noted in the subject of history. This situation seems to be common to all four large sections conducted by two different instructors. There may be two reasons for this. In the first place, history is a subject where the student may be left to himself, to read extensively, to write papers and to record the result of all this primarily in the final examinations. In other words, the daily assignments were not so definite or so similar to the practice drills of the preliminary course as in the other freshman subjects. Secondly, both history instructors placed a good deal of emphasis on library reference work and comprehensive written reports. Drill in this type of study has not been given until this past summer, so we may hope that from now on oral and written reports and the use of the library for reference may cause as much improvement in history as exists in the other subjects.

(5) In the freshman science subjects, it is interesting to notice that the difference in the results for the two courses corresponds to a difference in teaching methods of the two instructors. Although both are large classes, one

instructor holds to the lecture method, requires a good deal of work and gives stiff and frequent tests. The other instructor rambles in his lectures, is considered an easy teacher and surprises students at the end of the course by failing them in examinations.

This confirms our belief that it is the drill method in classroom work that is most adapted to improvement with preliminary coaching, noticeably more so than the more informal discussion classes where requirements do not seem to be so rigid. It is with the first instructor that the "how to study" group does so well relatively, with only 42 per cent. of D and F grades (compared to 60 per cent. of D and F grades for the middle fifth group), whereas with the more lenient instructor there were 20 per cent. of F and 40 per cent. of D, compared to 10 per cent. of F grades and 33 per cent. of D grades for the middle fifth group.

The question is frequently asked: If there are to be low or doubtful students admitted to college, and if a "how to study" course is advisable, should this be given before the college opens—in the summer, let us say—or should it be given during the fall term, in addition to the regular college work? We are inclined to favor the first plan. The student is not so apt to taste failure and give up. Then, too, a student who is doing poor work in any class is a retarding influence, interfering with the normal progress of the class. As one instructor from a western university remarked: "We can begin to really teach when we get rid of the dumb-bells around Christmas time."

EDWARD SAFFORD JONES
THE UNIVERSITY OF BUFFALO

A PLAN FOR THE IMPROVEMENT OF TEACHING IN THE HIGH SCHOOL

SUPERINTENDENT W. L. STEPHENS and his administrative associates of the Long Beach city schools had been considering for a long period of time the advisability of entering upon a pioneer experiment of securing a director of teaching whose function it should be to improve teaching in all the departments of the high school. The new Woodrow Wilson High School and Junior College, under the leadership of Principal John L. Lounsbury, was selected for the experiment, and the staff decided to confine the project to the high school alone. The director was given full authority to organize and initiate a plan of procedure without administrative responsibilities.

In the absence of information on this problem with regard to its organization and administration, the following plan of procedure was initiated and put into effect:

I. An analysis was made of the professional training of the teaching staff to determine the nature and character of their equipment for effective functioning in the activity assigned to them. For example, their exposure to educational psychology; tests and measurements; philosophy; general and special methods; work in their major and minor fields related directly and indirectly to the activity of present interest, etc. These facts formed the basis for determining the capacities of the teachers to make effective adjustments to the new technique to be assigned.

II. An analysis was then made of their teaching experience to determine the nature and character of their present assignment, it being considered an essential element in effective procedure to know what direct or indirect contributions such experience might make to the improvement of teaching.

III. Departmental conferences were then scheduled by the director to outline the plan of procedure for the teachers and interpret its application to the present situation. In these conferences teacher attitudes were discovered with regard to their present problems and needs, and their reaction to the plan as a possible solution. Inter-group as well as intra-group correlations of method and content were discussed in the light of the realization of the general and specific objectives for the purpose of establishing more effective coordination of aims and purposes. A secondary, though very significant, purpose was to place special departments on the same plane with the rest of the departments in the experiment, since all contributed to the general composite development of the work of the institution.

IV. After the general plan had been sold to the teaching staff, and before any attempt was made to do classroom supervision, a second conference, by departments, was called. The purpose of this conference was to interpret the course of study within the department so as to assume greater uniformity in the assignment and teaching of the minimum essentials, with special consideration of the time element involved and the character of the enrichment for the differentiated groups. No attempt was made to vary the course of study, this falling entirely within the sphere of the curriculum and research department. It was definitely understood that our significant problem was to "put over" the task assigned for us, with the tools and equipment offered, by the best technique available so that the objectives might be more fully realized by the pupils. With this goal in mind, the next step in the general procedure was to establish a "teaching unit." A teaching unit was defined as that portion of curricular content which the average teacher can and must cover in a certain period of time. For example: For U. S. history, 2B (first semester), a certain definite amount of material is assigned by the course of study to be covered in eighteen weeks. This material was divided into five periods or epochs with well-selected supplementary material for each period or epoch. One such period was called a "teaching unit."

The purpose of this "teaching unit" was not to mechanize teaching or rob the teacher of his initiative. It was rather to establish a basic unit of essentials around which he could build his enriched program and thereby prove his superior worth as a teacher. Another fundamental reason was to establish a basis for the measurement of intra-group progress. The elements of each teaching unit were carefully selected for an objective test. To these were added such other elements as would grow out of an enriched assignment. By this measure it was possible to determine the strength and weakness of the teaching technique within the department since all other criteria were available to rule out other variables.

The teaching unit forms the basis also for the determination of the qualifications of teachers to teach certain level courses within the department and makes adjustments obviously easy.

A composite distribution of results of the unit tests also aids in a more equitable distribution of intra-group grades. It is to be definitely understood that no autocracy is exercised in the interpretation of the results of such unit tests; rather do they form an excellent basis for group discussion on causes of existing variations, and thereby make adequate adjustments possible.

V. After the second conference by departments, together with many individual conferences, a schedule of supervision was established for the purpose of ascertaining by what method the teachers expected to effect mastery of the several teaching units. First semester, beginning classes, were taken up in order, so as to reach the greatest number of pupils during the first and second teaching units. Bulletins to teachers were issued outlining the purpose and plan of supervision so as to give the teacher every opportunity to do his best. It was the definite understanding that there was to be no "snupervision," but that a mutual understanding had been reached to welcome the director at any time for the purpose of effecting a better technique of classroom procedure so that higher standards of effective mastery might be reached.

The mechanics of classroom procedure, previously discussed at the general conferences, were checked first. This was followed by a specific analysis of the lesson assignment.

This is as far as we have progressed with the plan, and not all of the semester's teaching units will be completed before the end. However, it is our present plan to spend some time on the "lesson assignment" in small group and individual conferences before going into the field of special methods of teaching.

After the preliminary plan is well under way and the teachers are fully acquainted with the general plan, an experimental program will be discussed at group conferences in which definite technique will be formulated for controlled experimental work on methods in each department.

The reader may be interested to know that there are no heads of departments and no departmental chairmen. A counselor assists the administration in the plan of registration in departments, and the director of teaching is held responsible for the progress of each department.

W. J. Klopp

Woodrow Wilson High School,
Long Beach, California

EDUCATIONAL RESEARCH AND STATISTICS

THE EFFECT OF CHARACTER TRAITS ON SCHOLASTIC ACHIEVEMENT

A survey of the trend of recent educational literature indicates an increasing interest in character training in our schools. We are coming to believe that the schools must concern themselves more with the whole development of the child, mental, moral and physical, and abandon the narrower program of the mental training only. The physical development has come to occupy a recognized place in our educational objectives, but most educators are still looking hopefully to the homes and churches for the development of moral traits. Since the schools are the only agencies organized specifically for systematic child training, it would seem that more uniformly satisfactory results might be expected if these institutions were to accept more definitely the responsibility for the all-round training of children. Such a program must include character development along with mental and physical training.

The physical condition of the child is now recognized as an important factor in school work. A healthy body is more conducive to good work in school than an unhealthy condition. Is it possible that habits of character also have their effect on scholarship and that good character is more conducive to good school work than poor habits of conduct? If this can be shown, it would seem wise to reshape our educational objectives to include moral as well as mental and physical development.

There is little reported evidence that any important work has been done in studying the possible effect of character traits on scholastic accomplishment. One reason for this undoubtedly lies in the difficulty that has been encountered in attempting to measure character traits by objective methods. So far as I know, no satisfactory tests have yet been devised that successfully measure such traits on an objective basis. While scientifically accurate results can not be claimed when subjective judgments are used, still, a study based on such judgments should give results that are at least significant.

A recent study of this kind was made by the writer, and some interesting deductions obtained. All the ninth year pupils in two New York State high schools were used in the study and enough eighth and tenth year pupils from the same schools to make up about five hundred cases. Five hundred seven pupils of the median school age of nine years three months were used. Secondary pupils of eleventh and twelfth years were excluded because it was felt that these are a more select group, being survivals of earlier eliminations for various reasons.

An effort was made to find a few of the more basic traits which would seem to influence school success, rather than to attempt to search out all of the factors which make up what is called character. The ones finally selected for this study were initiative, control of attention, persistence, trustworthiness and sense of accuracy.

In each of the schools a carefully selected group of teachers was chosen to give the character ratings. In conference with these groups each character trait was defined and full instructions given about the ratings. The teachers gave these ratings only for those pupils who had been under their instruction for a sufficient time to make intelligent ratings possible. Only pupils who had been rated on all of the traits by at least three teachers were included in the study, and many of them had five or six separate ratings. All the various ratings for each pupil were then averaged for each trait, reducing them to a single composite rating. In this way a part at least of the errors due to subjective judgments was eliminated. These character trait ratings were then compared with the final scholarship ratings for the year for these pupils.

Both scholarship and character ratings were given in letter grades: A, excellent; B, good; C, fair or average; D, poor, and F, below passing. By assigning the usual percentage marks to these grades of 90, 80, 70, 60 and below 60, it was possible to obtain median marks and make comparisons.

In both schools from which these data were taken group intelligence tests were given regularly by persons well qualified for this work and IQ ratings placed on the permanent record cards. All these IQ ratings were obtained either from the Terman Group Test or the Otis Group Test.

The medians for scholarship and character ratings were not far apart:

Median scholarship for the whole group	77.
Median character trait rating for group	79.24

The slightly higher rating for character traits probably can be explained by the rather common tendency to be generous when in doubt regarding character judgment.

As one indication of the relation of character traits to scholarship, correlations were made between these and compared with a similar correlation between IQ ratings and scholarship:

Correlation of scholarship and IQ ratings .... .48
Correlation of scholarship and character ratings .73

These results indicate a much more substantial relation between character traits and scholarship than between IQ and scholarship. A check of these results by the partial correlation method clearly supported this conclusion.

When comparisons were made of median scholarship for various IQ levels between those rating well in character traits and those rating low in these traits, a still more convincing result was obtained. The whole group of pupils was divided into five groups according to IQ rank, those having an IQ below 95, between 95 and 105, between 105 and 115, between 115 and 125 and above 125. The pupils in each of these five groups were then divided on the basis of character rating median. Those rating above this median were placed in group I and compared with group II, made up of those who rated below the median in character. In this way comparisons were made between two groups of equal native ability or capacity for learning, but of different character development. The median scholarship for groups I and II for each of the five IQ levels is given below.

IQ Level	Below 95	95–105	105–115	115–125	Above 125
Median scholarship Group I	75.5	79.3	80.2	82.8	82.
Median scholarship Group II	68.5	72.5	73.9	74.1	78.5
Difference in median scholarship	7.	6.8	6.3	8.7	3.5

When we consider that groups I and II are alike in all except character development, the difference in median scholarship for these groups is pronounced.

The next tabulation gives a similar comparison between groups I and II on the basis of subjects failed during the year. These percentages are figured by taking the total number of subjects failed in each division compared with the total number attempted:

IQ Level	Below 95	95–105	105–115	115–125	Above 125
Per cent. of failures Group I	44	20	26	20	11
Per cent. of failures Group II	71	64	57	61	25

This comparison also is significant, for we see that pupils in group II fail in two to three times as much work as do pupils of their equal in all but character development.

Of course, no final conclusions are warranted from a study so limited in scope, but a careful consideration of the data given will lead directly into several fields of investigation that seem worthy of attention. While both of the schools from which the material for this study was taken rank well in the state and have well-trained teachers and officers, neither of them has classes divided according to ability. The data indicate a need of giving the low ability group more attention, and likewise indicate that the high ability group is not working up to capacity. However, this is outside of our present problem. The high percentage of failures in group II for each of the ability levels, and the wide difference in median scholarship between groups I and II for these different levels do fall within our problem.

If other investigations of the effect of character development on scholastic achievement reveal results similar to those presented in this study, then it is clear that the schools should look toward the inclusion of a more definite program of character development in connection with the regular school work. There are, of course, many other reasons for doing this, but on the evidence of the data given, such a program will pay worth-while dividends in terms of better school records.

H. J. STEERE

WEST TENNESSEE
STATE TEACHERS COLLEGE

EDUCATIONAL REVIEW

Edited by WILLIAM McANDREW

EDITORIAL COMMENT

As to Commissioner Cooper.—We ought to have William John Cooper in SCHOOL AND SOCIETY's gallery of notables. I can try to do a portrait of our commissioner of the U. S. Bureau of Education. I have known him pretty well for ten years and admired him much. He was particularly courteous to me on my California visits and refreshingly hail-fellow-well-met when we have happened together at the yearly meetings of the national department of superintendence. Once we spent a whole day touring schools in the Santa Rosa country north of San Francisco. Something set us to comparing our parents. Sitting in a golden afternoon on a hillside overlooking delicious little farms and fruit orchards near a wee white village clustered around a church, we enjoyed the luxury, so commonly forbidden, of talking about our own early days, our fathers, our mothers and our folks, each one of us saving the other from the charge of vanity and conceit. We both had fathers who came over from the old country with nothing to start on but the beginnings of their trades. We both had worked in drug-stores; we both had aimed at other careers than that of teaching. We both had been caught by the lure of it, the delight of it, the satisfaction that it gives. But, pardon me, I set out to paint Cooper, not myself.

His father, a half-orphan at five years old, got himself into California as a youth and came to be a teamster on the mountain roads. He was a popular chap and took the fancy of a bright girl who had lost one parent when but six years old and the other seven years later. At sixteen she passed the California examinations to teach and at twenty-four joined hands for life with the popular young Britisher, by that time so hearty an American that he had been elected a constable and a lieutenant in an artillery company of the State National Guard. There came the hundredth anniversary of the Declaration of Independence. The Fourth must be celebrated by cannon salutes at sunrise, by a procession, by speeches, by a big dinner in the grove. Bright and early the young artillerists haul their old-fashioned muzzle-loading piece to the vacant lot for the salute at sunrise. The powder is in cotton bags, one bag to a charge. It has to be pushed down the bore and wadding rammed down against it. After the first discharge the vent-hole must be kept closely shut by the thumb of an artilleryman lest the air getting in may enliven any spark left from a previous firing. Something goes wrong with the opening ceremony of July 4th, 1876, for a premature flash envelops Lieutenant Cooper. They pick him up from the ground, stunned and frightfully burned. That morning service cost him an arm. With his young wife and five-year-old William John, the plucky volunteer tries farming. You needed two good arms for that in California fifty-three years ago. But there was the painter's trade, learned before the teaming days. So here is Father Cooper in Red Bluff, freshening up the houses, doing the store signs, putting the luscious green on the Studebaker wagons, and the shiny black coats upon the buggies from Columbus. Here young William John gets his first taste of school and likes it. It's in his blood. That school-teacher mother talks geography with him and grammar and the delights that can be his who learns how really to read. He gets into high school. They have chemistry there and physiology. The town drugstore wants a boy for part-time work. Isn't chemistry done in bottles? Wash 'em. You're studying Latin? Here it is on the prescriptions. In due course, by carefully polishing the handle of the big front door the youthful Cooper gets as far as helping in the compounding of drugs, serving as general clerk, and managing the whole works when the owner is away. Then came a university scholarship and the big day when, as winner of it, the proud boy from Red Bluff found himself a freshman in the University of California, twenty-seven years ago. He found work that paid wages. He drove a header in the summer time—an amazing big machine hauled by a drove of horses. It snips the tops off the standing grain; it threshes the wheat from the chaff. The yellow kernels run down into bags. They accumulate upon a platform between the wheels. Wagons drive alongside like lighters coming to a steamer. Men toss the loads of wheat into the truck while all are moving ahead around the field. It's a good preparation for keeping a system of schools running.

It's in the blood.—The university thinks Cooper has teaching talent. Will he assist Professor William Scott Ferguson with the history courses? He will.

What sort of teachers did they have in the university at the beginning of the century? Ask Cooper.

They had real ones. There was Leon Richardson; he knew how to make Latin live. I read Virgil and Ovid with him. Not a dull minute. He's director of University Extension now. There was Prescott; he's on the faculty of the University of Chicago at present. I wanted to read Martial and Juvenal. I went to see him about it and told him what an awkward program I had so far as getting a period for this was concerned. He said he'd put the class on any of his free hours that suited me. He gave the course to me alone, in the study at his home. Believe me, it was a memorable course. Ferguson, when I studied with him, was already a well-recognized authority in ancient history and now is considered in the front rank of such scholars in the world. He's on the Harvard faculty now. These men certainly inspired us young fellows with appreciation of the beautiful in literature and gave us the experience of real delight in the work of a student. William Kemp guided me in my master's thesis and convinced me of the country's need of having students do research in educational theories and practice. We had Professor Lange, who was a student at Ann Arbor when you were. He had the real progressive, scientific spirit. He put us all through individual projects. That's the way to get the professional drive into education. California seems to me to have had and to be still using the university men who make education move ahead.

As I recall it, Cooper had ambition to enter the bar but wished to help his two sisters get the training necessary to enable them to take up teaching. For this reason he made his electives at the university in the field that would enable him to begin earning as soon as he got his degree.

The great earthquake came a few days before his diploma was due. The university had to close. The faculty organized a comprehensive campaign of relief on the campus. They elected Cooper its chairman. Secretary Taft, of the War Department and president of the Red Cross, sent Edward Devine as his representative. He took young Cooper on as secretary of the general relief office in San Francisco. Next we saw Cooper working for the Western Electric Company. He was getting on well with it. He had promotions that were gratifying to his self-respect and pleasing to his pocket. But whenever he went by a schoolhouse, whenever he met a troop of children with books, the lure of the big service gave him a twinge. It's in the blood. Some men are like that—Arthur Morgan, for instance, and Will Holmes, of Mount Vernon. I knew a man who offered Frank Boynton a fine money-making position. Frank Cody turned his back on tempting offers to join the industrial magnates. William John and the gentlewoman who is now Mrs. William John reasoned it out in this wise. If you had come to life in any corner of the earth except in the United States you would have, according to the actual mathematical chances involved, been practically doomed to stay on the level upon which you had been born. Instead of that you have been given a common-school education, a very valuable training in high school and four wonderful years in a splendid university. What is it in America that makes the chance of an immigrant's son so marvelous as compared with the opportunities elsewhere? It is education. Practically everybody says so. You know it. Why not, then, contribute to it? Why not boost it along? If you keep your health you'll have enough to eat and to wear and a shelter over your head. All the other things that you might get more of if you were a lawyer or a big business official are nothing unless you think that they are of the most importance.

That's the sort of reasoning every schoolmaster of ability has to repeat every once in a while to keep his spirit fresh and sweet when he sees some former classmate who didn't seem any brighter or more industrious advancing into a business paying a profit that makes the teacher's wages look like German currency in the bad days. That's the reasoning Washington Gladden used to give college men in commencement addresses: Many occupations offer fairly certain clothes, food and shelter. The calling of this kind whose processes are interesting, whose results are what the world needs, is the one that will give you the greatest satisfaction and happiness.

Cooper's services.—You can see, therefore, with approval, William John Cooper, aged twenty-five, turning his back on commercial business and teaching his favorite Latin and history in the high school of Stockton. Three years of it prepare him for becoming head of the history department in the senior and junior high schools at Berkeley. At thirty-three he is supervisor of social studies for the schools of Oakland; at thirty-six, district superintendent of schools, Piedmont region, organizing high-school service and working to get school bonds for that growing district on San Francisco Bay. At thirty-nine he is superintendent in Fresno and getting a $1,800,000 bond issue across. At forty-four he is superintendent of schools of San Diego. I recall that at the National Education Association meeting two years ago somebody asked: "Why would Cooper leave a $9,000 superintendency to become state school commissioner of California at $5,000 a year? Is it an easier place?"

Promptly a California schoolman shot back the answer: "It's twice as hard. That's the reason." No doubt there are state commissioners who make the position a very easy one. I happen to know that Cooper put into his two years in that office more travel, nerve strain and more mind-and-body-tax than five years of San Diego would have cost him. He knew this before he accepted the call. To return to Sacramento, the place of his birth, forty-five years after that event, as head of the great school department of a magnificent commonwealth is a picturesque achievement. Californians comment upon it with evident satisfaction. That he was called at the age of forty-six to be educational commissioner for the republic strikes schoolmen as a natural and propitious circumstance.

He is a public-school man, experienced in all grades of education from kindergarten through the university. As a student of procedures he has spent his professional life of twenty-five years applying progressive measures to the improvement of teaching.

As an organizer he is quiet and steady. His plans are laid carefully; his aids are made to feel the importance and responsibility of their duties. When he gets a thought-out scheme started he pushes it with notable vigor and tireless persistence. He has youth, enthusiasm, balance and a profound conviction that education really is the supreme good which the line of eminent Americans from Franklin through Lincoln and Roosevelt and Hoover declared it to be. We have a high-class commissioner.

Parent-teachers getting formidable.—At the last count on record in this office the parent-teacher associations in the United States numbered 1,134,714 persons, not including Hawaii and the District of Columbia. In 1920, twenty-three years after its origin, the movement had enrolled 190,000 people. Since then it has gained more than 400 per cent. This is a phenomenal growth. The association is formidable in that it is huge, great, wide-spread, active and growing. So many of us are exultant at seeing so large a number of intelligent people interested in boosting school service that we are inclined to brush aside the small percentage of principals, teachers and superintendents who express concern at an interference with their main business by an organization not legally empowered to direct the schools. When you try a questionnaire on superintendents, as Julian Butterworth did, less than 3 per cent. will recall any objection. When superintendents at educational conventions talk things over at those informal luncheons which they say give them as much help as the formal papers, the great majority are for the parent-teacher associations with complete enthusiasm. The fellow who is different, however, has had experience that counts for much. His reasons for opposition are respectable: "The association's aim is not the same as the objective of the public schools"; "the association is not the whole community"; "the association, amateurs, doesn't realize that education has become a profession based on a complex science"; "the association meddles"; "it is only another form of woman's club"; "it resolutes on every school matter without any investigation"; "it wants to dictate who shall be hired and fired," etc. But Mrs. Mason, official spokeswoman for the national organization, reminds us with much emphasis that the parent-teacher movement is not a crusade to reform the schools, that a local organization must not make the mistake of interfering with the school curriculum and that it must remember that school boards are the people's representatives to appoint superintendents, principals and teachers and to administer school affairs. If a school board proves unsatisfactory it is within the power of the people as individuals to make a better selection when the next opportunity comes. If school matters temporarily go wrong, the parent-teacher association should maintain its function as a cooperative body and not attempt to "run" the school. A controversy about school administration separates members of the parent-teacher group into unfriendly factions. An attempt by a few members to get the society to thwart a board or a school official or to depose a teacher or to bring personal grievances to the meetings results in bad feeling, lessened efficiency and a possible break-up of the organization. The movement must keep out of politics, remain non-partisan and non-sectarian. So writes Mrs. Mason to the members, all and sundry.

What fault schoolmen find.—Not everybody agrees to this. I notice in a recent number of *The School Parent,* organ of the United Parents Associations of New York City, an article by Eda Powers commenting on the domination of Chicago schools by the City Hall, with a history of political interference and graft. Miss Powers remarks:

> It seems significant and disconcerting that the parent-teacher associations of Chicago were not a strong enough force to be mentioned in accounts of the struggle for decent school administration. We know the parents were not a compelling force. Why not? Have they a poor city-wide organization? Were they afraid of overstepping the oft-repeated admonition that parents must not try to

shape school policies? Or had they allowed themselves to be so sidetracked on less important interests that they neglected to take a stand on the Chicago school issues? What might parents not accomplish if they banded together as parents?

One might fairly assume that Engleman, Corson, Ettinger, Finegan, Chadsey, Van Sickle, West and other superintendents deposed by corrupt politics from the successful and progressive management of schools might deplore too much pussyfoot policy by parents' associations formed of those who are the heaviest losers when the spoilsmen and grafters upset the schools. The parent-teacher movement is not militant; it is not a crusade. It is more gentle than that. It does not wish to enter into politics or to risk disrupting itself. So long as it maintains that policy the indications are that it will please 97 per cent., according to Mr. Butterworth's canvass, of the people concerned. Its aim is not the same as that of the public school. The statesmen who made schools the business of the whole people said nothing about parents. The founders of the system made it a charge on non-parents and soon got rid of the pre-Revolutionary practice of having fathers and mothers pay the cost. The public school is a community charge and therefore a community benefit, not an institution for the profit of children and their parents. That most parents still regard education as a means of pushing their children up in the social and financial scale, of giving children an ornamental possession or a distinction or a means of wealth is the fault of us schoolmasters who are affected by educational traditions dating from the gentleman-and-scholar days. Superintendents still issue circulars to grammar-school children urging them to go to high school because high-school graduates make more money when they enter employment. "Schools are for the children, not for the teachers," writes one superintendent in a rhetorical speech, epigrammatically untrue. Schools are not for children but for every person who spends a cent for anything. A part of his spending goes into the school tax. The schools are his, everybody's; they are not maintained that Johnny may learn to read but that everybody may share in a general welfare. This is old stuff. Each proponent for the school-tax laws called them investments in the safety and prosperity of the commonwealth.

What parent-teacherism is not.—Now, the parent-teacher organization began as a congress of mothers. Alice Birney originated it in 1896. Phoebe Hearst backed it with money. It was incorporated. Its main objects were the education of parents for child development and the training of young people for parenthood. By 1898 it had come so far in recognizing school as a valuable ally that the new name, National Congress of Mothers and Parent-Teacher Associations was adopted; twenty-six years later the National Congress of Parents and Teachers becomes its official title. Its objects, as given in its latest handbook, now are: first, child welfare; then, home betterment, laws for protection of women and children, cooperation with the school and development of public opinion so as to get for every child the highest advantages in education.

It is not a public education association composed of citizens organized to see that the community gets a fair deal from the politicians in so far as schools are concerned. You may wish you had a body of patriotic citizens realizing the immense importance of education as a civic force—men and women devoted to seeing that dirty politics keep away from school management. Every large city needs such a body. Otherwise, education becomes an institution for giving jobs to favorites and remunerative contracts to bosses' henchmen. Such an association has to be a fighting body.

In time such disgraces as have spoiled school management in Terre Haute, Baltimore, Cincinnati, Akron, Chicago, New York, Newark, Pennsylvania and elsewhere may lead to societies of citizens guarding their own schools from office-holders and bosses. Such public education associations will not be made up primarily of parents, but of civic defenders and promoters, whether they have any children or not.

Lacking such organizations, and because of its own specific purposes, the superintendent has in the parent-teacher association something eminently worth his support. Why? Because it comes nearer every year to being an honest-to-goodness public school society. Because it organizes and leads toward the support of the schools those citizens who, however traditional their ideas of the purpose of schools may be, have the strongest natural interest in them—that of parental devotion to children. Because it is a good thing for a schoolmaster to have some group of citizens keeping tab on his work. Few things wizen a man's work more than being surrounded by yes-yes companions who never give him the benefit of honest and open criticism. I had sooner have a meddlesome parent-teacher association at my heels than the listlessness a community usually shows in its municipal and political affairs. Obtrusiveness isn't so bad as indifference. It's good for you to have an organization which you can't manage watching you. Opposition can be met and, when wrong, often nullified. But neglect is already nullity and has no spur to put you on your mettle. Instead of complaining that parents and teachers interfere too much in school I hope they'll interfere more until membership on a board of education is forced by organized public opinion to concern itself with seeing that the present common use of the system for spoils politics is converted into protecting the best school workers in their service.

Whither the parent-teachers are tending.—As helps for a schoolman to know what this rapidly growing force is tending toward there are plenty of articles scattered through the educational magazines. There are a dozen separate booklets giving accounts of the work of the associations. There is *Child Welfare,* the monthly organ of the society. It has been published for twenty-three years. Two books have recently come out which are necessary to every school library. One covers the association's plans and work as outlined by its officials. The other does the same service from the schoolman's point of view.

"Parents and Teachers" is a handsome volume published by Ginn and Company. It is the work of a committee of the association on which are Mrs. Eugene Crutcher, Miss Frances Hays, Mrs. Laura Kohn, Mrs. A. H. Reeve, Mrs. Arthur Watkins, Miss Charl Williams and Mrs. Edward C. Mason, who is editor-in-chief. There seems to be apparent in its compilation a forestalling of criticism that the society has not had a sufficiently educational trend. Accordingly, the first 110 pages are dissertations on education written especially for this book by Henry Morrison, Sarah Arnold, Payson Smith, Joseph Lee and the Reverend Luther Weigle. Each of these chapters is followed by a bibliography of mostly modern works on the educational problems of the school. Then come the association's own doctrines, plans, activities and machinery. It is a decidedly readable account. The beginnings, the changes, the official objectives, the national body, the state and local branches, programs, activities, rural service and "What educators think" about it fill the book.

I recently read an article by the president of the parent-teacher association of the Ethical Culture Society of New York in which the statement was made that the question continues to be asked, "Of what use is a parent-teacher association?" "Parents, even those who have long worked in it, ask this. It lurks in the thoughts of some of our teachers. The one great purpose is to promote unity in guarding the life of the child.'' Mrs. Mason, in the official volume, elaborates this idea. It is our particular function not only to call attention to the value of all organized efforts to protect and educate the child, but also to provide a channel through which specialized information may reach fathers, mothers and other citizens who deal with children. In other places she says, ''The *child* is the center of interest, as indicated by the by-laws of all our departments, local, state and national.'' Bearing this in mind and the thought that public education is committed to the larger purpose, with society, not the child, as its central aim—a civic purpose, a social one, a political one—there is no justification in criticizing the parent-teachers. Their concern is only a part of the school's business. They are not a citizens' society but a parents' organization, recognizing that the teacher is *in loco parentis* and that fathers, mothers and teachers are parents in a legal sense and have enough in common to make association valuable to all of them for their interest in children.

What they do better than schools.—It is vital that the association undertake what schools neglect too much: the education of parents for parenthood. The Omaha public schools do this at their own instance in districts that have no parents' associations. In districts that do have them the public-school service furnishes teachers of home-training of children. Health, recreation, safety, thrift, art and religion, says Mrs. Mason, belong in every home. The society is working for this in all households in America. The average young mother comes to her task of child-rearing in blank ignorance because she has not been prepared for this vocation. Parenthood is the only important profession for which no preparation is demanded. ''We assemble the young mothers,'' continues Mrs. Mason, ''in the intimate company of others in the same situation. We have those who have studied the best procedure tell how often and how long a baby should be allowed to cry; what is the earliest time for discipline; when a baby should walk, talk, learn to read. We take up signs of deafness, sleep, open air, contagious diseases, obedience, vanity, precociousness.'' It seems to me that this service of itself is enough to put every school worker in the front row of those pushing for the parent-teachers. What an increased delight will come to schoolkeeping when we don't have to undo so much of the foolish spoiling of children that comes from neglect or from the wrong procedures in the impressionable preschool age. The suggested programs in the national handbook exhort the local clubs to study those traits which should have become habits by the time the child enters school. Obedience, self-reliance, washing hands and face, truthfulness, respect for the rights of others, it says, are home responsibilities. The school should be able to count on them. Our associations should study and appreciate what the school is doing for us. That's the right idea. Let our patron parents really discover what it means for a girl to take charge of forty youngsters—some of them little devils already—and to serve them the best part of the morning and the afternoon. Frequent opportunity, says this book, should be given to teachers, principals and superintendents to inform parents of the methods, activities and needs of the school and to acquaint citizens with progressive changes in the field of education. I'm for that. Aren't you? Few things clarify a complex process more than making it clear to those who know little about it. For teachers to tell, in half an hour, what the experimenters have found out regarding the damage of too prolonged oral reading or the deadening effect of memoriter recitation or the disappearance of the average child from the educational field or of the mesmerism of too much teacher talk or of what Lois Meek has discovered about failures, or to discourse on any chapter of the late books on teaching is to open the eyes of people whose ideas of instruction belong to the dark ages of 1919. More than that, if you get an audience of parents to ask questions about teaching methods you clarify your own mental processes as a good filter affects muddy water. The larger number of teacher participants you can coax to furnish educational programs, the better school you will have.

How they are dissolving the schoolman's opposition.—The association's leaders want it to be alive to the big duties to society at large. We are vitally concerned, says the book, with the quality of citizen that is produced by home and school for community service. All the year round the great school of the street and playground is in operation. The motion picture, the newsstand, the dance hall, the automobile were not considered when our traditions of home training were formed. It is the business of our organization to work for decency in these influences. Recreation, law observance, religion, civic duty—all are within our province. You must concede that this is a program worthy of your school people's support. In Chicago, when the newspapers announced that the school children, as guests of the mayor, were to be given free admission to a resort where obscene peep-show pictures of startling suggestiveness were a main attraction, the parent-teacher associations sent investigators to the grounds and issued a sturdy protest against the degradation of the schools. It is a sort of duty which lady-like literary and art clubs do not like to touch. But the handbook says that this association is not a lyceum course; it is a demonstration of moral reform by the people for the people.

It would be difficult for the most hardened objecting schoolman to read this entertaining book without experiencing a melting of his opposition or of his indifference to the movement. It is a development of more than thirty years. The women in charge of it have learned a lot of things that you know nothing of. They know what the organization may successfully do and what has endangered its usefulness in various localities. Their criticisms of their own organization are businesslike and to the point. So long, they say to the local branches, as you are merely a succession of afternoon teas with an interesting paper, so long as you are only sociable or an entertainment club, you are naught. Study your community, get facts, make a program on them, get an objective, make your work count. A gentle dig is given the fathers' meetings. "It seems to be generally conceded that they do not hold to the serious programs as well as the women." Too much tendency of the American male toward making fun of everything is the American man's fault. A kindergarten association in a city which was slow to put this feature into the public schools lured the superintendent to an exhibition of its teacher-training school. The madam president sat beside him. The girl students fluttered about, waving their arms in one of the kindergarten plays, imitating little birds. One becomes hurt and two others, with their arms around the young woman, tenderly conduct her to the home nest. "Isn't it beautiful!" exclaimed the lady president. "It is," replied the superintendent, "but don't you hate to see women doing a man's work?" Luigi Manzoni's "Impressions of the United States" notes an "itching of the average American man to say something funny. The presiding officer at every dinner tries to utter clownish things. The men teachers' banquet amused itself with songs ridiculing progressive ideas in education." Walter Lippmann says our political shame is treated by us as a jest. "Maybe," says the gentle author of our book, "the results of the men's meetings do not suffer from too much humor; the dart that is pointed with fun often sinks deepest." But, all the same, she lays down a program for fathers' nights that ought to make an ordinary man feel of some account. "Come back, sir," is the message, "to responsibilities. Fatherhood has been getting obscured. Your high respect for women, your reverence for mother have led you to leave in her hands power, authority and judgment which you should share. You have let your sense of responsibility deteriorate. Come to our fathers' clubs and get into the personal relation with your children which they deserve and give them the guidance which they need." Some of the most genuine father-stuff you could ask for is laid out in the association programs: father as companion in recreation, in gardening, in making swings, seesaws, flower boxes, in athletic diversions, in talking over science, literature and current events. Doesn't it bring up delicious pictures of the fathers of your boyhood days helping collect the specimens of rocks and shells, going on the boat trips, sleeping in the tent? O boys! What your youngsters of now are losing when there's no back yard for them and their dads, no fishing, no woods, nothing but streets, flats and the indoor movies. Come, father, says the association, stop saying you have no time. Don't be bankrupt of it. It's the most plentiful thing there is, flowing along, full stream, as ever it has from eternity. Time doesn't fly. You do. You flutter from one supplementary to another and the great things of life are untouched—friendship with your own, companionship, enjoyment of your children. What you need is organization to bring you back to normalcy. Our fathers' clubs are discussing boy nature. They are working out a scale of man's values in which the children are listed at the top where they belong. They are the most promising investment, they are the promise of your greatest profit and happiness. It is the law of nature. You can't go on breaking it without a grievous penalty.

The partnership idea.—These people are not going on blindly. Their programs are the work of high-class brains directed to a scheme of improvement perfected by these thirty years of experience. Mrs. Mason has a meaty chapter on what they have learned about leadership. It is too wasteful, she says, to go on making the same old mistakes. We are getting out of the early haphazard stage where each society had no precedents. We can look back and study how we wasted too much time. No organization can successfully meet the needs of the present circumstances except it be guided by leaders who have a clear vision of what should be done. We have those who are trained for the service. To me this seems the sure sign that this organization is a real force in the field. I can remember a sort of wild and glad atmosphere of our "home and school" societies forty years ago when some woman, avid of prominence, elected herself president and had a series of "inspirational" addresses by professional spellbinders imagining all sorts of mystical sacredness about "the child." There was enthusiasm without much use of a rudder. We worked the clubs for pictures, pianos and magic lanterns. We fended off the members from usurping our functions as directors of the schools committed to us. We regarded the associations as sort of annexes without anything to do other than what we suggested. But the parent-teachers have a policy. They know what it is. Courses of instruction in it are given in Teachers College, New York, in the Michigan State Normal College in Ypsilanti, at the Chautauqua Summer Assembly in Jamestown, and, according to our book, in growing numbers of normal schools, colleges and universities. In their own state convention, the associations devote a day to review of the essentials of leadership. The courses cover community organization, community needs, investigation of school service, principles of child nurture, programs and kindred matters. A cardinal principle emphasized in these classes and repeated in this book and in the association's various publications is cooperation. "Conference with school authorities first, last and always is essential. The schools are the greatest organization doing the kind of work for which our organization stands: promotion of child welfare. We are a partnership, home partners, school partners, parents, teachers. Since the home partners are more numerous they must be especially careful to keep in close touch with the others so that the activities of the association may be guided by the united good judgment of both. You should not throw the load of the work too heavily on the teachers. They are more burdened with children than parents are. Let the heaviest offices in the clubs be borne by parents." To load teachers with educational service outside of school, teaching church classes, running women's study clubs, and such like, breeds monotony for them. If you had a church sociable for all its members, waffles to be served hot, it might seem suitable to put the lady who runs the town waffle parlor in charge of that service. No doubt it would secure success as far as waffles are concerned, but it's no refreshment for her. The teacher members of the home-and-school society can run, probably, the best educational program, but, give these girls a rest. Let the others study education and write papers on it. It's good for them.

This will give you some idea of Mrs. Mason's enlightening book. It is direct, specific, official. It will correct the schoolman's notions derived from an outside, superficial view and likely to be obscured by local and unessential considerations and by conclusions based on his inner processes. A knowledge of this nation-wide service, rapidly permeating even rural communities, is essential to the intelligent supervision of education.

Parent-teachers as viewed by school people.—The other book I spoke of is an attractive little volume of 150 pages, "The Parent-Teacher Association and its Work," by Dr. Julian E. Butterworth, professor of rural education and chairman of the division of education, Cornell University, published by the Macmillan Company, New York. It is a view from outside the organization, and, in the modern style of educational writing, it avoids enthusiasm, propaganda and generalities. But, as is proper in considering the work of a public service such as that of the association is, Dr. Butterworth does not hesitate to give his opinions on what parent-teachers should and should not do. The parent-teacher movement is here, large, influential and growing, says Dr. Butterworth. It is no secret that professional school people are not unanimously in favor of it. Some would have it eliminated, others believe that if properly directed it would have an important constructive influence on education. Still others are enthusiastically for it. It ought to be studied. Accordingly, he asked the guardians of the university's research funds to pay the expenses of studying several hundred local parent-teacher associations distributed throughout the United States. He covered 797 in all. His book considers the origin, growth and present size of the movement, what it is doing, its programs, entertainments, receptions, use of school children, whether these clubs are doing what they ought, what American education is, how much of it is understood by the leaders of the parent-teacher associations, what school people think of the movement, a detailed account of the society's activities and objectives, how the programs are made, the membership, why it loses and gains, how a local may measure itself, its leadership, etc.

Schoolmen will be especially interested in Dr. Butterworth's canvass of superintendents and principals to ascertain what they think of the movement. He sent to them 797 inquiries and got 390 replies. Sixty-five per cent. of these approve the continuance of the association along present lines.

Twenty-eight per cent. approve it if re-directed in certain ways. Four per cent. dodged this question. Two per cent. said that in their communities they thought the work should be dropped. Of the 407 who kept the return postage and sent no reply of any sort it is, of course, only conjecture to estimate how many were conscientious objectors to questionnaires, how many were opposed to the association but wary of self-expression, and how many were in need of stamps. It is fair to assume that none of the non-respondents is at a white-heat of enthusiasm for the parent-teacher scheme. I am sorry. I think they are missing a big opportunity for pushing ahead the work of their schools and of making their own work easier and more enjoyable. If I could persuade you, gentle reader, to this view, it would be on the basis of what Mrs. Mason's outline contains and on what I have seen of the association's work in the locations which have allowed me to be their public-school teacher during the past forty-one delightful years.

Appraisal of the movement by educators.—Of the 390 good fellows who do help Butterworth make his study, 94 per cent. cite this desirable result—facilitating acquaintance among parents and teachers; 85 per cent., applying educational objectives and methods out of school; 81 per cent., helping educate the community in desirable aspects of the school's program; 66 per cent., raising money for school; 53 per cent., giving members an understanding of school aims and methods; 31 per cent., giving school officials an appraisal of the success or failure of school. From what you have read of the association's own purposes you readily see the discrepancy. The movement centers around parenthood and child-rearing, the school being one agency to assist in reaching the objectives. The schoolmen seem to regard it as a sort of school branch, and think that the school should be the center of the association's intentions. The parent-teachers' book emphasizes partnership; the schoolmen tend toward having the association as auxiliary. Over and over again the association's official statement is: "We don't want to run your school. We're for the children, so are you; in that field we want to help you and we need your help." It strikes me that the courteous and effective reply of the schoolman will be: "We, too, are in the child business, obligated to train him to make a better society and civic organization. Although we are not the servants of parents as such but of all citizens who pay us our wages, we are for parents. They keep the world alive. Whatever we can contribute of our experience and study toward the training of parents and children we shall give the association, so far as comports with our wider duty. We need the intelligent support of all citizens. We are for the service clubs, Rotary, Kiwanis, Lambs, Boosters, Lions and the others. We are for the churches, the chambers of commerce, the women's clubs and every organization that is for civic advance, child welfare, arts, sciences and civilization. We can't give ourselves wholly to each without neglecting our main business, but what we can reasonably do we will."

Some such idea as this is current in Butterworth's book, although it would be impertinent in me to formulate his ideas in my words. He considers the movement as momentous. He sees its value. It has gone through the first period of promotion. Its real test comes now, as to whether it will, by the scientific method of self-examination, criticism and correction, delimit its problems and discover effective means of attacking them. "Unless it does, the parent-teacher movement, like any that depends upon an emotional stimulus, is likely to decline. Wisely directed it has an important place in our scheme of education." With that belief he renders us all a distinct service by constructive criticism, pointing out good features and how they may be retained and bettered.

Parent-teachers measured.—By means of quantitative diagrams he holds a mirror up to the association and shows it devoting 20 per cent. more of its activity to money-raising than to educational objectives. Sixty-six per cent. of his schoolmen correspondents give that activity third place in their estimate of good deeds. It is unwise, comments the doctor, to endanger our conception of public support of schools by suggesting that parents should bear the financial burden. But, where the community is unable to raise the needed funds through taxes, the association may provide the desired facilities. It has put in new blackboards, modern heating and ventilating systems, beautified the school yards and even put teachers' salaries in a healthy state by direct contributions. It has bought books, magazines, pictures, sand tables, pianos, phonographs, moving-picture machines, scenery, footlights, drop curtains, band instruments, uniforms, cooking equipment, hot lunches, paid athletic coaches, dramatic directors and debating club instructors. It has donated Christmas trees and eyeglasses. This kind of service is alluring. You can point to the most of its gifts as something that shows. The amounts can be definitely measured. They make reports look good. The patient principal, refused modern equipment and beautification, turns to his association with the *argumentum ad matrem*: "This is your child's home. What you give not only makes him happier but cheers hundreds of others besides. Come on, be a good parent and a patriot. This is for your country. It's really better than buying a new car." When you visit those schools that have all these advantages that no school board will buy, when you consider the millions that are lavished on endowed colleges, the immense amount wasted on chewing gum, perfumery, jewelry and automobiles, it is hard to join the ranks of those who object to this activity of the parent-teachers. But in the official book entitled "Parents and Teachers," the classification of detailed objectives omits this service. On the contrary, the author reminds the local associations that money-raising has received more of praise and criticism than any other activity and has contributed most to the failure as well as to the success of the locals. Buying things for the school, she says, is not the main purpose of the movement. Taxation should provide the equipment, grounds and salaries of every school district in the United States. The public school is a community investment in citizenship. The failure of school authorities properly to equip a school will not be remedied by your buying what is needed. Let your locals study the finances. Educate the public to demand of its representatives what the schools need. Thus the association book goes farther than the outsider's volume in caution against too much centering on buying things for the school.

It is the same in the matter of studying education. "One is impressed," says Dr. Butterworth, "by the few activities, 2 per cent., given to studying the educational needs of the community. This should be increased." The official book's attention to this is constant. "No important work should be undertaken until a group of parents, teachers, principals, superintendent and members of the school board consider needs and agree that the activity contemplated is for the welfare of the children, that it is a feasible project for a parent-teacher association and that it is desirable. Attempt the most urgent first."

Dr. Butterworth shows by graphs the relative amount of attention given by his 937 sample associations to money-raising, educational and social objectives, non-educational, influencing boards, educating the community and studying school needs. He shows health and leisure as the chief educational ideas considered by the locals, with civic duties, home conduct, character and vocation much less attended to. In his study of the distribution of meetings he finds receptions and entertainments overtopping the educational work. Some of the associations, he says, are entirely neglecting certain significant problems. The official volume earnestly exhorts the locals to advance out of the stage of rummage sales and carnivals. "There will be a decrease in the purely entertainment features of the meetings and an increase in the attention to study. We are not an entertainment lyceum; we are not a social club; we are a school for parents and teachers studying the child and his welfare."

The bugaboo of interfering with the schools.—Mr. Butterworth's handling of the allegation that the locals interfere with the conduct of the schools is tactful and fair. "There is a difference between attempting to influence school officials and trying to interfere with their duties." We are restive when organized groups are pushing for what we don't want. A superintendent need not be. Continual pestering of school boards will turn them against a foolish project sooner than our opposition to it will. Butterworth was commendably persistent in tracking down this alleged interference. He studied 887 business sessions of different associations. He is surprised at finding only three or four cases that might be counted as interference. Some local associations, he believes, have in effect taken the position that they represent the communities more truly than the boards of education do. How about that? Miss Powers' article took the stand that the Chicago school board, appointed and controlled by Mayor Thompson, did not represent the community. Who shall say it did? Dr. Butterworth's argument is that the local association seldom, if ever, includes all citizens and is not the regular representative of them. The school board is that, by law. Confusion will surely result unless responsibility is exercised by those on whom it legally devolves. He discusses the question often raised—whether the association should take part in a school election. He thinks not. Mrs. Mason agrees. He quotes from her list of don'ts: "Don't try to dictate the policies of school administration." Probably they are right. I like to see my parent-teacher association, when a school board is debauching the schools at the behest of the big man in city hall, get out and fight for the rights of children, however disagreeable and unladylike it may seem. On a clear moral issue of that kind they'll gain more members than they lose, get more praise than blame and do more for "the child" than by taking the easier course of avoiding controversy. If escaping contention had been the rule of mankind we should still have a sun moving over a flat world of slaves, priest-ridden, which forbade women to organize in parent-teacher associations or anything else.

"Beware of becoming static," says Butterworth to the parent-teachers. "Organization tends to formalism. Education may easily get into a state of satisfaction with things as they are. It is not enough to train a boy up to the standard of the average citizen." We heard wiseacres define education as fitting for environment, introducing the child to the intellectual inheritance of the race. That isn't enough. That's static. The parent-teachers are awake to that. Hear one of their presidents, Margaretta Reeve, in the *Child-Welfare Magazine:* "Parent power plus teacher power may supply the force which is needed to revolutionize conditions as they are to-day and to develop new and better opportunities for the citizenship of to-morrow." And the Mason book opens with a quotation from Payson Smith: "The program of education will be a constantly expanding one."

Inside and outside, the same.—Dr. Butterworth's extensive study brings him to the conclusion that there is a place for such an organization as the parent-teacher association. This is the judgment he gets, not from its members nor from parents. The size and growth of it shows how they feel. It is the schoolmen that he was especially interested in. They are for it. "They are not unanimous that no other organization could serve the schools better nor that this one should not do its work better." But without Dr. Butterworth's canvass the association book relates the same fact. There are association objectives concerning parents and children which the schools have not yet undertaken. There are school duties which the association does not attempt to influence. The association's formal programs are really the course of study. It needs more educational content, says the Butterworth book. The association volume has emphasized the same. Both contain definite details of the improvement needed. Both remark that American public-school teachers are not given sufficient social recognition. Both urge more human sympathy to the end that teaching may be more enjoyable and children thereby better served. Both books desire teachers to talk to parents' clubs on school procedures. Both give suggested topics of real interest to every intelligent person. The association has standardized the activities so as to let the locals know what an up-to-grade local is and what is a superior one. Butterworth has put this into the form of an excellent self-measuring scale. He has tabulated a remarkably valuable list of reasons why members drop out and a supplementary one of what keeps members in. It is remarkable that working independently the makers of these two books have hit so closely upon the same ideas. Mrs. Mason had a canvass of the schoolmen made by Professor M. V. O'Shea. That and Butterworth's cover all the states. After a study of both books I could, I think, without doing much damage to either compiler, say that Mrs. Mason had written Dr. Butterworth's, and he, hers. Independently of both, Henry Morrison says what surely will appeal to you:

> Our education must aim to safeguard society. It must be the hope of social progress toward the goal of happiness and well-being for all men. Schools which really educate are attainable but only as intelligent and resolute citizens bend their energies to placing in the schools teachers who educate and school officials who are educators. The community can control the schools. It can do it through legislation. It can control the teaching of the home and the church only through the generation of an intelligent public opinion. Herein is the greatest single opportunity of the parent-teacher movement.

You're for it.—There you are. You now have a clearer idea of parent-teacherism than before. Any irritation that may have been disturbing your peace of mind has not been due to the real thing but to a distortion of it, due, perhaps, to personal strabismus or to a local branch of the association that is not living up to the spirit of its constitution. If you get Mrs. Mason's book you can quote to any members of your local organization who are straying from the path of organization rectitude the true gospel of the association scripture and with it gently shoo them back into their proper road. You will find so much in this manual that you believe, said so much better than you and I could express it, that you will want to thank the compiler and publisher for making it available. Within your generation the organizations that have come into being disposed to honor you and your service are a cause for you to rejoice. Here is one which more than most is respectful and sympathetic, resolved not to interfere with you, not to take your responsibilities from you, disposed to be guided by your experience in your own field. It is enroling the sort of people whose support you need in carrying out your progressive policies. If I were you I would hitch up with it and pull in the direction it is going.

SCHOOL AND SOCIETY

EDITED BY J. McKEEN CATTELL

WITH WHICH IS COMBINED THE

EDUCATIONAL REVIEW

EDITED BY WILLIAM McANDREW

Volume XXIX | SATURDAY, JUNE 8, 1929 | Number 754

HARVARD TEACHERS' ASSOCIATION

BUSINESS AND EDUCATION[1]

By Professor CARL FREDERICK TAEUSCH

HARVARD GRADUATE SCHOOL OF BUSINESS ADMINISTRATION

IT can safely be said that the most outstanding phenomenon of present-day social relations is the self-criticism and self-control of business. Criticism and control there have been in abundance before, and perhaps necessarily. But never before has a national body of business men, with voluntary membership, subscribed to the declaration that "Business should render restrictive legislation unnecessary through so conducting itself as to secure and inspire public confidence." This declaration is one of the fifteen "Principles of Business Conduct" initiated and sponsored by the Chamber of Commerce of the United States. Literally hundreds of groups of business and professional men have organized associations and formulated "codes of ethics" in conformity with the spirit of this declaration, partly as a means of group protection, to be sure, but partly also as a means of setting standards of conduct that are socially desirable as well as commercially, industrially and financially sound.

These business associations have outgrown the mere "code of ethics" stage, in which they were satisfied with declarations of meaningless platitudes or were guilty of disseminating a cloud of hypocritical camouflage. Trade practice conferences and other formulations of business policy are being sponsored by the Federal Trade Commission, the Department of Commerce, the Chamber of Commerce of the United States and the Better Business Bureau, and are now stating facts as well as theories, agreeing upon justifiable trade practices and defining trade terms so as to stabilize business methods, and business men themselves are accepting their responsibilities to the purchaser, the consumer, the laborer, the investor, the competitor—in short, to the general public. Trade disputes are no longer carried to the courts and there subjected to delay, expense and inexpert judgments; they are being arbitrated by business men themselves, speedily, economically and by men who are acquainted with justifiable trade practices.

The nearest previous approach to this phenomenon of the self-regulation of business has been the guild movement of the later Middle Ages. The earlier craft guilds and the later merchant guilds represented, in most cases, a positive necessity in that day and age. National governments did not then exist as such, nor was there a common law; there remained only the inadequate feudal control and the exotic influ-

[1] Address delivered at the annual meeting of the Harvard Teachers' Association, Cambridge, March 16, 1929.

ence of the church. The guilds supplied the regulation and control of quality, of workmanship, of bills of exchange and public finance that have since then become largely the functions of government and of law. As governments extended their jurisdictions over wider territories, and as the law became administered uniformly over such, the less powerful guilds succumbed. The extension of national law and its intensive development in succeeding centuries gave rise, however, to certain difficulties because of the heterogeneous character of territories or industries or peoples, difficulties that have given rise politically to the doctrines of "local option" and "states' rights." At the same time, business and industry have become increasingly variegated and complex, too much so for a centralized government and a *common* law adequately or accurately or expeditiously to administer. In contrast with this prevailing political centralization, there has developed a functional pluralism of business, expressed in trade associations, corporation policies and the differentiations among various individual businesses located in different parts of the country.

The result of these two conflicting tendencies in America has been a widening breach between government and business and a growing resentment among business men against "government interference." Much of this governmental attitude has been necessary and salutary; indeed much of it was fostered by business men themselves, who trained our national and state officials to assume such prerogatives: not only have business men secured valuable franchises, patents and trade-marks, tariff favors and the like from government, but our national proclivity to cure all evils by passing a law on the subject exhibits the same kind of social laziness on the part of business men that is expressed in the phrase, "Let George do it." George, the legislator, not only did it, but he afforded a beautiful illustration to pragmatic pedagogy: he "learned to do by doing," and the result of the past apathies and greed of the American business man has been the setting up of governmental agencies that hunger for more extensive functions and more intensive activities. Business, like Frankenstein, set up a monster whose all-consuming activities can now be inhibited only through the mystic charm, the still, small voice of self-regulation, prompted by the humble acknowledgment of evils discovered through honest and rigorous self-criticism and leading to the practical courses of action that prove effectively the sincerity of the confession.

It is this undercurrent of social movements that explains the present-day phenomenon of business ethics. Before plumbing still further the depths of this social undercurrent, it may be well to pause a moment to ask what bearing the phenomenon of business ethics has on educational theories or practices. We shall content ourselves with a single observation: If we allot the time in our schedules, and make a place in our curriculum, for the study of civil government and history in order to acquaint the child with his social environment, does it not seem apparent that economics and business are sufficiently important to warrant at least a place beside these two studies? At once the hands of many teachers are raised in despair or protest—our schedules and curricula are already overcrowded! The immediate answer to this is, of course, that so far as history is concerned, the question is one of relative values and emphasis. Certainly no one can defend a history which merely reflects the movements of political and military pawns, but such a recognition does not necessitate swinging to the opposite extreme of an economic interpretation of history. Certainly, however, nothing short of an adequate sociological point of view should govern the teaching of history; with such a point of view, colored by a really humanistic spirit, it is difficult to see how the study of modern business can be omitted. As for the study of civil government, it is doubtful—and this is said in all earnestness—it is doubtful whether the social relations studied in a course of civil government are as vital to the present and future interests of students, as real, as important, as valuable, as would be the study of business relations and principles, showing a child how one earns a living, what thrift means and production, what the difference is between capital and income and which govern expenditures, what honesty and integrity demand and what part is played by economic values in church and state and art and science and in the very educational processes from which he is benefiting.

Note that the present burden of the argument has taken this turn: Does our educational system give a true and adequate picture of society? If education purposes to make a boy or girl acquainted with the world in which he is to live, is it not necessary that our schools take account of one of the most vital factors in our life, the way in which people earn their living? Note also that this question is not one of values—we shall come to that later—but simply one of facts: Does our education recognize the world as it actually exists to-day? It is difficult to avoid anticipating the burden of the latter part of the argument by pointing out that the present vogue of "character education" can find few fields more fertile with concrete problems and practical idealism than modern business activities.

The argument of this paper has so far been concerned with the capacity of our educational system to portray the facts of life and to give to the pupil a true picture of the situation he will meet when he is once launched on his own voyage away from the protected harbors of the school, and the discussion so far has concerned itself with the part played by elementary schools in preparing a pupil for his life in the world. A reorganization in content and personnel faces the educational administrator of the future. The next step obviously would be to develop a scheme of vocational or practical education in which the pupil would be equipped with more highly tempered and better-sharpened tools for making his way in the world successfully. Inasmuch as this line of reasoning is the expected course to follow, it would perhaps be more interesting not to follow it. The implications are perfectly clear and the questions are largely of fact. The whole philosophy underlying our professional and business schools and our technological institutes is built upon the general proposition that, the world being so and so, the student should be fitted to master it.

But the remaining argument of this paper is to follow a totally different point of view, suggested, strangely enough, by the very requirements which some vocational schools themselves set as regards the preliminary training which is necessary and best adapted to specialized training. The law schools of the country have generally taken the attitude that a liberal arts education is a sufficient prerequisite for law school candidates, and it has been recognized by law school faculties and deans that a *thorough discipline* in mathematics or literature, Latin or biology or any subject is preferable to a *less thorough training* in any subject, including politics or government. The Harvard Business School pointedly advises a prospective graduate business student to study less rather than more business in college. Without assuming the burden of extending this principle to the preliminary training of the minister, the doctor, the engineer or the teacher, or to the still broader question as to whether college requirements shall dominate preparatory or high-school curricula—and I am rather inclined to think that such questions should be answered in the spirit of the law-school and business-school attitude—let us consider the problem in the philosophy of education which this question raises.

The problem is this: Shall the education of the child—rather of young men and young women, for we are now dealing with policies of secondary and collegiate education—shall education be directed exclusively in the direction, not of understanding life, but of training the student for the active or selfish part he shall play therein? The problem is a modified form of the old issue between those who would stress the encouragement of creative activity and those who emphasize the importance of cultivating appreciation. In order to clarify the issue we shall go back to the common-sense view that appreciation differs in kind from creative activity, that it is not merely an activity that differs in degree from creative production or that can be interpreted as an incipient or retrospective activity. Appreciation as spoken of here is more nearly akin to the attitude of tolerance than to that of reform or control, and may be likened to the joy one gets in seeing a kite or airplane aloft in the sky, in contrast with the desire or act of bringing it down, picking it apart and jumping on the pieces—acts which are so often identified with understanding.

It is easy to see the question here being raised: What is a liberal education? And the answer to this question may be in part anticipated when it is asserted that undeniably a part of liberal education consists in studying appreciatively many things which none of us can ever control—conspicuously among which are the past, with its rich coloring of traditions and meanings—indeed just the variegated pattern that it is—and the far-distant stars and places that even our fired imagination can not disturb. We are speaking here of the unattainables of life, and we beg leave to count ourselves among those who refuse to accept any pragmatic explanations of such appreciable values in terms of creation or control. The honest attempt to understand appreciatively a situation which is admittedly beyond our control may be criticized as being merely a modern form of totemism with its ritualistic and imitative dances; but if this is so, then the arrogance of science and the philosophical-psychological-pedagogical doctrines that emphasize exclusively the development of creative and controlling functions must be regarded as the lineal descendants of the ancient medicine man whose coat of arms contained chanticleer rampant on a field of amulets.

Appreciation is an attitude which is directed not only to unattainables or uncontrollables; it may be cultivated just as well in regard to matters which we ourselves can not control but which others do. Tolerance is a function which can well be made an educational objective, not to the exclusion of individual development but certainly as a compromise with the creativist theory. To know what another man is doing is to learn to tolerate both him and it. "I can't," said Charles Kingsley, "hate a man I know." And the situation is as true among the mutual relations of geniuses as it is in the relations between the genius and the mass.

The point at which the argument is directed is that education can ill afford to pin its faith exclusively to a program of directly fitting a student for his life work. The underlying difficulty with any scheme of vocational education is that it is apt to become too narrow and therefore self-destructive. Liberality in education is no more to be achieved by allowing individuals separately to pursue their chief interests exclusively than a general happiness can result from individual pursuits of pleasure; Carlyle once observed that such a doctrine was equivalent to expecting table manners to evolve by increasing the number of pigs at the trough. A liberal education consists, in part at least, in studying fields of activity that may not directly be connected with the objective of a life purpose.

In a recent article in the *Atlantic Monthly,* George Herbert Palmer pointed out what he regarded as a most significant contribution of the American college. In Europe prospective business men seldom go to college, and their intellectual contact with professional men and scholars is limited to the preparatory schools. Whatever critics may say of our inefficient collegiate training in America, such as there is is shared by business men. And no one denies the value of this state of affairs. One of the results of this situation is the munificence of business men in this country, especially towards colleges and universities, in striking contrast with the situation abroad. And much of the difference between the American and the European attitude is to be explained by the fact that the American business man, say what you will in criticism of him, has sensed the value of college and university ideals. The spirit of the article might lead us easily to the question: If the study of other than business subjects is already regarded as a necessary part of the liberal education of the business man, why can not the study of economics or business be likewise regarded as necessary in part to the liberal education of those who do not intend to enter the field of business?

The difficulty now becomes apparent. Traditionally we have regarded business as an inferior occupation and its activities as representative of values that play only a minor and instrumental rôle in the social pattern. To study business as a part of our cultural heritage seems like a contradiction in terms. This attitude we have inherited from the medieval church, which in turn derived the doctrine from Plato. It seems strange that Greek thought, whose secular clarity emancipated it from the superstitions of previous and other peoples, should have taken so seriously the mysteries of the East, and left us with a heritage that despises economic and business values. Whatever the cause, the event in Greek thought was an epistemological dualism between idea and reality that reflected the social attitudes of the time—in which the slave did the bidding of his master, and the observer sat far above the market-place and the competitors in the games. Critical reflection there no doubt had its origin, but one feels strongly with John Dewey that the situation was liable to become vicious in proportion to the superciliousness of the observer.

The attitude was transmitted through Plotinus to the church, which made "flesh" and "lucre" share alike in its condemnations. It is difficult to determine what would have happened if the guilds had continued independently to develop their own rules and regulations in opposition to this point of view. But they succumbed to the growing power of the state, in the form of newly arising, vigorous nationalities, and made way before the extension of the more rigorous Roman and common law. In spite of the temporary rebuffs of the church by the state, the former maintained its position of judging as to relative and absolute values, and in that capacity the church never gave much recognition to business and none at all to its autonomous capacities. Even with the coming of the Renaissance, the church retained its position of judging as to the values of the economic life, as is proved by the exception to the rule—for Calvinism has given capitalism and the modern business corporation their chief apologies. That such a complete reversal of affairs did not improve the situation may readily be seen, for whereas the medieval church unduly restricted business activities, Calvinism gave them a license which business itself could not venture to-day to assert and which still hinders business from achieving its highest intrinsic values. The whole matter resolves itself to this, that the exotic control of the church over business has not been the blessing it was intended to be; and as in the case of a similar disposition on the part of the state, the effect has been frequently mutually unsatisfactory.

But to-day we are faced with a new phenomenon, the self-assertion of business through the reactions of business men themselves. Not only have church and state failed to keep up with the growing complexities of industry and commerce, but business men themselves have shown an increasingly determined disposition to govern their own affairs. Are the objectives of business of such a character as to warrant their inclusion, beside those of church and state, science and art, in the pattern of justifiable absolute social values? Is there a sufficiently mutual interplay among the values of business and other social values as still further to accord a dignified place to the instrumental values of business activities? Certainly no one who has followed the history of an investment issue or of the organization of a corporation can deny that creative imagination of the first order is here at play. The tremendous increase in the responsibilities of bankers has sobered them into a realization of their social obligations, while the immortality of the corporation has enhanced the meaning of a reputation for reliable service and the dignity of a good name. Nowhere is the spoken word more rigorously kept than on the floor of the New York Stock Exchange; the Diamond Match Company presented to the American people without charge its exclusive patent for making non-poisonous matches, and General Motors Corporation has specifically indicated its unwillingness to purchase goods on terms which will not allow the selling company to make a reasonable profit. Following the leadership of Henry Ford, American industry has developed the most generous wage policy in history, while the main burden of trade association policies has been to safeguard the rights of the competitor. Are these facts known to the boys and girls, to young men and young women, to the teachers in our educational system? Not only are business facts a necessary part of the true picture of modern society, but business ethics can no longer be denied an important place in our pattern of social values.

I am not pleading for the introduction of business subjects into a crowded curriculum for young people who are later going to enter business or a business school. These students should indeed be encouraged to pursue other subjects. But the future minister, lawyer, politician, engineer, laborer, artist, scholar, teacher, would do well to get acquainted with the facts of the business world; not that he may learn to play the stock market, but for the same reason that admits the humanistic value of da Vinci's "Madonna of the Rocks" and Guicciardini's local histories. For once, a picture contained a real flower; for once, a historian wrote about the things that were happening about him. Tradition and history are necessary to any matured culture, but they are not sufficient; Greece and the Renaissance give the lie to him who despises the homely events of his contemporary environment.

The spirit of tolerance inevitably develops out of a study of alien fields, for the objective pattern will supplant the prejudiced opinion which so often prompts human beings to attempt to control what they do not understand. Tolerance and liberalism, in this sense, by reducing the desire to reform or control an alien field of activity, directs the attention to self-criticism and self-control. A study of modern business conditions will soon disclose the tremendous task that confronts the business administrator, and will imbue the non-business man with a sufficient sense of humility to encourage him to return to his own activity and interests if he be bent on reform or creative production. Business is rapidly freeing itself from exotic forms of control by self-attention and the discipline of self-correction. Is it too much to ask that church and state, art and science, which frequently have solaced themselves for their own shortcomings by criticizing economic values and business, return to their own tasks, some of which certainly have been much neglected?

If such a program be suggested, the question arises: Can business then be entrusted with the function of self-government? From the point of view of education, the question is: What content would a study of business include that would picture and justify such a social objective? It is the purpose of this article merely to call attention to the situation without indicating in detail the answers to the questions here raised.

The most subtle problem of business ethics consists in discovering the sanctions which prevail in business activities and which therefore must be relied upon in order to effect the appropriate measure of control over business conduct. Whether this control will be relatively extrinsic or intrinsic rests in large part with business men themselves and the educational processes to which they are subjected in the formative periods of their lives.

THE TEACHER'S PERSONAL INVESTMENT PROBLEM[1]

By A. VERE SHAW

THE relationship between education and modern business is a direct and vital one. Business looks to education to furnish a constant supply of sensible recruits. Education looks to business for the wherewithal to equip and train those recruits. If business wants still better recruits, if educators wish to improve their product, a greater degree of cooperation should be fostered between education and business. It is a matter of regret that at times the academic left hand of an educational institution is quite at a loss to understand what the administrative or business right hand is doing, and why; also *vice versa*.

A college in this neighborhood has an endowment fund containing a large proportion of sound common stocks, approximately 30 per cent. This policy has proved very profitable. Another well-known college has invested its fund 100 per cent. in bonds. Here are two opposed investment policies. Both can not be right. It is doubtful if the economic departments of these two colleges would disagree so greatly regarding investment policy as do their finance committees.

As a possible means of furnishing educators more and better equipment, of providing them more leisure and comfort, of helping them to accumulate the capital, ownership of which gives rise to a personal investment problem, I suggest a closer cooperation between economic departments and finance committees.

Investment is not a science and, if it deserves to be rated as an art, it is as yet without many exact definitions to cover its principal concepts. It is difficult for two persons to agree as to what an investor is, what conservatism is, what safety is. Generally, however, the investor is considered to be a capitalist who wishes to put his

[1] Address delivered at the annual meeting of the Harvard Teachers' Association, Cambridge, March 16, 1929.

funds to work with a high degree of safety and conservatism.

Contrary to general impression, but nevertheless quite reasonable when one comes to think of it, change, movement, revolution are more conservative, more to be expected than permanence. Permanence is never attained. Like perfection, it is only approached. Constant change has been the rule in all things since the world began. Safety is no exception. Think how our ideas of safety have changed as regards traveling, by carriage, by train, by automobile and by aeroplane! Thirty years ago the safest automobile was perhaps one which could travel at a speed not to exceed ten miles an hour. To-day a maximum speed of ten miles per hour would be entirely unsafe when cars on the average travel forty miles an hour. The safest automobile which could be imagined might be a motorless one standing in a ten-acre field. But it would not be an automobile because it could not accomplish what automobiles are designed for, that is, to afford transportation. Safety, therefore, in any activity must be defined reasonably in view of an objective to be accomplished. It can be taken for granted that the investor is a person who asks no more than reasonable safety under current conditions.

During the period from 1900 to 1921 we heard a great deal about the high cost of living. A change was going on during this period which affected invested capital. The "high cost of living" is another way of saying the "depreciated purchasing power of money." During this period, 1900 to 1921, the purchasing power of our dollar was constantly dwindling, and any one who had a fixed income during this period found that it decidedly was not fixed at all as far as purchasing power was concerned.

During this same period and for a long time before, another change had been going on which affected the investor and his problem and made it necessary that he have a constantly increasing purchasing power. During the last fifty years we have developed new needs and new luxuries; new methods of transportation, communication, amusement—automobiles, aeroplanes, refrigeration, the movies, the radio. In numerous ways we have raised our standard of living over that of our grandfathers. The increase in living standards and the constant fluctuation in the purchasing power of our currency are two of the most serious obstacles which the investor must overcome in solving his problem.

It must be recognized at the outset that absolute safety is unattainable and even undesirable. Every piece of property, every investment is subject to some hazard and may be destroyed or at least injured. The investor's problem, therefore, is how to minimize risk, how to secure certainty out of uncertainties. This is the problem of every business man and it varies from the investor's problem only in degree. The investor wishes the utmost reasonable safety.

The most widely known institution which has succeeded in securing maximum safety, or at least the best possible substitute for it, is the institution of insurance. Every piece of property, every contract, every life insured, is a risk upon which the company runs a chance of loss. Nevertheless, well-managed insurance companies are sound, profitable and successful, and there is no reason to believe they will not continue to be so. This building of a superstructure of safety upon a foundation of uncertainties has been accomplished by adherence to certain rules and principles which experience has proven to be reliable. Since investing, like insurance, is a business of risks, the investor can do no better than examine the principles followed by the insurance companies and apply them in the solution of his own problem. What are some of these principles?

Within twenty-four hours the fire bells of this city will be ringing, and somewhere there will be a loss by fire. No officer or stockholder of any insurance company, however, is sitting up worrying about that loss which is sure to come. One company or another has insured almost all the buildings in this city and other cities, and at rates which, regardless of losses here and there, assure each company reasonable profit on its business as a whole. The principle at work here is that of the law of averages, or, as the investor knows it, the principle of diversification of risk.

It will be recalled that the fire companies do not insure buildings indiscriminately. They examine each risk before it is taken, and grade it according to its quality and the territory in which it is located. Not only do the fire companies examine their risks originally, but they maintain departments constantly to scrutinize risks already insured to see that they *remain* good risks. The second important rule, therefore, of sound insurance practice is to secure good risks and to keep them good by regular inspection.

The insurance companies do not insist upon dealing only with the best risks. No company confines its business to fireproof buildings. Even the most disreputable building can be insured if the owner is willing to pay a large enough premium. While the losses on poorer risks are much greater than on good risks the increased premiums received on such risks are enough more than to offset the increased losses. Consequently, there is a grading of risks in insurance and an acceptance of some risks which are not the least hazardous.

The investor can profitably apply these principles in the solution of his problem. Diversification of risk should be practiced under every classification. The investor should spread his capital over several types of securities, over several industries, over a number of companies, over different territories, and, furthermore, he should average into the market, or, in other words, do his investing at different times so as to avoid the possibility of doing all his buying on a day which might mark the highest prices for a long time. Many an investor thinks that if he owns twenty different companies, even though they be all railroads, his fund is properly diversified. Most of us, however, should have at least five different industries represented among our investments, should have companies located in different parts of the country, and should at some time or other use bonds, preferred stocks and common stocks in our investment program.

Before buying a security, the investor investigates it. Business is so complicated nowadays that this business of analysis of securities is a profession in itself and is much better done by the expert than by the amateur. Where the amateur makes his greatest mistake, however, is in thinking that once a security has been approved and purchased it is likely to remain a good risk.

To dispose of a poor risk is just as important as to buy a good risk. In other words, selling is just as important a part of investing as buying. The expert recognizes this and cuts his losses before they grow.

The fire insurance companies do not prevent fires. They merely indemnify for loss by fire. There is no way of preventing investment losses. There is a way, however, of seeing that losses are more than offset by gain. Many capitalists who like to think they are conservative investors have the habit of saying, "I invest only for income and not for profit." This is an erroneous attitude. Profit is a substitute for safety. For the past six or seven years, a large New York bank has returned to its stockholders, in appreciation and income, an amount in excess of 50 per cent. per annum. The investor who has received any such treatment as this has no need to worry about his original principal. If it were all lost he would have had a handsome return in the meantime besides enough to replace his original principal. Given sufficient profit, safety, as it is ordinarily thought of, can be dispensed with entirely.

As to their immediate objectives, investors come under two classes. The bank or the insurance company is interested directly in dollars. These financial institutions can relieve themselves of all their obligations by paying to their depositors or stockholders a certain number of dollars, regardless of the value of those dollars. However, the individual investor and the college and the hospital are not interested primarily in dollars but in what dollars will buy. One can not eat a dollar or wear a dollar or sleep in a dollar. A dollar is good only for its exchange value into commodities which can be used for living purposes. This second type of investor has what might be termed a bread-and-butter liability, in contrast to the dollar liability of financial institutions. Here is an important point for individuals to bear in mind when seeking investment advice from men who are connected with financial institutions. Such men are raised in an atmosphere permeated with the idea that a dollar is a dollar, whereas any investor who has lived over the last fifteen years is thoroughly disabused of any such idea. He realizes that a dollar would not buy half as much in 1920 as it did in 1913, and, furthermore, he realizes that his living needs were not reduced but increased between 1913 and 1920.

One type of security, the bond, furnishes a fixed income in dollars. Fixed-dollar income, however, decidedly is not fixed in purchasing power. Another type of investment, the common stock, furnishes an income which varies in dollars as well as in purchasing power. But fortunately during a period of advancing commodity prices, corporations simultaneously advance the price of their products and thus afford their shareholders a greater number of dollars to offset the restricted purchasing power of the individual dollar. Consequently, for the individual, the hospital the college and other institutions with a bread-and-butter liability, the use of the common-stock medium is absolutely essential.

As a matter of fact, financial institutions are beginning to realize indirectly they also are interested in the purchasing power of their dollar. The insurance policy-holder and the insurance stockholder, upon whom the insurance company depends for its existence, are beginning to realize that investment safety lies only in the inclusion of a reasonable proportion of common stocks in any investment fund. Savings-bank depositors and insurance-policy holders have been told of the complete bankruptcy of savings banks and insurance companies in Germany at the time of the post-war inflation, due wholly to the fact that they were compelled to invest in bonds and other money obligations. It is my prediction that within five years life insurance companies of this country will be buying common stocks. Bonds, however, should never be neglected by the investor who wishes a reasonable back-log to protect him through times of depression and money deflation.

The term "common stocks" as defined by an investor means something entirely different from the ordinary garden variety of common stocks of all the hundreds of thousands of small locally owned corporations of the country. "Common stocks" to the investor should be limited in definition to "investment" common stocks, and no common stock achieves this distinction until the company it represents has a long record of successful management, good earnings and steady dividends, is a leader of its industry and has its ownership widely distributed. Many of the stocks listed on the New York Stock Exchange and on the Curb deserve this rating. In buying a stock, the investor should regard himself as about to become a partner in an established business conducted by successful managers. He should buy his partnership with the idea of its being to a large extent permanent. He should not think of selling it, if a few days after he has purchased, some one, as indicated by the prices in the quotation columns of the newspapers, offers him more than he paid for it. On the contrary, he should not feel badly if a few days after he has purchased he can find no one who will offer him as much as he paid. His chief endeavor should be to see that his business continues to be efficiently managed.

Finally, a few brief rules may be of help to the amateur investor. Every rule has its exceptions, and the expert will follow practices which it would be unsafe for the amateur to copy. Adherence to these few rules, however, will save the investor many losses and secure him many profits. The rules given apply to the selection of common stocks.

The first rule is to select an essential, sound industry. Many industries, the textile, for example, are essential but not sound. Without doubt there are excellent companies in the textile industry. What is the use, however, of the inexpert investor's attempting to select the best risk in a generally poor industry, when he can just as easily select a good risk in a good industry?

The second rule is to select the best company in the industry. But as the word "best" leaves us somewhat in the dark, I suggest selecting one of the two or three biggest companies in the industry. Usually a company leads its industry because it is soundly managed. Management is 90 per cent. responsible for the success of any company. Choose a good management.

To secure proper diversification one should own, if possible, ten or fifteen different companies in at least five different industries. This is rule three. To secure the necessary marketability, which is very important for small investors, rule four reads, "Confine the bulk of your common stock commitments to companies listed on one of the major stock exchanges."

The fifth and last rule is very important. Once a year sell at least one stock from your list, choosing the weakest and having no consideration whatever for its original cost; replace it by another good stock. This procedure will insure at least one careful inspection of each item annually.

An institution is now being developed in this country, which, when properly constructed and well managed, will be of inestimable benefit to the small investor. This is the investment trust. This institution pools the capital of numerous small investors in much the same manner as the savings bank does, but is not restricted in its investment policy as are savings banks. By building up a very large fund the investment trust can afford to retain expert management and can apply all the principles of diversification, examination and inspection. I commend the sound investment trust to your earnest consideration. Since many of these trusts have been organized in the interests of promoters and managers primarily, and only secondarily in the interests of investors, the investor should make his selection with great care and preferably upon advice of counsel.

There is no department of investing where ordinary common sense is not helpful. By following the rules stated, and tempering them with ordinary good judgment, any investor can do a creditable job for himself. Let him remember that investing is simply the application of insurance principles to the ownership of capital risks.

EDUCATION FOR LEADERSHIP IN BUSINESS[1]

By Dr. WILLIAM TRUFANT FOSTER
DIRECTOR, POLLAK FOUNDATION FOR ECONOMIC RESEARCH

YOUR chairman assures me that I shall commit no impropriety—since this is a kind of family party—if I illustrate what I have to say on education and business by telling you about the education of the business man whom I happen to know most intimately. He was graduated from Harvard College and from the Harvard Law School about a quarter of a century ago, having had no courses whatever in special preparation for a business career and no business experience. From the law school, he went to New York City, without money and without influence; and there he entered the employ of a law firm. Two or three years later, he represented this firm in connection with the receivership of a steel construction company which, just before it failed, had been doing a business of about forty million dollars a year. He knew nothing about this business; nothing about structural engineering. He had never even seen a rolling mill. Yet within six months he developed a plan for the reorganization of the entire company, and six months later he had reestablished the business on a sound basis, and was asked to take charge of it. Instead, he became receiver for another large concern, promptly put that concern upon its feet, and became its president.

Ever since that time, he has wrestled successfully with the problems of leading corporations in one industry after another. With apparent ease, he has stepped from one new field to another new field—from automobiles to wholesale drugs, from clothing to lumber, from shoes to typewriters, from department stores to rubber factories, from mail-order houses to motion pictures, from food products to investment trusts. And nearly every corporation which has had the benefit of his judgment has become a factor to be reckoned with, if not the commanding unit, in its field. Thus he has faced new situations as a part of his daily routine. Repeatedly, he has entered an industry of which he knew very little, and speedily solved some of the problems which had baffled men who had devoted their entire lives to that industry.

For such achievements, it goes without saying, his education was only in part responsible. Even so, his own judgment concerning the value of that education is at least interesting. He is convinced that, in so far as his formal schooling prepared him at all, that preparation consisted almost entirely in mental training. He believes that the most valuable part of his college life was the study of argumentation and the practice of debating, and that his law school prepared him for business chiefly through training him to think cogently on one problem after another. In college, it is true, he learned what many men had said about the principles of economics; but in actual business he did not find that information helpful. He found, on the contrary, that he had to do much of his economic thinking all over, before he could connect economics with the immediate, major problems of business and finance. It is true, also, that in the law school he learned much about law; but this information has not been of much help to him in business. As a business man, in fact, he has not practiced law at all, but has employed lawyers. Here, then, is one of the most successful business men of our time, who is convinced that the chief preparation for leadership in business is training in the processes of thought; and

[1] Notes from an address delivered at the annual meeting of the Harvard Teachers' Association, Cambridge, March 16, 1929.

that it matters little whether that training comes through wrestling with business problems or with entirely different problems.

Whether this busy man has ever found time to read the essays of Cardinal Newman, I do not know; but I do know that with Cardinal Newman he "holds very strongly that the first step in intellectual training is to impress upon a boy's mind the idea of science, method, order, principle, and system; of rule and exception."

"Let him once gain this habit of method," says Cardinal Newman, "of starting from fixed points, of making his ground good as he goes, of distinguishing what he knows from what he does not know, and I conceive he will be gradually initiated into the largest and truest philosophical views, and will feel nothing but impatience and disgust at the random theories and imposing sophistries and dashing paradoxes, which carry away half-formed and superficial intellects."

The point I am making is that in business, as in every other field, leadership depends largely upon the ability to solve *new* problems; and the first step in solving each new problem is the discovery of its main issue through the process of analysis. That is to say, in every emergency of business there is a main issue. Success in meeting the emergency requires the direction of efforts toward that issue. Without the ability to analyze the situation and thus discover the crux of the difficulty—the main issue—a man is almost sure to waste his energy in blind endeavor, like the fly which is now trying to escape from this room, unaware of the fact that only one of the windows is open. The fly bumps along from pane to pane until it either drops dead or by accident discovers the open window—the one direction in which its efforts count. The purpose of analysis is to find the opening intelligently, rather than by the method of trial and error.

A thousand blows *around* a nail will not move it; one blow *on the head* will drive it in. It is only by analysis—or by rare luck—that a business man hits the nail on the head.

If I were to be allowed a single remark concerning my own training at Harvard, I should say that I value most highly, not what Professor Taussig told me about economics, but the fact that he made me *think* about economics; not the information which I gained from Professor Baker, but the fact that he was not satisfied until I had done my best to see in, and around, and through every question upon which I attempted to argue; and, finally, not the theories which your beloved honorary president, Professor Hanus, passed on to me, but the fact that, opening up unexplored fields, he said to me, day after day, "Come, let us reason together. Let us discard all opinions, however respectable, and try to find solutions for the new problems of education which a rapidly changing world is constantly thrusting before us."

Nowhere are these changes now going on more rapidly than in the domain of business. Nowhere is independent thinking more essential. Any business man who depends to-day on the knowledge of business conditions and methods which he acquired yesterday is certain to be replaced to-morrow by some one who is doing his own thinking.

That is why preparation for leadership in business does take time. Nowadays, it is true, we are hurled through the air at one hundred and fifty miles an hour, and we try to take everything else at high speed—music, dancing, stockmarket profits, not to mention marriage and divorce. Some people expect to get trained for business at the same pace; just as others seem to think that they can "make culture hum," as a "realtor" booms a town. And do we not see advertisements every day which absolutely guarantee success to any one who attends the "Short Cut Business

School" for six months? Correspondence schools offer to do the job more quickly still. And no wonder, in this age when men make fortunes, almost overnight, by defacing the landscape with the astounding announcement that delighted consumers can now buy a package of chewing gum in a *pink* wrapper—and pay for it out of income instead of capital—a penny down and a penny a day. Chewing-gum types of education are also offered for sale in small packages—with deferred payments of effort. The buyer soon discovers that the flavor does *not* last, but he can keep up the motions until the alluring art of the advertiser startles him with a new kind—amazingly new, because now it is wrapped in a *lavender* paper!

You have all met the boy who says: "I want to become a writer. I have been told that I have real talent. I must not waste time. I don't want to study history and philosophy and sociology. My specialty is writing." It is difficult to convince such a person that if one wishes to write, it is extremely convenient to have something to say. Other persons are ambitious to become public speakers. They will not study logic and government and science in a broad way. Not at all; that is not their business. They wish to become public speakers; so they desire only a course in public speaking, and that a brief one. Why waste time? The man in the magazine cries out, "I can make you an effective speaker in fifteen minutes a day."

Well, why not become a leader in any vocation in fifteen minutes a day? Simply because specialization in any subject is ridiculous—a contradiction of terms—except on broad foundations. Specialization is thoroughness in one particular field; but no one field can be understood thoroughly except in its manifold relations to other fields; and those relations can not be discovered without the power of analysis—the means of finding the special issue. That is why there is no royal short-cut to preparation for leadership in business. A baseball pitcher ripens early, but Herbert Hoover is a rather mature product.

EDUCATIONAL EVENTS

EDUCATIONAL CONDITIONS IN CHINA

The Christian Science Monitor reports that unrest among the students in all the principal universities of Peiping, the student center of China, has seriously interfered with classroom work during the closing weeks of the school year. Mission and government schools alike have been affected. Political disturbances throughout the country have stirred the academic atmosphere, with unfortunate results.

The government schools have been most seriously affected, due largely to lack of funds. Teachers have not been paid on time, and endowment students have not received their remittances. Delay in remitting expenses from Nanking, said to be caused partly, at least, by the high costs of the military expedition against the Kwangsi militarists, has made those who rely upon the government for their livelihood uneasy.

An ominous tendency has been the so-called "anti-foreign aggression movement," which has affected the students at Yenching University, the principal Protestant mission school in China, and the Roman Catholic University, one of the leading Roman Catholic institutions. A minority group of students in both schools has agitated against some of the professors, on the ground that they are not sufficiently sympathetic with Chinese nationalism.

A Chinese president has been appointed at Yenching, the American president, Dr. Leighton Stuart, assuming a secondary position. It is noteworthy that a Chinese newspaper, the *Hsin Chen Pao,* commenting on the agitation in these schools, remarks: "If the students at Yenching and Roman Catholic universities opposed the two universities because of foreign control, they should not have taken their entrance examinations in the first place. The first duty of a student is to study, and our students should always bear this in mind."

With so much unrest among the general population as now prevails in China, however, it is considered inevitable that the students, who have been in the forefront of political agitation for years, should devote more attention to revolutionary movements than they do in better ordered countries.

INTERMEDIATE EDUCATION IN WALES

A REPORT of the Board of Education under the Welsh Intermediate Education Act, 1889, for the year 1928 on the problem of adjusting the academic and the practical sides of intermediate school education in Wales is summarized by the London *Times*, and it is suggested that the question should be examined afresh in view of the changed conditions and growth since 1916. The schools eligible to receive the treasury grant remained the same in 1928, totaling 99, and in all 101 county schools were inspected under the direction of the Central Welsh Board.

The pupils in the intermediate schools numbered 25,163, an increase of 289 over the previous year, and as the attendances at the other grant-earning schools also show considerable increases the number of scholars in the principality continued to grow. The average number of pupils at the intermediate schools was 248, and it is noted that no fewer than 2,481 pupils out of the total of 5,908 leavers, or 42 per cent., left before they attained the age of 16.

Considering the future, the report argues that in a large proportion of intermediate schools the question must soon be faced whether the curricula can be adapted to the present-day needs of industry, commerce and agriculture, or whether they are to be supplemented by other schools, and the board trusts that they have said enough to encourage the Central Welsh Board and the local education authorities, the governing bodies and the teachers of Wales to hammer and forge out of the old system a new instrument of education which will enable full justice to be done to the children of Wales, faced as they now are with conditions which are in so many vital respects rapidly changing in character along lines dictated by the march of events in the twentieth century.

It is said that one immediate and practicable step is to do a great deal more in assisting the pupils to choose suitable careers; the world is full of square pegs in round holes, and the schools can do something to remedy this wasteful condition of affairs. In equipping themselves with the knowledge that would enable them to offer the best and most complete information to their pupils heads of schools could with advantage enter into communication with the University Appointments Board, the Ministry of Labor and the various ministries concerned with life overseas.

THE SCHOOLS OF HAITI

ACCORDING to the correspondent of the New York *Sun* in Port au Prince, the development of a practical school system for Haiti is to be the outstanding factor of the next two years in the American program for rehabilitation of the country. Peace and order, sanitation and public works have all been emphasized in turn, but to-day the school plan is being stressed above all others.

While the treaty of September 16, 1915, was silent on American supervision or control of education, it did contain a provision for assistance in the development of Haitian resources. So when, eight years later, the "Service Technique," corresponding to a department of agriculture, was organized, full recognition was given to the fact that a system of industrial schools in the cities and of agricultural schools in the rural sections would constitute an important part of the development of Haiti's agricultural possibilities.

With an extraordinary credit of $705,000 available for this system and a budget of $236,133 for 1929, Dr. George E. Freeman, director of the Service Technique, has laid out a comprehensive program. Back of it lies the aim that before the expiration of the treaty in 1936 each graduate of the public schools will step into the world as the master of a trade.

The extra credit provides for twelve industrial schools in Port au Prince, two for girls with a capacity of 1,000 and ten for boys with a capacity of 5,000. In addition, the coffee port of St. Marc will join the ranks of Haitian cities that already boast industrial schools.

The credit will also make possible 25 new rural schools. Sixty such schools already exist with 110 teachers, seven supervisors and 5,253 pupils who have an average attendance of 74 per cent.

The existing eight industrial schools have enrolled 1,797 pupils with an average attendance of 86 per cent. Night schools have 1,056 pupils and an average attendance of 77 per cent. Tailoring, carpentry, electrical installation, automobile mechanics and shoe repairing are the favorite trades in these institutions.

In the rural farm schools the pupils learn planting and canalization in the school gardens. They also are taught to fashion furniture, mats, belts and cravats, tinware, trunks, baskets, pottery, hats and toys. All this in addition to practical farming.

SIGHT-SAVING CLASSES

BETWEEN 50,000 and 60,000 school children in the United States have such seriously defective vision as to require special educational methods and eye care in "sight-saving" classes, according to an estimate made by Mrs. Winifred Hathaway, associate director of the National Society for the Prevention of Blindness. There are only 318 of these classes in the entire country, although at least 5,000 are said to be necessary. Explaining the purpose and the need for more sight-saving classes for visually handicapped children, Mrs. Hathaway said:

> Through the use of special large type books, movable desks, ideal lighting and special teaching methods, children with little vision are not only given the same sort of education that children with full vision receive, but they are taught how to conserve their remaining sight. More than 4,000 of these partially-sighted students are now enrolled in sight-saving classes in the various states, but many thousands more are forced to attend schools for the blind, to struggle along in the regular classes intended for children with normal vision, or else to do without any sort of education.
>
> Educators have found that many children who had been accounted stupid, sullen, morose, mentally sub-normal and even criminal, displayed excellent intelligence and pleasing dispositions as soon as their defective vision was recognized and they were placed in sight-saving classes. The necessity for some children to take the same work over again, a serious educational waste, is frequently traced to eye difficulties.
>
> Although special training courses for sight-saving class teachers are given during the summer session at several universities, the demand for teachers with this training continues to be greater than the supply available. Such courses will be given this summer at Columbia University, the University of Chicago, the University of Cincinnati and the University of Southern California. Numerous inquiries and requests for advice concerning the establishment of sight-saving classes are received from public and private school authorities by the National Society for the Prevention of Blindness.

SELF-HELP FOR COLLEGE STUDENTS

THE Bureau of Education has issued a bulletin showing that half of the men and a fourth of the women in the colleges and universities in the United States are working to pay for their education.

To finance a college education over a period of years, many have found educational insurance a convenient method. Some form the habit of systematic savings. Building and loan associations have specific plans of financing education. Many high-school students are turning spare time into cash for the purpose of a college education.

The colleges and other agencies are offering scholarships for qualified students. Ex-service men and their blood relations are awarded scholarships in colleges in 16 different states. Colleges and universities to the number of 282 are lending over $4,000,000 annually to deserving students and 100 independent agencies maintain loan funds for the purpose of aiding students in college. They report $5,000,000 outstanding in student loans.

Besides these aids, the college students themselves, by their own efforts and labor, produced over $33,000,000 during term-time in a recent year. The jobs in which these students were employed include automobile repairing, office and clerical work, specialty selling, arts and crafts, professional and semi-professional employment, instruction, publishing, transportation, entertainment, recreation, hotel and summer resort jobs, food handling, household service, care and maintenance of buildings and grounds, agricultural pursuits and odd jobs.

In general, students and faculties both favor a reasonable amount of employment if a student needs financial assistance. The colleges and universities are aiding the employed student by installing college employment bureaus and service agencies, by arranging class schedules so that the worker may elect all morning classes or late afternoon classes to leave time free for employment, cooperative courses and many other means whereby the needy student may reduce college expenses.

ENTRANCE TO WEST POINT

A REVISION of regulations governing the admission of candidates to West Point to be put into effect with the class entering in 1930 has been approved by Secretary Good upon the recommendation of Major-General William R. Smith, superintendent of the academy.

The revisions are intended to provide a more thorough test of candidates, affecting, principally, those who are graduates of preparatory schools, public high schools or honor graduates of honor schools, accredited by the military academy.

General Smith's recommendation was made after an extensive study of the cause of failures of cadets after admission to the academy covering the period of 1890–1927. The largest proportion of failures was found to be due to deficiency in mathematics. There was a decided increase in the percentage of failures after the inauguration of admissions by certificate in 1915.

For the period from 1890 to 1914, 7.1 per cent. of the cadets were found deficient in mathematics at the end of the first term, while in the period 1915 to 1927 the percentage had risen to 12.45. Three times as many cadets admitted on certificate were found deficient as compared with those admitted on examination.

The revised regulations provide that honor graduates of honor schools may be admitted wholly on certificate provided they have been graded in their academic work in the upper 10 per cent. of their classes. Candidates from preparatory schools and from high schools, accredited by the United States Military Academy and honor graduates of honor schools not graded in the upper 10 per cent. in their academic work will no longer be admitted to the military academy wholly on certificate as under existing regulations. They must hereafter submit a certificate showing proficiency in subjects amounting to not less than fifteen units, eight required, and seven optional, the eight units including algebra, plane geometry, English grammar and composition, English literature and history. In addition, if their certificates are acceptable, they must pass a validating examination on the first Tuesday in March in three subjects—algebra, plane geometry and English. This validating examination is not identical with the regular entrance examination. It will be an examination of such a nature as to determine the knowledge of a candidate, but not so difficult as to require for the desirable student a special preparatory course.

The revised regulations make no material change in the requirements of those candidates who are regularly enrolled students in good standing without condition in a university, college or technical school accredited by the military academy. No change is made in the requirements of candidates from the United States at large, the Regular Army, the National Guard and other appointees who establish their qualifications for admission by taking the regular entrance examination. As in the past, the revised regulations require all candidates to submit to a physical examination.

LANGUAGE REQUIREMENTS IN THE HARVARD GRADUATE SCHOOL

STUDENTS in the graduate school of arts and sciences of Harvard University, candidates for the degree of A.M., entering on and after September, 1929, will be required to show a reading knowledge of either French or German, and an elementary knowledge of the other of these two languages. This new ruling will raise the standard of the language requirements for the higher degree to the level now existing in Harvard College for the degrees of A.B. and B.S.

Another ruling affecting graduate students in this department of the university has also been announced. It was voted that "All divisions and departments shall submit to the committee on instruction for approval, not later than two months in advance, any proposal to substitute some other form of test for the mid-year or final examination in courses under their jurisdiction, and the decision of the committee on instruction shall be final." This vote was passed in an effort to make the practice with regard to examinations in graduate courses more uniform, and was designed primarily to affect research courses in which the ordinary final examination was not consonant with the work of the course.

The ruling with respect to the language requirements will affect all those men entering the graduate school of arts and sciences this coming fall and thereafter, but it will apply principally to men entering from other colleges than Harvard, for all graduates of Harvard College have already been required to satisfy the requirement and will not be asked to take a second examination. Men already students in the university are not affected by the ruling. Previous courses in languages taken outside Harvard will not be counted toward this requirement, but all candidates for the degree except those named above will be asked to submit to these two examinations, one in French and one in German.

CONFERENCE ON TEACHING BY RADIO

THE possibilities of education by radio and the part the federal government should play in it were considered at a conference at the Department of the Interior May 24 on the call of the Secretary of the Interior, Ray Lyman Wilbur.

In announcing the conference on May 21, Secretary Wilbur stated that prominent educators and representatives of the radio industry had been invited. The announcement follows in full text:

Secretary Wilbur, of the Department of the Interior, has called a conference to discuss the possibilities of education by radio and what interest, if any, the United States Government should have in it. The meeting will be held in his office in the Department of the Interior Building at 3 o'clock on the afternoon of Friday, May 24.

The holding of this conference is in accordance with Secretary Wilbur's recently stated policy as to education to the effect that "the place of the national government is to develop methods, ideals and procedures, and to present them, to be taken on their merit." Heretofore, he points out, there have been certain methods. Pupils have studied from the printed page. They have sat in class and received instruction. They have followed with the eye demonstrations at the blackboard. Now there appears a new agency, radio, which conveys information in its own peculiar way. How can it be used?

The United States Bureau of Education, which is under the Department of the Interior, will participate in the conference. Invitations to attend have been sent to the following individuals: M. L. Aylesworth, president, National Broadcasting Corporation, New York; William S. Paley, president, Columbia Broadcasting Corporation, Paramount Building, New York; Dr. Charles R. Mann, president, American Council on Education, Washington; Dr. J. W. Crabtree, secretary, National Education Association, Washington, D. C.; Chairman Ira E. Robinson, of the Federal Radio Commission, Interior Building, Washington, D. C.; Commissioners Harold A. LaFount, Charles McK. Saltzman, William B. L. Starbuck and Eugene O. Sykes, of the Federal Radio Commission, Interior Building, Washington, D. C.; Frank Cody, superintendent of schools, Detroit, Mich.; H. Robinson Shipherd, New York City; J. L. Clifton, director of education, Columbus, Ohio; Dr. Harold Stonier, educational director, American Institute of Banking, New York City.

DES MOINES CONFERENCE OF THE BUREAU OF EDUCATION

A REGIONAL conference of Supervisors of Rural Schools of the mid-western states will be held at Des Moines, Iowa, on June 14 and 15. Participants in the conference will come from the District of Columbia and eleven states: Illinois, Indiana, Iowa, Kansas, Michigan, Minnesota, Missouri, Nebraska, North Dakota, South Dakota and Wisconsin. They will include, besides the U. S. Commissioner of Education, other representatives from the Bureau of Education; chief state education officers; the president of the department of rural education, National Education Association; state and county rural school supervisory officials; presidents of and professors of education in teachers colleges; an elementary principal and a county librarian.

The topics to be considered concern special types of assistance needed by beginning teachers; essentials of effective supervisory programs; educational needs of subnormal children in rural areas; duties of rural school principals, and contributions of teacher-preparing institutions, state departments of education and county libraries to the solution of supervisory problems.

The conference is the fifth regional supervisory conference called by the Bureau of Education. Preceding conferences were held in Nashville, Tennessee, Raleigh, North Carolina, New Orleans, Louisiana, and New York City. It is expected that the June, 1929, conference will point the way to an intensive attack upon the specific problems considered. The study and solution by supervisory officials of problems similar to those indicated above are urgently needed in the interests of equalization of educational opportunity for all rural children.

EDUCATIONAL NOTES AND NEWS

DR. JACOB GOULD SCHURMAN, ambassador to Germany, formerly president of Cornell University, celebrated his seventy-fifth birthday on May 22. An Associated Press despatch reads in part as follows: "The president sent the ambassador his autographed photograph, while Chancellor Mueller and Foreign Minister Stresemann sent congratulations. The latter sent a basket of flowers. From Heidelberg came as a birthday gift for its honorary citizen a portfolio containing two rare color prints of the city by Johann Jacob Struedt. Dr. Schurman spent the day at Halle, addressing the Kant Society on 'Kant and Peace,' and received a surprise birthday present by being made honorary member of the society of scientists and scholars."

A PLAQUE of Dr. David Starr Jordan, chancellor emeritus of Stanford University, has been made by Carleton B. Angell, to be hung in one of the halls of the new museum building of the University of Michigan. At a dinner last year in Tokyo of Stanford graduates, under the chairmanship of Yakanosuke Fukukita, of the class of 1904, at which about sixty Japanese were present, it was decided to secure and forward to Dr. Jordan a work of art symbolic of his efforts for world unity and peace. This gift arrived in due time. It is mainly of bronze with gold and silver overlays and consists of the figure of a dove, almost life-size, perched on an old broken temple-roof tile out of which a plant has grown. The piece is accompanied by a teakwood stand for its suitable display.

A TRIBUTE in the form of a letter from thousands of Tufts College alumni has been given to President John A. Cousens in recognition of his ten years as head of the institution. The letter, written by Fredwith R. MacKenzie, president of the Alumni Association, concludes with the words: "The burden of the responsibility is his; the glory of the achievement is forever ours. In appreciation of his ten years of successful management, it seems fitting for the alumni to join by voice and by written word, in conveying to him personally our satisfaction with his achievements of the past decade and our unanimous support of his plans for the future."

THE installation as president of Brown University of Dr. Clarence A. Barbour, formerly president of the Rochester-Colgate Theological Seminary, has been set for October 18. President W. H. P. Faunce made his last appearance at chapel on May 30, urging students and faculty members to give their support to Dr. Barbour. President Faunce will complete thirty years of service to Brown University next month, twenty-six years of which he has spent as president.

DRURY COLLEGE, Springfield, Missouri, conferred the LL.D. degree upon Dr. Stratton D. Brooks, president of the University of Missouri, on the occasion of the commencement exercises on May 22.

ON the occasion of its fifty-seventh commencement, Swarthmore College conferred honorary degrees on Mrs. Herbert Hoover, Dr. Marion Edwards Park, president of Bryn Mawr College; Dr. William F. G. Swann, director of the Bartol Foundation of the Franklin Institute, and Dr. Howard McClenahan, secretary of Franklin Institute. Dr. McClenahan delivered the commencement address.

MORDECAI WYATT JOHNSON, first Negro president of Howard University, Washington, D. C., has been awarded the fifteenth Spingarn medal for 1928, in consideration of his work. The Spingarn medal goes annually to a colored American for conspicuous achievement. Mr. Johnson during the past year has obtained legislation by which Howard University becomes a recognized institution by the United States government.

On the occasion of his leaving the faculty of the Columbia Law School after thirteen years of service, a portrait of Professor Underhill Moore by Edward B. Child was presented to the school at the Columbia commencement luncheon. Professor Moore leaves Columbia at the end of the present academic year to go to the Law School of Yale University. The portrait is the gift of students and faculty.

The trustees of Hampton Institute have announced the resignation of Dr. James Edgar Gregg as principal, to take effect on July 1, when Dr. Gregg will have served the institute for more than eleven years. In accepting his resignation the trustees issued a public statement thanking Dr. Gregg for his services. Dr. George P. Phenix, vice-principal, has been appointed acting-principal.

Professor Clark P. Bissett, of the faculty of law of the University of Washington, has become professor emeritus. Professor Caroline Ober, of the Spanish department, has also retired with the title of professor emeritus.

Narcisso Bassols, rector of the law school of the Mexican National University, has resigned as an outcome of the students' strike and riots. Dr. Bassols explained in resigning that he did not wish to be an obstacle to settlement of the dispute, which arose when the law students objected to newly introduced monthly written examinations.

Sir Gregory Foster, provost of University College, London, has presented his resignation to take effect in December. It is understood that although Sir Gregory is retiring from the office of provost, it is not his intention to give up active educational work.

A testimonial dinner in honor of Dr. Randall J. Condon, retiring superintendent of the schools of Cincinnati, will be given under the auspices of combined civic organizations on June 17. Dr. Condon sails for Europe on July 1 to study education in Denmark, Germany, Norway and Sweden.

Dr. Richard E. Day, assistant in the archives and history division of the State Education Department, retired on May 1 after a long service as editor of historical source material. Dr. Day was the guest of honor at a dinner given on April 10 in Albany by present and former associates in the department. Dr. A. C. Flick, state historian and director of the archives and history division, presided. Addresses were made by Regent William Leland Thompson, of Troy; Commissioner of Education Frank P. Graves, and others.

The resignation is announced of Henry Turner Bailey, dean of the Cleveland School of Art for twelve years.

After twenty years of service in the development of traveling libraries in the New York State Education Department, the Reverend Charles F. Porter has resigned.

Edward D. Myers will retire as superintendent of schools at Catskill, N. Y., on August 1. He went to Catskill in 1919, prior to which time he had been supervising principal at Tuxedo.

Miss Anna E. Logan, for the last fourteen years assistant superintendent of schools in Cincinnati, has asked for retirement because of failing sight. In submitting her request to the board Superintendent Condon said in part: "In presenting this request I wish to express my very deep appreciation of the great service which Miss Logan has rendered. Since 1915 she has given to the teachers and the schools and to the city a service of great value."

John G. Hulton, principal of the Latrobe, Pennsylvania, High School for the past seven years, has been elected superintendent of the public schools of Latrobe.

David A. Ward, superintendent of schools, Wilmington, Delaware, has been unanimously elected superintendent of the schools of Chester, Pennsylvania, at a salary of $7,500, effective June 1, to succeed George H. Weiss, resigned. In the interim, Samuel C. Miller, assistant superintendent, served as acting superintendent.

W. A. Grace, assistant master at Bembridge School, Isle of Wight, England, has been appointed headmaster of Halesowen Grammar School, Worcester.

Professor Heber H. Ryan, associate professor of education and principal of the university high school in the University of Michigan, has been appointed associate professor of education and principal of the Wisconsin high school. His appointment, as successor to the late Professor H. L. Miller, takes effect at the opening of the academic year. He has been at the University of Michigan since 1926.

DR. GEORGE W. STEPHENS, dean of freshmen at Washington University, St. Louis, is named to the newly created position of dean of students at the university.

DR. HENRY M. WINANS, of Dallas, Texas, has been appointed professor and chairman of the department of medicine at Baylor University College of Medicine.

THE REVEREND DR. HOWARD CHANDLER ROBBINS, formerly dean of the Cathedral of St. John the Divine, has been elected professor of pastoral theology at the General Theological Seminary of the Protestant Episcopal Church.

THE REVEREND JOHN W. DARR, of the First Congregational Church, Northampton, Massachusetts, has been appointed professor of religion at Scripps College, Claremont, California.

THE following have been added to the faculty of the college of liberal arts of the American University, Washington, D. C., for the coming year: Dr. W. M. Gewehr, of Denison University, professor of history; Mr. Walter H. Young, director of athletics and physical education; Mr. Edward L. McAdam, instructor in English, and Mr. Henry G. Statham, librarian.

HAROLD ROBERT ENSLOW, of the University of Pennsylvania, has been appointed assistant professor of political science at Union College, Schenectady, to assume direction of the work in American, national and local government, replacing Mr. Albert H. Hall, who has resigned as instructor in political science. Mr. Francis B. Stevens continues for another year as instructor in political science. Dr. W. Leon Godshall has received promotion from an associate professorship to a professorship and will devote practically all his time to international relations and to the direction of intercollegiate debating.

GIUSEPPE PREZZOLINI, professor of Italian, and Vittorio Macchioro, professor of religion, have been added to the summer session faculty of Columbia University. Signor Prezzolini is head of the information bureau of the League of Nations at Paris and has been active in the movements of Fascism, modernism and futurism. Signor Macchioro is an inspector of Italian museums and is an authority on Roman history. He is an officer of the University of Naples.

DR. ABRAHAM FLEXNER, who has made a prolonged stay in Europe, arrived in New York City on June 3.

DR. PERCIVAL R. COLE, of Sydney, Australia, has arrived in Seattle to give a series of lectures at the University of Washington under the Carnegie Endowment for International Peace.

PROFESSOR F. D. GARDNER, head of the department of agronomy at the Pennsylvania State College, and Professor J. W. White, in charge of soil research at the college agricultural experiment station, will accompany a party of fifteen agricultural college representatives on a tour of Germany, France, Belgium, Holland, Switzerland and England. The party sails on June 13.

PROFESSOR PORTEUS, of the University of Hawaii and formerly of the Department of Education in Victoria, will leave Melbourne early next month to investigate the aborigines in northwestern Australia.

DR. CARLETON R. BALL, principal agronomist in charge of the office of cereal crops and diseases of the U. S. Bureau of Plant Industry and regent-general of the honor society of Phi Kappa Phi, addressed the annual student convocation at the Virginia Polytechnic Institute on May 17. His subject was "Scholarship, Character and Leadership."

DR. ROBERT STEWART HYER, president emeritus of the Southern Methodist University, died on May 29 at the age of sixty-eight years.

THE U. S. Civil Service Commission announces the following open competitive examinations: Research specialist in agricultural education, $4,600 a year; specialist in agricultural education (teacher training), $3,800 a year; specialist in agricultural education (subject matter), $3,800 a year; specialist in agricultural education (part-time and evening schools), $3,800 a year; federal agent for home economics education, $4,600 a year; agent for home economics education, $3,800 a year; agent for trade and industrial education, $3,800 a year. Applications for specialist in agricultural education, home economics education, and trade and industrial education must be on file with the Civil Service Commission at Washington, D. C., not later than June 19. The examinations are to fill vacancies under the Federal Board for Vocational Education, Washington, D. C., and vacancies occurring in positions requiring similar qualifications. Competitors will not be required to report for examination at any place, but will be rated on their education, experience and a thesis and publications to be filed by the applicant.

THE feature of the convention of the National Education Association, which will be held at Atlanta from June 28 to July 4, will be a demonstration presented in the Atlanta Auditorium on the afternoon of July 1, by the department of school health and physical education under the direction of James E. Rogers, president of the department. One of the demonstrations will be under the direction of Miss Katharine Dozier, superintendent of schools which have been established by the Pacolet Manufacturing Company in connection with their plants at New Holland, Georgia, and Pacolet, South Carolina. Miss Dozier will bring a large group of children from New Holland who will demonstrate the educational value and physical developments of training in folk dancing as well as in the more formal exercises. Preceding the demonstration Miss Dozier will speak on "The Esthetic Value of Physical Education." Dr. Willis A. Sutton, superintendent of the Atlanta schools, and a local committee are arranging also for a demonstration by Atlanta school children. Dr. Sutton will speak on "Health Education in Education." It is expected that the auditorium will be crowded for this meeting.

SETTLEMENT of the long Princeton Seminary controversy was effected by the 141st Presbyterian General Assembly, when it decided to reorganize the government of the institution into a single board of thirty-three members. The assembly approved the report of its special committee of eleven, which provides that the new governing body of the Theological Seminary shall be made up of eleven members from the present board of trustees, eleven from the board of directors and eleven from the church at large. The committee's report, in addition, provides for increasing the authority of J. Ross Stevenson, president of the seminary. On the losing side is the faction which has attacked the policies of Dr. Stevenson as "too liberal." Although the report is said to reflect the more liberal sentiment in the church, theological policies of the seminary will not be affected by the action.

TRUSTEES of the Enoch Pratt Free Library, Baltimore, and Mayor William F. Broeing have approved plans for a new central library building which will be built from a $3,000,000 municipal loan recently approved by the voters. A total book capacity of 1,800,000 volumes will allow for expansion space for twenty-five years or more.

THE Grand Lodge of Masons of Pennsylvania is to receive a bequest of $200,000 for the erection of a home for boys or girls at Elizabethtown, Pennsylvania, under the terms of the will of Harry T. Porter. Mr. Porter expressed a desire that the building be called the Harry T. Porter Memorial Home for Boys or Girls, as the Grand Lodge shall elect, and that it be in keeping with other buildings and establishments of a similar character maintained by the order.

THE Lifwynn Foundation for Laboratory Research in Analytic and Social Psychiatry, Inc., a Maryland corporation, with New York offices in the Chanin Building, receives the entire $350,000 estate of John E. Huiskamp, of Baltimore and New York. "The reason for making the above devise and bequest," says the testament, which was executed on October 25, 1927, "is my lifelong interest in problems in human social behavior and years of service with the members of the above corporation in the social studies to which it is devoted. The aim and object of this devise and bequest is to enable the above corporation to continue this service."

BY the will of Evelyn May Bayly Tiffant, the University of Virginia receives $100,000.

THE coming year will mark the twenty-fifth anniversary of the College of Education at the

University of Minnesota. With a thought of making this milestone of progress in education a special occasion, Dean Haggerty called together, at the time of the Spring Short Course, members of the State Department of Education, officers of the Minnesota Education Association, representatives of the College of Education faculty and of its alumni, to discuss the value and possibilities of the event. Dean Haggerty and Commissioner McConnell were appointed as a steering committee to associate with themselves others to work out the plans. Further developments will be announced later.

INAUGURATING a plan which may become an annual event at the University of Washington, the registration department, under the direction of Registrar E. B. Stevens, recently held the first High School Preregistration Conference. The meeting was called with a view to establishing a correlation between high-school work and university requirements.

THROUGH a change in the general plan of enrolment in the arts and commerce law courses at the University of Kentucky, it has been made possible for new students who are contemplating taking the combined courses for the two degrees, to enroll for three years in either arts or commerce, as a preparation for the law course to follow, which is a three-year course. An arts or commerce degree may thus be awarded the student at the end of his first year in the law school, but his fourth year in college. This plan makes it possible for students who have determined on their college course to enter either the arts college or the commerce college and work off their requirements in the first three years of the course, thus taking freshman law in their fourth year in college, and receiving the arts or commerce degree, as the case may be, at the same time. The college of law has made complete plans for the summer session, the first term being from June 17 to July 20, and the second beginning July 22 and continuing through August 24. Three full summer sessions are equivalent to one long session. A student in the summer may thus obtain a degree by attending two long sessions and three summer sessions.

THE Philadelphia Census Committee was organized for the purpose of securing more complete social and economic statistics for the city of Philadelphia. It is composed of representatives from corporations, city departments and social agencies with city-wide interests. One of the first tasks of the committee will be to secure census data for areas of smaller size than those now used for the publications of the Bureau of the Census. It is believed that basic population data of this type will greatly facilitate the research activities of the department of sociology at the University of Pennsylvania. Mr. A. B. Bishop, of the Bell Telephone Company, is chairman of the committee, and Mr. W. Wallace Weaver, of the department of sociology at the University of Pennsylvania, is secretary.

DR. WILLIAM MACKAY SMITH, registrar of Lafayette College, announces that seventeen committees have been appointed in fifteen cities for the purpose of personally interviewing young men who apply for admission to the college. Each of these committees consists of three Lafayette graduates. New York City and Philadelphia, from which cities Lafayette draws a large number of its students, will each have two committees. It is planned to select men upon the basis of character and personality as well as scholarship. Whenever possible prospective students will meet with alumni groups at their weekly luncheon meetings, in various cities. Other cities in which these committees will be established are: Pittsburgh, New Haven, Johnstown, Los Angeles, Washington, D. C., Trenton, Newark, Reading, Wilkes-Barre, Harrisburg, Cleveland, Boston, Buffalo and Chicago.

ENTRANCE requirements for Princeton University will be changed to give applicants from high schools more favorable opportunities of entering the university without lowering the standard of admission. The new policy will allow those candidates for Princeton who come with high scholastic records to take examinations in the significant courses in the final preparatory year. In this way the school records of applicants will play a larger part than formerly, and the requirements of the College Entrance Examination Board will be more elastic. Certificates of excellence in work in the final preparatory year will be accepted in those subjects for which comprehensive examinations are not provided.

KING ALFONSO has signed a decree reestablishing normality of student life in the closed Spanish universities. Primo de Rivera stated that the government reserved the right to apply disciplinary measures against individual students or professors who had been prominent in public disorders, or had taken part in political activities against the government.

ALTHOUGH Peking is no longer the capital of China, it will retain its position as the student center of the nation, according to a decision made recently by the Nanking government. The nine official universities of China, which have attracted thousands of students from all parts of the country, have now, according to *The Christian Science Monitor*, resumed work after a delay of several weeks due to financial uncertainties. After a period of unrest following the Nationalist occupation of Peking, the students of Tsing Hua College, gift of the United States to China through remission of the Boxer indemnity, are also settling down now to regular study. Tsing Hua has an assured monthly income, so that its administration can plan for the future with confidence.

DISCUSSION

COLLEGE LIBRARY EXPENDITURES

QUITE unrestrained by the many observations about liars figuring and figures concealing facts the writer has been bold enough to do some figuring on the basis of statistics of thirty-one college and university libraries which appeared in the March 1929 *Bulletin* of the American Library Association. At the moment he is interested in adequate appropriations for the university library. This table gives in one column "total library budget" and in another "student enrolment, regular session." (Summer session enrolment is called for in another column.) In the following table the "total budget" of each institution has been divided by the "regular session enrolment" to get an "expenditure per year per student" figure by which the entire list has been arranged.

	Library budget	Enrolment regular session	Library expenditure per capita per year
Rochester	$106,327	1,403	$75.80
Princeton	171,877	2,488	69.00
Bryn Mawr	32,180	498	65.00
Bowdoin	31,253	554	56.40
Amherst	40,709	727	56.00
Chicago	376,994	*ca.* 7,000	53.80
Vassar	57,734	1,155	50.00
McGill	141,346	2,643	48.50
Dartmouth	101,118	2,244	45.00
North Carolina	107,848	2,504	43.00
Brown	92,976	2,199	42.30
Mills	25,340	600	42.20
Michigan	382,425	10,212	37.40
Wellesley	47,550	1,600	29.60
Oregon	84,304	3,008	28.00
Iowa State	101,000	4,200	24.30
Wyoming	26,286	1,172	22.40
Cornell	112,084	5,000 +	22.40
Illinois	276,451	12,738	21.70
California	215,902	9,994	21.70
Washington (St. Louis)	49,990	2,445	20.40
Texas	101,000	5,500	18.40
Kansas	65,210	3,854	17.00
Missouri	82,145	4,918	16.70
Minnesota	204,755	12,322	16.60
Washington (Seattle)	115,968	7,354	15.80
Ohio State	145,729	10,183	14.30
North Dakota	21,320	1,750	12.20
Syracuse	61,305	5,083	12.00
Purdue	31,214	3,824	8.20
Nebraska	80,094	*ca.* 11,000	7.30

Obviously some of these figures need explanation. The enrolment figures for Chicago, Cornell and Nebraska are avowedly round numbers. Those for Mills, Wellesley and Texas look like round figures. Nebraska's place at the bottom of the list is due to an enrolment figure which is so large that it must include all extension students. Purdue's reason for distinction is not so obvious. If one says that a school that is primarily concerned with engineering and mechanics needs laboratories rather than libraries he is given pause by the ranking of Iowa State College. Rochester's figure at the top appears very high. A letter from Librarian Gilchrist reveals that his 1927–28 budget included some rather large special expenditures. His own adjusted computation gives Rochester an expenditure per student per year of $52.20.

It is interesting to observe the grouping of institutions in this list. At the top appear a group of schools, all eastern except Chicago, which are well known for their careful attention to the development of the individual student. The center of the list is largely made up of the state institutions which attempt two tasks—on the one hand, a collegiate training for thousands of youths, and, on the other, high grade graduate instruction for smaller groups of advanced students. On the bottom of the list I will make no further comments. One would rather expect to find the larger institutions ranking low because of their numbers but this is not true, though the smaller institutions are close to the top. But Chicago, Michigan, Illinois and California rank well up in the list. Nor does the ranking seem to bear any direct relation to budget totals. There are $30,000 budgets near both ends of the list and the largest of all, that of Michigan, is almost in the middle. While probably all of these figures need some explanation before final conclusions should be drawn regarding any single institution, still the averages are very informing. The mean per capita expenditure, determined by dividing the total of all budgets by the total of all students, is $24.90. Fifteen schools are above this figure and sixteen below.

This mean figure should be compared with Mr. Jacobsen's finding (in the *Library Journal,* March 15, 1928, p. 263) of $12.00 per capita as the average for thirty-five small mid-western colleges and $18.44 for twenty listed in the library *Survey.* Even more interesting is the comparison with Professor Patton's ideal figure of $25.00 per student in his most informing article in *Libraries,* vol. 36, p. 151–155. Mr. W. P. Lewis (*Library Journal,* v. 51, p. 576) finds the average for fourteen New England colleges in 1926 was $23.69 per student.

EDWARD A. HENRY
VAN WORMER LIBRARY,
UNIVERSITY OF CINCINNATI

SPECIAL CORRESPONDENCE

COOPERATIVE SUPERVISION IN ST. LOUIS COUNTY, MISSOURI

TEN school systems of St. Louis County have initiated an interesting project in cooperative supervision which other suburban cities and closely grouped communities may do well to study.

For years large city schools have enjoyed an efficient supervision of both special and general activities which smaller cities have been unable to provide. The purpose of the cooperative undertakings in St. Louis County is to furnish the children and the teachers of the comparatively small communities similar supervision at a reasonable cost.

Regular monthly meetings of the superintendents of schools of St. Louis County, including the county superintendent and members of the department of education and of the extension division of Washington University, have been held during the past two years. At the initial meeting of this group in October, 1927, called to consider the possibility of adapting university courses to the needs of the teachers of the county, plans for cooperative supervision with Washington University as an integrating center were suggested.

For two years three of the cities, Clayton, Maplewood and Webster Groves, had cooperated in the supervision of handwriting. This experience served as an illustration of what might be achieved if a greater number of cities should cooperate in a supervisory program. Consequently, after discussion through several meetings, it was decided, for the year 1928–29, to employ a supervisor of primary reading, the expenses, aside from the amount paid by Washington University, to be prorated among the ten cooperating schools, Clayton, Ferguson, Jennings, Kirkwood, Maplewood, Normandy, Ritenour, University City, Webster Groves and Wellston, on the basis of the enrolment in the first and second grades on October 1, 1928. This supervising enterprise affects 150 teachers in the first and second grades and a total of 4,048 children in 37 buildings. The total cost for the year, including tests, bulletins, etc., will range from $60 for one school system to $550 for the largest. The annual cost borne by the school systems is less than eighty-five cents per pupil.

Miss Helen Laurie, a specialist in primary reading, formerly an elementary school principal and supervisor of primary work in the Seattle schools, was selected to offer one course in supervision and another in primary reading in the summer session, 1928, of Washington University, with the understanding that she would become supervisor of primary reading in the cooperating schools in September and at the same time offer courses in Washington University, which would be open to the teachers being supervised and others. During the summer session and the first semester of this year more than sixty teachers have enrolled in the course in reading. General meetings of principals and teachers were held at the opening of the year and plans were developed for a testing program. The Burr Classification Test was given to all beginning first-grade children and the Gates Primary Reading Test was given to the children in the 1A, 2B and 2A grades. Bulletins were distributed regarding the use which could be made of the test results and conferences were held with groups of teachers in this connection. Other bulletins—some thirty in number—have dealt with various phases of class organization, instructional materials and teaching technique.

From her office at Washington University Miss Laurie can reach any school over which she has supervision in less than thirty minutes. She has gone to the schools on call this first semester and has visited every school once and many of them several times. She has been asked to teach classes and to visit for the purpose of showing how to use the classroom library or of suggesting remedial measures. At other times she has been asked to hold meetings of the teachers of a school, to talk to parent-teachers' meetings or what not. A library of supplementary reading material is being assembled in Miss Laurie's office and careful attention is being given to the selection of classroom libraries in the various schools. Office hours are held each week on two afternoons and on Saturday for individual consultation with those desiring conference.

During the first semester the supervisor, in addition to the development of good classroom libraries, worked to show the great value in taking time to stimulate children's interests in reading and in discovering individual needs through the use of check-tests in the independent work-study period. In her university classes these same things were considered. The teachers planned, carried out and wrote up reading activities for a class project. This has resulted in the publishing of a bulletin of illustrative lessons for the use of all the teachers.

Four demonstration centers have been established in four different accessible suburbs. Enough schools use the Courtis-Smith material to warrant establishing one center for demonstrating the use of this material in the first grade. The other first-grade center was established to demonstrate no special method except modern and approved techniques.

One of the second-grade demonstration centers is a slow grade, composed of children from a low average and less than average environment, while the other consists of children from a high average and in some cases from exceptional environment. Principals and teachers observe the work in these classes in small groups and a conference is held after the session is concluded. Stenographic reports of some of these conferences have been made. Other demonstration centers will be established as the need develops.

Early in the second semester all children who were reported as not progressing satisfactorily in reading were retested with the Gates test, with group intelligence tests and eventually with individual tests when the case seemed to demand it. Miss Laurie has worked out a general bulletin of suggestions for the prevention of the need of remedial work and is visiting buildings to confer with principals and teachers regarding children having special difficulties. At the same time she is emphasizing in her class in reading in Washington University specific remedial measures. She plans early to begin a picture and slide library of reading activities in St. Louis County.

Two outstanding results have been accomplished thus far. In the first place, teachers have been greatly stimulated and their professional growth has been encouraged. One hears such remarks as these from teachers:

This work has been such an inspiration to me.

I never realized how far behind the procession I was until I began to study modern methods of teaching reading.

I know what's wrong with us. We don't have enough community life and other worth-while activities going on in our rooms. We don't do enough to develop the creative in children.

In the second place, the superintendents of schools in St. Louis County have discovered that more can be accomplished along many lines through cooperative effort than through individual labor, and at a very great reduction in cost. The hearing of all the pupils in the cooperating schools is being tested; uniform records are being considered, and a venture in cooperative purchasing is being undertaken.

Due to the open-mindedness and to the professional spirit of the teachers and of the supervisor and to the agreeable spirit of cooperation on the part of the administrators, the difficulties which might be predicted for supervision involving so many school systems have not been encountered. In fact, all the parties involved in this cooperative project seem to be enjoying their adventure.

FRANK L. WRIGHT
WASHINGTON UNIVERSITY,
ST. LOUIS, MISSOURI
JOHN L. BRACKEN
Superintendent of Schools
CLAYTON, MISSOURI

QUOTATIONS

EDUCATION BY RADIO

THE suggestion that a fact-finding commission be appointed to study what radio can do for education suggests many questions about the use of the radio to which no satisfactory answer has yet been found. Its popularity is largely due to its value as a source of entertainment. Some insist that this will always be its chief interest. But this same argument was advanced when the first efforts were made to broadcast symphony music. The listeners, said the radio companies, want only jazz. Experience showed, however, that the demand for good music has steadily increased, and that such features as the Damrosch concerts have won millions of regular "fans."

When first it was suggested that there might be "colleges of the air," the conservatives asserted that the people would not tune in on them. Experience has shown, however, that lectures—when they are interesting and well delivered—are eagerly heard. So also the early predictions that broadcasting sermons would not be well received have proved false.

If, then, there is a latent demand for educational matter of all sorts, the problem arises of determining what shall be offered. Heretofore the broadcasting companies or advertisers using their stations have supervised the selection of speakers and subjects. There are critics who say that this is a mistake, and that the educational programs should be worked out by our great universities or by the federal authorities. At once the practical matter of paying for the cost of broadcasting comes to the front. It has been said that unless special rates are made for educational programs they can not be made self-supporting.

These details deserve special study. But more important by far is the larger problem of how valuable, in actual practice, the radio can be made in educational work, and of in what field, besides music, it can be most effectively used. Certainly there has been a deficiency in the supply of good readers. This may be because the art of reading aloud is one which has never been cultivated in this country, and which is, in fact, possessed by only a very few persons. Of these some have voices which do not "get across" the ether as well as in a room or on a stage. Even among "popular" lecturers whose names are now familiar to large radio audiences there are only a few men who combine thorough culture with the ability to make themselves interesting to people by the loud-speaker. A better technique will in time be developed. But the very fact that so many lectures "on the air" meet with such little success shows that the entire subject is one which needs thorough investigation.—*The New York Times.*

EDUCATIONAL POLICY IN ENGLAND

ALL parties are agreed in principle on the main lines of educational progress, and, that being so, governments must be judged by performances rather than by promises. Recently we published the text of an official manifesto which sets out to describe "what the work of the present ministry means to the youth of England," and Mr. Baldwin has supplemented this in a pamphlet addressed "to all engaged in the work of education." In these documents there is a definite reliance on work accomplished, rather than a promise of work to be done. All that is promised is that, if the opportunity is given, the work will be continued on the lines laid down. Emphasis is laid on the belief that, if continuity is thus assured, results, national and individual, will be cumulative. Education is a slow process, and its reconstruction or reorganization is slower still. Unless some temporary crisis occurs which can be turned to party purposes, there is normally little party capital to be gained from an educational paragraph in electoral addresses. All that the candidate can hope to do is to influence the votes of electors endowed with longer sight than some by pointing to the record of his party in the past as evidence of its probable conduct of the future.

From this test the record of the last five years should emerge successfully. "So much to do, so little done" is the inevitable reflection of any educationist who looks back upon so brief a period as is covered by any one parliament; but it is something if the lines of progress are well and truly laid, so that the machine can travel along them steadily towards the goal. That goal is, in the words of the manifesto, "opportunity for every child." How far has the administration of the last few years promoted this ideal? The main step forward has been to make provision for a break in education at the age of eleven, and for a four years' course thereafter in some form of higher education, which may, or may not, according to the capacity of the child, lead to his completing a secondary or university course. This is the policy popularly known as "secondary education for all," long advocated in these columns and adopted by all parties and practically by all educational associations. It is one thing, however, to adopt a policy, and another to carry it out. What the present administration has done has been to set the ball actually rolling, or rather to kick it towards the goal. This is the most important step forward, since the Act of 1902, in the direction of providing what the manifesto calls "a complete and balanced system of education."—*The London Times.*

REPORTS

THE EXPERIMENTAL COLLEGE OF THE UNIVERSITY OF WISCONSIN

DESCRIPTIONS of teaching methods in the Experimental College of the University of Wisconsin, observations on the aims of the college and a recommendation for a thorough appraisal of the experiment next year are included in a report accepted by the faculty of the College of Letters and Science.

Information contributed by the report includes a description of studies of Greek civilization made during the first year of work in the college, of American civilization during the second year and of the system of instruction which is followed.

Two special observations and a recommendation supplement the data in the report.

The situation which the experimental college was designed to meet constitutes a major problem in contemporary education, reads the report. It is recognized as such by educational leaders throughout the country. Foremost universities and colleges are focusing attention upon it. In briefest form the problem may be summarized under these heads: (a) How to aid students to achieve, in some degree at least, a unified comprehension of the highly specialized types of knowledge which the advance of modern investigation inevitably entails, and to do so in spite of the diversified curricula which the rapid expansion of higher education has left in its train; (b) how to stimulate intellectual curiosity and to further the power to think objectively and creatively both in particular fields and in the more general contacts of life; (c) how to develop the sense of social responsibility and to put it in the way of becoming informed; (d) how to replace the existing credit and grade basis of appraisal by an arrangement more in accord with modern psychological and educational theory; (e) how to secure a more personal working relationship between teacher and student than our present conditions exemplify.

The fact that your committee refrains from passing judgment upon the present aims and practices of the experimental college should not be taken to mean that we assume a neutral attitude as regards this basic problem, or that we would suggest such an attitude as the proper one for university teachers to take. On the contrary, it is the very importance of this entire matter, a matter which may deeply influence future developments in undergraduate instruction, and which seems to us to demand long and profound study on the part of this faculty, that induces us to withhold judgment until that study has produced a larger body of fact and a clearer vision. Certainly it is apparent that a vital question of educational advance centers just at this point.

Efforts to solve this problem are, in general, most seriously being made by the older, endowed institutions of the country rather than by the tax-supported state or municipal universities. The former have greater liberty of action for educational experimentation in that they can control, and are very definitely controlling, undergraduate admission on the basis of intellectual fitness. Basically, of course, the aims of the two types of institutions are the same—to develop an ideal system of education. The endowed university finds itself less cramped; but the state university, accepting its handicap, will prove itself worthy in proportion as it rises to its common opportunity. We feel it to be a signal opportunity, as well as an unavoidable responsibility, for the University of Wisconsin resolutely to face this problem and to enlist the best abilities of the teaching and administration personnel for its solution.

The committee has been deeply impressed by the evidences of loyalty to the enterprise of the experimental college on the part of its staff. We have found at work upon the details of the experiment the collective intelligence of a superior body of teachers, and we believe them to have made substantial progress in the formulation of study content and teaching technique. We are under the impression, moreover, that the student population in the college has grown in its understanding of the experiment and shows an increasing tendency toward cooperative participation.

It appears desirable to your committee that a closer relationship than at present exists be brought about between the experimental college and the larger university project of which it forms a part. Whatever the ultimate fate of the experiment may be, it should be recognized as constituting for the time being a systematic effort on the part of the University of Wisconsin, as such, to meet a situation which is recognized as a major problem throughout the university world, and which is being dealt with in various ways by other universities and colleges. We therefore recommend the appointment of the committee referred to in the letters and science minutes for May 26, 1926, whose obligation it shall be to obtain such a complete insight into the theoretical aims and practical functioning of the experimental college as will justify an appraisal in May, 1930.

EDUCATIONAL RESEARCH AND STATISTICS

WHO HAVE CONTRIBUTED MOST TO THE EDUCATIONAL MEASUREMENT MOVEMENT?

For a number of years it has been more or less the fashion in education to determine the importance of items by counting their occurrences. Numerous word counts in English and other languages have been made; the frequency of use of arithmetical operations has been tabulated; references to historical dates, characters and events have been enumerated, and so on in many other fields. As a number of writers and speakers have pointed out, the results of such studies do not necessarily determine the most important items in the field dealt with. Nevertheless they do yield some indications along this line. Therefore when the writer wished to determine at least a tentative list of individuals who have made the most important contributions to the educational measurement movement, and whose work in this field is, therefore, most worth knowing about, he decided to resort to this method as probably the best single one.

The basis of the study was a selected list of recent publications in the field of educational measurements. Those examined included all books published within the last three years which deal with intelligence or achievement tests, or both, or with the new examination, in what might be called a general manner. Twenty[1] such publications, of which two are bibliographies, were found and the occurrences therein tabulated. Books which belong in the general field of educational measurements but deal with particular studies or investigations, such, for example, as Thorndike's "The Measurement of Intelligence,"[2] were not included. In addition to these twenty sources, the writer's rather complete file of standardized and near-standardized tests was also used. All occurrences of the names of individuals, whether in the form of discussions of their work, mentions of their writings or tests, or mere bibliographical references, found in the twenty-one sources were tabulated. An occurrence was defined as meaning a single complete reference to, or discussion of, an individual or his work. Thus, for example, if Ayres' Spelling Scale was just mentioned at one place and his Writing Scale at another, two occurrences were recorded. On the other hand, if a continuous discussion of his Writing Scale was several pages in length and mentioned his name a number of times, it was recorded as only one occurrence. Names of certain persons who, although mentioned in the sources used, had no connection with the educational measurements movement,[3] were included in the preliminary tabulations, but omitted from the final ones.

[1] The twenty publications consulted were as follows:

Buckingham, B. R. "Research for Teachers." New York: Silver, Burdett and Co., 1926. 386 pp.

Dearborn, W. F. "Intelligence Tests, Their Significance for School and Society." Boston: Houghton Mifflin Co., 1928. 336 pp.

Fenton, Norman, and Worcester, D. A. "An Introduction to Educational Measurements." Boston: Ginn and Co., 1928. 149 pp.

Freeman, F. N. "Mental Tests, Their History, Principles and Applications." Boston: Houghton Mifflin Co., 1926. 504 pp.

Greene, H. A., and Jorgensen, A. N. "The Use and Interpretation of Educational Tests." Longmans, Green and Co., 1929. 389 pp.

Hull, C. L. "Aptitude Testing." Yonkers: World Book Co., 1928. 535 pp.

Kelley, T. L. "Interpretation of Educational Measurements." Yonkers: World Book Co., 1927. 363 pp.

Levine, A. J., and Marks, Louis. "Testing Intelligence and Achievement." New York: Macmillan Co., 1928. 399 pp.

Monroe, W. S., Odell, C. W., Herriott, M. E., Engelhart, M. D., and Hull, M. R. "Research in Educational Measurement," *University of Illinois Bulletin*, Vol. 25, No. 51, Bureau of Educational Research Bulletin No. 42. Urbana: University of Illinois, 1928, Chapter IV.

Odell, C. W. "A Selected Annotated Bibliography Dealing with Examinations and School Marks," *University of Illinois Bulletin*, Vol. 26, No. 20, Bureau of Educational Research Bulletin No. 43. Urbana: University of Illinois, 1929. 42 pp.

Odell, C. W. "Traditional Examinations and New-Type Tests." New York: Century Co., 1928. 469 pp.

Orleans, J. S., and Sealy, G. A. "Objective Tests." Yonkers: World Book Co., 1928. 373 pp.

Ruch, G. M., and Stoddard, G. D. "Tests and Measurements in High School Instruction." Yonkers: World Book Co., 1927. 381 pp.

Russell, Charles. "Classroom Tests." Boston: Ginn and Co., 1926. 346 pp.

Smith, H. L., and Wright, W. W. "Second Revision of the Bibliography of Educational Measurements," *Bulletin of the School of Education*, Vol. 4, No. 2. Bloomington: Bureau of Cooperative Research, Indiana University, 1927. 251 pp.

Smith, H. L., and Wright, W. W. "Tests and Measurements." New York: Silver, Burdett and Co., 1928. 540 pp.

Symonds, P. M. "Measurement in Secondary Education." New York: Macmillan Co., 1927. 588 pp.

Van Wagenen, M. J. "Educational Diagnosis and the Measurement of School Achievement." New York: Macmillan Co., 1926. 276 pp.

Wells, F. F. "Mental Tests in Clinical Practice." Yonkers: World Book Co., 1927. 315 pp.

Wilson, G. M., and Hoke, K. J. "How to Measure, Revised and Enlarged." New York: Macmillan Co., 1928. 597 pp.

[2] Thorndike, E. L., *et al.* "The Measurement of Intelligence." New York: Bureau of Publications, Teachers College, Columbia University, 1926. 616 pp.

[3] The number of such persons mentioned was small. Most of them were historical characters such, for example, as Napoleon Bonaparte and U. S. Grant, who were referred to in some connection or other. A very few were educators, such as Plato and Horace Mann, to whose beliefs or writings references were made.

Before proceeding to give the names of those who were most frequently mentioned, the writer will give a few general figures concerning the results of the study. A total of 1,764 different persons was mentioned in the twenty-one sources, and the total number of occurrences of their names was 9,867. Of these persons, 859, or almost half, were mentioned in only one source, and 692 of the 859 only once in that source. Two hundred fifty-two individuals, or about one out of seven, were mentioned in five or more of the twenty-one sources, and 432, or slightly less than one in four, had their names occur five times or more in all. Only forty-eight had their names in more than half of the sources.

There was, of course, a very great difference among the different sources in the number of persons mentioned and the frequency for each. The writer's test file led in this regard, 832 persons being mentioned a total of 1,330 times therein. Among the other sources, the number of individuals named in each ranged from 16 to 506, and the number of total occurrences in each from 22 to 1,309. The number of persons named in the test file not found elsewhere was 239, whereas the numbers in the twenty other sources ranged from none to 78.

There are at least two bases which may be employed in such studies as this to determine the importance of the items dealt with. One is the number of sources in which each item occurs and the other the total number of occurrences. In this study both were tabulated, ranks given on each basis, and then averaged to determine the final order. In Table I will be found a list of the persons mentioned in the greatest number of sources; in Table II of those mentioned most often, and in Table III of those who stand highest when the rankings are averaged. The first twenty-five are included in each list, except that in Table I it is necessary to include three more because they are included in a tie with the four others needed to complete the number of twenty-five.

It will be noted from Table I that no one is mentioned in all or even all but one of the sources. Terman's name occurs in nineteen of the twenty-one sources, and those of McCall, Rugg and Thorndike in eighteen. Perhaps some readers will be surprised that the names of Terman and Thorndike, at least, do not occur in every source. The sources which do not mention these men deal with the new examination, a field in which neither Terman nor Thorndike has made very direct contributions, though their indirect influence has been felt therein. A glance at the list will show that on the whole it is composed of persons who have worked along several different lines within the field of educational measurements. The names of comparatively few persons, such as Binet, for example, whose work has been within rather narrowly restricted limits, occur. This is even more true with regard to Table II, in which it will be noted that Binet's name is not to be found.

TABLE I

NAMES OF INDIVIDUALS REFERRED TO IN THE MOST SOURCES AND NUMBER OF SOURCES MENTIONING EACH

Name	Number of sources
Terman	19
McCall	18
Rugg	18
Thorndike	18
Buckingham	17
Monroe	17
Pressey, S. L.	17
Ruch	17
Freeman	16
Gray, W. S.	16
Otis	16
Pintner	16
Starch	16
Trabue	16
Ayres	15
Binet	15
Chapman	15
Franzen	15
Paterson	15
Pressey, L. C.	15
Thurstone	15
Courtis	14
Dearborn	14
Kelley	14
Kelly	14
Odell	14
Wood	14
Woody	14

In connection with Table II, one of the facts which will probably be first noticed is the decided gap between Thorndike, who is first, and Ruch, who is second. The large number of occurrences of Thorndike's name, 252, is largely accounted for by the fact that in a single book he is mentioned seventy times, whereas no one else is mentioned more than forty times in any one source, and only three or four persons more than thirty. The fact that Thorndike's name occurs at the head of this list further emphasizes the point made above, that activity in many portions of the field, rather than intensive activity along a single line, is very influential in causing high rank.

TABLE II

NAMES OF INDIVIDUALS REFERRED TO MOST OFTEN AND NUMBER OF TIMES EACH IS MENTIONED

Name	Number of mentions
Thorndike	252
Ruch	198
Terman	184
Monroe	149
McCall	123
Otis	123
Kelley	112
Thurstone	109
Pressey, S. L.	106
Wood	93
Courtis	91
Starch	91
Trabue	88
Pressey, L. C.	86
Van Wagenen	84
Buckingham	82
Pintner	80
Rugg	75
Dearborn	71
Stoddard	67
Freeman	61
Gates	60
Odell	59
Haggerty	58
Toops	58

As would be expected, the lists of names in the three tables do not differ greatly. Gray, Ayres, Binet, Chapman, Franzen, Paterson, Kelly and Woody are listed in Table I, but not in Table II. The names appearing in the latter

TABLE III

AVERAGE RANKS OF THE TWENTY-FIVE HIGHEST RANKING PERSONS

Rank	Name
1.5	Terman
1.5	Thorndike
3.5	McCall
3.5	Ruch
5	Monroe
6	Pressey, S. L.
7	Otis
8	Rugg
9	Buckingham
10	Starch
11	Trabue
12	Thurstone
13	Pintner
14.5	Kelley
14.5	Pressey, L. C.
16	Freeman
17	Wood
18	Courtis
19	Dearborn
20	Binet
21.5	Chapman
21.5	Odell
23	Ayres
24	Woody
25	Van Wagenen

that are not in Table I are those of Van Wagenen, Stoddard, Gates, Haggerty and Toops. Van Wagenen is the only individual named in Table III who is not found in Table I, whereas Binet, Chapman, Ayres and Woody do not occur in Table II.

In closing, the writer would like to emphasize that he does not wish to be understood as believing that Table III necessarily contains the names of the twenty-five most important contributors in the field of educational measurements. He does believe, however, that the results of this study indicate that if these persons are not the first twenty-five, at least none of them falls very far below that position. Certainly one is justified in naming them as persons with whose work beginners in this field should become familiar.

C. W. ODELL

COLLEGE OF EDUCATION,
UNIVERSITY OF ILLINOIS

SCHOOL AND SOCIETY

EDITED BY J. McKEEN CATTELL

WITH WHICH IS COMBINED THE

EDUCATIONAL REVIEW

EDITED BY WILLIAM McANDREW

Volume XXIX | SATURDAY, JUNE 15, 1929 | Number 755

THE PHILOSOPHY AND ORGANIZATION OF RESEARCH[1]

By Dr. B. R. BUCKINGHAM

HARVARD UNIVERSITY

I SHOULD like, at the outset, to pay tribute to the group of persons who chose the topic for this convocation. The progress of the world rests squarely upon research; and as the boundaries of knowledge are extended, through its instrumentality, along one sector after another of the frontiers of human thought, and as a larger and ever larger number of workers join its ranks, the social significance of research is destined, as I verily believe, to exceed that of any other service yet entertained by the mind of man. It provides for nothing less than a new analysis and a new synthesis of human behavior and human relationships.

It therefore seems to me that the topic for the convocation this year has been happily chosen, and I feel it a privilege to take part in a program so admirably conceived.

In order that our generation may cope with the infinite detail of human activity and thought, it is necessary to divide the total field into areas within which conditions are more or less alike, and to call each of these areas by a distinctive name. Thus arise the various knowledges—the crafts, the sciences and the humanities. We say that this topic is classifiable under physics, that the other is in the field of aeronautics, that still another belongs to the subject of geography, and so on. We know quite well that the boundaries between these subjects are vague and shifting. We know that a given topic may belong to geology or physics or chemistry according to the way we think about it. Nevertheless, these means of classification are useful as pegs on which to hang our thoughts, and perhaps as crutches to sustain our faltering steps.

Research is a method applicable to all these areas of thought. Observe that I refer to research as a method. It is not, as I view it, a field of knowledge, although it is entirely possible to study it for what it is, namely, a way of establishing new facts, principles and procedures. The boundaries of research are precisely those of human knowledge itself. A student, therefore, who wants to "major in research," has the universe as his field of concentration. There is no domain of human thought which research may not reach and extend; there is no skill which it may not investigate and improve; there is no ideal which it may not examine and enrich.

The purpose of this universal method, we are agreed, is the *contribution of new*

[1] Address delivered before the sixty-fourth convocation of the University of the State of New York, October 18, 1928.

truth; and I submit there is no endeavor more worthy of the best efforts of a human being. I have just used three important words in the vocabulary of research, namely, "contribution," "new" and "truth." Truth as a concept is common enough, yet it is one of the noblest to which man attains. The Almighty is Himself described as the God of truth. In that supreme ethical triad, "the good, the beautiful and the true," it is *truth* which furnishes the climax. The research worker is nothing if he does not seek the truth wherever it may be found and in whatever form he may encounter it. Indeed, love of truth is the only thing from which, as a research worker, he can not be separated without losing his character. He may lack any virtue but that one, and survive. It has been pointed out that each calling has its special form of disqualification—a sort of negative test of fitness. The judge must not accept a bribe, the lawyer must not take a retainer from both sides, the doctor must not refuse to heal the sick; even the jockey must not "pull" the race, nor the pugilist "throw" the fight. The research worker must not fail to proclaim the truth as he finds it. Truth he can not tamper with and retain the respect of his confrères.

Although truth is at once the object of research and the touchstone of competence on the part of the research worker, it is not just any truth which may properly serve the purposes of research. The ideal is *new* truth, and it is right here that some of the critics of research pour forth the vials of their wrath. "Research," says one of them derisively, "is trying to find for the hundredth time what everybody knows and then explaining it in language nobody understands." Truth already established as such is not a proper object of research. Even here, however, a caution is necessary. "What everybody knows" may need revision. A fiction agreed upon is still a fiction. Not long ago I fancy everybody "knew" that small classes were being better taught than large classes, and I suspect that people of the mind of the man who made this satiric definition would have deprecated the early investigations of Boyce and Bachman and Elliott, who sought to find out forsooth whether small classes were actually being taught better than classes of larger size. It turns out—as "everybody" certainly did not know—that the advantages which small classes ought to afford are not in reality being attained, and that, with present teachers operating under present conditions, classes of twenty are not better taught, according to any measuring scheme that we can apply, than classes of thirty or thirty-five. The critic who dubs research workers mere putterers trying to find out for the hundredth time what everybody knows may be passing a very superficial judgment.

Nevertheless, I think we all get the force of the criticism. A great deal of so-called research is trivial; a great deal of it is stamping over old ground; a great deal of it could be better employed.

Yet I should like to point out that there is a place for repeating investigations that have already been made, and that such repetition often deserves to be crowned research by anybody competent to bestow the title. This is because one investigation, even if well conducted, is seldom a sufficient basis for the establishment of new truth. The first findings probably need to be confirmed. Sometimes the second trial, instead of confirming the first, modifies it or even contradicts it. Then many more investigations of the same kind must be made before we can be sure what the truth is. Each of these repetitions of the original investigation—as long as there is honest doubt as to the nature of the result—deserves the name of research. It may not be as interesting as an investigation never before attempted, it may not challenge the world; but we must remember that very few men indeed are capable of finding new problems. At a single memorable meeting in his Leipzig laboratory Wilhelm Wundt assigned thirty-eight new doctorate problems together with their key readings; but Wundt was almost unequaled as a frontier thinker. The criterion of newness as applicable to research is reasonably met as long as the study in question is not seeking to find out something which has in reality already been satisfactorily established.

Finally, returning to the definition in three words, I wish to point out that research has as its object the making of a *contribution*. If a research report were indeed written "in language nobody understands" there would obviously be no contribution. If the topic were so trivial as to be of no consequence whatever, there would again be no contribution. If the execution of the research were so faulty that its conclusions had no meaning, there would, from a third point of view, be no contribution. Evidently, therefore, the question of whether a contribution is made breaks up into several conditioning items. The problem must have some worth, the execution must be sufficiently competent to secure results of value and there must be a report which brings the findings to light in understandable form.

With this objective in mind, namely, the contribution of new truth, it is proper to consider the nature of research—in other words, its philosophy. For the philosophy of anything, I take it, is just that—its nature, its true meaning, its place in the scheme of things, its relation to life. Broadly speaking, research is a form of thinking. It can not arise until a problem is recognized. It can not proceed until data have been assembled. It requires the organization of these data so as to disclose their meaning and relationships. It ordinarily involves the setting up and frequently the tearing down of hypotheses or leads or "hunches." It organizes its data with reference to these hypotheses and pronounces them provisionally true or false, according to the meaning of the data when arrayed in accordance with these hypotheses. Finally, if the research worker is fortunate, a solution of the problem is attained, or in lieu of this an impasse is reached and recognized as such.

So far the procedure is scientific, and ordinarily this is as far as descriptions of research go. Yet the description is certainly incomplete. Suppose that a particular piece of research has advanced through the stages I have mentioned—stages which correspond to those of reflective thinking—and has arrived at a solution, provisional at least, of the initial problem. It is quite evident that something more is needed. Science has done its part, and philosophy must now take up the task. This no other than the interpretation of the scientific findings. This involves the determination of meanings and values. It raises the question, "What is this result worth?" In seeking to answer this question, philosophy, of course, views life as a whole and regards as of worth those things which serve the purposes of life. Moreover, philosophy attempts a higher synthesis than is available to science. Just as science uses observations—employing the term in its widest sense—for its data, so philosophy may use (among other things) the findings of science as *its* data. Accordingly there comes into view a hierarchy of activities ranging from the organizing of very simple observations, such as counting the legs of a beetle or the petals of a flower, to the organizing and evaluating of complex and far-reaching generalizations. I am not sure that any one can say at just what point science ceases and philosophy begins. I do know that philosophy goes deeper, although its techniques are less objective and less convincing. The findings of philosophy, although they lack the precision of science, possess a range and significance which science alone can not give.

I therefore view the matter somewhat as follows. As fields of human endeavor science and philosophy supplement each other. Science furnishes data for the use of philosophy, while philosophy gives these data meaning. Without philosophy, science is incomplete; without science, philosophy is barren. Of course, it goes without saying that the scientist and the philosopher may be the same man. In fact, if a scientist has no philosophy, he is an unsafe guide, while the philosopher who is without science is a mere speculative dreamer.

Just as I hold that both science and philosophy are needed in research, so I hold, too, that the methods of research are themselves applicable in the fields of science and philosophy. In other words, I recognize both scientific research and philosophical research. In fact it seems to me that the only creative work available to the philosopher is precisely of a research character—an activity in which he uses data just as certainly as the scientist uses data, and for the same purpose—namely, the establishment of truth.

I have said in an earlier paragraph that research provides a new analysis and a new synthesis of human behavior and human relationships. In making this statement I have in mind the fact that the research worker, whether in education or elsewhere, must select *specific* problems, and that in order to do this he must analyze the field. With further regard to analysis, it is my notion that if many workers devote themselves to a given field, each after he has thus selected specific problems, it is possible to approximate a condition whereby all attainable major problems within the field are identified, thus providing a sort of "spot" analysis of the field in question. This result would follow in education if the burning need for quantity production in research were generally realized and if large numbers of workers were organized to meet the need. My point is that to the extent that this is accomplished we shall have an analysis for purposes of research of the entire field of education.

But analysis is never sufficient. As long as the elements into which a whole may be broken up are all that we have at hand, our data are unorganized, refractory and difficult to control. Moreover, they may not even be true. At this point the philosopher plays his part. As each new problem reaches solution—or as each contribution of new truth is made—knowledge as it has hitherto existed must be modified. The newcomer has to be properly placed in the company which he has entered. Thus new alignments are made and new groupings, with new meanings for each of the alignments and groups. You have seen this process of integration going on in education with astonishing rapidity during the past twenty years. If the story were mine to tell at this moment, I could show not only that the accomplishment of the schools is quite different from what it used to be but even that our conception of method and our appraisal of results are distinctly new. What we are pleased to call progress—and I think we are justified in calling it progress—has been more rapid within the past twenty years than ever before. This is due to the research movement in education and to no other cause whatever. Research and research alone has made the scientific analysis and the philosophical synthesis which is the thing we call progress. For, after all, what is progress? Is it not truth ascertained and made meaningful? Is it not, in other words, science and philosophy operating through research methods?

In what I have thus far said I refer to research at its best. I mean research well organized and competently conducted; which is no more than to say, research of the kind that contributes new truth. It now becomes necessary, in the interest of presenting a whole thought, to examine the conditions under which research may be said to be "well organized and competently conducted," in other words the conditions under which it may merit what I have claimed for it.

About us on every hand are problems. The apprehension of these problems is the first necessary step in research. Let us suppose that a new consolidated school has been erected in a certain rural township. Apparently all the machinery of a modern school has been established and the children have been enrolled. It develops, however, that these children attend very irregularly. The work of the school is impaired. Something is evidently wrong. This is a problem and one of a very practical nature. Its solution may be attempted by speculation or by the use of authority. But the best way is by means of research. Probably the research worker will begin by studying the conditions in this school which are different from those in schools where the attendance is satisfactory, for he will think it probable that the cause of the poor attendance will be among these conditions. He may note that the distance between the pupils' homes and the school is greater in this instance than it is in schools otherwise similarly conditioned but having good attendance. The research worker may now formulate a hypothesis, at least in crude form, such as "the greater the distance from school the poorer the attendance."

A great many people stop right here. Moreover, some of them call their work research and their hypothesis the product of research. This is especially true if they have reached their conclusions by the use of elaborate questionnaires. This is what gives the critic a chance to say "Why, everybody knows that."

Dr. George H. Reavis in his study of attendance in rural schools reached this hypothesis; but he did not stop there. He went on and verified his hypothesis, defining and qualifying it as he proceeded. He showed among other things just what effect different distances from school had upon attendance—that, for example, there were three rather distinct zones of distance within each of which attendance was about the same, namely, distances up to a quarter of a mile, those from a quarter of a mile to a mile and a half, and those of more than a mile and a half. Again, in verifying and modifying his hypothesis he brought out in similar detail the bearing which the age of children has upon their attendance, when they come from homes of given distances from the schoolhouse.

By this time Dr. Reavis had shown that the causal relationship between distance and attendance which he had set up as a rough hypothesis was by no means simple. He had proved that the law embodying the solution was not at all the direct proportion which was formulated in the hypothesis and he had established the true solution in its multiple form with substantial reliability. The only step he left out was that of verification—the stage in which the solution is tried out, for further criticism and refinement. As he proceeded in his study, however, he came upon certain new problems such as the effect of different kinds of roads, of the presence or absence of a system of transportation, of different types of transportation, and of climatic and seasonal conditions. Since he could not make a systematic attack upon these problems with the data at his disposal he contented himself with suggesting the problems for future consideration.

I have used Dr. Reavis's study merely as a type. Any one of a large number of competent research reports would have done as well. I have used his report to show that in research we have first the realization of a problem and second the formulation of a crude hypothesis. This latter is often made after considerable preliminary study and is sometimes wrongly taken as the solution of the problem. The third step is the investigation itself designed to verify the hypothesis and at the same time to amplify it and subject it to critical examination. During the course of this investigation new problems usually emerge and these problems are stated. All along the way you will notice that these are the processes which Dewey has made familiar to us as the steps in thinking. In fact, as has already been suggested, it is not improper to regard research as a type of reflective thinking.

The essential difference between thinking which is not research and thinking which is research is in refinement of method—a refinement the purpose of which is to assure the truth of the result. Most of these refinements have to do with the nature of the data. First, they must be *relevant;* if we are concerned with twelve-year-olds, we must exercise due care to keep out returns from children of any other age. Second, the data must be *representative;* we must either secure all the twelve-year-olds or an unbiased sampling of them. Third, the data must be *abundant;* we must have enough cases of twelve-year-olds so that the addition of more cases will not materially alter the result. And fourth, the data must be *trustworthy;* if we are securing the record of the twelve-year-olds in reading we must use a measuring instrument which is valid, reliable, objective and accurate.

Probably the thinking ability of man has not improved within historical times. Certainly we have no right to suppose that we of to-day can think any better than our ancestors. Yet we do get more and better results. The improvement is not in the power to think but mainly in getting our data and safeguarding them from error. For example, there was a time when a citation from an authority—preferably the Bible or Aristotle—was admitted as an entirely sufficient datum, at once relevant, representative, abundant (because self-sufficient) and trustworthy beyond cavil. Speculation provided data especially acceptable in learned circles. The sterile philosophy of the middle ages and of the modern period almost to our own time was sterile because it cared little about its data and was concerned mainly in the quality of its speculative procedure. If we can ever enlist the amazing acumen of the philosopher in the consideration of the right kind of data we shall experience another renaissance.

Still other and even more questionable sources of data have been accepted in the past and are still accepted in some quarters as a basis for thinking. Custom or tradition, maxims or wise saws, folk-tales, dreams, fortune-telling, spiritualistic séances, political platforms, advertisements, campaign promises—in short any plausible hocus-pocus, especially if it emanates from a high place or is put into print or is dressed in attractive literary form—are accepted and actually used as the data of thought. It is no wonder that the culture even of the most enlightened nations has been honeycombed with taboos and superstitions. It is not, however, the thinking considered as a pure process of handling data that has been at fault. It is the data themselves. Our lamentable failure through the ages to make the best use of our power to think has been our failure to criticize the materials upon which the forms of thought were exercised. Thinking can rise no higher than its source; and if the data upon which it rests are vitiated the entire fabric is unsubstantial.

Thus it is the requirement of adequate data which, more than any other one thing, distinguishes the modern activity called research from the less fruitful thinking of an earlier and less scientifically critical day.

But if the adequacy of the data is of paramount importance, it is also regarded as essential to a research technique that the data should be handled so as to bring out their true meaning. Here statistics plays a prominent part. In fact Professor Simonds goes so far as to say that "all research involves the use of statistical methods." This does not seem to me to be true unless we give statistics a wider meaning than usual—a meaning so wide for example as to make it a part of all reflective thinking. Historical research investigates among other things the credibility of records. In doing so it can hardly be said to "involve the use of statistical methods." Nevertheless, the very fact that such a claim could be made indicates that the prevailing method of handling research data is statistical. It is certain that no research worker in education can proceed far without resort to this new science of numbers.

Statistics in reality represents a new type of logic. Professor George Boaz recently pointed out that according to the mode of thinking from Aristotle to Huxley everything belonged to an appropriate class. The camel, the bear and the humming-bird each had its fixed characteristics. A novel had certain features which made it a novel, a dollar was a dollar even if it would purchase but a third as much as formerly. Soldiers were invariably brave and women were always fair. The world was nicely marked off into types.

Our thinking, as Professor Boaz further points out, now comes more and more to center around the statistical class. We recognize that bravery is an attribute which may vary all the way from foolish, rash, romantic temerity to the timidity of those who "scenting the acrid perfume of the artillery, scuttled off to Washington and got jobs in the Judge Advocate General's Department." We realize that all women are fair only in theory and that if we were to arrange them in the order of fairness we should have at one end the face that launched a thousand ships and at the other the face that would stop a clock. Accordingly Professor Boaz says that thinking to-day is different from what it used to be. This, he believes, is not so much because we think of different things as it is because we think differently about the same things. Our very logic, he says, is different from that of our grandfathers.

We recognize therefore the presence of a new and powerful instrument to assist us in the organization of large masses of data. One of the stumbling-blocks in pursuing research of certain types has been the necessity of securing thousands of cases. On the one hand, without this abundance of data our results were unreliable; while on the other hand their mere bulk proved an unsurmountable obstacle. The new methods of handling numerical data have gone a long way toward making possible the authoritative conclusions which a wealth of raw material can alone ensure. In short, if it were not for the development of statistics, much of modern research would be impossible.

Sometimes, however, the very attractiveness of statistical technique leads to our undoing. Under the influence of statistical method our procedure tends to lose flexibility and to harden into set forms. When we decide to use measurement and the analysis that measurement permits, we put our trust in precision, accuracy and definition. This is desirable up to a certain point, and in some kinds of work it is desirable all the way. But there are wide areas of thought where precision is not possible or where it can only be attained by non-statistical methods. To let statistics aid our thinking is imperative as far as statistics applies, but to let it dominate all our thinking is to court disaster. Indeed there is in some quarters a lamentable tendency to substitute statistics for creative thought.

I believe this is true in some of our curriculum research. Let the work in spelling stand as a type. Here as in other subjects much labor has been expended in finding out the words most frequently used in written discourse. This is admirable so far as it goes. But quite clearly it does not suffice.

In the first place, we can not by any means be sure that the present determination of frequency of use is the true one. For example, in a list which purports to consist of the thousand commonest words, we do not find the names of our daily meals—neither *breakfast* nor *lunch, dinner* nor *supper.* Nor do we find the commonest articles of tableware, such as *plate, cup, knife, fork* and *spoon.* Many articles of food— *potatoes, beans, beets, peas, meat, fish, bread* and *butter*—are not named; nor are some of the commonest articles of clothing nor some of the most familiar colors. Only the *horse* is mentioned among domestic animals. The dog and the cat, the cow and the sheep find no place in the list.

One may contend that these may indeed be common words without being frequently used in written discourse. The contention, however, has little plausibility. A child can not write of his play without using such words as *hide, jump, swim, fish* or *sled,* and these words are omitted from the thousand said to be most frequently used. He can scarcely write of the barnyard without requiring such omitted words as *hen* and *egg;* he can not write about his *garden* nor the *baby* at home; nor about the *moon,* the *sun,* the *sky* nor the *stars.* Yet these are the things within his experience. They are, therefore, the sort of topics which we should expect him to write about.

On the other hand, among the "thousand commonest words" we actually find these: *preliminary, recommend, impossible, assure, committee, investigate, national;* and a number of terms of apparently legal meaning such as *property, judgment, testimony, complaint, agreement, witness* and *conviction.* This suggests that the source of our vocabulary studies must be very greatly widened and that an enormously greater amount of written material must be examined.

In the second place, even if true frequency of use has been determined, we assert that there are other tests of value than frequency of use. For example, although the word *bread* may be rightly excluded from the thousand commonest words, yet circumstances which, while they may be relatively infrequent are nevertheless inevitable, will make it at times indispensable in one's written vocabulary. Future research may conceivably confirm the present determination that *apple* and *banana, bright* and *beautiful, meat* and *drink* likewise do not belong to the thousand commonest words. But this is not a sufficient reason why they should be banished from our spelling curriculum. These are simple words and they stand for ideas common to the race. The ideas may not require expression quite often enough to secure for the words a place among those used with an assigned frequency; but when these ideas do require expression—and no one can escape the necessity for such expression—they become as "socially useful" as do their more frequently used competitors.

In the third place, in selecting material for the school curriculum, difficulty as well as frequency of use is a criterion. Indeed to a certain extent there is an inverse relationship between difficulty and frequency of use. Some elements of school subjects, precisely because they are frequently used and hence often repeated, do not need to be taught at all. Such is the case, for example, with most of the two and three letter words in our language. For example, no one who is in the least degree literate misspells *and* except by inadvertency—and correcting inadvertency is not a spelling problem. Some of the recent spellers in their attempts to adhere to the vocabulary studies have included a considerable group of words which do not constitute a spelling problem.

In the fourth place, whether with reference to spelling or any other subject of the curriculum, whatever the much-discussed aim of education may be it contemplates something more than the round of common experiences, something richer than the elemental facts of life. Moreover, it is only by providing for more than is now generally available that progress is possible. Here as elsewhere in the application of scientific procedure to education, a sound philosophy—as well as a sound common sense—must be invoked to save the scientific procedure from itself.

Four points may, therefore, be made with reference to the sufficiency of the idea of frequency of use. The first is that material far greater in amount and variety will have to be examined before we can be sure that frequency of use has been determined. The second is that certain material of relatively low frequency of occurrence has a social usefulness which renders it indispensable. The third is that difficulty, or need of being taught, is an important criterion—one which operates in particular to reject from the formal curriculum an appreciable amount of frequently used material. The fourth is that if we include in our curriculum only the materials which are found to be frequently used by children and adults we leave altogether out of account the material which they ought to use and would use if their lives were fuller and richer. This fulness and richness, we feel quite sure, the school must envisage. Moreover, to adjust the curriculum merely to current usage is to doom our educational system to a static condition wherein progress becomes impossible.

I have given this lengthy illustration because I wish to take a stand in the name of the integrity of the research movement for the use of interpretative thought, ranging from common sense to philosophy, to supplement the results of quantitative measurement. Never at any time shall we reach the point where the measurements will do all the work. If the perfectionists—be they purists within the ranks of the testers or obstructionists outside of them—demand this, they demand too much. Educational measurements will not automatically and unerringly sift children into compartments, and for my part I hope they never will. There will never be a time when our measurement processes will be so extensive that good judgment will not play a proper part after the results have been secured. Not infrequently the real function of measurement and statistics is to reduce the problem to dimensions such that reasonably good judgment can carry it to a solution.

But even if the test measures are fallible, this does not justify us in throwing up our hands in despair or lifting our voices in derision. Are we not better off than before? Is not the probability of being right greater than it has ever been? Why should any one prefer to think any less accurately than he has to about anything that can be the subject of thought?

As we become more and more capable of measuring our methods and results, we give closer attention to the discrepancies between our measurements. This does not mean that the discrepancies are really larger, but rather that the measurements have permitted us to detect them. Things which we never thought of before make themselves manifest. One reason why mistakes in the classification of pupils look so big is precisely because objective measurement serves to show up our blunders. Before we had measurements our failures in this respect were ghastly. But we were blind to them. Therefore we thought they did not exist.

Let's be sensible. Let us demand of the measurers that their system shall be clearly better than the one it seeks to supplant. Let us also call them to account when they are over-pretentious. But let us not demand of them a system which shall work with machine-like accuracy, for in so doing we shall not only ask the impossible, but also stand accused of seeking a desideratum of dubious value.

The position I have just taken has obvious practical meaning. It has close bearing upon the organization of research work which a superintendent may set up in his school system. Since research, to my way of thinking, is not throughout its entire course dependent upon measurement and statistics, there is a place among research workers for those who have not perfected their training in these matters. The common sense of the experienced teacher is not to be despised in assigning research work on a cooperative plan.

It is my belief that every educational institution from the kindergarten to the graduate school should be organized both for research and for teaching. We readily enough recognize that the university professor should contribute to the sum of knowledge within his field. The same expectation, however, should be entertained in the case of the secondary-school teacher, the elementary-school teacher and the various supervisors and administrators. They may indeed be expected to do less research in proportion to their other service than do university professors, but this is a difference in degree rather than in kind. Investigation *as well as* instruction, research *as well as* teaching, should be expected, planned for and paid for.

Indeed, teachers themselves should welcome this principle. Winch has well said, "Without the cooperation of teachers there will never be in any appreciable sense a science of education. If teachers stand aside and do not help, they will only have themselves to thank if methods are imposed upon them from the results of experiments which they do not understand, which are not really applicable to their work and in which they have no share."

In the movement to democratize education let us reflect how unwise it is to jam our nostrums down the throats of teachers, and how advantageous it is to give them that vital part in determining policies and procedures which research permits. We may honestly believe that a certain method is the best or at least better than a rival method now in operation. This we may call our hypothesis in a research project. What better way is there to enlist the interest of teachers than to have them try out the proposed method?

Suppose, for example, we wish our teachers to abandon the formal teaching of phonics and to resort to a "look and say" method of teaching reading. One way, of course, is to foist a "look and say" method upon the teachers by adopting a text-book committed to this method and requiring the text-book to be used. A far better plan would be to treat the teachers as intelligent participants in the educational enterprise and show them how to try out these rival methods of teaching reading. It may very likely become evident that our hypothesis is not valid, in other words that our particular method is not after all the better method. In that event we should clearly have been mistaken in requiring it.

We believe in creative work for children. We should have the same belief in regard to teachers. Research provides the opportunity. It is impersonal, unbiased and wholly genuine. It has no apologies to offer and no argument to make for its existence. It exists and grows among us on the basis of sheer worth and undisputed accomplishment.

RESEARCH IN CHILD DEVELOPMENT[1]

By ARNOLD GESELL, M.D.
DIRECTOR, YALE PSYCHO-CLINIC, YALE UNIVERSITY

POPE'S dictum that "the proper study of mankind is man" has in America been revised to read "the proper study of mankind is the child." Never before in the history of education has a people so deliberately and on such a large scale undertaken to investigate the nature and the potentialities of the child. With the partial exception of Russia, America leads in volume and in organization of child research. But the basic network of this research is international and is the product of modern science, which is quite irrespective of national boundaries and of national impulse. Fundamental research is in the last analysis the expression of individual scientists, and peculiar to no country.

In America, however, the study of the child has distinctive features which have been powerfully influenced by social forces. The material conquests of industry and of invention have made new social issues. There is a vague consciousness that the arrangements of society are altering under the pressure of economic and industrial changes so that even the old-time concepts of family and of school must modify in some measure with the newer form of civilization. It is highly significant that the great social movement of adult education in America finds itself closely linked with the whole problem of preschool education and with the development of child research. Even in the child study movement of the elegant eighties and the gay nineties it was so. It is this intermixture of popular and scientific expressions which will make the late Victorian child study movement, with all its shortcomings, significant to the historian.

The National Research Council in 1923 gave a certain official recognition to the scientific status of child research by the organization of a committee on child development to foster and coordinate such research. More recently, under similar auspices there was held a conference to outline the field of study represented by problems of family organization and of family life. Increasingly, the problems of child research are being approached from the standpoint of social organization and of the family institution. These problems are so interwoven that they can not be solved by the sciences of child psychology or of educational psychology in the traditional sense.

Child development is a useful, even though protean term. The problems of child development involve such varied scientific fields as biochemistry, developmental anatomy, nutrition, anthropometry, anthropology, psychiatry, pediatrics and genetic, experimental, comparative and clinical psychology. Child development is fundamentally a branch of human biology—a focal field for psychobiological and medical knowledge converging upon the central problem of early human growth. This is, of course, a prodigiously inclusive field of inquiry, but it is a legitimate one because the phenomena of growth are subject to general and unifying laws which can be formulated only by coordinated contribution from several scientific domains. Growth is itself a unifying concept which removes undue distinctions between mind and body, between heredity and environment, between health and disease and, we may add also, between separate scientific disciplines. In spite of their diversity and intricacy the problems of child development are organized and even simplified by the integrating concept of growth—a concept which will increasingly supplement and displace the concepts of education and of hygiene.

It seems important to emphasize the status of child development research as a branch of human biology. The study of the infant and the preschool child is not merely an extension downward of the prevailing concepts of mental testing, of psychometrics and of educational measurements with all their schoolroom implications of homogeneous grouping, classification according to abilities, promotion on the basis of achievement scores, etc. The orientations of research in child development are medical and

[1] Abstract of address at a meeting of the National Society for the Study of Education, Cleveland, February 26, 1929.

biological. They should remain so. The problems of early child development can not be envisaged in the conventional terms of learning, of school attendance and school organization. It is possible that even the nursery school, as a research device, has already made too much compromise with the traditional forms of elementary education.

It seems that the twenty-eighth yearbook of the National Society for the Study of Education[2] has taken a constructive and judicious attitude with reference to the educational status of the preschool child. It gives full recognition to the position of the public school, both from the standpoint of the kindergarten and of adolescent provision for preparental education. It recognizes, however, that the total welfare of the preschool child must take into account the field of infant hygiene represented in the home and in the consultation center.

A major division of the yearbook is devoted to critical and summary discussions of research activities in the field of child development. Over one hundred studies are abstracted in convenient form under the following headings: (1) Physical Growth. (2) Motor Development. (3) Language Development. (4) Intellectual Development. (5) Emotional and Social Development. Brief comments will be made on investigations in these five fields.

It is proper that the yearbook should contain a section on research studies in the field of physical growth. Although these studies have no immediate pertinence to the educator, they show how the basic physical welfare of the child rests upon a vast structure of research in animal and human biology. Indeed, discoveries which arise out of the field of physics and chemistry and of clinical medicine, as in the case of irradiated ergosterol, may be most significant for the developmental welfare of the preschool child. In this instance, a biochemical discovery points to the speedy extinction of the most prevalent handicap of early childhood, namely, rickets.

Studies in motor development thus far have been concerned chiefly with early infancy. These studies are important with regard to practical problems of posture and of motor skills which will fall increasingly within the purview of social control. In due time the foundational training of technical skills (possibly air-mindedness in the field of aviation!) will be anticipated in preschool measures which can only be defined by apparently remote researches in the fields of neurology and psychomotor development.

Studies in the field of language development seem to lie nearer to academic education, but even here genetic studies are necessary to establish the important fact that the language of early childhood, in spite of superficial resemblance, is psychologically not equivalent to the language of later years. The child has his own peculiar logic. Apparently he soliloquizes even when he talks to others. These researches into child logic are very important for the just appreciation of the preschool age. The yearbook reports an interesting study in the results of training a group of children in speaking French, a study which suggests that certain portions of the problem of modern language abilities may well be shifted to the preschool level, and even solved there with practicable rearrangements in the field of linguistic instruction. Speech, normal and defective, vernacular and foreign, is peculiarly a preschool problem, demanding continued research.

The section on intellectual development contains discussions of mental age and of intelligence quotient with reference to the preschool child. The studies, as a whole, show a drift away from the simpler psychometric concepts toward a descriptive, analytical interpretation of individual children, which aims to define their special talents and their patterns of ability and potency rather than degrees of a general capacity.

The section on studies of emotion and personality likewise shows a healthy trend toward a clinical individualization of child problems. Sufficiently fundamental emphasis has been placed upon intellectual gifts. It is now important to shift the emphasis to personality gifts. The nursery school has here perhaps its greatest opportunity to make a contribution which will radically influence procedures in the elementary grades.

[2] "Preschool and Parental Education." Prepared by the society's committee (Baldwin, Gesell, Hill, Thom, White, Woolley, Meek). Public School Publishing Company, Bloomington, 1929. x + 831 pp.

It is of course impossible to appraise the ultimate values of the researches reported in the yearbook. Some of the studies are relatively minor in importance and in quality. Some American child research is unfortunately a kind of imitative investigation which does not spring from genuine inquisitiveness. But, taken as a whole, the investigations show an encouraging tendency toward coordination of significant knowledge.

At present the research seems to be strongest in the psychological and psychobiological directions. It is weakest where, here in America, we might suppose it should be strongest, namely, in the field of social relations, including neighborhood and community organization. Even the nursery school is in danger of losing some of its full value as a research instrument if it fails to develop new social patterns of procedure. The organization of educational provisions for young children and their parents needs a fuller understanding of the social nature of the whole problem, which can only be defined by creating new social groupings and new experimental methods of approach. Here is a field for inventiveness which can not take its cue altogether from the present family, much less from the present day school. Inventiveness in this direction requires investigatory imagination in combination with great sanity of judgment. It is a challenging field for a non-academic type of child research, as essential to progress as strictly biological knowledge. In the long run, however, there can be no opposition between the study of child development from the standpoint of natural science and from the standpoint of social science.

The public school has a great responsibility in developing new administrative arrangements through research. It would be a sad waste of a natural resource if school administrators permitted the American kindergarten to congeal into a preprimary schoolroom in its organization, when it ought to be a free, adaptable instrument used frankly for experimental purposes to define new procedures in the field of preschool and parental education. The kindergarten is still on the frontier where pioneering is in order.

The amount of research in the field of child development is attaining stupendous proportions. It is almost impossible to follow the stream of investigation even by reading the bulletins, titles, abstracts and bibliographies. However, the magnitude of this research should not be dismaying. Though there is no superman, even in the National Society for the Study of Education, to integrate this knowledge, there are forces of social selection which bring the truth, and the best truth, to the surface. Science itself is shaped by laws of growth which apparently are similar to those which we are attempting to study in the child himself.

EDUCATIONAL EVENTS

PUBLIC PLAYING FIELDS IN HOLLAND

THE first Dutch National Congress to consider the provision of public playing fields, where necessary, was held in Amsterdam recently and is reported in *The Christian Science Monitor*. A resolution, put forward by the League of Amsterdam Playground Societies, was passed unanimously, stressing the necessity of spreading the movement throughout the whole of Holland. Also a committee was set up for the continuation of the work of the congress aiming at the forming of a National Playing Fields League.

The Dutch playground movement, which originated in Amsterdam, has shown a remarkable growth in the last quarter of a century. In 1902, Uilke J. Klaren, a man of the people and an inhabitant of one of the oldest quarters of the city, took the initiative in endeavoring to establish suitable playgrounds—play "gardens" as they are called in Holland—for the children.

And with a band of simple women and men of the people, Uilke Klaren founded the first playground society of parents in Amsterdam. The purpose was to provide occupation for the children in their leisure hours, through the medium of play and manual work, music and singing.

Now there are already more than thirty district societies in Amsterdam, and several more in other parts of the country. At present there are twenty-five play-gardens and four so-called "sand playgrounds," for which the municipality pays a subsidy of more than 140,000 florins per year. The municipal authorities, according to the *Monitor,* are well aware of the fact that this work on behalf of youth is of the utmost educational importance.

Investigation has already made plain that at least another thirty play-gardens are needed, involving an estimated expense of about 1,500,000 florins (as the town's share). This amount can not be voted at once, so the further development of the work must be carried on gradually.

EDUCATION IN ONTARIO

Announcement by the Premier of Ontario, G. Howard Ferguson, of his intention to reform the educational system of the province by means of legislation which he will introduce next session, was, according to *The Christian Science Monitor,* the high point of the Western Ontario Conservative Association convention. The premier's proposal is, in brief, to provide two years of high-school work in the public schools of the province, and one year of university course in the high schools. Back of the plan is the idea that such a system would enable young people in the rural districts to remain longer under the family roof and parental guidance than is now possible, and that it would also mean extensive saving in costs to rural people who send their children to high schools or universities.

The premier, who is also minister of education, set forth his ideal "to make possible for every child in the province, regardless of its location, equal educational opportunity." He believes that by extending the public-school course to provide for children up to 16 instead of 14 years, as at present, he will help to accomplish that purpose.

Since the lower school work now given in high schools would be given in public school under the new plan, the premier proposes to give the high schools new work, and to do that, he said, he would have high schools impart tuition for first-year university work. There are many failures now in first-year university work, he said, and the new plan would automatically do a lot of culling and sifting.

Concluding, Mr. Ferguson said that the new system would result in a great saving of money, since it costs the government $400 a year for each university student, and costs the parents from $800 to $1,000 more.

THE ROCKEFELLER FOUNDATIONS

A review of the activities of the Rockefeller Foundation in 1928, written by its president, Dr. George E. Vincent, will be issued in a few days. It summarizes the reorganization of the several boards which has already been reported. During 1928 a conference committee of four Rockefeller boards—the General Education Board, the Rockefeller Foundation, the Laura Spelman Rockefeller Memorial and the International Education Board—sought ways of bringing the work of these organizations into closer and more definitely cooperative relations. In the autumn the committee made a report embodying recommendations which were approved by all the groups, with the understanding that the new régime would go into effect at the beginning of 1929.

The essential features of the reorganization were these: (1) the merging of the Rockefeller Foundation and the Laura Spelman Rockefeller Memorial into a new corporation to be known as the Rockefeller Foundation, which should assume all the assets and liabilities of the two boards; (2) the extension of the scope of the new foundation's activities to include not only public health, but the advancement of knowledge in the medical sciences, in the natural sciences (taking over the foreign program of the International Education Board), in the social sciences (heretofore administered by the Memorial), and in the humanities; (3) the administration of the public health activities of the foundation through an international health division with a group of seven scientific directors; (4) the appointment of a director with necessary assistants for each of the fields—the natural sciences, the medical sciences, the social sciences and the humanities; (5) a clearly defined division of labor between the General Education Board and the foundation through frequent conferences of the officers; (6) the incorporation of a China Medical Board with independent self-perpetuating trustees to which the lands and buildings in Peking together with endowment funds and annual appropriations should be given.

From this reorganization two large and well-endowed Rockefeller boards emerge: the General Education Board with a Federal charter which limits expenditures to the United States, and the Rockefeller Foundation incorporated under the general laws of New York State. The book value of the combined resources of the new Rockefeller Foundation will be more than $203,000,000 with outstanding obligations of $35,000,000.

Since their founding the four Rockefeller boards have not only distributed all their incomes but have appropriated $225,000,000 of capital funds. Even when the increase in market value of securities has been taken into account, the appropriations from principal represent a substantial reduction in the endowments of these boards.

THE DITSON BEQUEST TO MUSICAL EDUCATION

A TOTAL sum of $800,000 is to be devoted to musical education in this country under the terms of the will of Charles H. Ditson, music publisher, of New York City. The will gives $100,000 each to Harvard, Yale, Princeton, Columbia, the College of Music of Cincinnati, the New England Conservatory of Music in Boston, the Chicago Musical College and the Ann Arbor School of Music of the University of Michigan.

The terms of bequest to each institution are similar except for the names of trust funds to be established with the money. The Harvard bequest, typical of the others, directs that the $100,000 be used as follows:

> In establishing a fund the income of which shall be used for any one or more of the purposes herein mentioned as shall be in the judgment of the officers of the said college of the greatest benefit musically to said college, to wit: in establishing and maintaining a chair or chairs of music or musical history or musical esthetics, or in establishing and maintaining scholarships or fellowships in music, or in giving public performances of the musical compositions of talented students and graduates of said college, and if preferred of other musical composers.
>
> Such fund is to be known as the James Edward Ditson Endowment, and any chair or scholarship or fellowship which is established, to bear his name; but nothing herein shall prevent said president and fellows of Harvard College from investing the money as part of their general fund and applying a proportionate part of the income of their general fund to the purpose of this bequest.

James Edward Ditson was a brother of the late music publisher. The Yale, Columbia and Princeton funds are to be known as the Charles H. Ditson Endowments, while the funds of New England Conservatory of Music, the Chicago Musical College and the College of Music of Cincinnati and the Ann Arbor School of Music are to be known as the Oliver Ditson Endowments, in memory of Mr. Ditson's father.

THE NURSERY SCHOOL OF WESTERN RESERVE UNIVERSITY

THE school of education of Western Reserve University will open in September a model nursery school of twenty-five children aged from twenty months to three and a half years, with the recommendation that children be enrolled at birth to ensure study by the staff of the school. Miss May Hill, associate professor of education and educational director, has been appointed director.

The school will represent cooperative efforts of the school of education, the school of nursing and the department of household administration of the college for women, the graduate school, the school of medicine of Western Reserve University and the Brush Foundation. The last-named organization will find in the school an observation laboratory station for its inquiry into and definition of the well-begotten child.

The staff of the school, which will work in cooperation with an advisory board, will include in addition to Miss Hill: Miss Amy Hostler, teacher in charge; Miss Dorothy Eisele, of the department of household administration, assistant teacher and dietician; Miss Helen Coe Clowes, psychologist; Miss Clara Robinson, director of parental education. The consultant staff will include: Charles W. Hunt, dean of the School of Education; Dr. T. Wingate Todd, director of research of the Brush Foundation; Miss Mary Eliza Parker, professor of household administration in the College for Women; Miss Nellie X. Hawkinson, dean of the school of nursing; Dr. Dewey Anderson, research psychologist of the Brush Foundation, and Dr. H.

J. Gerstenberger, professor of pediatrics in the school of medicine.

The three chief objects of the school are (1) To furnish an environment that will foster the all-round development of the child from two to four years old, (2) parental education, (3) the gradual accumulation and analysis of records of child behavior and child development, especially in those phases of child life about which we now have little objective evidence. These studies carried on under the Brush Foundation and the department of pediatrics of the school of medicine will record the child's progress in physical and mental development by means of measurements, radiographic determination of growth, estimation of muscular power, lung power, proper elimination, records of behavior and analysis of the developing mind.

GUGGENHEIM EXCHANGE FELLOWSHIPS BETWEEN THE UNITED STATES AND LATIN-AMERICA

A GIFT of $1,000,000 by former Senator and Mrs. Simon Guggenheim to the John Simon Guggenheim Memorial Foundation, to establish a system of exchange fellowships between the United States and the Latin-American countries, has been announced.

The gift is made through the Guggenheim Foundation set up in 1925 to provide fellowships between this and foreign countries. The foundation has a capital fund of $3,500,000 exclusive of the new gift. The existing fellowships are available for Latin-American as well as other foreign countries, but it was felt that the potential value of closer intellectual relations with the nations to the south made it advisable to create a separate department for them.

In offering the gift Mr. Guggenheim wrote:

> My brothers and I have long been engaged in commerce with many of the republics to the south of the United States, and we know that there are no longer any important factors of economic isolation separating us. But a similar commerce of things of the mind, of spiritual values, is yet to be accomplished. It is Mrs. Guggenheim's and my hope that this new fund may assist in supplying that great need.

Since the establishment of the foundation, 230 fellowships have been granted, and important work has been accomplished by the fellows, including the writing of the poem, "John Brown's Body," by Stephen Vincent Benet, and the work in physics by Professor A. H. Compton, of the University of Chicago, for which he received the Nobel prize in 1928.

The new fellowships will first be granted in Mexico in 1930, according to present plans. Thereafter they will be extended to the other countries where arrangements for the system have been made. Latin-American countries where such arrangements have not as yet been made will also be brought into the system as soon as its success appears assured.

The plan to be developed, as outlined by the trustees of the foundation, is as follows:

> The Latin-American Exchange Fellowships, in the first instance, shall be open to citizens of the United States and of the Argentine Republic, Bolivia, Brazil, Chile, Mexico, Peru and Uruguay, on terms generally similar to those hitherto governing the John Simon Guggenheim Memorial Fellowships in the United States. The new fellowships will be granted for independent research and also for training in the various professions, including engineering and teaching. Special consideration will be given to applicants who desire to study political, social or scientific problems which are common to the countries of North and South America. If the above outlined Latin-American Exchange Fellowships are successful, the trustees will consider extending them to the other countries of Latin-America as rapidly as proper arrangements can be made.
>
> The stipend for these fellowships, either for Latin-America or for the United States, will normally be $2,500 for twelve months plus a travel allowance proportionate to the distance which the fellows have to travel to the places of their study. The fellowships will be awarded in the first instance for one year, but with the possibility of renewal.

AMERICAN HOME ECONOMICS ASSOCIATION

THE twenty-second annual meeting of the American Home Economics Association will be held at the Hotel Statler, Boston, Massachusetts, from July 1 to 5.

The first session will be a public meeting on Monday evening, July 1, held jointly with the Fourth National Conference of Supervisors and Teachers of Home Economics called by the United States Commissioner of Education for that day. Dean Margaret Justin, of Kansas State Agricultural College, president of the association, will speak on "Twenty Years of Progress in Home Economics," and Dean John W. Withers, of New York University, on "What Is Progress in Education?"

At a second public meeting on Tuesday evening, July 2, the general topic will be "The Consumer and the Market"; the "Problems of the Homemaker as a Buyer" will be described by Dr. Faith Williams, and the point of view of the distributor will be expressed by Channing E. Sweitzer, managing director of the National Retail Dry Goods Association.

Special group meetings will provide for the interests of the various divisions of the association, such as those dealing with food and nutrition, clothing and textiles, household management and equipment, institution economics, child development and parental education, and the teaching of home economics in schools, colleges and extension services.

There will also be the usual business sessions of the association and its council, the latter open to all registrants.

Since the association is this year celebrating its twentieth anniversary, the program at the banquet on Thursday evening is planned to carry the members back to the days of its infancy and especially to its Boston friends who, under the leadership of Ellen H. Richards, of the Massachusetts Institute of Technology, played so important a part in launching this movement to improve conditions of every-day living by "the application of science to the problems of the home, the institution and the community."

TROUBLES AT CLARKSON COLLEGE OF TECHNOLOGY

AN Associated Press despatch under date of June 6 says that dismissal of two members of the faculty of Clarkson College of Technology "for insubordination," together with the resignation of a third professor in protest against the ousting of the two others, became known, following a mass meeting of students on June 5 to frame a formal protest to the board of trustees.

The dismissed faculty members are Professor Lynn L. Merrill, who has been at Clarkson nine years, and Professor George B. Lobdell, who has been there thirteen years. Professor Croskerry, with six years' service, resigned because of what he considered unfair treatment of his colleagues, and Mrs. Flora Laidler, secretary to President Joseph Eugene Rowe, resigned for the same reason.

Professor Merrill and Professor Lobdell were dismissed on the recommendation of Dr. Rowe, who went to Clarkson a year ago from William and Mary College, as a direct result, it is said, of a controversy over his abolition of student self-government. One of his first moves after taking office was to deprive students of all control—a step which was opposed by most of the faculty.

Specifically, the two dismissed faculty members were charged by Dr. Rowe with inciting opposition against him. They were reported to have been in New York attending a meeting of alumni called to consider the question of student government and to have expressed views contrary to Dr. Rowe's policies.

Dr. Rowe called the board of trustees together unexpectedly and the two professors were notified immediately after the meeting that "their resignations" had been accepted. Dismissal of the professors is reported to have aroused the student body to indignation, aimed especially at Dr. Rowe, and a meeting on the campus was attended by most of the undergraduates. A protest, to be sent to the board of trustees, was drafted and it was decided to await action by that body before taking other steps.

RETIREMENT OF MEMBERS OF THE FACULTIES OF THE UNIVERSITY OF CHICAGO

FIVE well-known members of the faculties of the University of Chicago, Professors Clyde W. Votaw, George W. Myers, Herbert L. Willett, Charles J. Chamberlain and Andrew C. McLaughlin, will retire at the close of the current academic year, each with the title of professor emeritus. The group has served the university for an average period of over thirty years.

Professors Votaw and Willett have served on the faculty of the Divinity School, the former as authority on the literature and interpretation of the New Testament and the latter on Semitic languages and literatures. A member of the first university faculty in 1892, Dr. Votaw has been associate editor of the *Journal of Religion* and has contributed four critical volumes on early Christian literature. Dr. Willett went to the University in 1894, and has been dean of the Disciples Divinity House, president of the Chicago Church Federation and associate editor of the *Christian Century*. He has written ten published works.

Professor A. C. McLaughlin went to the University of Chicago as a teacher of American history from the University of Michigan in 1906. He has been director of the Bureau of Historical Research of the Carnegie Foundation, managing editor of the *American Historical Review* and is a fellow of the Royal Historical Society of England. Seven books are credited to him, the most recent his *Steps in the Development of American Democracy*.

After serving at the University of Illinois as professor of astronomy and applied mathematics and director of the observatory, Professor George W. Myers went to the University of Chicago in 1901 as professor of the teaching of mathematics and astronomy in the school of education. He is the joint author of a series of text-books for grammar and high schools and editor and joint author of the Standard Mathematical Service.

Professor Charles J. Chamberlain joined the department of botany in 1897 as specialist in plant morphology and cytology. He is a leading authority on the cycad family, most primitive plant group still growing, and has ranged the world to gather the finest collection of cycads available. He is the author of "Methods in Plant Histology," of "The Morphology of Gymnosperms" and "The Morphology of Angiosperms," both with the late Dr. John M. Coulter, and of "The Living Cycads."

EDUCATIONAL NOTES AND NEWS

DR. JOSEPH S. AMES has been elected president of the Johns Hopkins University to succeed Dr. Frank J. Goodnow, who retires at the end of the academic year with the title of president emeritus. Dr. Goodnow will continue to lecture on municipal law at the university. Dr. Ames had filled the office of provost during the last three years. He first taught in the university in 1888, and before becoming provost had been professor of physics and director of the laboratory.

DR. HERMAN SCHNEIDER, dean of the college of engineering of the University of Cincinnati and acting president since the retirement of Dr. Frederick Charles Hicks, has been elected to the presidency.

DR. KATHARINE BLUNT, chemist and head of the department of home economics of the University of Chicago, has accepted the presidency of the Connecticut College for Women.

DR. EDWIN ANDERSON ALDERMAN completed a quarter century as president of the University of Virginia when the class of 1929 graduated on June 11. President Alderman was the guest of honor at the alumni luncheon and received as a gift a silver service and dining-room furniture of the early American period as an expression of the regard in which he is held by the alumni. Since Dr. Alderman became president the number of members of the faculty has risen from 48 to 290 and the student body has grown from 500 to more than 6,500.

A DINNER in honor of Dr. Aven Nelson, professor of botany and president emeritus of the University of Wyoming, was given on May 13 by his colleagues of the board of trustees, of the university faculty and of the administrative staff on the occasion of the completion of his seventieth year of life and forty-second in the service of the university.

A TESTIMONIAL dinner was recently tendered to Dr. James M. Kieran, newly elected president of Hunter College, New York City, by his fellow members of the New York Academy of Public Education. Many of his friends were there to voice their congratulations and good wishes, among them Dr. Frederick B. Robinson, president of the College of the City of New York; the Reverend William J. Duane, S.J., president of Fordham University, and the Reverend Brother Cornelius, president of Manhattan College. Superintendent of Schools William J. O'Shea told of Dr. Kieran's early teaching experiences in the city's public schools, and Dr. Harry P. Swift, president of the board of trustees, and Mrs. Maxwell H. Elliott, president of the Alumnae Association of Hunter College, voiced the esteem in which the new president is held by the Hunter authorities. President Olive M. Jones and Professor Albert Shiels, of Teachers College, were toastmasters.

DR. WILLIAM H. NICHOLS has been appointed acting chancellor of New York University, to serve during the absence of Chancellor Elmer Ellsworth Brown, who is ill.

THE Case School of Applied Science at its recent commencement conferred the degree of doctor of engineering on Dr. Charles S. Howe, who is retiring from the presidency after having served for twenty-seven years, and on Dr. William Elgin Wickenden, the newly elected president.

DEAN ROBERT MAYNARD HUTCHINS, of the Yale Law School and president-elect of the University of Chicago, delivered the commencement address at the ninety-fourth annual graduation exercises of Lafayette College and the honorary degree of doctor of laws was conferred on him.

DR. AUGUSTUS TROWBRIDGE, dean of Princeton University Graduate School, was the recipient of the degree of doctor of science at the recent commencement exercises of Columbia University.

THE University of Maine has conferred the doctorate of laws on the Reverend Everett Carleton Herrick, president of the Newton Theological Institution. Dr. Herrick was the commencement speaker.

THE degree of doctor of agriculture has been conferred by Rhode Island State College on Dr. Albert R. Mann, dean of the New York State College of Agriculture.

DR. CARL S. PATTON has been elected president of the Chicago Theological Seminary to succeed Dr. Ozora S. Davis, who recently resigned after a service of twenty years.

PROFESSOR ISABEL F. SMITH, of the department of geology at Smith College, has resigned to become dean of Scripps College, Claremont, California. She will be succeeded as dean of the class of 1932 by Professor Leona C. Gabel, of the history department.

DR. HAROLD R. PHALEN, professor of mathematics and instructor in physics at St. Stephen's College, Columbia University, has been appointed dean of the college.

DR. EDWARD POTTS CHEYNEY, professor of history at the University of Pennsylvania, has been appointed to the Henry Charles Lea professorship.

DR. HERBERT W. BRIGGS, associate professor of political science at Oberlin College, has been appointed assistant professor of government at Cornell University to succeed Professor Bruce Williams who returns to the University of Virginia.

THE Depew chair of oratory in the George Washington University, recently established through the gift of Mrs. Chauncey M. Depew, has been filled through the appointment of Hayes Yeager, acting head of the department of public speaking at the University of Illinois.

DR. P. P. CLAXTON has resigned as superintendent of schools at Tulsa, Oklahoma, and Merle Prunty, principal of the high school, has been elected to suceed him. Galen Jones, principal of the high school at Reading, Pennsylvania, has been elected director of the high schools.

HARRY B. FINE, for several years connected with the staff of the Princeton Preparatory School, has been selected to direct the school beginning with next autumn, succeeding his father, Dr. John Burchard Fine, who for forty years has been headmaster. Dr. Fine has been in poor health for several years. He will continue to serve in an advisory capacity, his son having the title of "acting headmaster."

HERBERT H. FRANKLIN, of Syracuse, president of the Franklin Automobile Company, has been elected a member of the board of trustees of Syracuse University.

PROFESSOR HENRY ELDRIDGE BOURNE has accepted the editorship of the *American Histor-*

ical Review and will go to Washington, D. C., with a year's leave of absence from Western Reserve University, where he has been professor of history since 1892 in the College for Women. A year ago, when Dr. J. F. Jameson, who for many years had been the editor of the *Review,* resigned to take charge of the manuscript division of the Library of Congress, Professor Dana C. Munro, of Princeton University, took the editorial chair with the understanding that he would occupy it for one year only.

Dr. Henry Raymond Mussey, who for more than seven years has been professor of economics at Wellesley College, will become managing editor of *The Nation* on June 17. The publication has not had a managing editor since last autumn. Dr. Mussey held the position in 1918 and 1919 and has continued his connection with it as a contributor.

The American Association of Teachers Colleges has appointed a committee of five, which will formulate plans for presenting to Congress a request for funds to make a study of teacher training in the United States. Members of the committee are as follows: D. B. Waldo, president of the Western State Teachers College, Kalamazoo, Michigan, *chairman;* J. L. Alger, president of the Rhode Island College of Education, Providence, Rhode Island; Ned H. Dearborn, president of the State College for Teachers, Albany, New York; Frank W. Thomas, president of the State Teachers College, Fresno, California, and Dr. L. A. Pittenger, president of Ball State Teachers College, Muncie, Indiana.

Dr. A. J. Jones, of the University of Pennsylvania, who has been acting chairman of the Commission on Secondary Schools, will be on the faculty of the school of education of the University of Washington for the summer term. The chairmanship of the commission will be resumed by Dr. E. D. Grizzell, who has been in England during 1928–29. He is returning to the University of Pennsylvania for the summer session. While in England, Dr. Grizzell has been organizing the study of English schools in connection with the comparative study of English and American secondary education which he and Dr. Jones are making. Dr. Grizzell has been made professor of secondary education at the University of Pennsylvania.

The daily papers report that Dr. Arthur W. Calhoun, instructor of economics at Brookwood Labor College, whose expulsion is sought by faculty members because of "his communistic activities," has stated that he would not resign. Dr. Calhoun, denying that he had any affiliation with the Workers' (Communist) Party, said that the faculty members had asked the executive committee not to reinstate him because he had opposed the policy of the college, expressed recently in the formation of the conference of progressive labor action.

Dr. Nicholas Murray Butler, president of Columbia University and of the Carnegie Endowment for International Peace, has sailed for Europe. He plans to confer with associates and representatives of the endowment in different countries, particularly with the members of the administrative committee for Europe, which has headquarters in Paris.

After thirty-one years of service, Professor A. H. Espenshade, head of the department of English composition of the Pennsylvania State College, will take a year's leave of absence, effective at the end of the present college year, during which he will teach English composition at the University of Hawaii.

Dr. William M. Davidson, superintendent of the Pittsburgh public schools, has been granted three months' leave of absence by the board of education, during which time he will travel in Europe, studying the school systems. He will leave Pittsburgh on July 1 and will return on September 30.

Dr. W. F. Book, of Indiana University, will during the summer give two special courses in psychology in the University of Hawaii.

Professor J. K. Hart, of the school of education of the University of Wisconsin, will speak at the Fifth International Conference of the New Education Fellowship, which will be held at Elsinore, Denmark, from August 8 to 21. His subjects will be "New Schools in Action," "Adult Schools" and "Social Conditions in Relation to School Reconstruction."

Dr. Frank P. Graves, New York State Commissioner of Education, gave the commencement address at the University of Buffalo on June 4.

Dr. Gordon Jennings Laing, professor of Latin and dean of the graduate school of arts and literature of the University of Chicago, gave the Phi Beta Kappa address in connection with the commencement exercises of the University of Virginia.

President Edward C. Elliott, of Purdue University, delivered the commencement address at Bradley Polytechnic Institute at Peoria, Illinois, June 14, and at the Rose Polytechnic Institute at Terre Haute, Indiana, on June 15. He delivered the commencement address at Kansas State Teachers College at Pittsburg, Kansas, on May 23 and two days later the address before the graduates of North Platte, Nebraska, High School, from which he was graduated thirty-eight years ago.

President-elect Robert M. Hutchins, dean of the Yale Law School, will give the address at the convocation of the University of Chicago. Acting-president Frederic Woodward will preside and confer the degrees.

Russell Gordon Smith, of the department of sociology in Columbia University, died, presumably by suicide, on June 7. Dr. Smith had been ill for some time.

Fred J. Bohlmann, of Peekskill, New York, for fifteen years superintendent of schools, has died at the age of fifty-four years.

DePauw University will receive the residue of an estate estimated to be worth somewhere between three quarters and a million dollars by the will of the late Mr. Frank L. Hall, of Kansas City.

Oberlin Graduate School of Theology has received a gift of $300,000 for a new building from John D. Rockefeller, Jr. It is the intention of the school to seek $200,000 more to increase the endowment and scholarship funds.

Rodney Sharp, of Wilmington, has added $100,000 to a former gift of $250,000 made a few months ago for the erection of an auditorium for the University of Delaware.

Gifts of $200,000 were announced at the close of the combined anniversary and commencement exercises of Abbot Academy at Andover, Massachusetts. Of this sum $160,000 was presented by President Constance Parker Chipman, '06, for the alumnae association and is to be known as the Alumnae Centennial Fund to be used to further worthy academic projects.

The name of the donor who has provided $500,000 for a student union building on the new campus of the University of California at Los Angeles has been made public by Dr. Ernest C. Moore as Mrs. William C. Kerckhoff, widow of one of Southern California's pioneers and capitalists. The building, which will be known as the Kerckhoff Student Union building, is to be a memorial to Mr. Kerckhoff.

Boston University School of Theology and the Garrett Biblical Institute are equal residuary legatees under the terms of the will of the late Lewis B. Alger, of Detroit. Each will receive in the neighborhood of $250,000.

Appropriations for education by the State of Pennsylvania involve the expenditure of $94,000,000 during the next two years, an increase of $19,500,000 over the state aid appropriation for 1927–29. State teachers' colleges will receive $6,000,000 as compared to their appropriation for the last biennium of $3,000,000. Nearly $3,000,000 has been added to the appropriations for universities and colleges, the bulk of which will benefit the Pennsylvania State College. School districts will be reimbursed to the amount of $52,000,000 for common school expenditures, an increase of $4,500,000. A state education building also is to be erected at Harrisburg at a cost of $4,500,000.

The daily papers report that Mayor Nichols, of Boston, rebuked the school committee when he returned its appropriation order for expenses for the current year without his approval and accompanied by the message that the committee's custom of appropriating in excess of requirements, in so far as it results in an unreasonable surplus, "is unfair to the taxpayer and ought to be discontinued." The mayor points out that the school budget of $15,407,891, exclusive of the additional appropriation order for alterations and repairs, is $827,596 above last year's expenditures. Taking into consideration the increased expenditures of the first five months of this year over a similar period last year, the mayor estimated that the school committee will have a surplus of $427,000 in the treasury on December 31. It is said that two years ago, at the mayor's demand, the school board cut $200,000 from its budget and still had a surplus of more than $500,000.

A CHAIR to be called the George Eastman Visiting Professorship at Oxford University has been established by George Eastman, of Rochester, New York, with an endowment of $200,000 to the Association of American Rhodes Scholars. The endowment was named for Mr. Eastman by the Oxford authorities. The incumbent must be a citizen of the United States, distinguished educator or research man. He will serve at Balliol College for from one to five years and will be eligible to reappointment. His task will be to lecture and teach the subject in which he has distinguished himself. In speaking of the gift, Mr. Eastman is reported to have said: "In the long run, I believe cooperation and civilization will be most effectively promoted if nations and those who form public opinion in them know and understand one another. I am desirous of doing something that will assist Englishmen and Colonials, and particularly the group destined to play an important part in government, science, scholarship, journalism and industry, to understand America—to study the vast and important experiments we are making in almost every field and to use their knowledge to advance civilization."

DISCUSSION

CONCERNING OVERLAPPING OF PROFESSIONAL COURSES IN TEACHER-TRAINING INSTITUTIONS

THE courses offered in departments of education in teacher-training institutions are frequently criticized as to overlapping in content. The alleged duplication of material in two or more different subjects, for each of which credit is given, furnishes one argument in support of the contention that professional courses are not equal in college grade to those of the academic departments either of the same institution or of the liberal arts college, and that, therefore, the teachers college degree is not equivalent to a degree from other colleges.

The accusation of repetition of subject-matter is perhaps most frequently made against the well-established technical courses wherein, it seems fair to assume, overlapping should have been reduced to the minimum. The assumption, valid or not, makes perfectly clear the only defensible attitude for institutions that are intent upon building up the department of education; namely, elimination or combination of courses which, on rigid investigation, show gross duplication. But the indictment is also brought against subjects more recently added to the curriculum, the content and objectives of which are, quite naturally, less clearly defined and therefore furnish ready opportunity for overlapping, new into the old, old into the new.

This criticism and the conditions supporting it are particularly true of that relatively new subject designated by various titles, of which perhaps the most common is "educational measurements." Not only are the limits of this field vaguely defined, a fact attested by the conversation and actual practice of many teachers of the subject, but the content involved is peculiarly susceptible to appropriation by teachers of other professional subjects such as the various psychologies and method courses common to all teacher-training curricula. Some teachers of the course seriously question whether the field offers a sufficiently large body of distinct material to justify a separate course. They maintain that acquaintance with standardized tests should be and often is made in the various courses on the teaching of reading, arithmetic and the like, and that the statistical treatment of data is a prerogative of the department of mathematics.

These and similar opinions expressed in good faith have influenced the writer to investigate the worth-while-ness of the course she gives in educational measurements in the State Teachers College, Milwaukee—a course which she regards as essential in the training of a teacher since it is the natural and logical one in which to develop the scientific attitude toward, and approach to, the study of education and its problems. With this as the main goal, the course not only will utilize the more concrete aspects of the field, that is the study of standardized tests and the interpretation of the data they yield to the end that classroom teaching may profit thereby, but it also should make a unique, direct and forceful contribution toward the attainment of the highest ends of all education, open-mindedness and independent thinking. These terms, often glibly quoted to idealize the work of the teacher, are not used here to epitomize an ethereal, mythical attainment. On the contrary, by the development of open-mindedness and independent thinking is meant the establishment of the habit of following logical thought processes in the study of school problems, wherein the tools of thinking, that is to say, ideas, are based upon the analysis of facts, not upon traditional opinion and practice, prejudice, superstition and the like. It means that conclusions, solutions, when accepted after due consideration of all phases of the question, will be regarded not as final, but tentative, subject to revision in the light of new objective evidence.

Applying this objective of the course to the evaluation of the course itself, the writer was constrained to make a simple investigation to collect evidence in regard to the amount of precourse knowledge of the subject which students bring to its study. This article deals with the experiment and its results.

A list of seventy true-false statements was submitted to forty-six students at the beginning of their course in educational measurements at the opening of the fall semester, 1928. This same list had been used as a part of the final examination given classes at the close of the course in previous semesters. From these former students a control group was taken consisting of the first forty-six on the class roll of the preceding semester, that is, the spring term, 1928. Since the mental ability of the members of the two groups was virtually the same, as that trait is measured by the Thorndike intelligence examination for high-school graduates which all students in the groups had taken in the freshman year; and since these students, all juniors or seniors, brought virtually the same type of previous academic training to this course, it seemed reasonable to infer that the main difference between the two groups in respect to knowledge of educational measurements would be due to the fact of having-had or not-having-had the course, and that, therefore, large overlapping in the two distributions of scores on this test would indicate a serious amount of overlapping of the content of this course with that of subjects taken previously by these students beginning the study; but that slight overlapping in the two distributions would indicate new knowledge and power gained from the course. The following comparison gives the results in condensed form.

Group I,	range,	2 to 45;	median, 18;	sigma, 9.1
" II,	"	31 " 58;	" 43;	" 5.8

This comparison of the data shows such a minimum of overlapping as is almost incredible. Moreover, inspection of the individual scores reveals that only two of the beginners made a score (34 and 45) as high as the lowest (31) of the control group. It should be added that these two scores were made by mature individuals, in C A, far above any other member of either group; both, teachers of experience; one of whom holds the A.B. from Northwestern University, and the other had a rich fund of information on tests and testing gleaned from the use of standardized material in his work as principal of a state graded school for three years. Thus it is seen that no *bona fide* beginner in the field scores as high as the lowest of those completing the course.

To investigate these results further, inspection was made of the record left by all former students who had taken this test as a part of the final examination at the end of the course. This brought out the fact that of 284 students who had received a passing mark in the course only sixteen made as low a score on this test as the highest (30) of the forty-four *bona fide* beginners.

These findings in no sense should be interpreted to justify sweeping conclusions. The important considerations of the relatively small population measured, the particular situation involved, the method of instruction, personality of the teacher—these and other elements are recognized as potent in their possible effect upon the results from any investigation in which classroom teaching is a conspicuous factor. Nevertheless it seems unquestionable that such a negligible amount of overlapping as is revealed by the comparison of the two groups and further substantiated by the record of nearly three hundred students may safely be regarded as trustworthy evidence of one, or both, of two simple, but important, facts which every instructor should know of the courses he teaches: (1) it does not draw upon the prerogatives of other fields, and *vice versa*, the courses taken previously by these students do not trespass seriously upon the domain of this subject; (2) whatever the nature of the content as respects duplication, the course is training the students in a type of mastery not formerly acquired.

The findings furthermore strongly indicate that where there obtains a defensible charge of serious overlapping of this course with others, the real cause of such duplication is to be found in other quarters than that of legitimate content, and that the remedy should be sought not in belittling or discarding the course but rather in a comprehensive grasp of its potential significance in the training of prospective teachers.

From the results of this simple investigation it appears that it should be a relatively easy matter for the teacher of any course that bears the odium of harboring duplications in content to prove or disprove, more or less conclusively, the validity of such an indictment. A concerted effort to do an honest job of housecleaning on the part of departments of education should go far in proving to the academic world that teacher-training institutions are not only becoming colleges in the best sense of the name, but also are pointing the way all higher institutions must follow eventually if we are to keep pace with the elementary school in shuffling off the dead-wood of traditional courses and in the selection of new ones on a basis of objective facts gathered by the application of scientific methods to the study of curriculum.

Lilian Hunsicker
State Teachers College, Milwaukee

THE ETHICAL TRAINING OF CHILDREN

The discussion in our journals as to how children in our public schools are to be trained in ethical and moral ideas and ideals is very interesting. In the discussion the teachers seem to throw the burden on the parents, and the parents to put it on the day schools and the Sunday Schools, and to urge the establishment of week-day schools of religion.

In this fundamental requirement for maintaining an honest and law-abiding population, we must use not one alone but every possible agency. First and foremost comes parental influence, and this finds its most effective use in the power of example and the atmosphere of the home which is created by the behavior of father and mother, in their attitude to each other and to their children. A very young child, in fact one too young to go to school, will recognize deceit in word or act and will react by showing the same trait. Similarly the destructiveness of careless habits, bad temper and lack of self-control appear. Whatever rules or instructions a parent gives are of little value unless supported by example. The same principle holds in regard to the teacher. No amount of technical training can take the place of fine character, high ideals and the atmosphere created by the personality of the teacher. With all due regard for the multitudes of noble-minded teachers in our schools, there is still need for the correction or the removal of those whose example is not uplifting and whose influence thus tends to nullify that of the high-minded.

A very helpful and easy way to instil high ideals in the schoolroom is to have a fine quotation written at the top of the blackboard or posted in some suitable place every day, or once a week, using appropriate ones for national holidays or special community events. There is, I believe, no question but that the vast majority of intelligent persons consider religion an essential factor in maintaining high ethical standards in face of the stress of temptation and bad example met with in daily life. Here, again, the religion of the home has the greatest influence, and that shown in the life more than belief or words. No hypocrisy can deceive the keen eyes of the young. The school, too, must have its influence. The fundamentals of religion, the "Fatherhood of God and the brotherhood of man," are justly recognized in the schools of a nation whose coins bear the words, "In God we trust." That true religious ideals may be presented without giving offence to sectarian ideas has been proved in many private educational institutions. In this matter the intelligence, sympathy and skill of the principal and his assistants are of essential importance.

A good Sunday School will help out the lack often found in home and school training. But for the millions who can not or will not attend Sunday School, surely the week-day school of religion, if it can attract them and give fine atmosphere as well as fine instruction, is greatly to be desired.

EMILY RAY GREGORY

SPECIAL CORRESPONDENCE

VIRGINIA POLYTECHNIC INSTITUTE'S SERVICE TO THE STATE

SERVICE to the state is a vital part of the program of Virginia Polytechnic Institute, for it has undertaken to advance in a very material and practical way the growing industrial development of Virginia. No longer is the institute content to confine its efforts—important as they are—to classroom instruction, but it intends to place its resources for research and experimentation at the disposal of business, both large and small.

The service of the institute is being offered in numerous spheres, but the ones which were started this fall relate particularly to the ceramics, wood utilizing and rayon industries, and to communities desiring industrial surveys. Three men were added to the faculty this year with the primary purpose of carrying on this work.

The way in which the engineering experiment station and the engineering extension division will serve the state is explained by Dean Earle B. Norris:

Through the engineering experiment station the laboratories in engineering and the allied sciences are used for studies of Virginia's natural resources and the technical problems of her industries. The departments of geology, mining engineering, chemical engineering, ceramics and wood technology are among those especially interested in the development and conservation of the resources of Virginia: development, by laboratory studies which seek to find economic methods of utilizing untouched resources; and conservation, by studies which search for better methods of utilization, whereby there may be improvements in quantity or quality of output or a reduction in the cost of production.

Some of the larger industries are able to maintain their own scientific staffs and laboratories, but even then occasional problems arise for which special equipment or facilities are needed or upon which outside scientific thought or advice is desired. The greatest opportunity for research service, however, appears to be in aiding smaller industries which are unable each to maintain its own research facilities. In many such cases groups or associations of industries in certain affiliated lines might join in the maintenance of research in fellowships for the study of their particular problem.

In order that our research and instruction may be effectively guided, it is important that we know our industries and their problems, as well as the technical problems of our civic and governmental organizations.

The engineering extension division is therefore set up as a service and contact organization to bring the facilities of the school of engineering into action in the service of the commonwealth.

The ceramic industries of Virginia are being surveyed by John W. Whittemore, who came to the Virginia Polytechnic Institute from Louisiana State College, where he made some important studies in Louisiana clay for the conservation commission of that state. Ceramic industries, especially in heavy clay products, are already of some importance in Virginia and are capable of great development, but thus far little has been done to develop the real possibilities of Virginia's ceramic resources.

In addition to the tabulation of ceramic resources, Professor Whittemore will study such industries as the manufacture of brick, drain tile, hollow building tile, sewer pipe, floor and wall tile, roofing tile, fire, brick, and similar refractory articles, dishes, glassware, enameled metals, abrasive wheels, pottery and cements. Tests of both the finished product and raw material from which the product is made have been made available to manufacturers. This survey will serve as a basis of courses in "ceramic materials," "ceramic technology," "ceramic manufacturing," which probably will not be given before next year.

Another service being offered industry in Virginia primarily affects wood-working industries, for Dr. J. E. Lodewick, formerly of the New York State College of Forestry, is at present conducting a state-wide survey in wood technology. The amount and kinds of wood in various sections, how best it can be utilized by local industry to obtain the best product at the lowest cost, and a careful plan of keeping the supply of raw material replenished are being studied by Dr. Lodewick in his investigation of the state, which is expected to take nearly a year to complete. Already Dr. Lodewick has done the field work in nearly all the counties. In all cases he has found excellent cooperation on the part of manufacturers, in several instances confidential data being freely furnished. In order to protect such, tabulations will not be published until the entire state has been studied.

The information thus gained will be used as a basis for courses in "wood technology," "industrial wood-fibers," "wood-using industries in Virginia," "forest products," which will be offered as part of the training of engineers who expect to enter this field.

One of the most important services being offered for the first time by the institute is an industrial survey of small cities. Reuben L. Humbert, who until August, 1928, was secretary of the Harrisonburg, Virginia, Chamber of Commerce, was added to the staff with the expressed purpose of making industrial surveys. While at Harrisonburg, Professor Humbert made a survey of that city of 7,000 persons, which has been used as a model all over the country for surveys of cities, some several times the size of Harrisonburg.

More than a score of Virginia cities have asked that the survey be made. The first one, made at Wytheville, has just been printed, while the field work of the Tazewell, Christiansburg-Cambria and Suffolk surveys has been completed. When a city asks that this semi-technical survey be made, members of the institute staff who are experts in gathering industrial data go there and determine such essential information as the number of industries already there, the kind, the number of persons engaged, the amount of weekly payrolls and what inducements are offered for a new industry to locate there.

In addition to this, certain primary factors, such as climate, amount and kind of raw materials, natural resources, type of labor, average wages offered, working conditions prevailing, living conditions, amount of power and its cost, kind of freight and express transportation, type of schools and churches, development of recreational facilities and the tax rate are tabulated. Other factors studied are municipal improvements, such as sewerage, water, light, police and fire protection. The type of hotels, restaurants, groceries and commercial establishments, newspapers, telegraph and postal facilities often influence new industries either to come or go elsewhere, so because of this such facts are given important consideration by those making the survey.

Major R. B. H. Begg, professor of civil engineering and director of the engineering extension division, and T. W. Knote, professor of business administration, have taken an active part in securing information. When the data have been gathered, the staff returns to the college, where all of the information is tabulated and printed in booklet form for the community. The only expense to the community is that of printing and distributing the booklet.

Producing rayon in the chemical laboratory of the institute will be part of the work of the present academic year. Equipment has been ordered and class work was started in January, in an effort to assist an industry nearly half of which is located in Virginia. Development of students trained in rayon productions is the primary object of this course. Dr. Robert E. Hussey, associate professor of chemistry, who gives the new course and supervises the manufacture of rayon on a small scale in the college laboratory, explains that the new course, which is believed to be the first of its kind in the country, includes lectures and laboratory work by covering the chemistry of cellulose, the basic principles involved in the manufacture and finishing of rayon and the chemistry of these processes, a study of raw materials used and the various factory tests.

Students will be required to produce rayon from the raw material during the course, and besides the actual instruction those in charge of the course are planning to conduct research work on rayon production and to keep in touch with the various rayon plants in the state.

In making industrial surveys, especially of smaller cities; in studying the wood technology and ceramic industries; in training rayon engineers and conducting research on this product; in making scientific tests especially for the smaller industries, Virginia Polytechnic Institute is directly serving the industries of its state, as well as training in the classroom the leaders of the future. Classroom work and practical assistance, research and application are being happily wedded.

R. H. McNEIL

VIRGINIA POLYTECHNIC INSTITUTE

REPORTS

THE RELATIONS OF THE NATIONAL GOVERNMENT TO EDUCATION[1]

PLANS for a study of the present relations of the National Government to education, to aid enactment of remedial legislation were discussed on June 7 by the Advisory Committee on Education, comprising representatives of national educational organizations, who met at the call of the Secretary of the Interior, Ray Lyman Wilbur.

In convening the conference, Secretary Wilbur outlined its scope and purpose. He announced that Charles R. Mann, director of the American Council on Education, was appointed general chairman of the advisory committee, and that J. W. Crabtree, of the National Education Association, was appointed general secretary. For the chairmanships of the three subcommittees, Secretary Wilbur appointed Dr. James E. Russell for the committee to consider the educational activities of the United States Government; President Lotus D. Coffman, of the University of Minnesota, for the committee to consider subsidies of the Federal Government to colleges, and Frank Cody, superintendent of the Detroit schools, for the committee to study other subsidies now granted.

Dr. Mann, in formally opening the discussions, outlined the present scope of government participation in education. He said that the task confronting the conference is "very difficult" because the whole question of organization of education in the Federal Government "is pretty well loaded with dynamite, as any one knows who has lived here and observed operations for any length of time."

The advisory committee adjourned without setting a date for another general meeting, after receiving reports from the three subcommittees indicating that they would be unable to formulate definite plans before next fall.

The chairmen of the subcommittees said they proposed to designate individual members to secure data to guide the groups in their further deliberations. By vote of the conference such a plan was agreed to, with the future procedure to be settled by a conference committee headed by Dr. Mann, and composed of three members of each subcommittee.

Dr. Mann said that Secretary Wilbur did not expect an early report, but preferred to have the advisory committee work out its plans in detail with a unanimity of opinion, even if it takes a year. All these factors, he said, should be left to the conference committee to decide.

The conference adjourned and the conference committee convened immediately to consider its preliminary plans.

When the meeting was called to order the Secretary of the Interior, Ray Lyman Wilbur, made an address of welcome. Dr. Charles R. Mann, director of the American Council of Education, who presided, made an introductory statement of the problems to be studied. The United States Commissioner of Education, William John Cooper, called attention to a list of official documents presented on various phases of education.

The conference considered Federal subsidies to education at college level, a paper on which was presented by Dr. Arthur J. Klein, chief of the division of higher education of the U. S. Bureau of Education, and to subsidies to education of less than college level. A paper on the latter subject was presented by Dr. J. C. Wright, director of the Federal Board of Vocational Education.

[1] Based on the report in the *U. S. Daily*.

Dr. Wright discussed in particular the crystalizing of public sentiment which resulted in the enactment of the Smith-Hughes Act for vocational education of less than college grades and traced the growth of vocational education since the law went into effect. The amount of State and local money for vocational education, he said, has been increasing much more rapidly than Federal funds.

The conference later divided into three groups to study various phases of education.

Group No. 1 will consider educational activities of the United States Government. This group consists of James E. Russell, chairman; S. P. Capen, W. M. Davidson, Frank P. Graves, J. C. Merriam, W. F. Willoughby, W. S. Thayer, Lois H. Meek, Lita Bane, George D. Strayer, Belle Sherwin, Walter L. Crocker, George Johnson, Mrs. F. P. Bagley.

This committee will give consideration in its studies to the following suggested issues:

On the basis of the present educational activities of the Federal Government and of their present administration, what are the next steps towards better organization for the future?

1. State the principle of local autonomy or decentralized responsibility.

2. What types of Federal activity strengthen local autonomy and responsibility? What types weaken them?

3. What organization of Federal educational activities best insures limitation of Federal activities to types that strengthen local autonomy?

4. What reorganization of present Federal activities in education best insures their effective coordination?

Group No. 2 will consider the subsidies of the Federal Government in colleges, their administration, results obtained and future policies. This group consists of Lotus D. Coffman, chairman; James R. Angell, Harry W. Chase, George H. Denny, Edward C. Elliott, Uel W. Lamkin, Cloyd H. Marvin, W. P. Morgan, Rt. Rev. Edward A. Pace, D. W. Springer, Mary E. Woolley, George F. Zook, Lida Lee Tall, E. P. Cubberley.

The list of suggested issues for this group to study is as follows:

On the basis of present Federal subsidies to colleges, of present administration, and of results obtained, what are the best policies for the future?

What is the procedure in paying these subsidies to colleges, disbursing them by colleges and auditing accounts?

What is the procedure in selecting candidates for subsidized positions, employing them and supervising their activities?

What constitutes an official appointment authorizing payment of Federal money for salaries?

Recognizing the value of Federal support in starting new enterprises, what are the present conditions that justify continuation of Federal subsidies?

When Federal subsidies were established, Federal taxation was indirect. What is the justification for continuing and extending these now that two-thirds of Federal taxes are direct income taxes?

What is the justification of Federal support of State engineering experiment stations?

What evidence shows whether Federal subsidies are or are not weakening local responsibility?

Group No. 3 will consider subsidies granted for education of less than college grade, how administered, results obtained and suggestions of future policy. This committee group consists of Frank Cody, chairman; J. B. Edmonson, Charles H. Judd, Mrs. S. M. N. Marrs, A. B. Meredith, Carl H. Milam, W. B. Munroe, W. F. Russell, Guy E. Snavely, William Green, T. E. Finegan, Mrs. L. W. Hughes, Mrs. Edith B. Joynes, Miss Agnes M. Samuelson, R. L. Cooley, Maurice Bisgyer.

The list of suggested issues for this group to study is as follows:

On the basis of present Federal subsidies to education of less than college grade, of present administration, and of results obtained, what are the best policies for the future?

What is the procedure in paying these subsidies to colleges, disbursing them by colleges and auditing accounts?

What is the procedure in selecting candidates for subsidized positions, employing them and supervising their activities?

What constitutes an official appointment authorizing payment of Federal money for salaries?

Recognizing the value of Federal support in starting new enterprises, what are the present conditions that justify continuation of Federal subsidies?

When Federal subsidies were established, Federal taxation was indirect. What is the justification for continuing and extending these now that two-thirds of Federal taxes are direct income taxes?

What is the justification of Federal support of State engineering experiment stations?

What evidence shows whether Federal subsidies are or are not weakening local responsibility?

On the basis of present Federal subsidies, what are the advantages and the disadvantages of gradually reducing and ultimately withdrawing Federal subsidies to a State as the State appropriations for the specified purpose increase?

In addressing the meeting Secretary Wilbur said:

The problems before you are more or less familiar to you all. They are fundamental—particularly fundamental to this country. Education has a unique significance in this republic. It has had a great history. The question is what shall its future history be in so far as the National Government is concerned. There has been since the very beginning here in the United States marked local development of the public school system, but we have had certain things develop in the National Capital and in different parts of the country. In the Department of the Interior, through the so-called Bureau of Education, there has been an attempt made to get a certain leadership in American education.

I think that while the history of that Department is somewhat checkered, on the whole it has done many good pieces of work and has provided sound leadership. But those of us who have studied it lately have felt that there is a great deal more that can be done. We have endeavored to increase the responsibility of the office by elevating somewhat the Commissioner of Education and by making room for an assistant commissioner of education. We are trying to find a suitable woman for assistant commissioner of education. It does not seem to be easy. Perhaps if we had left out the word suitable, we should have had no difficulty. No doubt, after I have mentioned it here, there will be a good many candidates. We want a first-class woman, for women, as you know, play a very important part in American education.

Aside from the activities of the bureau, certain responsibilities have been accepted in the Government for types of education of vocational character and otherwise. We feel that a very careful study should be made since there is a tendency at the present time in this country to bring to Washington all the various problems of the various parts of the country. If the Mediterranean fly makes trouble in Florida, there must be a resolution with appropriations passed by Congress. If an Act of God takes place in Oklahoma, and takes the form of a flood, Congress is expected to give relief. In other words, Congress is being looked upon as a sort of glorified Red Cross agency in many parts of the country.

There should be a limit to things of that kind—particularly in the field of education.

I want to express my appreciation of the fine spirit and interest which you all have shown. I doubt if there is any other field in the United States where one could send out as we did a considerable number of invitations, and not have a single declination. Some felt they could not come to the first conference, but expressed a desire to serve on the group.

If this committee can continue in the spirit in which it has begun, I feel that a historic document will finally be presented by Chairman Mann, to whom I now turn over the meetings.

QUOTATIONS

THE GOVERNMENT AND EDUCATION

SECRETARY WILBUR has declared that a separate Federal Department of Education with representation in the cabinet is not required, but has promptly taken steps toward assembling through expert assistance information about the results of the present educational activities of the federal government, with advice as to future policies. This is a much-needed study. It is fortunate that the Secretary of the Interior is himself so highly qualified to give general direction to the inquiry and to avail of its conclusions.

A joint committee of Congress on the reorganization of the executive departments made an extensive survey some years ago. It found that hardly a session of Congress passed without legislation creating new agencies, transposing old ones, or imposing new or larger duties, and that nearly every year some executive department organized a new bureau or division for carrying out the new requirements. Congress, for example, passes an insecticide and fungicide act and an Insecticide and Fungicide Board is forthwith set up. This great expansion has resulted in more or less duplicated or unrelated effort. The tendency was intensified during the war. Scores of new agencies came into being, some with departmental affiliation and many as virtually independent establishments. The number of employees in departmental service was trebled between June, 1916, and November, 1918.

The survey planned by Secretary Wilbur has a narrower range. It is concerned only with education. There was a chart in an outer room of Mr. Hoover's office when he was Secretary of Commerce showing the distribution of scattered functions throughout the departments—and some beyond. There are curious, not to say amusing incongruities. The mind of President Hoover has doubtless pondered over this chart. But the new committee will not only bring within view these varied educational activities, but will also consider projects under state or other control which receive subventions from the federal government. The personnel of this advisory committee is of the highest and gives promise that when the report comes it will be one on which an educational engineer can confidently build a system without duplication or waste—in which there will be a unifying of the federal educational agencies and a centralizing of the sources of information, without impairing local initiative and responsibility.—*New York Times.*

INTER-AMERICAN EDUCATION

Under the sponsorship of the National Education Association there is in process of formation an Inter-American Federation of Education Associations that promises to play an important part in the cementing of friendship between the nations of North and South America. Contacts are being established with all the Pan-American republics, either through representative educational associations or through the ministers of education of the various republics. In July there will be held at Atlanta an inter-American conference of education in which leading Latin-American educators will participate, and during which the aim and plan of the federation will be discussed. During the summer of 1930 a preliminary organization congress will be held at a Latin-American capital. The contacts thus far established definitely assure the creation of the federation.

In discussing, in connection with the creation of the federation the universal desire for understanding and accord among the peoples of the American continent, Dr. Glen Levin Swiggett, organizing secretary of the federation, speaks as follows: "Of all human interests, education is best fitted to promote fellowship. Political accord and mutual economic advantage can only come with informed public opinion and helpful technic which education alone can form and foster. It is for this reason that ministers of education in all participating countries have promised their cooperation, and the accredited representatives of these countries in Washington have given assurance of their interest and support."

The United States and the Latin-American nations will benefit alike through the creation of an Inter-American Federation of Education Associations. Matters of general concern can best be approached in a spirit of cooperation. Problems of individual interest can best be solved by bringing to bear the combined experience of the group. Isolation will be fought through the federation, and all the American nations brought to a more complete realization that they have so much in common that cooperation is not only desirable but necessary. The Inter-American Federation of Education Associations once established should develop into a powerful agency of good-will.—*Washington Post.*

EDUCATIONAL RESEARCH AND STATISTICS

ELUSIVE FACTORS TENDING TO REDUCE CORRELATIONS BETWEEN INTELLIGENCE TEST RANKS AND COLLEGE GRADES

For some years now investigators have been studying the predictive value of intelligence tests (or aptitude tests) for college freshmen. Their results have been expressed usually in terms of the coefficient of correlation, and not infrequently no other facts were considered. Few of the coefficients have been found to be greater than .60, and many were .50 or smaller.

Taken at their face value, these coefficients may be interpreted as being of marked significance because the correlations of college grades themselves for the same group of students from term to term are frequently no higher; or else because entrance examinations and secondary-school records seem to be somewhat less significant as criteria of college success, judged on the basis of correlations. These same coefficients of correlation, interpreted by one with a different bias, may be regarded as lacking significance because they are so far removed from unity or from a value approximating unity. Thus the evidence appears to be not unequivocal.

However, more recently, investigators of this problem have studied additional data, such as the number of hours spent in study (each day or week, or whatever the unit) and the number of honor points achieved. Thus, having three or more variables, the partial correlation and regression technique can be employed. Using this technique, it can be demonstrated, for instance, that with hours of study constant, the correlation between general intelligence and honor points is very high. Likewise it can be shown that when intelligence is constant, the correlation between the number of honor points and hours of study is almost as high.[1] The conclusions to be drawn from such data are clear. These same partial coefficients may then be employed in the derivation of a regression equation; and this equation, in turn, may be used to predict (within limits of error) the number of honor points a student will most likely achieve if his intelligence rating is known, together with the number of hours spent in study, per unit of time. If it were desired, numerical grades could be substituted for the number of honor points, and thus it would be possible to predict (within limits of error) a student's most likely average. But these predictions in any event would be dependent upon the reliability of the coefficients of correlation.

Data perhaps more useful than coefficients of correlation would be tables of chance based on the intelligence test rank and on college grades achieved over one, two or three or any number of semesters. Hence it would be possible to say that for a student ranking in the highest decile the chances for completing one, two or more years with a given grade are such and such; for a student in the second decile, the chances are such and such. Similarly, for students ranked in the lowest decile or quartile, or at any of the intermediate levels, the chances for successful completion of one or more years and for the achievement of certain grades can be stated.

Yet there are numerous factors contributing toward success or failure which are extremely difficult, if not impossible, of measurement for purposes of quantitative analysis. Among these elusive factors are interest in the work, motivation, extra-curricular activities, time spent in working for a living, health, disturbances of various sorts, time spent in study and reading independent of courses, poor habits of study, etc.

Because these are factors not capable of quantitative measure, and because they tend to lower the coefficients of correlation, is it to be concluded that the intelligence or aptitudes test is of less value? Quite the contrary seems true. Decreased correlations are due, of course, to the discrepancies which exist between rank in the intelligence test and rank in scholarship. But where significant differences do appear, some clear reason can usually be found for their presence. If this be so, then the discrepancies do not lessen the value of intelligence tests, providing that a careful study is made of individual cases where significant differences do exist.

In order to determine whether such clear reasons are usually present, sixty-eight sophomores were interviewed. These were students who fell in one of two groups: (1) those who ranked in the upper 30 per cent. on the intelligence tests, but who averaged less than 75 in their courses of the freshman year; (2) those who ranked in the lower half on the intelligence test, but whose freshman scholastic averages placed them in the upper 30 per cent. of their class. Of the former there were forty-two, and of the latter twenty-six. The freshman class numbered about 450. The test used was that published by the American Council on Education. It is felt that the testimony of these

[1] For example, M. A. May, "Predicting Academic Success," *Journal of Educational Psychology,* 1923, XIV, 7, pp. 429–440.

students is in every case reliable, for they were told that the information in no way affected their records in the college, and that we were merely seeking information by which to be guided.

Taking the first group—those whose scholastic records were poorer than the intelligence test results would lead us to expect—it was found that the reasons for their relatively poor scholarship could be grouped as shown in Table I. It will be noted, of course, that the total of the F column is greater than forty-two, for many students had more than one explanation to offer.

TABLE I

	F
Lack of interest	15
Poor habits of study	11
Loafing	8
Athletic competitions	7
Extra-curricular competitions	5
Work for self-support	5
Reading and study outside of courses	4
Social activities	4
Illness	1
No apparent reason	4

Only few of these need elaboration. The first reason—lack of interest—was given by students who were frequently doubtful of the wisdom of coming to college or who came into their courses without purpose and without any desire to study for the sake of study alone. The second—poor habits of study—includes such things as unfamiliarity with the lecture method, poor allotment of time and difficulty of adjustment to self-responsibility, as compared with the rather close supervision in the secondary school. There was also a small group who maintained that they did only enough in their courses to get a passing grade, but that they spent much of their time in reading books far afield of their courses.

The second group—composed of those whose intelligence test ranks were markedly below the level of their scholastic achievement—had the following reasons to offer for their poorer performance on the intelligence test.

With these freshmen the intelligence test is not used as a basis for admission: the test is given to students who have already entered, but it is administered during the first few days, when the strangeness of the new situation is very marked, and when many a freshman is still in an unsettled state. There is also a small group who felt that inasmuch as they had already been admitted to the university, their maximum effort was, therefore, not necessary. However, this unfortunate attitude frequently originates not with the freshman himself but rather with some of the upperclassmen, the self-constituted advisers of incoming students.

TABLE II

	F
Newness of conditions and nervousness during first days	15
Attached no importance to test	10
Handicapped by time limit	6
Illness	5
No apparent reason	1

Although it seems to be established that power and rate are very highly correlated and that they are, therefore, both functions of "general intelligence," there is nevertheless a small group who find time limits a handicap. They are the very small minority of slow, careful individuals who have probably given rise to the popular but erroneous belief that the slow worker is the more able and the rapid worker superficial and inaccurate. Yet the presence of this minority will to some degree lower correlations between intelligence tests and college marks, because the time factor is not nearly so effective in course work and course examinations, whereas it is an element of importance for some in taking the aptitudes test.

The correlation technique—including partial and multiple correlations—together with the regression equations, is of unquestionable assistance in studying predictive values; but it should also be clear that there are sufficiently frequent elusive factors which make it necessary, for a better understanding of a test's predictive value, to supplement the objective data with subjective reports in those instances where discrepancies exist between test rank and course grades.

Frank S. Freeman

Cornell University

SCHOOL AND SOCIETY

EDITED BY J. McKEEN CATTELL

WITH WHICH IS COMBINED THE

EDUCATIONAL REVIEW

EDITED BY WILLIAM McANDREW

Volume XXIX   SATURDAY, JUNE 22, 1929   Number 756

SELECTION AS A FUNCTION OF AMERICAN SECONDARY EDUCATION[1]

By Professor W. CARSON RYAN, JR.

SWARTHMORE COLLEGE

ONE who speaks on the selective function of American secondary education at the present juncture is under peculiar obligation to state promptly and unequivocally where he stands on the American public high school and its expansion. Let me say at the outset, therefore, that I believe in this expansion: that I regard the ideal of a high-school education or the equivalent for every boy and girl as not only feasible, but essential. We who are concerned with American education must not allow ourselves to be diverted from this goal of universal secondary schooling by the wails of those who complain on principle, in terms of "sanctified squander," about expenditures for public education. We must not be diverted from our goal by the comparatively few of the private secondary-school group who for commercial or social reasons resent the expansion of good secondary-school facilities at public expense; by the few remaining university presidents, chiefly in the east, who do not understand and apparently do not intend to understand the philosophy of American public education; by those who honestly but mistakenly confuse the older European goals with our present ones, or by that minority among American industrialists—I am convinced it is really a minority—who are so short-sighted as to wish to have large numbers of children leave school early, not realizing that a large part of American material prosperity—to say nothing of much that is even more precious—is directly due to the expansion of school opportunities upward for the great mass of our population.

We are clearly committed to a policy of universal secondary education in this country, much more clearly in practice than many of our own group seem to realize, so rapid has been the development. I remember Dr. Claxton's saying in 1913, "Think of it! We have a million boys and girls in high school!" It was an unheard of thing. If some one had said to Dr. Claxton and the rest of us in the Bureau of Education at that time that this enrolment was to double in a few short years and then more than double again, I doubt whether the most sanguine among us would have believed it; yet that is precisely what has happened. It is the upper reaches that are particularly significant. Of the seven and

[1] Address before the Department of Secondary School Principals, Cleveland, Ohio, on February 26, 1929.

a half million youth between fifteen and eighteen years of age in the United States more than two thirds are now in school. The 1920 census showed half the sixteen-year-olds in school, a third of the seventeen-year-olds, one fifth of the eighteen-year-olds. Next year's census will almost certainly show not less than three fourths of the sixteen-year-olds in school, half the seventeen-year-olds and at least a third of the eighteen-year-olds. What other nations are likely to term *selection* we are calling *pupil-mortality*. We actually try, and succeed measurably, in the task of keeping people in school—and even in college—rather than shoving them out. Not only do we have nearly five millions in secondary schools, but we have doubled our teaching force in these schools since 1920—less than a hundred thousand then, more than two hundred thousand now—and we are apparently already spending more annually for secondary education than our foremost authority in 1922 believed the public could ever be prevailed upon to spend.

From the point of view of comparative education this is of course stupendous. Literally nothing quite like it has ever happened before, so far as we know, though many people in other countries are watching our progress with very great interest, and far more important developments in this direction are coming in Europe than some school officials admit. One of our most competent observers recently said:

> There can be no question that suitable education during the adolescent years should devolve as a right and obligation on every child that comes to maturity within our borders. . . . It is becoming quite clear that the years between twelve and eighteen, or thereabouts, constitute the period during which proper education, combined with the development of sound health and normal habits, are of the utmost importance for the subsequent happiness of the individual and for the welfare of the nation.

This, by the way, is not a quotation from Professor Counts or any of the other of our best-known protagonists of universal secondary education. It is from a publication frequently cited on the other side of the controversy—Bulletin 20, of the Carnegie Foundation for the Advancement of Teaching, "The Quality of the Educational Process in the United States and in Europe," by W. S. Learned.

The Question of Selection

Is there, then, a real place for selection as a function of the secondary school? I believe that there is. To have faith in education for all is not to have faith in the same kind of education for all. Our real task is to use selection, but to see to it that this is not selection for elimination, but selection for further and better opportunity for each individual youngster. Somehow we must find a way of solving the very old question of mass education on an individual basis. Admitting the very great importance of going to school together through youth, of working, playing and living together, in schoolroom and on the playground, we must save these gains and yet help our people to realize that to have different interests, to be able to do different things, mentally, socially, emotionally, artistically, is not inconsistent with democracy, but is, on the contrary, a necessary part of real equality of opportunity and real cooperative effort for democracy.

If we are to have, in accordance with some of the principles underlying the articulation program presented at this Cleveland meeting, a genuine provision of secondary education for all between the ages of twelve and eighteen or twenty years of age, what are we going to do about it, and where does the selection come in? What are we going to do with these precious six or eight years through which Ross Finney says teachers are going to make the future as truly as soldiers and diplomats have made the past? Briefly, I believe the steps we are going to take will include at least these: (1) A genuine reorganization of the content of secondary education, to include both common material and specialized. (2) A real effort in the direction of individual and creative rather than mass and routine methods. (3) An insistence upon *quality* in the entire process that has so far been lost sight of in secondary education.

REORGANIZATION OF THE CURRICULUM

Any one who takes a long-time view of education is obliged to conclude that a real reorganization of content has only just begun. Somebody will have to do a blasting job on the secondary-school curriculum similar to the one Rugg began two years ago, mainly for elementary education, in the yearbook of the National Society, and has recently continued in "The Child-Centered School," which I believe is destined to be one of the significantly controversial books of our time. It is going to be more difficult to do it for the secondary period, for there are more intrenched absurdities and most of us do not see any fundamental reason for change. We go cheerfully along on the theory that if we only add new "subjects" (as we call them), that will suffice. The futility of this accretion method has been shown up convincingly in some recent books, notably in Thomas Jesse Jones' "Four Essentials of Education," but few of us are reached by this type of educational writing. We still think, most of us, in terms of the "regular" school subjects in the secondary school, not because these have ever been subjected to any real tests of cultural, social, practical or even intellectual values, but because they have been there a long time.

What we really eventually ought to do, but what nobody is yet ready to do, is to face the whole problem of content for the secondary school anew, without preconceived notions in favor of what we find there. We need to sit down and say to ourselves: What is this modern life of ours anyway? What are its beauties, its opportunities, its needs? What is this culture that we are to pass on, to use the words of Briggs in the 1929 yearbook? What are these heritages and these creative things as well that we are to put into the secondary school, and how shall we see that everybody—regardless of whether he is in the upper quartile, regardless of whether he can survive a linguistic Scholastic Aptitude Test—gets at least some glimpses of these richer things that are the only real excuse for modern civilization? If we did this conscientiously I think almost nothing of the traditional secondary-school content would remain. That it would have been the answer at one period probably nobody could deny—for it was a noble effort, and a successful effort, to open the accumulated cultures of at least two ancient civilizations to a newer age. To-day almost none of it could stand any such test. Apply to the current offerings in language and mathematics any real definition of the process of reflective thinking from Locke to Dewey and see how little of it is intellectual in any sense—to use the one last defense of those among us who would preserve the heritage only in its linguistic and mechanistic survivals. Think of the insistence upon language as an instrument of selection—which, by the way, appears to be on the increase, as a means of admission for college, at least, instead of on the wane, as we had thought. There is a tragic story here on the Greek and Latin side which I will refrain from telling, only reminding you that insistence on the mere verbal survivals of two once great civilizations, with no real effort to make the vital intellectual and emotional relation to our own, has cost us one of the most precious aids to an understanding of modern life. Instead I will take my example from modern foreign language, especially since there is a present crisis there that seems to be going almost unnoticed. As a modern language teacher for some years and still an interested amateur in that field (if the reports of the Modern Language Inquiry are correct I must be one of the few people who still read foreign languages after college days) I am convinced that we are at present going through a desperately barren period of foreign language teaching in the secondary schools. The teachers of French, for example, seem obsessed with the notion that nobody can learn to read French without first learning all the grammar that can be recorded. This is the same fallacy that the teachers of beginning reading in the primary school have fortunately worked themselves delightfully free from in good modern schools. Now language as language has practically no intellectual value; the content is the main thing. Professor Henmon, reviewing the results of the Modern Language Inquiry, points out that there is little correlation between teachers' marks and actual achievement as measured by tests in the foreign language, because the teachers tend to put all the emphasis upon the grammar in their marking, and he characterizes this as one of the real defects revealed in the investigation. I use the situation in modern language teaching merely as an example of the need for dynamiting followed by constructive rebuilding that will be necessary in the whole content situation, whether for determining and putting into operation a common basic material or arranging offerings of a specialized sort for groups and individuals beyond the common materials. Some of us may remember that the Classical Inquiry demonstrated the value of Latin as a secondary-school activity by asking the teachers of Latin throughout the country whether Latin was valuable or not. The other subject-matter inquiries have seldom been quite like that, but surely we must eventually come to a practical recognition of the fact that if we depend upon this method, even in the hands of capable and honest investigators, we shall never get anywhere in making a real content for the secondary school. Even in an activity like English we tend to take too much for granted. Though we have taken some real steps towards freedom here, on the whole we still think of English as a meticulous correctness rather than as creative expression and appreciation, thereby placing ourselves under the suspicion—which you will find quite audibly expressed at Adult Education Association meetings if not elsewhere—of sending out high-school graduates who do not read books any more because they have been so completely conditioned against reading as a result of assigned task-reading in school.

If the theory that I have tried to express has any validity it means that only those "constants" will eventually deserve a place in secondary education that can stand the test of modern usefulness in terms of cultural understandings or industrial and social needs. That even these constants, given as part of a mass educational provision, can be usefully adapted to different abilities, interests and needs, I believe can be demonstrated, but I shall postpone discussion of that for a minute or two. In any case, these constants, this common material, whatever we decide it shall be and however we decide it shall be given, must be supplemented by the widest possible offerings at public expense. However much synthesis may be found to be necessary, in the last analysis, proper economies of a practical nature being kept in mind, I see no reason why society, through public expenditure, should not provide any possible training that can be proved to have social value or the kind of value for the individual that ultimately contributes to the welfare of all. Furthermore, the possibilities of a varied offering, especially in small schools, are often not realized. Not caring much to make the change, we have not tried very hard to do it.

INDIVIDUALIZING SECONDARY EDUCATION

One of the real clues to securing attention to individual differences in a mass education program is *individual learning*. We are still so under the spell of rigid grades, rigid subject-matter stratification and formal class-teaching that we have so far declined to make on any really great scale the experiments in individualizing the secondary school that need to be tried. One may quarrel with certain of the accompanying philosophy of Winnetka and Dalton procedures as one finds them in different localities, but enough has been done to show that there are real possibilities here; that the individual method for certain things at least is not only desirable, but feasible and efficient—efficient and economical indeed, in the truest sense of the terms. At least one secondary school that I know of—a large secondary school in what some people would regard as a less favored environment—has demonstrated that the most gifted children can be accommodated under mass conditions, getting magnificent gains as individuals without in any way jeopardizing the democratic quality of the school or its essential standing as a cooperative enterprise. Such a plan, if worked out carefully, apparently avoids the social and emotional losses that so far have seemed to be inevitable accompaniments of the so-called homogeneous grouping method—there being, of course, no such thing as real homogeneous grouping in any sense, not even in the narrow academic activities usually covered by this practice.

Much of the despair over our supposed inability to provide differentiation in the thousands of smaller high schools in the United States is due, I am convinced, to our blindness to the possibilities of individualizing under superior leadership. E. E. Windes made a suggestion, when he was in the Bureau of Education two or three years ago, that has never had the attention it deserves. Apparently the plan as he advanced it sounded so radical that none of the several thousand school people who heard him gave it another thought. He proposed, as some of you may know, that instead of weak staffs of four and five underpaid, undereducated and overburdened teachers for these schools of from twenty to eighty pupils, one university man or woman of unusually good training and a salary several times what would ordinarily be paid in such a community be put in charge, with a very fine teacher-librarian as the other member of the staff. The job of this staff of two would be to direct, in a way none of the typical high-school teachers could have done, the enterprise of learning in that school. If this seems unduly fanciful to you, let me remind you that many of the most famous and successful academies of the early nineteenth century were organized on precisely this basis, except that present resources for directed learning are so superior to what they were a century ago that there is no comparison. Mr. Windes' proposal included professional supervision of a good type on a county or regional arrangement. It will be noticed that the plan would not be more costly than the present one, on the whole; it would provide expert direction instead of haphazard teaching; it would capitalize the individual initiative of pupils, not only in intellectual learnings of the book type, but in athletics and other similar activities, where at present so much is done in the wholly uneducational method of coaching from the side lines; it would make possible a synthesis, an interrelation of learnings quite impossible under any present plan of isolated departments and courses; it would emphasize achievement rather than "time-spent"—one of the curses of the present scheme of things, as Morrison has so well shown; it would allow considerable differentiation, in rates of learning, in kinds of material learned, in treatment for further learning opportunities or vocational opportunities—in other words, educational and vocational counseling.

If we are to carry all our youth through a secondary-school period, in city and country alike, we shall have to carry on experimentation with the types of individualized learning here described. There will always, for certain purposes, be advantages in grouping small units into somewhat larger ones, doubtless, but we have not begun to explore the possibilities of skilfully directed individual learning in the literally thousands of small country high schools that will always exist as well as in the large city high schools where differentiation, because of sheer numbers, has superficially seemed more practicable.

The Quality of the Educational Process

In the plan just suggested, attributed to Mr. Windes, the quality of the direction of the educational enterprise was the key to any possible success. We have certainly had to give our energies so much in the past to taking care of the numbers that we have had to pay less heed to the quality of the job we were doing. I do not mean that we should feel discouraged about it; quite the contrary. There are some very encouraging signs. Since I have put on record my personal conviction about the teaching of French and have called upon the Modern Language Inquiry to support my statement, I must be honest with you and state that the same investigation apparently shows that in actual achievement in foreign language the pupils in American secondary schools surpassed (on the same standard tests) corresponding pupils in both Canadian and English secondary schools. The North Central Association has for some time had from 90 to nearly 100 per cent. of its teaching staffs at least four-year college and university graduates, and has been able to insist upon some professional preparation besides. The Southern Association, with only a 75 per cent. requirement, recently announced a more than 90 per cent. achievement on the basis indicated—that is, college and university graduation.

But here, after all, is our real weakness. Those of us who are engaged in placing teachers know only too well about the alleged oversupply in certain regions—which turns out to be, as one might expect, an oversupply of poorly qualified candidates for teaching and a tragic undersupply of the kind of teachers that is needed to put genuine quality into American secondary education. Any real program in secondary education waits upon this. Every study of the qualifications of teachers shows how many are teaching with no real mastery of the materials. The richest potentialities of the junior high school go unrealized because of the lack of real teachers. Think how many general science courses, general social studies courses and other of the more hopeful efforts at new content are losing out because there are simply not enough real master-teachers to make them what they ought to be. We ought to face this squarely. If we are to profit by such individual plans as have been mentioned; if we are to take advantage of the study of seventh and eighth grade pupils Superintendent Davidson told the Vocational Guidance Association about the other day—a real experiment in differentiation; if we are to make the kind of progress in secondary content that will be comparable, for example, to the work of the Lincoln School elementary staff, we shall have to look more searchingly to the quality of our teachers.

AMERICA AND FOREIGN SCHOOLS

It is necessary to omit many important considerations in any such brief survey as this. One more point must, however, be mentioned. In our problem of furnishing universal secondary education and adequate differentiation it will be valuable for us to give careful study to the experience of nations other than our own. I hope I have shown that I am not interested in converting anybody to a European philosophy of education—or, for that matter, to an Indian, a Japanese or a West African philosophy of education. We need, however, to know very much more about foreign educational systems than we now know. If Europe has something in secondary education that we ought to know, by all means let us study it. It may not modify our practice at all, but at least it will help us to understand better what we are doing. I have always felt that one visit to a Glasgow school made me understand better something about the junior high school movement in America than I had ever been able to understand it from any American books on the subject. I would not study Germany and France and England alone. I would study Italy right now, with Mussolini's attempt to prove that the history of education is wrong when it says that no imposed civilization will endure; I would study the Balilla, that experiment in mass education for youth that is infinitely more significant than the school program; I would study Russia, *via* Mrs. Wilson, Dr. Counts, John Dewey, Lotus Coffman and other competent American investigators—that is, if I couldn't do it first hand; or I'd read the "Diary of a Communist Schoolboy." Surveys of education all over the world are making it easier than it ever has been before to understand what other countries are doing in the effort to educate youth and thereby understand better what we are trying to do. Is this undemocratic? On the contrary, it is essential to democracy. If our democracy and its philosophy of the greatest spread of education for all youth can not stand every possible scrutiny; if it can not make a place for studying methods used everywhere for giving individuals their best opportunity, then heaven help our democracy!

Selection is a function of American secondary education. It is not, and must not be, however, selection by elimination, but selection for additional opportunity. It needs to be based upon the broadest possible general provision, with as many common elements as possible; it must recognize the possibility of genuine intellectual interests among the entire group regardless of so-called levels of mental ability; it sees in individual learning a special way out for meeting individual differences, interests, aptitudes and needs; and it presupposes, whatever the method, a comprehensive remaking of the content of secondary education and a quality in the educational process hitherto not sufficiently insisted upon.

THE DRAMA IN EDUCATION[1]

By Dr. HENRY S. CURTIS
STATE DIRECTOR OF HYGIENE AND PHYSICAL EDUCATION FOR MISSOURI

AT different times and sometimes by large classes of people the theater has been regarded as evil. But drama is to be classed with speech, reading and the movie as a form of expression. It is the form which comes nearest to reproducing life. It is good or evil according to what it has to say.

There has always been some foundation for the criticism of the commercial drama. It is said that its scenes and characters are trivial,

[1] An address delivered before the Drama League of America.

that while it may represent life, it is life on its shallower and less desirable side, that it is often dominated by sex and that it gets a large part of its patronage from its sex appeal, that actors and actresses are not on the whole the best ideals to set before adolescent boys and girls.

THE MAKE-BELIEVE OF LITTLE CHILDREN

All little children are essentially dramatic and live in a world of make-believe. At least four phases of this impulse or instinct for acting and imitation have been noticed by every one. Little children tend to imitate every action of the people they see. So insistent is this tendency that people all over the world call them little monkeys. The educational purpose of this imitation is obvious. It is nature's great method of learning how. It is much stronger in the little child than it is in the child who is older.

The second phase in the acting of the little child is impersonation, the representing father, mother, doctor or clergyman in his play. So general is this tendency that it is not limited to the portrayal of persons, but the child transforms himself freely into a horse, a dog, a fire engine, or any other creature or object that wins his attention. In this play he does not need an audience, but is better or as well pleased when alone. Joseph Lee says that it is the child's effort to get inside the object and feel what it is really like. It is the great school of putting yourself in another's place, and teaches an understanding and sympathy that nothing else can give.

In the earliest stages of dramatization the child does not require scenery or costume, but, in older childhood, girls especially love to dress up and make calls and have tea parties and the like. There is scarcely any other activity which holds the attention longer.

Very early in this period before the kindergarten age children begin to play with puppets, marionettes or dolls. So vivid is their imagination that almost any form, a bottle, a block or even a stick of wood will serve to represent any character in the stories they have heard. Adults usually think of dolls as babies, and often speak of them as "doll babies." There have been several studies of dolls, and all of them show much the same things. A certain per cent. of dolls are always babies varying largely with the presence or absence of babies in the family and with the age of the child, but at no time are the majority of dolls babies. The doll is usually a marionette. The rag doll is usually better loved than the wax doll, primarily because the rag doll can take any part with equal ease, a giant, a dwarf, a wolf, a bear, or any other character that is needed. Little children usually have no self-consciousness in their acting and are not bothered by the lack of words. They make up passages freely to express their ideas.

DRAMATICS IN THE ELEMENTARY SCHOOL

Educators are coming to realize more and more how essentially dramatic is child nature, and are making more and more use of it in the elementary school.

One of the commonest readers in the schools of Missouri is the dramatic reader for the first and second grades. Where children have this reader, they usually act out a large part of the stories.

The public elementary school is nearly three hundred years old. It is our oldest public school. Its ideals, also, are old; its purpose has been to teach the three R's. Its teachers have had less training than the teachers in the high school and have been held by tradition and popular demand to a rigid curriculum.

The average elementary school building is probably about twenty-five years old. It is usually without an auditorium or a stage. There is no assembly or opportunity for one in most. There is, as a rule, no teacher who has had dramatic training.

These conditions are being rapidly modified at present. Most of the *new* elementary schools contain an auditorium and a stage and have at least a weekly assembly. The assembly program is often a drama, given by one of the grades. Many of the elementary schools now have at least one teacher who has had dramatic training.

DRAMATICS IN HIGH SCHOOL

The public high school is the newest of our educational institutions. As an institution it is about forty years old. There are nearly one hundred thousand high-school students in the state of Missouri, which is probably more than there are in Great Britain and France combined.

The average high-school building is not more than ten years old. It is often the finest building in the town. Some of the new ones have cost more than four millions of dollars, considerably more than the entire resources of the average college. In most states the teachers must be college graduates or have an equivalent training. In California they must have a year of graduate work beyond the college, and in New York City they must have two years unless they have had a considerable experience in teaching. The salaries paid in the large city high schools range up to $5,000 and compare favorably with college salaries. In laboratory equipment they are superior to the average college. The grade of work being given is about equal to that of the college of forty years ago.

Many of the city high schools contain a small theater. Nearly all have an auditorium which is usually ample to seat both the student body and as many more from the community. Most of them have a splendid stage with ample dressing rooms, costly curtains, fairly good scenery, excellent footlights and a growing costumery which gives them the equipment needed for presenting almost any kind of play.

There are four phases of dramatics to be distinguished in high school. Of these the first is the dramatics which is incidental to the study of literature. It is given by the English class as a method of English training and often to the class alone.

A second phase is the assembly program. Most high schools have a special program once a week which is in charge of the students. At this assembly a play is often presented to the student body. There are no, or at most, few outsiders and no admission is charged.

A third form is a play given by some high-school group for the public. The classic form of this is the senior play given at commencement time, but plays are now coming to be given at various times during the year. These plays are given primarily to parents and friends. Admission is generally charged and the profits may be several hundred dollars. The chief criticism of these two types of dramatics is that the plays are usually selected to win applause and may not be worthy of the time and effort required to give or hear them.

The fourth type is the dramatic contest. During the last few years these have been held in many states of the Union. In Missouri there is now a county contest in a good share of the counties each year. District contests are held at each of the teachers colleges and a state-wide contest at the university in May. These are all in one-act plays, which must not have more than eight actors or take more than fifteen minutes.

In Missouri each high school must submit the play it wishes to give in the district contest to the sponsor at the teachers college for approval before it may be given. In the state contest the play must be selected from a list that is sent out by the university. The standards set by the educational authorities are resulting in better plays.

A few years ago it was difficult to secure suitable plays and there was no one who had been trained to coach dramatics. There is now a much greater variety of plays, but the quality of the plays is still the greatest criticism. There is hardly a high school where some teacher has not had training in dramatics or at least some experience in this field.

There are several other factors which are being embodied in the school program which serve as accessories to the drama and increase its possibilities. In nearly all high schools various forms of the dance are taught, choruses and orchestras are trained and pageants are given.

There are two different types of objectives that are being secured or may be secured from high-school dramatics. One of these series of objectives results from dramatics almost inevitably whatever the nature of the plays. The second series of objectives will be secured only from certain plays.

Among objectives of the first class may be mentioned distinctness of speech. The average high-school pupil does not speak distinctly enough to be understood in a good-sized auditorium, but the person who presents a play in public has to learn to articulate and pronounce his words so that he can be heard.

Comparatively few high-school pupils habitually maintain good posture. But the one who is to appear on the stage must learn a dignified bearing and poise. The one who acts the part of a prince is apt to carry something princely into the posture of his daily life.

There is no easier way of teaching self-confidence in public. The actor need not go alone to face the audience, for he is with others and may be almost unconscious of those occupying the seats.

There is, also, a series of much larger objectives that will be secured only through appropriate plays and skilled coaching.

I have never seen dramatics given as a method of character education, but we commonly say that the most effective method is through imitation of a worthy example and through ideals. The child is indeed fortunate who has in father or mother, sister or brother, uncle or aunt, a worthy example to be copied. The effect of hero worship is due to the worshiper entering sympathetically into the life of another until he feels and understands that other's purpose and motives. Is there any better way to do this than through impersonation of worthy characters? It is easy to see that a series of dramas might be selected or written with this end in view which might yield wonderful results.

The drama has not been used so far as I know for vocational guidance. Yet a series of plays might be selected or written that would serve this purpose admirably. The young man who has taken the part of an engineer, a lawyer, a doctor or a farmer should be in a much better position to judge whether or not he wishes to follow one of these occupations.

The drama may be a great means to social understanding. If the native born sometimes takes the part of the recent immigrant, if the son of rich parents sometimes takes the part of the poor boy or poor man, if the capitalist takes the part of the laborer and the laborer takes the part of the capitalist, it should lead to a better attitude between the classes that make up America.

The drama might be made a great method of teaching American ideals and patriotisms. What better method can there be both for the actors and the audience than to portray or see portrayed upon the stage the lives of great Americans and great events from American history?

Dramatics at the Agricultural Colleges

One of the most notable and characteristic developments in this new educational drama is at the Agricultural College of North Dakota. Professor Arvold has been carrying on this work now for more than twenty years and has developed a real rural drama and several troupes of rural actors. For the most part the plays, all of which deal with rural life and its problems, are written by the students and are first presented in the auditorium or theater of the college. Afterwards they may be given during vacations in rural churches, lodge halls, barns, or any other available place.

Dramatics at the University

The next great professional school is apparently to be the school of drama and acting. Nearly all the larger universities have a beginning. Most of them have available a larger or smaller theater and are giving plays to the student body. In many cases these same plays are presented to the public during vacations in various places about the state where they serve both the purpose of advertising the school and as a worth-while entertainment to the public. At least five of these schools are worthy of consideration though time does not permit their being discussed in detail. Among these I would mention Cornell for its very fine theater and for the many plays given; Harvard for its drama writing; the University of North Carolina, under Professor Koch, for its reproductions in drama of local folk-tales and legend; Yale for its splendid school of drama, under Professor Baker, formerly at Harvard, and the School of Drama and Acting at the Pittsburgh School of Technology, under Professor Stevens.

There are two very notable results that are coming from this work in the universities and colleges. Courses in drama are given in practically all, and in nearly all plays are regularly presented with the result that a considerable number of the students are being trained in acting, and a large number are prepared to serve as dramatic coaches in high schools, churches and elsewhere and as amateur actors in the communities to which they go. More and more these university and college groups are going about the country during their vacations and presenting plays. With these new developments is coming a possibility of educational drama on a scope scarcely realized at present, which may give to America another great educational force comparable to what drama was to ancient Greece.

THE EDUCATIONAL DRAMA

The world to-day is faced with a new need. The hours of labor are being shortened every year. We have gone from a seventy-two-hour week to a forty-four-hour week in half a century. Ford has recently established a forty-hour week, and the Federation of Labor has taken the forty-hour week as one of its slogans. Everything seems to indicate that within less than a generation we shall have a week that is yet shorter than this. There is an increase in machines here such as the world has never seen before. There is an enormous increase of steam and electrical power. The efficiency movement has taught us how to do much more work in a shorter time and with less effort than formerly. Production is outrunning consumption everywhere. There seems to be no solution but a shorter day.

Henry Ford tells us that the secret of prosperity is a short working day and high wages. High wages in order that we may buy, short working hours in order that we may need. If labor does as much work in a four-hour day as it has been doing in eight, there is no reason why it should not be paid as much.

We have scarcely begun to train for this leisure. Continual attendance at the movies is little better than dissipation. Baseball, football and basketball do not carry over. What better recreation could we offer to the public than a worthy type of drama through amateur and professional players under the direction of our educational authorities? The theater in Greece and in Rome was a great public educational institution, offering free to the public great masterpieces of literature. Nearly every city of any importance in Europe has its municipal theater, publicly subsidized, which is giving high-type plays. France has its national theater in the *Théâtre Français*. But the difficulty with a national theater is that it is necessarily a local institution by whatever name we may call it, though it may influence powerfully drama throughout the country. Would it not be better to nationalize the players rather than the theater? The players can move about so as to reach the whole country, but the theater must remain where it is built. If we were to place under our national Bureau of Education troupes of actors to give in the high-school auditoriums such plays as Drinkwater's "Abraham Lincoln" and other great American dramas it might become a tremendous force both in education and Americanization.

Let the extension departments of our universities route its university troupes through the high-school auditoriums to give classic dramas to the high school in the afternoon and more popular plays to the public in the evening and we should bring into action a great new educational force that could be offered to the public at a price that the public could afford. It would make the literary dramas of the high school much more real and vital in the lives of the students and it would give to the public a better entertainment in the evening than is now available and at a lower cost.

To the university actor who is thus introduced to the public, this should be an experience that is comparable to the year of travel which is often prescribed for the completion of an education. It would give a familiarity with cities and a vital experience in meeting people. It should give breadth of view and self-confidence in public that would prepare the college man or woman to take his or her place as a leader in community life. A month or six months of such acting might properly be credited toward a college degree.

EDUCATIONAL EVENTS

PEKING UNION MEDICAL COLLEGE

IN his review of the activities of the Rockefeller Foundation President George E. Vincent says that in the foundation's program of medical education the Peking Union Medical College is unique. It is the only medical center for teaching and research to which the foundation has contributed the entire cost of land, buildings, equipment and maintenance. This policy was deemed necessary, since there were no universities or government agencies in a position to assume responsibility when the college was established. These were the only terms on which it then seemed possible to set up in China an adequately equipped and staffed school which would maintain high standards of teaching and investigation, train leaders in the medical sciences and in nursing, offer opportunities for graduate study, emphasize in the medical course the meaning of public health and gradually diffuse among leaders in China understanding and appreciation of modern scientific methods in the care and prevention of disease.

The work of the college has developed gradually without interruption or setback. In spite of disturbed conditions there has been no hostility shown towards the institution, which has scrupulously avoided any semblance of political partisanship.

During 1928 steps were taken towards the possibly remote but none the less steadily sought goal of making the Peking Union Medical College a Chinese institution, serving the Chinese people, staffed mainly by Chinese citizens and administered under Chinese auspices. The Rockefeller Foundation waived its right to appoint a majority of the board of trustees of the college, and with the consent of other organizations which previously appointed representatives on the board, the board of trustees was made self-perpetuating.

During the year the China Medical Board, Inc., with a self-perpetuating board of trustees, quite independent of the Rockefeller Foundation, was formed. To this board the foundation turned over an endowment of $12,000,000 for the maintenance of the Peking Union Medical College, but with the proviso that such funds may be used for the support of other educational institutions in China or in the United States, should it seem at any time in the future inadvisable to continue the present arrangement. The land, buildings and equipment held by the foundation for the Peking Union Medical College were also transferred to the China Medical Board, Inc. The latter board has leased the property to the college.

THE BRITISH SCHOOL AT YPRES

Field-Marshal Lord Plumer and Archbishop Lord Davidson have given their support, according to a report in the London *Times*, to a scheme providing for the education, at the cost of some of the schools of England, of a number of British children at the British School at Ypres in memory of those who fell in the defense of the Ypres Salient. An appeal, bearing their signatures, has been addressed to the headmasters of schools. It points out that the defense of the Ypres Salient was probably the most important and the most successful task entrusted to the British Army in the Great War, adding:

About 250,000 soldiers here gave their lives for their country. A church has been built at Ypres by public subscription. Close to the church Eton has built a school for the children of those British subjects who have the care of the British cemeteries there and in the neighborhood, whom we must all wish to see educated as citizens of their own country. The school was opened in April with about fifty children, and more are now joining from the neighborhood on the Imperial War Graves Commission undertaking to convey them free of charge from neighboring villages. The London County Council has lent to the school two excellent teachers, Mr. and Mrs. Morris, and a third, resident at Ypres, has been engaged as an assistant.

Each parent pays about 150f. per annum—the sum which he would pay at a Belgian school. Over and above this amount it is calculated that the education of each child will cost about £10 per annum. It has been decided that some of the schools of England should be asked to educate a fixed number of children, the boys' schools making the undertaking for the boys and the girls' schools for the girls. Eton is ready to be responsible for ten boys. Will you, after consultation with your boys, or your Old Boys' Association, or both, help on the lines here indicated? Such an enterprise would be a fine memorial made by their relations and friends of those who died in defending the Salient.

The trustees of the school are the Bishop of Fulham (North and Central Europe), the Chaplain-General to the Forces and the Provost of Eton. There is a local committee of management at Ypres consisting of the Rev. G. R. Milner, Chaplain at Ypres, and Captain Perrott and Mr. Melles, of the Imperial War Graves Commission. A committee of ladies has been formed to take a special interest in the girls attending the school, consisting of Lady Plumer (*chairman*); the Hon. Mrs. H. Adeane; Lady Pulteney and Lady Ware, with power to add to their number. We consider that the maintenance of such a school at Ypres would be a very appropriate gift from the schools of Britain. Any guaranteed support should be for a period of ten years, after which the whole situation would be reviewed.

LIBRARY EXTENSION IN BRITISH COLUMBIA

PROGRESS in library extension in British Columbia now hinges on the action the provincial government will take upon the report of the British Columbia Library Survey Council now before it. If the government will increase its appropriation for public library service, a grant of $100,000 from the Carnegie Corporation will be available for the carrying out of some of the projects suggested in the report of the council. This report, which includes a program for the future library development of British Columbia, recommends:

Unification of supervision of all public library affairs in a public library commission of seven members, including the superintendent of schools, the provincial librarian and five others to be appointed. As an educational agency, this commission should be responsible to the minister of education.

The carrying out of public library policy, as determined by this commission, through a capable director and professional staff qualified by ability, training and experience.

That the commission be given adequate authority to supervise all library work supported in whole or in part by provincial or local public grants, to administer the provincial grant in aid of public libraries, to promote and encourage the extension of public library service, to conduct a provincial library service where local organization and support is not yet possible and to cooperate with other libraries.

Recognition, in all plans for public library service, of the business principles of centralization of administration for both economy and efficiency, local distribution of books for the frequent interchange of book stock essential to satisfactory library service, and the assistance of the trained librarian for effective book use.

The development of local financial support and administration as early as possible.

Continuing the law relative to municipal public libraries and encouraging them through adequate assistance by provincial grant.

Using the principles of the county library system in a library district composed of municipal and school units cooperating for this purpose. The county library system is highly successful in Great Britain and the United States and is the only form of public library organization now known which can give adequate public library service in rural communities at reasonable cost.

Developing libraries for schools, with school collections and the use of all other available library facilities, under the direction of a supervisor of school libraries qualified for school library service.

Developing a library service for the sea-coast settlements through boat transportation.

Continuing the law relative to public library associations and developing them into agencies of a wider system for free public library service.

Continuing the traveling library system and developing it through the use of one or more depots in the interior with a trained librarian in charge.

An order for printing the report has been sent to the government printers.

The history of the report is a story of concerted action on the part of librarians, educators and laymen interested in the library movement in the province. Over 2,000 persons contributed information for it. The survey which is the basis for the report was initiated by the British Columbia Library Commission, headed by Dr. Norman J. Black. A research board, composed of the library commission and leading librarians, carried on the work and reported its findings to a survey council of representative and outstanding laymen. A grant from the Carnegie Corporation to the Library Commission made it possible to call in C. B. Lester, chairman of the American Library Association Committee on Library Extension, to complete the survey.

OFFENSES COMMITTED BY CONTINUATION SCHOOL BOYS IN NEW YORK STATE

THE working boy of 14, 15 and 16 years of age who is attending continuation school in New York State seldom falls into mischief, according to a report of the industrial education bureau of the State Education Department. In a recent investigation of 65,000 continuation school boys in the state, the bureau found that 89 per cent. of them had never been arrested. Of the eleven per cent. who had been arrested, theft was found to be the cause in 2 per cent. of the cases and trespassing, truancy, creating disturbance, crap shooting and "reasons not given" for one per cent. each. Over thirty reasons for arrests were reported by the boys, but most of them were for such slight offenses as having an unmuzzled dog, riding a bicycle on the sidewalk, playing Sunday baseball and staying out late at night. In addition to theft, arson and crimes against the person were the only serious offenses given.

The investigation showed that among the large cities of the state, New York City had proportionately the fewest number of continuation school boys who had been arrested, 7 per cent. as against 11 per cent. for the state. The chief offense in the metropolitan district was crap shooting, for which 1.1 per cent. had been arrested. Theft was second with approximately 1 per cent. Other causes of arrest in order of importance were: creating a disturbance, trespassing, truancy, selling without a permit, smashing windows and disorderly conduct.

The study showed a wide variation in what communities, through their police officers, consider offenses warranting arrest. In one community over one third of the boys reporting had been arrested, in another, only 7 per cent. Leniency might be shown in some cases and strictness in others. In some towns no objection is made to track walking, in others it may be subject to arrest.

So far as remedies are concerned, in some cases the school can help in providing wholesome recreation or make an effort to counteract a bad home environment with a line of work that will interest the boy, hold his attention and lead him into the occupation he is best fitted to do.

Cities and towns can help by providing playgrounds where the working boy can release his pent-up desire to "do something," and where the doing will be guided in the right direction. With few exceptions any boy of these ages can be interested in something that will lead to right instead of wrong. To discover that interest is our problem as educators.

SUMMERFIELD SCHOLARSHIPS AT THE UNIVERSITY OF KANSAS

THE newly established Summerfield scholarships at the University of Kansas are the gift of Solon E. Summerfield, New York manufacturer, who received degrees from the University of Kansas in 1899 and 1901. He is a native of Lawrence, and his father, a physician, was at one time a professor in the university's School of Law.

Nominations for the scholarships, according to an announcement made by Professor Olin Templin, chairman of the committee of award, are to be in the hands of the faculty committee by June 24, and examinations are to be held at a number of cities in Kansas on July 2 to select a group from which the final selection of five to ten scholars will be made.

Mr. Summerfield, in announcing the establishment of the scholarships, said that he was planning to give $5,000 for the academic year 1929–30; $10,000 for 1930–31; $15,000 for 1931–32, and $20,000 each year thereafter, and he added that provision would be made for an income of at least $20,000 annually in perpetuity.

His purpose is to enable young men graduating from Kansas high schools to pursue a college course unhampered by financial worries, and to this end he directs that the five or more scholarships awarded each year shall be renewable for a term of four years, provided the scholastic standards of the scholar merit it. Thus twenty and perhaps as many as forty Summerfield scholars will be on the campus at one time when the plan is in full operation.

The gift to the university was made through the University of Kansas Endowment Association, of which Mr. Summerfield is a trustee, and Professor Olin Templin is secretary. The amount is sufficient, Professor Templin said, to pay all expenses of at least five students, but in order to emphasize the scholastic phase of the awards, it is planned to make the stipend of each scholar dependent on his needs, and it is believed that as many as ten may be appointed at one time.

Upon announcement of the gift, Chancellor E. H. Lindley appointed this faculty committee to conduct examinations and determine the awarding of the scholarships: Professor Templin, chairman; Dr. E. B. Stouffer, dean of the Graduate School; Professor John Ise; Professor U. G. Mitchell; Professor Paul B. Lawson, associate dean of the College of Liberal Arts, and Irving Hill, of Lawrence, and Frank

G. Crowell, Kansas City, Mo., members of the Endowment Association trustees.

It is expected that contestants successful in the preliminary examinations in the cities of the state will be at the university about the middle of July for final examination, and for the selection of the first group of Summerfield scholars.

THE SUMMER SCHOOL OF HARVARD UNIVERSITY

THE director of the Harvard Summer School, Philip P. Chase, has made public a statement that Harvard is preparing the freshman dormitories, which front the Charles River, to receive the major part of the Harvard summer population of about 2,700 students.

Harvard is announcing a curriculum which is larger than ever, and affords a choice ranging from astronomy to post-war European history. Thirty-seven professors and instructors, a number of national reputation, are from other colleges and universities. In addition eighty members of the Harvard teaching staff will serve throughout the summer.

The scope of the summer courses has grown rapidly in recent years, particularly in the field of the graduate school of arts and sciences. While the courses in education have been growing with the rest, it is in the field of general academic studies, and particularly the humanities, that the greatest recent growth has come.

The summer school group is said to present many contrasts to that of the regular academic year. Almost half the students are women; the average age of the student body and the spread between the oldest and youngest is far greater in the summer, and the variety of previous educational experience of the students is naturally very great. Among these numbers are included two types of Harvard undergraduates, those making up courses in which they are deficient, and candidates for honors who desire to anticipate course-work in order to devote their senior year to study in their special field.

About half the students taking courses for credit aim for a degree, for which they have been studying while teaching. Another group has been rapidly increasing in recent years, the aggregation of graduate and undergraduate students of other institutions who have been attracted to Harvard by the special facilities offered by the collections in the libraries and museums. There are, in addition, men and women of mature years with no present academic connections, who see in such an educational center as Harvard an opportunity for general cultural development.

The four freshman dormitories are turned over to the students. The men are quartered in the Smith Halls quadrangle, and the women students in the other three freshman halls. The tennis courts of Soldiers Field, and the Weld Boat Club are available for the use of students. Many entertainments and excursions are planned for their benefit, with Yard concerts, special evening lectures and visits to important points of interest in and around Boston.

The school begins on July 8 and closes on August 17. From Monday to Friday the course instruction is uninterrupted throughout each week. Except in language courses, which are an hour and a half long, instruction is usually for a period of an hour a day, five days a week.

THE DEPARTMENT OF SUPERINTENDENCE AT ATLANTA

S. D. SHANKLAND, executive secretary, has addressed a letter to members of the Department of Superintendence, in which he calls attention to the sixty-seventh annual summer meeting of the National Education Association to be held at Atlanta, Georgia, from June 28 to July 4, with opening session in the Atlanta Auditorium on Friday evening, June 28. The convention will close with a patriotic meeting on Thursday morning, July 4.

On Monday afternoon, July 1, Superintendent Frank Cody, of Detroit, Michigan, president of the Department of Superintendence, will conduct a conference of superintendents of schools. A breakfast in honor of Superintendent Cody will be held in the Ansley Hotel, on Tuesday morning, July 2, at 7:30.

A conference of superintendents of schools will be held with the following program:

MONDAY, JULY 1, 2:00 P. M.
BALLROOM, CAPITAL CITY CLUB.

Chairman, Frank Cody, superintendent of schools, Detroit, Michigan, and president of the Department of Superintendence

General Theme: Equalization of Educational Opportunity—A Financial Problem.

How Methods of Finance Affect the Schools: A. L. Threlkeld, superintendent of schools, Denver, Colorado.

Educational Adjustments to Meet the Changing Economic and Industrial Conditions of the South: Robert E. Tidwell, state superintendent of education, Montgomery, Alabama.

Is the Elementary School Getting a Fair Share of the Public Money? Kate V. Wofford, county superintendent of schools, Laurens, South Carolina.

Signs of Progress—Reports from the Field: Nicholas Bauer, superintendent of schools, New Orleans, Louisiana; C. A. Brown, associate superintendent of schools, Birmingham, Alabama.

HONORARY DEGREES CONFERRED BY NEW YORK UNIVERSITY

Owing to the illness of Chancellor Elmer Ellsworth Brown, Dr. W. H. Nichols presided over the commencement exercises of New York University. Among the honorary degrees conferred was the doctorate of literature on Dr. Frank Parker Day, recently elected president of Union College; the doctorate of science on Dr. Robert A. Millikan, director of the Norman Bridge Laboratory of the California Institute of Technology, and the doctorate of commercial science on Mr. James Herbert McGraw, the publisher. In conferring these degrees Dr. Nichols spoke as follows:

Frank Parker Day—Graduate of Oxford University; colonel in command of Canadian forces in the Great War; scholar, educator, author; president of Union College, is presented for the degree of doctor of literature. You have had wide intercourse with books, with scholars, with men of affairs, yourself ''not least but honored of them all.'' This large experience is for you an arch wherethrough you look forth upon your great new enterprise. As executive of a great college and university, you are the successor of some of the greatest of American educators of an earlier day; a worthy and creative successor we confidently hope and believe.

Robert Andrews Millikan—Physicist; educated in Oberlin, Columbia and Berlin; recognized by many institutions of learning as a foremost leader in scientific research; a son of the manse whose discoveries in the physical world have not blinded him to spiritual realities, is presented for the degree of doctor of science.

James Herbert McGraw—Teacher, publisher of many technical periodicals, broad-minded and far-seeing man of business, is presented for the honorary degree of doctor of commercial science. Educator, transformed into publisher, you have never ceased to be an educator. Your notable career accentuates that tendency in commercial life through which, however private in its form, its operations have a public character and become an element in public education.

EDUCATIONAL NOTES AND NEWS

Dr. Robert G. Sproul has been elected president of the University of California to succeed Dr. W. W. Campbell who recently resigned, his resignation to take effect on July 1, 1930. Dr. Sproul has been comptroller of the university and secretary of the board of regents and since 1925 vice-president. Previously he had been engaged in business undertakings in San Francisco.

Professor Edward Wilber Berry, professor of paleontology in the Johns Hopkins University, has been appointed dean and provost in succession to Dr. Joseph S. Ames, whose election to the presidency was announced in School and Society last week.

Dr. Arlo Ayres Brown, president of the University of Chattanooga, who has been chosen president of Drew University, formerly the Drew Theological Seminary, at Madison, N. J., will be inaugurated on October 17. Dr. Brown succeeds President Ezra Squier Tipple, who announced his resignation last winter after seventeen years in office.

A. B. Ramsay, master of Magdalene College, has been elected vice-chancellor of the University of Cambridge for the academic year beginning October 1.

The Duke of Northumberland was recently installed as chancellor of Durham University in succession to the late Lord Durham. Sir Thomas Oliver, vice-chancellor, presided.

Among the degrees conferred by Columbia University at its recent commencement was the doctorate of letters on George A. Plimpton, president of the board of trustees of Amherst College and treasurer of the trustees of Barnard College.

DR. DANIEL L. MARSH, president of Boston University, was granted the honorary degree of doctor of the humanities at the commencement exercises of Cornell College, Mt. Vernon, Iowa. Dr. Marsh was the commencement speaker.

DR. ELIOT R. PAYSON, oldest member of the Rutgers University faculty and professor of the history of education since 1892, was awarded the degree of doctor of letters by the university on June 7.

AT the one hundred and sixty-first commencement of Brown University, the degree of doctor of education was conferred on Mr. Isaac O. Winslow, superintendent of the schools of Providence, Rhode Island.

ROLLINS COLLEGE has conferred on Harry Jewett Jeschke, of Benton Harbor, Michigan, the honorary degree of L.H.D., in recognition of his contribution to public-school education as author, editor and publisher of elementary textbooks.

OHIO WESLEYAN UNIVERSITY recently conferred the degree of doctor of laws upon Baron Shosuke Sato, president of the Hokkaido Imperial University, Japan.

A ROOSEVELT medal for distinguished service has been awarded to Dr. Herbert Putnam, for thirty years librarian of Congress, during which he has developed the library from an inadequately organized collection of little more than local importance "into an institution, national in its scope, international in its renown, whose contents place it beside the largest libraries in the world and whose range of activities is greater and more diversified than that of any other library."

THE Brown Club of Chicago has presented to Brown University a portrait of Dean Otis E. Randall, who will retire next year. He has been a teacher of mechanics and mechanical drawing at the university for forty-four years and has been dean since 1912.

AT the commencement exercises at the Johns Hopkins University on June 11, presentation was made to Dr. Frank J. Goodnow, its retiring president, of an appreciation of his fifteen years' service to the university by Judge Henry J. Harlan, on behalf of the trustees. Judge Harlan reviewed the many important achievements during Dr. Goodnow's administration and remarked that there had not been a single jarring note during his incumbency. A bronze medallion of Dr. Goodnow by Max Miller was presented to the retiring president by Dr. William H. Howell on behalf of the faculty.

AT the close of the commencement exercises at Brown University nearly 1,500 of the alumni gathered in the new Brown gymnasium at Aldrich Field for the luncheon, at which Dr. Faunce appeared for the last time as president of the university. He sat on the platform while alumni thanked him for his guidance, advice and friendship. An illuminated parchment, a testimonial of his leadership from the thirty classes graduated under him, and a book of autographs of corporation and faculty associates was presented to him. The testimonial from the thirty classes was presented to Dr. Faunce by Justice Fred T. Field, of the Massachusetts Supreme Court. Dr. Harry Lyman Koopman, librarian of the university, presented the volume of autographs in behalf of Dr. Faunce's colleagues. The speakers, all of whom paid tribute to the leadership of Dr. Faunce, were the Reverend Dr. Harry Emerson Fosdick, of New York; Bainbridge Colby, of New York, former secretary of state; Professor Zechariah Chafee, Jr., of the Harvard Law School, and Professor-emeritus Walter Goodnow Everett, who presided.

DR. EDWIN POST, dean of the college of liberal arts at De Pauw University, has completed fifty years as professor of Latin.

HERBERT F. GOODRICH, professor of law at the University of Michigan and adviser on professional and public relations of the American Law Institute, has been named dean of the University of Pennsylvania Law School. Dr. John Dickinson, of Princeton University, and Dr. Francis S. Philbrick, of the University of Illinois, have been appointed professors of law. Dr. William E. Mikell, who has been dean of the law school, and Professor Henry Wolfe Bikle will retire.

DR. KARL C. LEEBRICK, professor of political science and history at the University of Hawaii, has accepted the deanship of the college of liberal arts at Syracuse University, his appointment to take effect at once.

DR. JOHN RICHARD MEZ, for the past five years with the faculty of economics at the University of Arizona, has been appointed associate professor of economics and political science at the University of Oregon.

WILLIAM PEARSON TOLLEY, acting dean of Brothers College, Drew University, Madison, N. J., has been made dean of the college. Earl A. Aldrich, of Tufts College, has been made professor of English literature and head of the department.

ALLAN C. VALENTINE, assistant professor of English at Swarthmore College, has been made dean of men to succeed Dr. Detlev Bronk, who has been appointed director of the Eldridge R. Johnson Foundation for Research in Medical Physics at the University of Pennsylvania.

CLARK LEONARD HULL, professor of psychology and director of the psychological laboratory at the University of Wisconsin, has been elected professor of psychology in Yale University.

WAYNE DENNIS, of the department of psychology at Michigan State College, has been made acting assistant professor of psychology at the University of Virginia.

DR. DIXON RYAN FOX, professor of history at Columbia University, has been appointed visiting professor at Yale University.

HERBERT G. ESPY has been appointed assistant professor of education in the University of Rochester.

LINDSAY BROWN has been made librarian of the Free Public Library of New Haven, Connecticut, where he was assistant librarian from 1921 to 1925. For the past four years he has been librarian of the Silas Bronson Library, Waterbury, Connecticut.

PROFESSOR JOSEPH MAYER, of Tufts College, will be on leave of absence in the year 1929–30 in charge of the permanent office of the American Association of University Professors in Washington.

DR. WILLIAM WISTAR COMFORT, president of Haverford College and professor of Romance languages, has accepted an invitation to give two courses in the department of French during the coming summer session of the University of California, from July 1 to August 10. The subjects of his lectures are: "A Survey of French Literature and Culture" and "French Literature, 1789–1850."

DR. SIDNEY B. FAY, professor of European history at Smith College, will lecture at Harvard University and Radcliffe College next year on European history in the nineteenth and twentieth centuries.

PROFESSOR G. A. JAEDERHOLM, of the University of Gothenburg, recently arrived in New York City. He will deliver a series of lectures on psychology at the University of California.

DR. THOMAS S. BAKER, president of the Carnegie Institute of Technology, sailed on June 13 for Europe to consult scientific men in Europe in regard to developments at the institution. One of his objects is to establish at the institute a coal research laboratory.

DR. ROBERT M. YERKES, professor of psychology at the institute of psychology, Yale University, has started on an extended professional trip to Europe and Africa. He will go as far south as French Guinea and as far east as Moscow. He is traveling in the interest of his work on anthropoid apes, especially the chimpanzee.

SAILING June 21 from Montreal on the *S. S. Antonia,* a group of educators from all parts of the United States will start a new summer tour under the direction of Dr. Jesse B. Davis, professor of education at the school of education of Boston University. The group will travel through England, Germany, France and Sweden for observation of methods of education in the secondary schools of those countries. From the University of Heidelberg, they will proceed on July 26 to Geneva, Switzerland, where they will attend the conference of the World's Federation of Education Associations.

FOUR eminent authorities of the University of Chicago are lecturers at the sixth annual Institute of the Norman Wait Harris Memorial

Foundation at the University of Chicago, which opened on June 17 and continues to June 27. The institute is devoted to a discussion of the problems of population and migration in all its phases. The lecturers are: Corrado Gini, professor of economics at the University of Rome, director of the Central Statistical Bureau, Rome, and member of the Fascisti Grand Council; Shiroshi Nasu, professor of rural economics at the University of Tokyo and writer on Japanese food and population problems; Robert R. Kuczinski, professor of economics, Berlin Handelshochschule, formerly director of the Municipal Statistical Office, Berlin-Schoenberg, and author of numerous books on economic problems, and Oliver E. Baker, economic geographer, division of land economics of the U. S. Department of Agriculture, an authority on climate and geography in relation to agriculture. During the institute round tables consisting of a limited number of invited guests have been organized to discuss phases of the general problem. Among those who accepted invitations to attend are Dr. Raymond Pearl, professor of biology and director of the institute for biological research of the Johns Hopkins University; Dr. Charles B. Davenport, director of the Eugenics Laboratory, Cold Spring Harbor, New York; Dr. Warren S. Thompson, director of the Scripps Foundation for Population Research; Dr. Louis I. Dublin, statistician of the Metropolitan Life Insurance Company; Dr. H. P. Fairchild, professor of sociology, New York University; Mrs. Margaret Sanger, president of the American Birth Control League, and Mr. Robert H. Coats, statistician, Canada.

CORNELL UNIVERSITY has been given $1,500,000 by the General Education Board to assist in the development of a graduate center for scientific research in biophysics. It is conditional upon the university's obtaining a similar amount by June 30, 1930, and is the nucleus of a project which will require the addition of about $9,000,000 to the resources of the university.

A FORMAL announcement of the F. C. Austin Scholarship Foundation at Northwestern University for the training of business executives has been mailed recently to high schools. This foundation was created by F. C. Austin, a Chicago capitalist, by a gift to the university of more than $3,000,000, the income from which is to be used exclusively for scholarships. Five scholars will be assigned for the year 1929–30.

GIFTS amounting to nearly $5,000,000 were announced at the recent commencement exercises at Phillips Academy, Andover, Mass. Two gifts were for $1,000,000 each and one for $1,300,000, all from anonymous donors. The latter gift is for the building of an art gallery and for a collection of American paintings and art. In announcing the gifts, Dr. Alfred E. Stearns, the headmaster, stated that this is an entirely new departure in American secondary schools. One of the $1,000,000 gifts is for an unrestricted fund. The other, to be known as the Emily Cochrane endowment fund, will be used in caring for and maintaining the grounds of Phillips Academy. Other gifts ranging from $1,000 to $700,000 will be used for a new dining hall, a new heating plant, bird sanctuary now under construction, a science fund and a fund for sundry purposes amounting to $217,450.

THE sum of $500,000 has been provided by the will of Kennedy T. Friend, a lawyer of Pittsburgh, for the education of the children of members of the Allegheny County bar. They will be sent to Yale University and to the University of Paris.

THE Harvard Corporation has appropriated $200,000 for the erection of a faculty club which is to be ready in September, 1930.

COLONEL ROBERT W. STEWART, of Chicago, former chairman of the board of directors of the Standard Oil Company of Indiana, has given $200,000 to Coe College for a memorial library in honor of his father and mother.

PLANS for a second wing to be constructed to the new Burris School, which is being erected as a demonstration school at Ball State Teachers College, Muncie, Indiana, were completed on June 7. This south wing, which was planned before the main part of the building was completed and which will cost approximately $50,000, will house the physical education department. The contract for the construction of a north wing, which also had been planned before the completion of the main building, has been awarded to A. J. Glaser. This wing, which will cost $69,000, will house the industrial arts, home economics, chemistry, physics, music and arts departments. The entire building is being built at an approximate cost of $360,000. It is of English Gothic architecture and harmonizes with the other new buildings on the campus and with the new Ball Memorial Hospital, which adjoins the campus and which is being built at a cost of $1,000,000. The Ball brothers have been generous donors to the college, which they purchased in 1918 and gave to the state of Indiana.

A LIBRARY for all South Africa is the plan of Milton J. Ferguson, of California, and S. A. Pitt, of the Glasgow Library, who are on a visit to the Union and Rhodesia on behalf of the Carnegie Corporation. The proposals, which will probably be carried out in conjunction with the municipal and state libraries, teachers' associations and universities, involve a network of district libraries spreading from a central library in each province, which, in turn, would be served from a national library. There would be a free exchange of books to serve the demands of each district, and by utilizing the telephone and organizing a rapid service there would be no delay. How Johannesburg might form part of some such system was suggested in an address by Mr. Pitt. The small towns on the East and West Rand might cooperate with Johannesburg as a federated community for library services, he said. Having been found successful in Scotland and America, the system was now being established in England. Mr. Ferguson said that conditions in California, where he had been engaged in library work, were similar to South African conditions, and he claimed that through the public library Californians far removed from populous centers had ample facilities for obtaining books.

THE majority of the Australian commission appointed to inquire into the subject of child endowment has reported adversely on its establishment either as a commonwealth or state scheme. The minority, which consisted of two, advocated the payment of an endowment for all children exceeding two in a family and for all the dependent children of widows. Further ministerial action is unlikely. The subject of child endowment was raised at the Conference of State Premiers in June, 1927, and in the following September a committee was set up to inquire into its feasibility. The states were favorably inclined to the project, and New South Wales elaborated a scheme of its own, but all were agreed that a federal scheme was best.

THE American University Union in London sends to the Institute of International Education a request for cooperation in spreading a warning to American college students who entertain the idea of going to the British Isles with insufficient funds to maintain themselves or to buy a return passage, in the hope of securing remunerative employment there. Of late there has been a growing number of cases of Americans destitute in England and dependent upon the aid of the American Red Cross, the American Relief Society, or the American Consular Service, whose resources are inadequate to care for the number who apply for aid. The attention of the adventurous student who hopes to find employment when he reaches Europe is called to the fact of the general unemployment situation prevalent throughout the British Isles, and to the consequent strict practice of employing none but British subjects. So serious has become the situation of Americans stranded in Europe that general warnings have been issued through the Association of American Colleges, the National Association of State Universities and the Association of Land-Grant Colleges and Universities.

THE Universities Bureau of the British Empire has issued a report of the proceedings of the annual conference of the universities of Great Britain and Ireland, held this year at Liverpool. According to *Nature*, the only subject discussed was "The Contribution of the Universities to the Preparation of Teachers for their Vocation," considered under the heads—What is the essential service which a university can render to the education of the intending teacher, and what should be the relation of universities to the specialized professional training of teachers? The discussion revealed striking diversities of opinion. Sir Charles Robertson (Birmingham) maintained that not merely should there be nothing vocational whatever in the degree courses of would-be teachers, but while studying for their degrees these aspirants should forget their intention to become teachers. Mr. Culverwell (Dublin), on the contrary, held that they should all along realize the bearing of the degree course on their future work, and Professor Strong (Leeds) urged the institution of a degree course having a more definite relation to the work of teaching than any at present provided. Mrs. Simon (Manchester) proposed the abolition of university training departments; Professor Nunn (London), that they should confine themselves to the field of adolescent education; whilst Mr. Boyd (Glasgow) upheld the Scottish ideal of a university degree course for every teacher, and suggested "a rethinking of our training system along the lines of the medical analogy." There was a marked cleavage between the speakers who accepted and those who rejected this analogy between training for the medical profession and training for teaching. In answer to criticisms of the present system of training grants, Lord Eustace Percy said he would be glad to receive from any university a definite scheme for a ch[illegible]er from a grant for intending teachers [illegible]omething in the shape of an additional state scholarship scheme.

THE Federation of British Industries, as we learn from the London *Times*, has completed the compilation of a catalogue of educational films, which it is issuing to all educational authorities throughout the British Empire. The federation includes a film manufacturers' group, which has felt that a first and necessary step towards encouraging the use of the film as a medium for education would be the existence of a comprehensive catalogue of the educational films at present available. The book now issued has been compiled in consultation with representatives of leading educational bodies, and it is to be added to from time to time. In a preface the hope is expressed that it may be of assistance to teachers and others in adopting this type of visual education. While every care has been taken in the selection of films included in the catalogue, no guarantee can be given that every film will be considered by all teachers of educational value. The catalogue represents the best of the films, both of the standard size as used in picture theaters and the subnormal size suitable for the classroom. There is no pretension on the part of the federation to claim that the catalogue is complete, but it is felt that when manufacturers are assured of a market for the disposal of their goods by the support of educational authorities as a whole, they will be ready to fill every want that is likely to occur.

BY the terms of its concession, according to the *U. S. Daily,* the Hungarian Dutch Pedagogical Company must arrange for all primary, grammar and higher grade schools, excepting the municipal schools of Budapest, eight motion-picture exhibitions annually, one each month of the school year from October to June, inclusive. In the post-graduate schools five exhibitions must be held during the months of November to March. The programs shown are supervised by the Ministry of Public Education through its pedagogical film board and through the board of film censors. The Ministry of the Interior has directed that in those places where the schools are not equipped with proper exhibition halls or projectors, the motion-picture theater operators must provide facilities for the showing of these educational films. The films are exhibited during regular school hours and each pupil is required to pay an annual attendance fee of 2.24 pengo (approximately $0.40) annually, or $0.05 per film. Films were shown by the Hungarian Dutch Pedagogical Company during the first year of its concession in 170 communities.

THE *Journal* of the American Medical Association states that in connection with the installation of the new superior council on public instruction of Italy, Minister Belluzzo recently delivered an address in which he discussed the question of the organization and functioning of the universities. Some hold that Italy has too many universities, and that it is advisable to reduce the number, but the minister expressed himself as opposed to the suppression of the existing university seats, all of which were founded when the population of the realm was much less than now, and when the fields of science (technology in particular) were more restricted. It would appear to him more feasible to diminish in some of the universities the number of faculties, and, above all, to concentrate certain subjects that, to-day, are broken up, owing to the rather too large number of professorial chairs. The study of the question of reorganization of universities will be taken up by the new superior council. Another problem that the head of the government desires shall be given careful consideration and brought to a final solution is that concerning the university scientific laboratories, which should be equipped with more modern apparatus and have more adequate facilities, in order that they may be available for all the students pursuing subjects of a scientific and professional character, such as medicine and the natural sciences, agriculture, engineering and chemistry.

The report of the Royal Scottish Museum, Edinburgh, for 1928 states that, in spite of the steadily increasing facilities for entertainment in the city, the number of visitors to the museum continues to increase. The total for the year was 505,532, which shows that the museum maintains its position as one of the most attractive public institutions in the country. Thousands of working-class people visit the museum on Sunday afternoons. The Education Authority continues to take advantage of the museum for education by sending classes from their schools to attend special lantern lectures given by the staff, which are followed by case demonstration. Sixty-eight classes, containing in all 2,138 children, attended these lectures during the autumn and spring terms. A number of school classes also pay visits under their own teachers, some of them coming for instruction in art, engineering, or nature science and others for drawing.

The progress of education under the present régime in Mexico was recently outlined in the Community Church of New York City in an address by Dr. Moises Saenz, a member of the Mexican Ministry of Education. The Mexican government, since 1922, he said, has established 4,000 new rural schools which have become community social and cultural centers. One of the greatest benefits of the present government, Dr. Saenz declared, has been its devotion to educational problems, and its hope is to spend four or five times as much money on education in the future. Emphasis, he said, is laid on the rural schools because it is through them that the majority of the country's 4,000,000 Indians are reached. The government is endeavoring, he said, to incorporate the Indians into a homogeneous population.

According to a despatch to the New York *Times*, from Angora, Mustapha Kemal Pasha's major reform in the westernization of Turkey went into effect officially on June 1. Since that date Arabic writing has been entirely forbidden throughout the country and all Turks are required to use the Latin characters which they have been learning in special government schools. Although state papers have been written in the Latin alphabet ever since the reform was first inaugurated, Arabic letters were permitted in private commu[illegible]ange-ov[illegible] During this time all citizens between [illegible]s to s[illegible] of sixteen and forty have been required to attend the national schools to learn the new characters. The reform has proved so popular that people more than forty years of age have attended the classes, some of which have been taught by Kemal himself. The death of Nedjati Bey, the young Minister of Public Instruction, who had charge of the reform program, has not brought any relaxation in the government's efforts to teach the new alphabet to the 14,000,000 inhabitants. Premier Ismet Pasha temporarily took over the portfolio and continued the campaign. It is learned that Wasfi Bey, who has resigned as Ambassador to Moscow and who formerly was Minister of Public Instruction, will succeed Nedjati.

DISCUSSION

SOURCES OF INFORMATION COVERING RESEARCH IN PROGRESS AND UNIVERSITY DISSERTATIONS

Specific information covering research in progress in American universities in connection with the doctoral dissertations in the humanistic and social sciences is quite incomplete. At a time when exact information covering some fields of research is available, we also find several other fields where it is sometimes exceedingly difficult to find out exactly what is going on. The fields that are covered are taken care of in various periodical publications, scattered sources at best, and not always complete or up to date. These fields are history, political science, economics, Canadian history and economics, Oriental studies and medieval studies. In addition to these, a very few universities publish their own lists of research in progress at those universities.

A brief itemization of where these subject lists appear will serve to show how unsatisfactory is the present situation. History is taken care of in the "List of Doctoral Dissertations in History," now in progress at the chief American universities, published annually by the Department of Historical Research of the Carnegie Institution of Washington. Political science is covered by *The American Political Science Review,* where the latest list appeared in 1925. The one before that was published in 1922, and the preceding ones appeared at irregular intervals. Economics has been listed annually in *The American Economic Review* since 1911. From 1904 to 1910 this list first appeared separately and later in *Bulletins* of the American Economic Association. Canadian history and economics are covered by *The Canadian Historical Review.* This information appeared for the first time in 1927. Oriental studies are listed in *The Journal of the Linguistic Society of America.* Medieval studies are taken care of in "Progress of Medieval Studies in the United States of America." This publication, issued annually since 1923, is edited by Professor Willard, of the University of Colorado, and is now supported by the Medieval Academy of America.

The fact that it is found to be desirable to keep up these lists is significant, for it shows that there is a recognized need for information of this sort. We also see how few of the fields in the humanistic and social sciences are taken care of. When it comes to art and philosophy, for instance, information concerning research in progress can be had only through personal contacts. The secretaries of the various sections of the Modern Language Association often can give information concerning the dissertations in preparation in their respective fields, but no complete lists covering the modern languages exist.

This recital of present conditions seems to make it evident that there is need for systematic handling of the problem. You have, on the one hand, a group of subjects that are covered by lists, to be found in different places, and varying in method and completeness. On the other are subjects not at all covered in any systematic fashion. The logical remedy for this anomalous condition seems to be the publication of one annual list that will include all of the fields in the humanistic and social sciences. Such a list will remove the need for compiling the separate lists by subjects and will do away with the resultant duplication of effort that exists to a certain extent in the compilation of those lists. That list will fill a bad gap in our bibliographical literature. It will become a thing of the past to have a graduate student be compelled to abandon a partly completed dissertation because he has heard that some one else is doing the same subject. It will enable the members of the faculties to know exactly what is going on in the humanistic and social sciences. Such a list will have to omit the bulk of the work in the exact sciences for the simple reason that the student in science does not know what he will find when he starts an experiment. It should be possible, however, to include a few dissertations in science.

Some people will object to such a list on the ground that it will create "bibliographical ghosts," that is, that it will list titles of dissertations which will remain uncompleted. This is a valid criticism, but the same applies to publishers' announcement lists where at times titles are mentioned again and again, but the books fail to materialize. It is usually simple to run down such cases. Also, in the case of dissertations there have been instances where subjects have been staked out for future claims in order to reserve the circumscribed territories. If the proposed list comes into existence it should be understood that it will include only titles on which work is actually planned or under way. This will be a simple specification if everybody concerned will cooperate.

There is another problem closely allied to the one that I have just presented and that has to do with unpublished dissertations in all fields of research. There appears to be a growing tendency in the direction of publishing more and more abstracts of dissertations in annual collections of abstracts issued by the respective universities. In fact, a few universities require only the typed copy of the dissertation. These modified requirements help to reduce the amount of material to be published and handled, and also make it a great deal easier for the graduate student to meet them. The result, however, is that more and more results of research remain unlisted in a systematic fashion.

In addition to the annual collections of abstracts, there are various subject bibliographies in which are included several dissertations, published and unpublished. But you can not be sure of their completeness in this field. The well-edited "Bibliography of English Language and Literature," for instance, which is brought out by the Modern Humanities Research Association, is not complete so far as dissertations are concerned.

The Library of Congress List of Printed Doctoral Dissertations serves very well so far as it goes but it will become less useful as more dissertations remain unpublished. The logical way out of this difficulty points toward the publication of an annual list that will cover all the dissertations presented in American universities and not included in the Library of Congress List.

The two points presented here, therefore, will take care of the research in progress in connection with the preparation of doctoral dissertations in the humanistic and social sciences, as well as complete information covering unpublished dissertations in all fields. An annual volume containing these two lists, arranged by authors, subjects and universities, should fill a gap in our reference literature and will tell the scholar what is being done as well as what has been done.

Lawrence Heyl
Princeton University Library

INSURANCE ENDOWMENT

Endowment insurance has been adopted by a number of colleges and universities in the United States as a method of providing for gifts from the younger alumni. Members of each year's graduating class are asked to pledge themselves under a certain insurance plan ranging in value from $250 to $5,000 and to name their school as beneficiary. This furnishes an easy means by which individual students can aid their alma mater in school development, according to proponents of the plan.

The University of Nebraska, in order to determine whether or not this plan of endowment was working successfully enough in other schools to consider its adoption as a part of its program of developing scholarships, loan funds and prizes, recently sent a questionnaire to sixty-four schools reported to be using the plan.

Forty-four of these questionnaires were returned. On tabulating the replies, however, it was found that but twenty-five were available for tabulation, the other nineteen being necessarily excluded for various reasons. Despite previous information, ten schools reported that they did not have such a plan; one reported that it had been abandoned; one had no data; six used it for teachers' and employees' annuities, and one had a loan plan. Of the twenty-five schools which had tried the plan, five had used it for but one year and four had used it for two years, indicating that but few schools had used the scheme over a long period of time.

The form of policy and plan of insurance varied greatly among the various schools. Four schools had straight life policies, three had twenty-pay life, and nine had some form of endowment, three specifying twenty-year endowment, two twenty-five-year, one fifteen-year and one ten-year. Nine schools gave no information on the matter. A number of the schools gave no information regarding the size of the policies, the answers indicating a range from $250 per person to $5,000, more schools using an individual policy of $1,000 than any other size.

At sixteen of the schools, the insured were selected by their voluntary assumption of the risk; in three schools a limited number, such as class officers, were insured, and in two the entire class was insured. Four schools furnished no information on the subject. Statistics were not forthcoming regarding the exact number insured annually in the majority of cases, the figure varying greatly in the few answers given.

Another of the great points of difference was revealed in the percentage of lapsation, three schools reporting total lapsation of the policies and two reporting no lapsations. Six others reported that the percentage had been large, or more than 50 per cent., while nine replied that it was relatively small. Five furnished no information.

The question, "Has any effort been made by your institution to pay the premiums?" also brought widely divergent answers. Three schools said that efforts were made by the school to pay the premiums; seven replied that no effort was made; three said that some exceptional cases were carried for a short time; two followed a form of using dividends to pay premiums on lapsed policies, and ten schools gave no definite information, the tenor of the replies indicating that no effort had been made to meet the premiums.

At St. Viator College, with a twenty-year endowment policy plan, the percentage of lapsation has been less than 2 per cent., according to the reply, on which the school has paid premiums. At the Massachusetts Institute of Technology the plan has been adopted of keeping up all unpaid policies for a two-year period and of canceling the policy, taking the cash value thereof, in case the holder shows no further interest. Dividends are paid annually by the insurance company to the institute, which uses them to make good the lapses. At St. Olaf College, where the percentage of lapsation has been about 50 per cent., the college has paid all the lapses. Two other schools use some form of organization whereby the policy earnings protect the lapsed policies. At Princeton, which seems to have had the greatest success with this plan, lapsing is not permitted, as each class forms a special "reserve fund" from which all delinquent premiums are paid until accumulated dividends and death claims are sufficient to keep all in force. About 10 per cent. are delinquent each year.

The final question in the questionnaire, regarding the opinion of the official filling out the questionnaire as to the success or failure of the plan, naturally brought divergent views. Two had the opinion that the plan was a success; fifteen apparently considered it a failure; three were doubtful, and five believed that it was too soon to judge. Several had changed to other plans.

"Although we have been working on this plan for only three years, we consider it quite successful," reports St. Viator College, one of the schools supporting the plan.

"Success for the twelve classes which have used it. Enables class as a whole to participate by small gifts over a period of years, which means a good-sized gift collected from younger alumni who are usually the 'poor prospects,'" reports Princeton University.

"A failure," reports St. Olaf College. "The investment required to keep the policies in good standing would be too heavy a burden for most of the institutions if they should prevent lapses taking place, and the return would not be adequate."

"Complete failure due to our not having a class system or class organization after graduation," replied the secretary of the alumni association of the University of Virginia. "In our circumstances a graduating class gift should be paid in full before commencement. I do not approve asking alumni for annual gifts until they have been at least five years out of college."

"It is a failure," affirms Randolph-Macon College, also of Virginia. "People in their enthusiasm took insurance and afterwards got tired of paying the premium, and it would be rather risky for the institution to try to carry these premiums in the hope of ultimate gain."

A number of the schools reported that they know of alumni who are insured for the benefit of their alma mater through their own initiative, but these policies are not held by the colleges.

The plan in force at Princeton University, which seems to be operating favorably, is organized as follows: twenty- or twenty-five-year endowment, annual premiums, participating company, individual policies in amounts from $250 to $1,000 with the class memorial committee as beneficiary and also receiving all dividends. As many of the graduating class are insured as the committee can sign up, generally about 400, or 85 per cent. of the class. No physical examination is required for policies up to $1,000. Princeton University has nothing to do with this class insurance as an institution, the class committee also being the beneficiary.

A plan which apparently has been tried only by Doane College, Crete, Nebraska, appears to be a success as far as it has gone. This is a loan plan under which the college sells units of $300 each. For each unit purchased, the school, through an insurance company, issues life insurance of $600 on the life of the purchaser, or on the life of some person in whom he has an insurable interest. At the end of nineteen years the $300 is returned to the unit purchaser, or, in case of death during the period, $600 is paid to the purchaser or his beneficiary. No particular selection of risks has been made, the average age of the insured being forty-four years. In the short time that the plan has been in effect there have been no lapses, and the plan is considered by school authorities as a success.

One observation from a survey of bequest life insurance for educational purposes by Archie M. Palmer, assistant director of the Institute of International Education, is well worth noting: "In a small institution or in one where there is a well-knit, enthusiastically loyal undergraduate and class spirit the prospects of success are far more favorable than in a large institution where the classes are large and unwieldy, where the undergraduate spirit is at a low ebb or not well organized, or where there are many other conflicting activities and distractions."

Since the daily attendance at the University of Nebraska is approximately 6,500 students and class organization not closely knit, and since the experience of other schools has shown that the plan works best in a small, well-knit group, it has been decided that this form of making private gifts to the university is of a rather doubtful value.

LAWRENCE PIKE

UNIVERSITY OF NEBRASKA

SPECIAL CORRESPONDENCE

HONORS WORK IN SCHOOL AND COLLEGE

THE University of Buffalo inaugurated in 1923 the honors plan of individual instruction for superior students of the two upper classes. At this institution honors students are allowed considerably more freedom than in some other colleges. There are no restrictions whatever of a formal nature. Both the character of his tutorial work and the choice of whatever courses it seems best for him to take are settled by the student and his tutor. If this freedom seems to lead to undue specialization while the student is still an undergraduate, it is only because the attempt has already been made, during his first two years and during whatever summer work he has already taken, to introduce him as broadly as time can allow to the various fields of knowledge. Even if the specialization seems premature, the student involved is of the superior type who has already done more and better work as an underclassman than his fellows. Then, too, the entire honors group meets at frequent intervals to hear an informal address on some topic of general current interest either by a member of the faculty or by some authority on the subject outside the university. The address is so timed as to leave ample opportunity for discussion among the students.

This year 34 per cent. of the total enrolment of upperclassmen are ranked as honors students. For the first time a few sophomores of marked ability have been admitted, carrying the required subjects of their course but choosing as their electives work with a tutor in their major department instead of formal course attendance.

The success of the honors plan at the University of Buffalo will logically lead to two important extensions, each of which can be only tentatively touched on here inasmuch as no concrete beginning has yet been made.

(1) If the work is to be confined to upperclassmen, the decision will have to be made as to where to draw the line. Is it to be arbitrary or not? Is the method to be reserved for only superior students—if so, how superior; or to be extended to all upperclass students who have survived the spadework of the first two years? In other words, can not the method adapted to the superior student be extended to the average student, with perhaps not the same result as to brilliance of product, but with results which will still justify the individual method? If there is approval for the principle, the objection should be recognized that such an extension on a rather wholesale scale is extremely expensive. But that is an individual matter which

should not vitiate the theory. On the other side is the answer that only those upperclassmen should be retained in college after the sophomore year who are fitted to become honors students; all others should be shunted off into a professional school, into business life, or persuaded to transfer to a college of different, though not necessarily lower, standards.

(2) The other important extension of honors methods is downwards. It is undeniable that in every school, particularly, perhaps, in the large city high schools, there is a group of students taking the college preparatory course who by their environment or the average composition of the class in which they find themselves have no incentive to exert themselves to the full extent of their innate ability. Consequently they become lazy, inert, indifferent, carrying those attitudes over into college. If there were only sufficient motive, they would forget to follow the crowd. One such motive may well be the sectioning of school classes on the basis of ability. There has, of course, been marked progress along this line in the larger high schools. In New York City and in Buffalo, for instance, practically all the high schools are committed to the theory.

The liberal arts college is interested in the upper sections of these classes. If the school has differentiated, should not the college continue the good work? This is not the place for arguing the pros and cons of sectioning in college but simply for drawing attention to the fact that for this group the time factor is more important than is usually recognized; that time means not only money but also intellectual interest and motivation. These youngsters should not be forced beyond their best pace but opportunity should be given to let them show the college what their best pace is.

Urban universities, almost entirely dependent for moral support and financial aid upon their own city constituencies, must be particularly anxious that their educational policies may be generally understood and approved, and among the first people, outside the college faculty, to whom to take these policies for comment should be the administrative officers of the high schools. The University of Buffalo happens to have entrance regulations which, unless understood, may be regarded as discriminatory or restrictive. Accordingly, a year or so ago several of the officials of the university sent an invitation to the principals and assistant principals of all the local secondary schools, both public and private, for a conference on subjects of mutual concern. The meeting was cordial and achieved its purposes. The chancellor of the university was asked to appoint a permanent committee, consisting of representatives in equal numbers of the public and the private schools and of the university, whose function it would be to devise further ways of cooperation.

Such a committee should not be allowed to die of inanition. Something highly provocative was soon found for it to discuss, and the university representatives laid before it a proposal which carries further the attempts already made in Buffalo at better articulation between school and college. The university, for example, already gives college credit, by examination, for work done in school; it endeavors to express whatever entrance requirements it seems possible to treat not in terms of hours or units but rather in terms of standard of attainment. While this is particularly true of a tool subject such as a modern language, where the regulation can obviously be met by the acquirement in a variety of methods of what the faculty deems is in each individual case a satisfactory knowledge of the language, there is no reason to believe that in other fields also the mechanical requirement can not give way to the intellectual and the individual. Again, as in the case of honors students, the process is somewhat more laborious and expensive, but how can money and effort be better expended by the admissions office?

The student who comes with a brilliant school record deserves the interest of the college long before he knocks at its doors. It is the continuity of the educational process which is at stake. If that student knows two or three years in advance that he will apply for admission to X college, the college and the school should assume common guidance over his development. To be as concrete as is possible before the plan has received any trial, the Buffalo project aims at selecting a limited number of upper-level students in the junior year of their high school, so helping them in their selection of the remainder of their school program and also giving them such additional training both during their school course and especially during both summers, that they may enter college with a considerable amount of their junior college training completed. Such students would be admitted to the senior division of the college entirely on the basis of total accomplishment and ability rather than fulfilment of formal course requirements; the average of these students would perhaps spend one instead of two years in the junior division. They would then be treated in the senior college as honor students. At the end of that period they would be advised to go for the most part either into professional training or graduate academic work on the basis of their interests and abilities. Such students as elected the latter would be started on the field of investigation on which their graduate work would be conducted, before the completion of their undergraduate period, there being here as little break in continuity as possible, since the first year of graduate study would be made the ultimate objective rather than the completion of the undergraduate period.

Such a scheme as this is perhaps adapted only to an institution situated in a large city where it can have frequent contact with the schools which would furnish it its first material. One or more liaison officers would be appointed from the college faculty to consult on school programs from the university point of view. Obviously, tactfulness on their part would be the prime requisite. Such an officer, whether he be called a professor of education or by some more administrative title, should previously have secondary, as well as college experience. It should take practically all his time, and as the work grows others would be detailed. It would thus be expensive for the university.

JULIAN PARK

UNIVERSITY OF BUFFALO

QUOTATIONS

THE MILLION PUPILS OF NEW YORK CITY

THE report of the Superintendent of Schools for 1927–1928 shows that the average daily register for the school year of all the schools, exclusive of the continuation schools, passed the million mark (1,014,605), an increase of 18,262 over 1926–1927. We have thus come into the million-a-day period, though the average daily attendance still falls several tens of thousands short of that number. A certain ancient city was saved from extermination because there were "six score thousand who could not tell their right hand from their left hand—also much cattle." It was only a temporary salvation, however, and mere numbers of ignorance and innocence will not save a city from becoming ultimately "one with Nineveh and Tyre." By extension of the "polis" from the city to the nation, the existence of twenty or thirty million children without instruction in the common experience of those who have gone before, save through individual parental advice, would mean a loss of most if not all that the nation has won collectively.

The account of what has been undertaken for the million children of this city is most impressive in volume, and would be stirring reading if its significance could be appreciated. Spread through nearly five hundred pages, it will not be read by many in its entirety. It would be an added contribution of great value if there could be a brief interpretation of the report, through which the parents of these million could get a glimpse at least of what the city is attempting to do for their children, and the city itself might get a comprehensive view of its own vast and varied enterprise. When it is considered that no two children are alike, but that groups of them in classes of considerable size must be carried along together, it seems almost a miracle that democracy does as well as it does in carrying forward such a multitude to self-dependent and interdependent citizenship. It is, all in all, the greatest triumph of mankind over its past and the greatest promise of race progress, whatever disappointment there may be in the individual.

Older people will read some of the pages of this report with a sense that they in their training were imposed upon or wasted time and effort. Grammar is now limited to "the last two years of schools" and appears in simplified form. Parsing has long since vanished; the diagraming of sentences has also been eliminated. Writing has been "radically changed." Scientific study of penmanship now suggests the discarding of the "full-arm" system. Spelling is taught more scientifically and its range somewhat reduced. Nature study comes into a larger place in the urban child's life. These are but the beginnings of revisions that are going forward to give the oncoming generation advantages which those who went before have missed because of the excessive time spent on certain subjects.

As to the physical provision, the report shows that less than 5 per cent. of the elementary school pupils are on "short-time" and that the difficulty now is not in meeting the total need, but in following shifting needs. It is the continuation schools that seem most to demand attention. All in all, the city's educational work is of first importance and deserves a more general concern than is shown by the public.—*The New York Times.*

EDUCATIONAL RESEARCH AND STATISTICS

WHAT THE CHICAGO DOCTORS OF PHILOSOPHY ARE DOING

As we observe the members of a graduating class of college students marching across the stage and receiving diplomas from their respective deans on commencement day, a number of questions may arise. Each student, supposedly, has reached a certain degree of mastery and proficiency in the field in which he has made his major preparation. With his diploma in hand he confidently feels that he can successfully cope with the problems that may arise in his chosen line of activity. But the observer may wonder how many of the class will eventually find employment in the fields for which they have been especially trained. How many will be forced by circumstances or inclined by changed interests to follow a different line of intellectual activity? What proportion will enter into academic work and carry on the same type of service as did the instructors who made possible their training? To what extent will the graduates enter into non-academic types of service, either private or public, in which they can do a line of work which will be similar to that of their major department? Similarly, how many may enter non-academic fields which have little or nothing in common with the major training? And what proportion will pass from this life before their span of service should naturally come to a close?

In the brief study herein reported an attempt has been made to answer some of these questions. It deals, however, with only those graduates who have received the degree of doctor of philosophy. The data were taken from the "Register of Doctors of Philosophy of The University of Chicago," 1927. The period covered is from June, 1893, to June, 1927, or the period during which the institution has conferred the degree of doctor of philosophy. During this time the degree has been conferred upon 2,055 graduates.

In most instances the departments under which the graduates are classified are kept distinct. In some cases, however, when the work of several departments appears to be quite similar, they are combined under one heading. This is particularly true of those departments which make up the divinity group. As listed in the "Register" and in The University of Chicago Catalogue, this group consists of oriental languages and literatures, New Testament literature and interpretation, systematic theology, church history, practical theology and a department called sociology. And in addition to these, liberty has been taken to include the department of comparative religion, because it seems to be more closely related to the divinity group than to any other, although it is not so included in the "Register."

In the accompanying table most of the results of the study have been summarized. The column at the left shows the major department or department conferring the degree. Other columns show, in order, the year the first degree was conferred by a given department; the number receiving the degree; the percentages of doctorates employed in a given capacity at the present time, as teaching in the department of major preparation, teaching in a department other than the major department, serving in a non-academic activity which is similar in nature to work of the major department, serving in a non-academic activity which is dissimilar to the major department, serving in an activity which is non-specified, and the percentages deceased. Since the question of major interest in this study is concerned with the percentages of graduates who are continuing the work for which they made special preparation, the departments in the first column are arranged in order of these percentages which are shown in the fourth column.

Relative Frequency of Students Receiving the Degree in Different Departments

The order of departments with respect to the number of students receiving the degree in each is as follows: chemistry, 225; divinity, 188; botany, 172; mathematics, 143; classical languages, 115; earth sciences, 114; physics, 111; modern languages, 106; English, 98; history, 92; education, 81; physiology and physiological chemistry, 80; zoology, 77; sociology and anthropology, 75; psychology, 74; philosophy, 72; economics, 62; hygiene and bacteriology, 32; anatomy, 31; political science, 30; mathematical and practical astronomy, 28; pathology, 24; home economics and administration, 15; commerce and administration, 6, and social service administration, 4. The total number is 2,055.

In considering these frequencies, it should be kept in mind that the department of divinity is composed of several departments. It should be observed also that the degree of doctor of philosophy has been conferred in the department of commerce and administration only since 1922 and in social service administration only since 1924. In all other departments the first degree was conferred prior to 1904 and in most cases about 1895.

Concentration and Deflection in Placement

A scatter diagram whose axes represent on the one hand the major departments conferring the degree and on the other the academic departments and other activities in which the doctorates are at present engaged would show the degrees of concentration and deflection in vocational placement. However, such a diagram is too complicated for convenience of publication here. By degree of concentration is meant the tendency of a given departmental group of doctors to teach their major subject and by deflection is meant a corresponding tendency to teach some other subject or engage in some non-academic activity.

The five departments in which there is the highest degree of concentration in the major departments are as follows: mathematics, English, education, modern languages and botany. Social service administration is omitted from this ranking because the number of graduates from this department is very small. The greatest deflection is found in the departments of astronomy, pathology, divinity, philosophy and anatomy. However, as will be pointed out in the next section, pathology stands highest in the percentage of students engaged in non-academic activities which are similar to that of their major department. Astronomy stands high with respect to selection of a department for service which is closely related to it, namely, mathematics.

The most "versatile" group is the divinity group. They find employment in twelve of the academic departments, or practically 50 per cent. of all of the departments. These students are employed in all of the languages, in practically all of the social sciences and in mathematics. Likewise they have a wide range of choices in non-academic activities.

The department appropriated by the highest number of "outsiders" is education. Instructors in education are employed from graduates of the departments of philosophy, psychology, history, sociology, classical languages, botany and divinity. The department least appropriated by "outsiders" is astronomy. No one is at present employed in the department of astronomy who did not receive the degree in that department.

As will be shown by a glance at the last line in the table, 68.27 per cent. of all graduates are now engaged in teaching. This includes graduates who are engaged as instructors in major departments (60.29 per cent.) as well as those who are employed in non-major departments (7.99 per cent.). This total percentage is below that found by Charters,[1] namely, 75 per cent.

NON-ACADEMIC EXCURSIONS

Non-academic activities are of three kinds: those which are similar in nature to the work of the department of major preparation; those which are dissimilar to the work of the major department, and those which are non-specified. A total of 26.85 per cent. of the entire group are thus employed as follows: similar to major department, 13.77 per cent.; dissimilar to major department, 4.52 per cent., and non-specified, 8.56 per cent.

The departmental group of students which has the highest percentage of graduates engaged in non-academic activities similar to that for which they have made especial preparation is pathology, with a percentage of 62.50 per cent. Nearly all of these graduates are now practicing physicians and surgeons. Other departments which stand high in this respect are commerce and administration, chemistry, anatomy, and hygiene and bacteriology. No students are engaged in such activities from the departments of philosophy, home economics and administration, classical languages, modern languages, and English. This is presumably due to the fact that few if any kinds of public or private activities of a nature similar to the work of these departments are in existence.

The departments ranking highest in the percentages of graduates engaged in non-academic activities which are entirely different from the type of work for which they were trained are: home economics and administration, sociology and anthropology, classical languages, philosophy and history. Those ranking lowest in these respects are: physiology and physiological chemistry, pathology, hygiene and bacteriology, commerce and administration, and social service administration. Not one of these departments is represented in activities of this kind.

A large number of graduates who do not specify their present employment are women. Many of these have married since the degree was conferred, as indicated by the changes of name in the "Register," and are now engaged in home making. The departments ranking highest in the percentages of graduates whose present engagement is not specified are: classical languages, philosophy, psychology, political science, and home economics and administration. Those ranking lowest in this respect are: pathology, commerce and administration, social service administration, education, and economics, the first three of which are not so represented at all.

DECEASED

Over the thirty-four year period during which the degree of doctor of philosophy has been conferred by the University of Chicago, an even hundred graduates, or 4.86 per cent., are deceased. Deaths have occurred in every departmental group except philosophy and commerce and administration, the latter department having granted the degree only since 1922. The greatest mortality has occurred among the anatomists. Other groups which stand relatively high in the number deceased are: classical languages, modern languages, pathology and zoology. The departments ranking lowest aside from those which have offered the degree only recently are: philosophy, chemistry, psychology, political science, and earth sciences. The average time at which the first degree was offered in both the high group and the low group was the same, that is, 1897. Hence the difference in mortality of the two groups is due, presumably, to factors other than differences in ages.

SUMMARY

Some of the more important points brought out in this study may be summarized somewhat as follows:

(1) The total number of students upon whom the degree of doctor of philosophy has been conferred during a thirty-four year period is 2,055.

(2) Aside from the departments which began conferring the degree only recently, the department conferring the highest number of degrees is chemistry, and that conferring the lowest number is home economics and administration.

(3) At present, 68.28 per cent. of all graduates are employed in teaching. Of this per-

[1] W. W. Charters, "Graduate Schools and College Teaching." *Educ. Res. Bull.*, Univ. of Ohio, 1928, 7: 384–349.

VOCATIONAL PLACEMENT OF THE CHICAGO DOCTORS OF PHILOSOPHY

Major department	Year first degree conferred	No. receiving degree	Teaching in major department	Teaching in non-major department	Non-academic similar to major	Non-academic dissimilar to major	Non-specified	Percentage deceased
			Percentage of doctorates employed at present in a given capacity					
Mathematics	1896	143	88.81	00.00	2.79	1.39	2.79	4.19
English	1894	98	80.61	00.00	0.00	6.12	9.18	4.08
Education	1900	81	80.24	8.62	2.46	3.70	1.23	3.70
Social service	1924	4	75.00	00.00	0.00	0.00	0.00	25.00
Modern language	1894	106	70.75	7.60	0.00	6.60	7.54	8.49
Botany	1897	172	68.02	2.49	9.30	2.90	12.20	4.06
Earth science	1895	114	67.54	0.88	21.92	0.87	5.26	3.50
Political science	1898	30	66.66	0.00	13.33	3.33	13.33	3.33
Economics	1894	62	64.51	1.61	20.96	6.45	1.61	4.83
Psychology	1903	74	63.51	9.46	9.45	2.70	13.51	1.35
Zoology	1894	77	63.63	11.69	6.49	3.89	6.49	7.79
Physics	1897	111	63.06	00.00	26.12	0.90	6.30	3.60
Home economics	1895	15	60.00	6.66	00.00	13.33	13.33	6.66
History	1895	92	58.69	10.87	1.08	9.78	11.95	7.60
Physiology and physiological chemistry	1896	80	57.50	8.75	21.25	1.25	6.25	5.00
Classical language	1895	115	56.52	9.56	00.00	11.30	13.91	8.69
Sociology and anthropology	1895	75	53.33	17.33	2.66	11.99	10.69	3.99
Hygiene and bacteriology	1900	32	50.00	9.37	31.25	00.00	3.12	6.25
Commerce and administration	1922	6	50.00	00.00	50.00	00.00	00.00	0.00
Chemistry	1894	225	46.66	4.00	37.77	2.22	7.99	1.33
Anatomy	1899	31	41.93	9.68	25.80	0.00	9.67	12.90
Philosophy	1895	72	41.66	36.11	00.00	8.33	13.88	00.00
Divinity	1893	188	38.29	19.68	17.02	5.85	12.23	6.91
Pathology	1903	24	29.16	00.00	62.50	0.00	00.00	8.33
Astronomy	1900	28	25.00	32.14	17.85	7.14	10.71	7.14
Total		2055	60.29	7.99	13.77	4.52	8.56	4.86

centage, 60.29 are teaching the subjects of their major preparation and 7.99 per cent. are teaching subjects different from their major subjects. The department whose graduates are remaining truest to their preparation is mathematics.

(4) The department appropriated by the highest percentage of "outsiders" is education. Instructors are employed from graduates of seven different departments. The department least appropriated by "outsiders" is astronomy.

(5) Of those graduates who are engaged in non-academic activities, 13.77 per cent. are engaged in service similar in nature to that of the department of major preparation. The department ranking highest in this respect is pathology. The percentage of students engaged in non-academic work which is entirely different from that of the major department is 4.52. The department ranking highest is home economics and administration.

(6) A total of one hundred graduates, or 4.86 per cent., are deceased. The department ranking highest in the number of deaths is anatomy, with a percentage 12.90. The department ranking lowest is philosophy with no deaths. The period during which the degree was conferred in each of these departments is approximately the same, hence age difference is apparently not a factor.

Whether the relative frequency of Chicago doctors of philosophy who go into academic work, research activities, private enterprises and public service, represents the most desirable balance among these endeavors is problematical.

M. O. WILSON

THE UNIVERSITY OF OKLAHOMA

SCHOOL AND SOCIETY

EDITED BY J. McKEEN CATTELL

WITH WHICH IS COMBINED THE

EDUCATIONAL REVIEW

EDITED BY WILLIAM McANDREW

Volume XXIX SATURDAY, JUNE 29, 1929 Number 757

THE FUNCTION OF THE NATIONAL COUNCIL OF EDUCATION OF THE NATIONAL EDUCATION ASSOCIATION[1]

By JOHN K. NORTON

DIRECTOR OF RESEARCH, NATIONAL EDUCATION ASSOCIATION

THE original purposes of the National Council of Education are clearly set forth in early issues of the *Proceedings* of the National Education Association, particularly in the volumes of 1880, 1882 and 1906. Vision and clarity mark the thinking of Thomas W. Bicknell and other leaders who were instrumental in the creation of the council in 1880. No better guide can be found by one interested in clarifying the functions of the council in 1929 than the clear-cut statements of its purposes and functions given in the *Proceedings* just following 1880, particularly the 1882 volume. The assistance received from these early statements in the preparation of this paper is gladly acknowledged. The original 1880 constitution of the council states:

> In order to consider educational questions of general interest and of public importance, and to formulate such conclusions as may be reached, the National Council of Education is organized within the National Education Association.

The body created for this purpose was similar in its composition to the present national council although smaller as to numbers. It was a body of leading educators selected partly by the directors of the National Education Association and representatives of its various departments and partly by the council itself, representing all sections of the country and the principal fields of education.

What were the considerations which led to the formation of such a body in 1880 by the National Education Association, and to what extent are they still valid for 1929?

First, the founders of the national council had in mind that school organization in the United States is highly decentralized. The 1882 *Proceedings* state:

> The importance of such a council becomes more evident when we consider the present condition of American instruction in distinction from the school life of the Old World. . . It is a startling thought that the entire educational work of this nation today is really in the hands of teachers employed by the people, and responsible only to school committees and corporations whose fitness to formulate a consistent system of education and supervise its workings is not asserted by anybody.

Such being the case, it was contended fifty years ago that there was great need for an agency which would critically evalu-

[1] Address delivered before the National Council of Education, Cleveland, Ohio, February 25, 1929.

ate major educational procedures and trends and make available the results of their deliberations. Is this consideration still valid in 1929? Undoubtedly it is. Our system of school organization is still highly decentralized, and most of us hope it will continue to be so. There is still no common agreement, for example, as to what constitutes an elementary school. There are forty-eight independent school systems, and within each state from a hundred to a thousand or more school systems enjoying varying degrees of autonomy. This leads to a wide variety of practice. Elementary education in some communities begins with a nursery class and extends through the ninth grade. Or it may begin at the first grade and end at the fifth or sixth. There are many other variations as to point of beginning, ending and number of years included in the elementary school. This is merely one illustration of the diversity of practice which marks the organization of the school units of American education. When one goes over into the field of teaching methods, curriculum content or fundamental educational philosophy, the diversity of practice and thought is even greater.

Never was there greater need for a responsible group made up of mature educational thinkers to guide us through a welter of diverse educational practices and philosophies than there is to-day.

Second, the founders of the national council saw a need for such a body because of the relative intellectual immaturity but large professional zeal of the teaching profession. They pictured the 1880 situation as follows:

> Nine tenths of these teachers are in no way professionals. Their terms of service and places of occupation are short and changeful, and there are few communities in which the school life goes on with any marked consistency.

But it was pointed out that what the teaching profession lacked in maturity they made up for by the vigor and enthusiasm with which they developed new ways of doing things and adopted the ideas of others. It was stated in 1880 that these new departures in education were:

> Commonly wrought out by teachers whose original faculty and executive force are greater than their breadth of culture or philosophical habit of generalization. They are often achieved on such peculiar classes of children, under such unusual social conditions, that it is very difficult to estimate their relative value in a general system of national culture. . . . The man who has become famous as its representative is easily convinced that his plan includes the sum and substance of the matter. He appears in convention brandishing his brilliant essay, which, like the patent sweeper, cleans the street from curbstone to curbstone of everything in its path. . . . Everywhere among our ardent and successful teachers we find ourselves inspired as in the presence of prodigious, original power, assured that never were so many bright and beautiful things done with children since the foundation of the world; yet everywhere we are worried and confused by the narrow, partial, local and often merely personal point of view of this forcible man or woman, buried up to the eyes in one little section of school work, like the bee smothered in the honey of its own cell. . . . The teaching fraternity and the people of our country are failing to realize the value or appreciate the results of a great deal of the best school work now done, because there is no central body of superior schoolmen lifted above this turbulent region of transient work and heated controversy, devoted to the study of our national education in all its aspects, and prepared to pass intelligent judgment on its varied developments.

Is this statement still apropos? Does the teaching profession to-day include a considerable number of relatively immature thinkers, imbued with an abundant professional zeal? Is our attention too often caught by every educational will-o'-the-wisp? Do we too often accept the nostrum of some enthusiast as the sole panacea of educational progress and achievement?

Most of us will agree that the enthusiast of relatively limited vision is still with us. In evaluating a new educational procedure we are too often influenced more by the vigor of the personality and enthusiasm of its advocate than by the basic philosophy which underlies his device. There is great need for a group of mature, deliberate thinkers who will critically examine and pronounce upon the fundamental soundness of important educational innovations uninfluenced by the personality or enthusiasm of their advocates.

Third, the educational thinkers of 1880 established the national council because they were convinced of the great complexity of the educational process. They believed that if such a complex was to be viewed in its proper relationships and waste avoided, much hard thinking would have to be done. They expressed this view-point thus in 1882:

> There is no more pressing need in the national educational field to-day than the gathering of representative educators of the country into a deliberative body, with the object of surveying the entire field of operations and discussing every important fact and development in American school life, laboring to harmonize conflicting opinions, or, at least, to report how far rival methods are complementary and not destructive to each other, and at its own option, without haste or heat, announcing its conclusions to the public. . . . The very effort to accomplish an end so important is itself a worthy purpose for the ablest thinkers and teachers; it will help to soften pedagogic asperities and possibly check the growth of hostile schools and parties contending with the bitterness and bigotry that are the certain accompaniment of intense earnestness and narrow views.

Is this statement of 1882 pertinent in 1929? There was never a greater need for calm, deliberate thought in the field of education than there is to-day. The synthesis of the whole educational world is more difficult than ever before. Most of the factors of complexity existing in 1880 are still with us, and others have come in.

Since 1880 the place of the school as an instrument of social progress has taken on added significance. We are coming to hold the school partly responsible for correcting the shortcomings of contemporary civilization. Rather than merely limiting itself to conserving the best of the past, the school is expected to develop new and better cultures for the future. In the half decade since 1880 the school has become more of a dynamic and less of a static influence in social progress. To fulfil its function the school must properly evaluate and interpret into the lives of children the complex forces which make up modern civilization.

Since 1880 a promising start has been made in creating a science of education. Instruments of objective measurement have been developed, with the result that there may now be brought to bear upon most major educational problems at least some definite and tested knowledge. This is an eminently desirable development. But the scientific movement in education has some unfortunate by-products. Some persons appear to assume that if one uses a sufficient number of statistical formulas and instruments of educational measurement he is relieved of the obligation to think. The assembling of objective educational data should be preceded and particularly should be followed by thinking. In the last twenty-five years we have spent too much time in assembling new data and too little time in digesting it and interpreting its significance to educational evolution. This knowledge needs to be evaluated. The wheat needs to be winnowed from the chaff and properly used.

Walter S. Monroe sums up the point, and his statement is particularly significant coming as it does from a disciple of the scientific movement in education. He says:

> Objectivity is not synonymous with accuracy and accurate data may not be valid data. Furthermore, objective methods are not applicable to all problems. There is a need for subjective methods. There is urgent need for developing and employing technics of critical reflective thinking in which some or all of the data are subjective, and for reviving an interest in the philosophy of education

as a necessary supplement to the use of objective methods.[2]

Since 1880 the scope of public education has been extended. The secondary school has been developed and the battle to make it a democratic institution has been won. The field of conflict has now been transferred from the secondary to the college level, and the gage of battle has been thrown down between those who would make higher education a privilege of a selected few and those who would develop differentiated opportunities in the college so that all may have such talents as they possess developed on this level.

New movements have come upon the educational stage since 1880. I will mention but two. At one end, and before the traditional kindergarten and elementary school, we have the nursery school and the nascent preschool movement. At the other end is the tremendously significant postschool development—the adult education movement.

Education, like other fields, has been marked by a progressively rapid specialization since 1880. The official program of this convention shows that at the present moment no less than twenty-one separate and distinct educational meetings are in session in Cleveland. And there are perhaps a dozen more which are not recognized in the official program. Specialization always brings the danger that the tail will wag the dog.

The factors which made a National Council of Education desirable in 1880 are still with us, and others have come in. Ours is still a highly decentralized system of education. The teaching profession still includes many whose enthusiasm for new ideas is not equaled by their maturity of intellectual development. Education is still a highly complex field, and its complexity has been increased by the growing social significance of the school, by the birth of the science of education, by the extension of the scope of education and by progressively rapid specialization in education.

The question might be raised, are there not other agencies which offer the intellectual leadership and synthesized thinking needed in the field of education? The conventions of the National Education Association do not do it. I would be the last to depreciate the great value of these meetings. As a clearing-house of relatively undigested educational ideas they are unexcelled. But they are far too crowded, too hurried and too diverse to offer the opportunity for calm, deliberative discussion and thought on a few major problems as opposed to the brief consideration of a wide range of educational topics. The meetings of the National Education Association are agencies for the exchange of a tremendous amount of educational information which is carried back as a basis for practice and thought by individuals. This is all right, but something more is needed.

One might similarly take up each of the no less than 285 educational organizations listed in the 1928 Education Directory of the U. S. Bureau of Education. The American Educational Research Association, the National Society for the Study of Education, Section Q of the American Association for the Advancement of Science—these and other of the 285 organizations make their contributions to educational advance and have their more or less distinctive purposes. None of them is equipped, however, and none of them aims to make the contribution which should be expected from the national council.

Somewhat more specifically, just what is it that the national council should do? It should lead in reviving the importance of reflective thinking in education. It should aid in lifting educational philosophy to its rightful place in educational advance. We need an organization which will de-

[2] "Shall We Use Objective Methods Exclusively?" *The Nation's Schools*, May, 1928, p. 16.

velop an integrated philosophy or overview of education, which will see in their true perspective the numerous specialties, side issues and conflicting factors which play upon the schools to-day, which will evaluate the findings of scientific research in education, and which will fit each of these factors into its proper place, if it has one, in the whole educational scheme. The council should regularly bring together a few educational leaders to grind out of the mill of mind reacting on mind, taking into consideration all factors, certain mature conclusions on a few supreme educational issues. In short, we need a group of educational thinkers who are able to see the educational forest as a whole, who are able to enter the woods, to find their way about and to come out again unconfused by the multiplicity and variety of trees.

This the national council is admirably equipped to do. According to its constitution it is made up of 175 leaders in American educational thought and action. It brings together men of specialized as well as broad interests in education. It represents or should represent all phases of educational activity.

Under the leadership of its president the council has recently made encouraging progress in fulfilling the function discussed above. Papers such as those of Paul Monroe and others read at recent meetings of the council are the types of contributions which the national council should develop. Indeed, the progress made toward achieving the ideal in recent meetings of the council encourages one to hope that full attainment is possible. Without wishing to be presumptuous, may I suggest some of the positive and negative factors which it is believed will aid or hinder the council in achieving the ideal?

First, those who select the council membership should take their responsibility extremely seriously. If you will look over the present membership of the council you will agree that it includes most of the outstanding figures in education. But you will not find these men included: Lotus D. Coffman, Herbert S. West, Ellwood P. Cubberley, John W. Withers, Zenos E. Scott, Edward L. Thorndike, John Dewey, Leonard V. Koos, James E. Russell or Boyd H. Bode. I might have used still other names, but those named will serve the purpose. The 175 members of the national council should, as fully as this number will permit, include all the outstanding doers and thinkers in the field of education. It should seek out these leaders if they are not interested, and see that what goes on in the council is of interest to such men.

Second, the national council's principal activity should be the discussion of and interpretation of major educational issues. This discussion should be of an informal, unhurried, deliberative type which would search out the very roots of our educational evolution. Many of these deliberative sessions should come to nothing more than a clarification of the view-points of those deliberating. At other times the results of these discussions should eventuate in published statements representing the conclusions reached. At times, perhaps, one or two members of the council should be selected to bring together into well-written form the results of these discussions. The presentation of these statements at the summer and winter meetings of the National Education Association should be a feature of these sessions.

The council should keep itself relatively free from committee work, and particularly from the process which too often merely means that one man's opinion on a subject is made to look like that of several. The national council itself should carry on few, if any, research projects. To engage in these activities would absorb its energy in producing more educational opinion or objective data to be added to the already large unassimilated mass.

Rather, the council should concern itself with opinions already expressed and facts already available, and should seek to evaluate and bring some synthesis out of these materials. This does not mean that the council should not define major educational problems which call for scientific investigation. The council could render a significant service by pointing out problems which deserve the attention of the U. S. Bureau of Education, the National Education Association, graduate schools of education and other agencies for educational research.

The meetings of the national council should be open to members only. Also, it is doubtful if the meetings of the council will ever be what they should be if they are held at the same time as the summer and winter meetings of the National Education Association. These meetings are too hectic to permit reflective thinking. We should have what was aimed at in 1882, to quote from the volume of *Proceedings* of that date:

> A council organized with care, deliberating apart from the excitements of a popular audience with time and opportunity for comparison of views, and not compelled to premature declaration of opinions.

Such a council can not exist in the midst of a convention such as we are now attending. But if the council could meet at the headquarters of the National Education Association for two or three days at some stated time of the year, a proper environment for its thinking would be found. It might be that but a score or so would come. So much the better. If more came the group should be divided anyway.

The council sessions should not be given over to the presentation of a series of formal papers, with little or no time for discussion. This attitude is supported by the founders of the council, one of whom said in 1880:

> [The council should be] a conference for the discussion of living educational questions by those who have made such questions a study. Elaborate essays and speeches should be a subordinate incident rather than a leading feature.

There is a surfeit of opportunity to present formal papers at this and other conventions of our national, state and local educational organizations. Twenty-one such programs are going on in Cleveland at this identical hour. The council can make little contribution by merely contributing another program of prepared papers.

The typical session of the council should revolve about a few carefully worded, major educational issues. Here are the types of questions which might be raised:

(1) What are the criteria which should guide in determining which students shall be allowed to participate in post-secondary school offerings of our educational system?

(2) Does the present situation in the United States indicate that such educational progress as is to be achieved in the next few decades should or must be achieved without increasing the amount of financial support provided for education?

(3) Are some of the current shortcomings of contemporary civilization in the United States partly a result of a mistaken philosophy of education and of an application of that philosophy in public-school practice?

Previous to the discussion of each question a member should present a statement defining and clarifying the issue. The presentation of such papers, however, should be a subordinate rather than the major feature of the council sessions.

A council so constituted and so functioning could render an incalculable service in these days of rapid and often chaotic educational development. Its contributions to education might be few, but they would be of great significance. They would give to educational thinking a balance wheel which it at present badly needs.

The conclusions of the council would have no legal or official authority. But they would exercise a powerful, persuasive influence because of their innate worth. Like stones cast into a quiet pool the well-considered conclusions of the council would become the center of waves of thought extending throughout our educational system. These conclusions would not disturb the freedom of our school system, but they would do much to give it a desirable unity and coherence.

REMODELING OUR UNIVERSITY LIBRARIES

By JAMES GOODWIN HODGSON

INTERNATIONAL INSTITUTE OF AGRICULTURE, ROME, ITALY

HOWEVER one looks at education, or whatever his definition of its fundamental thesis, he must admit that the ability to evaluate carefully his independent reading is one of the keen tests of an educated person. All the numerous criticisms on our modern universities now being published touch that point with greater or less emphasis. It has been the gifted student who has been complaining that the university did not bring out the best that was in him, but quite possibly there is a considerable body of more nearly average students who have missed much that should have been theirs but who lack the voice to express their vague dissatisfaction.

Not long ago, in a western university, I attempted to interest the students in independent reading, only to find that in order to accomplish anything I had to cut across the whole system of required courses, four hours a week of this, fifty pages of text for to-morrow, or three references on the "Business Cycle" for next week—not to mention the host of "outside activities"—before I could reach any particular student who seemed to have possibilities as an independent reader. Now, about a third of the way around the world from the scene of that attempt, I have been running over in my mind the work that I used to do, checking it up with the ideals that I had with reference to those particular tasks and letting the new conditions under which I am now living suggest new points of view.

Surely we have a right to contend that some of our university students do get educated! But how? An English friend of mine who does know several whom he considers educated, once insisted to me that our formal university training could not educate a man, particularly not in how to study for himself. He added, however—a little facetiously because we had been talking of the educational functions of libraries —"Possibly it is your great university libraries that do that."

A sign of the times is to be seen in the frequency with which libraries are being mentioned in criticisms of American universities. Criticism has been negative in most cases, but it indicates that some solution of the educational problem may lie in that direction, suggesting that the rapidly growing collections of books are a provocative center for the next great experiment in educational methods. There is a tendency to look for broader and newer points of view in the relations of the library with the student body and faculty, in fact, in all those wider relations for which specialized technique serves as a basis.

We find examples of this tendency in several universities to-day, where the technical library work, uncriticized, has been placed or left in the hands of technical experts of long training or experience, but the direction of the broader policies of the library has been given to men, with broad outlook indeed, but without the formal library preparation which in these days of specialization might be expected for the chief as well as the subordinates. The appointments at Harvard, the Johns Hopkins, Columbia and Chicago within the last three years illustrate this point, while it is understood that the new librarian at Iowa, when appointed, is to be from outside the traditional library ranks.

These facts are a clear indication that the thoughtful educator feels that the modern university librarian is not living up to the possibilities of his post, that the library is not meeting the current needs of university instruction. Whether this inadequacy is due to poor training in the library schools now being copied so numerously in other parts of the world, or whether it is due to a lack of imagination in the librarians themselves, is a debatable question. It is clearly evident, however, that librarians themselves ought to become aware of the trend and meet this only too apparent lack of confidence.

And yet, in the last twenty-five years librarianship has come to be recognized as a profession. The accredited schools now number eighteen, and projects for new schools are constantly appearing. Within the last year the University of Chicago has opened an advanced graduate school of librarianship for which the Carnegie Corporation has granted a million-dollar endowment. The public library system of the United States, which is the outstanding contribution of our nation to the whole movement, is the leader of the world and is fast setting for itself new aims and standards of service as an educational instrument. Even technical methods are being restudied in an effort to make the library machine meet the needs that a broader vision is setting forth.

Why then, over against this growth, comes this display of a lack of confidence?

It is easy to conclude that low pay has been a big factor—but has it? The heads of many public libraries have set a progressive standard which has inspired confidence and consequent good salaries, while the figures for university librarians have at least equaled those of the public institutions.

Rather, the reason for the distrust in university libraries seems to lie in the fact that many important functions of the library as a part of formal instruction have only been suggested—never actually realized. Professors and librarians in number have referred to the library as the heart of the university; but for some reason the library has been left as one of the storerooms of the university administration and its part in instruction relegated to that of an auxiliary tool in the hands of professors engaged primarily in the immediate work of their own departments. Instruction, even when largely indirect, has been rigidly kept as the province solely of the departments of teaching.

Some time ago I discussed library administration and economics with a professor at Oxford. The walls of his office were literally lined with books. There were historic volumes which prompted me to ask the privilege of merely feeling their original, solid bindings, and there were newer ones that came into my hands when the professor spoke of some subject within his immediate interest. He scarcely made a point which did not call forth some book to be fingered.

So it is with European professors. They have at hand their own collections, built up piece by piece, their small departmental libraries, and the student who has once passed the very elementary stages is given a personal introduction to the things that are to be absorbed. Perhaps this is one telling reason why European university students, when compared with American students of the same school years, are found to be the better educated of the two.

From the American point of view, however, such a situation, with each professor acting as his own uncorrelated librarian, is hopeless. In Europe every man must begin afresh his personal collection, and cooperation between departments is impossible because no one knows what books really are on the campus. Worse, necessary but expensive books can not be had because all funds have been spent on too numerous and too widely distributed copies of less costly works. The Oxford professor admitted this criticism, but supposed that the system was one of their traditions. His own special collection was quite pleasant; and, after all, he had never tried any other method!

But if centralized American libraries have taken from the professor his function as a librarian, there is still no reason why the intimate connection which the European professor secures between his books and his teaching should not also form an integral part of the program of American libraries. May not the solution be found in a close correlation between the departments of instruction and the library, and the transformation of the library from a purely administrative element into a far more active agent in the instruction itself?

Suggestions of correlation are already in the air: better reference service, browsing rooms and even voluntary reading courses copied after the best in the "adult education projects" of the public library. All of these are needed, but they are not related closely enough to the first interest of the average student—his courses for credit—and therefore can never appeal to more than a very few.

The real solution must be some means which definitely connects the departments of instruction with the library as closely as are connected the European professor and the collection which he himself has gathered together.

The Library of Congress, by its newly appointed professorships in several subjects, has pointed out a part of the right solution. In the Library of Congress these professors are to act as guides to mature students working in the great collections there. To transfer this plan to the university would not make it into a modern counterpart of the famous "professorship of books" proposed so many years ago. It would make of the men functioning in it the coordinating link between the actual departments of instruction and the library; the difference would be not so much one of method or principle as of responsibility.

The other half of the solution has been pointed out by the recent action of some schools, such as the University of Iowa, in granting to certain exceptional students the permission to gain credit by independent study and browsing in the library.

Telling of experiments at Iowa in his "College and University Library Problems" (Chicago, Amer. Lib. Assoc., 1927, p. 110–11), Dr. G. A. Works writes:

> Two experiments are in progress at Iowa [University] that seem likely to influence materially the relation of the library to the work of instruction at least in that institution.
>
> Classes have been organized in certain of the humanities so as to reduce materially the periods devoted to the usual lectures and class discussions. Study periods are substituted for the lectures that have been omitted. Under this plan, instead of having students in a subject such as freshman English meet in relatively small groups three or four times a week, they would meet in a large class once a week for a lecture. This lecture would be given by the most stimulating and inspiring lecturer in the department. During the other two or three periods the students would spend their time in study. This studying would be done at appointed times and in a room with an instructor at hand to assist the student when help is needed.
>
> Walter A. Jessup, president of the State University of Iowa, holds the view that the laboratory sciences have outstripped the humanities in furnishing opportunity for students to do their work. He would materially reduce the number of lectures in the latter subjects and make provision for study periods under favorable conditions. These study periods would correspond to the usual laboratory periods of a science. The study rooms for the students in the humanities would be a part of the library building and studying would be done with instructors at hand to assist if help should be needed.
>
> The second experiment has to do with furnishing undergraduate study halls. Two such study places were established outside the library in the fall of 1924. One of the rooms is equipped with individual study desks and the other has study tables. Drawer space is provided so that students may leave the materials for their work without danger of losing them. The rooms are open from 7:50 A. M. to 10 P. M. They are open to undergraduates, with preference given to freshmen. Their use is entirely voluntary, but if a student desires he may have a desk assigned to him for definite hours each day. He is also given drawer space.
>
> In each study room there are some books for reserved readings, some books of general reference and some for general reading. The rooms are under the supervision of full-time assistants. In addition there is a reference assistant.
>
> The results have been so satisfactory that in the plans being drawn for a new library building provision is being made for a sufficient number of study rooms and desks to meet the needs of all students. The students in the humanities would then have the library as their place for laboratory work.

To my mind, the full solution is the appointment of a special corps of "library professors," one in each of the departments at least, and perhaps in some of the humanities more, who are responsible to the library for their knowledge of the collections and their technical acquaintance with library methods that makes the collection more of an open book to them than to the other faculty members, but who are responsible to the departments themselves for the actual instruction in their subject which they are to give to the free-lance students who become their special charge and interest. Such men and women would not give lectures, hold actual classes or in any way be bound to a curriculum. Their work would be purely individual and destined to supplement the elementary courses or the more advanced ones that needs must be taught in large part by the lecture method.

Let it not be supposed that these suggested library professors are to be glorified departmental librarians, for they must be free from technical duties so that they may give their undivided time to the students who ask their services. Assistance to the general staff on classification and cataloging, on handling the technical details, would be the work of the department librarian, who would be the professor's first assistant but who would be solely and directly responsible to the central administration of the library.

Some of this desired guidance to the student is now attempted by the reference or the department librarian, but their limitations are evident. A reference librarian is not a specialist in any one subject; he is a specialist in his breadth of knowledge. Besides, he is as fully occupied with bibliographical and reference work as would be the departmental librarian.

A "library professor" would not necessarily be a new member of the faculty, but he would be new to the library staff because he would belong primarily to a teaching department and would look for advancement in that department. Naturally, he could not be expected to be a specialist in library science in the sense that the librarian himself is; he should have his doctor's degree in his major subject. But he must have had some training in the technique of library work and in the use of library tools in order to do his new work.

Such men would be far ahead of the European professor, for they would have not only the books of their special interests at hand, but the whole library; and they would be versed in those labor-saving devices which the librarian has evolved to lighten his task of keeping the whole flood of the printed page before his eye without unduly taxing mind or memory.

We need not detail all the functions of such a professor or solve the various difficulties which arise in prospect because of his dual responsibility. We may note, however, that in this complicated world and particularly in universities there is already dual responsibility; and it has been adequately demonstrated that, with a clearly defined distinction of fields and a little spirit of cooperation, such a dual responsibility can be efficient.

University libraries which exist only as aids or laboratories for the departments definitely charged with instruction can only take as their unchallenged field training in the relatively narrow field of bibliography; the encouragement of general reading or browsing is an extra-curricular activity. But if American university instruction is going to reunite the process of getting educated with the love and use of the book itself, it must work by cooperative agreement with the library. Library professorships, entailing responsibility to both the library and the respective department, represent such cooperation.

EDUCATIONAL EVENTS

THE WORLD CONFERENCE OF LIBRARIANS

ACCORDING to an Associated Press dispatch, the World Congress of Librarians opened in Rome on June 15 with some of the most widely known librarians of the United States in attendance. Premier Mussolini delivered the inaugural address.

The congress spent ten days in discussions, interviews and visits. The delegates were received by the Pope, who is himself a librarian. He has spent more than twenty years in the Ambrosian Library at Milan and the Vatican Library.

June 16 was given to visiting libraries in and around Rome and the actual sessions began on Monday. The librarians remained in session until June 27, when they went to Venice, stopping *en route* to see exhibitions at Naples, Florence, Modena, Genoa, Milan and Turin.

Among the Americans attending the conference were Dr. Herbert Putnam, librarian of Congress, and a staff of assistant librarians, Herman H. B. Meyer, Dr. E. C. Richardson and John T. Vance; Charles Belden, director of the Public Library of Boston; William W. Bishop, librarian of the University of Michigan; Arthur Elmore Bostwick, of St. Louis; Miss Winifred Gregory, of New York City; Andrew Keogh, president of the American Library Association and librarian of Yale University; Theodore Wesley Koch, of Northwestern University; H. George Locke, of Toronto, Canada; Carl H. Milam, secretary of the American Library Association of Chicago; Miss Emily V. D. Miller, editor of the publications, the American Library Association of Chicago, and George Watson Cole, of Pasadena, Calif.

Premier Mussolini in his inaugural address welcomed the delegates to Italy and outlined briefly the program which had been prepared. He said it would afford a complete résumé of the art of book-making from ancient times up to the Fascist régime, which, he said, was working in full cooperation with the best intellectual forces of the country.

Contrary to his usual custom of speaking French at international gatherings, the Premier gave his address in Italian. He was greeted with a salvo of applause as he familiarly bade his audience sit down. His reference to the Pope as "master of the book of knowledge" brought resounding cheers.

THE EDUCATION OF ARCHITECTS

To raise the educational standards for architects and encourage high ideals in architectural training, the American Institute of Architects has, according to Professor William Emerson, chairman of the institute committee on education, instituted a program of nation-wide cooperation with universities, libraries, art and technical schools.

Chaotic conditions resulting in great diversity in the length and scope of the courses leading to a degree in architecture exist in schools throughout the country. Professor Emerson, who is head of the department of architecture of the Massachusetts Institute of Technology, states that one of the objects of the work undertaken by the institute is to clear up this situation, which tends to lessen the prestige of the architect and the confidence of the general public.

"Architectural degrees vary as the colors of leaves of the trees in the fall," says Professor Emerson. "There are degrees of every kind, based on every kind and length of college course. The institute will endeavor to determine the basic essentials and the degrees which can significantly express these different categories of training."

Many scholarships are open to the architectural student. In addition, the institute, through an appropriation of the Carnegie Corporation, pays all the expenses of representative professors from colleges throughout the country at the summer courses of the Art Institute at Chicago.

Describing the institute's plan of cooperation with the American Library Association, Professor Emerson declares that its object is to place in the principal libraries of the United States a collection of approved books on architecture, lists of architectural reading and an assistant capable of giving advice to those pursuing a definite course of study. Its purpose is to bridge the gap between the layman's appreciation of what is meant by architecture and what the architect means by it, and to provide guidance for young architects, architectural draftsmen and craftsmen wishing to supplement their training in this field.

The committee on education of the institute reports:

> It is our belief that it is unwise to standardize teaching methods. Organization, conformity to accepted requirements, and good intentions will not make a school. Environment, atmosphere, the personality of the staff, are intangible but essential features, and a great teacher is a law unto himself.
>
> Definite effort should be made to promote during the years of active service, and particularly during those years that follow immediately upon college studies, the continued development of those imaginative ideas that comprised so high a percentage in time and in value of our school and college effort.
>
> An ever closer relation should exist between the office and the school, to the end that there may be a better understanding between these two essential

elements in our professional education, and that they may better cooperate in perfecting that balance between theory and practice that is essential to the best accomplishments in architecture.

THE AMERICAN-SCANDINAVIAN FOUNDATION

AMERICAN and Scandinavian students received scholarships amounting to $72,000 for the academic year 1928–1929 from the American-Scandinavian Foundation, according to its recent award report, which is summarized in the New York *Times*. Twenty-six university fellows and thirty-three industrial fellows were named. The aim of the organization is "to draw the American and Scandinavian peoples closer in bonds of intellectual kinship, to keep the lamp of international friendship burning and to dispel ignorance."

The first two American industrial fellows were appointed in 1928, posts for them having been obtained in Sweden through the allied organization of the foundation in Sweden, the Sverige-Amerika Stiftelsen, the report announces. Meanwhile in America several new appointments have been made available for Scandinavian students. In San Francisco the Bank of Italy has agreed to accept two industrial fellows of the association, one from Sweden and one from Denmark. The Swedish fellow has already taken up his work at the bank.

These fellowships were arranged by E. H. Frisell, president of the California Chapter of Foundation Associates. The Detroit Public Library is giving a year's training to a Swedish librarian. B. Altman and Co. and the Bankers Trust Company last year received their first industrial fellows.

It has been customary for some of the American universities to grant remission of tuition to fellows of the foundation. In 1928 a fellowship valued at $800 was appropriated by the University of Pittsburgh for a Norwegian. A special scholarship in sculpture was donated by Frederic Schaefer, of Pittsburgh, and awarded to Trygve Hammer, sculptor.

The report announces the sending to Sweden of an American art exhibition. It will be opened in Stockholm at the Royal Academy of Art in March, 1930, and will be under the patronage of Crown Prince Gustaf Adolf of Sweden.

Owen D. Young has been elected a trustee of the foundation to succeed William H. Short, resigned. Following a revision of the constitution to permit the enlargement of the board to twenty-one members the following have been elected trustees: Hans Christian Sonne, of New York; Frederic Schaefer, of Pittsburgh, and George N. Jeppson, of Worcester, Massachusetts.

James Creese, secretary of the foundation since 1921, presented his resignation from that office but was requested to continue as secretary until the close of the year. Mr. Creese retired from the foundation to become vice-president of Stevens Institute of Technology. Neilson Abeel was assistant secretary from August 1 until February 2 this year when he was elected secretary of the foundation.

GRANTS AND FELLOWSHIPS OF THE AMERICAN COUNCIL OF LEARNED SOCIETIES

GRANTS in aid of research, available at once, and of post-doctoral fellowships, available from July, 1930, are offered in the humanities by the American Council of Learned Societies.

The stipends aggregate many thousands of dollars. The fields of study are: Philosophy, philology, linguistics, literature, art, archeology, musicology, Oriental studies, including Sinology, Indology, Semitics, Assyriology and Egyptology; history and auxiliary sciences, except those branches that are essentially economic, social and political history, such as history of religion, thought, science, learning and the fine arts, paleography, diplomacy and chronology.

Grants in aid of research are of two categories—small grants and larger grants. The small grants are normally of the maximum of $300, but they may be increased to $500 when, in the judgment of the committee on aid to research, such increase is justified by unusual expenses, as of foreign travel.

The small grants are available to scholars of all ages, except for assistance in fulfilling the requirements for any academic degree, who are citizens of the United States or permanently employed or domiciled therein, and who are engaged in specific projects of research for which aid is actually needed and not obtainable from any other source.

The larger grants range in amount from $750 to $2,000, and are reserved for mature scholars of demonstrated ability who are engaged in important enterprises of research to which they are able to devote at least six months without interruption. The same conditions as to citizenship, residence or employment obtain as for the small grants. The object of the larger grants is to assist in the advancement of knowledge through aiding individual undertakings of fundamental importance.

The fellowships are of the post-doctoral type already offered by the Social Science Research Council and the National Research Council. Their object is to assist the better training of research and teaching personnel, and they are limited to scholars, citizens of the United States, who have received the Ph.D. degree or have acquired its equivalent, and who are still in the "training period." The amounts of the fellowships will be determined by individual needs.

Applications for both grants and fellowships must be made by January 15, 1930, on special forms that will be furnished after October 1 by the permanent secretary of the American Council of Learned Societies, 907 Fifteenth Street, N. W., Washington, D. C., to whom preliminary inquiries may be addressed.

At the same time, attention is called to the grants-in-aid and fellowships offered by the Social Science Research Council, New York Central Building, 230 Park Avenue, New York City, in economics, statistics, political science, sociology, anthropology, psychology, social, economic and political history and related subjects, such as law and human geography.

RADIO EDUCATION

The Advisory Committee on Radio Education appointed by the Secretary of the Interior to investigate radio as a medium for education held its first meeting in Chicago on June 19. According to a statement made by the department many institutions and school organizations have experimented with radio as a medium of instruction, and the results have been difficult to measure, although the possibilities are conceded to be great. Thorough study of the whole question is contemplated by the committee.

The members present at the conference were: Miss Judith Waller, representing William S. Paley, president of the Columbia Broadcasting Company; Mr. John W. Elwood, representing M. H. Aylesworth, president of the National Broadcasting Company; Dr. H. Robinson Shipherd, Business Training Corporation, New York, N. Y.; Professor W. W. Charters, bureau of educational research, Ohio State University, Columbus, Ohio; James A. Moyer, director of division of university extension, department of education, Boston, Mass.; George B. Zehmer, University of Virginia; Miss Alice Keith, director of educational department, Radio Corporation of America, New York, N. Y., Mrs. Howell Moorhead, Foreign Policy Association, New York, N. Y.

Dr. William John Cooper, United States Commissioner of Education, who, is chairman of the advisory committee, presided over the conference.

The committee took steps to raise $25,000 to finance its investigations. It proposes to submit a report of facts to the Secretary of the Interior not later than January 1, 1930, which will show the scope of radio instruction so far, and what appears to be its most significant features; will describe actual programs, methods and costs; and will set forth plans for recording educational activities which utilize radio. Dr. Shipherd was named as chairman of the fact-finding committee.

Supplementing the study of facts will be research in possibilities of further utilization of radio, by a committee of which Dr. W. W. Charters is chairman. This committee will measure, if practicable, the results already accomplished, will study techniques and will cooperate with authorities which are now broadcasting educational programs.

An executive committee with the commissioner of education as chairman was constituted to correlate the work of the several subcommittees, and to prepare recommendations for action by the advisory committee as a whole.

SUMMER LIBRARY CONFERENCE AT THE UNIVERSITY OF WISCONSIN

President Glenn Frank, of the University of Wisconsin, and Zona Gale Breeze, Wisconsin author, will open the fourth Summer Library Conference conducted by the Wisconsin Free Library Commission from July 1 to 15. President Frank will formally welcome the delegates to the university and Mrs. Breeze will speak on "Implications" on the evening of July 1.

An intensive program throughout the conference will include lectures by professors at the University of Wisconsin and by persons who are familiar with the problems of library work.

The conference, like its three predecessors in 1911, 1915 and 1923, each of which had an attendance of more than two hundred, is designed to give trustees, librarians and assistants an opportunity to consider through lectures, discussions and exhibits the changing and enlarging phases of library work.

Opportunities will be given delegates to study technical and professional subjects, sociology and community life, rural sociology, farm relief programs and problems, and library business and management.

In addition to regular courses at the University of Wisconsin, which will be open to the delegates, lectures by prominent men, exhibits to supplement the various courses and round-table discussion groups have been planned by the commission.

The program as arranged carries the following subjects and speakers:

"Writing Library News and Writing Special Articles on the Library," Professor W. G. Bleyer, director of the School of Journalism; "Adult Education," M. S. Dudgeon, of the Milwaukee Public Library; "Economic Value of Human Beings from the Viewpoint of School and Library," Samuel H. Ranck, of the Grand Rapids Public Library; "The New School Organization," Frank O. Holt, registrar, University of Wisconsin; "What the School Needs from the Library in History," Professor B. W. Phillips, of the Wisconsin High School; "What the School Needs from the Library in Biography," E. G. Doudna, secretary of the Board of Normal Regents. "Registration and Its Significance," Clara F. Baldwin, director of the Minnesota Library Commission; "Fundamentals of Organization and Management," F. O. Holt; "What the School Needs from the Library in Science," Professor Ira C. Davis, Wisconsin High School; "What the School Needs from the Library in Geography," Leavelva Bradbury, of the State Department of Education; "What the Library Can Do for Employed Youth," Mrs. Jennie M. Turner, of the State Board of Vocational Education; "Means of Encouraging Young People to Read Good Literature," Letha M. Davidson, supervisor of children's work, Des Moines Public Library; "Equipment and Planning of the School Library," Mary A. Smith, Madison Free Library; Question Box on School Libraries, M. H. Jackson, supervisor of school libraries.

Among the speakers on books are:

Philosophy, Professor Max Otto; religion, Rev. Robins W. Barstow, pastor of the First Congregational Church, Madison; biography, Carl Russell Fish; domestic arts, Abby L. Marlatt, director of course in home economics; agriculture and farm life, Clarence S. Hean, librarian, College of Agriculture; current problems, Dr. E. E. White, chief, Legislative Reference Library.

One evening of the conference will be devoted to a dramatic reading of "The Devil in the Cheese," by a group of university faculty readers, and one to an illustrated lecture on "Rambles Among Old Books," by Professor W. A. Sumner, of the department of agricultural journalism.

APPROPRIATIONS FOR THE CHICAGO PUBLIC SCHOOLS

Chicago's public schools, according to *The Christian Science Monitor,* are to get an additional $35,000,000 income for the next two years. A bill for a tax rate increase in 1929 and 1930 passed the Legislature and the Governor has announced he will allow it to become law without his signature.

This extra school money is granted for the limited period to tide the board of education over a tight place reached because it has struck the limit of its borrowing power.

Instead of paying 98 cents on every $100 of assessed valuations, Chicago will pay $1.47 in 1929. The next year it will pay $1.35. Then it will return to the old 98-cent rate unless there is new legislation.

Louis L. Emmerson, Governor, said he would not put his name to it chiefly "because it increases taxes without a referendum and does not provide any guarantee that the relief will be permanent." His reason for not using his veto power, he said, was because he realized that the schools had to have money.

The legal department of the board of education holds that the present situation is an emergency due to the delay in collecting taxes. Revaluation of property has been ordered here and the 1928 taxes, normally collectable in 1929, may not come in until 1930.

If the new valuations prove fair, however, the board should find its problems solved, for certain expected increases in assessments ought to bring in enough money to pay the educational bills, according to Ralph Condee, assistant attorney for the board. Financial experts on the other hand point out that a better budget system is needed.

THE MURRY AND LEONIE GUGGENHEIM FOUNDATION

MR. MURRY GUGGENHEIM has announced the establishment of the Murry and Leonie Guggenheim Foundation, Inc., for "the promotion through charitable and benevolent activities of the well-being of mankind throughout the world." Free clinics for dental relief work among children in New York City is the immediate aim of the foundation. The first clinic, on which work is to be started immediately, will cost between $3,000,000 and $4,000,000. Besides Mr. and Mrs. Guggenheim, charter members of the foundation are: Their son, Edmond A. Guggenheim, Carroll A. Wilson, attorney; Mr. Robbins and Dr. S. S. Goldwater, former commissioner of health of New York City. The announcement of the foundation as outlined by Mr. Guggenheim is in part:

> Mrs. Guggenheim and I, having become thoroughly convinced of the great necessity for dental relief work, especially among children, have decided to do what we can along this line. We are prepared to contribute a large sum of money for the construction, equipment and endowment of non-sectarian clinics for the treatment of children whose parents are not in a position to pay for this most important and essential work, and Dr. Goldwater has consented to formulate a suitable program. It is our intention to push the work vigorously, with the idea of placing the first unit in operation at the earliest date possible.
>
> General realization of the import of preventive dentistry, and of the lifelong benefits of dental care for young children, has quickened interest in the creation of a growing number of public or semi-public agencies, chiefly under auspices of educational and health organizations, for the wider extension of dental service, especially to children of pre-school age, to children in public schools and to children of parents who are financially unable to pay the conventional fees of the private practitioners.
>
> Benefactions such as the Forsyth Dental Infirmary for Children in Boston and the Rochester Dental Dispensary are needed in all parts of the country for the solution of health problems that involve the cooperation of dentistry.

In addition to preventive and reparative work, including departments for the straightening of crooked teeth, the new Guggenheim Foundation plans to provide for the training of dental hygienists for employment in public schools and industrial establishments. This is recognized as of the first importance, as only by the periodic cleansing and inspection of the teeth can many defects be discovered in their early stages and corrected. Efforts will be made to follow the example of the Rochester Dispensary in its close affiliation with the municipal school authorities.

The maintenance of the health of school children has long been a recognized part of the program of the New York City Board of Education, whose experts, together with those of the Department of Health, will be asked to assist in the formulation of an effective program.

Mr. Guggenheim said that he was counting on the cooperation and support of the dental societies. It is his opinion, instead of taking from the practicing dentists work which otherwise would be theirs, the result will be directly opposite. The proposed clinics will also benefit the dental profession by affording a valuable field for graduate study and training.

EDUCATIONAL NOTES AND NEWS

PRESIDENT WILLIAM A. MADDOX, of Rockford College, having completed ten years as president of that institution, the faculty and board of trustees, the general alumnae association and several of the branch associations extended to him at the recent commencement votes of thanks and appreciation for the ten years of progress.

THE degree of doctor of laws was conferred at the commencement exercises of the University of Michigan on Dr. Robert A. Millikan, director of the Norman Bridge Laboratory and chairman of the executive council of the California Institute of Technology.

Bowdoin College has conferred honorary degrees on Dr. James F. Norris, professor of organic chemistry at the Massachusetts Institute of Technology, and on William E. Lunt, professor of English history at Haverford College.

The honorary doctorate of science was conferred by Beloit College on June 17 on Dr. Walter Van Dyke Bingham, director of the Personnel Research Federation, New York City, for his contributions to industrial psychology.

Among honorary degrees conferred at the commencement exercises on June 12 of Marquette University was the doctorate of humane letters on Carlton Joseph Huntley Hayes, professor of history at Columbia University.

Loyola University, Chicago, has conferred the doctorate of laws on Dr. Edward A. Fitzpatrick, dean of the graduate school of Marquette University.

Professor James H. Breasted, of the University of Chicago, was awarded the Rosenberger medal at the university's one hundred and fifty-fifth convocation. The medal is given annually to the person connected with the university who has performed the greatest service "through research, in authorship, in invention, for discovery, for unusual public service or for anything deemed of great benefit to humanity."

Dr. T. Franklin Sibly, principal of the University of London, becomes vice-chancellor of the University of Reading, in succession to Dr. W. M. Childs, who is retiring from the vice-chancellorship in September.

Dr. Lewis H. Weed has retired as dean of the faculty of medicine of the Johns Hopkins University. He will remain head of the department of anatomy.

Dr. Richard G. Tyler, of the Massachusetts Institute of Technology, has been appointed professor of sanitary engineering and dean of the college of engineering at the University of Washington.

Dr. Robert Riegel has been appointed professor of statistics and insurance in the school of business administration of the University of Buffalo. For some time he has been a member of the faculty of the Wharton School at the University of Pennsylvania. At the University of Buffalo he will also be director of research in the bureau of business and social research.

William Leonard Crum, professor of statistics in the graduate school of business, Stanford University, has been elected professor of economics in Harvard College, to serve from September 1.

Dr. B. Youngblood, for seventeen years director of the Texas Experiment Station and for the past three years principal economist in the division of cotton marketing of the bureau of agricultural economics of the U. S. Department of Agriculture, has been appointed principal economist in the office of experiment stations. He will give his attention primarily to studying the status of research in this field, the nature of the complex problems presented and the organization of definite projects to advance their solution.

Dr. A. G. Black, of the University of Minnesota, will become head of the department of agricultural economics in the Iowa State College, and chief of the agricultural economics section of the experiment station on July 1, succeeding Dr. C. L. Holmes.

Dr. John Lee Coulter, president of the North Dakota Agricultural and Mechanical College at Fargo, North Dakota, who has specialized in rural economics, has been appointed chief economist of the Tariff Commission. He succeeds to the post made vacant by Dr. Charles R. Turner, resigned.

John G. Rossman, assistant superintendent of the schools of Gary, Indiana, has been elected head of the East Chicago school system, the appointment to take effect on August 1.

Howard G. Spalding, superintendent of the Ticonderoga, New York, High School, has become principal of the Junior-Senior High School at Balboa Heights, Canal Zone.

C. M. Workman, for the past five years head of the schools at Hamburg, Iowa, has been elected superintendent of schools at Carbondale, Pennsylvania, at an increase in salary of $2,000 a year. Mr. Workman will take up his new work on July 1.

DAVID J. SLEICHER, for the past five years supervising principal of the schools of Fleetwood, Pennsylvania, has resigned to accept a position as a representative for Allyn and Bacon, publishers, in western New York.

A. W. Yawberg, who was recently elected superintendent of Cuyahoga County, Ohio, has decided to remain at Berea, where he has lived for twenty-two years.

THE *School Board Journal* reports that Mr. Gustav J. Provo, a member of the school board of East Cleveland, Ohio, for the past thirteen years, was recently awarded a medal for outstanding work on the board of education and other civic organizations, and for his unselfish service to the city. Superintendent W. H. Kirk, of the local school system, presented Mr. Provo with a wreath of flowers in behalf of the teachers of the East Cleveland schools. The presentation was made at a dinner given in one of the local churches by Mr. E. M. Sprague, president of the East Cleveland commission.

IN recognition of the great value to this nation and to the public school system of the qualities of motherhood as exhibited by Mrs. Evangeline L. L. Lindbergh, a teacher in the public schools, the Board of Education of Detroit conferred upon her, in June, a medal of honor. The medal, designed by George W. Styles, equipment engineer of the Board of Education and well-known Detroit artist, in accordance with a resolution passed by the board in December, 1927, will bear the inscription: "Presented to Mrs. Evangeline L. L. Lindbergh by the Detroit Board of Education for national service as an educator and to commemorate the achievements of her son, Colonel Charles A. Lindbergh, in the advancement of international goodwill through aviation."

COLONEL M. D. HALL, for forty-three years division superintendent of schools of Fairfax County, Virginia, who retired at the close of the school year in June, was the guest of honor at a banquet in the Madison School, given by the members of the Fairfax County Teachers' Association. Mr. Hall was presented with a large sterling silver bowl.

GOVERNOR ALLEN, of Massachusetts, has named B. Preston Clark, of Boston; Dr. Zenos E. Scott, superintendent of schools in Springfield, and Martin T. Joyce, of Quincy, labor leader, as members of a special unpaid commission for the study of the general question of increasing the educational requirements of the commonwealth and of certain related matters. In his inaugural message the governor recommended that the compulsory school age be raised to fifteen years and the present study was authorized as a result of this recommendation.

DR. CLARENCE A. BARBOUR, recently named president of Brown University, has been elected chairman of the board of education of the Northern Baptist convention.

DR. ALLEN ROGERS BENHAM, professor of English at the University of Washington, has been granted a leave of absence for the academic year 1929–30.

DR. JOHN GRIER HIBBEN, president of Princeton University, and Mrs. Hibben have sailed for London. Dr. Hibben will speak at the annual dinner of the American Society in London at the Hotel Savoy on July 4. His subject will be on the relations between the United States and Great Britain.

MRS. SIDONIE MATSNER GRUENBERG, director of the Child Study Association of America and consultant in parental education of the child development institute, Teachers College, Columbia University, left on June 7 to attend the Home and School Conference in London to be held June 28 and 29. Mrs. Gruenberg will remain in Europe to take part in the conference of the World Federation of Education Associations, which will be held July 25 to August 4 in Geneva, and the World Conference on New Education, which will be held August 8 to 21 at Elsinore, Denmark. She will then go to Cambridge to participate in the Adult Education Conference, which will be held from August 22 to 29.

DR. M. LYLE SPENCER, president of the University of Washington, delivered the commencement address at the University of Idaho on June 10.

DR. JOHN A. H. KEITH, Pennsylvania State Superintendent of Public Instruction, gave the commencement address at the Pennsylvania State College on June 18.

AT the tenth annual Industrial Conference of Pennsylvania State College and the Personnel Research Federation held at Pennsylvania State College, on May 16, the opening address was by Dr. David A. Robertson, American Council on Education, "Recent Developments of Educational Personnel Practice," and was discussed by General R. I. Rees, assistant vice-president of the American Telephone and Telegraph Company.

STRATTON D. BROOKS, president of the University of Missouri, delivered the commencement address at Drury College, Springfield, Missouri; at the South Dakota State College of Agriculture and Mechanic Arts, Brookings, South Dakota, and at the Oklahoma Agricultural and Mechanical College, Stillwater, Oklahoma.

DR. FREDERICK GEORGE DONNAN, professor of general chemistry at University College, London, gave the commencement address at the Johns Hopkins University. He spoke on the relation of chemistry to modern life.

THE Archibald Cary Coolidge Memorial was unveiled in the hallway of the Harvard College Library on commencement day. The memorial was presented by Jerome D. Greene, of New York City, to the president and fellows of Harvard College on behalf of the group of friends of Professor Coolidge who had contributed to make this gift. President Lowell responded on behalf of the university. The memorial is the work of a Boston sculptor, Joseph A. Coletti. The Harvard College Library was chosen as the location of this memorial for the sake of commemorating Professor Coolidge's labors in helping to make that library the greatest university library in the world. He became director of the library in 1910.

DR. VERNON LOUIS PARRINGTON, professor of English in the University of Washington, died suddenly in London on June 17. He was fifty-eight years old.

ACCORDING to an announcement in the *Journal* of the American Mathematical Association the thirteenth summer meeting will be held at the University of Colorado, on Monday afternoon and Tuesday morning, August 26 and 27. A program of interest to college and university teachers of mathematics is being prepared. It will include the retiring presidential address of Professor W. B. Ford. Immediately following this meeting and lasting for the remainder of the week, there will be a colloquium and summer meeting of the American Mathematical Society. The colloquium will consist of a series of five lectures, beginning Tuesday afternoon, by Professor R. L. Moore, of the University of Texas, on "Point-set Theory." On Thursday afternoon, Professor Virgil Snyder will give his address as the retiring president of the society on "The Problem of Cubic Variety in Four-way Space." This meeting will offer an unusual opportunity to combine mathematical activities with a pleasant outing. Boulder is a beautiful city with a population of about 15,000, delightfully located at the entrance to the Rocky Mountains.

AT the annual congress of the Southeastern Union of Scientific Societies, which was held at Brighton, from June 5 to 8, Sir Arthur Keith gave his presidential address on "Southern Englishmen of the Pre-Roman and Roman Period."

THE fourteenth annual conference of the British Museums Association will be held at Worthing from July 1 to 5, under the presidency of Sir Henry Miers. The presidential address, on "Cooperation—the Association's Task," will be delivered on July 2, and will be open to discussion. In connection with the conference there will be an exhibition of museum furniture and requirements.

THE first assembly of the Pan-American Geographical and Historical Institute will convene at Mexico City in August, according to an announcement made recently at the Pan-American Union. The institute was created by resolution of the sixth International Conference of American States, which met at Havana in 1928, and by resolution of the Governing Board of Pan-American Union Mexico City was selected as the seat of the institute.

GROUND was broken on June 16 for the new buildings of the New York Hospital-Cornell Medical College Association's new buildings at York Avenue and East Sixty-ninth Street. The site of the new medical center includes the property from Sixty-eighth to Seventy-first Streets between York Avenue and Exterior Street and is just north of the Rockefeller Institute for Medical Research. Mr. Edward W. Sheldon, president of the board of governors of New York Hospital, turned the first spadeful of earth.

A GRANT of $1,000,000 has been given to Princeton University by the General Education Board.

THE Oberlin Graduate School of Religion has received a gift of $300,000 for a new building from Mr. John D. Rockefeller, Jr. It is the intention of the school to seek $200,000 more to increase the endowment and scholarship funds.

THE University of Denver has received gifts amounting to $200,000 from Paul T. Mayo for the salary fund. The money is to be spent in eight years at the rate of $25,000 per year.

ARRANGEMENTS have been made to start construction on a new men's gymnasium, to cost about $600,000, at the University of Southern California. The work will begin soon and it is hoped the building may be completed by the opening of the fall semester. The new gymnasium will replace the old basketball pavilion which was destroyed by fire recently.

ANNOUNCEMENT was made at the commencement exercises of Wellesley College of gifts to the semi-centennial fund amounting to $472,000, making the total to date $8,057,000 and leaving $943,000 to be raised to complete the $9,000,000 program. The largest single item was the conditional gift of $175,000 from Edward S. Harkness, of New York, if the college can raise $525,000 by July 1. To date $300,000 of this amount has been obtained.

A GIFT of $100,000 to Hotchkiss School has been made by Paul Block, newspaper publisher.

UNDER terms of the will of James B. Wilbur, Chicago banker and summer resident of Manchester, Vt., a trust fund of between $2,000,000 and $3,000,000 has been left the University of Vermont, subject to certain conditions. A trust fund of $500,000 has been set aside for a son, James B. Wilbur, of New Britain, Conn., and upon his death this additional fund will also go to the university. In his will Mr. Wilbur requires the university to limit its attendance to one thousand students annually, preference to be given to Vermont boys. The quota may be increased at the rate of 250 for every 100,000 increase in the state's population since the federal census in 1920. Should the University of Vermont fail to meet the restrictions imposed under the trust, the bequests go to the trust fund board of the Library of Congress. Bequests are also made as follows: $100,000 to the Vermont Historical Society; $25,000 to the Putnam Memorial Hospital, Bennington, Vt.; $25,000 to Western Reserve Historical Society, Cleveland; $100,000 to the trust fund board of the Library of Congress; $100,000 to the New York Historical Society, and $100,000 to the New York *Times* for the Hundred Neediest Cases Fund.

THE Association to Aid Scientific Research by Women announces its continued support of the American Woman's Table at the Zoological Station at Naples for the years 1929–1930 and 1930–1931. Applications for the use of the table must be made to the secretary of the Association, Mrs. Samuel F. Clarke, Williamstown, Massachusetts. There is no required limit of occupancy, but it is always hoped that a worker can arrange to stay for three months. No financial help is given—merely the opportunity to occupy a research room; but the American Woman's Table is fully equipped with apparatus so that none need be carried by the student. Since no instruction is given the table is only awarded to those who are ready to carry on independent investigation, and preferably to those who have a definite piece of work in mind which can best be carried on by the facilities offered at Naples. The American Woman's Table was first supported in 1898 on the suggestion of Dr. Ida Hyde, one of the first American women to study there, and as a courtesy to Dr. Dohrn on the twenty-fifth anniversary of the opening of the laboratory. With the exception of one war year, and a few years at a later period during reorganization of the support of the station, the table has been continuously maintained by the Association to Aid Scientific Research by Women.

THE United States Civil Service Commission announces an open competitive examination for supervisor of vocational rehabilitation for the District of Columbia. Applications must be on file with the commission at Washington, D. C., not later than July 17. The entrance salary is $3,800 a year. Higher-salaried positions are filled through promotion. The duties are, under general administrative direction, to supervise and promote the vocational rehabilitation program for the District of Columbia under the Act of February 23, 1929, providing for the vocational rehabilitation of persons disabled in the District of Columbia; to establish and maintain contacts and relations with governmental, commercial, industrial and civic cooperative agencies, to contract for training facilities, both public and private, and to organize and maintain systematic and comprehensive statistical and financial records; to make studies, investigations and reports as required to promote the welfare of the service, and to perform related work as required. For this position men are desired. Competitors will not be required to report for examination at any place, but will be rated on their education, training and experience, and on a thesis or publication to be filed by the applicant.

The graduate faculty of the University of Iowa has adopted a new optional method of pursuing graduate work, to be known as the "Individual Plan." The purpose of this plan is to place greater responsibility on the student for scholarly initiative and self-help; and in turn, to grant freedom from such procedures as taking courses, course examinations and earning credits in terms of grades. The plan is open to candidates for the doctorate who pass a qualifying examination, usually combined with the master's examination, at the end of the first year of graduate work and are recommended by the committee for this privilege. They must present an accepted program for a unified field of study and must secure the approval of sponsors and of the Individual Plan Committee. The sponsors are responsible for preliminary advice, organization and program, and constant guidance in consultation. In view of this freedom, the candidate, at the time he qualifies for the degree, must pass a final comprehensive examination, both written and oral, covering his field of study.

The British Medical Research Council, after consultation with the Ministry of Health and the Board of Education, have appointed the following committee to inquire into the prevalence and mode of spread of minor epidemics in residential schools, especially those believed to be spread by "droplet infection," and to report upon the means by which they may be prevented or restricted: Sir George Newman, *chairman;* Dame Janet Campbell; Dr. R. H. Crowley; Surgeon-Commander S. F. Dudley, M.D.; Dr. J. A. Glover; Professor M. Greenwood; Mr. L. R. Lempriere; Miss E. M. Newbold; Professor W. W. C. Topley; Mrs. Joyce Wilson, *secretary.*

DISCUSSION

THE RESPONSIBILITY OF APPOINTING STATE SUPERINTENDENTS

A vital, abiding interest in any system built up by a democracy demands a consideration of its origin and evolution to see how its conserved assets may serve the future. That consideration will ripen a judgment which can select the best means to chart the channel of the greatest continuing usefulness of that system. The question of how education became a state function, rather than a local function, is of interest because of a recent attack on a plan splendidly evolved in the State and, secondly, because of an equally important question that is being discussed as to the best method of appointing a state superintendent of education. Both questions find their answers in a review of educational practices which began with our republic and which have resulted in the various school codes of the States.

When our constitution was adopted in 1789, there had been no discussion as to education. The great task of our statesmen was to establish a stable government for the nation, with as many matters of vital importance as possible left in the hands of the States. The reason is manifest. In 1791, the tenth amendment to the constitution was passed. It specifically states that "powers not delegated to the United States by the Constitution, nor prohibited by it to the States, are reserved to the States respectively, or to the people." Thus, education and control of it passed historically to each State, to develop according to its peculiar needs. In

Pennsylvania, after forty-three years, the first school law was made in 1834, and the public-school system of the State was born. Free schools were established. When the system was attacked, Thaddeus Stevens, the great champion of the Pennsylvania public schools, defended the integrity of the state program that secured equal educational opportunity in all parts of that greatly diversified state.

Many laws, at first, were permissive in character. People were permitted by the State to meet, organize and tax themselves to maintain schools. The practices found good through experimentation became fixed by State enactment into laws, and the State secured those good results to all parts of the State by legislation. The approved custom became mandatory. In other words, state control said to citizens, try out your local plans; if they are good, they may become fixed for school guidance. The collection of these enactments is called the school code. The State thus maintained its right, as the largest governmental unit, to experiment and, in the course of time, to select only those results which would promote the general welfare in education, and to fix them by legislative enactment as a part of the code. Each section of the state is thereby represented in the State code by its *best approved practice.*

This brief review of the origin and development of the Pennsylvania school code helps us to realize how state control has secured the best results from past experience with which to chart future effective school management. This accumulated wisdom prevents great vagaries in education, prevents insular and community inbreeding and liberates to a whole State the best from each part of the State. Each State has thus gradually developed a system of laws relating to education for the evolution of which those interested in education have been responsible.

The State now vests responsibility in a state department of education, with a state superintendent at its head. He must present a program of education to the governor for his approval, and the governor, in turn, to the legislature, the taxing body, for the financial support of that program. Education is truly a larger thing than a local interest. The people, as a whole, in the State, have been supremely responsible in the matter of educational legislation, including taxation for education, methods of administration and the proper appointment of the state superintendent.

Those who judge hastily are inclined to think that legislative enactment is vested in the legislature alone; that the school code has been the product of the legislative body. They fail to see that current practice, current sanction, has preceded the presentation of an act to the legislature. If an act is not good, two sources are responsible: first, the people, whose money pays for education through taxation and who should see that educational plans prepare for social, industrial and economic welfare; second, the state superintendent. These two factors should be involved in any change.

In a democracy, the great trouble lies in delegating power and then not watching to see that the power is functioning properly. Increasingly, the lay body has delegated all interest in education to the teachers. The great mass of citizens has functioned less and less in its rightful, critical attitude toward the State's greatest interest and expense, *i.e.,* education. To counteract this, and to replace responsibility again in the citizen body, a council of education, which should consist of lay members, has been appointed to suggest policies, to advise from the citizens' standpoint, so that the will of the people is expressed in all things educational. This appointive body respects citizen approval or censure. It seeks to secure lay reaction to educational policy. It functions as the voice of the people interested in education, as opposed to that of technical educators. It represents the employer agency, the State, in contradistinction to the employee attitude, the teacher. As people become less interested in educational policies and outcomes, they increasingly become dependent on the advice of technically trained teachers. The result is not conducive to the best progress of education. To safeguard the citizens' interest, then, our best practice has evolved the appointment of a council of education from among the people. This group is peculiarly responsible as the testing body, the suggesting group, the guarding group, which sees that education bought and paid for by the State produces that kind of education which shall develop self-guidance, self-control, and which shall be worthy of that freedom for which the State has nurtured it. For citizens to safeguard education thus is the highest and best expression of our belief in education.

When the council of education functions, it seeks the best State superintendent, and secures to him the right of a permanent continuance of educational policy without the injection of politics as such, and without the interference of unseasoned judgment which seeks an opportunity to attack rather than to construct. The integrity of the State council lies not only in its outlook and grasp of educational needs, but also in its lay personnel. With the appointment of one technical educator again begins the weakness of delegating more power to the technician. If more than one educator should be in the council the bias is more noticeable, and again the responsibility is delegated farther away from its rightful source, the people. The people never sanction professional educators on a local board of education, hence a State should never sanction professional administrators or educators on a state council of education. The state council should function for the citizens' welfare. It should not merely sanction administrative expediency suggested by educators. It should be the auditing committee for the department of education. For these reasons the chief function of the council should be the appointment of the state superintendent who should receive suggestions relating to education from them. He, in turn, should give them technical significance. Thus should be formulated a State program of education for which the State superintendent is responsible to the governor.

We are now making school history. The thing to decide from recent experimentation is this: Is it better for the council of education to select and appoint a State superintendent of instruction and retain him as long as his program is constructive and economically progressive? Or is it better for the governor of a State to appoint and select a state superintendent each term to express a program that may seem expedient during one term and inexpedient during another? The economic loss of the latter method is apparent. In no great business does a specially trained individual function according to his politics. In the greatest business of the State, that of education for useful citizenship, no specially trained and fit person should be State superintendent during one term only—his appointment should be continuing in order to secure the best development and growth of education in the State. By making him responsible to the State through the council of education this may be accomplished. Any other method of appointment means defeat of purpose. For this reason it is desirable that the council of education should appoint the state superintendent and that he should be directly responsible to them for a program that will best fit a State for its greatest participation in securing national progress and welfare.

JESSIE GRAY

A PHASE OF RECORD KEEPING

A PIECE of string tied around the finger, an empty salt jar set toward the front of the kitchen table, a few words jotted down on a piece of memo paper, an unanswered letter laid in the center of the desk—all are forms of record keeping. Record keeping is as old as civilization and it is as varied too. In fact civilization itself has been dependent upon record keeping for its progress. If we have nothing to remind us of what has gone before we can not benefit by our experiences or the experiences of others. It is most interesting to trace record keeping throughout the ages and note particularly the factors that influenced both the type and the volume. Although time forbids a résumé of such a study, we necessarily call attention to the conclusion—namely, that to-day we are recording more than was ever recorded in the history of humankind. We record masterpieces of music, we record masterpieces of drama, we record the courses of the stars, we record quakes of the earth, we record speed, altitude, temperature, pressure, color, beauty, efficiency, intelligence, industry and a thousand and one other things, some of which we did not even know existed a few years ago. Now the question which presents itself, is—"What's the use of all this?"

Our discussion must naturally be limited to a phase of record keeping which directly concerns us as fellow workers in the field of education. In this matter of child accounting three questions rightly suggest themselves:

(1) What records shall we keep?
(2) Why shall we keep them?
(3) How shall we keep them?

Questions 1 and 2—the what and the why—are possibly so closely allied and so dovetailed that we may necessarily have to answer them jointly. But before we dare begin our task it seems that we must start at the beginning and answer still another question which is fundamentally essential to these other three. The question is, "What is the ultimate object of education?" I suggest that query—not to discuss it, for I am sure I may take for granted that although we may each express it differently, we do in the main agree—I suggest the question, rather that we may start thinking from the same point and consider the "record keeping" in the light of that ultimate conception. However we may wish to express that ultimate objective, I think we agree that at the center of all stands the child. We no longer make courses of study and expect children to adapt themselves to them—we try now to fit the curricula to children. We admit individual differences, whether we do anything about them or not. Education, we say, is the art of producing useful changes in individuals. We agree that these changes can not in all likelihood be produced in two individuals by the same method. Whether we admit it or not, I believe our general impression of boyhood and girlhood is based upon those qualities which are immeasurable or at least extremely difficult to score, such as honesty, reliability, resourcefulness, loyalty, enthusiasm, etc. We believe that attitude is one of the biggest factors in the learning process, and that environment and health both exert a most potent influence. We know that industry plays a big part in a youngster's success, and we often wonder whether certain students are living up to the best of their ability. These are some of the factors which consciously or unconsciously influence our ultimate conception of what education should do.

Now to go back to question number one. "What records should we keep?" From the standpoint of the number of records that should be kept, there are in vogue at the present time three classes of record systems: first, a system inadequate because of its incompleteness; second, the opposite extreme, a system which calls for a laborious compilation of much more data than can ever practically be used; and third, a system which attempts to hit the happy medium. I am certain that we would readily vote for system number three, and we say to ourselves, "Well that's another place where I check." But how are we ever going to know what data should compose this "just enough" record.

Possibly I can make my point a bit clearer by suggesting an analogy. Say, for instance, you are a physician. A patient comes to you and tells you he is ill. He does not know what the trouble is but he knows he is losing weight; he has lost his appetite and he just feels miserable all over. What do you believe you as a skilled physician would do?

"Well," you say, "that's easy. I'd first get his family history as much in detail as I could. Then I'd give him a thorough examination. If I had the facilities, I would undoubtedly ask him to remain for a few days, so that I might study his case more carefully. In fact, to make the most reliable diagnosis I would collect all the data that might have a bearing upon his condition."

In short, that is the guiding principle which must influence us in deciding the character and the amount of data that should constitute our record systems. To be sure, we want permanent records so that we may have the data on hand when another institution or a prospective employer requests it. But were that the only reason for compiling data, I am afraid schools could by no means justify the amount of time and expense that record keeping demands. As men and women entrusted with the sacred task of developing childhood and casting destiny, it is most certainly our first responsibility to understand and to diagnose. Our permanent records ought to mean to us what an X-ray negative means to a medical man. Only in so far as an X-ray negative is carefully studied in an effort to understand the body conditions is it worth anything. Likewise, only in so far as a record is used and most scrutinizingly studied is its compiling justifiable.

"What records shall we keep?" Testing by this criterion, we wish to suggest the following:

(1) *General Information:* school address, home address, telephone number, place of birth, nationality, parent or guardian, occupation and place of

employment, previous schools attended, vocational choice. Under this same general heading of "General Information," we suggest withdrawal data, *i.e.*, if withdrawn to work, form of occupation, name of employer, location; if transferred to another school, name of city and school; if ill, name of attending physician; if graduated, name of college or place of employment. This withdrawal data should prove most valuable in gradually moulding the curricula, especially the vocational.

(2) *Attendance:* days absent, times tardy, with period or semester summaries.

(3) *Scholarship:* subjects and grades, results and credits, with a grand summary showing standing in graduating class.

(4) *Educational and Mental Tests:* a subject tabulation of achievement tests, grouped by departments, so that a quick inspection would reveal the trend; also a tabulation of individual and group intelligence tests, either showing standard norm as basis of comparison, or a translation into the IQ.

(5) *Health:* including only the items that will and can be profitably used. Careful follow-up on every deficiency should be made and recorded.

(6) *Discipline:* any disciplinary difficulty or difficulties serious enough to be of any diagnostic value.

(7) *Character:* each teacher shall rate each of her students twice a year on as many items of a set of character qualities as shall be agreed upon. This rating shall be merely tallied, irrespective of teacher, and kept permanently.

Impracticable as this latter item may seem, I wish to say that of all the records just enumerated, the character record is of most interest from the standpoint of student diagnosis, as well as from the fact that this is the type of data that is in constant demand by prospective employers.

The "why" of these records has been covered previously and so now we come to the "how."

The difficulty with so many record systems is that the data are so scattered that it is a real task, which takes a considerable amount of time, to collect from the files all the information about a single individual. Experience seems to point toward a single cumulative record, including in some convenient form blanks for all these different kinds of data.

The record should be compact, easily accessible and readily comprehensible. Above all things it should include only such data as will be used and will be valuable to the teacher or administrator who attempts to better understand the child in an effort to be of greater service.

A. R. KEPPEL

SENIOR-JUNIOR HIGH SCHOOL,
MARIETTA, OHIO

SPECIAL CORRESPONDENCE

THE SUMMER SESSION OF COLUMBIA UNIVERSITY

THE Summer Session of Columbia University, both through its student group and through its faculty, enables the university to bring together a body of American educators that is distinctly national in character.

The summer faculty includes more men of professorial rank than at any other period of the year. It constitutes the university's opportunity to invite eminent scholars of other institutions who are not free the rest of the year to lecture here for the six-week period. More than two hundred professors from other institutions will take part in the work this summer.

The curriculum stresses education and psychology courses. They include a psychology seminar under the direction of Professor Richard Maurice Elliott, of the University of Minnesota, formerly instructor in psychology at Harvard and at Yale Universities. Experimental psychology, human behavior and psychopathology will be offered.

A course in abnormal psychology, planned for those intending to enter the field of psychiatric social work, will be conducted by Dr. A. M. Phillips and Dr. Oswald Boltz, with the cooperation of the staff of the Manhattan State Hospital, Ward's Island, where clinical demonstrations will be given.

Professor Clark Leonard Hull, recently called from the University of Wisconsin to Yale University, will conduct lectures and practice work in the principles of aptitude testing.

Architecture, theology, law, library service, journalism, music and Romance languages are among the subjects for which special programs have been arranged.

The courses in architecture have been designed to bring students in contact with types of buildings in New York City and to encourage them to utilize the experience directly in their studies. Visits under the guidance of the teaching staff will be made to the finest examples of office buildings, hotels, apartment houses, hospitals, theaters, churches, public buildings and private estates in the suburbs.

Graduate courses in theology will be given at the Union Theological Seminary, Broadway and 120th Street. They include the Old and the New Testament, Philosophy of Religion, Christian Ethics, Religious Education, Practical Theology and Foreign Service.

A special feature of the courses in library service is the three weeks' program of intensive training for workers in the book trade. Three hours of lectures each morning beginning July 8 will be followed by afternoon visits of observation to establishments representing the various aspects of the trade, from printing house, through publishing office and wholesale house, to bookshops of various kinds.

A survey of publishers' lines will be made, with suggestions for buying stock, choice of editions to suit various markets, quantities, discounts, terms and other practical problems. There will also be a series of lectures on locating and equipping a bookshop, arrangement of stock, display and advertising, bookkeeping and sales records.

Graduate courses in modern languages include English, German, French, Italian and Spanish. Dr. Fortunat Strowski, visiting professor from the University of Paris and member of the Institute of France, will lecture on French civilization and French literature.

Dr. Guido Ferrando, professor of English literature in Florence, Italy, will give a series of lectures on the history of Italian literature and on the relations between Italian and English literature in the nineteenth century.

The university's foreign cultural centers, the Casa Italiana, the Deutsches Haus and the Maison Française, will cooperate with summer-session students of modern languages.

An extensive program of musical education forms an integral part of the summer-session work. It is adapted particularly to the needs of teachers of vocal and instrumental music in public or private schools. Music demonstration classes meet daily in the Lincoln School Building. Song leading and community music will be considered with respect to group activities suitable for communities of various sizes, and will embrace elementary instruction on simple instruments for camps and playgrounds.

The teaching of music in the primary grades, including singing, rhythmic games and interpretative movements, will be offered in connection with demonstration classes in the Horace Mann School. Music for the grammar grades and for high schools will develop methods of organizing school choruses, glee clubs, orchestras and bands. Problems of music supervision in cities of 30,000 and over will be treated in special lectures.

There will also be several courses in the history and appreciation of music and in methods of teaching music appreciation, in the psychology of music and in Dalcroze eurythmics.

In addition to the many free concerts and entertainments offered on the campus, Morningside's summer community will be encouraged to profit by the cultural advantages of New York City. Excursions to places of historic and literary interest will be conducted under the university's auspices. Visits will be made to the Metropolitan Museum, to the financial section, to a metropolitan newspaper plant, to churches and cathedrals, to Sleepy Hollow, the cottage of Edgar Allan Poe, the Statue of Liberty, Fraunce's Tavern and other points of interest. Last year 12,000 summer-session students participated in these excursions.

John J. Coss,
Director

QUOTATIONS

EDUCATION AND THE BRITISH LABOR GOVERNMENT

The net result of the general election seems to be that the country is anxious that the labor party, after an interval of four and a half years, should have another term of office, but a term of office limited by the condition that no violent political experiments should be tried. Continuity of general policy seems to be indicated, with other hands to carry that policy out.

Mr. MacDonald appears to have expressed in his post-election declaration a general policy of peace, good-will and progressive social effort that might almost have come from the lips of Mr. Baldwin. These columns do not concern themselves with general politics, but they are concerned with the effect of substantial political changes on the national subject of education, a subject that in common with foreign affairs is now regarded as existing in a plane above, or rather independent of, the politics of the hour. Lord Rosebery strove with success to place the conduct of foreign affairs in a position where continuity of policy could be relied upon by foreign governments, and it may be said that Lord Eustace Percy and his immediate predecessors have placed the conduct of national education in a position where continuity of policy can be relied upon by the Board of Education, the local education authorities, the teaching profession, and (not least) the parents. Cautious but definite progress has been the policy of the last Minister of Education, and he has shown that such progress is consistent with reasonable economy of expenditure. His successor will find the whole educational system in good working order and ready for such expansion as is consistent with the educational policy put forward by the labor party, a policy that is largely identical with that adumbrated by the other parties.

On one point, however, it may be that the new ministry will be found inclined to move faster than the last ministry. Lord Eustace Percy was tempted to delay the raising of the compulsory school age to fifteen years until, in the judgment of the local authorities, the country is ready for it. In these columns that Fabian policy has always been opposed, and for the simple reason that it leaves progress in the hands of the backward authorities. The Hadow scheme can not be at work until the age of leaving is postponed to fifteen years, and it is the business of the Board of Education to provide the basis on which the Hadow scheme can be worked. The leaving age of fifteen will give a four-year course in which the new system of secondary education can have full play. The four-year course will make clear what children are fit for advanced secondary education, what children should be transferred to the regions of purely technical education, and the classes of children who are ready to enter this or that form of industry or commerce. The sooner the new administration can fix a date for the operation throughout the country of a new compulsory leaving age the better. It will give the local authorities a time limit in which to fix the forms of their local schemes in accordance with the new four-year course, and it will give the additional advantage that the school medical service can replan that service on the basis of the examination of children above the age of fourteen. No party, indeed, would object to a system by which the school medical service would have the duty to inspect all school leavers up to the age of sixteen. A provision to that effect would show at once whether the employment into which the children enter on leaving school at fifteen is or is not beneficial employment.

A second problem with which the new administration will have to deal is that of reconditioning the schools. It has become clear that the financial position of some local authorities and practically of all the diocesan authorities is such that many years must pass, if treasury aid is not granted, before the black lists are wiped out. The late administration had come to the conclusion, the obviously right conclusion, that the black lists of ineffective school buildings must be wiped out at once, and that the only way to do it is the making of non-recurring special building or reconditioning treasury grants. In that way, and in that way only, can the school buildings of the country be made fit for the children, and in that way only can the Hadow scheme of universal secondary education be made effective. The voluntary schools have for a century and a quarter borne the burden in most rural districts of elementary education. Local grants of this kind will not be grants in favor of this or that denomination, but grants that will make possible a universal national system of primary and secondary education. The matter is one that fortunately can be dealt with at once, since every school that is on the black lists—provided and non-provided—has schemes on paper which can at once be carried out if the funds are provided. The condition of the grant should be that the work will be completed at the latest for the opening of the new school term in the autumn of 1930. Whatever the other political prospects of the immediate future may be, the future of national education ought to be safe. The lines of progress were long since laid down in Mr. Fisher's day, so that all three parties in the state can claim a share in the most significant movement of modern times.—*The London Times Educational Supplement.*

REPORTS

FEDERAL AND LOCAL SUPPORT OF SCHOOLS

SECRETARY RAY LYMAN WILBUR, of the Department of the Interior, delivered the following speech on "Local Self-government in Education" on May 3, before the twelfth annual meeting of the American Council on Education, held at the National Research Council in Washington.

I have often wished that I might have had the pleasure of sitting in at the discussions when the basic principles underlying the organization of the United States of America were being thought out loud by men like Thomas Jefferson and Benjamin Franklin. It seems to me that the wisest and shrewdest thing that was done was to encourage universal public education as the basis upon which citizenship should rest. The schoolhouse and the church have been the earliest community enterprises throughout the history of our gradual conquest of a great continent. They came just as soon as sustenance and defense had been mastered. In themselves, they were most significant because they brought local self-government and self-control into play.

There has been a unique distribution of the taxing power so that the majority of the expenditures for taxation have been raised and spent in the local districts and only a modest percentage outside of those for war and its after effects has come from the central government in Washington. This, together with the organization of the state governments, has permitted of a wide range of development in the public schools. Fortunately, too, there were no national universities, and the state universities followed a prolonged period of privately operated and later privately endowed institutions of higher learning. When the state universities appeared they were under the constant stimulation of private and independent institutions of equal rank. This kept the hand of centralized government largely off of the school-teacher and the schoolroom. Of course, there have been marked inadequacies in districts without a proper sense of self-government, without natural organizing power and without financial strength. Some of those who have looked over our educational system have noticed only these dark spots and have thought that a national mechanism should be devised that would be nationwide in scope and would bring these weaker or dark spots at least up to the average level of the country. Correction of abuses is a poor method of developing proper administration. It seems to me that there is a distinct menace in the centralization in the national government of any large educational scheme with extensive financial resources available. Abnormal power to mold and standardize and crystallize education, which would go with the dollars, would be more damaging to local government, local aspiration and self-respect and to state government and state self-respect, than any assistance that might come from the funds.

We cannot rise higher than our source. That source in government with us is local. The family and the local community must be the places where citizenship is built and where the fiber of the nation is strengthened and its forces recruited. Too much help from afar is harmful to the initiative and self-reliance requisite for character in a community.

The place of the national government is not that of supplying funds in large amounts for carrying on the administrative functions of education in the communities, but to develop methods, ideals and procedures, and to present them, to be taken on their merits. The national government, too, can give wide-spread information on procedures, can report on what is actually going on in different parts of the country and in the world and can unify to some extent the objects of those in the field of education in so far as unification is desirable. There is a distinct place for this sort of thing in the administrative side of the national government, but it should not be recognized as an administrative position with large funds at its disposal. A department of education similar to the other departments of the government is not required. An adequate position for education within a department and with sufficient financial support for its research, survey and other work, is all that is needed.

Great gains are possible in our whole educational scheme through national leadership provided in this way. Education is preparation for the future, and there must be constant change to keep in step with the advances made. Our conceptions regarding the mental make-up of children are shifting and the requirements of life are changing with a civilization which is being revamped by the practical applications of science and invention. The object of those of us who seek the greatest possible advantages for all from education can, it seems to me, be accomplished without disturbing the initiative and responsibility of local and state units of government.

A DEPARTMENT OF EDUCATION

Dr. Thos. E. Finegan, educational director of the Eastman Kodak Company, formerly state superintendent of public instruction for Pennsylvania, has addressed the following open letter to the president of the United States:

In your address before the Department of Superintendence of the National Education Association, in the winter of 1926, and in other public addresses and documents since that time, you have spoken with such clearness and effectiveness upon the relation of education to the cultural and material interests of the country and upon the scope of the educational facilities which America should provide for her children, that you have given great encouragement and satisfaction to administrators and students of education.

These views expressed by you have also stimulated the educational workers of the country to increase their efforts in behalf of the movement which seeks the establishment of a federal department of education, having a secretary at its head who shall possess the rank of a cabinet officer.

The traditions and practices in education in our country have fortunately established education as a subject of state and not national direction and control. Nevertheless, the federal government has always shown a vital concern in the development of education and for years has appropriated funds for its support, and has otherwise provided for an extension of its service. There has been no inconsistency in this action of the federal government and no conflict with the established usages and practices of the nation in educational affairs.

Speaking from an experience of more than thirty years in state educational administration in the state departments of New York and Pennsylvania, and being hostile, therefore, to any thought, even, of federal domination, control, or interference with education, I am writing to express the opinion that no measure could be inaugurated which would contribute so much to the improvement and effectiveness of our state educational systems and to the development of the types of education essential to our civilization as the establishment of a federal department of education.

The states generally can not afford to expend the funds which must be made available to do the research work that is required to supply the information and knowledge on the basic aspects of modern education which must be placed at the disposal of state administrators before they can intelligently organize and administer state education systems adapted to the needs of their respective states. States should not be expected to render this service. Such research service should not be provided solely through private sources or by foundations.

Education is a public function. It serves industry, labor, professional life, scientific endeavor and every citizen of the land. The sources which influence its organization and administration should be public in nature. The purpose of research in education is to obtain basic data and knowledge upon which to build a solid foundation in harmony with the American philosophy of life and government, and to develop practices and procedure which will enable each state to erect a superstructure upon this foundation which will best serve the social and economic needs of its people.

The benefits flowing from a state system of education are not limited to the people of the state which maintains such system. The benefits radiate throughout the whole land, and each of the forty-eight states profits therefrom. The federal government may properly, therefore, provide the facilities for scientific research in education, and make the results available for state and local systems of education and for educational institutions in general. I do not believe adequate research service will ever be provided through any other agency.

A nation whose people, through state initiative and local and state taxation, expend $2,500,000,000 annually on a project so vital to its cultural interests and industrial and commercial supremacy, should afford the several states adequate guidance in the operation of the enterprise upon which this vast sum is expended.

The amount invested in the maintenance of a federal department of education, functioning as a national clearing house in the field of education and as a great research institution, would not only result in the maintenance in each of the forty-eight states of a school system meeting the needs of the country, but it would also be the means of diverting large sums of money now expended upon education with ineffective results into channels upon which every dollar invested could be made to yield much larger returns to the public.

The teacher-training institutions of the country would be greatly strengthened and would be sending into the schools a body of teachers of greater vision, increased mental power, and a clearer conception of human relationships; health programs could be vitalized and human happiness increased; school attendance organizations could be transformed from police agencies into those engaged in accounting and conserving the rights of childhood; rural schools could be made a great asset to the agricultural interests of the nation; and in fact every vital aspect of state education and all the problems growing out of the adjustments of education to our complicated civilization would receive the scientific study and consideration which their importance demands by the establishment of a federal department of education.

This service would be provided without contravening in any way the sound American principle that education is a state function. In cooperation with existing educational institutions and agencies, with leading industrial and commercial corporations, with health departments and other health agencies, with city and state governmental departments, and with many of the bureaus and departments of the federal government which contain a wealth of material bearing upon the educational needs of the land, a federal department of education could place at the disposal of each state and each community the basic data and knowledge upon which a system of education should rest.

This department would never speak with the voice of official authority or legal mandates. It would, however, speak with knowledge born of the experiences of mankind, and with such professional and scientific understanding that its opinion would be sought by all educational interests of the nation. The possibilities of its service are not limited to America.

EDUCATIONAL RESEARCH AND STATISTICS

FACTORS AFFECTING ABILITY IN HANDWRITING

THE nature of handwriting as a subject taught in our schools is such as to set it apart from the major branches. The task of the child learning to write has been compared to that of an adult learning to trace a star in the mirror-drawing experiment. The work is preeminently one of building new eye-hand coordinations, of muscular control in response to visual and kinesthetic sensations. This training of muscles, making automatic an organization of motor responses in the midbrain, calls for quite different abilities from those employed in learning to spell a word or to multiply by a two-place number—skills which draw upon associative centers of the cerebrum.

Evidence is not lacking which indicates that ability in muscular control does not develop *pari passu* with ability to form symbolic connections with words and figures. A study of the scores of young children in the four-year-old tests of the Binet Scale shows that subjects who earn fairly high average scores often fail in the fourth test, that of copying the square. In revising Binet's 1911 scale Terman shifted the diamond-copying test from year VI to year VII, explaining that he had found too low a proportion of successes at six years to warrant its location at that age, an age, however, at which school practice does not hesitate to introduce the child to verbal, *i.e.*, symbolic learning. Miss Margaret Baxter, a student at Harvard Graduate School of Education, in a study of the diamond-copying test, found that children frequently lag in this test behind their attainment in other tests of the same age group. Finally, a study made by Dr. E. A. Lincoln of the achievement of under-age children in their first three years in the Winchester, Massachusetts, public schools revealed 23.7 per cent. of these superior children ranking in the bottom quarter of achievement in penmanship as against 15.8 per cent., 13.2 per cent. and 7.9 per cent. respectively in arithmetic, spelling and reading. The conclusion is natural that success in writing and probably also drawing is conditioned upon abilities other than general intelligence as measured by the tests.

The study here reported undertook to discover what special functions occur most often in connection with good penmanship. A guess was made that anatomic age as measured by the degree of ossification of the wrist bones might indicate physical maturity as a factor. Measurement of carpal development has found favor with a number of investigators, among whom Dearborn and B. T. Baldwin have carried on studies of the same children over a period of years, and may be said to have taken its place beside mental age as one of the major quantitative measures of growth. A student of Dearborn's, D. A. Prescott, in 1923 originated and standardized an objective method of measuring the development of the wrist bones. This measure, known as the anatomic index, is found by dividing the sum of the diameters of the carpal bones by the width of the hand at its base.

The first intent of the present study was to ascertain what correlation exists between anatomic age as expressed by the anatomic index (AI) and the two measures of writing ability commonly used, rate and quality. Secondary questions included (*a*) What other functions appear to influence quality and rapidity of handwriting in children? and (*b*) How are rate and quality of writing related to each other? A study of the rôle played by the IQ is indispensable to an understanding of other relationships in school achievement. The second question is important to the teaching of penmanship, particularly if it can be shown that the writing of school children can be speeded up without marked loss to legibility.

This study is based upon samples of handwriting taken from 550-odd children in grades III, IV, V and VI in the public schools of a city of 50,000 people suburban to Boston. As this city is one of those which contribute annually measurements in a wide variety of traits to Dearborn's ten-year project known as the Harvard Growth Study, records were available at the Harvard Psychoeducational Clinic of the AI and IQ for the same children over a five-year period. The most recent measures of anatomic age had been taken within a few weeks of the date of the handwriting tests. The fourth variable, the intelligence quotient, was computed from an average of IQ's taken over the five-year period and based upon results of Binet tests, the Dearborn Group Test of Intelligence and the Otis Group Intelligence Scale. Handwriting samples were secured by giving the Holmes Penmanship Test, which provides both a rate and a quality test. As it seemed desirable to secure specimens truly representative of each child's writing, the directions for the quality section of the Holmes Test were changed from "I am going to give you a test in penmanship from dictation," to "I am going to give you a story to write from dictation," followed by the injunction to write neatly. Failure on the part of the young testees to observe directions caused a shrinkage of usable samples to a total of 490. This fact emphasizes the importance of carefully worded instructions, a feature frequently overlooked in the giving of penmanship tests. As accurate scoring of the handwriting samples required experienced markers, four judges underwent a course of preliminary training with the Ayres Scale covering a period of twelve weeks. A subsidiary study was made of the effects of this training and of the factors making for improvement of technique and accuracy.

Coefficients of correlation were obtained between the four variables for the group as a whole, also for the boys and girls taken separately. In order to eliminate chronological age as a variable the scores were then divided into six-month age groups, separated also as to sex, and intercorrelations obtained. Division according to sex and age furnished four half year groups for each sex of size sufficient for dependable correlation. Their numbers are given in Table I.

TABLE I

Whole group, 490 cases

Boys, whole number, 269 Girls, whole number, 221

HALF YEAR GROUPS

	Age	Number		Age	Number
Boys	10–0 to 10–5	44	Girls	10–0 to 10–5	44
	10–6 to 10–11	61		10–6 to 10–11	43
	11–0 to 11–5	48		11–0 to 11–5	54
	11–6 to 11–11	38		11–6 to 11–11	28

Four smaller age groups containing from twenty-five to sixteen cases each yielded intercorrelations which were deemed unreliable owing to their small numbers. Coefficients obtained were not materially greater than the probable error of each. A scattering few cases outside any of these age groups were included only in the computations of the whole numbers.

Results of intercorrelations of the four variables appear to argue somewhat conclusively against anatomic age as a determining factor in either rate or quality of penmanship. As will be seen from Table II, which gives intercorrelations for each sex as a whole as well as for the entire group, anatomic index stood lowest in its relation both to rate and to quality of writing.

A glance at Table III will show that in the six-month age groups the anatomic index fared worse, while intercorrelations of the other three functions tended to be higher than in the group as a whole.

TABLE II

CORRELATIONS FOR EACH SEX AND FOR THE WHOLE GROUP

		Cases	r
AI and rate	(boys)	269	.13 ± .04
	(girls)	221	.13 ± .045
	(whole)	490	.21 ± .029
AI and quality	(boys)		−.009 ± .04
	(girls)		.054 ± .045
	(whole)		.18 ± .029
IQ and rate	(boys)		.28 ± .038
	(girls)		.47 ± .036
	(whole)		.35 ± .027
IQ and quality	(boys)		.28 ± .038
	(girls)		.37 ± .039
	(whole)		.31 ± .028
Rate and quality	(boys)		.39 ± .035
	(girls)		.33 ± .041
	(whole)		.41 ± .025

TABLE III

HALF YEAR AGE GROUPS

		Range	Mean Coefficient	Mean P. E.
AI and rate	(boys)	−.07 to .02	−.018	± .099
	(girls)	−.21 to .21	.012	± .103
AI and quality	(boys)	−.24 to .14	−.087	± .096
	(girls)	−.19 to .16	.005	± .102
IQ and rate	(boys)	.35 to .47	.41	± .082
	(girls)	.36 to .74	.53	± .072
IQ and quality	(boys)	.21 to .44	.31	± .088
	(girls)	.28 to .55	.44	± .085
Rate and quality	(boys)	.31 to .58	.44	± .079
	(girls)	.07 to .47	.39	± .095

In place of a spectacular performance by the anatomic index we find the intelligence quotient taking its usual place in the center of the stage. And for good reason. For superior intelligence, translated into neural terms, is nothing else but superiority of the nerve fibers and their synapses, whether they be located in the association areas of the cortex or in the afferent-efferent connections to the skeletal muscles. To date no measure of physical development has been found to compare with the IQ in prognostic value of school success.

The relatively higher correlation of IQ with each of the two penmanship functions in the case of girls as against the boys is less readily explained. A combination of intelligence and interest among girls may furnish a good guess, increased mental ability being attended by the joy of interesting activity—leading to rapid achievement—and the pride in neatly executed work—tending toward improvement in quality of writing. Or it might be due to the tendency of girls to excel in tasks calling for dexterity of hand and finger muscles, accepting for the moment the contention that this tendency has been proved. Rather to be expected is the lag of ten points in mean coefficient of IQ and quality behind the mean coefficient of IQ and rate. What writer of exceptionally graceful hand but has been twitted by his friends with the byword that "pretty" writing goes with a small mind? Case studies in connection with the present investigation furnish ample illustration, among them a girl scoring near the top in quality who proved to have an IQ of 66.

Correlations of rate and quality, while high enough to be notable, offer little help in answering the latter of the two secondary questions cited above. With a single exception no coefficient was found above .50, which Hull has recently pronounced practically useless for forecasting purposes.[1] Moreover, a disconcerting variance from the norms was found when grade medians were computed, the group as a whole exceeding Ayres' standards for rate and running below them in quality to the degree shown in Table IV.

TABLE IV

SHOWING PER CENT. IN TERMS OF AYRES' NORMS IN WHICH PRESENT MEDIANS EXCEEDED AYRES' STANDARDS IN RATE, AND FAILED TO EQUAL THEM IN QUALITY

	III	IV	V	VI
Rate by grades	.02	.16	.27	.28
Quality by grades	.33	.28	.24	.24

[1] Clark L. Hull, "The Correlation Coefficient and its Prognostic Significance," *Journal of Educational Research*, Vol. 15, May, 1927.

It is apparent that rapid writing had been stressed in the school system studied, evidently at the expense of legibility.

A comparison of sex differences in the four functions studied is given below.

TABLE V

SEX DIFFERENCES IN FOUR FUNCTIONS

	Mean score	Difference	Per cent. of boys' mean	Range
AI—				
Boys	2.55 ± .13	.32 ± .18	.126	1.60
Girls	2.87 ± .12			1.30
IQ—				
Boys	101.54 ± .12	.60 ± .17	.006	90.
Girls	102.14 ± .12			85.
Rate*—				
Boys	75.80 ± .15	9.96 ± .23	.130	100.
Girls	85.76 ± .17			105.
Quality—				
Boys	35.85 ± .067	6.30 ± .11	.176	50.
Girls	42.15 ± .085			50.

* Number of letters per minute.

A search for factors appearing to affect rate and quality of handwriting other than those used as variables in the correlations described was made in case studies of twenty-four children who deviated to a marked degree from the average in one or other pertinent trait. Among these, two seem to deserve further study: manual dexterity and attitude. The highest rate score among the boys was won by the son of a skilled machine worker. This youngster is noted in his school for practical efficiency; in absence of a time clock the principal has entrusted him with the ringing of every class bell during the school day. He is quick and efficient in his bodily movements, though he has a strong distaste for study. Conversely a girl of eleven years was found in the fifth grade, of average mentality and average school achievement, who scored the median for girls in rate of writing and stood in quality at the very bottom of girl writers. In height she was two years over age, in weight more than five years advanced. Her movements in general were ungainly and deliberate; her gait rolling and elephantine. She is one of a number of children in the present study whose aspect and scores suggest a comparative study of bodily age-weight with tasks calling for quick and exact muscular execution.

Regarding attitude, abundant instances were found of children denied by reason of poor mental endowment the hope of success in the major school studies, who had compensated by falling back upon neat writing, the one thing in the school program in which they could find self-expression. At the other end of the intelligence range was found a boy of ten years and three months in the sixth grade, whose IQ ranked him among the three highest in the city, who was found in the bottom quarter for quality of writing. His class record at the close of the year studied was five A's, two B's and one D—in penmanship. He confessed to the writer that he was aware of the inferiority of his writing, but had not regarded it as worth while to develop a better.

To summarize on the basis of the data studied: anatomic age as expressed in skeletal development appears irrelevant as a determiner of either rate or quality of penmanship. Superior mental ability is a more important correlate. The bright child is usually a rapid writer; he may or may not turn out a more legible product than his less gifted classmate: IQ correlated roughly about 20 per cent. lower with quality than with rate of writing. Rate and quality, though showing coefficients ranging from .07 to .58, gave no conclusive answer to the question of how fast children may be expected to write without detriment to the product. There is evidence of the existence of that unidentified quantum known as manual aptitude, motor coordination or muscular control, with the probability that it does affect scores in penmanship. Apparently quite as important, if not exerting a larger influence, is the subjective attitude of the child to his task. And since it is not uncommon for their elders to show indifference to bad writing, if not even to take a certain pride in the illegibility of their own script, we can not expect school children to be strongly motivated toward graceful writing until some change is made in our American folkways.

MILTON WITTLER

GRINNELL COLLEGE